M000284114

BaseBall america®
PROSPECT
HANDBOOK
2008

BASEBALL AMERICA INC. • DURHAM, N.C.

FOR GREAT PROSPECTS COVERAGE ALL YEAR, VISIT ...

Baseball america
PROSPECT HANDBOOK
2008

Editors
JIM CALLIS, WILL LINGO, JOHN MANUEL

Assistant Editors
BEN BADLER, J.J. COOPER, MATT EDDY, AARON FITT, CHRIS KLINE, JOSH LEVENTHAL, ALAN MATTHEWS, NATHAN RODE

Contributing Writers
ANDY BAGGARLY, BILL BALLEW, MIKE BERARDINO, DERRICK GOOLD, TOM HAUDRICOURT, JON PAUL MOROSI, JOHN PERROTTO, TRACY RINGOLSBY, PHIL ROGERS

Photo Editor
NATHAN RODE

Editorial Assistant
JIM SHONERD

Design & Production
DANIEL BEDEN, SARA HIATT, LINWOOD WEBB

Jacket Photos
JAY BRUCE BY STAN DENNY; FRANKLIN MORALES BY LARRY GOREN; CLAYTON KERSHAW BY BILL MITCHELL; CAMERON MAYBIN BY BRIAN BISSELL; JIMMY ROLLINS BY RODGER WOOD; C.C. SABATHIA BY RICH ABEL

Cover Design
LINWOOD WEBB

Baseball america

PRESIDENT/PUBLISHER: LEE FOLGER
EDITORS IN CHIEF: WILL LINGO, JOHN MANUEL
EXECUTIVE EDITOR: JIM CALLIS
DESIGN & PRODUCTION DIRECTOR: SARA HIATT

DISTRIBUTED BY SIMON & SCHUSTER
ISBN-10: 1-932391-19-3   ISBN-13: 978-1-932391-19-0

STATISTICS COMPILED AND PROVIDED BY MAJOR LEAGUE BASEBALL ADVANCED MEDIA.

BaseballAmerica.com

TABLE OF CONTENTS

478

Chris Marrero leads the way for a resurgent Nationals farm system that has added talent in the field and on the mound

Foreword by Theo Epstein	5
Introduction	6
Profiling Prospects	7
Depth Chart Overview	8
Staff Top 50s	9
Organization Rankings	12
Arizona Diamondbacks	14
Atlanta Braves	30
Baltimore Orioles	46
Boston Red Sox	62
Chicago Cubs	78
Chicago White Sox	94
Cincinnati Reds	110
Cleveland Indians	126
Colorado Rockies	142
Detroit Tigers	158
Florida Marlins	174
Houston Astros	190
Kansas City Royals	206
Los Angeles Angels	222
Los Angeles Dodgers	238
Milwaukee Brewers	254
Minnesota Twins	270
New York Mets	286
New York Yankees	302
Oakland Athletics	318
Philadelphia Phillies	334
Pittsburgh Pirates	350
St. Louis Cardinals	366
San Diego Padres	382
San Francisco Giants	398
Seattle Mariners	414
Tampa Bay Rays	430
Texas Rangers	446
Toronto Blue Jays	462
Washington Nationals	478
APPENDIX: Extra scouting reports	494
2005-2007 Signing bonuses	495
2008 Draft Prospects	499
Minor League Top 20s	503
Index	506

FOREWORD

Working under Kevin Towers in the Padres' baseball operations department from 1997 to 2002, one of my primary responsibilities was to keep track of the other 29 organizations' farm systems. Using our pro scouts' reports and some statistical analysis, my job was to monitor each club's prospects, provide summary descriptions of the players and, most important, get them in the right order on organizational pref lists I produced for Kevin. Trying to keep the lists—we called them "zebra sheets" for their striped look—updated throughout the season was a challenge, but it was also a lot of fun, an invaluable education and one of the most rewarding parts of my job.

Every time I pick up Baseball America's Prospect Handbook, I think back to my time cranking out the zebra sheets. These days, it's not just front offices that put in the resources and effort to track prospects and get them in the right order. Baseball America is on the job as well, and the result is a great read and valuable reference for any hardcore baseball fan. We don't always agree with them—that's what makes this fun—but it's impossible to deny the Baseball America writers' thoroughness, commitment to accuracy, feel for prospects and dedication to getting their evaluations right.

The Prospect Handbook is a great opportunity for baseball fans to follow the game the way insiders do. With the Handbook at your side, you can track prospects through the natural ups and downs of a player-development path, find out for yourself who might be a sleeper and who might be overrated, and start to get a feel for what makes a prospect truly valuable. Instead of viewing a trade as "John Doe for an A-ball player" as it appears in the headlines, you can use the Prospect Handbook to dig deeper into the prospect's actual value and make your own assessment of the deal. You can think along with your favorite organization as it not only builds its 2008 team but also plans its roster for 2013. Use the book enough, and you can familiarize yourself with the entire prospect landscape. When today's minor leaguers are populating major league rosters in a few years, you'll have a much deeper understanding of an entire generation of players' backgrounds, tools and track records.

Prospects never have been more valuable than they are in today's game. It's virtually impossible to understand how the industry operates today without getting to know the game's best prospects. Unless you have time to crank out some zebra sheets of your own, I can think of no better resource to develop this knowledge than Baseball America's Prospect Handbook.

THEO EPSTEIN
EXECUTIVE VICE PRESIDENT, GENERAL MANAGER
BOSTON RED SOX

INTRODUCTION

n retrospect, what's amazing is not that the Prospect Handbook has become such a signature publication for Baseball America. It's amazing that we didn't think of it sooner.

Baseball America has been ranking prospects almost since the magazine began publishing in 1981. People have a natural affinity for lists, and baseball fans in particular love to stack players up against one another. With the way baseball development is set up, with players working their way through what is usually years of development before making a mark in the big leagues, prospect rankings are just that much more appealing.

The first BA prospect lists were top 10s, of course, because that's just the natural order of things. As people started thirsting for more, we added a list of prospects Nos. 11-15. Then we got the crazy idea to put all the lists in a book, with even more information. Eventually the number we settled on was 30, which seemed crazy at the time but now sometimes seems like it's not enough—at least for the strong organizations.

The first Prospect Handbook came out before the 2001 season, and while we tweak the format of the book each year—this year you get a review of what happened to everyone on last year's top 30, for example—the basic format has remained unchanged. Our rankings and the accompanying scouting reports make up the backbone of the book, and that will always be true. They're the product of a year's worth of information-gathering and the culmination of everything Baseball America does. The people who write up each organization talk to scouts, managers and coaches, instructors and coordinators, farm directors, scouting directors and anyone else with an educated opinion about the players in each organization.

And it's not just the people who write up each organization who contribute this information. When I write up the Diamondbacks, for example, I'm relying on Jim Callis to provide me additional information on Diamondbacks prospects from the Midwest League, because he did our prospect list for that league and talked to managers and scouts about the talent. And that's true of every league where the Diamondbacks had prospects. We want as many viewpoints as we can find, particularly those from outside the organization.

Performance also matters, a lot, and it always mystifies me when people think it doesn't. The major exception to this, if you want to call it that, comes with recently drafted players, who have a limited professional track record. But in almost all of those cases, the players have a track record of performance in amateur baseball, often against high-quality competition. And while we're willing to overlook a down year from a prospect who has tools, when that becomes a trend you'll see a player start to slide on our lists. On the flip side, yes, we do value tools enough that a player who puts up big numbers in the minors but doesn't have the skills to indicate he'll repeat his performance in the majors won't be high on our lists.

We also rely on Jim to coordinate all the information in the book, so that it all fits together and so every list is of the quality you expect. Jim discusses every list with each writer, and he and John Manuel in particular debate the rankings and help line the players up. There are a lot of reasons why this book is so good, and one is that we actually care where Dennis Sarfate slotted into the Orioles prospect list when he came over in a trade with the Astros.

The three of us get our names on the top line of the book, but we're just part of a huge team of people who help make this massive collection of information come together into an attractive, readable book. Big thanks to Sara Hiatt and our production and design team for their great work; Greg Levine and our technology team for helping us move all the data, particularly the stats; all our correspondents and full-time writers and editors for their incredible hard work; and of course you, for continuing to buy this book. We think it's great, but that wouldn't matter unless you kept reading it.

A few housekeeping notes: Transactions for this book go through Dec. 12, so the last major deal included here was Miguel Tejada going from the Orioles to the Astros for five players. As always, you can find players even if they change organizations by using the handy index in the back. We also have supplemental scouting reports for three late-signing Japanese players on Page 494. And for the purposes of this book, a prospect is anyone who has no more than 50 innings pitched or 130 at-bats in the big leagues, regardless of service time. Finally, the grades you'll find for each team's drafts are based solely on the quality of the players signed, with no consideration for who players were traded for or how many picks a team might have lost.

Enough of my yakkin'. Dive in and find your own favorite big leaguer of tomorrow.

WILL LINGO
EDITOR IN CHIEF
BASEBALL AMERICA

PROFILING PROSPECTS

Among all the scouting lingo you'll come across in this book, perhaps no terms are more telling and prevalent than "profile" and "projection."

When scouts evaluate a player, their main objective is to identify—or project—what the player's future role will be in the major leagues. Each organization has its own philosophy when it comes to grading players, so we talked to scouts from several teams to provide general guidelines.

The first thing to know is what scouts are looking for. In short, tools. These refer to the physical skills a player needs to be successful in the major leagues. For a position player, the five basic tools are hitting, hitting for power, fielding, arm strength and speed. For a pitcher, the tools are based on the pitches he throws. Each pitch is graded, as well as a pitcher's control, delivery and durability.

For most teams, the profiling system has gone through massive changes in recent years because of the offensive explosion in baseball. Where arm strength and defense used to be a must in the middle of the diamond, there has been an obvious swing toward finding players who can rake, regardless of their gloves. In the past, players like Jeff Kent and Chase Utley wouldn't have been accepted as second basemen, but now they are the standard for offensive-minded second basemen.

While more emphasis is placed on hitting—which also covers getting on base—fielding and speed are still at a premium up the middle. As teams sacrifice defense at the corner outfield slots, they look for a speedy center fielder to make up ground in the alleys. Most scouts prefer at least a 55 runner (on the 20-80 scouting scale; see chart) at short and center field, but as power increases at those two positions, running comes down. Shortstops need range and at least average arm strength, and second basemen need to be quick on the pivot. Teams are more willing to put up with an immobile corner infielder if he can mash.

Arm strength is the one tool moving way down preference lists. For a catcher, it was always the No. 1 tool, though in today's game, scouts are looking for more offensive production from the position. Receiving skills, including game-calling, blocking pitches and release times, can make up for the lack of a plus arm.

On the mound, it doesn't just come down to pure stuff. While a true No. 1 starter on a first-division team should have a couple of 70 or 80 pitches in his repertoire, like Johan Santana and Josh Beckett, they also need to produce 200-plus innings, 30 starts and 15-plus wins.

A player's overall future potential is also graded on the 20-80 scale, though some teams use a letter grade. This number is not just the sum of his tools, but rather a profiling system and a scout's ultimate opinion of the player.

70-80 (A): This category is reserved for the elite players in baseball. This player will be a perennial all-star, the best player at his position, one of the top five starters in the game or a frontline closer. Alex Rodriguez, Ichiro Suzuki and Santana reside here.

60-69 (B) You'll find all-star-caliber players here: No. 2 starters on a championship club and first-division players. See John Lackey, Torii Hunter and Carl Crawford.

55-59 (C+) The majority of first-division starters are found in this range, including quality No. 2 and 3 starters, frontline set-up men and second-tier closers.

50-54 (C) Solid-average everyday major leaguers. Most are not first-division regulars. This group also includes No. 4 and 5 starters.

45-49 (D+) Fringe everyday players, backups, some No. 5 starters, middle relievers, pinch-hitters and one-tool players.

40-44 (D) Up-and-down roster fillers, situational relievers and 25th players.

38-39 (O) Organizational players who provide depth for the minor leagues but are not considered future major leaguers.

20-37 (NP) Not a prospect.

THE SCOUTING SCALE

When grading a player's tools, scouts use a standard 20-80 scale. When you read that a pitcher throws an above-average slider, it can be interpreted as a 60 pitch, or a plus pitch. Plus-plus is 70, or well-above-average, and so on. Scouts don't throw 80s around very freely. Here's what each grade means:

80	Outstanding
70	Well-above-average
60	Above-average
50	Major league average
40	Below-average
30	Well-below-average
20	Poor

An Overview

Another feature of the Prospect Handbook is a depth chart of every organization's minor league talent. This shows you at a glance what kind of talent a system has and provides even more prospects beyond the top 30. Each depth chart is accompanied by a quick take on a system's strengths and weaknesses, as well as where it ranks in baseball (see facing page for the complete list). The rankings are based on the quality and quantity of talent in each system, with higher marks to clubs that have more high-ceiling prospects or a deep system. The best systems have both.

Players are usually listed on the depth charts where we think they'll ultimately end up. To help you better understand why players are slotted at particular positions, we show you here what scouts look for in the ideal candidate at each spot, with individual tools ranked in descending order.

LF
Hitting
Power
Fielding
Arm Strength
Speed

CF
Fielding
Hitting
Speed
Power
Arm Strength

RF
Hitting
Power
Arm Strength
Fielding
Speed

3B
Hitting
Power
Fielding
Arm Strength
Speed

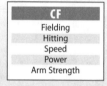

SS
Fielding
Arm Strength
Hitting
Speed
Power

2B
Hitting
Fielding
Power
Speed
Arm Strength

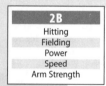

1B
Hitting
Power
Fielding
Arm Strength
Speed

C
Fielding
Arm Strength
Hitting
Power
Speed

STARTING PITCHERS

No. 1 starter	No. 2 starter	No. 3 starter	No. 4-5 starters
• Two plus pitches	• Two plus pitches	• One plus pitch	• Command of two major league pitches
• Average third pitch	• Average third pitch	• Two average pitches	• Average velocity
• Plus-plus command	• Average command	• Average command	• Consistent breaking ball
• Plus makeup	• Average makeup	• Average makeup	• Decent changeup

CLOSER

- One dominant pitch
- Second plus pitch
- Plus command
- Plus-plus makeup

TOP 50 PROSPECTS

When Baseball America ranks prospects, there's almost always a byline attributing who finally put the players in order, who decided, "OK, this guy's 6 and this guy's 7." But all our rankings are more than one person's opinion. They are most often a reflection of the consensus of sources on the subject—managers, coaches, scouts, front-office personnel, the whole spectrum.

Except here, really. In this section of the Handbook, we get personal. Sifting through all the information we've gathered to this point, four of our top prospect writers and editors give their own personal takes on the game's Top 50 prospects. This helps form the basis of the arguments that shape Baseball America's Top 100 Prospects. That list comes out during spring training, and we consider it the definitive guide to the best talent in the minor leagues.

The rules for these lists are the same for any prospect who appears in the handbook: rookie standards of no more than 130 at-bats or 50 innings in the major leagues. We do not consider service time in our eligibility requirements.

Red Sox phenom Clay Buchholz already has tossed a big league no-hitter

As with any prospect list, these rankings represent how each person regarded the top minor league talent in the game at a moment in time. Ask us again in a few months—or even tomorrow—how these prospects stack up, and you'll get a different answer.

Jim Callis

1. Jay Bruce, of, Reds
2. Clay Buchholz, rhp, Red Sox
3. Joba Chamberlain, rhp, Yankees
4. Evan Longoria, 3b, Rays
5. Clayton Kershaw, lhp, Dodgers
6. Mike Moustakas, ss, Royals
7. Colby Rasmus, of, Cardinals
8. Cameron Maybin, of, Marlins
9. Travis Snider, of, Blue Jays
10. Homer Bailey, rhp, Reds
11. Franklin Morales, lhp, Rockies
12. David Price, lhp, Rays
13. Rick Porcello, rhp, Tigers
14. Brandon Wood, 3b/ss, Angels
15. Matt Wieters, c, Orioles
16. Jacoby Ellsbury, of, Red Sox
17. Jake McGee, lhp, Rays
18. Wade Davis, rhp, Rays
19. Angel Villalona, 3b/1b, Giants
20. Jason Heyward, of, Braves
21. Brett Anderson, lhp, Diamondbacks
22. Jose Tabata, of, Yankees
23. Fernando Martinez, of, Mets
24. Andy LaRoche, 3b, Dodgers
25. Matt LaPorta, of, Brewers
26. Reid Brignac, ss, Rays
27. Andrew McCutchen, of, Pirates
28. Carlos Gonzalez, of, Diamondbacks
29. Lars Anderson, 1b, Red Sox
30. Nick Adenhart, rhp, Angels
31. Jordan Schafer, of, Braves
32. Jeff Clement, c, Mariners
33. Joey Votto, 1b/of, Reds
34. Johnny Cueto, rhp, Reds
35. Chris Marrero, 1b/of, Nationals
36. Deolis Guerra, rhp, Mets
37. Elvis Andrus, ss, Rangers
38. Adam Miller, rhp, Indians
39. Gio Gonzalez, lhp, White Sox
40. Austin Jackson, of, Yankees
41. Daniel Cortes, rhp, Royals
42. Luke Hochevar, rhp, Royals
43. Josh Vitters, 3b, Cubs
44. Chin-Lung Hu, ss, Dodgers
45. Ross Detwiler, lhp, Nationals
46. Geovany Soto, c/1b, Cubs
47. J.R. Towles, c, Astros
48. Jair Jurrjens, rhp, Braves
49. Desmond Jennings, of, Rays
50. Chase Headley, 3b, Padres

Will Lingo

1. Jay Bruce, of, Reds
2. Evan Longoria, 3b, Rays
3. Clay Buchholz, rhp, Red Sox
4. Cameron Maybin, of, Marlins
5. Homer Bailey, rhp, Reds
6. Franklin Morales, lhp, Rockies
7. Colby Rasmus, of, Cardinals
8. Joba Chamberlain, rhp, Yankees
9. Clayton Kershaw, lhp, Dodgers
10. Elvis Andrus, ss, Rangers
11. Andrew McCutchen, of, Pirates
12. Carlos Gonzalez, of, Diamondbacks
13. Andy LaRoche, 3b, Dodgers
14. Chase Headley, 3b, Padres
15. Chris Marrero, 1b/of, Nationals
16. Brandon Wood, 3b, Angels
17. Nick Adenhart, rhp, Angels
18. Travis Snider, of, Blue Jays
19. Carlos Carrasco, rhp, Phillies
20. David Price, lhp, Rays
21. Matt Wieters, c, Orioles
22. Ian Stewart, 3b, Rockies
23. Rick Porcello, rhp, Tigers
24. Jordan Schafer, of, Braves
25. Jacoby Ellsbury, of, Red Sox
26. Jake McGee, lhp, Rays
27. Mike Moustakas, 3b, Royals
28. Wade Davis, rhp, Rays
29. Jason Heyward, of, Braves
30. Matt LaPorta, of, Brewers
31. Chris Volstad, rhp, Marlins
32. Fernando Martinez, of, Mets
33. Radhames Liz, rhp, Orioles
34. Gio Gonzalez, lhp, White Sox
35. Adam Miller, rhp, Indians
36. Jarrod Parker, rhp, Diamondbacks
37. Lars Anderson, 1b, Red Sox
38. Jeff Clement, c, Mariners
39. Josh Vitters, 3b, Cubs
40. Brett Anderson, lhp, Diamondbacks
41. Matt Antonelli, 2b, Padres
42. Angel Villalona, 3b/1b, Giants
43. Brett Sinkbeil, rhp, Marlins
44. Nick Blackburn, rhp, Twins
45. Austin Jackson, of, Yankees
46. Ross Detwiler, lhp, Nationals
47. Geovany Soto, c/1b, Cubs
48. Joey Votto, 1b, Reds
49. Chin-Lung Hu, ss, Dodgers
50. Max Scherzer, rhp, Diamondbacks

John Manuel

1. Joba Chamberlain, rhp, Yankees
2. Jay Bruce, of, Reds
3. Evan Longoria, 3b, Rays
4. Colby Rasmus, of, Cardinals
5. Cameron Maybin, of, Marlins
6. Clayton Kershaw, lhp, Dodgers
7. Clay Buchholz, rhp, Red Sox
8. David Price, lhp, Rays
9. Franklin Morales, lhp, Rockies
10. Jacob McGee, lhp, Rays
11. Wade Davis, rhp, Rays
12. Jacoby Ellsbury, of, Red Sox
13. Andrew McCutchen, of, Pirates
14. Mike Moustakas, ss, Royals
15. Matt Wieters, c, Orioles
16. Homer Bailey, rhp, Reds
17. Elvis Andrus, ss, Rangers
18. Travis Snider, of, Blue Jays
19. Fernando Martinez, of, Mets
20. Austin Jackson, of, Yankees
21. Brandon Wood, 3b, Angels
22. Jordan Schafer, of, Braves
23. Gio Gonzalez, lhp, White Sox
24. Rick Porcello, rhp, Tigers
25. Jose Tabata, of, Yankees
26. Matt LaPorta, of, Brewers
27. Chris Marrero, 1b/of, Nationals
28. Nick Blackburn, rhp, Twins
29. Johnny Cueto, rhp, Reds
30. Ian Kennedy, rhp, Yankees
31. Ian Stewart, 3b, Rockies
32. Nick Adenhart, rhp, Angels
33. Deolis Guerra, rhp, Mets
34. Daric Barton, 1b, Athletics
35. Jason Heyward, of, Braves
36. Carlos Gomez, of, Mets
37. Carlos Gonzalez, of, Diamondbacks
38. Reid Brignac, ss, Rays
39. Chase Headley, 3b, Padres
40. Adam Miller, rhp, Indians
41. Andy LaRoche, 3b, Dodgers
42. Jeff Clement, c, Mariners
43. Matt Antonelli, 2b, Padres
44. Lars Anderson, 1b, Red Sox
45. Jair Jurrjens, rhp, Braves
46. Brett Anderson, lhp, Diamondbacks
47. Chris Volstad, rhp, Marlins
48. Angel Villalona, 3b/1b, Giants
49. J.R. Towles, c, Astros
50. Tim Alderson, rhp, Giants

Rockies infielder Ian Stewart could earn a spot on the pennant winners' roster

Righthander Johnny Cueto contributes to an improved Reds farm system

Chris Kline

1. Evan Longoria, 3b, Rays
2. Jay Bruce, of, Reds
3. Colby Rasmus, of, Cardinals
4. Joba Chamberlain, rhp, Yankees
5. Cameron Maybin, of, Marlins
6. Franklin Morales, lhp, Rockies
7. Clay Buchholz, rhp, Red Sox
8. Clayton Kershaw, lhp, Dodgers
9. David Price, lhp, Rays
10. Travis Snider, of, Blue Jays
11. Matt Wieters, c, Orioles
12. Jacoby Ellsbury, of, Red Sox
13. Andrew McCutchen, of, Pirates
14. Fernando Martinez, of, Mets
15. Adam Miller, rhp, Indians
16. Johnny Cueto, rhp, Reds
17. Jacob McGee, lhp, Rays
18. Homer Bailey, rhp, Reds
19. Carlos Gonzalez, of, Diamondbacks
20. Deolis Guerra, rhp, Mets
21. Wade Davis, rhp, Rays
22. Brandon Wood, 3b, Angels
23. Elvis Andrus, ss, Rangers
24. Rick Porcello, rhp, Tigers
25. Nick Adenhart, rhp, Angels
26. Engel Beltre, of, Rangers
27. Matt LaPorta, of, Brewers
28. Mike Moustakas, ss, Royals
29. Carlos Triunfel, ss, Mariners
30. Josh Vitters, 3b, Cubs
31. Angel Villalona, 1b/3b, Giants
32. Ian Kennedy, rhp, Yankees
33. Carlos Carrasco, rhp, Phillies
34. Matt Harrison, lhp, Rangers
35. Jordan Schafer, of, Braves
36. Daric Barton, 1b, Athletics
37. Jair Jurrjens, rhp, Braves
38. Chase Headley, 3b, Padres
39. Brett Anderson, lhp, Diamondbacks
40. Jason Heyward, of, Braves
41. Chris Marrero, of/1b, Nationals
42. Nick Blackburn, rhp, Twins
43. Chuck Lofgren, lhp, Indians
44. Neil Walker, 3b, Pirates
45. Reid Brignac, ss, Rays
46. Hector Gomez, ss, Rockies
47. Max Scherzer, rhp, Diamondbacks
48. Andy LaRoche, 3b, Dodgers
49. Joey Votto, 1b/of, Reds
50. Neftali Feliz, rhp, Rangers

TALENT RANKINGS

	2007	2006	2005	2004	2003
1 Tampa Bay Rays	1	10	9	9	10

With back-to-back seasons ranking at No. 1, the Rays have the talent to finally turn the corner. The difference the last two years has been improved quality of pitching talent, with power arms throughout the organization.

	2007	2006	2005	2004	2003
2 Boston Red Sox	9	8	21	23	27

That $100 million player development machine Theo Epstein talked about has come to pass, with a pair of World Series championships thrown in for good measure. Boston has depth, variety and impact talent. It's a nice mix.

	2007	2006	2005	2004	2003
3 Cincinnati Reds	12	30	23	26	24

The biggest mover on the list from 2006 to 2007, the Reds again rank among the biggest movers in 2008. Their top talents from '07 remain prospect-eligible, they've drafted well of late and have found more talent internationally.

	2007	2006	2005	2004	2003
4 Texas Rangers	28	16	16	16	19

No one has improved their system like the Rangers, who shot up our rankings after a productive draft and the five-player Mark Teixeira deal with the Braves. Texas has become an aggressive player internationally, and it's reflected in their system's talent.

	2007	2006	2005	2004	2003
5 New York Yankees	7	17	24	27	17

The Yankees' 2006 draft brought in premium pitchers Joba Chamberlain and Ian Kennedy, and the organization continues to emphasize pitching, with 20 of its Top 30 prospects doing their work on the mound.

	2007	2006	2005	2004	2003
6 Los Angeles Dodgers	6	2	2	2	14

See why we ranked the Dodgers so high—have Russ Martin, Chad Billingsley, Matt Kemp and James Loney been convincing enough? Now lefthander Clayton Kershaw leads another pack of premium talents.

	2007	2006	2005	2004	2003
7 Colorado Rockies	2	11	6	15	25

The Rockies will trade moving down our rankings a smidge in exchange for being the 2007 Organization of the Year and National League champions. Colorado's playoff roster was peppered with homegrown talent, including current No. 1 prospect Franklin Morales.

	2007	2006	2005	2004	2003
8 Atlanta Braves	16	7	5	4	2

How about the Braves, who traded five prospects to the Rangers for Mark Teixeira, yet move up our rankings and back into their customary spot in the top 10? Good drafts, especially a slew of talented draft-and-follows, have restocked the farm.

	2007	2006	2005	2004	2003
9 Washington Nationals	30	24	26	30	29

After the last three exceptional classes of big league rookies, talent in the minor leagues looks thinner this offseason, making it easier for organizations like the Nationals to skyrocket up the rankings after one good, deep draft.

	2007	2006	2005	2004	2003
10 Los Angeles Angels	4	4	1	3	5

The Angels drop out of the top five in our rankings for the first time since 2003, the first book after they won the World Series. A bit of impatience has crept in, as the Angels will lack a first-round pick for the third time in four years in 2008.

	2007	2006	2005	2004	2003
11 Seattle Mariners	24	27	11	12	9

The Mariners make one of the biggest moves up our rankings, thanks to retaining top prospects at upper levels such as Jeff Clement and Wladimir Balentien and the maturation of teen phenoms such as Carlos Triunfel and Chris Tillman.

	2007	2006	2005	2004	2003
12 San Diego Padres	29	29	27	25	20

The Padres made a huge leap up the rankings thanks to back-to-back strong drafts under Grady Fuson's leadership. Impressively, San Diego has two big league-ready hitters in Matt Antonelli and Chase Headley.

	2007	2006	2005	2004	2003
13 St. Louis Cardinals	23	21	30	28	28

The Cardinals break into the upper half of our rankings for the first time in Handbook history. Ownership threw its weight behind scouting and player-development chief Jeff Luhnow, and the result was Walt Jocketty's ouster as general manager.

	2007	2006	2005	2004	2003
14 Florida Marlins	15	3	14	14	8

After trading Miguel Cabrera and Dontrelle Willis—twin youthful heroes of their 2003 World Series title—the Marlins officially are done with the slash-and-burn part of their latest talent cycle. Landing Cameron Maybin was crucial for a hitting-starved system.

	2007	2006	2005	2004	2003
15 Arizona Diamondbacks	3	1	13	13	21

Only Colorado rivaled Arizona for talent graduated to the major leagues in 2007, and less talent was left behind by the Diamondbacks. The Diamondbacks had a college-heavy draft in 2007 as well, restocking the thinned-out system.

	2007	2006	2005	2004	2003
16 Baltimore Orioles	17	12	25	18	30

The Andy MacPhail regime made its first real impact with the go-ahead to sign first-round pick Matt Wieters for $6 million. The O's hope the '07 draft had depth to help a system with power arms but plenty of question marks.

17 New York Mets	13	28	19	10	13

General manager Omar Minaya's international emphasis has paid dividends, but the Mets seem to realize they can't rely on Latin America alone for young talent and hint that they will draft more aggressively in 2008.

18 Minnesota Twins	8	6	4	5	4

The Twins fell in the majors, with their first losing season since 2000, and in the minors, ranking outside our top 10 in terms of talent for the first time since the first Prospect Handbook back in 2001. The system has few sure things, particularly among hitters.

19 Cleveland Indians	10	9	7	6	1

Past high rankings again proved prophetic, as Cleveland won 96 games featuring a young lineup of players from its fertile Latin American program and others such as Grady Sizemore and Travis Hafner, acquired as minor leaguers.

20 Chicago Cubs	18	15	10	7	3

The Cubs have perhaps the most volatile system in the minors, as first-rounder Josh Vitters had a difficult, if short, debut, and the system has several boom-or-bust players such as pitchers Jeff Samardzija and Donald Veal and outfielder Tyler Colvin.

21 Milwaukee Brewers	5	5	3	1	16

The Brewers finally drop out of our top five for the right reason—graduating talent to the majors. The replacement talent on the farm is mostly in A-ball, but Executive of the Year Jack Zduriencik figures to replenish the system.

22 Philadelphia Phillies	21	22	20	21	7

The Phillies have an approach reminiscent of the Angels of the late '90s, adding impact young players one at a time. While Jimmy Rollins and Ryan Howard have won MVP awards, the current system looks bereft of such impact.

23 San Francisco Giants	20	18	17	24	11

The Giants have dipped in the rankings while dipping in the major leagues the last four seasons. One culprit—not having a pick during the first three rounds of the 2005 draft, one of the strongest drafts ever.

24 Kansas City Royals	11	23	28	19	26

A star-laden system last season graduated several key talents—Billy Butler, Alex Gordon, Brian Bannister and Joakim Soria among them—to the majors last year. The Royals need to start hitting on some later draft picks to develop depth.

25 Toronto Blue Jays	25	25	15	8	6

Call 'em the Hold Steady. J.P. Ricciardi's club has averaged 80 wins a year in his tenure as GM and can't seem to find its player-development footing. A large 2007 draft class, which produced mixed early results, could help this ranking improve next year.

26 Pittsburgh Pirates	19	19	18	11	18

The Pirates hit rock bottom in 2007, when their big league team had its 15th straight losing season and their farm system's talent reached its thinnest level in years. After a clutch of four or five prospects, the Pirates have little if anything to count on.

27 Oakland Athletics	27	26	8	17	22

GM Billy Beane was shopping his best commodities—young righthanders Joe Blanton and Dan Haren—aggressively during the Winter Meetings, seeking affordable talent the team's drafts have not provided.

28 Chicago White Sox	26	14	12	20	15

The White Sox approached the draft conservatively in recent years while aggressively trading prospects to help the big league club. With an aging roster in Chicago that stumbled in '07, the White Sox could be in for a long dry spell.

29 Detroit Tigers	14	13	29	22	12

Must . . . win . . . now . . . The Tigers decided to go for it in the offseason, trading seven prospects who would have been in the Handbook to the Marlins and Braves for Miguel Cabrera, Edgar Renteria and Dontrelle Willis.

30 Houston Astros	22	20	22	29	23

Owner Drayton McLane is getting what he paid for, with several years of thrifty draft spending, a dried-up pipeline to Latin America and several win-now, develop-later trades contributing to the game's weakest system.

Arizona Diamondbacks

BY WILL LINGO

The Diamondbacks system looks much thinner than it did a year ago, but it's a price the organization was only too happy to pay.

Arizona used an influx of young talent to carry it to the National League West title, not to mention a Division Series victory over the Cubs. The season ended with a sweep in the NL Championship Series at the hands of the Rockies, but that didn't dent the Diamondbacks' optimism about their future.

Their playoff rosters featured 14 homegrown players, including eight of the top nine prospects on this list a year ago. Chris Young nearly had the first 30-30 season ever by a rookie, hitting 32 home runs with 27 stolen bases, while Mark Reynolds had 17 homers in 366 at-bats. Micah Owings was a lifesaver in the rotation, eating 153 innings and patching the big hole left by Randy Johnson's back injury. Tony Pena pitched a team-high 85 relief innings and earned 30 holds.

Justin Upton ranked as the minors' top prospect when Arizona summoned him in August to fill in for an injured Carlos Quentin. Upton, the No. 1 pick in 2005 who became the youngest big leaguer in franchise history at age 19, showed flashes of his prodigious talent and went 5-for-14 in the postseason.

The impressive group of rookies added to a young core of everyday players who had already gotten their feet wet, including Stephen Drew, Conor Jackson and Chris Snyder in the lineup, rotation ace Brandon Webb and closer Jose Valverde. Webb improved on his Cy Young Award-winning numbers from 2006 by going 18-10, 3.01 and Valverde led the NL with 47 saves.

While most of these players were acquired by people who are no longer with the organization—most notably former scouting director Mike Rizzo, now with the Nationals—it's worth noting that general manager Josh Byrnes has made several astute deals since taking over after the 2005 season. Byrnes traded for Doug Davis, Orlando Hudson and Johnson, and he also signed sparkplug Eric Byrnes.

Many of Arizona's young players aren't finished products. That's why even though the Diamondbacks led the NL with 90 wins, they did so with a negative run differential. The pitching staff finished fifth in the NL by allowing 732 runs, but the offense ranked 14th by scoring just 712. Arizona finished last in the league in on-base percentage, though that has been an emphasis of the new administration.

Brandon Webb was the ace of a young staff that boosted Arizona into the NLCS

LARRY GOREN

TOP 30 PROSPECTS

1. Carlos Gonzalez, of	16. Esmerling Vasquez, rhp
2. Jarrod Parker, rhp	17. Dallas Buck, rhp
3. Brett Anderson, lhp	18. Doug Slaten, lhp
4. Max Scherzer, rhp	19. Ed Easley, c
5. Gerardo Parra, of	20. Tyrell Worthington, of
6. Emilio Bonifacio, 2b/ss	21. Matt Green, rhp
7. Aaron Cunningham, of	22. Sean Morgan, rhp
8. Chris Carter, 1b	23. Emiliano Fruto, rhp
9. Reynaldo Navarro, ss	24. Clayton Conner, 3b
10. Barry Enright, rhp	25. Cyle Hankerd, of
11. Wes Roemer, rhp	26. Javier Brito, 1b
12. Brooks Brown, rhp	27. Hector Ambriz, rhp
13. Greg Smith, lhp	28. Alex Romero, of
14. Wilkin Castillo, c/inf	29. Pedro Ciriaco, ss
15. Daniel Stange, rhp	30. Leyson Septimo, lhp

In the meantime, the scouting and player-development staffs are working on the next wave of prospects. Pitching has been the emphasis of the past couple of drafts, and the system's five best mound prospects are products of those efforts. The Diamondbacks grabbed Max Scherzer and Brett Anderson in 2006, followed by Jarrod Parker, Wes Roemer and Barry Enright last June, all in the first two rounds. The only position prospect close to big league-ready is outfielder Carlos Gonzalez, and Arizona has no obvious opening for him.

General Manager: Josh Byrnes. **Farm Director:** A.J. Hinch. **Scouting Director:** Tom Allison.

Class	Team	League	W	L	PCT	Finish*	Manager	Affiliated
Majors	Arizona	National	90	72	.556	1st (16)	Bob Melvin	—
Triple-A	Tucson Sidewinders	Pacific Coast	75	67	.528	5th (16)	Bill Plummer	1998
Double-A	Mobile BayBears	Southern	71	68	.511	5th (10)	Brett Butler	2007
High A	Visalia Oaks	California	77	63	.550	1st (10)	Hector de la Cruz	2007
Low A	South Bend Silver Hawks	Midwest	68	70	.493	9th (14)	Mark Haley	1997
Short-season	Yakima Bears	Northwest	33	43	.434	8th (8)	Mike Bell	2001
Rookie	Missoula Osprey	Pioneer	27	49	.355	7th (8)	Damon Mashore	1999
Overall 2007 Minor League Record			351	360	.494	16th		

*Finish in overall standings (No. of teams in league) ^League champion

LAST YEAR'S TOP 30

Player, Pos.		Status
1.	Justin Upton, of	Majors
2.	Chris Young, of	Majors
3.	Carlos Gonzalez, of	No. 1
4.	Alberto Callaspo, 2b	Majors
5.	Miguel Montero, c	Majors
6.	Micah Owings, rhp	Majors
7.	Mark Reynolds, 3b	Majors
8.	Dustin Nippert, rhp	Majors
9.	Tony Pena, rhp	Majors
10.	Ross Ohlendorf, rhp	(Yankees)
11.	Brett Anderson, lhp	No. 3
12.	Emilio Bonifacio, 2b/ss	No. 6
13.	Alberto Gonzalez, ss	(Yankees)
14.	Gerardo Parra, of	No. 5
15.	Greg Smith, lhp	No. 13
16.	Cyle Hankerd, of	No. 25
17.	Chris Carter, 1b	(Red Sox)
18.	Chris Rahl, of	Dropped out
19.	Brooks Brown, rhp	No. 12
20.	Brian Barden, inf	(Cardinals)
21.	Andrew Fie, 3b	Dropped out
22.	Hector Ambriz, rhp	No. 27
23.	Daniel Stange, rhp	No. 15
24.	Danny Richar, 2b	(White Sox)
25.	Pedro Ciriaco, ss	No. 29
26.	Dallas Buck, rhp	No. 17
27.	Kyler Newby, rhp	Dropped out
28.	Evan MacLane, lhp	Dropped out
29.	Leyson Septimo, of	No. 30
30.	Matt Torra, rhp	Dropped out

BEST TOOLS

Best Hitter for Average	Gerardo Parra
Best Power Hitter	Carlos Gonzalez
Best Strike-Zone Discipline	Javier Brito
Fastest Baserunner	Emilio Bonifacio
Best Athlete	Tyrell Worthington
Best Fastball	Max Scherzer
Best Curveball	Jarrod Parker
Best Slider	Brett Anderson
Best Changeup	Esmerling Vasquez
Best Control	Brett Anderson
Best Defensive Catcher	Wilkin Castillo
Best Defensive Infielder	Emilio Bonifacio
Best Infield Arm	Pedro Ciriaco
Best Defensive Outfielder	Gerardo Parra
Best Outfield Arm	Carlos Gonzalez

PROJECTED 2011 LINEUP

Catcher	Chris Snyder
First Base	Conor Jackson
Second Base	Orlando Hudson
Third Base	Mark Reynolds
Shortstop	Stephen Drew
Left Field	Carlos Gonzalez
Center Field	Chris Young
Right Field	Justin Upton
No. 1 Starter	Brandon Webb
No. 2 Starter	Jarrod Parker
No. 3 Starter	Micah Owings
No. 4 Starter	Brett Anderson
No. 5 Starter	Barry Enright
Closer	Max Scherzer

TOP PROSPECTS OF THE DECADE

Year	Player, Pos.	2007 Org.
1998	Travis Lee, 1b	Out of baseball
1999	Brad Penny, rhp	Dodgers
2000	John Patterson, rhp	Nationals
2001	Alex Cintron, ss	White Sox
2002	Luis Terrero, of	White Sox
2003	Scott Hairston, 2b	Padres
2004	Scott Hairston, 2b	Padres
2005	Carlos Quentin, of	Diamondbacks
2006	Stephen Drew, ss	Diamondbacks
2007	Justin Upton, of	Diamondbacks

TOP DRAFT PICKS OF THE DECADE

Year	Player, Pos.	2007 Org.
1998	Darryl Conyer, of (3rd)	Out of baseball
1999	Corey Myers, ss	Angels
2000	Mike Schultz, rhp (2nd)	Diamondbacks
2001	Jason Bulger, rhp	Angels
2002	Sergio Santos, ss	Blue Jays
2003	Conor Jackson, of	Diamondbacks
2004	Stephen Drew, ss	Diamondbacks
2005	Justin Upton, of	Diamondbacks
2006	Max Scherzer, rhp	Diamondbacks
2007	Jarrod Parker, rhp	Diamondbacks

LARGEST BONUSES IN CLUB HISTORY

Travis Lee, 1996	$10,000,000
Justin Upton, 2005	$6,100,000
John Patterson, 1996	$6,075,000
Stephen Drew, 2004	$4,000,000
Max Scherzer, 2006	$3,000,000

ARIZONA DIAMONDBACKS

Top 2008 Rookie: Max Scherzer, rhp. Arizona showed with Micah Owings that it's not afraid to move college pitchers quickly, and this will be particularly true if Scherzer moves to the bullpen.

Breakout Prospect: Tyrell Worthington, of. A fifth-round pick last June, he was a two-sport high school star and has the tools to be an impact player.

Sleeper: Matt Torra, rhp. His 2007 numbers were ugly, but scouts who saw him in the second half of the year liked his stuff and thought he might finally be over his shoulder woes.

SOURCE OF TOP 30 TALENT			
Homegrown	26	Acquired	4
College	12	Trades	3
Junior college	1	Rule 5 draft	0
High school	4	Independent leagues	0
Draft-and-follow	1	Free agents/waivers	1
Nondrafted free agents	0		
International	8		

Numbers in parentheses indicate prospect rankings.

LF
Cyle Hankerd (25)
Alex Romero (28)
Chris Rahl
Danny Perales
Pete Clifford

CF
Aaron Cunningham (7)
Tyrell Worthington (20)
Evan Frey
Jereme Milons

RF
Carlos Gonzalez (1)
Gerardo Parra (5)

3B
Clayton Conner (24)
Jamie D'Antona
Steve Mena
Andrew Fie
Brandon Burgess

SS
Reynaldo Navarro (9)
Pedro Ciriaco (29)
Mark Hallberg

2B
Emilio Bonifacio (6)
Taylor Harbin

1B
Chris Carter (8)
Javier Brito (26)
Brad Miller
Bryan Byrne

C
Wilkin Castillo (14)
Ed Easley (19)
Josh Ford
Justin Brashear

RHP

Starters	Relievers
Jarrod Parker (2)	Max Scherzer (4)
Barry Enright (10)	Daniel Stange (15)
Wes Roemer (11)	Matt Green (21)
Brooks Brown (12)	Sean Morgan (22)
Esmerling Vasquez (16)	Emiliano Fruto (23)
Dallas Buck (17)	Hector Ambriz (27)
Matt Torra	Leo Rosales
Josh Collmenter	Jailen Peguero
Bryant Thompson	Bryan Augenstein
	Kyler Newby
	Eric Butler
	Jorge Perez
	Reid Mahon
	Ty Davis

LHP

Starters	Relievers
Brett Anderson (3)	Doug Slaten (18)
Greg Smith (13)	Leyson Septimo (30)
Jordan Norberto	Evan MacLane
Scott Maine	

DRAFT ANALYSIS

Best Pro Debut: RHP Josh Collmenter (15) led the short-season Northwest League with a 2.71 ERA. SS Mark Hallberg (9) earned NWL all-star honors after hitting .313 with six homers and 12 steals. None of the draftees had a better debut than draft-and-follow 3B Clayton Conner (45 in 2006), who hit .351 with nine homers in the NWL.

Best Athlete: OF Tyrell Worthington (5) was an all-state prep running back in North Carolina, landing a football scholarship from East Carolina. Speed is his standout tool.

Best Pure Hitter: The Diamondbacks like the hitting prowess of C Ed Easley (1s), who was hampered by a jammed left thumb in his debut, Hallberg and OF Evan Frey (10). SS Reynaldo Navarro (3) has a line-drive approach and bat speed, and he started switch-hitting after turning pro.

Best Power Hitter: OF Pete Clifford (20), a fifth-year senior sign, hit 10 homers at Rookie-level Missoula in his pro debut.

Fastest Runner: Worthington and OF Jimmy Principe (37) have 60-65 speed on the 20-80 scouting scale.

Best Defensive Player: Navarro is a flashy defender with plenty of range and enough arm to make plays from the hole. Easley is very athletic for his position, while C Bill Mussleman (30) is a catch-and-throw specialist who threw out 39 percent of basestealers in his debut.

Best Fastball: RHP Jarrod Parker (1) hit 97 mph with his first pitch of the high school season and didn't let up all year, sitting at 93-96 mph and touching 98. LHP Scott Maine (6) worked at 90-93 mph when pitching out of the bullpen.

Best Secondary Pitch: Parker has a hard curveball and also unveils a mid-80s slider from time to time. Morgan and Wes Roemer (1s) both have good sliders.

Most Intriguing Background: OF Mike Mee's (16) uncle Darryl Scott pitched briefly in the majors and his father Tom directs Cardinals television broadcasts. Mee's grandfather Tom Sr. was the first employee the Twins hired after moving to Minnesota in 1961, and was the club's longtime public-relations director and official scorer.

Closest To The Majors: The D-backs landed two of the most polished college pitchers in the draft in Roemer and RHP Barry Enright (2).

Best Late-Round Pick: Collmenter doesn't have overwhelming stuff, but his command, deception and savvy have allowed him to succeed at every level during his career.

The One Who Got Away: LHP Sammy Solis (18) sits at 89-90 mph but had an inconsistent spring. He's at San Diego.

Assessment: Parker had the most electric arm in the draft, yet the Diamondbacks were able to nab him with the No. 9 overall pick. Tom Allison's first draft as Arizona scouting director focused on the mound, with six pitchers taken in the first seven rounds.

The Diamondbacks may have overpaid for RHP Max Scherzer (1), but he could help them in a hurry. RHP Brooks Brown (1s) and LHP Brett Anderson (2) also are on the fast track.

GRADE: B+

OF Justin Upton (1) has lived up to his billing as the No. 1 overall pick, reaching the majors sooner than expected. RHP Micah Owings (3) also has made a swift impact—with his bat as well as his arm.

GRADE: A

SS Stephen Drew (1) and 3B Mark Reynolds (16) anchored the left side of the infield for the National League West champs. RHPs Garrett Mock (3) and Ross Ohlendorf (4) proved useful in trades for Livan Hernandez and Randy Johnson.

GRADE: A

1B Conor Jackson (1) and OF Carlos Quentin (1) haven't been as productive as hoped, though Jackson remains Arizona's starter at first base. Upton's rapid development made Quentin expendable.

GRADE: B

Draft analysis by Jim Callis. Numbers in parentheses indicate draft rounds. Budgets are bonuses in first 10 rounds.

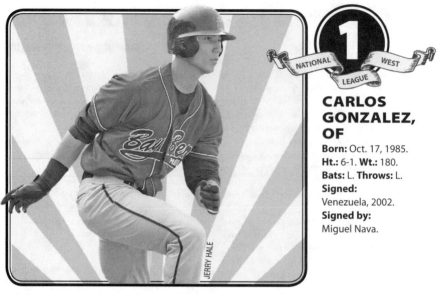

1 NATIONAL LEAGUE WEST

CARLOS GONZALEZ, OF

Born: Oct. 17, 1985.
Ht.: 6-1. **Wt.:** 180.
Bats: L. **Throws:** L.
Signed:
Venezuela, 2002.
Signed by:
Miguel Nava.

Gonzalez burst onto the scene by winning the low Class A Midwest League MVP award in 2005, and he has followed that with two straight appearances in the Futures Game. He also was Baseball America's Winter Player of the Year after the 2006 season, batting .318/.393/.530 with nine home runs in 198 at-bats in his native Venezuela. He was back with Zulia this winter as its starting right fielder after an up-and-down season in the minors. Gonzalez got off to his traditional slow start, batting .210 in April, before coming around later in the season, batting .335 with eight of his nine homers in the final two months. He earned a promotion to Triple-A Tucson for the final week of the season. Scouts loved working Double-A Mobile games when both Justin Upton and Gonzalez were in the outfield, as the two seemed to play off each other and enjoyed a friendly rivalry at the plate and in the field.

Gonzalez lacks nothing in the way of physical tools. He has tremendous bat speed, with a pure easiness to his swing that generates plus raw power to all fields. The strength and leverage in his natural inside-out stroke makes the ball jump off his bat. A prototype right fielder, he has an above-average arm and enough speed to play in center field if need be–and in fact he played there quite a bit when Upton was with Mobile. Gonzalez is becoming more comfortable in right field as he gets more time there, learning better routes and whether to uncork a rocket or just hit the cutoff man. In general, his feel for the game has improved.

Scouts and managers often have been turned off by Gonzalez' approach to the game, accusing him of giving away at-bats or not hustling at times. The Diamondbacks have addressed this concern in the past and say it's a case of immaturity and lack of focus but not bad makeup. To the contrary, they say he's a bright, outgoing person who wants to be a star. On a more tangible level, he needs to have a plan every time he goes to the plate, so he doesn't expand his strike zone and get himself out. He gets himself in trouble when he tries to pull the ball too much. He's still an erratic defender, leading the high Class A California and Double-A Southern league in outfield miscues the last two years with 12 each time.

Gonzalez is knocking on the door of the big leagues at age 22, but he needs more at-bats and the Diamondbacks have no opening for him. He'll spend most of 2008 in Triple-A unless injuries create a need for him in Arizona. He could be a valuable trade chip, as it seems unlikely Gonzalez would displace Upton or Chris Young, and Eric Byrnes just signed a $30 million contract extension.

Year	Club (League)	Class	AVG	G	AB	R	H	2B	3B	HR	RBI	BB	SO	SB	OBP	SLG
2003	Missoula (Pio)	R	.258	72	275	45	71	14	4	6	25	16	61	12	.308	.404
2004	South Bend (MWL)	A	.275	14	51	5	14	4	0	1	8	1	13	0	.288	.412
	Yakima (NWL)	A	.273	73	300	44	82	15	2	9	44	22	70	2	.327	.427
2005	South Bend (MWL)	A	.307	129	515	91	158	28	6	18	92	48	86	7	.371	.489
2006	Lancaster (Cal)	A	.300	104	403	82	121	35	4	21	94	30	104	15	.356	.563
	Tennessee (SL)	AA	.213	18	61	11	13	6	0	2	5	7	12	1	.294	.410
2007	Mobile (SL)	AA	.286	120	458	63	131	33	3	16	75	32	103	9	.330	.476
	Tucson (PCL)	AAA	.310	10	42	9	13	5	0	1	11	6	6	1	.396	.500
MINOR LEAGUE TOTALS			.286	540	2105	350	603	140	19	74	354	162	455	47	.341	.476

2 JARROD PARKER, RHP

Born: Nov. 24, 1988. **B-T:** R-R. **Ht.:** 6-2. **Wt.:** 175. **Drafted:** HS—Norwell, Ind., 2007 (1st round). **Signed by:** Mike Daughtry.

Parker drew his first widespread notice pitching for the U.S. junior national team in September 2006, and he continued to shoot up draft boards as a high school senior. He overmatched inferior high school competition in Indiana, going 7-0, 0.20 with 68 strikeouts in 34 innings. The Diamondbacks grabbed him with the ninth overall pick and signed him just before the Aug. 15 deadline for a $2.1 million bonus. Though he didn't pitch during the summer, Parker showed the Diamondbacks his stuff in instructional league, flashing the easy 93-97 mph fastball that so excited scouts. His hard curveball already rates as the best in the system, and he also has a mid-80s slider. He earns comparisons to Tim Lincecum and Scott Kazmir for his quick arm, smooth mechanics and small frame. The Diamondbacks also like his intelligence, attitude, athleticism and how easily he repeats his delivery. Parker is working on getting more separation between his curveball and slider. Though he has a feel for the strike zone and for throwing a changeup, he still needs to work on both. He hasn't thrown a professional pitch yet, but Arizona already believes Parker was worth the price it paid to sign him. He'll make his professional debut at low Class A South Bend.

Year	Club (League)	Class	W	L	ERA	G	GS	CG	SV	IP	H	R	ER	HR	BB	SO	AVG
2007	Did Not Play—Signed Late																

3 BRETT ANDERSON, LHP

Born: Feb. 1, 1988. **B-T:** L-L. **Ht.:** 6-4. **Wt.:** 215. **Drafted:** HS—Stillwater, Okla., 2006 (2nd round). **Signed by:** Joe Robinson.

Anderson's 2.21 ERA would have led the Midwest League had he stuck around long enough to qualify, but he earned a promotion to high Class A Visalia in June. His season effectively ended at the end of July when he and six teammates were in a car accident. Anderson pitched four more innings after sustaining a concussion. You can never say stuff doesn't matter, but with Anderson it's not the most important thing. The son of Oklahoma State coach Frank Anderson, a noted mentor of pitchers, Brett has smooth mechanics and always pitches with a plan. He throws two breaking balls for strikes, and both can be plus pitches, as can his changeup. His fastball usually sits at 90 mph, but his command of it is impeccable. He played some center field in high school, so Anderson has some athleticism. But he has not maintained his conditioning. His body has gotten soft and he doesn't move well around the mound. Anderson has rare command and polish for a pitcher his age, so he could move quickly. He'll get a chance to earn a spot in the Double-A rotation in spring training and profiles as a middle-of-the-rotation innings-eater.

Year	Club (League)	Class	W	L	ERA	G	GS	CG	SV	IP	H	R	ER	HR	BB	SO	AVG
2007	South Bend (MWL)	A	8	4	2.21	14	14	0	0	81	76	26	20	3	10	85	.248
	Visalia (Cal)	A	3	3	4.85	9	9	0	0	39	50	23	21	6	11	40	.311
MINOR LEAGUE TOTALS			11	7	3.07	23	23	0	0	120	126	49	41	9	21	125	.270

4 MAX SCHERZER, RHP

Born: July 27, 1984. **B-T:** R-R. **Ht.:** 6-2. **Wt.:** 210. **Drafted:** Missouri, 2006 (1st round) **Signed by:** Joe Robinson.

The 11th overall pick in 2006, Scherzer pitched for the independent Fort Worth Cats and held out before he would have re-entered the draft pool. Though he projected as no more than a mid-first-rounder the second time around, Arizona gave him a $3 million bonus, $4.3 million in guaranteed money and another $1.5 million in easily reachable incentives. Scherzer's fastball can overmatch batters, arriving in the mid-90s with sinking action at its best. His slider also can be a plus pitch, though he's working on its command and plane. Some scouts who saw Scherzer as a starter at midseason wondered what the fuss was about. His fastball sat at 89-93 mph range, and his overall stuff, command, feel and delivery all drew questions. Then they saw him relieving in the Arizona Fall League and he was a different pitcher, touching 98 mph. Arizona's official opinion is that Scherzer is a starter. If he continues in the rotation, he'll likely open 2008 back in Double-A. If he moves to the bullpen, he could provide immediate help in the big leagues and has the pure stuff to eventually close games.

Year	Club (League)	Class	W	L	ERA	G	GS	CG	SV	IP	H	R	ER	HR	BB	SO	AVG
2007	Visalia (Cal)	A	2	0	0.53	3	3	0	0	17	5	1	1	0	2	30	.089
	Mobile (SL)	AA	4	4	3.91	14	14	0	0	73	64	38	32	3	40	76	.235
MINOR LEAGUE TOTALS			6	4	3.28	17	17	0	0	90	69	39	33	3	42	106	.210

5 GERARDO PARRA, OF

Born: May 6, 1987. **B-T:** L-L. **Ht.:** 6-1. **Wt.:** 186. **Signed:** Venezuela, 2004. **Signed by** Miguel Nava.

Parra followed up his strong U.S. debut in 2006 with the Midwest League (.320) batting title in 2007, also earning a promotion to high Class A for the last month of the minor league season. He capped his year by starting in the outfield alongside Carlos Gonzalez for Zulia in the Venezuelan winter league. Parra leads the next wave of Latin American talent coming through the system, and his tools draw comparisons to Gonzalez in every phase except power. He's the best pure hitter in the system and sprays balls all over the field, showing sound mechanics and a good approach. He has a plus arm and good defensive instincts, and he always plays with energy. Parra hasn't yet shown the power to fit the ideal profile for right field, but his bat speed suggests it could come as he matures. His speed is a tick below-average, though he was playing center field in winter ball, so he'll have to drive more balls out of the park to be a regular. In an organization loaded with talented young outfielders, it's hard to see where Parra will fit. But the logjam also means he'll have time to develop his game. He'll begin 2008 back in Visalia but should move to Double-A at some point during the season.

Year	Club (League)	Class	AVG	G	AB	R	H	2B	3B	HR	RBI	BB	SO	SB	OBP	SLG
2005	Diamondbacks (DSL)	R	.384	64	237	53	91	14	5	6	45	22	25	26	.444	.561
2006	Missoula (Pio)	R	.328	69	271	46	89	18	4	4	43	25	42	30	.386	.469
2007	South Bend (MWL)	A	.320	110	444	64	142	25	4	6	57	30	51	24	.370	.435
	Visalia (Cal)	A	.284	24	102	11	29	2	1	2	14	4	17	2	.303	.382
MINOR LEAGUE TOTALS			.333	267	1054	174	351	59	14	18	159	81	123	75	.385	.467

6 EMILIO BONIFACIO, 2B/SS

Born: April 23, 1985. **B-T:** B-R. **Ht.:** 5-11. **Wt.:** 180. **Signed:** Dominican Republic, 2001. **Signed by:** Junior Noboa.

After four so-so pro seasons, Bonifacio moved into the fast lane by batting .321 with 61 steals in high Class A in 2006. He followed up with a good year in Double-A and made his major league debut in September. Bonifacio's speed rates as either a 70 or 80 on the 20-80 scouting scale, and he plays with energy and passion. He continues to refine his basestealing, picking pitches and counts and getting good breaks, and he has no fear of getting thrown out (though he did get caught 13 times in 54 Double-A attempts). He's an above-average defender at second base, with sure hands, great range and enough arm for shortstop. While Bonifacio draws comparisons to Luis Castillo, he doesn't have Castillo's approach at the plate. Bonifacio's swing isn't conducive to the small-ball game he needs to play, and he still doesn't have a good idea of the strike zone. He also hasn't shown the strength to drive the ball, which could be a problem against quality fastballs at higher levels. Bonifacio is the kind of player managers love to have in the lineup, but if he doesn't improve at the plate he could end up as a utility player. He'll open the season in Triple-A, with Orlando Hudson and Alberto Callaspo ahead of him in the organization's pecking order.

Year	Club (League)	Class	AVG	G	AB	R	H	2B	3B	HR	RBI	BB	SO	SB	OBP	SLG
2002	Diamondbacks (DSL)	R	.300	68	227	60	68	9	5	1	15	51	55	51	.428	.396
2003	Missoula (Pio)	R	.199	54	146	20	29	1	1	0	16	18	43	15	.298	.219
2004	South Bend (MWL)	A	.260	120	411	59	107	9	6	1	37	25	122	40	.306	.319
2005	South Bend (MWL)	A	.270	127	522	81	141	14	7	1	44	56	90	55	.341	.330
2006	Lancaster (Cal)	A	.321	130	546	117	175	35	7	7	50	44	104	61	.375	.449
2007	Mobile (SL)	AA	.285	132	551	84	157	21	5	2	40	38	105	41	.333	.352
	Arizona (NL)	MLB	.217	11	23	2	5	1	0	0	2	4	3	0	.333	.261
MINOR LEAGUE TOTALS			.282	631	2403	421	677	89	31	12	202	232	519	263	.347	.360
MAJOR LEAGUE TOTALS			.217	11	23	2	5	1	0	0	2	4	3	0	.333	.261

7 AARON CUNNINGHAM, OF

Born: April 24, 1986. **B-T:** R-R. **Ht.:** 5-11. **Wt.:** 195. **Drafted:** Everett (Wash.) CC, 2005 (6th round). **Signed by:** Joe Butler/Adam Virchis (White Sox).

DAVID STONER

After earning high Class A Carolina League midseason all-star honors, Cunningham came to the Diamondbacks in a June trade for Danny Richar. A corner outfielder with the White Sox, he played mostly center field after changing organizations. Cunningham is a natural hitter who has a knack for getting the fat part of the bat on the ball, and he can drive pitches from gap to gap. He's a throwback player who always gets his uniform dirty and plays an instinctive game. He has an above-average arm and has enough speed to get by in center field. While Cunningham does everything well, he doesn't do anything exceptionally, leading to questions about whether he'll end up as a tweener. He has a long swing and better pitchers have been able to get inside on him. He also has a tendency to get out of his comfort zone and try to drive the ball too much. Unless Cunningham adds power or shows he can play center field every day, he has the long-term look of a fourth outfielder or platoon player. He'll start 2008 back in Double-A.

Year	Club (League)	Class	AVG	G	AB	R	H	2B	3B	HR	RBI	BB	SO	SB	OBP	SLG
2005	Bristol (Appy)	R	.315	56	222	41	70	10	2	5	25	16	45	6	.392	.446
	Kannapolis (SAL)	A	.115	10	26	7	3	0	0	0	2	3	7	1	.207	.115
2006	Kannapolis (SAL)	A	.305	95	341	58	104	26	3	11	41	34	72	19	.386	.496
2007	Winston-Salem (Car)	A	.294	67	252	51	74	12	5	8	37	34	39	22	.376	.476
	Visalia (Cal)	A	.358	29	123	25	44	11	2	3	20	5	23	5	.386	.553
	Mobile (SL)	AA	.288	31	118	25	34	8	3	5	20	12	27	1	.364	.534
MINOR LEAGUE TOTALS			.304	288	1082	207	329	67	15	32	145	104	213	54	.378	.482

8 CHRIS CARTER, 1B

Born: Dec. 18, 1986. **B-T:** R-R. **Ht.:** 6-4. **Wt.:** 210. **Drafted:** HS—Las Vegas, 2005 (15th round). **Signed by:** George Kachigian/Joe Butler (White Sox).

RODGER WOOD

Not to be confused with the Chris Carter whom the Diamondbacks traded to acquire Emiliano Fruto from the Nationals in August, this slugger joined Arizona in a December deal that sent Carlos Quentin to the White Sox. Carter dropped to the 15th round of the 2005 draft because he was considered a raw project, but he has shown more aptitude more quickly than expected, slugging 51 homers in 273 career games. Carter's calling card is the ability to hit the ball a long way, and he's also showing that he can hit for average and not get himself out chasing bad pitches. An opposing manager who saw him in the low Class A South Atlantic League said that Carter's approach reminded him of a young Jermaine Dye. He has a natural, fluid swing from the right side and generally looks to use the whole field instead of to pull the ball. He has shown the ability to make adjustments from one at-bat to the next. Carter has nothing going for him except for his bat. Drafted as a third baseman, he has migrated across the infield and will have to work hard to become even an adequate defender at first base. He made 11 errors in just 73 games there last season. Carter doesn't run well, has little agility around the bag and has below-average hands. Offensively, strikeouts will be a tradeoff for his power. The California League notoriously favors hitters, and Carter could put up huge numbers at Visalia in 2008. He needs to improve markedly on defense, however, as he doesn't have the option of being a DH now that he's with a National League organization.

Year	Club (League)	Class	AVG	G	AB	R	H	2B	3B	HR	RBI	BB	SO	SB	OBP	SLG
2005	Bristol (Appy)	R	.283	65	233	33	66	17	0	10	37	17	64	2	.350	.485
2006	Kannapolis (SAL)	A	.130	13	46	4	6	3	0	1	5	5	17	0	.231	.261
	Great Falls (Pio)	R	.299	69	251	37	75	21	1	15	59	34	70	4	.398	.570
2007	Kannapolis (SAL)	A	.291	126	467	84	136	27	3	25	93	67	112	3	.383	.522
MINOR LEAGUE TOTALS			.284	273	997	158	283	68	4	51	194	123	263	9	.373	.514

9 REYNALDO NAVARRO, SS

Born: Dec. 22, 1989. **B-T:** B-R. **Ht.:** 5-9. **Wt.:** 160. **Drafted:** HS—Guaynabo, P.R., 2007 (3rd round). **Signed by:** Ray Blanco.

BILL MITCHELL

A product of the Puerto Rico Baseball Academy, Navarro drew interest at a work-out on the island in May. He sealed his match with Arizona by attending a predraft workout in Phoenix, where he looked comfortable in a major league environment. The Diamondbacks took him in the third round and gave him a $330,000 bonus. Navarro has all the tools scouts look for in a shortstop, with plus range as well as quickness, great actions and an average arm. Navarro also showed promise at the plate, with good bat speed and a line-drive stroke. He started switch-hitting full-time during instructional league. Navarro committed a Pioneer League-high 28 errors and will work to become more consistent on routine plays. He needs to get stronger and develop a better approach to become a productive hitter. He's too aggressive at the plate at this point. Ideally, Navarro could become a slick-fielding shortstop who bats in the No. 2 hole and moves the ball around the field. Navarro was sometimes overmatched in the Pioneer League, but the Diamondbacks have no complex team so they had to throw him in the fire. He'll try to win a starting job in low Class A but could spend 2008 at short-season Yakima.

Year	Club (League)	Class	AVG	G	AB	R	H	2B	3B	HR	RBI	BB	SO	SB	OBP	SLG
2007	Missoula (Pio)	R	.250	60	212	21	53	4	0	1	17	6	41	6	.274	.283
MINOR LEAGUE TOTALS			.250	60	212	21	53	4	0	1	17	6	41	6	.274	.283

10 BARRY ENRIGHT, RHP

BILL MITCHELL

Born: March 30, 1986. **B-T:** R-R. **Ht.:** 6-2. **Wt.:** 200. **Drafted:** Pepperdine, 2007 (2nd round). **Signed by:** Hal Kurtzman.

The Diamondbacks made a point of taking Friday night college starters in their 2007 draft, and Enright outperformed them all. He signed quickly for $441,000 as a second-rounder after compiling a 35-8 record in three years at Pepperdine, then didn't allow an earned run in 10 pro appearances. Arizona kept his workload light after he threw 131 innings in the spring. Enright dominated hitters all spring and summer with an average fastball that sits at 88-91 mph and peaks at 92 mph. Command is his forte, but Arizona also loved his willingness to attack hitters and put them away early. He has a great feel for pitching and clean arm action. He also tightened his slider, making it an effective second pitch, and shows a knack for adding and subtracting velocity. None of Enright's offerings are legitimate out pitches, and his curveball and changeup are a notch behind his fastball and slider. He'll have to prove he has the stuff to get more advanced hitters out. Some scouts saw Enright as a middle reliever coming out of the draft, but the Diamondbacks are expecting more. He'll probably open the season in high Class A, where he finished his pro debut.

Year	Club (League)	Class	W	L	ERA	G	GS	CG	SV	IP	H	R	ER	HR	BB	SO	AVG
2007	Yakima (NWL)	A	0	0	0.00	5	0	0	0	8	4	0	0	0	3	12	.148
	South Bend (MWL)	A	0	0	0.00	1	0	0	1	2	1	0	0	0	0	1	.167
	Visalia (Cal)	A	0	0	0.00	4	0	0	1	5	3	1	0	0	2	4	.167
MINOR LEAGUE TOTALS			0	0	0.00	10	0	0	2	15	8	1	0	0	5	17	.157

11 WES ROEMER, RHP

Born: Oct. 7, 1986. **B-T:** R-R. **Ht.:** 6-0. **Wt.:** 200. **Drafted:** Cal State Fullerton, 2007 (1st round supplemental). **Signed by:** Mark Baca.

Roemer had an outstanding season at Cal State Fullerton in 2006, going 13-2, 2.38 as a sophomore. His stock slipped a bit after he went 11-7, 3.19 for the Titans in 2007, getting off to a slow start in part because of a broken pinky. Arizona still took him with the 50th overall pick and signed him for $620,000, then limited his innings after he pitched 144 during the spring. An aggressive, fearless pitcher, Roemer commands the ball effectively and never gives in to hitters. He allowed 44 walks in three college seasons, yet hit 62 batters. His fastball can touch 93 mph, but the Diamondbacks emphasized to him in instructional league that it's more effective when he throws it at 89 with sink. His slider can be a plus pitch. The Diamondbacks are working with Roemer on being more efficient with his pitches, working both sides of the plate and dialing down his stuff to get more grounders. They also want him to pitch more to contact. While he can command his changeup, it still needs work, as does his slider, which remains inconsistent. Roemer has a bit more stuff than polish right now, but if he refines his package he could be an effective back-end starter. He and Barry Enright should open the season together in the Visalia rotation.

Year	Club (League)	Class	W	L	ERA	G	GS	CG	SV	IP	H	R	ER	HR	BB	SO	AVG
2007	Yakima (NWL)	A	1	0	4.50	8	0	0	0	12	11	6	6	1	2	18	.234
MINOR LEAGUE TOTALS			1	0	4.50	8	0	0	0	12	11	6	6	1	2	18	.234

12 BROOKS BROWN, RHP

Born: June 20, 1985. **B-T:** L-R. **Ht.:** 6-3. **Wt.:** 205. **Drafted:** Georgia, 2006 (1st round supplemental **Signed by:** Howard McCullough.

After getting a light workload in 2006 following a busy college season at Georgia that included a trip to the College World Series, Brown occupied what the Diamondbacks hope will be his professional role last season. He ate innings at two minor league stops to finish with 146 in his first full pro year. He's a sinker/

slider pitcher who knows his game and usually pitches to his strengths. He shows plus stuff at times, but his fastball sat more frequently in the high 80s than the low 90s last season, and scouts also thought his slider was fringy at times. His changeup is an average pitch, though he'll need to improve his command of it. Brown's command of all three pitches was shakier in Double-A, but in general he shows a mature approach and a good idea of how to set up hitters. He throws from a three-quarters slot, creating a little bit of deception for hitters, and his strong frame and athletic ability mean he should be durable. In order to pitch in the middle or even the back of a big league rotation, however, he'll have to show more zip on his pitches and sharpen his command. Otherwise he looks more like a middle reliever. Brown will open the season back in Double-A.

Year	Club (League)	Class	W	L	ERA	G	GS	CG	SV	IP	H	R	ER	HR	BB	SO	AVG
2006	Yakima (NWL)	A	0	2	3.42	13	1	0	0	23	23	11	9	2	12	30	.250
2007	Visalia (Cal)	A	6	3	2.81	14	14	0	0	80	66	30	25	2	23	74	.224
	Mobile (SL)	AA	4	4	3.66	12	12	0	0	66	64	30	27	2	36	54	.261
MINOR LEAGUE TOTALS			10	9	3.23	39	27	0	0	170	153	71	61	6	71	158	.242

13 GREG SMITH, LHP

Born: Dec. 22, 1983. **B-T:** L-L. **Ht.:** 6-2. **Wt.:** 190. **Drafted:** Louisiana State, 2005 (6th round). **Signed by:** Matt Valarezo.

Smith pitched his way into prominence in his first full pro season in 2006, reaching Double-A and then emerging as one of Team USA's best starters in its Olympic qualifying tournament in Panama. The extra work caused him to get off to a slow start in 2007, however, and he spent the first month of the season in extended spring training with a tired arm. Once he got into action, he pitched well all year, including a 2.61 ERA in 21 innings in the Arizona Fall League. Smith doesn't have dominant stuff, but he gets hitters out with good command and a great feel for his craft. He's perceptive and knows how to keep batters off balance, skillfully adding and subtracting velocity. He has four legitimate pitches with an 88-91 mph fastball, a cutter, a curveball and a changeup, and he has focused on improving his offspeed offerings. He also has what may be the best pickoff move in the minors. Only 12 runners tried to steal on him in 2007, and just four succeeded. Smith's margin for error is small because he has no out pitch, so it will be important for him to command all his pitches if he's to succeed in the big leagues. He projects as a back-of-the-rotation starter, and while he'll likely open the season in Triple-A, he'll likely get a big league opportunity sometime in 2008.

Year	Club (League)	Class	W	L	ERA	G	GS	CG	SV	IP	H	R	ER	HR	BB	SO	AVG
2005	Missoula (Pio)	R	8	5	4.15	16	14	0	0	82	69	40	38	8	18	100	.231
2006	Lancaster (Cal)	A	9	0	1.63	13	13	2	0	88	57	21	16	3	31	71	.190
	Tennessee (SL)	AA	5	4	3.90	11	11	0	0	60	65	32	26	4	23	38	.284
2007	Mobile (SL)	AA	5	3	3.36	12	12	2	0	69	64	30	26	7	14	62	.251
	Tucson (PCL)	AAA	4	2	3.78	10	10	1	0	52	61	27	22	4	18	34	.296
MINOR LEAGUE TOTALS			31	14	3.27	62	60	5	0	352	316	150	128	26	104	305	.245

14 WILKIN CASTILLO, C/INF

Born: June 1, 1984. **B-T:** B-R. **Ht.:** 6-0. **Wt.:** 170. **Signed:** Dominican Republic, 2003. **Signed by:** Junior Noboa.

Castillo has played all over the diamond for the Diamondbacks, and the organization rewarded his versatility by adding him to the 40-man roster in November. His main position is catcher, and he played 70 games there last season in Double-A. He also played at second base, shortstop, third base and right field, and he was named the utilityman on the Southern League's postseason all-star team. Castillo has the tools to be at least an average defender at every position he plays, and he also could play first base if needed. As a catcher, he's quick and loose behind the plate, and his arm is slightly above-average. His footwork on the exchange is good and he threw out 45 percent of basestealers last year to rank second in the SL, though he can improve his receiving. Castillo also offers versatility at the plate, as a switch-hitter with speed and a little bit of pop. He has good hand-eye coordination and uses the whole field, but he's a free swinger who will expand his zone. He tends to drift through his stroke at times, which limits his power. While he runs well and especially well for a catcher, he needs to be more judicious as a basestealer after getting caught 14 times in 32 tries last year. Castillo's only real plus tool is his versatility, but that makes him an ideal role player on a big league team. He'll move up to Triple-A for 2008.

Year	Club (League)	Class	AVG	G	AB	R	H	2B	3B	HR	RBI	BB	SO	SB	OBP	SLG
2003	Diamondbacks (DSL)	R	.301	59	196	32	59	9	4	1	29	17	28	6	.356	.403
2004	Missoula (Pio)	R	.272	63	243	32	66	13	5	4	32	8	40	5	.308	.416
	Tucson (PCL)	AAA	.150	6	20	2	3	1	0	0	2	3	3	0	.261	.200
2005	South Bend (MWL)	A	.302	113	411	65	124	21	3	6	53	26	38	9	.346	.411
2006	Tucson (PCL)	AAA	.238	6	21	3	5	1	0	1	4	0	8	1	.273	.429

Lancaster (Cal)	A	.285	56	200	25	57	10	1	3	19	13	24	9	.329	.390
Tennessee (SL)	AA	.250	27	76	7	19	3	0	0	5	6	10	1	.314	.289
2007 Mobile (SL)	AA	.302	109	410	50	124	31	3	6	46	17	62	18	.333	.437
MINOR LEAGUE TOTALS		.290	439	1577	216	457	89	16	21	190	90	213	49	.332	.406

15 DANIEL STANGE, RHP

Born: Dec. 22, 1985. **B-T:** R-R. **Ht.:** 6-3. **Wt.:** 185. **Drafted:** UC Riverside, 2006 (7th round). **Signed by** Mark Baca.

Stange was a 33rd-round pick of the Braves coming out of a California high school in 2003, but he didn't sign and instead ended up at UC Riverside, where he became the closer by his junior season. The Diamondbacks drafted him in 2006 and he looked to be on the fast track as a reliever until he got hurt in 2007. He opened the season as the closer in high Class A and saved 16 games before earning a promotion to Double-A in mid-July. He made just five appearances there before getting shut down, then had Tommy John surgery in August. When healthy, Stange has the body and power stuff to pitch at the back of a big league bullpen. He throws his lively fastball at 93-97 mph and can touch 99, and his slider may be an even better pitch. He also has the mentality to take the ball at the end of the game and go right at hitters. Stange throws from a low three-quarters slot, and it was his violent delivery that sent him to the bullpen in the first place. He may have to tone it down to stay healthy. Aside from returning to health, he'll need to refine his command as he moves up. Stange will begin throwing by midsummer but probably won't see any meaningful action until the 2009 season.

Year	Club (League)	Class	W	L	ERA	G	GS	CG	SV	IP	H	R	ER	HR	BB	SO	AVG
2006	Missoula (Pio)	R	5	2	4.25	27	0	0	13	36	39	19	17	2	17	48	.267
2007	Visalia (Cal)	A	4	5	3.19	38	0	0	16	42	37	26	15	3	18	53	.230
	Mobile (SL)	AA	1	0	5.40	5	0	0	1	6	9	4	4	1	2	5	.321
MINOR LEAGUE TOTALS			10	7	3.81	70	0	0	30	85	85	49	36	6	37	106	.254

16 ESMERLING VASQUEZ, RHP

Born: Nov. 7, 1983. **B-T:** R-R. **Ht.:** 6-1. **Wt.:** 168. **Signed:** Dominican Republic, 2003. **Signed by:** Junior Noboa.

A dream season turned into a potential nightmare for Vasquez when he injured his right shoulder diving for a ball in the Arizona Fall League. An MRI revealed a torn labrum, and he was scheduled to rest his shoulder before beginning a strengthening program in January. Before that, he had pitched his way onto the 40-man roster by leading the organization in ERA (2.99), innings (165), strikeouts (151) and opponent average (.217). Vasquez did it with a fastball that usually ranged from 88-93 mph and touched 95, and an effective changeup, complemented by a slurvy breaking ball. He throws all three pitches for strikes, and shows polish even though he spent his first three seasons in the system as a reliever. He now understands that he doesn't have to strike every batter out, and he's learning how to attack hitters. He's wiry but has proven durable as a starter. Scouts, however, don't see a major league out pitch and say he'll have to improve his command as well as his breaking ball. Of more concern in the short team is his health. The Diamondbacks hope Vasquez will bounce back without surgery, but won't know if he can until spring training.

Year	Club (League)	Class	W	L	ERA	G	GS	CG	SV	IP	H	R	ER	HR	BB	SO	AVG
2003	Diamondbacks (DSL)	R	6	2	2.08	12	12	0	0	69	53	21	16	0	19	80	.204
2004	Missoula (Pio)	R	3	2	3.52	19	0	0	5	30	22	15	12	1	21	33	.193
	Yakima (NWL)	A	0	0	6.35	5	0	0	1	5	10	6	4	1	0	7	.370
2005	South Bend (MWL)	A	6	4	3.64	53	0	0	3	71	63	33	29	2	47	79	.238
2006	Lancaster (Cal)	A	4	9	5.89	34	18	0	0	117	129	89	77	9	51	115	.271
2007	Mobile (SL)	AA	10	6	2.99	29	29	0	0	165	125	61	55	11	60	151	.217
MINOR LEAGUE TOTALS			29	23	3.77	152	59	0	9	460	402	225	193	24	198	465	.234

17 DALLAS BUCK, RHP

Born: Nov. 11, 1984. **B-T:** R-R. **Ht.:** 6-3. **Wt.:** 210. **Drafted:** Oregon State, 2006 (3rd round). **Signed by:** Ed Gustafson.

Courage and guile had become Buck's trademarks, but he finally faced reality in the middle of last season and had Tommy John surgery in August. Something had obviously been wrong with his arm for a while, because he had been one of the top prospects for the 2006 draft until his velocity dropped during his junior season. He gutted it out and played a major role in Oregon State's 2006 College World Series championship, but doctors found a partial ligament tear in his elbow after the draft. Signed for a discounted $250,000, he opted for rehab over surgery and made it through 16 starts in high Class A last year. Again it was obvious he wasn't at full strength, however, as he still was throwing at 85-88 mph with a lot of effort. When he's healthy, Buck's fastball is more in the 89-91 mph range, touching 94, and he complements it with a slider and changeup. Interestingly, scouts still liked his pitches when they saw him last year, particularly his changeup and the sink on his fastball, so he still could be a premium pitcher if he gets the power back in his arm. Unfortunately, trying to pitch through the injury now means that both 2007 and 2008 will essentially be lost seasons for him. Depending on how his arm responds, Buck should get some work at the end of this year, but he probably won't do anything meaningful until 2009.

Year	Club (League)	Class	W	L	ERA	G	GS	CG	SV	IP	H	R	ER	HR	BB	SO	AVG
2007	Visalia (Cal)	A	4	4	3.41	16	16	0	0	97	84	49	37	10	31	88	.231
MINOR LEAGUE TOTALS			4	4	3.41	16	16	0	0	97	84	49	37	10	31	88	.231

18 DOUG SLATEN, LHP

Born: Feb. 4, 1980. **B-T:** L-L. **Ht.:** 6-5. **Wt.:** 190. **Drafted:** Pierce (Calif.) JC, 2000 (17th round). **Signed by:** Hal Kurtzman.

Slaten was inconsistent as a starter, and more significant, he couldn't stay healthy, battling shoulder problems in his first few seasons in the system. He moved to the bullpen full-time in 2004, then made the major league club out of spring training last year. He was the primary lefty in an unheralded bullpen that helped carry the Diamondbacks into the playoffs. He still qualifies for this list because he amassed just 36 innings in his 61 appearances. Slaten attacks hitters with a fastball that ranges from 88-92 mph and a slurvy breaking ball. The breaking ball has good depth, and he can add and subtract from it. Both pitches become more effective because he throws them on a good downward plane and he locates well to both sides of the plate. He also improved his focus and confidence last season. Slaten must slow down his changeup to establish himself as more than just a situational lefty. His change runs in the mid-80s now, and he uses it only as a chase pitch for righthanders. He may also add a cut fastball to combat righties. Arizona used him in more than just left-on-left situations last year, and he pitched anywhere from the fifth inning to the end of the game, though the bulk of his appearances were in the seventh and eighth. Slaten will return to a setup role in 2008, and the Diamondbacks hope he's not done improving.

Year	Club (League)	Class	W	L	ERA	G	GS	CG	SV	IP	H	R	ER	HR	BB	SO	AVG
2000	Diamondbacks (AZL)	R	0	0	0.96	9	4	0	0	9	7	1	1	0	3	7	.200
2001	Lancaster (Cal)	A	9	8	4.79	28	27	1	0	157	207	105	84	16	45	110	.312
2002	Lancaster (Cal)	A	1	6	9.00	8	8	0	0	35	59	43	35	4	12	23	.360
	South Bend (MWL)	A	0	0	4.40	7	0	0	0	14	18	8	7	0	4	5	.310
2003	Lancaster (Cal)	A	6	7	6.03	32	19	0	0	119	156	94	80	13	47	78	.316
2004	El Paso (TL)	AA	0	1	10.00	11	0	0	0	9	16	13	10	1	10	6	.390
	South Bend (MWL)	A	5	2	2.25	36	0	0	5	44	44	13	11	2	13	40	.250
2005	Tennessee (SL)	AA	2	2	4.26	58	0	0	1	61	61	45	29	2	26	72	.262
2006	Tennessee (SL)	AA	2	3	1.88	40	0	0	8	43	31	12	9	1	15	59	.209
	Tucson (PCL)	AAA	2	1	0.45	18	0	0	2	20	10	2	1	0	7	21	.152
	Arizona (NL)	MLB	0	0	0.00	9	0	0	0	6	3	0	0	0	2	3	.167
2007	Arizona (NL)	MLB	3	2	2.72	61	0	0	0	36	41	15	11	4	14	28	.275
MINOR LEAGUE TOTALS			27	30	4.68	247	58	1	16	513	609	336	267	39	182	421	.293
MAJOR LEAGUE TOTALS			3	2	2.36	70	0	0	0	42	44	15	11	4	16	31	.263

19 ED EASLEY, C

Born: Dec. 21, 1985. **B-T:** R-R. **Ht.:** 6-0. **Wt.:** 192. **Drafted:** Mississippi State, 2007 (1st round supplemental). **Signed by:** Mike Valarezo.

Easley was a second-team high school All-American in 2004, but he went undrafted because of his strong commitment to Mississippi State. He had a successful career in Starkville, taking the Bulldogs to the College World Series and winning the Johnny Bench award as the nation's top college catcher in 2007. He compiled career highs in most offensive categories as a junior, batting .358 with 12 home runs, and led the Southeastern Conference by throwing out 29 basestealers. The Diamondbacks liked his athleticism and offensive potential, so they took him 61st overall and gave him a $531,000 bonus. He jammed his left thumb early in his pro debut, so he didn't show a lot with the bat. But Arizona sees a solid approach at the plate, with good bat speed and good hands, and they expect him to hit .260-.275 with 15-20 homers each year. He moves well behind the plate, though his arm is just average. He earns high marks for the way he handles a staff. He also runs well for a catcher. Easley could jump to high Class A for his first full season, but there's no need to rush him because of Arizona's young catching depth in the big leagues.

Year	Club (League)	Class	AVG	G	AB	R	H	2B	3B	HR	RBI	BB	SO	SB	OBP	SLG
2007	Yakima (NWL)	A	.250	33	124	21	31	1	1	6	20	9	30	1	.319	.419
MINOR LEAGUE TOTALS			.250	33	124	21	31	1	1	6	20	9	30	1	.319	.419

20 TYRELL WORTHINGTON, OF

Born: Aug. 2, 1988. **B-T:** R-R. **Ht.:** 6-0. **Wt.:** 190. **Drafted:** HS—Winterville, N.C., 2007 (5th round)
Signed by: Howard McCullough.

Worthington looked like a likely college football player after his senior season in high school, when he rushed for 2,591 yards and committed to East Carolina. Most teams considered him a tough sign, but the Diamondbacks got a good read on his commitment to baseball and what it would take to get him under contract. They took him in the fifth round and signed him for $220,000, which was above MLB's slot recommendation but wasn't a bank-breaker by any means. Worthington profiles as a center fielder with legitimate power if everything comes together for him, but that's going to take patience. After watching him in action in a brief stint at short-season Missoula and in instructional league, Arizona saw a lot of bad swings but also signs that he uses his hands well and can put a charge in the ball. He's obviously athletic and is an above-average runner, drawing comparisons to Chris Young. Worthington is also raw in center field, but there too he has the tools, including an average arm, to be a strong defender. He'll probably open the 2008 season in extended spring training before reporting to Yakima. It will be a slow road, but he has as much upside as anyone in the organization.

Year	Club (League)	Class	AVG	G	AB	R	H	2B	3B	HR	RBI	BB	SO	SB	OBP	SLG
2007	Missoula (Pio)	R	.135	13	37	6	5	0	1	0	2	5	11	1	.238	.189
MINOR LEAGUE TOTALS			.135	13	37	6	5	0	1	0	2	5	11	1	.238	.189

21 MATT GREEN, RHP

Born: Jan. 5, 1982. **B-T:** R-R. **Ht.:** 6-5. **Wt.:** 195. **Drafted:** Louisiana-Monroe, 2005 (2nd round). **Signed by:** Mike Valarezo.

Some thought Green was a reach in the second round when the Diamondbacks drafted him in 2005, and in his first two seasons he certainly looked like a bust. He developed slowly at Louisiana-Monroe and wasn't a full-time starter until his redshirt junior year in '05, when he finished fifth in NCAA Division I with 141 strikeouts in 105 innings. Arizona signed him for $500,000, but he didn't show the same stuff and struggled with his command, posting 5.55 and 5.14 ERAs at his first two minor league stops. But Green reinvigorated his prospect status in 2007, again showing a 91-93 mph fastball that peaked a few miles an hour faster, backed by a power slider. Scouts also were impressed by how he competed in the Mobile rotation, as he and Esmerling Vasquez provided a potent 1-2 punch and finished among the Southern League leaders in ERA, innings and strikeouts. Green's mechanics aren't smooth or easy, and his changeup still needs work, as does his command. But with his fastball/slider combo, he should at least end up as a quality reliever. He'll compete for a Triple-A rotation spot this spring and he'll get a big league look soon if he has another strong season.

Year	Club (League)	Class	W	L	ERA	G	GS	CG	SV	IP	H	R	ER	HR	BB	SO	AVG
2005	Missoula (Pio)	R	4	3	5.55	15	12	0	0	60	77	41	37	6	26	59	.316
2006	Lancaster (Cal)	A	5	12	5.14	27	27	0	0	136	182	99	78	18	51	96	.318
2007	Mobile (SL)	AA	12	6	3.95	28	28	0	0	148	151	75	65	15	55	128	.265
MINOR LEAGUE TOTALS			21	21	4.70	70	67	0	0	344	410	215	180	39	132	283	.296

22 SEAN MORGAN, RHP

Born: Jan. 15, 1986. **B-T:** L-R. **Ht.:** 6-3. **Wt.:** 225. **Drafted:** Tulane, 2007 (4th round). **Signed by:** Mike Valarezo.

Diamondbacks scouting director Tom Allison had plenty of background on Morgan because the Brewers, Allison's former organization, drafted him in 2004 out of a Texas high school. He shared outstanding pitcher honors with Yovani Gallardo at the 2003 Perfect Game/Baseball America World Wood Bat Championship, but he fell to the 25th round of the '04 draft because of his strong commitment to Tulane. Allison grabbed him again in 2007 as part of the group of Friday-night college pitchers he took at the top of the draft. A fourth-rounder, Morgan signed for $202,500. He long has been recognized for his outstanding slider, which was one of the best in the 2007 draft, and that pitch and his big body draw comparisons to fellow Texan Jason Jennings. Morgan's fastball sits at 88-92 mph, though he operates at the high end of that range when working out of the bullpen. He hasn't used a changeup much. Morgan has a maximum-effort delivery that affects his command, so the Diamondbacks are trying to smooth it out a bit. He worked in relief in his pro debut after pitching 103 innings for Tulane, and that may be the role he's best suited for down the road. But he'll start his first full season in the rotation at one of Arizona's Class A affiliates.

Year	Club (League)	Class	W	L	ERA	G	GS	CG	SV	IP	H	R	ER	HR	BB	SO	AVG
2007	Yakima (NWL)	A	1	1	5.46	17	0	0	0	28	31	19	17	3	15	29	.277
MINOR LEAGUE TOTALS			1	1	5.46	17	0	0	0	28	31	19	17	3	15	29	.277

23 EMILIANO FRUTO, RHP

Born: June 6, 1984. **B-T:** R-R. **Ht.:** 6-3. **Wt.:** 235. **Signed:** Colombia, 2000. **Signed by:** Curtis Wallace (Mariners).

Fruto continues to show the flashes of pure stuff that have put him on prospect lists for years, mixed with the inconsistency that has him with his third organization in a year. He was originally signed by the Mariners and reached the big leagues in 2006, but Seattle traded him and outfielder Chris Snelling to the Nationals for Jose Vidro after that season. Despite an open casting call for starters last spring, Fruto couldn't make Washington's big league roster, and he went to the Diamondbacks in a three-team trade that sent first baseman Chris Carter (not the No. 8 prospect on this list) from Arizona to Boston and Wily Mo Pena from the Red Sox to the Nationals. Fruto has three quality pitches, with a 92-96 mph fastball, a true curveball and a changeup that at times is his best pitch. He also throws a slider. The problem is that he hasn't developed consistent mechanics to command any of his pitches reliably. He particularly needs to establish better fastball command. He has to back off on his velocity to try to get better control, which makes him more hittable. He's athletic for his size, but both his conditioning and his competitiveness leave something to be desired. Fruto made just six appearances after his trade to the Diamondbacks, so they'll take a longer look at him in spring training and give him a shot to make their big league bullpen.

Year	Club (League)	Class	W	L	ERA	G	GS	CG	SV	IP	H	R	ER	HR	BB	SO	AVG
2001	Mariners (AZL)	R	5	3	5.84	12	12	0	0	61	73	45	40	3	22	51	.291
2002	Wisconsin (MWL)	A	6	6	3.55	33	13	0	1	111	101	57	44	6	55	99	.239
2003	Tacoma (PCL)	AAA	1	0	0.00	1	0	0	0	4	1	0	0	0	2	2	.083
	Inland Empire (Cal)	A	7	8	3.78	42	4	0	7	78	80	43	33	5	38	83	.267
2004	San Antonio (TL)	AA	3	3	5.66	43	1	0	1	68	77	47	43	6	37	56	.277
2005	San Antonio (TL)	AA	2	3	2.57	40	0	0	12	66	56	22	19	6	22	63	.231
	Tacoma (PCL)	AAA	1	2	13.09	9	0	0	0	11	11	17	16	1	11	12	.268
2006	Tacoma (PCL)	AAA	1	3	3.18	28	0	0	10	45	33	23	16	1	21	55	.204
	Seattle (AL)	MLB	2	2	5.50	23	0	0	1	36	34	24	22	4	24	34	.246
2007	Columbus (IL)	AAA	3	9	5.26	18	16	0	0	87	78	52	51	6	59	68	.249
	Tucson (PCL)	AAA	0	1	2.45	6	0	0	0	11	8	3	3	0	10	14	.216
MINOR LEAGUE TOTALS			29	38	4.37	232	46	0	31	545	518	309	265	34	277	503	.252
MAJOR LEAGUE TOTALS			2	2	5.50	23	0	0	1	36	34	24	22	4	24	34	.246

24 CLAYTON CONNER, 3B

Born: Oct. 8, 1986. **B-T:** R-R. **Ht.:** 6-2. **Wt.:** 205. **Drafted:** Wallace State (Ala.) CC, D/F 2006 (45th round). **Signed by:** Mike Valarezo.

Conner was a 31st-round draft pick of the Nationals in 2005 out of a Florida high school, and he went to Okaloosa-Walton (Fla.) CC but didn't sign with Washington as a draft-and-follow. So the Diamondbacks took him in the 2006 draft, then signed him after he spent a season at Wallace State (Ala.) CC, where he batted .466 with 13 home runs in 161 at-bats and nearly won the triple crown in the Alabama Community College Conference. He kept performing in his pro debut, leading Yakima in the triple-crown categories, and his 1.026 OPS would have led the Northwest League if he had enough at-bats to qualify. Conner's most intriguing asset is his combination of big raw power and a good approach at the plate. He's quick to the ball and can drive it to all parts of the park, and he has a feel for the strike zone. He's a big, physical player, but his body has some looseness to it. Still, he's a slightly below-average runner. Defense is the big question for Conner. He made 11 errors in just 36 games at third base in his debut, so he might be better off at first base, where he also saw some action. Arizona also thinks he could handle left field, a position he played as an amateur. For now he'll stay at third and see how far his bat takes him. He'll open 2008 back in low Class A.

Year	Club (League)	Class	AVG	G	AB	R	H	2B	3B	HR	RBI	BB	SO	SB	OBP	SLG
2007	Yakima (NWL)	A	.351	45	171	35	60	12	4	9	45	11	44	0	.400	.626
	South Bend (MWL)	A	.143	11	42	2	6	0	0	1	3	1	16	0	.178	.214
MINOR LEAGUE TOTALS			.310	56	213	37	66	12	4	10	48	12	60	0	.357	.545

25 CYLE HANKERD, OF

Born: Jan. 24, 1985. **B-T:** R-R. **Ht.:** 6-3. **Wt.:** 180. **Drafted:** Southern California, 2006 (3rd round). **Signed by:** Hal Kurtzman.

Hankerd had an auspicious pro debut, winning the Northwest League MVP award and batting title (.384), hitting .369 in 18 games in high Class A and becoming the only 2006 draftee to top 100 hits in his first summer. His first full season in 2007 was a major step down because he was bothered by a sore left wrist all season, and his numbers declined across the board. The injury was diagnosed as tendinitis for much of the year, but he sat out almost all of July and finally had surgery after the season. When healthy, Hankerd is a pure hitter who can drive the ball to all fields and has a great approach at the plate. He showed his desire to get on base last year even when his swing wasn't working, getting hit by a pitch 19 times in 103 games to tie for the California League lead. He should have enough power for an outfield corner, though he's limited to left field because of his below-average speed and arm. He'll have to work to be an average defender there. Hankerd's value is all in his bat, so he'll have to prove his wrist is fine and his swing is back to keep moving through the organization. He's expected to be healthy in spring training and could make the Mobile roster if that's the case.

Year	Club (League)	Class	AVG	G	AB	R	H	2B	3B	HR	RBI	BB	SO	SB	OBP	SLG
2006	Yakima (NWL)	A	.384	54	216	24	83	17	0	4	38	13	54	0	.424	.519
	Lancaster (Cal)	A	.369	18	65	15	24	4	0	8	23	8	9	0	.474	.800
2007	Visalia (Cal)	A	.285	103	386	55	110	27	1	8	54	35	60	2	.368	.422
MINOR LEAGUE TOTALS			.325	175	667	94	217	48	1	20	115	56	123	2	.396	.490

26 JAVIER BRITO, 1B

Born: March 25, 1983. **B-T:** R-R. **Ht.:** 6-2. **Wt.:** 230. **Signed:** Venezuela, 2002. **Signed by:** Miguel Nava.

Brito always has shown a good batting eye since signing out of Venezuela in 2002, but he didn't show much power to speak of until 2006 at the hitter's haven of Lancaster, the Diamondbacks' former high Class A affiliate. He came back to earth a bit in Double-A but still had double figures in home runs, and he was added to the 40-man roster after the season. Brito has the type of approach that the Diamondbacks love, giving him a career .404 on-base percentage. He has a good idea of the strike zone and uses the whole field. To get to the big leagues, he'll have to put balls over the fence more often. Some scouts say he doesn't have enough bat speed to do so, and his swing can get long when he tries to focus on power. That leaves him short of the profile at first base, and moving isn't an option. Even his defense at first is below average, as he's a slow, big-bodied player with heavy legs around the bag. Brito's on-base production will keep earning him opportunities, but unless he develops more power he looks like a backup or a second-division regular. He'll compete for the first-base job in Triple-A this spring.

Year	Club (League)	Class	AVG	G	AB	R	H	2B	3B	HR	RBI	BB	SO	SB	OBP	SLG
2002	Diamondbacks (DSL)	R	.295	59	207	28	61	11	3	4	38	26	42	7	.391	.435
2003	Missoula (Pio)	R	.258	38	97	11	25	3	0	1	7	6	27	2	.324	.320
2004	Missoula (Pio)	R	.310	68	232	36	72	17	1	8	44	16	37	0	.365	.496
2005	South Bend (MWL)	A	.296	78	284	43	84	18	1	5	52	41	37	1	.389	.419
	Lancaster (Cal)	A	.292	25	89	17	26	6	0	2	11	10	17	0	.376	.427
2006	Lancaster (Cal)	A	.356	85	264	63	94	20	1	16	60	44	48	1	.448	.621
2007	Mobile (SL)	AA	.327	127	440	72	144	29	2	11	72	78	90	1	.433	.477
MINOR LEAGUE TOTALS			.314	480	1613	270	506	104	8	47	284	221	298	12	.404	.476

27 HECTOR AMBRIZ, RHP

Born: May 24, 1984. **B-T:** L-R. **Ht.:** 6-1. **Wt.:** 210. **Drafted:** UCLA, 2006 (5th round). **Signed by:** Hal Kurtzman.

Ambriz was one of seven Visalia players (including Brett Anderson) involved in an August car accident that forced the postponement of an Oaks game, but he wasn't injured. It was a bit of good fortune for a player who battled injuries throughout his college career, though Ambriz has been healthy as a pro and was a workhorse in the Visalia rotation. He finished fourth in the California League in strikeouts (133 in 150 innings) and sixth in ERA (4.08). He also won both of his postseason starts, running his innings total to 165 in his first full season. Ambriz throws three pitches for strikes, including a fastball that sits in the low 90s, a splitter and a curveball. His changeup made progress last season to potentially give him a fourth pitch. Scouts, however, don't like his arm action or his big body, and they worry that only his splitter will remain effective at higher levels. He'll also have to tighten up his control against more advanced hitters. Ambriz certainly looked the part of a middle-of-the-rotation workhorse last season, and he'll try to show that again in Double-A.

Year	Club (League)	Class	W	L	ERA	G	GS	CG	SV	IP	H	R	ER	HR	BB	SO	AVG
2006	Missoula (Pio)	R	1	3	1.91	15	4	0	3	42	29	10	9	1	11	52	.192
2007	Visalia (Cal)	A	10	8	4.08	28	26	2	0	150	137	79	68	12	50	133	.241
MINOR LEAGUE TOTALS			11	11	3.60	43	30	2	3	192	166	89	77	13	61	185	.231

28 ALEX ROMERO, OF

Born: Sept. 9, 1983. **B-T:** B-R. **Ht.:** 6-0. **Wt.:** 190. **Signed:** Venezuela, 2000. **Signed by:** Rudy Hernandez (Twins).

Romero came up through the Twins system but got bumped off the 40-man roster after the 2006 season, so the Diamondbacks snatched him up on waivers. He posted career-best numbers in several categories in 2007, and again was one of the toughest batters to strike out in his league. But he didn't earn a callup at the end of the season because fellow waiver pickup Jeff Salazar was a little better than him in just about every area. Romero has a good approach at the plate and clearly is adept at making contact, though he could take more walks. He can play all three outfield positions, though he's best suited for a corner, but he doesn't have enough power to profile as a regular there. With Romero's all-around skills and switch-hitting ability, yet the lack of one dominant tool, he profiles as an ideal fourth outfielder. With the depth in Arizona's outfield, however, it's not clear he'll get that opportunity with the Diamondbacks.

Year	Club (League)	Class	AVG	G	AB	R	H	2B	3B	HR	RBI	BB	SO	SB	OBP	SLG
2001	San Joaquin (VSL)	R	.347	49	167	22	58	9	0	2	30	11	9	10	.388	.437
2002	Twins (GCL)	R	.333	56	186	31	62	13	2	2	42	29	14	16	.423	.457
2003	Quad City (MWL)	A	.296	120	423	50	125	16	3	4	40	43	43	11	.359	.376
2004	Fort Myers (FSL)	A	.292	105	380	59	111	21	2	6	42	54	47	6	.387	.405
2005	New Britain (EL)	AA	.301	139	509	65	153	31	2	15	77	36	69	12	.354	.458
2006	New Britain (EL)	AA	.281	48	167	29	47	11	2	5	16	26	19	15	.384	.461
	Rochester (IL)	AAA	.250	71	236	20	59	8	2	0	26	15	22	6	.300	.301
2007	Tucson (PCL)	AAA	.310	131	535	82	166	32	6	5	66	37	53	12	.354	.421
MINOR LEAGUE TOTALS			.300	719	2603	358	781	141	19	39	339	251	276	88	.365	.414

29 PEDRO CIRIACO, SS

Born: Sept. 27, 1985. **B-T:** R-R. **Ht.:** 6-0. **Wt.:** 150. **Signed:** Dominican Republic, 2003. **Signed by:** Junior Noboa.

Ciriaco remains a raw package of tools—which is pretty much what he was when the Diamondbacks signed him—but he shows enough progress each season that they continue to push him up the ladder. He did make progress at the plate last season, batting .284 in the second half, and he was much more comfortable at the bottom of the order than the top, even showing the willingness to take a walk. He still needs to cut down on his strikeouts, and he'll have to get stronger as well. He also needs to make better use of his above-average speed, as he got caught in 11 of 31 basestealing attempts last season. Ciriaco reduced his errors from 45 in 2006 to 32 in 2007, but consistency on defense remains one of his biggest challenges. He has the tools, including an above-average arm, to play shortstop, but he'll have to continue to cut down on his errors to stay there. Arizona worked Ciriaco out at second and third base in instructional league, and unless he makes significant improvements this season he's probably looking at a career as a utilityman.

Year	Club (League)	Class	AVG	G	AB	R	H	2B	3B	HR	RBI	BB	SO	SB	OBP	SLG
2003	Diamondbacks (DSL)	R	.231	57	221	40	51	10	2	0	16	16	34	14	.290	.294
2004	Diamondbacks (DSL)	R	.349	67	252	45	88	11	4	1	18	19	33	29	.401	.437
2005	Missoula (Pio)	R	.240	69	254	28	61	9	4	2	31	7	50	7	.264	.331
2006	South Bend (MWL)	A	.264	128	550	77	145	15	5	2	32	32	96	19	.308	.320
2007	Visalia (Cal)	A	.251	119	463	61	116	14	5	3	39	20	81	20	.286	.322
MINOR LEAGUE TOTALS			.265	440	1740	251	461	59	20	8	136	94	294	89	.307	.336

30 LEYSON SEPTIMO, LHP

Born: July 7, 1985. **B-T:** L-L. **Ht.:** 6-0. **Wt.:** 150. **Signed:** Dominican Republic, 2003. **Signed by:** Junior Noboa.

Septimo never figured it out at the plate, though he wasn't completely hopeless, as so many conversion cases are. He always rated as the best outfield arm in every league he played in, so the Diamondbacks finally made the move in instructional league after the 2007 season and put him on the mound. Septimo promptly became one of the most talked-about names in advance of the major league Rule 5 draft in December, with reports he had thrown 94-96 mph in his first experience as a pitcher. Teams also had clocked his throws before games from the outfield in the triple digits in the past. Those clubs ultimately decided the gamble wasn't worth a major league roster spot for all of next season, however, and Arizona was happy to sneak him through the Rule 5 process. The decision also will be beneficial to Septimo, who clearly needs plenty of mound time and wouldn't have received it in the big leagues. He showed a plus fastball, particularly for a lefthander, but his entire repertoire is a work in progress. He's working on a slider that shows potential, though his control is a question mark. He'll work out of the bullpen to begin 2008, as a way of controlling his workload and potentially speeding him through the system. He'll likely open the season in high Class A.

Year	Club (League)	Class	AVG	G	AB	R	H	2B	3B	HR	RBI	BB	SO	SB	OBP	SLG
2003	Diamondbacks (DSL)	R	.214	52	182	20	39	10	3	0	21	23	57	1	.319	.302
2004	Diamondbacks (DSL)	R	.276	63	221	29	61	9	3	2	25	14	41	8	.335	.371
2005	Yakima (NWL)	A	.241	67	237	20	57	11	2	2	21	10	51	2	.272	.329
2006	South Bend (MWL)	A	.251	132	529	79	133	22	5	6	51	36	112	10	.310	.346
2007	Visalia (Cal)	A	.271	100	362	54	98	18	2	5	42	23	67	12	.322	.373
MINOR LEAGUE TOTALS			.253	414	1531	202	388	70	15	15	160	106	328	33	.312	.348

Atlanta Braves

BY BILL BALLEW

One of the most successful general managerial runs in baseball history runs came to an end after the 2007 season, when John Schuerholz moved up to team president with the Braves. In 17 years at the helm of the baseball operation, Schuerholz presided over teams that won 14 division titles, five National League pennants and one World Series championship. Frank Wren, who had been Schuerholz' right-hand man and earlier served a one-year stint as Orioles GM, was promoted to replace him.

Change has become commonplace recently in Atlanta, beginning in May 2006 when assistant GM Dayton Moore left to become GM of the Royals. Liberty Media acquired the franchise from Time Warner in a corporate trade in February 2007. Longtime scouting and player development guru Paul Snyder, who was named director of baseball operations after Moore's departure, planned to retire this winter. Bobby Cox, who has managed the club for the last 17-plus seasons, has hinted that he too may step down soon.

Moves under the new ownership suggest the Braves will continue their commitment to player development. In the last year when draft-and-follows were in play, Atlanta signed seven, most notably lefthander Cole Rohrbough for $675,000. They dropped another $4.9 million on the draft and made a splash on the international market by signing Colombian righthander Julio Tehran for $850,000.

Wren also acted quickly to keep continuity in the player development and scouting departments, giving two-year contract extensions to scouting director Roy Clark, farm director Kurt Kemp and director of Latin American operations Johnny Almaraz.

As with the front office, the farm system also has gone through upheaval. The Braves used 18 rookies when they won the NL East in 2005, and they've continued to incorporate young talent the last two seasons. They also shipped five prospects to the Rangers for Mark Teixeira at the trading deadline, including the top three prospects on this list a year ago—catcher Jarrod Saltalamacchia, shortstop Elvis Andrus, lefthander Matt Harrison—and one of their most electric arms, righty Neftali Feliz.

Yet Atlanta hasn't gutted its system. They may not have as many big names, but the Braves still have plenty of promising lefthanded starters and sluggers with all-around games. The first three players the Braves signed out of the 2007 draft (Jason

Cole Rohrbough reflects the Braves' continued commitment to player development

BILL SETLIFF

TOP 30 PROSPECTS

1. Jordan Schafer, of	16. Chad Rodgers, lhp
2. Jason Heyward, of	17. Joey Devine, rhp
3. Jair Jurrjens, rhp	18. Josh Anderson, of
4. Brandon Jones, of	19. Freddie Freeman, 1b
5. Gorkys Hernandez, of	20. Eric Campbell, 3b
6. Brent Lillibridge, ss	21. Van Pope, 3b
7. Cole Rohrbough, lhp	22. Erik Cordier, rhp
8. Jeff Locke, lhp	23. Cory Rasmus, rhp
9. Tommy Hanson, rhp	24. Kris Medlen, rhp
10. Julio Teheran, rhp	25. Kala Ka'aihue, 1b
11. Cody Johnson, of	26. Clint Sammons, c
12. Tyler Flowers, 1b/c	27. Jairo Cuevas, rhp
13. Jon Gilmore, 3b	28. Eric Barrett, lhp
14. Brandon Hicks, ss	29. Diory Hernandez, ss/2b
15. Steve Evarts, lhp	30. Phillip Britton, c

Heyward, Jon Gilmore and Freddie Freeman) added to their collection of athletes with power bats, which already included outfielders Jordan Schafer and Brandon Jones.

Wren added to the system with his first major move, which sent Edgar Renteria to the Tigers for two prospects the day after the World Series ended. Righthander Jair Jurrjens should provide help for the back of the rotation, while Gorkys Hernandez will compete with Schafer to be Andruw Jones' long-term replacement in center field.

General Manager: Frank Wren. **Farm Director:** Paul Snyder. **Scouting Director:** Roy Clark.

Class	Team	League	W	L	PCT	Finish*	Manager	Affiliated
Majors	Atlanta	National	84	78	.519	7th (30)	Bobby Cox	—
Triple-A	Richmond Braves	International	77	64	.546	4th (14)^	Dave Brundage	1966
Double-A	Mississippi Braves	Southern	67	72	.482	5th (10)	Phillip Wellman	2005
High A	Myrtle Beach Pelicans	Carolina	59	80	.424	7th (8)	Rocket Wheeler	1999
Low A	Rome Braves	South Atlantic	66	74	.471	11th(16)	Randy Ingle	2003
Rookie	Danville Braves	Appalachian	48	20	.706	2nd (9)	Paul Runge	1993
Rookie	GCL Braves	Gulf Coast	17	43	.283	15th (16)	Luis Ortiz	1998
Overall 2007 Minor League Record			334	353	.486	21st		

*Finish in overall standings (No. of teams in league) ^League champion

LAST YEAR'S TOP 30

Player, Pos.		Status
1.	Jarrod Saltalamacchia, c	(Rangers)
2.	Elvis Andrus, ss	(Rangers)
3.	Matt Harrison, lhp	(Rangers)
4.	Brandon Jones, of	No. 4
5.	Van Pope, 3b	No. 21
6.	Eric Campbell, 3b	No. 20
7.	Scott Thorman, 1b/of	Majors
8.	Jo-Jo Reyes, lhp	Majors
9.	Joey Devine, rhp	No. 17
10.	Yunel Escobar, ss	Majors
11.	Kala Ka'aihue, 1b	No. 25
12.	Anthony Lerew, rhp	Dropped out
13.	Steve Evarts, lhp	No. 15
14.	Beau Jones, lhp	(Rangers)
15.	Jeff Lyman, rhp	Dropped out
16.	Cory Rasmus, rhp	No. 23
17.	Tommy Hanson, rhp	No. 9
18.	Neftali Feliz, rhp	(Rangers)
19.	Jeff Locke, lhp	No. 8
20.	Chad Rodgers, lhp	No. 16
21.	Dan Smith, lhp	Dropped out
22.	Brayan Pena, c	Dropped out
23.	Jamie Romak, of	(Pirates)
24.	Jamie Richmond, rhp	Dropped out
25.	Chase Fontaine, ss	Dropped out
26.	Clint Sammons, c	No. 26
27.	Jordan Schafer, of	No. 1
28.	Kris Medlen, rhp	No. 24
29.	Kevin Gunderson, lhp	Dropped out
30.	Cody Johnson, of	No. 11

BEST TOOLS

Best Hitter for Average	Jordan Schafer
Best Power Hitter	Jason Heyward
Best Strike-Zone Discipline	Jason Heyward
Fastest Baserunner	Gorkys Hernandez
Best Athlete	Brandon Jones
Best Fastball	Julio Teheran
Best Curveball	Cole Rohrbough
Best Slider	Joey Devine
Best Changeup	Steve Evarts
Best Control	Cole Rohrbough
Best Defensive Catcher	Clint Sammons
Best Defensive Infielder	Van Pope
Best Infield Arm	Van Pope
Best Defensive Outfielder	Jordan Schafer
Best Outfield Arm	Jordan Schafer

PROJECTED 2011 LINEUP

Catcher	Brian McCann
First Base	Mark Teixeira
Second Base	Kelly Johnson
Third Base	Jon Gilmore
Shortstop	Yunel Escobar
Left Field	Jason Heyward
Center Field	Jordan Schafer
Right Field	Jeff Francoeur
No. 1 Starter	Tim Hudson
No. 2 Starter	Jair Jurrjens
No. 3 Starter	Cole Rohrbough
No. 4 Starter	Jeff Locke
No. 5 Starter	Jo-Jo Reyes
Closer	Rafael Soriano

TOP PROSPECTS OF THE DECADE

Year	Player, Pos.	2007 Org.
1998	Bruce Chen, lhp	Rangers
1999	Bruce Chen, lhp	Rangers
2000	Rafael Furcal, ss	Dodgers
2001	Wilson Betemit, ss	Yankees
2002	Wilson Betemit, ss	Yankees
2003	Adam Wainwright, rhp	Cardinals
2004	Andy Marte, 3b	Indians
2005	Jeff Francoeur, of	Braves
2006	Jarrod Saltalamacchia, c	Rangers
2007	Jarrod Saltalamacchia, c	Rangers

TOP DRAFT PICKS OF THE DECADE

Year	Player, Pos. 2007 Org.	
1998	Matt Beslisle, rhp (2nd)	Reds
1999	Matt Butler, rhp (2nd)	Out of baseball
2000	Adam Wainwright, rhp	Cardinals
2001	Macay McBride, lhp	Tigers
2002	Jeff Francoeur, of	Braves
2003	Luis Atilano, rhp	Nationals
2004	Eric Campbell, 3b (2nd)	Braves
2005	Joey Devine, rhp	Braves
2006	Cody Johnson, of	Braves
2007	Jason Heyward, of	Braves

LARGEST BONUSES IN CLUB HISTORY

Jeff Francoeur, 2002	$2,200,000
Matt Belisle, 1998	$1,750,000
Jung Bong, 1997	$1,700,000
Jason Heyward, 2007	$1,700,000
Cody Johnson, 2006	$1,375,000

ATLANTA BRAVES

Top 2008 Rookie: Josh Anderson, of. He hit .358 in a September callup with the Astros and is the heir apparent after coming over in a trade for Oscar Villareal.

Breakout Prospect: Tyler Flowers, 1b/c. Now that he's healthy again, his power could be ready to blossom and he should be able to move back behind the plate.

Sleeper: Phillip Britton, c. Yet another Braves draft-and-follow, Britton is more advanced offensively than defensively.

SOURCE OF TOP 30 TALENT			
Homegrown	25	Acquired	5
College	3	Trades	5
Junior college	2	Rule 5 draft	0
High school	10	Independent leagues	0
Draft-and-follow	6	Free agents/waivers	0
Nondrafted free agents	1		
International	3		

Numbers in parentheses indicate prospect rankings.

LF
Brandon Jones (4)
Cody Johnson (11)
Carl Loadenthal
Matt Young
Chase Fontaine
Concepcion Rodriguez

CF
Jordan Schafer (1)
Gorkys Hernandez (5)
Josh Anderson (18)
Gregor Blanco
Dennis Dixon
Rashod Henry

RF
Jason Heyward (2)
Quentin Davis
Jon Mark Owings

3B
Jon Gilmore (13)
Eric Campbell (20)
Van Pope (21)
Adam Coe
Danny Brezeale

SS
Brent Lillibridge (6)
Brandon Hicks (14)
Samuel Sime

2B
Diory Hernandez (29)
Martin Prado
Michael Fisher
J.C. Holt
Cole Miles

1B
Freddie Freeman (19)
Kala Ka'aihue (25)

C
Tyler Flowers (12)
Clint Sammons (26)
Phillip Britton (30)
Brayan Pena

RHP

Starters	Relievers
Jair Jurrjens (3)	Joey Devine (17)
Tommy Hanson (9)	Kris Medlen (24)
Julio Teheran (10)	Cody Gearrin
Erik Cordier (22)	Blaine Boyer
Cory Rasmus (23)	Charlie Morton
Jairo Cuevas (27)	Ryan Basner
Jamie Richmond	Manny Acosta
Jeff Lyman	Michael Broadway
Anthony Lerew	Benino Pruneda
James Parr	

LHP

Starters	Relievers
Cole Rohrbough (7)	Dan Smith
Jeff Locke (8)	Kevin Gunderson
Steve Evarts (15)	Royce Ring
Chad Rodgers (16)	Lee Hyde
Eric Barrett (28)	
Jose Ortegano	
Kelvin Villa	
Jonny Venters	
Jake Stevens	

2007 SIGNING BUDGET: $4 MILLION

Best Pro Debut: Using a slider as his out pitch, RHP Nick Fellman (12) led the Rookie-level Appalachian League with 12 saves and had a 46-7 K-BB ratio in 28 innings. LHP Cole Rohrbough (22, 2006), one of the game's top draft-and-follows this spring, went 5-2, 1.17 with 96 strikeouts in 61 innings and advanced to low Class A.

Best Athlete: OF Dennis Dixon (5) hadn't played baseball in the last three years and is better known as the quarterback at Oregon, where he had accounted for 21 touchdowns while leading the Ducks to a 5-1 start this fall. He's rusty on the diamond, but Dixon has plenty of arm strength and speed.

Best Pure Hitter: OF Jason Heyward (1) has everything scouts look for in a young hitter. He has a very quick bat and advanced pitch recognition and plate discipline for an 18-year-old. Atlanta also has high hopes for two more high school bats, 3B Jon Gilmore (1s) and 1B Freddie Freeman (2).

Best Power Hitter: Heyward again gets the nod over Gilmore and Freeman.

Fastest Runner: OF Rashod Henry (28) turned down a Southern Mississippi football scholarship to sign for $100,000. Henry has run sub-4.0 times from the right side of the plate to first base.

Best Defensive Player: SS Brandon Hicks (3) has solid speed and range to go with a plus arm.

Best Fastball: Though he's just 5-foot-9 and 170 pounds, RHP Benino Pruneda (31) touches 97 mph. He had the best arm on a loaded San Jacinto (Texas) Junior College staff.

Best Secondary Pitch: RHP Cory Gearrin's (4) sweeping slider, which he throws from a side-arm slot that makes him tough on righthanders. Rohrbough's best pitch, a power curveball, grades better than Gearrin's slider.

Most Intriguing Background: RHP Mitch Harris (24) is the best pitcher in Naval Academy history, capable of reaching 94 mph, but his military commitment precluded him from signing. Gilmore is the brother-in-law of Devil Rays shortstop Ben Zobrist and Dallas Baptist hitting coach Dan Heefner.

Closest To The Majors: Hicks batted .313 in low Class A and went to the Arizona Fall League

to expedite his development. As a reliever, Gearrin could move quicker than Hicks.

Best Late-Round Pick: Henry and Pruneda.

The One Who Got Away: RHP Joshua Fields (2) wouldn't have fallen to the 69th pick if he hadn't lost his command and slider during the spring. The Braves thought he would sign for slot money, but he took his 93-96 mph fastball back to Georgia.

Assessment: As usual, the Braves focused on the Southeast and weren't afraid to take high school players at the top of the draft. They got their top-rated position player with Heyward at No. 14, and Rohrbough might have been a sandwich pick had he re-entered the draft.

2006 BUDGET: $6.2 MILLION

The Braves got an impressive haul of LHPs in Cole Rohrbough (22), Jeff Locke (2), Steve Evarts (1s) and Chad Rodgers (3). OF Cody Johnson (1) rebounded from a bad debut with a big 2007.

GRADE: B

2005 BUDGET: $4.2 MILLION

Atlanta found two potential up-the-middle starters in SS Yunel Escobar (3) and OF Jordan Schafer (3), and stole RHP Tommy Hanson (22) in the late rounds. RHP Joey Devine (1) has been up and down since being rushed to the majors.

GRADE: B+

2004 BUDGET: $1.8 MILLION

The Braves didn't have a first-rounder, and 3Bs Eric Campbell (2) and Van Pope (5) took giants steps backward in 2007.

GRADE: D

2003 BUDGET: $5.0 MILLION

Atlanta already has dealt four of its top seven picks, including C Jarrod Saltalamacchia (1s) and LHP Matt Harrison (3) in the Mark Teixeira trade. OF Brandon Jones (24) and LHP Jo-Jo Reyes (2) are the best of their keepers.

GRADE: B+

Draft analysis by Jim Callis. Numbers in parentheses indicate draft rounds. Budgets are bonuses in first 10 rounds.

ROBERT GURGANUS

JORDAN SCHAFER, OF

Born: Sept. 4, 1986.
Ht.: 6-1. **Wt.:** 190.
Bats: L. **Throws:** L.
Drafted: HS—
Winter Haven, Fla,
2005 (3rd round).
Signed by:
Greg Kilby.

Schafer may have made more progress than anyone in the minor leagues in 2007. After struggling to hit his weight for much of the 2006 season at low Class A Rome, he made adjustments and improvements to lead the minors with 176 hits last year. He also ranked third in the minors with 49 doubles, tied for sixth with 74 extra-base hits and missed nary a beat following his early May promotion to high Class A Myrtle Beach. Schafer first attracted attention when Baseball America rated him the nation's top 13-year-old in 2000, when he started at first base for his high school team as a seventh-grader. He drew some interest as a pitcher, but the Braves wanted to put his solid tools across the board to use in the outfield when they drafted him 107th overall in 2005. After signing for $320,000, Schafer struggled with the bat in his first season and a half. He was hitting just .214 at the end of June 2006, but started to find his groove during the last two months, when he raised his batting average 26 points and hit six of his eight home runs. A baseball rat, he focused nearly every waking moment on his game in the offseason and reaped the rewards in 2007. He batted a combined .312/.374/.513 and was rated the top prospect in the high Class A Carolina League and the sixth-best prospect in the low Class A South Atlantic League.

Schafer has a line-drive stroke from the left side of the plate and the ability to drive and loft the ball. He took off in 2007 after improving his pitch recognition as well as his understanding of what pitchers are trying to do against him. Though projected to be a leadoff hitter, he has the ability to hit anywhere in the top third in the batting order. Schafer's defensive wizardry has been evident since he signed with Atlanta. He has advanced instincts in center field with immediate recognition of the ball off the bat, a lightning-quick first step and impeccable routes. He frequently makes highlight-reel catches. The owner of a high-80s fastball as a high school pitcher, Schafer has a plus-plus arm as an outfielder. He has solid speed and should be at least a 20-20 man in his major league prime.

Despite making solid adjustments at the plate, Schafer still swings and misses more often than a leadoff hitter should. If he can cut down on his strikeouts, he'll be even more dangerous at the plate. Though he ranked fifth in the system with 23 steals in 2007, he also was caught 15 times and must learn how to read pitchers better so he can improve his jumps.

Despite the arrival of Gorkys Hernandez in the Edgar Renteria trade, Schafer eventually should be Andruw Jones' long-term replacement in center field, and some club officials believe he could take over in 2008. But he has yet to play above high Class A and may struggle to make consistent contact against big league pitchers. He's ready to make the jump from a defensive standpoint, but he'd benefit from another full season in the minors, starting at Double-A Mississippi.

Year	Club (League)	Class	AVG	G	AB	R	H	2B	3B	HR	RBI	BB	SO	SB	OBP	SLG
2005	GCL Braves (GCL)	R	.203	49	182	18	37	12	3	3	19	13	49	13	.256	.352
2006	Rome Braves (SAL)	A	.240	114	388	49	93	15	7	8	60	28	95	15	.293	.376
2007	Rome Braves (SAL)	A	.372	30	129	16	48	15	2	5	20	16	31	4	.441	.636
	Myrtle Beach Pelicans (Car)	A	.294	106	436	70	128	34	8	10	43	40	95	19	.354	.477
MINOR LEAGUE TOTALS			.270	299	1135	153	306	76	20	26	142	97	270	51	.328	.441

2 JASON HEYWARD, OF

Born: Aug. 9, 1989. **B-T:** L-L. **Ht.:** 6-4. **Wt.:** 220. **Drafted:** HS—McDonough, Ga., 2007 (1st round). **Signed by:** Brian Bridges.

DAVID STONER

Another high-profile Braves pick from the Atlanta area, Heyward led Henry County to its first state title as a junior and batted .520 with eight home runs in 52 at-bats as a senior. He slipped to Atlanta with the 14th pick, mostly because opponents pitched around him so much in the spring that clubs had difficulty getting a good look at him. Signed for $1.7 million, he homered in his first professional game. Heyward has the physical attributes and instincts to be a star. His raw power is off the charts and his bat speed is nearly as good. He shows impressive plate discipline and pitch recognition. He's a good baserunner and has a plus arm with good carry. Heyward just needs to fine-tune his game. His patience leads to Frank Thomas comparisons, though he could be more productive by turning up his aggressiveness. He's discovering how to use his hands to drive the ball and will improve his batting average by using the entire field. His routes and ability to move back on fly balls need work. Though only 18, Heyward looks like a man among boys. He profiles well as a right fielder and should move quickly through the system, and he will open his first full season in low Class A.

Year	Club (League)	Class	AVG	G	AB	R	H	2B	3B	HR	RBI	BB	SO	SB	OBP	SLG
2007	Braves (GCL)	R	.296	8	27	1	8	4	0	1	5	2	4	1	.355	.556
	Danville (Appy)	R	.313	4	16	3	5	1	0	0	1	1	5	0	.353	.375
MINOR LEAGUE TOTALS			.302	12	43	4	13	5	0	1	6	3	9	1	.354	.488

3 JAIR JURRJENS, RHP

Born: Jan. 29, 1986. **B-T:** R-R. **Ht.:** 6-1. **Wt.:** 160. **Signed:** Curacao, 2003. **Signed by:** Greg Smith (Tigers).

STEVE MOORE

Jurrjens became the first Curacao native to pitch in the majors last August when he held the Indians to one hit in seven innings. In need of a shortstop, the Tigers swapped him and Gorkys Hernandez for Edgar Renteria after the season. Jurrjens goes after hitters with a two-seam fastball with plenty of sink or a four-seamer than ranges from 92-95 mph with late life and armside run. He has good arm speed and sinking action on his changeup. His curveball can be inconsistent but has good downer action. Both his changeup and curve are plus pitches when they're on. He's athletic and throws strikes with a fluid delivery. He's fearless on the mound. Jurrjens' command isn't as fine as his control, and at times he leaves pitches up in the strike zone. Durability is his primary concern. He missed the end of 2006 with shoulder spasms, and was sidelined for two weeks in June (groin) and again in September (shoulder inflammation). He failed to record an out in the fourth inning of his final two starts with the Tigers, and his workload was enough of a concern that they scratched him from the Arizona Fall League for a second consecutive year. It's not easy to trade for a quality young starter these days, but Atlanta did that thanks to its depth at shortstop. Jurrjens will get every opportunity to crack the big league rotation in spring training and profiles as a No. 3 starter with a ceiling as a No. 2.

Year	Club (League)	Class	W	L	ERA	G	GS	CG	SV	IP	H	R	ER	HR	BB	SO	AVG
2003	Tigers (GCL)	R	2	1	3.21	7	2	0	0	28	33	16	10	3	3	20	.292
2004	Tigers (GCL)	R	4	2	2.27	6	6	2	0	39	25	16	10	2	10	39	.171
	Oneonta (NYP)	A	1	5	5.31	7	7	0	0	39	50	25	23	0	10	31	.311
2005	West Michigan (MWL)	A	12	6	3.41	26	26	0	0	142	132	62	54	5	36	108	.246
2006	Lakeland (FSL)	A	5	0	2.08	12	12	0	0	73	53	23	17	4	10	59	.198
	Erie (EL)	AA	4	3	3.36	12	12	0	0	67	71	30	25	7	21	53	.277
2007	Erie (EL)	AA	7	5	3.20	19	19	1	0	112	112	43	40	7	31	94	.257
	Detroit (AL)	MLB	3	1	4.70	7	7	0	0	30	24	16	16	4	11	13	.220
MINOR LEAGUE TOTALS			35	22	3.20	89	84	3	0	502	476	215	179	28	121	404	.248
MAJOR LEAGUE TOTALS			3	1	4.70	7	7	0	0	30	24	16	16	4	11	13	.220

4 BRANDON JONES, OF

Born: Dec. 10, 1983. **B-T:** L-R. **Ht.:** 6-1. **Wt.:** 210. **Drafted:** Tallahassee (Fla.) CC, D/F 2003 (24th round). **Signed by:** Al Goetz.

ED WOLFSTEIN

A three-sport standout in high school who had offers to play college football, Jones took his game to the next level in 2007. After battling injuries the previous two seasons, he drove in 100 runs between the top two levels in the system and made his major league debut in September. His managers and coaches rave about Jones' presence and even-keel approach on the field. He carries himself with confidence and works tirelessly. He has budding power with a quick line-drive swing and a feel for the strike zone. An all-around athlete, he has improved his ability to use the entire field as well as the patience to wait for his pitch. He has plus speed and solid arm strength. While Jones' bat is ready for the majors, he needs to upgrade his defense in left field. He's taking better routes on fly balls, but he has to improve his throwing accuracy. While he runs the bases well, he can become a more proficient basestealer after getting caught seven times in 24 tries in 2007. The Braves consider Jones their long-term answer in left field, where Matt Diaz and Willie Harris split time last season. Jones probably will get another few months at Triple-A Richmond.

Year	Club (League)	Class	AVG	G	AB	R	H	2B	3B	HR	RBI	BB	SO	SB	OBP	SLG
2004	Danville (Appy)	R	.297	57	209	35	62	6	5	3	33	23	33	4	.366	.416
2005	Braves (GCL)	R	.125	2	8	0	1	0	0	0	2	0	2	0	.125	.125
	Danville (Appy)	R	.286	2	7	0	2	0	0	0	1	1	0	0	.375	.286
	Rome (SAL)	A	.308	43	156	37	48	12	3	8	27	29	29	4	.423	.577
	Myrtle Beach (Car)	A	.350	17	60	7	21	4	0	0	5	9	9	0	.437	.417
2006	Myrtle Beach (Car)	A	.257	59	226	27	58	10	3	7	35	25	49	11	.329	.420
	Mississippi (SL)	AA	.273	48	176	18	48	9	3	7	25	15	38	4	.326	.477
2007	Mississippi (SL)	AA	.293	94	365	58	107	21	6	15	74	44	84	12	.368	.507
	Richmond (IL)	AAA	.300	44	170	26	51	12	1	4	26	17	36	5	.363	.453
	Atlanta (NL)	MLB	.158	5	19	0	3	1	0	0	4	0	8	0	.190	.211
MINOR LEAGUE TOTALS			.289	366	1377	208	398	74	21	44	228	163	280	40	.364	.469
MAJOR LEAGUE TOTALS			.158	5	19	0	3	1	0	0	4	0	8	0	.190	.211

5 GORKYS HERNANDEZ, OF

PAUL GIERHART

Born: Sept. 7, 1987. **B-T:** R-R. **Ht.:** 6-0. **Wt.:** 175. **Signed:** Venezuela, 2005. **Signed by:** Ramon Pena (Tigers).

While in the Tigers organization, Hernandez had an impressive encore after winning the Rookie-level Gulf Coast League batting crown in his 2006 U.S. debut. He played in the Futures Game and served as the catalyst for the low Class A Midwest League champions. He won the league's MVP award and stolen base title. Hernandez draws comparisons to a young Kenny Lofton as a speedster with gap power. He makes good contact and has shown the ability to make adjustments against experienced pitchers. His well-above-average speed makes him a threat on the basepaths and allows him to run down fly balls in the gaps. He even has a strong arm for a center fielder. Hernandez needs to add muscle for more power. He has tools to bat leadoff, but needs to use his speed better on the bases and continue to improve his plate discipline. The Tigers wanted to upgrade at shortstop and Hernandez became expendable with Curtis Granderson and Cameron Maybin ahead of him. Hernandez likely will open 2008 in high Class A, with a chance for a midseason promotion to Double-A. He has a lot of upside, but he also has a lot of young outfielders to contend with in the Braves system.

Year	Club (League)	Class	AVG	G	AB	R	H	2B	3B	HR	RBI	BB	SO	SB	OBP	SLG
2005	Tigers (DSL)	R	.265	63	211	44	56	10	0	4	19	30	38	10	.377	.370
2006	Tigers (GCL)	R	.327	50	205	41	67	9	2	5	23	10	27	20	.356	.463
2007	West Michigan (MWL)	A	.293	124	481	84	141	25	5	4	50	36	69	54	.344	.391
MINOR LEAGUE TOTALS			.294	237	897	169	264	44	7	13	92	76	134	84	.355	.402

6 BRENT LILLIBRIDGE, SS

STEVE MOORE

Born: Sept. 18, 1983. **B-T:** R-R. **Ht.:** 5-11. **Wt.:** 180. **Drafted:** Washington, 2005 (4th round). **Signed by:** Greg Hopkins (Pirates).

Acquired from Pittsburgh in the deal that sent Adam LaRoche to the Pirates last offseason, Lillibridge served as a catalyst on Richmond's International League championship club. He led the system with 42 steals and posted a hit in each of his nine playoff games. R-Braves manager Dave Brundage said Lillibridge improved more over the course of the season than any player on his club. Lillibridge has the tools to hit leadoff, plus the range and arm strength to play shortstop in the major leagues. His hands work well at the plate and he's adept at using the entire field. He also drives the ball well for a player his size. With above-average speed and savvy, he has succeeded in 79 percent of his pro steal attempts. Lillibridge thinks of himself as a middle-of-the-lineup hitter too often. He needs to reduce his strikeouts by shortening his swing and controlling the zone better. He also needs to upgrade his bunting ability and become more of a small-ball player. He doesn't always deal with failure well, though he's doing better as he matures. Once Lillibridge plays to his strengths he'll be ready to contribute at the major league level. He'll open 2008 in Triple-A.

Year	Club (League)	Class	AVG	G	AB	R	H	2B	3B	HR	RBI	BB	SO	SB	OBP	SLG
2005	Williamsport (NYP)	A	.243	42	169	19	41	12	4	4	18	14	35	10	.305	.432
2006	Hickory (SAL)	A	.299	74	274	59	82	18	5	11	43	51	61	29	.414	.522
	Lynchburg (Car)	A	.313	54	201	47	63	10	3	2	28	36	43	24	.426	.423
2007	Mississippi (SL)	AA	.275	52	204	31	56	8	3	3	17	20	60	14	.355	.387
	Richmond (IL)	AAA	.287	87	321	47	92	14	2	10	41	20	59	28	.331	.436
MINOR LEAGUE TOTALS			.286	309	1169	203	334	62	17	30	147	141	258	105	.369	.445

7 COLE ROHRBOUGH, LHP

BILL SETLIFF

Born: May 23, 1987. **B-T:** L-L. **Ht.:** 6-3. **Wt.:** 205. **Drafted:** Western Nevada CC, D/F 2006 (22nd round). **Signed by:** Tim Moore.

After earning all-tournament honors at the Junior College World Series, Rohrbough capped Atlanta's final class of draft-and-follows by signing for $675,000. Rohrbough ranked as the No. 1 prospect in the Rookie-level Appalachian League and was just as dominant in six starts in low Class A after getting promoted. Danville pitching coach Jim Czajkowski realized that Rohrbough became untouchable when his arm slot rose and was more hittable when he dropped down. When he maintained the higher angle, his fastball went from sitting in the high 80s to regularly touching 94. He also has a plus power curveball with sharp, late break. He studies hitters and already mixes his pitches like a veteran. Rohrbough needs to improve his changeup consistency and repeat his delivery. Experience should take care of both flaws. Rohrbough has the best fastball-curveball combination in the system. He moved quickly in his debut and could continue at that same rapid rate. Though he may return to Rome to begin 2008, he should reach high Class A by midseason.

Year	Club (League)	Class	W	L	ERA	G	GS	CG	SV	IP	H	R	ER	HR	BB	SO	AVG
2007	Danville (Appy)	R	3	2	1.08	8	7	0	0	33	20	8	4	1	8	58	.167
	Rome (SAL)	A	2	0	1.29	6	6	0	0	28	13	7	4	1	12	38	.138
MINOR LEAGUE TOTALS			5	2	1.17	14	13	0	0	61	33	15	8	2	20	96	.154

8 JEFF LOCKE, LHP

BILL SETLIFF

Born: Nov. 20, 1987. **B-T:** L-L. **Ht.:** 6-2. **Wt.:** 180. **Drafted:** HS—Conway, N.H., 2006 (2nd round). **Signed by:** Lonnie Goldberg.

The 51st overall pick in the 2006 draft, Locke looks like the best pitcher from New Hampshire since Chris Carpenter was drafted in 1993. He lost his first outing at Rookie-level Danville last summer before going 7-0 the rest of the way, allowing just 10 earned runs over his last 10 starts. Locke's command is as impressive as his fastball, which usually ranges from 90-94 mph with significant movement. He also pounds the strike zone with a hard-breaking curveball (which has the makings of a plus pitch) and an improved changeup. He has confidence in all three pitches. His herky-jerky delivery creates deception. As a high school pitcher from the Northeast, Locke was more raw than most pitchers when he signed. He still gets out of sync with his delivery and needs to repeat it more consistently. He must do a better job of handling the finer points of pitching, such as fielding his position and backing up bases. Locke is a fearless competitor who shows every indication of developing into a premier lefthanded starter. He'll start 2008 in the low Class A rotation.

Year	Club (League)	Class	W	L	ERA	G	GS	CG	SV	IP	H	R	ER	HR	BB	SO	AVG
2006	Braves (GCL)	R	4	3	4.22	10	5	0	0	32	38	18	15	4	5	38	.299
2007	Danville (Appy)	R	7	1	2.66	13	11	0	1	61	48	23	18	2	8	74	.213
MINOR LEAGUE TOTALS			11	4	3.19	23	16	0	1	93	86	41	33	6	13	112	.244

9 TOMMY HANSON, RHP

TOM PRIDDY

Born: Aug. 28, 1986. **B-T:** R-R. **Ht.:** 6-6. **Wt.:** 210. **Drafted:** Riverside (Calif.) CC, D/F 2005 (22nd round). **Signed by:** Tom Battista.

Hanson entered pro ball a year before Rohrbough, passing up the chance to attend Arizona State to sign for $325,000. Hanson won just five games in his first full pro season, but pitched well at two Class A stops. Hanson throws three pitches for strikes: an 89-92 fastball with above-average life, a nasty overhand curveball with tight spin and 12-to-6 break, and an average changeup that continues to improve. He has a strong mound presence, the frame to throw on a steep downhill angle and isn't afraid to challenge hitters. He changes planes well and uses both sides of the plate. Hanson tends to rely too much on one pitch, particularly his fastball, when his other offerings aren't working. He also tends to pitch up in the strike zone, leaving him vulnerable to home runs. He gave up 10 longballs in just 60 innings in high Class A. A potential middle-of-the-rotation starter, Hanson has moved quickly while making adjustments against experienced competition. He will likely return to Myrtle Beach, but could earn a midseason promotion.

Year	Club (League)	Class	W	L	ERA	G	GS	CG	SV	IP	H	R	ER	HR	BB	SO	AVG
2006	Danville (Appy)	R	4	1	2.09	13	8	0	0	51	42	15	12	2	9	56	.218
2007	Rome (SAL)	A	2	6	2.59	15	14	0	0	73	51	28	21	6	26	90	.194
	Myrtle Beach (Car)	A	3	3	4.20	11	11	0	0	60	53	33	28	10	32	64	.243
MINOR LEAGUE TOTALS			9	10	2.97	39	33	0	0	184	146	76	61	18	67	210	.217

10 JULIO TEHERAN, RHP

Born: Jan. 28, 1991. **B-T:** R-R. **Ht.:** 6-2. **Wt.:** 160. **Signed:** Colombia, 2007.
Signed by: Miguel Teheran/Carlos Garcia.

The Braves believe they signed the top amateur pitcher in Latin America when they inked Teheran for $850,000. His cousin Miguel is one of the scouts who signed him for the Braves, and he reportedly turned down a higher offer from the Yankees. He showed every indication during instructional league that he'll be as good as advertised. Teheran is a mature teenager with a vast repertoire, great makeup and tremendous upside. Scouts love how easily the ball comes out of his hand and how loose his arm works. His fastball sat at 94-95 during instructional league. He throws an advanced changeup at 81-82 with good sinking action. His 78-79 mph curveball has late, hard bite. Teheran has a pump delivery and struggles at times with his command. His arm action is a little short in the backside and he needs to get stronger, which should occur naturally as he matures physically. Teheran has a chance to move rapidly through the system and become a standout at the major league level. The Braves have no plans to rush him, and likely will send him to the Gulf Coast League in 2008 in order to help him adapt to pro ball and a new culture.

Year	Club (League)	Class	W	L	ERA	G	GS	CG	SV	IP	H	R	ER	HR	BB	SO	AVG
Has Not Played—Signed 2008 Contract																	

11 CODY JOHNSON, OF

Born: Aug. 18, 1988. **B-T:** L-R. **Ht.:** 6-4. **Wt.:** 200. **Drafted:** HS—Lynn Haven, Fla., 2006 (1st round).
Signed by: Al Goetz.

Criticism was commonplace a year ago after the Braves' 2006 first-round draft pick struggled mightily in all aspects of the game in his pro debut. Johnson quieted the critics in his second season, however, after brutalizing Appalachian League pitchers and pacing the loop in homers, extra-base hits and slugging percentage. Johnson admits he employs the swing-hard-in-case-you-hit-it strategy, and the result is screaming 2-iron line drives to all fields. He gets good extension with his long arms and drives balls long distances. He has solid-average speed and is an underrated baserunner who takes the extra base and went 7-for-7 stealing bases last summer. No one doubts his power, but Johnson is streaky and some scouts still question how much he'll hit for average at higher levels. He still struggles with pitch recognition and rarely tones down his aggressiveness. His big swing has holes and he doesn't adjust with two strikes. After struggling at first base in his debut, he moved to left field in 2007 and still has a lot of work to do with his routes and throwing accuracy. The Braves realized Johnson was a work in progress when they drafted him and will be patient. They're hoping he'll make more progress this year in low Class A.

Year	Club (League)	Class	AVG	G	AB	R	H	2B	3B	HR	RBI	BB	SO	SB	OBP	SLG
2006	Braves (GCL)	R	.184	32	114	13	21	6	1	1	16	12	49	2	.260	.281
2007	Danville (Appy)	R	.305	63	243	51	74	18	5	17	57	26	72	7	.374	.630
MINOR LEAGUE TOTALS			.266	95	357	64	95	24	6	18	73	38	121	9	.338	.518

12 TYLER FLOWERS, 1B/C

Born: Jan. 24, 1986. **B-T:** R-R. **Ht.:** 6-4. **Wt.:** 220. **Drafted:** Chipola (Fla.) JC, D/F 2005 (33rd round).
Signed by: Al Goetz.

The fourth draft-and-follow on this Top 10, Flowers began his pro career in inauspicious fashion. He tested positive for performance-enhancing drugs shortly after signing in May 2006, and his 50-game suspension cost him the first month of the 2007 season. After returning, he ranked among the system's leaders in most offensive categories, including second-place finishes in doubles and RBIs. Flowers has a disciplined approach and hits line drives with authority to all fields. He trusts his hands and drives through the ball. His home run total could increase significantly as he develops more loft in his swing. The Braves consider him the best receiver in their system behind Clint Sammons. Flowers has excellent lateral movement for his size, with consistent hands and a strong arm. In part because he had knee surgery last March and spent much of his first full season at first base, Flowers has little experience handling professional pitchers. He wasn't 100 percent behind the plate in 2007, as evidenced by throwing out just four of 24 basestealers. He moves well for a big man but is still a below-average runner. The Braves aren't concerned about future performance-enhancing drug use and say he simply made a bad decision while still at Chipola (Fla.) JC. Flowers has shown what he's capable of accomplishing from an offensive perspective, and he'll be even more valuable if he returns behind the plate on a full-time basis in 2008. After catching and playing first base in Hawaii Winter Baseball, he'll make the jump to high Class A.

Year	Club (League)	Class	AVG	G	AB	R	H	2B	3B	HR	RBI	BB	SO	SB	OBP	SLG
2006	Danville (Appy)	R	.279	34	129	24	36	9	0	5	16	16	30	0	.373	.465
2007	Rome (SAL)	A	.298	106	389	65	116	34	2	12	70	49	74	3	.378	.488
MINOR LEAGUE TOTALS			.293	140	518	89	152	43	2	17	86	65	104	3	.376	.483

13 JON GILMORE, 3B

Born: Aug. 23, 1988. **B-T:** R-R. **Ht.:** 6-3. **Wt.:** 195. **Drafted:** HS—Iowa City, Iowa, 2007 (1st round supplemental). **Signed by:** Terry Tripp.

After taking Cody Johnson in the first round in 2006 and Jason Heyward with the 14th overall pick in 2007, the Braves continued to add power bats by drafting Gilmore with the 33rd overall selection last June. Gilmore jumped on the national radar with an impressive showing at the 2006 Area Code Games before a hamstring injury limited him as a high school senior. Since signing with Atlanta for a $900,000 bonus, Gilmore has shown the tools to be an old-school power-hitting third baseman. A solid athlete who drew interest from college football programs as a quarterback, he has a quick bat that can drive the ball out of the park to all fields. In addition to his sweet, smooth swing, he displays outstanding balance at the plate and a great approach. He played shortstop in high school but shifted to third base in his pro debut, making a relatively smooth transition. While he has soft hands and a strong, accurate arm, he needs to improve his footwork and shorten his arm action in order to become a plus defender. Gilmore has a strong desire to succeed and can be excessively hard on himself when he fails to live up to his high expectations. His brothers-in-law include Devil Rays shortstop Ben Zobrist and Dallas Baptist hitting coach Dan Heefner. Because he's a young player from the Upper Midwest, Atlanta won't rush Gilmore. He'll likely open 2008 at Danville though he has a chance to see low Class A at some point during the season.

Year	Club (League)	Class	AVG	G	AB	R	H	2B	3B	HR	RBI	BB	SO	SB	OBP	SLG
2007	Braves (GCL)	R	.284	43	162	11	46	5	1	1	29	4	28	0	.296	.346
MINOR LEAGUE TOTALS			.284	43	162	11	46	5	1	1	29	4	28	0	.296	.346

14 BRANDON HICKS, SS

Born: Sept. 14, 1985. **B-T:** R-R. **Ht.:** 6-2. **Wt.:** 200. **Drafted:** Texas A&M, 2007 (3rd round). **Signed by:** Chris Knabenshue.

For a player who went undrafted after leading San Jacinto (Texas) to the Junior College World Series in 2006, Hicks proved that he can have a significant impact at higher levels. The shortstop helped Texas A&M turn its program around with a solid junior season before signing with Atlanta for $283,500 as a third-round pick in June. Following a brief stint in Rookie ball, Hicks and fellow 2007 draftee Travis Jones brought a winning attitude to Rome, helping the young club compete for a playoff spot late in the season before falling short. An excellent all-around athlete who also showed a low-90s fastball as a pitcher at San Jacinto, Hicks is a consistent defender at shortstop with solid range and a strong arm. Though some scouts questions his ability to hit with wood, his bat has shown steady development and he has proven capable of making adjustments. He answered many of those doubts during his pro debut, but he still needs to improve at maintaining his overall balance and keeping his head in against breaking balls. The Braves envision Hicks remaining at shortstop for the long haul, and he could open 2008 in high Class A after spending the offseason in the Arizona Fall League.

Year	Club (League)	Class	AVG	G	AB	R	H	2B	3B	HR	RBI	BB	SO	SB	OBP	SLG
2007	Danville (Appy)	R	.224	18	58	14	13	3	1	3	13	12	18	1	.370	.466
	Rome (SAL)	A	.313	37	128	26	40	11	0	4	15	27	26	5	.433	.492
MINOR LEAGUE TOTALS			.285	55	186	40	53	14	1	7	28	39	44	6	.413	.484

15 STEVE EVARTS, LHP

Born: Oct. 13, 1987. **B-T:** L-L. **Ht.:** 6-3. **Wt.:** 180. **Drafted:** HS—Tampa, 2006 (1st round supplemental). **Signed by:** Gregg Kilby.

The 43rd overall pick in the 2006 draft, Evarts continued to impress last year with his ability to pound the strike zone. After a strong pro debut, he overcame some legal problems to post an impressive follow-up at Danville, where he had a 34-4 K-BB ratio and didn't allow a homer in 37 innings. Evarts has an excellent feel for pitching, throws strikes with three pitches and consistently stays ahead in the count. His velocity was a little down last summer, as his fastball sat at 87-89 mph compared to 89-91 mph in 2006, but Atlanta has no concerns in that regard. A changeup that acts like a screwball is his best pitch. He's the quintessential lanky lefty with smooth mechanics and the ability to repeat his delivery. The biggest thing he's working on is keeping his arm slot consistent, especially staying on top of his slurvy breaking ball instead of dropping down, which tends to flatten the pitch. Some scouts questioned Evarts' makeup prior to the draft, and he was charged with criminal mischief in December 2006 after police said he damaged a vehicle with a baseball bat. However, the Braves believe he has made strides with his overall maturity. Evarts has the ability to become a No. 3 starter, and he'll take the next step in low Class A this year.

Year	Club (League)	Class	W	L	ERA	G	GS	CG	SV	IP	H	R	ER	HR	BB	SO	AVG
2006	Braves (GCL)	R	2	2	2.93	11	9	0	0	43	42	19	14	0	12	33	.255
2007	Danville (Appy)	R	4	0	1.95	8	7	0	0	37	29	11	8	0	4	34	.213
MINOR LEAGUE TOTALS			6	2	2.48	19	16	0	0	80	71	30	22	0	16	67	.236

16 CHAD RODGERS, LHP

Born: Nov. 23, 1987. **B-T:** L-L. **Ht.:** 6-2. **Wt.:** 185. **Drafted:** HS—Stow, Ohio, 2006 (3rd round). **Signed by:** Nick Hostetler.

Along with Jeff Locke and Steve Evarts, Rodgers is another lefty from the 2006 draft who's on the verge of moving quickly through the system. The consensus top mound prospect in Ohio in 2006, he has lived up to his reputation as one of the more polished high school pitchers to emerge from the Midwest in recent years. Rodgers has terrific athleticism for a pitcher and above-average movement with his three primary pitches. His fastball sits at 88-90 mph and reaches 92 mph, and the Braves believe he'll add velocity as his slender frame continues to mature. In addition to throwing both a two-seam and four-seam fastball, he also has a hard curveball with impressive bite. He has shown steady improvement with the depth of his changeup. He used to roll his wrist when he threw his changeup, but he has made some minor adjustments and it now has the makings of a solid-average major league offering. Quiet and reserved off the field, Rodgers is a tremendous competitor on the mound. He suffered from shoulder tendinitis late in the season, though he proved he was healthy during instructional league. He's expected to spend this year in the low Class A rotation with Locke and Evarts.

Year	Club (League)	Class	W	L	ERA	G	GS	CG	SV	IP	H	R	ER	HR	BB	SO	AVG
2006	Braves (GCL)	R	3	2	2.31	11	5	0	1	39	31	14	10	1	13	30	.217
2007	Danville (Appy)	R	3	1	3.88	11	10	0	1	48	40	21	21	2	11	46	.220
MINOR LEAGUE TOTALS			6	3	3.18	22	15	0	2	87	71	35	31	3	24	76	.218

17 JOEY DEVINE, RHP

Born: Sept. 29, 1983. **B-T:** R-R. **Ht.:** 6-0. **Wt.:** 212. **Drafted:** North Carolina State, 2005 (1st round). **Signed by:** Billy Best.

Devine returned to the mechanics he employed while at North Carolina State and re-emerged as a potential set-up man or closer at the major league level in 2007. Rushed to the big leagues by the Braves less than three months after going 27th overall in the 2005 draft, he gave up grand slams in his first two appearances and a Division Series-ending home run to Chris Burke. His confidence took a hit, and he also battled a lingering back injury in 2006. He found a comfort zone with his old delivery in spring training last year and the result was his best season yet, including a couple of trips to Atlanta and a 1.89 ERA and 20 saves in the minors. He also contributed mightily to Richmond's Governors' Cup title by saving four postseason games in as many opportunities. Devine's success is centered on a sinking fastball that sits in the low 90s and can touch 96. He also has a hard slider that he throws from a three-quarters angle and can be unhittable for righthanders. He owns righties, holding them to a .154 average in the minors last year while fanning 62 of the 127 he faced. Lefthanders, however, hit .267 against him because he has had limited success in developing a changeup. He has the resiliency and makeup to pitch at the end of games in the majors. With Rafael Soriano expected to become Atlanta's closer, Devine will be a strong candidate for a set-up role with the Braves this spring.

Year	Club (League)	Class	W	L	ERA	G	GS	CG	SV	IP	H	R	ER	HR	BB	SO	AVG
2005	Myrtle Beach (Car)	A	0	0	0.00	4	0	0	1	5	0	0	0	0	3	7	.000
	Mississippi (SL)	AA	1	1	2.70	18	0	0	5	20	19	13	6	2	12	28	.250
	Richmond (IL)	AAA	0	0	18.00	1	0	0	0	1	3	2	2	0	1	1	.600
	Atlanta (NL)	MLB	0	1	12.60	5	0	0	0	5	6	7	7	2	5	3	.286
2006	Richmond (IL)	AAA	0	0	—	1	0	0	0	0	1	1	1	0	1	0	1.000
	Myrtle Beach (Car)	A	1	3	5.89	13	2	0	0	18	13	12	12	1	11	28	.203
	Mississippi (SL)	AA	2	0	0.82	6	0	0	0	11	2	1	1	1	4	20	.065
	Atlanta (NL)	MLB	0	0	9.95	10	0	0	0	6	8	7	7	1	9	10	.308
2007	Mississippi (SL)	AA	2	4	2.06	33	0	0	16	35	26	9	8	1	13	51	.211
	Richmond (IL)	AAA	3	0	1.64	17	0	0	4	22	15	5	4	1	6	27	.188
	Atlanta (NL)	MLB	1	0	1.08	10	0	0	0	8	7	1	1	0	8	7	.241
MINOR LEAGUE TOTALS			9	8	2.72	93	2	0	26	112	79	43	34	6	51	162	.201
MAJOR LEAGUE TOTALS			1	1	6.86	25	0	0	0	19	21	15	15	3	22	20	.276

18 JOSH ANDERSON, OF

Born: Aug. 10, 1982. **B-T:** L-R. **Ht.:** 6-2. **Wt.:** 195. **Drafted:** Eastern Kentucky, 2003 (4th round). **Signed by:** Nick Venuto (Astros).

After deciding they wouldn't negotiate with free agent Andruw Jones, who had been their center fielder since late 1996, the Braves had no obvious replacement for 2008. Jordan Schafer and Gorkys Hernandez are two of the more talented center-field prospects in the minors but neither figures to be ready to step in this year. Enter Anderson, who came to Atlanta in a November deal that sent Oscar Villareal to Houston. Though Anderson led the minors with 78 steals in 2004, topped the Double-A Texas League with 50 swipes in 2005 and 43 in 2006, and hit .358 after his callup last September, the Astros never believed Anderson was an everyday player. His speed has slipped, though it's still above-average, and he doesn't drive the ball very often. He'll have to prove he won't be overpowered by quality pitching, and he needs to improve his on-base skills and bunting ability so he can get on base more often. Anderson's speed allows him to outrun his mistakes in center field, but he still makes too many goofs. He led Triple-A Pacific Coast League outfielders with seven errors in 2007. His arm is playable and accurate in center. Anderson may be nothing more than a one-year bridge between Jones and Schafer, but the Braves will give him the opportunity to win a starting job in spring training.

Year	Club (League)	Class	AVG	G	AB	R	H	2B	3B	HR	RBI	BB	SO	SB	OBP	SLG
2003	Tri-City (NYP)	A	.286	74	297	44	85	11	4	3	30	16	53	26	.339	.380
2004	Lexington (SAL)	A	.324	73	299	69	97	12	3	4	31	33	47	47	.402	.425
	Salem (Car)	A	.268	66	280	45	75	13	6	2	21	13	53	31	.314	.379
2005	Corpus Christi (TL)	AA	.282	127	524	67	148	16	9	1	26	29	80	50	.329	.353
2006	Corpus Christi (TL)	AA	.308	130	561	83	173	26	4	3	50	27	73	43	.349	.385
2007	Round Rock (PCL)	AAA	.273	132	513	64	140	17	6	2	43	32	75	40	.325	.341
	Houston (NL)	MLB	.358	21	67	10	24	3	0	0	11	5	6	1	.413	.403
MINOR LEAGUE TOTALS			.290	602	2474	372	718	95	32	15	201	150	381	237	.341	.373
MAJOR LEAGUE TOTALS			.358	21	67	10	24	3	0	0	11	5	6	1	.413	.403

19 FREDDIE FREEMAN, 1B

Born: Sept. 12, 1989. **B-T:** L-R. **Ht.:** 6-5. **Wt.:** 220. **Drafted:** HS—Orange, Calif., 2007 (2nd round). **Signed by:** Mike Baker.

The Braves' willingness to let him hit, along with a signing bonus of $409,500, contributed to Freeman's decision to bypass Cal State Fullerton and sign with Atlanta as the 78th overall pick in the 2007 draft. A former member of USA Baseball's youth and junior national teams, Freeman attracted strong interest from many teams for his abilities on the mound. He showed two plus pitches—a heavy, low-90s fastball and a hard slider—while working as a closer in high school, but Freeman always has preferred mashing the ball as opposed to throwing it. Only 17 when drafted, he has an ideal hitter's frame that projects extremely well. He has above-average power with a smooth stroke from the left side that produces hits that sound different coming off the bat. He shows a good feel for the strike zone and his hands work very well, helping to give him above-average raw power. Though not the fleetest afoot, Freeman handles first base well, displaying good footwork and excellent reactions. He also has an exceedingly strong arm for the position. His performance in spring training will determine whether he opens 2008 in low Class A or in extended spring training.

Year	Club (League)	Class	AVG	G	AB	R	H	2B	3B	HR	RBI	BB	SO	SB	OBP	SLG
2007	Braves (GCL)	R	.268	59	224	24	60	7	0	6	30	7	33	1	.295	.379
MINOR LEAGUE TOTALS			.268	59	224	24	60	7	0	6	30	7	33	1	.295	.379

20 ERIC CAMPBELL, 3B

Born: Aug. 6, 1985. **B-T:** R-R. **Ht.:** 6-0. **Wt.:** 200. **Drafted:** HS—Owensville, Ind., 2004 (2nd round). **Signed by:** Sherard Clinkscales.

Campbell had a year to forget in 2007. A broken thumb followed by a series of minor injuries prevented him from building on the momentum he generated with a co-MVP award in the Appalachian League in 2005 and a home run crown (with 22) in the South Atlantic League in 2006. Equally as disappointing as his performance was Campbell's overall attitude. Though frustrated by the injuries, he showed little intensity in his rehab efforts. That led to his being sent home in August, marking the second time in the past year the Braves had to discipline him. An intense competitor when the lights come on, Campbell has above-average power as well as the ability to drive the ball to all fields. He showed progress last season with his plate discipline, drawing walks at a better rate than ever before. A former shortstop, Campbell has relatively soft hands and a strong arm at third base, but his lateral movement rates no better than average. An attempted shift to second base in 2006 in Hawaii Winter Baseball proved fruitless, and he could land in the outfield down the road. Atlanta remains confident it still has a prospect in Campbell, who marches to the beat of a different drummer. But he'll have to show an improved attitude and approach in 2008, when he'll likely repeat high Class A.

Year	Club (League)	Class	AVG	G	AB	R	H	2B	3B	HR	RBI	BB	SO	SB	OBP	SLG
2004	Braves (GCL)	R	.251	56	211	30	53	7	0	7	29	15	47	3	.306	.384
	Rome (SAL)	A	.136	7	22	0	3	0	0	0	1	2	7	0	.240	.136
2005	Danville (Appy)	R	.313	66	262	77	82	26	2	18	64	28	64	15	.383	.634
2006	Rome (SAL)	A	.296	116	449	83	133	27	3	22	77	23	68	18	.335	.517
2007	Myrtle Beach (Car)	A	.221	81	298	47	66	13	0	14	49	36	48	6	.312	.406
MINOR LEAGUE TOTALS			.271	326	1242	237	337	73	5	61	220	104	234	42	.333	.486

21 VAN POPE, 3B

Born: Feb. 26, 1984. **B-T:** R-R. **Ht.:** 6-0. **Wt.:** 200. **Drafted:** Meridian (Miss.) CC, 2004 (4th round). **Signed by:** Don Thomas.

After a solid season in high Class A in 2006, Pope received a promotion to Mississippi, where Trustmark Park in Pearl is located in a suburb of his hometown of Jackson. Playing at home didn't work well for Pope, as he pressed too much. He batted just .150 in the first two months and didn't climb above .200 for good until June 1. In the past, he had shown some raw power as well as the ability to hit for average, yet did neither with consistency in 2007. His pitch recognition leaves something to be desired, and scouts have wondered if he'll produce enough power at higher levels to profile as a starter at the hot corner. Pope is a premier defender with soft hands and a plus arm. His footwork is flawless and he moves well in all directions. That ability also translates into good baserunning skills, though his speed is only slightly above-average. The Braves hope that Pope will adjust and bounce back in 2008, when he'll return to Double-A.

Year	Club (League)	Class	AVG	G	AB	R	H	2B	3B	HR	RBI	BB	SO	SB	OBP	SLG
2004	Danville (Appy)	R	.270	60	233	39	63	18	2	5	39	11	44	5	.333	.429
2005	Rome (SAL)	A	.277	100	386	48	107	24	7	6	60	42	70	0	.347	.422
	Myrtle Beach (Car)	A	.167	25	84	7	14	1	0	1	5	9	21	0	.253	.214
2006	Myrtle Beach (Car)	A	.263	127	467	78	123	31	1	5	74	58	92	7	.353	.430
2007	Mississippi (SL)	AA	.223	123	421	48	94	23	4	6	43	36	77	10	.298	.340
MINOR LEAGUE TOTALS			.252	435	1591	220	401	97	14	33	221	156	304	22	.329	.393

22 ERIK CORDIER, RHP

Born: Feb. 25, 1986. **B-T:** R-R. **Ht.:** 6-3. **Wt.:** 215. **Drafted:** HS—Sturgeon Bay, Wis., 2004 (2nd round). **Signed by:** Phil Huttman (Royals).

It was considered a minor transaction at the time, but the trade that sent Tony Pena to the Royals for Cordier could pay off for both teams. Pena became Kansas City's starting shortstop, while the Braves are excited about Cordier's power arm. They have yet to see it in action, however, because he was sidelined for all of 2007 while recovering from Tommy John surgery. He also missed 2005 following knee surgery and has pitched just 87 innings since signing as a second-round pick in 2004—making him the highest-drafted player out of Wisconsin since the Angels selected Jarrod Washburn 31st overall in 1995. During instructional league this fall, Cordier got back on the mound and showed the potential for three quality pitches. He didn't have all of his velocity back, but he eventually should regain a fastball that sat at 92-95 mph and clocked as high as 98. His heater has nice armside run, allowing him to jam righthanders and get grounders. He also has a plus changeup and has shown signs of an above-average curveball when his release point is in sync. Equally impressive is the way Cordier attacks hitters. He's not afraid to throw inside and has shown an excellent feel for setting up hitters to make his offspeed offerings that much more effective. Cordier could figure prominently in Atlanta's plans provided he stays healthy. The first step back will be an assignment to low Class A.

Year	Club (League)	Class	W	L	ERA	G	GS	CG	SV	IP	H	R	ER	HR	BB	SO	AVG
2004	Royals (AZL)	R	2	4	5.19	11	11	0	0	35	38	27	20	1	21	22	.279
2005	Did Not Play—Injured																
2006	Idaho Falls (Pio)	R	1	0	3.38	3	3	0	0	16	11	6	6	0	3	19	.186
	Burlington (MWL)	A	3	1	2.70	7	7	0	0	37	27	17	11	3	14	23	.203
2007	Did Not Play—Injured																
MINOR LEAGUE TOTALS			6	5	3.81	21	21	0	0	87	76	50	37	4	38	64	.232

23 CORY RASMUS, RHP

Born: Nov. 6, 1987. **B-T:** R-R. **Ht.:** 6-1. **Wt.:** 220. **Drafted:** HS—Seale, Ala., 2006 (1st round supplemental). **Signed by:** Al Goetz.

The younger brother of top Cardinals prospect Colby Rasmus, Cory missed the entire 2007 season. The Braves hoped rest and rehab would cure his shoulder problems, but he wound up having surgery in July to tighten the muscles his shoulder. He has pitched just seven pro innings since signing for $900,000 as the 38th overall pick in the 2006 draft. Rasmus, who teamed with Colby to help lead Russell County (Ala.) High to the 2005 national championship and also was the valedictorian of his class, declined a full ride to Auburn to turn pro. Before he got hurt, he featured a low- to mid-90s fastball that has been clocked as high as 97 mph along with a sharp overhand 11-to-5 curveball that can buckle the knees of righthanders. His two-seamer has good late movement, and his changeup has the makings of a plus pitch. Scouts were concerned about Rasmus' full-effort delivery during his high school days, and he's not very big or project-able. He'll have to iron out his mechanics, which should improve his durability and his command. While shoulder injuries are more troublesome than elbow problems, Atlanta is confident that Rasmus can bounce back and develop into a middle-of-the-rotation starter. If he's healthy this spring, he'll open the season in low Class A.

Year	Club (League)	Class	W	L	ERA	G	GS	CG	SV	IP	H	R	ER	HR	BB	SO	AVG
2006	Braves (GCL)	R	0	0	8.59	3	1	0	0	7	7	7	7	0	5	3	.280
2007	Did Not Play—Injured																
MINOR LEAGUE TOTALS			0	0	8.59	3	1	0	0	7	7	7	7	0	5	3	.280

24 · KRIS MEDLEN, RHP

Born: Oct. 7, 1985. **B-T:** B-R. **Ht.:** 5-10. **Wt.:** 175. **Drafted:** Santa Ana (Calif.) JC, 2006 (10th round). **Signed by:** Tom Battista.

After posting a 0.81 ERA at three stops in the lower minors, Medlen reached Double-A a little more than a year after signing as a 10th-round pick out of the 2006 draft. An aggressive pitcher with a quick and resilient arm, he doubled as a shortstop in junior college. He isn't afraid to challenge hitters with his low-90s fastball and does an excellent job of mixing his sharp curveball, which often serves as his strikeout pitch. He continues to work on his changeup, which shows promise, but he doesn't use it much out of the bullpen. While his size is less than ideal in the eyes of many scouts, Medlen pitches with great confidence and has ideal makeup for a closer. He also repeats his compact delivery well and has an easy arm action. He dominated in Hawaii Winter Baseball, striking out 27 in 14 innings, though he was shut down in November with a sore elbow. He should be healthy by spring training and could claim a role in the Atlanta bullpen in 2008.

Year	Club (League)	Class	W	L	ERA	G	GS	CG	SV	IP	H	R	ER	HR	BB	SO	AVG
2006	Danville (Appy)	R	1	0	0.41	20	0	0	10	22	14	2	1	0	2	36	.175
2007	Rome (SAL)	A	0	1	0.87	17	0	0	8	20	13	4	2	1	3	33	.169
	Myrtle Beach (Car)	A	2	0	1.13	18	0	0	2	24	22	7	3	1	7	28	.239
	Mississippi (SL)	AA	0	0	11.57	3	0	0	1	2	4	3	3	0	2	2	.444
MINOR LEAGUE TOTALS			3	1	1.17	58	0	0	21	69	53	16	9	2	14	99	.205

25 · KALA KA'AIHUE, 1B

Born: March 29, 1985. **B-T:** R-R. **Ht.:** 6-2. **Wt.:** 230. **Signed:** NDFA/South Mountain (Ariz.) CC, 2005. **Signed by:** Tom Battista/Lonnie Goldberg.

During the first two-thirds of the 2007 season, the big first baseman known as "KK" lived up to his frequent comparisons to Andres Galarraga. After going hitless in his first five games, Ka'aihue crushed Carolina League pitching to the tune of 22 homers by mid-July. By the time he received a promotion to Double-A, he easily led the CL in homers and slugging percentage (.583). Yet as productive as he was in high Class A, Ka'aihue struggled that much and more against Double-A pitchers. He hit just .127 with no homers and just one multihit game in 33 outings. Just as he had when he had a midseason promotion in 2006, he put excessive pressure on himself to live up to his reputation as an offensive force. When in a zone, he has an excellent eye that leads to an impressive number of walks. While his strikeout totals will reach triple digits, he's capable of making consistent hard contact and uses the entire field. He's a below-average runner but moves well for a big man and has developed into an above-average first baseman with soft hands and quick feet. Ka'aihue hails from a baseball family, as his father Kala Sr. reached Triple-A with the Pirates and his brother Kila is a first baseman in the Royals system. Kala Jr. will head back to Double-A to start 2008.

Year	Club (League)	Class	AVG	G	AB	R	H	2B	3B	HR	RBI	BB	SO	SB	OBP	SLG
2005	Braves (GCL)	R	.283	40	127	18	36	8	2	6	22	15	38	0	.358	.520
	Danville (Appy)	R	.438	5	16	4	7	3	0	2	3	0	5	0	.438	1.000
2006	Rome (SAL)	A	.329	67	228	44	75	16	2	15	49	52	66	3	.458	.614
	Myrtle Beach (Car)	A	.223	53	188	37	42	8	0	13	31	30	49	0	.342	.473
2007	Myrtle Beach (Car)	A	.298	89	309	57	92	20	1	22	61	53	92	2	.410	.583
	Mississippi (SL)	AA	.127	33	118	14	15	5	1	0	8	11	51	0	.211	.186
MINOR LEAGUE TOTALS			.271	287	986	174	267	60	6	58	174	161	301	5	.380	.520

26 CLINT SAMMONS, C

Born: May 15, 1983. **B-T:** R-R. **Ht.:** 6-0. **Wt.:** 200. **Drafted:** Georgia, 2004 (6th round). **Signed by:** Al Goetz.

A logjam behind the plate throughout the system meant Sammons had to return to high Class A to start the 2007 season, but he finished it by making his major league debut and going 2-for-3 in his lone start. The leader of Georgia's 2004 College World Series team, he has emerged as one of the premier defensive catchers in the minors. Having fine-tuned his ability under Myrtle Beach pitching coach Bruce Dal Canton, Sammons handles pitchers with aplomb and calls a near-flawless game. His footwork and exchange are off the charts. He has a pop time of 1.89 seconds from mitt to glove on throws to second base and led the Southern League by throwing out 48 percent of basestealers last summer. Sammons is just adequate with the bat, which is why he projects as a backup. He tries to pull the ball too much, preventing him from hitting for a high average. He has occasional pop and below-average speed. He's the leading candidate to caddy for Brian McCann in Atlanta in 2008.

Year	Club (League)	Class	AVG	G	AB	R	H	2B	3B	HR	RBI	BB	SO	SB	OBP	SLG
2004	Danville (Appy)	R	.288	40	132	19	38	7	2	0	17	18	26	5	.368	.371
2005	Rome (SAL)	A	.286	121	427	61	122	29	0	4	62	55	66	4	.368	.382
2006	Myrtle Beach (Car)	A	.258	103	360	36	93	21	0	8	56	32	65	4	.323	.383
2007	Myrtle Beach (Car)	A	.269	23	78	13	21	6	0	4	13	10	14	1	.363	.500
	Mississippi (SL)	AA	.243	83	296	27	72	10	0	5	36	26	72	1	.304	.328
	Atlanta (NL)	MLB	.667	2	3	0	2	1	0	0	0	0	0	0	.667	1.000
MINOR LEAGUE TOTALS			.268	370	1293	156	346	73	2	21	184	141	243	15	.341	.376
MAJOR LEAGUE TOTALS			.667	2	3	0	2	1	0	0	0	0	0	0	.667	1.000

27 JAIRO CUEVAS, RHP

Born: Jan. 24, 1984. **B-T:** R-R. **Ht.:** 6-4. **Wt.:** 230. **Signed:** Dominican Republic, 2003. **Signed by:** Roberto Aquino/Julian Perez.

Cuevas was streaky in 2007, opening the season with eight straight losses before bouncing back with six consecutive victories in June and July. Wins proved fleeting thereafter, however, as he dropped his last four decisions over a span of six starts. Despite his 6-12 record, he pitched well for most of the season and ranked seventh in the Carolina League with a 3.55 ERA. Cuevas' fastball sits at 92-93 mph and can touch 96, and it also has good movement. His curveball and changeup show flashes of potential. While he has promising stuff, he counteracts it with a tendency to overthrow and an inability to command his pitches. He opens up too much on the front side of his delivery, which causes his arm to drag behind. His release point is also inconsistent, particularly from the stretch, when he tends to rush his lower half. Cuevas has the strong build and could develop into a workhorse starter. After getting added to the 40-man roster in November, he'll start 2008 in Double-A.

Year	Club (League)	Class	W	L	ERA	G	GS	CG	SV	IP	H	R	ER	HR	BB	SO	AVG
2003	Braves2 (DSL)	R	2	4	3.21	12	4	0	1	28	21	20	10	0	21	27	.210
2004	Braves (GCL)	R	2	3	3.09	9	7	0	1	35	29	13	12	1	7	39	.218
	Danville (Appy)	R	0	0	0.00	1	1	0	0	4	1	0	0	0	4	3	.077
2005	Danville (Appy)	R	6	1	1.95	12	10	0	0	55	35	20	12	3	22	69	.179
2006	Rome (SAL)	A	7	12	5.55	27	23	0	0	129	123	87	80	10	65	117	.248
2007	Myrtle Beach (Car)	A	6	12	3.55	25	25	0	0	132	113	74	52	9	71	116	.225
MINOR LEAGUE TOTALS			23	32	3.89	86	70	0	2	384	322	214	166	23	190	371	.224

28 ERIC BARRETT, LHP

Born: Dec. 12, 1986. **B-T:** L-L. **Ht.:** 6-2. **Wt.:** 180. **Drafted:** John A. Logan (Ill.) CC, D/F 2006 (31st round). **Signed by:** Stu Cann.

The Indians took Barrett as a draft-and-follow out of an Illinois high school in 2005, but his velocity dipped into the mid-80s at John A. Logan (Ill.) CC the next spring. The Braves made him a 31st-round pick in 2006 and followed him last year, when his fastball rose to 88-92 mph during his sophomore season. He signed before the draft for $150,000, one of seven draft-and-follows to ink with Atlanta. Barrett was the most consistent pitcher on the GCL Braves, showing a sound delivery with an easy arm action. His fastball peaks at 93-94 mph and has nice late tailing life. His changeup has good depth and fade, while his sweeping curveball is sharp with late break and has the potential to be his best offering. Barrett is a free spirit off the field, but he's one of the system's more competitive pitchers once he crosses the white lines. He'll need to continue to make adjustments against more advanced hitters while sharpening the command and consistency of all his pitches. He's expected to spend 2008 in low Class A.

Year	Club (League)	Class	W	L	ERA	G	GS	CG	SV	IP	H	R	ER	HR	BB	SO	AVG
2007	Braves (GCL)	R	1	2	1.36	8	5	0	0	33	33	14	5	0	11	46	.262
	Danville (Appy)	R	2	0	2.28	5	3	0	0	23	14	9	6	0	9	25	.173
MINOR LEAGUE TOTALS			3	2	1.75	13	8	0	0	56	47	23	11	0	20	71	.227

29 DIORY HERNANDEZ, SS/2B

Born: April 8, 1984. **B-T:** R-R. **Ht.:** 5-11. **Wt.:** 180. **Signed:** Dominican Republic, 2002. **Signed by:** Roberto Aquino.

A change in attitude last year altered Hernandez' performance as well as his standing within the organization. After acting sullen and lethargic at Myrtle Beach for most of 2005 and 2006, Hernandez returned to high Class A with a fresh determination to succeed. He batted .378 in April and received an early promotion to Double-A, where he continued to show plenty of tools as well as the ability to play second base in addition to shortstop. Offensively, Hernandez' strength is his ability to put the ball in play. He uses the entire field with his short swing, solid bat speed and outstanding hand-eye coordination. His plate discipline and overall approach tend to fluctuate, but his ability to make consistent contact helps him avoid prolonged slumps. Hernandez has plus speed and good lateral movement on defense. He also has soft hands with a quick first step. His arm is fringe-average for short but plays well at second. For all his tools, Hernandez continues to learn the finer points of the game, particularly in understanding game situations when at the plate and running the bases. He got caught 20 times in 42 steal attemps last season. If he maintains his recent momentum and has a strong season in Triple-A in 2008, he could factor into Atlanta's infield plans in the near future.

Year	Club (League)	Class	AVG	G	AB	R	H	2B	3B	HR	RBI	BB	SO	SB	OBP	SLG
2003	Braves (GCL)	R	.221	54	190	26	42	9	2	1	12	14	24	2	.287	.305
2004	Rome (SAL)	A	.271	90	306	40	83	20	1	3	38	26	67	7	.325	.373
2005	Braves (GCL)	R	.357	7	28	5	10	1	0	1	4	0	2	0	.357	.500
	Myrtle Beach (Car)	A	.253	73	265	30	67	15	1	5	30	18	53	5	.314	.374
2006	Braves (GCL)	R	.267	8	30	6	8	1	0	1	2	3	5	0	.371	.400
	Myrtle Beach (Car)	A	.238	76	286	37	68	10	0	6	47	19	51	11	.295	.336
2007	Myrtle Beach (Car)	A	.313	17	64	9	20	8	2	0	9	2	11	2	.343	.500
	Mississippi (SL)	AA	.307	115	433	50	133	25	1	7	59	29	68	22	.370	.418
MINOR LEAGUE TOTALS			.269	440	1602	203	431	89	7	24	201	111	281	49	.328	.378

30 PHILLIP BRITTON, C

Born: Sept. 25, 1984. **B-T:** R-R. **Ht.:** 6-0. **Wt.:** 220. **Drafted:** Olney Central (Ill.) CC, D/F 2004 (36th round). **Signed by:** Stu Cann.

Britton is in many ways the polar opposite of fellow receiver Clint Sammons. Whereas Sammons came from a major college program with incredible defensive skills, Britton arrived from the junior college ranks with a reputation for being able to put the ball in play. The 2007 campaign was his first full season in pro ball and Britton put together a productive and consistent year with the bat, showing the ability to drive pitches into the gaps. The Braves also were pleased with the progress Britton made behind the plate. He has above-average athleticism and does a good job of moving laterally and knocking down pitches. While his game-calling ability is showing significant progress, he's still learning the nuances of working with a staff. He spent the offseason in Hawaii Winter Baseball to work on his exchange and footwork as well as to become more consistent with his throws to second. He threw out 29 percent of basestealers last season. Britton has a great passion for the game and an impressive desire to be a top-flight catcher. He'll advance to high Class A in 2008.

Year	Club (League)	Class	AVG	G	AB	R	H	2B	3B	HR	RBI	BB	SO	SB	OBP	SLG
2005	Braves (GCL)	R	.231	18	39	3	9	1	0	1	2	2	7	0	.318	.333
2006	Danville (Appy)	R	.296	58	223	34	66	18	0	7	35	7	31	1	.321	.471
2007	Rome (SAL)	A	.287	89	345	54	99	22	3	10	44	9	44	4	.322	.455
	Mississippi (SL)	AA	.000	2	5	1	0	0	0	0	0	0	1	0	.000	.000
MINOR LEAGUE TOTALS			.284	167	612	92	174	41	3	18	81	18	83	5	.319	.449

Baltimore Orioles

BY WILL LINGO

Could it finally be the beginning of a turn-around for the Orioles?

The team hired Andy MacPhail as president of baseball operations in June, effectively making him the team's new general manager. MacPhail came from the Cubs, where he was team president from 1994-2006, and before that he had been GM of the Twins since August 1985.

MacPhail, who knows Orioles owner Peter Angelos from major league labor negotiations in 2002 and '06, may finally be the executive who can isolate the Angelos family from the daily functions of the baseball operation. He got assurances to that effect when he took the job, and when asked at his introductory press conference if Angelos had promised not to interfere, MacPhail said: "If I didn't feel that way, I wouldn't be here. It's just that simple."

MacPhail's first major step, other than replacing manager Sam Perlozzo, was signing off on two huge draft deals. The first was catcher Matt Wieters, the fifth overall pick who signed for a draft-record $6 million in up-front bonus money. Baltimore also signed fifth-rounder Jake Arrieta for $1.1 million, making up for the team's lack of a second- or third-round pick. Wieters and Arrieta were the first Scott Boras clients ever signed by the Orioles during Angelos' tenure. They also continued a trend of stronger drafts under scouting director Joe Jordan, who was overseeing his third draft for Baltimore.

After another dismal regular season ended, MacPhail began work on remaking the roster. The first major step was unloading Miguel Tejada to the Astros for five players, most notably young arms Matt Albers and Troy Patton, who will compete for big league rotation spots in spring training.

He also hired Rick Kranitz as the team's new pitching coach, ending a failed two years under Leo Mazzone, who couldn't work the same magic he did with the Braves. Kranitz has much less of a major league track record but quickly gained respect with the Marlins, and he was Baseball America's 2006 Major League Coach of the Year.

Those are small steps but hopeful signs for Orioles fans who have grown weary of watching a string of 10 straight losing seasons following the team's last playoff appearance in 1997. Years of poor decisions have led to the smallest crowds ever at Camden Yards, an organization that has fallen far

Dealing Miguel Tejada for young players signaled a new era for the Orioles

TOP 30 PROSPECTS

1. Matt Wieters, c	16. Bob McCrory, rhp
2. Radhames Liz, rhp	17. Brandon Tripp, of
3. Troy Patton, lhp	18. Randor Bierd, rhp
4. Nolan Reimold, of	19. James Hoey, rhp
5. Bill Rowell, 3b	20. Dennis Sarfate, rhp
6. Brandon Snyder, 1b/3b	21. Zach Britton, lhp
7. Jake Arrieta, rhp	22. Tyler Henson, ss
8. Chorye Spoone, rhp	23. Jeff Fiorentino, of
9. Pedro Beato, rhp	24. Matt Angle, of
10. Brandon Erbe, rhp	25. Chris Vinyard, 1b
11. Mike Costanzo, 3b	26. Brad Bergesen, rhp
12. Garrett Olson, lhp	27. Tyler Kolodny, 3b
13. Tim Bascom, rhp	28. Luis Lebron, rhp
14. Scott Moore, 3b/of	29. James Johnson, rhp
15. David Hernandez, rhp	30. Kieron Pope, of

behind the Red Sox and Yankees in the AL East and the demise of the Oriole Way. MacPhail appreciates the history of the franchise because his father Lee, a Hall of Famer, was GM of the Orioles from 1959-65.

"The Orioles (of the past) had their Oriole Way and we need to find ours," MacPhail said. "You have to do what you have to do to get this franchise to the postseason and get them to the World Series. I don't have a goal of getting over .500. We shouldn't be here for that. No team should be here for that."

But it wouldn't be a bad place to start.

General Manager: Mike Flanagan. **Farm Director:** David Stockstill. **Scouting Director:** Joe Jordan.

Class	Team	League	W	L	PCT	Finish*	Manager	Affiliated
Majors	Baltimore	American	69	93	.426	11th (14)	Tom Trebelhorn	—
Triple-A	Norfolk Tides	International	69	74	.483	9th (14)	Gary Allenson	2007
Double-A	Bowie Baysox	Eastern	72	68	.514	4th (12)	Bien Figueroa	1993
High A	Frederick Keys	Carolina	64	74	.464	5th (8)^	Tommy Thompson	1989
Low A	Delmarva Shorebirds	South Atlantic	68	68	.500	9th (16)	Gary Kendall	1997
Short-season	Aberdeen IronBirds	New York-Penn	34	42	.447	9th (14)	Andy Etchebarren	2002
Rookie	Bluefield Orioles	Appalachian	32	36	.471	6th (9)	Alex Arias	1958
Rookie	GCL Orioles	Gulf Coast	32	24	.571	5th (16)	Ramon Sambo	2007

Overall 2007 Minor League Record   371   386   .490   18th
*Finish in overall standings (No. of teams in league) ^League champion

LAST YEAR'S TOP 30

Player, Pos.		Status
1.	Bill Rowell, 3b	No. 5
2.	Brandon Erbe, rhp	No. 10
3.	Nolan Reimold, of	No. 4
4.	Pedro Beato, rhp	No. 9
5.	Radhames Liz, rhp	No. 2
6.	Garrett Olson, lhp	No. 12
7.	Brandon Snyder, c	No. 6
8.	James Hoey, rhp	No. 19
9.	Jeff Fiorentino, of	No. 23
10.	Kieron Pope, of	No. 30
11.	Ryan Adams, 2b	Dropped out
12.	Luis Lebron, rhp	No. 28
13.	James Johnson, rhp	No. 29
14.	Zach Britton, lhp	No. 21
15.	Sendy Rleal, rhp	Dropped out
16.	Jason Berken, rhp	Dropped out
17.	Val Majewski, of/1b	Dropped out
18.	Marino Salas, rhp	(Pirates)
19.	Chris Vinyard, 1b	No. 25
20.	Adam Stern, of	Dropped out
21.	Kurt Birkins, lhp	Majors
22.	Luis Hernandez, ss/2b	Dropped out
23.	Beau Hale, rhp	(Free agent)
24.	Pedro Florimon, ss	Dropped out
25.	Chorye Spoone, rhp	No. 8
26.	J.R. House, c/1b	(Free agent)
27.	Anderson Garcia, rhp	(Phillies)
28.	Luis Montanez, of	Dropped out
29.	Brian Burres, lhp	Majors
30.	Adam Donachie, c	(Royals)

BEST TOOLS

Best Hitter for Average	Brandon Snyder
Best Power Hitter	Nolan Reimold
Best Strike-Zone Discipline	Matt Angle
Fastest Baserunner	Calvin Lester
Best Athlete	Tyler Henson
Best Fastball	Radhames Liz
Best Curveball	Chorye Spoone
Best Slider	David Hernandez
Best Changeup	Radhames Liz
Best Control	Garrett Olson
Best Defensive Catcher	Matt Wieters
Best Defensive Infielder	Luis Hernandez
Best Infield Arm	Billy Rowell
Best Defensive Outfielder	Matt Angle
Best Outfield Arm	Nolan Reimold

PROJECTED 2011 LINEUP

Catcher	Matt Wieters
First Base	Brandon Snyder
Second Base	Brian Roberts
Third Base	Bill Rowell
Shortstop	Luis Hernandez
Left Field	Nolan Reimold
Center Field	Matt Angle
Right Field	Nick Markakis
Designated Hitter	Mike Costanzo
No. 1 Starter	Erik Bedard
No. 2 Starter	Adam Loewen
No. 3 Starter	Radhames Liz
No. 4 Starter	Jeremy Guthrie
No. 5 Starter	Matt Albers
Closer	Chris Ray

TOP PROSPECTS OF THE DECADE

Year	Player, Pos.	2007 Org.
1998	Ryan Minor, 3b	Out of baseball
1999	Matt Riley, lhp	Dodgers
2000	Matt Riley, lhp	Dodgers
2001	Keith Reed, of	Newark (Atlantic)
2002	Richard Stahl, lhp	Out of baseball
2003	Erik Bedard, lhp	Orioles
2004	Adam Loewen, lhp	Orioles
2005	Nick Markakis, of	Orioles
2006	Nick Markakis, of	Orioles
2007	Bill Rowell, 3b	Orioles

TOP DRAFT PICKS OF THE DECADE

Year	Player, Pos.	2007 Org.
1998	Rick Elder, of	Out of baseball
1999	Mike Paradis, rhp	Out of baseball
2000	Beau Hale, rhp	Orioles
2001	Chris Smith, lhp	Out of baseball
2002	Adam Loewen, lhp	Orioles
2003	Nick Markakis, of	Orioles
2004	*Wade Townsend, rhp	Devil Rays
2005	Brandon Snyder, c	Orioles
2006	Bill Rowell, 3b	Orioles
2007	Matt Wieters, c	Orioles

*Did not sign.

LARGEST BONUSES IN CLUB HISTORY

Matt Wieters, 2007	$6,000,000
Adam Loewen, 2002	$3,200,000
Beau Hale, 2000	$2,250,000
Chris Smith, 2001	$2,175,000
Bill Rowell, 2006	$2,100,000

BALTIMORE ORIOLES

Top 2008 Rookie: Troy Patton, lhp. The new acquisition from the Astros is the best-equipped of the organization's young pitchers to succeed right away.

Breakout Prospect: Tyler Henson, ss. The high school two-sport star is showing signs that his athleticism will translate on the diamond.

Sleeper: Joe Mahoney, 1b. A sixth-round pick 2007, he offers well above-average power if he can clean up his swing.

SOURCE OF TOP 30 TALENT

Homegrown	24	Acquired	6
College	9	Trades	4
Junior college	3	Rule 5 draft	1
High school	9	Independent leagues	1
Draft-and-follow	1	Free agents/waivers	0
Nondrafted free agents	0		
International	2		

Numbers in parentheses indicate prospect rankings.

LF
Kieron Pope (30)
Kraig Binick
Arturo Rivas
Val Majewski

CF
Jeff Fiorentino (23)
Matt Angle (24)
Adam Stern
Danny Figueroa

RF
Nolan Reimold (4)
Brandon Tripp (17)
Luis Montanez

3B
Mike Costanzo (11)
Scott Moore (14)
Tyler Henson (22)
Tyler Kolodny (27)
Oscar Salazar
Ryan Finan

SS
Luis Hernandez
Pedro Florimon

2B
Ryan Adams
Paco Figueroa
Miguel Abreu

1B
Bill Rowell (5)
Brandon Snyder (6)
Chris Vinyard (25)
Joe Mahoney
Mark Fleisher

C
Matt Wieters (1)
Luis Bernardo
Dashenko Ricardo

RHP

Starters	Relievers
Radhames Liz (2)	Bob McCrory (16)
Jake Arrieta (7)	Randor Bierd (18)
Chorye Spoone (8)	James Hoey (19)
Pedro Beato (9)	Dennis Sarfate (20)
Brandon Erbe (10)	Luis Lebron (28)
Tim Bascom (13)	Rocky Cherry
David Hernandez (15)	Freddy Deza
Brad Bergesen (26)	Jason Berken
James Johnson (29)	Cory Doyne
Kyle Schmidt	
Jeff Moore	
Justin Moore	
John Mariotti	

LHP

Starters	Relievers
Troy Patton (3)	Brett Bordes
Garrett Olson (12)	Wilfredo Perez
Zach Britton (21)	

2007   SIGNING BUDGET: $7.7 MILLION

Best Pro Debut: OF Matt Angle (7) hit .301 for short-season Aberdeen and ranked second in the New York-Penn League with 34 stolen bases. 3B Tyler Kolodny (16) ranked in the top five in the Rookie-level Gulf Coast League in on-base and slugging percentage during his .318/.406/.530 debut. OF Kraig Binick (27) was an Appalachian League all-star and hit .301/.396/.449 overall in 272 at-bats with 15 stolen bases.

Best Athlete: Matt Wieters (1) is as athletic as any catcher, and was an outstanding two-way player at Georgia Tech in his first two seasons. He hit 96 mph off the mound, and the Major League Scouting Bureau at one time had a higher grade for him as a pitcher than as a hitter.

Best Pure Hitter: Wieters can handle velocity and trusts his hands to stay back on breaking balls.

Best Power Hitter: While Wieters has 25-homer potential, 1B Joe Mahoney (6) produces top-of-the-scale raw power from a 6-foot-6, 260-pound frame. The Orioles are working to help him simplify his swing, which has too much going on.

Fastest Runner: Angle is an above-average runner with good instincts, but OF Calvin Lester (36) is a true burner with 70 speed.

Best Defensive Player: Wieters has premium arm strength and the agility to be a well-above-average catcher despite his big 6-foot-5 frame.

Best Fastball: With Wieters catching, RHP Jake Arrieta (5) earns the honor, touching 95 and pitching comfortably in the 91-93 mph range. RHP John Mariotti (18) surprised the Orioles by showing a heavy low-90s sinker, with more velocity than he had in college.

Best Secondary Pitch: Tim Bascom (4) had one of the best changeups by a righthander in the draft, and his slider also is the best of this draft class.

Most Intriguing Background: The Padres drafted Bascom in the sixth round in 2006 and had him signed, but Bascom didn't pass his physical due to a knee injury. Central Florida then declared him ineligible for having negotiated a contract, leaving Bascom to pitch in the independent South Coast League leading up to the draft. OF/2B Eric Perlozzo (35) is the son of ex-O's manager Sam Perlozzo.

Closest To The Majors: Wieters got a $6 million bonus to make it to the majors, not to thrill the fans in Frederick.

Best Late-Round Pick: Kolodny, a grinder with energy who can hit, and Binick.

The One Who Got Away: RHP Dan Klein (24), an athletic high school quarterback with a good breaking ball and projectable 6-foot-3, 200-pound frame, chose to attend UCLA.

Assessment: Even with solid finds such as Angle, Bascom and Kolodny, the Orioles' efforts will be judged by Arrieta and Wieters, in whom $7.1 million is invested.

2006   BUDGET: $5.0 MILLION

3B Billy Rowell (1) and RHP Pedro Beato (1s) had pedestrian first full seasons but still offer a lot of upside. So does sleeper SS Tyler Henson (5).

GRADE: C+

2005   BUDGET: $4.2 MILLION

The Orioles' first four picks have become four of the system's very best prospects: 1B/3B Brandon Snyder (1), LHP Garrett Olson (1s), OF Nolan Reimold (2) and RHP Brandon Erbe (3). So too has RHP Chorye Spoone (8).

GRADE: B

2004   BUDGET: $1.3 MILLION

Baltimore failed to sign RHP Wade Townsend (1) and didn't have a second-rounder. OF Jeff Fiorentino (3) was rushed to the majors, and this crop's best player looks like RHP Kevin Hart (11)—who blossomed after getting traded to the Cubs.

GRADE: C

2003   BUDGET: $4.0 MILLION

Most teams were on OF Nick Markakis (1) more as a pitcher, but the Orioles rightly saw him as their No. 3 hitter of the future. They also found a closer in RHP Chris Ray (3) and two more live arms in RHPs Bob McCrory (4) and James Hoey (13).

GRADE: B+

Draft analysis by John Manuel (2007) and Jim Callis (2003-06). Numbers in parentheses indicate draft rounds. Budgets are bonuses in first 10 rounds.

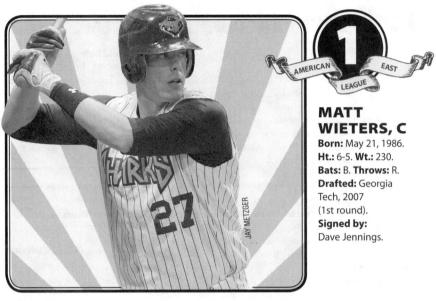

1

MATT WIETERS, C

Born: May 21, 1986.
Ht.: 6-5. **Wt.:** 230.
Bats: B. **Throws:** R.
Drafted: Georgia Tech, 2007 (1st round).
Signed by: Dave Jennings.

Baseball America rated Wieters the best position player available in the 2007 draft and the No. 2 prospect overall. He would have been a premium pick in the 2004 draft coming out of high school in suburban Charleston, S.C., if not for his strong commitment to Georgia Tech. He hit in the middle of the order and was the closer for the Yellow Jackets from the time he was a freshman. Wieters was an All-American in both 2006 and '07, batting .358 with 10 homers as a junior. He started sliding in the draft as teams worried about his price tag—agent Scott Boras compared him to former Georgia Tech star Mark Teixeira, who turned pro for a $9.5 million contract—but the Orioles took a rare draft gamble with the fifth overall pick. Baltimore signed him just before the Aug. 15 deadline for a $6 million bonus, the largest up-front payment in draft history. He signed too late to play during the regular season, but he went to Hawaii Winter Baseball in the fall and ranked as the league's top prospect, batting .283/.364/.415 in 106 at-bats.

Talk about the total package. Wieters offers plus tools both at the plate and behind it, yet the Orioles might be most excited about his intangibles. He's an impressive person, the type who looks like he can lead not only a pitching staff but a clubhouse. He was the most polished offensive player in the 2007 draft class, with plus bat speed and a line-drive approach to all fields. He has a good approach at the plate, and shows both discipline and pitch recognition. A switch-hitter, his swing is shorter from the right side and offers more power from the left. And even on days when his bat's not producing, he'll help his club with his catching. One scout said Wieters was the best defensive catcher he had seen since Charles Johnson, and he has soft hands and good footwork and receives the ball well. He obviously has plus-plus arm strength, having touched 96 mph as a closer.

Pitchers constantly worked away from Wieters in college, and he developed a bad habit of stepping toward the plate to cover the outer half, which short-circuits his power a bit and leaves him vulnerable to inside pitches. The Orioles worked with him to get his lower half in better position and have him step toward the pitcher to free his swing up inside, and they expect he'll be able to make that adjustment. Though he's exceptionally big for a catcher, his size hasn't worked against him behind the plate so far. His worst tool is his below-average speed, but that's a given for a catcher.

Wieters was a little rusty after holding out all summer, but his time in Hawaii should allow him to hit the ground running in the spring. All his tools are playable now yet he still offers projection, so he has the makings of a legitimate star. He'll officially open his pro career at high Class A Frederick and should move through the system quickly.

Year	Club (League)	Class	AVG	G	AB	R	H	2B	3B	HR	RBI	BB	SO	SB	OBP	SLG
2007	Did Not Play—Signed Late															

2 RADHAMES LIZ, RHP

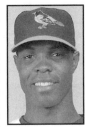

Born: Oct. 6, 1983. **B-T:** R-R. **Ht.:** 6-2. **Wt.:** 170. **Signed:** Dominican Republic, 2003. **Signed by:** Carlos Bernhardt.

Liz was part of a combined no-hitter in high Class A in 2006, and he added another last season at Double-A Bowie on the way to his major league debut. He got knocked around in the big leagues because he consistently fell behind hitters. Once seen as a possible reliever, Liz now looks like he has the stamina and pitches to work at the front of a major league rotation. His fastball still clocks in at 94-97 mph with life, and he has a curveball and changeup that are plus pitches when he commands them. If he gets ahead of hitters and uses all three pitches, he can be devastating. The keys for Liz are commanding his fastball in the strike zone and using his other pitches regularly. When he falls behind and starts leaning too much on his heater, it tends to drift up in the zone. He also needs to be more consistent with his mechanics, which will allow him to improve his overall command. Ideally he would get at least part of one more season in the minors, but he'll compete for a spot in the big league rotation in spring training.

Year	Club (League)	Class	W	L	ERA	G	GS	CG	SV	IP	H	R	ER	HR	BB	SO	AVG
2003	Orioles (DSL)	R	2	2	3.18	9	7	1	0	45	40	16	16	1	12	43	.233
2004	Orioles (DSL)	R	8	4	2.62	15	14	2	0	82	53	32	24	2	28	109	.177
2005	Aberdeen (NYP)	A	5	4	1.77	11	11	0	0	56	36	14	11	1	19	82	.188
	Delmarva (SAL)	A	2	3	4.46	10	10	0	0	38	33	23	19	2	23	55	.231
2006	Frederick (Car)	A	6	5	2.82	16	16	0	0	83	57	32	26	8	44	95	.196
	Bowie (EL)	AA	3	1	5.36	10	10	0	0	50	55	31	30	9	31	54	.281
2007	Bowie (EL)	AA	11	4	3.22	25	25	2	0	137	101	60	49	13	70	161	.204
	Baltimore (AL)	MLB	0	2	6.93	9	4	0	0	24	25	21	19	3	23	24	.260
MINOR LEAGUE TOTALS			37	23	3.20	96	93	5	0	492	375	208	175	36	227	599	.210
MAJOR LEAGUE TOTALS			0	2	6.93	9	4	0	0	24	25	21	19	3	23	24	.260

3 TROY PATTON, LHP

Born: Sept. 3, 1985. **B-T:** B-L. **Ht.:** 6-1. **Wt.:** 185. **Drafted:** HS—Magnolia, Texas, 2004 (9th round). **Signed by:** Rusty Pendergrass (Astros).

The Astros spent $900,000 in 2004 to lure Patton away from a Texas scholarship, and he made his big league debut with Houston at age 21 in August. The Orioles then acquired him and four other players in a December deal for Miguel Tejada. Patton enhances his solid stuff with outstanding command. He can touch 94 mph with his four-seam fastball and gets good sink on a two-seamer that sits in the high 80s. He has ditched a slow curveball he used in high school for a slider that he runs in on righthanders. He isn't afraid to use his changeup, which has nice fade. Patton has had minor shoulder issues for three straight seasons. He'll drop down to give batters another look, though that often causes his pitches to flatten out and hang in the strike zone. He likes to challenge hitters inside, which is good, but he has little margin for error. Patton should be healthy for spring training and is expected to crack Baltimore's rotation right away. His upside is as a No. 3 starter at best, but he's also a pretty safe bet to reach his ceiling.

Year	Club (League)	Class	W	L	ERA	G	GS	CG	SV	IP	H	R	ER	HR	BB	SO	AVG
2004	Greeneville (Appy)	R	2	2	1.93	6	6	0	0	28	23	8	6	1	5	32	.225
2005	Lexington (SAL)	A	5	2	1.94	15	15	0	0	78	59	24	17	3	20	94	.211
	Salem (Car)	A	1	4	2.63	10	9	0	0	41	34	12	12	2	8	38	.227
2006	Salem (Car)	A	7	7	2.93	19	19	1	0	101	92	49	33	4	37	102	.240
	Corpus Christi (TL)	AA	2	5	4.37	8	8	0	0	45	48	26	22	6	13	37	.271
2007	Corpus Christi (TL)	AA	6	6	2.99	16	16	0	0	102	96	38	34	10	33	69	.247
	Round Rock (PCL)	AAA	4	2	4.59	8	8	0	0	49	44	26	25	5	11	25	.247
	Houston (NL)	MLB	0	2	3.55	3	2	0	0	12	10	6	5	3	4	8	.213
MINOR LEAGUE TOTALS			27	28	3.01	82	81	1	0	445	396	183	149	31	127	397	.239
MAJOR LEAGUE TOTALS			0	2	3.55	3	2	0	0	12	10	6	5	3	4	8	.213

4 NOLAN REIMOLD, OF

Born: Oct. 12, 1983. **B-T:** R-R. **Ht.:** 6-4. **Wt.:** 210. **Drafted:** Bowling Green State, 2005 (2nd round). **Signed by:** Marc Ziegler.

Reimold has been the Orioles' best power prospect from the time he signed out of the 2005 draft, but he has battled nagging injuries that have slowed his progress in the last couple of years. It was foot and back injuries in 2006, then a strained oblique last year. He got 106 at-bats in the Arizona Fall League to make up some of his lost time. The injuries haven't dented Reimold's power, as he hit 17 home runs between Double-A and the AFL in just 292 at-bats. His bat speed and the leverage in his swing allow him to drive the ball out to any part of the park, and he should be a good hitter for average as well. He has the best outfield arm in the system, average speed and enough athleticism to play right field. The most important thing for Reimold is to stay healthy and get at-bats. He's now 24 and has just 186 at-bats in Double-A, so he needs to get moving. He still has holes in his swing that more advanced pitchers can exploit. The Orioles are anxious for Reimold to move through the upper levels of the system. He'll probably start the season back in Double-A, but if he plays well he could become a big league option quickly.

Year	Club (League)	Class	AVG	G	AB	R	H	2B	3B	HR	RBI	BB	SO	SB	OBP	SLG
2005	Aberdeen (NYP)	A	.294	50	180	33	53	15	2	9	30	29	44	2	.392	.550
	Frederick (Car)	A	.265	23	83	17	22	6	0	6	11	12	27	3	.371	.554
2006	Frederick (Car)	A	.255	119	415	73	106	26	0	19	75	76	107	14	.379	.455
2007	Orioles (GCL)	R	.233	9	30	4	7	4	1	0	8	6	4	0	.410	.433
	Bowie (EL)	AA	.306	50	186	30	57	15	0	11	34	17	47	2	.365	.565
MINOR LEAGUE TOTALS			.274	251	894	157	245	66	3	45	158	140	229	21	.379	.506

5 BILL ROWELL, 3B

RODGER WOOD

Born: Sept. 10, 1988. **B-T:** L-R. **Ht.:** 6-5. **Wt.:** 205. **Drafted:** HS—Pennsauken, N.J., 2006 (1st round). **Signed by:** Dean Albany.

Rowell received a $2.1 million bonus as the first high school position player selected in the 2006 draft, the most Baltimore had given a hitter out of the draft until Matt Wieters in 2007. Rowell strained his right oblique in spring training and didn't report to low Class A Delmarva until the end of May, and he struggled all year to catch up. Rowell has a big frame and a sweet lefthanded swing, and the Orioles still have no doubt it will add up to a power hitter in the middle of their lineup within a few seasons. Rowell has the bat speed to drive any pitch out to any part of a ballpark, and the aptitude to make adjustments. The Orioles say Rowell has made progress with his defense at third, showing improved footwork and using his arm better. But he still made 21 errors in 82 games last year, and it's not clear he'll have the range to stay there. He also needs to improve his approach against lefthanders after batting .185 against them in 2007. Though he's athletic for his size, he's a below-average runner. He didn't have a great year statistically, but Rowell learned a lot in his first full pro season despite missing more than a month of action. Baltimore has no doubts about his bat, whether he stays at third base or has to move to first base or the outfield. He'll take the next step to high Class A this season.

Year	Club (League)	Class	AVG	G	AB	R	H	2B	3B	HR	RBI	BB	SO	SB	OBP	SLG
2006	Bluefield (Appy)	R	.329	42	152	38	50	15	3	2	26	25	47	3	.422	.507
	Aberdeen (NYP)	A	.326	11	43	8	14	4	0	1	6	4	12	0	.388	.488
2007	Delmarva (SAL)	A	.273	91	352	47	96	21	3	9	57	31	104	3	.335	.426
MINOR LEAGUE TOTALS			.293	144	547	93	160	40	6	12	89	60	163	6	.365	.453

6 BRANDON SNYDER, 1B/3B

BRIAN BISSELL

Born: Nov. 23, 1986. **B-T:** R-R. **Ht.:** 6-2. **Wt.:** 205. **Drafted:** HS—Centreville, Va., 2005 (1st round). **Signed by:** Ty Brown.

Snyder was the Orioles' minor league comeback player of the year in 2007, rebounding from shoulder surgery to repair a torn rotator cuff in 2006. He then went to Hawaii Winter Baseball and batted .378 to win the batting title. He's the son of former big league pitcher Brian Snyder. A healthy Snyder again showed the swing that made him the 13th overall pick in 2005, with his bat head getting a better path to the ball. He also became more aggressive in the strike zone. He stays on breaking balls well and shows opposite-field power. Most of his adjustments were mental, however, after he got very low emotionally during 2006. He's a good athlete with decent speed, but he's not a basestealing threat. Though he was drafted as a catcher, that now appears to be out of the picture, putting even more emphasis on his bat. He made significant improvements at first base last season. He played third base in Hawaii and will get time there in 2008. He has the arm for third but will need to improve his footwork. He's still refining his strike-zone discipline. Now healthy and with his swing back in a groove, Snyder should move quickly. He should be fine at either first or third base, where his value will be tied to his run production. He should open the season in high Class A with the chance for a midseason promotion if he hits.

Year	Club (League)	Class	AVG	G	AB	R	H	2B	3B	HR	RBI	BB	SO	SB	OBP	SLG
2005	Bluefield (Appy)	R	.271	44	144	26	39	8	0	8	35	28	36	7	.380	.493
	Aberdeen (NYP)	A	.393	8	28	4	11	2	0	0	6	2	7	0	.419	.464
2006	Delmarva (SAL)	A	.194	38	144	12	28	12	0	3	20	9	55	0	.237	.340
	Aberdeen (NYP)	A	.234	34	124	14	29	8	1	1	11	5	43	2	.267	.339
2007	Delmarva (SAL)	A	.283	118	448	63	127	23	3	11	58	44	107	0	.354	.422
MINOR LEAGUE TOTALS			.264	242	888	119	234	53	4	23	130	88	248	9	.331	.410

7 JAKE ARRIETA, RHP

BILL MITCHELL

Born: March 6, 1986. **B-T:** R-R. **Ht.:** 6-3. **Wt.:** 210. **Drafted:** Texas Christian, 2007 (5th round). **Signed by:** Jim Richardson.

Arrieta was a candidate for the top of the first round after a standout sophomore season at Texas Christian and a 4-0, 0.27 summer for Team USA, but a disappointing junior season and high bonus demands drove him down in the draft. The Orioles took a chance on him in the fifth round and signed him just before the deadline for $1.1 million. Arrieta's fastball has run from 91-95 mph in the past, though he lost some velocity and life during the college season. His heater was better in the Arizona Fall League, though still not at its best. He also throws a hard slider with good bite. He has an ideal pitcher's body and an aggressive approach. The Orioles took Arrieta despite his down spring because they thought his problems were mechanical. His lines to the plate got off and he was throwing across his body and not transferring his weight properly, so he lost velocity and left balls up in the zone. The player-development staff thinks those flaws can be fixed with minor adjustments, not a major overhaul. He flashed a promising changeup as a sophomore but wasn't consistent with it in 2007. Even though he wasn't stretched out, Arrieta impressed scouts in the AFL, going right after hitters and performing well. The Orioles expect even better things once he fixes his mechanics. He could make his pro debut in high Class A.

Year	Club (League)	Class	W	L	ERA	G	GS	CG	SV	IP	H	R	ER	HR	BB	SO	AVG
2007	Did Not Play—Signed Late																

8 CHORYE SPOONE, RHP

RODGER WOOD

Born: Sept. 16, 1985. **B-T:** R-R. **Ht.:** 6-1. **Wt.:** 215. **Drafted:** Catonsville (Md.) CC, 2005 (8th round). **Signed by:** Ty Brown.

A local product, Spoone had been on the fringes of prospect status the previous two seasons, based on the promise of his live arm. He delivered on that promise in 2007, capping the year with a playoff MVP award as Frederick won the Carolina League title. He had two complete-game victories in the postseason, allowing just two runs while striking out 17. Spoone always has had a live fastball, sitting at 93-95 mph, and an outstanding curveball that has become much more consistent. His changeup also is getting better and ranks as a plus pitch at times. He has been very durable, leading the CL with three complete games and finishing fifth with 152 innings. While his command has improved significantly, Spoone will have to sharpen it further and consistently locate all his pitches as he advances. His biggest improvement has come with mound presence, as he now tunes out extraneous things like bad calls and focuses on the matter at hand. Spoone took the biggest leap forward of anyone in the system last year, maturing into a pitcher who now seems to have a clear future in a big league rotation. He'll take the next step to Double-A to open 2008.

Year	Club (League)	Class	W	L	ERA	G	GS	CG	SV	IP	H	R	ER	HR	BB	SO	AVG
2005	Bluefield (Appy)	R	2	5	8.03	15	3	0	0	24	27	25	22	3	13	27	.273
2006	Delmarva (SAL)	A	7	9	3.56	26	25	0	0	129	118	72	51	5	80	90	.241
2007	Frederick (Car)	A	10	9	3.26	26	25	3	0	152	108	65	55	8	67	133	.200
MINOR LEAGUE TOTALS			19	23	3.77	67	53	3	0	305	253	162	128	16	160	250	.224

9 PEDRO BEATO, RHP

MIKE JANES

Born: Oct. 27, 1986. **B-T:** R-R. **Ht.:** 6-5. **Wt.:** 210. **Drafted:** St. Petersburg (Fla.) JC, 2006 (1st round supplemental). **Signed by:** Nick Presto.

After the Mets failed to sign Beato as a draft-and-follow, the Orioles took him 31st overall and signed him for $1 million in 2006. He jumped to low Class A in his first full season and got knocked around a bit as he tried to work with a narrowed repertoire in order to improve his breaking pitches and changeup. Beato's stuff compares with that of anyone in the system, starting with a mid-90s fastball that has good movement and sink. He throws both a curveball and slider, with the curve the better pitch right now. His changeup has also made progress. He's intelligent and confident. While his stuff is good, Beato's pitchability still needs work. He's still inexperienced in knowing sequences and how to set hitters up. Baltimore took away his cutter, which he regards as his best offspeed pitch, and it was sometimes hard for him to pitch without it. He's too inventive with new pitches and actually makes it easier on hitters when he comes off his best stuff. His command also suffers when he tries to be too perfect. He had Tommy John surgery in high school, though he has shown no ill effects since. Beato will take the move up to high Class A this season, and he should be more effective with the cutter back in his arsenal. He'll need some time to develop but should be worth the wait.

Year	Club (League)	Class	W	L	ERA	G	GS	CG	SV	IP	H	R	ER	HR	BB	SO	AVG
2006	Aberdeen (NYP)	A	3	2	3.63	14	10	0	0	57	47	31	23	6	23	52	.222
2007	Delmarva (SAL)	A	7	8	4.05	27	27	0	0	142	139	75	64	10	59	106	.256
MINOR LEAGUE TOTALS			10	10	3.93	41	37	0	0	199	186	106	87	16	82	158	.246

10 BRANDON ERBE, RHP

STEVE MOORE

Born: Dec. 25, 1987. **B-T:** R-R. **Ht.:** 6-4. **Wt.:** 180. **Drafted:** HS—Baltimore, 2005 (3rd round). **Signed by:** Ty Brown.

There's no getting around Erbe's numbers for 2007, as he got knocked around all year and reached the system's single-inning pitch limit of 30 five times in his 25 starts. But the Orioles focus on how he made every turn in the rotation as a 19-year-old in the Carolina League. Erbe's stuff is still there, led by a mid-90s fastball that peaks at 96 mph, a slider with bite that's sometimes a plus pitch and an improving changeup. He shows good aptitude for his craft and for taking instruction. He smoothed out his delivery in instructional league. Command problems are the root of Erbe's struggles, and Baltimore thinks that comes down to being able to repeat his delivery and improving his overall confidence and mound presence. When he starts doubting his stuff, he tries to nibble and winds up leaving pitches over the middle of the plate. It wouldn't be surprising for Erbe to go back to high Class A to have some success, but his progress in instructional league gives him a chance to make the Double-A rotation out of spring training. He needs to show better command if he wants to stay in a starting role.

Year	Club (League)	Class	W	L	ERA	G	GS	CG	SV	IP	H	R	ER	HR	BB	SO	AVG
2005	Bluefield (Appy)	R	1	1	3.09	11	3	0	1	23	8	10	8	1	10	48	.103
	Aberdeen (NYP)	A	1	1	7.71	3	1	0	0	7	6	6	6	0	4	9	.261
2006	Delmarva (SAL)	A	5	9	3.22	28	27	0	0	114	88	47	41	2	47	133	.217
2007	Frederick (Car)	A	6	8	6.26	25	25	0	0	119	127	95	83	14	62	111	.273
MINOR LEAGUE TOTALS			13	19	4.70	67	56	0	1	264	229	158	138	17	123	301	.236

11 MIKE COSTANZO, 3B

Born: Sept. 9, 1983. **B-T:** L-R. **Ht.:** 6-3. **Wt.:** 215. **Drafted:** Coastal Carolina, 2005 (2nd round). **Signed by:** Roy Tanner (Phillies).

Costanzo had a busy offseason, moving from the Phillies to the Astros in the Brad Lidge trade in November, then staying with Houston just over a month before going to the Orioles as part of the five-player package for Miguel Tejada. Costanzo has enormous raw power, especially to the pull side, and ranked second in the Double-A Eastern League in homers last season. He typically has struggled against lefthanders, but he made huge strides late in 2007. If pitchers won't challenge him, Costanzo is more than willing to take a walk. A two-way player at Coastal Carolina, he has a plus arm at third base. He's an average runner once he gets underway. Some scouts believe Costanzo will have to move to first base because of poor agility and footwork at third, while others wonder whether he has too many holes in his swing to be an everyday player. He has 379 strikeouts in 345 pro games, and it's unlikely he'll hit for much of an average. Though he arrived in camp last spring in the best shape of his life, his lateral movement and first-step quickness remain fringy at best. The Orioles have had just four players hit 30 homers or more in the last decade, so while Costanzo has flaws, his power has value to them. Younger corner infielders Billy Rowell and Brandon Snyder could affect his future in his new organization, but Costanzo has the advantage of being more advanced and could see big league time in 2008 if he plays well at Triple-A Norfolk.

Year	Club (League)	Class	AVG	G	AB	R	H	2B	3B	HR	RBI	BB	SO	SB	OBP	SLG
2005	Batavia (NYP)	A	.274	73	281	47	77	17	3	11	50	35	89	0	.356	.473
2006	Clearwater (FSL)	A	.258	135	504	72	130	33	1	14	81	74	133	3	.364	.411
2007	Reading (EL)	AA	.270	137	508	92	137	29	1	27	86	75	157	2	.368	.490
MINOR LEAGUE TOTALS			.266	345	1293	211	344	79	5	52	217	184	379	5	.364	.456

12 GARRETT OLSON, LHP

Born: Oct. 18, 1983. **B-T:** R-L. **Ht.:** 6-1. **Wt.:** 200. **Drafted:** Cal Poly, 2005 (1st round supplemental). **Signed by:** Gil Kubski.

Olson continued his mastery of minor league hitters in 2007, but his first major league experience was considerably less impressive. He made his major league debut in July and held his own in two spot starts, but he got knocked around when he came up for good in August. Orioles officials said it was a simple function of getting behind hitters in the big leagues. Olson is intelligent and has confidence in every facet of his game, but sometimes he gives hitters too much credit and tries to come up with the perfect pitch early in the count, instead of just rearing back and getting strike one. When he gets ahead of hitters, he's a completely different pitcher. His fastball ranges from 88-93 mph, and it plays up because of his command.

He has a sharp, late-breaking slider, and his changeup has come along, though he still doesn't throw it enough. The key for him this year will be commanding all his pitches better in the strike zone, and using his changeup more so that he can completely master it. Olson's tough major league debut was the first time he had struggled as a pro, and he should learn from the experience. He'll compete for a rotation spot in spring training and go back to Triple-A for more minor league innings if he doesn't make it.

Year	Club (League)	Class	W	L	ERA	G	GS	CG	SV	IP	H	R	ER	HR	BB	SO	AVG
2005	Aberdeen (NYP)	A	2	1	1.58	11	6	0	1	40	22	7	7	1	13	40	.164
	Frederick (Car)	A	0	0	3.14	3	3	0	0	14	10	5	5	0	7	19	.192
2006	Frederick (Car)	A	4	4	2.77	14	14	0	0	81	81	32	25	7	19	77	.266
	Bowie (EL)	AA	6	5	3.42	14	14	0	0	84	78	33	32	5	31	85	.249
2007	Norfolk (IL)	AAA	9	7	3.16	22	22	1	0	128	95	49	45	13	39	120	.208
	Baltimore (AL)	MLB	1	3	7.79	7	7	0	0	32	42	28	28	4	28	28	.326
MINOR LEAGUE TOTALS			21	17	2.95	64	59	1	1	348	286	126	114	26	109	341	.227
MAJOR LEAGUE TOTALS			1	3	7.79	7	7	0	0	32	42	28	28	4	28	28	.326

13 TIM BASCOM, RHP

Born: Jan. 4, 1985. **B-T:** R-R. **Ht.:** 6-1. **Wt.:** 190. **Drafted:** Bradenton (South Coast), 2007 (4th round). **Signed by:** John Martin.

Bascom followed a winding road to professional baseball, and the Orioles are happy to be the beneficiaries. The Padres drafted Bascom in the sixth round out of Central Florida in 2006, and agreed to a $140,000 bonus before discovering he had damage in his right knee. He had been pitching on a torn anterior cruciate ligament, making his junior season (5-6. 2.47 with a 90-25 K-BB ratio in 80 innings) all the more impressive. San Diego lowered its bonus offer and Bascom passed, then returned to Florida to have surgery and return to school. Central Florida declared him ineligible because of his negotiations with a pro club and rescinded his scholarship, so he rehabbed his knee and then pitched for about three weeks in the independent South Coast League before the draft. The Orioles had liked him when scouting him for the 2006 draft, and he also worked out at their Sarasota complex in the spring, so they took him with their second pick in 2007 after losing their second- and third-rounders as free-agent compensation. They liked what they saw after signing Bascom for $200,000, even though he wasn't at his best as he worked himself back into game shape. He has a good feel for pitching and is willing to throw any pitch in any count, keeping hitters off balance. His fastball is 93-94 mph at its best, though it was more in the 89-91 range last summer. He also throws a curveball and slider for strikes, and his changeup can be a plus pitch. The Orioles put Bascom on a throwing program and expect to see him back to 100 percent in 2008, when he'll open the season in high Class A. He has the stuff and feel for pitching to move quickly.

Year	Club (League)	Class	W	L	ERA	G	GS	CG	SV	IP	H	R	ER	HR	BB	SO	AVG
2007	Delmarva (SAL)	A	3	3	3.74	12	12	0	0	67	60	30	28	6	24	55	.229
	Frederick (Car)	A	1	0	3.00	2	1	0	0	6	6	2	2	0	0	4	.250
MINOR LEAGUE TOTALS			4	3	3.68	14	13	0	0	73	66	32	30	6	24	59	.231

14 SCOTT MOORE, 3B/OF

Born: Nov. 17, 1983. **B-T:** L-R. **Ht.:** 6-2. **Wt.:** 180. **Drafted:** HS—Long Beach, 2002 (1st round). **Signed by:** Rob Wilfong (Tigers).

Moore looked like a first-round bust after three seasons in the Tigers system, but a trade to the Cubs for Kyle Farnsworth before the 2005 season gave his career a jumpstart. He was blocked at third base there by Aramis Ramirez, however, so Chicago included him and minor league righthanders Rocky Cherry and Jake Renshaw in a late-season deal for Steve Trachsel. Moore jumped right to the big leagues after the trade and held his own in September. Moore offers above-average lefthanded power at the plate, and he has hit at least 20 home runs in each of the last three seasons. His .260 career minor league average is about what scouts expect him to hit in the big leagues, as he strikes out a lot and has trouble with breaking balls. He has become a solid defensive third baseman, with a strong arm, though he occasionally has trouble with his accuracy. The Cubs gave him some Triple-A time in the outfield to increase his versatility and his chances of making their roster, and he was decent out there. He's an average runner whose instincts help him get the most of his speed. The Orioles were in full roster makeover mode in the offseason, and depending on how things shake out Moore could end up as the everyday third baseman. He should at least make the team as a backup, because he can also play at first base or on the outfield corners. Another recent trade acquisition, Mike Costanzo, could push him for playing time at the hot corner later in the year.

Year	Club (League)	Class	AVG	G	AB	R	H	2B	3B	HR	RBI	BB	SO	SB	OBP	SLG
2002	Tigers (GCL)	R	.293	40	133	18	39	6	2	4	25	10	31	1	.349	.459
2003	West Michigan (MWL)	A	.239	107	372	40	89	16	6	6	45	41	110	2	.325	.363
2004	Lakeland (FSL)	A	.223	118	391	52	87	13	4	14	56	49	125	2	.322	.384
2005	Daytona (FSL)	A	.281	128	466	77	131	31	2	20	82	55	134	22	.358	.485

Year	Club	Class	AVG	G	AB	R	H	2B	3B	HR	RBI	BB	SO	SB	OBP	SLG
2006	West Tenn (SL)	AA	.276	132	463	52	128	28	0	22	75	55	126	12	.360	.479
	Iowa (PCL)	AAA	.250	1	4	1	1	1	0	0	0	0	1	0	.250	.500
	Chicago (NL)	MLB	.263	16	38	6	10	2	0	2	5	2	10	0	.317	.474
2007	Iowa (PCL)	AAA	.265	103	321	61	85	19	4	19	69	48	100	4	.373	.526
	Chicago (NL)	MLB	.000	2	5	0	0	0	0	0	0	0	2	0	.000	.000
	Baltimore (AL)	MLB	.255	17	47	2	12	2	0	1	11	1	15	0	.260	.362
MINOR LEAGUE TOTALS			.260	629	2150	301	560	114	18	85	352	258	627	43	.348	.449
MAJOR LEAGUE TOTALS			.244	35	90	8	22	4	0	3	16	3	27	0	.271	.389

15 DAVID HERNANDEZ, RHP

Born: May 13, 1985. **B-T:** R-R. **Ht.:** 6-2. **Wt.:** 180. **Drafted:** Cosumnes River (Calif.) JC, 2005 (16th round). **Signed by:** James Keller.

Hernandez was drafted three times before he began his professional career. The Rockies took him in the 29th round out of a California high school in 2003, but failed to sign him as a draft-and-follow. The Diamondbacks took him in the 34th round in 2004 but couldn't sign him either. The Orioles took him in 2005 and signed him after he put his name all over the Cosumnes River (Calif.) JC record book. He holds school records for single-season (119) and career strikeouts (224), as well as career wins (20). Hernandez draws interest because he has a quick arm that generates 91-93 mph fastballs with amazing deception that allows him to generate high strikeout totals. The ball comes out quick from behind Hernandez' head, and batters don't pick it up. He easily outdistanced Chorye Spoone for the Carolina League strikeout lead last season (168 in 145 innings) and finished tied for eighth in the minors. Hernandez' breaking pitch is a big, sharp curveball, and his changeup has become a usable third offering. His numbers aren't better because he struggles with his command at times and tends to leave the ball up, resulting in too many baserunners and home runs. Command in the strike zone will tell the tale, and Hernandez will take the next step to Double-A for 2008.

Year	Club (League)	Class	W	L	ERA	G	GS	CG	SV	IP	H	R	ER	HR	BB	SO	AVG
2005	Aberdeen (NYP)	A	1	2	3.89	12	8	0	0	41	41	21	18	2	17	47	.255
2006	Delmarva (SAL)	A	7	8	4.15	28	28	0	0	145	134	83	67	13	71	154	.244
2007	Frederick (Car)	A	7	11	4.95	28	27	0	0	145	139	86	80	16	47	168	.249
MINOR LEAGUE TOTALS			15	21	4.47	68	63	0	0	332	314	190	165	31	135	369	.247

16 BOB McCRORY, RHP

Born: May 3, 1982. **B-T:** R-R. **Ht.:** 6-1. **Wt.:** 205. **Drafted:** Southern Mississippi, 2003 (4th round). **Signed by:** Mike Tullier.

Now that he has elbow problems out of the way, McCrory is in a hurry to get to the big leagues. He didn't pitch after getting drafted in 2003 because of a strained elbow, then had Tommy John surgery in 2005. He came back in 2006 and showed his arm was healthy, but he wasn't at full strength until last year, when he showed a fastball that peaked at 98-99 mph out of the bullpen during the summer and then drew good reviews in the Arizona Fall League, where he led the league with five saves and had a 1.50 ERA. McCrory is a pure power arm, coming at hitters with his live fastball and a sharp slider. He throws both two-seamers and four-seamers and keeps the ball down, making it tough for hitters to elevate. He has a nice delivery and good mound presence. Now that McCrory has established that his arm is sound, he'll have to get consistent with his command. He has the stuff and the makeup to pitch in the late innings. Because of his injuries, he has logged just 171 pro innings at age 25. The Orioles will bring him up from Triple-A as soon as he shows he's ready.

Year	Club (League)	Class	W	L	ERA	G	GS	CG	SV	IP	H	R	ER	HR	BB	SO	AVG
2003	Did Not Play—Injured																
2004	Delmarva (SAL)	A	0	1	7.59	8	0	0	0	10	13	16	9	3	15	11	.295
	Bluefield (Appy)	R	4	3	1.92	11	11	0	0	51	42	21	11	3	32	51	.226
	Aberdeen (NYP)	A	0	1	27.00	1	1	0	0	1	3	3	3	1	2	1	.500
2005	Aberdeen (NYP)	A	2	1	3.28	5	5	0	0	24	21	9	9	2	8	21	.233
2006	Aberdeen (NYP)	A	2	2	2.33	20	1	0	2	38	32	12	10	2	16	57	.230
2007	Frederick (Car)	A	0	0	1.23	22	0	0	14	22	16	4	3	1	12	22	.205
	Bowie (EL)	AA	1	2	3.91	22	0	0	13	23	23	17	10	0	16	22	.247
MINOR LEAGUE TOTALS			9	10	2.88	89	18	0	29	171	150	82	55	12	101	185	.236

17 BRANDON TRIPP, OF

Born: April 2, 1985. **B-T:** L-R. **Ht.:** 6-2. **Wt.:** 215. **Drafted:** Cal State Fullerton, 2006 (12th round). **Signed by:** Mark Ralston.

Orioles scouting director Joe Jordan has had an eye on Tripp since he was in high school in southern California, picking him in the 21st round in 2003 when Jordan was the Marlins' national crosschecker. Tripp went to Cal State Fullerton instead of signing, so Jordan grabbed him again in 2006. He wasn't a hotter pro prospect because of a funky swing, but roving hitting instructor Denny Walling made a small adjustment during spring training that helped him take off in 2007. He was the organization's minor league player of the year after establishing himself as one of the farm system's best run producers. He belted 19 home runs despite missing three weeks in May with a wrist injury. Walling made a small change in Tripp's lower half that got him in a better position to hit, and it allowed him to tap into his plus raw power while hitting for a better average as well. His pitch recognition needs improvement, but that should happen with continued at-bats. Tripp spent most of his time in right field last season, and he has enough arm to play there, and he also can play in center. His slightly above-average speed allows him to steal the occasional base. After the progress he made last season, the Orioles wouldn't be surprised by anything. He'll advance to high Class A in 2008.

Year	Club (League)	Class	AVG	G	AB	R	H	2B	3B	HR	RBI	BB	SO	SB	OBP	SLG
2006	Aberdeen (NYP)	A	.221	43	145	20	32	8	0	2	15	16	49	1	.345	.317
2007	Delmarva (SAL)	A	.288	104	371	72	107	25	4	19	79	43	112	7	.377	.531
MINOR LEAGUE TOTALS			.269	147	516	92	139	33	4	21	94	59	161	8	.368	.471

18 RANDOR BIERD, RHP

Born: March 14, 1984. **B-T:** R-R. **Ht.:** 6-4. **Wt.:** 190. **Signed:** Dominican Republic, 2003. **Signed by:** Ramon Pena (Tigers).

Two years after his promising 2005 season was cut short by Tommy John surgery, Bierd established himself as one of the Tigers' top relief pitching prospects, but they couldn't find room for him on their 40-man roster. The Orioles gladly took him with the third pick of the major league Rule 5 draft in December. Bierd began the 2007 season as a reliever in low Class A and earned a promotion all the way to Double-A in June. He walked only 10 batters thereafter while displaying the stuff and mound presence you'd hope to see in a reliable, sinker/slider setup man. His fastball, which ranges from 90-93 mph, has average velocity but plays up because of sharp sinking movement. His hard slider has good downward tilt and changes planes, and it also induces a lot of groundballs. He has made progress with his changeup, but it's still below average. Bierd has shown good durability since his surgery and has the stamina to pitch on back-to-back days. He averaged 5.2 strikeouts per walk in Double-A, a testament to his impeccable control. Detroit loved his work ethic and believed in his ability, and it's reasonable to think he could stick in the big leagues all season with the Orioles. If he doesn't, they'll have to expose him to waivers or offer him back to the Tigers.

Year	Club (League)	Class	W	L	ERA	G	GS	CG	SV	IP	H	R	ER	HR	BB	SO	AVG
2003	Tigers (DSL)	R	2	2	4.61	9	5	0	0	27	24	18	14	1	12	31	.240
2004	Tigers (GCL)	R	1	3	2.78	11	1	0	0	32	23	11	10	3	5	39	.197
	Lakeland (FSL)	A	0	3	6.52	4	4	0	0	19	22	15	14	2	9	18	.301
2005	West Michigan (MWL)	A	4	1	2.64	7	7	0	0	44	30	14	13	2	10	42	.194
	Lakeland (FSL)	A	1	3	5.66	4	4	0	0	20	22	14	13	4	4	18	.268
	Erie (EL)	AA	1	3	5.40	4	4	0	0	21	28	19	13	2	8	10	.315
2006	Oneonta (NYP)	A	5	0	6.57	20	2	0	0	38	48	30	28	2	15	41	.298
2007	West Michigan (MWL)	A	1	1	2.05	15	0	0	0	22	17	8	5	1	6	29	.210
	Erie (EL)	AA	3	2	3.35	27	3	0	1	45	31	18	17	1	10	52	.188
MINOR LEAGUE TOTALS			18	18	4.21	101	30	0	1	271	245	147	127	18	79	280	.239

19 JAMES HOEY, RHP

Born: Dec. 30, 1982. **B-T:** R-R. **Ht.:** 6-6. **Wt.:** 200. **Drafted:** Rider, 2003 (13th round). **Signed by:** Jim Howard.

Hoey jumped into the Orioles' plans in 2006, flying through three levels of the minors and making his major league debut after recovering from Tommy John surgery in 2004. He pitched just as well in the minors last year, including 20 scoreless appearances in Double-A, but again got hit hard in the big leagues. Hoey has shown plus stuff ever since coming back from his surgery, with a fastball that consistently sits at 94-97 mph and has touched 100. He gets a good downhill plane to the plate from his 6-foot-6 frame, and it's hard for hitters to elevate the ball. He backs up his heat with a sharp slider. While Hoey goes right after hitters in the minors, he has tried to be too fine in the majors, losing command of both his pitches and falling behind in the count. When he goes to the fastball in those situations, big league hitters turn it around. Hoey has all the tools to pitch in the late innings at the big league level, so the Orioles hope his stints at the end of the last two seasons have taught him what he needs to do to have success there. They've worked him in multiple innings and on back-to-back days to prepare him for a middle-relief role for the near future. He'll compete for a job in the Baltimore bullpen in spring training.

Year	Club (League)	Class	W	L	ERA	G	GS	CG	SV	IP	H	R	ER	HR	BB	SO	AVG
2003	Bluefield (Appy)	R	2	3	2.79	11	8	0	0	42	33	19	13	3	19	20	.219
2004	Aberdeen (NYP)	A	0	1	9.45	2	2	0	0	6	12	8	7	1	1	6	.375
2005	Aberdeen (NYP)	A	1	1	4.80	9	0	0	0	15	11	10	8	1	10	15	.216
2006	Delmarva (SAL)	A	2	1	2.54	27	0	0	18	28	17	8	8	2	10	46	.175
	Frederick (Car)	A	0	0	0.64	14	0	0	11	14	13	3	1	0	5	16	.228
	Bowie (EL)	AA	0	0	4.00	8	0	0	4	9	9	5	4	1	3	11	.243

	Club (League)	Class	W	L	ERA	G	GS	CG	SV	IP	H	R	ER	HR	BB	SO	AVG
	Baltimore (AL)	MLB	0	1	10.24	12	0	0	0	9	14	11	11	1	5	6	.359
2007	Bowie (EL)	AA	1	0	0.00	20	0	0	14	18	13	0	0	0	4	28	.200
	Norfolk (IL)	AAA	2	0	1.33		0	0	2	27	15	4	4	1	10	41	.161
	Baltimore (AL)	MLB	3	4	7.30	23	0	0	0	24	25	21	20	2	18	18	.272
MINOR LEAGUE TOTALS			8	6	2.52	111	10	0	49	160	123	57	45	9	62	183	.211
MAJOR LEAGUE TOTALS			3	5	8.13	35	0	0	0	34	39	32	31	3	23	24	.298

20 DENNIS SARFATE, RHP

Born: April 9, 1981. **B-T:** R-R. **Ht.:** 6-4. **Wt.:** 220. **Drafted:** Chandler-Gilbert (Ariz.) CC, 2001 (9th round). **Signed by:** Brian Johnson (Brewers).

Sarfate finally found his niche in the bullpen, and now he's hoping he has found an organization that has a role for him. After coming up through the Brewers system, he was sold to the Astros in September and made seven appearances in Houston, giving up one run. The Astros then included him in the five-player package they used to acquire Miguel Tejada in December. Sarfate's professional future became much brighter when he moved into a full-time relief role in 2006. He could focus solely on his 93-96 mph fastball and power slider, and no longer had to worry about his curveball or changeup. Some scouts have seen his fastball up to 100 mph, and when he commands both his fastball and slider, he can be untouchable. His slider breaks down more than most, with three-quarter tilt. Sarfate always had a great arm, big frame and easy motion, but showed little feel for pitching as a starter, and he has been much more confident in relief. The Brewers didn't trust his command enough to throw Sarfate into a pennant race last season, but Baltimore should give him ample opportunity to work out the kinks in the big league bullpen in 2008.

Year	Club (League)	Class	W	L	ERA	G	GS	CG	SV	IP	H	R	ER	HR	BB	SO	AVG
2001	Ogden (Pio)	R	1	2	4.63	9	4	0	1	23	20	13	12	4	10	32	.230
2002	Brewers (AZL)	R	0	0	2.57	5	5	0	0	14	6	4	4	0	7	22	.125
	Ogden (Pio)	R	0	0	9.00	1	0	0	0	1	2	1	1	0	1	2	.400
2003	Beloit (MWL)	A	12	2	2.84	26	26	0	0	139	114	50	44	11	66	140	.227
2004	Huntsville (SL)	AA	7	12	4.05	28	25	0	0	129	128	71	58	12	78	113	.278
2005	Huntsville (SL)	AA	9	9	3.88	24	24	1	0	130	120	65	56	13	59	110	.245
	Nashville (PCL)	AAA	0	1	2.25	2	1	0	0	12	6	3	3	1	4	10	.150
2006	Nashville (PCL)	AAA	10	7	3.67	34	21	0	0	125	125	63	51	7	78	117	.265
	Milwaukee (NL)	MLB	0	0	4.32	8	0	0	0	8	9	4	4	0	4	11	.265
2007	Nashville (PCL)	AAA	2	7	4.52	45	1	0	4	61	61	35	31	6	47	68	.270
	Houston (NL)	MLB	1	0	1.08	7	0	0	0	8	5	1	1	0	1	14	.172
MINOR LEAGUE TOTALS			41	40	3.68	174	107	1	5	635	582	305	260	54	350	614	.250
MAJOR LEAGUE TOTALS			1	0	2.70	15	0	0	0	16	14	5	5	0	5	25	.222

21 ZACH BRITTON, LHP

Born: Dec. 22, 1987. **B-T:** L-L. **Ht.:** 6-2. **Wt.:** 180. **Drafted:** HS—Weatherford, Texas, 2006 (3rd round). **Signed by:** Jim Richardson.

Britton has the Orioles looking for big things as he heads into his first experience in a full-season league. They've kept a pretty tight leash on him through his first year and a half in the organization. He signed for $435,000 out of the 2006 draft and spent last year in the short-season Aberdeen rotation, showing the live low-90s fastball that made him a third-round pick. He featured a good curveball during the summer, then turned the corner with his slider in instructional league. Baltimore thinks the slider could elevate his entire repertoire. It's a sharp, late breaker, and Britton got excited about it when he saw what it did to hitters in instructional league. He never been able to get good action on the slider before. His changeup also looks promising but still needs work. He has good mound presence and will have to improve his command as he moves up.

Year	Club (League)	Class	W	L	ERA	G	GS	CG	SV	IP	H	R	ER	HR	BB	SO	AVG
2006	Bluefield (Appy)	R	0	4	5.29	11	11	0	0	34	35	22	20	4	20	21	.271
2007	Aberdeen (NYP)	A	6	4	3.68	15	15	0	0	63	64	33	26	1	22	45	.256
MINOR LEAGUE TOTALS			6	8	4.24	26	26	0	0	97	99	55	46	5	42	66	.261

22 TYLER HENSON, SS

Born: Dec. 15, 1987. **B-T:** R-R. **Ht.:** 6-1. **Wt.:** 190. **Drafted:** HS—Tuttle, Okla., 2006 (5th round). **Signed by:** Jim Richardson.

Henson was a three-sport standout at Tuttle High in Oklahoma, a school with a proud athletic history and the alma mater of 2003 Heisman Trophy winner Jason White. As a quarterback, he led the football team to a 14-0 record and state title in the fall of his senior year, then led the baseball team to a state championship in the spring. He looked overmatched by pro pitching in his pro debut, but he showed athleticism and the ability to make adjustments last season. He hit the ball all over the field and showed some power as well, handling lefthanders and righthanders equally well. He'll need to improve his approach as he moves up and cut down on his strikeouts. He offers above-average speed and puts it to use on the basepaths, stealing 20 bases in 22 attempts in 2007. Henson made 30 errors in 67 games at shortstop last year, most of them related to poor footwork. The Orioles say the problems can be overcome, but he's also still growing, so it's more likely he'll move over to third base in time. He has plenty of arm for the hot corner. Henson has an interesting package of skills, and Baltimore is curious to see how he'll do in a full-season league in 2008.

Year	Club (League)	Class	AVG	G	AB	R	H	2B	3B	HR	RBI	BB	SO	SB	OBP	SLG
2006	Bluefield (Appy)	R	.230	43	148	21	34	5	2	0	13	18	49	1	.314	.291
2007	Aberdeen (NYP)	A	.289	67	256	44	74	18	4	5	31	22	68	20	.353	.449
	Frederick (Car)	A	.059	6	17	0	1	0	0	0	1	1	8	0	.105	.059
MINOR LEAGUE TOTALS			.259	116	421	65	109	23	6	5	45	41	125	21	.329	.378

23 JEFF FIORENTINO, OF

Born: April 14, 1983. **B-T:** L-R. **Ht.:** 6-1. **Wt.:** 185. **Drafted:** Florida Atlantic, 2004 (3rd round). **Signed by:** Nick Presto.

While getting to the big leagues is usually a cause for celebration, getting there so quickly hasn't been a boon for Fiorentino. The Orioles jumped him from high Class A to Baltimore in 2005 and it has stunted his progress since, raising expectations unnecessarily. He got off to a horrible start in 2007, batting .160 in April, but hit .298 or better in every month after that and had 10 home runs in July and August. At the plate, Fiorentino uses the whole field when he's at his best and has power in his bat. He has an unorthodox approach, relying on his hands to do the work in his swing, but he succeeds with it. He struggles when he tries to pull the ball, and he didn't perform well against lefthanders last season, batting .217. Fiorentino has a wide range of skills, offering above-average defense at all three outfield positions with good speed, range and arm strength. He plays hard every day. While Fiorentino seems to have stalled, the Orioles still believe he can be an everyday player, though he would also seem to be an ideal fourth outfielder. Pleased with his performance last year, they'll move him up to Triple-A and see if he can earn his way back to the big leagues.

Year	Club (League)	Class	AVG	G	AB	R	H	2B	3B	HR	RBI	BB	SO	SB	OBP	SLG
2004	Aberdeen (NYP)	A	.348	14	46	9	16	7	1	2	12	9	4	3	.474	.674
	Delmarva (SAL)	A	.302	49	179	40	54	15	2	10	36	20	50	2	.379	.575
2005	Frederick (Car)	A	.286	103	413	70	118	18	4	22	66	34	90	12	.346	.508
	Baltimore (AL)	MLB	.250	13	44	7	11	2	0	1	5	2	10	1	.277	.364
2006	Bowie (EL)	AA	.275	104	385	63	106	14	0	13	62	53	58	9	.365	.413
	Baltimore (AL)	MLB	.256	19	39	8	10	2	0	0	7	7	3	1	.375	.308
2007	Bowie (EL)	AA	.282	126	436	68	123	18	4	15	65	44	89	8	.346	.445
MINOR LEAGUE TOTALS			.286	396	1459	250	417	72	11	62	241	160	291	34	.360	.478
MAJOR LEAGUE TOTALS			.253	32	83	15	21	4	0	1	12	9	13	2	.326	.337

24 MATT ANGLE, OF

Born: Sept. 10, 1985. **B-T:** L-R. **Ht.:** 5-10. **Wt.:** 175. **Drafted:** Ohio State, 2007 (7th round). **Signed by:** Rich Morales.

Orioles area scouts and crosscheckers fell in love with Angle's game at Ohio State, seeing a legitimate center fielder who not only could play the little man's game but actually relished the role. He had also impressed scouts in the Cape Cod League in the summer of 2006, finishing eighth in the league in batting (.298). Baltimore took him in the seventh round, signed him for $110,000 and found him to be exactly as advertised. Angle has legitimate leadoff skills, highlighted by his willingness to work counts and take walks. He focuses on getting on base and is a skillful bunter, and he also uses his hands well in his swing and shows gap power. He's an above-average runner with good instincts on the bases, and he was caught just four times in 38 basestealing attempts in his pro debut. He also uses his speed in center field to play good defense and shows plenty of arm for the position. Angle's game is all about getting on base and using his legs, and the Orioles are interested to see how it will play at higher levels. He should open his first full season in low Class A.

Year	Club (League)	Class	AVG	G	AB	R	H	2B	3B	HR	RBI	BB	SO	SB	OBP	SLG
2007	Aberdeen (NYP)	A	.301	66	236	60	71	4	4	0	14	47	40	34	.421	.352
MINOR LEAGUE TOTALS			.301	66	236	60	71	4	4	0	14	47	40	34	.421	.352

25 CHRIS VINYARD, 1B

Born: Dec. 15, 1985. **B-T:** R-R. **Ht.:** 6-4. **Wt.:** 230. **Drafted:** Chandler-Gilbert (Ariz.) CC, D/F 2005 (38th round). **Signed by:** Bill Bliss/John Gillette.

Vinyard signed as a draft-and-follow in May 2006 and immediately attracted attention by hitting 26 doubles and eight home runs at Aberdeen, establishing himself as a power prospect in a system that didn't have many. He continued driving the ball last season in low Class A, though his slugging percentage dropped by

49 points, and proved himself as a run producer. Vinyard is a skilled hitter who can drive the ball all over the field and shows legitimate plus power. The tradeoff is high strikeout numbers, and while the Orioles are willing to accept that to a point, they would like him to become more selective. The big question for Vinyard, though, is whether he can handle a position. He doesn't move well around the bag at first base, so he'll have to work to be an adequate defender there. A fringy arm and below-average speed mean the outfield isn't an option, so DH is the only other place for him to go. Vinyard split time between first base and DH last year and should do the same this year in high Class A. He'll have to keep hitting home runs to have value.

Year	Club (League)	Class	AVG	G	AB	R	H	2B	3B	HR	RBI	BB	SO	SB	OBP	SLG
2006	Aberdeen (NYP)	A	.284	73	264	40	75	26	2	8	47	28	62	0	.366	.489
2007	Delmarva (SAL)	A	.269	129	480	61	129	34	0	16	82	48	115	1	.340	.440
MINOR LEAGUE TOTALS			.274	202	744	101	204	60	2	24	129	76	177	1	.349	.457

26 BRAD BERGESEN, RHP

Born: Sept. 25, 1985. **B-T:** L-R. **Ht.:** 6-2. **Wt.:** 205. **Drafted:** HS—Foothill, Calif., 2004 (4th round). **Signed by:** Ed Sprague.

Bergesen struggled with mononucleosis in 2006, and the illness not only kept him out of action for a month but also sapped his strength for much of the year. He bounced back with a strong performance in low Class A, then was hit in the head by a line drive during batting practice after a promotion to high Class A. He missed only one start but never got untracked, though he pitched better in the Carolina League playoffs. Bergesen succeeds with command and movement, though his velocity improved last season from 89-90 to 91-93 mph. He throws a four-seam fastball that peaks at 95, but is better off using his two-seamer with good sink. He also throws a low-80s slider and a solid changeup. Bergesen gets in trouble when he doesn't command his pitches in the strike zone, and he has a tendency to overthink and try to be too precise at times. As one scout said, "He's not sexy, but he can pitch." Bergesen probably will return to high Class A to open 2008 but could earn another midseason promotion if he performs well.

Year	Club (League)	Class	W	L	ERA	G	GS	CG	SV	IP	H	R	ER	HR	BB	SO	AVG
2004	Bluefield (Appy)	R	0	0	7.94	5	0	0	0	5	7	5	5	1	3	6	.292
2005	Aberdeen (NYP)	A	1	3	4.82	15	15	0	0	71	89	45	38	5	14	54	.308
2006	Delmarva (SAL)	A	5	4	4.27	18	14	1	0	86	97	44	41	6	10	49	.280
2007	Delmarva (SAL)	A	7	3	2.19	15	15	1	0	94	75	30	23	3	17	73	.214
	Frederick (Car)	A	3	6	5.75	10	10	1	0	56	78	38	36	4	9	35	.332
MINOR LEAGUE TOTALS			16	16	4.10	63	54	3	0	313	346	162	143	19	53	217	.278

27 TYLER KOLODNY, 3B

Born: March 9, 1988. **B-T:** R-R. **Ht.:** 6-2. **Wt.:** 210. **Drafted:** HS—Woodland Hills, Calif., 2007 (16th round). **Signed by:** Gil Kubski.

Baltimore went with a college-heavy approach in the 2007 draft. Kolodny was the first high school player it picked, and one of just two it signed out of the entire draft. After turning pro for a $39,000 bonus, he instantly endeared himself to the Orioles by playing all-out every minute of every game, bringing great energy to the ballpark every day. Scouts and coaches said he was easy to identify because he was the one who always had the dirty uniform. Kolodny is a big, physical kid who loves to play and has a knack for hitting. He makes consistent hard contact and showed good power in his pro debut. He has a good approach for his age and loves to work on his swing. He's an average runner and shows decent range at third base, but he needs to work on his throws. He made 15 errors in 36 games at third base, and his motion costs him strength and accuracy. He made progress in instructional league, but he could end up at first base. There's no doubt he'll put in the work to try to stay at third base, though. Kolodny will open the season at 20, old for a high school player in his first full season, so he'll get the chance to jump to low Class A.

Year	Club (League)	Class	AVG	G	AB	R	H	2B	3B	HR	RBI	BB	SO	SB	OBP	SLG
2007	Orioles (GCL)	R	.318	43	151	33	48	10	2	6	30	15	30	6	.406	.530
MINOR LEAGUE TOTALS			.318	43	151	33	48	10	2	6	30	15	30	6	.406	.530

28 LUIS LEBRON, RHP

Born: March 13, 1985. **B-T:** R-R. **Ht.:** 6-1. **Wt.:** 170. **Signed:** Dominican Republic, 2004. **Signed by:** Carlos Bernhardt.

Lebron drew raves in 2006 when he moved to the bullpen full-time and overmatched hitters as a closer in the short-season New York-Penn League, but the results weren't as good last season. He didn't bring his ERA below 5.00 until the end of July. A poor final month took it back up to 5.04. Lebron struggled with his command all season, a function of his mechanics and an inability to repeat his delivery. The Orioles also think he lost confidence in his first exposure to cold weather, as he had a hard time getting a feel for the ball and subsequently lost his confidence. The stuff is still there, however. Lebron throws a lively mid-90s fastball that peaks at 98 mph. His slider is a legitimate second offering now, and he can get by with just those two pitches coming out of the bullpen, though he does mix in an occasional changeup. His control problems not only create baserunners in droves, but also drive up his pitch counts. Lebron is young and has a lot of learning to do, but his stuff means he'll get every opportunity. He should move up to high Class A this year.

Year	Club (League)	Class	W	L	ERA	G	GS	CG	SV	IP	H	R	ER	HR	BB	SO	AVG
2005	Bluefield (Appy)	R	2	4	11.16	14	7	0	0	25	34	37	31	2	22	45	.318
2006	Delmarva (SAL)	A	1	0	27.00	2	0	0	0	1	3	4	4	1	1	1	.500
	Aberdeen (NYP)	A	0	2	1.17	32	0	0	20	30	17	6	4	2	15	46	.163
2007	Delmarva (SAL)	A	1	2	5.04	46	0	0	5	55	48	35	31	1	55	86	.233
	Bowie (EL)	AA	0	0	3.86	2	0	0	0	2	1	1	1	0	1	4	.125
MINOR LEAGUE TOTALS			4	8	5.57	96	7	0	25	114	103	83	71	6	94	182	.239

29 JAMES JOHNSON, RHP

Born: June 27, 1983. **B-T:** R-R. **Ht.:** 6-5. **Wt.:** 224. **Drafted:** HS—Endicott, N.Y., 2001 (5th round). **Signed by:** Jim Howard.

Johnson continued his systematic progression through the system in 2007, moving up to Triple-A and again taking his turn like clockwork all season long. His numbers were about the same as the year before in Double-A, but he pitched a little better and was done in by a few disastrous starts. Johnson has three major league pitches, highlighted by an 88-92 mph fastball that maintains its velocity all season long. His curveball has become a reliable second pitch, and his changeup is average as well. The key is getting better command in the strike zone, because more advanced hitters have been able to lay off his chase pitches and wait for something in the fat part of the plate. He also has run up high pitch counts as he tries to pick his way through a batting order. Johnson has proven his durability and the quality of his pitches, and the Orioles are ready to see if he can pitch in the big leagues or if his command issues will keep him from fulfilling his potential. He'll compete for a major league bullpen job in spring training.

Year	Club (League)	Class	W	L	ERA	G	GS	CG	SV	IP	H	R	ER	HR	BB	SO	AVG
2001	Orioles (GCL)	R	0	1	3.86	7	4	0	0	18	17	10	8	3	7	19	.239
2002	Bluefield (Appy)	R	4	2	4.37	11	9	0	0	55	52	36	27	5	16	36	.250
2003	Bluefield (Appy)	R	3	2	3.68	11	11	0	0	51	62	24	21	2	18	46	.291
2004	Delmarva (SAL)	A	8	7	3.29	20	17	0	0	106	97	44	39	9	30	93	.246
2005	Bowie (EL)	AA	0	0	0.00	1	1	0	0	7	3	0	0	0	2	6	.136
	Frederick (Car)	A	12	9	3.49	28	27	2	1	159	139	77	62	11	64	168	.231
2006	Bowie (EL)	AA	13	6	4.44	27	26	0	0	156	165	80	77	13	57	124	.274
	Baltimore (AL)	MLB	0	1	24.00	1	1	0	0	3	9	8	8	1	3	0	.563
2007	Norfolk (IL)	AAA	6	12	4.07	26	25	2	0	148	164	79	67	15	48	109	.278
	Baltimore (AL)	MLB	0	0	9.00	1	0	0	0	2	3	2	2	0	2	1	.375
MINOR LEAGUE TOTALS			46	39	3.85	131	120	4	1	703	699	350	301	58	242	601	.259
MAJOR LEAGUE TOTALS			0	1	18.00	2	1	0	0	5	12	10	10	1	5	1	.500

30 KIERON POPE, OF

Born: Oct. 3, 1986. **B-T:** R-R. **Ht.:** 6-1. **Wt.:** 195. **Drafted:** HS—Gay, Ga., 2005 (4th round). **Signed by:** Dave Jennings.

Pope is a poster boy for the kinds of players whom scouting director Joe Jordan is trying to bring into the organization, but his progress has been stunted by shoulder problems. After unsuccessfully trying to rehabilitate a shoulder injury, Pope finally had surgery last spring and got just 66 at-bats during the season. He was closer to full health in instructional league, but he had to DH because his arm still wasn't ready. The bad news is that he has missed valuable development time, but the good news is that in 2008, he'll be at full strength for the first time in two years. Pope's raw power is his most impressive tool, and he shows plenty of ability in flashes. He needs to stay healthy and establish some consistency in his game. The key to his advancement is simply getting the bat and ball together more, and the main area of emphasis there is adjusting to breaking balls. His speed and defensive tools all rate about average, but he should be a fine left fielder. It's simply too early to judge Pope, who just needs a full season of at-bats. He'll probably open at low Class A.

Year	Club (League)	Class	AVG	G	AB	R	H	2B	3B	HR	RBI	BB	SO	SB	OBP	SLG
2005	Bluefield (Appy)	R	.228	41	149	23	34	3	1	5	22	8	62	5	.297	.362
2006	Bluefield (Appy)	R	.341	37	135	20	46	16	1	5	29	10	36	4	.411	.585
	Aberdeen (NYP)	A	.107	20	75	9	8	0	0	0	7	2	33	1	.160	.107
2007	Bluefield (Appy)	R	.197	20	66	4	13	2	0	0	5	5	22	0	.284	.227
MINOR LEAGUE TOTALS			.238	118	425	56	101	21	2	10	63	25	153	10	.308	.367

Boston Red Sox

BY JIM CALLIS

When the Red Sox introduced Theo Epstein as their general manager in November 2002, he talked of building a "$100 million player-development machine." Epstein may have come in low on his estimate for big league payroll, but otherwise consider his goal a mission accomplished.

The Red Sox' first World Series championship of Epstein's tenure—and their first in 86 years—came in 2004. Just one fully homegrown player, Trot Nixon, was on the roster for the entire postseason.

By contrast, the club that swept the Rockies in 2007 highlighted Boston's scouting and development aptitude. Rookies Jacoby Ellsbury and Dustin Pedroia batted atop the lineup in the last two games, and the only reason that second-year starter Kevin Youkilis wasn't in the heart of the order was that David Ortiz moved to first with the DH scrapped at Coors Field. Second-year pitchers Jon Lester, Manny Delcarmen and Jonathan Papelbon did most of the pitching in the clincher.

Clay Buchholz, who no-hit the Orioles in his second big league start in September, wasn't even needed. He sat out the playoffs with a tired arm.

The Red Sox' continued aggressive pursuit of talent on both the free-agent and amateur markets has them poised to be a World Series favorite for at least the next few years. Their deep, balanced farm system offers both position players and pitchers, with talent spread throughout all levels.

Though cracking the Boston roster will be difficult, righthanders Justin Masterson and Michael Bowden, shortstop Jed Lowrie and outfielder Brandon Moss are just about ready for prime-time duty. Deeper down, first baseman Lars Anderson, outfielder Ryan Kalish, lefty Nick Hagadone and shortstop Oscar Tejeda are loaded with promise.

The Red Sox aren't afraid to buck MLB and spend what they deem necessary on the draft. That's an advantage, to be sure, but it still can't take away from the success scouting director Jason McLeod has had running drafts from 2005-07. His draftees inclued the first eight prospects on this list: Buchholz, Ellsbury, Anderson, Masterson, Lowrie, Kalish, Bowden and Hagadone.

Boston also is becoming a leader on the international front. Besides signing Japanese big leaguers Daisuke Matsuzaka and Hideki Okajima, the Sox have bolstered the system with the likes of Tejeda, outfielder Engel Beltre (sent to the Rangers in the

Homegrown lefty Jon Lester helped Boston win its second championship in four years

TOP 30 PROSPECTS

1. Clay Buchholz, rhp	16. Michael Almanzar, 3b
2. Jacoby Ellsbury, of	17. Anthony Rizzo, 1b
3. Lars Anderson, 1b	18. Craig Hansen, rhp
4. Justin Masterson, rhp	19. Daniel Bard, rhp
5. Jed Lowrie, ss	20. Mark Wagner, c
6. Ryan Kalish, of	21. Aaron Bates, 1b
7. Michael Bowden, rhp	22. Dustin Richardson, lhp
8. Nick Hagadone, lhp	23. Jason Place, of
9. Oscar Tejeda, ss	24. Che-Hsuan Lin, of
10. Josh Reddick, of	25. Bubba Bell, of
11. Brandon Moss, of	26. Chris Carter, 1b/of
12. Argenis Diaz, ss	27. Hunter Jones, lhp
13. Kris Johnson, lhp	28. Reid Engel, of
14. Will Middlebrooks, ss	29. Yamaico Navarro, ss/3b
15. Ryan Dent, 2b/ss	30. Bryce Cox, rhp

Eric Gagne trade) and infielder Michael Almanzar from the Dominican Republic and outfielder Che-Hsuan Lin from Taiwan.

Besides restocking the big league club, the depth of talent also provides Boston with plenty of trade fodder. The Red Sox gave up Hanley Ramirez and Anibal Sanchez in a November 2005 swap that landed ace Josh Beckett and World Series MVP Mike Lowell. They also appear to be in as good a position as any club to acquire Johan Santana if the Twins decide to deal the best pitcher in baseball.

General Manager: Theo Epstein. **Farm Director:** Mike Hazen. **Scouting Director:** Jason McLeod.

Class	Team	League	W	L	PCT	Finish*	Manager	Affiliated
Majors	Boston	American	96	66	.593	1st (14)	Terry Francona	—
Triple-A	Pawtucket Red Sox	International	67	75	.472	10th (14)	Ron Johnson	1973
Double-A	Portland Sea Dogs	Eastern	71	72	.497	6th (12)	Arnie Beyeler	2003
High A	Lancaster JetHawks	California	83	57	.593	1st (10)	Chad Epperson	2007
Low A	Greenville Drive	South Atlantic	58	81	.417	14th (16)	Gabe Kapler	2005
Short-season	Lowell Spinners	New York-Penn	40	36	.526	5th (14)	Jon Deeble	1996
Rookie	GCL Red Sox	Gulf Coast	30	26	.536	6th (16)	Dave Tomlin	1993
Overall 2007 Minor League Record			349	347	.501	12th		

*Finish in overall standings (No. of teams in league) ^League champion

LAST YEAR'S TOP 30

Player, Pos.		Status
1.	Daisuke Matsuzaka, rhp	Majors
2.	Jacoby Ellsbury, of	No. 2
3.	Clay Buchholz, rhp	No. 1
4.	Michael Bowden, rhp	No. 7
5.	Daniel Bard, rhp	No. 19
6.	Lars Anderson, 1b	No. 3
7.	Dustin Pedroia, ss/2b	Majors
8.	Bryce Cox, rhp	No. 30
9.	Craig Hansen, rhp	No. 18
10.	Kris Johnson, lhp	No. 13
11.	Jason Place, of	No. 23
12.	George Kottaras, c	Dropped out
13.	Justin Masterson, rhp	No. 4
14.	Brandon Moss, of	No. 11
15.	David Murphy, of	(Rangers)
16.	Jed Lowrie, ss	No. 5
17.	Ryan Kalish, of	No. 6
18.	Felix Doubront, lhp	Dropped out
19.	Caleb Clay, rhp	Dropped out
20.	Engel Beltre, of	(Rangers)
21.	Oscar Tejeda, ss	No. 9
22.	Hideki Okajima, lhp	Majors
23.	Devern Hansack, rhp	Dropped out
24.	Jon Egan, c	Dropped out
25.	Aaron Bates, 1b	No. 21
26.	Edgar Martinez, rhp	Dropped out
27.	Ty Weeden, c/1b	Dropped out
28.	Chad Spann, 3b	Dropped out
29.	Kris Negron, ss/3b	Dropped out
30.	Jeff Natale, 2b	Dropped out

BEST TOOLS

Best Hitter for Average	Lars Anderson
Best Power Hitter	Lars Anderson
Best Strike-Zone Discipline	Jeff Natale
Fastest Baserunner	Jacoby Ellsbury
Best Athlete	Jacoby Ellsbury
Best Fastball	Justin Masterson
Best Curveball	Clay Buchholz
Best Slider	Nick Hagadone
Best Changeup	Clay Buchholz
Best Control	Michael Bowden
Best Defensive Catcher	Mark Wagner
Best Defensive Infielder	Argenis Diaz
Best Infield Arm	Will Middlebrooks
Best Defensive Outfielder	Jacoby Ellsbury
Best Outfield Arm	Che-Hsuan Lin

PROJECTED 2011 LINEUP

Catcher	Mark Wagner
First Base	Lars Anderson
Second Base	Dustin Pedroia
Third Base	Kevin Youkilis
Shortstop	Jed Lowrie
Left Field	Ryan Kalish
Center Field	Jacoby Ellsbury
Right Field	Josh Reddick
Designated Hitter	David Ortiz
No. 1 Starter	Josh Beckett
No. 2 Starter	Clay Buchholz
No. 3 Starter	Daisuke Matsuzaka
No. 4 Starter	Jon Lester
No. 5 Starter	Michael Bowden
Closer	Jonathan Papelbon

TOP PROSPECTS OF THE DECADE

Year	Player, Pos.	2007 Org.
1998	Brian Rose, rhp	Out of baseball
1999	Dernell Stenson, of	Deceased
2000	Steve Lomasney, c	Out of baseball
2001	Dernell Stenson, of/1b	Deceased
2002	Seung Song, rhp	Out of baseball
2003	Hanley Ramirez, ss	Marlins
2004	Hanley Ramirez, ss	Marlins
2005	Hanley Ramirez, ss	Marlins
2006	Andy Marte, 3b	Indians
2007	Daisuke Matsuzaka, rhp	Red Sox

TOP DRAFT PICKS OF THE DECADE

Year	Player, Pos.	2007 Org.
1998	Adam Everett, ss	Astros
1999	Rick Asadoorian, of	Reds
2000	Phil Dumatrait, lhp	Reds
2001	Kelly Shoppach, c (2nd round)	Indians
2002	Jon Lester, lhp (2nd round)	Red Sox
2003	David Murphy, of	Rangers
2004	Dustin Pedroia, ss (2nd round)	Red Sox
2005	Jacoby Ellsbury, of	Red Sox
2006	Jason Place, of	Red Sox
2007	Nick Hagadone, lhp (1st supp.)	Red Sox

LARGEST BONUSES IN CLUB HISTORY

Daisuke Matsuzaka, 2006	$2,000,000
Rick Asadoorian, 1999	$1,725,500
Adam Everett, 1998	$1,725,000
Mike Rozier, 2004	$1,575,000
Daniel Bard, 2006	$1,500,000

BOSTON RED SOX

Top 2008 Rookie: Jacoby Ellsbury, of. He eliminated any doubt that he was ready by hitting .361 in September and .438 in the World Series.

Breakout Prospect: Will Middlebrooks, ss. He has all the tools to be an offensive and defensive standout, though he may eventually move to third base.

Sleeper: Austin Bailey, rhp. The Red Sox gave him $285,000 as a 16th-rounder at the signing deadline because they love his arm and competitiveness.

SOURCE OF TOP 30 TALENT

Homegrown	29	Acquired	1
College	12	Trades	1
Junior college	2	Rule 5 draft	0
High school	9	Independent leagues	0
Draft-and-follow	0	Free agents/waivers	0
Nondrafted free agents	1		
International	5		

Numbers in parentheses indicate prospect rankings.

LF
Zach Daeges
Jeff Corsaletti
Carlos Fernandez-Oliva

CF
Jacoby Ellsbury (2)
Ryan Kalish (6)
Jason Place (23)
Che-Hsuan Lin (24)
Bubba Bell (25)
Reid Engel (28)
Ronald Bermudez

RF
Josh Reddick (10)
Brandon Moss (11)
David Mailman
Mickey Hall
Kade Keowen

3B
Michael Almanzar (16)
Jorge Jimenez

SS
Jed Lowrie (5)
Oscar Tejeda (9)
Argenis Diaz (12)
Will Middlebrooks (14)
Yamaico Navarro (29)
Christian Lara

2B
Ryan Dent (15)
Chih-Hsein Chiang

1B
Lars Anderson (3)
Anthony Rizzo (17)
Aaron Bates (21)
Chris Carter (26)
Jon Still
Jeff Natale
Michael Jones
Ricardo Burgos

C
Mark Wagner (20)
George Kottaras
Dusty Brown
Tyler Weeden
Jon Egan

RHP

Starters	Relievers
Clay Buchholz (1)	Craig Hansen (18)
Justin Masterson (4)	Daniel Bard (19)
Michael Bowden (7)	Bryce Cox (30)
Devern Hansack	Kyle Jackson
David Pauley	Beau Vaughan
Brock Huntzinger	Edgar Martinez
Austin Bailey	Chris Province
Jordan Craft	Josh Papelbon
Adam Mills	
Stolmy Pimentel	

LHP

Starters	Relievers
Nick Hagadone (8)	Dustin Richardson (22)
Kris Johnson (13)	Hunter Jones (27)
Drake Britton	
Felix Doubront	
Jose Alvarez	
Ryan Phillips	

2007   SIGNING BUDGET: $3.5 MILLION

Best Pro Debut: After giving up five runs in his pro debut, LHP Nick Hagadone (1s) threw 23 consecutive scoreless innings, allowing eight hits and seven walks while striking out 32.

Best Athlete: From a pure physical standpoint, it's OF Kade Keowen (9). He's a 6-foot-6, 230-pounder with plus raw power, arm strength and speed. SS Will Middlebrooks (5) does a better job of translating his athleticism into baseball production. Middlebrooks, who had NFL potential as a punter, is a big athlete at 6-foot-4, 215 pounds.

Best Pure Hitter: 1B Anthony Rizzo (6), who signed for $325,000, reminds the Red Sox of another first baseman whom they gave above-slot money last year—Lars Anderson.

Best Power Hitter: Rizzo not only has considerable raw power, but it's usable power. He rates an edge over Middlebrooks.

Fastest Runner: 2B Ryan Dent (1s) can get from the right side of the plate to first base in 4.1 seconds. Dent and 2B Kenneth Roque (10) are well-above-average runners under way.

Best Defensive Player: While most teams projected Middlebrooks as a third baseman in the mold of Cal Ripken Jr. and Scott Rolen, the Red Sox believe he has a chance to stick at shortstop. He has good actions and body control, and plenty of arm. C Peter Gilardo (45) has a plus-plus arm.

Best Fastball: Hagadone works consistently at 92-94 mph. RHP Chris Province (4) has a nastier fastball at times, sitting at 91-92 mph and touching 95 with good life and downward plane, but he doesn't throw strikes consistently.

Best Secondary Pitch: Hagadone's hard slider.

Most Intriguing Background: Middlebrooks and unsigned C Mike Bourdon (41) both were recruited by college football programs as quarterbacks. Bourdon is at Fairfield, which doesn't have a football program.

Closest To The Majors: Hagadone. He may start 2008 in low Class A to avoid the launching pad at high Class A Lancaster, but he's on the fast track.

Best Late-Round Pick: LHP Drake Britton (23) had an inconsistent spring but signed for $700,000 after pitching in the low 90s during the summer.

The One Who Got Away: Coming back from Tommy John surgery, RHP Scott Green (15) pitched just 18 innings at Kentucky in the spring. He showed enough in the Cape Cod League this summer to get an $800,000 offer from Boston, but he returned to the Wildcats in hopes of becoming a first-round pick.

Assessment: The Red Sox' draft wasn't as splashy or expensive as their 2006 effort, but they still hauled in some talent. They were delighted to get Hagadone and Dent with their top two picks in the sandwich round, and Middlebrooks was a borderline first-rounder who dropped because of signability.

2006   BUDGET: $6.8 MILLION

Both first-rounders, OF Jason Place and RHP Daniel Bard, struggled mightily in 2007. But the Red Sox are more than thrilled by RHP Justin Masterson (2), OFs Ryan Kalish (9) and Josh Reddick (17), and 1B Lars Anderson (18).

GRADE: B+

2005   BUDGET: $6.2 MILLION

The system's two best prospects are RHP Clay Buchholz (1s), who threw a no-hitter in his second big league start, and OF Jacoby Ellsbury (1), who starred in the World Series. There's more talent coming in RHPs Craig Hansen (1) and Michael Bowden (1s) and SS Jed Lowrie (1s).

GRADE: A

2004   BUDGET: $1.8 MILLION

Boston didn't have a first-rounder and used its top pick on 2B Dustin Pedroia (2). RHP Cla Meredith (6) was a nice find, too, but was given away to the Padres.

GRADE: B+

2003   BUDGET: $5.1 MILLION

RHP Jonathan Papelbon (4) is on his way to becoming the best closer in franchise history. OFs David Murphy (1) and Matt Murton (1s) were used in stretch-drive deals in years the Red Sox won the World Series.

GRADE: A

Draft analysis by Jim Callis. Numbers in parentheses indicate draft rounds. Budgets are bonuses in first 10 rounds.

KEVIN PATAKY

CLAY BUCHHOLZ, RHP

Born: Aug. 14, 1984.
Ht.: 6-3. **Wt.:** 190.
Bats: R. **Throws:** R.
Drafted: Angelina (Texas) JC, 2005 (1st round supplemental).
Signed by: Jim Robinson.

No pitching prospect had a more decorated 2007 than Buchholz. He ranked as the No. 1 prospect in the Double-A Eastern League, where he outpitched Roger Clemens in a May matchup. From there he went to the Futures Game and then on to Triple-A Pawtucket, making five starts before getting summoned to Boston. Buchholz went six innings to beat the Angels in his big league debut, but the best was still yet to come. Called back up in September, he became the 21st rookie in modern baseball history to throw a no-hitter, dominating the Orioles in just his second start. He might have made Boston's playoff roster had he not come down with a tired arm, which led the club to shut him down as a precaution. Buchholz led all minor league starters by averaging 12.3 strikeouts per nine innings and won the organization's minor league pitcher of the year for the second straight season. His accomplishments are all the more impressive considering that he was a backup infielder at McNeese State in 2004 and didn't become a full-time pitcher until 2005. Buchholz emerged as a prospect that spring at Angelina (Texas) JC, though some clubs backed off him because he had been arrested in April 2004 and charged with stealing laptop computers from a middle school. Red Sox general manager Theo Epstein and scouting director Jason McLeod grilled him about the incident during a Fenway Park workout and decided it was a one-time lapse in judgment. Boston drafted him 42nd overall and signed him for $800,000. Buchholz has gone 22-11, 2.39 with 378 strikeouts in 308 innings since.

Buchholz has a low-90s fastball that tops out at 95 mph, and it's just his third-best pitch. His 12-to-6 curveball and his changeup both rate as 70s on the 20-80 scouting scale and are better than anyone's on Boston's big league staff. With terrific athleticism and hand speed, he used an overhand delivery to launch curves that drop off the table. His changeup can make hitters look even sillier. He'll also mix in a handful of sliders during a game, and that's a plus pitch for him at times. Buchholz improved his mechanics in 2007 and now operates more under control. He showed during his no-hitter that he won't be fazed by pressure.

His secondary pitches are so outstanding that Buchholz doesn't use his fastball enough. He needs to throw more fastball strikes early in counts and improve his command of the pitch. Clearly gassed after throwing a career-high 149 innings last season, he needs to get stronger. Working toward that goal, he trained at the Athlete's Performance Institute in Florida during the offseason.

Buchholz is Boston's best pitching prospect since Clemens and has everything he needs to become a No. 1 starter. He'll join Josh Beckett, Daisuke Matsuzaka and Jon Lester in the big league rotation in 2008, giving the Red Sox four quality starters aged 27 and younger. Buchholz is the baby of the group at 23.

Year	Club (League)	Class	W	L	ERA	G	GS	CG	SV	IP	H	R	ER	HR	BB	SO	AVG
2005	Lowell (NYP)	A	0	1	2.61	15	15	0	0	41	34	15	12	2	9	45	.219
2006	Greenville (SAL)	A	9	4	2.62	21	21	0	0	103	78	34	30	10	29	117	.211
	Wilmington (Car)	A	2	0	1.13	3	3	0	0	16	10	4	2	0	4	23	.182
2007	Portland (EL)	AA	7	2	1.77	16	15	1	0	86	55	18	17	4	22	116	.180
	Pawtucket (IL)	AAA	1	3	3.96	8	8	0	0	38	32	21	17	5	13	55	.221
	Boston (AL)	MLB	3	1	1.59	4	3	1	0	22	14	6	4	0	10	22	.184
MINOR LEAGUE TOTALS			19	10	2.46	63	62	1	0	285	209	92	78	21	77	356	.203
MAJOR LEAGUE TOTALS			3	1	1.59	4	3	1	0	22	14	6	4	0	10	22	.184

2 JACOBY ELLSBURY, OF

Born: Sept. 11, 1983. **B-T:** L-L. **Ht.:** 6-1. **Wt.:** 185. **Drafted:** Oregon State, 2005 (1st round). **Signed by:** John Booher.

Ellsbury electrified Red Sox fans by scoring from second base on a wild pitch in his third big league game in July, and there was more to come. After setting a Pawtucket record with a 25-game hitting streak, he batted .361 while subbing for an injured Manny Ramirez in September and hit .438 in the World Series. Ellsbury puts his plus-plus speed to good use on the bases and in center field. At the plate, he focuses on getting on base with an easy live-drive swing and outstanding bat control. He's a prolific and efficient basestealer, swiping 50 bases in 57 tries in 2007, including a perfect 9-for-9 in the majors. He may not be as spectacular in center field as Coco Crisp, but he's a Gold Glover waiting to happen. Ellsbury has just 10 homers in 1,017 minor league at-bats, but Boston believes he has the deceptive strength to hit 10-15 homers per season. He can launch balls in batting practice and did go deep three times in September. Like Clay Buchholz, he spent time at API during the offseason to add strength. Ellsbury's arm is below average, but he compensates by getting to balls and unloading them quickly. The Red Sox have tried to downplay the expectations and the Johnny Damon comparisons for Ellsbury since drafting him in 2005's first round, but that's impossible now. He's clearly their center fielder of the future, and the future is soon.

Year	Club (League)	Class	AVG	G	AB	R	H	2B	3B	HR	RBI	BB	SO	SB	OBP	SLG
2005	Lowell (NYP)	A	.317	35	139	28	44	3	5	1	19	24	20	23	.418	.432
2006	Wilmington (Car)	A	.299	61	244	35	73	7	5	4	32	25	28	25	.379	.418
	Portland (EL)	AA	.308	50	198	29	61	10	3	3	19	24	25	16	.387	.434
2007	Portland (EL)	AA	.452	17	73	16	33	10	2	0	13	6	7	8	.518	.644
	Pawtucket (IL)	AAA	.298	87	363	66	108	14	5	2	28	32	47	33	.360	.380
	Boston (AL)	MLB	.353	33	116	20	41	7	1	3	18	8	15	9	.394	.509
MINOR LEAGUE TOTALS			.314	250	1017	174	319	44	20	10	111	111	127	105	.390	.426
MAJOR LEAGUE TOTALS			.353	33	116	20	41	7	1	3	18	8	15	9	.394	.509

3 LARS ANDERSON, 1B

Born: Sept. 25, 1987. **B-T:** L-L. **Ht.:** 6-4. **Wt.:** 215. **Drafted:** HS—Carmichael, Calif., 2006 (18th round). **Signed by:** Blair Henry.

Anderson led California high schoolers with 15 homers in 2006, but his inexperienced agent didn't understand baseball's slotting system and scared teams off with a $1 million price tag. The Red Sox took an 18th-round flier on him and landed him in August for $825,000. He went to low Class A Greenville at age 19 for his pro debut, where he showed that he has the best bat and best power in the system. He's extremely disciplined, recognizes pitches well and lets balls travel deep before drilling them to the opposite field. He generates tremendous raw power with just an easy flick of the wrists. His glove was better than expected, as he worked hard and managers rated him the best defensive first baseman in the South Atlantic League. Boston loves Anderson's approach but wants him to get more aggressive with two strikes. He takes too many borderline pitches in those situations. His power will explode once he starts to pull more pitches. All but one of his 11 homers last year went to left or center field. Once he fills out, he'll be a below-average runner. The next step is the launching pad at high Class A Lancaster, where Anderson could put up some crazy numbers in 2008. Corner infielders Kevin Youkilis and Mike Lowell are under Red Sox control through 2010, but Anderson may be ready before then.

Year	Club (League)	Class	AVG	G	AB	R	H	2B	3B	HR	RBI	BB	SO	SB	OBP	SLG
2007	Greenville (SAL)	A	.288	124	458	69	132	35	3	10	69	71	112	2	.385	.443
	Lancaster (Cal)	A	.343	10	35	13	12	2	0	1	9	11	9	0	.489	.486
MINOR LEAGUE TOTALS			.292	134	493	82	144	37	3	11	78	82	121	2	.393	.446

4 JUSTIN MASTERSON, RHP

Born: March 22, 1985. **B-T:** R-R. **Ht.:** 6-6. **Wt.:** 250. **Drafted:** San Diego State, 2006 (2nd round). **Signed by:** Dan Madsen.

After beginning his high school career as a catcher, Masterson first blossomed as a prospect in the Cape Cod League in the summer of 2005. He transferred from Bethel (Ind.) to San Diego State, went in the second round of the 2006 draft and reached Double-A in his first full pro season. Using a low three-quarters arm slot, Masterson unleashes a special sinker. With its combination of low-90s velocity and heavy movement, batters feel like they're trying to hit a bowling ball. His No. 2 pitch is a slider that improved last season. He showed his toughness by not giving in when he went

2-3, 6.31 in his first nine starts at hitter-friendly Lancaster, making adjustments so he could survive the wind tunnel there. Because he throws from a lower arm angle, Masterson doesn't always stay on top of his slider. His changeup is getting better but also is inconsistent and he doesn't use it enough. He worked a career-high 154 innings and tired down the stretch, so he'll need to get stronger. The Red Sox will send Masterson to Triple-A as a starter but envision him becoming a big league reliever. He has the power sinker and the mentality to close games, though in Boston he'd be a setup man for Jonathan Papelbon.

Year	Club (League)	Class	W	L	ERA	G	GS	CG	SV	IP	H	R	ER	HR	BB	SO	AVG
2006	Lowell (NYP)	A	3	1	0.85	14	0	0	0	31	20	4	3	0	2	33	.174
2007	Lancaster (Cal)	A	8	5	4.33	17	17	0	0	95	103	56	46	4	22	56	.275
	Portland (EL)	AA	4	3	4.34	10	10	0	0	58	49	29	28	4	18	59	.225
MINOR LEAGUE TOTALS			15	9	3.74	41	27	0	0	185	172	89	77	8	42	148	.243

5 JED LOWRIE, SS

KEVIN PATAKY

Born: April 17, 1984. **B-T:** B-R. **Ht.:** 6-0. **Wt.:** 180. **Drafted:** Stanford, 2005 (1st round supplemental). **Signed by:** Nakia Hill.

Following a strong pro debut in 2005, when he was a supplemental first-round pick, Lowrie slumped to .262 with three homers in his high Class A encore. He hit just .170 last April and seemed destined for another down year, but he improved dramatically afterward and wound up being Boston's minor league offensive player of the year. Lowrie is a switch-hitter with a patient approach and pop from both sides of the plate. He started to make adjustments at the end of 2006 and they helped him recover from his season-opening slump last year. He improved even more dramatically on defense, becoming an average shortstop. Lowrie improved his fielding percentage there to .965 from .938 the year before and demonstrated enough speed and range to stay there. His hands and arm weren't in question. While Lowrie can play shortstop and his offensive production makes his glove more tolerable, a contender probably would want a better defender at the position. As with most of their best prospects, the Red Sox would like to see him get stronger. Luckily for Lowrie, his bat will play at second or third base, but there are no infield openings in Boston. That's why his name repeatedly surfaced in offseason trade talks. If he's still with the organization in 2008, he'll go to Triple-A to get regular playing time and be on call to fill any infield need that arises.

Year	Club (League)	Class	AVG	G	AB	R	H	2B	3B	HR	RBI	BB	SO	SB	OBP	SLG
2005	Lowell (NYP)	A	.328	53	201	36	66	12	0	4	32	34	30	7	.429	.448
2006	Wilmington (Car)	A	.262	97	374	43	98	21	6	3	50	54	65	2	.352	.374
2007	Portland (EL)	AA	.297	93	337	61	100	31	7	8	49	65	58	5	.410	.501
	Pawtucket (IL)	AAA	.300	40	160	21	48	16	1	5	21	12	33	0	.356	.506
MINOR LEAGUE TOTALS			.291	283	1072	161	312	80	14	20	152	165	186	14	.386	.448

6 RYAN KALISH, OF

Born: March 28, 1988. **B-T:** L-L. **Ht.:** 6-1. **Wt.:** 205. **Drafted:** HS—Red Bank, N.J., 2006 (9th round). **Signed by:** Ray Fagnant.

It may be apocryphal, but legend has it that Kalish didn't swing and miss at a single pitch as a high school senior. Because he was strongly committed to Virginia, he dropped to the ninth round, where the Red Sox signed him for $600,000. He was hitting .368 at short-season Lowell when an errant pitch broke the hamate bone in his right wrist in mid-July, ending his year and necessitating surgery in September. Kalish's approach and plate discipline are quite advanced for his age, which combined with his sweet lefty swing mean that he should have little trouble hitting for average. He already pulls his share of pitches and could develop into a 15-20 homer threat, perhaps more if he adds some loft to his swing. He's a plus runner with good instincts in center field. He has a strong work ethic and constant energy. Kalish is still growing and if he loses a step, he wouldn't profile as a leadoff hitter or center fielder. He'll need to improve his arm strength if he shifts to right field. Because he signed late in 2006 and got hurt last year, he has accumulated just 142 pro at-bats in parts of two seasons. Kalish began hitting again after Thanksgiving and should be 100 percent for spring training, where an assignment to low Class A awaits. He's most often compared to J.D. Drew, whom he eventually could succeed as Boston's right fielder.

Year	Club (League)	Class	AVG	G	AB	R	H	2B	3B	HR	RBI	BB	SO	SB	OBP	SLG
2006	Red Sox (GCL)	R	.300	6	20	6	6	2	0	1	2	1	2	0	.333	.550
	Lowell (NYP)	A	.200	11	35	8	7	0	1	0	4	2	14	2	.275	.257
2007	Lowell (NYP)	A	.368	23	87	27	32	4	1	3	13	16	12	18	.471	.540
MINOR LEAGUE TOTALS			.317	40	142	41	45	6	2	4	19	19	28	20	.406	.472

7 MICHAEL BOWDEN, RHP

Born: Sept. 9, 1986. **B-T:** R-R. **Ht.:** 6-3. **Wt.:** 215. **Drafted:** HS—Aurora, Ill., 2005 (1st round supplemental). **Signed by:** Danny Haas.

STEVE MOORE

While most of his fellow pitchers were shellshocked by Lancaster last year, Bowden's fine command allowed him to overcome the dreadful pitching environment. He wasn't as spectacular following a promotion to Portland in mid-May, but he acquitted himself well for a 20-year-old in Double-A. The Rangers could have taken him in the Eric Gagne trade last July, but chose Kason Gabbard instead. Bowden has uncanny feel for pitching, pounding both sides of the plate and commanding the bottom of the strike zone with his low-90s fastball. His curveball has big 12-to-6 break and he throws his changeup with deceptive arm speed. He uses a high arm slot to throw all of his pitches on a steep downhill plane. He's durable and a tough competitor. Bowden needs to get more consistent with his secondary pitches. His offerings all move down in the strike zone, so he may try to add a slider to give him something with lateral break. Scouts have quibbled with his delivery, which is long in back, short in front and reminiscent of former all-star Ken Hill's mechanics. But Bowden repeats it well and never has had any injury problems. Bowden is a workhorse with the ceiling of a No. 3 starter. He'll probably open 2008 in Double-A and move up to Triple-A by the end of the year. The Red Sox don't have any rotation openings, so they may use him as trade bait.

Year	Club (League)	Class	W	L	ERA	G	GS	CG	SV	IP	H	R	ER	HR	BB	SO	AVG
2005	Red Sox (GCL)	R	1	0	0.00	4	2	0	0	6	4	0	0	0	4	10	.190
2006	Greenville (SAL)	A	9	6	3.51	24	24	0	0	107	91	50	42	9	31	118	.224
	Wilmington (Car)	A	0	0	9.00	1	1	0	0	5	9	5	5	0	1	3	.391
2007	Lancaster (Cal)	A	2	0	1.37	8	8	0	0	46	35	10	7	1	8	46	.212
	Portland (EL)	AA	8	6	4.28	19	19	1	0	96	105	51	46	9	33	82	.279
MINOR LEAGUE TOTALS			20	12	3.44	56	54	1	0	261	244	116	100	19	77	259	.246

8 NICK HAGADONE, LHP

Born: Jan. 1, 1986. **B-T:** L-L. **Ht.:** 6-5. **Wt.:** 230. **Drafted:** Washington, 2007 (1st round supplemental). **Signed by:** John Booher.

MIKE JANES

Hagadone has a nondescript fastball and performance in his first two years at Washington before suddenly blossoming in 2007, becoming Boston's top draft pick (55th overall) and signing for $571,500. He allowed five runs in his first pro game, then slammed the door and threw 23 straight shutout innings afterward, allowing just eight hits. A big-bodied lefthander, Hagadone has two plus pitches in a 92-94 mph fastball and a hard slider that ranks as the best in the system. He uses a high three-quarters arm slot to stay on top of his pitches and drive them down in the strike zone. The Red Sox love his makeup and believe he can handle any role they throw at him. Hagadone's changeup isn't as good as his other two pitches, though it has potential and he showed some feel for it at Lowell and in instructional league. His mechanics aren't picture-perfect and when they get out of whack, his stuff flattens out. The short-term plan is to send Hagadone to low Class A as a starter, allowing him to have success and build up some innings. Long term, Boston isn't sure whether it wants to deploy Hagadone as a possible No. 3 starter or as a power lefty reliever. If he moves to the bullpen, he could rocket to the majors quickly.

Year	Club (League)	Class	W	L	ERA	G	GS	CG	SV	IP	H	R	ER	HR	BB	SO	AVG
2007	Lowell (NYP)	A	0	1	1.85	10	10	0	0	24	14	5	5	1	8	33	.163
MINOR LEAGUE TOTALS			0	1	1.85	10	10	0	0	24	14	5	5	1	8	33	.163

9 OSCAR TEJEDA, SS

Born: Dec. 12, 1989. **B-T:** R-R. **Ht.:** 6-1. **Wt.:** 180. **Signed:** Dominican Republic, 2006. **Signed by:** Luis Scheker.

DAVID STONER

When Tejeda signed for $525,000 out of the Dominican Republic in 2006, a rival international scouting director described him as Alfonso Soriano with better hands. That hyperbole elicited chuckles from the Red Sox, but they didn't hesitate to challenge him as a 17-year-old last season. He ranked among the Top 10 Prospects in both the Rookie-level Gulf Coast and the short-season New York-Penn leagues, and he was the latter circuit's youngest player. With a projectable frame and a fluid swing that imparts backspin, Tejeda could develop considerable power once he matures physically and as a hitter. He has quick hands and plenty of bat speed. His arm strength attracted scouts when he was 14, and he makes accurate throws as well. His speed and range are solid. A leader on the field, he made tremendous strides learning English in 2007. Tejeda is aggressive at the plate, and while he makes enough contact now, it's going to take him a while to incorporate Boston's emphasis on plate discipline. He's thin and needs to get stronger, and it's possible he'll outgrow shortstop. Like many young shortstops, Tejeda will have to become more reliable with his glove. He made 22 errors in 63 games at short last year. The Red Sox have an abundance of gifted middle infielders at the lower levels of their system. They're trying to figure out where everyone will play in 2008, but the one sure thing is that Tejeda will be the regular shortstop in low Class A.

Year	Club (League)	Class	AVG	G	AB	R	H	2B	3B	HR	RBI	BB	SO	SB	OBP	SLG
2007	Red Sox (GCL)	R	.295	45	173	23	51	13	1	1	21	15	27	6	.344	.399
	Lowell (NYP)	A	.298	22	94	14	28	5	2	0	12	6	26	4	.347	.394
MINOR LEAGUE TOTALS			.296	67	267	37	79	18	3	1	33	21	53	10	.345	.397

10 JOSH REDDICK, OF

Born: Feb. 19, 1987. **B-T:** L-R. **Ht.:** 6-2. **Wt.:** 180. **Drafted:** Middle Georgia JC, 2006 (17th round). **Signed by:** Rob English.

When the Red Sox selected Reddick in the 17th round in 2006, they intended on making him a draft-and-follow. But when they watched him homer off Team USA's Ross Detwiler (who became the No. 6 overall pick in 2007), they moved to sign Reddick immediately for $140,000. Boston didn't have an opening for him at the start of last season, so he punished pitchers in extended spring training and then did the same when he got to low Class A. Reddick will consistently hit for average because he has a smooth lefty stroke, strong wrists and great feel for putting the bat on the ball. He doesn't chase pitches and drives them with little effort. He's a solid right fielder with good arm strength and precision accuracy, which enabled him to lead the South Atlantic League with 19 outfield assists. He's a smart baserunner. Reddick is so aggressive at the plate and makes so much contact that he rarely walks. Boston doesn't want to tone him down too much, but he needs to learn that he's better off letting pitches on the black go by and waiting for something more hittable. He's still filling out his frame, and his speed is already fringy. Lancaster features perhaps the best hitting environment in the minors, so Reddick could have a monster year in 2008. The Red Sox have no need to rush him but may not be able to hold his bat back for long.

Year	Club (League)	Class	AVG	G	AB	R	H	2B	3B	HR	RBI	BB	SO	SB	OBP	SLG
2007	Greenville (SAL)	A	.306	94	369	60	113	17	6	18	72	26	51	8	.352	.531
	Portland (EL)	AA	.000	1	1	0	0	0	0	0	0	0	0	0	.000	.000
MINOR LEAGUE TOTALS			.305	95	370	60	113	17	6	18	72	26	51	8	.351	.530

11 BRANDON MOSS, OF

Born: Sept. 16, 1983. **B-T:** L-R. **Ht.:** 6-0. **Wt.:** 205. **Drafted:** HS—Monroe, Ga., 2002 (8th round). **Signed by:** Rob English.

At the all-star break last year, Moss was hitting .303 with 31 doubles and 13 homers in Triple-A, numbers that usually would merit big league playing time in the second half. But with the Red Sox, he got just 25 at-bats. That's the dilemma facing Moss, who has nothing left to prove at Pawtucket but is blocked in Boston. Moss broke out as a prospect by winning the MVP award and batting title (.339) in the South Atlantic League in 2004, then struggled to find offensive consistency the next two years in Double-A. His swing got long when he tried to take advantage of the short right-field porch in Portland, but he made adjustments in the second half of 2006, which he capped by winning Eastern League playoff MVP honors. In 2007, Moss demonstrated more opposite-field power than ever before and led his league in doubles for the second straight season. He has strong hands, a quick bat, leverage in his swing and a greater understanding that he should just let his power come naturally. He imparts nice backspin on his drives, and though he'll swing and miss, he does a good job of covering both sides of the plate. Though Moss isn't as streaky as he used to be, he still can get inconsistent with his approach and gives too many at-bats away. He projects as a .270 hitter with 20 homers a year. Despite slightly below-average speed, he's a solid right fielder with a good arm. Moss will be a reserve outfielder this season for the Red Sox, unless they use him as trade bait.

Year	Club (League)	Class	AVG	G	AB	R	H	2B	3B	HR	RBI	BB	SO	SB	OBP	SLG
2002	Red Sox (GCL)	R	.204	42	113	10	23	6	2	0	6	13	40	1	.295	.292
2003	Lowell (NYP)	A	.237	65	228	29	54	15	4	7	34	15	53	7	.290	.430
2004	Augusta (SAL)	A	.339	109	433	66	147	25	6	13	101	46	75	19	.402	.515
	Sarasota (FSL)	A	.422	23	83	16	35	2	1	2	10	7	15	2	.462	.542
2005	Portland (EL)	AA	.268	135	503	87	135	31	4	16	61	53	129	6	.337	.441
2006	Portland (EL)	AA	.285	133	508	76	145	36	3	12	83	56	108	8	.357	.439
2007	Pawtucket (IL)	AAA	.282	133	493	66	139	41	2	16	78	61	148	3	.363	.471
	Boston (AL)	MLB	.280	15	25	6	7	2	1	0	1	4	6	0	.379	.440
MINOR LEAGUE TOTALS			.287	640	2361	350	678	156	22	66	373	251	568	46	.357	.456
MAJOR LEAGUE TOTALS			.280	15	25	6	7	2	1	0	1	4	6	0	.379	.440

12 ARGENIS DIAZ, SS

Born: Feb. 12, 1987. **B-T:** R-R. **Ht.:** 5-11. **Wt.:** 155. **Signed:** Venezuela, 2003. **Signed by:** German Robles/Miguel Garcia.

As soon as Diaz made his U.S. debut in 2006, Boston realized he's the best defensive shortstop its system has seen in years. His actions, instincts and first step are so good that he has above-average range to both sides despite owning slightly below-average speed. His hands are reliable, his exchange is quick and his arm is strong. He can wow scouts just by making routine plays. The Red Sox compare his defensive skills to those of Alex Gonzalez, who played a slick shortstop for them in 2006. Diaz isn't as strong physically as Gonzalez, but he made some encouraging progress with the bat in 2007. He hit a career-high .279 during the regular season, then challenged for the Hawaii Winter Baseball batting title before slumping late and finishing at .358. It's still unclear what Diaz will bring to the table offensively. He doesn't offer much power and speed, so he needs to focus on making contact and getting on base. His approach is fairly sound for his age, though he can get too aggressive at times. He took such a huge cut at a pitch in late April that he hurt his shoulder and missed most of May. He speaks English very well, which makes it easier for him to receive instruction. Boston believes Diaz will develop into a Gold Glover who hits for a high average. Though he hasn't progressed past low Class A, he was eligible for the Rule 5 draft this offseason, so the Red Sox didn't hesitate to add him to their 40-man roster. He'll advance to high Class A this year.

Year	Club (League)	Class	AVG	G	AB	R	H	2B	3B	HR	RBI	BB	SO	SB	OBP	SLG
2004	Ciudad Alianza (VSL)	R	.236	50	165	28	39	12	0	0	22	20	29	7	.333	.309
2005	Red Sox/Padres (VSL)	R	.266	58	203	37	54	10	2	2	26	38	25	14	.390	.365
2006	Red Sox (GCL)	R	.263	37	133	16	35	2	1	0	11	6	23	3	.300	.293
2007	Greenville (SAL)	A	.279	99	405	62	113	25	5	2	40	36	92	5	.342	.380
MINOR LEAGUE TOTALS			.266	244	906	143	241	49	8	4	99	100	169	29	.346	.351

13 KRIS JOHNSON, LHP

Born: Oct. 14, 1984. **B-T:** L-L. **Ht.:** 6-4. **Wt.:** 170. **Drafted:** Wichita State, 2006 (1st round supplemental). **Signed by:** Ernie Jacobs.

Johnson got a huge wakeup call in his first full pro season with an assignment to the wind tunnel that is Lancaster. Like most of the JetHawks pitchers, he struggled to adapt, going 2-3, 8.76 in his first nine starts. Then he realized that he had to challenge hitters because nibbling and falling behind in the count had been disastrous. He turned his season around, going 7-4, 4.32 the rest of the way. Johnson wouldn't have lasted 40 picks in the 2006 draft if he hadn't been at less than full strength after having Tommy John surgery the year before. He's a tall lefthander who uses his size to throw lively low-90s fastballs down in the strike zone. Though he's still skinny, he generates his velocity with an easy delivery and has no trouble throwing 91-92 mph in the seventh inning. His changeup is a solid second pitch, but he has yet to regain the plus curveball with power and depth that he showed before getting hurt at Wichita State. A breaking ball and command are often the last two things to return after Tommy John surgery, so the Red Sox are hoping his curve will improve in 2008, when the operation will be three years behind him. Command isn't an issue, as Johnson can pitch to both sides of the plate and most of his walks last year came when he was afraid to go after hitters. He also did a better job of maintaining his delivery last year than he did in 2006. Though he made a nice comeback at Lancaster, Boston wants Johnson to show mental toughness from the outset in 2008. He could be ready for a breakout year in Double-A.

Year	Club (League)	Class	W	L	ERA	G	GS	CG	SV	IP	H	R	ER	HR	BB	SO	AVG
2006	Lowell (NYP)	A	0	2	0.88	14	13	0	0	30	25	7	3	0	7	27	.229
2007	Lancaster (Cal)	A	9	7	5.56	27	27	0	0	136	148	91	84	20	57	100	.279
MINOR LEAGUE TOTALS			9	9	4.70	41	40	0	0	166	173	98	87	20	64	127	.271

14 WILL MIDDLEBROOKS, SS

Born: Sept. 9, 1988. **B-T:** R-R. **Ht.:** 6-4. **Wt.:** 215. **Drafted:** HS—Texarkana, Texas, 2007 (5th round). **Signed by:** Jim Robinson.

Middlebrooks received $925,000, the highest bonus of any 2007 Red Sox draftee, despite lasting until the fifth round. He only dropped that far because he priced himself above his consensus draft slot, but Boston was thrilled to grab him with its last pick on the first day of the draft. He's a tremendous athlete who drew college football interest as a quarterback and punter, and he might have had an NFL future as a punter. Nagged by shoulder tendinitis, he didn't play in a minor league game after signing at the Aug. 15 deadline and didn't take balls at shortstop until the final week of instructional league. His bat will need some polish, but he has the size and leverage to hit for power. Most clubs projected Middlebrooks as a third baseman because of his size, but the Red Sox will give him every opportunity to remain at shortstop despite their burgeoning depth at the position. He has average speed and range, plus the actions and body control to pull it off. His arm isn't a question, as he was a legitimate prospect as a pitcher with a low-90s fastball and an occasional plus curveball. He'll still have plenty of value if he does wind up at the hot corner. For scouts, the high-end comparisons are Cal Ripken Jr. if he sticks at shortstop and Scott Rolen if he moves to third. Oscar Tejeda, Ryan Dent and Yamaico Navarro all are ready for Class A and need time at shortstop as well, so it's unclear what Middlebrooks' assignment will be for 2008. He may begin the year in extended spring and then play shortstop for Lowell in June.

Year	Club (League)	Class	AVG	G	AB	R	H	2B	3B	HR	RBI	BB	SO	SB	OBP	SLG
2007	Did Not Play—Signed Late															

15 RYAN DENT, 2B/SS

Born: March 15, 1989. **B-T:** R-R. **Ht.:** 6-0. **Wt.:** 190. **Drafted:** HS—Long Beach, Calif., 2007 (1st round supplemental). **Signed by:** Jim Woodward.

The Red Sox slotted Nick Hagadone at No. 18 and Dent at No. 19 on their draft board, but didn't have a pick in the first round after giving theirs up as compensation for free agent Julio Lugo, so they weren't sure they'd get either player. They got both, however, taking Hagadone 55th overall and Dent 62nd. Dent had starred on the showcase circuit the previous year, helping the Reds' scout team win the World Wood Bat Association championship. He signed two days before the Aug. 15 signing deadline for $571,000, which was slightly over slot and $500 less than Hagadone's bonus. Dent was one of the best athletes in the draft. He can go from the right side of the plate to first base in 4.1 seconds, and he's also strong enough to drive balls into the gaps. He could develop 15-20 homer power in time. He has a quick stroke and sound hitting mechanics, and he should hit for average if he tones down his aggressiveness. Despite his speed and athleticism, he's not smooth at shortstop. His actions, range and arm are all just average, unlike the rest of his physical tools. The Red Sox see him as a shortstop and would like to play him there, but they also have more shortstops than they know what to do with. With Oscar Tejeda ticketed for low Class A, Dent will get the bulk of his playing time at second base if he's assigned there as well. Center field is another option for him, though Boston definitely will keep him in the infield for now.

Year	Club (League)	Class	AVG	G	AB	R	H	2B	3B	HR	RBI	BB	SO	SB	OBP	SLG
2007	Red Sox (GCL)	R	.371	10	35	7	13	1	2	1	2	5	5	4	.463	.600
	Lowell (NYP)	A	.178	11	45	5	8	1	0	0	3	1	13	4	.196	.200
MINOR LEAGUE TOTALS			.263	21	80	12	21	2	2	1	5	6	18	8	.322	.375

16 MICHAEL ALMANZAR, 3B

Born: Dec. 2, 1990. **B-T:** R-R. **Ht.:** 6-5. **Wt.:** 180. **Signed:** Dominican Republic, 2007. **Signed by:** John DiPuglia/Pablo Lantigua.

To sign Almanzar out of the Dominican Republic last summer, Boston gave him a $1.5 million bonus, a club record for a Latin American player. He's the son of former big leaguer Carlos Almanzar, who pitched in the Red Sox system in 2007. Michael is lanky and athletic, with the bat speed and leverage to hit for a ton of power once he matures physically. He's just 6-foot-5 and 180 pounds now, so there's room for him to add a significant amount of strength—and he already had legitimate gap power as a 16-year-old. He has a good load and trigger in his swing, and though there's some bat wrap in the back of his stroke, it doesn't hamper him. Almanzar played shortstop in the Dominican but will play third base in pro ball. He runs well, but at his size he'd almost certainly outgrow shortstop. He's more fluid and has better actions at the hot corner. He has the arm to make the longer throws, as it's plenty strong. He needs to remember to keep his elbow up so his tosses will be more accurate. Almanzar will need plenty of time to develop because he's so young and skinny. Given his background in baseball and his makeup, Boston believes he can handle an assignment to the Gulf Coast League this year at age 17.

Year	Club (League)	Class	AVG	G	AB	R	H	2B	3B	HR	RBI	BB	SO	SB	OBP	SLG
2007	Did Not Play															

17 ANTHONY RIZZO, 1B

Born: Aug. 8, 1989. **B-T:** L-L. **Ht.:** 6-3. **Wt.:** 220. **Drafted:** HS—Parkland, Fla., 2007 (6th round). **Signed by:** Laz Gutierrez.

No one with the Red Sox is quite comparing Rizzo to Lars Anderson yet, but for the second year in a row, they're excited about a high school first baseman out of the most recent draft. Rizzo had performed well with wood bats on the showcase circuit, yet his $325,000 price tag caused him to slide in the 2007 draft. Boston anted up on the Aug. 15 signing deadline and got more than it bargained for. They knew he had raw strength and usable power, but they didn't realize he had such an advanced approach. Rizzo surprised them even more with his better-than-expected agility at first base. Though he's easily a below-average runner, he has soft hands and moves wells around the bag. He also pitched in high school, so his arm is an asset at first base. In the Red Sox' minds, getting Rizzo more than makes up for not signing Alabama high school first baseman Hunter Morris, their second-round pick. They like Rizzo's maturity, too, and think he'll be able to handle low Class A in 2008.

Year	Club (League)	Class	AVG	G	AB	R	H	2B	3B	HR	RBI	BB	SO	SB	OBP	SLG
2007	Red Sox (GCL)	R	.286	6	21	6	6	0	0	1	3	1	2	0	.375	.429
MINOR LEAGUE TOTALS			.286	6	21	6	6	0	0	1	3	1	2	0	.375	.429

18 CRAIG HANSEN, RHP

Born: Nov. 15, 1983. **B-T:** R-R. **Ht.:** 6-5. **Wt.:** 185. **Drafted:** St. John's, 2005 (1st round). **Signed by:** Ray Fagnant.

In the final two months last season, the Red Sox finally started to see glimpses of the pitcher they thought they were getting when they spent the 26th overall pick and a $4.4 million big league contract on Hansen in 2005. After making some adjustments to his mechanics and mental approach, Hansen had a 1.23 ERA and a 25-9 K-BB in his final 22 innings, and he again started flashing the slider that made him so dominant in college. It's still inconsistent, but Boston hadn't seen that killer slider since he turned pro. He also worked with a 93-96 mph fastball that had good life down in the strike zone. Before Jonathan Papelbon emerged as the Red Sox' closer in 2006, there was talk that Hansen might assume that role in his first full pro season. The pressure got to Hansen, who kept tinkering with his mechanics while trying to find the slider that had deserted him. He started throwing with more effort and a lower arm slot, and it hurt his fastball command. Now he's back up to a true three-quarters angle and looking more like his old self. Hansen did hit a couple of speed bumps after his resurgence, missing three weeks in August after he banged his forearm when he slipped and fell against a nightstand. He also left the Arizona Fall League early to have surgery to correct his sleep apnea. As soon as Hansen gets more consistent with his slider, he'll be pitching in Boston again.

Year	Club (League)	Class	W	L	ERA	G	GS	CG	SV	IP	H	R	ER	HR	BB	SO	AVG
2005	Red Sox (GCL)	R	1	0	0.00	2	1	0	0	3	2	0	0	0	0	4	.182
	Portland (EL)	AA	0	0	0.00	8	0	0	1	9	9	0	0	0	1	10	.243
	Boston (AL)	MLB	0	0	6.00	4	0	0	0	3	6	2	2	1	1	3	.429
2006	Portland (EL)	AA	1	0	0.82	5	0	0	0	11	4	1	1	0	4	12	.105
	Pawtucket (IL)	AAA	1	2	2.75	14	4	0	0	36	31	14	11	0	19	26	.238
	Boston (AL)	MLB	2	2	6.63	38	0	0	0	38	46	32	28	5	15	30	.305
2007	Pawtucket (IL)	AAA	3	1	3.86	40	0	0	3	51	58	29	22	2	32	48	.275
MINOR LEAGUE TOTALS			6	3	2.76	69	5	0	4	111	104	44	34	2	56	100	.244
MAJOR LEAGUE TOTALS			2	2	6.59	42	0	0	0	41	52	34	30	6	16	33	.315

19 DANIEL BARD, RHP

Born: June 25, 1985. **B-T:** R-R. **Ht.:** 6-4. **Wt.:** 200. **Drafted:** North Carolina, 2006 (1st round). **Signed by:** Jeff Zona.

No pitcher struggled with the hitting environment at Lancaster last year more than Bard did. After surrendering four runs in 2⅔ innings in his first start, he completely lost his confidence and stopped challenging hitters. He gave up 21 walks and 19 runs over 10⅓ innings in his next four starts, then went on the disabled list for what was described as a triceps injury but may have been a mental health break as much as anything. He spent some time in extended spring training before being shipped to low Class A. Bard wasn't much better at the lower level, as he continued to fall out of whack with his mechanics, lose his release point and miss the strike zone. He did a better job of repeating his delivery in Hawaii Winter Baseball, but still has a considerable ways to go to find consistent command. The Red Sox will remain patient because Bard has an electric arm even if he can't harness it. He throws 96-98 mph without breaking a sweat, breaking bats with his combination of velocity and heavy life. He never has had a reliable breaking ball. He's now working with a slurvy pitch that's more curve than slider, and while it's a plus offering at times, he doesn't locate it very well. His changeup is less dependable than his breaking ball. Bard posted a 1.08 ERA in Hawaii, though he still walked 15 batters and hit five in 17 innings. Though they drafted him as a starter—and gave him a $1.55 million bonus—the Red Sox are starting to think they should just put him in the bullpen. He seems to challenge hitters more and just let his pitches go in that role, and he has a history of success in shorter stints in venues such as Team USA, the Cape Cod League and his relief role in Hawaii.

Year	Club (League)	Class	W	L	ERA	G	GS	CG	SV	IP	H	R	ER	HR	BB	SO	AVG
2007	Lancaster (Cal)	A	0	2	10.13	5	5	0	0	13	21	23	15	2	22	9	.350
	Greenville (SAL)	A	3	5	6.42	17	17	0	0	61	55	49	44	3	56	38	.250
MINOR LEAGUE TOTALS			3	7	7.08	22	22	0	0	75	76	72	59	5	78	47	.271

20 MARK WAGNER, C

Born: June 11, 1984. **B-T:** R-R. **Ht.:** 6-1. **Wt.:** 205. **Drafted:** UC Irvine, 2005 (9th round). **Signed by:** James Orr.

The only unsettled long-term position on the Red Sox is catcher, where there's no clear heir apparent to Jason Varitek. Wagner is the leading candidate to fill that role, as he has the most well-rounded game among a group of catching prospects that also includes Dusty Brown, Jon Egan, George Kottaras, Jon Still and Tyler Weeden. A ninth-round pick in 2005, Wagner has improved in each of his seasons in the system. He initially stood out with his work behind the plate. Wagner may not have a plus defensive tool, but he's solid across the board. With average arm strength and a hair-trigger release, he threw out 35 percent of basestealers in 2007. He also gets the job done as a receiver and game-caller. When Wagner first signed, his stance was too spread out and he had a defensive swing. He now stands more upright and has become more aggressive without sacrificing any of his tremendous plate discipline. Lancaster did help his power numbers (which included a career-high 14 homers) but he did hit .281 with 36 doubles the previous season. He's not going to be an offensive force, but Wagner will hit at least enough to be a big league backup. He's a typical catcher in that he doesn't run well. His blue-collar makeup helps Wagner get the most out of his abilities. He'll move up to Double-A for 2008.

Year	Club (League)	Class	AVG	G	AB	R	H	2B	3B	HR	RBI	BB	SO	SB	OBP	SLG
2005	Lowell (NYP)	A	.203	24	69	1	14	2	1	0	6	9	7	1	.309	.261
2006	Greenville (SAL)	A	.301	96	355	49	107	32	1	7	45	42	52	1	.386	.456
	Wilmington (Car)	A	.169	17	65	8	11	4	0	1	5	7	9	0	.243	.277
2007	Lancaster (Cal)	A	.318	95	368	71	117	35	1	14	82	55	46	0	.406	.533
MINOR LEAGUE TOTALS			.291	232	857	138	249	73	3	22	138	113	114	2	.378	.460

21 AARON BATES, 1B

Born: March 10, 1984. **B-T:** R-R. **Ht.:** 6-4. **Wt.:** 232. **Drafted:** North Carolina State, 2006 (3rd round). **Signed by:** Jeff Zona.

On May 19, Bates became the first player in the 64 seasons of the high Class A California League to hit four homers in a game. Teammate Brad Correll matched him five weeks later, another indication of how ridiculous Lancaster can get. For someone like Bates, who has legitimate hitting ability and power, it's an opportunity to put up crazy numbers and he did just that, leading the league with a .456 on-base percentage and posting a 1.048 OPS. Bates has a patient approach, waiting for a pitch he can pound and using the whole field. His biggest issue at the plate is that he takes an exceedingly long stride and doesn't always get his front foot down in time, messing up his stroke. It's a compact swing at times and long at others. He has good pitch recognition and hammers fastball and offspeed pitches alike. Bates' value rests totally with his bat. He's a below-average runner and athlete who's working hard to become an acceptable first baseman. He needs to adjust his stride after Double-A pitchers ate him up at the end of 2007, and he'll return to Portland to begin the season.

Year	Club (League)	Class	AVG	G	AB	R	H	2B	3B	HR	RBI	BB	SO	SB	OBP	SLG
2006	Lowell (NYP)	A	.360	27	100	17	36	8	0	3	14	9	21	2	.436	.530
	Greenville (SAL)	A	.270	43	152	13	41	7	0	4	16	17	26	0	.351	.395
2007	Lancaster (Cal)	A	.332	98	373	89	124	21	2	24	88	69	83	0	.456	.592
	Portland (EL)	AA	.198	27	91	16	18	9	0	4	13	17	29	0	.348	.429
MINOR LEAGUE TOTALS			.306	195	716	135	219	45	2	35	131	112	159	2	.418	.521

22 DUSTIN RICHARDSON, LHP

Born: Jan. 9, 1984. **B-T:** L-L. **Ht.:** 6-5. **Wt.:** 195. **Drafted:** Texas Tech, 2006 (5th round). **Signed by:** Jim Robinson.

Richardson competed on ESPN's reality show "Knight School," where Texas Tech students tried to make coach Bob Knight's basketball team as a walk-on. Richardson would have won the competition if he had been able to join the team, but that would have conflicted with his baseball responsibilities. Though he was a lefthander with an 89-92 mph fastball, he lasted until the fifth round in 2006 because he was a one-pitch pitcher and not the easiest guy to see because he pitched his home games in Lubbock. Richardson gets terrific extension out front of his delivery, and his low three-quarters arm slot adds deception. He has continued to get swings and misses with his heater in pro ball. His fastball plays above its velocity more than any other starter's in the system, with the exception of Justin Masterson. Richardson even tamed Lancaster in four starts at the end of the season—including three at home, with five no-hit innings in his last outing. Because he relied almost exclusively on his fastball in college, his secondary pitches are still works in progress. His curveball has loopy break and not much power, while his changeup is inconsistent. He may try to replace the changeup with a splitter in the future. The Red Sox envision him as a starter and will continue that development path, though it's easy to see him becoming a reliever and working mostly off his fastball. He could open the year in Double-A.

Year	Club (League)	Class	W	L	ERA	G	GS	CG	SV	IP	H	R	ER	HR	BB	SO	AVG
2006	Lowell (NYP)	A	4	1	3.18	16	1	0	2	39	28	16	14	2	13	44	.199
2007	Greenville (SAL)	A	5	7	3.34	21	21	0	0	99	86	46	37	4	47	98	.235
	Lancaster (Cal)	A	4	0	2.74	4	4	0	0	23	14	8	7	1	5	25	.173
MINOR LEAGUE TOTALS			13	8	3.22	41	26	0	2	162	128	70	58	7	65	167	.218

23 JASON PLACE, OF

Born: May 8, 1988. **B-T:** R-R. **Ht.:** 6-3. **Wt.:** 205. **Drafted:** HS—Piedmont, S.C., 2006 (1st round). **Signed by:** Rob English.

The Red Sox knew Place's hitting mechanics would need an overhaul, but they couldn't resist his athleticism and chose him with the 27th overall pick in the 2006 draft. He signed for $1.3 million. Place struggled in his first full season, which wasn't unexpected. Place came into pro ball with a funny load to his swing, with his hands starting in the middle of his body and circling back. Boston has fixed his load and spread out his stance, giving him a shorter stride and better balance in his lower half. He further smoothed out his swing in Hawaii Winter Baseball, albeit with similar results. Now it's up to him to make consistent contact so he can take advantage of his above-average raw power and speed. Place has lots of bat speed and power to all fields, though he'll get pull-conscious at times. Besides his speed, he also has the instincts and route-running ability to play center field. He has a strong, accurate arm that would easily play in right field if needed. Lancaster would boost Place's numbers and confidence, but he may repeat low Class A this year.

Year	Club (League)	Class	AVG	G	AB	R	H	2B	3B	HR	RBI	BB	SO	SB	OBP	SLG
2006	Red Sox (GCL)	R	.292	33	113	14	33	3	1	4	21	17	35	3	.386	.442
2007	Greenville (SAL)	A	.214	129	459	60	98	23	4	12	55	52	160	9	.298	.359
MINOR LEAGUE TOTALS			.229	162	572	74	131	26	5	16	76	69	195	12	.316	.376

24 CHE-HSUAN LIN, OF

Born: Sept. 21, 1988. **B-T:** R-R. **Ht.:** 6-1. **Wt.:** 183. **Signed:** Taiwan, 2007. **Signed by:** Jon Deeble/Louie Lin.

While Daisuke Matsuzaka and Hideki Okajima were helping to pitch Boston to a World Series championship, the club made another Asian investment on a smaller scale. In June, the Red Sox signed Lin out of Taiwan for $400,000. He held his own as an 18-year-old in his U.S. debut while showing off some exciting tools. Chief among them are his plus-plus arm, his instincts and above-average play in center field and his plus speed. Lin has some ability at the plate, too. He holds his hands high and employs a big leg kick, drilling line drives to the gap. He has some strength and projectable power, and he does a nice job of imparting backspin on the ball. Lin generally uses a whole-field approach, though he sometimes gets pull-conscious. He'll need to adjust to breaking balls down and away, which led to many of his strikeouts in his debut. Boston could challenge him by sending him to low Class A in 2008.

Year	Club (League)	Class	AVG	G	AB	R	H	2B	3B	HR	RBI	BB	SO	SB	OBP	SLG
2007	Red Sox (GCL)	R	.263	43	175	33	46	10	6	4	22	17	42	14	.330	.457
	Lowell (NYP)	A	.163	11	43	7	7	2	0	0	3	5	10	3	.265	.209
MINOR LEAGUE TOTALS			.243	54	218	40	53	12	6	4	25	22	52	17	.317	.408

25 BUBBA BELL, OF

Born: Oct. 9, 1982. **B-T:** L-R. **Ht.:** 6-0. **Wt.:** 195. **Drafted:** Nicholls State, 2005 (39th round). **Signed by:** Danny Watkins.

Of all the hitters who thrived at Lancaster last year, none could top Bell. He was named MVP, rookie of the year and all-star game MVP in the California League, which he led in batting (.370), slugging (.665), homers per at-bat (one every 14.6) and plate appearances per strikeout (9.7). He likely would have paced the Cal League in several counting stats had he not been promoted to Double-A in early July, as he was tops in all three triple-crown categories at the time. Bell clearly benefited from playing his home games at Clear Channel Stadium, but the Red Sox say he's not a fluke. He has a short lefthanded swing, tremendous plate discipline and a willingness to use the entire field, so there's no reason he can't keep hitting for average. His power was inflated by Lancaster, but he has enough juice to hit 10-15 homers per year under normal conditions. Bell has solid speed and plays a better center field than Boston thought, and he has an average arm. He may be more fourth outfielder than regular, but his ability can take him to the majors. He was slowed by back and quadriceps injuries once he got to Double-A, and he'll head back there to start 2008.

BOSTON RED SOX

Year	Club (League)	Class	AVG	G	AB	R	H	2B	3B	HR	RBI	BB	SO	SB	OBP	SLG
2005	Red Sox (GCL)	R	.317	43	164	18	52	13	2	2	27	10	14	2	.363	.457
2006	Lowell (NYP)	A	.429	23	91	22	39	9	2	2	13	13	13	3	.495	.637
	Greenville (SAL)	A	.231	59	208	30	48	7	1	3	28	27	31	5	.326	.317
	Wilmington (Car)	A	.283	19	60	8	17	4	1	1	9	8	7	2	.368	.433
2007	Lancaster (Cal)	A	.370	76	322	95	119	27	1	22	83	48	39	10	.455	.665
	Portland (EL)	AA	.265	34	147	23	39	5	2	4	22	14	17	4	.337	.408
MINOR LEAGUE TOTALS			.317	254	992	196	314	65	9	34	182	120	121	26	.395	.503

26 — CHRIS CARTER, 1B/OF

Born: Sept. 16, 1982. **B-T:** L-L. **Ht.:** 6-0. **Wt.:** 210. **Drafted:** Stanford, 2004 (17th round). **Signed by:** Fred Costello (Diamondbacks).

With Wily Mo Pena rotting on their bench, the Red Sox shipped him to the Nationals in a three-way deal that netted Carter from the Diamondbacks, who got righthander Emiliano Fruto from Washington. Carter is similar in many ways to Pena, as he's a defensively challenged slugger who may find at-bats hard to come by in Boston. Carter was a top recruit when he arrived at Stanford, but he left as a 17th-round pick in 2004 following a disappointing, injury-plagued career. He has been anything but disappointing in pro ball, reaching Triple-A in his second full season and putting up a career .906 OPS. With tremendous bat speed, Carter can knock a ball out of any part of any park. He also has the discipline to wait until pitchers challenge him before turning his bat loose. The rest of his game is substandard. He's a well below-average runner who hasn't thrown well since having surgery to repair a torn labrum in college. The Red Sox played Carter solely at first base after the trade, though he did see extensive time in the outfield during his time in the Arizona system. He's bad in both spots and really best suited to become a DH. Boston protected him on its 40-man roster but has no way to get him at-bats. The best Carter can hope for is to serve as a lefty bat off the bench, and he may be looking at a third straight year in Triple-A.

Year	Club (League)	Class	AVG	G	AB	R	H	2B	3B	HR	RBI	BB	SO	SB	OBP	SLG
2004	Yakima (NWL)	A	.336	70	256	47	86	15	1	15	63	46	34	2	.438	.578
2005	Lancaster (Cal)	A	.296	103	412	71	122	26	2	21	85	46	66	0	.370	.522
	Tennessee (SL)	AA	.297	36	128	21	38	4	0	10	30	19	11	0	.397	.563
2006	Tucson (PCL)	AAA	.301	136	509	87	153	30	3	19	97	78	69	10	.395	.483
2007	Tucson (PCL)	AAA	.324	126	503	74	163	39	3	18	84	50	68	2	.383	.521
	Pawtucket (IL)	AAA	.234	12	47	6	11	1	0	1	4	4	7	0	.308	.319
MINOR LEAGUE TOTALS			.309	483	1855	306	573	115	9	84	363	243	255	14	.390	.516

27 — HUNTER JONES, LHP

Born: Jan. 10, 1984. **B-T:** L-L. **Ht.:** 6-4. **Wt.:** 235. **Signed:** NDFA/Florida State, 2005. **Signed by:** Jason McLeod.

Jones pitched with a misdiagnosed broken arm as a sophomore at Florida State, eventually developing a fracture through his ulnar bone in his elbow. He had a pin inserted into the elbow to prevent further damage, then decided not to redshirt and went just 4-3, 5.05 as a junior in 2005. Given his performance and medical history, he went undrafted. Jones pitched well that summer in the Cape Cod League, however, and the Red Sox signed him as a nondrafted free agent. Jones' stuff won't wow anyone, but he gets outs with his 87-88 mph fastball. His heater peaks at 91 but still gets a lot of swings and misses because he's deceptive, throws downhill and can spot it on both sides of the plate. He also uses a slow curveball with deep break and a changeup but mostly works with his fastball. Jones is an especially versatile reliever because he gets righthanders out and can pitch up to three innings in an outing. He'll start 2008 in Triple-A and should make his major league debut at some point during the summer.

Year	Club (League)	Class	W	L	ERA	G	GS	CG	SV	IP	H	R	ER	HR	BB	SO	AVG
2005	Lowell (NYP)	A	1	1	3.21	12	1	0	1	28	29	12	10	2	5	30	.257
2006	Greenville (SAL)	A	4	5	3.34	35	5	0	5	94	87	41	35	8	20	100	.246
2007	Lancaster (Cal)	A	4	1	2.11	24	0	0	0	47	35	16	11	2	21	40	.212
	Portland (EL)	AA	2	1	3.19	23	0	0	2	42	35	17	15	3	16	43	.226
MINOR LEAGUE TOTALS			11	8	3.02	94	6	0	8	211	186	86	71	15	62	213	.236

28 — REID ENGEL, OF

Born: May 7, 1987. **B-T:** L-R. **Ht.:** 6-2. **Wt.:** 175. **Drafted:** HS—Monument, Colo., 2005 (5th round). **Signed by:** Darryl Milne.

Engel's Baylor commitment led most teams to believe he was unsignable in 2005, but the Red Sox took him in the fifth round and signed him for slot money ($154,000) plus money to cover his tuition if he does attend Baylor ($96,000). He just hit .243 in his first two pro seasons and didn't reach full-season ball until his third, but he had a nice little breakout in 2007. He made adjustments to his approach and to his swing, showing more patience while putting his hands more out in front of his body, giving him a better trigger. He has decent power, though his best tool is plus-plus speed that he's still learning to use on the basepaths. He has enough range to play center field and enough arm to play in right, but he was a left fielder at Greenville because Jason Place and Josh Reddick were also there. Engel endured a scary incident at the end of May, when he fouled a ball off the plate and it bounced up and hit him in the jaw. But after spending 10 days on the disabled list, he returned and kept on hitting. He'll enjoy playing in hospitable Lancaster this year.

Year	Club (League)	Class	AVG	G	AB	R	H	2B	3B	HR	RBI	BB	SO	SB	OBP	SLG
2005	Red Sox (GCL)	R	.233	27	103	9	24	2	1	2	8	11	36	2	.313	.330
2006	Red Sox (GCL)	R	.200	6	20	2	4	0	1	0	0	3	5	1	.304	.300
	Lowell (NYP)	A	.251	56	231	20	58	8	2	4	26	10	48	4	.280	.355
2007	Greenville (SAL)	A	.292	112	411	60	120	20	6	9	49	38	78	13	.361	.436
MINOR LEAGUE TOTALS			.269	201	765	91	206	30	10	15	83	62	167	20	.329	.393

29 YAMAICO NAVARRO, SS/3B

Born: Oct. 31, 1987. **B-T:** R-R. **Ht.:** 5-11. **Wt.:** 170. **Signed:** Dominican Republic, 2006. **Signed by:** Pablo Lantigua.

Yet another shortstop prospect who emerged for the Red Sox in 2007, Navarro slid over to third base once Oscar Tejeda was promoted to Lowell. Navarro is more offensive-minded than most of the other young shortstops. He squares up fastballs well and already shows some opposite-field power. Navarro takes violent cuts and chases pitches, and Boston would like him to use his two-strike approach (more selectivity, shorter swing) throughout his entire at-bats. He has good speed but doesn't always run hard, and he needs to mature and show more professionalism. Navarro isn't as fluid as some of the other shortstops, but he has the range and arm to make most of the plays. He needs work on balls in the hole. Navarro is slated to play with Tejeda again this year in low Class A, and Tejeda once again will man shortstop.

Year	Club (League)	Class	AVG	G	AB	R	H	2B	3B	HR	RBI	BB	SO	SB	OBP	SLG
2006	Red Sox (DSL)	R	.279	53	201	29	56	13	5	3	37	21	29	5	.344	.438
2007	Lowell (NYP)	A	.289	62	225	36	65	10	1	5	37	22	52	12	.357	.409
MINOR LEAGUE TOTALS			.284	115	426	65	121	23	6	8	74	43	81	17	.351	.423

30 BRYCE COX, RHP

Born: Aug. 10, 1984. **B-T:** R-R. **Ht.:** 6-4. **Wt.:** 205. **Drafted:** Rice, 2006 (3rd round). **Signed by:** Jim Robinson.

With shoulder problems putting Jonathan Papelbon's career as a closer in jeopardy, the Red Sox were searching for a new closer in spring training last year. Given his spectacular success down the stretch with Rice and in his pro debut the year before, there was talk that Cox might even take over the role at some point during his first full season. That didn't happen, of course, and not just because Papelbon proved healthy enough to keep the job. After finally finding a compact delivery and a three-quarters arm slot that not only worked for him but also produced spectacular results, Cox lost them again in 2007. He missed time in Double-A and again after a demotion to low Class A with hamstring strains, and he never got his mechanics back. The Red Sox tried everything, even hitting him groundballs at third base like the Rice coaching staff had. By the end of the year, Cox had regained the 92-94 mph velocity on his fastball, but it didn't have its previous ride and sink. His wipeout slider also remained AWOL. The logical next step for him in 2008 would be high Class A, but Boston doesn't want to expose him to Lancaster while he's struggling. He's an enigma with huge upside, but the fact remains that in five years of college and pro ball, he has dominated for just four months.

Year	Club (League)	Class	W	L	ERA	G	GS	CG	SV	IP	H	R	ER	HR	BB	SO	AVG
2006	Lowell (NYP)	A	0	1	1.59	3	0	0	0	5	6	2	1	0	2	3	.261
	Wilmington (Car)	A	2	0	0.74	13	0	0	0	24	14	4	2	0	9	25	.165
2007	Portland (EL)	AA	1	1	4.91	9	0	0	0	14	15	14	8	1	11	3	.273
	Greenville (SAL)	A	1	1	5.40	21	0	0	0	33	31	23	20	4	10	24	.238
MINOR LEAGUE TOTALS			4	3	3.58	46	0	0	0	78	66	43	31	5	32	55	.225

Chicago Cubs

BY JIM CALLIS

After coming within five outs of making the World Series in 2003, the Cubs spiraled downward. They blew the National League wild card in the final week of the 2004 season, then dropped to 79 victories in 2005 and 66 in 2006 after expecting to contend in both years.

The farm system regressed as well. Chicago topped Baseball America's minor league talent rankings at the outset of the 2002 season, then slipped to third, seventh, 10th, 15th and 18th as injuries, trades and attrition took their toll.

Desperate to reverse their fortunes in 2007, the Cubs had no other choice last offseason but to plunge into the free agent market. Chicago doled out contracts totaling $297.7 million to 10 free agents—and it worked. Returnee Aramis Ramirez and newcomers Alfonso Soriano, Ted Lilly, Jason Marquis, Mark DeRosa and Cliff Floyd played significant roles as the Cubs won 85 games, just enough to squeak by in the NL Central.

The farm system also played a role, as several homegrown products who had debuted in recent seasons took steps forward. Carlos Marmol went from a 5.99 ERA as a starter in 2006 to a 1.43 ERA as a set-up man in 2007. Rich Hill and Sean Marshall solidified the rotation by posting identical 3.92 ERAs and combining for 18 wins.

Ryan Theriot claimed the shortstop job, and along with former Louisiana State double-play partner Mike Fontenot, injected energy into the lineup. Geovany Soto performed so well during his September callup that he started two of three playoff games behind the plate. Kevin Hart also earned a postseason roster spot after opening eyes in September.

Chicago will continue to rely on veterans as it builds on its 2007 turnaround, though a few youngsters will get opportunities. The catching job is Soto's to lose. Hart, Sean Gallagher and Billy Petrick also will factor into the big league staff. Felix Pie, who lost his rookie status while serving as an extra outfielder, could play a more prominent role.

The Cubs haven't signed a position player who developed into an all-star for them since Joe Girardi in 1986, but they have high hopes for Soto, Pie and four players taken by scouting director Tim Wilken in his two drafts for the team. Both of Wilken's first-rounders—third baseman Josh Vitters and outfielder Tyler Colvin—and two other 2006 draftees—catcher Josh Donaldson and second baseman Tony Thomas—rank

Ryan Theriot was one of the minor leaguers who provided unexpected help in Chicago

TOP 30 PROSPECTS

1. Josh Vitters, 3b	16. Dae-Eun Rhee, rhp
2. Geovany Soto, c/1b	17. Robert Hernandez, rhp
3. Tyler Colvin, of	18. Sam Fuld, of
4. Jose Ceda, rhp	19. Jake Fox, of/1b/c
5. Sean Gallagher, rhp	20. Larry Suarez, rhp
6. Donald Veal, lhp	21. Ryan Acosta, rhp
7. Josh Donaldson, c	22. James Russell, lhp
8. Jeff Samardzija, rhp	23. Alex Maestri, rhp
9. Tony Thomas, 2b	24. Darwin Barney, ss
10. Kevin Hart, rhp	25. Jose Ascanio, rhp
11. Billy Petrick, rhp	26. Rocky Roquet, rhp
12. Eric Patterson, 2b/of	27. Mark Holliman, rhp
13. Kyler Burke, of	28. Josh Lansford, 3b
14. Chris Huseby, rhp	29. Steve Clevenger, c/1b
15. Welington Castillo, c	30. Tim Lahey, rhp

among the organization's top 10 prospects.

While general manager Jim Hendry and his crew are on firmer ground after the reversal of fortune, change is still afoot. Innovative club president John McDonough resigned in November to take the same position with the NHL's Chicago Blackhawks. The Tribune Co., which bought the team from the Wrigley Family in 1981, plans on selling the club in order to relieve some of its debt. The process is moving slower than expected and is unlikely to occur before the start of the 2008 season.

General Manager: Jim Hendry. **Farm Director:** Oneri Fleita. **Scouting Director:** Tim Wilken.

Class	Team	League	W	L	PCT	Finish*	Manager	Affiliated
Majors	Chicago	National	85	77	.525	6th (16)	Lou Piniella	—
Triple-A	Iowa Cubs	Pacific Coast	79	65	.549	3rd (16)	Buddy Bailey	1981
Double-A	Tennessee Smokies	Southern	73	65	.529	3rd (10)	Pat Listach	2007
High A	Daytona Cubs	Florida State	57	80	.416	11th (12)	Jody Davis	1993
Low A	Peoria Chiefs	Midwest	71	68	.511	7th (14)	Ryne Sandberg	2005
Short-season	Boise Hawks	Northwest	37	39	.487	3rd (8)	Tom Byers	2001
Rookie	AZL Cubs	Arizona	27	29	.482	6th (9)	Ricardo Medina	1997

Overall 2007 Minor League Record | | | 344 | 346 | .499 | 13th

*Finish in overall standings (No. of teams in league) ^League champion

LAST YEAR'S TOP 30

Player, Pos.		Status
1.	Felix Pie, of	Majors
2.	Donald Veal, lhp	No. 6
3.	Tyler Colvin, of	No. 3
4.	Jeff Samardzija, rhp	No. 8
5.	Sean Gallagher, rhp	No. 5
6.	Eric Patterson, 2b	No. 12
7.	Scott Moore, 3b	(Orioles)
8.	Ryan Harvey, of	Dropped out
9.	Chris Huseby, rhp	No. 14
10.	Mark Pawelek, lhp	Dropped out
11.	Juan Mateo, rhp	Dropped out
12.	Brian Dopirak, 1b	Dropped out
13.	Jae-Kuk Ryu, rhp	(Rays)
14.	Mark Reed, c	Dropped out
15.	Drew Rundle, of	Dropped out
16.	Rocky Cherry, rhp	(Orioles)
17.	Geovany Soto, c	No. 2
18.	Billy Petrick, rhp	No. 11
19.	Dylan Johnston, ss	Dropped out
20.	Josh Lansford, 3b	No. 28
21.	Sammy Baez, ss	Dropped out
22.	Chris Robinson, c	Dropped out
23.	Mark Holliman, rhp	No. 27
24.	Jake Fox, c	No. 19
25.	Larry Suarez, rhp	No. 20
26.	Rocky Roquet, rhp	No. 26
27.	Sam Fuld, of	No. 18
28.	Scott Taylor, rhp	Dropped out
29.	Mitch Atkins, rhp	Dropped out
30.	Mike Fontenot, 2b	Majors

BEST TOOLS

Best Hitter for Average	Tony Thomas
Best Power Hitter	Josh Vitters
Best Strike-Zone Discipline	Sam Fuld
Fastest Baserunner	Leon Johnson
Best Athlete	Tyler Colvin
Best Fastball	Jose Ceda
Best Curveball	Casey Lambert
Best Slider	Alex Maestri
Best Changeup	James Russell
Best Control	Mark Holliman
Best Defensive Catcher	Welington Castillo
Best Defensive Infielder	Josh Lansford
Best Infield Arm	Josh Lansford
Best Defensive Outfielder	Sam Fuld
Best Outfield Arm	Kyler Burke

PROJECTED 2011 LINEUP

Catcher	Geovany Soto
First Base	Derrek Lee
Second Base	Tony Thomas
Third Base	Aramis Ramirez
Shortstop	Ronny Cedeno
Left Field	Alfonso Soriano
Center Field	Felix Pie
Right Field	Tyler Colvin
No. 1 Starter	Carlos Zambrano
No. 2 Starter	Rich Hill
No. 3 Starter	Sean Gallagher
No. 4 Starter	Ted Lilly
No. 5 Starter	Donald Veal
Closer	Carlos Marmol

TOP PROSPECTS OF THE DECADE

Year	Player, Pos.	2007 Org.
1998	Kerry Wood, rhp	Cubs
1999	Corey Patterson, of	Orioles
2000	Corey Patterson, of	Orioles
2001	Corey Patterson, of	Orioles
2002	Mark Prior, rhp	Cubs
2003	Hee Seop Choi, 1b	Kia (Korea)
2004	Angel Guzman, rhp	Cubs
2005	Brian Dopirak, 1b	Cubs
2006	Felix Pie, of	Cubs
2007	Felix Pie, of	Cubs

TOP DRAFT PICKS OF THE DECADE

Year	Player, Pos.	2007 Org.
1998	Corey Patterson, of	Orioles
1999	Ben Christensen, rhp	Out of baseball
2000	Luis Montanez, ss	Orioles
2001	Mark Prior, rhp	Cubs
2002	Bobby Brownlie, rhp	Newark (Atlantic)
2003	Ryan Harvey, of	Cubs
2004	Grant Johnson, rhp (2nd)	Cubs
2005	Mark Pawelek, lhp	Cubs
2006	Tyler Colvin, of	Cubs
2007	Josh Vitters, 3b	Cubs

LARGEST BONUSES IN CLUB HISTORY

Mark Prior, 2001	$4,000,000
Corey Patterson, 1998	$3,700,000
Josh Vitters, 2007	$3,200,000
Luis Montanez, 2000	$2,750,000
Bobby Brownlie, 2002	$2,500,000

CHICAGO CUBS

Top 2008 Rookie: Geovany Soto, c. His performance during his September callup earned him two playoff starts—and Chicago's catching job for 2008.

Breakout Prospect: Robert Hernandez, rhp. With two potential plus pitches, he's ready to take on high Class A hitters at age 19.

Sleeper: Brandon Guyer, of. A fifth-round pick last June, he hit just .245 in his pro debut, but he had a huge instructional league and has one of the best power-speed combinations in the system.

SOURCE OF TOP 30 TALENT			
Homegrown	25	Acquired	5
College	11	Trades	4
Junior college	2	Rule 5 draft	1
High school	6	Independent leagues	0
Draft-and-follow	0	Free agents/waivers	0
Nondrafted free agents	1		
International	5		

Numbers in parentheses indicate prospect ranking.

LF
Jake Fox (19)

CF
Sam Fuld (18)
Brandon Guyer
Ty Wright
Leon Johnson
Jonathan Wyatt

RF
Tyler Colvin (3)
Kyler Burke (13)
Josh Kroeger
Ryan Harvey
Yusuf Carter
Drew Rundle

3B
Josh Vitters (1)
Josh Lansford (28)
Kyle Reynolds
Marquez Smith
Jovan Rosa
Casey McGehee

SS
Darwin Barney (24)
Dylan Johnston
Jonathan Mota

2B
Tony Thomas (9)
Eric Patterson (12)
Matt Camp
Nate Spears

1B
Brian Dopirak
Micah Hoffpauir

C
Geovany Soto (2)
Josh Donaldson (7)
Welington Castillo (15)
Steve Clevenger (29)
Carlos Perez
Chris Robinson
Mark Reed

RHP

Starters	Relievers
Sean Gallagher (5)	Jose Ceda (4)
Jeff Samardzija (8)	Billy Petrick (11)
Kevin Hart (10)	Alex Maestri (23)
Chris Huseby (14)	Jose Ascanio (25)
Dae-Eun Rhee (16)	Rocky Roquet (26)
Robert Hernandez (17)	Tim Lahey (30)
Larry Suarez (20)	Justin Berg
Ryan Acosta (21)	Audy Santana
Mark Holliman (27)	Juan Mateo
Mitch Atkins	Matt Avery
Adam Harben	Grant Johnson

LHP

Starters	Relievers
Donald Veal (6)	Casey Lambert
James Russell (22)	Edward Campusano
Mark Pawelek	Jeremy Papelbon
	Carmen Pignatiello

2007   SIGNING BUDGET: $4.9 MILLION

Best Pro Debut: C Josh Donaldson (1s) batted .335 with nine homers and OF Ty Wright (7) hit .308 with 10 longballs and 11 steals, as both spent most of the summer in the short-season Northwest League. LHP Casey Lambert (6) struck out 47 in 41 innings and limited opponents to a .176 average while getting to low Class A.

Best Athlete: OF Leon Johnson (10) was a four-sport star and Arizona state 100-meter champion in high school. RHP Ryan Acosta (12) qualified for the Florida state finals in the 100 meters and played point guard on his high school basketball team.

Best Pure Hitter: Forget about 3B Josh Vitters' (1) 6-for-51 pro debut. The No. 3 overall pick was one of the best pure hitters in the entire draft. 2B Tony Thomas (3) hit .430 this spring, seventh in Division I.

Best Power Hitter: Vitters' power may be more impressive than his pure hitting ability. Both project as at least a 70 on the 20-80 scouting scale.

Fastest Runner: Johnson, who stole 23 bases in 27 pro attempts, covers 60 yards in 6.4 seconds. OFs Brandon Guyer (6), Wright and Jonathan Wyatt (13) all have plus speed.

Best Defensive Player: OF Clark Hardman (9) is a true center fielder with a plus arm who makes defense look easy.

Best Fastball: The Cubs didn't take a pitcher before the sixth round and didn't land any fire-ballers. LHP Chris Siegfried (11), Acosta and RHP Stephen Vento (23) touch 92-93 mph.

Best Secondary Pitch: Lambert's curveball, ahead of LHP James Russell's (14) changeup.

Most Intriguing Background: Johnson spent two years on a Mormon mission in Siberia. Speed runs in his family, as brothers Elliott (a Devil Rays infield prospect) and Cedric (Philadelphia's 19th-round pick) also can fly. Acosta's father Oscar is a former Cubs pitching coach who died in a car accident in 2006 while working for the Yankees in the Dominican Republic. Russell's father Jeff and unsigned OF Jordan Herr's (41) dad Tommy were big league all-stars. Vitters' brother Christian is a third baseman in the Athletics system.

Closest To The Majors: SS Darwin Barney (4) and Lambert get the most out of their ability

because they're intelligent and instinctive.

Best Late-Round Pick: The Cubs spent $225,000 on Acosta and $350,000 on Russell, who showed improved velocity this summer.

The One Who Got Away: 3B/C Victor Sanchez (25) ranked as the No. 1 prospect in the collegiate Northwoods League. He's now at San Diego. C Preston Clark (33) returned to Texas and should go much higher in the 2008 draft.

Assessment: The Cubs were set to take prep righty Jarrod Parker at No. 3 until the Royals made a late decision to pass on Vitters. That set the tone for Chicago, which took position players with nine of its first 10 choices.

2006   BUDGET: $2.3 MILLION

OF Tyler Colvin (1) reached Double-A in his first pro season. But $10 million RHP Jeff Samardzija (5) and $1.3 million RHP Chris Huseby (11) have yet to live up to the money invested in them.

GRADE: C

2005   BUDGET: $3.8 MILLION

LHP Mark Pawelek (1) is looking more and more like a bust, and LHP Donald Veal (2) took a step back in 2007.

GRADE: D

2004   BUDGET: $2.8 MILLION

The Cubs didn't have a first-rounder and have gotten little out of RHP Grant Johnson (2), who got first-round money. But they did a nice job in later rounds with 2B/OF Eric Patterson (8), OF Sam Fuld (10), RHP Sean Gallagher (12) and since-traded RHP Jerry Blevins (17).

GRADE: C+

2003   BUDGET: $3.9 MILLION

High-ceiling OF Ryan Harvey (1) has gone more bust than boom. LHP Sean Marshall (6) has filled a rotation slot, but Chicago surely wishes it had signed OF/1B Matt LaPorta (14) and RHP Tim Lincecum (48).

GRADE: C

Draft analysis by Jim Callis. Numbers in parentheses indicate draft rounds. Budgets are bonuses in first 10 rounds.

BILL MITCHELL

1
NATIONAL CENTRAL LEAGUE

JOSH VITTERS, 3B

Born: Aug. 27, 1989.
Ht.: 6-3. **Wt.:** 200.
Bats: R. **Throws:** R.
Drafted: HS—
Cypress, Calif., 2007
(1st round.)
Signed by:
Denny Henderson.

Vitters cemented his status as a first-rounder in the summer before his senior year. After failing to make the U.S. junior national team, he lit up the showcase circuit instead. He won MVP honors at the Cape Cod Classic, ranked as the top prospect at the Area Code Games and smacked three doubles at the Aflac Classic, all in the span of two weeks. Vitters didn't disappoint last spring, either, hitting .390 with nine homers in 24 games despite a bout with pneumonia, and earning first-team All-America honors. The only question was how high he'd go in the 2007 draft. Both the Cubs (picking third) and Pirates (fourth) coveted him, but the Royals seemed set on taking him at No. 2 the night before the draft. Then Kansas City took California prep infielder Mike Moustakas, allowing Vitters to fall to Chicago. He became the highest draft pick in Cypress (Calif.) High history, going five spots higher than Scott Moore (a former Cubs farmhand) did to the Tigers five years earlier. Vitters held out all summer before officially signing minutes before the Aug. 15 deadline expired, landing a $3.2 million bonus. Rusty after his long layoff, he went just 6-for-51 (.118), but that didn't diminish the Cubs' enthusiasm about him. His brother Christian is an infielder in the Athletics system.

You can debate which tool is more impressive, Vitters' hitting ability or his power, but the consensus is that his future potential grades as a 70 on the 20-80 scouting scale in both categories. He's the rare righthanded hitter whose swing is described as pretty, and his bat speed and feel for putting the barrel on the ball are also uncommon. He can crush the ball to all fields and hammers fastballs and offspeed pitches alike. Defense doesn't come as easily to Vitters, but he has plenty of arm strength and reliable hands, so he should become an average third baseman. His work ethic will drive him to put in the time he needs at the hot corner. The Cubs also love his makeup, and he fit in well with teammates at his two minor league stops and in instructional league.

Vitters made five errors in nine pro games at third base, and his biggest defensive shortcomings are his agility and his ability to read hops. He addressed both areas in instructional league, doing a lot of jump-rope work to quicken his lower half and taking hundreds of ground balls. Chicago writes off his lackluster debut to being more gung-ho than prepared after three months without game action. He got a little pull-conscious, but his stroke looked as sound as ever. Once he fills out, he'll be a below-average runner, though he shouldn't be a liability on the bases.

Aramis Ramirez is signed through 2011, which could create a dilemma because Vitters' bat should be ready for the majors well before then. But the presence of Ramirez and the depth of third basemen in the system also will make it easy for the Cubs to let Vitters develop at his own pace. He'll begin his first full pro season at low Class A Peoria.

Year	Club (League)	Class	AVG	G	AB	R	H	2B	3B	HR	RBI	BB	SO	SB	OBP	SLG
2007	Cubs (AZL)	R	.067	7	30	0	2	0	0	0	2	1	9	0	.094	.067
	Boise (NWL)	A	.190	7	21	2	4	0	0	0	1	2	5	1	.261	.190
MINOR LEAGUE TOTALS			.118	14	51	2	6	0	0	0	3	3	14	1	.164	.118

2 GEOVANY SOTO, C/1B

Born: Jan. 20, 1983. **B-T:** R-R. **Ht.:** 6-1. **Wt.:** 200. **Drafted:** HS—Rio Piedras, P.R., 2001 (11th round). **Signed by:** Sam Hughes.

Soto had done little to distinguish himself in the first two years after the Cubs put him on their 40-man roster, but he exploded in 2007. He led the minors in batting average by a catcher (.353) and overall slugging percentage (.652), and won the Triple-A Pacific Coast League MVP award. Chicago's minor league player of the year, he upped his production after a September callup. The key for Soto was losing 30 pounds after spring training started, allowing him to maintain his bat speed and get to inside fastballs better than he had in the past. He also showed a knack for driving outside pitches the other way, and while his 2007 numbers may be a bit crazy, he has the ability to annually hit .275 with 20 homers in the majors. He provides good defense as well, with a strong arm, good receiving skills and improved agility behind the plate. Now that he has seen what it can do for him, Soto must remain in top shape. He's a below-average runner, but not bad for a catcher. Soto has raised his ceiling from likely backup to potential all-star. He'll be the Cubs' regular catcher in 2008 and eventually should become their best all-around catcher since Jody Davis two decades ago.

Year	Club (League)	Class	AVG	G	AB	R	H	2B	3B	HR	RBI	BB	SO	SB	OBP	SLG
2001	Cubs (AZL)	R	.260	41	150	18	39	16	0	1	20	15	33	1	.339	.387
2002	Cubs (AZL)	R	.269	44	156	24	42	10	2	3	24	13	35	0	.333	.417
	Boise (NWL)	A	.400	1	5	1	2	0	0	0	0	0	1	0	.400	.400
2003	Daytona (FSL)	A	.242	89	297	26	72	12	2	2	38	31	58	0	.313	.316
2004	West Tenn (SL)	AA	.271	104	332	47	90	16	0	9	48	40	71	1	.355	.401
2005	Iowa (PCL)	AAA	.253	91	292	30	74	14	0	4	39	48	77	0	.357	.342
	Chicago (NL)	MLB	.000	1	1	0	0	0	0	0	0	0	0	0	.000	.000
2006	Iowa (PCL)	AAA	.272	108	342	34	93	21	0	6	38	41	74	0	.353	.386
	Chicago (NL)	MLB	.200	11	25	1	5	1	0	0	2	0	5	0	.231	.240
2007	Iowa (PCL)	AAA	.353	110	385	75	136	31	3	26	109	53	94	0	.424	.652
	Chicago (NL)	MLB	.389	18	54	12	21	6	0	3	8	5	14	0	.433	.667
MINOR LEAGUE TOTALS			.280	588	1959	255	548	120	7	51	316	241	443	2	.360	.426
MAJOR LEAGUE TOTALS			.325	30	80	13	26	7	0	3	10	5	19	0	.368	.525

3 TYLER COLVIN, OF

ROBERT GURGANUS

Born: Sept. 5, 1985. **B-T:** L-L. **Ht.:** 6-3. **Wt.:** 200. **Drafted:** Clemson, 2006 (1st round). **Signed by:** Antonio Grissom.

Colvin was the surprise of the first round in the 2006 draft, going 13th overall and signing for $1.475 million. He has made the Cubs look good by drawing comparisons to Steve Finley and Shawn Green while shooting to Double-A in his first full season. Colvin missed time in August with a minor shoulder injury that also limited him with Team USA at the World Cup. The best athlete in the system, he has average or better tools across the board. With his smooth swing and bat speed, he projects to hit for average and power. He's a slightly above-average runner whose speed plays up on the basepaths and in center field. He has average arm strength and good accuracy on his throws. Colvin drew just 15 walks in 125 games, and more advanced pitchers will exploit his anxiousness. He has trouble with offspeed stuff, and he must learn to trust his hands. He's content to serve balls to the opposite field, though he'll have more power once he gets stronger. If Felix Pie doesn't take over center field in 2008, Colvin could get a crack at it after a year at Triple-A Iowa. At-bats to hone his approach and pitch recognition are all he needs.

Year	Club (League)	Class	AVG	G	AB	R	H	2B	3B	HR	RBI	BB	SO	SB	OBP	SLG
2006	Boise (NWL)	A	.268	64	265	50	71	12	6	11	53	17	55	12	.313	.483
2007	Daytona (FSL)	A	.306	63	245	38	75	24	3	7	50	10	47	10	.336	.514
	Tennessee (SL)	AA	.291	62	247	34	72	11	2	9	31	5	54	7	.313	.462
MINOR LEAGUE TOTALS			.288	189	757	122	218	47	11	27	134	32	156	29	.320	.486

4 JOSE CEDA, RHP

RODGER WOOD

Born: Jan. 28, 1987. **B-T:** R-R. **Ht.:** 6-5. **Wt.:** 247. **Signed:** Dominican Republic, 2004. **Signed by:** Felix Francisco/Randy Smith (Padres).

Cubs special assistant Steve Hinton spotted Ceda in Padres instructional league camp in 2005, and Chicago grabbed him in a deal for Todd Walker in mid-2006. Ceda opened 2007 as a starter in low Class A before missing two months with shoulder stiffness. He returned as a reliever in mid-July and didn't allow a hit, striking out 42 in 23 innings in that role. The Cubs could have another Lee Smith on their hands. When he came out of the bullpen, Ceda's fastball sat in the mid-90s and reached 99 mph. His slider also tightened up and could be a 65 pitch on the 20-80 scouting scale. Ceda is still figuring out his mechanics, so his control and command are erratic. He carried 280 pounds when he arrived in the trade, and he needs to keep the extra weight off so that he can repeat his delivery. He doesn't have much of a changeup and didn't hold up well as a starter, but those aren't issues now that he's a reliever. Chicago may jump Ceda to Double-A Tennessee so he can face better hitters. He has big league stuff and will head to Wrigley Field once he figures out how to locate his pitches better.

Year	Club (League)	Class	W	L	ERA	G	GS	CG	SV	IP	H	R	ER	HR	BB	SO	AVG
2005	Padres (DSL)	R	4	2	1.50	13	9	2	2	60	38	18	10	2	29	83	.174
2006	Padres (AZL)	R	2	0	5.09	8	4	0	0	23	20	14	13	1	13	31	.235
	Cubs (AZL)	R	0	0	0.75	5	3	0	0	12	6	2	1	0	7	21	.154
	Boise (NWL)	A	1	0	3.27	3	3	0	0	11	5	4	4	1	2	11	.139
2007	Cubs (AZL)	R	0	0	2.45	2	1	0	0	3	2	1	1	0	3	3	.182
	Peoria (MWL)	A	2	2	3.11	21	6	0	0	46	14	18	16	1	31	66	.093
MINOR LEAGUE TOTALS			9	4	2.60	52	26	2	2	156	85	57	45	5	85	215	.157

5 SEAN GALLAGHER, RHP

Born: Dec. 30, 1985. **B-T:** R-R. **Ht.:** 6-2. **Wt.:** 225. **Drafted:** HS—Fort Lauderdale, Fla., 2004 (12th round). **Signed by:** Rolando Pino.

Most clubs considered Gallagher unsignable in the 2004 draft, but the Cubs nabbed him with a 12th-round pick and a $60,000 bonus. He has been a bargain, reaching double figures in wins in each of his three full seasons and making his major league debut in June at age 21. Gallagher has added fastball velocity since signing, reaching 90-94 mph last season, and he can spot it wherever he wants. It has surpassed his 11-to-5 curveball as his best pitch. His changeup is an effective third pitch and he mixes his offerings well. Gallagher can get into trouble with the softer version of his curveball,  which arrives at 69-74 mph. Typical of most rookies, he nibbled too much in his first taste of the majors. He'll have to watch the weight, though dropping 10 pounds in the Arizona Fall League is a good sign. Gallagher will compete for a spot as a No. 5 starter or long reliever. Spending most of 2008 at Triple-A wouldn't be a setback, however. He has the makings of a No. 3 starter along the lines of Jon Lieber.

Year	Club (League)	Class	W	L	ERA	G	GS	CG	SV	IP	H	R	ER	HR	BB	SO	AVG
2004	Cubs (AZL)	R	1	2	3.12	10	9	0	0	34	38	19	12	0	11	44	.275
2005	Peoria (MWL)	A	14	5	2.71	26	26	0	0	146	107	53	44	10	55	139	.206
	Daytona (FSL)	A	0	0	1.80	1	1	0	0	5	6	1	1	1	0	7	.286
2006	Daytona (FSL)	A	4	0	2.30	13	13	0	0	78	75	24	20	5	21	80	.260
	West Tenn (SL)	AA	7	5	2.71	15	15	0	0	86	74	30	26	4	55	91	.239
2007	Tennessee (SL)	AA	7	2	3.39	11	11	0	0	61	54	25	23	3	24	54	.233
	Iowa (PCL)	AAA	3	1	2.66	8	8	0	0	40	33	12	12	1	13	37	.232
	Chicago (NL)	MLB	0	0	8.59	8	0	0	1	14	19	15	14	3	12	5	.317
MINOR LEAGUE TOTALS			36	15	2.75	84	83	0	0	452	387	164	138	24	179	452	.235
MAJOR LEAGUE TOTALS			0	0	8.59	8	0	0	1	14	19	15	14	3	12	5	.317

6 DONALD VEAL, LHP

Born: Sept. 18, 1984. **B-T:** L-L. **Ht.:** 6-4. **Wt.:** 230. **Drafted:** Pima (Ariz.) CC, 2005 (2nd round). **Signed by:** Steve McFarland.

After Veal led minor league starters with a .175 opponent average in 2006, he had trouble getting untracked last season. He went 0-4, 10.57 in his first four starts and battled his control throughout the year, leading the Double-A Southern League with 73 walks. Hitters don't see many pitchers like Veal, a big lefthander with quality stuff and an unorthodox delivery. He has a swing-and-miss fastball in the low 90s and works both corners with it. His curveball shows flashes of being a plus pitch, while his changeup is  solid at times. Veal has a tough time maintaining his delivery, which includes a big leg kick, and his arm slot. When he falls behind, he'll short-arm the ball and try to aim it. He has trouble staying on top of his curveball, and some scouts wonder if he might need to go to a splitter. He has a ceiling as a No. 2 starter, but Veal could wind up as a reliever in the mold of Arthur Rhodes. The Cubs sent him to instructional league so he could build up confidence, and they'll probably send him back to Double-A to start 2008.

Year	Club (League)	Class	W	L	ERA	G	GS	CG	SV	IP	H	R	ER	HR	BB	SO	AVG
2005	Cubs (AZL)	R	0	1	5.06	4	3	0	0	10	8	6	6	2	5	14	.205
	Boise (NWL)	A	1	2	2.48	7	6	0	0	29	18	11	8	2	15	34	.180
2006	Peoria (MWL)	A	5	3	2.69	14	14	0	0	73	45	26	22	4	40	86	.179
	Daytona (FSL)	A	6	2	1.67	14	14	0	0	80	46	18	15	3	42	88	.170
2007	Tennessee (SL)	AA	8	10	4.97	28	27	0	0	130	126	80	72	11	73	131	.256
MINOR LEAGUE TOTALS			20	18	3.41	67	64	0	0	324	243	141	123	22	175	353	.211

7 JOSH DONALDSON, C

Born: Dec. 8, 1985. **B-T:** R-R. **Ht.:** 6-0. **Wt.:** 195. **Drafted:** Auburn, 2007 (1st round supplemental). **Signed by:** Bob Rossi.

A former third baseman, Donaldson started catching as a sophomore at Auburn in 2006. The position shift and a strong summer in the Cape Cod League sent his draft stock skyrocketing, and he went 48th overall in June. After signing for $652,500, he rated as the short-season Northwest League's top position prospect. Donaldson provides more offense and athleticism than most catchers. He's aggressive and looks to pull pitches for power early in counts, but can shorten his stroke and use the opposite field. He controls the strike zone and projects as a .280 hitter with 15-20 homers a season. He has slightly above-average arm strength and threw out 38 percent of basestealers in his pro debut. His speed is average. His inexperience shows behind the plate, though the Cubs believe he'll become a solid defender. He had 11 passed balls in 45 games and sometimes hurried his release and undermined his arm strength. Chicago has built up its catching depth, so it may take things slow with Donaldson and let him concentrate on his work behind the plate. He'll probably open 2008 in low Class A.

Year	Club (League)	Class	AVG	G	AB	R	H	2B	3B	HR	RBI	BB	SO	SB	OBP	SLG
2007	Cubs (AZL)	R	.182	4	11	1	2	2	0	0	0	2	4	0	.308	.364
	Boise (NWL)	A	.346	49	162	37	56	11	2	9	35	37	34	6	.470	.605
MINOR LEAGUE TOTALS			.335	53	173	38	58	13	2	9	35	39	38	6	.460	.590

8 JEFF SAMARDZIJA, RHP

Born: Jan. 23, 1985. **B-T:** R-R. **Ht.:** 6-5. **Wt.:** 220. **Drafted:** Notre Dame, 2006 (5th round). **Signed by:** Stan Zielinski.

Samardzija set every significant receiving record at Notre Dame, and the Cubs, who signed him for $250,000 as a fifth-rounder in 2006, ponied up a five-year major league contract worth $10 million last January to get him to give up football. In his first outing in big league camp, he retired Eric Chavez, Mark Ellis and Travis Buck on eight pitches and broke two bats. It's easy to dream on Samardzija, who has size, athleticism, makeup and a nasty fastball. His heater has a rare combination of velocity (low to mid-90s, touching 98 mph) and sink. His slider could also be a plus-plus pitch, though it's inconsistent. He stayed healthy, maintained his velocity and threw strikes in 2007 despite pitching far more than ever before. For a guy with Samardzija's stuff, his statistics don't add up, including a .306 opponent average and 4.1 strikeouts per nine innings last season. His slider and changeup need a lot of polish. Samardzija is an enigma, still capable of becoming a frontline starter, a closer or a bust. After pitching better following a promotion to Double-A, he'll return to Tennessee to start 2008.

Year	Club (League)	Class	W	L	ERA	G	GS	CG	SV	IP	H	R	ER	HR	BB	SO	AVG
2006	Boise (NWL)	A	1	1	2.37	5	5	0	0	19	18	5	5	1	6	13	.247
	Peoria (MWL)	A	0	1	3.27	2	2	0	0	11	6	5	4	1	6	4	.167
2007	Daytona (FSL)	A	3	8	4.95	24	20	1	0	107	142	69	59	8	35	45	.323
	Tennessee (SL)	AA	3	3	3.41	6	6	0	0	34	33	15	13	8	9	20	.250
MINOR LEAGUE TOTALS			7	13	4.25	37	33	1	0	171	199	94	81	18	56	82	.293

9 TONY THOMAS, 2B

Born: July 10, 1986. **B-T:** R-R. **Ht.:** 5-10. **Wt.:** 180. **Drafted:** Florida State, 2007 (3rd round). **Signed by:** Keith Stohr.

Thomas hit just .265 in his first two seasons at Florida State, prompting him to adopt a more open stance in 2007. The results were spectacular, as he batted .430 and led NCAA Division I in runs (91), doubles (33) and total bases (189). The Cubs were elated to grab him in the third round for $360,000. The consensus in the organization is that Thomas has more pure batting ability than Josh Vitters. He employs a level swing to make consistent line-drive contact to all fields. He's strong for his size and doesn't have to cheat to catch up to fastballs, which allows him to stay back on offspeed stuff. He has average speed and outstanding instincts. Thomas isn't as instinctive at second base as he is at the plate or on the bases, and his defensive ceiling is average at best. He has adequate range and a fringy arm. There's not another good fit for him elsewhere on the diamond, but Chicago thinks roving infield instructor Bobby Dickerson will be able to help him out. Thomas will jump to high Class A Daytona. If he can make progress with his glove, he could reach Chicago by the end of 2009.

Year	Club (League)	Class	AVG	G	AB	R	H	2B	3B	HR	RBI	BB	SO	SB	OBP	SLG
2007	Cubs (AZL)	R	.176	5	17	7	3	0	2	0	6	2	5	0	.286	.412
	Boise (NWL)	A	.308	46	182	44	56	12	8	5	33	25	41	28	.404	.544
MINOR LEAGUE TOTALS			.296	51	199	51	59	12	10	5	39	27	46	28	.393	.533

10 KEVIN HART, RHP

RODGER WOOD

Born: Dec. 29, 1982. **B-T:** R-R. **Ht.:** 6-4. **Wt.:** 215. **Drafted:** Maryland, 2004 (11th round). **Signed by:** Ty Brown (Orioles).

The biggest surprise in the system last season, Hart hadn't pitched above high Class A when the Cubs acquired him for Freddie Bynum in December 2006. But he responded to Tennessee pitching coach Dennis Lewallyn and finished the year on the playoff roster. Lewallyn taught Hart a cut fastball that made all the difference in the world. Once he mastered it, he allowed just 13 earned runs over his final nine Double-A starts and pitched better as he moved up the ladder. He also improved his fastball, which sat at 91-92 mph in the minors and 93-94 mph when he relieved in the majors, as well as his changeup. He has a durable frame and throws strikes. A quality cutter should allow a righthander to hold lefty hitters at bay, but they batted .316/.383/.453 against Hart in the minors. He has a curveball, but it's nothing more than a show-me pitch. Hart thrived as a big league reliever in September, but the Cubs haven't given up on him as a starter. He could open the season in their rotation if he pitches well in spring training.

Year	Club (League)	Class	W	L	ERA	G	GS	CG	SV	IP	H	R	ER	HR	BB	SO	AVG
2004	Aberdeen (NYP)	A	3	0	3.77	9	0	0	1	14	10	7	6	0	7	16	.189
	Delmarva (SAL)	A	2	0	3.77	4	2	0	0	14	13	6	6	0	5	16	.232
2005	Delmarva (SAL)	A	9	8	4.55	28	28	0	0	152	170	101	77	9	54	164	.278
2006	Frederick (Car)	A	6	11	4.61	28	27	0	0	148	149	97	76	18	65	122	.258
2007	Iowa (PCL)	AAA	4	1	3.54	9	8	1	0	56	56	23	22	6	23	39	.271
	Tennessee (SL)	AA	8	5	4.24	18	17	0	0	102	100	59	48	13	27	92	.255
	Chicago (NL)	MLB	0	0	0.82	8	0	0	0	11	7	1	1	0	4	13	.189
MINOR LEAGUE TOTALS			32	25	4.34	96	82	1	1	487	498	293	235	46	181	449	.263
MAJOR LEAGUE TOTALS			0	0	0.82	8	0	0	0	11	7	1	1	0	4	13	.189

11 BILLY PETRICK, RHP

Born: April 29, 1984. **B-T:** R-R. **Ht.:** 6-6. **Wt.:** 240. **Drafted:** HS—Morris, Ill., 2002 (3rd round). **Signed by:** Bob Hale.

Petrick was developing nicely as one of the Cubs' top starting pitching prospects before going down with a small tear in his labrum in May 2005. Following arthroscopic surgery, he returned to the mound in the second half of 2006 and took off after moving to the bullpen last season. He started 2007 in high Class A and advanced to the majors by June. Petrick's best pitch when he was coming up as a starter was a heavy 91-92 mph sinker, but he showed a mid-90s four-seam fastball that touched 97-98 in multiple big league outings. His slider also played up, reaching as high as 86-87 mph while he was with the Cubs. In the minors, he worked mostly with a 91-94 mph heater and a low-80s slider. A former Washington State football recruit as a long snapper, he always has exhibited an aggressive demeanor that served him well as a reliever. Petrick went more with his four-seamer last year, trading velocity for movement. That decision left him more vulnerable to homers, as he gave up nine in 65 innings after surrendering just 10 in 332 frames in his previous five seasons. He fell behind too many hitters during his two big league stints, but throwing strikes wasn't an issue in the minors, so it was more a matter of rookie jitters than anything. Chicago brought him back slowly, never using him on consecutive days all season, though he still ran out of gas toward the end. He permitted 11 runs in his final seven innings and made just four Triple-A appearances in August. Petrick should be ready for a full workload in 2008, and he'll be back with the Cubs once he shows some consistency at Triple-A.

Year	Club (League)	Class	W	L	ERA	G	GS	CG	SV	IP	H	R	ER	HR	BB	SO	AVG
2002	Cubs (AZL)	R	2	1	1.71	6	6	0	0	31	21	8	6	0	6	35	.189
2003	Boise (NWL)	A	2	5	4.76	14	14	0	0	64	60	49	34	4	27	64	.241
2004	Lansing (MWL)	A	13	7	3.50	26	24	0	0	146	149	66	57	3	43	113	.276
2005	Daytona (FSL)	A	1	4	5.59	9	9	0	0	37	39	23	23	0	19	25	.275
2006	Boise (NWL)	A	5	0	2.23	7	7	0	0	36	37	10	9	0	12	28	.266
	Daytona (FSL)	A	1	2	6.06	3	3	0	0	16	24	11	11	3	2	9	.343
2007	Daytona (FSL)	A	0	1	3.09	6	0	0	0	11	12	4	4	0	2	10	.267
	Tennessee (SL)	AA	1	1	2.37	18	0	0	2	30	22	10	8	3	8	33	.202
	Chicago (NL)	MLB	0	0	7.45	8	0	0	0	9	8	8	8	3	7	6	.229
	Iowa (PCL)	AAA	1	1	5.11	9	0	0	0	12	17	8	7	3	2	7	.354
MINOR LEAGUE TOTALS			26	22	3.70	98	63	0	2	386	381	189	159	16	121	324	.262
MAJOR LEAGUE TOTALS			0	0	7.45	8	0	0	0	9	8	8	8	3	7	6	.229

12 ERIC PATTERSON, 2B/OF

Born: April 8, 1983. **B-T:** L-R **Ht.:** 5-11. **Wt.:** 170. **Drafted:** Georgia Tech, 2004 (8th round). **Signed by:** Sam Hughes.

Patterson entered 2007 as the Cubs' second baseman of the future but now looks more like a utilityman. Mark DeRosa and Mike Fontenot shared Chicago's second-base job during the season, and though Patterson earned Pacific Coast League all-star recognition, the Cubs looked outside for additional options during the offseason. He got his first taste of the big leagues in August, and when he returned for a September callup, he lasted just two days before arriving late at the ballpark. Because he did the same thing at Iowa, the Cubs made a point to him by demoting him to Double-A. Patterson's tools are similar to but not as good as those of his older brother Corey. Eric's best tool is his plus speed and he has surprising pop for his size, though sometimes it is too much for his own good. While he'd be better off focusing on getting on base, he can get caught up in trying to hit for power. Despite his athleticism, Patterson never has gotten the hang of playing second base. He doesn't read balls well off the bat or range well to his right. He began seeing time in left and center field in May and played there exclusively in August. He has solid center-field range but a below-average arm for the outfield. He doesn't have the arm to play shortstop, third base or right field, so he's somewhat limited as a utilityman. Patterson figures to return to Triple-A at the outset of 2008, and he could be most useful to Chicago as a trade chip.

Year	Club (League)	Class	AVG	G	AB	R	H	2B	3B	HR	RBI	BB	SO	SB	OBP	SLG
2005	Peoria (MWL)	A	.333	110	432	90	144	26	11	13	71	53	94	40	.405	.535
	West Tenn (SL)	AA	.200	9	30	5	6	2	0	0	2	6	7	3	.324	.267
2006	West Tenn (SL)	AA	.263	121	441	66	116	22	9	8	48	46	89	38	.330	.408
	Iowa (PCL)	AAA	.358	17	67	14	24	1	1	2	12	6	9	8	.395	.493
2007	Iowa (PCL)	AAA	.297	128	516	94	153	28	6	14	65	54	85	24	.362	.455
	Chicago (NL)	MLB	.250	7	8	0	2	1	0	0	0	0	3	0	.250	.375
MINOR LEAGUE TOTALS			.298	385	1486	269	443	79	27	37	198	165	284	113	.366	.462
MAJOR LEAGUE TOTALS			.250	7	8	0	2	1	0	0	0	0	3	0	.250	.375

13 KYLER BURKE, OF

Born: April 20, 1988. **B-T:** L-L. **Ht.:** 6-3. **Wt.:** 205. **Drafted:** HS—Ooltewah, Tenn., 2006 (1st round supplemental). **Signed by:** Ash Lawson (Padres).

The 35th overall pick in the 2007 draft, Burke never got untracked in the Padres system after signing for $950,000. He batted just .210 with two homers in 107 games, and San Diego soured on him enough that it included him in a June trade for the embattled Michael Barrett. Burke got off to a less than auspicious start with the Cubs, going 0-for-22 at short-season Boise before recovering to hit .282/.361/.495 for the remainder of the summer. The key to his resurgence was getting more aggressive at the plate. Burke has a sound knowledge of the strike zone and good patience, but he would get too passive at times, taking strikes down the middle and then chasing offspeed pitches once he fell behind in the count. Athletic and strong, he should develop at least 20-homer power, though he needs to make contact and use the whole field more often. Burke has slightly below-average speed but is better once he gets underway. He's a solid right fielder with the best arm strength among the system's outfielders. He built on his progress in Hawaii Winter Baseball, where he hit .333 but also struck out 37 times in 87 at-bats. He's ready to give the low Class A Midwest League another shot in 2008, this time at Peoria.

Year	Club (League)	Class	AVG	G	AB	R	H	2B	3B	HR	RBI	BB	SO	SB	OBP	SLG
2006	Padres (AZL)	R	.209	45	163	24	34	3	4	1	15	26	56	1	.313	.294
2007	Fort Wayne (MWL)	A	.211	62	213	24	45	7	1	1	21	26	73	3	.305	.268
	Boise (NWL)	A	.254	63	224	35	57	11	1	10	41	24	63	1	.340	.446
MINOR LEAGUE TOTALS			.227	170	600	83	136	21	6	12	77	76	192	5	.320	.342

14 CHRIS HUSEBY, RHP

Born: Jan. 11, 1988. **B-T:** R-R. **Ht.:** 6-7. **Wt.:** 215. **Drafted:** HS—Stuart, Fla., 2006 (11th round). **Signed by:** Rolando Pino.

Huseby landed the most stunning bonus in the 2006 draft, signing for an 11th-round-record $1.3 million after barely pitching as a high school senior. He had pitched for Team USA's youth team and was laying the groundwork for being an early-round pick before he needed Tommy John surgery in the spring of 2005. Though he didn't pitch much between then and the draft, the Cubs monitored him closely and saw enough in a workout to make a seven-figure investment. Though Huseby pitched at 86-90 mph for much of 2007, Chicago doesn't regret that decision. He's still ultraprojectable at 6-foot-7 and 215 pounds. He throws his hard-breaking curveball at 78-80 mph, an indication that he has plenty of arm speed and that more fastball velocity should be in his future. His delivery is sound and he uses his big frame to pitch downhill. Because he barely pitched in 2005 and 2006, Huseby is less experienced than most 20-year-olds and still has much improvement to make with his changeup, control and command. He spent most of the summer shooting for strikeouts—and falling behind in counts—but did a better job of pitching to contact during instructional league. The Cubs believe he could be poised for a breakout this year in low Class A.

Year	Club (League)	Class	W	L	ERA	G	GS	CG	SV	IP	H	R	ER	HR	BB	SO	AVG
2006	Cubs (AZL)	R	0	2	5.19	6	6	0	0	17	21	10	10	1	6	14	.296
2007	Boise (NWL)	A	2	5	3.39	15	15	0	0	66	61	39	25	7	31	53	.245
MINOR LEAGUE TOTALS			2	7	3.76	21	21	0	0	83	82	49	35	8	37	67	.256

15 WELINGTON CASTILLO, C

Born: April 24, 1987. **B-T:** R-R. **Ht.:** 6-0. **Wt.:** 200. **Signed:** Dominican Republic, 2004. **Signed by:** Jose Serra.

After an aborted U.S. debut in 2006, during which he played in just three games before missing two months with a high ankle sprain, Castillo established himself as the best defensive catcher in the Midwest League as well as the Cubs system last season. A short, stocky catcher in the mold of Yadier Molina, Castillo has quick feet and a strong arm. He threw out 37 percent of basestealers in 2007 and also improved as a receiver, though he needs to be more consistent. He led MWL backstops with 15 errors and also committed 13 passed balls. He has the defensive package to be at least a big league backup, and Castillo's bat will determine if he eventually becomes a regular. He has some strength in his swing, though his approach and plate discipline are still works in progress. He's still figuring out how to hit breaking balls, which is why righties limited him to a .249 average and .690 OPS last year (compared to .323 with a .911 OPS against lefties). He's a below-average runner, no surprise for a catcher. Castillo will advance to high Class A this year and is at least two years away from being ready for the majors.

Year	Club (League)	Class	AVG	G	AB	R	H	2B	3B	HR	RBI	BB	SO	SB	OBP	SLG
2005	Cubs (DSL)	R	.289	60	204	29	59	14	0	1	28	19	28	1	.370	.373
2006	Boise (NWL)	A	.167	3	6	1	1	0	0	0	0	1	0	0	.286	.167
	Cubs (AZL)	R	.192	7	26	4	5	0	0	0	0	1	6	0	.250	.192
2007	Peoria (MWL)	A	.271	98	317	41	86	11	2	11	44	23	77	1	.334	.423
MINOR LEAGUE TOTALS			.273	168	553	75	151	25	2	12	72	44	111	2	.343	.391

16 DAE-EUN RHEE, RHP

Born: March 23, 1989. **B-T:** L-R. **Ht.:** 6-2. **Wt.:** 190. **Signed:** Korea, 2007. **Signed by:** Steve Wilson.

The Cubs invested heavily in Koreans Hee-Seop Choi ($1.2 million in 1999) and Jae-Kuk Ryu ($1.6 million in 2001), neither of whom did much in the majors, though they did trade Choi for Derrek Lee. Chicago's latest Korean bonus baby is Rhee, who signed for $525,000 last July. He didn't pitch in any games during the summer but he did open eyes with his performance in instructional league. Rhee's fastball ranged from 90-94 mph, and his best pitch was a changeup that dives at the plate like a splitter. He also showed a hard curveball and exceptional control and feel for an 18-year-old. Rhee still has room to easily add strength, as he carries just 190 pounds on his broad-shouldered, 6-foot-2 frame. He has a balanced delivery, which bodes well for his future health. As intriguing as Rhee is, he still has yet to prove anything in pro ball. He'll get his first chance to do that in 2008, either in the Rookie-level Arizona League or at Boise.

Year	Club (League)	Class	W	L	ERA	G	GS	CG	SV	IP	H	R	ER	HR	BB	SO	AVG
2007	Did Not Play																

17 ROBERT HERNANDEZ, RHP

Born: Oct. 7, 1988. **B-T:** R-R. **Ht.:** 6-2. **Wt.:** 165. **Signed:** Venezuela, 2005. **Signed by:** Hector Ortega.

Carlos Zambrano has taken his Venezuelan countryman Hernandez under his wing and already has started touting him to the Cubs' press corps. Hernandez is still a few years away from joining his booster at Wrigley Field, but he's further along then most players his age. He began 2007 in extended spring training before being summoned to Peoria in May, and he stayed there for the remainder of the season. The Midwest League's youngest regular starting pitcher at 18, Hernandez showed the potential for two plus pitches with his 88-92 mph fastball and his advanced changeup. Extremely young and skinny, he has plenty of time and room to add strength and velocity. He wasn't intimidated by older hitters and had no difficulties throwing strikes. Besides maturing physically, Hernandez' biggest need is to come up with a breaking ball. He has messed around with both a curveball and a slider, but both remain below average for now. After handling low Class A with surprising ease, Hernandez faces another challenge in 2008 as a 19-year-old in high Class A.

Year	Club (League)	Class	W	L	ERA	G	GS	CG	SV	IP	H	R	ER	HR	BB	SO	AVG
2006	Cubs (AZL)	R	5	2	3.20	14	5	0	0	39	42	27	14	1	16	18	.266
2007	Peoria (MWL)	A	8	9	4.34	20	20	0	0	103	106	60	50	11	28	71	.266
MINOR LEAGUE TOTALS			13	11	4.03	34	25	0	0	143	148	87	64	12	44	89	.266

18 SAM FULD, OF

Born: Nov. 20, 1981. **B-T:** L-L. **Ht.:** 5-10. **Wt.:** 180. **Drafted:** Stanford, 2004 (10th round). **Signed by:** Steve Hinton.

Eric Patterson's loss was Fuld's gain. When Patterson arrived late to the ballpark on the third day of his September callup, Chicago demoted him to Double-A and brought up Fuld. Though he went hitless in six big league at-bats, he scored the winning run in one game against the Reds and made a spectacular catch up against the ivy against the Pirates. He already was an organization favorite for his energy and effort, and Fuld helped his cause further. He graduated from Stanford with an economics degree and still holds the College World Series record with 24 career hits. He has the best strike-zone judgment in the system, drawing more than his share of walks and making consistent line-drive contact. He doesn't have much power and his speed is just a tick above average, though his tremendous instincts allow him to steal a few bases and play a quality center field. Fuld's arm rates as below average, but his savvy and quick release helped him lead the Southern League with 13 outfield assists in just 87 games last year. He plays so hard that it's difficult for him to hold up over a full season. He jammed his shoulder on a headfirst slide during his 2005 pro debut, then battled back and hip problems before having offseason surgery to repair a sports hernia in 2006. He missed the first two weeks of last season after tweaking an oblique muscle in spring training. Fuld has boosted his profile from quality organization player to a big league reserve outfielder, and some scouts who saw him in the Arizona Fall League thought he could be more than that. He batted .402 and led the AFL in hits (43), doubles (11), extra-base hits (16), total bases (67), on-base percentage (.492) and slugging percentage (.626). He also won the league's Dernell Stenson Award for leadership. He could push Felix Pie for the Cubs' center-field job in spring training, but Fuld is more likely to stick in the majors as a backup or head to Triple-A.

Year	Club (League)	Class	AVG	G	AB	R	H	2B	3B	HR	RBI	BB	SO	SB	OBP	SLG
2005	Peoria (MWL)	A	.300	125	443	82	133	32	6	5	37	50	44	18	.377	.433
2006	Daytona (FSL)	A	.300	89	353	63	106	19	6	4	40	40	54	22	.378	.422
2007	Iowa (PCL)	AAA	.269	14	52	13	14	4	1	1	2	9	5	2	.397	.442
	Tennessee (SL)	AA	.290	90	335	56	97	23	2	2	27	41	38	10	.372	.388
	Chicago (NL)	MLB	.000	14	6	3	0	0	0	0	0	3	3	0	.333	.000
MINOR LEAGUE TOTALS			.296	318	1183	214	350	78	15	12	106	140	141	52	.377	.418
MAJOR LEAGUE TOTALS			.000	14	6	3	0	0	0	0	0	3	3	0	.333	.000

19 JAKE FOX, OF/1B/C

Born: July 20, 1982. **B-T:** R-R. **Ht.:** 6-0. **Wt.:** 210. **Drafted:** Michigan, 2003 (3rd round). **Signed by:** Stan Zielinski.

Fox generates split opinions both inside and outside of the organization. Those who like him point to his righthanded power and believe he could be a regular at first base or left field. Those who don't think he sells out for homers, an approach that won't work in the major leagues, and question whether he'll ever be effective against breaking pitches. One thing both sides do agree on is that Fox won't make it as a catcher, his full-time position before 2007. Fox undermined decent arm strength with subpar footwork and a slow transfer, and his receiving skills were even shakier. While he's a good athlete for a catcher, he has below-average speed, range, hands and arm strength, which makes it a stretch that he can play an outfield corner on a regular basis. Fox' background as an offensive-minded catcher who had to move from behind the plate is similar to Ryan Garko's. He's a better defender at first base and has as much power as Garko, but Fox isn't as polished a hitter. He can hit fastballs early in the count, but he doesn't have much patience and is susceptible to offspeed pitches. Though the Cubs will give Fox a look in spring training, he'll probably open the year in Triple-A.

Year	Club (League)	Class	AVG	G	AB	R	H	2B	3B	HR	RBI	BB	SO	SB	OBP	SLG
2003	Cubs (AZL)	R	.240	15	50	4	12	5	0	1	6	5	14	0	.321	.400
	Lansing (MWL)	A	.260	29	100	13	26	8	0	5	12	8	19	0	.330	.490
2004	Lansing (MWL)	A	.287	97	366	49	105	19	3	14	55	17	75	2	.331	.470
2005	Daytona (FSL)	A	.281	83	270	37	76	20	0	9	40	26	48	5	.357	.456
2006	Daytona (FSL)	A	.313	66	249	45	78	15	1	16	61	27	49	4	.383	.574
	West Tenn (SL)	AA	.269	55	193	20	52	17	0	5	25	9	44	0	.304	.435
2007	Tennessee (SL)	AA	.284	91	359	60	102	23	1	18	60	17	72	6	.327	.504
	Chicago (NL)	MLB	.143	7	14	3	2	2	0	0	1	1	2	0	.200	.286
	Iowa (PCL)	AAA	.283	25	99	18	28	7	0	6	19	5	23	2	.343	.535
MINOR LEAGUE TOTALS			.284	461	1686	246	479	114	5	74	278	114	344	19	.340	.489
MAJOR LEAGUE TOTALS			.143	7	14	3	2	2	0	0	1	1	2	0	.200	.286

20 LARRY SUAREZ, RHP

Born: Dec. 20, 1989. **B-T:** R-R. **Ht.:** 6-4. **Wt.:** 245. **Signed:** Venezuela, 2006. **Signed by:** Hector Ortega.

Since he signed for $850,000 as the top Venezuelan amateur in the summer of 2006, Suarez has drawn comparisons to Carlos Zambrano. They're not only from the same nation, but they also have similar builds and strong arms. Suarez first drew notice when he flashed a 91-mph fastball as a 15-year-old, and he worked regularly at 88-92 at age 16. The Cubs admit that Suarez was better prepared to face Rookie-level Dominican Summer League hitters in his pro debut last year, but they brought him to the Arizona League to speed up his learning of English and his adjusting to the United States. He displayed an 89-91 mph fastball early in the summer before running out of gas and pitching with more effort in his delivery in August. He also elevated his heater too often. Suarez did make some progress tightening his curveball and gaining more command of the pitch. His changeup can become a solid third offering if he can consistently throw it with the same arm speed he uses with his fastball. He already carries a lot of weight and must guard against his body getting away from him, though Chicago is encouraged by his work ethic. After rushing Suarez a bit in 2007, the Cubs will keep him in extended spring training to start this season before shipping him to Boise in June.

Year	Club (League)	Class	W	L	ERA	G	GS	CG	SV	IP	H	R	ER	HR	BB	SO	AVG
2007	Cubs (AZL)	R	1	4	5.31	14	9	0	0	40	37	33	24	4	26	35	.248
MINOR LEAGUE TOTALS			1	4	5.31	14	9	0	0	40	37	33	24	4	26	35	.248

21 RYAN ACOSTA, RHP

Born: Nov. 4, 1988. **B-T:** R-R. **Ht.:** 6-2. **Wt.:** 170. **Drafted:** HS—Clearwater, Fla., 2007 (12th round). **Signed by:** Rolando Pino.

Rolando Pino has a knack for finding quality late-round arms as a Florida area scout. Pino signed Sean Gallagher as a 12th-rounder in 2004 and Chris Huseby as an 11th-rounder in 2006. His latest coup is Acosta, a 12th-rounder in June who signed for $225,000. The son of former Cubs pitching coach Oscar Acosta, who died in an April 2006 auto accident while working for the Yankees in the Dominican Republic, Ryan pitched in a high school game the night his father was killed, and continues to display maturity and mound presence beyond his years. He was mostly a shortstop until his senior year, and the Cubs think he'll develop rapidly now that he's focusing on pitching. Acosta's fastball sits at 88-90 mph and touches 93, and he should develop plus velocity once his skinny frame fills out. He's more about pitchability than pure stuff, though his stuff is fine. He can backdoor his fastball for strikes, and he shows good command of his curveball, slider and changeup, all of which could be at least average pitches. Acosta also plays around with a splitter, and Chicago probably will have him concentrate on working with just three pitches in 2008. He'll probably eschew his slider in favor of his curve. He repeats his delivery well in part because he's more athletic than most pitchers. He qualified for the Florida state 100-meter finals but had to bow out because of a baseball playoff conflict, and he also played point guard on his high school basketball team. Acosta is so advanced that the Cubs will have no qualms about sending him to low Class A as a 19-year-old.

Year	Club (League)	Class	W	L	ERA	G	GS	CG	SV	IP	H	R	ER	HR	BB	SO	AVG
2007	Cubs (AZL)	R	0	0	3.00	3	1	0	0	6	5	2	2	0	3	6	.263
	Boise (NWL)	A	0	2	3.00	3	3	0	0	12	9	4	4	2	3	8	.209
MINOR LEAGUE TOTALS			0	2	3.00	6	4	0	0	18	14	6	6	2	6	14	.226

22 JAMES RUSSELL, LHP

Born: Jan. 8, 1986. **B-T:** L-L. **Ht.:** 6-4. **Wt.:** 205. **Drafted:** Texas, 2007 (14th round). **Signed by:** Trey Forkerway.

Russell turned down the Mariners as a 37th-round pick out of high school and again as a 17th-rounder after his first season at Navarro (Texas) JC, and there was no guarantee he'd sign with the Cubs as a 14th-rounder. But he saw his velocity increase over the summer, and Chicago anted up $350,000 to get him to turn pro. During the spring at Texas, Russell stood out with his changeup and an 84-88 mph fastball and a marginal breaking ball, didn't excite scouts. After the Longhorns' season ended, Russell worked with independent pitching coach Tom House to shape up his curveball before heading to the Texas Collegiate League. In the TCL, his fastball jumped to 88-92 mph and his curve was more usable. Russell's changeup is the best in the system and helps his other pitches play up. He throws strikes on a good downhill plane, and he has the know-how befitting the son of a former big leaguer, all-star closer Jeff Russell. James should team up with the other pitching sleeper of the Cubs' 2007 draft, Ryan Acosta, in low Class A this year.

Year	Club (League)	Class	W	L	ERA	G	GS	CG	SV	IP	H	R	ER	HR	BB	SO	AVG
2007	Cubs (AZL)	R	0	0	0.00	1	1	0	0	2	0	0	0	0	0	2	.000
	Peoria (MWL)	A	0	0	0.00	2	2	0	0	7	3	0	0	0	4	9	.136
MINOR LEAGUE TOTALS			0	0	0.00	3	3	0	0	9	3	0	0	0	4	11	.107

23 ALEX MAESTRI, RHP

Born: June 1, 1985. **B-T:** R-R. **Ht.:** 6-1. **Wt.:** 180. **Signed:** Italy, 2006. **Signed by:** Bill Holmberg.

The first Italian pitcher ever signed by a major league organization, Maestri has pitched for his nation at the World Baseball Classic (where he gave up a homer to Moises Alou) and most recently at the World Cup in Taiwan in November. The Cubs first noticed Maestri at MLB's inaugural European Baseball Academy in Tirrenia, Italy, in the summer of 2005 and signed him in January 2006. He's more than a novelty act, as he has a legitimate chance to reach the big leagues. Maestri has surprising feel for pitching considering his background, and his fastball has risen from 87-90 mph when he signed to 90-94 last season. His out pitch is a hard slider that ranks as the best in the system and is death on righthanders, who hit just .139 with 62 strikeouts in 187 at-bats against him in 2007. He's athletic, repeats his delivery well and throws strikes. Maestri even has the potential for an average changeup, so Chicago decided to try him as a starter last May. The move didn't work out, as he went 0-3, 7.04 in four outings before returning to the bullpen. He's more comfortable in that role and led Midwest League relievers in opponent average (.156) and baserunners per nine innings (6.9). He pitches almost exclusively with hard stuff, so he needs to refine his changeup or learn to subtract from his fastball in order to give hitters an offspeed look. Because he's handled everything the Cubs have thrown at him so far, not to mention that he'll turn 23 in June, he may skip a level and jump to Double-A in 2008.

Year	Club (League)	Class	W	L	ERA	G	GS	CG	SV	IP	H	R	ER	HR	BB	SO	AVG
2006	Boise (NWL)	A	4	3	3.80	22	0	0	1	42	36	20	18	4	13	35	.232
2007	Peoria (MWL)	A	6	3	2.26	48	4	0	12	83	57	24	21	7	15	83	.186
MINOR LEAGUE TOTALS			10	6	2.78	70	4	0	13	126	93	44	39	11	28	118	.201

24 DARWIN BARNEY, SS

Born: Nov. 8, 1985. **B-T:** R-R. **Ht.:** 5-10. **Wt.:** 175. **Drafted:** Oregon State, 2007 (4th round). **Signed by:** John Bartsch.

Barney doesn't have a single tool that grades out as plus, but his instincts and intelligence make him a winner. An integral part of Oregon State's back-to-back College World Series championships, he signed for $227,500 as a fourth-round pick. His best physical attribute is his slightly above-average speed, though he's more of a savvy baserunner than a significant basestealing threat. Offensively, he's a contact hitter with modest power, and he could fit into the No. 2 slot in a batting order if he draws more walks. He got underneath a lot of pitches when using wood bats with Team USA in 2006, but the Cubs worked with him at instructional league to get his top hand over the ball. He made harder contact and stopped hitting as many balls in the air, and they're curious to see how much the adjustment will pay off in the future. Barney's arm and range are nothing special at shortstop, but he reads balls well and unloads his throws in a hurry, enabling him to get the job done. Chicago plans on bringing up Barney and 2007 third-rounder Tony Thomas together as a double-play combination through the minors, and they'll head to high Class A this year.

Year	Club (League)	Class	AVG	G	AB	R	H	2B	3B	HR	RBI	BB	SO	SB	OBP	SLG
2007	Cubs (AZL)	R	.444	5	18	6	8	3	0	0	2	4	0	0	.545	.611
	Peoria (MWL)	A	.273	44	176	27	48	9	3	2	21	11	22	5	.323	.392
MINOR LEAGUE TOTALS			.289	49	194	33	56	12	3	2	23	15	22	5	.346	.412

25 JOSE ASCANIO, RHP

Born: May 2, 1985. **B-T:** R-R. **Ht.:** 6-0. **Wt.:** 175. **Signed:** Venezuela, 2001. **Signed by:** Rolando Petit/Julian Perez (Braves).

The Cubs added another potential arm for their big league bullpen when they grabbed Ascanio from the Braves in a December deal for Will Ohman and Omar Infante. After a back injury limited him to five appearances in 2005 and character issues hampered his progress in 2006, Atlanta tried to trade Ascanio prior to last season but found no takers. He wound up making his big league debut in July and held his own in 13 games with the Braves. He showed added maturity and the potential to be a dominating reliever. He has clocked as high as 97 mph with his fastball, yet relies too heavily on the pitch at the expense of developing his breaking ball and changeup. His heater sits in the mid-90s and he commands it well. He has shown some feel for his changeup but the pitch lacks consistent depth. Ascanio probably could use some more seasoning in the upper minors, but he should contribute to the Cubs at some point in 2008.

Year	Club (League)	Class	W	L	ERA	G	GS	CG	SV	IP	H	R	ER	HR	BB	SO	AVG
2002	Braves2 (DSL)	R	1	4	3.38	12	9	0	0	42	38	21	16	1	21	35	.253
2003	Braves (GCL)	R	4	0	1.37	8	0	0	0	26	26	4	4	0	5	17	.271
2004	Rome (SAL)	A	3	3	3.84	34	0	0	9	65	58	39	28	6	15	64	.227
2005	Myrtle Beach (Car)	A	3	1	6.10	5	3	0	0	20	26	17	14	5	9	12	.310

Year	Club (League)	Class	W	L	ERA	G	GS	CG	SV	IP	H	R	ER	HR	BB	SO	AVG
2006	Myrtle Beach (Car)	A	1	1	4.94	8	6	0	0	31	38	18	17	0	20	23	.314
	Mississippi (SL)	AA	4	2	4.26	24	0	0	0	38	37	20	18	2	17	37	.253
2007	Mississippi (SL)	AA	2	2	2.54	44	1	0	10	78	66	26	22	1	18	71	.234
	Atlanta (NL)	MLB	1	1	5.06	13	0	0	0	16	17	11	9	3	6	13	.254
MINOR LEAGUE TOTALS			18	13	3.54	135	19	0	19	302	289	145	119	15	105	259	.255
MAJOR LEAGUE TOTALS			1	1	5.06	13	0	0	0	16	17	11	9	3	6	13	.254

26 ROCKY ROQUET, RHP

Born: Nov. 6, 1982. **B-T:** R-R. **Ht.:** 6-2. **Wt.:** 205. **Signed:** NDFA/Cal Poly, 2006. **Signed by:** Steve Fuller.

Few college careers have been more circuitous than Roquet's. He went to Florida State as an outfielder, then redshirted as a freshman after converting to the mound that spring. He subsequently spent one year each at Santa Ana (Calif.) JC and Northeast Texas CC, then two at Cal Poly before signing as a fifth-year senior free agent prior to the 2006 draft. He reached Double-A by June in his first full pro season, in part because the Cubs were trying to advance him quickly because he already was 24. Roquet is a two-pitch reliever, operating with a 90-94 mph fastball that touches 97 on occasion and an 80-83 mph slider. His fastball doesn't have much life and his easy delivery lacks deception, so it's not as overpowering as its velocity might suggest. Hitters also can gear up for hard stuff because Roquet doesn't have an offspeed option, and his command wavers. He's still picking up the nuances of pitching, such as fielding his position and holding runners. Opponents stole 15 bases in as many tries against him in 2007. Chicago tried to further expedite Roquet's development by sending him to the Arizona Fall League, but he had to leave early after coming down with a sports hernia that required surgery. He should be ready for spring training and an assignment to Triple-A.

Year	Club (League)	Class	W	L	ERA	G	GS	CG	SV	IP	H	R	ER	HR	BB	SO	AVG
2006	Boise (NWL)	A	0	0	5.49	19	0	0	3	19	21	13	12	1	5	31	.273
2007	Peoria (MWL)	A	0	0	0.36	19	0	0	11	25	17	1	1	0	11	29	.200
	Daytona (FSL)	A	1	0	1.50	3	0	0	0	6	5	1	1	0	1	9	.217
	Tennessee (SL)	AA	4	0	3.63	28	0	0	7	39	32	16	16	4	18	42	.224
MINOR LEAGUE TOTALS			5	0	2.99	69	0	0	21	90	75	31	30	5	35	111	.229

27 MARK HOLLIMAN, RHP

Born: Sept. 19, 1983. **B-T:** R-R. **Ht.:** 6-0. **Wt.:** 200. **Drafted:** Mississippi, 2005 (3rd round). **Signed by:** Bob Rossi.

Holliman has the best command in the system, and never was it more on display than on June 21. Though he worked at 84-85 mph with his fastball, he threw a seven-inning no-hitter, with a lone walk all that stood between him and a perfect game. Holliman had a low-90s fastball in college but now operates at 84-88 mph. When he first broke into pro ball, he tried to overpower hitters with his fastball, and now he feels more comfortable pacing himself in cruise control. At times he can reach back for a 92-mph heater when he needs one, and at others he'll find that he can't just dial up plus velocity at will. Holliman mixes his fastball with a curveball, slider and changeup. There's divided opinion as to which of his breaking balls is better, but all three of his secondary offerings are mostly average at best. Holliman has a short-arm delivery, but it doesn't affect his ability to locate his pitches. He helps his cause by doing all the little things well, such as fielding his position (one error in 40 chances last year), holding runners (40 percent of basestealers were thrown out on his watch) and even hitting (he batted .229 with two homers, including one in his no-hitter). Holliman is on the small side, but he hasn't missed a start while pitching 305 innings in his first two pro seasons. He did fade in August, going 2-3, 5.50, so the Cubs would like to see him get stronger. Projected as a No. 5 starter or a middle reliver, Hollman will pitch in Triple-A this season.

Year	Club (League)	Class	W	L	ERA	G	GS	CG	SV	IP	H	R	ER	HR	BB	SO	AVG
2006	Daytona (FSL)	A	8	11	4.38	26	26	0	0	144	129	76	70	12	58	121	.241
2007	Tennessee (SL)	AA	10	11	3.57	27	26	2	0	161	157	68	64	15	57	108	.257
MINOR LEAGUE TOTALS			18	22	3.95	53	52	2	0	305	286	144	134	27	115	229	.250

28 JOSH LANSFORD, 3B

Born: July 3, 1984. **B-T:** R-R. **Ht.:** 6-3. **Wt.:** 210. **Drafted:** Cal Poly, 2006 (6th round). **Signed by:** Steve Fuller.

Lansford has outstanding bloodlines. His father Carney won an American League batting title, his uncles Jody and Phil were first-round draft picks and his brother Jared was a second-round choice of the Athletics in 2005. One of three players Chicago signed out of Cal Poly in 2006, Lansford has a higher ceiling than hard-throwing reliever Rocky Roquet or defensive-minded catcher Matt Canepa. The question will be whether he can get his bat into gear so he can reach his potential. Though Lansford has strength and bat speed and makes consistent contact, he has batted .266 with 33 extra-base hits in 146 games in the lower minors. Most of his power currently comes from gap to gap, and he should hit more homers once he stops hitting most of his long drives to the deepest part of the pack. He focuses well with runners in scoring position, yet maddeningly throws away at-bats in less crucial situations. Lansford has stood out more with his defense to this point of his career. Managers rated him the best defensive third baseman in the Midwest League last year, and he has the best infield skills and infield arm in the system. His arm rates as a 70 on the 20-80 scouting scale and he has good agility for his size, especially to his right. He's a below-average runner but not a baseclogger. The Cubs believe Lansford can develop into a .280 hitter with 15-plus homers per season and Gold Glove defense at the hot corner. He lost six weeks worth of at-bats after spraining his knee in an infield collision in mid-July, but he didn't require surgery and got some of them back with time in the Arizona Fall League. He'll open 2008 in high Class A.

Year	Club (League)	Class	AVG	G	AB	R	H	2B	3B	HR	RBI	BB	SO	SB	OBP	SLG
2006	Boise (NWL)	A	.255	62	235	32	60	7	1	5	35	24	43	4	.333	.357
2007	Peoria (MWL)	A	.273	84	322	29	88	17	0	3	42	16	33	2	.305	.354
MINOR LEAGUE TOTALS			.266	146	557	61	148	24	1	8	77	40	76	6	.317	.355

29 STEVE CLEVENGER, C/1B

Born: April 5, 1986. **B-T:** L-R. **Ht.:** 6-0. **Wt.:** 185. **Drafted:** Chipola (Fla.) JC, 2006 (7th round). **Signed by:** Keith Stohr.

After hitting .347 as a freshman at Southeastern Louisiana, Clevenger planned on transferring to Texas but a problem with his credits landed him at Chipola (Fla.) JC instead. The move made him draft-eligible a year early, and the Cubs signed him as a seventh-rounder in 2006 for $130,000. He moved from shortstop in college to second base in his pro debut, and Chicago worked him behind the plate in instructional league that fall. Clevenger continued to work on the transition to catching in extended spring training, then hit .340 with just 11 strikeouts in 65 games between Boise and Daytona. The Cubs had catchers who needed to play on both clubs, so Clevenger saw more time at first base, but they plan on developing him as a backstop. His ability to put the bat on the ball and spray line drives is intriguing, and he started to incorporate his legs more into his swing late in the year so he could develop some more power. Clevenger doesn't have the bat for first base, so his chances on reaching the majors hinge on his ability to catch. He moves well for a catcher, has some arm strength and threw out 33 percent of basestealers in 2007. His receiving skills are more shaky and he committed four passed balls in 18 games. Realistically, he has a ceiling as an offensive-minded backup. But Chicago will give him the chance to prove he can be more than that, and Clevenger could begin 2008 in Double-A so he can get regular time behind the plate.

Year	Club (League)	Class	AVG	G	AB	R	H	2B	3B	HR	RBI	BB	SO	SB	OBP	SLG
2006	Boise (NWL)	A	.286	63	220	35	63	8	1	2	21	26	28	5	.363	.359
2007	Boise (NWL)	A	.373	22	83	10	31	9	0	0	18	4	6	0	.398	.482
	Daytona (FSL)	A	.323	43	164	21	53	8	1	2	24	13	5	0	.368	.421
MINOR LEAGUE TOTALS			.315	128	467	66	147	25	2	4	63	43	39	5	.371	.403

30 TIM LAHEY, RHP

Born: Feb. 7, 1982. **B-T:** R-R. **Ht.:** 6-4. **Wt.:** 250. **Drafted:** Princeton, 2004 (20th round). **Signed by:** John Wilson (Twins).

The Cubs traded up to get the No. 1 overall pick in the 2007 Rule 5 draft, having the Rays select Lahey from the Twins on their behalf and then sending $150,000 to Tampa Bay. Minnesota originally drafted him as a catcher, but he shifted to the mound after hitting .202 in Rookie ball in his first pro summer. Chicago has success making the same move with Carlos Marmol, and Lahey's huge frame is reminiscent of that of Troy Percival, another backstop-turned-reliever. Lahey still throws with a short catcher's arm action, but that doesn't prevent him form throwing strikes with a 90-92 mph sinker that tops out at 95. He also throws a solid slider and a changeup, and because he only has pitched for three years, there's still room for improvement at age 26. His frame is built for durability and he's also a good athlete for his size. Lahey is more of a groundball guy than a strikeout machine, posting a 2.0 groundout/airout ratio in 2007. He'll have to stick on the Cubs' 25-man roster, or else they'll have to run him through waivers and offer him back to the Twins for half his $50,000 draft price.

Year	Club (League)	Class	AVG	G	AB	R	H	2B	3B	HR	RBI	BB	SO	SB	OBP	SLG
2004	Elizabethton (Appy)	R	.202	26	84	7	17	2	0	3	11	13	38	0	.333	.317
MINOR LEAGUE TOTALS			.202	26	84	7	17	2	0	3	11	13	38	0	.333	.317

Year	Club (League)	Class	W	L	ERA	G	GS	CG	SV	IP	H	R	ER	HR	BB	SO	AVG
2005	Elizabethton (Appy)	R	0	1	3.55	26	0	0	15	25	21	13	10	0	8	30	.212
2006	Fort Myers (FSL)	A	7	1	4.33	45	0	0	9	72	74	36	35	1	27	57	.264
2007	New Britain (EL)	AA	8	4	3.45	50	0	0	13	78	78	42	30	8	33	56	.255
	Rochester (IL)	AAA	0	0	9.00	2	0	0	1	3	4	3	3	0	2	3	.308
MINOR LEAGUE TOTALS			15	6	3.91	123	0	0	38	179	177	94	78	9	70	146	.254

Chicago White Sox

BY PHIL ROGERS

ew owners in baseball are more loyal than Jerry Reinsdorf. Few general managers are more aggressive than Ken Williams. Those two personalities came to a crossroads in 2007—making it impossible to overlook the deterioration of the White Sox since their World Series victory two years earlier.

After 35 years with the organization, including 14 as scouting director, Duane Shaffer was fired by Williams after he oversaw the draft in June. It was a painful move for Reinsdorf to sign off on, but one that Williams convinced him was necessary after a painfully unproductive period for the farm system, especially in terms of producing position players.

Had Shaffer wanted to engage in public mudslinging, he could have pointed out how it was the work of White Sox scouts that was primarily responsible for a 17-year stretch in which the big league club never performed poorly enough to earn a top-10 pick in the draft. That streak will end in 2008, when the Sox will pick eighth after a late surge that took them to a 72-90 finish and past the Royals for fourth place in the American League Central. Or Shaffer could have pointed out how it was the work of scouts that gave Williams a chance to pull off so many of the high-profile trades he has made.

In seven years since replacing the scout-friendly Ron Schueler as general manager, Williams has often dealt tomorrow for today with his trades. For Roberto Alomar, Bartolo Colon, Freddy Garcia, Mike MacDougal, Todd Ritchie, Jim Thome, Javier Vazquez, David Wells and others, Williams repeatedly has undercut the depth of his farm system.

Williams always knew he was taking a risk that a young player would come back to bite him in a big way, and one did in 2007. Chris Young, part of the package for Vazquez, hit 32 homers and stole 27 bases as a rookie to help the Diamondbacks reach the playoffs.

But it wasn't just losing a player here or a player there that put the Sox at risk. Chicago has had a run of conservative and unproductive drafts, and the last impact pick they made was Young—a 16th-rounder in 2001. The White Sox also have done little in Latin America. None of their full-season affiliates managed a winning record last year, and their six farm clubs combined to go 334-369 (.475), the seventh-worst record in baseball.

Josh Fields led American League rookies with 23 home runs in 2007

TOP 30 PROSPECTS

1. Gio Gonzalez, lhp	16. Charlie Haeger, rhp
2. Fautino de los Santos, rhp	17. Christian Marrero, 1b
3. Aaron Poreda, lhp	18. Sergio Morales, of
4. Lance Broadway, rhp	19. Justin Cassel, rhp
5. Jack Egbert, rhp	20. Sergio Miranda, ss
6. Ryan Sweeney, of	21. Francisco Hernandez, c
7. Jose Martinez, of	22. Ehren Wasserman, rhp
8. Chris Getz, 2b	23. Donny Lucy, c
9. John Ely, rhp	24. Oneli Perez, rhp
10. Juan Silverio, ss	25. Brian Omogrosso, rhp
11. John Shelby Jr., of	26. Dewon Day, rhp
12. Adam Russell, rhp	27. Brandon Allen, 1b
13. Kyle McCulloch, rhp	28. Sal Sanchez, of
14. Nevin Griffith, rhp	29. Robert Valido, ss
15. Lucas Harrell, rhp	30. Lyndon Estill, of

There were some positive signs. Josh Fields led American League rookies with 23 home runs after a June promotion, and speedster Jerry Owens finished strong in the big leagues. Down on the farm, Dominican righthander Fautino de los Santos was a revelation in his first season in the United States. Lefty Gio Gonzalez, reacquired from the Phillies in a rare Williams deal that sent a veteran (Garcia) packing, led the minors in strikeouts, while righty Jack Egbert, a former 13th-round pick, continued to exceed expectations.

General Manager: Ken Williams. **Farm Director:** Alan Regier. **Scouting Director:** Doug Laumann.

Class	Team	League	W	L	PCT	Finish*	Manager	Affiliated
Majors	Chicago	American	72	90	.444	10th (14)	Ozzie Guillen	—
Triple-A	Charlotte Knights	International	63	80	.441	13th (14)	Marc Bombard	1999
Double-A	Birmingham Barons	Southern	62	78	.443	8th (10)	Rafael Santana	1986
High A	Winston-Salem Warthogs	Carolina	64	74	.464	5th (8)	Tim Blackwell	1997
Low A	Kannapolis Intimidators	South Atlantic	69	70	.496	7th (16)	Chris Jones	2001
Rookie	Great Falls White Sox	Pioneer	51	24	.680	1st (8)	Chris Cron	2003
Rookie	Bristol Sox	Appalachian	25	43	.368	8th (9)	Omer Munoz	1995
Overall 2007 Minor League Record			334	369	.475	24th		

*Finish in overall standings (No. of teams in league) ^League champion

LAST YEAR'S TOP 30

Player, Pos.		Status
1.	Ryan Sweeney, of	No. 6
2.	Josh Fields, 3b	Majors
3.	Gio Gonzalez, lhp	No. 1
4.	Lance Broadway, rhp	No. 4
5.	Kyle McCulloch, rhp	No. 13
6.	Charlie Haeger, rhp	No. 16
7.	Aaron Cunningham, of	(Diamondbacks)
8.	Adam Russell, rhp	No. 12
9.	Lucas Harrell, rhp	No. 15
10.	Matt Long, rhp	Dropped out
11.	Chris Carter, 1b	(Diamondbacks)
12.	Heath Phillips, lhp	Free agent
13.	Jerry Owens, of	Majors
14.	Ray Liotta, lhp	(Royals)
15.	Oneli Perez, rhp	No. 24
16.	Jack Egbert, rhp	No. 5
17.	Justin Edwards, lhp	Dropped out
18.	Boone Logan, lhp	Majors
19.	Robert Valido, ss	No. 29
20.	Pedro Lopez, ss/2b	Dropped out
21.	John Shelby Jr., 2b/ss	No. 11
22.	Dewon Day, rhp	No. 26
23.	Chris Stewart, c	(Rangers)
24.	Anderson Gomes, of	Dropped out
25.	Francisco Hernandez, c	No. 21
26.	Sean Tracey, rhp	(Orioles)
27.	Brian Omogrosso, rhp	No. 25
28.	Paulo Orlando, of	Dropped out
29.	Wes Whisler, lhp	Dropped out
30.	Ricardo Nanita, of	Dropped out

BEST TOOLS

Best Hitter for Average	Ryan Sweeney
Best Power Hitter	Brandon Allen
Best Strike-Zone Discipline	Chris Getz
Fastest Baserunner	Paulo Orlando
Best Athlete	Lyndon Estill
Best Fastball	Aaron Poreda
Best Curveball	Gio Gonzalez
Best Slider	Fautino de los Santos
Best Changeup	Lance Broadway
Best Control	Jack Egbert
Best Defensive Catcher	Donny Lucy
Best Defensive Infielder	Robert Valido
Best Infield Arm	Juan Silverio
Best Defensive Outfielder	Ryan Sweeney
Best Outfield Arm	Ryan Sweeney

PROJECTED 2011 LINEUP

Catcher	A.J. Pierzynski
First Base	Paul Konerko
Second Base	Chris Getz
Third Base	Joe Crede
Shortstop	Orlando Cabrera
Left Field	Josh Fields
Center Field	Ryan Sweeney
Right Field	Carlos Quentin
Designated Hitter	Jermaine Dye
No. 1 Starter	Mark Buehrle
No. 2 Starter	Javier Vazquez
No. 3 Starter	Gio Gonzalez
No. 4 Starter	Fautino de los Santos
No. 5 Starter	Aaron Poreda
Closer	Bobby Jenks

TOP PROSPECTS OF THE DECADE

Year	Player, Pos.	2007 Org.
1998	Mike Caruso, ss	South Georgia (South Coast)
1999	Carlos Lee, 3b	Astros
2000	Kip Wells, rhp	Cardinals
2001	Jon Rauch, rhp	Nationals
2002	Joe Borchard, of	Marlins
2003	Joe Borchard, of	Marlins
2004	Joe Borchard, of	Marlins
2005	Brian Anderson, of	White Sox
2006	Bobby Jenks, rhp	White Sox
2007	Ryan Sweeney, of	White Sox

TOP DRAFT PICKS OF THE DECADE

Year	Player, Pos.	2007 Org.
1998	Kip Wells, rhp	Cardinals
1999	Jason Stumm, rhp	Out of baseball
2000	Joe Borchard, of	Marlins
2001	Kris Honel, rhp	White Sox
2002	Royce Ring, lhp	Braves
2003	Brian Anderson, of	White Sox
2004	Josh Fields, 3b	White Sox
2005	Lance Broadway, rhp	White Sox
2006	Kyle McCulloch, rhp	White Sox
2007	Aaron Poreda, lhp	White Sox

LARGEST BONUSES IN CLUB HISTORY

Joe Borchard, 2000	$5,300,000
Jason Stumm, 1999	$1,750,000
Royce Ring, 2002	$1,600,000
Brian Anderson, 2003	$1,500,000
Lance Broadway, 2005	$1,570,000

CHICAGO WHITE SOX

Top 2008 Rookie: Gio Gonzalez, lhp. The White Sox may have some openings in their rotation, and the 2007 minor league strikeout leader is best equipped to make the most of an opportunity.

Breakout Prospect: Brian Omogrosso, rhp. The further he puts 2005 Tommy John surgery behind him, the stronger he gets.

Sleeper: Paulo Orlando, of. He's the fastest player in the system, though he needs to get his bat going.

SOURCE OF TOP 30 TALENT			
Homegrown	28	Acquired	2
College	12	Trades	1
Junior college	1	Rule 5 draft	0
High school	6	Independent leagues	0
Draft-and-follow	3	Free agents/waivers	1
Nondrafted free agents	1		
International	5		

Numbers in parentheses indicate prospect rankings.

LF
Jimmy Gallagher
Thomas Collaro
Ricardo Nanita
Lee Cruz
Maurice Gartrell

CF
Jose Martinez (7)
Sergio Morales (18)
Lyndon Estill (30)
Kent Gerst
Paulo Orlando

RF
Ryan Sweeney (6)
Sal Sanchez (28)
Anderson Gomes

3B
Javier Castillo
C.J. Retherford
Michael Grace

SS
Juan Silverio (10)
Sergio Miranda (20)
Robert Valido (29)
C.J. Lang

2B
Chris Getz (8)
John Shelby Jr. (11)
Scott Madsen

1B
Christian Marrero (17)
Brandon Allen (27)
Micah Schnurstein

C
Francisco Hernandez (21)
Donny Lucy (23)
Matt Inouye
Tyler Reves
Cole Armstrong
Adam Ricks

RHP

Starters	Relievers
Fautino de los Santos (2)	Adam Russell (12)
Lance Broadway (4)	Ehren Wasserman (22)
Jack Egbert (5)	Oneli Perez (24)
John Ely (9)	Brian Omogrosso (25)
Kyle McCulloch (13)	Dewon Day (26)
Nevin Griffith (14)	Nick Masset
Lucas Harrell (15)	Matt Long
Charlie Haeger (16)	Leroy Hunt
Justin Cassel (19)	Charlie Shirek
Jacob Rasner	Clevelan Santeliz
	Kanekoa Teixeira
	Charlie Burdie
	John Lujan

LHP

Starters	Relievers
Gio Gonzalez (1)	Carlos Vasquez
Aaron Poreda (3)	Wes Whisler
Justin Edwards	
Clayton Richard	
Po-Yu Lin	
Kevin Skogley	

DRAFT ANALYSIS

Best Pro Debut: LHP Aaron Poreda (1) ranked as the No. 4 prospect in the Rookie-level Pioneer League after winning all four of his decisions and striking out 48 in 46 innings. SS Sergio Miranda (13) jumped straight to low Class A Kannapolis and shored up the middle infield while batting .301/.397/.380 overall.

Best Athlete: Poreda was a high school football player as a tight end/defensive end. OF Lyndon Estill (8), a football safety and quarterback in high school, is raw but has a strong, 6-foot-3, 215-pound body reminiscent of a young Bobby Bonilla.

Best Pure Hitter: When OF Jimmy Gallagher (7) gets in a rhythm, he makes his high hands and upright stance work for him, producing line drives to all fields. He hit .332/.418/.534 at Great Falls.

Best Power Hitter: Estill played in a wood-bat junior-college league and has present strength and power that showed through as an amateur.

Fastest Baserunner: Estill and Gallagher are solid-average runners.

Best Defensive Player: Greg Paiml (15) isn't flashy at shortstop, but he makes all the routine plays with smooth hands, good footwork and an accurate, solid-average arm.

Best Fastball: The deepest spot in the Sox' draft class starts with top pick Poreda; some of the Great Falls' game reports had him touching 100 mph. He pitches at times at 95-97, giving him the edge on RHP Johnnie Lowe (6), who can sit between 92-95. RHP Leroy Hunt (4) has excellent sinking life on his 90-93 mph heater.

Best Secondary Pitch: RHP John Ely (3) has more than enough fastball at 91-93 mph, but his changeup is a plus-plus pitch that he sinks and commands.

Most Intriguing Background: The White Sox drafted a slew of players with dads who played big league ball and have organization ties, such as 2B Oney Guillen (36), son of manager Ozzie Guillen. The best prospect of the bunch is RHP Grant Monroe (38), a projected two-way player at Duke.

Closest To The Majors: Poreda, even though his secondary pitches need work. Ely has the stuff and poise to move quickly.

Best Late-Round Pick: RHP Charlie Shirek (23) had a nightmare season at Nebraska, but his stuff was back to normal in the summer in the M.I.N.K. League and in his brief stint with the White Sox. He's shown a plus fastball, touching 96, with a solid-average slider.

The One Who Got Away: Athletic SS Brian Guinn (10) should start as a freshman at California, while RHP Ryan Sharpley (34) joined his brother Evan, a football quarterback, at Notre Dame.

Assessment: In Duane Shaffer's last draft before being let go by the organization, the White Sox stocked up on power arms and are extremely excited about Poreda's upside, considering how late in the first round they got him. A system in need of impact bats, though, got little help.

RHP Kyle McCulloch (1) doesn't have a high ceiling. Most of the rest of these draftees took a step back in their first full season.

GRADE: D

OF Aaron Cunningham (6) and 1B Chris Carter (15) may be the two best picks, and they've both been traded to Arizona. RHP Lance Broadway (1) and 2B Chris Getz (4) can be complemenary players.

GRADE: C+

3B Josh Fields (1) hit 23 homers as a rookie last summer, while LHP Gio Gonzalez (1s) is the system's top prospect. RHP Jack Egbert (13) continues to exceed expectations.

GRADE: B+

Brian Anderson (1) and Ryan Sweeney (2) were supposed to be playing together in Chicago's outfield by now, but they've both been disappointments.

GRADE: D

Draft analysis by John Manuel (2007) and Jim Callis (2003-06). Numbers in parentheses indicate draft rounds. Budgets are bonuses in first 10 rounds.

JERRY HALE

GIO GONZALEZ, LHP

Born: Sept. 19, 1985.
Ht.: 5-11. **Wt.:** 185.
Bats: R. **Throws:** L.
Drafted: HS—Miami, 2004 (1st round supplemental).
Signed by: Jose Ortega.

A supplemental first-round pick of the White Sox out of a Miami high school in 1985, Gonzalez signed for $850,000. He had been projected to go in the first round until he was dismissed from his high school team after his mother got into a dispute with his coach over her other son's playing time. Gonzalez had barely turned 20 when he was traded for the first time, going to the Phillies as a key piece in the Jim Thome trade after the 2005 season. He was back with Chicago 13 months later, returning as part of a deal for Freddy Garcia. Gonzalez has spent the last two seasons in Double-A and should benefit from the experience. He was as close to overpowering as anyone in the Southern League last year, striking out a minors-best 185 in only 150 innings and holding hitters to a .216 batting average and 10 homers—down from 24 at Reading the year before. He also cut his walks significantly, showing better command and confidence.

Gonzalez' bread and butter is a sharp-breaking two-plane curveball that he doesn't hesitate to throw in any count. It complements a fastball that generally parks in the low 90s but can spike upward to 96 mph. His fastball has some natural sink, allowing him to get his share of groundballs. He can change speeds with his fastball, adding and subtracting throughout the game and sometimes saving his best velocity for the late innings. Gonzalez is as effective against righthanded hitters as he is against lefties, making it difficult for opposing managers to stack a lineup to face him. He has a fundamentally simple, smooth and repeatable delivery from a high three-quarters arm slot. His changeup isn't at the same level of his other two pitches but improved considerably in 2007, largely because he was committed to throwing it.

At times when he throws across his body, Gonzalez will miss his intended location. His command is merely average and will be tested as he faces more advanced hitters, though he should be able to throw enough strikes. When the White Sox traded him away, some club officials questioned his makeup, especially a tendency to come unraveled on the mound when things got tough. He also carried some baggage from his suspension at the end of his senior season. Chicago has no makeup concerns at this point because he has matured as a pitcher and as a person.

Gonzalez will go to big league camp for the third time in the spring. He's in a good situation, as he'll get a look but won't be especially under the gun. The likelihood is that he'll will open 2008 in the rotation at Triple-A Charlotte, though there does figure to be at least one opening for a starter in Chicago. Gonzalez figures to make his major league debut at some point this year and has the ability to develop into a No. 2 or 3 starter.

Year	Club (League)	Class	W	L	ERA	G	GS	CG	SV	IP	H	R	ER	HR	BB	SO	AVG
2004	Bristol (Appy)	R	1	2	2.25	7	6	0	0	24	17	8	6	0	8	36	.207
	Kannapolis (SAL)	A	1	1	3.03	6	6	0	0	32	30	13	11	1	13	27	.229
2005	Kannapolis (SAL)	A	5	3	1.87	11	10	0	0	57	36	16	12	3	22	84	.175
	Winston-Salem (Car)	A	8	3	3.56	13	13	0	0	73	61	33	29	5	25	79	.228
2006	Reading (EL)	AA	7	12	4.66	27	27	0	0	154	140	88	80	24	81	166	.239
2007	Birmingham (SL)	AA	9	7	3.18	27	27	0	0	150	116	57	53	10	57	185	.216
MINOR LEAGUE TOTALS			31	28	3.49	91	89	0	0	492	400	215	191	43	206	577	.221

2 FAUTINO DE LOS SANTOS, RHP

Born: Feb. 15, 1986. **B-T:** R-R. **Ht.:** 6-2. **Wt.:** 190. **Signed:** Dominican Republic, 2006. **Signed by:** Denny Gonzalez.

The White Sox haven't done well signing and developing players from the Dominican Republic in recent years, but de los Santos is the type of prospect who makes the effort worthwhile. He flashed his potential in the Rookie-level Dominican Summer League in 2006, then burst onto the U.S. scene last year. He made the low Class A Kannapolis roster to open the season, flashed a 96-97 mph fastball and a plus slider in the Futures Game and finished by pitching well at high Class A Winston-Salem. De los Santos has a collection of plus pitches and the innate ability to use them. He has developed four pitches at a young age, including a fastball, slider and curveball that all rate among the best in the system, and he'll throw them all whether he's ahead or behind in the count. His fastball can overpower hitters, buzzing into the top of the strike zone in the mid-90s or at the bottom of the zone with sink in the low 90s. He has been poised on the mound and coachable on the sidelines, and made the often-difficult transition to the United States with impressive grace. De los Santos improved his changeup greatly over the course of the season but it remains a pitch in progress. He often throws it in the high 80s, not achieving enough differential from his fastball. More advanced hitters are more likely to lay off his breaking pitches, and he'll have to prove he can throw quality strikes when they do. He needs to polish his pickoff move. His high ceiling as a frontline starter could force him into major league consideration in a hurry. He could open 2008 at Double-A Birmingham and Chicago may break him into the majors as a reliever, as it did at a young age with Mark Buehrle and Jon Garland.

Year	Club (League)	Class	W	L	ERA	G	GS	CG	SV	IP	H	R	ER	HR	BB	SO	AVG
2006	White Sox (DSL)	R	3	3	1.86	10	9	0	0	48	44	20	10	0	10	61	.232
2007	Kannapolis (SAL)	A	9	4	2.40	21	15	0	0	97	49	33	26	5	36	121	.148
	Winston-Salem (Car)	A	1	1	3.65	5	5	0	0	24	20	12	10	3	7	32	.220
MINOR LEAGUE TOTALS			13	8	2.43	36	29	0	0	170	113	65	46	8	53	214	.184

3 AARON POREDA, LHP

Born: Oct. 1, 1986. **B-T:** L-L. **Ht.:** 6-6. **Wt.:** 240. **Drafted:** San Francisco, 2007 (1st round). **Signed by:** Joe Butler/Adam Virchis.

The White Sox went into the 2007 draft needing to improve the depth of their position prospects but still took pitchers with their first six picks. They landed the Poreda with the 25th overall pick and signed him for $1.2 million. He went from walk-on to No. 1 starter at San Francisco, then posted a 0.93 ERA (counting two scoreless playoff starts) in his pro debut. Poreda has a rare fastball for a lefthander. He pitched in the low- to mid-90s in college but actually gained velocity late in the season, hitting 98 mph multiple times in an August start and topping out at 100. He has the body to handle the stress of throwing hard—he played on both sides of the line as a high school footballer—and still could develop more physically. A lack of secondary pitches was the primary reason Poreda was still available when Chicago drafted. Both his slider and a changeup are works in progress. The White Sox were encouraged with his efforts improving the slider in instructional league, though he still needs to consistently throw it for strikes. He's raw for a college pitcher, needing work on the fine points of his craft. Poreda will open his first full season as a starter in Class A, but he eventually could wind up as a bigger version of Billy Wagner coming out of the bullpen. The Sox will monitor his secondary pitches closely this season as they try to settle on a career path for him. If they move him to relief, he could get to Chicago quickly—possibly even at season's end.

Year	Club (League)	Class	W	L	ERA	G	GS	CG	SV	IP	H	R	ER	HR	BB	SO	AVG
2007	Great Falls (Pio)	R	4	0	1.17	12	8	0	0	46	29	7	6	1	10	48	.181
MINOR LEAGUE TOTALS			4	0	1.17	12	8	0	0	46	29	7	6	1	10	48	.181

4 LANCE BROADWAY, RHP

Born: Aug. 20, 1983. **B-T:** R-R. **Ht.:** 6-2. **Wt.:** 210. **Drafted:** Texas Christian, 2005 (1st round). **Signed by:** Keith Staab.

Broadway never has blown away scouts with his stuff but he knows how to pitch. He went 15-1 as a junior at Texas Christian to pitch his way up to the 15th overall pick in the 2005 draft, and he won his first major league start last September by shutting out the Royals for six innings. He needed just 63 minor league starts to reach Chicago. Broadway can throw strikes with four pitches, including a plus changeup. He impressed manager Ozzie Guillen by getting strikeouts on 3-2 sliders against Kansas City, showing surprising confidence considering he hadn't started in almost a month. His curveball is also considered a plus pitch. He learned a cut fastball from pitching coach Don Cooper while spending most of September in the White Sox bullpen. He's a workout freak who has proven durable in his two full seasons as a pro. Broadway's fastball rarely gets above 90 mph, leaving him in trouble on the days when he can't command his other pitches. He was inconsistent throughout most of 2007, as his walk rate rose to 4.5 per nine innings in Triple-A, up from 2.3 in Double-A the year before. By trading Jon Garland, Chicago increased Broadway's chances of making its Opening Day rotation. He'll compete with Gavin Floyd, Gio Gonzalez and others for the No. 5 slot in the rotation. He doesn't have a high ceiling but can be a serviceable back-end starter.

Year	Club (League)	Class	W	L	ERA	G	GS	CG	SV	IP	H	R	ER	HR	BB	SO	AVG
2005	Winston-Salem (Car)	A	1	3	4.58	11	11	0	0	55	68	31	28	4	20	58	.306
2006	Birmingham (SL)	AA	8	8	2.74	25	25	2	0	154	160	59	47	10	40	111	.269
	Charlotte (IL)	AAA	0	0	3.00	1	1	0	0	6	5	2	2	0	1	6	.217
2007	Charlotte (IL)	AAA	8	9	4.65	26	26	2	0	155	155	86	80	17	78	108	.264
	Chicago (AL)	MLB	1	1	0.87	4	1	0	0	10	5	2	1	0	5	14	.143
MINOR LEAGUE TOTALS			17	20	3.82	63	63	4	0	370	388	178	157	31	139	283	.272
MAJOR LEAGUE TOTALS			1	1	0.87	4	1	0	0	10	5	2	1	0	5	14	.143

5 JACK EGBERT, RHP

STEVE MOORE

Born: May 12, 1983. **B-T:** R-R. **Ht.:** 6-3. **Wt.:** 200. **Drafted:** Rutgers, 2004 (13th round). **Signed by:** Chuck Fox.

Lightly regarded while at Rutgers, Egbert has gotten better in each of his three full pro seasons. He has gone 35-24 in a system that isn't doing a lot of winning in the minors, putting himself within one rung of the big leagues. Consistently praised for his competitiveness, he quietly has improved the quality of his pitches and ranked second in the Southern League in victories (12) and strikeouts (165 in 162 innings) last season. Egbert throws strikes and puts pressure on hitters by coming right at them. His rapid-fire pace is a hit with everyone in the park except the hitters. He gets a lot of groundballs with his two-seam fastball, which parks in the high 80s, and his slider can be a go-to pitch at times. He has refined his changeup into a plus pitch. Egbert's fastball is fringe-average and he gets hurt when he throws it up in the strike zone. Some think his delivery can get a little long, but he makes adjustments on the fly. His performance could have dictated a second-half promotion to Triple-A, but Egbert benefited from a full year in Double-A. Projected as a No. 5 starter or swingman, he should open 2008 in Triple-A and could put himself into position to be an early callup with a strong showing in spring training.

Year	Club (League)	Class	W	L	ERA	G	GS	CG	SV	IP	H	R	ER	HR	BB	SO	AVG
2004	Great Falls (Pio)	R	4	1	3.38	17	9	0	0	58	51	25	22	2	33	52	.244
2005	Kannapolis (SAL)	A	10	5	3.12	30	24	4	0	147	127	66	51	5	48	107	.236
2006	Winston-Salem (Car)	A	9	8	2.94	25	25	0	0	140	131	57	46	2	46	120	.246
	Birmingham (SL)	AA	0	2	0.86	4	4	0	0	21	17	4	2	0	8	24	.215
2007	Birmingham (SL)	AA	12	8	3.06	28	28	0	0	161	138	63	55	3	44	165	.232
MINOR LEAGUE TOTALS			35	24	2.99	104	90	4	0	529	464	215	176	12	179	468	.237

6 RYAN SWEENEY, OF

SPORTS ON FILM

Born: Feb. 20, 1985. **B-T:** L-L. **Ht.:** 6-4. **Wt.:** 215. **Drafted:** HS—Cedar Rapids, Iowa, 2003 (2nd round). **Signed by:** Nathan Durst.

After the White Sox traded slugger Chris Carter to the White Sox for Carlos Quentin, Sweeney once again became the top position player in the system. No. 1 on this list a year ago—in a split decision over Josh Fields—he has stalled. He has hit .213 in 80 big league at-bats and received a wakeup call when he was denied a promotion last September. Sweeney is a skilled fielder who has hit .289 in five minor league seasons, including three in the high minors. He came to the big leagues with a sweet swing and a willingness to hit the ball the other way and should be able to hit for a solid average when he gets regular playing time at the highest level. He has a plus arm and average speed, and he can play all three outfield positions. When Sweeney was in Double-A, manager Razor Shines projected he would develop 30-homer power, but he never has hit more than 13 in a season. Some believe he's the victim of overcoaching, having had his ability to hit line drives all over the park compromised by Chicago's overzealous attempts to help him hit for more power. He showed tremendous confidence as a teenager but appeared to beat himself up mentally last year. Sweeney had been projected to stick in the big leagues in 2007 and develop into a fixture in the Sox outfield by 2008, but he failed to seize the opportunity. Instead of trading Jermaine Dye, Chicago re-signed him and then dealt for Quentin. It's up to Sweeney to put himself back on the radar.

Year	Club (League)	Class	AVG	G	AB	R	H	2B	3B	HR	RBI	BB	SO	SB	OBP	SLG
2003	Bristol (Appy)	R	.313	19	67	11	21	3	0	2	5	7	10	3	.387	.448
	Great Falls (Pio)	R	.353	10	34	0	12	2	0	0	4	2	3	0	.389	.412
2004	Winston-Salem (Car)	A	.283	134	515	71	146	22	3	7	66	40	65	8	.342	.379
2005	Birmingham (SL)	AA	.298	113	429	64	128	22	3	1	47	35	53	6	.357	.371
2006	Charlotte (IL)	AAA	.296	118	449	64	133	25	3	13	70	35	73	7	.350	.452
	Chicago (AL)	MLB	.229	18	35	1	8	0	0	0	5	0	7	0	.229	.229
2007	Chicago (AL)	MLB	.200	15	45	5	9	3	0	1	5	4	5	0	.265	.333
	Charlotte (IL)	AAA	.270	105	397	50	107	17	2	10	47	48	71	8	.348	.398
MINOR LEAGUE TOTALS			.289	499	1891	260	547	91	11	33	239	167	275	32	.351	.401
MAJOR LEAGUE TOTALS			.213	33	80	6	17	3	0	1	10	4	12	0	.250	.288

7 JOSE MARTINEZ, OF

Born: July 25, 1988. **B-T:** R-R. **Ht.:** 6-5. **Wt.:** 170. **Signed:** Venezuela, 2006. **Signed by:** Amador Arias/Dave Wilder.

Like Fautino de los Santos, Martinez made an early impact in his first season in the United States. He benefited from opening in 2007 in extended spring training before showing signs that he could develop into a complete outfielder. He wore down late in the summer at Rookie-level Bristol. Martinez is a good athlete with a body reminiscent of a young Juan Gonzalez. Martinez has shown the skills to hit for average but is most intriguing to scouts in batting practice, when he displays his power potential. He has a lot of room to add strength as his body matures, making it easy to see him as a middle-of-the-order hitter. He runs well, stealing 12 bases in 14 tries last season, and is a solid outfielder. He has a plus arm that plays well in right field and he also covers enough ground to play center. Martinez is a raw package of skills. He was willing to use the whole field against righthanders but often looked to pull lefties, getting himself out on bad pitches. His plate discipline is encouraging for his age but he still strikes out too much. As he fills out, he'll slow down and most likely lose his ability to play center field. Martinez should be ready for low Class A at age 19. He's not nearly as polished as Ryan Sweeney or Chris Getz, but he has a higher ceiling.

Year	Club (League)	Class	AVG	G	AB	R	H	2B	3B	HR	RBI	BB	SO	SB	OBP	SLG
2006	Orioles/White Sox (VSL)	R	.278	54	158	26	44	8	0	4	30	25	29	5	.384	.405
2007	Bristol (Appy)	R	.282	65	245	34	69	11	3	7	37	22	53	12	.348	.437
MINOR LEAGUE TOTALS			.280	119	403	60	113	19	3	11	67	47	82	17	.363	.424

8 CHRIS GETZ, 2B

Born: Aug. 30, 1983. **B-T:** L-R. **Ht.:** 6-0. **Wt.:** 175. **Drafted:** Michigan, 2005 (4th round). **Signed by:** Mike Shirley.

Drafted by Chicago in the sixth round out of a Michigan high school and again in the fourth round after a college career split between Wake Forest and Michigan, Getz doesn't fit the mold of sleeper. Yet he flew under the radar until a breakout season in 2007, when he showed leadoff skills in Double-A. He missed two months with a leg injury and one manager noted that Birmingham wasn't the same without him. A baseball rat, Getz is fundamentally strong in all phases of the game, which allowed him to advance to Double-A in his first full season as a pro, and he's especially adept at getting on base and putting the ball in play. He struck out only 46 times in his three seasons of college ball and almost always has more walks than whiffs, showing that he's not afraid to hit with two strikes. He has a short, quick swing. His arm is strong enough that he was a closer for his high school team and even pitched at Michigan. He has average speed. Despite the strong arm, Getz profiles exclusively as a second baseman. He doesn't have great range despite having worked hard on his first-step quickness. He has no power, having hit just five homers in 202 Double-A games. He has good baserunning instincts but won't be a basestealing threat. For the moment, Getz is below Danny Richar on the White Sox' depth chart. He'll almost certainly start 2008 at Triple-A but figures to push Richar for the big-league job.

Year	Club (League)	Class	AVG	G	AB	R	H	2B	3B	HR	RBI	BB	SO	SB	OBP	SLG
2005	Great Falls (Pio)	R	.333	6	24	3	8	1	0	0	4	1	2	2	.346	.375
	Kannapolis (SAL)	A	.304	55	214	38	65	13	2	1	28	35	10	11	.407	.397
2006	Birmingham (SL)	AA	.256	130	508	67	130	15	6	2	36	52	47	19	.326	.321
2007	Birmingham (SL)	AA	.299	72	278	40	83	10	2	3	29	36	30	13	.382	.381
MINOR LEAGUE TOTALS			.279	263	1024	148	286	39	10	6	97	124	89	45	.359	.354

9 JOHN ELY, RHP

Born: May 17, 1986. **B-T:** R-R. **Ht.:** 6-1. **Wt.:** 190. **Drafted:** Miami (Ohio), 2007 (3rd round). **Signed by:** Mike Shirley/Keith Staab.

A product of Chicago's far South Side, Ely emerged as a prospect during his college career at Miami (Ohio). He boosted his standing for the 2007 draft with a strong showing in the Cape Cod League after his sophomore season, and did nothing to hurt it with a junior season that included a complete-game at Texas. Signed for $240,750 as a third-round pick, he has won wherever he has pitched, amassing a 59-13 record between high school, college and pro ball. Ely is a strike thrower who works quickly and comes right at hitters with three quality pitches—a low-90s fastball with good movement, a plus-plus changeup with sink and a curveball that improved throughout his pro debut. His fastball and changeup have a lot of life, inducing batters to beat them into the ground. He's a fierce competitor. Ely's lack of size and his max-effort delivery lead to concerns about his durability. But he has never had arm problems and his mechanics add to his deception without ruining his control. The White Sox would be best served to leave Ely's delivery alone. He should reach high Class A at some point this year and could be the first player from Chicago's 2007 draft class to reach the majors.

Year	Club (League)	Class	W	L	ERA	G	GS	CG	SV	IP	H	R	ER	HR	BB	SO	AVG
2007	Great Falls (Pio)	R	6	1	3.86	13	12	0	0	56	55	26	24	6	14	56	.259
MINOR LEAGUE TOTALS			6	1	3.86	13	12	0	0	56	55	26	24	6	14	56	.259

10 JUAN SILVERIO, SS

Born: April 18, 1991. **B-T:** R-R. **Ht.:** 6-1. **Wt.:** 175. **Signed:** Dominican Republic, 2007. **Signed by:** Victor Mateo/Dave Wilder.

Given the way the White Sox historically have thrown around nickels like they were manhole covers in their pursuit of international players, it speaks highly of Silverio that he was deemed worthy of a $600,000 bonus based on the recommendation of scout Victor Mateo and special assistant Dave Wilder. In trying to restock a position of weakness, Chicago signed two other teenage shortstops from the Dominican, but Alexander Adame and Daurys Mercedes don't have Silverio's ceiling. Silverio shows all five tools at shortstop. He combines a quick bat with upper-body strength, enabling him to drive the ball around the park. He has a strong arm and a quick first step in the infield. He runs well, though he projects more as a Miguel Tejada-type shortstop than a true basestealer. There's still a lot of projection remaining in Silverio's frame, so there's concern he could outgrow shortstop and have to move to third base. His skills are untested because he has yet to make his pro debut, but Chicago was encouraged that he held his own as a 16-year-old in instructional league. Silverio figures to open 2008 in extended spring training, preparing to play at Rookie-level Bristol. The White Sox will need to develop him patiently, but the payoff could be huge. He's already by far the best shortstop prospect in the system.

Year	Club (League)	Class	AVG	G	AB	R	H	2B	3B	HR	RBI	BB	SO	SB	OBP	SLG
2007	Did Not Play															

11 JOHN SHELBY JR., OF

Born: Aug. 6, 1985. **B-T:** L-R. **Ht.:** 5-10. **Wt.:** 190. **Drafted:** Kentucky, 2006 (5th round). **Signed by:** Mike Shirley.

It wasn't a surprise that Shelby hit during his first full season of pro ball. The biggest development for the son of former big league outfielder John "T-Bone" Shelby was that he showed signs of making a successful transition to center field after playing mostly second base in college and in his first pro season. His athleticism played well in center field. He struggled at times with his routes to balls but had the speed to run down most of his mistakes and the instincts to know what to do with the ball when he got to it. His only defensive drawback is an arm that will challenge opponents to run on him, but the belief is he can be an above-average center fielder in time. Shelby's bat was the tool that caused the White Sox to select him in the fifth round of the 2006 draft, and he continued to hit in low Class A. He flashed his power, compiling 60 extra-base hits, while getting on base enough to project as a possible No. 2 hitter. He runs well and is a solid worker and teammate. He's expected to open 2008 in high Class A, but he could get a look in Double-A before the season is over.

Year	Club (League)	Class	AVG	G	AB	R	H	2B	3B	HR	RBI	BB	SO	SB	OBP	SLG
2006	Great Falls (Pio)	R	.272	66	250	37	68	12	3	8	36	18	55	8	.332	.440
2007	Kannapolis (SAL)	A	.301	122	488	83	147	35	9	16	79	35	77	19	.352	.508
MINOR LEAGUE TOTALS			.291	188	738	120	215	47	12	24	115	53	132	27	.345	.485

12 ADAM RUSSELL, RHP

Born: April 14, 1983. **B-T:** R-R. **Ht.:** 6-8. **Wt.:** 250. **Drafted:** Ohio, 2004 (6th round). **Signed by:** Nathan Durst/Larry Grefer.

Following his breakout season in 2006, Russell's development slowed a little in what may have been a confusing season. He became one of the flavors of the month in spring training, when his 95-mph fastball and sharply breaking curveball made him a favorite of scouts in Arizona, but seemed to suffer a letdown when he wound up back in Double-A. He seemed his own worst enemy at times, opening the year in the rotation and ending it in the bullpen. He pitched well as a reliever in the Arizona Fall League. Russell throws a 91-94 mph fastball from a variety of arm slots, emulating Jose Contreras after a suggestion in mid-2006 from from Winston-Salem pitching coach J.R. Perdew. Russell's curveball is a plus pitch at times but hitters don't chase it out of the strike zone. He is about as subtle as a lumberjack, using his build to gain some intimidation and durability. Russell's secondary pitches lag behind his fastball. He can get out of whack mechanically in a hurry and has a hard time getting himself back on track. The Sox would like him to work faster as he can think too much on the mound. While Russell has pitched primarily as a starter in the minors, the bullpen appears his most likely path to the big leagues. The White Sox need help in that area, and he figures to be a candidate for a job in spring training. He also could benefit from spending at least half a year in Triple-A.

Year	Club (League)	Class	W	L	ERA	G	GS	CG	SV	IP	H	R	ER	HR	BB	SO	AVG
2004	Great Falls (Pio)	R	4	0	2.37	15	4	0	0	38	31	11	10	2	18	33	.228
	Kannapolis (SAL)	A	0	2	9.00	2	2	0	0	10	18	11	10	3	7	3	.409
2005	Kannapolis (SAL)	A	9	7	3.78	24	24	0	0	126	116	61	53	10	55	82	.246
2006	Winston-Salem (Car)	A	7	3	2.66	17	17	0	0	94	80	35	28	5	39	61	.235
	Birmingham (SL)	AA	3	3	4.75	10	10	0	0	55	59	33	29	5	19	47	.269
2007	Birmingham (SL)	AA	9	11	4.80	38	20	0	1	138	159	81	74	8	58	95	.290
MINOR LEAGUE TOTALS			32	26	3.97	106	77	0	1	462	463	232	204	33	196	321	.263

13 KYLE McCULLOCH, RHP

Born: Dec. 2, 1985. **B-T:** R-R. **Ht.:** 6-3. **Wt.:** 190. **Drafted:** Texas, 2006 (1st round). **Signed by:** Keith Staab.

By the nature of their status and signing bonuses, first-round picks almost always create a buzz in a farm system. However, the low-key McCulloch has been almost buzzproof since the White Sox selected him 29th overall in 2006 and handed him a $1.05 million bonus. He's a winner and an innings-eater, but he lacks the stuff to become a front-of-the-rotation starter. His best pitch is his plus changeup, which he throws in the high 70s to complement a fastball that generally sits in the high 80s, occasionally climbing to 91 mph. McCulloch used a new splitter last season in high Class A, where he was named Carolina League pitcher of the week three times, but rarely got into counts to use it after being promoted to Double-A. He has had problems with his delivery, which has some stabbing action toward the plate when it gets long. He does get a lot of groundouts, a point of emphasis for the White Sox. A former shortstop, he shows athleticism and competitiveness. He'll get another test from Double-A hitters this season, and he'll need to have more success against them to generate some buzz.

Year	Club (League)	Class	W	L	ERA	G	GS	CG	SV	IP	H	R	ER	HR	BB	SO	AVG
2006	Great Falls (Pio)	R	1	1	1.61	6	5	0	0	22	19	15	4	1	7	27	.213
	Winston-Salem (Car)	A	2	5	4.08	7	7	0	0	35	37	20	16	4	17	21	.266
2007	Winston-Salem (Car)	A	7	7	3.64	22	22	0	0	121	116	62	49	7	42	88	.251
	Birmingham (SL)	AA	1	2	6.41	6	6	0	0	26	38	25	19	4	11	16	.333
MINOR LEAGUE TOTALS			11	15	3.86	41	40	0	0	205	210	122	88	16	77	152	.261

14 NEVIN GRIFFITH, RHP

Born: March 23, 1989. **B-T:** R-R. **Ht.:** 6-2. **Wt.:** 165. **Drafted:** HS—Tampa, 2007 (2nd round). **Signed by:** Scott Bikowski/Warren Hughes.

Griffith was regarded as a premium prospect as an underclassman in Florida, and his stock spiked after he pitched well in two outings against Tampa-area rival Hillsborough High and outfielder Michael Burgess, a supplemental first-round pick by the Nationals. A second-rounder in his own right, Griffith signed for $382,500. He's long, lean and athletic with a whippy arm action. He improved his balance over the rubber and incorporated his lower half more in his delivery as a high school senior, causing his velocity to spike. He can reach the mid-90s with a four-seamer that's very straight, or he can work at 90-92 mph with natural sink with a two-seamer. All of Griffith's other pitches need work. His slider can be tough to hit but lacks consistency. Ditto for his curveball and his changeup, which needs more work than the breaking pitches. His command is a question as well, with the White Sox working to smooth out a long delivery. The raw stuff is there and he's in an organization with a history of helping pitchers develop consistency. He'll try to win a spot in the low Class A rotation to open 2008.

Year	Club (League)	Class	W	L	ERA	G	GS	CG	SV	IP	H	R	ER	HR	BB	SO	AVG
2007	Bristol (Appy)	R	0	0	5.19	8	1	0	0	8	14	8	5	0	6	7	.359
MINOR LEAGUE TOTALS			0	0	5.19	8	1	0	0	8	14	8	5	0	6	7	.359

15 LUCAS HARRELL, RHP

Born: June 3, 1985. **B-T:** S-R. **Ht.:** 6-2. **Wt.:** 200. **Drafted:** HS—Ozark, Mo., 2004 (4th round). **Signed by:** Alex Slattery.

Ranked among the system's best pitching prospects coming into 2007, Harrell missed the season after relatively minor repairs on his elbow. He also missed the end of the previous season with a strained trapezius muscle. The timing of the elbow injury was bad because he had put himself onto the map in 2006 and had been ticketed to work alongside Gio Gonzalez and Jack Egbert in the Birmingham rotation. Instead, he wound up watching them and Fautino de los Santos jump past him. Harrell wasn't standing still, however, working hard on both his rehabilitation and his overall conditioning. The White Sox credited his strong showing in instructional league to his work ethic. He has a low-90s fastball with life, getting a lot of groundballs on his sinker. He has developed a plus changeup and continues to work on a slider as his third pitch. He'll have to continue to hone his control. Harrell ended instructional league healthy and ready to handle a starter's workload in 2008, most likely in Double-A.

Year	Club (League)	Class	W	L	ERA	G	GS	CG	SV	IP	H	R	ER	HR	BB	SO	AVG
2004	Bristol (Appy)	R	3	5	5.59	13	9	0	0	48	53	39	30	5	32	33	.282
2005	Kannapolis (SAL)	A	7	11	3.65	26	26	0	0	133	128	86	54	8	71	85	.248
2006	Winston-Salem (Car)	A	7	2	2.45	17	17	0	0	91	58	29	25	3	44	70	.182
	Birmingham (SL)	AA	0	2	10.24	3	3	0	0	9	12	12	11	1	14	4	.316
2007	Did Not Play—Injured																
MINOR LEAGUE TOTALS			17	20	3.82	59	55	0	0	283	251	166	120	17	161	192	.237

16 CHARLIE HAEGER, RHP

Born: Sept. 19, 1983. **B-T:** R-R. **Ht.:** 6-1. **Wt.:** 220. **Drafted:** HS—Plymouth, Mass., 2001 (25th round). **Signed by:** Ken Stauffer/Nathan Durst.

On the surface, Haeger appeared to take a major step backward in 2007. He was hit hard in too many of his eight big league outings and went 5-16 for Triple-A Charlotte. But it's far too early to write off a guy who might have the best knuckleball this side of Tim Wakefield. Haeger, who started throwing the knuckler full-time after a self-imposed one-year retirement in 2003, got out of whack with his mechanics during spring training. He didn't get them back under control until the second half of the season, when he finished strong. He had gotten long in his delivery but made a major adjustment, working almost exclusively out of the stretch in the second half. Haeger can mix in a mid-80s fastball and a decent curve, though he throws the knuckleball about 75 percent of the time. He did nothing to tarnish his reputation as a workhorse, topping 150 innings for the third straight season. Haeger is a good athlete who fields his position well. He clearly has fallen on Chicago's depth charts since the end of the 2006 season and could need a trade to get a long look as a big league starter.

Year	Club (League)	Class	W	L	ERA	G	GS	CG	SV	IP	H	R	ER	HR	BB	SO	AVG
2001	White Sox (AZL)	R	0	3	6.39	13	4	0	0	31	44	29	22	2	17	17	.336
2002	White Sox (AZL)	R	1	4	4.17	25	0	0	6	41	46	25	19	2	13	24	.295
2003	Did Not Play—Restricted List																
2004	Bristol (Appy)	R	1	6	5.18	10	10	0	0	57	70	41	33	6	22	23	.303
	Kannapolis (SAL)	A	1	3	2.01	5	5	0	0	31	31	17	7	0	12	21	.270
2005	Winston-Salem (Car)	A	8	2	3.20	14	13	0	0	81	82	33	29	3	40	64	.267
	Birmingham (SL)	AA	6	3	3.78	13	13	3	0	85	84	43	36	1	45	48	.263
2006	Charlotte (IL)	AAA	14	6	3.07	26	25	2	0	170	143	71	58	9	78	130	.231
	Chicago (AL)	MLB	1	1	3.44	7	1	0	1	18	12	10	7	0	13	19	.182
2007	Charlotte (IL)	AAA	5	16	4.08	24	23	3	0	147	138	82	67	16	67	126	.250
	Chicago (AL)	MLB	0	1	7.15	8	0	0	0	11	17	11	9	3	8	1	.354
MINOR LEAGUE TOTALS			36	43	3.78	130	93	8	6	645	638	341	271	39	294	453	.262
MAJOR LEAGUE TOTALS			1	2	4.85	15	1	0	1	29	29	21	16	3	21	20	.254

17 CHRISTIAN MARRERO, 1B

Born: July 30, 1986 **B-T:** L-L. **Ht.:** 6-1. **Wt.:** 185. **Drafted:** Broward (Fla.) CC, D/F 2005 (22nd round). **Signed by:** Jose Ortega.

A draft-and-follow from the 2005 draft, Marrero is the older brother of Nationals No. 1 prospect Chris Marrero. Christian's offensive ceiling isn't as high as his brother's but he shares the same understanding of the art of hitting, which showed when he repeated the Rookie-level Pioneer League. League managers praised his smooth stroke, the result of his work with White Sox coaches. The ball seemed to jump off his bat last season. Marrero is a disciplined hitter, seldom getting himself out on bad pitches. He has gap power and could develop into a true power hitter as he matures. He has few outstanding tools other than his bat, however. His arm is excellent but he doesn't run well enough or cover enough ground in the outfield. He played most of 2007 at first base, his likely home in the future. Club officials praise his love for the game. Marrero probably will open 2008 in low Class A and could earn a swift promotion if he continues to hit like he did last season.

Year	Club (League)	Class	AVG	G	AB	R	H	2B	3B	HR	RBI	BB	SO	SB	OBP	SLG
2006	Great Falls (Pio)	R	.252	72	242	24	61	17	0	3	24	30	37	1	.337	.360
2007	Great Falls (Pio)	R	.305	69	269	53	82	21	6	12	63	36	43	3	.383	.561
MINOR LEAGUE TOTALS			.280	141	511	77	143	38	6	15	87	66	80	4	.362	.466

18 SERGIO MORALES, OF

Born: Dec. 17, 1987. **B-T:** R-R. **Ht.:** 6-1. **Wt.:** 190. **Drafted:** Broward (Fla.) CC, D/F 2006 (12th round). **Signed by:** Jose Ortega.

A raw talent with lots of room for projection, Morales gave just a hint of his ability during his pro debut. He opted to attend Broward (Fla.) CC when he wasn't happy with what the Rangers offered after selecting him in the 28th round of the 2005 draft, and the White Sox took him in the 12th round a year later. It took $180,000 to sign him as a draft-and-follow. Morales hasn't been a great hitter for average since he was in high school, but Chicago loves his bat speed and believes he needs only time to develop into a guy who produces for both average and power. While he's strong, he's also a hacker, and he needs to improve his strike-zone discipline to reach the expectations for him. Morales has good speed and could develop into a major stolen-base threat. He played a quality center field in his debut and the Sox believe he has the athleticism and instincts to remain there. He should open 2008 in low Class A.

Year	Club (League)	Class	AVG	G	AB	R	H	2B	3B	HR	RBI	BB	SO	SB	OBP	SLG
2007	Bristol (Appy)	R	.270	55	196	35	53	8	2	6	24	14	67	11	.326	.423
MINOR LEAGUE TOTALS			.270	55	196	35	53	8	2	6	24	14	67	11	.326	.423

19 JUSTIN CASSEL, RHP

Born: Sept. 25, 1984. **B-T:** R-R. **Ht.:** 6-2. **Wt.:** 200. **Drafted:** UC Irvine, 2006 (7th round). **Signed by:** Danny Ontiveros.

Before leaving a May 6 start with an unusual strain on the underside of his right shoulder, Cassel had made the White Sox look wise for taking him in the 2006 draft. His emergence was no surprise to anyone who knows his family history. Older brother Matt has been a longtime backup quarterback for the New England Patriots. Another brother, Jack, pitched in the big leagues for the Padres in September. Even his mother Barbara has won an Emmy for her work as a set decorator. Justin has had plenty of success himself, having gone 15-0 as a senior to help Chatsworth (Calif.) High finish the 2003 season as the national high school champion. He got off to a fast start in high Class A in 2007 before missing more than half a season while rehabilitating his shoulder. Cassel was healthy at the end of 2007, pitching so well in instructional league that he'll have a chance to open 2008 in the Double-A rotation. He has a smooth delivery but isn't overpowering. His fastball rarely gets out of the high 80s but has great natural sink, getting hitters to put it on the ground. Both his curveball and changeup grade as average to plus. Cassel works fast and comes at hitters. He'll have to improve his command as he moves up, but durability is the biggest question for him at this point.

Year	Club (League)	Class	W	L	ERA	G	GS	CG	SV	IP	H	R	ER	HR	BB	SO	AVG
2006	Great Falls (Pio)	R	3	2	2.97	13	4	0	0	39	38	17	13	1	10	37	.252
	Winston-Salem (Car)	A	1	1	5.12	4	4	0	0	19	28	15	11	2	4	8	.333
2007	Winston-Salem (Car)	A	4	2	2.27	10	6	0	0	39	31	13	10	1	17	31	.215
	Bristol (Appy)	R	0	0	6.75	2	2	0	0	2	5	2	2	0	0	3	.357
MINOR LEAGUE TOTALS			8	5	3.21	29	16	0	0	101	102	47	36	4	31	79	.260

20 SERGIO MIRANDA, SS

Born: March 5, 1987. **B-T:** B-R. **Ht.:** 5-9. **Wt.:** 169. **Drafted:** Virginia Commonwealth, 2007 (13th round). **Signed by:** Chuck Fox

Sometimes good things come in small packages. The White Sox believe that's true with Miranda, whose stature contributed to him sliding to the 13th round in the 2007 draft. Like Duke outfielder Jimmy Gallagher, Chicago's 2007 seventh-rounder, he came out of college as a polished performer lacking the tools that get scouts excited. But there's no doubt he knows how to play the game, as he won a college Gold Glove last spring and then more than held his own with the bat in low Class A after signing for $25,000. Miranda is a switch-hitter with impressive bat control and a good knowledge of the strike zone, which allowed him to walk more than he struck out in his debut. He had batted .376 as a three-year starter at Virginia Commonwealth, but scouts expected him to have trouble adjusting to a wood bat. He's a better hitter lefthanded than righthanded but will continue to work as a switch-hitter. Miranda has been groomed to play pro ball, attending the Puerto Rico Baseball Academy before college. His arm is average, but he had the range to set a school record for assists last year at VCU. Miranda will open 2008 with one of the Class A teams and could move quickly. He has replaced Robert Valido as the best bet to become the organization's first homegrown regular at shortstop since Bucky Dent was traded to the Yankees after the 1976 season.

Year	Club (League)	Class	AVG	G	AB	R	H	2B	3B	HR	RBI	BB	SO	SB	OBP	SLG
2007	Great Falls (Pio)	R	.464	7	28	2	13	3	1	0	1	3	4	1	.516	.643
	Kannapolis (SAL)	A	.282	61	238	45	67	9	2	1	30	37	27	5	.384	.349
MINOR LEAGUE TOTALS			.301	68	266	47	80	12	3	1	31	40	31	6	.397	.380

21 FRANCISCO HERNANDEZ, C

Born: Feb. 4, 1986. **B-T:** S-R. **Ht.:** 5-9. **Wt.:** 160. **Signed:** Dominican Republic, 2002. **Signed by:** Denny Gonzalez.

Farm director Alan Regier made an interesting decision in the spring, essentially demoting a handful of prospects in hopes they would enjoy a level of success that had previously eluded them. It paid dividends with Hernandez, along with outfielder Sal Sanchez and first baseman Micah Schnurstein. The undersized Hernandez performed well in what was his fourth taste of low Class A, and followed up on that by getting off to a solid start in the Dominican Winter League. The 21-year-old switch-hitter opened as a reserve for Estrellas but hit his way into regular playing time. His above-average arm is still what gets Hernandez noticed—though he threw out a pedestrian 29 percent of basestealers in 2007—but he has made strides at the plate, drawing more walks than strikeouts for the first time in his career. He has the bat control to put the ball in play and offers some gap power, but his bat will be tested as he climbs the ladder. His pitch-calling and handling of a pitching staff need improvement if he's to play in the majors. Hernandez has the potential to be a regular in the big leagues, but only if he continues to improve in all phases of the game.

Year	Club (League)	Class	AVG	G	AB	R	H	2B	3B	HR	RBI	BB	SO	SB	OBP	SLG
2003	White Sox (DSL)	R	.296	66	216	34	64	14	0	6	29	39	23	9	.412	.444
2004	Bristol (Appy)	R	.326	53	181	32	59	13	1	5	30	13	32	0	.372	.492
	Kannapolis (SAL)	A	.333	3	12	0	4	1	0	0	0	0	3	0	.333	.417
2005	Kannapolis (SAL)	A	.222	44	153	15	34	5	0	3	18	13	29	0	.292	.314
	Great Falls (Pio)	R	.349	58	212	37	74	19	0	6	34	19	25	0	.405	.524
2006	Kannapolis (SAL)	A	.247	92	316	29	78	16	1	6	34	22	31	3	.305	.361
2007	Kannapolis (SAL)	A	.277	80	271	42	75	23	1	4	36	35	29	0	.362	.413
MINOR LEAGUE TOTALS			.285	396	1361	189	388	91	3	30	181	141	172	12	.358	.422

22 EHREN WASSERMAN, RHP

Born: Dec. 6, 1980. **B-T:** B-R. **Ht.:** 6-0. **Wt.:** 185. **Signed:** NDFA, Samford, 2003. **Signed by:** Warren Hughes.

During a season-long bullpen breakdown in Chicago, many relievers were called but few stuck around. Wasserman might have been the least likely of those who did. An undrafted college player who was signed out of a tryout camp, he earned his way to the big leagues by succeeding at every level in the minors. He's a strike thrower who gets deception from a sidearm delivery, using his fearlessness to overcome a lack of velocity. Wasserman relies on a high-80s sinker and a curveball that ties up righthanders. He held righties to a .174 average in his 33 big league outings but had trouble getting lefties out. Still, he managed not to allow a homer all season, getting batters to beat the ball into the ground. Pitching coach Don Cooper will spend spring training trying to better equip Wasserman to face lefties. Regardless, he's good enough against righties to earn a spot in the White Sox bullpen.

Year	Club (League)	Class	W	L	ERA	G	GS	CG	SV	IP	H	R	ER	HR	BB	SO	AVG
2003	Bristol (Appy)	R	0	1	14.73	4	0	0	0	3	9	6	6	0	3	4	.474
	Kannapolis (SAL)	A	1	1	1.00	6	0	0	0	9	8	1	1	0	3	10	.267
2004	Kannapolis (SAL)	A	2	3	2.75	50	0	0	30	55	44	20	17	1	16	42	.211
	Winston-Salem (Car)	A	1	0	2.70	10	0	0	1	10	11	4	3	1	5	5	.268
2005	Winston-Salem (Car)	A	4	2	1.37	42	0	0	20	46	41	10	7	0	9	37	.247
	Birmingham (SL)	AA	2	0	2.14	14	0	0	0	21	23	6	5	0	7	18	.291
2006	Birmingham (SL)	AA	4	8	2.56	61	0	0	22	63	60	26	18	3	25	47	.253
2007	Charlotte (IL)	AAA	2	4	2.11	38	0	0	5	42	34	13	10	0	18	33	.230
	Chicago (AL)	MLB	1	1	2.74	33	0	0	0	23	20	9	7	0	7	14	.238
MINOR LEAGUE TOTALS			16	19	2.40	225	0	0	78	251	230	86	67	5	86	196	.248
MAJOR LEAGUE TOTALS			1	1	2.74	33	0	0	0	23	20	9	7	0	7	14	.238

23 DONNY LUCY, C

Born: Aug. 8, 1982. **B-T:** R-R. **Ht.:** 6-3. **Wt.:** 210. **Drafted:** Stanford, 2004 (2nd round). **Signed by:** Rick Ingalls/Adam Virchis.

Highly decorated as a high school and college player, Lucy got to the big leagues in his third full season out of Stanford. But he may never develop into more than a solid, defensive-oriented backup. Some in the organization compare him to Chris Stewart, a former minor league standout who has stalled on the threshold of the big leagues, but others argue that Lucy still could hit enough to have a long career in the big leagues. Despite his college success, Lucy had to overhaul his mechanics at the plate and behind it after the White Sox selected him in the second round in 2004. The results have started to show, as he hit .269 in the first half of last season in Double-A, though he seemed overmatched after advancing to Triple-A and then Chicago for a September callup. His strength is pitch-calling and handling a staff. He has an average arm but has quickened his release and threw out 34 percent of minor league basestalers in 2007. He runs well for a catcher, albeit below average overall. He needs more at-bats against advanced pitchers and should be a regular in Triple-A this season.

Year	Club (League)	Class	AVG	G	AB	R	H	2B	3B	HR	RBI	BB	SO	SB	OBP	SLG
2004	Great Falls (Pio)	R	.239	50	176	19	42	7	1	1	26	17	36	13	.312	.307
2005	Kannapolis (SAL)	A	.264	54	178	25	47	5	0	1	22	21	41	6	.353	.309
2006	Winston-Salem (Car)	A	.262	97	332	48	87	17	1	7	32	33	67	12	.341	.383
	Birmingham (SL)	AA	.283	18	60	2	17	1	0	0	3	4	15	1	.358	.300
2007	Birmingham (SL)	AA	.269	87	290	42	78	17	0	6	27	30	59	13	.343	.390
	Charlotte (IL)	AAA	.200	19	75	5	15	3	0	0	3	3	25	0	.231	.240
	Chicago (AL)	MLB	.200	8	15	0	3	0	0	0	0	0	6	0	.200	.200
MINOR LEAGUE TOTALS			.257	325	1111	141	286	50	2	15	113	108	243	45	.333	.347
MAJOR LEAGUE TOTALS			.200	8	15	0	3	0	0	0	0	0	6	0	.200	.200

24 ONELI PEREZ, RHP

Born: May 26, 1983. **B-T:** R-R. **Ht.:** 6-2. **Wt.:** 163. **Signed:** Dominican Republic, 2001. **Signed by:** Denny Gonzalez.

Perez started out as a hitter in the Padres organization, but he never made it out of the Rookie-level Dominican Summer League with them, even after moving to the mound in 2003. He was released, and the White Sox signed him in May 2004. Based purely on results, he has been one of the best pitchers in the system. He has gone 10-4, 1.45 with 25 saves between three levels the last two years, and was one of the top closers in the Dominican League in 2007-08. But the reality is that he's something of an afterthought for the White Sox. That's not because he's 24 and only now reaching Triple-A, or because he's like Antonio Alfonseca and was born with six fingers on each hand. It's because Perez can drive his managers a little loopy with his laid-back approach to conditioning and preparation, and because he always has been a flyball pitcher, which doesn't project well for U.S. Cellular Field. His approach on the mound is simple. He comes at hitters with a low-90s fastball and an average slider, thrown from a three-quarters arm slot. His key to success is getting ahead of hitters. His ratios have been excellent the last two seasons: 10.5 strikeouts per nine innings and 4.6 whiffs per walk. The only place he pitched badly was in big league camp before the 2007 season, where he got shelled. Perez could put himself in the picture for a bullpen spot this spring but has to erase the poor first impression.

Year	Club (League)	Class	AVG	G	AB	R	H	2B	3B	HR	RBI	BB	SO	SB	OBP	SLG
2001	Padres (DSL)	R	.276	59	196	27	54	6	2	1	18	20	35	7	.344	.342
2002	Padres (DSL)	R	.216	62	199	19	43	7	3	1	30	20	38	8	.286	.296
MINOR LEAGUE TOTALS			.246	121	395	46	97	13	5	2	48	40	73	15	.314	.319

Year	Club (League)	Class	W	L	ERA	G	GS	CG	SV	IP	H	R	ER	HR	BB	SO	AVG
2003	Padres (DSL)	R	3	0	1.77	15	0	0	3	40	33	11	8	0	7	33	.213
2004	White Sox (DSL)	R	7	5	2.08	20	1	1	5	65	53	17	15	1	17	52	.227
2005	Kannapolis (SAL)	A	4	2	3.71	36	2	0	2	80	84	41	33	7	32	62	.265
2006	Kannapolis (SAL)	A	3	1	0.99	30	0	0	8	36	23	5	4	1	8	42	.172
	Winston-Salem (Car)	A	1	0	0.72	17	0	0	0	25	17	5	2	1	5	29	.181
	Birmingham (SL)	AA	0	1	0.55	7	0	0	1	16	6	1	1	1	6	20	.115
2007	Birmingham (SL)	AA	6	2	2.10	59	0	0	16	77	62	19	18	5	20	89	.219
MINOR LEAGUE TOTALS			24	11	2.14	184	3	1	35	340	278	99	81	16	95	327	.219

25 BRIAN OMOGROSSO, RHP

Born: April 24, 1984. **B-T:** R-R. **Ht.:** 6-4. **Wt.:** 230. **Drafted:** Indiana State, 2006 (6th round). **Signed by:** Mike Shirley.

On course to be a top draft pick after his sophomore season at Indiana State, Omogrosso wound up being sidelined by an elbow injury that would require Tommy John surgery in 2005. He has been climbing back ever since and looks like he may be ready to have a breakout season in 2008. A barrel-chested kid with a tough attitude, he projects as a late-inning reliever. Omogrosso's best pitch is a mid-90s fastball with good movement that he can throw from a low three-quarters or sidearm delivery. He flashed a plus slider as a college sophomore, but it hasn't had quite the same tilt or depth since his surgery. The White Sox put him in the rotation last year to get him some more work. Omogrosso handled the switch well, throwing one shutout and ending the year with three consecutive quality starts, but the real benefit was that he used his improved changeup with regularity. That could be a big pitch for him, as he has been far more effective against righthanders than lefties. He's a good athlete who lettered in football and basketball in high school. Omogrosso is ticketed for Double-A, either as a starter or a closer.

Year	Club (League)	Class	W	L	ERA	G	GS	CG	SV	IP	H	R	ER	HR	BB	SO	AVG
2006	Kannapolis (SAL)	A	1	2	3.19	22	0	0	2	36	27	14	13	2	13	23	.209
2007	Winston-Salem (Car)	A	8	8	3.74	40	14	1	5	120	94	60	50	7	57	108	.211
MINOR LEAGUE TOTALS			9	10	3.61	62	14	1	7	157	121	74	63	9	70	131	.210

26 DEWON DAY, RHP

Born: Sept. 29, 1980. **B-T:** R-R. **Ht.:** 6-4. **Wt.:** 210. **Drafted:** Southern, D/F 2002 (26th round). **Signed by:** Jaymie Bane (Blue Jays).

At 27 it's hard to see Day as a premium prospect, though he still has the look of a late bloomer who could establish himself in the big leagues. He got his first chance in 2007, getting summoned after destroying Double-A hitters, but he lost command of the plus slider he uses to set up his fastball. He hung around for 13 outings as manager Ozzie Guillen reached for straws in his disintegrating bullpen, but Day eventually needed time in Triple-A to get himself back on track. He finished strong there and then added a solid performance in the Arizona Fall League. In his work for four teams in 2007, the big righthander struck out 87 in 64 innings while allowing only one homer. That's the kind of performance that should guarantee him a second chance at some point in 2008. He's a classic two-pitch reliever, with a low-90s fastball and a slider that has textbook tilt and depth. It's a good pitch against lefties and righties alike when it's sharp. Day could open the season as a closer in Triple-A if he doesn't win a spot in the big league bullpen.

Year	Club (League)	Class	W	L	ERA	G	GS	CG	SV	IP	H	R	ER	HR	BB	SO	AVG
2003	Pulaski (Appy)	R	2	0	1.80	26	0	0	12	30	21	8	6	0	9	26	.184
	Auburn (NYP)	A	0	0	0.00	2	0	0	0	1	1	0	0	0	0	1	.200
2004	Auburn (NYP)	A	0	3	1.50	27	0	0	8	24	24	8	4	0	10	28	.250
2005	Auburn (NYP)	A	0	0	3.00	3	0	0	0	3	4	2	1	0	3	4	.286
	Lansing (MWL)	A	0	0	4.05	9	0	0	0	13	15	6	6	2	9	14	.300
2006	Winston-Salem (Car)	A	1	4	3.40	40	0	0	8	47	40	23	18	3	21	63	.222
2007	Birmingham (SL)	AA	2	3	3.60	20	0	0	3	25	26	13	10	1	12	48	.257
	Chicago (AL)	MLB	0	1	11.25	13	0	0	0	12	19	15	15	1	9	7	.352
	Charlotte (IL)	AAA	0	2	6.28	14	0	0	0	14	10	10	10	0	20	15	.192
MINOR LEAGUE TOTALS			5	12	3.12	141	0	0	31	158	141	70	55	6	84	199	.230
MAJOR LEAGUE TOTALS			0	1	11.25	13	0	0	0	12	19	15	15	1	9	7	.352

27 BRANDON ALLEN, 1B

Born: Feb. 12, 1986. **B-T:** L-R. **Ht.:** 6-2. **Wt.:** 235. **Drafted:** HS—Montgomery, Texas, 2004 (5th round). **Signed by:** Paul Provas/Keith Staab.

Allen drew Division I-A football interest as a linebacker but decided to turn pro in baseball out of high school for a $175,000 bonus as a fifth-round pick. With his size, strength and power potential, he would have gone higher in the draft had he not had a dismal senior season, striking out all too frequently and hitting just two homers. He has been more consistent as a pro and improved in his second try at low Class A in 2007, but he still strikes out too much. Offspeed stuff and pitches low in the strike zone can give him trouble. Allen has some surprising athleticism and speed for his size, but he has found the going rough at first base. The White Sox at one point considered trying him in the outfield, though those plans have been scrapped and he spent almost as much time at DH as in the field last year. After the trade of Chris Carter to the Diamondbacks, Allen now has more power than any hitter in the system, so Chicago will remain patient. He'll move up to high Class A in 2008.

Year	Club (League)	Class	AVG	G	AB	R	H	2B	3B	HR	RBI	BB	SO	SB	OBP	SLG
2004	Bristol (Appy)	R	.205	58	185	17	38	9	1	3	23	16	60	2	.280	.314
2005	Great Falls (Pio)	R	.264	66	231	41	61	11	2	11	42	32	69	7	.366	.472
2006	Kannapolis (SAL)	A	.213	109	395	36	84	17	2	15	68	22	126	6	.257	.380
2007	Kannapolis (SAL)	A	.283	129	516	84	146	39	5	18	93	39	124	7	.337	.483
MINOR LEAGUE TOTALS			.248	362	1327	178	329	76	10	47	226	109	379	22	.311	.427

28 SAL SANCHEZ, OF

Born: Sept. 13, 1985. **B-T:** R-R. **Ht.:** 6-6. **Wt.:** 195. **Signed:** Dominican Republic, 2004. **Signed by:** Denny Gonzalez.

After seemingly stalling as a hitter, Sanchez revived his stock with a strong showing following a demotion to Rookie ball in 2007. He flashed his big-time power and the full collection of five tools, leading the Pioneer League with 97 hits while uncorking showcase throws from right field. Then again, he was old for the league at 21 and took a step back after failing in low Class A in 2006. The book on Sanchez so far remains a story of untapped potential, and time is beginning to run out. He has range in right field but doesn't always take good routes to the ball. He has the speed to steal 30-plus bases but hasn't learned how to read pitchers and get a good jump. He has never had much plate discipline, though he did make a huge leap in on-base percentage last year. Sanchez was projected to develop into a Juan Gonzalez type physically when he signed out of the Dominican in 2004, but he has yet to fill out. He still has a high ceiling but needs to start moving faster toward the big leagues.

Year	Club (League)	Class	AVG	G	AB	R	H	2B	3B	HR	RBI	BB	SO	SB	OBP	SLG
2004	White Sox (DSL)	R	.326	56	215	35	70	14	2	4	37	8	21	4	.363	.465
2005	Bristol (Appy)	R	.260	64	246	38	64	17	1	4	30	17	62	14	.313	.386
2006	Kannapolis (SAL)	A	.209	88	287	36	60	9	0	8	37	16	76	17	.264	.324
2007	Great Falls (Pio)	R	.343	70	283	57	97	16	10	7	51	18	59	18	.394	.544
MINOR LEAGUE TOTALS			.282	278	1031	166	291	56	13	23	155	59	218	53	.332	.429

29 ROBERT VALIDO, SS

Born: May 16, 1985. **B-T:** R-R. **Ht.:** 6-2. **Wt.:** 180. **Drafted:** HS—Miami, 2003 (4th round). **Signed by:** Jose Ortega.

Only the most patient player-development sorts would still consider Valido a prospect, but his defense at shortstop is too strong to overlook, even if he hit himself back into high Class A after opening each of the last two seasons in Double-A. He appeared to have a breakout season with his bat in 2005, but hasn't looked like the same hitter since serving a suspension after a positive test for a performance-enhancing substance. The mention of his name sometimes brings an agonized look from general manager Ken Williams, who had counted on him to be ready to take over for Juan Uribe at shortstop in 2008, but Valido still has supporters in the organization. They point out that he already has the range, arm strength and experience to play shortstop in the big leagues, and that he has a strong work ethic and carries himself like a leader wherever he plays. That won't matter unless he makes major strides with the bat. He developed bad habits while dealing with a wrist injury in 2006 and may have aggravated his problems by experimenting with different stances at the plate. He has plus speed but doesn't get on base enough to use it, and his pop has disappeared since his suspension. Valido will be 22 when the 2008 season begins, and it's probably time to produce or be gone.

Year	Club (League)	Class	AVG	G	AB	R	H	2B	3B	HR	RBI	BB	SO	SB	OBP	SLG
2003	Bristol (Appy)	R	.307	58	215	39	66	15	2	6	31	17	28	17	.364	.479
2004	Kannapolis (SAL)	A	.252	122	456	65	115	25	0	4	43	35	59	28	.313	.333
2005	Winston-Salem (Car)	A	.288	119	513	86	148	28	7	8	59	21	64	52	.320	.417
2006	Birmingham (SL)	AA	.208	45	168	15	35	9	3	1	11	13	24	8	.269	.315
	Winston-Salem (Car)	A	.222	9	36	5	8	1	1	1	5	3	3	0	.282	.389
2007	Birmingham (SL)	AA	.177	70	266	23	47	8	1	0	17	9	43	10	.210	.214
	Winston-Salem (Car)	A	.252	57	234	30	59	8	0	3	16	14	36	20	.296	.325
MINOR LEAGUE TOTALS			.253	480	1888	263	478	94	14	23	182	112	257	135	.300	.354

30 LYNDON ESTILL, OF

Born: March 29, 1987. **B-T:** R-R. **Ht.:** 6-3. **Wt.:** 200. **Drafted:** Lower Columbia (Wash.) CC, 2007 (8th round). **Signed by:** Joe Butler/Adam Virchis.

Estill immediately became one of the better athletes in the system when he signed last June for $82,000 as an eight-round pick. He was drawing interest from Pacific-10 Conference football recruiters as a quarterback/safety before an injury in his senior season of high school. He instead spent two years playing baseball in junior college before turning pro. Estill is a potential five-tool player, with speed and power and the ability to play at least an average center field. But he's a project for the organization's hitting coaches, as he can look great in one plate appearance and awful in the next. He has a lot of extraneous movement at the plate and seems to pick up pitches late, leading to an overabundance of strikeouts. The walks he draws are largely from pitchers who work around him after seeing him drive the ball into the gaps or over the fence. He could be headed for an extended-spring assignment in 2008, but could get a crack at low Class A to start the year.

Year	Club (League)	Class	AVG	G	AB	R	H	2B	3B	HR	RBI	BB	SO	SB	OBP	SLG
2007	Great Falls (Pio)	R	.247	54	186	34	46	8	7	7	38	21	84	3	.338	.478
MINOR LEAGUE TOTALS			.247	54	186	34	46	8	7	7	38	21	84	3	.338	.478

Cincinnati Reds

BY J.J. COOPER

I n hindsight, the Reds' success during the first part of the 2006 season was the worst thing that could have happened to them.

A new ownership group led by Bob Castellini took over in January 2006 and hired Wayne Krivsky as general manager a month later. Krivsky quickly went to work fixing a roster with some clear deficiencies, swinging preseason deals for Bronson

Arroyo, Brandon Phillips and David Ross. Those moves helped Cincinnati jump to a 17-8 start that put it atop the National League Central at the end of April, and it appeared that Krivsky had a Midas touch for talent acquisition.

The reality was that the hot start was more a matter of luck than any actual improvement. The Reds were tied for first place in the division as late as Aug. 24, but they collapsed in September and have been trying to live up to unrealistic expectations ever since. Cincinnati finished fifth with a 72-90 record in 2007, and the rotation and bullpen are still as problematic as they were when Krivsky arrived. The Reds have tried to fix the bullpen problem by signing righthander Francisco Cordero to a four-year, $46 million deal. The Reds went into the Winter Meetings looking for rotation help, but left Nashville believing improvement will have to come from within.

After 12 years without a playoff appearance, Reds fans are understandably restless for some signs of success. Krivsky is facing discontent even though the team is actually closer to contending for a prolonged period of time than it has been in years. A farm system that has produced very little over the past decade has four top prospects ready to contribute.

Outfielder Jay Bruce became the first Cincinnati prospect to win Baseball America's Minor League Player of the Year award. He and first baseman Joey Votto should take up residence in the heart of the Reds' batting order in the very near future, while Homer Bailey and Johnny Cueto are the organization's best pair of pitching prospects in several decades.

Behind them, Cincinnati has more depth in its system than it has had in recent years, especially at third base, in the outfield and in the bullpen.

When the Reds' Fab Four make it to the big leagues, they'll join a club that has succeeded in turning other team's castoffs into solid regulars. Picking up Phillips for righthander Jeff Stevens

Second baseman Brandon Phillips has proven to be Wayne Krivsky's best acquisition

TOP 30 PROSPECTS

1. Jay Bruce, of	16. Sean Watson, rhp
2. Homer Bailey, rhp	17. Craig Tatum, c
3. Joey Votto, 1b/of	18. Zack Cozart, ss
4. Johnny Cueto, rhp	19. Paul Janish, ss/2b
5. Drew Stubbs, of	20. Carlos Fisher, rhp
6. Devin Mesoraco, c	21. Travis Wood, lhp
7. Todd Frazier, ss	22. Adam Rosales, 1b/3b
8. Juan Francisco, 3b	23. Brandon Waring, 3b
9. Josh Roenicke, rhp	24. Sam LeCure, rhp
10. Matt Maloney, lhp	25. Jose Castro, ss
11. Kyle Lotzkar, rhp	26. Tyler Pelland, lhp
12. Jared Burton, rhp	27. Chris Dickerson, of
13. Chris Valaika, ss	28. Danny Dorn, of
14. Neftali Soto, ss	29. Justin Turner, 2b/ss
15. Pedro Viola, lhp	30. Sergio Valenzuela, rhp

was a masterstroke, as the young second baseman finally realized his considerable promise with a 30-30 season in 2007.

Cincinnati also poached former No. 1 overall pick Josh Hamilton from the Devil Rays via the major league Rule 5 draft at the 2006 Winter Meetings. Hamilton became one of the stories of the 2007 season with his amazing return from a nearly four-year layoff because of drug suspensions. Another Rule 5 pickup, Jared Burton, has become one of the club's most reliable relievers.

General Manager: Wayne Krivsky. **Farm Director:** Terry Reynolds. **Scouting Director:** Chris Buckley.

Class	Team	League	W	L	PCT	Finish*	Manager	Affiliated
Majors	Cincinnati	National	72	90	.444	13th (16)	J. Narron/P. Mackanin	—
Triple-A	Louisville Bats	International	74	70	.514	7th (14)	Rick Sweet	2000
Double-A	Chattanooga Lookouts	Southern	67	73	.479	7th (10)	Jayhawk Owens	1988
High A	Sarasota Reds	Florida State	81	59	.579	3rd (12)	Joe Ayrault	2005
Low A	Dayton Dragons	Midwest	78	62	.557	6th (14)	Billy Gardner	2000
Rookie	Billings Mustangs	Pioneer	37	38	.493	4th (8)	Joe Krunzel	1974
Rookie	GCL Reds	Gulf Coast	15	41	.268	16th (16)	Pat Kelly	1999

Overall 2007 Minor League Record   352   343   .506   10th
*Finish in overall standings (No. of teams in league) ^League champion

LAST YEAR'S TOP 30

Player, Pos.		Status
1.	Homer Bailey, rhp	No. 2
2.	Jay Bruce, of	No. 1
3.	Joey Votto, 1b	No. 3
4.	Johnny Cueto, rhp	No. 4
5.	Drew Stubbs, of	No. 5
6.	Travis Wood, lhp	No. 21
7.	Sean Watson, rhp	No. 16
8.	Milton Loo, ss	Restricted list
9.	Paul Janish, ss	No. 19
10.	Chris Valaika, ss	No. 13
11.	Cody Strait, of	Dropped out
12.	Sam LeCure, rhp	No. 24
13.	Josh Ravin, rhp	Dropped out
14.	James Avery, rhp	Dropped out
15.	Chris Dickerson, of	No. 27
16.	Phil Dumatrait, lhp	(Pirates)
17.	Tyler Pelland, lhp	No. 26
18.	Daryl Thompson, rhp	Dropped out
19.	Camilio Vazquez, lhp	Dropped out
20.	David Shafer, rhp	(Athletics)
21.	Miguel Perez, c	Dropped out
22.	Jon Coutlangus, lhp	Dropped out
23.	Jordan Smith, rhp	Dropped out
24.	Justin Reed, of	Dropped out
25.	Brad Salmon, rhp	Dropped out
26.	Juan Francisco, 3b	No. 8
27.	Norris Hopper, of	Majors
28.	Rafael Gonzalez, rhp	Dropped out
29.	B.J. Szymanski, of	Dropped out
30.	Josh Hamilton, of	Majors

BEST TOOLS

Best Hitter for Average	Jay Bruce
Best Power Hitter	Jay Bruce
Best Strike-Zone Discipline	Paul Janish
Fastest Baserunner	Chris Dickerson
Best Athlete	Chris Dickerson
Best Fastball	Homer Bailey
Best Curveball	Homer Bailey
Best Slider	Johnny Cueto
Best Changeup	Travis Wood
Best Control	Johnny Cueto
Best Defensive Catcher	Craig Tatum
Best Defensive Infielder	Zach Cozart
Best Infield Arm	Juan Francisco
Best Defensive Outfielder	Drew Stubbs
Best Outfield Arm	Cody Strait

PROJECTED 2011 LINEUP

Catcher	Devin Mesoraco
First Base	Joey Votto
Second Base	Brandon Phillips
Third Base	Todd Frazier
Shortstop	Chris Valaika
Left Field	Adam Dunn
Center Field	Josh Hamilton
Right Field	Jay Bruce
No. 1 Starter	Homer Bailey
No. 2 Starter	Aaron Harang
No. 3 Starter	Johnny Cueto
No. 4 Starter	Bronson Arroyo
No. 5 Starter	Matt Maloney
Closer	Francisco Cordero

TOP PROSPECTS OF THE DECADE

Year	Player, Pos.	2007 Org.
1998	Damian Jackson, ss/2b	Out of baseball
1999	Rob Bell, rhp	Orioles
2000	Gookie Dawkins, ss	Phillies
2001	Austin Kearns, of	Nationals
2002	Austin Kearns, of	Nationals
2003	Chris Gruler, rhp	Out of baseball
2004	Ryan Wagner, rhp	Nationals
2005	Homer Bailey, rhp	Reds
2006	Homer Bailey, rhp	Reds
2007	Homer Bailey, rhp	Reds

TOP DRAFT PICKS OF THE DECADE

Year	Player, Pos.	2007 Org.
1998	Austin Kearns, of	Nationals
1999	Ty Howington, lhp	Out of baseball
2000	David Espinosa, ss	Tigers
2001	*Jeremy Sowers, lhp	Indians
2002	Chris Gruler, rhp	Out of baseball
2003	Ryan Wagner, rhp	Nationals
2004	Homer Bailey, rhp	Reds
2005	Jay Bruce, of	Reds
2006	Drew Stubbs, of	Reds
2007	Devin Mesoraco, c	Reds

*Did not sign.

LARGEST BONUSES IN CLUB HISTORY

Chris Gruler, 2002	$2,500,000
Homer Bailey, 2004	$2,300,000
Drew Stubbs, 2006	$2,000,000
Austin Kearns, 1998	$1,950,000
Jay Bruce, 2005	$1,800,000

CINCINNATI REDS

Top 2008 Rookie: Homer Bailey, rhp. He still has ace stuff and should make everyone forget his first-year struggles in his second shot at the majors.

Breakout Prospect: Kyle Lotzkar, rhp. He already has one of the best fastballs in the system, and both his curveball and changeup are promising.

SOURCE OF TOP 30 TALENT			
Homegrown	25	Acquired	5
College	15	Trades	3
Junior college	0	Rule 5 draft	2
High school	7	Independent leagues	0
Draft-and-follow	0	Free agents/waivers	0
Nondrafted free agents	0		
International	3		

Sleeper: Denis Phipps, of. He's very raw because he has played baseball for only four years, but his tools are exceptional.

Numbers in parentheses indicate prospect rankings.

LF
Danny Dorn (28)
Chris Heisey

CF
Drew Stubbs (5)
Chris Dickerson (27)
Justin Reed
Brandon Menchaca
Sean Henry
B.J. Syzmanski

RF
Jay Bruce (1)
Cody Strait
Denis Phipps
Alexis Oliveras
Brett Bartles

3B
Todd Frazier (7)
Juan Francisco (8)
Neftali Soto (14)
Adam Rosales (22)
Brandon Waring (23)
Michael Griffin

SS
Zack Cozart (18)
Paul Janish (19)
Jose Castro (25)

2B
Chris Valaika (13)
Justin Turner (29)

1B
Joey Votto (3)
Logan Parker

C
Devin Mesoraco (6)
Craig Tatum (17)
Alvin Collina
Jordan Wideman
Eddy Rodriguez

RHP
Starters	Relievers
Homer Bailey (2)	Josh Roenicke (9)
Johnny Cueto (4)	Jared Burton (12)
Kyle Lotzkar (11)	Sean Watson (16)
Sam Lecure (24)	Carlos Fisher (20)
Josh Ravin	Sergio Valenzuela (30)
Daryl Thompson	Ramon Ramirez
Richie Gardner	David Shafer
Jordan Smith	Brad Salmon
Rafael Gonzalez	Scott Carroll
Evan Hildenbrandt	Evan Hildenbrandt
Derrick Conatser	Derrick Lutz
Efrain Rodriguez	Marcus McBeth
Chiu Tzu-Kai	

LHP
Starters	Relievers
Matt Maloney (10)	Pedro Viola (15)
Travis Wood (21)	Tyler Pelland (26)
Camilio Vazquez	Philippe Valiquette
Ben Jukich	Jon Coutlangus
Drew Bowman	Alexander Smit

2007

Best Pro Debut: SS Todd Frazier (1s) ranked as the No. 1 prospect in the Rookie-level Pioneer League where he hit .319/.409/.513, and he added a two-homer game in low Class A. 3B Brandon Waring (7) batted .311 with a Pioneer League-leading 20 homers, including 10 in a 10-game stretch.

Best Athlete: Devin Mesoraco (1) is a rare five-tool catcher. He has plus potential to hit for average and power, plus catch-and-throw skills and average speed. Frazier is a good athlete for a 6-foot-4, 215-pounder, though most scouts think he'll have to move off shortstop.

Best Pure Hitter: Mesoraco, despite his .219 debut in the Gulf Coast League.

Best Power Hitter: Frazier, who owns the Rutgers records for season (22) and career homers (47), has the best current power. He's followed closely by Waring, who set a Southern Conference record with 27 homers this spring.

Fastest Runner: OFs Brendan Menchaca (13) and Alexis Oliveras (9) are plus runners.

Best Defensive Player: Zack Cozart (2) was arguably the best defensive shortstop in college baseball this year, and he has drawn comparisons to Adam Everett for his glovework (high praise) and his bat (not so much).

Best Fastball: RHP Kyle Lotzkar (1s) pitches comfortably from 91-94 mph. RHP Scott Carroll (3), LHP Drew Bowman (5) and RHP Ty Rhoden (22) all top out at 93.

Best Secondary Pitch: RHP Evan Hildenbrandt's (6) tight curveball beats out RHP Heath Honeycutt's (10) changeup.

Most Intriguing Background: Carroll once started at quarterback for Missouri State, while unsigned RHP Jordan Chambless (50, back at Texas A&M) is a former defensive back/punt returner for the Aggies. Frazier started for Toms River's (N.J.) Little League World Series championship team in 1998, and his brothers Jeff (an outfielder in the Mariners system) and Charlie (a retired pitcher) also played pro ball. 3B Drew Benes (47), now at Arkansas State, is the son of former No. 1 overall pick Andy Benes.

Closest To The Majors: The Reds don't want to rush Cozart's bat, but his defense will tempt them to advance him quickly. Conversely, Frazier's offense may be ready before he finds a defensive home.

Best Late-Round Pick: Menchaca. 3B Brett Bartles (30) opened some eyes by batting .322 in his debut. RHP Derrick Conatser (28), a Tommy John surgery survivor, has a solid sinker-slider combination.

The One Who Got Away: 3B/OF Blake Stouffer (4), who offers athleticism and some bat potential, returned to Texas A&M for his senior season.

Assessment: In both of their drafts with Chris Buckley as scouting director, the Reds have spent three of their first four picks on up-the-middle players. While focusing on premium positions, Cincinnati also raked in a lot of power potential this time.

2006

Athletic OF Drew Stubbs (1) made strides with the bat in 2007. RHPs Sean Watson (2) and Josh Roenicke (10) and SS Chris Valaika (3) could beat Stubbs to the majors, while 2B/SS Justin Turner (7) and OF Danny Dorn (32) are sleepers.

GRADE: B

2005

This crop has started to thin out quickly, but that doesn't matter with OF Jay Bruce (1) at the forefront. The Reds have uses four signees as trade fodder, most notably getting Brandon Phillips for RHP Jeff Stevens (6).

GRADE: A

2004

RHP Homer Bailey (1) continues to project as Cincinnati's future ace and flashed that talent in his big league debut last year. C Craig Tatum (3) and SS Paul Janish (5) could be complementary players.

GRADE: B

2003

The Reds once had high hopes for RHPs Ryan Wagner (1/since traded), Thomas Pauly (2) and Richie Gardner (6) before injuries struck. Toolsy but raw OF Chris Dickerson (16) is now the best of this group.

GRADE: F

Draft analysis by Jim Callis. Numbers in parentheses indicate draft rounds. Budgets are bonuses in first 10 rounds.

JAY BRUCE, OF

Born: April 3, 1987.
Ht.: 6-2. **Wt.:** 218.
Bats: L. **Throws:** L.
Drafted: HS—
Beaumont, Texas,
2005 (1st round).
Signed by:
Brian Wilson.

exas has been very good to the Reds. In successive years, they used first-round picks on Lone Star State products Homer Bailey, Bruce and Drew Stubbs, who occupy three of the first five spots on this list. The 12th overall pick in 2005, Bruce signed for $1.8 million and has met every expectation, while drawing comparisons to the likes of Larry Walker, Jeremy Hermida, Jim Edmonds and even Ken Griffey Jr. When he was 9, Bruce called the Seattle Kingdome and asked to speak to Griffey, but he couldn't get past the switchboard operator. Now he has a chance to play beside Griffey in Cincinnati's outfield. After ranking ahead of fellow 2005 first-round picks Cameron Maybin, Colby Rasmus and Justin Upton as the top prospect in the low Class A Midwest League in 2006, Bruce figured to split 2007 between high Class A Sarasota and Double-A Chattanooga. But when he moved up to Triple-A Louisville in July for what was supposed to be a brief injury fill-in, he homered in his first game and never looked back. He finished the season with a .319 average and 80 extra-base hits, and he would have earned a September callup had he been on the 40-man roster. He did travel to Cincinnati to receive Baseball America's Minor League Player of the Year award.

Bruce combines tremendous bat speed with an excellent swing plane. He has a knack for deciphering and correcting flaws in his swing between at-bats and sometimes even between pitches. He has the natural ability to hit for average and power even if he didn't work hard, but he does have the drive of a baseball rat–he's the first person to the ballpark and the last to leave. Every one of Bruce's tools is better than average. On the 20-80 scouting scale, his bat rates as a 65, his power as a 65-70, his speed as a 55, his defense in center field as a 55 (60 if he moves to right field) and his arm as a 60. As impressive as his tools are, he also has exceptional instincts and exceptional makeup. He's a leader in the clubhouse and has the aw-shucks humbleness to be the public face of the franchise.

Bruce has few faults. He strikes out a lot, but the whiffs are an acceptable tradeoff for his production. Some Triple-A teams busted him inside, but that doesn't appear to be a long-term problem. While he's capable of playing center field, he still projects to end up in right as he fills out. Staying in center also might hinder his ability to add the weight that will bring extra home runs in his late 20s. He has enough speed and savvy to steal 15-20 bases a season, but he wasn't aggressive on the bases in 2007.

Bruce is ready for the big leagues, but there isn't a clear spot for him after the Reds picked up Adam Dunn's option. All three of their regular outfielders from 2007 return, so they could let Bruce ripen a little more in Triple-A, especially considering he doesn't have to be protected on the 40-man roster until after the 2009 season.

Year	Club (League)	Class	AVG	G	AB	R	H	2B	3B	HR	RBI	BB	SO	SB	OBP	SLG
2005	Reds (GCL)	R	.270	37	122	29	33	9	2	5	25	11	31	4	.331	.500
	Billings (Pio)	R	.257	17	70	16	18	2	0	4	13	11	22	2	.358	.457
2006	Dayton (MWL)	A	.291	117	444	69	129	42	5	16	81	44	106	19	.355	.516
2007	Sarasota (FSL)	A	.325	67	268	49	87	27	5	11	49	24	67	4	.379	.586
	Chattanooga (SL)	AA	.333	16	66	10	22	7	1	4	15	8	20	2	.405	.652
	Louisville (IL)	AAA	.305	50	187	28	57	12	2	11	25	15	48	2	.358	.567
MINOR LEAGUE TOTALS			.299	304	1157	201	346	99	15	51	208	113	294	33	.362	.543

2 HOMER BAILEY, RHP

Born: May 3, 1986. **B-T:** R-R. **Ht.:** 6-3. **Wt.:** 190. **Drafted:** HS—LaGrange, Texas, 2004 (1st round). **Signed by:** Mike Powers.

No. 1 on this list after his first three seasons in pro ball, Bailey wouldn't have qualified again had a lingering groin injury not sidelined him for most of the second half of 2007. Once he was healthy again in September, Bailey was back throwing in the mid-90s with his fastball and buckling knees with his curveball. They're both already well above-average major league pitches, and he has shown the ability to take a little off his heater. He's also added a high-80s cutter to give him a pitch with more lateral movement. Bailey has no shortage of pure stuff, but he still has to refine his control and command to get big league hitters out and to work deeper into games. He threw strikes on only 58 percent of pitches in the majors. His changeup is still below average. The groin injury meant that his route to the front end of Cincinnati's rotation was delayed by a year. Bailey has all the ingredients to become the Reds' first homegrown ace since Mario Soto.

Year	Club (League)	Class	W	L	ERA	G	GS	CG	SV	IP	H	R	ER	HR	BB	SO	AVG
2004	Reds (GCL)	R	0	1	4.38	6	3	0	0	12	14	7	6	0	3	9	.275
2005	Dayton (MWL)	A	8	4	4.43	28	21	0	0	103	89	64	51	5	62	125	.232
2006	Sarasota (FSL)	A	3	5	3.31	13	13	0	0	70	49	35	26	6	22	79	.189
	Chattanooga (SL)	AA	7	1	1.59	13	13	0	0	68	50	13	12	1	28	77	.208
2007	Louisville (IL)	AAA	6	3	3.07	12	12	0	0	67	49	29	23	4	32	59	.204
	Sarasota (FSL)	A	0	1	10.13	2	2	0	0	8	15	9	9	2	5	7	.385
	Cincinnati (NL)	MLB	4	2	5.76	9	9	0	0	45	43	32	29	3	28	28	.257
MINOR LEAGUE TOTALS			24	15	3.46	74	64	0	0	330	266	157	127	18	152	356	.219
MAJOR LEAGUE TOTALS			4	2	5.76	9	9	0	0	45	43	32	29	3	28	28	.257

3 JOEY VOTTO, 1B/OF

Born: Sept. 10, 1983. **B-T:** L-L. **Ht.:** 6-3. **Wt.:** 200. **Drafted:** HS—Toronto, 2002 (2nd round). **Signed by:** John Castleberry.

Votto was the Double-A Southern League's MVP in 2006 and the Triple-A International League's rookie of the year in 2007. He didn't watch any Reds games or highlights in 2007 because he vowed to see the Great American Ballpark in person by earning a promotion, then went 3-for-3 with a homer in his first big league start in September. Votto has turned himself into a tough out. He uses the entire field, has natural power to both power alleys and has developed a feel for the strike zone that allows him to lay off pitches off the plate. He makes good adjustments, which allowed him to fix his swing after he hit .197 in April. He shortened his stroke and closed off some holes. He projects as a .270-280 hitter with 25 home runs. Votto does most of his damage against righthanders, but he has been decent against lefties. His speed is slightly below average. Though Votto has done everything he can in the minors, the Reds picked up the 2008 option on starting first baseman Scott Hatteberg. Votto will challenge for Hatteberg's job in spring training.

Year	Club (League)	Class	AVG	G	AB	R	H	2B	3B	HR	RBI	BB	SO	SB	OBP	SLG
2002	Reds (GCL)	R	.269	50	175	29	47	13	3	9	33	21	45	7	.342	.531
2003	Dayton (MWL)	A	.231	60	195	19	45	8	0	1	20	34	64	2	.348	.287
	Billings (Pio)	R	.317	70	240	47	76	17	3	6	38	56	80	4	.452	.488
2004	Dayton (MWL)	A	.302	111	391	60	118	26	2	14	72	79	110	9	.419	.486
	Potomac (Car)	A	.298	24	84	11	25	7	0	5	20	11	21	1	.385	.560
2005	Sarasota (FSL)	A	.256	124	464	64	119	23	2	17	83	52	122	4	.330	.425
2006	Chattanooga (SL)	AA	.319	136	508	85	162	46	2	22	77	78	109	24	.408	.547
2007	Louisville (IL)	AAA	.294	133	496	74	146	21	2	22	92	70	110	17	.381	.478
	Cincinnati (NL)	MLB	.321	24	84	11	27	7	0	4	17	5	15	1	.360	.548
MINOR LEAGUE TOTALS			.289	708	2553	389	738	161	14	96	435	401	661	68	.385	.476
MAJOR LEAGUE TOTALS			.321	24	84	11	27	7	0	4	17	5	15	1	.360	.548

4 JOHNNY CUETO, RHP

Born: Feb. 15, 1986. **B-T:** R-R. **Ht.:** 5-10. **Wt.:** 192. **Signed:** Dominican Republic, 2004. **Signed by:** Johnny Almaraz.

Cueto was the first player signed out of the Dominican Republic after Cincinnati reworked its international scouting department in 2004. Thanks in part to working with former Reds star Mario Soto, Cueto hasn't taken long to become one of the system's gems. Cueto pitches like a 10-year major league veteran, not a fresh-faced 21-year-old. He features a 93-94 mph fastball that touches 96, a tight 83-88 mph slider and a solid changeup that he learned from Soto. His makeup is impeccable, which

STAN DENNY

is why the Reds have felt comfortable keeping him on the fast track. Cueto has above-average control but he sometimes struggles with command in the strike zone. He found in his brief exposure to Triple-A that more advanced hitters will punish pitches up in the strike zone, even 94-mph fastballs. The Reds plan on acquiring a veteran starter this offseason, which would leave Cueto without a clear spot in the rotation. He could bide his time waiting for an opening by helping out the Cincinnati bullpen.

Year	Club (League)	Class	W	L	ERA	G	GS	CG	SV	IP	H	R	ER	HR	BB	SO	AVG
2004	Reds (DSL)	R	3	6	2.58	18	10	0	0	76	66	35	22	2	26	69	.222
2005	Reds (GCL)	R	2	2	5.02	13	6	0	1	43	49	31	24	2	8	38	.285
	Sarasota (FSL)	A	0	1	3.00	2	1	0	0	6	5	2	2	0	2	6	.217
2006	Dayton (MWL)	A	8	1	2.59	14	14	2	0	76	52	22	22	5	15	82	.191
	Sarasota (FSL)	A	7	2	3.50	12	12	1	0	61	48	25	24	6	23	61	.214
2007	Sarasota (FSL)	A	4	5	3.33	14	14	1	0	78	72	34	29	3	21	72	.238
	Louisville (IL)	AAA	2	1	2.05	4	4	0	0	22	22	5	5	2	2	21	.259
	Chattanooga (SL)	AA	6	3	3.10	10	10	0	0	61	52	24	21	6	11	77	.231
MINOR LEAGUE TOTALS			32	21	3.16	87	71	4	1	425	366	178	149	26	108	426	.229

5 DREW STUBBS, OF

RODGER WOOD

Born: Oct. 4, 1984. **B-T:** R-R. **Ht.:** 6-5. **Wt.:** 190. **Drafted:** Texas, 2006 (1st round). **Signed by:** Brian Wilson.

After winning a College World Series championship at Texas, Stubbs went eighth overall in the 2006 draft and signed for $2 million. Stubbs' athleticism jumps out at first glance. He combines plus raw power with a gliding stride that swallows up giant swaths of real estate in the outfield. Though his speed was limited in 2007 by a nagging turf-toe injury, he's a plus-plus runner when healthy and has excellent instincts on the basepaths. For a college product, Stubbs still has an extremely raw bat, which explains why the Reds left him at low Class A Dayton all season. He never has made consistent contact and he has struck out 206 times in 185 pro games. A late-season switch to choking up on the bat gave him better bat control. He fanned just twice in his first 42 at-bats after the switch and hit .366 with four homers in 24 games after the adjustment. If Stubbs' improvement was for real, he has a chance to be a superstar because his power, speed and defense are all above-average. If he continues to strike out, he still should be a big leaguer, albeit with a lower ceiling and average. He'll open 2008 in high Class A.

Year	Club (League)	Class	AVG	G	AB	R	H	2B	3B	HR	RBI	BB	SO	SB	OBP	SLG
2006	Billings (Pio)	R	.252	56	210	39	53	7	3	6	24	32	64	19	.368	.400
2007	Dayton (MWL)	A	.270	129	497	93	134	29	5	12	43	69	142	23	.364	.421
MINOR LEAGUE TOTALS			.264	185	707	132	187	36	8	18	67	101	206	42	.365	.414

6 DEVIN MESORACO, C

Born: June 19, 1988. **B-T:** R-R. **Ht.:** 6-1. **Wt.:** 195. **Drafted:** HS—Punxsutawney, Pa., 2007 (1st round). **Signed by:** Lee Seras.

Limited to DH duty in 2006 while recovering from Tommy John surgery, Mesoraco flew up teams' draft boards with an outstanding senior year that culminated in Punxsutawney Area High's first-ever Pennsylvania state title. It's a stretch to call Mesoraco a five-tool player, but he stands out as a catcher who doesn't have a below-average tool. He has the bat speed to hit for average and power. He used his plus-plus arm to throw out 33 percent of basestealers in his pro debut, and he also has soft hands and good footwork. He won't be a stolen-base threat, but he does have average speed. He's a leader on the field. Mesoraco showed a tendency to pull off the ball in his pro debut, when he seemed to press after he got off to a bad start. Despite his struggles, the Reds aren't concerned that it was anything more than a rough introduction to pro ball. Injuries to both thumbs didn't help his cause and limited him to 28 games behind the plate. Cincinnati doesn't plan on rushing Mesoraco, a potential all-star. He'll get every opportunity to earn a spot in low Class A Dayton, but he coud begin the season in extended spring training.

Year	Club (League)	Class	AVG	G	AB	R	H	2B	3B	HR	RBI	BB	SO	SB	OBP	SLG
2007	Reds (GCL)	R	.219	40	137	16	30	4	0	1	8	15	26	2	.310	.270
MINOR LEAGUE TOTALS			.219	40	137	16	30	4	0	1	8	15	26	2	.310	.270

7 TODD FRAZIER, SS

R. DEAN HENDRICKSON

Born: Feb. 12, 1986. **B-T:** R-R. **Ht.:** 6-3. **Wt.:** 215. **Drafted:** Rutgers, 2007 (1st round supplemental). **Signed by:** Jeff Brookens.

Frazier comes from a successful baseball family (older brothers Jeff and Charlie both were drafted) and first made a name for himself by homering in each of the final three games of the 1998 Little League World Series to lead Toms River, N.J., to the title. A supplemental first-round pick in June, he signed for $825,000 and ranked as the No. 1 prospect in the Rookie-level Pioneer League. Frazier has above-average raw power, and if he can make some tweaks to his swing, he has the size and strength to hit 20-25 home runs per year. His drive to succeed and his instincts have allowed him to exceed expectations wherever he's played. Frazier could quicken his path to the ball if he quieted his hands, leading to concerns about his swing, and he also could use his legs more. Scouts give him little chance to stay at shortstop because he lacks the first-step quickness, range and actions for the position. The Reds like prospects to play their way off a position, so Frazier will remain at shortstop in 2008. With his advanced pedigree, he should be able to handle high Class A in his first full pro season.

Year	Club (League)	Class	AVG	G	AB	R	H	2B	3B	HR	RBI	BB	SO	SB	OBP	SLG
2007	Billings (Pio)	R	.319	41	160	29	51	6	5	5	25	18	22	3	.409	.513
	Dayton (MWL)	A	.318	6	22	4	7	3	0	2	5	2	4	0	.375	.727
MINOR LEAGUE TOTALS			.319	47	182	33	58	9	5	7	30	20	26	3	.405	.538

8 JUAN FRANCISCO, 3B

DAN ARNOLD

Born: June 24, 1987. **B-T:** L-R. **Ht.:** 6-2. **Wt.:** 180. **Signed:** Dominican Republic, 2004. **Signed by:** Juan Peralta.

One of the products of the Reds' renewed emphasis in pursuing Latin American talent, Francisco led the Midwest League with 25 homers. A temporary requirement that he choke up on the bat helped improve his bat control, and he hit 10 homers in the final month. Francisco has long arms that generate exceptional leverage and raw power that compares with that of Jay Bruce and Joey Votto. He also has the system's best infield arm, a cannon that allows him to turn infield hits into outs. He also has good first-step quickness and is an average to slightly above-average runner. When pitchers don't challenge Francisco, he's so aggressive that he'll get himself out by chasing pitches out of the zone. He'll have to cut down on his strikeouts to keep his average up as he faces more advanced pitching. As he fills out, he'll lose some of his speed and will have to watch his weight if he's to remain at third base. Francisco is developing nicely and will head to high Class A at age 20. The Reds are shaping up to have a logjam at the hot corner, with Edwin Encarnacion in the majors and Todd Frazier, Francisco and Pioneer League home run champ Brandon Waring in the minors.

Year	Club (League)	Class	AVG	G	AB	R	H	2B	3B	HR	RBI	BB	SO	SB	OBP	SLG
2006	Reds (GCL)	R	.280	45	182	24	51	14	0	3	30	6	35	2	.305	.407
	Billings (Pio)	R	.333	9	36	6	12	3	0	0	2	0	8	2	.333	.417
2007	Dayton (MWL)	A	.268	135	534	69	143	21	4	25	90	23	161	12	.301	.463
MINOR LEAGUE TOTALS			.274	189	752	99	206	38	4	28	122	29	204	16	.303	.447

9 JOSH ROENICKE, RHP

Born: Aug. 4, 1982. **B-T:** R-R. **Ht.:** 6-3. **Wt.:** 195. **Drafted:** UCLA, 2006 (10th round). **Signed by:** Rex de la Nuez.

Roenicke originally went to UCLA as a wide receiver, but after failing to catch a pass in two seasons he chose to emulate his father Gary and uncle Ron, former major league outfielders. After signing for $20,000, Roenicke has flown through the system, reaching Double-A in his first full pro season. Roenicke dominates hitters with a live 93-95 mph fastball that he'll run up to 98 mph on occasion. His fastball has late movement that adds to its effectiveness. He pairs it with an 87-89 mph cutter that has so much action that one opposing manager described it as a splitter. He's an excellent athlete and has the fearless approach to close games. As expected from a recently converted outfielder, Roenicke is still an unpolished pitcher. His control is just adequate and he'll have to sharpen his command before he makes it to the big leagues. He's still learning about setting up batters and proper pitch selection. He's already 25, but Roenicke is making up for a lot of lost time with his rapid rise. He could be in Cincinnati by September and should be at least a big league set-up man with a chance to develop into a closer.

Year	Club (League)	Class	W	L	ERA	G	GS	CG	SV	IP	H	R	ER	HR	BB	SO	AVG
2006	Reds (GCL)	R	1	0	1.17	7	0	0	0	7	8	2	1	0	3	9	.258
	Billings (Pio)	R	1	0	6.32	14	0	0	6	15	10	11	11	1	12	24	.179
2007	Sarasota (FSL)	A	2	1	3.25	27	0	0	16	27	23	10	10	1	15	41	.225
	Chattanooga (SL)	AA	1	1	0.95	19	0	0	8	19	12	3	2	0	6	15	.185
MINOR LEAGUE TOTALS			5	2	3.09	67	0	0	30	70	53	26	24	2	36	89	.209

10 MATT MALONEY, LHP

Born: Jan. 16, 1984. **B-T:** L-R. **Ht.:** 6-4. **Wt.:** 220. **Drafted:** Mississippi, 2005 (3rd round). **Signed by:** Mike Stauffer (Phillies).

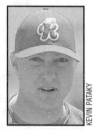

After acquiring Kyle Lohse for the 2006 stretch drive, the Reds sent him to the Phillies last July in exchange for Maloney, who immediately became the system's top lefthander. The deal seemed to energize him, as he struck out 62 in 45 innings afterward. Maloney is the typical crafty lefty who knows how to pitch. His 87-91 mph fastball has enough sink to keep hitters honest, especially since he combines it with a plus changeup and a slightly above-average slider. He does a good job of pitching downhill and keeps hitters off balance with his outstanding feel for pitching. He has solid command to both sides of the plate. Though he hit 92-93 mph in college, Maloney's fastball straightens out and his command suffers when he tries to muscle up to that kind of velocity now. As a lefty who's around the plate without overwhelming stuff, he's prone to giving up longballs. Maloney is nearly ready for the big leagues but lacks much upside, profiling as a back-of-the-rotation starter.

Year	Club (League)	Class	W	L	ERA	G	GS	CG	SV	IP	H	R	ER	HR	BB	SO	AVG
2005	Batavia (NYP)	A	2	1	3.89	8	8	0	0	37	38	20	16	2	15	36	.277
2006	Lakewood (SAL)	A	16	9	2.03	27	27	2	0	168	120	54	38	5	73	180	.194
2007	Reading (EL)	AA	9	7	3.94	21	21	1	0	125	117	70	55	13	45	115	.246
	Chattanooga (SL)	AA	2	2	2.57	4	4	0	0	28	17	9	8	4	3	39	.175
	Louisville (IL)	AAA	2	1	3.18	3	3	0	0	17	10	6	6	2	6	23	.169
MINOR LEAGUE TOTALS			31	20	2.94	63	63	3	0	376	302	159	123	26	142	393	.218

11 KYLE LOTZKAR, RHP

Born: Nov. 24, 1989. **B-T:** L-R. **Ht.:** 6-4. **Wt.:** 200. **Drafted:** HS—Delta, B.C., 2007 (1st round supplemental). **Signed by:** Bill Byckowski.

Lotzkar was one of the biggest risers in the 2007 draft, climbing draft boards after adding 15 pounds of muscle before his senior season. He showed off his improved physique with a fastball that touched 96 mph against Cuba in the World Junior Championships in the fall of 2006, and also was impressive while touring with a Canadian team in April. When he pitched well in front of several scouts in Florida, he became a possible first-rounder, then cooled off a little and went 53rd overall, signing for $594,000. Lotzkar maintained his stuff in the humidity of the Rookie-level Gulf Coast League, showing a 91-94 mph fastball, a potential plus changeup and a promising 78-82 mph curveball. Lotzkar's feel for pitching was surprising considering his youth and his relative inexperience. He sometimes struggles to command his stuff partly because it has outstanding life. He's a long ways from the big leagues, but Lotzkar's stuff, frame and pitchability give the Reds reason to believe he could develop into a middle-of-the-rotation starter. He'll likely start 2008 in low Class A.

Year	Club (League)	Class	W	L	ERA	G	GS	CG	SV	IP	H	R	ER	HR	BB	SO	AVG
2007	Reds (GCL)	R	0	2	3.86	7	7	0	0	21	21	10	9	2	7	24	.263
	Billings (Pio)	R	0	0	1.13	2	2	0	0	8	1	1	1	1	3	12	.040
MINOR LEAGUE TOTALS			0	2	3.10	9	9	0	0	29	22	11	10	3	10	36	.210

12 JARED BURTON, RHP

Born: June 2, 1981. **B-T:** R-R. **Ht.:** 6-5. **Wt.:** 230. **Drafted:** Western Carolina, 2002 (8th round). **Signed by:** Kelly Heath (Athletics).

After seeing him in the Arizona Fall League in 2006, the Reds were thrilled to get the chance to pick up Burton in the major league Rule 5 draft. He may not be as big a coup as fellow Rule 5 pickup Josh Hamilton, but Burton also proved to be an outstanding addition. He walked all three batters he faced in his major league debut and missed time early in the season with back and hamstring problems. But once he settled down, he became Cincinnati's most reliable set-up man. Burton pairs a 93-96 mph fastball with a hard 86-89 mph slider. He has thrown a changeup in the past, but as a one-inning reliever he's most effective when he sticks with his power stuff. His command is still somewhat shaky, and he sometimes has trouble finding his release point. Nevertheless, Burton has the stuff and composure to continue to provide reliable relief.

Year	Club (League)	Class	W	L	ERA	G	GS	CG	SV	IP	H	R	ER	HR	BB	SO	AVG
2002	Vancouver (NWL)	A	0	4	3.58	13	5	0	1	37	32	22	15	0	14	38	.221
2003	Kane County (MWL)	A	2	1	2.27	15	2	0	1	31	19	9	8	2	7	33	.174
2004	Athletics (AZL)	R	1	0	4.15	5	5	0	0	21	21	12	10	2	4	15	.247
	Modesto (Cal)	A	3	2	4.78	10	3	0	0	32	34	19	17	6	20	25	.270
2005	Stockton (Cal)	A	4	4	2.60	52	0	0	24	55	44	21	16	2	20	67	.212
2006	Midland (TL)	AA	6	5	4.14	53	0	0	1	74	71	36	34	7	27	66	.255
2007	Chattanooga (SL)	AA	0	1	11.81	4	0	0	0	5	10	7	7	0	5	3	.400
	Louisville (IL)	AAA	1	0	0.64	10	0	0	1	14	11	1	1	0	4	13	.224
	Cincinnati (NL)	MLB	4	2	2.51	47	0	0	0	43	28	15	12	2	22	36	.187
MINOR LEAGUE TOTALS			17	17	3.58	162	15	0	28	271	242	127	108	19	101	260	.236
MAJOR LEAGUE TOTALS			4	2	2.51	47	0	0	0	43	28	15	12	2	22	36	.187

13 CHRIS VALAIKA, SS

Born: Oct. 14, 1985. **B-T:** R-R. **Ht.:** 6-1. **Wt.:** 180. **Drafted:** UC Santa Barbara, 2006 (3rd round). **Signed by:** Rex de la Nuez.

Like fellow 2006 draftees Drew Stubbs, Justin Turner and Danny Dorn, Valaika was a college product with a long track record of success against high-level competition. He was an honorable-mention selection for the top 15-year-old player in the nation in Baseball America's Baseball for the Ages feature and was a fixture on USA Baseball teams for years. He has bounced back from a torn elbow ligament during his freshman year in high school and a blown anterior cruciate ligament during his sophomore season at UC Santa Barbara. Valaika stands out most for his bat and his makeup. He has slightly above-average hitting skills and power. He'll need to tighten his strike zone against more advanced pitching, but the bigger question is his defense. A tick below-average runner, he lacks the range to be a full-time shortstop in the majors, though he could fill in there. He moved over to second base while playing in Hawaii Winter Baseball and showed aptitude for the position. His average arm plays well at second base, while his feet and pivot are quick enough to get the job done. He has some previous experience at the position, as he was named the all-star second baseman at the 2001 World Youth Championships. Valaika's bat should pave his way to the big leagues, where he profiles as an offensive second baseman or utilityman. His performance in spring training and the Reds' decision on what position to play him at in 2008 will determine whether he returns to high Class A or advances to Double-A.

Year	Club (League)	Class	AVG	G	AB	R	H	2B	3B	HR	RBI	BB	SO	SB	OBP	SLG
2006	Billings (Pio)	R	.324	70	275	58	89	22	4	8	60	24	61	2	.387	.520
2007	Dayton (MWL)	A	.307	79	300	38	92	20	3	10	56	17	72	1	.353	.493
	Sarasota (FSL)	A	.253	57	217	26	55	9	1	2	23	13	42	0	.310	.332
MINOR LEAGUE TOTALS			.298	206	792	122	236	51	8	20	139	54	175	3	.353	.458

14 NEFTALI SOTO, SS

Born: Feb. 28, 1989. **B-T:** R-R. **Ht.:** 6-2. **Wt.:** 180. **Drafted:** HS—Manati, P.R., 2007 (3rd round). **Signed by:** Tony Arias.

Soto broke Juan Gonzalez' youth home run record in Puerto Rico, and he showed off his power potential during his pro debut. Scouts considered his bat relatively polished for a Puerto Rican high schooler, and he showed that by displaying the ability to work counts to go along with excellent hand-eye coordination. He has above-average bat speed to go with a smooth stroke and should develop into a 25-30 homer threat as he fills out and matures. Soto will stick at shortstop until he proves he can't play the position, but it's hard to find anyone who believes he won't have to move. He's an average runner at best, and as he matures, he'll likely outgrow the position. His average arm might be enough to allow him to slide over to third base, but if not, his bat has enough potential to allow him to be a corner outfielder. In that way, he's much like Reds first-rounder Todd Frazier. Soto may be able to handle a jump to low Class A this season.

Year	Club (League)	Class	AVG	G	AB	R	H	2B	3B	HR	RBI	BB	SO	SB	OBP	SLG
2007	Reds (GCL)	R	.303	40	152	18	46	7	5	2	28	11	31	2	.355	.454
MINOR LEAGUE TOTALS			.303	40	152	18	46	7	5	2	28	11	31	2	.355	.454

15 PEDRO VIOLA, LHP

Born: June 29, 1983. **B-T:** R-L. **Ht.:** 6-1. **Wt.:** 185. **Signed:** Dominican Republic, 2005. **Signed by:** Luis Baez/Maximo Rombley.

Viola took a long and winding road to prospectdom. He originally used a cousin's birth certificate to shave three years off his age when he originally signed for $20,000 as an outfielder with the Giants, but they released him after discovering his subterfuge. The Reds subsequently signed him for $1,000 as a 22-year-old lefthander and quickly discovered they had nabbed an intriguing arm. Because he's older, Cincinnati was aggressive in promoting Viola during his U.S. debut in 2007, and he rocketed all the way to Double-A while posting a 1.42 ERA. His calling card is a 92-95 mph fastball with some life, and he complements it with an average slider and fringy changeup. He was especially nasty against lefties last year, holding them to a .167 average with 45 strikeouts in 107 at-bats, and righties weren't much more successful. Viola did show signs of fatigue in the Arizona Fall League and he sometimes drops down and struggles to maintain his release point, but he established himself as a promising reliever who isn't that far away from the big leagues. If he were younger he would get a shot as a starter, because he has three pitches and a solid frame, but the Reds are going to move him quickly as a reliever. He could open 2008 in Triple-A and make his major league debut later in the year.

Year	Club (League)	Class	W	L	ERA	G	GS	CG	SV	IP	H	R	ER	HR	BB	SO	AVG
2006	Reds (DSL)	R	3	5	2.04	15	12	0	0	61	50	25	14	0	20	77	.214
2007	Dayton (MWL)	A	3	1	1.87	22	0	0	2	43	29	14	9	3	17	49	.190
	Sarasota (FSL)	A	0	1	0.90	10	0	0	2	20	14	2	2	0	7	28	.187
	Chattanooga (SL)	AA	0	0	0.95	14	0	0	2	19	12	3	2	2	6	17	.176
MINOR LEAGUE TOTALS			6	7	1.69	61	12	0	6	144	105	44	27	5	50	171	.198

16 SEAN WATSON, RHP

Born: July 24, 1985. **B-T:** R-R. **Ht.:** 6-3. **Wt.:** 215. **Drafted:** Tennessee, 2006 (2nd round). **Signed by:** Perry Smith.

Watson had top-five-round talent coming out of high school, but concerns about his signability and his makeup caused him to slip to the 21st round. He turned down the Giants to attend Tennessee, where he began his career as a weekend starter and ended it as the team's closer. After drafting him in the second round, the Reds have moved him back into the rotation, though he still projects as a reliever in the big leagues. Watson's fastball sat at 89-92 mph last season when he was a starter, though he added 2 mph when he worked out of the bullpen late in the year to keep his innings down. He showed improved command of his heavy fastball to both sides of the plate. His knuckle-curve was his calling card in college, but he struggled with the feel of it in 2007 and largely junked it in favor of an average slider. He also throws a fringy changeup. Watson's biggest concern is his body. He has a tendency to put on weight and needs to take a more professional attitude and stay in shape. Because of his weight issues, he has a tendency to wear down. Cincinnati has to decide how long it wants to leave him in the rotation. He'll move quicker once he moves to the bullpen for good, and could start the season in Double-A and possibly finish it in the majors if that shift comes in 2008.

Year	Club (League)	Class	W	L	ERA	G	GS	CG	SV	IP	H	R	ER	HR	BB	SO	AVG
2006	Billings (Pio)	R	0	0	1.52	7	4	0	1	23	16	7	4	0	5	19	.190
	Dayton (MWL)	A	1	2	8.59	10	0	0	0	14	22	14	14	2	5	16	.349
2007	Dayton (MWL)	A	5	2	1.88	13	13	0	0	71	58	20	15	7	13	85	.226
	Sarasota (FSL)	A	4	4	5.43	14	10	0	0	54	54	34	33	8	21	50	.257
MINOR LEAGUE TOTALS			10	8	3.61	44	27	0	1	164	150	75	66	17	44	170	.244

17 CRAIG TATUM, C

Born: March 18, 1983. **B-T:** R-R. **Ht.:** 6-0. **Wt.:** 220. **Drafted:** Mississippi State, 2004 (3rd round). **Signed by:** Jerry Flowers.

Tatum's career hit a detour in his first full pro season in 2005, when he went down with an elbow injury that required Tommy John surgery. But he regained his prospect status with a strong 2007 season that carried over into a solid Arizona Fall League performance. The Reds always have liked Tatum's defensive work. He has soft hands, blocks balls in the dirt and handles pitchers well. His arm has bounced back fully from elbow reconstruction, as he was ripping off 1.90-1.95 second pop times again and threw out 32 percent of basestealers last season. Cincinnati believes his defense will be enough to earn him a backup big league job, and his bat will determine whether he can play a larger role. Tatum has a short, quick swing and does a good job of using the entire field, which should allow him to hit for average, but he doesn't have much power potential. He's a well below-average runner. Tatum struggled in a late-season promotion to Double-A, so he'll likely return to Chattanooga to see if he can build off his AFL stint.

Year	Club (League)	Class	AVG	G	AB	R	H	2B	3B	HR	RBI	BB	SO	SB	OBP	SLG
2004	Billings (Pio)	R	.221	42	149	19	33	8	3	2	21	21	36	2	.322	.356
2005	Dayton (MWL)	A	.188	37	128	16	24	7	1	1	12	21	30	0	.311	.281
2006	Dayton (MWL)	A	.277	98	343	41	95	21	0	8	37	32	70	3	.344	.408
2007	Sarasota (FSL)	A	.320	58	219	29	70	15	0	10	39	9	41	0	.348	.525
	Chattanooga (SL)	AA	.231	46	173	21	40	10	1	2	22	17	49	0	.299	.335
MINOR LEAGUE TOTALS			.259	281	1012	126	262	61	5	23	131	100	226	5	.329	.397

18 ZACK COZART, SS

Born: Aug. 12, 1985. **B-T:** R-R. **Ht.:** 6-1. **Wt.:** 185. **Drafted:** Mississippi, 2007 (2nd round). **Signed by:** Jerry Flowers.

Cozart could stake a claim to being the best defensive shortstop in college baseball last spring, and after he signed for $407,250 as a second-round pick, he became the best the system has had since the days of Gookie Dawkins. But as there were with Dawkins, there are plenty of questions about Cozart's bat. His pull-happy approach doesn't fit well with his below-average power. He has a tick above-average speed and would be better served if he stopped looking to yank everything and used the entire field. He'll have to make adjustments, as he's easy meat for good pitching right now and has a tendency to chase pitches off the plate. Defensively, he's already an excellent shortstop with fluid actions, soft hands and a quick first step. As a heady baseball rat with good instincts, he fits the profile of many other recent Reds draftees. He's also durable, as he never missed a game during his three years at Mississippi. Cincinnati believes his bat will catch up to his glove, and he'll get a second chance in low Class A to get comfortable at the plate.

Year	Club (League)	Class	AVG	G	AB	R	H	2B	3B	HR	RBI	BB	SO	SB	OBP	SLG
2007	Dayton (MWL)	A	.239	53	184	28	44	7	2	2	18	11	36	3	.288	.332
MINOR LEAGUE TOTALS			.239	53	184	28	44	7	2	2	18	11	36	3	.288	.332

19 PAUL JANISH, SS/2B

Born: Oct. 12, 1982. **B-T:** R-R. **Ht.:** 6-2. **Wt.:** 190. **Drafted:** Rice, 2004 (5th round). **Signed by:** Mike Powers.

Janish was the system's best defensive shortstop from the day he signed in 2004 until Zach Cozart joined the organization last June. As with Cozart, no one questions Janish's glove, yet questions about his bat have followed him since he turned pro. He was supposed to spend 2007 in Double-A, but injuries led to a July promotion to Triple-A, where he looked over-matched. His 14 homers the season before were an aberration, as he doesn't profile as anything more than a contact hitter at best. His strikeout rate rose last year, and he also looked helpless against righthanders, batting just .204 against them. He does draw some walks and can steal an occasional base with his savvy and average speed. Janish has only average first-step quickness and range, but he plays well at shortstop because he almost never takes a false step, reads balls off the bat, has solid footwork and uses his plus arm well. In addition to above-average pure arm strength—he has made a full recovery from Tommy John surgery in 2005—he has a quick release and good accuracy. But his defensive prowess will go for naught if he can't improve offensively. He figures to return to Double-A in an attempt to get his bat going.

Year	Club (League)	Class	AVG	G	AB	R	H	2B	3B	HR	RBI	BB	SO	SB	OBP	SLG
2004	Billings (Pio)	R	.263	66	205	39	54	11	0	2	22	45	45	7	.406	.346
2005	Dayton (MWL)	A	.245	55	208	30	51	10	2	5	29	29	38	5	.346	.385
2006	Dayton (MWL)	A	.398	26	98	19	39	6	0	5	18	7	10	0	.435	.612
	Sarasota (FSL)	A	.278	91	335	53	93	17	2	9	55	38	39	8	.355	.421
	Chattanooga (SL)	AA	.267	4	15	1	4	1	0	0	2	1	5	0	.313	.333
2007	Chattanooga (SL)	AA	.244	88	324	46	79	21	2	1	20	50	54	10	.358	.330
	Louisville (IL)	AAA	.221	55	199	20	44	8	1	3	19	14	31	2	.278	.317
MINOR LEAGUE TOTALS			.263	385	1384	208	364	74	7	25	165	184	222	32	.357	.381

20 CARLOS FISHER, RHP

Born: Feb. 22, 1983. **B-T:** R-R. **Ht.:** 6-3. **Wt.:** 210. **Drafted:** Lewis-Clark State (Idaho), 2005 (11th round). **Signed by:** Howard Bowens.

As a high school outfielder, Fisher went to the Padres in the 15th round of the 2001 draft. He opted for college, and after realizing he couldn't hit pitching at that level, he moved to the mound as a sophomore at Citrus (Calif.) JC to take advantage of his above-average arm. The Reds signed him as an 11th-rounder in 2005 after he spent two years at NAIA power Lewis-Clark State (Idaho). When he's on, Fisher's 90-93 mph heavy sinker and cutter are enough to completely handcuff hitters. He knows how to work down in the zone and induces plenty of grounders. Though he has worked primarily as a starter in his three pro seasons, Fisher's high-effort delivery and arm action are better suited for relief. He wore out in the second half of 2007, posting a 1.58 ERA through his first 14 starts and a 6.14 ERA in his final 14. Coming out of the pen, Fisher could simplify his repertoire and junk his fringy changeup. He'd also probably add 2-3 mph to his fastball. He'll return to Double-A this year.

Year	Club (League)	Class	W	L	ERA	G	GS	CG	SV	IP	H	R	ER	HR	BB	SO	AVG
2005	Billings (Pio)	R	4	4	4.19	15	8	0	1	53	56	30	25	3	19	45	.268
2006	Dayton (MWL)	A	12	5	2.76	27	27	0	0	150	133	53	46	5	38	122	.237
2007	Sarasota (FSL)	A	4	1	2.20	7	7	0	0	41	34	12	10	1	7	41	.221
	Chattanooga (SL)	AA	5	9	4.29	21	21	0	0	113	127	61	54	11	42	94	.291
MINOR LEAGUE TOTALS			25	19	3.39	70	63	0	1	358	350	156	135	20	106	302	.257

21 TRAVIS WOOD, LHP

Born: Feb. 6, 1987. **B-T:** R-L. **Ht.:** 6-0. **Wt.:** 165. **Drafted:** HS—Alexander, Ark., 2005 (2nd round). **Signed by:** Mike Keenan.

Wood has been one of the system's most polished young pitchers from the day he signed for $600,000, but with every year there are more concerns as to whether he'll ever develop the stuff to complement his outstanding changeup. He has a small, skinny frame, and he battled shoulder problems that dropped his fastball into the mid-80s for much of 2007. Even at his best, Wood walks a tightrope. His fastball, which touched 94-95 mph just before the 2005 draft, is now fringe-average at 88-91 mph when he's healthy. He bounced back to that range during instructional league. If he can just maintain that velocity, he could be a big leaguer, because his changeup is still a plus-plus pitch with excellent deception, consistent arm speed and sink that can induce strikeouts or groundouts. His curveball still hasn't developed into an average pitch, which is another worry. After a lost season, he'll try to get back on track when he returns to high Class A.

Year	Club (League)	Class	W	L	ERA	G	GS	CG	SV	IP	H	R	ER	HR	BB	SO	AVG
2005	Reds (GCL)	R	0	0	0.75	8	7	0	0	24	13	3	2	0	7	45	.157
	Billings (Pio)	R	2	0	1.82	6	4	0	0	24	15	6	5	0	13	22	.174
2006	Dayton (MWL)	A	10	5	3.66	27	27	0	0	140	108	65	57	14	56	133	.215
2007	Sarasota (FSL)	A	3	2	4.86	12	12	0	0	46	49	33	25	6	27	54	.268
MINOR LEAGUE TOTALS			15	7	3.41	53	50	0	0	235	185	107	89	20	103	254	.217

22 ADAM ROSALES, 1B/3B

Born: May 20, 1983. **B-T:** R-R. **Ht.:** 6-1. **Wt.:** 191. **Drafted:** Western Michigan, 2005 (12th round). **Signed by:** Mike Sellers.

Don't be misled by the fact that Rosales spent most of the 2007 season playing first base. It was a temporary move to rest his sore throwing elbow. He had another good year at the plate and was able to return to third base full-time in the Arizona Fall League. That's good news because his righthanded bat doesn't profile nearly as well at first base. Area scout Rick Sellers sold the Reds on Rosales when he was a senior at Western Michigan. His swing isn't particularly pretty with a downward cut to it, but it's relatively quick and his discerning batting eye helps him to work into counts where he can get pitches to drive. A shortstop during his first two pro season, Rosales has just average speed and his lack of range forced a move. He has enough lateral quickness to stick at third base. When healthy, his arm is one of his best tools, as it's above-average with good accuracy. Rosales profiles more as an offensive-minded utilityman but has exceeded expectations ever since he signed. It's not out of the question that he could develop into a regular third baseman.

Year	Club (League)	Class	AVG	G	AB	R	H	2B	3B	HR	RBI	BB	SO	SB	OBP	SLG
2005	Billings (Pio)	R	.321	34	140	29	45	14	0	5	25	13	37	2	.396	.529
	Dayton (MWL)	A	.328	32	134	24	44	8	0	9	21	10	24	3	.378	.590
2006	Sarasota (FSL)	A	.213	34	122	15	26	8	2	2	14	20	27	3	.329	.361
	Dayton (MWL)	A	.270	55	222	36	60	9	3	6	29	15	40	5	.328	.419
2007	Sarasota (FSL)	A	.294	69	248	47	73	23	5	5	48	31	46	9	.393	.488
	Chattanooga (SL)	AA	.278	67	255	51	71	18	6	13	31	37	66	4	.377	.549
MINOR LEAGUE TOTALS			.285	291	1121	202	319	80	16	40	168	126	240	26	.368	.492

23 BRANDON WARING, 3B

Born: Jan, 2, 1986. **B-T:** R-R. **Ht.:** 6-4. **Wt.:** 195. **Drafted:** Wofford, 2007 (7th round). **Signed by:** Steve Kring.

In each of the past three years, the Reds have seen an unheralded college draftee turn into a star at Rookie-level Billings. Adam Rosales came first in 2005 and was followed by Chris Valaika and then Waring. After a broken wrist ruined his sophomore season in 2006, Waring finished second in NCAA Division I with 27 homers last spring. Five came during the Southern Conference tournament as he led ninth-seeded Wofford to the title. Signed for $94,000 as a seventh-round pick, Waring continued his power display in his debut. He led the Pioneer League with 20 homers, including 10 in a span of 10 games. He generates above-average bat speed from his large frame and can catch up to quality fastballs. He has a level swing, but he's prone to chasing pitches out of the zone. He also can get pull-happy at times, which is unnecessary because he has shown opposite-field power. Waring's speed is below-average and his athleticism is fringy, so he'll have to work to stay at third base. He has enough agility and arm strength, though he'll have to improve his footwork to avoid a move to first base or an outfield corner. Cincinnati sent Rosales and Valaika to low Class A after their big debuts, and likely will do the same with Waring.

Year	Club (League)	Class	AVG	G	AB	R	H	2B	3B	HR	RBI	BB	SO	SB	OBP	SLG
2007	Billings (Pio)	R	.311	68	267	63	83	17	2	20	61	21	83	1	.369	.614
	Dayton (MWL)	A	1.000	1	1	0	1	0	0	0	2	0	0	0	1.000	1.000
MINOR LEAGUE TOTALS			.313	69	268	63	84	17	2	20	63	21	83	1	.372	.616

24 SAM LeCURE, RHP

Born: May 4, 1984. **B-T:** R-R. **Ht.:** 6-1. **Wt.:** 195. **Drafted:** Texas, 2005 (4th round). **Signed by:** Brian Wilson.

LeCure was supposed to be Texas' ace in 2005, but while the Longhorns were winning the College World Series, he was stocking gas stations with beer for a local distributor. He was declared academically ineligible before the season, and an appeal citing a learning disability caused by attention deficit hyperactivity disorder was denied. The Reds looked past that setback and signed him for $260,000 as a fourth-round pick. If LeCure were ice cream, he'd be a scoop of vanilla. There's not a whole lot to get excited about but, like America's favorite ice cream flavor, he's very reliable. He throws three pitches, all of which grade out as average. His 87-91 mph fastball, his slider and his changeup are enough to keep hitters off balance, largely because he has clever pitch selection to go with solid command. More advanced hitters have given him more trouble because he lacks a true out pitch, which causes him nibble too much. A strained oblique muscle forced him to miss most of May, but his solid frame and clean delivery have allowed him to be very durable otherwise. LeCure profiles as no more than a No. 5 starter or swingman, but his makeup and feel for pitching make it likely he'll reach that low ceiling. He'll get his first exposure to Triple-A in 2008.

Year	Club (League)	Class	W	L	ERA	G	GS	CG	SV	IP	H	R	ER	HR	BB	SO	AVG
2005	Billings (Pio)	R	5	1	3.27	13	6	0	0	41	43	18	15	2	15	44	.272
2006	Sarasota (FSL)	A	7	12	3.43	27	27	0	0	141	130	63	54	12	46	115	.243
2007	Sarasota (FSL)	A	1	0	1.80	1	1	0	0	5	2	1	1	0	0	8	.125
	Chattanooga (SL)	AA	7	5	4.17	21	21	0	0	110	119	55	51	12	46	104	.281
MINOR LEAGUE TOTALS			20	18	3.65	62	55	0	0	298	294	137	121	26	107	271	.260

25 JOSE CASTRO, SS

Born: Nov. 5, 1986. **B-T:** B-R. **Ht.:** 5-11. **Wt.:** 172. **Drafted:** Miami-Dade CC North, 2005 (32nd round). **Signed by:** Joe Salermo (Mets).

A year ago, Castro was an afterthought in the Mets system. But after he returned to switch-hitting, Castro turned himself into a prospect and caught the eye of the Reds, who picked him up along with Sean Henry in an August trade for Jeff Conine. Resuming switch-hitting did wonders for Castro's bat, as he was hitting .348 before he hurt his hand (an injury that had bothered him before this year as well) at the end of June and hit .312 overall, including a stint in Double-A. Helpless to the tune of a .206 average against righthanders in 2006, he batted .321 from the left side against them last year. One opposing manager thought Castro's lefty swing even looked smoother and more natural than his righty stroke. He's a tremendous contact hitter, though he offers no power (three homers in three pro seasons) and lacks the instincts and pure speed to be a basestealing threat. A slightly above-average runner, he was caught 10 times in 18 steal attempts last year. Defensively, Castro has the loose actions that scouts look for in a shortstop. He has enough arm for the position, shows a quick first step and reads balls off the bat well. He turned the double play effectively as a second baseman in Rookie ball before moving back to his natural position in 2006. Castro has the defensive ability to make it to the big leagues as a middle infielder, though his lack of power and blazing speed make it more likely he'll be a utilityman than a regular. He'll open 2008 in Double-A.

Year	Club (League)	Class	AVG	G	AB	R	H	2B	3B	HR	RBI	BB	SO	SB	OBP	SLG
2005	Kingsport (Appy)	R	.286	8	14	1	4	0	0	0	1	2	1	0	.412	.286
	Mets (GCL)	R	.293	31	116	15	34	3	2	1	10	6	9	2	.359	.379
2006	Hagerstown (SAL)	A	.219	118	434	38	95	12	1	0	38	21	52	6	.286	.251
2007	St. Lucie (FSL)	A	.318	77	308	47	98	12	1	2	25	11	21	7	.363	.383
	Chattanooga (SL)	AA	.278	13	54	5	15	2	1	0	1	2	8	1	.328	.352
MINOR LEAGUE TOTALS			.266	247	926	106	246	29	5	3	75	42	91	16	.325	.317

26 TYLER PELLAND, LHP

Born: Oct. 9, 1983. **B-T:** L-L. **Ht.:** 5-11. **Wt.:** 203. **Drafted:** HS—Bristol, Vt., 2002 (9th round). **Signed by:** Ray Fagnant (Red Sox).

In November, the Reds faced decisions on both lefthanders they acquired in the trade that sent Scott Williamson to Boston in 2003. They placed former first-round pick Phil Dumatrait on waivers to remove him from the 40-man roster and lost him to the Pirates. Meanwhile, they added Pelland to the roster after he had succeeded following a full-time move to the bullpen in May. His new role allowed him to junk his fringy changeup and rely primarily on his 90-92 mph fastball and tight slider. Durability also became less of an issue, and he responded better to short stints as a reliever. His command issues and his lack of an adequate third pitch always kept him from reaching his potential as a starter. Pelland's fastball/slider combination proved nearly unhittable for lefthanders (.130 batting average with 32 strikeouts in 80 at-bats) last year, but he didn't have nearly the same success against righthanders (.275). Pelland has a future as a lefty reliever, though his ceiling is much less than it was when Cincinnati envisioned him as a future No. 3 starter. The Reds have multiple lefty bullpen options, so Pelland figures to begin the season in Triple-A.

Year	Club (League)	Class	W	L	ERA	G	GS	CG	SV	IP	H	R	ER	HR	BB	SO	AVG
2003	Red Sox (GCL)	R	3	4	1.62	11	8	0	0	39	26	12	7	0	18	34	.186
	Reds (GCL)	R	0	0	0.00	1	1	0	0	2	3	0	0	0	0	1	.273
2004	Dayton (MWL)	A	1	7	8.66	14	10	0	0	44	66	49	43	6	20	38	.328
	Billings (Pio)	R	9	3	3.42	18	12	0	0	73	67	36	28	3	39	82	.248
2005	Sarasota (FSL)	A	5	8	4.05	30	15	0	0	102	103	52	46	5	63	103	.270
2006	Chattanooga (SL)	AA	9	5	3.99	28	28	0	0	142	144	78	63	11	89	107	.275
2007	Chattanooga (SL)	AA	5	4	3.95	35	5	0	2	66	63	40	29	6	32	71	.251
	Louisville (IL)	AAA	1	1	3.04	19	0	0	0	23	17	9	8	1	7	27	.213
MINOR LEAGUE TOTALS			33	32	4.08	156	79	0	2	494	489	276	224	32	268	463	.263

27 CHRIS DICKERSON, OF

Born: April 10, 1982. **B-T:** L-L. **Ht.:** 6-4. **Wt.:** 212. **Drafted:** Nevada, 2003 (16th round). **Signed by:** Keith Chapman.

The Reds have been extremely patient with Dickerson, largely because it's easy to dream about the system's best athlete. A cousin of NFL Hall of Famer Eric Dickerson and former college teammate of Kevin Kouzmanoff at Nevada, Dickerson has the best combination of strength and speed among Cincinnati farmhands, though his baseball skills never have caught up to his raw tools. When he puts the ball in play, he has outstanding raw power. When he gets on base, he can take advantage with his plus speed and his ability to read pitchers and get good jumps. He also plays an outstanding center field and his average arm allows him to play all three outfield slots. But Dickerson doesn't put the ball in play very often. He struck out once every 2.7 at-bats in Triple-A and has whiffed once every 3.2 at-bats in pro ball. At times he shows a short, quick swing, but too often he gets pull-happy and lengthens his stroke in an attempt to hit home runs. Dickerson's defense, speed and ability to hit righthanders eventually should earn him a spot on a big league roster as a backup outfielder, but even after five years in the system he still has a long way to go to develop into a big league regular.

Year	Club (League)	Class	AVG	G	AB	R	H	2B	3B	HR	RBI	BB	SO	SB	OBP	SLG
2003	Billings (Pio)	R	.244	58	201	36	49	6	4	6	38	39	66	9	.376	.403
2004	Dayton (MWL)	A	.303	84	314	50	95	15	3	4	34	51	92	27	.410	.408
	Potomac (Car)	A	.200	15	45	5	9	2	0	0	5	7	14	3	.321	.244
2005	Sarasota (FSL)	A	.236	119	436	68	103	17	7	11	43	53	124	19	.325	.383
2006	Chattanooga (SL)	AA	.242	115	389	65	94	21	7	12	48	65	129	21	.355	.424
2007	Chattanooga (SL)	AA	.272	30	114	11	31	4	1	1	11	7	31	7	.325	.351
	Louisville (IL)	AAA	.260	104	354	58	92	11	6	13	44	52	131	23	.361	.435
MINOR LEAGUE TOTALS			.255	525	1853	293	473	76	28	47	223	274	587	109	.359	.403

28 DANNY DORN, OF

Born: July 20, 1984. **B-T:** L-L. **Ht.:** 6-2. **Wt.:** 190. **Drafted:** Cal State Fullerton, 2006 (32nd round). **Signed by:** Mike Misuraca.

Dorn teamed with fellow Reds prospect Justin Turner to help Cal State Fullerton win the 2004 College World Series title in 2004. Dorn drew Garrett Anderson comps early in his college career, but a nagging shoulder injury and concerns about his effort led him to drop to the Devil Rays in the 23rd round in 2005. Tampa Bay made him a competitive offer, but he returned to help Fullerton to another CWS appearance and became a steal as the Reds' 32nd-round pick. Signed for $1,000, Dorn has proven to be a much better hitter and a better competitor than scouts expected. His solid lefthanded stroke should allow him to hit for average with gap power. His bat will have to carry him, because his speed, left-field defense and arm strength are all slightly below-average, though he does have good instincts. Dorn projects as a platoon left fielder/first baseman and will return to Double-A after a strong final month there in 2007.

Year	Club (League)	Class	AVG	G	AB	R	H	2B	3B	HR	RBI	BB	SO	SB	OBP	SLG
2006	Billings (Pio)	R	.354	60	206	48	73	17	2	8	40	36	36	3	.457	.573
2007	Sarasota (FSL)	A	.281	92	338	49	95	21	1	12	66	32	69	3	.359	.456
	Chattanooga (SL)	AA	.311	26	90	20	28	6	1	8	21	15	23	1	.422	.667
MINOR LEAGUE TOTALS			.309	178	634	117	196	44	4	28	127	83	128	7	.401	.524

29 JUSTIN TURNER, 2B/SS

Born: Nov. 23, 1984. **B-T:** R-R. **Ht.:** 5-11. **Wt.:** 180. **Drafted:** Cal State Fullerton, 2006 (7th round). **Signed by:** Mike Misuraca.

Like Chris Valaika and former Cal State Fullerton teammate Danny Dorn, Turner is a pure baseball player with outstanding instincts, a love of the game and an ability to turn every ounce of his potential into production. Turner's father John was a childhood friend of former Titans assistant coach Rick Vanderhook and Justin served as a Fullerton batboy, so there was no question as to where he would go to school. Turner helped Fullerton reach three College World Series and win the 2004 national title, and former coach George Horton compared him to Titans great Mark Kotsay for his leadership and baseball savvy. A relatively inexpensive senior sign for $50,000, Turner quickly has established himself with his solid bat and above-average defense. He's an average runner but knows how to take an extra base. Turner turns the double play well and his range is good enough to fill in at shortstop, though his fringy arm plays much better at second. He likely never will hit for much power, but his ability to produce for average while doing all of the little things gives him a chance to make it to the big leagues as a second baseman or utilityman.

Year	Club (League)	Class	AVG	G	AB	R	H	2B	3B	HR	RBI	BB	SO	SB	OBP	SLG
2006	Billings (Pio)	R	.338	60	231	53	78	16	3	6	41	23	38	12	.411	.511
2007	Dayton (MWL)	A	.311	117	466	70	145	25	4	10	59	39	72	12	.374	.446
	Sarasota (FSL)	A	.200	6	20	2	4	0	0	0	0	1	2	0	.238	.200
MINOR LEAGUE TOTALS			.317	183	717	125	227	41	7	16	100	63	112	24	.383	.460

30 SERGIO VALENZUELA, RHP

Born: Sept. 15, 1984. **B-T:** R-R. **Ht.:** 6-3. **Wt.:** 215. **Signed:** Mexico, 2001. **Signed by:** Victor Favela/Julian Perez (Braves).

Valenzuela's beauty is in the eye of the beholder. The Braves didn't bother to protect him on their 40-man roster because they thought his stuff was average and he posted a 7.00 ERA in 2007 while getting his first taste of full-season ball. The Reds pounced on him in the major league phase of the Rule 5 draft, however, because their reports gave Valenzuela the chance to have three above-average pitches. They clocked his fastball at 91-96 mph—Atlanta had him at 86-93—and graded his changeup as plus and his slider as having the potential to get to that level. A pitcher with that arsenal seemingly would have to have more success than Valenzuela, whose stats remained uninspiring in the Mexican Pacific League this winter (3.78 ERA, 12-13 K-BB ratio in 33 innings). The Braves weren't upset at all to lose Valenzuela, while Cincinnati thinks he can develop into a big league starter. The Reds will stash him in their bullpen this season, as they have to keep him on their 25-man roster. Before they could send him to the minors, he'd have to clear waivers and be offered back to Atlanta for half of the $50,000 draft price.

Year	Club (League)	Class	W	L	ERA	G	GS	CG	SV	IP	H	R	ER	HR	BB	SO	AVG
2003	Braves1 (DSL)	R	6	2	0.96	11	11	0	0	65	34	9	7	1	12	56	.152
2004	Braves (GCL)	R	1	2	3.00	5	3	0	0	21	15	9	7	3	3	16	.188
2005	Braves (GCL)	R	1	4	3.60	8	7	0	0	35	35	16	14	1	4	16	.259
2006	Danville (Appy)	R	3	4	6.04	13	11	0	0	50	57	44	34	5	18	29	.286
2007	Myrtle Beach (Car)	A	0	0	6.88	18	2	0	0	35	47	33	27	3	18	19	.318
	Rome (SAL)	A	1	3	7.12	14	3	0	0	36	55	33	29	5	19	19	.350
MINOR LEAGUE TOTALS			12	15	4.35	69	37	0	0	244	243	144	118	18	74	155	.258

Cleveland Indians

BY CHRIS KLINE

While their season ended in disappointing fashion, the Indians completed their rebuilding project by returning to the top of the American League Central. The organization had been pointing toward that goal since Mark Shapiro took over as general manager after the 2001 season, the last time Cleveland had gone to the playoffs. Shapiro's administration immediately tore down an expensive roster and began assembling younger talent.

The Indians won 93 games in 2005 and looked well on their way back, but a faulty bullpen contributed to a 78-84 finish in 2006. Their young core matured last season and showed that the step back in '06 was the anomaly.

What will linger in Cleveland fans' memories, however, is how much better it could have been. The Tribe knocked off the Yankees in the Division Series, then pushed the Red Sox to seven games in the AL Championship Series. The most frustrating part was that the Indians had Boston on the ropes with a 3-1 series lead and a chance to clinch at Jacobs Field. But Josh Beckett turned the tide in Game Five, starting a run of three straight wins for the Red Sox that dashed the Indians' hopes of their first World Series title since 1948.

The good news is that the remade Indians are equipped to go on the same kind of run they enjoyed from 1995-2001, when they went to the playoffs six times in seven years. While a primary focus of Shapiro's rebuilding efforts centered around homegrown contributors such as Fausto Carmona, Victor Martinez, Jhonny Peralta and C.C. Sabathia, the pro scouting department helped build the club as much, if not more, than the amateur department.

Recognizing the talent of Grady Sizemore while he was in Class A or Travis Hafner when he was in Triple-A paid huge dividends. So did stealing Asdrubal Cabrera from the Mariners in a trade for Eduardo Perez.

After graduating several players to the big leagues, the farm system is at a crossroads. The system still has depth, but aside from oft-injured righthander Adam Miller, no true blue-chip prospects are waiting in the wings.

And aside from holdovers liked Miller, no new faces outside of Double-A first baseman Jordan Brown separated themselves from the pack in 2007. The system was wracked by injury and lack of

Homegrown product Victor Martinez played a huge role in the Tribe's 2007 run

TOP 30 PROSPECTS

1. Adam Miller, rhp	16. Scott Lewis, lhp
2. Chuck Lofgren, lhp	17. Sung-Wei Tseng, rhp
3. Beau Mills, 3b/1b	18. Carlos Rivero, ss
4. Wes Hodges, 3b	19. Jeff Stevens, rhp
5. Aaron Laffey, lhp	20. Josh Rodriguez, ss
6. Nick Weglarz, of	21. Ryan Miller, lhp
7. Jordan Brown, 1b	22. Michael Aubrey, 1b
8. David Huff, lhp	23. John Drennen, of
9. Ben Francisco, of	24. Wyatt Toregas, c
10. Jensen Lewis, rhp	25. Brad Snyder, of
11. Masahide Kobayashi, rhp	26. Frank Herrmann, rhp
12. Tony Sipp, lhp	27. Chris Nash, 1b
13. Matt McBride, c	28. Hector Rondon, rhp
14. Trevor Crowe, of	29. Reid Santos, lhp
15. Chris Jones, lhp	30. Joey Mahalic, rhp

performance last year, as lefthander Tony Sipp had Tommy John surgery, outfielder Brad Snyder went down with a broken thumb in July and the two top draft picks from 2005 (outfielders Trevor Crowe and John Drennen) were disappointments.

The Indians had just one pick in the first three rounds in the 2007 draft, selecting Beau Mills 13th overall. Two of their later-round picks have a lot of upside, as the club went over slot to sign lefthander Chris Jones (15th round) for $350,00 and righthander Joey Mahalic (32nd round) for $123,000.

General Manager: Mark Shapiro. **Farm Director:** Ross Atkins. **Scouting Director:** Brian Grant.

Class	Team	League	W	L	PCT	Finish*	Manager	Affiliated
Majors	Cleveland	American	96	66	.593	1st (14)	Eric Wedge	—
Triple-A	Buffalo Bisons	International	75	67	.528	6th (14)	Torey Lovullo	1995
Double-A	Akron Aeros	Eastern	80	61	.567	3rd (12)	Tim Bogar	1997
High A	Kinston Indians	Carolina	87	52	.626	1st (8)	Mike Sarbaugh	1987
Low A	Lake County Captains	South Atlantic	64	74	.464	12th (16)	Chris Tremie	2003
Short-season	Mahoning Valley Scrappers	New York-Penn	37	37	.500	7th (14)	Tim Laker	1999
Rookie	GCL Indians	Gulf Coast	28	31	.475	8th (16)	Rouglas Odor	2006
Overall 2007 Minor League Record			371	322	.535	5th		

*Finish in overall standings (No. of teams in league) ^League champion

LAST YEAR'S TOP 30

Player, Pos.		Status
1.	Adam Miller, rhp	No. 1
2.	Chuck Lofgren, lhp	No. 2
3.	Trevor Crowe, of	No. 13
4.	Tony Sipp, lhp	No. 11
5.	Brian Barton, of	(Cardinals)
6.	John Drennen, of	No. 22
7.	Scott Lewis, lhp	No. 17
8.	Brad Snyder, of	No. 21
9.	Wes Hodges, 3b	No. 4
10.	David Huff, lhp	No. 8
11.	Rafael Perez, lhp	Majors
12.	Sung-Wei Tseng, rhp	No. 15
13.	J.D. Martin, rhp	Dropped out
14.	Juan Lara, lhp	Dropped out
15.	Asdrubal Cabrera, ss	Majors
16.	Matt McBride, c	No. 9
17.	Brian Slocum, rhp	Dropped out
18.	Edward Mujica, rhp	Dropped out
19.	Kelly Shoppach, c	Majors
20.	Wyatt Toregas, c	No. 19
21.	Max Ramirez, c	(Rangers)
22.	Aaron Laffey, lhp	No. 5
23.	Josh Rodriguez, ss	No. 18
24.	Jordan Brown, 1b	No. 7
25.	Jensen Lewis, rhp	No. 12
26.	Jose Constanza, of	Dropped out
27.	Tom Mastny, rhp	Majors
28.	Frank Herrmann, rhp	No. 24
29.	Stephen Wright, rhp	Dropped out
30.	Stephen Head, 1b	Dropped out

BEST TOOLS

Best Hitter for Average	Jordan Brown
Best Power Hitter	Beau Mills
Best Strike-Zone Discipline	Jordan Brown
Fastest Baserunner	Jose Constanza
Best Athlete	Brad Snyder
Best Fastball	Adam Miller
Best Curveball	Scott Lewis
Best Slider	Adam Miller
Best Changeup	David Huff
Best Control	David Huff
Best Defensive Catcher	Wyatt Toregas
Best Defensive Infielder	Adam Davis
Best Infield Arm	Josh Rodriguez
Best Defensive Outfielder	Brad Snyder
Best Outfield Arm	Brad Snyder

PROJECTED 2011 LINEUP

Catcher	Victor Martinez
First Base	Ryan Garko
Second Base	Asdrubal Cabrera
Third Base	Beau Mills
Shortstop	Jhonny Peralta
Left Field	Nick Weglarz
Center Field	Grady Sizemore
Right Field	Franklin Gutierrez
Designated Hitter	Travis Hafner
No. 1 Starter	C.C. Sabathia
No. 2 Starter	Fausto Carmona
No. 3 Starter	Adam Miller
No. 4 Starter	Chuck Lofgren
No. 5 Starter	Aaron Laffey
Closer	Rafael Perez

TOP PROSPECTS OF THE DECADE

Year	Player, Pos.	2007 Org.
1998	Sean Casey, 1b	Tigers
1999	Russell Branyan, 3b	Cardinals
2000	C.C. Sabathia, lhp	Indians
2001	C.C. Sabathia, lhp	Indians
2002	Corey Smith, 3b	Newark (Atlantic)
2003	Brandon Phillips, ss/2b	Reds
2004	Grady Sizemore, of	Indians
2005	Adam Miller, rhp	Indians
2006	Adam Miller, rhp	Indians
2007	Adam Miller, rhp	Indians

TOP DRAFT PICKS OF THE DECADE

Year	Player, Pos.	2007 Org.
1998	C.C. Sabathia, lhp	Indians
1999	Will Hartley, c (2nd round)	Out of baseball
2000	Corey Smith, 3b	Newark (Atlantic)
2001	Dan Denham, rhp	Athletics
2002	Jeremy Guthrie, rhp	Orioles
2003	Michael Aubrey, 1b	Indians
2004	Jeremy Sowers, lhp	Indians
2005	Trevor Crowe, of	Indians
2006	David Huff, lhp	Indians
2007	Beau Mills, 3b/1b	Indians

LARGEST BONUSES IN CLUB HISTORY

Danys Baez, 1999	$4,500,000
Jeremy Guthrie, 2002	$3,000,000
Jeremy Sowers, 2004	$2,475,000
Michael Aubrey, 2003	$2,010,000
Dan Denham, 2001	$1,860,000

CLEVELAND INDIANS

Top 2008 Rookie: Masahide Kobayashi, rhp. The Tribe initially will use him in a sixth- or seventh-inning role, and he's also an insurance policy at closer if Joe Borowski falters.

Breakout Prospect: Sung-Wei Tseng, rhp. He hit a wall in the second half last year, but should bounce back after pitching much less on the international scene in the offseason.

SOURCE OF TOP 30 TALENT			
Homegrown	28	Acquired	2
College	14	Trades	1
Junior college	2	Rule 5 draft	0
High school	7	Independent leagues	0
Draft-and-follow	1	Free agents/waivers	1
Nondrafted free agents	1		
International	3		

Sleeper: Mike Pontius, rhp. Strong, durable and armed with a 93-95 mph fastball and a 12-to-6 curve, he was the Tribe's best pitcher during instructional league.

Numbers in parentheses indicate prospect rankings.

LF
Nick Weglarz (6)
John Drennen (23)

CF
Ben Francisco (9)
Trevor Crowe (14)
Jose Constanza
Adam White

RF
Nick Weglarz (6)
Brad Snyder (25)
Roman Pena
Matt Brown

3B
Beau Mills (3)
Wes Hodges (4)

SS
Carlos Rivero (18)
Josh Rodriguez (20)
Brandon Pinckney
Mark Thompson

2B
Jared Goedert
Adam Davis
Chris de la Cruz

1B
Jordan Brown (7)
Michael Aubrey (22)
Chris Nash (27)
Ryan Mulhern
Stephen Head
Todd Martin

C
Matt McBride (13)
Wyatt Toregas (24)
Chris Gimenez

RHP

Starters	Relievers
Adam Miller (1)	Jensen Lewis (10)
Sung-Wei Tseng (17)	Masahide Kobayashi (11)
Frank Herrmann (26)	Jeff Stevens (19)
Hector Rondon (28)	Juan Lara
Joey Mahalic (30)	Edward Mujica
Sean Smith	Dallas Cawiezell
J.D. Martin	Bubbie Buzachero
James Deters	Mike Finocchi
Josh Tomlin	T.J. Burton
Steven Wright	
Jonathan Holt	

LHP

Starters	Relievers
Chuck Lofgren (2)	Tony Sipp (12)
Aaron Laffey (5)	Reid Santos (29)
David Huff (8)	Matt Meyer
Chris Jones (15)	Rich Rundles
Scott Lewis (16)	
Ryan Miller (21)	
T.J. McFarland	
Ryan Edell	
Shawn Nottingham	
Heath Taylor	

2007

Best Pro Debut: LHP Heath Taylor (10) didn't allow a home run and posted a 2.35 ERA in 57 innings for short-season Mahoning Valley; his ERA would have ranked fourth in the league had he qualified. Scrappers LHP Garrett Rieck (29) also allowed no homers and walked four with a 2.00 ERA in 36 relief innings.

Best Athlete: The Indians tried to get more athletic, leading them to draft OF Adam White (9), a former prep wrestler and football star who's learning to switch-hit in an effort to take advantage of his speed. OF Bo Greenwell (6) was an outstanding prep football player.

Best Pure Hitter: 3B/1B Beau Mills (1) hit .261/.337/.424 with 20 doubles overall and finished the year in high Class A. He has a feel for hitting and smells RBI situations.

Best Power Hitter: Mills, who set an NAIA record with 38 homers while leading Lewis-Clark State (Idaho) to another NAIA championship.

Fastest Runner: White has work to do offensively but is an 80 runner. He hit .260/.362/.361 for Mahoning Valley with 22 steals in 30 attempts.

Best Defensive Player: Mills' old Warriors teammate, SS Mark Thompson (8), has above-average speed and range. C Michael Valadez (26) has a plus arm and athleticism behind the plate.

Best Fastball: RHP Dallas Cawiezell (40) signed as a summer follow after dominating the summer collegiate Northwoods League and flashed 96 mph as a pro. LHP T.J. McFarland (4) touched 93 mph as an amateur.

Best Secondary Pitch: McFarland has shown a plus power breaking ball at times; the Indians call it a slider with two-plane break. Rieck's best pitch is his plus changeup.

Most Intriguing Background: Mills' father Brad is the Red Sox' bench coach and a former big leaguer. Greenwell's dad Mike batted .303 and played in two All-Star Games for the Red Sox from 1985-96. RHP Joey Mahalic (32), who has a projectable fastball and athleticism, is the son of Drew Mahalic, an NFL linebacker in the mid-1970s.

Closest To The Majors: RHP Jonathan Holt (5) has fringe-average velocity but should move quickly due to his above-average command and movement on his fastball.

Best Late-Round Pick: The Indians found several keepers after the 10th round, none better than RHP Chris Jones (15), who's ahead of where Aaron Laffey was at the same stage of development. Among the position players, OF Matt Brown (13) has the most all-around ability.

The One Who Got Away: The Indians made serious runs at LHP Cole St.Clair (7), who returned to Rice, and 3B/OF Matt Hague (11), who transferred to Oklahoma State.

Assessment: The success of this draft depends more on late-round picks than any other, as most of Cleveland's power arms arrived in the double-digit rounds. It also hinges in part on Mills, who could be a steal at 13 if he can play third base.

2006 BUDGET: $5.2 MILLION

LHP David Huff (1s) and 3B Wes Hodges (2) are talented but need to stay healthy. Matt McBride (2s) is the system's top catching prospect.

GRADE: B

2005 BUDGET: $4.9 MILLION

RHP Jensen Lewis (3) is already helping out in the big league bullpen, while OF Nick Weglarz (3) and 1B Jordan Brown (4) are exceeding expectations. But OFs Trevor Crowe (1) and John Drennen (1s) are headed in the other direction.

GRADE: C+

2004 BUDGET: $4.9 MILLION

LHP Jeremy Sowers (1) regressed in 2007, but Chuck Lofgren (4) ranks with the best lefty prospects in the game. LHP Tony Sipp (45) eventually could be Cleveland's closer, but he missed all of last year with Tommy John surgery.

GRADE: C+

2003 BUDGET: $6.0 MILLION

RHP Adam Miller (1s) should be the stud of this group, but he keeps getting hurt. He's still the Tribe's No. 1 prospect. 1B Ryan Garko (3) and since-traded 3B Kevin Kouzmanoff (6) have mashed, while LHP Aaron Laffey (16) was a steal.

GRADE: A

Draft analysis by John Manuel (2007) and Jim Callis (2003-06). Numbers in parentheses indicate draft rounds. Budgets are bonuses in first 10 rounds.

MIKE JANES

1 AMERICAN CENTRAL LEAGUE

ADAM MILLER, RHP

Born: Nov. 26, 1984.
Ht.: 6-4. **Wt.:** 195.
Bats: R. **Throws:** R.
Drafted: HS—
McKinney, Texas,
2003 (1st round
supplemental).
Signed by:
Matt Ruebel.

After spending 2005 rehabbing an elbow strain, Miller bounced back in 2006 to re-establish himself as one of the top pitching prospects in the game. But his health again faltered last season, as finger and elbow woes kept him out of action for nearly two months. When he returned to Triple-A Buffalo, the Tribe kept him in the bullpen to limit his innings and closely monitored his work between outings. He went down to Double-A Akron for the Eastern League playoffs, and allowed five runs on eight hits in just six innings. Miller went to instructional league before heading to the Arizona Fall League for the second time in three seasons, again with mixed results. While Cleveland raved about his AFL stint, several scouts were less than impressed with his secondary pitches and Miller finished with a 9.00 ERA in 13 innings.

When he's healthy, Miller has proven to be dominant with two plus pitches. His 93-97 mph fastball has natural late life and he works all four quadrants of the strike zone with it. His hard 86-88 mph slider can be devastating at times with late break and power. His slider is by far his best pitch. With the addition of a two-seamer, Miller also has a weapon to attack lefthanders and it has emerged as an out pitch over the last two seasons, boosting his groundball ratio in the process. His delivery is free and easy and his work ethic and makeup never have been questioned. After wanting to just blow his fastball by hitters early in his career, Miller has shown exceptional maturity, understanding the value of his secondary pitches.

Miller struggled with the arm speed and location of his changeup in the AFL, and it always has lagged behind his other offerings. He made significant progress with his changeup in Double-A in 2006, but with the layoff and the move to the bullpen last year, he didn't get much opportunity to use it. While his mechanics are easily repeatable, Miller struggled to maintain his arm slot in the AFL. His arm dragged behind his body at times, elevating his pitches and leaving them lifeless, which made him extremely hittable. The Indians hope he can pitch out of the major league bullpen, but in order to do that, he's going to need to refine his pickoff move and do a better job of controlling the running game.

Though his medical history is beginning to become somewhat worrisome, Miller will have the opportunity to begin 2008 in the Cleveland bullpen. The club still views him as a starter down the road, but he has the stuff to make an impact in a relief role now. How well he can stay healthy and further develop his changeup ultimately will determine his ceiling. Miller still has the arsenal of pitches and the makeup to be a legitimate frontline starter.

Year	Club (League)	Class	W	L	ERA	G	GS	CG	SV	IP	H	R	ER	HR	BB	SO	AVG
2003	Burlington (Appy)	R	0	4	4.96	10	10	0	0	32	30	20	18	2	9	23	.250
2004	Lake County (SAL)	A	7	4	3.36	19	19	1	0	91	79	39	34	7	28	106	.240
	Kinston (Car)	A	3	2	2.08	8	8	0	0	43	29	17	10	1	12	46	.193
2005	Mahoning Valley (NYP)	A	0	0	5.06	3	3	0	0	10	17	6	6	0	4	6	.405
	Kinston (Car)	A	2	4	4.83	12	12	0	0	59	76	43	32	5	17	45	.318
2006	Buffalo (IL)	AAA	0	0	5.79	1	1	0	0	4	4	3	3	0	3	4	.235
	Akron (EL)	AA	15	6	2.75	26	24	1	0	153	129	56	47	9	43	157	.226
2007	Buffalo (IL)	AAA	5	4	4.82	19	11	1	0	65	68	39	35	4	21	68	.265
MINOR LEAGUE TOTALS			32	24	3.61	98	88	3	0	461	432	223	185	28	137	455	.251

2 CHUCK LOFGREN, LHP

Born: Jan. 29, 1986. **B-T:** L-L. **Ht.:** 6-4. **Wt.:** 200. **Drafted:** HS—San Mateo, Calif., 2004 (4th round). **Signed by:** Don Lyle.

Several teams liked Lofgren more for his lefthanded bat than his ability on the mound in the 2004 draft, but the Indians persuaded him that his future was on the mound after letting him serve as a two-way player during his pro debut. Though he wasn't nearly as dominant in 2007 as he had been in the past, Lofgren still led the system with 123 strikeouts in 146 innings and ranked second with 12 wins. Lofgren adds and subtracts with his full arsenal of pitches, beginning with a fastball that ranges anywhere from 87-93 mph and tops out at 95. He added a slider in 2006 and developed it into a true out pitch last year. He also throws a spike curveball in the upper 70s and a changeup that grades out as average. An imposing presence on the mound, he gets downhill easily and pounds the bottom of the strike zone. He kept his composure when things went poorly, and the Tribe loves his makeup. Lofgren struggled with runners on base last year, rushing his lower half in his delivery, which threw off his command. His changeup wasn't the weapon it was during his breakout campaign in 2006 when he led the minors with 17 wins, but it still has considerable upside. He needs to consistently command his fastball to maximize his effectiveness. Lofgren likely will make a few starts in Double-A before getting his first taste of Triple-A. Projected as a No. 3 starter, he could make his big league debut later in the year.

Year	Club (League)	Class	W	L	ERA	G	GS	CG	SV	IP	H	R	ER	HR	BB	SO	AVG
2004	Burlington (Appy)	R	0	0	6.04	9	9	0	0	22	25	16	15	4	13	23	.294
2005	Lake County (SAL)	A	5	5	2.81	18	18	0	0	93	73	31	29	6	43	89	.218
2006	Kinston (Car)	A	17	5	2.32	25	25	1	0	139	108	51	36	5	54	125	.217
2007	Buffalo (IL)	AAA	0	1	10.80	1	1	0	0	5	7	6	6	1	3	7	.350
	Akron (EL)	AA	12	7	4.37	26	26	0	0	146	153	79	71	14	68	123	.270
MINOR LEAGUE TOTALS			34	18	3.48	79	79	1	0	406	366	183	157	30	181	367	.243

3 BEAU MILLS, 3B/1B

Born: Aug. 15, 1986. **B-T:** L-R. **Ht.:** 6-3. **Wt.:** 205. **Drafted:** Lewis-Clark State (Idaho), 2007 (1st round). **Signed by:** Greg Smith.

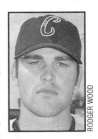

After hitting 36 homers in two years at Fresno State, Mills got suspended for academic shortcomings and code-of-conduct violations in 2006. He decided to transfer to NAIA power Lewis-Clark State (Idaho) after playing for Warriors coach Ed Cheff in the Alaska League, which Mills led with seven homers and 33 RBIs. Mills led Lewis-Clark State to its 15th national title, hitting an NAIA-record 38 homers and driving in 123 runs. The son of former big leaguer and current Red Sox bench coach Brad Mills, Beau went 13th overall in the draft and signed for $1.575 million. With a leveraged, balanced swing and excellent strength, Mills generates well above-average power to all fields. He has the bat speed and pitch recognition to hit for average as well. His hands and his footwork are his best defensive tools, and he has enough athleticism and work ethic to have a chance to become an adequate third baseman. Many scouts who have evaluated Mills give him no chance to stick at the hot corner, and he spent his debut alternating between there and first base. A shoulder impingement in 2006 didn't require surgery but has limited his arm strength, and the Indians have put him on an extensive throwing program. He's going to strike out, but his offensive production will be well worth it. His speed is fringy at best. His arm strength improved during instructional league, so the Tribe will leave Mills at third base when he returns to high Class A Kinston. But first base or possibly left field appears to be his ultimate destination.

Year	Club (League)	Class	AVG	G	AB	R	H	2B	3B	HR	RBI	BB	SO	SB	OBP	SLG
2007	Mahoning Valley (NYP)	A	.179	8	28	5	5	2	0	0	1	3	7	0	.303	.250
	Lake County (SAL)	A	.271	44	177	32	48	12	1	5	36	14	38	0	.333	.435
	Kinston (Car)	A	.275	10	40	7	11	6	0	1	5	4	8	0	.375	.500
MINOR LEAGUE TOTALS			.261	62	245	44	64	20	1	6	42	21	53	0	.337	.424

4 WES HODGES, 3B

Born: Sept. 14, 1984. **B-T:** R-R. **Ht.:** 6-1. **Wt.:** 205. **Drafted:** Georgia Tech, 2006 (2nd round). **Signed by:** Jerry Jordan.

Hodges always has shown a gamer mentality. When he broke the hamate bone in his left wrist as a high school senior, he taught himself to bat lefthanded and hit .430. A 13th-round pick of the White Sox in 2003, he opted to attend Georgia Tech and played through a leg injury that was ultimately diagnosed as a stress fracture during his draft year. Injuries again hampered him during his pro debut in 2007, as a broken toe and hamstring injury cost him three weeks in May. Hodges has an easy, fluid stroke that produces line drives to all fields. His swing has good leverage and he has opposite-field power. He grades out as an average defender with soft hands and average arm strength. He worked with Kinston manager Mike Sarbaugh and infield coordinator Ted Kubiak to push off his back leg and get better extension on his throws. He has a reputation for good plate discipline, but Hodges didn't show it in 2007. He struggled to recognize breaking balls, especially against righthanders. While his throws improved, he struggled charging grounders and ranging to his right, and some in the organization question whether he can stick at third base. Hodges will begin 2008 as the everyday third baseman in Double-A. He's a better defender than Beau Mills, but he needs to stay healthy to be the club's long-term answer at the hot corner.

Year	Club (League)	Class	AVG	G	AB	R	H	2B	3B	HR	RBI	BB	SO	SB	OBP	SLG
2007	Kinston (Car)	A	.288	104	393	60	113	22	3	15	71	44	90	0	.367	.473
MINOR LEAGUE TOTALS			.288	104	393	60	113	22	3	15	71	44	90	0	.367	.473

5 AARON LAFFEY, LHP

Born: April 15, 1985. **B-T:** L-L. **Ht.:** 6-0. **Wt.:** 180. **Drafted:** HS—Allegany, Md., 2003 (16th round). **Signed by:** Bob Mayer.

Laffey fell to the 16th round in the 2003 draft because of his commitment to Virginia Tech, but the Indians took a gamble on him and signed him for $363,000. After bouncing between the bullpen and a starting role throughout his career, he moved back to the rotation for good in 2006 and hurried to the big leagues after just 22 starts in 2007. Laffey wound up winning four of his nine starts in the majors. A groundball machine, Laffey pounds the bottom of the strike zone with three quality pitches. His 86-89 mph sinker has outstanding downward movement and his mid-80s slider has developed into an out pitch with late break. His changeup also improved significantly in 2007, with much better fade and command to both sides of the plate. Lefthanders hit .322 with power against Laffey in the majors, which doesn't make sense because he has the platoon advantage to go with his nasty slider. The Indians think it was more a fluke than anything and aren't concerned. His velocity is below average, but his slider and changeup help his fastball play up. Laffey has surpassed fellow lefties Cliff Lee and Jeremy Sowers in Cleveland's plans. A future No. 3 or 4 starter, he'll compete for a rotation job this spring.

Year	Club (League)	Class	W	L	ERA	G	GS	CG	SV	IP	H	R	ER	HR	BB	SO	AVG
2003	Burlington (Appy)	R	3	1	2.91	9	4	0	0	34	22	13	11	0	15	46	.183
2004	Lake County (SAL)	A	3	7	6.53	19	15	0	1	73	79	58	53	6	44	67	.274
	Mahoning Valley (NYP)	A	3	1	1.24	8	8	0	0	43	38	15	6	1	10	30	.229
2005	Lake County (SAL)	A	7	7	3.22	25	23	1	1	142	123	62	51	5	52	69	.239
	Akron (EL)	AA	1	0	3.60	1	1	0	0	5	8	2	2	0	2	6	.364
2006	Kinston (Car)	A	4	1	2.18	10	4	1	1	41	38	16	10	0	6	24	.241
	Akron (EL)	AA	8	3	3.53	19	19	0	0	112	121	50	44	9	33	61	.286
2007	Akron (EL)	AA	4	1	2.31	6	6	0	0	35	29	13	9	2	7	24	.225
	Buffalo (IL)	AAA	9	3	3.08	16	15	2	0	96	89	36	33	5	23	75	.243
	Cleveland (AL)	MLB	4	2	4.56	9	9	0	0	49	54	26	25	2	12	25	.287
MINOR LEAGUE TOTALS			42	24	3.38	113	95	4	3	583	547	265	219	28	192	402	.250
MAJOR LEAGUE TOTALS			4	2	4.56	9	9	0	0	49	54	26	25	2	12	25	.287

6 NICK WEGLARZ, OF

Born: Dec. 16, 1987. **B-T:** L-L. **Ht.:** 6-3. **Wt.:** 215. **Drafted:** HS—Stevensville, Ontario, 2005 (3rd round). **Signed by:** Les Pajari.

Weglarz was the first Canadian selected in the 2005 draft, going in the third round after being touted as the best power hitter his country had to offer. He struggled in his pro debut, then missed nearly all of 2006 after breaking the hamate bone in his right wrist in spring training. He bounced back last season, ranking among the low Class A South Atlantic League leaders with 23 homers and 82 RBIs as a 19-year-old. Weglarz is comparable to fellow Canadian slugger Justin Morneau for his size and power. Weglarz' long arms allow him to have plenty of plate coverage and he has outstanding natural leverage and loft in his swing. He has good instincts, and he has shown the ability to shorten his stroke and use the opposite field. He's a patient hitter with advanced strike-zone discipline. Weglarz still has trouble getting extended with his swing at times. He'll cut it off at the point of contact and not follow through consistently. He was drafted as a first baseman and played right field during his debut, but his limited arm strength and range will relegate him to left field. He's a below-average runner. Weglarz' bat will have to carry him, and the Tribe thinks it will. He'll begin 2008 in high Class A.

Year	Club (League)	Class	AVG	G	AB	R	H	2B	3B	HR	RBI	BB	SO	SB	OBP	SLG
2005	Burlington (Appy)	R	.231	41	147	22	34	11	0	2	13	17	42	2	.313	.347
2006	Indians (GCL)	R	.000	1	2	0	0	0	0	0	0	0	2	0	.000	.000
2007	Lake County (SAL)	A	.276	125	439	75	121	28	0	23	82	82	129	1	.395	.497
	Kinston (Car)	A	.143	2	7	1	1	0	0	1	1	1	2	0	.250	.571
MINOR LEAGUE TOTALS			.262	169	595	98	156	39	0	26	96	100	175	3	.373	.459

7 JORDAN BROWN, 1B

MIKE JANES

Born: Dec. 18, 1983. **B-T:** L-L. **Ht.:** 6-0. **Wt.:** 205. **Drafted:** Arizona, 2005 (4th round). **Signed by:** Joe Graham.

Often compared to Wally Joyner in college for his aggressive approach and fluid stroke from the left side, Brown has improved his stock by winning back-to-back league MVP awards in the high Class A Carolina and the Eastern leagues the past two seasons. He led the CL with 87 RBIs in 2006 and the EL with a .333 batting average in 2007. Brown uses the whole field with a compact, line-drive swing and he wears out the opposite field. His bat speed is just average, but it plays up because of outstanding plate discipline and pitch recognition. He has good instincts on the bases and stole 11 bases in 13 attempts last year. He's an average defender at first base with good footwork and reactions. The Indians praise his leadership skills. Brown played much of the second half of 2007 with knee problems and had minor arthroscopic surgery in September. He's a below-average runner, which is why he returned to first base after playing left field in 2006. Brown profiles as a first baseman in the mold of Sean Casey or Lyle Overbay. With Ryan Garko's emergence in Cleveland, he'll likely play all of 2008 in Triple-A.

Year	Club (League)	Class	AVG	G	AB	R	H	2B	3B	HR	RBI	BB	SO	SB	OBP	SLG
2005	Mahoning Valley (NYP)	A	.253	19	75	15	19	1	0	3	7	3	7	2	.291	.387
2006	Kinston (Car)	A	.290	125	473	71	137	26	7	15	87	51	59	4	.362	.469
2007	Akron (EL)	AA	.333	127	483	85	161	36	2	11	76	63	56	11	.421	.484
MINOR LEAGUE TOTALS			.307	271	1031	171	317	63	9	29	170	117	122	17	.385	.470

8 DAVID HUFF, LHP

CARL KLINE

Born: Aug. 24, 1984. **B-T:** L-L. **Ht.:** 6-2. **Wt.:** 210. **Drafted:** UCLA, 2006 (1st round supplemental). **Signed by:** Vince Sagisi.

Huff attended UC Irvine, Cypress (Calif.) JC and finally UCLA before signing with the Tribe for $900,000 as a supplemental first-rounder in 2006. Coming out of the draft, the Indians compared him to Jeremy Sowers for his ability to command four pitches, but Huff may have better mound presence. His first full season was a disappointment after elbow soreness shut him down in May, but he returned for the Arizona Fall League. Huff's major strength is the ability to command all parts of the strike zone with a full arsenal of pitches. He can pound the bottom of the zone with an upper-80s sinker that tops out at 91 mph. The sink and depth on his changeup are well above average, and he showed a little cut slider and a deeper curveball during his AFL stint. Huff's velocity is fringy. His secondary pitches still aren't consistently effective against lefthanders, who raked him at a .314 clip in high Class A and then hit .360 against him in the AFL. His changeup can keep lefties off balance, but he can't put them away. Huff's elbow troubles set off an alarm for the Indians, who didn't want to risk any further injury. He could return to high Class A to begin 2008, though Double-A is a more likely destination.

Year	Club (League)	Class	W	L	ERA	G	GS	CG	SV	IP	H	R	ER	HR	BB	SO	AVG
2006	Mahoning Valley (NYP)	A	0	1	5.87	4	4	0	0	7	9	5	5	0	7	8	.300
2007	Kinston (Car)	A	4	2	2.72	11	11	0	0	59	57	23	18	4	15	46	.251
MINOR LEAGUE TOTALS			4	3	3.07	15	15	0	0	67	66	28	23	4	22	54	.257

9 BEN FRANCISCO, OF

MIKE JANES

Born: Oct. 23, 1981. **B-T:** R-R. **Ht.:** 6-1. **Wt.:** 190. **Drafted:** UCLA, 2002 (5th round). **Signed by:** Jason Smith.

Aside from a down year in 2004, when he skipped a level up to Double-A, Francisco has been one of the most consistent hitters in the system since he was drafted in 2002. His track record extends beyond pro ball, as he hit .330 in two seasons at Cypress (Calif.) JC before earning all-Pacific-10 Conference honors in each of his two years at UCLA. One of the best athletes in the system, Francisco drew comparisons to Torii Hunter from Triple-A International League managers for his bat speed, energy and defensive prowess. Scouts aren't completely sold on Francisco's power, but it's at least average. He's a well above-average runner with good instincts on the bases. He has the range and arm to play all three outfield spots. Lefthanders give Francisco a tough time, and he has trouble picking up pitches against them. While he is a patient hitter, he needs to do a better job at working deeper counts. When he gets behind in the count, he seldom works out of it with positive results. Francisco has a wide skill set of tools, but hasn't been given a full-time opportunity with Cleveland, mainly due to their deluge of outfield talent. He'll provide an insurance policy as a fourth outfielder or return to Triple-A again to wait in the wings.

Year	Club (League)	Class	AVG	G	AB	R	H	2B	3B	HR	RBI	BB	SO	SB	OBP	SLG
2002	Mahoning Valley (NYP)	A	.349	58	235	55	82	23	2	3	23	22	28	22	.416	.502
2003	Lake County (SAL)	A	.287	80	289	57	83	21	1	11	48	31	50	15	.359	.481
2004	Akron (EL)	AA	.254	133	497	72	126	29	3	15	71	50	86	21	.326	.414
2005	Akron (EL)	AA	.307	83	323	45	99	19	7	7	46	24	59	15	.357	.474
	Buffalo (IL)	AAA	.500	4	16	4	8	1	0	0	3	1	3	1	.500	.563
2006	Buffalo (IL)	AAA	.278	134	515	80	143	32	4	17	59	45	72	25	.345	.454
2007	Buffalo (IL)	AAA	.318	95	377	60	120	27	2	12	51	36	66	22	.382	.496
	Cleveland (AL)	MLB	.274	25	62	10	17	5	0	3	12	3	19	0	.303	.500
MINOR LEAGUE TOTALS			.294	587	2252	373	661	152	19	65	301	209	364	121	.359	.464
MAJOR LEAGUE TOTALS			.274	25	62	10	17	5	0	3	12	3	19	0	.303	.500

10 JENSEN LEWIS, RHP

Born: Sept. 26, 1983. **B-T:** R-R. **Ht.:** 6-0. **Wt.:** 185. **Drafted:** Vanderbilt, 2005 (3rd round). **Signed by:** Scott Barnsby.

RICH ABEL

The Indians drafted Lewis twice, in the 33rd round out of high school and again in the third round out of Vanderbilt, where he was a teammate of Jeremy Sowers. Prior to 2007, Lewis was as well known in the organization for his Bob Uecker impressions and his lack of a third pitch as anything. But he broke through in his new role as a setup man in 2007, making seven appearances for Cleveland in the playoffs. As a reliever, Lewis attacks hitters with a 91-93 mph sinker that he spots well. He does a good job of varying speeds, and his changeup ranks among the best in the system. It helped him limit big league lefthanders to a .244 average with no extra-base hits in 44 at-bats. He scrapped his slider in 2006 in favor of a softer, deeper curveball that's much more effective. His mechanics create some deception on the front side and are easily repeatable. Lewis can still rush with his lower half in his delivery at times. When that happens he gets under his pitches, flattening them out and leaving them high in the strike zone. Moving to the bullpen proved to be the best thing for Lewis. The Indians are counting on him to once again be an integral part of their relief corps in 2008.

Year	Club (League)	Class	W	L	ERA	G	GS	CG	SV	IP	H	R	ER	HR	BB	SO	AVG
2005	Mahoning Valley (NYP)	A	4	2	3.20	13	11	0	0	59	58	24	21	6	11	59	.253
2006	Kinston (Car)	A	7	6	3.99	21	20	0	0	108	110	59	48	11	29	94	.261
	Akron (EL)	AA	1	2	3.89	7	7	0	0	39	41	21	17	4	12	44	.270
2007	Akron (EL)	AA	2	0	1.85	24	0	0	1	39	27	12	8	2	13	49	.196
	Buffalo (IL)	AAA	1	0	1.38	10	0	0	1	13	5	2	2	1	4	12	.116
	Cleveland (AL)	MLB	1	1	2.15	26	0	0	0	29	26	8	7	1	10	34	.234
MINOR LEAGUE TOTALS			15	10	3.34	75	38	0	2	258	241	118	96	24	69	258	.245
MAJOR LEAGUE TOTALS			1	1	2.15	26	0	0	0	29	26	8	7	1	10	34	.234

11 MASAHIDE KOBAYASHI, RHP

Born: May 24, 1974. **B-T:** R-R. **Ht.:** 6-0. **Wt.:** 195. **Signed:** Japan, 2007. **Signed by:** Nate Minchey.

The Indians were active on the Pacific Rim in 2006 and made a bigger splash in 2007, when they signed Kobayashi in November for $6 million over two years. A nine-year veteran in Japan, Kobayashi left the Chiba Lotte Marines with 227 career saves, after notching more than 20 saves in each of the last seven seasons. Kobayashi throws three pitches for strikes, and unlike a lot of Japanese pitchers, his 90-94 mph fastball has good life in the zone. His slider could be his best pitch with short late action, power and bite. Kobayashi uses his forkball to finish off hitters, but will throw it in any count. The Indians plan on using him as a sixth- or seventh-inning reliever, but Kobayashi also provides insurance if Lewis or veteran closer Joe Borowski falters. He has plenty of big game experience and Tribe officials rave about his poise and mound presence.

Year	Club (League)	Class	W	L	ERA	G	GS	CG	SV	IP	H	R	ER	HR	BB	SO	AVG
1999	Chiba Lotte (PL)	JAP	5	5	2.68	46	7	3	0	124	93	42	37	8	55	107	—
2000	Chiba Lotte (PL)	JAP	11	6	2.13	65	3	0	14	110	87	34	26	4	37	72	—
2001	Chiba Lotte (PL)	JAP	0	4	4.33	48	0	0	33	52	54	25	25	7	13	47	—
2002	Chiba Lotte (PL)	JAP	2	1	0.83	43	0	0	37	43	26	4	4	1	6	41	—
2003	Chiba Lotte (PL)	JAP	0	2	2.87	44	0	0	33	47	45	18	15	2	11	30	—
2004	Chiba Lotte (PL)	JAP	8	5	3.90	51	0	0	20	58	51	25	25	4	19	50	—
2005	Chiba Lotte (PL)	JAP	2	2	2.58	46	0	0	29	45	49	14	13	6	9	33	—

2006	Chiba Lotte (PL)	JAP	6	2	2.68	53	0	0	34	54	49	16	16	4	8	48	—
2007	Chiba Lotte (PL)	JAP	2	7	3.61	49	0	0	27	47	53	24	19	4	12	35	—
JAPAN LEAGUE TOTALS			36	34	2.79	445	10	3	227	580	507	202	180	40	170	463	—

12 TONY SIPP, LHP

Born: July 12, 1983. **B-T:** L-L. **Ht.:** 6-0. **Wt.:** 185. **Drafted:** Clemson, 2004 (45th round). **Signed by:** Tim Moore.

A two-way player at Meridian (Miss.) JC and at Clemson, Sipp had a modest season as a college junior, and the Indians took a flier on him in the 45th round in 2004 and then signed him for $130,000 after a strong showing in the Cape Cod League. Sipp was moving through the system quickly and was considered for a major league bullpen spot ahead of lefthander Rafael Perez last spring before breaking down and needing Tommy John surgery. When he's right, Sipp is a funky, deceptive late-inning reliever with the ability to attack lefthanders and righthanders. His 89-93 mph fastball is a swing-and-miss pitch, and he mixes in an above-average slider and plus changeup. Sipp relied on his changeup too much at times before he got hurt, and needs to focus on fastball command. He'll be out of action until at least June, and even if his stuff returns, he likely won't factor into the major league club's needs until 2009. Nevertheless, Cleveland protected him on its 40-man roster in November.

Year	Club (League)	Class	W	L	ERA	G	GS	CG	SV	IP	H	R	ER	HR	BB	SO	AVG
2004	Mahoning Valley (NYP)	A	3	1	3.16	10	10	0	0	42	33	23	15	5	13	74	.212
2005	Lake County (SAL)	A	4	1	2.22	13	12	0	0	69	47	19	17	5	19	71	.196
	Kinston (Car)	A	2	2	2.66	22	5	0	2	47	34	19	14	4	23	59	.205
2006	Akron (EL)	AA	4	2	3.13	29	4	0	3	60	44	23	21	2	21	80	.201
2007	Did Not Play—Injured																
MINOR LEAGUE TOTALS			13	6	2.75	74	31	0	5	219	158	84	67	16	76	284	.202

13 MATT McBRIDE, C

Born: May 23, 1985. **B-T:** R-R. **Ht.:** 6-3. **Wt.:** 205. **Drafted:** Lehigh, 2006 (2nd round supplemental). **Signed by:** Brent Urcheck.

After Victor Martinez graduated to the big leagues in 2002, the Indians had trouble developing catching depth in their system. They addressed the shortage in 2006, drafting McBride and trading for Kelly Shoppach and Max Ramirez (whom they later included in a deal for Kenny Lofton last year). Cleveland loves the leverage and loft in McBride's swing. He makes consistent hard contact and his strike-zone discipline and pitch recognition are both assets. He's a natural leader who runs a pitching staff well. He's more athletic and runs better than most catchers. One of the organization's hardest workers, he arrived at the Tribe's complex at 6 a.m. every morning during spring training to work on his core strength. Though McBride has solid-average arm strength, he threw out just 14 percent of basestealers last season. He also struggled with his receiving skills, committing 16 passed balls. Then he had minor surgery on his throwing shoulder during the offseason. He should be ready for spring training. There's no talk of moving him from behind the plate just yet, and Cleveland's logjam at first base would make it tough to find a spot for McBride. The tools are there, and he'll be challenged to improve defensively in high Class A this season.

Year	Club (League)	Class	AVG	G	AB	R	H	2B	3B	HR	RBI	BB	SO	SB	OBP	SLG
2006	Mahoning Valley (NYP)	A	.272	52	184	24	50	12	0	4	31	16	22	5	.355	.402
2007	Lake County (SAL)	A	.283	105	421	66	119	35	2	8	66	38	54	1	.348	.432
	Akron (EL)	AA	.571	2	7	2	4	2	0	0	0	0	0	0	.625	.857
MINOR LEAGUE TOTALS			.283	159	612	92	173	49	2	12	97	54	76	6	.354	.428

14 TREVOR CROWE, OF

Born: Nov. 17, 1983. **B-T:** B-R. **Ht.:** 6-0. **Wt.:** 200. **Drafted:** Arizona, 2005 (1st round). **Signed by:** Joe Graham.

Jordan Brown was considered the second-best prospect the Indians signed out of Arizona in 2005, but after Crowe endured an ill-advised move to second base at the end of 2006 and an atrocious first half last year, Brown appears to have a higher ceiling than his college teammate. Crowe's numbers were on par or better than Red Sox outfielder Jacoby Ellsbury's when both were in the Carolina League in 2006, but after being promoted to Double-A and being asked to move to the infield, all facets of Crowe's game fell apart. Crowe spent the bulk of last spring in major league camp and had an outside chance of making the roster. When he was instead sent to Double-A, he lacked confidence, began swinging at bad breaking balls out of the zone and took his struggles with him to the field. Crowe eventually put things together and hit .318 over the season's final two months. He had a lot more hand movement in his approach than he ever had, but quieted things down significantly by midseason. There are a lot of questions about Crowe's ceiling. While scouts projected average power for him coming out of college, he seems likely to fall short of that now, and he won't play center field in Cleveland anytime soon. A strained chest muscle cut Crowe's Arizona Fall League stint short but isn't a long-term concern. He will likely move up to Triple-A, but a return trip to Double-A might be in order.

Year	Club (League)	Class	AVG	G	AB	R	H	2B	3B	HR	RBI	BB	SO	SB	OBP	SLG
2005	Mahoning Valley (NYP)	A	.255	12	51	9	13	2	1	1	6	6	8	4	.345	.392
	Lake County (SAL)	A	.258	44	178	18	46	8	2	0	23	18	25	7	.327	.326
	Akron (EL)	AA	.100	3	10	1	1	0	0	0	0	0	3	0	.100	.100
2006	Kinston (Car)	A	.329	60	219	51	72	15	2	4	31	48	46	29	.449	.470
	Lake County (SAL)	A	.000	2	5	0	0	0	0	0	0	0	1	0	.000	.000
	Akron (EL)	AA	.234	39	154	20	36	7	2	1	13	20	24	16	.318	.325
2007	Akron (EL)	AA	.259	133	518	87	134	26	4	5	50	62	71	28	.341	.353
MINOR LEAGUE TOTALS			.266	293	1135	186	302	58	11	11	123	154	178	84	.355	.366

15 CHRIS JONES, LHP

Born: Sept. 19, 1988. **B-T:** L-L. **Ht.:** 6-2. **Wt.:** 165. **Drafted:** HS—Tampa, Fla., 2007 (15th round). **Signed by:** Mike Soper.

Jones fully expected to attend South Florida this past fall, but the Indians selected him in the 15th round. They decided to go over slot to sign him for $350,000 after seeing him extensively last summer with the Midland (Ohio) Redskins, an elite travel team. Several members of the organization like Jones better than big league lefty Aaron Laffey at the same stage of their development for his ability to pitch to the bottom of the strike zone and roll up ground balls. Pitching from a three-quarters arm slot, Jones' fastball has good natural life, currently sitting at 88-92 mph, and he projects to add velocity as he fills out physically. The life and action on his fastball through the zone is above-average as well. His two other pitches lag behind his fastball at this point, but he's shown the ability to spin a slurvy breaking ball and a good feel for his changeup. Jones will likely make his full-season debut at low Class A Lake County this season and profiles as a power lefty reliever, though like Laffey, the Indians will give him every opportunity to start.

Year	Club (League)	Class	W	L	ERA	G	GS	CG	SV	IP	H	R	ER	HR	BB	SO	AVG
2007	Indians (GCL)	R	0	0	2.45	1	1	0	0	3	4	1	1	0	2	5	.267
	Lake County (SAL)	A	0	1	6.75	1	1	0	0	4	4	3	3	1	3	2	.286
MINOR LEAGUE TOTALS			0	1	4.70	2	2	0	0	7	8	4	4	1	5	7	.276

16 SCOTT LEWIS, LHP

Born: Sept. 26, 1983. **B-T:** B-L. **Ht.:** 6-0. **Wt.:** 190. **Drafted:** Ohio State, 2004 (3rd round). **Signed by:** Bob Mayer.

After recovering from Tommy John surgery in college and biceps tendinitis that plagued him his first two seasons as a pro, Lewis maximized his 60-75 pitch counts in 2006 and led the minors in ERA. He took the next step last season, working nearly as many innings in 2007 as his first three years combined. A command/control deceptive lefthander, Lewis' fastball sits at 86-90 mph when he's at his best, and his changeup improved in depth and fade over the course of the season. He needs to command both pitches better with his modest velocity. His only plus pitch since college was always a 12-to-6 curveball, but Lewis lost confidence in the pitch last year after he lacked command of it early in the season. He's learning a slider to help deepen his repertoire. His delivery is simple and easy to repeat, but he still throws across his body at times. Lewis still projects as a No. 4 or No. 5 starter, and the Indians see last season as a major step in the right direction. But Lewis will need to prove he's durable based on his medical history. Added to the 40-man roster during the offseason, he'll start in the Triple-A rotation in 2008.

Year	Club (League)	Class	W	L	ERA	G	GS	CG	SV	IP	H	R	ER	HR	BB	SO	AVG
2004	Mahoning Valley (NYP)	A	0	2	5.06	3	3	0	0	5	5	3	3	0	1	13	.250
2005	Mahoning Valley (NYP)	A	0	1	4.60	7	6	0	0	15	13	8	8	2	6	24	.224
2006	Kinston (Car)	A	3	3	1.48	27	26	0	0	115	84	24	19	3	28	123	.203
2007	Akron (EL)	AA	7	9	3.68	27	25	0	0	134	135	58	55	13	34	121	.262
MINOR LEAGUE TOTALS			10	15	2.82	64	60	0	0	271	237	93	85	18	69	281	.235

17 SUNG-WEI TSENG, RHP

Born: Dec. 28, 1985. **B-T:** R-R. **Ht.:** 5-11. **Wt.:** 180. **Signed:** Taiwan, 2006. **Signed by:** Jason Lee.

Taiwan's top amateur pitcher in 2006, the Indians signed Tseng for $300,000. He'd spent the summer of 2005 pitching in the summer collegiate Alaska League, where he ranked as that league's No. 4 prospect. The Indians expressed their concern with Tseng's workload by the national team in last year's Intercontinental Cup, and assistant GM John Mirabelli closely monitored Tseng's outings again during Taiwan's appearances in the '07 World Cup and Olympic Qualifier, and he was used less aggressively this time around. While Tseng had a solid debut during the first half of last year, he wore down over the course of the year and posted a 5.21

ERA in August. Tseng works in the low 90s with an explosive fastball, and is very aggressive on the mound. He has good command of the fastball and slider, but his best pitch is his split-finger fastball. The pitch features tight, down spiral and he commands it to both sides of the plate, giving him a weapon against lefties and righties. His delivery is simple and compact and he creates good natural deception. Tseng profiles as a solid No. 3 starter, but he'll have to hold up for a full season in 2008, which he'll begin in Double-A.

Year	Club (League)	Class	W	L	ERA	G	GS	CG	SV	IP	H	R	ER	HR	BB	SO	AVG
2007	Kinston (Car)	A	6	9	4.05	26	26	0	0	140	130	71	63	10	47	92	.250
MINOR LEAGUE TOTALS			6	9	4.05	26	26	0	0	140	130	71	63	10	47	92	.250

18 CARLOS RIVERO, SS

Born: May 20, 1988. **B-T:** R-R. **Ht.:** 6-3. **Wt.:** 200. **Signed:** Venezuela, 2005. **Signed by:** Henry Centeno.

Several clubs passed on Rivero as a 16-year-old in 2005 when the Indians signed him for $100,000. That could wind up being a bargain-basement price if Rivero's performance matches his tools. For his size, Rivero still shows good hands, range and a plus arm at short, though as he continues to fill into his body, he might have to move to third base. Rivero has big raw power and hitting ability to go with his defensive tools. His bat speed is above-average and he features an easy, fluid stroke. Rivero's ceiling will ultimately be determined by his offensive approach. Plate discipline is the first and foremost concern, as Rivero struggles to recognize breaking balls. But overall discipline and his maturity will also play a large role. Several front-office personnel and managers around the South Atlantic League dropped points from Rivero's game because he's too flashy and appears lackadaisical at times. He'll head to high Class A for 2008, where he's sure to see a steady diet of offspeed stuff.

Year	Club (League)	Class	AVG	G	AB	R	H	2B	3B	HR	RBI	BB	SO	SB	OBP	SLG
2005	Indians1 (DSL)	R	.257	66	237	21	61	6	0	0	31	12	26	7	.295	.283
2006	Indians (GCL)	R	.284	37	134	17	38	6	0	2	22	10	20	0	.338	.373
	Burlington (Appy)	R	.212	16	66	3	14	3	0	1	7	5	11	0	.264	.303
2007	Lake County (SAL)	A	.261	115	436	59	114	26	0	7	62	47	84	1	.332	.369
MINOR LEAGUE TOTALS			.260	234	873	100	227	41	0	10	122	74	141	8	.318	.341

19 JEFF STEVENS, RHP

Born: Sept. 5, 1983. **B-T:** R-R. **Ht.:** 6-1. **Wt.:** 200. **Drafted:** Loyola Marymount, 2005 (6th round). **Signed by:** Mike Misuraca (Reds).

In college Stevens outpitched his more celebrated teammate (and Mariners fifth-rounder) Stephen Kahn before the 2005 draft, going 6-7, 3.97 with 76 strikeouts in 100 innings. After a year and a half in the Reds system, Stevens was the player to be named in the Brandon Phillips deal, coming over in June 2006. Stevens finished the year in Double-A and moved on briefly to the Arizona Fall League before pitching for Team USA in the World Cup. He got the save for the Americans as they beat Cuba to win the gold medal. Stevens creates good down angle and deception on his 92-94 mph fastball, touching 95. He's adept at missing bats with his fastball, elevating it and hitting his spots while maintaining velocity. He also features a power mid-80s curveball that has tremendous depth at times, though it lacks consistency. He also throws a changeup and has toyed with a cutter. Stevens had trouble maintaining his composure at times on the mound, but normally has good presence and poise. He'll start in Triple-A, but several scouts who saw Stevens in 2007 think he has the stuff to pitch in the majors now.

Year	Club (League)	Class	W	L	ERA	G	GS	CG	SV	IP	H	R	ER	HR	BB	SO	AVG
2005	Billings (Pio)	R	4	4	2.98	13	8	0	0	54	44	20	18	4	15	58	.220
2006	Dayton (MWL)	A	2	4	4.43	14	6	0	0	42	42	22	21	6	16	43	.261
	Lake County (SAL)	A	7	3	4.42	16	15	0	0	73	65	40	36	4	23	60	.232
2007	Kinston (Car)	A	3	2	2.31	15	0	0	0	35	18	13	9	2	9	37	.150
	Akron (EL)	AA	3	1	3.17	34	0	0	2	48	40	17	17	4	16	65	.223
MINOR LEAGUE TOTALS			19	14	3.58	92	29	0	2	253	209	112	101	20	79	263	.222

20 JOSH RODRIGUEZ, SS

Born: Dec. 18, 1984. **B-T:** R-R. **Ht.:** 6-0. **Wt.:** 180. **Drafted:** Rice, 2006 (2nd round). **Signed by:** Les Pajari.

Considered one of the top shortstops available in the 2006 draft, Rodriguez's stock plummeted during his junior season at Rice due to a nagging elbow injury. When he returned to the Owls, he lost his position to Brian Friday (the Pirates' 2007 third-round pick) and finished the season at third base. Area scouts in Texas were skeptical of Rodriguez's quickness and range at shortstop, but the Indians left him there during his first full season and he made 32 errors, tied for most in the Carolina League. Consistency was Rodriguez' biggest difficulty defensively, as he'd make a highlight-reel play look easy, then struggle with average ground balls.

Offensively, a huge month of August—which included 10 homers in 117 at-bats as well as a game with nine RBIs on Aug. 2—boosted his overall numbers. He tied for third in the CL in homers, ranked fourth in RBIs and first in runs, and was the league's only 20-homers, 20-steals man. Rodriguez has surprising strength and gets a lot of leverage out of his compact swing. He showed above-average power, mostly to the pull side at Kinston, but organization officials praised him during the season for starting to use the whole field. He's a tick below average runner. His arm strength is also above-average and should allow him to move to third as a pro if he can't handle shortstop. He'll open 2008 as an everyday shortstop in Double-A.

Year	Club (League)	Class	AVG	G	AB	R	H	2B	3B	HR	RBI	BB	SO	SB	OBP	SLG
2006	Mahoning Valley (NYP)	A	.268	45	157	26	42	11	4	4	24	14	33	2	.337	.465
2007	Kinston (Car)	A	.262	133	493	84	129	20	9	20	82	68	95	21	.351	.460
MINOR LEAGUE TOTALS			.263	178	650	110	171	31	13	24	106	82	128	23	.348	.462

21 RYAN MILLER, LHP

Born: Dec. 14, 1986. **B-T:** L-L. **Ht.:** 6-0. **Wt.:** 195. **Drafted:** Blinn (Texas) JC, D/F 2006 (36th round). **Signed by:** Les Pajari.

One of the top lefties on the last-ever draft-and-follow market last spring, Miller returned to Blinn (Texas) JC for his sophomore season after the Indians drafted him in the 36th round. After he went 9-0, 2.05 and ranked among the national juco leaders with 115 strikeouts in 92 innings, Cleveland anted up $450,000 to keep him from re-entering the 2007 draft. Miller, who turned down an Arkansas scholarship to go pro, has very good stuff for a lefthander. He goes after hitters with a 91-93 mph fastball and a hard 78-81 mph breaking ball. He's still somewhat raw and needs to work on things such as not tipping off his marginal changeup by slowing down his arm speed. While he throws strikes, he needs to locate his pitches better in the strike zone. He's not very big, and after fading late in his pro debut, he'll need to get stronger before his first full season. He'll open 2008 in low Class A.

Year	Club (League)	Class	W	L	ERA	G	GS	CG	SV	IP	H	R	ER	HR	BB	SO	AVG
2007	Mahoning Valley (NYP)	A	0	2	18.69	3	3	0	0	4	9	10	9	1	8	3	.409
	Indians (GCL)	R	4	2	2.40	9	9	1	0	45	26	15	12	1	12	44	.160
MINOR LEAGUE TOTALS			4	4	3.83	12	12	1	0	49	35	25	21	2	20	47	.189

22 MICHAEL AUBREY, 1B

Born: April 15, 1982. **B-T:** L-L. **Ht.:** 6-0. **Wt.:** 190. **Drafted:** Tulane, 2003 (1st round). **Signed by:** Scott Meaney.

Chronic back problems caused Aubrey to drop almost completely off the prospect radar in 2006, when he was limited to just 54 at-bats. The injuries extend into Aubrey's college career at Tulane, where he was a standout two-way player and the 2001 Freshman of the Year. However, back problems forced him off the mound in college, and Aubrey went down in May 2005 with what was diagnosed as a stress fracture in his back, and has been rehabbing the injury ever since. After getting just 250 at-bats during the 2007 regular season, Aubrey reported to the Arizona Fall League, where he boosted his stock significantly, hitting five homers while showing his usual outstanding plate discipline. His performance earned him a spot on the 40-man roster. When he's healthy, Aubrey is the best natural hitter in the system with plus bat speed, quick hands and uncanny bat control. He's also the best first baseman in the organization, ranking as a premium defender with Gold Glove potential. As has been his story, his ceiling is extremely high, but his health will have the final say if he reaches it. A healthy Aubrey will challenge for a role in Triple-A this year, and the Indians would settle for getting him 500 at-bats at any level.

Year	Club (League)	Class	AVG	G	AB	R	H	2B	3B	HR	RBI	BB	SO	SB	OBP	SLG
2003	Lake County (SAL)	A	.348	38	138	22	48	13	0	5	19	14	22	0	.409	.551
2004	Kinston (Car)	A	.339	60	218	34	74	14	1	10	60	27	26	3	.438	.550
	Akron (EL)	AA	.261	38	134	13	35	7	0	5	22	15	18	0	.340	.425
2005	Akron (EL)	AA	.283	28	106	17	30	5	1	4	20	7	18	1	.336	.462
2006	Kinston (Car)	A	.286	8	28	8	8	3	0	2	10	5	5	0	.417	.607
	Akron (EL)	AA	.269	6	26	3	7	2	0	1	2	2	4	0	.345	.462
2007	Kinston (Car)	A	.400	13	50	15	20	5	0	5	11	6	7	0	.492	.800
	Akron (EL)	AA	.248	52	206	22	51	11	0	7	34	10	35	0	.290	.403
MINOR LEAGUE TOTALS			.301	243	906	134	273	60	2	39	178	86	135	4	.375	.501

23 JOHN DRENNEN, OF

Born: Aug. 26, 1986. **B-T:** L-L. **Ht.:** 5-11. **Wt.:** 185. **Drafted:** HS—San Diego, 2005 (1st round supplemental). **Signed by:** Jason Smith.

Drennen was one of the most highly touted high school hitters in the 2005 draft, and he made national headlines during his first full pro season when he homered off a rehabbing Roger Clemens in 2006. Since then, however, Drennen stalled out in high Class A and hasn't been able to get untracked. He has good strength for an undersized hitter and produces above-average raw power. His other tools all grade out as average. Drennen fell in love with his power too much the past two seasons and stopped shortening his stroke to use the whole field to his advantage. He started pulling everything as a result, and his swing became too long. Drennen had no chance against lefthanders in 2007, hitting .153/.240/.241, and must improve in that area to become a big league regular. Managers in the Carolina League in 2007 also thought he'd lost some of his bat speed, though Tribe officials disagree with that assessment. They want Drennen to develop his power naturally, and he'll have another opportunity to do that when he starts 2008 in Kinston for a repeat performance.

Year	Club (League)	Class	AVG	G	AB	R	H	2B	3B	HR	RBI	BB	SO	SB	OBP	SLG
2005	Burlington (Appy)	R	.238	51	168	24	40	7	1	8	29	18	37	6	.325	.435
2006	Lake County (SAL)	A	.321	67	240	33	77	12	3	6	30	31	52	6	.409	.471
	Kinston (Car)	A	.239	31	113	15	27	6	2	0	8	12	21	2	.328	.327
2007	Kinston (Car)	A	.254	131	496	72	126	25	2	13	77	53	104	6	.336	.391
MINOR LEAGUE TOTALS			.265	280	1017	144	270	50	8	27	144	114	214	20	.351	.410

24 WYATT TOREGAS, C

Born: Dec. 2, 1982. **B-T:** R-R. **Ht.:** 5-11. **Wt.:** 200. **Drafted:** Virginia Tech, 2004 (24th round). **Signed by:** Bob Mayer.

A versatile performer at Virginia Tech who played infield and outfield as well as catcher, Toregas has emerged as a prospect since switching positions and becoming a full-time catcher. The Indians added him to their 40-man roster in November. He became the complete package behind the plate in 2006 and took another step forward last year, continuing to hone his game-calling skills and maintain some offensive upside. A contact hitter with good plate discipline, Toregas hits line drives to all fields, showing surprising power as well. He reads pitches well and can turn on inside fastballs, though he can get too pull-happy at times. Toregas' gregarious demeanor can sometimes rub pitchers the wrong way, but he's a natural leader who handles a staff well. Toregas has the best catch-and-throw skills in the system, and threw out 51 percent of basestealers last year, tops in the Eastern League. He possesses well-above-average arm strength, posting 1.85 pop times consistently. Though the organization is split on how much upside Toregas has, he's at least a solid backup in the majors. He'll likely spend all of 2008 in Triple-A.

Year	Club (League)	Class	AVG	G	AB	R	H	2B	3B	HR	RBI	BB	SO	SB	OBP	SLG
2004	Mahoning Valley (NYP)	A	.294	59	214	38	63	18	1	7	48	11	26	1	.338	.486
2005	Lake County (SAL)	A	.231	104	411	57	95	22	0	5	42	37	76	0	.302	.321
2006	Kinston (Car)	A	.336	44	146	25	49	14	0	4	23	20	28	0	.418	.514
	Akron (EL)	AA	.258	48	163	21	42	10	0	4	29	14	33	1	.319	.393
2007	Akron (EL)	AA	.250	86	284	36	71	16	0	6	39	27	45	3	.317	.370
MINOR LEAGUE TOTALS			.263	341	1218	177	320	80	1	26	181	109	208	5	.328	.394

25 BRAD SNYDER, OF

Born: May 25, 1982. **B-T:** L-L. **Ht.:** 6-3. **Wt.:** 200. **Drafted:** Ball State, 2003 (1st round). **Signed by:** Bob Mayer/Chuck Ricci.

Snyder's brother Ben, a lefthander who followed him at Ball State, ranks as the Giants' No. 21 prospect. Brad has better tools, is in a deeper organization and is considered a better prospect, but his younger brother out-performed him in 2007. In 2006, the Indians experimented with Snyder, batting him in the leadoff spot at Akron to push him to work deeper counts and improve his two-strike approach. Snyder still ranked 10th in the minors in strikeouts that season, and hasn't improved much since moving back down the lineup. He was on pace to top his career-high 158 strikeouts before a broken thumb put him out of action at the end of July. Still, the Indians believe in Snyder's wide tool set. He runs extremely well for his size, has plus bat speed, above-average power and outstanding arm strength that profile him as an everyday right-field candidate. His lack of ability to control the strike zone is particularly acute against lefthanders—he struck out in 32 of 79 at-bats against them in 2007, batting just .203. His propensity for striking out likely means Snyder will never hit for much of an average, and it seems as though the Tribe is willing to live with the whiffs. The more contact he makes, though, the more his power comes into play. He did return late in the year in the Arizona Fall League, replacing Trevor Crowe after his injury. The Indians chose to keep Snyder on the 40-man roster this winter over outfielder Brian Barton, and are hopeful Snyder can turn it around.

Year	Club (League)	Class	AVG	G	AB	R	H	2B	3B	HR	RBI	BB	SO	SB	OBP	SLG
2003	Mahoning Valley (NYP)	A	.284	62	225	52	64	11	6	6	31	41	82	14	.393	.467
2004	Lake County (SAL)	A	.280	79	304	52	85	15	5	10	54	48	78	11	.382	.461
	Kinston (Car)	A	.355	29	110	20	39	7	1	6	21	13	28	4	.424	.600
2005	Kinston (Car)	A	.278	58	209	36	58	10	2	6	28	24	64	12	.365	.431

	Akron (EL)	AA	.280	75	304	56	85	21	5	16	54	25	94	5	.345	.539
2006	Akron (EL)	AA	.270	135	523	86	141	28	5	18	72	62	158	20	.351	.446
2007	Buffalo (IL)	AAA	.263	86	259	41	68	12	3	10	35	36	91	12	.355	.448
MINOR LEAGUE TOTALS			.279	524	1934	343	540	104	27	72	295	249	595	78	.366	.473

26 FRANK HERRMANN, RHP

Born: May 30, 1984. **B-T:** L-R. **Ht.:** 6-4. **Wt.:** 220. **Drafted:** Harvard, NDFA 2005. **Signed by:** Phil Rossi.

One of the most intelligent players in the organization, Herrmann is also one of its greatest success stories. After struggling with elbow tendinitis in college, Herrmann was passed over in the 2005 draft and eventually signed for $35,000 with the Indians after they saw him in the Hawaii Collegiate Baseball League. The Tribe also agreed to pay Herrmann's final two semesters at Harvard, and he graduated last spring with an economics degree. He also kept a diary of his first year in pro ball on the website of Harvard's student newspaper, The Crimson. He's proved a quick study on the field as well, though he has work to do. After revamping his delivery in 2006 with the help of Lake County pitching coach Ruben Niebla, Herrmann made major strides in the Carolina League. Herrmann features a low-90s power sinker, slurvy breaking ball and changeup. His changeup was his best weapon to both work ahead in counts and put hitters away. He struggled to maintain his arm slot at times and his pitches elevated, which led to 15 home runs allowed. Herrmann has tackled each challenge thrown his way since he signed, and will begin 2008 in the Double-A rotation.

Year	Club (League)	Class	W	L	ERA	G	GS	CG	SV	IP	H	R	ER	HR	BB	SO	AVG
2006	Lake County (SAL)	A	4	6	3.90	26	26	0	0	122	122	61	53	8	47	89	.261
2007	Kinston (Car)	A	11	5	4.01	26	26	3	0	146	163	75	65	15	28	88	.285
MINOR LEAGUE TOTALS			15	11	3.96	52	52	3	0	268	285	136	118	23	75	177	.274

27 CHRIS NASH, 1B

Born: Feb. 22, 1987. **B-T:** R-R. **Ht.:** 6-4. **Wt.:** 230. **Drafted:** Johnson County (Mo.) CC, 2006 (24th round). **Signed by:** Steve Abney.

Courted more for his football background as an amateur, Nash was pursued by major college football programs such as Southern California, Michigan and Kansas State to play tight end. But a foot injury affected his football future and draft status in baseball as he fell to the 22nd round in 2005, when the Angels picked him as a draft-and-follow. He didn't sign, and the Indians drafted him the next year in the 24th round, after an all-conference season as a freshman that included nine home runs in 136 at-bats at Johnson County (Mo.) CC. Nash is one of the better athletes in the system and has above-average raw power to all fields. His swing can get a little long and he becomes too pull-conscious at times, but he held his own with wood in the Rookie-level Gulf Coast League. He's somewhat raw defensively, but infield coordinator Ted Kubiak worked extensively on his hands and footwork around the bag, and Nash made improvements. His arm strength is just average, but his bat should be enough to carry him. Nash will move to low Class A in 2008.

Year	Club (League)	Class	AVG	G	AB	R	H	2B	3B	HR	RBI	BB	SO	SB	OBP	SLG
2006	Did Not Play—Signed Late															
2007	Indians (GCL)	R	.313	47	166	28	52	16	0	3	21	17	35	4	.372	.464
	Mahoning Valley (NYP)	A	.274	16	62	4	17	4	1	0	12	7	18	0	.352	.371
MINOR LEAGUE TOTALS			.303	63	228	32	69	20	1	3	33	24	53	4	.367	.439

28 HECTOR RONDON, RHP

Born: Feb. 26, 1988. **B-T:** R-R. **Ht.:** 6-3. **Wt.:** 165. **Signed:** Venezuela, 2004. **Signed by:** Stewart Ruiz.

The highlight of Rondon's first full season came on July 3 when he combined with Neil Wagner on a no-hitter against Delmarva. Signed out of Venezuela in 2004, Rondon has a wiry frame with a lively 90-93 mph fastball. He has a loose, easy delivery and his projectable body could add more velocity. He pounds the zone aggressively and has good mound presence. His curveball grades as average, and he can get around on it at times. He has decent feel for a changeup, but it's definitely his third-best pitch. His arm speed isn't quite where it needs to be, as he'll slow it down too much and miss his spots as a result. Despite having good life to his arm, Rondon doesn't miss a lot of bats. That should change in time as his breaking ball develops. Rondon will start 2008 in the high Class A rotation.

Year	Club (League)	Class	W	L	ERA	G	GS	CG	SV	IP	H	R	ER	HR	BB	SO	AVG
2005	Indians1 (DSL)	R	3	3	1.65	15	12	1	1	65	60	24	12	2	8	55	.230
2006	Indians (GCL)	R	3	4	5.13	11	11	0	0	52	62	34	30	6	3	32	.286
2007	Lake County (SAL)	A	7	10	4.37	27	27	0	0	136	143	78	66	13	27	113	.269
MINOR LEAGUE TOTALS			13	17	3.83	53	50	1	1	254	265	136	108	21	38	200	.262

29 REID SANTOS, LHP

Born: Aug. 24, 1982. **B-T:** L-L. **Ht.:** 6-1. **Wt.:** 170. **Drafted:** Saddleback (Calif.) CC, 2002 (13th round). **Signed by:** Don Lyle.

Santos looked more like organizational fodder as a starter over his first three seasons before the Indians moved him to the bullpen in high Class A in 2006. Santos always had a penchant for missing bats, and when he moved to a relief role his stuff played up in shorter stints. Santos worked in his native Hawaii during the Hawaii Winter Baseball season in each of the last two years, which has only added to his profile. His fastball sits anywhere from 87-91, topping out at 92 with good deception in his delivery. He also features a short slider, but his changeup is his best pitch, grading out as plus at times with depth and fade. Like Sipp, Santos' changeup gives him a weapon to attack both lefthanders and righthanders, and he's shown the ability to extend into multiple-inning stints. He had some success starting at Double-A and could fill a fifth-starter role, but he's been better in relief. Freshly added to the 40-man roster, he could be in Cleveland as a long reliever before the end of the 2008 season if the need arises.

Year	Club (League)	Class	W	L	ERA	G	GS	CG	SV	IP	H	R	ER	HR	BB	SO	AVG
2003	Burlington (Appy)	R	1	0	4.40	14	0	0	2	28	29	15	14	1	6	25	.264
2004	Burlington (Appy)	R	3	5	3.07	11	11	0	0	58	48	26	20	3	17	60	.229
	Lake County (SAL)	A	0	0	6.75	3	3	0	0	13	20	13	10	1	5	12	.377
2005	Lake County (SAL)	A	5	8	4.94	27	27	0	0	147	168	93	81	17	46	127	.288
2006	Kinston (Car)	A	2	0	3.44	35	2	0	4	70	55	28	27	2	28	65	.223
	Akron (EL)	AA	1	0	2.61	9	0	0	0	10	11	4	3	0	0	20	.262
2007	Akron (EL)	AA	8	3	2.72	39	10	0	2	96	80	39	29	10	30	85	.223
MINOR LEAGUE TOTALS			20	16	3.89	138	53	0	8	425	411	218	184	34	132	394	.256

30 JOEY MAHALIC, RHP

Born: Nov. 28, 1988. **B-T:** R-R. **Ht.:** 6-3. **Wt.:** 205. **Drafted:** HS—Portland, Ore., 2007 (32nd round). **Signed by:** Greg Smith.

One of the most publicized prep baseball players in Oregon history, Mahalic led Wilson High to the state title in 2006 and was named the 6-A player of the year in 2007. A three-sport prep standout, Mahalic also played football, which his father Drew did at Notre Dame and for four seasons in the NFL, and basketball. He quit football to focus on baseball prior to his senior year, and quit basketball after his freshman season after achieving his goal of dunking in a game. The athletic Mahalic already features three average pitches with a 88-91 sinking fastball, hard slider and a changeup. Mahalic had signed a commitment to play at Oregon State under head coach Pat Casey, who said he could have come in and seen consistent playing time as a middle reliever for the two-time defending national champion Beavers in 2008. Instead, Mahalic signed as a 32nd-rounder for $123,000 and wound up pitching in the Rookie-level Gulf Coast League. The Indians raved about him during instructional league for his makeup and advanced feel to pitch. He'll likely start off 2008 in extended spring before heading to short-season Mahoning Valley.

Year	Club (League)	Class	W	L	ERA	G	GS	CG	SV	IP	H	R	ER	HR	BB	SO	AVG
2007	Indians (GCL)	R	2	0	4.88	7	4	0	0	24	28	16	13	0	7	21	.277
MINOR LEAGUE TOTALS			2	0	4.88	7	4	0	0	24	28	16	13	0	7	21	.277

Colorado Rockies

BY TRACY RINGOLSBY

Ten years ago, the Rockies were a non-factor in Latin America. In 2007, their impact there was a significant reason that they won the first pennant in franchise history and had just their second winning season in the last decade.

Manny Corpas, who converted 19 of 20 save opportunities after seizing the closer's role in July, signed out of Panama. Franklin Morales and Ubaldo Jimenez, who stabilized the rotation at midseason and keyed the team's remarkable late-season run, were found in Venezuela and the Dominican Republic, respectively. Shortstop Hector Gomez and righthander Pedro Strop, both from the Dominican Republic, join No. 1 prospect Morales among the Rockies' top up-and-coming prospects.

Before the recent surge of talent, the only Latin Americans whom Colorado originally signed and brought to the big leagues were Neifi Perez and Juan Uribe. "It takes a long time to build a Latin program, but we now have a solid infrastructure," Rockies general manager Dan O'Dowd said.

Getting to this point has been a challenge. Under O'Dowd's predecessor Bob Gebhard, the Rockies budgeted $50,000 for their entire Latin American operation. In the last year alone, they spent $1.9 million on signing bonuses for Latin players.

The change began in 1999, Gebhard's final year as GM, when ownership hired legendary scout Gary Hughes. Colorado moved out of the three-bedroom home it had been using as its Dominican "academy" and began sharing a top-flight facility with the Diamondbacks that included well-groomed fields, a dormitory for housing, a weight room and a cafeteria. Next, Hughes promoted Rolando Fernandez from roving coordinator in charge of Latin instruction to director of Latin American operations.

"For us, the Latin program is integrated into the rest of the organization," Rockies vice president of baseball operations Bill Geivett said. "We treat it just like we treat any of our minor league teams. We send all our roving instructors down there to work with the players, providing consistency in the message we are sending to everyone in our system."

The program's impact has been most apparent in pitching, and with strong Latin arms matriculating to the majors, scouting director Bill Schmidt has targeted position players with recent early draft picks. The Rockies have spent first-rounders on infielders Jayson Nix (2001), Ian Stewart (2003), Chris Nelson

Panamanian closer Manny Corpas was one of the Rockies' Latin success stories

TOP 30 PROSPECTS

1. Franklin Morales, lhp	16. Michael McKenry, c
2. Ian Stewart, 3b	17. Joe Koshansky, 1b
3. Dexter Fowler, of	18. Jhoulys Chacin, rhp
4. Hector Gomez, ss	19. Ryan Speier, rhp
5. Greg Reynolds, rhp	20. Daniel Mayora, 2b
6. Casey Weathers, rhp	21. Darren Clarke, rhp
7. Chris Nelson, ss	22. Eric Young Jr., 2b
8. Brandon Hynick, rhp	23. Helder Velazquez, ss/2b
9. Pedro Strop, rhp	24. Corey Wimberly, 2b
10. Chaz Roe, rhp	25. Jonathan Herrera, ss
11. Juan Morillo, rhp	26. Lars Davis, c
12. Seth Smith, of	27. Keith Weiser, lhp
13. Esmil Rogers, rhp	28. Aneury Rodriguez, rhp
14. Brian Rike, of	29. Connor Graham, rhp
15. Jayson Nix, 2b	30. Cory Riordan, rhp

(2004) and Troy Tulowitzki (2005). The Rockies originally signed six of the eight regulars in their postseason lineup, including Matt Holliday, a seventh-rounder in 1998. Holliday hit just .271 in six minor league seasons before blossoming into the National League's batting and RBI champion.

Four of the five pitchers who started postseason games for the Rockies were originally signed by the club, including ace Jeff Francis, a first-rounder in 2002. Sixteen of the 25 players on the World Series roster were homegrown.

General Manager: Dan O'Dowd. **Farm Director:** Marc Gustafson. **Scouting Director:** Bill Schmidt.

Class	Team	League	W	L	PCT	Finish*	Manager	Affiliated
Majors	Colorado	National	90	73	.552	^2nd (16)	Clint Hurdle	—
Triple-A	Colorado Springs Sky Sox	Pacific Coast	69	75	.479	11th (16)	Tom Runnells	1993
Double-A	Tulsa Drillers	Texas	69	69	.500	4th (8)	Stu Cole	2003
High A	Modesto Nuts	California	76	64	.543	3rd (10)	Jerry Weinstein	2005
Low A	Asheville Tourists	South Atlantic	80	58	.580	4th (16)	Joe Mikulik	1994
Short-season	Tri-City Dust Devils	New York-Penn	37	39	.487	3rd (8)	Fred Ocaio	2001
Rookie	Casper Rockies	Pioneer	22	53	.293	8th (8)	Tony Diaz	2001
Overall 2007 Minor League Record			353	358	.496	15th		

*Finish in overall standings (No. of teams in league) ^League champion

LAST YEAR'S TOP 30

Player, Pos.		Status
1.	Troy Tulowitzki, ss	Majors
2.	Franklin Morales, lhp	No. 1
3.	Jason Hirsh, rhp	Majors
4.	Dexter Fowler, of	No. 3
5.	Ian Stewart, 3b	No. 2
6.	Ubaldo Jimenez, rhp	Majors
7.	Greg Reynolds, rhp	No. 5
8.	Chris Iannetta, c	Majors
9.	Jeff Baker, 3b	Majors
10.	Chaz Roe, rhp	No. 10
11.	Manny Corpas, rhp	Majors
12.	Juan Morillo, rhp	No. 11
13.	Joe Koshansky, 1b	No. 17
14.	Jonathan Herrera, 2b	No. 25
15.	Hector Gomez, ss/3b	No. 4
16.	Seth Smith, of	No. 12
17.	Samuel Deduno, rhp	Dropped out
18.	Shane Lindsay, rhp	Dropped out
19.	Chris Nelson, ss	No. 7
20.	Brandon Hynick, rhp	No. 8
21.	Aneury Rodriguez, rhp	No. 28
22.	Corey Wimberly, 2b	No. 24
23.	Ching-Lung Lo, rhp	Dropped out
24.	Darren Clarke, rhp	No. 21
25.	Alvin Colina, c	(Reds)
26.	Matt Miller, of	Dropped out
27.	Eric Young Jr., 2b	No. 22
28.	Pedro Strop, rhp	No. 9
29.	Andrew Johnston, rhp	Dropped out
30.	David Christensen, of	Dropped out

BEST TOOLS

Best Hitter for Average	Ian Stewart
Best Power Hitter	Joe Koshansky
Best Strike-Zone Discipline	Michael McKenry
Fastest Baserunner	Corey Wimberly
Best Athlete	Dexter Fowler
Best Fastball	Juan Morillo
Best Curveball	Chaz Roe
Best Slider	Pedro Strop
Best Changeup	Brandon Hynick
Best Control	Brandon Hynick
Best Defensive Catcher	Mike McKenry
Best Defensive Infielder	Hector Gomez
Best Infield Arm	Hector Gomez
Best Defensive Outfielder	Dexter Fowler
Best Outfield Arm	Brian Rike

PROJECTED 2011 LINEUP

Catcher	Chris Iannetta
First Base	Todd Helton
Second Base	Ian Stewart
Third Base	Garrett Atkins
Shortstop	Troy Tulowitzki
Left Field	Matt Holliday
Center Field	Dexter Fowler
Right Field	Brad Hawpe
No. 1 Starter	Ubaldo Jimenez
No. 2 Starter	Jeff Francis
No. 3 Starter	Franklin Morales
No. 4 Starter	Aaron Cook
No. 5 Starter	Greg Reynolds
Closer	Manny Corpas

TOP PROSPECTS OF THE DECADE

Year	Player, Pos.	2007 Org.
1998	Todd Helton, 1b	Rockies
1999	Choo Freeman, of	Dodgers
2000	Choo Freeman, of	Dodgers
2001	Chin-Hui Tsao, rhp	Dodgers
2002	Chin-Hui Tsao, rhp	Dodgers
2003	Aaron Cook, rhp	Rockies
2004	Chin-Hui Tsao, rhp	Dodgers
2005	Ian Stewart, 3b	Rockies
2006	Ian Stewart, 3b	Rockies
2007	Troy Tulowitzki, ss	Rockies

TOP DRAFT PICKS OF THE DECADE

Year	Player, Pos.	2007 Org.
1998	Choo Freeman, of	Dodgers
1999	Jason Jennings, rhp	Astros
2000	*Matt Harrington, rhp	(American Assoc.)
2001	Jayson Nix, 2b	Rockies
2002	Jeff Francis, lhp	Rockies
2003	Ian Stewart, 3b	Rockies
2004	Chris Nelson, ss	Rockies
2005	Troy Tulowitzki, ss	Rockies
2006	Greg Reynolds, rhp	Rockies
2007	Casey Weathers, rhp	Rockies

*Did not sign.

LARGEST BONUSES IN CLUB HISTORY

Greg Reynolds, 2006	$3,250,000
Jason Young, 2000	$2,750,000
Troy Tulowitzki, 2005	$2,300,000
Chin-Hui Tsao, 1999	$2,200,000
Chris Nelson, 2004	$2,150,000

COLORADO ROCKIES

Top 2008 Rookie: Franklin Morales, lhp. He already shares the franchise record for consecutive scoreless innings by a starter (20), so it's safe to say he'll be in the rotation.

Breakout Prospect: Michael McKenry, c. He's improving defensively and slugged 27 homers between low Class A and Hawaii Winter Baseball.

Sleeper: Zack Murry, ss. A draft-and-follow signed last spring, he has a live bat and defensive awareness.

SOURCE OF TOP 30 TALENT			
Homegrown	30	Acquired	0
College	12	Trades	0
Junior college	0	Rule 5 draft	0
High school	6	Independent leagues	0
Draft-and-follow	2	Free agents/waivers	0
Nondrafted free agents	1		
International	9		

Numbers in parentheses indicate prospect rankings.

LF
Seth Smith (12)
Sean Barker
Cole Garner
Justin Nelson
Joe Gaetti
Matt Miller

CF
Dexter Fowler (3)
Eric Young Jr. (22)
Mike Mitchell

RF
Brian Rike (14)
David Christensen
Daniel Carte

3B
Ian Stewart (2)
Christian Colonel
Darin Holcomb

SS
Hector Gomez (4)
Chris Nelson (7)
Helder Velazquez (23)
Jonathan Herrera (25)
Zack Murry
Carlos Martinez

2B
Jayson Nix (15)
Daniel Mayora (20)
Corey Wimberly (24)

1B
Joe Koshansky (17)
Michael Paulk
Jeff Cunningham

C
Michael McKenry (16)
Lars Davis (26)
Neil Wilson

RHP

Starters	Relievers
Greg Reynolds (5)	Casey Weathers (6)
Brandon Hynick (8)	Pedro Strop (9)
Chaz Roe (10)	Juan Morillo (11)
Esmil Rogers (13)	Ryan Speier (19)
Jhoulys Chacin (18)	Darren Clarke (21)
Aneury Rodriguez (28)	Connor Graham (29)
Cory Riordan (30)	William Harris
Ching-Lung Lo	Ethan Katz
Bruce Billings	Jarret Grube
Samuel Deduno	Andrew Johnston
Shane Lindsay	Ryan Mattheus
Xavier Cedeno	Andy Groves
Alan Johnson	
Robinson Fabian	
Parker Frazier	

LHP

Starters	Relievers
Franklin Morales (1)	Josh Newman
Keith Weiser (27)	Adam Bright
Isaiah Froneberger	

2007

Best Pro Debut: RHP Bruce Billings (30) went 4-2, 2.97 and led the short-season Northwest League with 89 strikeouts in 79 innings. OF Mike Mitchell (25) topped the NWL with 32 steals. 3B Darin Holcomb (12) batted .303 with 12 homers in the NWL.

Best Athlete: OF Brian Rike (2) has solid if not spectacular tools across the board. He added 25 pounds of muscle and went from a below-average to plus runner in three years at Louisiana Tech. The Rockies also clocked him at 92 mph off the mound. C Lars Davis (3) was a standout volleyball player as a Canadian high schooler.

Best Pure Hitter: Davis hit .400 at Illinois during the spring, but dipped to .219 in his debut as he made a slow transition to wood bats. He still might be the best pure hitter in this crop, rivaling Rike and Holcomb.

Best Power Hitter: 1B Jeff Cunningham (7) set a South Alabama record with 22 homers in the spring and then bashed eight more in his pro debut.

Fastest Runner: Mitchell is a plus-plus runner, though he's still learning how to take full advantage of his speed on the basepaths.

Best Defensive Player: Mitchell uses his speed to cover the gaps well as a center fielder.

Best Fastball: RHP Casey Weathers (1) began his college career as an outfielder at Sacramento (Calif.) CC, but his arm strength led to a move to the mound. Now he sits at 96-97 mph and reaches 99. RHP Connor Graham (5) has touched 98, RHP Andy Groves (11) has peaked at 95 and RHP Cory Riordan (6) has topped out at 94.

Best Secondary Pitch: Weathers has a dastardly slider that can creep into the low 90s. LHP Isaiah Froneberger (4) has a plus curve; RHP Jeff Fischer (10) has the best changeup.

Most Intriguing Background: RHP Parker Frazier (8) and unsigned 2B Nick Gallego (37, now at UCLA) have fathers who played in the majors and now work with the Rockies. George Frazier is a television broadcaster, while Mike Gallego is the third-base coach. OF Kenny Williams Jr. (32), who returned to Wichita State, is the son of the White Sox general manager.

Closest To The Majors: Weathers finished his first pro summer with a scoreless inning in high Class A and could open his first full-season in Double-A.

Best Late-Round Pick: Holcomb and Billings.

The One Who Got Away: OF Kentrail Davis (14) was considered a supplemental first-round talent, an athlete with lots of power potential. Colorado never got close to signing the Scott Boras client, and he's now at Tennessee.

Assessment: The Rockies concentrated on power pitchers and offensive-minded position players. They took Weathers at No. 8 for the express purpose of getting him to the majors quickly.

2006

BUDGET: $5.4 MILLION

RHP Greg Reynolds (1), the No. 2 overall pick, has been impressive but slowed by shoulder problems. Surprising RHP Brandon Hynick (8) could beat him to Colorado.

GRADE: C+

2005

BUDGET: $6.0 MILLION

SS Troy Tulowitzki (1) looks like an all-star for years to come. RHP Chaz Roe's (1s) curveball could make him a No. 3 starter.

GRADE: A

2004

BUDGET: $4.0 MILLION

SS Chris Nelson (1) got his career back on track in 2007, and he and OF Dexter Fowler (14) are two of the best all-around talents in the system. OF Seth Smith (2), C Chris Iannetta (4) and 1B Joe Koshansky (6) have reached the majors and could start for other teams.

GRADE: B

2003

BUDGET: $4.0 MILLION

The Rockies are still figuring out how they can squeeze 3B Ian Stewart (1) into their lineup. 2B Eric Young Jr. (30) is the next-best player in this group, but speed alone won't make him a regular.

GRADE: C+

Draft analysis by Jim Callis. Numbers in parentheses indicate draft rounds. Budgets are bonuses in first 10 rounds.

NATIONAL **1** WEST
LEAGUE

FRANKLIN MORALES, LHP

Born: Jan. 24, 1986.
Ht.: 6-0 . **Wt.:** 190.
Bats: L. **Throws:** L.
Signed:
Venezuela, 2002.
Signed by:
Francisco Cartaya.

After leading the high Class A California League with a 3.68 ERA and 179 strikeouts in 154 innings in 2006, Morales found success harder to come by at the beginning of the 2007 season. Thirteen starts into the year, he was winless at Double-A Tulsa and had just given up six runs in two-thirds of an inning when he learned that he had been named to the World Team in the Futures Game. There, he hit 97 mph with his fastball and struck out fellow Rockies farmhand Ian Stewart, Twins second baseman Matt Tolbert and Reds outfielder Jay Bruce in an inning of work. He went 3-0 in four starts at Tulsa afterward, then won two of his three starts at Triple-A Colorado Springs before becoming the fourth-youngest player in Rockies history at 21. He tied a franchise record for starters by spinning 20 straight scoreless innings. Morales wasn't as sharp in the postseason, getting tagged for 11 earned runs in 10 innings. The Rockies first spotted him as an outfielder but immediately converted him to the mound after signing him for $40,000. He is the first big league lefthander to come out of Colorado's replenished Latin American program.

Morales can reach the upper 90s with his fastball, but he achieves his best command and life when he pitches at 92-93 mph, more than enough velocity for a lefty. He features two curveballs, a slower version that he throws for strikes, and a harder, sweepier pitch that hitters will chase. He made major strides with his changeup in 2007. The Rockies consider Morales a big-game pitcher who gets better with a challenge. He has a short-term memory and is able to shake off struggles, make adjustments and move on in his next start. He shows the athleticism of a position player, and his experience as an outfielder is evident.

Morales still has to work on throwing more consistent and better quality strikes. He can make a pitch when he has to, but he can cut down on his walks and refine his command. His hard curveball isn't as reliable as his slower bender. He needs to smooth out his arm action and add deception to his changeup to help him against righthanders, who hit .273 off him in the majors. Morales can get a little too emotional at times on the mound. When he first got to the majors, he got himself into trouble by becoming so obsessed with videos and scouting reports that he lost touch with his own strengths.

Morales has the ability to be a top-of-the-rotation starter. He projects as Colorado's No. 4 starter in 2008, but the spot won't be handed to him. Because he's young and has spent only one year above Class A, the Rockies would have no qualms about sending him to Triple-A if he doesn't have a strong spring.

Year	Club (League)	Class	W	L	ERA	G	GS	CG	SV	IP	H	R	ER	HR	BB	SO	AVG
2003	Rockies (DSL)	R	9	3	2.18	13	13	0	0	78	58	24	19	0	34	69	.211
2004	Casper (Pio)	R	6	4	7.62	15	15	1	0	65	92	61	55	8	39	82	.338
2005	Asheville (SAL)	A	8	4	3.08	21	15	0	1	96	73	40	33	6	48	108	.214
2006	Modesto (Cal)	A	10	9	3.68	27	26	0	0	154	126	77	63	9	89	179	.223
2007	Tulsa (TL)	AA	3	4	3.48	17	17	1	0	95	77	41	37	8	45	77	.226
	Colorado Springs (PCL)	AAA	2	0	3.71	3	3	0	0	17	20	8	7	1	13	16	.323
	Colorado (NL)	MLB	3	2	3.43	8	8	0	0	39	34	15	15	2	14	26	.241
MINOR LEAGUE TOTALS			38	24	3.80	96	89	2	1	506	446	251	214	32	268	531	.240
MAJOR LEAGUE TOTALS			3	2	3.43	8	8	0	0	39	34	15	15	2	14	26	.241

2 IAN STEWART, 3B

Born: April 5, 1983. **B-T:** L-R. **Ht.:** 6-3. **Wt.:** 210. **Drafted:** HS—La Quinta, Calif., 2003 (1st round). **Signed by:** Todd Blyleven.

Teaming with Ian Kennedy to help La Quinta High win the 2003 California Southern section title, Stewart set Orange County records with 16 homers and 61 RBIs. The 10th overall pick that June, he signed for $1.95 million and ranked No. 1 on this list in 2005 and 2006. He made his big league debut late last season, primarily serving as a pinch-hitter in the Rockies' pennant drive. Stewart hasn't had a strong followup to his 2004 breakout in low Class A Asheville (.319, 30 homers), but he has big-time power potential along the lines of Matt Holliday, who failed to put up big numbers in the minors. Stewart has a quick bat and good plate coverage. Because he grew up hitting against his father, a lefty, he had good feel against southpaws and hit .312 with a .522 slugging percentage against them in 2007. He's a gifted athlete with a strong arm, allowing him to make spectacular plays at third base. He has average speed and some basestealing instincts. Stewart's swing can get a bit long and he can become too pull-conscious. He needs to develop more patience and trust his ability to drive balls to the opposite field. He gets lackadaisical on routine plays, leading to careless errors. Because Garrett Atkins is at the hot corner in Colorado, Stewart has worked out at second base and the outfield. He fits best as a run-producing third baseman, however, and soon may force the Rockies to make room for him. He'll return to Triple-A to begin 2008.

Year	Club (League)	Class	AVG	G	AB	R	H	2B	3B	HR	RBI	BB	SO	SB	OBP	SLG
2003	Casper (Pio)	R	.317	57	224	40	71	14	5	10	43	29	54	4	.401	.558
2004	Asheville (SAL)	A	.319	131	505	92	161	31	9	30	101	66	112	19	.398	.594
2005	Modesto (Cal)	A	.274	112	435	83	119	32	7	17	86	52	113	2	.353	.497
2006	Tulsa (TL)	AA	.268	120	462	75	124	41	7	10	71	50	103	3	.351	.452
2007	Colorado Springs (PCL)	AAA	.304	112	414	72	126	23	2	15	65	49	92	11	.379	.478
	Colorado (NL)	MLB	.209	35	43	3	9	4	0	1	9	1	17	0	.261	.372
MINOR LEAGUE TOTALS			.295	532	2040	362	601	141	30	82	366	246	474	39	.374	.514
MAJOR LEAGUE TOTALS			.209	35	43	3	9	4	0	1	9	1	17	0	.261	.372

3 DEXTER FOWLER, OF

STEVE MOORE

Born: March 12, 1986. **B-T:** B-R. **Ht.:** 6-4. **Wt.:** 175. **Drafted:** HS—Milton, Ga., 2004 (14th round). **Signed by:** Damon Iannelli.

Fowler projected as a possible first-round talent in the 2004 draft, but teams shied away from him because his college options included playing basketball at Harvard or baseball at Miami. The Rockies took a flier in the 14th round, and after they saved $2 million by dealing Larry Walker to the Cardinals that August, they signed Fowler for $925,000. He has played in just 164 games the last two years because of injuries. Fowler is a graceful athlete, particularly in center field, where he has plus range and a slightly above-average arm. He began switch-hitting after signing and now has a technically stronger swing from the left side. He has well-above-average speed, intriguing power potential and a willingness to draw walks. An ankle sprain in 2006 and a broken hand in 2007 have cost Fowler much-needed at-bats. He needs to make more consistent contact, and quieting his swing would be a step in that direction. He still needs to get stronger, which would allow him to drive balls more often. He can make better use of his speed by bunting more. Fowler will move to Double-A, and a strong first half could put him in Triple-A. Colorado's center fielder of the future, he could be ready by mid-2009.

Year	Club (League)	Class	AVG	G	AB	R	H	2B	3B	HR	RBI	BB	SO	SB	OBP	SLG
2005	Casper (Pio)	R	.273	62	220	43	60	10	4	4	23	27	73	18	.357	.409
2006	Asheville (SAL)	A	.296	99	405	92	120	31	6	8	46	43	79	43	.373	.462
2007	Modesto (Cal)	A	.273	65	245	43	67	7	5	2	23	44	64	20	.397	.367
MINOR LEAGUE TOTALS			.284	226	870	178	247	48	15	14	92	114	216	81	.376	.422

4 HECTOR GOMEZ, SS

BILL MITCHELL

Born: March 5, 1988. **B-T:** R-R. **Ht.:** 6-1. **Wt.:** 160. **Signed:** Dominican Republic, 2004. **Signed by:** Felix Feliz.

In his first year in a full-season league, Gomez was a low Class A South Atlantic League all-star at age 19. The best of a deep crop of Rockies shortstop prospects, he recovered from a .227 start in April to bat .317 over the next three months before tiring in August. Gomez has the physical tools to be an exceptional shortstop. His range and arm strength are both above-average. He has plus speed, getting from the right side of the plate to first base in 4.2 seconds. His bat isn't as advanced as his glove, but he has some pop and should have average power once he fills out. At this point, Gomez is too aggressive and pull-happy at the plate. As long as he can reach a pitch, he's not worried if it's a strike, limiting his power potential. He needs to improve his basestealing after getting caught 10 times in 30 tries, and his defensive consistency after making 39 errors. With Troy Tulowitzki entrenched in the majors, Colorado has no need to rush Gomez. He'll move one level at a time, with high Class A Modesto his next step.

Year	Club (League)	Class	AVG	G	AB	R	H	2B	3B	HR	RBI	BB	SO	SB	OBP	SLG
2005	Rockies (DSL)	R	.335	67	242	49	81	16	1	6	43	24	38	15	.423	.483
2006	Casper (Pio)	R	.327	50	202	24	66	9	4	5	35	11	26	5	.364	.485
	Tri-City (NWL)	A	.244	12	45	4	11	3	0	0	6	0	14	0	.255	.311
2007	Asheville (SAL)	A	.266	124	534	89	142	34	8	11	61	29	120	20	.309	.421
MINOR LEAGUE TOTALS			.293	253	1023	166	300	62	13	22	145	64	198	40	.346	.444

5 GREG REYNOLDS, RHP

Born: July 3, 1985. **B-T:** R-R. **Ht.:** 6-7. **Wt.:** 225. **Drafted:** Stanford, 2006 (1st round). **Signed by:** Todd Blyleven.

Recruited to play quarterback by several college programs, Reynolds opted instead to pitch at Stanford. That decision paid off when he went second overall in the 2006 draft and signed for $3.25 million. He made just eight starts in 2007 because of rotator-cuff inflammation that led to minor surgery in August. Reynolds has a 91-93 mph that he can spot to both sides of the plate and elevate in the strike zone when he wants. His curveball gives him a second plus pitch, and his changeup is an effective third offering. He's athletic and repeats his delivery easily, giving him good command. He has a good sense of himself and how good he can become. After working once a week in college, Reynolds must adapt to pitching every fifth day in pro ball. He can aggravate his shoulder problem when he puts too much torque on the joint when he throws his curveball. His fastball doesn't have a great deal of movement, so he doesn't get a lot of strikeouts. If he hadn't gotten hurt, Reynolds would have been called up to Colorado for the stretch drive. A likely No. 3 starter, he's expected to be fully healthy for spring training and could open the season in Triple-A.

Year	Club (League)	Class	W	L	ERA	G	GS	CG	SV	IP	H	R	ER	HR	BB	SO	AVG
2006	Modesto (Cal)	A	2	1	3.33	11	11	0	0	48	51	22	18	1	14	29	.271
2007	Tulsa (TL)	AA	4	1	1.42	8	8	0	0	50	32	10	8	2	9	35	.180
MINOR LEAGUE TOTALS			6	2	2.36	19	19	0	0	99	83	32	26	3	23	64	.227

6 CASEY WEATHERS, RHP

Born: June 10, 1985. **B-T:** R-R. **Ht.:** 6-1. **Wt.:** 200. **Drafted:** Vanderbilt, 2007 (1st round). **Signed by:** Scott Corman.

Originally an outfielder at Sacramento (Calif.) CC, Weathers began to blossom on the mound in the summer of 2006, when he was named closer of the year in the summer Alaska League. The highest-drafted college senior in 2007, he went eighth overall after an All-America season at Vanderbilt and signed for $1.8 million. Weathers has a power arm with two swing-and-miss pitches. His fastball sits at 96-97 mph and becomes even nastier because he throws it on a nice downhill plane despite his short stature. His power slider can reach the low 90s. He has the confidence, cockiness and aggressiveness needed to be a closer. Weathers can get long with his arm action and too quick with his delivery, costing him command and life on his pitches. He doesn't have a changeup or a third pitch, but won't need one in a bullpen role. He needs to work on controlling the running game, so in instructional league he broke out a slide step. Weathers is on the fast track. He most likely will open the 2008 in Double-A Tulsa and could reach the big leagues later in the year. He eventually can become a closer but figures to break into the majors as a setup man to Manny Corpas.

Year	Club (League)	Class	W	L	ERA	G	GS	CG	SV	IP	H	R	ER	HR	BB	SO	AVG
2007	Asheville (SAL)	A	0	1	4.61	13	0	0	2	13	6	7	7	2	7	19	.130
	Modesto (Cal)	A	0	0	0.00	1	0	0	0	1	0	0	0	0	2	2	.000
MINOR LEAGUE TOTALS			0	1	4.30	14	0	0	2	14	6	7	7	2	9	21	.122

7 CHRIS NELSON, SS

Born: Sept. 3, 1985. **B-T:** R-R. **Ht.:** 5-11. **Wt.:** 180. **Drafted:** HS—Redan, Ga., 2004 (1st round). **Signed by:** Damon Iannelli.

A two-way star in high school, Nelson concentrated on shortstop after having Tommy John surgery as a junior. The Georgia state player of the year in 2004, he went ninth overall in the draft and signed for $2.15 million. He struggled in two years in low Class A in 2005-06, but had a breakout season in the hitter-friendly high Class A California League in 2007. Nelson has excellent bat speed, drawing comparisons to a young Gary Sheffield. Once he lowered and quieted his hands in his stance in July, he hit .333 with 13 homers in the last two months. He showed marked improvement looking for a pitch to hit and not missing it when he got it. He has plus speed and arm strength, as well as excellent work habits. Nelson needs to smooth out his footwork defensively, particularly when he gets into throwing position. The Rockies say he improved his range and reliability at shortstop and no longer seems on the verge of moving to second base or center field. In his fifth pro season, he's ready for Double-A. He'll continue to stay at shortstop, though Tulowitzki ahead of him and Gomez behind make it unlikely Nelson will play there in Colorado. He has more upside than Clint Barmes and Jayson Nix, who figure to be the Rockies' second basemen in 2008.

Year	Club (League)	Class	AVG	G	AB	R	H	2B	3B	HR	RBI	BB	SO	SB	OBP	SLG
2004	Casper (Pio)	R	.347	38	147	36	51	6	3	4	20	20	42	6	.432	.510
2005	Asheville (SAL)	A	.241	79	315	51	76	13	3	3	38	25	88	7	.304	.330
2006	Asheville (SAL)	A	.260	118	466	69	121	38	1	11	76	32	101	14	.313	.416
2007	Modesto (Cal)	A	.289	133	529	97	153	42	7	19	99	55	92	27	.358	.503
MINOR LEAGUE TOTALS			.275	368	1457	253	401	99	14	37	233	132	323	54	.340	.439

8 BRANDON HYNICK, RHP

Born: March 7, 1985. **B-T:** R-R. **Ht.:** 6-3. **Wt.:** 205. **Drafted:** Birmingham-Southern, 2006 (8th round). **Signed by:** Damon Iannelli.

A two-way star at Birmingham-Southern, Hynick has won pitcher of the year honors in the Rookie-level Pioneer League in his pro debut and again in the California League last season. He led the Cal League with 16 wins and a 2.52 ERA, and led all minor leaguers with 182 innings. Hynick's stuff won't wow anybody, but he makes up for that with command, poise and preparation. He develops a plan of attack and stays with it, and his ability to throw quality strikes is the key to his success. He can locate his fastball where he wants, and mixes in a splitter, a straight changeup and a curveball. Hynick operates with little margin for error. He'll flash above-average velocity at times, but he usually pitches at 87-89 mph with his fastball. His curveball isn't very good but his splitter makes up for it by serving as his out pitch. He'll have to keep proving himself at higher levels in the system, but Hynick isn't far from the majors. He was next in line for a big league callup in September if the Rockies had another injury. He'll probably open 2008 in Double-A but could force his way to Triple-A with a solid spring.

Year	Club (League)	Class	W	L	ERA	G	GS	CG	SV	IP	H	R	ER	HR	BB	SO	AVG
2006	Casper (Pio)	R	4	3	2.39	12	12	0	0	64	55	23	17	3	8	70	.227
	Tri-City (NWL)	A	0	0	2.57	2	1	0	0	7	5	2	2	0	1	9	.208
2007	Modesto (Cal)	A	16	5	2.52	28	28	3	0	182	170	64	51	13	31	136	.243
MINOR LEAGUE TOTALS			20	8	2.49	42	41	3	0	253	230	89	70	16	40	215	.238

9 PEDRO STROP, RHP

Born: June 13, 1985. **B-T:** R-R. **Ht.:** 6-0. **Wt.:** 190. **Signed:** Dominican Republic, 2002. **Signed by:** Rolando Fernandez/Felix Feliz.

Signed as a shortstop, Strop hit .212 with 231 strikeouts in 221 games in his first four pro seasons, playing just four games above the short-season level. Noting his live arm, the Rockies moved him to the mound prior to the 2006 season. After successfully sneaking him through the Rule 5 draft that year, they protected him on their 40-man roster after the 2007 season. Having pitched just 81 pro innings, Strop has a fresh arm that delivers power stuff. His fastball ranges from 92-96 mph, while his slider runs from 85-88 mph. He can make hitters look silly with his splitter, giving him three swing-and-miss pitches. He has adapted quickly to the nuances of pitching, most likely because of the feel for the game he showed at shortstop, and remains an elite fielder. Strop needs to polish his mechanics and throw more strikes. He'll open up too soon and also cock his arm like a catcher and use a dart-throwing motion. He has made some adjustments to lengthen his delivery. He's still learning to keep his emotions in check. Strop figures to start 2008 in Double-A and can reach Colorado later in the year. Along with Manny Corpas and Casey Weathers, he gives the Rockies three strong closer options for the future.

Year	Club (League)	Class	AVG	G	AB	R	H	2B	3B	HR	RBI	BB	SO	SB	OBP	SLG
2002	Rockies (DSL)	R	.227	60	194	28	44	9	3	0	20	12	32	6	.286	.304
2003	Casper (Pio)	R	.172	40	128	13	22	4	1	1	11	15	43	1	.284	.242
2004	Tri-City (NWL)	A	.200	55	190	20	38	6	1	3	20	17	64	2	.286	.289
2005	Asheville (SAL)	A	.167	4	12	2	2	0	0	0	0	0	6	0	.167	.167
	Tri-City (NWL)	A	.236	62	229	26	54	11	2	3	25	6	86	7	.261	.341
MINOR LEAGUE TOTALS			.212	221	753	89	160	30	7	7	76	50	231	16	.277	.299

Year	Club (League)	Class	W	L	ERA	G	GS	CG	SV	IP	H	R	ER	HR	BB	SO	AVG
2006	Casper (Pio)	R	1	0	2.08	11	0	0	0	13	9	3	3	1	2	22	.188
	Asheville (SAL)	A	2	1	4.73	11	0	0	0	13	10	7	7	3	5	13	.213
2007	Modesto (Cal)	A	5	2	4.28	48	0	0	7	54	43	28	26	4	29	75	.215
MINOR LEAGUE TOTALS			8	3	4.00	70	0	0	7	81	62	38	36	8	36	110	.210

10 CHAZ ROE, RHP

BILL MITCHELL

Born: Oct. 9, 1986. **B-T:** R-R. **Ht.:** 6-5. **Wt.:** 180. **Drafted:** HS—Lexington, Ky., 2005 (1st round supplemental). **Signed by:** Scott Corman.

Roe turned down a chance to follow in his father's footsteps as a quarterback at Kentucky, signing instead for $1.025 million as a supplemental first-round pick. The Rockies have developed Roe patiently, limiting his innings in his first two seasons before turning him loose in 2007. He finished strong in high Class A with a 4-0, 2.15 record in his final eight starts. Roe has a big-time curveball that's a swing-and-miss pitch. His low-90s fastball plays off his curve well. He still has a lot of projection remaining in his 6-foot-5, 180-pound frame and should develop into a workhorse with two consistent plus pitches. He's very tough when he uses his height to pitch with a steep downward angle to his pitches. Roe is walking that fine line of trying to harness his power without losing command of his pitches. He tends to slip into a more side-to-side motion, causing and his pitches flatten out. He still has a lot of work to do with his changeup. Roe will continue to move one level at a time, advancing to Double-A in 2008. A potential No. 3 starter, he should be ready for the majors by 2010.

Year	Club (League)	Class	W	L	ERA	G	GS	CG	SV	IP	H	R	ER	HR	BB	SO	AVG
2005	Casper (Pio)	R	5	2	4.17	12	12	0	0	49	31	25	23	2	36	55	.175
2006	Asheville (SAL)	A	7	4	4.06	19	19	0	0	99	105	54	45	4	47	80	.273
2007	Modesto (Cal)	A	7	11	4.33	29	29	2	0	170	148	93	82	17	73	131	.235
MINOR LEAGUE TOTALS			19	17	4.22	60	60	2	0	319	284	172	150	23	156	266	.238

11 JUAN MORILLO, RHP

Born: Nov. 5, 1983. **B-T:** R-R. **Ht.:** 6-3. **Wt.:** 190. **Signed:** Dominican Republic, 2001. **Signed by:** Rolando Fernandez.

Morillo is at a turning point in his career. He has drawn attention ever since the Rockies clocked him at 104 mph in 2004, but he has yet to harness his electric arm. He's out of options, which means he has to make the big league roster out of spring training or be placed on waivers. While Morillo's fastball frequently hits triple digits, he best commands the pitch when he throws it at 95 mph. He still lacks a second plus pitch. His slider did go from inconsistent at the start of 2007 to average by season's end. He had been working on a splitter, but tightness in the top of his forearm had him back off that pitch last season. Once he put the splitter on hold, he returned to throwing a changeup. Morillo needs to throw strikes more consistently. If he can do that and develop a reliable second pitch, he could be a power closer. For now, Colorado would be content if he could make the club as a sixth- or seventh-inning reliever.

Year	Club (League)	Class	W	L	ERA	G	GS	CG	SV	IP	H	R	ER	HR	BB	SO	AVG
2001	Rockies (DSL)	R	2	4	6.81	14	7	0	0	35	35	31	27	1	38	20	.248
2002	Rockies (DSL)	R	1	5	4.75	14	11	0	0	55	49	44	29	1	33	43	.230
2003	Casper (Pio)	R	1	6	5.91	15	15	0	0	64	85	73	42	6	40	44	.318
2004	Tri-City (NWL)	A	3	2	2.98	14	14	0	0	66	56	34	22	0	41	73	.226
2005	Asheville (SAL)	A	1	3	4.54	7	7	0	0	33	40	24	17	2	13	43	.290
	Modesto (Cal)	A	6	5	4.41	20	20	0	0	112	107	69	55	10	65	101	.258
2006	Tulsa (TL)	AA	12	8	4.62	27	27	1	0	140	128	82	72	13	80	132	.248
	Colorado (NL)	MLB	0	0	15.75	1	1	0	0	4	8	7	7	3	3	4	.421
2007	Tulsa (TL)	AA	6	4	2.35	46	0	0	0	57	44	19	15	2	27	59	.210
	Colorado Springs (PCL)	AAA	0	1	3.72	7	0	0	0	9	7	4	4	0	4	12	.200
	Colorado (NL)	MLB	0	0	9.82	4	0	0	0	3	3	4	4	1	1	3	.214
MINOR LEAGUE TOTALS			32	38	4.43	164	101	1	0	574	551	380	283	35	341	527	.252
MAJOR LEAGUE TOTALS			0	0	12.91	5	1	0	0	7	11	11	11	4	4	7	.333

12 SETH SMITH, OF

Born: Sept. 30, 1982. **B-T:** L-L. **Ht.:** 6-3. **Wt.:** 215. **Drafted:** Mississippi, 2004 (2nd round). **Signed by:** Damon Iannelli.

A backup quarterback to Eli Manning at Mississippi—he never took a snap in three years—Smith has made rapid strides in baseball since signing with the Rockies and concentrating on one sport. He played a key role down the stretch in 2007, going 8-for-14 as a pinch-hitter. He provided a crucial triple in the wild-card playoff against the Padres and the game-winning double in the pennant-clincher against the Diamondbacks. Smith has a pure swing and was able to maintain his mechanics even while coming off the bench. He has shown more power as he has advanced to higher levels, setting new career highs for homers in each of the last two years, though he doesn't get caught up trying to drive the ball over the fence. His plate discipline has improved as well. He can fall into slumps when he gets too carried away with the leg lift he uses as a timing mechanism. Smith has above-average speed but needs to work on his baserunning. He can play center field on at least a part-time basis but fits better in right field. He has a strong arm and has recorded 44 assists in the last three seasons. Blocked by Matt Holliday and Brad Hawpe in Colorado, Smith will have to be content as a backup in 2008.

Year	Club (League)	Class	AVG	G	AB	R	H	2B	3B	HR	RBI	BB	SO	SB	OBP	SLG
2004	Casper (Pio)	R	.369	56	233	46	86	21	3	9	61	25	47	9	.427	.601
	Tri-City (NWL)	A	.259	9	27	6	7	1	1	2	5	1	3	0	.276	.593
2005	Modesto (Cal)	A	.300	129	533	87	160	45	6	9	72	44	115	5	.353	.458
2006	Tulsa (TL)	AA	.294	130	524	79	154	46	4	15	71	51	74	4	.361	.483
2007	Colorado Springs (PCL)	AAA	.317	129	451	68	143	32	6	17	82	39	73	7	.381	.528
	Colorado (NL)	MLB	.625	7	8	4	5	0	1	0	0	0	1	0	.625	.875
MINOR LEAGUE TOTALS			.311	453	1768	286	550	145	20	52	291	160	312	25	.371	.504
MAJOR LEAGUE TOTALS			.625	7	8	4	5	0	1	0	0	0	1	0	.625	.875

13 ESMIL ROGERS, RHP

Born: Aug. 14, 1985. **B-T:** R-R. **Ht.:** 6-1. **Wt.:** 170. **Signed:** Dominican Republic, 2003. **Signed by:** Felix Feliz.

Of the top eight pitchers on this list, Rogers is the fourth who began his pro career as a position player, and that doesn't include Brandon Hynick, a two-way star in college. Originally a shortstop, Rogers hit just .209 in three years in the Rookie-level Dominican Summer League before moving to the mound in 2006. He advanced to low Class A in 2007 and established himself as a legitimate pitching candidate. For a converted infielder, Rogers has a surprisingly solid delivery and startling command of a curveball. He also showcases his arm strength with a 92-94 mph fastball that has late life. The Rockies kept him in extended spring training last year to keep his innings down, and he's still working on building his durability. He also has to develop a changeup if he's to remain in the rotation. Though he was placed on the 40-man roster, Rogers doesn't project to be in Colorado's big league plans until 2010. He'll move up to high Class A this year.

Year	Club (League)	Class	W	L	ERA	G	GS	CG	SV	IP	H	R	ER	HR	BB	SO	AVG
2006	Casper (Pio)	R	3	6	6.96	15	15	1	0	63	78	53	49	8	24	40	.306
2007	Asheville (SAL)	A	7	4	3.75	19	18	1	0	117	125	60	49	6	42	90	.272
MINOR LEAGUE TOTALS			10	10	4.87	34	33	2	0	181	203	113	98	14	66	130	.284

14 BRIAN RIKE, OF

Born: Dec. 13, 1985. **B-T:** L-L. **Ht.:** 6-2. **Wt.:** 200. **Drafted:** Louisiana Tech, 2007 (2nd round). **Signed by:** Damon Iannelli.

A walk-on at Louisiana Tech, Rike exploded as a junior and became the 72nd overall pick in the 2007 draft, signing for $450,000. A conditioning program helped him add 25 pounds after arriving at Louisiana Tech, and he led the Western Athletic Conference with 20 homers last spring after totaling nine in his first two seasons. He also cut his 60-yard-dash time from 7.1 seconds as a freshman to 6.7 seconds as a junior. Rike reminds the Rockies of a young Brad Hawpe, showing power potential that will develop as he starts to get a book on how pitchers are working him. He has an idea of the strike zone and will draw walks, though he'll need to make more consistent contact. Rike played some center field at Louisiana Tech and in his pro debut, but he's more of a right fielder and has the arm to play there. He needs to focus better on his defense, as his routes and angles can get him in trouble. He could put up impressive power numbers at hitter-friendly Asheville in 2008.

Year	Club (League)	Class	AVG	G	AB	R	H	2B	3B	HR	RBI	BB	SO	SB	OBP	SLG
2007	Tri-City (NWL)	A	.296	49	186	36	55	13	1	4	29	32	54	7	.404	.441
MINOR LEAGUE TOTALS			.296	49	186	36	55	13	1	4	29	32	54	7	.404	.441

15 JAYSON NIX, 2B

Born: Aug. 26, 1982. **B-T:** R-R. **Ht.:** 5-11. **Wt.:** 185. **Drafted:** HS—Midland, Texas, 2001 (1st round supplemental). **Signed by:** Dar Cox.

The Rockies' top draft pick (supplemental first round) in 2001, Nix was in line to be their second baseman of his future after his first three seasons in the minors. Then he hit the wall hard, batting .213 and .236 in back-to-back seasons in Double-A and doing little better in his first taste of Triple-A. He got back on track in 2007, which he capped by earning MVP honors as Team USA won the World Cup for the first time since 1974. He batted .387, scored a team-high nine runs, drilled two homers (including one in the championship game) and played terrific defense. Nix is an excellent situational hitter, though he doesn't trust his hands as much as he should. He tends to go into funks when he hits home runs, seeming caught up in trying to hit more longballs rather than letting his gap power come naturally. A shortstop and pitcher in high school, he developed excellent game awareness from those experiences. He has solid speed and good baserunning instincts. Carney Lansford, his hitting coach in Triple-A, called him the best defensive second baseman he has ever seen. Nix has brilliant instincts and reactions, as well as a solid arm for his position. He's fearless turning the double play and led Triple-A Pacific Coast League second basemen with a .986 fielding percentage last season. Now that Kaz Matsui has left as a free agent, Nix has pushed himself to the front of the line to take over at second base.

Year	Club (League)	Class	AVG	G	AB	R	H	2B	3B	HR	RBI	BB	SO	SB	OBP	SLG
2001	Casper (Pio)	R	.294	42	153	28	45	10	1	5	24	21	43	1	.385	.471
2002	Asheville (SAL)	A	.246	132	487	73	120	29	2	14	79	62	105	14	.340	.400
2003	Visalia (Cal)	A	.281	137	562	107	158	46	0	21	86	54	131	24	.351	.475
2004	Tulsa (TL)	AA	.213	123	456	58	97	17	1	14	58	40	101	14	.292	.346
2005	Tulsa (TL)	AA	.236	131	501	68	118	27	0	11	47	29	92	10	.289	.355
2006	Colorado Springs (PCL)	AAA	.251	103	358	39	90	14	1	2	26	32	61	15	.317	.313
2007	Colorado Springs (PCL)	AAA	.292	124	439	80	128	33	2	11	58	31	79	24	.342	.451
MINOR LEAGUE TOTALS			.256	792	2956	453	756	176	7	78	378	269	612	102	.326	.399

16 MICHAEL MCKENRY, C

Born: March 4, 1985. **B-T:** R-R. **Ht.:** 5-10. **Wt.:** 200. **Drafted:** Middle Tennessee State, 2006 (7th round). **Signed by:** Scott Corman.

McKenry was a bit disappointed that he slipped to the seventh round in the 2006 draft, but signed quickly because he was the first catcher the Rockies drafted that year and he figured that meant he'd get plenty of playing time. He was correct and capitalized on that opportunity in his first full season. He made the South Atlantic League's midseason and postseason all-star teams, and he earned the same honors in Hawaii Winter Baseball, where he hit .281 with five homers. McKenry has a good all-around game. While Asheville's McCormick Field is a nice hitter's park, his 22 homers were eight more than any other player on the club and he showed power in Hawaii as well. He has a good idea of the strike zone, draws walks and doesn't panic when he gets behind in the count. Though he has below-average speed, he runs better than most catchers. Roving catching instructor Marv Foley worked with McKenry on his mechanics, helping him shorten his arm action in the back and finishing his throws better rather than hurrying them. Though he's still straightening out his footwork, he has a strong arm and threw out 34 percent of basestealers in 2007. His receiving skills are solid as well. He's ready to move up to high Class A.

Year	Club (League)	Class	AVG	G	AB	R	H	2B	3B	HR	RBI	BB	SO	SB	OBP	SLG
2006	Tri-City (NWL)	A	.216	66	245	28	53	16	1	4	23	22	49	3	.303	.339
2007	Asheville (SAL)	A	.287	113	408	79	117	35	1	22	90	66	84	8	.392	.539
MINOR LEAGUE TOTALS			.260	179	653	107	170	51	2	26	113	88	133	11	.359	.464

17 JOE KOSHANSKY, 1B

Born: May 26, 1982. **B-T:** L-L. **Ht.:** 6-4. **Wt.:** 225. **Drafted:** Virginia, 2004 (6th round). **Signed by:** Jay Matthews.

Primarily a pitcher his first two years at Virginia, Koshansky took to playing first base so well that he became the first Cavalier to be named Atlantic Coast Conference player of the year. That came in 2004, when he hit 16 homers while going 8-3 on the mound as a senior after going undrafted the previous year. Koshansky's main tool is his raw power. He'll hit home runs at the big league level, but he's going to have to make better adjustments if he's going to be a true threat. He went just 1-for-12 with five strikeouts as pitchers weren't afraid to bust him inside. He sometimes falls into the trap of guessing too much at the plate. He will strike out, a tradeoff for his power, but he also draws a healthy share of walks. His biggest problem is the one that Ryan Shealy once dealt with: Todd Helton owns Colorado's first-base job and Koshansky can't play another position. He's a good athlete for his size and has some arm strength, but his below-average speed would make playing the outfield a stretch. He also needs to be pushed to become a better first baseman. His footwork and throwing mechanics get loose, and it's a challenge for him to make the toss to second base.

Year	Club (League)	Class	AVG	G	AB	R	H	2B	3B	HR	RBI	BB	SO	SB	OBP	SLG
2004	Tri-City (NWL)	A	.234	66	239	41	56	18	0	12	43	31	84	1	.330	.460
2005	Asheville (SAL)	A	.291	120	453	92	132	31	1	36	103	53	122	6	.373	.603
	Tulsa (TL)	AA	.267	12	45	5	12	3	0	2	12	2	15	0	.292	.467
2006	Tulsa (TL)	AA	.284	132	500	84	142	28	0	31	109	64	134	3	.371	.526
2007	Colorado Springs (PCL)	AAA	.295	136	498	79	147	30	2	21	99	67	128	4	.380	.490
	Colorado (NL)	MLB	.083	17	12	0	1	1	0	0	2	2	5	0	.200	.167
MINOR LEAGUE TOTALS			.282	466	1735	301	489	110	3	102	366	217	483	14	.366	.525
MAJOR LEAGUE TOTALS			.083	17	12	0	1	1	0	0	2	2	5	0	.200	.167

18 JHOULYS CHACIN, RHP

Born: Jan. 7, 1988. **B-T:** R-R. **Ht.:** 6-1. **Wt.:** 175. **Signed:** Venezuela, 2004. **Signed by:** Francisco Cartaya.

After two years in the Rookie-level Dominican Summer League, Chacin came to the United States for the first time last summer and quickly established himself as one of the premier pitchers in the Pioneer League. He went 5-2, 1.20 in his final 10 starts, allowing more than one earned run only once in that stretch, and tied for the league strikeout lead with 77 in 92 innings. Chacin already has a solid fastball at 89-92 mph and can touch 94. The key is that he can command his heater to both sides of the plate. He still needs to develop his secondary pitches, though he does throw his curveball and changeup for strikes and they do have plus potential. His changeup is more reliable at this point. Chacin figures to fill out and add more strength and durability. He's a good athlete, though he can get into a hurry with his mechanics and must be reminded to stay closed and finish his delivery. He'll advance to low Class A this year, though the Rockies may limit his workload by keeping him in extended spring training at the start of the season.

Year	Club (League)	Class	W	L	ERA	G	GS	CG	SV	IP	H	R	ER	HR	BB	SO	AVG
2005	Rockies (DSL)	R	3	1	4.32	16	4	0	0	50	43	32	24	5	16	48	.219
2006	Rockies (DSL)	R	4	1	1.49	12	11	1	0	72	60	20	12	4	18	67	.226
2007	Casper (Pio)	R	6	5	3.13	16	16	0	0	92	85	45	32	5	26	77	.248
MINOR LEAGUE TOTALS			13	7	2.85	44	31	1	0	214	188	97	68	14	60	192	.234

19 RYAN SPEIER, RHP

Born: July 24, 1979. **B-T:** R-R. **Ht.:** 6-7. **Wt.:** 210. **Signed:** Radford, NDFA 2001. **Signed by:** Jay Matthews.

After missing the 2006 season when he tore the labrum in his shoulder during an offseason basketball game, Speier was a pleasant surprise last year. He bounced back strong and the Rockies called him up multiple times and kept him on their postseason roster. He made a scoreless appearance in each of the first two rounds of the playoffs before walking three straight Red Sox in a disastrous World Series outing. Speier went just 8-14, 5.09 at Radford and went unselected in the 2001 draft, signing with Colorado as a free agent after a strong performance in the Cape Cod League. He forced his way to the majors by steadily proving himself at each level in the system. Speier most often works from a sidearm slot but he'll use as many as four different arm angles in a single inning. His funky delivery throws hitters off but also can create some command problems. Despite his low slot, he can hit 91 mph with his fastball, though he achieves better sink when he works at 88-89. He attacks lefthanders with his hard slider and also has confidence in his changeup. He has a sweeping curveball that isn't very effective. As long as he can throw strikes, Speier can continue to help Colorado out of the bullpen.

Year	Club (League)	Class	W	L	ERA	G	GS	CG	SV	IP	H	R	ER	HR	BB	SO	AVG
2001	Casper (Pio)	R	1	2	3.16	17	0	0	1	25	19	12	9	2	9	24	.196
2002	Asheville (SAL)	A	3	1	3.93	28	0	0	1	36	32	21	16	3	13	39	.235
	Salem (Car)	A	2	2	3.94	24	0	0	4	32	35	21	14	0	11	33	.285
2003	Visalia (Cal)	A	4	2	1.53	56	0	0	18	58	50	14	10	2	17	73	.226
2004	Tulsa (TL)	AA	3	1	2.04	61	0	0	37	61	33	14	14	3	25	70	.151
2005	Colorado Springs (PCL)	AAA	2	2	4.99	45	0	0	6	52	70	30	29	2	18	45	.327
	Colorado (NL)	MLB	2	1	3.65	22	0	0	0	24	26	12	10	0	13	10	.277
2007	Colorado Springs (PCL)	AAA	1	4	4.38	50	0	0	33	49	47	26	24	3	23	40	.253
	Colorado (NL)	MLB	3	1	4.00	20	0	0	0	18	20	8	8	1	8	13	.299
MINOR LEAGUE TOTALS			16	14	3.30	281	0	0	100	316	286	138	116	15	116	324	.239
MAJOR LEAGUE TOTALS			5	2	3.80	42	0	0	0	42	46	20	18	1	21	23	.286

20 DANIEL MAYORA, 2B

Born: July 27, 1985. **B-T:** R-R. **Ht.:** 5-11. **Wt.:** 160. **Signed:** Venezuela, 2003. **Signed by:** Francisco Cartaya.

Mayora has been a league postseason all-star in each of the last two seasons. After primarily playing shortstop in 2006, he made a smooth transition to second base because the Rockies have so much depth at short and had Hector Gomez stationed there in Asheville. Mayora maintained consistent production throughout the year, batting third for much of 2007 and showing good pop for a middle infielder. His plate discipline is still developing and his swing can get long when he tries to power up, leading to strikeouts. He has above-average speed underway but a slow initial step, which limits him down the line and as a basestealer, though he did swipe 26 bags in 35 tries. Mayora made a quick adjustment to second base, showing impressive range, especially to his left, and the ability to turn the double play. He and Gomez will move up to high Class A together in 2008.

Year	Club (League)	Class	AVG	G	AB	R	H	2B	3B	HR	RBI	BB	SO	SB	OBP	SLG
2003	Rockies (DSL)	R	.192	23	78	7	15	2	1	0	4	7	19	1	.297	.244
2004	Rockies (DSL)	R	.261	69	261	35	68	14	6	1	35	21	51	24	.332	.372
2005	Casper (Pio)	R	.265	47	151	20	40	12	1	1	14	9	36	4	.325	.377
2006	Tri-City (NWL)	A	.304	74	276	40	84	19	2	5	30	23	70	8	.375	.442
2007	Asheville (SAL)	A	.312	127	516	88	161	42	1	14	78	41	124	26	.367	.479
MINOR LEAGUE TOTALS			.287	340	1282	190	368	89	11	21	161	101	300	63	.353	.423

21 DARREN CLARKE, RHP

Born: March 18, 1981. **B-T:** R-R. **Ht.:** 6-8. **Wt.:** 235. **Drafted:** South Florida CC, D/F 2000 (35th round). **Signed by:** John Cedarburg.

The question with Clarke is whether he can ever stay healthy enough to get more than the two-game cameo he had with the Rockies last May. He had Tommy John surgery in 2004 and has yet to make more than 25 appearances in a season since becoming a full-time reliever in 2005. He strained his elbow that season and his right lat muscle in 2006, and the lat muscle knocked him out for three months last year. Clarke has a 1.98 ERA since moving to the bullpen but has worked just 59 innings in that time. He has overpowering stuff and could contribute to the Colorado bullpen if he could remain on the active roster. Clark's fastball consistently registers in the mid-90s, and he backs it up with an 85-88 mph slider. He also has a changeup that elicits swings and misses from lefthanders. With his size, Clark throws on a downhill plane that adds some movement to his pitches. He has learned to control his emotions and doesn't let even tight situations faze him. He pleased the Rockies by dedicating himself to conditioning in 2006, but he still hasn't been able to stay on the mound.

Year	Club (League)	Class	W	L	ERA	G	GS	CG	SV	IP	H	R	ER	HR	BB	SO	AVG
2001	Casper (Pio)	R	3	6	6.02	14	14	0	0	55	76	47	37	3	33	42	.336
2002	Tri-City (NWL)	A	4	3	6.98	12	9	0	0	40	51	34	31	3	19	38	.305
2003	Asheville (SAL)	A	8	6	3.83	27	25	1	0	157	155	80	67	22	59	107	.259
2004	Visalia (Cal)	A	1	3	7.39	8	7	0	0	35	54	35	29	6	16	27	.342
2005	Tri-City (NWL)	A	0	0	0.64	12	0	0	3	14	9	1	1	0	2	18	.184
	Modesto (Cal)	A	0	0	9.00	5	0	0	0	6	13	8	6	2	3	4	.433
2006	Modesto (Cal)	A	1	1	1.35	25	0	0	5	26	13	5	4	1	7	37	.140
2007	Colorado (NL)	MLB	0	0	0.00	2	0	0	0	1	2	0	0	0	1	1	.333
	Tulsa (TL)	AA	1	1	1.64	10	1	0	0	11	5	2	2	2	1	16	.139
MINOR LEAGUE TOTALS			18	20	4.61	113	56	1	8	345	376	212	177	39	140	289	.277
MAJOR LEAGUE TOTALS			0	0	0.00	2	0	0	0	1	2	0	0	0	1	1	.333

22 ERIC YOUNG JR., 2B

Born: May 25, 1985. **B-T:** B-R. **Ht.:** 5-10. **Wt.:** 180. **Drafted:** Chandler-Gilbert (Ariz.) CC, D/F 2003 (30th round). **Signed by:** Mike Garlatti.

Much like his father Eric, a 43rd-round draft pick who became an all-star for the Rockies, Eric Jr. is driven to be successful. Seeing no value in sitting at home after the 2007 season, he invited himself to instructional league and offered to pay his own expenses so he could spend six weeks continuing to refine his game. Young has game-changing speed, and thanks to tutoring from his father, he uses it aggressively. He led the minors with 87 steals in 2006 and finished second with 73 last season, improving his success rate to 80 percent, up from 74 the year before. He already has made bunting a staple in his offensive game, and realizes that trying to hit for power only will get him into trouble. His plate discipline slipped in 2007, however, and he needs to tighten his strike zone in order to be a true leadoff hitter. Though Young showed better range and footwork at second base, his future could be in center field. He has a questionable arm and stiff hands, which will limit his opportunity to play in the middle infield for a contender. He'll move up to Double-A in 2008.

Year	Club (League)	Class	AVG	G	AB	R	H	2B	3B	HR	RBI	BB	SO	SB	OBP	SLG
2004	Casper (Pio)	R	.264	23	87	20	23	5	1	0	7	20	13	14	.407	.345
2005	Casper (Pio)	R	.301	63	219	48	66	7	7	3	25	35	52	25	.404	.438
2006	Asheville (SAL)	A	.295	128	482	92	142	28	6	5	49	67	75	87	.391	.409
2007	Modesto (Cal)	A	.291	130	540	113	157	29	11	8	63	46	105	73	.359	.430
MINOR LEAGUE TOTALS			.292	344	1328	273	388	69	25	16	144	168	245	199	.382	.418

23 HELDER VELAZQUEZ, SS/2B

Born: Oct. 14, 1988. **B-T:** R-R. **Ht.:** 6-3. **Wt.:** 165. **Drafted:** HS—Gurabao, P.R., 2006 (5th round). **Signed by:** Jorge Posada.

One of the younger players in the 2006 draft, Velazquez played his first two seasons in pro ball before turning 19 and already has displayed big league defensive ability. He has exceptional arm strength that allows him to make plays from a variety of angles. He has soft hands and shows agility that belies his gangly body. Though he has a big frame and has seen time at second and third base, he should be able to stay at shortstop. Velazquez' challenge is going to be his bat. He has a long swing and lacks the strength to survive that approach. He should get stronger as he fills out and has the hands to hit for some power, but his utter lack of plate discipline is a problem. He has walked just eight times in 113 pro games, and more advanced pitchers will exploit his impatience. Velazquez' speed rates as average to a tick above, and he has the instincts to steal a few bases. He likely will advance to low Class A in 2008, but at his age a return to short-season Tri-City wouldn't be a setback.

Year	Club (League)	Class	AVG	G	AB	R	H	2B	3B	HR	RBI	BB	SO	SB	OBP	SLG
2006	Casper (Pio)	R	.255	40	157	12	40	7	1	2	19	3	27	3	.272	.350
2007	Tri-City (NWL)	A	.262	73	317	44	83	19	4	1	43	5	62	13	.280	.356
MINOR LEAGUE TOTALS			.259	113	474	56	123	26	5	3	62	8	89	16	.277	.354

24 COREY WIMBERLY, 2B

Born: Oct. 26, 1983. **B-T:** B-R. **Ht.:** 5-8. **Wt.:** 180. **Drafted:** Alcorn State, 2005 (6th round). **Signed by:** Damon Iannelli.

Wimberly won two batting titles in 2005, leading NCAA Division I with a .462 average and then topping the Pioneer League with a .381 mark in his pro debut. He has become one of the Rockies' more advanced middle-infield prospects, but repeated muscle pulls in his legs have restricted him to a total of 179 games over the last two years. Wimberly understands that his value is based on his elite speed and that his job is to get on base. The fastest runner in the system, he works counts, makes contact, puts the ball on the ground and lets his quickness do the rest. His bunting is an asset but he needs to take more walks, something that shouldn't be an issue for someone whose listed height of 5-foot-8 may be two inches too generous. He has no power and pitchers showed little fear of him in Double-A, where his average dipped to .268 and his OBP to .323, which won't cut it. Wimberly also needs to improve his defense, which was the focus of his efforts after the season in the Arizona Fall League, where he hit .407. He has the range to get to balls but drops his arm angle and doesn't finish his throws. He needs to pay more attention to detail this year, when he may return to Tulsa at the outset.

Year	Club (League)	Class	AVG	G	AB	R	H	2B	3B	HR	RBI	BB	SO	SB	OBP	SLG
2005	Casper (Pio)	R	.381	67	281	58	107	10	0	1	22	18	27	36	.427	.427
2006	Modesto (Cal)	A	.325	87	342	72	111	6	4	2	24	30	42	50	.404	.383
2007	Tulsa (TL)	AA	.268	92	365	63	98	15	1	4	33	19	52	36	.323	.348
MINOR LEAGUE TOTALS			.320	246	988	193	316	31	5	7	79	67	121	122	.381	.383

25 JONATHAN HERRERA, SS

Born: Nov. 3, 1984. **B-T:** B-R. **Ht.:** 5-9. **Wt.:** 160. **Signed:** Venezuela, 2002. **Signed by:** Francisco Cartaya.

Herrera rebounded from a 15-game suspension for violating baseball's performance-enhancing drug policy in 2005 to become a California League all-star while repeating high Class A in 2006. His batting average dropped 53 points last year in his first shot at Double-A, though he was selected to play in the Texas League all-star game. A natural righthander before he started switch-hitting, Herrera was better from the left side of the plate in 2007. He's decent but nothing special with the bat. He makes contact but has only modest power, and he has above-average speed but isn't much of a basestealing threat. He was caught 12 times in 30 attempts last year. Though he played solely at shortstop in 2007, Herrera's biggest asset is his ability to also handle second and third base, and he projects as more of a utilityman than a regular on a contender. He has good range and enhances his plus arm with a quick release. Herrera tends to wear down over the course of a long season and lose his focus. He didn't show much progress in the Venezuelan

Winter League this offseason and could benefit from repeating Double-A, but fellow shortstop prospect Chris Nelson is ready to move up.

Year	Club (League)	Class	AVG	G	AB	R	H	2B	3B	HR	RBI	BB	SO	SB	OBP	SLG
2002	Rockies (DSL)	R	.300	61	230	39	69	10	2	0	22	25	27	23	.371	.361
2003	Casper (Pio)	R	.308	39	159	27	49	7	1	1	25	10	25	12	.355	.384
2004	Asheville (SAL)	A	.279	95	380	71	106	20	2	6	35	26	80	21	.335	.389
2005	Asheville (SAL)	A	.310	19	87	17	27	2	0	0	5	8	11	6	.384	.333
	Modesto (Cal)	A	.258	73	310	48	80	9	4	2	30	23	52	9	.315	.332
2006	Modesto (Cal)	A	.310	127	487	87	151	20	8	7	77	58	67	34	.382	.427
2007	Tulsa (TL)	AA	.257	131	509	65	131	24	4	3	40	36	69	18	.315	.338
MINOR LEAGUE TOTALS			.284	545	2162	354	613	92	21	19	234	186	331	123	.346	.372

26 LARS DAVIS, C

Born: Nov. 7, 1985. **B-T:** L-R. **Ht.:** 6-3. **Wt.:** 205. **Drafted:** Illinois, 2007 (3rd round). **Signed by:** Mark Germann.

An all-province volleyballer as a high schooler in Grand Prairie, Alberta, Davis is very athletic for a catcher. He became a part-time backstop at Lethbridge (Alberta) CC in 2005 and didn't move behind the plate full-time until he transferred to Illinois. The Big 10 Conference player of the year last spring, he hit .400 with 13 homers before going in the third round of the draft and signing for $337,000. He struggled learning to use wood bats in his pro debut and must tighten up his swing to stay back on offspeed pitches. He still projects as an offensive catcher with some pop, and as a bonus, he bats lefthanded. His speed is below average but good for a catcher. Defensively, Davis has solid arm strength which will improve as he smooths out his throwing mechanics. He threw out 30 percent of basestealers in his debut. His receiving skills are adequate, but with his work ethic—he was a microcellular biology major at Illinois—they should get better. Davis will spend his first full season in low Class A.

Year	Club (League)	Class	AVG	G	AB	R	H	2B	3B	HR	RBI	BB	SO	SB	OBP	SLG
2007	Tri-City (NWL)	A	.219	52	187	17	41	5	3	3	27	14	49	2	.284	.326
MINOR LEAGUE TOTALS			.219	52	187	17	41	5	3	3	27	14	49	2	.284	.326

27 KEITH WEISER, LHP

Born: Sept. 21, 1984. **B-T:** R-L. **Ht.:** 6-3. **Wt.:** 200. **Drafted:** Miami (Ohio), 2006 (3rd round). **Signed by:** Ed Santa.

After going 10-0, 2.73 as a sophomore at Miami, Weiser had a relatively disappointing junior season but that didn't deter the Rockies from taking him in the third round. He repaid their faith in his first full season in 2007, leading the South Atlantic League with 17 victories and 175 innings. The typical crafty lefthander, Weiser has excellent command of an 86-88 mph fastball that occasionally hits 90. His secondary pitches are a slurvy breaking ball and a changeup. He has excellent feel for adjusting to hitters and setting them up. Weiser has little margin for error, however, and he's susceptible to homers if he leaves pitches up in the strike zone. He won't turn heads with his stuff, which is why he stayed in low Class A all season despite his success. He'll have to keep proving himself as he moves up the ladder, and the hitter's haven that is the California League will provide a stern test in 2008.

Year	Club (League)	Class	W	L	ERA	G	GS	CG	SV	IP	H	R	ER	HR	BB	SO	AVG
2006	Tri-City (NWL)	A	1	2	3.79	12	11	0	0	57	63	25	24	6	8	53	.283
2007	Asheville (SAL)	A	17	7	3.75	28	28	1	0	175	195	86	73	18	30	126	.283
MINOR LEAGUE TOTALS			18	9	3.76	40	39	1	0	232	258	111	97	24	38	179	.283

28 ANEURY RODRIGUEZ, RHP

Born: Dec. 13, 1987. **B-T:** R-R. **Ht.:** 6-3. **Wt.:** 180. **Signed:** Dominican Republic, 2005. **Signed by:** Felix Feliz.

Rodriguez has been on the fast track since signing, coming to the United States as a 17-year-old and taking a regular turn in the low Class A rotation last year at age 19. His 160-48 K-BB ratio was a more telling statistic than his 5.15 ERA. Rodriguez has good stuff, with a fastball that already ranges from 88-94 mph and should pick up more velocity as he continues to grow and fill out. With his bone structure and the size of his hands, the Rockies think he could wind up as tall as 6-foot-6. His curveball has a chance to become a power breaking ball, and his changeup is advanced for his age. Rodriguez just needs to get stronger and more consistent with his delivery. He's still in the beginning stages of his education as a pitcher and can't always fight his way out of jams. He's doing well in English classes and Colorado praises his work habits. Because he's still so young and the California League is hard on pitchers, Rodriguez could return to Asheville to start 2008. Once he matures physically, he could become a dominant pitcher.

Year	Club (League)	Class	W	L	ERA	G	GS	CG	SV	IP	H	R	ER	HR	BB	SO	AVG
2005	Casper (Pio)	R	3	4	7.55	15	15	0	0	62	77	54	52	7	26	47	.309
2006	Tri-City (NWL)	A	4	4	4.14	15	15	1	0	76	78	42	35	2	30	69	.261
2007	Asheville (SAL)	A	9	9	5.15	28	28	1	0	152	182	105	87	19	48	160	.298
MINOR LEAGUE TOTALS			16	17	5.40	58	58	2	0	290	337	201	174	28	104	276	.291

29 CONNOR GRAHAM, RHP

Born: Dec. 30, 1985. **B-T:** R-R. **Ht.:** 6-7. **Wt.:** 235. **Drafted:** Miami (Ohio), 2007 (5th round). **Signed by:** Ed Santa.

A year after drafting Keith Weiser out of Miami (Ohio) in the third round, the Rockies went back to the Redhawks for Graham in the fifth round last June. Signed for $143,000, he was a project when he arrived at Tri-City. It wasn't until the end of the summer that he started to get in shape, and he drew attention when he hit 98 mph with his fastball in his final outing. He pitched at 93-94 mph for most of his debut and also flashed a swing-and-miss slider. Graham also throws a curveball, and his changeup ranks as his fourth-best pitch. He was a reliever in his first two college seasons and most area scouts projected him to eventually return to that role, but Colorado will give him a chance to develop as a starter. To remain in the rotation, Graham will need to find a trustworthy offspeed offering and improve his control so he can keep his pitch counts down. He does throw on a steep downhill angle, but his delivery relies too much on his arm and not enough on lower body, which will have to be addressed to ease strain on his shoulder. He'll probably move up one step to low Class A this year.

Year	Club (League)	Class	W	L	ERA	G	GS	CG	SV	IP	H	R	ER	HR	BB	SO	AVG
2007	Tri-City (NWL)	A	1	0	2.37	6	4	0	0	19	23	7	5	2	6	18	.303
MINOR LEAGUE TOTALS			1	0	2.37	6	4	0	0	19	23	7	5	2	6	18	.303

30 CORY RIORDAN, RHP

Born: May 25, 1986. **B-T:** R-R. **Ht.:** 6-4. **Wt.:** 200. **Drafted:** Fordham, 2007 (6th round). **Signed by:** Mike Garlatti.

Last spring Riordan became just the third Fordham pitcher ever to strike out 100 batters in a season. The first two, Dick Egan and Hank Borowy, went on to long big league careers, and Riordan has the raw stuff to do the same. He was inconsistent in his junior season with the Rams, allowing the Rockies to draft him in the sixth round and sign him for $120,000. He led the Northwest League in ERA until fading late in the summer. Riordan's fastball ranges from 88-94 mph, and when he's on he'll show a hard curveball with good tilt and an average changeup. He has a smooth delivery and throws strikes, but his command comes and goes. Scouts questioned his desire and focus while he was at Fordham, but if Riordan becomes more consistent he can reach his ceiling as a No. 3 or 4 starter.

Year	Club (League)	Class	W	L	ERA	G	GS	CG	SV	IP	H	R	ER	HR	BB	SO	AVG
2007	Tri-City (NWL)	A	2	3	4.25	14	11	0	1	65	69	34	31	5	17	65	.265
MINOR LEAGUE TOTALS			2	3	4.25	14	11	0	1	65	69	34	31	5	17	65	.265

Detroit Tigers

BY JON PAUL MOROSI
DETROIT FREE PRESS

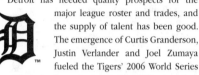

The Tigers are clearly in the midst of a win-now era, after back-to-back winning seasons for the first time since 1987-88. The farm system, supported by an ample draft budget, is shouldering great responsibility in their pursuit of sustainable success.

Detroit has needed quality prospects for the major league roster and trades, and the supply of talent has been good. The emergence of Curtis Granderson, Justin Verlander and Joel Zumaya fueled the Tigers' 2006 World Series run. Their depth was tested during 2007, when they tried, unsuccessfully, to reach the postseason for a second consecutive year.

With injuries to key players, several prospects made their major league debuts, led by star-in-the-making Cameron Maybin and righthanders Eulogio de la Cruz, Jair Jurrjens and Virgil Vasquez. Others with little big league experience entering the season, such as lefthander Andrew Miller, righthander Yorman Bazardo, catcher Mike Rabelo and outfielder Ryan Raburn, were relied upon at various times during the year.

During the offseason, the Tigers used many of those players to bolster their big league club via trades. They addressed their biggest need less than 24 hours after the World Series, when they dealt Jurrjens and fleet center fielder Gorkys Hernandez to the Braves for all-star shortstop Edgar Renteria. That was merely a prelude to a blockbuster.

Detroit's willingness to surrender Maybin and Miller allowed it to pry both Miguel Cabrera and Dontrelle Willis from the Marlins. The Tigers also included de la Cruz, Rabelo and righthanders Dallas Trahern and Burke Badenhop. Now they'll have seven former all-stars in the 2008 lineup, not to mention three in their rotation.

Those deals, along with the trade that sent three pitching prospects to the Yankees for Gary Sheffield after the 2006 season, have had an obvious effect on the system. Detroit has attempted to fill any gaps by spending big in the amateur draft. On Aug. 15, the first signing deadline day in draft history, the Tigers invested $9.4 million to sign righthander Rick Porcello (first round), lefthander Casey Crosby (fifth), shortstop Cale Iorg (sixth) and lefthander Matt Hoffman (26th).

The expenditure demonstrated two things: Detroit owner Mike Ilitch's willingness to sustain

Justin Verlander followed his rookie of the year campaign with a solid 2007 season

TOP 30 PROSPECTS

1. Rick Porcello, rhp	16. Brent Clevlen, of
2. Cale Iorg, ss	17. Jeff Gerbe, rhp
3. Scott Sizemore, 2b	18. Virgil Vasquez, rhp
4. Michael Hollimon, 2b/ss	19. Tony Giarratano, ss
5. Yorman Bazardo, rhp	20. Brent Dlugach, ss
6. Jeff Larish, 1b	21. Charlie Furbush, lhp
7. Matt Joyce, of	22. Jonah Nickerson, rhp
8. Danny Worth, ss	23. Jeramy Laster, of
9. Francisco Cruceta, rhp	24. Brennan Boesch, of
10. Brandon Hamilton, rhp	25. Clay Rapada, lhp
11. Jordan Tata, rhp	26. Duane Below, lhp
12. Clete Thomas, of	27. James Skelton, c
13. Casey Crosby, lhp	28. Ryan Strieby, 1b
14. Wilkin Ramirez, of	29. Freddy Dolsi, rhp
15. Freddy Guzman, of	30. Preston Larrison, rhp

a winning team, and confidence the club has in scouting director David Chadd, whose draft picks during his tenure with the Red Sox included Jonathan Papelbon and Dustin Pedroia. Similar over-slot spending landed Maybin and Miller, making the Cabrera/Willis deal possible.

"You can spend your money toward talent in various ways," general manager Dave Dombrowski said. "One place we can compete–and I feel like we do an outstanding job–is scouting at the amateur level, and developing those players."

General Manager: Dave Dombrowski. **Farm Director:** Dan Lunetta. **Scouting Director:** David Chadd.

Class	Team	League	W	L	PCT	Finish*	Manager	Affiliated
Majors	Detroit	American	88	74	.543	4th (14)	Jim Leyland	—
Triple-A	Toledo Mud Hens	International	82	61	.573	2nd (14)	Larry Parrish	1987
Double-A	Erie SeaWolves	Eastern	81	59	.579	2nd (12)	Matt Walbeck	2001
High A	Lakeland Flying Tigers	Florida State	53	87	.379	12th (12)	Kevin Bradshaw	1967
Low A	West Michigan Whitecaps	Midwest	83	57	.593	1st (14)^	Tom Brookens	1997
Short-season	Oneonta Tigers	New York-Penn	44	32	.579	4th (14)	Andy Barkett	1999
Rookie	GCL Tigers	Gulf Coast	28	32	.467	9th (16)	Benny Castillo	1995
Overall 2007 Minor League Record			371	328	.531	6th		

*Finish in overall standings (No. of teams in league) ^League champion

LAST YEAR'S TOP 30

Player, Pos.		Status
1.	Cameron Maybin, of	(Marlins)
2.	Andrew Miller, lhp	(Marlins)
3.	Brent Clevlen, of	No. 16
4.	Jair Jurrjens, rhp	(Braves)
5.	Jordan Tata, rhp	No. 11
6.	Eulogio de la Cruz, rhp	(Marlins)
7.	Gorkys Hernandez, of	(Braves)
8.	Dallas Trahern, rhp	(Marlins)
9.	Jeff Larish, 1b	No. 6
10.	Scott Sizemore, ss/2b	No. 3
11.	Kody Kirkland, 3b	Dropped out
12.	Sendy Vasquez, rhp	Dropped out
13.	Wilkin Ramirez, 3b	No. 14
14.	Tony Giarratano, ss	No. 19
15.	Michael Hollimon, ss	No. 4
16.	Brennan Boesch, of	No. 24
17.	Edward Campusano, lhp	(Cubs)
18.	Mike Rabelo, c	(Marlins)
19.	P.J. Finigan, rhp	Dropped out
20.	Ronnie Bourquin, 3b	Dropped out
21.	Jeff Frazier, of	(Mariners)
22.	Burke Badenhop, rhp	(Marlins)
23.	Matt Joyce, of	No. 7
24.	Virgil Vasquez, rhp	No. 18
25.	Jonah Nickerson, rhp	No. 22
26.	Preston Larrison, rhp	No. 30
27.	Ryan Raburn, of/2b	Majors
28.	Audy Ciriaco, ss	Dropped out
29.	Clete Thomas, of	No. 12
30.	Kyle Sleeth, rhp	Dropped out

BEST TOOLS

Best Hitter for Average	Scott Sizemore
Best Power Hitter	Jeff Larish
Best Strike-Zone Discipline	Scott Sizemore
Fastest Baserunner	Freddy Guzman
Best Athlete	Cale Iorg
Best Fastball	Rick Porcello
Best Curveball	Brandon Hamilton
Best Slider	Rick Porcello
Best Changeup	Yorman Bazardo
Best Control	Virgil Vasquez
Best Defensive Catcher	Dusty Ryan
Best Defensive Infielder	Danny Worth
Best Infield Arm	Kody Kirkland
Best Defensive Outfielder	Matt Joyce
Best Outfield Arm	Brent Clevlen

PROJECTED 2011 LINEUP

Catcher	James Skelton
First Base	Carlos Guillen
Second Base	Placido Polanco
Third Base	Cale Iorg
Shortstop	Edgar Renteria
Left Field	Miguel Cabrera
Center Field	Curtis Granderson
Right Field	Matt Joyce
Designated Hitter	Magglio Ordonez
No. 1 Starter	Justin Verlander
No. 2 Starter	Rick Porcello
No. 3 Starter	Dontrelle Willis
No. 4 Starter	Jeremy Bonderman
No. 5 Starter	Nate Robertson
Closer	Joel Zumaya

TOP PROSPECTS OF THE DECADE

Year	Player, Pos.	2007 Org.
1998	Juan Encarnacion, of	Cardinals
1999	Gabe Kapler, of	Out of baseball
2000	Eric Munson, 1b/c	Astros
2001	Brandon Inge, c	Tigers
2002	Nate Cornejo, rhp	Out of baseball
2003	Jeremy Bonderman, rhp	Tigers
2004	Kyle Sleeth, rhp	Tigers
2005	Curtis Granderson, of	Tigers
2006	Justin Verlander, rhp	Tigers
2007	Cameron Maybin, of	Tigers

TOP DRAFT PICKS OF THE DECADE

Year	Player, Pos.	2007 Org.
1998	Jeff Weaver, rhp	Mariners
1999	Eric Munson, 1b/c	Astros
2000	Matt Wheatland, rhp	Out of baseball
2001	Kenny Baugh, rhp	Marlins
2002	Scott Moore, ss	Orioles
2003	Kyle Sleeth, rhp	Tigers
2004	Justin Verlander, rhp	Tigers
2005	Cameron Maybin, rhp	Tigers
2006	Andrew Miller, lhp	Tigers
2007	Rick Porcello, rhp	Tigers

LARGEST BONUSES IN CLUB HISTORY

Rick Porcello, 2007	$3,580,000
Andrew Miller, 2006	$3,550,000
Eric Munson, 1999	$3,500,000
Kyle Sleeth, 2003	$3,350,000
Justin Verlander, 2004	$3,120,000

DETROIT TIGERS

Top 2008 Rookie: Yorman Bazardo, rhp. Acquired from the Mariners in a minor league trade last year, he should make the Tigers out of spring training and could be their No. 5 starter.

Breakout Prospect: Wilkin Ramirez, of. Moving him off third base kept him healthier and should allow his promising bat to take off.

Sleeper: Justin Henry, 2b. A ninth-round pick last June, he batted .340 with 14 steals in his pro debut.

SOURCE OF TOP 30 TALENT			
Homegrown	27	Acquired	3
College	17	Trades	2
Junior college	1	Rule 5 draft	0
High school	6	Independent leagues	0
Draft-and-follow	0	Free agents/waivers	1
Nondrafted free agents	1		
International	2		

Numbers in parentheses indicate prospect rankings.

LF
Clete Thomas (12)
Wilkin Ramirez (14)
Jeramy Laster (23)
Michael Hernandez

CF
Freddy Guzman (15)
Deik Scram
Chris White
Londell Taylor

RF
Matt Joyce (7)
Brent Clevlen (16)
Brennan Boesch (24)
Jason Perry

3B
Kody Kirkland
Ronnie Bourquin
Santo DeLeon

SS
Cale Iorg (2)
Danny Worth (8)
Tony Giarratano (19)
Brent Dlugach (20)
Audy Ciriaco
Hernan Perez

2B
Scott Sizemore (3)
Michael Hollimon (4)
Will Rhymes
Justin Henry

1B
Jeff Larish (6)
Ryan Strieby (28)
Ryan Roberson

C
James Skelton (27)
Dusty Ryan
Jordan Newton
Devin Thomas
Jeff Kunkel

RHP

Starters	Relievers
Rick Porcello (1)	Francisco Cruceta (9)
Yorman Bazardo (5)	Jeff Gerbe (17)
Brandon Hamilton (10)	Jonah Nickerson (22)
Jordan Tata (11)	Freddy Dolsi (29)
Virgil Vasquez (18)	Preston Larrison (30)
Eddie Bonine	Casey Fien
Chris Lambert	Luis Marte
Angel Castro	Brett Jensen
Alfredo Figaro	P.J. Finigan
Guillermo Moscoso	Josh Rainwater
Andrew Kown	Noah Krol
Matt O'Brien	Erik Crichton
Ben Fritz	Brendan Wise

LHP

Starters	Relievers
Casey Crosby (13)	Clay Rapada (25)
Charlie Furbush (21)	Santo Franco
Duane Below (26)	Danny Zell
Matt Hoffman	Juan Cedeno
Lucas French	

2007 | SIGNING BUDGET: $7.3 MILLION

Best Pro Debut: SS Danny Worth (3), known for his glove, debuted in the high Class A Florida State League and finished the year in the Double-A Eastern League playoffs; counting playoff games, he went 13-for-31 for Erie. LHP Charlie Furbush (4) went 6-1, 2.34 in 62 innings, most of them at low Class A West Michigan, with a 69-14 K-BB ratio. 2B Justin Henry (9) hit .340 for Oneonta in the short-season New York-Penn League.

Best Athlete: SS Cale Iorg (6) spent two years on a Mormon mission, but came back looking much like the middle-of-the-diamond talent he was as a freshman at Alabama back in 2005. An excellent prep football player, LHP Casey Crosby (5) was an all-state wide receiver, but OF Londell Taylor (13) had signed a football scholarship to play wide receiver at Oklahoma.

Best Pure Hitter: Henry, also a plus runner from the left side, has a line-drive, all-fields approach.

Best Power Hitter: Iorg and Taylor have above-average raw power, which Iorg is closer to tapping into.

Fastest Runner: OF Kyle Peter (34), from NCAA Division II Washburn (Kan.), is a 70 runner.

Best Defensive Player: Scouts describe Worth as a smooth, instinctive shortstop with good hands and an accurate arm.

Best Fastball: RHP Rick Porcello (1) was sitting in the 94-97 mph range with his fastball in instructional league, while Crosby was bumping 95. RHP Brandon Hamilton (2) runs his fastball up to 96, and it sits in the low-to-mid 90s.

Best Secondary Pitch: Porcello has an excellent hard, power slider that he throws in the low 80s. Hamilton's power curve is thrown just as hard.

Most Intriguing Background: Iorg's dad Garth and uncle Dane played in the big leagues, while brother Eli is an Astros farmhand. The Tigers drafted six other players with big league relatives; the most intriguing are 2B Colin Kaline (25), grandson of Tigers Hall of Famer Al; Matt Robertson (42), brother of Tigers lefthander Nate; and RHP Richard Zumaya (43), brother of Tigers reliever Joel. Kaline and Robertson did not sign.

Closest To The Majors: Worth. Furbush, who rediscovered some velocity late this summer, touching 92, and could be fast-tracked.

Best Late-Round Pick: Athletic LHP Matt Hoffman (26) got $175,000 to forgo his Oklahoma scholarship; he's touched 92 mph.

The One Who Got Away: RHP Barret Loux (24) was fulfilling some of the projection his 6-foot-5, 215-pound frame lends this summer, sitting at 92-95 mph with his fastball. He's at Texas A&M.

Assessment: In Porcello, the Tigers got one of the highest-ceiling players in the draft for the fourth straight season, despite picking 27th. If Crosby and Iorg or even Taylor come through on their prodigious talent, the Tigers will have had a tremendous effort.

2006 | BUDGET: $5.7 MILLION

The Tigers got LHP Andrew Miller (1), the top prospect in the draft, with the sixth overall pick and used him a year later to get Miguel Cabrera and Dontrelle Willis from the Marlins. 2B Scott Sizemore (5) may have the most consistent bat in the system.

GRADE: B+

2005 | BUDGET: $3.8 MILLION

OF Cameron Maybin (1), a steal with the No. 10 choice, was the other key part of the Cabrera/Willis trade, while RHP Kevin Whelan (4) became part of the package for Gary Sheffield. 2B/SS Michael Hollimon (16) and 1B Jeff Larish (5) are the best players Detroit has kept.

GRADE: A

2004 | BUDGET: $5.4 MILLION

If it's possible, RHP Justin Verlander (1) has exceeded expectation as the No. 2 pick. RHP Dallas Trahern (34) was another component in the blockbuster deal with the Marlins.

GRADE: A

2003 | BUDGET: $5.6 MILLION

Injuries have harmed the best pitcher, RHP Kyle Sleeth (1), and the best position player, SS Tony Giarratano (3) from this draft. RHP Jordan Tata (16) is now the best hope.

GRADE: D

Draft analysis by John Manuel (2007) and Jim Callis (2003-06). Numbers in parentheses indicate draft rounds. Budgets are bonuses in first 10 rounds.

BILL SETLIFF

RICK PORCELLO, RHP

Born: Dec. 27, 1988.
Ht.: 6-5. **Wt.:** 195.
Bats: R. **Throws:** R.
Drafted: HS—West Orange, N.J., 2007 (1st round).
Signed by: Bill Buck.

Porcello first was tabbed as a can't-miss prospect as early as age 15, and he maintained that status for the rest of his high school career. He entered 2007 ranking with Connecticut's Matt Harvey as the top prep arms in the draft class, then clearly separated himself. Porcello went 10-0, 1.18 with 112 strikeouts in 71 innings, leading Seton Hall Prep (West Orange, N.J.) to a 32-1 record, a state championship and a final No. 2 national ranking. Porcello was considered the best high school pitching prospect since Josh Beckett, but signability concerns caused him to drop to the Tigers with the 27th overall pick in the draft. Detroit hadn't planned to exceed MLB's slot recommendations again but decided it couldn't pass on Porcello. He and Harvey had planned to room together at North Carolina, and while Harvey became a Tar Heel, Porcello signed on the Aug. 15 deadline day. The Tigers made the decision easy for him, doling out a club-record $3.58 million bonus as part of a $7 million major league contract, matching Beckett's record guarantee for a high school pitcher. By MLB calculations, Porcello received the richest deal in the 2007 draft. Though No. 1 overall pick David Price got an $8.5 million big league contract, it's so backloaded that it's net present value was $4.8 million—which pales next to the $6.1 million present value of Porcello's pact. Now he'll try to become the second member of his family to reach the majors, following grandfather Sam Dente, who played for the Indians in the 1954 World Series.

Porcello could be another Justin Verlander in the making. His clean, repeatable delivery resembles Verlander's, and his power stuff is also reminiscent of the Tigers ace. Porcello's fastball rides up on righthanders and sits at 94-97 mph. He's able to keep that velocity deep into games. He throws two breaking balls, a power slider in the low 80s and a big-breaking curveball at 70-74 mph. He also shows good arm speed on his promising changeup. For a teenager, he has very good feel of multiple pitches and mixes them effectively. He has a tall, athletic body and good mound presence. The Tigers believe very strongly in Porcello's makeup, and he reinforced all the lofty comparisons with a strong showing in instructional league.

Porcello's command isn't major league average yet—but he's also 19 and has yet to throw his first official pro pitch. He harnesses his fastball better than his secondary offerings at this point. He tends to throw across his body slightly, and with better extension out front he could add more life to his pitches.

The Tigers are looking forward to the day when they can pitch Porcello and Verlander in the same big league rotation, giving them two youngsters with filthy stuff. Porcello didn't sign in time to pitch in the minors last summer, but there's no reason he can't handle an assignment to a full-season club. Low Class A West Michigan would be a logical fist step, though Detroit may send him to high Class A Lakeland so he can pitch in warmer weather. While the Tigers won't rush him, it will be difficult to hold his undeniable talent back. Beckett reached the major leagues at the end of his second minor league season, and Porcello could do the same.

Year	Club (League)	Class	W	L	ERA	G	GS	CG	SV	IP	H	R	ER	HR	BB	SO	AVG
2007	Did Not Play—Signed Late																

2 CALE IORG, SS

Born: Sept. 6, 1985. **B-T:** R-R. **Ht.:** 6-2. **Wt.:** 175. **Drafted:** Alabama, 2007 (6th round). **Signed by:** David Chadd.

Iorg's father Garth and uncle Dane played in the major leagues, and his brother Eli is an outfielder in the Astros system. Cale hadn't played since hitting .280 as a freshman at Alabama in 2005, taking two years off to go on a Mormon mission to Portugal. Believing he'd blossom into a first-round pick in 2008 if he returned to school, the Tigers drafted him in the sixth round and signed him for $1,497,500. Iorg has the body frame and actions of a natural shortstop. He's an instinctive player with enough power to hit between 15-20 homers per year in the majors. He has a smooth swing and should hit for average as well. He's a plus runner who showed an average to slightly above-average arm during workouts last summer. He has the tools to be an everyday shortstop, but it's unclear how long it will take Iorg to compensate for the long layoff. The Tigers hoped he would gain experience in Hawaii Winter Baseball, but he injured his hamstring in early October. Detroit believes Iorg's bloodlines and good makeup will offset his inexperience. He should begin his first full pro season in low Class A.

Year	Club (League)	Class	AVG	G	AB	R	H	2B	3B	HR	RBI	BB	SO	SB	OBP	SLG
2007	Tigers (GCL)	R	.182	3	11	1	2	0	0	0	0	1	6	0	.308	.182
	Lakeland (FSL)	A	.278	5	18	0	5	2	0	0	5	1	5	0	.316	.389
MINOR LEAGUE TOTALS			.241	8	29	1	7	2	0	0	5	2	11	0	.313	.310

3 SCOTT SIZEMORE, 2B

DAVID STONER

Born: Jan. 4, 1985. **B-T:** R-R. **Ht.:** 6-0. **Wt.:** 185. **Drafted:** Virginia Commonwealth, 2006 (5th round). **Signed by:** Bill Buck.

Sizemore overcame a slow start last year to reinforce his projection as a sound hitter with good bat control. The most polished position player in Detroit's 2006 draft class, he played second base on West Michigan's Midwest League championship club and saw action at shortstop (where he played during his pro debut) in the Arizona Fall League, where he hit .356. Sizemore demonstrated strong makeup by preventing an early slump from disrupting his confidence. He batted .311 in the second half, thanks to a short swing path, impeccable eye and sound approach. He walked more than he struck out, showed good hit-and-run ability, and generally looked like a classic No. 2 hitter. He has average speed and can steal a few bases thanks to good instincts. Sizemore's arm and hands are just adequate at second, and his range is average at best. With his line-drive, gap-to-gap stroke, Sizemore should hit his way to the big leagues, even if he becomes a utility player. He could reach Double-A Erie this year if he continues performing.

Year	Club (League)	Class	AVG	G	AB	R	H	2B	3B	HR	RBI	BB	SO	SB	OBP	SLG
2006	Oneonta (NYP)	A	.327	70	294	49	96	15	4	3	37	32	47	7	.394	.435
2007	West Michigan (MWL)	A	.265	125	438	78	116	33	5	4	48	73	60	16	.376	.390
MINOR LEAGUE TOTALS			.290	195	732	127	212	48	9	7	85	105	107	23	.383	.408

4 MICHAEL HOLLIMON, 2B/SS

KEVIN PATAKY

Born: June 14, 1982. **B-T:** B-R. **Ht.:** 6-1. **Wt.:** 185. **Drafted:** Oral Roberts, 2005 (16th round). **Signed by:** Steve Taylor.

Since signing for $5,000 as 16th-round pick in 2005, Hollimon has demonstrated the early-round ability he showed in high school. The Tigers love his makeup, and he has performed at every stop he has made in the system. Hollimon was an all-star in the Double-A Eastern League last year, finished the season at Triple-A Toledo and served as a backup as Team USA won the World Cup in November. Hollimon is a patient hitter whose at-bats often culminate with walks, strikeouts, or extra-base hits. He swings well from both sides of the plate and could have double-digit totals in doubles, triples, homers and steals if he plays everyday in the majors. He's an average runner with decent range as an infielder. Though he's adept at hitting outside fastballs, Hollimon can be pitched to inside. The Tigers lack depth on the left side of the infield, but it doesn't appear that Hollimon has the arm to play at shortstop or third base on an everyday basis. Second base would be his best position, but the Tigers have Placido Polanco under contract through 2009. Hollimon is athletic enough to play in the outfield, but Detroit has no plans to move him there this year in Triple-A.

Year	Club (League)	Class	AVG	G	AB	R	H	2B	3B	HR	RBI	BB	SO	SB	OBP	SLG
2005	Oneonta (NYP)	A	.275	72	255	66	70	13	10	13	53	50	76	8	.391	.557
2006	West Michigan (MWL)	A	.278	128	449	69	125	29	13	15	54	77	124	19	.386	.501
2007	Erie (EL)	AA	.282	127	471	91	133	34	8	14	76	64	121	17	.371	.478
	Toledo (IL)	AAA	.211	5	19	2	4	1	1	0	2	1	4	0	.250	.368
MINOR LEAGUE TOTALS			.278	332	1194	228	332	77	32	42	185	192	325	44	.379	.502

5 YORMAN BAZARDO, RHP

Born: July 11, 1984. **B-T:** R-R. **Ht.:** 6-2. **Wt.:** 220. **Signed:** Venezuela, 2000. **Signed by:** Miguel Garcia (Marlins).

Bazardo already has pitched for three organizations—and he's only 23. He was a top prospect with the Marlins before being sent to the Mariners in a deal for Ron Villone in 2005. During spring training last year the Tigers acquired him from Seattle in exchange for minor league outfielder Jeff Frazier. Detroit assistant general manager Al Avila was Florida's scouting director when Bazardo signed with the Marlins, so the Tigers had a good history with him. Bazardo had a solid season in the Triple-A rotation and pitched effectively as a starter and reliever for the Tigers. His fastball ranges from 90-94 mph with good sink, and his primary out pitch is a changeup with depth and armside run. His arm action is similar on both pitches and his herky-jerky delivery keeps hitters off balance. He has good command to both sides of the plate and throws a lot of first-pitch strikes. Because he lacks a consistent breaking ball, Bazardo doesn't rack up strikeouts. Without an improved slider, his ceiling likely will be as a middle reliever. He still was able to limit righthanders to a .143 average in the majors with his fastball and changeup alone. He's out of minor league options, so the Tigers will give Bazardo every opportunity to make the Opening Day roster in the bullpen.

Year	Club (League)	Class	W	L	ERA	G	GS	CG	SV	IP	H	R	ER	HR	BB	SO	AVG
2001	Ciudad Alianza (VSL)	R	7	2	2.43	12	12	1	0	70	59	26	19	0	18	62	—
2002	Jamestown (NYP)	A	5	0	2.72	25	0	0	6	36	39	11	11	0	6	26	.275
2003	Greensboro (SAL)	A	9	8	3.12	21	21	4	0	130	132	56	45	8	26	70	.261
2004	Jupiter (FSL)	A	5	9	3.27	25	25	2	0	154	161	78	56	3	30	95	.274
2005	Florida (NL)	MLB	0	0	21.60	1	0	0	0	1	5	5	4	0	2	2	.500
	Carolina (SL)	AA	8	7	3.99	19	19	0	0	108	108	60	48	12	36	73	.263
	San Antonio (TL)	AA	3	1	4.28	6	6	0	0	33	38	16	16	4	11	26	.295
2006	San Antonio (TL)	AA	6	5	3.64	25	25	0	0	138	144	65	56	10	45	80	.275
2007	Toledo (IL)	AAA	10	6	3.75	23	21	2	0	136	134	66	57	8	43	69	.263
	Detroit (AL)	MLB	2	1	2.28	11	2	0	0	23	19	7	6	2	5	15	.218
MINOR LEAGUE TOTALS			53	38	3.43	156	129	9	6	808	815	378	308	45	215	501	.290
MAJOR LEAGUE TOTALS			2	1	3.55	12	2	0	0	25	24	12	10	2	7	17	.247

6 JEFF LARISH, 1B

Born: Oct. 11, 1982. **B-T:** L-R. **Ht.:** 6-2. **Wt.:** 200. **Drafted:** Arizona State, 2005 (5th round). **Signed by:** Brian Reid.

What was true of Larish at Arizona State remains true today. There's no consensus among the scouting community about him, yet everyone seems to have an opinion. Scouts are divided on his unorthodox stance, and many wonder whether his home runs will turn into pop-outs once he reaches the big leagues. He keeps his chin turned completely to his right shoulder and both eyes focused on the pitcher, with his hands remaining still until the ball is on its way to the plate. His style worked just fine in Double-A, as he led the Eastern League with 28 homers and 101 RBIs and was Detroit's minor league player of the year in 2007. Larish has tremendous raw power and can hit the ball out from foul pole to foul pole. He patiently waits for a pitch to hammer and won't give in if pitchers don't challenge him, as evidenced by his 87 walks last season. He has soft hands at first base and a good arm for the position. Though he's selective, Larish won't alter his approach with two strikes, leading to whiffs. He's susceptible to good breaking pitches and gets too pull-happy. The key for him is swinging hard without overswinging. He has below-average speed. There's not a lot of projection involved with Larish. He simply has to keep hitting. Detroit's new everyday first baseman, Carlos Guillen, is signed through 2011, so Larish's path to becoming a big league regular is blocked for now. Larish also played third base and left field in college, but the Tigers will keep him at first in Triple-A.

Year	Club (League)	Class	AVG	G	AB	R	H	2B	3B	HR	RBI	BB	SO	SB	OBP	SLG
2005	Tigers (GCL)	R	.222	6	18	1	4	1	0	0	4	4	5	0	.375	.278
	Oneonta (NYP)	A	.297	18	64	16	19	3	0	6	13	13	6	0	.430	.625
2006	Lakeland (FSL)	A	.258	135	457	76	118	34	2	18	65	81	101	9	.379	.460
2007	Erie (EL)	AA	.267	132	454	71	121	25	2	28	101	87	108	6	.390	.515
MINOR LEAGUE TOTALS			.264	291	993	164	262	63	4	52	183	185	220	15	.387	.492

7 MATT JOYCE, OF

Born: Aug. 3, 1984. **B-T:** L-R. **Ht.:** 6-2. **Wt.:** 185. **Drafted:** Florida Southern, 2005 (12th round). **Signed by:** Steve Nichols.

KEVIN PATAKY

Joyce helped West Michigan win the Midwest League title in 2006, then skipped a level and helped Erie make the Eastern League playoffs. He was pulling off the ball early in the season and batted .193 during the first two months. But then he settled back into his overachieving ways, started allowing the ball to travel deeper into the zone and batted .293 with 13 homers over the final three months. Joyce has a smooth left-handed stroke and a knack for driving in runs. He generally hits gap-to-gap but possesses some home run power and has the potential to top last year's career high of 17. A well-above-average right fielder, he gets great jumps and has a strong, accurate arm. He can play an adequate center field if needed. Like many of the Tigers' top position prospects, Joyce needs to cut down his strikeouts. He chases low changeups from righthanders. He doesn't use his average speed as well on the bases as he does in the outfield. Joyce has moved swiftly since signing in 2005, and he'll move up to Triple-A this season. If all goes well, he'll challenge for a big league job in 2009.

Year	Club (League)	Class	AVG	G	AB	R	H	2B	3B	HR	RBI	BB	SO	SB	OBP	SLG
2005	Oneonta (NYP)	A	.332	65	247	51	82	10	4	4	46	28	29	9	.394	.453
2006	West Michigan (MWL)	A	.258	122	465	75	120	30	5	11	86	56	70	5	.338	.415
2007	Erie (EL)	AA	.257	130	456	61	117	33	3	17	70	51	127	4	.333	.454
MINOR LEAGUE TOTALS			.273	317	1168	187	319	73	12	32	202	135	226	18	.348	.438

8 DANNY WORTH, SS

Born: Sept. 30, 1985. **B-T:** R-R. **Ht.:** 6-1. **Wt.:** 180. **Drafted:** Pepperdine, 2007 (2nd round). **Signed by:** Tim McWilliam.

JERRY HALE

Others may have received more acclaim, but no one in the Tigers' 2007 draft class made a greater immediate impact than Worth. He signed for $378,000 as a second-round pick, became the starting shortstop in high Class A and finished his pro debut with a late promotion to Double-A. He picked up even more professional experience in Hawaii Winter Baseball, where he hit .292. Worth is a consistent, confident defender with reliable hands. A natural shortstop, he has an average arm that plays up because of his quick release and above-average range. He's not flashy but makes all the routine plays. A gap hitter, he has a quick bat and a good sense of the strike zone. Worth has limited power, projecting to hit some doubles but not many homers. Like many young hitters, he's susceptible to good breaking balls. His speed is maybe a tick below average, though he looks faster on the bases because of good instincts. His ceiling is comparable to that of Jason Bartlett, as a smooth-fielding shortstop who bats in the bottom third of an American League lineup and hits around .270 without much power. Worth will return to Lakeland or Erie to begin 2008, and his polished skills could enable him to move quickly in a system that lacks depth at shortstop in the upper minors.

Year	Club (League)	Class	AVG	G	AB	R	H	2B	3B	HR	RBI	BB	SO	SB	OBP	SLG
2007	Lakeland (FSL)	A	.251	51	171	22	43	9	2	2	21	18	39	6	.325	.363
	Erie (EL)	AA	.429	5	14	4	6	2	1	0	4	1	1	1	.438	.714
MINOR LEAGUE TOTALS			.265	56	185	26	49	11	3	2	25	19	40	7	.333	.389

9 FRANCISCO CRUCETA, RHP

Born: July 4, 1981. **B-T:** R-R. **Ht.:** 6-2. **Wt.:** 215. **Signed:** Dominican Republic, 1999. **Signed by:** Pablo Peguero (Dodgers).

STEVE MOORE

Cruceta already spent time in four organizations when he signed a major league contract in November with the Tigers, who believe he's ready to reach his high ceiling. He possesses above-average stuff but has performed inconsistently throughout his career because of command problems. He tested positive for a performance-enhancing substance while in Triple-A with the Rangers in 2007, and the 50-game suspension didn't help his development. Cruceta throws a sinking fastball that sits in the low 90s and tops out at 94 mph. He has featured two secondary pitches since moving to the bullpen full-time, a sharp splitter that he usually throws out of the zone and a 12-to-6 curveball that should become at least an average pitch. Cruceta has a reputation for throwing hittable pitches up in the zone, but giving up two homers in 66 innings last year suggests that he has made adjustments. His arm slot wandered in the past and his command is still erratic at times. He appears to have little confidence in his slider and changeup and has removed those pitches from his repertoire. It would be useful to bring one of them back so he could break his pattern of two-strike splitters. Detroit signed Cruceta with the idea that he'd pitch for their big league club in 2008. He's out of minor league options, so he has to clear waivers before he could be farmed out. If he throws enough strikes, he could become a reliable middle reliever.

Year	Club (League)	Class	W	L	ERA	G	GS	CG	SV	IP	H	R	ER	HR	BB	SO	AVG
1999	Dodgers (DSL)	R	3	2	7.56	14	1	0	0	25	33	34	21	4	15	21	.308
2000	Dodgers (DSL)	R	4	2	3.31	21	6	0	3	49	33	29	18	1	36	49	.180
2001	Dodgers (DSL)	R	0	4	1.50	11	9	0	0	48	35	24	8	1	24	47	.200
2002	South Georgia (SAL)	A	8	5	2.80	20	20	3	0	112	98	42	35	7	34	111	.231
	Kinston (Car)	A	2	0	2.50	7	7	0	0	39	31	13	11	2	25	37	.217
2003	Akron (EL)	AA	13	9	3.09	27	25	6	0	163	141	70	56	7	66	134	.232
2004	Akron (EL)	AA	4	8	5.28	15	15	1	0	88	89	58	52	11	33	45	.261
	Buffalo (IL)	AAA	6	5	3.25	14	14	1	0	83	78	35	30	6	36	62	.259
	Cleveland (AL)	MLB	0	1	9.39	2	2	0	0	7	10	9	8	1	4	9	.303
2005	Buffalo (IL)	AAA	6	4	5.19	30	13	1	0	102	123	65	59	16	32	92	.297
	Tacoma (PCL)	AAA	1	1	5.00	2	2	0	0	9	11	6	5	3	3	10	.297
2006	Tacoma (PCL)	AAA	13	9	4.38	28	28	1	0	160	150	81	78	25	76	185	.247
	Seattle (AL)	MLB	0	0	10.80	4	1	0	0	6	10	8	8	2	6	2	.370
2007	Oklahoma (PCL)	AAA	3	0	3.02	25	5	0	1	65	38	25	22	2	40	70	.164
MINOR LEAGUE TOTALS			63	49	3.76	214	145	13	4	946	860	482	395	85	420	863	.241
MAJOR LEAGUE TOTALS			0	1	10.05	6	3	0	0	14	20	17	16	3	10	11	.333

10 BRANDON HAMILTON, RHP

JERRY HALE

Born: Dec. 25, 1988. **B-T:** R-R. **Ht.:** 6-2. **Wt.:** 205. **Drafted:** HS—Millbrook, Ala., 2007 (1st round supplemental). **Signed by:** Jim Rough.

The Tigers have rebuilt their franchise on power pitching, and Hamilton, their second pick in the 2007 draft fits the prototype. Detroit officials liked what they saw in his athleticism, durability and projectability, and signed him for $540,000 with the 60th overall pick, compensation for losing free agent Jamie Walker to Baltimore. Hamilton isn't as polished as 2007 first-rounder Rick Porcello but has the better curveball of the two. It's a power downer, and he throws it at 80-83 mph with hard, late, three-quarters break. He has shown an ability to repeat the curve and throw it for strikes, which bodes well for his long-term development. His fastball is an average pitch now, sitting in the low 90s, and more velocity should come. He has a strong, lean frame and clean mechanics. His changeup is promising but inconsistent, and his command is still below-average. The Tigers will take their time with Hamilton, but still may send him to low Class A as a 19-year-old.

Year	Club (League)	Class	W	L	ERA	G	GS	CG	SV	IP	H	R	ER	HR	BB	SO	AVG
2007	Tigers (GCL)	R	1	1	3.10	7	5	0	0	20	12	9	7	2	12	23	.171
MINOR LEAGUE TOTALS			1	1	3.10	7	5	0	0	20	12	9	7	2	12	23	.171

11 JORDAN TATA, RHP

Born: Sept. 20, 1981. **B-T:** R-R. **Ht.:** 6-6. **Wt.:** 220. **Drafted:** Sam Houston State, 2003 (16th round). **Signed by:** Tim Grieve.

After making the Tigers' 2006 Opening Day roster after an injury to Todd Jones, Tata began last year on the disabled list in Triple-A with shoulder inflammation. He joined Detroit's rotation in late July, when Kenny Rogers went on the disabled list, and earned his first big league win at Oakland. But Tata wasn't as sharp in his second start and a quick exit from the third sent him back to the minors. Still, there's hope for him to reach his ceiling as a fifth starter or long reliever. His best pitch is a natural cut fastball that runs from 89-93 mph, which he could have success with out of the bullpen. He throws it frequently, but predictability wouldn't be a problem if he commanded it better. He has incorporated a two-seam fastball, which he throws in the high 80s with some armside run, and a slurvy breaking ball at 79-80 mph. The breaking ball has good depth when Tata is throwing well but is average at best on most days. The Tigers didn't bring Tata back as a September callup last year, casting some doubt on his chances to make the club this spring.

Year	Club (League)	Class	W	L	ERA	G	GS	CG	SV	IP	H	R	ER	HR	BB	SO	AVG
2003	Oneonta (NYP)	A	4	3	2.58	16	12	0	1	73	64	32	21	1	20	60	.236
2004	West Michigan (MWL)	A	8	11	3.35	28	28	1	0	166	167	77	62	7	68	116	.272
2005	Lakeland (FSL)	A	13	2	2.79	25	25	2	0	155	138	55	48	12	41	134	.239
2006	Detroit (AL)	MLB	0	0	6.14	8	0	0	0	14	14	11	10	1	7	6	.250
	Toledo (IL)	AAA	10	6	3.84	21	21	1	0	122	117	58	52	11	49	86	.252
2007	Toledo (IL)	AAA	4	5	3.05	14	14	0	0	82	67	31	28	8	28	50	.220
	Detroit (AL)	MLB	1	1	7.71	3	3	0	0	14	16	12	12	1	8	8	.302
MINOR LEAGUE TOTALS			39	27	3.17	104	100	4	1	599	553	253	211	39	206	446	.248
MAJOR LEAGUE TOTALS			1	1	6.91	11	3	0	0	28	30	23	22	2	15	14	.275

12 CLETE THOMAS, OF

Born: Nov. 14, 1983. **B-T:** L-R. **Ht.:** 5-11. **Wt.:** 195. **Drafted:** Auburn, 2005 (6th round). **Signed by:** Jerome Cochran.

Thomas' tools began to take shape during a productive 2007 season in Double-A. He demonstrated better plate discipline and made more contact than he had the year before. He's a smart, determined hitter from the left side who uses the whole field. He still strikes out a little too much because he doesn't handle breaking balls well from either lefties or righties. Thomas probably won't be a double-digit home run hitter but has some power to the gaps and his pull side. He runs very well but must do a better job of picking his spots to steal after getting caught 11 times in 29 tries last season. Thomas takes good angles and routes and can play all three outfield positions with a slightly above-average arm. At this point, his ceiling appears to be as a platoon outfielder. He would need to cut down on his strikeouts and perform better against lefthanders in order to be an everyday player in the major leagues, but his defensive ability and baseball instincts could make him a valuable extra outfielder for the Tigers. Brett Clevlen and Matt Joyce also will be pushing for big league jobs, so Thomas has his work cut out for him. He'll likely begin this season in Triple-A.

Year	Club (League)	Class	AVG	G	AB	R	H	2B	3B	HR	RBI	BB	SO	SB	OBP	SLG
2005	Oneonta (NYP)	A	.386	18	70	19	27	5	1	1	14	12	11	9	.488	.529
	West Michigan (MWL)	A	.284	51	194	39	55	8	5	0	11	21	37	11	.356	.376
2006	Lakeland (FSL)	A	.257	132	529	67	136	30	5	6	40	56	127	34	.333	.367
2007	Erie (EL)	AA	.280	137	528	97	148	30	6	8	53	59	110	18	.359	.405
MINOR LEAGUE TOTALS			.277	338	1321	222	366	73	17	15	118	148	285	72	.356	.392

13 CASEY CROSBY, LHP

Born: Sept. 17, 1988. **B-T:** R-L. **Ht.:** 6-5. **Wt.:** 200. **Drafted:** HS—Maple Park, Ill., 2007 (5th round). **Signed by:** Marty Miller.

The Tigers faced scrutiny from the commissioner's office after signing some of their top draft picks for well above MLB's slot recommendations. But if Crosby becomes a top-of-the-rotation starter—and they believe he will—it will be well worth the trouble. Detroit ranked him among the draft's top 25 players, so it was happy to sign him for $748,500 when he dropped into the fifth round because of a high price tag. However, the Tigers will have to wait for returns on their investment, as Crosby required Tommy John surgery after coming down with an elbow injury in instructional league. There aren't many 6-foot-5 lefthanders who reach 95 mph as high school seniors like Crosby did. He's raw, but the Tigers love his athleticism. He was an all-state wide receiver in football and played center field before moving to the mound full-time in 2006. His delivery has some deception, and the ball jumps on hitters because of his long limbs. He has broad shoulders, a good body and a high three-quarters arm slot. While the success rate for Tommy John surgery is strong, it's not a given that his stuff will come back. When healthy, he hasn't shown good command with his tailing fastball. He throws an inconsistent, slurvy breaking ball and has yet to develop a changeup. His mechanics need polish, too, but that's common among young pitchers from cold-weather states. The Tigers believe Crosby has great potential, which is one reason they'll be cautious with him coming back from his injury. If he throws in instructional league in 2008, he'll be ahead of schedule.

Year	Club (League)	Class	W	L	ERA	G	GS	CG	SV	IP	H	R	ER	HR	BB	SO	AVG
2007	Did Not Play—Signed Late																

14 WILKIN RAMIREZ, OF

Born: Oct. 25, 1985. **B-T:** R-R. **Ht.:** 6-2. **Wt.:** 190. **Signed:** Dominican Republic, 2003. **Signed by:** Ramon Pena.

Ramirez was struggling at third base and had played more than 70 games only once since signing with the Tigers in 2003. Last year, the Tigers decided to solve both issues by moving him to left field, where his defense would be less of an issue and he wouldn't suffer as much wear and tear. It worked, as Ramirez wasn't as much of a liability with the glove and nearly established a new career high with 122 games. He has plus power and a high ceiling, but he must improve his pitch recognition in order to have consistent success at the upper levels. Because of a tendency to chase breaking pitches, he has more strikeouts than games played in his career. Still, he has a good work ethic, which bodes well for his chances to make the necessary adjustments. Ramirez possesses plus speed but had difficulty judging balls in the outfield because of inexperience. He has a strong throwing arm that has bounced back from labrum surgery that cost him the entire 2004 season. His athleticism should enable him to be a close-to-average defender once he has more repetitions in the outfield. Ramirez has an intriguing blend of power and speed but lacks polish. He seems likely to return to Double-A for 2008.

Year	Club (League)	Class	AVG	G	AB	R	H	2B	3B	HR	RBI	BB	SO	SB	OBP	SLG
2003	Tigers (GCL)	R	.275	54	200	34	55	6	7	5	35	13	51	6	.321	.450
2004	Did Not Play—Injured															
2005	West Michigan (MWL)	A	.262	131	493	69	129	21	2	16	65	35	143	21	.317	.410
2006	Lakeland (FSL)	A	.225	66	249	31	56	10	4	8	33	10	69	8	.259	.394
2007	Lakeland (FSL)	A	.273	88	319	48	87	7	4	10	41	20	86	28	.315	.414
	Erie (EL)	AA	.215	34	121	15	26	3	1	2	14	8	38	6	.273	.306
MINOR LEAGUE TOTALS			.255	373	1382	197	353	47	18	41	188	86	387	69	.303	.404

15 FREDDY GUZMAN, OF

Born: Jan. 20, 1981. **B-T:** B-R. **Ht.:** 5-10. **Wt.:** 165. **Signed:** Dominican Republic, 2000. **Signed by:** Bill Clark/Modesto Ulloa (Padres).

Detroit manager Jim Leyland has often said that he would like to have more speed on his team, and Guzman is among the fastest players in the game. The Tigers are eager to see what Guzman can do after acquiring him from the Rangers in exchange for first baseman Chris Shelton during the Winter Meetings. Guzman is an older prospect, but he still has plus-plus speed and very good baserunning instincts. He stole 90 bases during the 2003 season, when he played for three San Diego affiliates, and led the Pacific Coast League in 2007 with 56. Guzman has become a free swinger over time and must make more consistent contact in order to stick in the big leagues. He has a quick bat and some doubles power to the pull field but isn't strong or physical. His bunting ability is only average. He has good range in the outfield but his arm is erratic. He fits best in center field and profiles as a useful bench player. Guzman could force his way into the competition for a reserve role in Detroit if he has an impressive spring.

Year	Club (League)	Class	AVG	G	AB	R	H	2B	3B	HR	RBI	BB	SO	SB	OBP	SLG
2000	Padres (DSL)	R	.210	49	167	38	35	6	1	1	10	46	38	24	.386	.275
2001	Idaho Falls (Pio)	R	.348	12	46	11	16	4	1	0	5	2	10	5	.388	.478
2002	Lake Elsinore (Cal)	A	.259	21	81	13	21	3	0	1	6	8	12	14	.326	.333
	Fort Wayne (MWL)	A	.279	47	190	35	53	7	5	0	18	18	37	39	.341	.368
	Eugene (NWL)	A	.225	21	80	14	18	2	1	0	8	7	15	16	.293	.275
2003	Lake Elsinore (Cal)	A	.285	70	281	64	80	12	3	2	22	40	60	49	.375	.370
	Mobile (SL)	AA	.271	46	177	30	48	5	2	1	11	26	34	38	.368	.339
	Portland (PCL)	AAA	.300	2	10	1	3	0	0	0	0	0	1	3	.300	.300
2004	Mobile (SL)	AA	.283	35	138	21	39	5	2	1	7	16	28	17	.359	.370
	Portland (PCL)	AAA	.292	66	264	48	77	12	4	0	19	30	46	48	.365	.379
	San Diego (NL)	MLB	.211	20	76	8	16	3	0	0	5	3	13	5	.250	.250
2006	Portland (PCL)	AAA	.274	30	124	15	34	7	2	2	14	14	19	11	.348	.411
	Texas (AL)	MLB	.286	9	7	1	2	0	0	0	0	1	1	0	.444	.286
	Oklahoma (PCL)	AAA	.282	69	252	45	71	9	2	1	14	36	36	31	.375	.345
2007	Oklahoma (PCL)	AAA	.269	133	535	92	144	22	8	4	34	62	88	56	.348	.363
	Texas (AL)	MLB	.167	8	6	2	1	0	0	1	1	0	2	0	.167	.667
MINOR LEAGUE TOTALS			.272	601	2345	427	639	94	31	14	168	305	424	351	.359	.357
MAJOR LEAGUE TOTALS			.213	37	89	11	19	3	0	1	6	4	16	5	.263	.281

16 BRENT CLEVLEN, OF

Born: Oct. 27, 1983. **B-T:** R-R. **Ht.:** 6-2. **Wt.:** 190. **Drafted:** HS—Cedar Park, Texas, 2002 (2nd round). **Signed by:** Tim Grieve.

Clevlen's performance fell decidedly short of his tools again last year, the continuation of a disappointing trend. His shortcomings are almost exclusively at the plate, as Detroit manager Jim Leyland has said Clevlen might be the best outfield defender in the organization. Clevlen has tremendous raw power and has struggled with plate discipline and pitch recognition for much of his pro career. He has good speed but doesn't steal many bases. He can play all three outfield positions, and his strong, accurate arm plays well in right. Clevlen's window to earn playing time may have reopened a bit after top prospect Cameron Maybin went to the Marlins in the Miguel Cabrera and Dontrelle Willis deal, as his defense could make him a valuable reserve. Unless he learns to make more consistent contact, a reserve role is his ceiling.

Year	Club (League)	Class	AVG	G	AB	R	H	2B	3B	HR	RBI	BB	SO	SB	OBP	SLG
2002	Tigers (GCL)	R	.330	28	103	14	34	2	3	3	21	8	24	2	.372	.495
2003	West Michigan (MWL)	A	.260	138	481	67	125	22	7	12	63	72	111	6	.359	.410
2004	Lakeland (FSL)	A	.224	117	420	49	94	23	6	6	50	44	127	2	.300	.350
2005	Lakeland (FSL)	A	.302	130	494	77	149	28	4	18	102	65	118	14	.387	.484
2006	Erie (EL)	AA	.230	109	395	47	91	17	0	11	45	47	138	6	.313	.357
	Detroit (AL)	MLB	.282	31	39	9	11	1	2	3	6	2	15	0	.317	.641
2007	Toledo (IL)	AAA	.220	90	322	33	71	14	5	7	36	39	113	4	.304	.360
	Tigers (GCL)	R	.313	14	48	10	15	1	0	2	8	3	8	1	.346	.458
	Detroit (AL)	MLB	.100	13	10	2	1	0	0	0	0	0	7	0	.100	.100
MINOR LEAGUE TOTALS			.256	626	2263	297	579	107	25	59	325	278	639	35	.339	.403
MAJOR LEAGUE TOTALS			.245	44	49	11	12	1	2	3	6	2	22	0	.275	.531

17 JEFF GERBE, RHP

Born: July 4, 1984. **B-T:** R-R. **Ht.:** 6-3. **Wt.:** 200. **Drafted:** Michigan State, 2006 (16th round). **Signed by:** Tom Osowski.

The Tigers appear to have found a late-round gem in Gerbe, who had a local-boy-does-good season. He grew up in suburban Detroit, was a senior sign from Michigan State in 2006 and excelled while pitching for the club's lone in-state affiliate last year. Shoulder tendinitis had limited him to eight starts in his pro debut, but he was quickly noticed. Gerbe commands a sinking fastball that tops out around 94 mph and features plus movement. He gets a lot of ground balls and also can miss bats with his slider. His changeup has also improved. He's a competitor who showed tremendous makeup by pitching well in two spot starts at Double-A Erie and was one of the most reliable pitchers on a West Michigan team that won the Midwest League title. Gerbe spent some time on the disabled list with more shoulder inflammation, but the Tigers believe they have resolved the issue. They were confident enough in his health that they sent him to pitch in the Arizona Fall League, where he mixed in four scoreless outings with five putrid ones, posting a 9.42 ERA overall. He projects as a middle reliever and could return to Double-A in that role this year.

Year	Club (League)	Class	W	L	ERA	G	GS	CG	SV	IP	H	R	ER	HR	BB	SO	AVG
2006	Oneonta (NYP)	A	1	4	5.08	8	8	0	0	39	52	30	22	1	8	23	.325
2007	West Michigan (MWL)	A	2	2	2.34	19	9	0	2	73	65	26	19	2	12	40	.243
	Erie (EL)	AA	0	1	4.50	2	2	1	0	12	8	8	6	1	6	5	.190
MINOR LEAGUE TOTALS			3	7	3.41	29	19	1	2	124	125	64	47	4	26	68	.266

18 VIRGIL VASQUEZ, RHP

Born: June 7, 1982. **B-T:** R-R. **Ht.:** 6-3. **Wt.:** 205. **Drafted:** UC Santa Barbara, 2003 (7th round). **Signed by:** Tom Hinkle.

After an attention-getting performance in the 2006 Arizona Fall League and a steady start to his 2007 season in Triple-A, Vasquez made his big league debut in 2007. He was called up to make three starts and pitched twice out of the bullpen in September. Detroit lost each time he started, and he was hit especially hard in his debut at Minnesota, but Vasquez still could develop into a fifth starter. His biggest problem was that he left too many pitches up and allowed seven home runs in just 17 innings pitched. The quality of his breaking balls and location on all his pitches must improve in order for Vasquez to succeed in the majors. He's not a hard thrower, which makes command that much more important. His fastball is consistently at 90 mph, and he throws a sinker in the upper 80s. Both are good pitches when Vasquez keeps them on the corners, but they become hittable when he doesn't locate. His low-to-mid 80s slider has some potential, and he mixes in a slower curveball and a changeup. His pitches have some late movement in on righthanders. He'll start the season in Triple-A unless he has an overwhelming spring.

Year	Club (League)	Class	W	L	ERA	G	GS	CG	SV	IP	H	R	ER	HR	BB	SO	AVG
2003	Oneonta (NYP)	A	3	4	6.92	11	11	0	0	53	76	43	41	5	10	35	.328
2004	West Michigan (MWL)	A	14	6	3.64	27	27	0	0	168	156	73	68	14	34	120	.252
2005	Lakeland (FSL)	A	4	1	4.21	8	8	1	0	47	52	23	22	6	7	31	.289
	Erie (EL)	AA	2	8	5.27	15	15	0	0	83	93	59	49	10	14	53	.281
2006	Erie (EL)	AA	7	12	3.73	27	27	3	0	173	174	79	72	21	50	129	.265
2007	Toledo (IL)	AAA	12	5	3.48	25	25	2	0	155	139	64	60	18	33	127	.241
	Detroit (AL)	MLB	0	1	8.64	5	3	0	0	17	27	16	16	7	5	7	.360
MINOR LEAGUE TOTALS			42	36	4.12	113	113	6	0	681	690	341	312	74	148	495	.266
MAJOR LEAGUE TOTALS			0	1	8.64	5	3	0	0	16	27	16	16	7	5	7	.360

19 TONY GIARRATANO, SS

Born: Nov. 29, 1982. **B-T:** B-R. **Ht.:** 6-0. **Wt.:** 180. **Drafted:** Tulane, 2003 (3rd round). **Signed by:** Steve Taylor.

Giarratano ranked No. 8 on this list as recently as two years ago, but injuries have sidetracked his promising career. Giarratano was limited to 67 games in 2006 because of a wrist injury and surgery on a torn anterior cruciate ligament in his right knee. His rehabilitation from the knee injury went well and Giarratano reported early to spring training. Even before the Grapefruit League opened, though, he felt pain in his throwing shoulder. He had surgery to repair a torn labrum soon afterward and missed the entire 2007 season. At this point, it's impossible to know how much the shoulder and knee injuries will compromise a good throwing arm and above-average defensive tools. Giarratano had projected as an everyday shortstop because of his brilliant glove and plus range, and might have been a candidate to start for the Tigers in 2008 if he had remained healthy. He makes good contact from both sides of the plate and runs well enough to turn some doubles into triples and steal some occasional bases. He's expected to participate in spring training this season, a good sign. More than anything else, he needs to stay healthy.

Year	Club (League)	Class	AVG	G	AB	R	H	2B	3B	HR	RBI	BB	SO	SB	OBP	SLG
2003	Oneonta (NYP)	A	.328	47	189	31	62	11	4	3	27	12	22	9	.369	.476
2004	West Michigan (MWL)	A	.285	43	165	20	47	6	1	1	13	25	22	11	.383	.352
	Lakeland (FSL)	A	.376	53	202	30	76	11	0	5	25	16	38	14	.421	.505
2005	Detroit (AL)	MLB	.143	15	42	4	6	0	0	1	4	5	7	1	.234	.214
	Erie (EL)	AA	.266	89	346	40	92	22	3	3	32	32	75	12	.334	.373
2006	Erie (EL)	AA	.283	67	269	35	76	19	5	0	19	22	45	16	.340	.390
2007	Did Not Play—Injured															
MINOR LEAGUE TOTALS			.301	299	1171	156	353	69	13	12	116	107	202	62	.363	.413
MAJOR LEAGUE TOTALS			.143	15	42	4	6	0	0	1	4	5	7	1	.234	.214

20 BRENT DLUGACH, SS

Born: March 3, 1983. **B-T:** R-R. **Ht.:** 6-4. **Wt.:** 195. **Drafted:** Memphis, 2004 (6th round). **Signed by:** Harold Zonder.

Dlugach impressed some of the Tigers' top officials—including manager Jim Leyland—with his smooth, confident play at shortstop last spring. He also acquitted himself well at the plate, with a .316 average during his first big league camp. He got off to a strong start in Double-A, hitting .304 in his first 20 games, and appeared on his way to a breakthrough season. On May 2, however, he jarred his shoulder while diving for a ball. He attempted to play in two games after that, but the pain persisted. He had rotator-cuff surgery in August, and Detroit doesn't expect him to be quite ready when the 2008 season begins. Dlugach's glove looked big league-ready last spring, and he showed above-average arm strength before the injury. There were some questions about his bat before the injury, and the missed time certainly won't help his development as a hitter. He has good bat speed but doesn't project to hit for much power. His defensive ability could allow him to play every day on a team with good production at other key positions. His 2008 role hinges on his health, but with Edgar Renteria's arrival, Dlugach has time to recooperate after his injury.

Year	Club (League)	Class	AVG	G	AB	R	H	2B	3B	HR	RBI	BB	SO	SB	OBP	SLG
2004	Oneonta (NYP)	A	.213	47	183	17	39	7	2	1	12	8	59	5	.256	.290
2005	West Michigan (MWL)	A	.283	124	488	55	138	26	5	5	61	19	121	13	.317	.387
2006	Lakeland (FSL)	A	.256	125	465	51	119	24	6	5	52	27	144	13	.299	.366
	Toledo (IL)	AAA	.000	2	6	0	0	0	0	0	0	0	2	0	.000	.000
2007	Erie (EL)	AA	.292	22	72	12	21	4	3	1	7	6	25	1	.346	.472
MINOR LEAGUE TOTALS			.261	320	1214	135	317	61	16	12	132	60	351	32	.301	.367

21 CHARLIE FURBUSH, LHP

Born: April 11, 1986. **B-T:** L-L. **Ht.:** 6-5. **Wt.:** 215. **Drafted:** Louisiana State, 2007 (4th round). **Signed by:** Jim Rough.

Furbush was a fine NCAA Division III pitcher but relatively unknown, then had two strong seasons in the Cape Cod League, winning pitcher-of-the-year honors in 2006. He transferred to Louisiana State as a junior, but a modest 3-9, 4.95 season dropped him out of first-round consideration. A hard-throwing lefthander, he rekindled memories of his outstanding Cape League effort with his strong pro debut. Signed for $153,000 as a fourth-rounder, he seemed to regain his velocity after the draft, touching 92 mph while helping West Michigan to a second consecutive league title. His fastball sits at 89-90 mph, and his slurvy breaking ball is more advanced than those of many lefthanders his age. His changeup is still in the developmental stages. Furbush has a tall, lean frame and showed good poise in low Class A, especially considering his lack of pro experience. He has sound mechanics, good balance in his windup and a nice angle to his three-quarters release. Furbush has major league average command, and, if he gains strength, he could move quickly through the system. He'll open 2008 with one of the Tigers' Class A affiliates.

Year	Club (League)	Class	W	L	ERA	G	GS	CG	SV	IP	H	R	ER	HR	BB	SO	AVG
2007	Tigers (GCL)	R	2	0	2.81	4	3	0	0	16	11	5	5	2	3	23	.186
	West Michigan (MWL)	A	4	1	2.17	8	7	0	0	45	40	14	11	2	11	46	.237
MINOR LEAGUE TOTALS			6	1	2.34	12	10	0	0	61	51	19	16	4	14	69	.224

22 JONAH NICKERSON, RHP

Born: March 9, 1985. **B-T:** R-R. **Ht.:** 6-1. **Wt.:** 200. **Drafted:** Oregon State, 2006 (7th round). **Signed by:** Brian Reid.

It took about one calendar year, but it seems Nickerson has finally recovered from his 323-pitch marathon at the 2006 College World Series, where he was the most outstanding player after leading Oregon State to the national championship. He returned to form near the middle of his first full season as a pro, and his ERA dropped from 5.80 before the all-star break to 2.95 thereafter. His overhand curveball had been slow and loopy during the first half, but it became sharper down the stretch. He battled back stiffness at times but was a vital part of West Michigan's championship run. Nickerson showed plus command with his fastball and spotted it at the knees and on the corners at 89-90 mph. Terrific control enabled Nickerson to be efficient with his pitches, and he finished as the team leader with 151 innings. When he misses with a pitch, he tends to do so down in the strike zone, which limits home runs and big innings. Great makeup and sound mechanics should aid his development, but Nickerson is a back-of-the-rotation starter at best as he lacks a true plus pitch. He'll move up to high Class A this year.

Year	Club (League)	Class	W	L	ERA	G	GS	CG	SV	IP	H	R	ER	HR	BB	SO	AVG
2006	Oneonta (NYP)	A	0	0	2.77	5	0	0	2	13	8	4	4	1	4	12	.190
2007	West Michigan (MWL)	A	11	7	4.24	25	25	2	0	151	156	74	71	8	38	116	.271
MINOR LEAGUE TOTALS			11	7	4.12	30	25	2	2	164	164	78	75	9	42	128	.266

23 JERAMY LASTER, OF

Born: April 5, 1985. **B-T:** R-R. **Ht.:** 6-1. **Wt.:** 185. **Drafted:** HS—Nashville, 2003 (12th round). **Signed by:** Harold Zonder.

The Tigers wanted Laster to repeat low Class A last year so he could play more often. The plan worked to perfection, as he had by far his most consistent pro season. He has a long uppercut swing that continues to result in high strikeout totals, but last year he produced 16 homers while playing his home games in a pitcher-friendly park. He followed that with an impressive showing in Hawaii Winter Baseball, where he ranked among the league leaders with six homers. He still didn't control the strike zone in Hawaii, with a 36-3 K-BB ratio in 82 at-bats. The ball jumps off Laster's bat, and he has tremendous raw power to all fields. He's adequate in the outfield, with average speed and arm strength. Even after the breakthrough season, Laster has plenty of untapped potential and must continue improving his pitch recognition. The Tigers could have something special with Laster if he continues developing at this rate, and his ceiling and early-career development path resembles that of Marcus Thames. Laster will start the season in high Class A with the chance for a midseason promotion.

Year	Club (League)	Class	AVG	G	AB	R	H	2B	3B	HR	RBI	BB	SO	SB	OBP	SLG
2003	Tigers (GCL)	R	.240	42	121	27	29	4	1	1	17	10	35	9	.295	.314
2004	Tigers (GCL)	R	.242	43	149	23	36	6	4	4	17	17	63	10	.317	.416
2005	Oneonta (NYP)	A	.208	43	120	19	25	3	2	2	14	13	53	6	.287	.317
2006	West Michigan (MWL)	A	.233	75	253	31	59	11	4	9	31	21	107	4	.305	.415
2007	West Michigan (MWL)	A	.276	110	391	68	108	21	3	16	72	37	141	16	.348	.468
MINOR LEAGUE TOTALS			.249	313	1034	168	257	45	14	32	151	98	399	45	.320	.412

24 BRENNAN BOESCH, OF

Born: April 12, 1985. **B-T:** L-L. **Ht.:** 6-6. **Wt.:** 210. **Drafted:** California, 2006 (3rd round). **Signed by:** Scott Cerny.

Boesch wasn't as impressive over his first full season as he had been in his 2006 pro debut, but he showed flashes of his potential as a run-producing outfielder. He has long arms and a tall frame to help leverage a promising-yet-inconsistent line-drive swing. He has shown power to his pull side, thanks to good bat speed, but his swing does get long from time to time. Boesch started taking pitches the other way late in the year and needs to do so more often. He runs into trouble when he extends his arms too much and tries to pull outside pitches. Boesch has average speed and arm strength. He isn't graceful in right field, though he does hustle after balls. Boesch currently projects as a reserve because he lacks the plus power expected from a corner outfielder. He'll play in high Class A this year.

Year	Club (League)	Class	AVG	G	AB	R	H	2B	3B	HR	RBI	BB	SO	SB	OBP	SLG
2006	Oneonta (NYP)	A	.291	70	292	27	85	15	6	5	54	21	42	3	.344	.435
2007	West Michigan (MWL)	A	.267	126	513	52	137	19	4	10	86	23	81	15	.297	.378
MINOR LEAGUE TOTALS			.276	196	805	79	222	34	10	15	140	44	123	18	.314	.399

25 CLAY RAPADA, LHP

Born: March 9, 1981. **B-T:** R-L. **Ht.:** 6-5. **Wt.:** 200. **Signed:** NDFA/Virginia State, 2002. **Signed by:** Billy Swoope (Cubs).

The Tigers dealt struggling outfielder Craig Monroe to the Cubs in August, and received Rapada as the player to be named. The sidearming Rapada profiles as a lefty specialist and struggled to retire righthanders with any regularity during a brief callup to Detroit at the end of the season. He has a quirky, scissors-like delivery, which hinders his ability to hold runners but also adds deception. Keeping hitters off balance is key for Rapada, who sits in the upper 80s with his fastball, which has some cutting action. His fastball command is average at best, but it gets on hitters quickly. He has had some success throwing his heater up in the zone. Rapada throws a sweeping 76-79 mph slider and he's in the early stages of developing a changeup. He'll start the season in Triple-A, but a return to the majors during the year is very possible.

Year	Club (League)	Class	W	L	ERA	G	GS	CG	SV	IP	H	R	ER	HR	BB	SO	AVG
2002	Boise (NWL)	A	0	0	1.50	12	0	0	1	18	18	7	3	0	8	12	.250
2003	Boise (NWL)	A	0	0	0.00	1	0	0	0	3	2	0	0	0	1	3	.200
	Lansing (MWL)	A	1	2	5.31	21	4	0	0	42	46	29	25	3	19	24	.274
2004	Lansing (MWL)	A	6	6	2.33	57	0	0	3	85	65	30	22	2	30	91	.204
2005	Daytona (FSL)	A	1	3	3.83	27	0	0	5	42	40	21	18	2	16	61	.245
2006	West Tenn (SL)	AA	3	2	0.82	33	0	0	21	43	30	7	4	1	10	45	.192
	Iowa (PCL)	AAA	3	2	3.04	28	0	0	0	23	27	8	8	0	15	21	.310
2007	Iowa (PCL)	AAA	7	2	3.58	55	0	0	17	55	55	24	22	4	25	50	.272
	Chicago (NL)	MLB	0	0	0.00	1	0	0	0	0	0	0	0	0	0	0	.000
	Toledo (IL)	AAA	0	0	11.57	2	0	0	0	2	5	3	3	0	1	3	.417
	Detroit (AL)	MLB	0	0	11.57	4	0	0	0	2	3	3	3	2	2	4	.300
MINOR LEAGUE TOTALS			21	17	2.99	236	4	0	47	315	288	129	105	12	125	310	.242
MAJOR LEAGUE TOTALS			0	0	10.13	5	0	0	0	2	3	3	3	2	2	4	.273

26 DUANE BELOW, LHP

Born: Nov. 15, 1985. **B-T:** L-L. **Ht.:** 6-2. **Wt.:** 205. **Drafted:** Lake Michigan CC, 2006 (19th round). **Signed by:** Tom Osowski.

Much like Jeff Gerbe and since-traded Burke Badenhop—two fellow pitchers from the Midwest—Below has moved quickly to prospect status. The Tigers named him their minor league pitcher of the year in 2007, after he led the Midwest League with 13 wins and 160 strikeouts. Below's fastball averages 89-90 mph and tops out in the low 90s with armside run. It seems to jump on hitters and force late swings. When he's on, righthanders foul high fastballs toward the first-base side. His arching curveball is a swing-and-miss pitch that he throws at two different speeds. His changeup remains a work in progress. A mechanically sound pitcher, Below has shown the durability to take a regular turn in the rotation and last deep into games. He works quickly and controls the running game, thanks to a good pickoff move and athleticism on the mound. Even though he didn't turn 22 until after the season, he seemed comfortable in his role as a staff ace. He showed great makeup, stamina, and work ethic, and the result was a 2.31 ERA in the second half. Below projects as a back-end starter and should begin this season in high Class A.

Year	Club (League)	Class	W	L	ERA	G	GS	CG	SV	IP	H	R	ER	HR	BB	SO	AVG
2006	Tigers (GCL)	R	2	0	1.60	15	4	0	0	33	27	8	6	1	10	30	.216
	Oneonta (NYP)	A	0	0	3.86	2	2	0	0	9	11	6	4	0	5	8	.282
2007	West Michigan (MWL)	A	13	5	2.97	26	26	0	0	145	128	54	48	6	58	160	.236
MINOR LEAGUE TOTALS			15	5	2.77	43	32	0	0	188	166	68	58	7	73	198	.235

27 JAMES SKELTON, C

Born: Oct. 28, 1985. **B-T:** L-R. **Ht.:** 5-11. **Wt.:** 165. **Drafted:** HS—West Covina, Calif., 2004 (14th round). **Signed by:** Rob Wilfong.

For an organization with little catching depth, Skelton has been a revelation—and a lefthanded-hitting one at that. Skelton was rarely mentioned among the Tigers' top prospects during his first three years in the system, but he put together a 2007 season that was too impressive to ignore. With a pure swing, sound approach and good eye, he finished fifth in the Midwest League batting race at .309. He hasn't hit for much power but takes pitches the other way and gets the most out of his below-average speed. The Tigers aren't sure about Skelton's defensive projection, and he did play briefly at first base last year. Given the catching shortage across baseball today, though, Skelton will likely have every chance to continue at the position. He has a slender build, which raises questions about his durability. His arm strength is average at best, but his throws have good backspin and he erased 43 percent of basestealers last year. He needs to improve on blocking balls, though he has soft hands and calls a good game. Skelton is a smart player whose physical tools should improve over time. He'll advance to high Class A in 2008.

Year	Club (League)	Class	AVG	G	AB	R	H	2B	3B	HR	RBI	BB	SO	SB	OBP	SLG
2004	Tigers (GCL)	R	.140	23	43	3	6	1	0	0	2	7	11	0	.260	.163
2005	Lakeland (FSL)	A	.000	1	1	0	0	0	0	0	0	0	1	0	.000	.000
	Tigers (GCL)	R	.182	17	33	6	6	1	0	0	1	13	9	0	.413	.212
2006	Oneonta (NYP)	A	.300	42	130	20	39	8	1	1	22	21	29	1	.403	.400
2007	West Michigan (MWL)	A	.309	101	353	60	109	24	2	7	52	55	53	18	.402	.448
MINOR LEAGUE TOTALS			.286	184	560	89	160	34	3	8	77	96	103	19	.392	.400

28 RYAN STRIEBY, 1B

Born: Aug. 9, 1985. **B-T:** R-R. **Ht.:** 6-5. **Wt.:** 235. **Drafted:** Kentucky, 2006 (4th round). **Signed by:** Harold Zonder.

Strieby didn't sign with the Dodgers when they drafted him in the 29th round out of Edmonds (Wash.) CC in 2004, and a year later he transferred to Kentucky. It turned into a wise move, as he was the Southeastern

Conference player of the year in 2006, leading Kentucky to a surprise regular season title before the Tigers made him a fourth-round pick. He has continued his winning ways as a pro and was one of the most consistent players on a West Michigan team that won the 2007 Midwest League championship. Strieby has a polished, sound approach that enables him to work the count and take walks. He's rarely fooled by breaking pitches, a rare trait among power hitters in the low minors, and his actions are fluid for a player his size. He stays on the ball very well, but at 6-foot-5, his lengthy swing probably will prevent him from hitting for a high average. Strieby has plus raw power and hit 16 home runs last year in a pitcher-friendly park. He grew accustomed to swinging with a wood bat during his junior college career, which seems to have helped his adjustment to pro ball. He has good baseball instincts but is a below-average runner. He'll likely continue moving one level at a time and should begin this season in high Class A Lakeland.

Year	Club (League)	Class	AVG	G	AB	R	H	2B	3B	HR	RBI	BB	SO	SB	OBP	SLG
2006	Oneonta (NYP)	A	.241	61	224	26	54	9	0	4	25	25	58	1	.319	.335
2007	West Michigan (MWL)	A	.253	123	443	65	112	23	2	16	76	63	78	6	.347	.422
MINOR LEAGUE TOTALS			.249	184	667	91	166	32	2	20	101	88	136	7	.338	.393

29 FREDDY DOLSI, RHP

Born: Jan. 9, 1983. **B-T:** R-R. **Ht.:** 6-0. **Wt.:** 160. **Signed:** Dominican Republic, 2003. **Signed by:** Ramon Pena.

He may be short in stature, but Dolsi has a big arm and projects as a late-inning reliever if his command and one of his offspeed pitches can become at least average. He spent almost all of the 2007 season in high Class A, where he was an effective closer for a last-place Lakeland team that didn't give him many save opportunities. Dolsi throws a four-seam fastball from 92-96 mph with late life in the zone, but his secondary pitches are iffy. His 85-87 mph slider lacks depth. He tends to get under it, making the pitch spin more than break. He's still working on his changeup, which he throws around 84 mph with good arm speed. Dolsi has below-average command but comes at hitters with a quick, three-quarters delivery. He may lack size and polish, but his quick arm and plus fastball give the Tigers something to work with. He's headed to Double-A for 2008.

Year	Club (League)	Class	W	L	ERA	G	GS	CG	SV	IP	H	R	ER	HR	BB	SO	AVG
2003	Tigers (GCL)	R	1	1	4.70	8	2	0	0	23	27	20	12	1	12	19	.281
	Tigers (DSL)	R	3	1	1.96	4	4	0	0	23	18	10	5	0	5	21	.202
2004	Tigers (DSL)	R	6	7	2.39	14	14	0	0	83	60	40	22	2	31	97	.199
2005	West Michigan (MWL)	A	1	0	2.43	23	0	0	0	37	36	16	10	5	14	27	.247
2006	Lakeland (FSL)	A	4	4	4.01	30	0	0	1	42	47	25	19	5	17	29	.278
2007	Lakeland (FSL)	A	5	3	3.48	48	0	0	23	51	52	24	20	3	17	44	.267
	Erie (EL)	AA	0	0	0.00	1	0	0	0	1	1	0	0	0	1	0	.250
MINOR LEAGUE TOTALS			20	16	3.03	128	20	0	24	261	241	135	88	16	97	237	.241

30 PRESTON LARRISON, RHP

Born: Nov. 19, 1980. **B-T:** R-R. **Ht.:** 6-4. **Wt.:** 235. **Drafted:** Evansville, 2001 (2nd round). **Signed by:** Harold Zonder.

Once a promising starter, Larrison never reached his middle-of-the-rotation ceiling because of lack of command and Tommy John surgery in 2004. Moved to the bullpen in 2006, he has taken to the role. Larrison became a minor league free agent after the season but elected to re-sign with Detroit. He has very good life on his sinking fastball, which sits in the low 90s and touches 94 mph. He allowed just two home runs last season and had an excellent 3.0 groundout/airout ratio, thanks to the movement of his heater. He relies on the power sinker to the exclusion of his other pitches, but he's effective when he changes speeds. Larrison could re-emerge as a prospect, but only if he improves his command and refines his mechanics. He's still walking and hitting too many batters. He also uncorked a Toledo-high 12 wild pitches last year. His release point is very inconsistent, especially with his slider, which he rarely throws. Larrison ended the year on the disabled list with a sore shoulder but should be ready for spring training.

Year	Club (League)	Class	W	L	ERA	G	GS	CG	SV	IP	H	R	ER	HR	BB	SO	AVG
2001	Oneonta (NYP)	A	1	3	2.47	10	8	0	0	47	37	22	13	1	21	50	.208
2002	Lakeland (FSL)	A	10	5	2.39	21	19	3	0	120	86	39	32	6	45	92	.200
2003	Toledo (IL)	AAA	0	1	3.38	1	1	0	0	5	3	3	2	1	2	3	.158
	Erie (EL)	AA	4	12	5.61	24	24	0	0	126	161	89	79	10	59	53	.322
2004	Erie (EL)	AA	5	4	3.05	20	20	0	0	118	122	54	40	12	36	59	.265
2005	Lakeland (FSL)	A	1	2	4.70	9	9	0	0	38	48	22	20	0	12	25	.318
	Erie (EL)	AA	4	3	5.23	7	7	0	0	32	38	21	19	3	9	11	.290
2006	Erie (EL)	AA	4	10	3.92	26	15	1	1	105	108	48	46	10	40	48	.272
	Toledo (IL)	AAA	1	0	1.74	6	0	0	0	10	12	3	2	1	5	3	.324
2007	Toledo (IL)	AAA	2	2	3.84	45	0	0	1	58	54	28	25	2	29	37	.248
MINOR LEAGUE TOTALS			32	42	3.77	169	103	4	2	663	669	329	278	46	258	381	.265

Florida Marlins

BY MIKE BERARDINO

MORRIS FOSTOFF

Hanley Ramirez has emerged as one of the best offensive shortstops in baseball

Stop us if you've heard this before: The Marlins continue their push for a new baseball-only stadium but haven't let that fruitless pursuit interrupt their quest to stockpile young talent for the future.

While the major league club suffered through an injury-marred season under first-year manager Fredi Gonzalez, dropping to 71-92 and last place in the National League East for the first time in eight years, the top levels of the organization enjoyed rare stability. Owner Jeffrey Loria followed the disappointment of 2007 by locking up four key members of his baseball operations staff through 2015. Loria promoted general manager Larry Beinfest to president of baseball operations, with assistant general manager Michael Hill moving up to the titular role of GM. Beinfest and Hill will retain the same basic duties, with the new titles merely an attempt to head off potential inquiries about future positions elsewhere. Player-personnel guru Dan Jennings and scouting-and-development czar Jim Fleming also received identical extensions.

This was Loria's way of letting his top advisers know he believes they're on the right track, even if the results on the field in 2007 failed to show that. Despite fielding the majors' second-lowest payroll at $32 million, the Marlins again boasted some of the top young talent in the game. Hanley Ramirez, in particular, built on the gains of his rookie-of-the-year season, putting himself in the same sentence as Jose Reyes and Jimmy Rollins for shortstop supremacy in the National League.

Beinfest and Co. pulled off the biggest blockbuster of the Winter Meetings, trading the franchise's two most established stars for two of the most promising young players in baseball. In order to get Miguel Cabrera and Dontrelle Willis, the Tigers gave up outfielder Cameron Maybin and lefthander Andrew Miller in a six-player package that also included catcher Mike Rabelo and righthanders Burke Badenhop, Eulogio de la Cruz and Dallas Trahern. Hard as it may have been to lose Cabrera and Willis, Florida finally filled its center-field hole and got a lefty with more upside than Willis.

On draft day, the Marlins picked 12th and added a player who one day could play alongside Ramirez: California prep third baseman Matt Dominguez. It was the first time since taking Jeremy Hermida with the 11th overall selection in 2002 that Florida had

TOP 30 PROSPECTS

1. Cameron Maybin, of	16. Logan Morrison, 1b
2. Chris Volstad, rhp	17. Henry Owens, rhp
3. Brett Sinkbeil, rhp	18. Eulogio de la Cruz, rhp
4. Ryan Tucker, rhp	19. Chris Leroux, rhp
5. Sean West, lhp	20. Brett Hayes, c
6. Gaby Hernandez, rhp	21. Kyle Winters, rhp
7. Chris Coghlan, 2b	22. Greg Burns, of
8. Matt Dominguez, 3b	23. Brett Carroll, of
9. Aaron Thompson, lhp	24. Harvey Garcia, rhp
10. Dallas Trahern, rhp	25. Scott Nestor, rhp
11. Mike Stanton, of	26. Jacob Marceaux, rhp
12. Gaby Sanchez, 1b	27. Jesus Delgado, rhp
13. Hector Correa, rhp	28. Tom Hickman, of
14. John Raynor, of	29. Graham Taylor, lhp
15. Scott Cousins, of	30. Jai Miller, of

gone away from its pitching-first approach to the draft. Scouting director Stan Meek called out names of position players with his first four selections.

The attempt to restock the organization with position talent seemed wise, especially considering the mound-heavy flavor of the Marlins' prospects list. Florida again struggled to produce victories as many of its top prospects were pushed along or even promoted to the majors. The farm system produced a cumulative mark of .468, with no affiliate reaching the playoffs and only three managing winning records.

General Manager: Larry Beinfest. **Farm Director:** Brian Chattin. **Scouting Director:** Stan Meek.

Class	Team	League	W	L	PCT	Finish*	Manager	Affiliated
Majors	Florida	National	71	91	.438	14th (16)	Fredi Gonzalez	—
Triple-A	Albuquerque Isotopes	Pacific Coast	72	70	.507	8th (16)	Dean Treanor	2003
Double-A	Carolina Mudcats	Southern	60	80	.429	10th (10)	Brandon Hyde	2003
High A	Jupiter Hammerheads	Florida State	63	76	.453	9th (12)	Luis Dorante	2002
Low A	Greensboro Grasshoppers	South Atlantic	71	69	.507	8th (16)	Edwin Rodriguez	2003
Short-season	Jamestown Jammers	New York-Penn	28	47	.373	13th (14)	Daren Everson	2002
Rookie	GCL Marlins	Gulf Coast	29	25	.537	7th (16)	Tim Cossins	1992
Overall 2007 Minor League Record			323	367	.468	25th		

*Finish in overall standings (No. of teams in league) ^League champion

LAST YEAR'S TOP 30

Player, Pos.		Status
1.	Chris Volstad, rhp	No. 2
2.	Brett Sinkbeil, rhp	No. 3
3.	Gaby Hernandez, rhp	No. 6
4.	Sean West, lhp	No. 5
5.	Gaby Sanchez, 1b/c	No. 12
6.	Taylor Tankersley, lhp	Majors
7.	Aaron Thompson, lhp	No. 9
8.	Ryan Tucker, rhp	No. 4
9.	Chris Coghlan, 3b/2b	No. 7
10.	Kris Harvey, of	Dropped out
11.	Renyel Pinto, lhp	Majors
12.	Jose Garcia, rhp	Dropped out
13.	Rick Vanden Hurk, rhp	Majors
14.	Henry Owens, rhp	No. 17
15.	Yusmeiro Petit, rhp	(Diamondbacks)
16.	Jesus Delgado, rhp	No. 27
17.	Harvey Garcia, rhp	No. 24
18.	Matt Lindstrom, rhp	Majors
19.	Tom Hickman, of	No. 28
20.	Robert Andino, ss	Dropped out
21.	Brett Carroll, of	No. 23
22.	Kyle Winters, rhp	No. 21
23.	John Raynor, of	No. 14
24.	Brett Hayes, c	No. 20
25.	Jacob Marceaux, rhp	No. 26
26.	Jose Campusano, of	Dropped out
27.	Greg Burns, of	No. 22
28.	Jason Stokes, 1b	(Athletics)
29.	Brad McCann, 1b	(Royals)
30.	Todd Doolittle, rhp	Dropped out

BEST TOOLS

Best Hitter for Average	Chris Coghlan
Best Power Hitter	Cameron Maybin
Best Strike-Zone Discipline	Chris Coghlan
Fastest Baserunner	Cameron Maybin
Best Athlete	Cameron Maybin
Best Fastball	Ryan Tucker
Best Curveball	Gaby Hernandez
Best Slider	Brett Sinkbeil
Best Changeup	Aaron Thompson
Best Control	Graham Taylor
Best Defensive Catcher	Brett Hayes
Best Defensive Infielder	Matt Dominguez
Best Infield Arm	Robert Andino
Best Defensive Outfielder	Cameron Maybin
Best Outfield Arm	Brett Carroll

PROJECTED 2011 LINEUP

Catcher	Brett Hayes
First Base	Logan Morrison
Second Base	Chris Coghlan
Third Base	Dan Uggla
Shortstop	Hanley Ramirez
Left Field	Josh Willingham
Center Field	Cameron Maybin
Right Field	Jeremy Hermida
No. 1 Starter	Andrew Miller
No. 2 Starter	Anibal Sanchez
No. 3 Starter	Chris Volstad
No. 4 Starter	Brett Sinkbeil
No. 5 Starter	Josh Johnson
Closer	Ryan Tucker

TOP PROSPECTS OF THE DECADE

Year	Player, Pos.	2007 Org.
1998	Mark Kotsay, of	Athletics
1999	A.J. Burnett, rhp	Blue Jays
2000	A.J. Burnett, rhp	Blue Jays
2001	Josh Beckett, rhp	Red Sox
2002	Josh Beckett, rhp	Red Sox
2003	Miguel Cabrera, 3b	Marlins
2004	Jeremy Hermida, of	Marlins
2005	Jeremy Hermida, of	Marlins
2006	Jeremy Hermida, of	Marlins
2007	Chris Volstad, rhp	Marlins

TOP DRAFT PICKS OF THE DECADE

Year	Player, Pos.	2007 Org.
1998	Chip Ambres, of	Mets
1999	Josh Beckett, rhp	Red Sox
2000	Adrian Gonzalez, 1b	Padres
2001	Garrett Berger, rhp (2nd)	Atlantic Lg.
2002	Jeremy Hermida, of	Marlins
2003	Jeff Allison, rhp	Marlins
2004	Taylor Tankersley, lhp	Marlins
2005	Chris Volstad, rhp	Marlins
2006	Brett Sinkbeil, rhp	Marlins
2007	Matt Dominguez, 3b	Marlins

LARGEST BONUSES IN CLUB HISTORY

Josh Beckett, 1999	$3,625,000
Adrian Gonzalez, 2000	$3,000,000
Livan Hernandez, 1996	$2,500,000
Jason Stokes, 2000	$2,027,000
Jeremy Hermida, 2002	$2,012,500

MINOR LEAGUE DEPTH CHART

FLORIDA MARLINS

Top 2008 Rookie: Gaby Hernandez, rhp. There's more opportunity in the young Marlins rotation than you might think, and this durable workhorse is poised to take full advantage.

Breakout Prospect: Logan Morrison, 1b. The former draft-and-follow from Albert Pujols' alma mater shows the potential to hit for power and be a plus defender.

Sleeper: Kyle Kaminska, rhp. The Marlins believe they got a 25th-round steal last June in Kaminska, who has a low-90s fastball and the makings of a solid three-pitch repertoire.

SOURCE OF TOP 30 TALENT

Homegrown	23	Acquired	7
College	10	Trades	7
Junior college	1	Rule 5 draft	0
High school	11	Independent leagues	0
Draft-and-follow	1	Free agents/waivers	0
Nondrafted free agents	0		
International	0		

Numbers in parentheses indicate prospect rankings.

LF
John Raynor (14)
Tom Hickman (28)

CF
Cameron Maybin (1)
Greg Burns (22)
Jai Miller (30)
Eric Reed
Dante Brinkley

RF
Mike Stanton (11)
Scott Cousins (15)
Brett Carroll (23)
Kris Harvey
Bryan Petersen

3B
Matt Dominguez (8)
Jacob Blackwood
Lee Mitchell
Jesus Rojas

SS
Robert Andino
Agustin Septimo
Smelin Perez

2B
Chris Coghlan (7)
Ryan Curry
Carlos Piste

1B
Gaby Sanchez (12)
Logan Morrison (16)
Ernie Banks

C
Brett Hayes (20)
Jose Ceballos
Chris Hatcher
Torre Langley
Jameson Smith
Brad Davis

RHP

Starters	Relievers
Chris Volstad (2)	Henry Owens (17)
Brett Sinkbeil (3)	Eulogio de la Cruz (18)
Ryan Tucker (4)	Chris Leroux (19)
Gaby Hernandez (6)	Harvey Garcia (24)
Dallas Trahern (10)	Scott Nestor (25)
Hector Correa (13)	Jacob Marceaux (26)
Kyle Winters (21)	Jesus Delgado (27)
Kyle Kaminska	Todd Doolittle
Steve Cishek	Alberto Mendez
Garrett Parcell	Ross Wolf
Daniel Barone	Derek Blacksher
Chaz Gilliam	Rodolfo Encarnacion

LHP

Starters	Relievers
Sean West (5)	Jeff Gogal
Aaron Thompson (9)	Matt Yourkin
Graham Taylor (29)	Kristhiam Linares

Best Pro Debut: RHPs Steven Cishek (5), Garrett Parcell (12) and Derek Blacksher (33) all posted sub-2.00 ERAs and 90-plus mph readings on radar guns. Blacksher had 11 saves and the best K-BB ratio (33-9 in 26 innings) of the trio.

Best Athlete: Southern California's football program recruited OF Mike Stanton (2) as a wide receiver/defensive back, and he was also an all-conference basketball player who averaged double figures in points and rebounds. On the diamond, he has light-tower power and plus arm strength and speed.

Best Pure Hitter: 3B Matt Dominguez (1) has the bat speed to hit for power and average. He hit .158 in his debut but started to make adjustments in a postseason minicamp.

Best Power Hitter: Stanton hit some bombs in the same minicamp, with one approaching an estimated 500 feet.

Fastest Runner: OF Marcus Crockett (9), a product of MLB's Urban Youth Academy, gets down the first-base line in 4.0 seconds from the left side of the plate.

Best Defensive Player: Some veteran scouts said Dominguez was one of the best high school third basemen they'd seen. He has tremendous hands and a strong arm.

Best Fastball: Cishek threw just 82-84 mph as a high school senior, but now he sits at 92-93 mph and tops out at 95 with good life on his fastball. He's still gangly at 6-foot-6 and 200 pounds and could add more velocity.

Best Secondary Pitch: Parcell has a power curveball. He falls in love with it at times, and the Marlins have encouraged him to use his 90-93 mph fastball more often.

Most Intriguing Background: Dominguez and Royals No. 2 overall pick Mike Moustakas were the sixth pair of high school teammates (Chatsworth, Calif., High) to be taken in the first round of the same draft. Dominguez' agent is his uncle Gus, who was convicted in April of smuggling Cuban players into the United States. OF Taiwan Easterling (6) turned down the Marlins to play wide receiver at Florida State.

Closest To The Majors: Florida likes OF Bryan Petersen's (4) feel for hitting and work ethic. Cishek and Parcell probably will be developed as relievers, which could push them past Petersen.

Best Late-Round Pick: RHP Kyle Kaminska (25) has a lot of projection remaining and already

has a lively low-90s fastball, short slider and solid changeup.

The One Who Got Away: The Marlins made a strong push for Easterling, whom they compared to Giants first-rounder Wendell Fairley. Easterling has 6.4-second speed in the 60-yard dash and threw 93 mph off the mound in a Mississippi state playoff game.

Assessment: The Marlins switched gears after loading up on pitchers in recent drafts, going for well-rounded position players with their first four choices this time. Dominguez could become their version of Ryan Zimmerman.

2006   BUDGET: $4.6 MILLION

RHP Brett Sinkbeil (1) was slowed by injuries in his first full pro season but still could move quickly. 2B Chris Coghlan (1s) is the best position prospect in the system, while RHP Hector Correa (4) and OF John Raynor (9) were good mid-round finds.

GRADE: B

2005   BUDGET: $7.7 MILLION

The Marlins' Fab Five of pitchers drafted before the second round took a collective step back in 2007, but they're still optimistic about RHPs Chris Volstad (1) and Ryan Tucker (1s) and LHPs Aaron Thompson (1) and Sean West (1s). RHP Jacob Marceaux (1) continues to scuffle. 1B Gaby Sanchez (4) continues to hit.

GRADE: C+

2004   BUDGET: $3.0 MILLION

Florida already has gotten four draftees to the majors, but only LHP Taylor Tankersley (1) looks like more than a role player. The others are since-traded LHP Jason Vargas (2), OF Brett Carroll (10) and RHP Daniel Barone (11).

GRADE: C

2003   BUDGET: $3.9 MILLION

Repeated drug problems have all but killed the career of RHP Jason Allison (1), who had the best arm in the entire 2003 draft. Unless OF Jai Miller (4) continues to make improvement, RHP Logan Kensing (2) will be the best of this crop.

GRADE: D

Draft analysis by John Manuel (2007) and Jim Callis (2003-06). Numbers in parentheses indicate draft rounds. Budgets are bonuses in first 10 rounds.

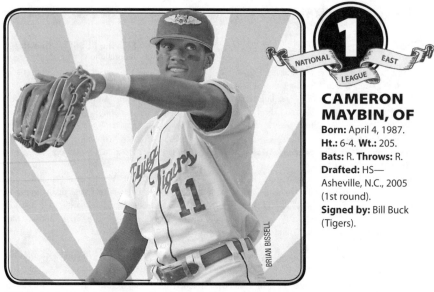

NATIONAL **1** EAST
LEAGUE

CAMERON MAYBIN, OF

Born: April 4, 1987.
Ht.: 6-4. **Wt.:** 205.
Bats: R. **Throws:** R.
Drafted: HS—
Asheville, N.C., 2005
(1st round).
Signed by: Bill Buck
(Tigers).

The Marlins have been looking for a center fielder since jettisoning Juan Pierre in their fire sale following the 2005 season, and they found one who should become the best in the franchise's short history. In an eight-player blockbuster with the Tigers and former Florida general manager Dave Dombrowski, the Marlins got Maybin, Andrew Miller and four lesser prospects for Miguel Cabrera and Dontrelle Willis. The 10th overall pick in the 2005 draft, Maybin signed for $2.65 million. One of the best athletes in that draft, he slid slightly because of a perception that his bat lacked polish and would need time to develop. He put that notion to rest by reaching the majors at age 20 in 2007, just his second pro season. He was in over his head in Detroit, but he did single and homer off Roger Clemens for his first two big league hits. Maybin accelerated his timetable despite losing a month of time with a partial dislocation of his right shoulder. That cost him his second straight Futures Game appearance. The Tigers sent Maybin to the Arizona Fall League, where he was the youngest player on the Peoria Saguaros. His AFL work was curtailed by a slight strain of his left shoulder that wasn't considered serious.

Maybin remained remarkably composed throughout 2007, a tribute to his makeup. Of course, it helps to have five-tool ability. He has a big frame and tremendous overall strength, which is evident in his raw power to all fields. Still, he's not afraid to hit the ball on the ground and use his plus-plus speed to beat out infield singles. He's also comfortable taking pitches up the middle and to the opposite field. Maybin has 30-30 potential, as he has succeeded in 80 percent of his steal attempts in the minors. Defensively, he has plus range in center field and a strong arm that would fit nicely in right. All the tools are there for Maybin to be an all-star.

Maybin's stint in the majors brought out flaws in his game that should be corrected in time. He has trouble recognizing breaking pitches, which partially explains his elevated strikeout totals. He takes bad reads in the outfield, though his straight-ahead speed usually allows him to recover. He has good arm strength, but his throws lacked consistency and accuracy last year, perhaps a result of the shoulder injury.

The comparisons to Torii Hunter seem fair, and scouts highest on Maybin see him as a young Andre Dawson. He handled his struggles in Detroit and earned immediate respect from the team's veterans, which bodes well for his long-term success. There will be pressure on him in Florida to justify the trade, and he should be up to the challenge. The Tigers planned to have him start 2008 in Double-A, but the Marlins likely will make Maybin their starting center fielder. They need to validate the deal as well.

Year	Club (League)	Class	AVG	G	AB	R	H	2B	3B	HR	RBI	BB	SO	SB	OBP	SLG
2006	West Michigan (MWL)	A	.304	101	385	59	117	20	6	9	69	50	116	27	.387	.457
2007	Tigers (GCL)	R	.571	2	7	1	4	0	0	0	1	2	2	0	.667	.571
	Lakeland (FSL)	A	.304	83	296	58	90	14	5	10	44	43	83	25	.393	.486
	Erie (EL)	AA	.400	6	20	9	8	1	0	4	8	6	6	0	.538	1.050
	Detroit (AL)	MLB	.143	24	49	8	7	3	0	1	2	3	21	5	.208	.265
MINOR LEAGUE TOTALS			.309	192	708	127	219	35	11	23	122	101	207	52	.397	.487
MAJOR LEAGUE TOTALS			.143	24	49	8	7	3	0	1	2	3	21	5	.208	.265

2 CHRIS VOLSTAD, RHP

Born: Sept. 23, 1986. **B-T:** R-R. **Ht.:** 6-7. **Wt.:** 190. **Drafted:** HS—Palm Beach Gardens, Fla., 2005 (1st round). **Signed by:** John Martin.

STEVE MOORE

Volstad committed to Miami out of high school. Though education was important to the family, it surprised no one when his stock rose to such an extent that he virtually had to turn pro. The first prep pitcher selected at No. 16 overall, Volstad quickly signed for $1.6 million. He pitched effectively at high Class A Jupiter for the first four months of 2007 and received a late promotion to Double-A Carolina. Volstad keeps his fastball in the zone, typically at 89-92 mph, and hitters routinely drive the pitch into the ground. He will touch 94 mph occasionally with his four-seamer and he could add another tick or two. Pitching coordinator Wayne Rosenthal and Jupiter pitching coach Reid Cornelius changed Volstad's curve to a modified spike grip, and the early results were outstanding. He also has the makings of a plus changeup. Extensive experience as a high school basketball player helped him improve his footwork and agility, and his makeup and intelligence draw rave reviews. Volstad gave up an alarming number of hits in 2007, and you'd expect to see more strikeouts. He needs to do a better job of elevating his fastball to make young hitters chase. Though he shows good coordination, Volstad's big frame makes maintaining his delivery more of a challenge. But he's right on schedule. He'll spend the first half of 2008 in Double-A, with a chance at a second-half callup to the majors. Whenever he arrives, he projects as a solid No. 3 starter for years to come.

Year	Club (League)	Class	W	L	ERA	G	GS	CG	SV	IP	H	R	ER	HR	BB	SO	AVG
2005	Marlins (GCL)	R	1	1	2.33	6	6	0	0	27	25	14	7	1	4	26	.243
	Jamestown (NYP)	A	3	2	2.13	7	7	0	0	38	43	19	9	0	11	29	.279
2006	Greensboro (SAL)	A	11	8	3.08	26	26	0	0	152	161	73	52	12	36	99	.275
2007	Jupiter (FSL)	A	8	9	4.50	21	20	2	0	126	152	76	63	8	37	93	.293
	Carolina (SL)	AA	4	2	3.16	7	7	0	0	42	41	19	15	4	10	25	.252
MINOR LEAGUE TOTALS			27	22	3.41	67	66	2	0	385	422	201	146	25	98	272	.277

3 BRETT SINKBIEL, RHP

Born: Dec. 26, 1984. **B-T:** R-R. **Ht.:** 6-2. **Wt.:** 170. **Drafted:** Missouri State, 2006 (1st round). **Signed by:** Ryan Wardinsky.

MIKE JANES

Because Sinkbeil missed three weeks with a strained oblique, he slipped to the 19th pick in the 2006 draft, where he signed for $1.525 million. He missed time with elbow and lower back concerns in his first full pro season, the latter a herniated disc suffered in weight training that cost him six weeks at the end of the year. It responded well to rest and rehab and he headed to Hawaii Winter Baseball. A hard worker, Sinkbeil has two plus pitches. His fastball sits between 91-94 mph with late life and his slider is the best in the system. He has made significant strides with his changeup, especially after Marlins officials felt his early elbow troubles were the result of leaning too heavily on his slider. Sinkbeil's injuries have led to concerns about his durability, and some see him as a future reliever as a result. Some scouts don't like his pendulum-style arm action and feel that could contribute to his physical problems.He has to be careful to work down in the zone because his stuff tends to straighten out when he elevates his pitches. After missing 10 weeks at Jupiter, Sinkbeil figures to return to high Class A for the start of 2008. His strong showing in Hawaii indicates he should get to Double-A at some point this season.

Year	Club (League)	Class	W	L	ERA	G	GS	CG	SV	IP	H	R	ER	HR	BB	SO	AVG
2006	Jamestown (NYP)	A	2	0	1.23	5	5	0	0	22	14	4	3	1	8	22	.192
	Greensboro (SAL)	A	1	1	4.99	8	8	0	0	39	45	22	22	5	14	32	.290
2007	Jupiter (FSL)	A	6	4	3.42	14	14	1	0	79	82	41	30	8	14	49	.268
MINOR LEAGUE TOTALS			9	5	3.52	27	27	1	0	140	141	67	55	14	36	103	.264

4 RYAN TUCKER, RHP

Born: Dec. 6, 1986. **B-T:** R-R. **Ht.:** 6-2. **Wt.:** 190. **Drafted:** HS—Temple City, Calif., 2005 (1st round supplemental). **Signed by:** John Cole.

MORRIS FOSTOFF

A huge senior season, highlighted by 69 strikeouts in 43 innings, moved Tucker into the sandwich round of the 2005 draft, and he signed for $975,000. He was suspended last season after disputes with Jupiter pitching coach Reid Cornelius, but Marlins officials chalked that up to a natural flareup between two strong personalities. Armed with the biggest fastball in the system, Tucker runs it up there at 93-96 mph and has touched 98. He has gotten better at holding runners, thanks to a slide step he has been able to incorporate. His changeup is solid and he's learned to use it effectively as a second pitch. His mound presence is excellent and he doesn't lack for confidence. Tucker could go straight to the big leagues if he just develops a legitimate slider. His success rate with the pitch remains down in the 20-30 percent range, and that must improve markedly. That's why pitching coordinator Wayne Rosenthal mandated a minimum of 10-15 sliders per game late in 2007. Previous attempts at mastering a curveball or a cutter were scrapped. Tucker should move up the ladder and open the year in Double-A. While some still see him as a future closer, the Marlins plan to keep him in the rotation until he proves otherwise.

Year	Club (League)	Class	W	L	ERA	G	GS	CG	SV	IP	H	R	ER	HR	BB	SO	AVG
2005	Marlins (GCL)	R	3	3	3.69	8	7	0	0	31	35	13	13	0	16	23	.315
	Jamestown (NYP)	A	1	1	8.36	4	4	0	0	14	21	14	13	3	8	18	.323
2006	Greensboro (SAL)	A	7	13	5.00	25	25	2	0	131	123	86	73	14	67	133	.246
2007	Jupiter (FSL)	A	5	8	3.71	24	24	1	0	138	142	64	57	6	46	104	.264
MINOR LEAGUE TOTALS			16	25	4.45	61	60	3	0	315	321	177	156	23	137	278	.264

5 SEAN WEST, LHP

MORRIS FOSTOFF

Born: June 15, 1986. **B-T:** L-L. **Ht.:** 6-8. **Wt.:** 200. **Drafted:** HS—Shreveport, La., 2005 (1st round supplemental). **Signed by:** Ryan Fox.

After signing for $775,000 out of high school, West showed he might have the highest ceiling of any of the five pitchers Florida took in the first 44 picks in June 2005. Signed away from San Jacinto (Texas) JC, he could become the tallest pitcher in Marlins big league history, but his timetable was set back when he had season-ending surgery to repair a torn labrum last March. Aggressive and competitive, West can overwhelm hitters with a 90-93 mph fastball that touched 96 mph and showed good tail before he got hurt. He has a Randy Johnson-type look with his height and three-quarters arm slot. He has two different sliders, one tight and the other with a larger break. His changeup has shown plus potential at times. Considered immature in the past, he worked hard on his conditioning during his rehab, adding additional trunk strength. West's secondary pitches didn't get a chance to improve, because he not only missed a season but was restricted from using them when he was able to return to the mound. Durability will be a concern. He still has a tendency to rush his delivery, letting his arm drag behind that big frame. While the rest of his draft class moves on to Double-A, West will have to head to high Class A and show he can stay healthy.

Year	Club (League)	Class	W	L	ERA	G	GS	CG	SV	IP	H	R	ER	HR	BB	SO	AVG
2005	Marlins (GCL)	R	2	3	2.35	9	8	0	0	38	33	12	10	2	7	40	.229
	Jamestown (NYP)	A	0	2	5.73	3	3	0	0	11	17	7	7	1	5	14	.362
2006	Greensboro (SAL)	A	8	5	3.74	21	21	0	0	120	115	55	50	13	40	102	.255
2007	Did Not Play—Injured																
MINOR LEAGUE TOTALS			10	10	3.55	33	32	0	0	169	165	74	67	16	52	156	.257

6 GABY HERNANDEZ, RHP

STEVE MOORE

Born: May 21, 1986. **B-T:** R-R. **Ht.:** 6-3. **Wt.:** 210. **Drafted:** HS—Miami, 2004 (3rd round). **Signed by:** Joe Salermo (Mets).

Acquired from the Mets in the Paul LoDuca salary dump, the hometown Miami kid keeps impressing as he climbs the ladder. Hernandez annually has been among the youngest players at each level, but that has yet to catch up with him. Hernandez' tight curveball comes and goes but still ranks as the best in the system. His fastball sits at 88-92 mph and touches 94 mph with good deception. His changeup is improving and shows plus life at times. He has proven to be durable, missing time in 2006 with a minor toe injury but having no other physical problems of note. He has a well-developed frame and good athleticism. Hernandez wore down in the final month, when he posted an 8.48 ERA, and may have put too much pressure on himself with a potential big league callup dangling in front of him. He needs to be more consistent and do a better job of resisting the urge to pitch backward. He can overthink at times and be too self-critical. Hernandez will come to spring training with a chance to make the Marlins rotation, but more likely he will go to Triple-A Albuquerque for a few additional months of seasoning. Once he makes it to Florida, he profiles as a back-of-the-rotation piece who can eat up valuable innings.

Year	Club (League)	Class	W	L	ERA	G	GS	CG	SV	IP	H	R	ER	HR	BB	SO	AVG
2004	Mets (GCL)	R	3	3	1.09	10	9	2	0	49	25	10	6	1	12	58	.151
	Brooklyn (NYP)	A	1	0	0.00	1	0	0	0	3	2	0	0	0	0	6	.200
2005	Hagerstown (SAL)	A	6	1	2.43	18	18	1	0	92	59	29	25	4	30	99	.179
	St. Lucie (FSL)	A	2	5	5.74	10	10	0	0	42	48	28	27	1	10	32	.298
2006	Jupiter (FSL)	A	9	7	3.68	21	20	0	0	120	120	60	49	7	35	115	.259
2007	Carolina (SL)	AA	9	11	4.22	28	28	1	0	153	144	87	72	14	56	113	.245
MINOR LEAGUE TOTALS			30	27	3.49	88	85	4	0	461	398	214	179	27	143	423	.232

7 CHRIS COGHLAN, 2B

Born: June 18, 1985. **B-T:** L-R. **Ht.:** 6-1. **Wt.:** 190. **Drafted:** Mississippi, 2006 (1st round supplemental). **Signed by:** Mark Willoughby.

Coghlan hit the radar by winning a Cape Cod League batting title (.346) the summer before he went 36th overall in the 2006 draft and signed for $950,000. While at Mississippi, he drew comparisons to Bill Mueller for his dirtbag playing style and ability to put the barrel on the ball. Coghlan's plate discipline is rated the best in the organization, and Marlins owner Jeffrey Loria considers him one of his favorites. After playing mostly third base in college, Coghlan adapted well to second. He has improved his pivot and footwork around the bag, and his aptitude and work habits are excellent. He has an average arm. Coghlan struggled at the plate after a second-half promotion to high Class A, but he had hernia surgery before reporting to the Arizona Fall League and showed better movement and balance after recovering. He had an extreme inside-out swing, and hitting coordinator John Mallee has taught him to stay behind the ball better and use the whole field, which also improved his gap power. He's an average runner at best, but has good instincts on the bases. Coghlan got his bat going again in the AFL, which should serve as a springboard to Double-A. He's on track to reach the majors by 2009.

Year	Club (League)	Class	AVG	G	AB	R	H	2B	3B	HR	RBI	BB	SO	SB	OBP	SLG
2006	Marlins (GCL)	R	.286	2	7	2	2	0	0	0	3	0	1	0	.286	.286
	Jamestown (NYP)	A	.298	28	94	14	28	5	1	0	12	13	9	5	.373	.372
2007	Greensboro (SAL)	A	.325	81	305	60	99	26	4	10	64	47	43	19	.419	.534
	Jupiter (FSL)	A	.200	34	130	17	26	5	3	2	18	15	19	5	.277	.331
MINOR LEAGUE TOTALS			.289	145	536	93	155	36	8	12	97	75	72	29	.376	.453

8 MATT DOMINGUEZ, 3B

Born: August 28, 1989. **B-T:** R-R. **Ht.:** 6-2. **Wt.:** 180. **Drafted:** HS—Chatsworth, Calif., 2007 (1st round). **Signed by:** Tim McDonnell.

A standout on the same Chatsworth (Calif.) High School team that produced No. 2 overall pick Mike Moustakas, Dominguez played for the U.S. junior national team that played in Cuba the summer before his senior year. Dominguez signed on the Aug. 15 deadline for $1.8 million. Dominguez is a tremendous defender, slick of glove and smooth of hands. He has drawn comparisons to Ryan Zimmerman and Mike Lowell for his work at the hot corner, as well as a bat that should add gap power as he matures and gains strength. He has a strong arm and is judicious about showing it off. He shows loose hands at the plate and good whip in his swing, plus the ability to put the bat on the ball. Dominguez was lunging at the plate upon first signing, but hitting coordinator John Mallee helped him concentrate on staying back to better handle the inside pitch. He tended to tinker too much with his swing in high school, rather than maintaining a consistent stroke. He doesn't run well. Dominguez should head to Greensboro, where the forgiving conditions for hitters should help him gain confidence. His glove is advanced, but his bat will dictate how quickly he moves through the minors.

Year	Club (League)	Class	AVG	G	AB	R	H	2B	3B	HR	RBI	BB	SO	SB	OBP	SLG
2007	Marlins (GCL)	R	.100	5	20	0	2	0	0	0	2	1	2	0	.136	.100
	Jamestown (NYP)	A	.189	10	37	3	7	2	0	1	4	1	12	0	.211	.324
MINOR LEAGUE TOTALS			.158	15	57	3	9	2	0	1	6	2	14	0	.183	.246

9 AARON THOMPSON, LHP

Born: Feb. 7, 1987. **B-T:** L-L. **Ht.:** 6-3. **Wt.:** 195. **Drafted:** HS—Houston, 2005 (1st round). **Signed by:** Dennis Cardoza.

Thompson signed with the Marlins for $1.225 million in 2005 after coaching upheaval at Texas A&M changed his mind about his college commitment. Marlins owner Jeffrey Loria was struck by his rare polish during predraft film sessions, at one point blurting out how much he looked like Whitey Ford. Part of a standout Jupiter rotation in 2007, Thompson more than held his own by comparison. His fastball sat at 88-91 mph and touched 93 mph, showing good run and effectiveness against righties. His changeup is among the best in the system, and both his curveball and slider show plus potential. He keeps the ball down, allowing just two home runs all season. He holds runners well and shows excellent poise. Thompson needs to do a better job of pitch selection, as he too often tries to make a perfect pitch or trick hitters rather than simply working the plate. He still overthrows at times as well, and he must do a better job of maintaining his arm slot on the curve. Thompson is pretty close to his ceiling as a No. 3 or 4 starter now. With a little experience at Double-A in 2008, he could be ready for a shot at the big leagues.

Year	Club (League)	Class	W	L	ERA	G	GS	CG	SV	IP	H	R	ER	HR	BB	SO	AVG
2005	Marlins (GCL)	R	2	4	4.50	8	8	0	0	32	42	20	16	1	10	41	.316
	Jamestown (NYP)	A	1	2	3.10	5	5	0	0	20	25	13	7	1	10	17	.301
2006	Greensboro (SAL)	A	8	8	3.63	24	24	0	0	134	139	68	54	12	35	114	.270
2007	Jupiter (FSL)	A	4	6	3.37	20	19	0	0	115	121	64	43	2	35	84	.266
MINOR LEAGUE TOTALS			15	20	3.58	57	56	0	0	301	327	165	120	16	90	256	.276

10 DALLAS TRAHERN, RHP

STEVE MOORE

Born: Nov. 29, 1985. **B-T:** R-R. **Ht.:** 6-3. **Wt.:** 190. **Drafted:** HS—Owasso, Okla., 2004 (34th round). **Signed by:** Steve Taylor (Tigers).

Trahern's commitment to Oklahoma scared teams off in the 2004 draft, but the Tigers signed him for $160,000 in the 34th round after the Sooners fired pitching coach Ray Hayward. The best of the secondary prospects the Marlins received in the Miguel Cabrera/Dontrelle Willis trade with Detroit, Trahern won 13 games in the high minors last season at age 21. His best asset is a low-90s sinker with great movement. When he's going well, he pitches to early contact and gets a lot of routine grounders. To continue as a starter, Trahern will need to improve his secondary pitches. His changeup has some sink, though lefthanders batted .308 against him in 2007. His slider eventually could become average, but for now it's a short spinner that needs to improve. A better slider would be a great complement to his sinker. For all his talent, Trahern has not missed many bats as a pro, averaging just 4.9 strikeouts per nine innings. Whether he can succeed at the highest levels with that strikeout rate remains to be seen, though he does have strong mound presence and makeup, and he's a good athlete. Trahern will pitch at Triple-A this season and could earn a callup to Florida before the year is through.

Year	Club (League)	Class	W	L	ERA	G	GS	CG	SV	IP	H	R	ER	HR	BB	SO	AVG
2004	Tigers (GCL)	R	1	2	0.59	7	6	0	0	30	22	8	2	1	7	24	.198
2005	West Michigan (MWL)	A	7	11	3.58	26	26	2	0	156	158	78	62	9	50	66	.265
2006	Lakeland (FSL)	A	6	11	3.30	25	25	4	0	144	129	66	53	9	41	86	.238
2007	Toledo (IL)	AAA	1	0	2.84	1	1	0	0	6	5	2	2	0	3	2	.217
	Erie (EL)	AA	12	6	3.87	26	26	3	0	162	177	81	70	12	51	92	.284
MINOR LEAGUE TOTALS			27	30	3.40	85	84	9	0	500	491	235	189	31	152	270	.259

11 MIKE STANTON, OF

Born: Nov. 8, 1989. **B-T:** R-R. **Ht.:** 6-5. **Wt.:** 205. **Drafted:** HS—Sherman Oaks, Calif., 2007 (2nd round). **Signed by:** Tim McDonnell.

A former three-sport star at Notre Dame Academy, Stanton was offered a baseball scholarship by Southern California and a chance to walk on in football as a receiver/defensive back. Nevada-Las Vegas wanted him to play two sports as well, but the Marlins signed him for $475,000 as a second-round pick in 2007. Stanton wasted little time showing his raw power. He hit a couple of homers that traveled close to 500 feet in a post-season minicamp, reminding some of a young Pat Burrell. Others saw Dave Winfield in his setup and loose swing. He shows good intelligence and work ethic. He ran better than the Marlins expected, flashing plus speed and arm strength. Though he shows the ability to put the barrel of the bat on the ball, Stanton is still raw. He struck out 21 times in 56 pro at-bats, though he should be able to make quicker adjustments now that he's focusing on baseball full-time. More repetitions also should help him improve as a right fielder. Despite struggling badly in his debut, Stanton still should begin 2008 at low Class A. He likely will need a year at each level for his first few pro seasons, but his ceiling is as high as any position player in the system.

Year	Club (League)	Class	AVG	G	AB	R	H	2B	3B	HR	RBI	BB	SO	SB	OBP	SLG
2007	Marlins (GCL)	R	.269	8	26	6	7	2	0	0	1	1	6	0	.321	.346
	Jamestown (NYP)	A	.067	9	30	2	2	1	0	1	2	3	15	0	.147	.200
MINOR LEAGUE TOTALS			.161	17	56	8	9	3	0	1	3	4	21	0	.226	.268

12 GABY SANCHEZ, 1B

Born: Sept. 2, 1983. **B-T:** R-R. **Ht.:** 6-2. **Wt.:** 225. **Drafted:** Miami, 2005 (4th round). **Signed by:** John Martin.

Suspended for undisclosed reasons as a junior at Miami, Sanchez signed with the Marlins for $250,000 as a fourth-round pick in 2005. The recommendation of East Coast scouting supervisor Mike Cadahia, who had known Sanchez for years, was a key factor in the decision to draft him. Sanchez has excellent plate discipline and a solid understanding at the plate. He makes adjustments and uses the whole field. Thanks to hard work with infield coordinator Ed Romero, Sanchez has made himself into a solid first baseman. He's getting better jumps and reading contact better, and his hands even look a little softer. He moves laterally much better than he did even a year ago and still shows a strong arm. Sanchez fell into some bad habits, diving for pitches and struggling against top-quality stuff. He uncharacteristically started to chase bad pitches in the first half but got back to his normal approach in the final two months, when he hit .287 with seven of his nine homers. A below-average runner, his body is still a work in progress and could be an issue for him. Sanchez should advance to Double-A in 2008 and with continued improvement, he could push Mike Jacobs for Florida's first-base job in 2009.

Year	Club (League)	Class	AVG	G	AB	R	H	2B	3B	HR	RBI	BB	SO	SB	OBP	SLG
2005	Jamestown (NYP)	A	.355	62	234	34	83	16	0	5	42	16	24	11	.401	.487
2006	Greensboro (SAL)	A	.317	55	189	43	60	12	0	14	40	39	20	6	.447	.603
	Marlins (GCL)	R	.333	3	6	1	2	1	0	0	3	5	0	0	.636	.500
	Jupiter (FSL)	A	.182	16	55	13	10	3	1	1	7	12	12	1	.324	.327
2007	Jupiter (FSL)	A	.279	133	473	89	132	40	3	9	70	64	74	6	.369	.433
MINOR LEAGUE TOTALS			.300	269	957	180	287	72	4	29	162	136	130	24	.393	.474

13 HECTOR CORREA, RHP

Born: March 18, 1988. **B-T:** R-R. **Ht.:** 6-3. **Wt.:** 170. **Drafted:** HS—Hatillo, P.R., 2006 (4th round). **Signed by:** Carlos Berroa.

Fast-tracking a pitcher can work to his advantage or mess him up for years to come. The way Correa handled the beating he took after getting jumped to low Class A to begin his first full pro season says a lot about him and his future. Demoted to short-season Jamestown after eight painful starts for Greensboro, he took off and finished second in the New York-Penn League with 83 strikeouts in just 59 innings. Correa has a clean delivery, a loose arm and a lean, projectable frame. His fastball sits at 91-94 mph and touches 95 mph, though command can be an issue. The Marlins took away his curve and gave him a power slider, one reason he struggled at Greensboro. As he got more comfortable with the slider, he was able to keep it tight in the low 80s and sometimes threw it as hard as 85 mph. At this point, he has more confidence in his changeup, which has excellent action. Pitching coordinator Wayne Rosenthal required him to throw at least 10-15 sliders in every outing at Florida's fall minicamp in an effort to sharpen the pitch even further. Correa needs to hold runners better, but he's a good athlete with outstanding makeup and a pleasant personality. He should get another crack at low Class A to start 2008.

Year	Club (League)	Class	W	L	ERA	G	GS	CG	SV	IP	H	R	ER	HR	BB	SO	AVG
2006	Marlins (GCL)	R	1	2	1.76	10	5	0	0	41	38	13	8	1	15	38	.244
2007	Greensboro (SAL)	A	1	5	9.29	8	8	0	0	31	55	40	32	7	16	20	.401
	Jamestown (NYP)	A	6	2	3.22	11	11	0	0	59	61	25	21	5	13	83	.261
MINOR LEAGUE TOTALS			8	9	4.20	29	24	0	0	130	154	78	61	13	44	141	.292

14 JOHN RAYNOR, OF

Born: Jan. 4, 1984. **B-T:** R-R. **Ht.:** 6-2. **Wt.:** 185. **Drafted:** UNC Wilmington, 2006 (9th round). **Signed by:** Joel Matthews.

The Marlins named Raynor their 2007 minor league player of the year after his boffo season in low Class A. He also earned South Atlantic League MVP honors after topping the circuit in runs (110) and finishing second in batting (.333) and steals (54). Florida signed him in 2006 for the bargain price of $17,500 as a college senior in the ninth round, three rounds earlier than he went to the Orioles the year before. Timed at 6.3 seconds in the 60-yard dash, Raynor is a tremendous weapon on the bases. Going back to college, he has been caught just 14 times in his past 129 steal attempts, an 89 percent success rate. Raynor became much more selective at the plate in his first full pro season, showing true leadoff qualities. He's a good bunter, too. He has some gap power but mostly employs a smooth inside-out swing to rip line drives to right and right-center. His arm is below-average and he moved over to left in Greensboro to make room for fellow speedster Greg Burns, but the Marlins haven't shut the door on Raynor as a potential center fielder. Because he has had so much success and also will be 24 to open the 2008 season, he could skip a level and jump to Double-A.

Year	Club (League)	Class	AVG	G	AB	R	H	2B	3B	HR	RBI	BB	SO	SB	OBP	SLG
2006	Jamestown (NYP)	A	.286	54	199	36	57	8	4	4	21	17	51	21	.356	.427
2007	Greensboro (SAL)	A	.333	116	445	110	148	28	8	13	57	66	98	54	.429	.519
MINOR LEAGUE TOTALS			.318	170	644	146	205	36	12	17	78	83	149	75	.408	.491

15 SCOTT COUSINS, OF

Born: Jan. 22, 1985. **B-T:** L-L. **Ht.:** 6-2. **Wt.:** 190. **Drafted:** San Francisco, 2006 (3rd round). **Signed by:** John Hughes.

One of the best athletes in the system, Cousins took a huge step forward in his first full pro season. Playing mostly right field in an all-prospect Greensboro outfield that boasted Greg Burns in center and John Raynor in left, Cousins finished third on the team with 18 homers, stole 16 bases and made several leaping highlight catches at the wall. Some teams liked Cousins better as a pitcher out of college, but the Marlins never were tempted to bypass his bat. There's a Chipper Jones-style looseness to his lefthanded swing, and he improved his plate discipline as the year developed. Cousins made some mechanical adjustments with hitting coordinator John Mallee to bring his stride under control and keep him from jumping at pitches. A potential five-tool player, he should get more out of his speed once he learns to read pitchers and get better jumps. Defensively, his arm strength and accuracy are both above-average, and he could play center full-time if needed. Cousins shows solid makeup and should open the year in high Class A.

Year	Club (League)	Class	AVG	G	AB	R	H	2B	3B	HR	RBI	BB	SO	SB	OBP	SLG
2006	Jamestown (NYP)	A	.211	21	90	11	19	1	0	1	6	4	17	3	.253	.256
2007	Greensboro (SAL)	A	.292	110	421	69	123	25	0	18	74	38	92	16	.358	.480
MINOR LEAGUE TOTALS			.278	131	511	80	142	26	0	19	80	42	109	19	.340	.440

16 LOGAN MORRISON, 1B

Born: Aug. 25, 1987. **B-T:** L-L. **Ht.:** 6-2. **Wt.:** 215. **Drafted:** Maple Woods (Mo.) CC, D/F 2005 (22nd round). **Signed by:** Mark Willoughby.

In his first full pro season, Morrison opened eyes throughout the organization. A draft-and-follow, he signed out of Maple Woods (Mo.) CC—Albert Pujols' alma mater—just before the 2006 draft. The Marlins were pleasantly surprised by Morrison's tremendous raw power along with his ability to make consistent hard contact. He has a reliable inside-out stroke and the ability to use the whole field, and some believe he could become a .300 hitter with 30-homer power. He did have trouble against lefthanders, hitting .195 (albeit with six homers) in 113 at-bats in 2007, but Florida thinks he'll make adjustments with experience. Defensively, he has made great strides at first base in very little time, though his speed and range are still somewhat limited. He worked with former infield coordinator Ed Romero to improve his positioning, footwork and hands. His throwing arm is a plus weapon and he can nab lead runners with ease. Morrison has a solid frame, a tremendous work ethic and a rapidly earned reputation as a gamer. He figures to open 2008 in high Class A and could put himself on the fast track with another year of improvement like the one he just enjoyed.

Year	Club (League)	Class	AVG	G	AB	R	H	2B	3B	HR	RBI	BB	SO	SB	OBP	SLG
2006	Marlins (GCL)	R	.270	26	89	10	24	4	0	1	7	10	12	1	.343	.348
	Jamestown (NYP)	A	.203	23	74	6	15	3	0	1	11	11	17	0	.295	.284
2007	Greensboro (SAL)	A	.267	128	453	71	121	22	2	24	86	48	96	2	.343	.483
MINOR LEAGUE TOTALS			.260	177	616	87	160	29	2	26	104	69	125	3	.337	.440

17 HENRY OWENS, RHP

Born: April 23, 1979. **B-T:** R-R. **Ht.:** 6-3. **Wt.:** 230. **Signed:** NDFA/Barry (Fla.), 2001. **Signed by:** Delvy Santiago (Pirates).

Owens has come a long way from his days as a backup college catcher at Miami's Barry University. Intelligent and coachable, he still has thoughts of a career in medicine, but baseball should pay the bills for a while longer. After the Pirates originally signed him as a nondrafted free agent, the Mets claimed him in the Triple-A phase of the 2004 Rule 5 draft and gave him a brief taste of the majors in 2006. He got his big break when his hometown Marlins acquired him and Matt Lindstrom last offseason in exchange for Jason Vargas and Adam Bostick—a deal that heavily favors Florida thus far. Owens opened the year on the Marlins' big league roster and worked his way into the closer's role when Jorge Julio flopped, but elbow issues forced him to the disabled list. He made several abortive attempts to return to the mound before finally shutting it down. Before getting hurt, Owens showed a 92-94 mph fastball that touched 96 mph. He creates good deception with an unusual delivery and a short, quick arm action. He also has a sweeping slider and has worked to add a splitter to his arsenal. He also can fine-tune his command and control. Owens should be ready for the start of spring training, where he'll compete with Lindstrom for primary setup chores behind new closer Kevin Gregg.

Year	Club (League)	Class	W	L	ERA	G	GS	CG	SV	IP	H	R	ER	HR	BB	SO	AVG
2001	Pirates (GCL)	R	1	0	1.29	6	0	0	1	7	5	1	1	0	2	8	.192
2002	Williamsport (NYP)	A	0	3	2.62	23	0	0	7	44	26	18	13	4	16	63	.166
2003	Hickory (SAL)	A	2	1	2.91	22	0	0	9	34	21	14	11	1	17	52	.176
	Lynchburg (Car)	A	1	2	2.45	13	0	0	5	14	9	6	4	0	11	21	.176
2004	Lynchburg (Car)	A	3	4	4.28	39	0	0	4	54	46	26	26	4	26	49	.219
2005	St. Lucie (FSL)	A	2	5	3.15	38	1	0	4	54	49	29	19	2	24	74	.233
2006	New York (NL)	MLB	0	0	9.00	3	0	0	0	4	4	4	4	0	4	2	.286
	Binghamton (EL)	AA	2	2	1.58	37	0	0	20	40	19	9	7	1	10	74	.137
2007	Jupiter (FSL)	A	1	0	0.00	3	0	0	0	3	1	0	0	0	0	5	.100
	Florida (NL)	MLB	2	0	1.96	22	0	0	4	23	19	7	5	3	10	16	.216
MINOR LEAGUE TOTALS			12	17	2.89	181	1	0	50	252	176	103	81	12	106	346	.191
MAJOR LEAGUE TOTALS			2	0	3.00	25	0	0	4	27	23	11	9	3	14	18	.225

18 EULOGIO DE LA CRUZ, RHP

Born: March 12, 1984. **B-T:** R-R. **Ht.:** 5-11. **Wt.:** 177. **Signed:** Dominican Republic, 2001. **Signed by:** Ramon Pena (Tigers).

Another piece in the Miguel Cabrera/Dontrelle Willis trade with the Tigers, de la Cruz has spent the last three years shuffling between the rotation and bullpen. He opened 2007 as a starter in Double-A, moved up to Triple-A as a reliever and made six relief appearances for Detroit. Though he's short, de la Cruz has a big-time arm and averages 92-94 mph with his fastball, which peaks at 96. He also has an 82-85 mph changeup with terrific sinking action that takes it out of the strike zone. His third pitch is a hard curveball that is a plus pitch at times and sometimes gets confused with a slider. He also throws a cutter, and his repertoire is deep enough for him to remain a starter. But de la Cruz' command is below-average and his pitch selection can be poor, and he might just be better off working in relief and letting the ball fly. The Marlins will try to determine his best role during big league camp, where he'll get a fair chance to make the club.

Year	Club (League)	Class	W	L	ERA	G	GS	CG	SV	IP	H	R	ER	HR	BB	SO	AVG
2002	Tigers (GCL)	R	1	1	2.63	20	0	0	1	37	40	24	11	0	21	46	.260
	Oneonta (NYP)	A	0	0	23.14	2	0	0	0	2	7	8	6	0	4	4	.500
2003	Tigers (GCL)	R	2	2	2.59	22	0	0	7	24	18	10	7	0	15	30	.205
	Oneonta (NYP)	A	0	0	10.80	2	0	0	0	3	6	4	4	0	1	4	.400
2004	West Michigan (MWL)	A	2	4	3.83	54	0	0	17	54	51	30	23	2	33	44	.239
2005	Erie (EL)	AA	0	1	16.20	1	0	0	0	1	2	3	3	0	4	0	.286
	Lakeland (FSL)	A	4	3	3.39	40	10	0	5	95	66	46	36	5	36	97	.191
2006	Erie (EL)	AA	5	6	3.43	38	12	0	2	105	103	46	40	3	45	87	.258
	Toledo (IL)	AAA	0	0	11.57	1	1	0	0	2	4	3	3	1	2	3	.333
2007	Detroit (AL)	MLB	0	0	6.75	6	0	0	0	6	10	8	5	1	4	5	.357
	Erie (EL)	AA	4	5	3.41	11	11	2	0	66	54	31	25	5	19	57	.224
	Toledo (IL)	AAA	3	0	3.52	22	1	0	0	38	41	17	15	0	18	25	.289
MINOR LEAGUE TOTALS			21	22	3.62	213	35	2	32	430	392	222	173	16	198	397	.240
MAJOR LEAGUE TOTALS			0	0	6.75	6	0	0	0	6	10	8	5	1	4	5	.357

19 CHRIS LEROUX, RHP

Born: April 14, 1984. **B-T:** L-R. **Ht.:** 6-6. **Wt.:** 210. **Drafted:** Winthrop, 2005 (7th round). **Signed by:** Joel Matthews.

You've heard of the Joba Rules, of course, but did you know about the Leroux Doctrine? In 2007, his first full healthy pro season, the Marlins mandated two days of rest for Leroux after each of his two-inning stints. The hulking Canadian never threw back-to-back outings as Florida did all it could to protect his intriguing young arm. A former catcher, he converted to the mound at Winthrop and showed a big-breaking curveball. Unfortunately, he threw it so much some believe that led directly to his Tommy John surgery two months before the 2005 draft. The Marlins weren't deterred, making him their 12th pick (seventh round) in their pitching-heavy harvest. He signed for $152,000, and they let him rehab fully before making his pro debut midway through 2006. The Marlins made sure to take away that overwrought curve and give him a tight slider instead, which he throws at 84-86 mph. Leroux also boasts a 91-94 mph fastball that touches 96. He profiles as a future closer, though the Marlins will be careful to move him along slowly, likely in a setup role this year in high Class A. He joined the Canadian national team for the World Cup in Taiwan, pitching a perfect inning in his lone appearance.

Year	Club (League)	Class	W	L	ERA	G	GS	CG	SV	IP	H	R	ER	HR	BB	SO	AVG
2006	Greensboro (SAL)	A	0	3	6.10	3	3	0	0	10	13	7	7	2	6	9	.325
	Marlins (GCL)	R	0	0	4.09	4	4	0	0	11	10	9	5	0	1	9	.250
	Jamestown (NYP)	A	0	1	7.94	4	4	0	0	11	13	13	10	0	12	4	.283
2007	Greensboro (SAL)	A	2	3	4.14	46	0	0	0	71	72	38	33	6	29	76	.261
MINOR LEAGUE TOTALS			2	7	4.74	57	11	0	0	104	108	67	55	8	48	98	.269

20 BRETT HAYES, C

Born: Feb. 13, 1984. **B-T:** R-R. **Ht.:** 6-1. **Wt.:** 200. **Drafted:** Nevada, 2005 (2nd round supplemental). **Signed by:** John Hughes.

The Marlins haven't drafted and developed an everyday catcher since selecting Charles Johnson with the very first pick in franchise history in 1992. There's hope that Hayes could soon end that drought. He reported to the Arizona Fall League at season's end, which gave him a chance to make up for some of the experience he's missed due to nagging injuries and health setbacks. A broken thumb and broken hamate bone cost him valuable time during his first two full seasons, and an infected tooth slowed him over the final six weeks in 2007. He wound up dropping close to 15 pounds and struggled to maintain his strength and bat speed. Offense is the primary question mark with Hayes, who profiles as a Brad Ausmus type in terms of his glove-first toolset. Hayes never has hit higher than .254 in three pro seasons, though Florida believes he would hit for a higher average with more gap power if he could stay healthy. He's an excellent receiver and has a stronger arm than his success rate catching basestealers (21 percent last year) would indicate. Intelligent and fiery, he isn't afraid to knock a pitcher back into line when necessary. More athletic and a better runner than most catchers, Hayes played seven positions for Team USA's college team in 2004. He'll probably repeat Double-A at the start of 2008, but he might not be much more than a year away from the majors.

Year	Club (League)	Class	AVG	G	AB	R	H	2B	3B	HR	RBI	BB	SO	SB	OBP	SLG
2005	Marlins (GCL)	R	.417	3	12	2	5	1	0	0	2	0	2	0	.417	.500
	Jamestown (NYP)	A	.239	36	117	11	28	6	1	1	12	12	21	3	.313	.333
2006	Greensboro (SAL)	A	.245	82	278	39	68	13	1	9	38	29	61	4	.321	.396
2007	Jupiter (FSL)	A	.338	17	65	10	22	3	1	1	11	9	10	2	.413	.462
	Carolina (SL)	AA	.234	74	273	22	64	16	0	3	31	18	51	2	.280	.326
MINOR LEAGUE TOTALS			.251	212	745	84	187	39	3	14	94	68	145	11	.315	.368

21 KYLE WINTERS, RHP

Born: April 22, 1987. **B-T:** R-R. **Ht.:** 6-4. **Wt.:** 190. **Drafted:** HS—Arvada, Colo., 2005 (5th round). **Signed by:** Scott Stanley.

Easily overlooked because of the starting pitching depth ahead of him in the system, Winters nonetheless has his supporters. Some view him as the sleeper of the mound crop, but he'll have to overcome some minor elbow issues first. Elbow soreness caused him to be shut down for seven weeks in May and June, but he returned and surpassed 100 innings for the first time as a pro. Smart and extremely coachable, Winters has an 88-91 mph fastball that he works down in the zone for strikes. He commands both his slider and curveball, with his slider more of an out pitch and likely the breaking ball that will win out in the future. His changeup could become a plus pitch as well. Due to his Colorado upbringing, he remains relatively raw with a lean, projectable frame that evokes comparisons to a young Roy Halladay or Brandon McCarthy. He should open 2008 in high Class A.

Year	Club (League)	Class	W	L	ERA	G	GS	CG	SV	IP	H	R	ER	HR	BB	SO	AVG
2005	Marlins (GCL)	R	0	4	3.64	11	10	0	0	42	37	26	17	4	12	33	.237
2006	Jamestown (NYP)	A	6	6	2.45	15	15	0	0	88	63	31	24	2	15	60	.194
2007	Greensboro (SAL)	A	8	4	3.95	19	19	1	0	111	105	55	49	13	20	68	.245
MINOR LEAGUE TOTALS			14	14	3.35	45	44	1	0	242	205	112	90	19	47	161	.226

22 GREG BURNS, OF

Born: Nov. 7, 1986. **B-T:** R-R. **Ht.:** 6-2. **Wt.:** 185. **Drafted:** HS—West Covina, Calif., 2004 (3rd round). **Signed by:** Robby Corsaro.

Part of an all-prospect outfield at Greensboro last year, Burns may have an even higher ceiling than those who flanked him, John Raynor and Scott Cousins. Burns' bat is still developing, but he did establish career highs for batting average (.280) and slugging percentage (.401) while repeating low Class A. He stayed in much better against lefthanders, actually faring significantly better (.318 average, .892 OPS) against them than against righties (.267, .698 OPS). He's growing into his body, adding muscle through the legs and shoulders, and that should add to his gap power. He has strong hands and a flat swing, and he does a good job of keeping the ball on the ground to take advantage of his speed. He has been clocked at 3.9 seconds to first base. Burns still must improve his bunting, but he has shown a strong work ethic and a willingness to try anything. He's a plus center-field defender with excellent range and closing speed. Once wary of walls, he now crashes into them in pursuit of fly balls. His arm is average despite a funky throwing motion. He managed to stay healthy, avoiding the sort of minor injuries that cost him time in the past. Next up should be a shot at high Class A as he progresses step by step up the organizational ladder.

Year	Club (League)	Class	AVG	G	AB	R	H	2B	3B	HR	RBI	BB	SO	SB	OBP	SLG
2004	Marlins (GCL)	R	.243	42	136	28	33	5	4	0	7	26	48	7	.372	.338
2005	Jamestown (NYP)	A	.257	65	241	43	62	5	2	1	11	39	84	17	.366	.307
2006	Greensboro (SAL)	A	.231	105	342	44	79	13	8	2	23	38	109	20	.307	.333
2007	Greensboro (SAL)	A	.280	120	414	70	116	21	4	7	54	40	122	39	.347	.401
MINOR LEAGUE TOTALS			.256	332	1133	185	290	44	18	10	95	143	363	83	.343	.353

23 BRETT CARROLL, OF

Born: Oct. 3, 1982. **B-T:** R-R. **Ht.:** 6-0. **Wt.:** 190. **Drafted:** Middle Tennessee State, 2004 (10th round). **Signed by:** Brian Bridges.

Few players expend more effort than Carroll, who willed himself to the big leagues for the first time in 2007. He wasn't able to win an everyday job, but he showed enough to put himself in the mix as a versatile fourth outfielder. Teammates call him "The Maniac," and his wall-banging approach to defense is straight out of the Eric Byrnes catalog. Marlins manager Fredi Gonzalez raved about Carroll's energy and looked for ways to get him into the lineup. Barrel-chested and outgoing, he shows well-above-average raw power and has gotten a little more selective at the plate with the help of hitting coordinator John Mallee and Triple-A hitting coach Steve Phillips. Carroll still strikes out too much as he struggles to learn a zone-hitting approach. He's a slightly above-average runner. Mainly a right fielder, he again flashed the strongest outfield arm in the system. He saw some time in center after his June callup, and though he struggled at times with his jumps and reads, he makes up for those deficiencies with hustle. Carroll won't beat out Cameron Maybin or Jeremy Hermida for playing time, so his long-term future in Florida is as a fourth outfielder.

Year	Club (League)	Class	AVG	G	AB	R	H	2B	3B	HR	RBI	BB	SO	SB	OBP	SLG
2004	Jamestown (NYP)	A	.251	60	211	27	53	16	1	6	28	15	57	1	.321	.422
2005	Greensboro (SAL)	A	.243	118	412	57	100	28	1	18	54	17	108	10	.296	.447
2006	Jupiter (FSL)	A	.241	59	216	31	52	12	1	8	30	18	48	9	.324	.417
	Carolina (SL)	AA	.231	74	251	29	58	15	3	9	30	18	62	4	.303	.422
2007	Carolina (SL)	AA	.270	30	100	9	27	13	0	3	12	12	20	0	.359	.490
	Albuquerque (PCL)	AAA	.314	88	318	60	100	21	6	19	70	18	69	0	.361	.597
	Florida (NL)	MLB	.184	23	49	10	9	1	0	0	2	3	15	0	.231	.204
MINOR LEAGUE TOTALS			.259	429	1508	213	390	105	12	63	224	98	364	24	.323	.469
MAJOR LEAGUE TOTALS			.184	23	49	10	9	1	0	0	2	3	15	0	.231	.204

24 HARVEY GARCIA, RHP

Born: March 16, 1984. **B-T:** R-R. **Ht.:** 6-2. **Wt.:** 170. **Signed:** Venezuela, 2000. **Signed by:** Louie Eljaua/ Miguel Garcia.

Dumped by the current Marlins regime after it took over in 2002, Garcia was reacquired from the Red Sox in the Josh Beckett trade in November 2005. He served as Jupiter's primary closer in 2006, but served in a setup role in the upper minors last season. A late-season audition with the Marlins went well enough to give him a decent shot at breaking camp in their bullpen this year. Garcia comes right at hitters with a 93-95 mph fastball he sometimes tries to overthrow, leaving it up in the zone. He has developed two different sliders, one a conventional type he throws for strikes and another he throws with a spike grip that features a bigger break. He has the makings of an excellent changeup but rarely uses it. Garcia can be demonstrative on the mound, sometimes to his own detriment, and struggles to maintain his confidence. He has broad shoulders and a lean, projectable frame but must sharpen his command in order to stick in the majors for good.

Year	Club (League)	Class	W	L	ERA	G	GS	CG	SV	IP	H	R	ER	HR	BB	SO	AVG
2001	Ciudad Alianza (VSL)	R	2	2	3.58	12	4	0	0	32	36	20	13	0	18	23	—
2002	San Joaquin (VSL)	R	0	2	6.08	4	3	0	0	13	16	11	9	3	8	12	.320
	Ciudad Alianza (VSL)	R	2	3	2.68	9	7	0	0	40	32	15	12	0	14	31	.221
2003	Red Sox (GCL)	R	3	0	1.89	9	8	0	0	33	21	11	7	2	12	32	.179
	Red Sox2 (DSL)	R	0	2	1.20	3	3	0	0	15	10	4	2	0	3	10	.172
2004	Lowell (NYP)	A	4	6	5.16	14	14	0	0	61	61	40	35	8	30	54	.268
2005	Greenville (SAL)	A	3	5	2.01	32	0	0	6	44	49	18	10	3	18	54	.275
2006	Jupiter (FSL)	A	0	7	2.92	55	0	0	21	64	54	27	21	5	32	83	.221
2007	Carolina (SL)	AA	2	2	4.07	18	0	0	0	24	21	14	11	3	17	25	.231
	Albuquerque (PCL)	AAA	4	1	6.19	42	0	0	1	48	59	35	33	9	22	45	.303
	Florida (NL)	MLB	0	1	4.38	8	0	0	0	12	14	6	6	3	7	15	.298
MINOR LEAGUE TOTALS			20	30	3.65	198	39	0	28	377	359	195	153	33	174	369	.275
MAJOR LEAGUE TOTALS			0	1	4.38	8	0	0	0	12	14	6	6	3	7	15	.298

25 SCOTT NESTOR, RHP

Born: Aug. 20, 1984. **B-T:** R-R. **Ht.:** 6-4. **Wt.:** 225. **Drafted:** Chaffey (Calif.) JC, 2003 (14th round). **Signed by:** Robby Corsaro.

Nestor may have the best pure arm strength in the system. He's all about power, starting with a fastball that sits at 93-95 mph and has touched 98. He also throws a hard slider at 85-86 mph and a cutter at 88-89. The slider in particular has a chance to be a plus pitch once he learns to throw it for strikes. Big and durable, Nestor has no trouble taking the ball several days in a row, although he did have some minor elbow issues in 2004 and again in 2006. Used primarily as a setup man in Double-A, he struggled with command at times but was lights-out when things were clicking. He goes right after hitters and has averaged better than a strikeout per inning for his career. Nestor has a very intense personality, on and off the mound, and sometimes that affects him adversely when things start to snowball against him. The Marlins added him to their 40-man roster and sent him to the Arizona Fall League to prepare him for challenging for a big league bullpen spot out of spring training.

Year	Club (League)	Class	W	L	ERA	G	GS	CG	SV	IP	H	R	ER	HR	BB	SO	AVG
2003	Marlins (GCL)	R	4	1	2.49	13	0	0	0	25	20	11	7	0	16	27	.211
2004	Greensboro (SAL)	A	2	0	6.35	23	0	0	0	39	46	33	28	3	25	34	.282

2005	Greensboro (SAL)	A	4	6	3.96	58	0	0	2	72	59	40	32	7	46	80	.227
2006	Jupiter (FSL)	A	2	2	2.52	33	0	0	10	39	19	12	11	0	26	48	.142
	Carolina (SL)	AA	2	2	7.43	12	0	0	0	13	18	15	11	1	13	13	.310
2007	Carolina (SL)	AA	2	4	4.44	58	0	0	1	75	65	44	37	5	41	86	.233
MINOR LEAGUE TOTALS			16	15	4.27	197	0	0	13	265	227	155	126	16	167	288	.230

26 JACOB MARCEAUX, RHP

Born: Feb. 14, 1984. **B-T:** R-R. **Ht.:** 6-2. **Wt.:** 195. **Drafted:** McNeese State, 2005 (1st round). **Signed by:** Dennis Cardoza.

Of the five pitchers the Marlins drafted before the second round in the 2005 draft, four landed among the top eight spots on this list while Marceaux remains the enigma. See him one day and he might appear overpowering, with an 89-91 mph fastball that touches 94 and has good movement, a 12-to-6 curveball, a potential plus slider and a changeup. Come back for his next outing, and you can't be sure you're seeing the same guy. His fastball tends to flatten out as Marceaux lifts his arm slot and tries to overthrow it, and the same goes for the secondary stuff. A devout tinkerer, he just needs to trust his stuff and stick with the basics. Toward that end, roving pitching coordinator Wayne Rosenthal worked with Marceaux on a few minor mechanical adjustments during a fall minicamp. Strong enough to start, Marceaux will remain in the bullpen, in large part because of his problems repeating his delivery. He went to Hawaii Winter Baseball in hopes he might emulate the rapid Hawaii-to-bigs rise of Rick Vanden Hurk, but Marceaux continued to battle inconsistency. With a $1 million investment in him, the Marlins will give Marceaux plenty of chances to figure things out. After repeating high Class A in 2007, he'll advance to Double-A this year.

Year	Club (League)	Class	W	L	ERA	G	GS	CG	SV	IP	H	R	ER	HR	BB	SO	AVG
2005	Jamestown (NYP)	A	3	5	5.55	10	10	0	0	47	56	33	29	5	13	32	.287
	Greensboro (SAL)	A	0	3	12.36	5	5	0	0	19	40	32	27	4	9	12	.426
2006	Jupiter (FSL)	A	4	11	3.99	22	22	1	0	117	115	65	52	8	49	80	.254
2007	Jupiter (FSL)	A	3	5	5.22	30	0	0	0	39	35	26	23	0	23	29	.238
MINOR LEAGUE TOTALS			10	24	5.27	67	37	1	0	223	246	156	131	17	94	153	.277

27 JESUS DELGADO, RHP

Born: April 19, 1984. **B-T:** R-R. **Ht.:** 6-1. **Wt.:** 198. **Signed:** Venezuela, 2001. **Signed by:** Ben Cherington (Red Sox).

Durability remains a concern for Delgado, who again landed on the disabled list in 2007. He missed all of 2002 and 2003 following Tommy John surgery while in the Red Sox system, and most of the second half of 2006 with a pulled muscle under his armpit. Last season, a strained shoulder muscle knocked him out for two weeks at the end of June, an injury believed to be related to his return to the rotation. Part of the Josh Beckett trade with Boston, Delgado embraced the idea of starting for the first time in three years but couldn't handle it physically, frequently tiring in the middle innings. He returned to the bullpen, where he will remain for the foreseeable future. Delgado had a 1.59 ERA in relief last year, and a 5.83 mark as a starter. He profiles as a seventh-inning setup arm, thanks to his low-90s fastball that touches 95 mph and his hard curveball. He also owns a potential plus changeup that he must learn to trust. Originally spotted as an outfielder, Delgado made a quick conversion to the mound after the Red Sox signed him. He shows a solid makeup and work ethic, but he can beat himself up on the mound at times. If he can stay healthy and get on a roll, he could push for a spot in the Marlins' bullpen at some point in 2008.

Year	Club (League)	Class	W	L	ERA	G	GS	CG	SV	IP	H	R	ER	HR	BB	SO	AVG
2001	Red Sox (DSL)	R	0	2	5.34	10	8	0	0	32	31	25	19	1	14	19	.240
2003	Did Not Play—Injured																
2004	Red Sox (GCL)	R	0	0	10.80	1	0	0	0	1	4	2	2	0	0	2	.500
	Augusta (SAL)	A	1	5	5.22	21	16	0	0	58	61	40	34	10	26	34	.275
2005	Greenville (SAL)	A	7	3	3.50	33	0	0	2	72	57	30	28	3	39	69	.215
2006	Jupiter (FSL)	A	2	4	2.58	28	0	0	0	38	33	19	11	0	18	40	.231
2007	Carolina (SL)	AA	5	7	4.80	31	16	0	1	93	97	59	50	6	45	75	.266
MINOR LEAGUE TOTALS			15	21	4.37	124	40	0	3	296	283	175	144	20	142	239	.250

28 TOM HICKMAN, OF

Born: April 18, 1988. **B-T:** L-L. **Ht.:** 6-0. **Wt.:** 170. **Drafted:** HS—Lindale, Ga., 2006 (2nd round). **Signed by:** Brian Bridges.

The Jeremy Hermida comparisons seemed a bit farfetched in 2007, as Hickman struggled against more experienced competition in the New York-Penn League. The advanced grasp of the strike zone he showed in his first pro summer wasn't as evident in his followup campaign, when he also battled with a nagging groin injury. His diving into pitches was so pronounced that assistant GM Jim Fleming brought out the 4-by-4 he'd previously used with Greg Burns and had Hickman take batting practice with the board at his feet. A product of the storied East Cobb (Ga.) amateur program that also spawned Hermida, Hickman was a star athlete in high school. He played basketball, which led to a slow start on the diamond in his senior year that helped drop him to the second round, and also pitched, hitting 91 mph with his fastball. With his build and ability to handle the bat, he could develop into a classic No. 2 hitter if he can regain his plate discipline and stay back better on pitches. Despite average speed, Hickman played center field in his pro debut and reminded some club officials of Mark Kotsay with his instinctive jumps and routes. He moved to left field in 2007 in part because of his arm, which now rates as fringe-average. He'll get a chance to get back on track offensively with a move up the ladder to Greensboro, a hitter's paradise.

Year	Club (League)	Class	AVG	G	AB	R	H	2B	3B	HR	RBI	BB	SO	SB	OBP	SLG
2006	Marlins (GCL)	R	.263	50	175	28	46	12	4	2	20	30	43	4	.377	.411
2007	Jamestown (NYP)	A	.183	51	164	15	30	7	1	1	17	19	63	3	.278	.256
MINOR LEAGUE TOTALS			.224	101	339	43	76	19	5	3	37	49	106	7	.330	.336

29 GRAHAM TAYLOR, LHP

Born: May 25, 1984. **B-T:** L-L. **Ht.:** 6-3. **Wt.:** 225. **Drafted:** Miami (Ohio), 2006 (10th round). **Signed by:** Matt Anderson.

If the commissioner's office hadn't blocked the Cubs from including a significant amount of money in a proposed Jacque Jones trade in June, Taylor reportedly would have been the player going from Florida to Chicago. He doesn't have overpowering stuff, which makes him easy to overlook in a pitching-rich system, yet his command is something to behold. Through his first two pro seasons, the underwhelming lefty has posted a 186-27 K-BB ratio in 240 innings. He has done it with a sneaky 85-89 mph fastball that has excellent movement, as well as a much-improved slurve for which he learned a new grip last season. His improving changeup shows good tailing action, and when he gets on a roll he's a groundball machine. There's a little funk to his delivery, as Taylor hides the ball well enough to make his stuff play up. He works fast, follows the gameplan and has strong mound presence. The Marlins were pleased when Taylor followed their suggestion to drop 15 pounds after his first pro season, but he'll always carry the bad-body tag. He shows good intelligence and makeup. As a college senior sign, Taylor has been older than most of the other players at each level he has pitched. That tends to knock him down a peg, especially after he got shelled in a two-start audition at high Class A at the end of 2007. That's where he'll start in 2008.

Year	Club (League)	Class	W	L	ERA	G	GS	CG	SV	IP	H	R	ER	HR	BB	SO	AVG
2006	Jamestown (NYP)	A	3	5	2.47	13	13	0	0	65	59	26	18	2	4	48	.243
2007	Greensboro (SAL)	A	11	3	2.68	25	25	3	0	164	135	59	49	16	18	135	.222
	Jupiter (FSL)	A	1	1	8.10	2	2	0	0	10	16	9	9	0	5	3	.356
MINOR LEAGUE TOTALS			15	9	2.85	40	40	3	0	240	210	94	76	18	27	186	.235

30 JAI MILLER, OF

Born: Jan. 17, 1985. **B-T:** R-R. **Ht.:** 6-4. **Wt.:** 195. **Drafted:** HS—Selma, Ala., 2003 (4th round). **Signed by:** Dave Dangler.

The first three-sport all-state athlete in Alabama high school history, Miller was headed to Stanford as a wide receiver and basketball guard until the Marlins signed him for $250,000 as a fourth-round pick in 2003. He never hit better than .209 in any of his first four pro seasons, but something seemed to finally click for him and he took a huge step forward in 2007. The five-tool threat made strides with his plate discipline, began to drive balls with more authority and appeared more confident in all areas of the game. The owner of as much bat speed as anyone in the organization, Miller learned to stay back on pitches and drive the ball to right-center. Timed at 4.1 seconds to first base from the right side of the plate, he's still learning to use his plus-plus speed on the bases. He has plenty of range and a strong arm in center field, though he must continue to improve his routes and the accuracy of his throws. His doubters still wonder whether Miller isn't merely the next Reggie Abercrombie, a tools-laden player whose skills never fully transferred to the diamond, and he still has work to do with his bat. But the Marlins are more than willing to be patient while they await the answer. After earning a trip to the Arizona Fall League and a spot on the 40-man roster, Miller figures to open the year in Triple-A.

Year	Club (League)	Class	AVG	G	AB	R	H	2B	3B	HR	RBI	BB	SO	SB	OBP	SLG
2003	Marlins (GCL)	R	.199	46	146	17	29	4	1	1	15	15	45	9	.279	.260
	Jamestown (NYP)	A	.233	11	43	5	10	3	0	0	6	3	15	1	.292	.302
2004	Greensboro (SAL)	A	.205	113	390	51	80	15	3	12	49	32	163	11	.273	.351
2005	Greensboro (SAL)	A	.207	115	415	69	86	14	2	13	34	57	139	16	.305	.345
2006	Jupiter (FSL)	A	.209	111	344	40	72	16	2	0	24	45	115	24	.308	.267
2007	Carolina (SL)	AA	.261	129	406	54	106	26	2	14	58	55	127	12	.354	.438
MINOR LEAGUE TOTALS			.220	525	1744	236	383	78	10	40	186	207	604	73	.308	.345

Houston Astros

BY JIM CALLIS

I n two years, the Astros went from World Series participant to a total rebuilding job. Their 73-89 finish marked just their second losing season since 1992, but it wasn't an anomaly. Though owner Drayton McLane expects his team to contend again in 2008, Houston's rise won't be as swift as its fall.

The Astros built a consistent winner through their farm system. Few teams worked the now-defunct draft-and-follow system or the Venezuelan market as well, and they also had a knack for finding quality, low-cost college seniors. But the talent has dried up this decade, and Houston has had to invest heavily in free agents to keep winning. That approach has proved costly, not only in terms of big league salaries but also in its effect on the club's drafts.

By signing Carlos Lee and Woody Williams, the Astros surrendered their first two draft choices in 2007. They couldn't compensate by drafting players with high price tags because McLane refused to exceed MLB's slots. Offering arbitration to their own free agents—Aubrey Huff, Andy Pettitte and Russ Springer—was a low-risk proposition that could have yielded three first-round picks and three supplemental first-rounders, but the Astros balked.

Houston thought it had signing parameters in place with its first two choices, third baseman Derek Dietrich (third round) and righthander Brett Eibner (fourth), as well as righty Chad Bettis (eighth). But they all asked for more than slot money and wound up opting for college over pro ball. The Astros spent just $1.584 million on the draft, $3.6 million below the average of the other 29 teams.

They also haven't been aggressive internationally, especially since former director of Venezuelan scouting and development Andres Reiner left the organization in February 2006. Reiner, a pioneer in establishing a Venezuelan pipeline, helped sign players such as Bobby Abreu, Carlos Guillen and Johan Santana, as well as the club's current top pitching prospect, Felipe Paulino. The Astros haven't brought in any comparable foreign talents in recent years.

Disappointed with his club's performance, McLane has cleaned house. He fired general manager Tim Purpura and manager Phil Garner in August. Former Phillies GM Ed Wade assumed control of the front office in September and appointed interim manager Cecil Cooper on a permanent basis. Wade also

The Astros have stopped developing impact talent from Venezuela such as Carlos Guillen

TOP 30 PROSPECTS

1. J.R. Towles, c	16. Paul Estrada, rhp
2. Felipe Paulino, rhp	17. Max Sapp, c
3. Juan Gutierrez, rhp	18. Jordan Parraz, of
4. Michael Bourn, of	19. Brian Bogusevic, lhp
5. Bud Norris, rhp	20. Yordany Ramirez, of
6. Brad James, rhp	21. Wesley Wright, lhp
7. Chad Reineke, rhp	22. Devon Torrence, of
8. Eli Iorg, of	23. Lou Santangelo, c
9. Josh Flores, of	24. Mark McLemore, lhp
10. Mitch Einertson, of	25. Robert Bono, rhp
11. Collin DeLome, of	26. Koby Clemens, 3b
12. Sergio Perez, rhp	27. Josh Muecke, lhp
13. Chris Johnson, 3b/1b	28. Jonny Ash, 2b
14. Samuel Gervacio, rhp	29. Matt Cusick, 2b
15. Tommy Manzella, ss	30. Jimmy Van Ostrand, of/1b

restructured the scouting department, tabbing former Brewers crosschecker Bobby Heck as scouting director and reassigning senior director of player personnel Paul Ricciarini and coordinator of amateur scouting Tad Slowik.

Wade's early personnel moves were made with the intent of returning to contention, when the club would be better off trying to rebuild for the future. Wade traded Brad Lidge to the Phillies for a substandard return, then jettisoned five young players in deals for a declining Miguel Tejada.

STAN DENNY

General Manager: Ed Wade. **Farm Director:** Ricky Bennett. **Scouting Director:** Bobby Heck.

Class	Team	League	W	L	PCT	Finish*	Manager	Affiliated
Majors	Houston	National	73	89	.451	11th (16)	P. Garner/C. Cooper	—
Triple-A	Round Rock Express	Pacific Coast	61	81	.430	14th (16)	Jackie Moore	2005
Double-A	Corpus Christi Hooks	Texas	67	73	.479	6th (8)	Dave Clark	2005
High A	Salem Avalanche	Carolina	79	60	.568	2nd (8)	Jim Pankovits	2003
Low A	Lexington Legends	South Atlantic	59	81	.421	13th (16)	Gregg Langbehn	2001
Short-season	Tri-City Valley Cats	New York-Penn	27	47	.365	14th (14)	Pete Rancont	2001
Rookie	Greeneville Astros	Appalachian	17	51	.250	9th (9)	Rodney Linares	2004
Overall 2007 Minor League Record			310	393	.441	30th		

* Finish in overall standings (No. of teams in league) ^League champion

LAST YEAR'S TOP 30

Player, Pos.		Status
1.	Hunter Pence, of	Majors
2.	Troy Patton, lhp	(Orioles)
3.	Matt Albers, rhp	(Orioles)
4.	Jimmy Barthmaier, rhp	(Pirates)
5.	Juan Gutierrez, rhp	No. 3
6.	J.R. Towles, c	No. 1
7.	Paul Estrada, rhp	No. 16
8.	Felipe Paulino, rhp	No. 2
9.	Max Sapp, c	No. 17
10.	Chad Reineke, rhp	No. 7
11.	Sergio Perez, rhp	No. 12
12.	Chris Sampson, rhp	Majors
13.	Eli Iorg, of	No. 8
14.	Brian Bogusevic, lhp	No. 19
15.	Brooks Conrad, 2b/3b	(Athletics)
16.	Josh Anderson, of	(Braves)
17.	Chance Douglass, rhp	Dropped out
18.	Lou Santangelo, c	No. 23
19.	Josh Flores, of	No. 9
20.	Jordan Parraz, of	No. 18
21.	Lincoln Holdzkom, rhp	(Phillies)
22.	Bud Norris, rhp	No. 5
23.	Tommy Manzella, ss	No. 15
24.	Chris Johnson, 3b	No. 13
25.	Koby Clemens, 3b	No. 26
26.	Sergio Severino, lhp	Dropped out
27.	Hector Gimenez, c	Dropped out
28.	Ronald Ramirez, ss/2b	Dropped out
29.	Mike Rodriguez, of	(Free agent)
30.	Chris Salamida, lhp	Dropped out

BEST TOOLS

Best Hitter for Average	Jonny Ash
Best Power Hitter	Chris Johnson
Best Strike-Zone Discipline	Jonny Ash
Fastest Baserunner	Michael Bourn
Best Athlete	Devon Torrence
Best Fastball	Felipe Paulino
Best Curveball	Bud Norris
Best Slider	Chad Reineke
Best Changeup	Samuel Gervacio
Best Control	Polin Trinidad
Best Defensive Catcher	J.R. Towles
Best Defensive Infielder	Tommy Manzella
Best Infield Arm	Chris Johnson
Best Defensive Outfielder	Yordany Ramirez
Best Outfield Arm	Jordan Parraz

PROJECTED 2011 LINEUP

Catcher	J.R. Towles
First Base	Lance Berkman
Second Base	Kaz Matsui
Third Base	Chris Johnson
Shortstop	Miguel Tejada
Left Field	Carlos Lee
Center Field	Michael Bourn
Right Field	Hunter Pence
No. 1 Starter	Roy Oswalt
No. 2 Starter	Matt Albers
No. 3 Starter	Felipe Paulino
No. 4 Starter	Juan Gutierrez
No. 5 Starter	Wandy Rodriguez
Closer	Chad Qualls

TOP PROSPECTS OF THE DECADE

Year	Player, Pos.	2007 Org.
1998	Richard Hidalgo, of	Out of baseball
1999	Lance Berkman, of	Astros
2000	Wilfredo Rodriguez, lhp	Out of baseball
2001	Roy Oswalt, rhp	Astros
2002	Carlos Hernandez, lhp	Out of baseball
2003	John Buck, c	Royals
2004	Taylor Buchholz, rhp	Rockies
2005	Chris Burke, 2b	Astros
2006	Jason Hirsh, rhp	Rockies
2007	Hunter Pence, of	Astros

TOP DRAFT PICKS OF THE DECADE

Year	Player, Pos.	2007 Org.
1998	Brad Lidge, rhp	Astros
1999	Mike Rosamond, of	Out of baseball
2000	Robert Stiehl, rhp	Astros
2001	Chris Burke, ss	Astros
2002	Derick Grigsby, rhp	Out of baseball
2003	Jason Hirsh, rhp (2nd)	Rockies
2004	Hunter Pence, of (2nd)	Astros
2005	Brian Bogusevic, lhp	Astros
2006	Max Sapp, c	Astros
2007	*Derek Dietrich, 3b (3rd)	Georgia Tech

*Did not sign.

LARGEST BONUSES IN CLUB HISTORY

Chris Burke, 2001	$2,125,000
Max Sapp, 2006	$1,400,000
Brian Bogusevic, 2005	$1,375,000
Robert Stiehl, 2000	$1,250,000
Derick Grigsby, 2002	$1,125,000

HOUSTON ASTROS

Top 2008 Rookie: Felipe Paulino, rhp. One of the few young pitchers the Astros haven't traded, he can help them as a starter or reliever.

Breakout Prospect: Chris Johnson, 3b/1b. He provides power and quality defense, and he just needs to be left alone at the hot corner.

Sleeper: Brandon Barnes, of. Despite limited baseball experience, he was short-season Tri-City's MVP after bashing 10 homers in 2007.

SOURCE OF TOP 30 TALENT			
Homegrown	27	Acquired	3
College	14	Trades	1
Junior college	4	Rule 5 draft	1
High school	5	Independent leagues	0
Draft-and-follow	0	Free agents/waivers	1
Nondrafted free agents	0		
International	4		

Numbers in parentheses indicate prospect rankings

LF
Mitch Einertson (10)
Collin DeLome (11)
Jimmy Van Ostrand (30)

CF
Michael Bourn (4)
Josh Flores (9)
Yordany Ramirez (20)
Devon Torrence (22)
Nick Moresi

RF
Eli Iorg (8)
Jordan Parraz (18)
Brandon Barnes
Russell Dixon
Travis Sweet

3B
Chris Johnson (13)
Koby Clemens (26)
Ebert Rosario
Billy Hart

SS
Tommy Manzella (15)
Ronald Rosario
Edwin Maysonet
Wladimir Sutil
Cat Everett

2B
Jonny Ash (28)
Matt Cusick (29)

1B
Mark Saccomano

C
J.R. Towles (1)
Max Sapp (17)
Lou Santangelo (23)
Ernesto Genoves

RHP	
Starters	**Relievers**
Felipe Paulino (2)	Bud Norris (5)
Juan Gutierrez (3)	Chad Reineke (7)
Brad James (6)	Samuel Gervacio (14)
Sergio Perez (12)	Paul Estrada (16)
Robert Bono (25)	David Dinelli
Leandro Cespedes	Raymar Diaz
Chance Douglass	Jason Dominguez
Kyle Greenwalt	

LHP	
Starters	**Relievers**
Brian Bogusevic (19)	Wesley Wright (21)
Polin Trinidad	Mark McLemore (24)
	Josh Muecke (27)
	Sergio Severino

2007 — SIGNING BUDGET: $0.5 MILLION

Best Pro Debut: OF Collin DeLome (5), the highest pick signed by the Astros, hit .300 with six homers in the New York-Penn League. RHP Jason Dominguez (31) saved 10 games and had a 1.35 ERA in the NY-P.

Best Athlete: OF Devon Torrence (16) will juggle pro baseball and college football, playing wide receiver for Ohio State. He's so enthusiastic about the national pastime that he called the Astros in October to discuss a training program for baseball. DeLome was one of the best all-around athletes among college players in the draft.

Best Pure Hitter: DeLome has a solid swing plus a willingness to use the opposite field.

Best Power Hitter: DeLome, OF/2B Russell Dixon (7) and 1B Brian Pellegrini (12) all have the chance to develop average or better power.

Fastest Runner: If there's one thing Houston got out of this draft, it's speed. Torrence, 2B Albert Cartwright (36) and OFs Chris Turner (42) and Marques Williams (43) are all well-above-average runners. Williams ran track at Cal State Fullerton before migrating to MLB's Urban Youth Academy.

Best Defensive Player: SS Cat Everett (44), whom the Astros were surprised was signable with their last pick.

Best Fastball: RHP David Dinelli (6), the highest-drafted pitcher signed by the Astros, pitched at 92-93 mph and topped out at 96 before the draft. RHP Roberto Bono (11) preferred catching but his future is on the mound, where he has hit 94 mph.

Best Secondary Pitch: RHP Kyle Greenwalt (20) has a sharp breaking ball. Bono flashes a nasty curveball but can't match Greenwalt's feel for his breaking ball.

Most Intriguing Background: Unsigned OF/LHP Chad Jones (13) is playing defensive back for Louisiana State. Unsigned 3B Derek Dietrich's (3, now at Georgia Tech) grandfather Steve Demeter and unsigned 3B/OF Brian Fletcher's (39, now at Auburn) father Scott played in the majors.

Closest To The Majors: DeLome, though he'll need a couple of years in the minors.

Best Late-Round Pick: Torrence, provided he sticks with baseball. Torrence's brother Devoe will join him at Ohio State next fall, which could strengthen football's hold on him.

The One Who Got Away: The Astros yielded their picks in the first two rounds as free-agent compensation, which made their failure to sign Dietrich and RHPs Brett Eibner (4, now at Arkansas) and Chad Bettis (8, now at Texas Tech) all the more glaring.

Assessment: Houston became the first team since the 1980 Yankees to fail to sign a player before the fifth round, an utter disaster for a farm system in need of talent. Owner Drayton McLane wouldn't let his club go over slot for a single player and spent a big league-low $1.584 million on the draft. The Astros got what they paid for and reassigned scouting director Paul Ricciarini after the season.

2006 — BUDGET: $3.1 MILLION

C Max Sapp (1) went backward in his first full pro season. But the Astros are happy with the early returns on RHPs Sergio Perez (2) and Bud Norris (6) and 3B/1B Chris Johnson (4).

GRADE: C

2005 — BUDGET: $4.1 MILLION

OF Eli Iorg (1s) was starting to put things together when he got hurt last summer. LHP Brian Bogusevic (1) has shown little consistency. At least 3B Koby Clemens (8) got his dad to play an extra year in Houston.

GRADE: D

2004 — BUDGET: $2.2 MILLION

The Astros didn't have a first-round pick, but they made an astute choice with OF Hunter Pence (2) and stole since-traded LHP Troy Patton (9). Their deepest recent draft class also includes C J.R. Towles (20), the system's No. 1 prospect, plus OF Mitch Einerston (5) and RHPs Chad Reineke (13) and Brad James (29).

GRADE: A

2003 — BUDGET: $1.5 MILLION

Again without a first-rounder, Houston snagged RHP Jason Hirsh (2) but included him in the foolish Jason Jennings trade. The Astros were set to sign OF Drew Stubbs (3) but MLB talked owner Drayton McLane into toeing the line.

GRADE: C

Draft analysis by Jim Callis. Numbers in parentheses indicate draft rounds. Budgets are bonuses in first 10 rounds.

**J.R.
TOWLES, C**

Born: Feb 11, 1984.
Ht.: 6-2. **Wt.:** 190.
Bats: R. **Throws:** R.
Drafted: North Central Texas JC, 2004 (20th round).
Signed by: Pat Murphy.

The Athletics were the first team on Towles, drafting him in the 32nd round out of Crosby (Texas) High in 2002 and in the 23rd round out of Collin County (Texas) Community College a year later. Towles ranked fourth among national juco hitters with a .484 batting average as a freshman, then transferred to North Central Texas Junior College after Collin County disbanded its program. Towles turned down an Oklahoma State scholarship to sign for $100,000. In his first three pro seasons, he had problems staying healthy and played just 165 games. He needed surgery after catching a foul tip off his right index finger in instructional league in 2004 and had tendinitis in his right knee in 2006. The Astros hoped he could catch 110-120 games at high Class A Salem in 2007, and he reached that playing-time goal—while unexpectedly climbing to the major leagues. He took off after moving up to Double-A Corpus Christi out of necessity when Lou Santangelo drew a 50-game suspension for performance-enhancing drugs in May. Towles performed well enough to keep the job when Santangelo returned, then moved up to Triple-A Round Rock in August and Houston in September. In his fourth big league start, he set a club record with eight RBIs in an 18-1 rout of the Cardinals.

Towles has a chance to have average or better skills across the board. He has good pitch recognition, handles the bat well and controls the strike zone, so he should hit for average. He's adding strength and starting to pull the ball more often, so he could develop into a 15-20 home run threat. He's more agile and runs better than most catchers, with average speed and double-digit steal totals in each of his three full seasons. Behind the plate, Towles moves and receives well and calls a good game. He has a strong arm and his athleticism gives him a quick release.

Because he has played the equivalent of just two full minor league seasons, Towles still needs polish. His primary goal is to get stronger, so he can tap into more of his power potential and be more durable. He can get pull-happy at times and should drive more balls to the opposite field. Despite his quickness, he must be more judicious about stealing bases after getting caught 14 times in 28 tries in 2007. He can improve the accuracy of his throws after throwing out 28 percent of basestealers last season.

Houston re-signed Brad Ausmus yet again, but only as a mentor and backup to Towles. The Astros have sent only one catcher to the All-Star Game in franchise history (Craig Biggio, 1991) and believe Towles can become their second.

Year	Club (League)	Class	AVG	G	AB	R	H	2B	3B	HR	RBI	BB	SO	SB	OBP	SLG
2004	Greeneville (Appy)	R	.243	39	111	17	27	6	0	0	8	12	23	4	.370	.297
2005	Lexington (SAL)	A	.346	45	162	35	56	14	2	5	23	16	29	11	.436	.549
2006	Lexington (SAL)	A	.317	81	284	39	90	19	2	12	55	21	46	13	.382	.525
2007	Salem (Car)	A	.200	26	90	14	18	3	2	0	11	12	15	3	.339	.278
	Corpus Christi (TL)	AA	.324	61	216	47	70	12	2	11	49	23	35	9	.425	.551
	Round Rock (PCL)	AAA	.279	13	43	5	12	0	0	0	2	4	7	2	.354	.279
	Houston (NL)	MLB	.375	14	40	9	15	5	0	1	12	3	1	0	.432	.575
MINOR LEAGUE TOTALS			.301	265	906	157	273	54	8	28	148	88	155	42	.395	.471
MAJOR LEAGUE TOTALS			.375	14	40	9	15	5	0	1	12	3	1	0	.432	.575

2 FELIPE PAULINO, RHP

Born: Oct. 5, 1983. **B-T:** R-R. **Ht.:** 6-3. **Wt.:** 245. **Signed:** Dominican Republic, 2001. **Signed by:** Andres Reiner/Omar Lopez.

Originally signed as a shortstop, Paulino quickly moved to the mound and could be the next in the Astros' long tradition of flamethrowers. Houston has seen Paulino's fastball hit 100 mph, while other clubs have had him up to 102. Paulino has consistently gotten better in making the transition from thrower to pitcher. He's improved at maintaining his athletic delivery and locating his fastball. He likes to bust hitters inside, then make them look silly with a hammer 80-85 mph curveball. Paulino works up in the strike zone with his four-seam fastball, and major league hitters turned it around for five homers in 19 innings. His improved curveball and changeup are still not consistently reliable. He'll fly open in his delivery at times, costing him command. He's an adventure as a fielder, having led his minor leagues in errors by a pitcher the last two seasons. The Astros still haven't determined Paulino's long-term role. He'll compete for a rotation spot in spring training, but he eventually could emerge as their closer if Chad Qualls doesn't seize the job.

Year	Club (League)	Class	W	L	ERA	G	GS	CG	SV	IP	H	R	ER	HR	BB	SO	AVG
2002	Venoco (VSL)	R	0	0	1.29	4	0	0	0	7	4	1	1	1	6	4	.182
2003	Venoco (VSL)	R	1	0	5.59	5	0	0	0	9	6	6	6	0	12	13	.194
	Martinsville (Appy)	R	2	2	5.61	16	0	0	1	25	23	20	16	0	19	27	.235
2004	Greeneville (Appy)	R	1	3	7.59	10	10	0	0	32	30	30	27	4	22	37	.246
2005	Tri-City (NYP)	A	2	2	3.82	13	2	0	1	30	21	15	13	2	11	34	.189
	Lexington (SAL)	A	1	1	1.85	7	5	0	0	24	21	8	5	2	6	30	.233
2006	Salem (Car)	A	9	7	4.35	27	26	0	0	126	119	67	61	13	59	91	.250
2007	Corpus Christi (TL)	AA	6	9	3.62	22	21	0	0	112	103	55	45	6	49	110	.238
	Houston (NL)	MLB	2	1	7.11	5	3	0	0	19	22	15	15	5	7	11	.289
MINOR LEAGUE TOTALS			22	24	4.26	104	64	0	2	367	327	202	174	28	184	346	.237
MAJOR LEAGUE TOTALS			2	1	7.11	5	3	0	0	19	22	15	15	5	7	11	.289

3 JUAN GUTIERREZ, RHP

Born: July 14, 1983. **B-T:** R-R. **Ht.:** 6-3. **Wt.:** 200. **Signed:** Venezuela, 2000. **Signed by:** Andres Reiner/Pablo Torrealba/Rafael Lara.

Gutierrez spent four years in Rookie ball, which meant that he had to be protected on Houston's 40-man roster before he even reached a full-season league. But the Astros haven't regretted that decision or their patience, and he made his big league debut in August. Gutierrez has one of the better fastballs in the system, both in terms of its low-90s velocity and its sink. He'll flash a plus changeup at times, allowing him to keep hitters off balance. He has a sturdy frame and has missed time just once in seven years as a pro, when he had a tender elbow in 2006. His command regressed last season, as did his secondary pitches. Gutierrez doesn't finish his curveball consistently and it's probably going to be an average pitch at best. He's unflappable on the mound, but he's also too happy-go-lucky at times. Gutierrez could wind up as a reliever. He pitched better in that role during his big league stint, and he may not have enough command or pitches to stick in the rotation. Houston isn't ready to make that move yet, however, and will give him a long look in spring training.

Year	Club (League)	Class	W	L	ERA	G	GS	CG	SV	IP	H	R	ER	HR	BB	SO	AVG
2001	Venoco (VSL)	R	1	0	1.78	10	3	0	4	25	23	8	5	0	8	17	—
2002	Venoco (VSL)	R	3	2	2.13	13	7	0	1	38	35	14	9	0	12	28	.252
2003	Martinsville (Appy)	R	1	2	4.76	16	3	0	2	34	42	22	18	2	13	30	.302
2004	Greeneville (Appy)	R	8	2	3.70	13	13	0	0	65	74	31	27	4	30	59	.294
2005	Lexington (SAL)	A	9	5	3.21	22	21	1	0	120	106	55	43	10	43	100	.239
	Salem (Car)	A	1	1	3.00	3	2	0	0	12	10	4	4	1	8	9	.233
2006	Corpus Christi (TL)	AA	8	4	3.04	20	20	0	0	103	94	39	35	10	34	106	.237
2007	Round Rock (PCL)	AAA	5	10	4.15	26	25	0	0	156	154	84	72	17	63	108	.261
	Houston (NL)	MLB	1	1	5.91	7	3	0	0	21	25	14	14	3	6	16	.298
MINOR LEAGUE TOTALS			36	26	3.45	123	94	1	7	555	538	257	213	44	211	457	.269
MAJOR LEAGUE TOTALS			1	1	5.91	7	3	0	0	21	25	14	14	3	6	16	.298

4 MICHAEL BOURN, OF

Born: Dec. 27, 1982. **B-T:** L-R. **Ht.:** 5-11. **Wt.:** 180. **Drafted:** Houston, 2003 (4th round). **Signed by:** Dave Owen (Phillies).

Houston acquired Bourn and Mike Costanzo along with Geoff Geary in a November trade that sent Brad Lidge to Philadelphia. Bourn spent all of 2007 in the majors but got just 15 starts and 119 at-bats while serving mainly as a pinch-runner and defensive replacement. Upon his arrival, Bourn immediately became the fastest runner and one of the best defensive outfielders among Houston prospects. One club official joked that Bourn's speed rated a 90 on the 20-80 scouting scale, and he was caught just once in 19 steal attempts last season. He knows how to make best use of his quickness, spraying line drives from gap to gap and showing an eye for drawing walks. He has a strong arm for a center fielder. Bourn never will hit for much power and needs to make more consistent contact to be a truly effective leadoff man. He hit just .154 against lefthanders in 2007, though battling southpaws hadn't been a problem in the past. The best-case scenario is Bourn develops into the younger version of Juan Pierre. It will be an upset if he's not batting leadoff and playing center field for Houston in 2008, shifting Hunter Pence to right.

Year	Club (League)	Class	AVG	G	AB	R	H	2B	3B	HR	RBI	BB	SO	SB	OBP	SLG
2003	Batavia (NYP)	A	.280	35	125	12	35	0	1	0	4	23	28	23	.404	.296
2004	Lakewood (SAL)	A	.317	109	413	92	131	20	14	5	53	85	88	57	.433	.470
2005	Reading (EL)	AA	.268	135	544	80	146	18	8	6	44	63	123	38	.348	.364
2006	Reading (EL)	AA	.274	80	318	62	87	5	6	4	26	36	67	30	.350	.365
	Scranton/W-B (IL)	AAA	.283	38	152	34	43	5	7	1	15	20	33	15	.368	.428
	Philadelphia (NL)	MLB	.125	17	8	2	1	0	0	0	0	1	3	1	.222	.125
2007	Philadelphia (NL)	MLB	.277	105	119	29	33	3	3	1	6	13	21	18	.348	.378
MINOR LEAGUE TOTALS			.285	397	1552	280	442	48	36	16	142	227	339	163	.379	.393
MAJOR LEAGUE TOTALS			.268	122	127	31	34	3	3	1	6	14	24	19	.340	.362

5 BUD NORRIS, RHP

Born: March 2, 1985. **B-T:** R-R. **Ht.:** 6-0. **Wt.:** 195. **Drafted:** Cal Poly, 2006 (6th round). **Signed by:** Dennis Twombley.

Thanks in part to a strong performance in Hawaii Winter Baseball, Norris rates as the best prospect from the Astros' 2006 draft despite lasting until the sixth round. He struck out 33 in 25 innings and opponents hit .184 against him in Hawaii. Norris worked in the mid-90s and topped out at 97 mph as a reliever, and he sat in the low 90s as a starter. His fastball also has late life, making it that much more difficult to hit. He has the best curveball in the system, a power downer that he throws in the low 80s. Norris still lacks polish. His control of his curveball comes and goes, while his changeup is still very much a work in progress. He's still honing his feel for pitching, and when he rushes his delivery he loses rhythm and command. He's not very big, so there are questions about his long-term durability as a starter. The Astros will continue to start Norris to give him more innings, but he profiles better as a reliever. He likely will begin 2008 in high Class A Salem, and he could develop into Houston's closer of the future.

Year	Club (League)	Class	W	L	ERA	G	GS	CG	SV	IP	H	R	ER	HR	BB	SO	AVG
2006	Tri-City (NYP)	A	2	0	3.79	15	3	0	2	38	28	20	16	1	13	46	.200
2007	Lexington (SAL)	A	2	8	4.75	22	22	0	0	96	85	58	51	8	41	117	.233
	Salem (Car)	A	1	0	1.50	1	1	0	0	6	4	1	1	0	1	2	.190
MINOR LEAGUE TOTALS			5	8	4.35	38	26	0	2	140	117	79	68	9	55	165	.222

6 BRAD JAMES, RHP

Born: June 19, 1984. **B-T:** R-R. **Ht.:** 6-2. **Wt.:** 200. **Drafted:** North Central Texas JC, 2004 (29th round). **Signed by:** Pat Murphy.

A teammate of J.R. Towles at North Central Texas, James took longer to emerge as a true prospect. Once he found a consistent delivery and release point at low Class A in 2006, his stock surged upward. He tore up high Class A in the first half of 2007, then got hit harder in Double-A and the Arizona Fall League. James relies heavily on a low-90s sinker that generated a 2.1 groundout/flyout ratio last season. His slider serves as a fine complement to his sinker. He has the mental toughness to pitch in any role the Astros throw at him. He depends on his sinker too much at times, which caused trouble against more advanced hitters. He has yet to come up with an effective changeup; he doesn't have enough command or arm speed on his current model. He's starting to realize that he has to have the changeup to remain a starter. After he pitched in the AFL, James was diagnosed with a fracture in his right foot. He had a screw inserted in the foot but still was expected to be ready for spring training. Added to the 40-man roster in November, James will head back to Double-A as a starter to begin 2008. There's a good chance that he'll eventually wind up in the bullpen, and he has enough stuff and the makeup to become a setup man.

Year	Club (League)	Class	W	L	ERA	G	GS	CG	SV	IP	H	R	ER	HR	BB	SO	AVG
2004	Greeneville (Appy)	R	2	6	4.44	13	10	0	0	52	49	36	26	1	26	38	.245
2005	Greeneville (Appy)	R	3	3	4.97	13	13	0	0	63	65	42	35	2	24	48	.265
2006	Lexington (SAL)	A	6	2	1.36	17	14	1	0	92	75	24	14	3	28	51	.220
2007	Salem (Car)	A	9	2	1.98	16	16	0	0	95	72	27	21	5	33	55	.207
	Corpus Christi (TL)	AA	1	5	5.17	9	9	0	0	47	53	27	27	2	20	22	.294
MINOR LEAGUE TOTALS			21	18	3.15	68	62	1	0	351	314	156	123	13	131	214	.239

7 CHAD REINEKE, RHP

Born: April 9, 1982. **B-T:** R-R. **Ht.:** 6-6. **Wt.:** 210. **Drafted:** Miami (Ohio), 2004 (13th round). **Signed by:** Nick Venuto.

ANDREW WOOLLEY

Reineke had the size and stuff to warrant an early-round selection, but a spotty track record in four years at Miami (Ohio) dropped him to the 13th round of the 2004 draft. He has bounced between starting and relieving in each of his three full seasons. He spent April and May in Round Rock's rotation, moved to the bullpen in June and July and started again in August. Reineke's fastball and slider both grade as average to plus pitches, though they both slipped a bit in 2007. His fastball sat closer to 90 mph more often and his slider wasn't as hard or as sweeping as it had been in the past. He delivers both pitches on a steep angle that's tough on hitters. Houston keeps starting Reineke in an attempt to develop his changeup. It will dive at times but still remains inconsistent. So do his mechanics and his command, which is a problem because his fastball is fairly straight. He relies on his slider too heavily. Ticketed for another half-season at Round Rock after being placed on the 40-man roster, Reineke could be another Chad Qualls. Qualls had only intermittent success until the Astros made him a full-time reliever in Triple-A, and they'll probably wind up making the same move with Reineke.

Year	Club (League)	Class	W	L	ERA	G	GS	CG	SV	IP	H	R	ER	HR	BB	SO	AVG
2004	Tri-City (NYP)	A	1	2	2.45	23	0	0	3	36	27	13	10	0	23	52	.197
2005	Lexington (SAL)	A	10	8	3.52	42	11	0	4	102	84	46	40	5	49	108	.230
2006	Salem (Car)	A	6	5	2.98	17	17	1	0	99	82	42	33	5	29	87	.220
	Corpus Christi (TL)	AA	1	3	3.05	15	4	0	0	44	33	17	15	3	26	45	.209
2007	Round Rock (PCL)	AAA	5	5	4.68	32	16	0	0	100	99	61	52	7	52	95	.261
MINOR LEAGUE TOTALS			23	23	3.52	129	48	1	7	383	325	179	150	20	179	387	.230

8 ELI IORG, OF

Born: March 14, 1983 **B-T:** R-R. **Ht:** 6-3. **Wt.:** 200. **Drafted:** Tennessee, 2005 (1st round supplemental). **Signed by:** Mike Rosamond Sr.

STEVE MOORE

Iorg comes from an extended baseball family, as his father Garth and uncle Dane played in the majors, older brother Isaac played in the minors and younger brother Cale signed with the Tigers in August. Eli's 2007 season ended in late May when he tore a ligament in his right elbow diving into first base. Iorg has the tools to be a 20-20 man and play a solid right field. He chased fewer pitches, made more consistent contact and used the opposite field more often in 2007. He has slightly above-average speed and a plus arm. He has good instincts on the bases and in the outfield. He was less stubborn and quicker to make adjustments this season. Because he went on a Mormon mission while in college, Iorg is already 24 and losing three months of at-bats was costly. He still doesn't trust his swing enough and tries to drive balls from a dead start. He's still not very adept at working counts. Iorg hit well enough in two months in high Class A to open 2008 in Double-A. He'll likely play DH to ease his return from Tommy John surgery. The Astros are strong on the outfield corners with Carlos Lee and Hunter Pence, but Iorg has the upside to force his way into the picture.

Year	Club (League)	Class	AVG	G	AB	R	H	2B	3B	HR	RBI	BB	SO	SB	OBP	SLG
2005	Greeneville (Appy)	R	.333	35	138	36	46	7	2	7	34	9	27	12	.391	.565
2006	Lexington (SAL)	A	.256	125	469	68	120	32	4	15	85	33	119	42	.313	.437
2007	Salem (Car)	A	.296	44	162	35	48	12	4	5	24	14	36	14	.350	.512
MINOR LEAGUE TOTALS			.278	204	769	139	214	51	10	27	143	56	182	68	.335	.476

9 JOSH FLORES, OF

BILL MITCHELL

Born: Nov. 18, 1985. **B-T:** R-R. **Ht.:** 6-0. **Wt.:** 195. **Drafted:** Triton (Ill.) JC, 2005 (4th round). **Signed by:** Kevin Stein.

The Braves tried to sign Flores before and after he won the national juco batting title with a .519 average at Triton (Ill.) JC in 2005, but he declined six-figure offers on both occasions. He turned pro for $217,500 after the Astros made him a fourth-round pick that June. Flores has been inconsistent since signing, but he still has the best package of tools among the club's center-field prospects. He's a more well-rounded player than Michael Bourn, acquired from the Phillies in the offseason. Flores' most obvious tool is his speed, which grades as a 65 on the 20-80 scouting scale. Managers rated him the best baserunner in the high Class A Carolina League last year, when he stole 39 bases in 44 tries between two levels. Houston would like to see him get more aggressive and improve his reads of pitchers so he could steal more often. Similarly, he can get more out of his speed in center field once he learns to take better routes on flyballs. He has fringe-average arm strength, but that's fine for center field and he registered 12 assists last year. Flores' offensive performance has been up and down, typified in 2007 when he hit well in high Class A but couldn't solve Double-A pitching. He has a short stroke and good jump for a speedster, but he's vulnerable to being set up by advanced pitchers and slow to adjust when that happens. He has some grasp of the strike zone but needs better discipline, especially if he's to bat at the top of the order. Flores is a gifted athlete but doesn't have the best instincts. He'll give Double-A another try in 2008.

Year	Club (League)	Class	AVG	G	AB	R	H	2B	3B	HR	RBI	BB	SO	SB	OBP	SLG
2005	Greeneville (Appy)	R	.335	59	248	49	83	12	5	8	25	16	57	20	.384	.520
	Lexington (SAL)	A	.278	5	18	1	5	2	0	0	1	1	4	4	.316	.389
2006	Lexington (SAL)	A	.253	125	475	81	120	19	2	11	35	33	107	28	.313	.371
2007	Salem (Car)	A	.325	63	246	49	80	16	6	5	30	23	47	25	.392	.500
	Corpus Christi (TL)	AA	.219	60	192	29	42	8	3	2	12	18	40	14	.284	.323
MINOR LEAGUE TOTALS			.280	312	1179	209	330	57	16	26	103	91	255	91	.340	.422

10 MITCH EINERTSON, OF

STEVE MOORE

Born: April 4, 1986. **B-T:** R-R. **Ht.:** 5-10. **Wt.:** 178. **Drafted:** HS—Oceanside, Calif., 2004 (5th round). **Signed by:** Mark Ross.

Will the real Mitch Einertson please step forward? Is he the guy who has won league MVP awards in the Appalachian (2004) and Carolina leagues (2007), and tied a 44-year-old Appy record with 24 homers in his pro debut? Or is he the guy who batted .222 in two years in low Class A, taking four weeks off in 2005 to deal with off-field issues? The Astros sure hope he's the first one, though there's mixed opinion within the organization. Einertson says his Appy League homer binge was the worst thing that could have happened to him, because it fouled up his approach. Last year, he finally realized that he had to shorten his swing and use the whole field rather than taking a huge hack and trying to pull everything out of the park. He also looked more balanced at the plate and understood that he can just let his power, which is at least average, come naturally. He's making more consistent hard contact now, though he still doesn't walk much. Einertson is a decent runner but not a basestealing threat. He played all three outfield positions in 2007, spending the most time in center field, but scouts who saw him play in the Arizona Fall League didn't like his routes and jumps. He has the arm for right field but may wind up in left, and an experiment at second base in instructional league in 2004 didn't go well. Houston will watch with fingers crossed to see if Einertson can continue to make progress in Double-A this year.

Year	Club (League)	Class	AVG	G	AB	R	H	2B	3B	HR	RBI	BB	SO	SB	OBP	SLG
2004	Greeneville (Appy)	R	.308	63	227	53	70	15	0	24	67	32	70	4	.413	.692
	Tri-City (NYP)	A	.143	2	7	1	1	0	0	1	1	0	2	0	.143	.571
2005	Lexington (SAL)	A	.234	101	355	52	83	19	1	7	45	52	99	5	.353	.352
2006	Lexington (SAL)	A	.211	122	426	51	90	25	1	12	62	31	77	6	.276	.359
2007	Salem (Car)	A	.305	122	446	68	136	40	3	11	87	35	75	5	.365	.482
MINOR LEAGUE TOTALS			.260	410	1461	225	380	99	5	55	262	150	323	20	.344	.448

11 COLLIN DeLOME, OF

Born: Dec. 18, 1985. **B-T:** L-R. **Ht.:** 6-2. **Wt.:** 195. **Drafted:** Lamar, 2007 (5th round). **Signed by:** Rusty Pendergrass.

The Astros' 2007 draft was a debacle, as they forfeited their first two choices as free-agent compensation for Carlos Lee and Woody Williams, then failed to sign the top two picks they held onto, third-rounder Derek Dietrich (now at Georgia Tech) and fourth-rounder Brett Eibner (now at Arkansas). That made fifth-rounder DeLome the highest selection they actually got under contract. Signed for $135,000, he was considered one of the best college athletes in the draft. A former middle infielder at a small-town Texas high school, DeLome was considered more raw than most collegians, but he surprised Houston by showing more polish than expected in his debut. He hit fastballs and lefthanders (.324 versus southpaws) better than the Astros' reports indicated he might. He'll still need time to develop but has the tools to become a well-rounded player. He has a compact swing and good balance, stays back on offspeed pitches and has the bat speed for at least average power. His ability to hit for average will be tied to how much progress he can make with his strike-zone discipline. He has above-average speed but lacks instincts in the outfield and will drop some catchable flyballs. Bothered by shoulder tendinitis in his debut, he played mostly left field and Houston may leave him there even though he has enough arm strength to play anywhere in the outfield. DeLome has the quickness to steal bases, but he's still figuring that part of the game out too. The Astros' conservative approach to promoting college players will be good for him, because he doesn't need to be rushed. He'll move up to high Class A in 2008.

Year	Club (League)	Class	AVG	G	AB	R	H	2B	3B	HR	RBI	BB	SO	SB	OBP	SLG
2007	Tri-City (NYP)	A	.300	65	243	31	73	17	6	6	28	23	65	9	.374	.494
MINOR LEAGUE TOTALS			.300	65	243	31	73	17	6	6	28	23	65	9	.374	.494

12 SERGIO PEREZ, RHP

Born: Dec. 5, 1984. **B-T:** R-R. **Ht.:** 6-3. **Wt.:** 230. **Drafted:** Tampa, 2006 (2nd round). **Signed by:** Jon Bunnell.

Perez was the Astros' backup plan for their first-round choice in the 2006 draft, so they were delighted to get him 44 picks later in the second round. He was a star at NCAA Division II Tampa, throwing the Spartans' first no-hitter in a decade and helping them win the national title in his draft year with a win as a starter in the semifinals and a save in the clincher. Houston eased him into pro ball as a reliever that summer but returned him to the rotation in 2007. There's nothing subtle about Perez. He likes to go after hitters with his 91-93 mph fastball, which tops out at 95 and peaked at 97 in college. His heater has late life, and he backs it up with an 83-85 mph slider. The Astros liked his changeup when he was at Tampa, but he uses his slider too much at the expense of it now. He also tips off the changeup by slowing down his arm action. Perez' arm action isn't pretty, with a wrist wrap in the back, but it gives him some deception and Houston doesn't want to change him too much. He's working on a two-seam fastball to go with his four-seamer, because hitters don't tend to miss his mistakes. Perez has a high-maintenance body and must remain dedicated to his conditioning. He still could wind up a reliever in the long run and has the mentality to work the late innings. The Astros have moved him aggressively and will send him to Double-A this year.

Year	Club (League)	Class	W	L	ERA	G	GS	CG	SV	IP	H	R	ER	HR	BB	SO	AVG
2006	Lexington (SAL)	A	3	0	2.20	11	0	0	0	16	9	6	4	0	8	21	.153
2007	Salem (Car)	A	7	10	4.00	25	25	0	0	128	129	67	57	9	43	84	.265
MINOR LEAGUE TOTALS			10	10	3.79	36	25	0	0	144	138	73	61	9	51	105	.253

13 CHRIS JOHNSON, 3B/1B

Born: Oct. 1, 1984. **B-T:** R-R. **Ht.:** 6-3. **Wt.:** 220. **Drafted:** Stetson, 2006 (4th round). **Signed by:** Jon Bunnell.

With Mike Costanzo included in a trade for Miguel Tejada a month after the Astros acquired him in a deal for Brad Lidge, Johnson is once again the franchise's third baseman of the future. Not all scouts were sold on Costanzo and Johnson may be on the verge of a breakout, so he may have passed him anyway. The son of former big leaguer and current Red Sox Triple-A manager Ron Johnson, Chris holds the Stetson career batting mark with a .379 average. He hit just .261 in his first full pro season, though there were extenuating circumstances. The Astros didn't help him by playing him out of position for 19 games at shortstop in low Class A, and he injured a wrist on a checked swing in high Class A. Houston thinks he'll hit for more power than average anyway, as he shows above-average pop to all fields. He needs to show more patience and make pitchers challenge him to unlock his offensive potential. Despite a thick lower half, Johnson has average speed and can make some spectacular plays at third base. He has quick feet, good actions and range to both sides. He has one of the strongest infield arms in the system, though it sometimes leads to errors when he tries to make throws he shouldn't. Johnson reinjured his wrist during his fourth game in Hawaii Winter Baseball but should be ready for spring training. He'll open 2008 back in Salem with a good chance for a midseason promotion.

Year	Club (League)	Class	AVG	G	AB	R	H	2B	3B	HR	RBI	BB	SO	SB	OBP	SLG
2006	Tri-City (NYP)	A	.212	60	222	18	47	7	1	1	29	11	35	7	.251	.266
2007	Lexington (SAL)	A	.259	64	255	37	66	14	0	8	44	17	38	3	.304	.408
	Salem (Car)	A	.263	60	224	24	59	11	0	6	38	8	41	1	.292	.393
MINOR LEAGUE TOTALS			.245	184	701	79	172	32	1	15	111	36	114	11	.283	.358

14 SAMUEL GERVACIO, RHP

Born: Jan. 10, 1985. **B-T:** R-R. **Ht.:** 6-0. **Wt.:** 170. **Signed:** Dominican Republic, 2002. **Signed by:** Julio Linares.

Gervacio has been consistently successful in his five years as a pro, striking out more than one batter per inning at every stop and limiting opponents to a .190 average overall. He's the rare prospect who has been a full-time reliever since signing, which in some ways is odd because he has three pitches and a resilient arm. He's not physical but he has a quick arm that produces low-90s sinkers that seem to jump out of his hand. He also shows a plus changeup that he'll throw in any count, and a slider that he commands well. There's a lot of deception and guile to Gervacio, who will vary his arm angles from three-quarters all the way down to sidearm. He's impossible to fluster and he'll throw any pitch in any count. On the right day, he'll flash three above-average pitches. His stuff isn't as consistent as his results, but it's not short either. The Astros haven't tried to start him because they don't believe his slight frame would hold up, but his repertoire and durability as a reliever at least make it a possibility worth considering. Houston added him to the 40-man roster this offseason and he could get his first taste of the majors at some point in 2008.

Year	Club (League)	Class	W	L	ERA	G	GS	CG	SV	IP	H	R	ER	HR	BB	SO	AVG
2003	Astros (DSL)	R	4	0	2.01	24	0	0	6	44	34	13	10	3	14	50	.206
2004	Astros (DSL)	R	1	4	1.92	29	0	0	13	51	30	18	11	2	29	81	.160
2005	Greeneville (Appy)	R	3	2	2.67	21	0	0	8	33	24	10	10	1	6	53	.190
	Lexington (SAL)	A	1	0	0.96	5	0	0	0	9	4	1	1	0	1	11	.125
2006	Lexington (SAL)	A	7	5	2.58	47	0	0	10	83	58	28	24	8	28	89	.197
2007	Salem (Car)	A	1	3	2.44	39	0	0	18	55	42	16	15	1	15	80	.204
	Corpus Christi (TL)	AA	3	2	1.99	13	0	0	0	22	15	7	5	1	11	24	.197
MINOR LEAGUE TOTALS			20	16	2.27	178	0	0	55	301	207	93	76	16	104	388	.190

15 TOMMY MANZELLA, SS

Born: April 16, 1983. **B-T:** R-R. **Ht.:** 6-2. **Wt.:** 190. **Drafted:** Tulane, 2005 (3rd round). **Signed by:** Mike Rosamond.

Manzella's future with the Astros took a hit when they traded five players for Miguel Tejada in December. However, he still could surface as a starter if Tejada's declining range leads him to third base in the future. Manzella also could soon become an Eric Bruntlett-style utilityman after Bruntlett was sent to the Phillies in the Brad Lidge deal. Manzella draws comparisons from inside and outside the organization to Adam Everett, Houston's starting shortstop for five years until getting nontendered in December. He's a better hitter than Everett though not as spectacular as a fielder. Nevertheless, defense is Manzella's best tool. He has range to both sides, as well as the arm and body control to make difficult plays. He had a long, metal-bat swing when he signed in 2005 and now has shortened it somewhat. He makes good contact and uses the opposite field, but he has no power and pitchers have no reason to walk him. He has average speed and good baserunning instincts. Last season was his first relatively healthy year as a pro after he battled elbow and ankle problems in his first two years. He's ready to play defensively in the majors right now, but with Tejada on board he'll get a much-needed year in Triple-A to work on his bat.

Year	Club (League)	Class	AVG	G	AB	R	H	2B	3B	HR	RBI	BB	SO	SB	OBP	SLG
2005	Tri-City (NYP)	A	.232	53	220	24	51	6	4	0	18	9	39	5	.260	.295
2006	Lexington (SAL)	A	.275	99	338	50	93	22	1	7	43	33	80	16	.340	.408
2007	Salem (Car)	A	.238	57	223	28	53	13	0	0	24	19	30	5	.305	.296
	Corpus Christi (TL)	AA	.289	64	228	35	66	12	3	1	15	19	40	10	.343	.382
MINOR LEAGUE TOTALS			.261	273	1009	137	263	53	8	8	100	80	189	36	.316	.353

16 PAUL ESTRADA, RHP

Born: Sept. 10, 1982. **B-T:** R-R. **Ht.:** 6-1. **Wt.:** 220. **Signed:** Venezuela, 1999. **Signed by:** Andres Reiner.

In a season of disappointments for the Astros, Estrada was the biggest downer in the farm system. He pitched spectacularly in 2006, nearly leading the Texas League in strikeouts while pitching out of the bullpen. He topped all minor league relievers by averaging 13.6 whiffs per nine innings and looked like he should have been pitching in Houston. Hitters had little clue how they were supposed to handle a downer curveball that looks like a hard knuckler, a sick 83-86 mph splitter or a 92-94 mph fastball with sink and armside run. If there was a knock on Estrada, it was that he could fall deeply in love with his curve and splitter. The Astros forced him to use his fastball more in 2007, and the net effect was disastrous. He maintained his 92-94 mph velocity, but his long arm action creates little deception or movement on his heater. When it got hit, he became more tentative throwing his fastball over the plate, and his control deteriorated. His splitter was still good but his curve was much more hittable. Estrada didn't exhibit much poise while getting pounded, and he let an already less-than-ideal body get softer. Estrada clearly needs to pitch backward to succeed, and he'll try to pick up the pieces in 2008.

Year	Club (League)	Class	W	L	ERA	G	GS	CG	SV	IP	H	R	ER	HR	BB	SO	AVG
2000	Venoco (VSL)	R	1	0	7.14	16	1	0	0	29	38	33	23	1	28	27	.311
2001	Venoco (VSL)	R	2	2	4.20	14	9	0	3	40	35	24	19	0	29	50	—
2002	Martinsville (Appy)	R	2	2	11.65	14	6	0	0	31	45	45	41	2	36	42	.326
2003	Martinsville (Appy)	R	1	0	5.48	12	1	0	1	21	19	17	13	2	22	25	.235
2004	Tri-City (NYP)	A	5	1	2.81	23	0	0	8	41	26	13	13	4	17	56	.172
2005	Lexington (SAL)	A	6	7	2.69	46	3	0	3	90	65	31	27	6	34	94	.202
2006	Corpus Christi (TL)	AA	8	5	3.05	56	0	0	15	88	61	33	30	10	37	134	.191
2007	Round Rock (PCL)	AAA	1	8	5.12	53	0	0	8	70	72	49	40	6	42	69	.264
MINOR LEAGUE TOTALS			26	25	4.48	234	20	0	38	413	361	245	206	31	245	497	.257

17 MAX SAPP, C

Born: Feb. 21, 1988. **B-T:** L-R. **Ht.:** 6-2. **Wt.:** 220. **Drafted:** HS—Windermere, Fla., 2006 (1st round). **Signed by:** Jon Bunnell.

Signed for $1.4 million as the 23rd overall pick in the 2006 draft, Sapp held his own as the youngest regular in the short-season New York-Penn League during his pro debut. Drafted for his exceptional offensive potential for a catcher, he enthused the Astros by hitting .337 with 10 doubles last May. But that was his only good month in 2007, as he battled hip and back injuries and hit .207 with just 15 extra-base hits over the rest of the season. Sapp's thick, barrel-chested frame has a big lower half, and his body was a point of contention. He has lost some weight and committed to conditioning, but while he has a good work ethic, it may take an exceptional effort to keep that body in shape. Houston believes in his bat and his power but acknowledges that his value will be reduced drastically if he has to move to first base. He has reduced a high leg kick that he used as a timing mechanism and is willing to take walks, but he'll need to make more consistent contact. He's obviously a liability on the basepaths. Despite a minor shoulder tear in high school (it didn't require surgery), Sapp has a strong arm. He led NY-P catchers by throwing out 42 percent of basestealers in 2006, though his success rate dipped to 28 percent last year. He's not very agile behind the plate and struggles to block pitches in the dirt. The Astros still think he can make catching work and that he can hit if he can get into the best shape possible. He'll repeat low Class A in 2008.

Year	Club (League)	Class	AVG	G	AB	R	H	2B	3B	HR	RBI	BB	SO	SB	OBP	SLG
2006	Tri-City (NYP)	A	.229	50	166	20	38	9	0	1	20	22	37	0	.317	.301
2007	Lexington (SAL)	A	.241	86	315	25	76	23	0	2	32	38	70	0	.330	.333
MINOR LEAGUE TOTALS			.237	136	481	45	114	32	0	3	52	60	107	0	.325	.322

18 JORDAN PARRAZ, OF

Born: Oct. 8, 1984. **B-T:** R-R. **Ht.:** 6-3. **Wt.:** 212. **Drafted:** CC of Southern Nevada, 2004 (3rd round). **Signed by:** Doug Deutsch.

Parraz creates a lot of debate within the organization. Though he has moved at a snail's pace, he has been one of the system's most productive hitters. He led the New-York Penn League in batting (.336), slugging (.494) and on-base percentage (.421) in 2006, then topped Lexington in most offensive categories and was the team's MVP last year. Those who like him say he's a multitooled athlete similar to Eli Iorg. Those who don't say he has holes in his swing that will be exposed by advanced pitching. No one questions his athletic ability and he works hard, but the game doesn't come easily to Parraz. He does have raw power and slightly above-average speed, but he still hasn't gained control of the strike zone against lower-level pitchers. He plays out of control on the bases and in the outfield. His arm is a cannon, as he was clocked up to 96 mph at the CC of Southern Nevada—where he couldn't demonstrate enough command to stick in the rotation. Managers rated his arm the best among low Class A South Atlantic League outfielders last year, when he recorded 13 assists. High Class A should be a good test in 2008 for Parraz.

Year	Club (League)	Class	AVG	G	AB	R	H	2B	3B	HR	RBI	BB	SO	SB	OBP	SLG
2004	Greeneville (Appy)	R	.244	53	180	35	44	6	5	4	21	24	44	8	.349	.400
2005	Tri-City (NYP)	A	.262	71	282	31	74	11	2	5	35	12	45	17	.310	.369
2006	Tri-City (NYP)	A	.336	70	253	46	85	18	2	6	38	33	44	23	.421	.494
2007	Lexington (SAL)	A	.281	122	462	69	130	28	3	14	76	47	89	33	.364	.446
MINOR LEAGUE TOTALS			.283	316	1177	181	333	63	12	29	170	116	222	82	.360	.431

19 BRIAN BOGUSEVIC, LHP

Born: Feb. 18, 1984. **B-T:** L-L. **Ht.:** 6-3. **Wt.:** 215. **Drafted:** Tulane, 2005 (1st round). **Signed by:** Mike Rosamond.

The Astros hoped to draft Jacoby Ellsbury with the 24th overall pick in the 2005 draft, but the Red Sox grabbed him right ahead of them. Houston's consolation prize was Bogusevic, who figured to improve as a full-time pitcher after starring as a two-way player at Tulane. But he only has flashed the ability that earned him a $1.375 million bonus. He battled some elbow tendinitis in 2006 and has been inconsistent with his stuff, command and ability to repeat his delivery. Bogusevic has solid velocity for a lefthander, but his 88-91 mph fastball lacks life and hitters pick it up easily. He's still working to find a reliable breaking ball, and his slider is currently ahead of his curveball. He did make some progress with his changeup last season. There's some thought within the organization that Bogusevic would have more success as a reliever, but he'll remain a starter in Double-A this year. There's no talk yet of trying him as an outfielder—his bat, power, raw speed and right-field arm were all plus tools at Tulane—though that idea has occurred to some club officials.

Year	Club (League)	Class	W	L	ERA	G	GS	CG	SV	IP	H	R	ER	HR	BB	SO	AVG
2005	Tri-City (NYP)	A	0	2	7.59	13	0	0	3	21	30	20	18	2	9	17	.316
2006	Tri-City (NYP)	A	0	0	4.09	3	3	0	0	11	10	8	5	1	5	6	.233
	Lexington (SAL)	A	2	5	4.73	17	17	0	0	70	76	44	37	6	24	60	.274
2007	Salem (Car)	A	9	7	4.01	21	21	1	0	114	133	57	51	7	39	91	.296
	Corpus Christi (TL)	AA	1	1	7.40	6	6	0	0	24	29	21	20	1	14	17	.296
MINOR LEAGUE TOTALS			12	15	4.89	60	47	1	3	241	278	150	131	17	91	191	.289

20 YORDANY RAMIREZ, OF

Born: July 31, 1984. **B-T:** R-R. **Ht.:** 6-1. **Wt.:** 187. **Signed:** Dominican Republic, 2001. **Signed by:** Felix Francisco (Padres).

When the Astros traded outfield prospect Josh Anderson to the Braves for Oscar Villareal, new Astros GM Ed Wade said he wouldn't have made the deal if he hadn't signed Ramirez as a six-year minor league free agent. Several teams pursued Ramirez, but Houston sweetened its offer with the promise of a spot on the 40-man roster and a long look in big league camp this spring. There's little doubt about Ramirez' defensive ability, as he's the best center fielder in the system. He has exceptional range thanks to his first-step quickness and ability to read balls off the bat, and he has a plus arm as a bonus. The question is whether Ramirez can hit enough to be a productive big leaguer. Though he set personal bests in many categories last year, he's still a career .251 hitter with modest power and little plate discipline. The ball does jump off his bat at times, but not on any kind of consistent basis. Ramirez is too aggressive at the plate, but he's starting to figure out that his chances of playing in the majors depend on making more contact and getting on base more often to take advantage of his above-average speed. The Astros may start Ramirez at Double-A this year, but they'd like him to be ready in 2009 as insurance in case new center fielder Michael Bourn can't get the job done.

Year	Club (League)	Class	AVG	G	AB	R	H	2B	3B	HR	RBI	BB	SO	SB	OBP	SLG
2002	Idaho Falls (Pio)	R	.179	23	78	8	14	1	0	0	5	3	24	0	.244	.192
2003	Idaho Falls (Pio)	R	.266	22	79	7	21	3	0	0	5	3	17	7	.301	.304
2004	Padres (AZL)	R	.264	39	159	23	42	7	5	1	21	4	26	16	.300	.390
	Eugene (NWL)	A	.200	4	15	1	3	0	0	1	3	1	5	0	.250	.400
2005	Fort Wayne (MWL)	A	.222	104	369	50	82	19	3	8	46	18	71	15	.263	.355
2006	Lake Elsinore (Cal)	A	.252	78	278	36	70	16	5	3	38	12	50	23	.285	.378
2007	Lake Elsinore (Cal)	A	.269	82	286	45	77	17	2	4	43	9	43	22	.298	.385
	Portland (PCL)	AAA	.315	30	127	18	40	3	0	4	18	6	21	6	.353	.433
MINOR LEAGUE TOTALS			.251	382	1391	188	349	66	15	21	179	56	257	89	.288	.365

21 WESLEY WRIGHT, LHP

Born: Jan. 28, 1985. **B-T:** L-L. **Ht.:** 5-11. **Wt.:** 160. **Drafted:** HS—Goshen, Ala., 2003 (7th round). **Signed by:** Clarence Johns (Dodgers).

The best lefthanded pitching prospect in the system didn't become an Astro until the Winter Meetings. Houston selected Wright from the Dodgers in the major league Rule 5 draft. Now he'll have to stick on the 25-man roster all season, or else be put through waivers and be offered back to Los Angeles for half his $50,000 draft price. Wright has steadily pitched his way to prospect status, though he was left off the Dodgers' 40-man roster and they feared losing him in the Rule 5. He got hammered in his first taste of Triple-A last year but finished with 16 straight scoreless innings in Double-A after a demotion. Wright pitches off his deft command of an 88-91 mph fastball that has late, riding life. His solid-average spike-curveball is his best secondary pitch, and he'll mix in a below-average slider and changeup as well. Wright offers good feel for pitching and consistency, two things major league managers covet. As a middle reliever or situational man, his ceiling is modest, but he could be a useful part of a bullpen.

Year	Club (League)	Class	W	L	ERA	G	GS	CG	SV	IP	H	R	ER	HR	BB	SO	AVG
2003	Dodgers (GCL)	R	3	1	3.58	14	5	0	0	37	37	15	15	1	19	26	.270
2004	Ogden (Pio)	R	3	3	6.29	17	2	0	0	44	56	43	31	3	23	66	.299
2005	Columbus (SAL)	A	1	5	1.93	30	0	0	1	60	38	21	13	2	33	68	.178
	Vero Beach (FSL)	A	0	0	9.45	6	0	0	0	6	8	7	7	0	10	8	.296
2006	Vero Beach (FSL)	A	3	3	1.49	26	0	0	0	42	29	11	7	0	23	51	.197
	Jacksonville (SL)	AA	1	1	4.64	15	0	0	1	21	14	13	11	2	11	28	.189

2007	Las Vegas (PCL)	AAA	1	2	9.18	14	1	0	0	16	28	23	17	4	18	18	.406
	Jacksonville (SL)	AA	6	2	2.49	30	1	0	2	61	45	19	17	4	31	68	.204
MINOR LEAGUE TOTALS			18	17	3.65	152	9	0	4	291	255	152	118	16	168	333	.237

22 DEVON TORRENCE, OF

Born: Oct. 21, 1988. **B-T:** B-R. **Ht.:** 5-11. **Wt.:** 185. **Drafted:** HS—Canton, Ohio, 2007 (16th round). **Signed by:** Nick Venuto.

Torrence has spent this fall as a reserve wide receiver and punt returner for Ohio State. While Ohio State was marching toward the national championship game, Torrence was calling farm director Ricky Bennett and area scout Nick Venuto, asking about a baseball training regimen and the organization's plans for him this summer. After falling to the 16th round of the 2007 draft because of his commitment to the Buckeyes, Torrence turned pro in baseball for $123,000. He emerged as a baseball prospect when he hit 14 homers as a high school sophomore, though that has led him to sell out for power ever since. He'll have to overhaul his approach after striking out 48 times in 87 at-bats in his pro debut. The best athlete in the system, he has well-above-average speed but still is learning to use it on the diamond. He's definitely quick enough to play center, though he'll have to improve his reads and jumps. His arm is below-average. When he rejoins the Astros in mid-2008, he'll head to either Rookie-level Greeneville or to Lexington.

Year	Club (League)	Class	AVG	G	AB	R	H	2B	3B	HR	RBI	BB	SO	SB	OBP	SLG
2007	Greeneville (Appy)	R	.149	30	87	8	13	2	0	0	3	23	48	5	.330	.172
MINOR LEAGUE TOTALS			.149	30	87	8	13	2	0	0	3	23	48	5	.330	.172

23 LOU SANTANGELO, C

Born: March 16, 1983. **B-T:** R-R. **Ht.:** 6-1. **Wt.:** 200. **Drafted:** Clemson, 2004 (4th round). **Signed by:** Brian Keegan.

Santangelo didn't do his career any favors when he got busted for using performance-enhancing drugs last May. The Astros already considered J.R. Towles a superior catching prospect, but Santangelo's 50-game suspension enabled Towles to take his job in Double-A and move up once Santangelo returned. Houston believes Santangelo has learned his lesson, but didn't bother to protect him from the Rule 5 draft, where he drew some interest but ultimately wasn't selected. He does two things well: hit for power and throw. He has as much raw power as anyone in the system and can drive balls out to dead-center. However, he doesn't make full use of his pop because he's not a very good hitter. Teams will pitch around his power and give him some walks, but he's mostly a dead-fastball hitter with little patience. He doesn't work counts or recognize pitches well, and he also gets too pull-happy. Fully recovered from a labrum tear in 2005, Santangelo has plus arm strength and threw out 30 percent of basestealers last year. He can get lazy behind the plate, though, which limits his ability as a receiver and blocker. He doesn't project as more than a backup, but his power and arm could make him a useful reserve. He figures to return to Double-A to open the season.

Year	Club (League)	Class	AVG	G	AB	R	H	2B	3B	HR	RBI	BB	SO	SB	OBP	SLG
2004	Tri-City (NYP)	A	.201	47	164	28	33	5	2	6	20	21	58	2	.299	.366
2005	Lexington (SAL)	A	.268	70	239	43	64	14	2	14	39	24	86	4	.336	.519
2006	Salem (Car)	A	.241	98	357	48	86	19	5	18	57	36	112	0	.310	.473
2007	Corpus Christi (TL)	AA	.243	58	206	30	50	9	2	5	17	23	57	2	.317	.379
MINOR LEAGUE TOTALS			.241	273	966	149	233	47	11	43	133	104	313	8	.316	.446

24 MARK McLEMORE, LHP

Born: Oct. 9, 1980. **B-T:** L-L. **Ht.:** 6-2. **Wt.:** 220. **Drafted:** Oregon State, 2002 (4th round). **Signed by:** Dan Houston.

McLemore's stuff has come back since he missed a year following labrum surgery in mid-2005, and last year he posted his first winning record since he was a high school senior in 1999. All three of his victories came in the majors, where he had decent success as a middle reliever. He works with an 89-92 mph fastball with natural sink and backs it up with a tight, late-breaking slider and a changeup. He never has done a good job of maintaining his release point. He'll fly open early in his delivery and lose command, leading to too many deep counts, walks and pitches up in the zone. McLemore may start incorporating a true two-seamer so he can keep the ball down in the zone more often. His mental toughness has been in question throughout his college and pro careers, but he proved something by competing well with Houston. He's not going to be the three-pitch starter the Astros once hoped he could become. He'll head to Houston as a lefty reliever this year unless he bombs in spring training.

Year	Club (League)	Class	W	L	ERA	G	GS	CG	SV	IP	H	R	ER	HR	BB	SO	AVG
2002	Martinsville (Appy)	R	0	1	1.80	4	2	0	0	10	9	3	2	0	5	11	.237
	Tri-City (NYP)	A	1	5	14.09	9	6	0	0	23	42	37	36	2	17	16	.393
2003	Lexington (SAL)	A	2	11	4.58	36	7	0	0	92	84	57	47	4	55	101	.243

2004	Salem (Car)	A	7	7	3.66	37	14	1	6	93	80	38	38	8	44	79	.231
2005	Corpus Christi (TL)	AA	5	6	2.81	15	15	1	0	73	59	34	23	5	34	65	.220
2006	Round Rock (PCL)	AAA	2	3	2.81	21	9	0	0	57	48	27	18	5	38	52	.226
2007	Round Rock (PCL)	AAA	0	1	2.77	21	9	0	0	52	34	20	16	2	35	52	.185
	Houston (NL)	MLB	3	0	3.86	29	0	0	0	35	38	17	15	5	18	35	.270
MINOR LEAGUE TOTALS			17	34	4.03	143	62	2	6	402	356	216	180	26	228	376	.237
MAJOR LEAGUE TOTALS			3	0	3.86	29	0	0	0	35	38	17	15	5	18	35	.270

25 ROBERT BONO, RHP

Born: Dec. 12, 1988. **B-T:** R-R. **Ht.:** 6-2. **Wt.:** 175. **Drafted:** HS—Waterford, Conn., 2007 (12th round). **Signed by:** Tim Harrington.

Most teams thought Bono wanted to catch and figured he'd play both ways while attending Connecticut. But the Astros took him in the 12th round and gave him a $105,000 bonus to convince him to pitch. Though Bono didn't exactly put up big numbers in his pro debut, Houston knew he would be a work in progress. His fastball sits at 89-91 mph and tops out at 94. He works from a three-quarters arm slot and has a surprisingly clean delivery for someone who just became a full-time pitcher. Bono can flash a dastardly curveball, but he doesn't have much feel, command or consistency with the pitch. He has also begun messing around with a slider. He actually has made more progress with his changeup than with his breaking pitches. Bono will need a lot of time to add some polish, but he's unquestionably one of Houston's better hopes from its disappointing 2007 drat. He may not be ready for a full-season assignment at the start of 2008.

Year	Club (League)	Class	W	L	ERA	G	GS	CG	SV	IP	H	R	ER	HR	BB	SO	AVG
2007	Greeneville (Appy)	R	0	4	7.34	11	8	0	0	34	39	31	28	6	20	18	.285
MINOR LEAGUE TOTALS			0	4	7.34	11	8	0	0	34	39	31	28	6	20	18	.285

26 KOBY CLEMENS, 3B

Born: July 2, 1986. **B-T:** R-R. **Ht.:** 5-11. **Wt.:** 193. **Drafted:** HS—Houston, 2005 (8th round). **Signed by:** Rusty Pendergrass.

Even if he doesn't play in the majors, Clemens will have made some significant contributions to the Astros. His presence in the system helped entice his father Roger to pitch an additional season for Houston in 2006. Koby also has made a positive impression on several farmhands with his leadership, work ethic and utter lack of any sense of entitlement. The Astros say he has some talent, too, though they were the only club that would have popped him in the eighth round of the 2005 draft. He doesn't have his father's natural ability, but he does have a sound swing and legitimate raw power. He boosted his slugging percentage 66 points while repeating low Class A in 2007, but his strikeout rate spiked in the process. He does have the patience to draw some walks. Clemens is going to have to hit because his athleticism, speed and range at third base are all well-below-average. He works very hard on his defense and has made some progress, but he's still not going to get to balls that other third basemen will gobble up. If he gets any thicker or slower, he'll have to play first base. Clemens will remain at third base and move up to high Class A this year.

Year	Club (League)	Class	AVG	G	AB	R	H	2B	3B	HR	RBI	BB	SO	SB	OBP	SLG
2005	Greeneville (Appy)	R	.297	33	111	14	33	8	0	4	17	18	26	4	.398	.477
	Tri-City (NYP)	A	.281	9	32	3	9	1	2	0	6	4	5	1	.361	.438
2006	Lexington (SAL)	A	.229	91	306	40	70	19	1	5	39	32	67	2	.313	.346
2007	Lexington (SAL)	A	.252	115	413	65	104	21	0	15	56	53	112	8	.344	.412
MINOR LEAGUE TOTALS			.251	248	862	122	216	49	3	24	118	107	210	15	.341	.398

27 JOSH MUECKE, LHP

Born: Jan. 9, 1982. **B-T:** L-L. **Ht.:** 6-3. **Wt.:** 195. **Drafted:** Loyola Marymount, 2003 (3rd round). **Signed by:** Doug Deutsch.

The Astros always thought Muecke had enough stuff to pitch in the majors, and he may get that opportunity in 2008 after posting a 1.56 ERA as a reliever in the Arizona Fall League. He has a solid arsenal for a lefthander, with an 88-92 mph fastball, a cutter he'll run in on righthanders and a useful slider and a changeup. He also possesses a curveball, but it's not very effective. His control improved in 2007 because he started to challenge hitters more aggressively than he had in the past. Muecke's mental toughness had been in question and he tried to pitch away from contact in the past, but work with a sports psychologist has changed him for the better. Though he has worked as a swingman the last two years, he projects as a big league reliever. His first taste of Triple-A wouldn't hurt Muecke.

Year	Club (League)	Class	W	L	ERA	G	GS	CG	SV	IP	H	R	ER	HR	BB	SO	AVG
2003	Tri-City (NYP)	A	3	3	4.14	14	11	0	0	54	58	28	25	2	25	43	.284
2004	Lexington (SAL)	A	9	1	3.97	37	8	0	2	104	81	48	46	8	48	91	.217
2005	Salem (Car)	A	10	12	3.67	28	28	1	0	159	164	81	65	10	47	98	.268

2006	Corpus Christi (TL)	AA	0	7	7.40	25	9	0	0	62	92	54	51	8	27	43	.351
2007	Corpus Christi (TL)	AA	9	5	3.90	32	16	1	0	131	133	60	57	18	45	78	.263
MINOR LEAGUE TOTALS			31	28	4.29	136	72	2	2	511	528	271	244	46	192	353	.270

28 JONNY ASH, 2B

Born: Sept. 11, 1982. **B-T:** L-R. **Ht.:** 5-9. **Wt.:** 185. **Drafted:** Stanford, 2004 (11th round). **Signed by:** Gene Wellman.

Ash is the best pure hitter in the system. He has a career .310 average in pro ball and never has batted less than .297 in any of his five pro stops. He's one of the minors' most difficult batters to strike out, fanning just once every 13.4 at-bats, and managers rated his strike-zone judgment the best in the Texas League last year. But he's more of an overachieving organization player than a true prospect, because the rest of his game is fringy at best. Though he stunned Chad Cordero with a memorable College World Series homer while at Stanford, there's no power in Ash's bat and he doesn't project to do much damage in the majors. His speed is below-average, as are his range and arm at second base. He has reliable hands but doesn't have the tools to play other positions. Ash's 2007 season ended in July with a knee infection that required surgery, which won't help his tools. He'll advance to Triple-A this year, but his ceiling is limited to that of a reserve and reliable pinch-hitter.

Year	Club (League)	Class	AVG	G	AB	R	H	2B	3B	HR	RBI	BB	SO	SB	OBP	SLG
2004	Tri-City (NYP)	A	.297	61	239	50	71	7	3	2	25	25	16	5	.388	.377
2005	Lexington (SAL)	A	.320	67	256	44	82	11	2	8	38	25	20	3	.395	.473
	Salem (Car)	A	.320	59	225	32	72	19	2	1	25	14	15	3	.365	.436
2006	Corpus Christi (TL)	AA	.314	112	392	40	123	22	5	1	28	25	36	5	.370	.403
2007	Corpus Christi (TL)	AA	.300	79	280	33	84	16	2	3	33	26	17	2	.374	.404
MINOR LEAGUE TOTALS			.310	378	1392	199	432	75	14	15	149	115	104	18	.378	.417

29 MATT CUSICK, 2B

Born: May 5, 1986. **B-T:** L-R. **Ht.:** 5-10. **Wt.:** 190. **Drafted:** Southern California, 2007 (10th round). **Signed by:** Dennis Twombley.

Cusick is a newer version of Jonny Ash. Like Ash a product of the Pacific-10 Conference, Cusick went in the 10th round of the 2007 draft and signed for $75,000. He hit better than .300 with more walks than strikeouts in each of his three years at Southern California, then did the same in his pro debut. He first demonstrated his aptitude with wood bats by hitting .304 in the Cape Cod League in 2006. As with Ash, the question becomes what else Cusick can bring to the table. He makes contact, though not as much as Ash, and doesn't drive the ball consistently. His speed is below-average as are his defensive tools, with the exception of his hands. Cusick can't play other positions well enough to become a utilityman. He'll advance to Class A this year and try to develop some skills to complement his contact hitting ability.

Year	Club (League)	Class	AVG	G	AB	R	H	2B	3B	HR	RBI	BB	SO	SB	OBP	SLG
2007	Tri-City (NYP)	A	.306	61	222	42	68	14	4	3	35	38	25	5	.422	.446
MINOR LEAGUE TOTALS			.306	61	222	42	68	14	4	3	35	38	25	5	.422	.446

30 JIMMY VAN OSTRAND, OF/1B

Born: Aug. 7, 1984. **B-T:** R-R. **Ht.:** 6-4. **Wt.:** 210. **Drafted:** Cal Poly, 2006 (8th round). **Signed by:** Dennis Twombley.

When Mets outfielder Fernando Martinez had to miss the Futures Game with a hand injury, Van Ostrand replaced him on the World roster. He provided one of the prospect showcase's highlights when he homered off the Dodgers' Clayton Kershaw. It was a nice moment for Van Ostrand, but he's not really in the same prospect stratosphere as Kershaw and Martinez. Van Ostrand offers average raw power as his best tool. He has a line-drive stroke and uses the whole field, but he's more of a gap hitter than a true home run threat. His speed is well-below-average and limits him defensively. While his average arm would play in right field, he's a left fielder at best and may have to be a first baseman. Hamstring problems last year forced him to spend time on the disabled list and at DH. Van Ostrand finished 2007 as a 23-year-old in low Class A, so he really hasn't been challenged. He should see Double-A at some point this year, though he may start off in high Class A.

Year	Club (League)	Class	AVG	G	AB	R	H	2B	3B	HR	RBI	BB	SO	SB	OBP	SLG
2006	Tri-City (NYP)	A	.215	40	149	14	32	6	0	2	13	9	36	2	.272	.295
2007	Lexington (SAL)	A	.289	98	363	42	105	18	3	12	60	38	64	4	.360	.455
MINOR LEAGUE TOTALS			.268	138	512	56	137	24	3	14	73	47	100	6	.335	.408

Kansas City Royals

BY JOSH LEVENTHAL

The Royals completed the 2007 season in the same fashion they had in 12 of the previous 13 years—with a losing record. Yet unlike years past, optimism could be found in Kansas City's 69-93 mark and fourth consecutive last-place finish in the American League Central.

That hope is tied to a restructured player-development system and draft philosophy modeled after one of baseball's most successful franchises, the Braves.

It's no coincidence that general manager Dayton Moore and farm director J.J. Picollo worked for Atlanta before coming to Kansas City. Senior adviser Art Stewart, who has been with the franchise since its inception, said the team's renewed efforts to build from within under Moore reminded him of the Royals' early days, when they swiftly assembled a contender through shrewd trades and homegrown talent.

"The most important thing we have done is staff our front office and development departments with good people and a full staff," said Moore, who noted that when scouting director Derric Ladnier arrived (also from the Braves) in 2000, he had just two cross-checkers. "Certainly scouting and player development are the most important things we can do, and it doesn't matter if it is in a small or large market."

Kansas City made clear its commitment to the future by spending $6.6 million on the 2007 draft—the seventh-biggest outlay in baseball—starting with $4 million for No. 2 overall pick Mike Moustakas, the best hitter available.

The Royals have yet to show much improvement at the big league level, but they are putting more talent on the field. Four rookies who should be cornerstones for their future successfully made the transition to the big leagues in 2007. First-round picks Billy Butler and Alex Gordon had steady debuts. Brian Bannister, stolen from the Mets in a trade for Ambiorix Burgos, won 12 games, while Joakim Soria, a Rule 5 draft coup, earned 17 saves.

Luke Hochevar, the No. 1 overall pick in the 2006 draft, made his major league debut in September. Daniel Cortes has been a revelation after coming over from the White Sox in a deal for Mike MacDougal. But other than counting on improvement from its young big leaguers, a Royals offense that finished 13th in the AL in scoring can't count on any immediate help.

The makeup of his team spurred Moore's decision to go off the beaten path to find a replacement for

Alex Gordon showed that he belongs in the big leagues after a solid rookie season

Photo credit: JOHN WILLIAMSON

TOP 30 PROSPECTS

1. Mike Moustakas, ss	16. Chris Lubanski, of
2. Daniel Cortes, rhp	17. Justin Huber, of/1b
3. Luke Hochevar, rhp	18. Jeff Bianchi, ss
4. Billy Buckner, rhp	19. Brett Fisher, lhp
5. Blake Wood, rhp	20. Neal Musser, lhp
6. Danny Duffy, lhp	21. Fernando Cruz, 3b
7. Carlos Rosa, rhp	22. David Lough, of
8. Julio Pimentel, rhp	23. Mitch Maier, of
9. Matt Mitchell, rhp	24. Chris McConnell, ss
10. Yasuhiko Yabuta, rhp	25. Jose Duarte, of
11. Derrick Robinson, of	26. Joe Dickerson, of
12. Sam Runion, rhp	27. Keaton Hayenga, rhp
13. Tyler Lumsden, lhp	28. Dusty Hughes, lhp
14. Blake Johnson, rhp	29. Mike Aviles, inf
15. Ryan Braun, rhp	30. Rowdy Hardy, lhp

manager Buddy Bell, who resigned at the end of the season. Trey Hillman takes over after five seasons in Japan managing the Hokkaido Nippon Ham Fighters. In Kansas City, Hillman will try to implement many of the same values that worked with his 2006 Japan Series champions, an offensively challenged club that won with pitching, defense and fundamentals.

The Royals showed that they'll explore every avenue for talent by also going to Japan to land reliever Yasuhiko Yabuta with a two-year, $6 million contract.

General Manager: Dayton Moore. **Farm Director:** J.J. Picollo. **Scouting Director:** Deric Ladnier.

Class	Team	League	W	L	PCT	Finish*	Manager	Affiliated
Majors	Kansas City	American	69	93	.426	12th (14)	Buddy Bell	—
Triple-A	Omaha Royals	Pacific Coast	73	71	.507	8th (16)	Mike Jirschele	1969
Double-A	Wichita Wranglers	Texas	56	84	.400	8th (8)	Tony Tijerina	1995
High A	Wilmington Blue Rocks	Carolina	75	62	.547	3rd (8)	John Mizerock	2007
Low A	Burlington Bees	Midwest	61	77	.442	13th (16)	Jim Gabella	2001
Rookie	Idaho Falls Chukars	Pioneer	46	30	.605	3rd (8)	Brian Rupp	2001
Rookie	Burlington Royals	Appalachian	38	30	.559	3rd (9)	Darryl Kennedy	2007
Rookie	AZL Royals	Arizona	28	28	.500	t-4th (9)	Lloyd Simmons	2004
Overall 2007 Minor League Record			377	382	.497	14th		

*Finish in overall standings (No. of teams in league) ^League champion

LAST YEAR'S TOP 30

Player, Pos.		Status
1.	Alex Gordon, 3b	Majors
2.	Luke Hochevar, rhp	No. 3
3.	Billy Butler, of	Majors
4.	Chris Lubanski, of	No. 16
5.	Tyler Lumsden, lhp	No. 13
6.	Mitch Maier, of	No. 23
7.	Brian Bannister, rhp	Majors
8.	Justin Huber, of/1b	No. 17
9.	Billy Buckner, rhp	No. 4
10.	Brent Fisher, lhp	No. 19
11.	Jeff Bianchi, ss	No. 18
12.	Ryan Braun, rhp	No. 15
13.	Joakim Soria, rhp	Majors
14.	Blake Wood, rhp	No. 5
15.	Erik Cordier, rhp	(Braves)
16.	Jason Taylor, 3b	Dropped out
17.	Blake Johnson, rhp	No. 14
18.	Julio Pimentel, rhp	No. 8
19.	Carlos Rosa, rhp	No. 7
20.	Luis Cota, rhp	Dropped out
21.	Derrick Robinson, of	No. 11
22.	Chris Nicoll, rhp	Dropped out
23.	Jarod Plummer, rhp	Dropped out
24.	Danny Christensen, lhp	(Tigers)
25.	Angel Sanchez, ss	Dropped out
26.	Kurt Mertins, 2b	Dropped out
27.	Chris McConnell, ss	No. 24
28.	Joe Dickerson, of	No. 26
29.	Jason Godin, rhp	Dropped out
30.	Daniel Cortes, rhp	No. 2

BEST TOOLS

Best Hitter for Average	Mike Moustakas
Best Power Hitter	Mike Moustakas
Best Strike-Zone Discipline	Kila Kaaihue
Fastest Baserunner	Patrick Norris
Best Athlete	Derrick Robinson
Best Fastball	Daniel Cortes
Best Curveball	Daniel Cortes
Best Slider	Neal Musser
Best Changeup	Julio Pimentel
Best Control	Rowdy Hardy
Best Defensive Catcher	Matt Tupman
Best Defensive Infielder	Chris McConnell
Best Infield Arm	Mike Moustakas
Best Defensive Outfielder	Jose Duarte
Best Outfield Arm	Jose Duarte

PROJECTED 2011 LINEUP

Catcher	John Buck
First Base	Justin Huber
Second Base	Jeff Bianchi
Third Base	Alex Gordon
Shortstop	Tony Pena
Left Field	Jose Guillen
Center Field	David DeJesus
Right Field	Mike Moustakas
Designated Hitter	Billy Butler
No. 1 Starter	Zack Greinke
No. 2 Starter	Daniel Cortes
No. 3 Starter	Luke Hochevar
No. 4 Starter	Gil Meche
No. 5 Starter	Brian Bannister
Closer	Joakim Soria

TOP PROSPECTS OF THE DECADE

Year	Player, Pos.	2007 Org.
1998	Dee Brown, of	Athletics
1999	Carlos Beltran, of	Mets
2000	Dee Brown, of	Athletics
2001	Chris George, lhp	Marlins
2002	Angel Berroa, ss	Royals
2003	Zack Greinke, rhp	Royals
2004	Zack Greinke, rhp	Royals
2005	Billy Butler, of	Royals
2006	Alex Gordon, 3b	Royals
2007	Alex Gordon, 3b	Royals

TOP DRAFT PICKS OF THE DECADE

Year	Player, Pos.	2007 Org.
1998	Jeff Austin, rhp	Out of baseball
1999	Kyle Snyder, rhp	Red Sox
2000	Mike Stodolka, lhp	Royals
2001	Colt Griffin, rhp	Out of baseball
2002	Zack Greinke, rhp	Royals
2003	Chris Lubanski, of	Royals
2004	Billy Butler, of	Royals
2005	Alex Gordon, of	Royals
2006	Luke Hochevar, rhp	Royals
2007	Mike Moustakas, ss	Royals

LARGEST BONUSES IN CLUB HISTORY

Alex Gordon, 2005	$4,000,000
Mike Moustakas, 2007	$4,000,000
Luke Hochevar, 2006	$3,500,000
Jeff Austin, 1998	$2,700,000
Mike Stodolka, 2000	$2,500,000

KANSAS CITY ROYALS

Top 2008 Rookie: Luke Hochevar, rhp. The No. 1 overall pick in the 2006 draft had a so-so season, but he looked good in Kansas City in September and probably has seen his last of the minor leagues.

Breakout Prospect: Jose Duarte, of. The Royals' best defensive outfielder has made steady improvements at the plate.

Sleeper: Mario Lisson, 3b. A good athlete, he put together a 20-game hitting streak late in the year in high Class A, then finished among the home run leaders in the Venezuelan Winter League.

SOURCE OF TOP 30 TALENT			
Homegrown	24	Acquired	6
College	6	Trades	4
Junior college	0	Rule 5 draft	0
High school	13	Independent leagues	1
Draft-and-follow	0	Free agents/waivers	1
Nondrafted free agents	1		
International	4		

Numbers in parentheses indicate prospect rankings.

LF
Chris Lubanski (16)

CF
Derrick Robinson (11)
David Lough (22)
Mitch Maier (23)
Jose Duarte (25)
Adrian Ortiz
Patrick Norris
Hilton Richardson

RF
Joe Dickerson (26)
Brian McFall

3B
Fernando Cruz (21)
Mario Lisson
Jason Taylor

SS
Mike Moustakas (1)
Chris McConnell (24)
Mike Aviles (29)
Yowill Espinal
Guelin Beltre

2B
Jeff Bianchi (18)
Kurt Mertins
Marc Maddox

1B
Justin Huber (17)
Kila Kaaihue
Mike Stodolka
Clint Robinson

C
Sean McCauley
Matt Tupman
Salvador Perez
Brad McCann

RHP

Starters	Relievers
Daniel Cortes (2)	Ryan Braun (15)
Luke Hochevar (3)	Jarrod Plummer
Billy Buckner (4)	Luis Cota
Blake Wood (5)	Ivor Hodgson
Carlos Rosa (7)	Tyler Chambliss
Julio Pimentel (8)	Greg Holland
Matt Mitchell (9)	Mike Lehmann
Sam Runion (12)	
Blake Johnson (14)	
Keaton Hayenga (27)	
Mitch Hodge	
Harold Mozingo	
Daniel Gutierrez	
Jacob Rodriguez	
Jason Godin	

LHP

Starters	Relievers
Danny Duffy (6)	Yasuhiko Yabuta (10)
Tyler Lumsden (13)	Neal Musser (20)
Brent Fisher (19)	Dusty Hughes (28)
Ray Liotta	Rowdy Hardy (30)
	Gilbert de la Vara

2007   SIGNING BUDGET: $3.3 MILLION

Best Pro Debut: 1B Clint Robinson (25) led the Rookie-level Pioneer League with 66 RBIs while batting .336/.388/.593 and slugging 15 homers. RHP Matt Mitchell (14) led the Rookie-level Arizona League in ERA and ranked fourth in strikeouts (72); teammate LHP Danny Duffy (3) ranked sixth in Ks (63) in just 37 innings, and posted a 1.45 ERA.

Best Athlete: A Utah baseball recruit, OF Hilton Richardson (7) has a long, lanky body with some present strength and blazing speed. RHP Keaton Hayenga (31), like Richardson, was an excellent prep basketball player in Washington.

Best Pure Hitter: Most scouts like his power better, but SS Mike Moustakas (1) has the smooth, compact stroke to hit for average as well as power.

Best Power Hitter: Moustakas has 80 raw power and set California high school records for single-season (24) and career (52) home runs this spring.

Fastest Runner: OFs Adrian Ortiz (5) and Patrick Norris (16) both grade as 80 runners. Norris gets to first base in 3.8 seconds from the right side.

Best Defensive Player: 3B Fernando Cruz (6) needs to add some first-step quickness as he moves from shortstop to third, but he has the arm, hands and reactions to be a plus defender. C Sean McCauley (12) has a knack for game-calling and good athleticism. His plus arm delivers 1.9-second pop times from behind the plate to the second base bag.

Best Fastball: Duffy and RHP Sam Runion (2) have hit 95 mph since signing, and both have good life; Runion has slightly more projection. RHP Mitch Hodge (4) can hit 94.

Best Secondary Pitch: Duffy (with both a curve-ball and slider) and Mitchell (changeup, curve) have solid-average secondary stuff, which Mitchell commands better.

Most Intriguing Background: Moustakas is the nephew of former big league hitting coach Tom Robson; he and Marlins first-rounder Matt Dominguez became the sixth pair of prep team-mates picked in the first round of the same draft. Cruz was home-schooled in Puerto Rico and peti-tioned the commissioner's office successfully to enter the draft a year early.

Closest To The Majors: Moustakas. The Royals intend to try him at shortstop, even if his range is a step shy.

Best Late-Round Pick: Hayenga got a $300,000

bonus because of his athleticism, projectable 6-foot-4, 195-pound body and three-pitch mix that includes a fastball reaching 91 mph. Shoulder surgery in the spring allowed him to fall to the 31st round.

The One Who Got Away: RHP Zach Kenyon (9) touched 91 in the summer but kept to his Iowa commitment.

Assessment: Moustakas has superstar potential, and the organization acquired needed pitching depth. This draft offers more possibilities in the late rounds than usual in the form of talents such as McCauley, Hayenga and OF David Lough (11).

2006   BUDGET: $6.3 MILLION

The jury is out a little bit on RHP Luke Hochevar (1) after the No. 1 overall pick got knocked around in the minors. OF Derrick Robinson (4) is the best athlete in the system.

GRADE: C+

2005   BUDGET: $6.0 MILLION

3B Alex Gordon (1) continues to fuel George Brett comparisons, right down to the early-season slump and second-half improvements in his rookie season. No other member of this class has distinguished himself.

GRADE: A

2004   BUDGET: $5.8 MILLION

The Royals' faith in OF Billy Butler (1) has been justified. They had four other picks in the first two rounds, but only RHP Billy Buckner (2) looks like he'll pan out.

GRADE: B+

2003   BUDGET: $5.6 MILLION

Kansas City once had high hopes for OFs Chris Lubanski (1) and Mitch Maier (1), but those have passed. OF Shane Costa (2) and RHP Ryan Braun (6) have reached the majors but haven't done much there. RHP Luis Cota (10) was a $1.05 million draft-and-follow bust.

GRADE: D

Draft analysis by John Manuel (2007) and Jim Callis (2003-06). Numbers in parentheses indicate draft rounds. Budgets are bonuses in first 10 rounds.

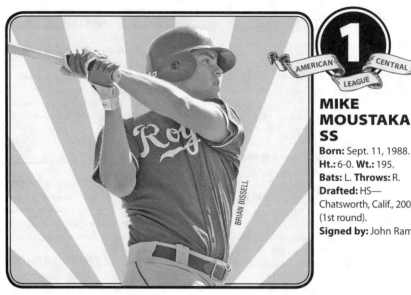

1
AMERICAN LEAGUE CENTRAL

MIKE MOUSTAKAS, SS

Born: Sept. 11, 1988.
Ht.: 6-0. **Wt.:** 195.
Bats: L. **Throws:** R.
Drafted: HS—Chatsworth, Calif., 2007 (1st round).
Signed by: John Ramey.

Moustakas stepped into the spotlight during his junior season, when he set the Chatsworth (Calif.) High single-season home record with 14 as a somewhat pudgy 5-foot-11, 175-pounder. Moustakas tightened his physique before his senior season and hit a state-record 24 homers, upping his career total to 52—another California mark. His performance earned him Baseball America's High School Player of the Year award and consensus acclaim as the best hitter available in the 2007 draft. After almost backing away because of signability concerns, the Royals chose him with the No. 2 overall pick. Chatsworth third baseman Matt Dominguez, went 10 choices later to the Marlins, making them the sixth pair of high school teammates to go in the first round of the same draft. Kansas City didn't sign Moustakas until just before the Aug. 15 deadline, when it gave him a $4 million bonus that matched the club record established by Alex Gordon in 2005. Agent Scott Boras said he thought Moustakas was worth considerably more and advised his client to attend Southern California rather than turning pro. Though he didn't come cheap, the Royals believe they locked up a future middle-of-the-order hitter, though perhaps not a middle infielder. But they will allow him to begin his pro career as a shortstop. He's the nephew of former Mets hitting coach Tom Robson.

There are few holes in Moustakas' offensive game. He has a short, quick swing that he repeats easily, plus an advanced approach for his age. He lets the ball travel deep into the strike zone before cutting loose, and it jumps off his bat to all fields. In his first pro at bat, he drove a two-strike pitch for an opposite-field double. He shows off tremendous bat speed and strength and simply has the look of a major league hitter. Assistant general manager Brian Murphy compared Moustakas' Major League Scouting Bureau video to a hitting clinic in which he did everything correct. A mature hitter, he already stays back on offspeed pitches. Also a quarterback and a pitcher in high school, Moustakas has good athleticism, average speed and some baserunning aptitude. He was clocked throwing as hard as 98 mph off the mound—he also flashed a two-plane slider—and that arm strength is an asset at shortstop. He has sure hands and makes accurate throws. He has tremendous makeup and understanding of the game.

Moustakas projects to be too bulky to stay at shortstop. He's still filling out and his range is already less than ideal for the position. His best position might be third base, though that's currently occupied by Gordon in Kansas City. Some clubs were intrigued by the possibilities of making him a catcher, but that would delay the arrival of his bat in the major leagues. Right field is another possibility. His positioning and instincts will determine how long Moustakas stays at shortstop. After dominating in high school, he sometimes got frustrated with any lack of success during his brief pro debut.

The only thing that will slow Moustakas' ascent to the big leagues is finding him a defensive home. He'll stay at shortstop this year at low Class A Burlington. His athleticism and arm strength will make switching positions easy when that time comes. His bat will play anywhere on the diamond.

Year	Club (League)	Class	AVG	G	AB	R	H	2B	3B	HR	RBI	BB	SO	SB	OBP	SLG
2007	Idaho Falls (Pio)	R	.293	11	41	6	12	4	1	0	10	4	8	0	.383	.439
MINOR LEAGUE TOTALS			.293	11	41	6	12	4	1	0	10	4	8	0	.383	.439

2 DANIEL CORTES, RHP

Born: March 4, 1987. **B-T:** R-R. **Ht.:** 6-6. **Wt.:** 225. **Drafted:** HS—Pomona, Calif., 2005 (7th round). **Signed by:** Dan Ontiveros (White Sox).

CARL KLINE

Cortes has passed lefty Tyler Lumsden as the best prospect the Royals received from the White Sox in the Mike MacDougal trade in mid-2006. No player in the system made a bigger leap in 2007 than Cortes, who has grown an inch and added 20 pounds since changing organizations. He was held back in spring training to work on slowing down the tempo of his delivery and steadily progressed after joining high Class A Wilmington at the end of April. Slowing down Cortes' delivery resulted in his fastball velocity increasing from 89-92 to 93-96 mph, and it seems to jump out of his hand. His heater has late life, currently grades as a 70 on the 20-80 scouting scale and has the potential to get better. He mixes in a sharp, 12-to-6 curveball that could become a dominant strikeout pitch. For a pitcher of his age and size, he does a good job of throwing strikes. Cortes still has a tendency to be quick in his delivery and will sometimes overthrow his fastball and curveball. He relies heavily on those two pitches and is hesitant to mix in his changeup, which lags well behind in his repertoire. The Royals envision Cortes as a frontline starter and will send him to their new Double-A Northwest Arkansas affiliate in 2008.

Year	Club (League)	Class	W	L	ERA	G	GS	CG	SV	IP	H	R	ER	HR	BB	SO	AVG
2005	Bristol (Appy)	R	1	4	5.17	15	7	0	0	38	44	23	22	2	13	38	.289
2006	Kannapolis (SAL)	A	3	9	4.01	20	19	0	0	107	109	61	48	6	38	96	.260
	Burlington (MWL)	A	1	2	6.69	7	7	0	0	35	40	27	26	7	17	30	.284
2007	Wilmington (Car)	A	8	8	3.07	24	24	0	0	123	102	50	42	7	45	120	.226
MINOR LEAGUE TOTALS			13	23	4.09	66	57	0	0	304	295	161	138	22	113	284	.253

3 LUKE HOCHEVAR, RHP

Born: Sept. 15, 1983. **B-T:** R-R. **Ht.:** 6-5. **Wt.:** 205. **Drafted:** Fort Worth (American Association), 2006 (1st round). **Signed by:** Phil Huffman/Gerald Turner.

Hochevar took a winding path to professional baseball. Selected 40th overall by the Dodgers in 2005, he backed out of a $2.98 million bonus deal that September and showcased himself with a stint in the independent American Association the following spring. The Royals made him the No. 1 overall pick in 2006 and signed him for a $5.25 million big league contract that included a $3.5 million bonus. Hochevar's stuff was impressive in his first full pro season, though he went just 4-9, 4.86 in the minors before getting a September callup. Hochevar pitches off a 92-93 mph fastball that reaches 95 and also mixes in a two-seamer with heavy sink. His big, late-breaking curveball will become an above-average pitch once he shows the ability to command it better. He throws his curve in the mid-80s and can use it to freeze hitters or to bury it in the dirt. He used his slider more when he was in college and still employs it as a chase pitch. Hochevar battled wildness at times in 2007, primarily because of his tendency to spin off the mound toward first base. When he does that, he leaves his pitches up in the strike zone and they flatten out. He largely corrected the problem by the end of the season by focusing on landing in line with the plate. His changeup still needs fine-tuning. Armed with a five-pitch arsenal, Hochevar needs to improve his command to become a frontline starter. His performance in spring training will determine whether he opens 2008 in Kansas City or Triple-A Omaha.

Year	Club (League)	Class	W	L	ERA	G	GS	CG	SV	IP	H	R	ER	HR	BB	SO	AVG
2006	Fort Worth (A-A)	IND	1	1	2.38	4	4	0	0	23	20	7	6	1	11	34	.244
	Burlington (MWL)	A	0	1	1.17	4	4	0	0	15	8	3	2	2	2	16	.148
2007	Wichita (TL)	AA	3	6	4.69	17	16	0	0	94	110	62	49	13	26	94	.286
	Omaha (PCL)	AAA	1	3	5.12	10	10	0	0	58	53	34	33	11	21	44	.244
	Kansas City (AL)	MLB	0	1	2.13	4	1	0	0	12	11	4	3	1	4	5	.239
MINOR LEAGUE TOTALS			4	9	4.52	31	30	0	0	167	171	99	84	26	49	154	.261
MAJOR LEAGUE TOTALS			0	1	2.13	4	1	0	0	12	11	4	3	1	4	5	.239

4 BILLY BUCKNER, RHP

Born: Aug. 27, 1983. **B-T:** R-R. **Ht.:** 6-2. **Wt.:** 215. **Drafted:** South Carolina, 2004 (2nd round). **Signed by:** Spencer Graham.

Buckner is the most advanced pitcher in the system, yet where he fits remains a bit of a question. He made 12 relief appearances in Triple-A so that he'd be better prepared for a callup, then worked primarily as a starter when he did join the Royals in late August. Like many pitchers getting their first taste of the majors, he didn't challenge hitters as aggressively as he did in the minors. Buckner mixes an 89-92 mph fastball with an above-average knuckle-curve and a changeup that could grade equally high down the road. Buckner's curve is his go-to pitch. He shows good arm action with his changeup, which he also uses as a strikeout pitch. When he's going good, he gets ahead with an easy two-seam fastball that has some sink or a four-seamer that moves away from righthanders to setup his offspeed pitches. His mechanics are sound. Buckner relied too much on his curve in college, and as a result he has an underdeveloped fastball. He needs better command of his heater to reach his potential. He didn't establish his curveball and changeup in the majors as well as he did in the minors. At times, he tries to be too fine with his pitches. Buckner projects as a possible No. 3 starter if he can refine his fastball command. The Royals would like him to earn a big league rotation job in spring training.

Year	Club (League)	Class	W	L	ERA	G	GS	CG	SV	IP	H	R	ER	HR	BB	SO	AVG
2004	Idaho Falls (Pio)	R	2	1	3.30	7	5	0	0	30	36	14	11	4	4	37	.303
2005	Burlington (MWL)	A	3	7	3.88	11	11	0	0	60	66	36	26	9	17	60	.268
	High Desert (Cal)	A	5	6	5.36	17	17	0	0	94	105	65	56	10	46	92	.285
2006	High Desert (Cal)	A	7	1	3.90	16	16	0	0	90	92	44	39	6	47	85	.271
	Wichita (TL)	AA	5	3	4.64	13	13	0	0	75	78	40	39	7	39	63	.265
2007	Wichita (TL)	AA	1	3	4.66	4	3	0	0	19	20	10	10	4	6	13	.253
	Omaha (PCL)	AAA	9	7	3.78	27	15	0	0	104	108	49	44	11	26	83	.271
	Kansas City (AL)	MLB	1	2	5.29	7	5	0	0	34	37	20	20	5	16	17	.294
MINOR LEAGUE TOTALS			32	28	4.27	95	80	0	0	474	505	258	225	51	185	433	.274
MAJOR LEAGUE TOTALS			1	2	5.29	7	5	0	0	34	37	20	20	5	16	17	.294

5 BLAKE WOOD, RHP

BILL MITCHELL

Born: Aug. 8, 1985. **B-T:** R-R. **Ht.:** 6-4. **Wt.:** 225. **Drafted:** Georgia Tech, 2006 (3rd round). **Signed by:** Spencer Graham.

Wood missed the first half of 2007 after having surgery to repair a herniated disc in his back but made up for lost time with a stellar second half. Wood described the operation as instant relief, and he improved with seemingly every start. His success carried over to Hawaii Winter Baseball, where he went 2-1, 3.55 with 57 strikeouts in 33 innings. Wood throws a heavy 94-95 mph fastball with some natural bore and an above-average curveball with true 12-to-6 break. He gained velocity on his fastball last year after learning not to overthrow it. He continues to improve an average changeup with good action down in the zone. Mechanics continue to be Wood's biggest obstacle. Though he doesn't rely on blowing the ball past hitters as he did in 2006—which caused him to hurry his delivery—he still needs to improve his balance and trust that he has plenty of arm strength and life in his fastball to overwhelm hitters. Once he got going, Wood had the look of a frontline starter, and he should provide a better look at his ceiling with a full season in 2008. He'll start the year in high Class A and figures to get a midseason promotion.

Year	Club (League)	Class	W	L	ERA	G	GS	CG	SV	IP	H	R	ER	HR	BB	SO	AVG
2006	Idaho Falls (Pio)	R	3	1	4.50	12	12	0	0	52	50	28	26	1	15	46	.258
2007	Royals (AZL)	R	0	0	0.00	4	4	0	0	9	9	2	0	0	0	15	.250
	Burlington (MWL)	A	2	1	3.03	7	7	0	0	35	32	12	12	3	14	26	.239
	Wilmington (Car)	A	0	1	4.66	2	2	0	0	9	9	5	5	1	3	11	.257
MINOR LEAGUE TOTALS			5	3	3.62	25	25	0	0	107	100	47	43	5	32	98	.251

6 DANNY DUFFY, LHP

BILL MITCHELL

Born: Dec. 21, 1988. **B-T:** L-L. **Ht.:** 6-2. **Wt.:** 185. **Drafted:** HS—Lompoc, Calif., 2007 (3rd round). **Signed by:** Rick Schroeder.

After signing for $365,000 as a third-round pick in June, Duffy couldn't have been more dominant in the Rookie-level Arizona League. He struck out 15.2 batters per nine innings, posted a 1.45 ERA and went 37 innings without allowing a homer. Duffy already has an 89-92 mph fastball that tops out at 95, and he should add more velocity as he develops physically and fills out his frame. His curveball has the potential to give him a second plus pitch, while his slider can become solid-average. He hides the ball well in his delivery. Duffy's mechanics are extremely raw and hamper his command. He struggles at times to get extension in his delivery and to repeat his arm slot. He also has a tendency to rush toward the plate. His curveball remains inconsistent, and he doesn't have much of a changeup. Duffy should fit in the middle of a major league rotation, though not any time soon. He could open the season in low Class A but will be held back in extended spring training if he struggles in minor league camp.

Year	Club (League)	Class	W	L	ERA	G	GS	CG	SV	IP	H	R	ER	HR	BB	SO	AVG
2007	Royals (AZL)	R	2	3	1.45	11	9	0	0	37	24	14	6	0	17	63	.178
MINOR LEAGUE TOTALS			2	3	1.45	11	9	0	0	37	24	14	6	0	17	63	.178

7 CARLOS ROSA, RHP

Born: Sept. 21, 1984. **B-T:** R-R. **Ht.:** 6-1. **Wt.:** 185. **Signed:** Dominican Republic, 2001. **Signed by:** Luis Silverio.

After an impressive spring training that prompted some consideration for Rosa to break camp with the big league club, the Royals sent him to high Class A with the intention of promoting him in June. But he needed just four starts before it became apparent he was ready for a new challenge in Double-A. He has made a full recovery from Tommy John surgery in 2004. Rosa's fastball operates at 93-95 mph and touches 97, and it seems quicker because he has such an effortless delivery. His heater has late arm-side run, and he backs it up with a sharp curveball and a changeup. Both are effective secondary pitches, though he trusts his curve more. By focusing on pitching down and away, Rosa has developed a hesitancy to work inside on hitters. More advanced hitters in Double-A took advantage and knocked him around until he made some adjustments in August. He doesn't have much feel for his slider and would be better off just scrapping it. Rosa could make the Royals out of spring training as a reliever, but likely will open 2008 in the Double-A rotation.

Year	Club (League)	Class	W	L	ERA	G	GS	CG	SV	IP	H	R	ER	HR	BB	SO	AVG
2002	Royals (GCL)	R	0	4	6.19	10	9	0	0	32	52	32	22	3	12	11	.361
	Royals (DSL)	R	1	0	1.80	1	1	0	0	5	3	1	1	0	0	2	.167
2003	Royals (AZL)	R	5	3	3.63	15	11	0	0	69	79	36	28	4	18	54	.288
2004	Royals (AZL)	R	0	0	4.91	4	4	0	0	11	14	6	6	1	9	8	.326
	Burlington (MWL)	A	0	5	4.67	8	8	0	0	34	41	24	18	1	17	23	.297
2006	Burlington (MWL)	A	8	6	2.53	24	24	1	0	138	121	50	39	6	54	102	.239
	High Desert (Cal)	A	0	1	7.15	3	3	0	0	11	20	12	9	1	4	13	.392
2007	Wilmington (Car)	A	2	1	0.39	4	4	0	0	23	18	2	1	0	3	15	.209
	Wichita (TL)	AA	6	6	4.36	21	17	0	1	97	101	50	47	8	43	70	.272
MINOR LEAGUE TOTALS			22	26	3.65	90	81	1	1	422	449	213	171	24	160	298	.275

8 JULIO PIMENTEL, RHP

Born: Dec. 14, 1985. **B-T:** R-R. **Ht.:** 6-1. **Wt.:** 190. **Signed:** Dominican Republic, 2003. **Signed by:** Pablo Peguero/Angel Santana (Dodgers).

Pimentel completed his tour of high Class A with a 2007 stint in the Carolina Leauge. He previously made stops in the Florida State League as a Dodger, and in the California League after joining the Royals in the July 2006 Elmer Dessens trade. Primarily a reliever in 2006, Pimentel pitched almost exclusively as a starter last year. Pimentel has two above-average pitches in a lively 90-93 mph fastball and a changeup with late fade that can be a swing-and-miss pitch. He mixes in an improved curveball that has some sharp, late break. He showed his competitiveness by pitching out of a no-out, bases-loaded jam in the decisive CL playoff game, though he eventually took the loss. Pimentel's curveball is average at best and he struggles to control it at times. He needs better command, pitches too much to contact and has a bafflingly low strikeout rate for someone with two plus pitches. Pimentel's improving curveball should keep him in the rotation for now, but he may profile best as a late-inning reliever. He'll pitch out of the Double-A rotation in 2008.

Year	Club (League)	Class	W	L	ERA	G	GS	CG	SV	IP	H	R	ER	HR	BB	SO	AVG
2003	Dodgers N (DSL)	R	1	1	4.09	8	3	0	0	22	17	12	10	1	13	24	.221
2004	Columbus (SAL)	A	10	8	3.48	23	23	2	0	111	106	56	43	14	47	102	.260
2005	Vero Beach (FSL)	A	8	10	5.08	26	24	1	0	124	149	79	70	9	43	105	.305
2006	Vero Beach (FSL)	A	3	8	5.69	30	9	0	2	74	85	56	47	4	45	77	.290
	High Desert (Cal)	A	2	1	3.18	12	0	0	2	22	21	8	8	3	10	26	.244
2007	Wilmington (Car)	A	12	4	2.65	27	22	0	0	152	145	56	45	8	43	73	.250
MINOR LEAGUE TOTALS			36	32	3.96	126	81	3	4	507	523	267	223	39	201	407	.271

9 MATT MITCHELL, RHP

Born: March 31, 1989. **B-T:** R-R. **Ht.:** 6-2. **Wt.:** 205. **Drafted:** HS—Barstow, Calif., 2007 (14th round). **Signed by:** John Ramey.

The Royals might come away with one of the steals of the 2007 draft after finding Mitchell in the small southern California town of Barstow and signing him for $100,000 as a 14th-rounder. The secret was out once he won the Arizona League ERA title (1.80). Mitchell was able to correct an early tendency of pitching up in the strike zone by getting better extension in his delivery and throwing on more of a downhill plane. Advanced for a high school pitcher, Mitchell locates an 88-92 mph fastball to both sides of the plate and shows an ability to throw it for strike one. He uses his secondary pitches a lot for a young pitcher, including a palm changeup and a curveball with 11-to-5 break when it's on. He hides the ball well with a smooth delivery, similar to Curt Schilling's, which makes it hard for hitters to time his arm speed. Mitchell is still working on feel for his curveball, which has inconsistent trajectory and rotation. He's still figuring out his mechanics and needs to repeat his delivery on a more regular basis. Kansas City is thrilled with Mitchell so far and thinks it could have a future mid-rotation starter. He'll compete with fellow 2007 high school draftees Daniel Duffy and Sam Runion for spots in the low Class A rotation this year.

Year	Club (League)	Class	W	L	ERA	G	GS	CG	SV	IP	H	R	ER	HR	BB	SO	AVG
2007	Royals (AZL)	R	5	1	1.80	14	7	0	1	55	34	16	11	0	25	72	.183
MINOR LEAGUE TOTALS			5	1	1.80	14	7	0	1	55	34	16	11	0	25	72	.183

10 YASUHIKO YABUTA, RHP

Born: June 19, 1973. **B-T:** R-R. **Ht.:** 6-2. **Wt.:** 190. **Signed:** Japan, 2007. **Signed by:** Louie Medina/Rene Francisco.

The first Japanese free agent ever signed by the Royals, Yabuta agreed to a two-year contract worth $6 million in December. He spent his first eight years in Japan as a starter, but found more success when Bobby Valentine moved him to the bullpen in 2004. Yabuta registered 86 holds for the Chiba Lotte Mariners over the past three seasons and drew attention by striking out Alex Rodriguez, Derrek Lee and Johnny Damon during the World Baseball Classic. Royals director of international operations Rene Francisco and special assistant Louie Medina discovered Yabuta while spending considerable time in Japan as part of the team's increased Pacific Rim presence. New manager Trey Hillman, who spent the past five years skippering the Hokkaido Nippon Ham Fighters, confirmed their positive reports. Yabuta throws a 90-92 mph fastball and controls the pitch down in the strike zone. His out pitch is a plus changeup with some late fade. It's deceptive because he deploys it with the same arm action as his fastball. He use his changeup and a forkball to keep lefthanders at bay. He throws strikes with ease. Yabuta struggled as a starter because he didn't have a good breaking ball. Coming out of the bullpen, he doesn't use his slider as much. The track record of Japanese relievers in the U.S. majors is strong, but he still has to adjust to big league hitters and an entirely new culture. The Royals will immediately plug Yabuta into their big league bullpen. With David Riske departing as a free agent, Yubota will be the primary setup man for Joakim Soria.

Year	Club (League)	Class	W	L	ERA	G	GS	CG	SV	IP	H	R	ER	HR	BB	SO	AVG
1996	Chiba Lotte (PL)	JAP	4	6	3.62	18	10	1	0	92	79	39	37	8	29	58	—
1997	Chiba Lotte (PL)	JAP	5	9	3.94	25	20	4	0	146	144	69	64	16	48	74	—
1998	Chiba Lotte (PL)	JAP	2	9	4.84	17	14	2	0	100	123	61	54	15	40	45	—
1999	Chiba Lotte (PL)	JAP	5	4	4.89	12	10	0	0	57	68	33	31	9	30	33	—
2000	Chiba Lotte (PL)	JAP	0	1	13.50	2	2	0	0	7	9	10	10	3	2	3	—
2001	Chiba Lotte (PL)	JAP	4	6	3.88	27	13	0	0	97	94	46	42	15	40	70	—
2002	Chiba Lotte (PL)	JAP	1	2	8.74	3	3	0	0	11	16	11	11	4	4	8	—
2003	Chiba Lotte (PL)	JAP	5	6	5.90	17	13	0	0	69	74	45	45	12	27	44	—
2004	Chiba Lotte (PL)	JAP	3	4	2.79	66	1	0	2	77	62	26	24	4	34	71	—
2005	Chiba Lotte (PL)	JAP	7	4	3.07	51	0	0	2	56	42	20	19	7	13	54	—
2006	Chiba Lotte (PL)	JAP	4	2	2.62	47	0	0	1	55	43	19	16	3	26	48	—
2007	Chiba Lotte (PL)	JAP	4	6	2.73	58	0	0	4	63	64	21	19	5	10	45	—
JAPAN LEAGUE TOTALS			44	59	4.03	343	86	7	9	830	818	400	372	101	303	553	—

11 DERRICK ROBINSON, OF

Born: Sept. 28, 1987. **B-T:** B-L. **Ht.:** 5-11. **Wt.:** 170. **Drafted:** HS—Gainesville, Fla., 2006 (4th round). **Signed by:** Cliff Pastornicky.

The best athlete in the system, Robinson abandoned a football scholarship to Florida to sign with the Royals for $850,000 in 2006. Speed is Robinson's biggest tool and it is beginning to show on the basepaths. He's a slightly above-average basestealer now but has good instincts and should continue to improve as his timing and jumps get better. He stole 35 bases in 42 attempts in 2007 after being caught 14 times in 34 attempts in 2006. Robinson's ceiling is that of a prototypical leadoff hitter with a little extra pop in his bat, with one Royals official comparing him to a young Kenny Lofton. He's still raw offensively, however, and did not work counts well as the Royals encouraged him to learn to hit the ball first and develop discipline later. He did improve his approach at the plate by spreading out his stance and creating a better base. Robinson is an above-average defender and continues to improve his routes. The team had him play a shallow center field last year to get a better feel for going back on the ball. The Royals believe Robinson has the potential to be a special player and will take their time with his development. He may begin 2008 back in Burlington but should move up to high Class A quickly.

Year	Club (League)	Class	AVG	G	AB	R	H	2B	3B	HR	RBI	BB	SO	SB	OBP	SLG
2006	Royals (AZL)	R	.233	54	176	25	41	6	3	1	24	24	55	20	.335	.318
2007	Burlington (MWL)	A	.243	102	407	42	99	11	3	2	26	32	100	34	.299	.300
	Wilmington (Car)	A	.385	3	13	1	5	1	0	0	0	1	0	1	.429	.462
MINOR LEAGUE TOTALS			.243	159	596	68	145	18	6	3	50	57	155	55	.313	.309

12 SAM RUNION, RHP

Born: Nov. 9, 1988. **B-T:** R-R. **Ht.:** 6-4. **Wt.:** 220. **Drafted:** HS—Asheville, N.C., 2007 (2nd round). **Signed by:** Steve Connelly.

Runion was the first of three consecutive high school pitchers taken by the Royals in the 2007 draft, an indication of the team's commitment to developing young arms. Though outshone by fellow '07 selections Danny Duffy (third) and Matt Mitchell (14th) in the Arizona League last summer, Runion's stuff was better than his lofty ERA indicated. Signed for $504,000 as a second-rounder, he showed one of the better fastballs in the Arizona League, a 90-94 mph offering that jumps on hitters with late life and movement. And he may have more in the tank as he fills out. His secondary pitches remain a work in progress, including a changeup, slider and a sloppy curveball. Runion throws from a three-quarters arm slot and was working in instructional league to get tighter rotation on his offspeed and breaking pitches while maintaining his arm speed. Though his stuff may play better out of the bullpen in the short term, the Royals want to give him a chance to develop his secondary pitches and think he'll have the durability to be a starter. He'll likely join Duffy and Mitchell in the low Class A rotation in 2008.

Year	Club (League)	Class	W	L	ERA	G	GS	CG	SV	IP	H	R	ER	HR	BB	SO	AVG
2007	Royals (AZL)	R	3	4	5.82	12	9	0	0	51	61	36	33	4	17	51	.310
MINOR LEAGUE TOTALS			3	4	5.82	12	9	0	0	51	61	36	33	4	17	51	.310

13 TYLER LUMSDEN, LHP

Born: May 9, 1983. **B-T:** R-L. **Ht.:** 6-4. **Wt.:** 215. **Drafted:** Clemson, 2004 (1st round supplemental). **Signed by:** Nick Hostetler (White Sox).

Lumsden appeared on the verge of the major leagues after a stellar 2006 campaign, and he was the key component of a midseason deal that also brought Daniel Cortes from the White Sox for Mike MacDougal. But he unraveled last season, frustrating team officials by occasionally showing off the best stuff in the system but often struggling with his command. Lumsden has an easy and seemingly effortless delivery. His fastball clocks at 91-92 mph, and he has a legitimate 12-to-6 curveball and a changeup that he can throw for strikes. Locating his pitches on a consistent basis was a challenge last season, however, particularly his fastball. He also was hesitant to throw his fastball inside to righthanders. In general he was too concerned with strikeouts and didn't pitch enough to contact. While he missed all of 2005 after arthroscopic surgery to remove bone chips from his elbow, Lumsden has shown no ill effects and his mechanics are fine. His command should improve as he matures. Lumsden will be a longshot to make the major league rotation out of spring training, but Kansas City did put him on the 40-man roster in November.

Year	Club (League)	Class	W	L	ERA	G	GS	CG	SV	IP	H	R	ER	HR	BB	SO	AVG
2004	Winston-Salem (Car)	A	3	1	4.12	15	3	0	0	39	45	25	18	2	20	31	.280
2005	Did Not Play—Injured																
2006	Birmingham (SL)	AA	9	4	2.69	20	20	0	0	123	114	47	37	9	40	72	.252
	Wichita (TL)	AA	2	1	3.06	7	6	0	0	35	35	12	12	3	20	24	.276
2007	Omaha (PCL)	AAA	9	6	5.88	25	24	0	0	119	141	89	78	11	59	74	.306
MINOR LEAGUE TOTALS			23	12	4.11	67	53	0	0	317	335	173	145	25	139	201	.279

14 BLAKE JOHNSON, RHP

Born: June 14, 1985. **B-T:** R-R. **Ht.:** 6-5. **Wt.:** 200. **Drafted:** HS—Baton Rouge, La., 2004 (2nd round). **Signed by:** Clarence Johns (Dodgers).

Dayton Moore made his focus on developing pitchers obvious from the time he took over as Royals general manager, and one of his first deals was getting Johnson and Odalis Perez in July 2006 for Elmer Dessens. After struggling in high Class A in 2006, Johnson spent all of last season with Wilmington and saw his ERA dip from 6.19 in six May starts to 1.40 in 26 innings in August. He corrected a flaw in which he collapsed a little in the back of his delivery, resulting in his arm slot getting too low and his pitches flattening out. By staying taller in his delivery he got more leverage and threw on more of a downhill plane, adding velocity to a 92 mph fastball that now reaches 94 and has improved by a full grade from 2006. Johnson mixes in a mid-70s curveball with good downward bite and an improving changeup with late sink that he throws with good arm action. Johnson can still be inconsistent with his command and struggles when he becomes too reliant on his curveball. He's ready to make the jump to Double-A.

Year	Club (League)	Class	W	L	ERA	G	GS	CG	SV	IP	H	R	ER	HR	BB	SO	AVG
2004	Ogden (Pio)	R	3	3	6.47	13	12	0	0	57	73	46	41	5	19	57	.324
2005	Columbus (SAL)	A	9	4	3.33	24	17	1	0	100	83	47	37	4	36	88	.226
2006	Vero Beach (FSL)	A	4	5	4.92	20	18	0	0	106	121	70	58	11	19	73	.285
	High Desert (Cal)	A	1	1	5.73	3	2	0	0	11	15	7	7	1	0	9	.319
2007	Wilmington (Car)	A	9	6	3.28	26	22	1	1	131	119	52	48	7	33	80	.244
MINOR LEAGUE TOTALS			26	19	4.24	86	71	2	1	405	411	222	191	28	107	307	.265

15 RYAN BRAUN, RHP

Born: July 29, 1980. **B-T:** R-R. **Ht.:** 6-1. **Wt.:** 220. **Drafted:** Nevada-Las Vegas, 2003 (6th round). **Signed by:** Mike Brown.

For the second straight year, Braun overwhelmed minor league hitters with an arsenal that features a fastball that reaches 97 mph, a top-to-bottom curveball and a low-90s, late-breaking slider. He still has yet to translate that success to the major leagues, however, and he struggled after making the team out of spring training and again in a late-July callup. His major league ERA is a full four runs higher than his minor league mark. Command in the strike zone and overall inconsistency have been at the root of his problems. He can bury hitters by keeping his pitches down in the zone one inning and then get hit around by leaving those same pitches up the next inning. Key to his future role will be his ability to stay down in the zone and establish command in the majors, where he had a 24-22 K-BB ratio compared to 36-12 in Triple-A. Control problems have limited his projection. Once considered a closer in the making, Braun now looks more like a setup man.

Year	Club (League)	Class	W	L	ERA	G	GS	CG	SV	IP	H	R	ER	HR	BB	SO	AVG
2003	Royals (AZL)	R	0	0	2.95	18	0	0	3	21	15	9	7	0	10	25	.185
2004	Wilmington (Car)	A	2	3	2.21	51	0	0	23	57	48	25	14	2	25	58	.219
2005	Wichita (TL)	AA	0	1	17.36	6	0	0	0	4	15	10	9	0	7	1	.536
	High Desert (Cal)	A	1	0	4.50	2	0	0	0	4	3	2	2	0	2	6	.214
2006	Wichita (TL)	AA	1	6	2.21	26	0	0	10	40	30	11	10	2	16	58	.204
	Omaha (PCL)	AAA	0	2	2.16	17	0	0	3	25	23	9	6	0	13	22	.247
	Kansas City (AL)	MLB	0	1	6.75	9	0	0	0	10	13	8	8	2	3	6	.317
2007	Omaha (PCL)	AAA	2	2	1.09	23	0	0	9	33	19	7	4	1	12	36	.173
	Kansas City (AL)	MLB	2	0	6.64	26	0	0	0	39	46	32	29	4	22	24	.299
MINOR LEAGUE TOTALS			6	14	2.52	143	0	0	48	185	153	73	52	5	85	206	.221
MAJOR LEAGUE TOTALS			2	1	6.66	35	0	0	0	50	59	40	37	6	25	30	.303

16 CHRIS LUBANSKI, OF

Born: March 24, 1985. **B-T:** L-L. **Ht.:** 6-3. **Wt.:** 206. **Drafted:** HS—Schwenksville, Pa., 2003 (1st round). **Signed by:** Sean Rooney.

After getting off to slow starts before making second-half surges in each of his first three full seasons, Lubanski came out swinging last season in his return to the Texas League. A midseason leap to Triple-A was not so smooth, and he once again struggled in unfamiliar surroundings. He didn't fare much better in the Arizona Fall League, hitting just .200/.266/.412, and was left off the 40-man roster. Lubanski has long boasted one of the smoothest swings in the Royals system and has continued to add power as he filled out, though at the cost of speed. He showed an improved ability to drive the ball to all fields last season and better plate discipline. Lubanski now bears little resemblance to the speedy center fielder the Royals selected fifth overall in 2003. His bulk has pushed him to left field, where he's an average defender at best, and he's no longer a threat on the basepaths. Always trying to improve with a tireless work ethic, he also tends to doubt himself when things go wrong and guesses at the plate rather than trusting his swing. He should improve upon last year's performance while repeating Triple-A and make his major league debut.

Year	Club (League)	Class	AVG	G	AB	R	H	2B	3B	HR	RBI	BB	SO	SB	OBP	SLG
2003	Royals (AZL)	R	.326	53	221	41	72	4	6	4	27	18	50	9	.382	.452
2004	Burlington (MWL)	A	.275	127	483	64	133	26	7	9	56	43	104	16	.336	.414
2005	High Desert (Cal)	A	.301	126	531	91	160	38	6	28	116	38	131	14	.349	.554
2006	Wichita (TL)	AA	.282	137	524	93	148	34	11	15	70	72	112	11	.369	.475
2007	Wichita (TL)	AA	.295	64	241	33	71	14	3	9	34	28	43	3	.361	.490
	Omaha (PCL)	AAA	.208	49	168	20	35	6	1	6	22	16	48	0	.273	.363
MINOR LEAGUE TOTALS			.286	556	2168	342	619	122	34	71	325	215	488	53	.350	.471

17 JUSTIN HUBER, OF/1B

Born: July 1, 1982. **B-T:** R-R. **Ht.:** 6-2. **Wt.:** 205. **Signed:** Australia, 2000. **Signed by:** Fred Mazzuca/Omar Minaya (Mets).

Huber missed significant time for a second straight season, leaving Royals officials to ponder numbers that would project to 30-plus home runs over a full season. A productive enough player at the plate, Huber remains on the prospect map despite not really profiling anywhere with the Royals after a third season in

Triple-A. Knee injuries forced him from behind the plate after he was acquired from the Mets in 2004. He split time last season between right field and first base but is not great at either position. He has plenty of arm to play either corner outfield position but lacks instincts. He showed improved footwork and a better understanding of first base, and that could be where he ultimately lands. It's Huber's bat that will determine his big league success. One team official compared him to a Matt Diaz, a player without an obvious position who can hit .300 with power if given 300 at-bats. Huber has good strike-zone discipline and drives the ball to all fields and would be a DH candidate if Billy Butler could play first base. Out of options, Huber needs to make the big league club out of spring training or else be exposed to waivers.

Year	Club (League)	Class	AVG	G	AB	R	H	2B	3B	HR	RBI	BB	SO	SB	OBP	SLG
2001	St. Lucie (FSL)	A	.000	2	6	0	0	0	0	0	0	0	2	0	.000	.000
	Kingsport (Appy)	R	.314	47	159	24	50	11	1	7	31	17	42	4	.415	.528
	Brooklyn (NYP)	A	.000	3	9	0	0	0	0	0	0	0	4	0	.000	.000
2002	St. Lucie (FSL)	A	.270	28	100	15	27	2	1	3	15	11	18	0	.370	.400
	Columbia (SAL)	A	.291	95	330	49	96	22	2	11	78	45	81	1	.408	.470
2003	St. Lucie (FSL)	A	.284	50	183	26	52	15	0	9	36	17	30	1	.370	.514
	Binghamton (EL)	AA	.264	55	193	16	51	13	0	6	36	19	54	0	.350	.425
2004	St. Lucie (FSL)	A	.245	14	49	10	12	2	0	2	8	5	8	1	.327	.408
	Binghamton (EL)	AA	.271	70	236	44	64	16	1	11	33	46	57	2	.414	.487
	Norfolk (IL)	AAA	.313	5	16	3	5	2	0	0	3	3	3	0	.421	.438
2005	Wichita (TL)	AA	.343	88	335	68	115	22	3	16	74	51	70	7	.432	.570
	Omaha (PCL)	AAA	.274	32	113	19	31	6	1	7	23	16	33	3	.374	.531
	Kansas City (AL)	MLB	.218	25	78	6	17	3	0	0	6	5	20	0	.271	.256
2006	Kansas City (AL)	MLB	.200	5	10	1	2	1	0	0	1	1	4	1	.273	.300
	Omaha (PCL)	AAA	.278	100	352	47	98	22	2	15	44	40	94	2	.358	.480
2007	Royals (AZL)	R	.360	7	25	4	9	4	0	2	7	2	4	0	.414	.760
	Omaha (PCL)	AAA	.276	77	286	39	79	13	1	18	68	20	48	1	.336	.517
	Kansas City (AL)	MLB	.100	8	10	2	1	0	0	0	0	0	2	0	.100	.100
MINOR LEAGUE TOTALS			.288	673	2392	364	689	150	12	107	456	292	548	22	.383	.495
MAJOR LEAGUE TOTALS			.204	38	98	9	20	4	0	0	7	6	26	1	.255	.245

18 JEFF BIANCHI, SS

Born: Oct. 5, 1986. **B-T:** R-R. **Ht.:** 6-0. **Wt.:** 175. **Drafted:** HS—Lampeter, Pa., 2005 (2nd round). **Signed by:** Sean Rooney.

Expectations have dipped for Bianchi since back and shoulder injuries spoiled a sparkling pro debut in 2005. Once compared to Michael Young and expected to shoot through the farm system, Bianchi had mixed results in his first full professional season after missing most of 2006 due to labrum surgery. The Royals held him back in spring training to keep him out of cold weather in the Midwest League, and by season's end he started to show the form team officials once considered the best offensive approach they had seen by a high school player. He has a tendency to get out on his front foot too much, but can have a short, explosive swing when he lets the ball travel deep into the zone. Bianchi didn't hit his first home run until July and didn't show much power in the pitcher-friendly Midwest League, though he did hit .330 over 91 at-bats in August and September and hit in 12 of his first 13 games in Hawaii Winter Baseball. Bianchi has a strong enough arm to play shortstop and has average range. Injuries have sapped some of his flair and confidence since he was first drafted, and his long-term future may be at second base. Going into spring training, he'll compete with fellow prospect Chris McConnell for the shortstop gig in high Class A.

Year	Club (League)	Class	AVG	G	AB	R	H	2B	3B	HR	RBI	BB	SO	SB	OBP	SLG
2005	Royals (AZL)	R	.408	28	98	29	40	7	4	6	30	16	22	5	.484	.745
2006	Royals (AZL)	R	.429	12	42	13	18	4	0	2	6	9	3	1	.537	.667
2007	Burlington (MWL)	A	.247	99	368	43	91	19	0	2	36	25	72	15	.296	.315
MINOR LEAGUE TOTALS			.293	139	508	85	149	30	4	10	72	50	97	21	.358	.427

19 BRENT FISHER, LHP

Born: Aug. 6, 1987. **B-T:** L-L. **Ht.:** 6-2. **Wt.:** 190. **Drafted:** HS—Goodyear, Ariz., 2005 (7th round). **Signed by:** Mike Brown.

Fisher didn't get a lot of attention as an amateur because he didn't have an overpowering fastball, but he drew attention in his first two seasons in the organization with strong performances. He made just nine appearances for Burlington in 2007, however, before being shut down with a strained rotator cuff. The Royals had high hopes for him after he won the strikeout title in his second season in the Arizona League in 2006, and because of his youth they expect him to bounce back this season. Fisher features a 90-92 mph fastball that plays up because of his deceptive delivery, to the point that teammates have labeled it the "invisi-ball." He keeps his front side closed and the ball behind him for a long time, making it difficult for hitters to time him. He mixes in an average curveball that he can spot well, and a changeup that he still needs improvement. The team is eager to see how he fares against higher-level hitters, but he'll go back to low Class A to start 2008.

Year	Club (League)	Class	W	L	ERA	G	GS	CG	SV	IP	H	R	ER	HR	BB	SO	AVG
2005	Royals (AZL)	R	5	2	3.04	13	8	0	1	50	48	20	17	2	13	69	.249
2006	Royals (AZL)	R	3	1	2.11	14	14	0	0	68	41	18	16	2	19	98	.171
	Idaho Falls (Pio)	R	0	0	2.25	1	0	0	1	4	2	1	1	1	0	9	.143
2007	Burlington (MWL)	A	1	4	5.09	9	5	0	1	35	46	24	20	3	14	28	.322
MINOR LEAGUE TOTALS			9	7	3.08	37	27	0	3	158	137	63	54	8	46	204	.232

20 NEAL MUSSER, LHP

Born: Aug. 25, 1980. **B-T:** L-L. **Ht.:** 6-1. **Wt.:** 235. **Drafted:** HS—Oxford, Ind., 1999 (2nd round). **Signed by:** Joe Morlan (Mets).

The Mets had visions of the next Tom Glavine when they drafted Musser with the 73rd overall pick in 1999, but a variety of injuries and control problems limited his development and they finally released him following the 2005 season. The Royals signed Musser following his brief stint with the Diamondbacks and moved him to the bullpen, a role in which he has thrived. His strong 2006 Arizona Fall League performance prompted Kansas City to add him to the 40-man roster. Musser earned big league promotions three times in 2007, the last ending when he broke his right hand punching a chair in the clubhouse after giving up a game-winning run. He recovered in time to help Team USA win gold in the World Cup. Rather than focus on conserving energy as a starter, Musser lets it all out in each relief appearance and has seen his fastball velocity increase from 88-92 mph to 92-95. Musser dominated as a Triple-A reliever and didn't give up an earned run until his 27th appearance. He pitches exclusively out of the stretch and displays a lively fastball that tails late from a three-quarters arm slot. His go-to pitch is a slider that has some width and depth and that he can control down in the zone. He's added a cut fastball and his changeup is serviceable. Musser should make the big league team out of spring training as the first or second reliever out of the bullpen.

Year	Club (League)	Class	W	L	ERA	G	GS	CG	SV	IP	H	R	ER	HR	BB	SO	AVG
1999	Mets (GCL)	R	2	1	2.01	8	7	0	0	31	26	13	7	1	18	22	.224
2000	Kingsport (Appy)	R	3	2	2.10	7	7	0	0	34	33	10	8	1	6	21	.252
2001	Columbia (SAL)	A	7	4	2.84	17	17	1	0	95	86	38	30	3	18	98	.240
	St. Lucie (FSL)	A	3	4	3.55	9	9	0	0	45	45	24	18	2	19	40	.257
2002	Brooklyn (NYP)	A	0	0	0.69	4	4	0	0	13	7	2	1	0	5	12	.163
	St. Lucie (FSL)	A	2	0	1.42	4	4	0	0	19	20	4	3	1	5	12	.274
2003	St. Lucie (FSL)	A	3	0	4.67	7	6	0	0	34	41	20	18	5	9	16	.293
	Binghamton (EL)	AA	5	9	4.57	20	20	0	0	100	108	57	51	9	39	76	.282
2004	Norfolk (IL)	AAA	2	4	6.25	7	7	0	0	36	39	30	25	4	17	24	.291
	Binghamton (EL)	AA	9	6	3.41	19	19	0	0	108	103	52	41	7	40	70	.257
2005	Norfolk (IL)	AAA	6	11	5.02	24	24	0	0	123	140	75	69	12	52	89	.287
2006	Tucson (PCL)	AAA	1	3	5.45	8	7	0	0	36	44	26	22	4	24	18	.306
	Omaha (PCL)	AAA	1	0	1.86	2	2	0	0	9	7	2	2	0	2	6	.200
	Wichita (TL)	AA	6	3	4.95	18	11	0	2	83	80	53	46	12	48	67	.255
2007	Omaha (PCL)	AAA	4	1	0.49	32	0	0	8	55	32	5	3	1	11	47	.173
	Kansas City (AL)	MLB	0	1	4.38	17	0	0	0	24	32	13	12	5	14	19	.314
MINOR LEAGUE TOTALS			54	48	3.75	186	144	1	10	826	811	411	344	64	314	618	.260
MAJOR LEAGUE TOTALS			0	1	4.38	17	0	0	0	24	32	13	12	5	14	19	.314

21 FERNANDO CRUZ, 3B

Born: March 28, 1990. **B-T:** B-R. **Ht.:** 6-2. **Wt.:** 184. **Signed:** HS—Dorado, P.R., 2007 (6th round). **Signed by:** Johnny Ramos.

Cruz successfully petitioned the commissioner's office to enter the draft a year early after meeting high school diploma requirements as a 17-year-old home-schooled student. That meant he was late coming onto the draft scene, first drawing wide attention at a May scouting combine in Puerto Rico. Some scouts believed he could be a first- or second-rounder if he had to wait until the 2008 draft, so the Royals think he could be a steal after signing him for $125,000. Cruz has the tools to be above-average at the plate and in the field. A converted shortstop, he has a 70 arm (on the 20-80 scouting scale) and soft hands, but needs to improve his first-step quickness. He has the swing and power potential that draw comparisons to Carlos Beltran, with tremendous bat speed from both sides of the plate, projectable power and a smooth swing with some natural loft. He generates his power from a strong lower half, and as his upper-body fills out he should show it more in games. Cruz is raw and often struggles with plate discipline and pitch selection, and can look like a different player from one pitch to the next. The Royals consider his time on the practice field and with hitting instructors as valuable at-bats at this point, and he'll stay in extended spring training before reporting to a short-season affiliate.

Year	Club (League)	Class	AVG	G	AB	R	H	2B	3B	HR	RBI	BB	SO	SB	OBP	SLG
2007	Royals (AZL)	R	.210	48	181	14	38	5	1	1	15	8	43	0	.254	.265
MINOR LEAGUE TOTALS			.210	48	181	14	38	5	1	1	15	8	43	0	.254	.265

22 DAVID LOUGH, OF

Born: Jan. 20, 1986. **B-T:** L-L. **Ht.:** 6-0. **Wt.:** 180. **Drafted:** Mercyhurst (Pa.), 2007 (11th round). **Signed by:** Jason Bryans.

The athletic outfielder doubled as a wide receiver/kickoff return specialist for Mercyhurst's football team before matching the school's single-season hits record (74) while slugging .689 in the spring. One of several speedy outfielders selected by the Royals in the 2007 draft, Lough went in the 11th round and signed for $49,500. He's a well-above-average runner with a promising, though raw, approach at the plate. His impressive pro debut was slowed by a hamstring strain that factored in his stealing just six bases in seven attempts. He showed a consistent lefthanded swing path with raw power potential. He was a little too pull-conscious, but when he stayed back on the ball he showed power to the opposite field with backspin and carry. Lough has the speed to bat leadoff but could move down the lineup as his power develops. He was more polished in center field, where he showed plenty of range and an above-average arm. Lough will compete with fellow rookie outfielders Patrick Norris and Adrian Ortiz for a spot in the high Class A lineup.

Year	Club (League)	Class	AVG	G	AB	R	H	2B	3B	HR	RBI	BB	SO	SB	OBP	SLG
2007	Burlington (Appy)	R	.337	24	86	15	29	6	0	2	12	4	13	6	.380	.477
MINOR LEAGUE TOTALS			.337	24	86	15	29	6	0	2	12	4	13	6	.380	.477

23 MITCH MAIER, OF

Born: June 30, 1982. **B-T:** L-R. **Ht.:** 6-2. **Wt.:** 210. **Drafted:** Toledo, 2003 (1st round). **Signed by:** Jason Bryans.

Maier has been able to match the offensive promise of his professional debut following his first-round selection in 2003. And after playing catcher and third base early in his pro career, Maier has emerged as a steady defensive center fielder. But he has not been consistent enough at the plate to settle the question of whether he's more than a fourth outfielder. He worked with Omaha hitting coach Terry Bradshaw to get his hands in a better load position. The change—he now has the bat off his left shoulder when it was previously wrapped with the barrel pointed to center field—has helped him get ready to hit and shorten a swing that tended to get a little long. He hovered around .300 for most of the season before an August slump in which he hit .222. He still strikes out too much, but the organization may accept that as part of his profile. Maier has defensive instincts, gets good reads on balls, and has enough arm to play any outfield position. Though not a basestealer, Maier has average speed and is a competent baserunner. A hard worker with good makeup, he'll have a shot to make the big league club out of spring training.

Year	Club (League)	Class	AVG	G	AB	R	H	2B	3B	HR	RBI	BB	SO	SB	OBP	SLG
2003	Royals (AZL)	R	.350	51	203	41	71	14	6	2	45	18	25	7	.403	.507
2004	Burlington (MWL)	A	.300	82	317	41	95	24	3	4	36	27	51	34	.354	.432
	Wilmington (Car)	A	.264	51	174	25	46	9	2	3	17	15	29	9	.326	.391
2005	High Desert (Cal)	A	.336	50	211	42	71	26	1	8	32	12	43	6	.370	.583
	Wichita (TL)	AA	.255	80	322	55	82	21	5	7	49	15	47	10	.289	.416
2006	Wichita (TL)	AA	.306	138	543	95	166	35	7	14	92	41	96	13	.357	.473
	Kansas City (AL)	MLB	.154	5	13	3	2	0	0	0	0	2	4	0	.267	.154
2007	Omaha (PCL)	AAA	.279	140	544	75	152	29	5	14	62	33	89	7	.320	.428
MINOR LEAGUE TOTALS			.295	592	2314	374	683	158	29	52	333	161	380	86	.342	.456
MAJOR LEAGUE TOTALS			.154	5	13	3	2	0	0	0	0	2	4	0	.267	.154

24 CHRIS McCONNELL, SS/2B

Born: Dec. 18, 1985. **B-T:** R-R. **Ht.:** 5-11. **Wt.:** 175. **Drafted:** HS—Franklinville, N.J., 2004 (9th round). **Signed by:** Sean Rooney.

The Royals were too late finding McConnell in 2004 to send a crosschecker to see him. Instead area scout Sean Rooney borrowed a home video of McConnell's at-bats filmed by his mother, and team officials were impressed enough to give him a bargain bonus of $40,000. The team thought it had a steal after McConnell's tremendous pro debuts in 2004 and '05, but then tinkered with his awkward swing and McConnell responded by hitting just .211 in 2006. He may have turned the corner in re-establishing himself at the plate last season despite hitting just .233. McConnell's defense is what will get him to the big leagues, and the Royals would like to see him take a more conservative approach at the plate to help his advancement, learning to hit behind runners and bunt. While he has some power for a player his size, his swing gets a little long and he needs to stay on top of the ball. Defensively, McConnell could be ready for the big leagues. He has a plus arm that has improved significantly since he was drafted, and he can throw from three different angles. He has above-average range and made just three errors in Wilmington after his promotion. He split time at short with Bianchi in low Class A and the two will compete for the job in high Class A this year.

Year	Club (League)	Class	AVG	G	AB	R	H	2B	3B	HR	RBI	BB	SO	SB	OBP	SLG
2004	Royals (AZL)	R	.339	37	124	22	42	5	0	3	11	17	19	8	.420	.452
2005	Idaho Falls (Pio)	R	.331	70	275	56	91	17	8	6	39	31	34	7	.403	.516
2006	Burlington (MWL)	A	.172	69	239	23	41	4	0	1	18	17	47	8	.254	.201
	Idaho Falls (Pio)	R	.262	47	183	25	48	8	4	4	35	15	35	8	.320	.415
2007	Burlington (MWL)	A	.231	57	212	25	49	12	1	1	14	20	36	14	.311	.311
	Wilmington (Car)	A	.236	66	208	20	49	9	2	3	20	16	43	6	.303	.341
MINOR LEAGUE TOTALS			.258	346	1241	171	320	55	15	18	137	116	214	51	.332	.370

25 JOSE DUARTE, OF

Born: March 7, 1985. **B-T:** R-R. **Ht.:** 5-10. **Wt.:** 165. **Signed:** Venezuela, 2004. **Signed by:** Juan Indriago.

Duarte stole more than 30 bases for the second consecutive season and turned in his most consistent season at the plate as a professional, earning recognition from the organization as the top position player on the Wilmington squad. Duarte has a quick bat and a good path to the ball but needs to improve his plate discipline and pitch recognition. Thin and lanky with a physique that draws comparisons to Doug Glanville, Duarte is still developing physically and does not project to hit for much power. He has above-average speed, though not considered a burner, and is an advanced basestealer. His speed translates best in center field, where he has above-average range and is an instinctive defender who gets jumps and reads on balls. Duarte ranks as the best defensive outfielder and has the best outfield arm in the system, and is advanced enough to fill the position in Kansas City. Duarte's future depends on his development at the plate. He'll begin next season in Double-A.

Year	Club (League)	Class	AVG	G	AB	R	H	2B	3B	HR	RBI	BB	SO	SB	OBP	SLG
2004	Royals (DSL)	R	.317	58	221	51	70	12	4	2	40	42	39	10	.428	.434
2005	Royals (AZL)	R	.309	47	178	33	55	7	6	3	36	25	32	11	.388	.466
2006	Burlington (MWL)	A	.266	127	466	65	124	24	5	1	38	49	99	31	.338	.345
2007	Wilmington (Car)	A	.290	128	493	82	143	26	5	1	42	48	77	34	.356	.369
MINOR LEAGUE TOTALS			.289	360	1358	231	392	69	20	7	156	164	247	86	.367	.384

26 JOE DICKERSON, OF

Born: Oct. 3, 1986. **B-T:** L-L. **Ht.:** 6-1. **Wt.:** 190. **Drafted:** HS—Yorba Linda, Calif., 2005 (4th round). **Signed by:** John Ramey.

After a pair of standout seasons in the Rookie-level Arizona and Pioneer leagues, Dickerson made a fine full-season debut as a 20-year-old, ranking among the Midwest League leaders in batting. An early-season adjustment, in which Dickerson steadied his base by correcting a tendency to move his feet in the batter's box, paid off when he batted .302 after the all-star break. The adjustment allowed him to use his hands better and turn on balls on the inside half of the plate. He has average to above-average speed but is not an advanced basestealer, indicated by being caught 13 times in 39 steal attempts. Dickerson is still filling out and his power numbers should improve over time. Where Dickerson fits in the outfield is a question. He may not have the speed and range for center field and would need to develop significantly more power at the plate to stick at a corner outfield spot. Dickerson has drawn comparisons to Brad Wilkerson as a potential corner outfielder who can play center, and he will begin 2008 in high Class A.

Year	Club (League)	Class	AVG	G	AB	R	H	2B	3B	HR	RBI	BB	SO	SB	OBP	SLG
2005	Royals (AZL)	R	.294	56	214	27	63	12	9	4	40	27	46	9	.371	.491
2006	Idaho Falls (Pio)	R	.281	63	242	36	68	14	3	7	38	19	34	9	.338	.450
2007	Burlington (MWL)	A	.289	115	419	50	121	23	2	3	43	38	76	26	.354	.375
MINOR LEAGUE TOTALS			.288	234	875	113	252	49	14	14	121	84	156	44	.354	.424

27 KEATON HAYENGA, RHP

Born: July 10, 1988; **B-T:** R-R. **Ht.:** 6-5. **Wt.:** 180. **Drafted:** HS—Eastlake, Wash., 2007 (31st round). **Signed by:** Scott Ramsay.

Hayenga was considered among the top high school pitchers in Washington before tearing his labrum sliding into third base last spring. Washington State still considered him one of its most important signings in years, but the Royals went well above the slot recommendation for picks after the fifth round with a $300,000 bonus to lure him away from college. A good athlete who led his high school basketball team in scoring and rebounding, Hayenga has a projectable body and was considered an early-round pick before the injury. He throws a lively 88-92 mph fastball and mixes in an average sweeping curve with good deception and late bite that could develop into a plus pitch. His changeup is a work in progress. The Royals have been impressed with his makeup and dedication to his offseason rehab program and he'll likely make his pro debut in short-season ball.

Year	Club (League)	Class	W	L	ERA	G	GS	CG	SV	IP	H	R	ER	HR	BB	SO	AVG
2007	Did Not Play—Injured																

28 DUSTY HUGHES, LHP

Born: June 29, 1982. **B-T:** L-L. **Ht.:** 5-10. **Wt.:** 187. **Drafted:** Delta State (Miss.), 2003 (11th round). **Signed by:** Mark Willoughby.

Hughes tossed a complete-game win at an NCAA Division II regional in his collegiate finale and combined on a no-hitter in his full-season debut in 2004, retiring 22 consecutive batters for Burlington. Since then he's had to battle to keep his career going. Hughes missed 2006 after undergoing Tommy John surgery at the end of 2005, but he rebounded in 2007 with his best pro season. He was named Double-A Wichita's pitcher of the year and went 1-0, 2.45 in the Arizona Fall League. The Royals did not protect him on the 40-man roster, however. Hughes mixes an average 88-91 mph fastball with a plus changeup that is equally effective against lefties and righties. He's still working to establish a reliable breaking ball. Hughes may profile best as a reliever, but the Royals plan to keep him in the rotation next season, beginning in Triple-A.

Year	Club (League)	Class	W	L	ERA	G	GS	CG	SV	IP	H	R	ER	HR	BB	SO	AVG
2003	Royals (AZL)	R	5	2	2.84	11	6	0	0	50	38	21	16	4	18	54	.207
2004	Burlington (MWL)	A	4	2	1.56	8	8	0	0	52	39	12	9	2	15	36	.213
	Wilmington (Car)	A	5	5	2.41	18	18	0	0	108	95	37	29	5	31	68	.245
2005	High Desert (Cal)	A	5	7	5.67	19	19	0	0	92	119	74	58	13	45	87	.319
2006	Did Not Play—Injured																
2007	Wichita (TL)	AA	6	2	3.08	25	16	1	1	108	98	44	37	5	45	77	.240
MINOR LEAGUE TOTALS			25	18	3.26	81	67	1	1	411	389	188	149	29	154	322	.253

29 MIKE AVILES, INF

Born: March 13, 1981. **B-T:** R-R. **Ht.:** 5-9. **Wt.:** 205. **Drafted:** Concordia (N.Y.), 2003 (7th round). **Signed by:** Steve Connelly.

The former Division II player of the year has moved level-to-level through the Royals system after signing for $1,000 out of the 2003 draft, part of an organization cost-cutting effort that focused around drafting college seniors. Aviles has always displayed a short, compact swing and quick bat, and turned in his best year as a professional in his second stint in Triple-A. He's a gap hitter with some power who has the potential to balance a big league lineup in a utility role. Though Aviles has plenty of arm to play shortstop, he lacks range and touch for the position and profiles best as an offensive-minded second baseman. The Royals left him off the 40-man roster but still feel he could be a contributor in the big leagues. He'll compete for a major league job in spring training but is more likely headed back for another year in Triple-A, waiting for an opportunity to open up.

Year	Club (League)	Class	AVG	G	AB	R	H	2B	3B	HR	RBI	BB	SO	SB	OBP	SLG
2003	Royals (AZL)	R	.363	52	212	51	77	19	5	6	39	13	28	11	.404	.585
2004	Wilmington (Car)	A	.300	126	463	66	139	40	4	6	69	39	57	2	.352	.443
2005	Wichita (TL)	AA	.280	133	521	79	146	33	6	14	80	30	64	11	.318	.447
2006	Omaha (PCL)	AAA	.264	129	469	52	124	21	3	8	47	28	48	14	.307	.373
2007	Omaha (PCL)	AAA	.296	133	538	78	159	27	6	17	77	30	59	5	.332	.463
MINOR LEAGUE TOTALS			.293	573	2203	326	645	140	24	51	312	140	256	43	.335	.448

30 ROWDY HARDY, LHP

Born: Oct. 26, 1982. **B-T:** L-L. **Ht.:** 6-4. **Wt.:** 170. **Signed:** NDFA/Austin Peay State, 2006. **Signed by:** Spencer Graham.

Hardy won an Ohio Valley Conference-record 32 games with Austin Peay State and signed with the Royals for $1,000 as a fifth-year senior prior to the 2006 draft. He has continued to win as a professional, leading the Carolina League in victories and innings and ranking second in ERA last season, compiling one of the best seasons of any pitcher in the minor leagues. He succeeds with below-average stuff but with the best control in the system, evidenced by a 91-16 K-BB ratio last season and just 21 walks in 247 career innings. Hardy's fastball sits at just 82-84 mph and tops out at 86. He has plenty of movement on the pitch, locates it to both sides of the plate and has shown he's not afraid to pitch inside with it. He keeps hitters off balance with an above-average changeup with late sink that he uses almost as a variation of his fastball. Hardy's curveball is still developing and is not quite average, but he can locate it on the outer half or throw it as a backdoor pitch. Velocity is Hardy's biggest hurdle in developing as a starter, and how he fares against Double-A hitters this season will be telling. Scouts will always doubt him because his stuff is so short. Though compared by some to Jamie Moyer, Hardy may profile best a lefty specialist out of the bullpen because he may have difficulty making it through a lineup more than once.

Year	Club (League)	Class	W	L	ERA	G	GS	CG	SV	IP	H	R	ER	HR	BB	SO	AVG
2006	Idaho Falls (Pio)	R	5	3	2.80	15	15	0	0	80	79	29	25	4	5	52	.262
2007	Wilmington (Car)	A	15	5	2.48	26	22	3	1	167	144	52	46	6	16	91	.239
MINOR LEAGUE TOTALS			20	8	2.58	41	37	3	1	247	223	81	71	10	21	143	.247

Los Angeles Angels

BY ALAN MATTHEWS

Stability is something every major league organization strives for. But in the case of the Angels, stability already has gotten old.

With an excellent bullpen, improved defense and a resourceful manager orchestrating the offense, Los Angeles had the majors' best record at times last season before finishing with 94 wins, clinching its third American League West crown in four years.

But after being swept by the Red Sox in the first round, it was more than just the fans who were feeling frustrated. In five years since their 2002 World Series championship, the Angels have won four postseason games.

In 2007, Mike Scioscia may have done his best managerial job yet, filling out 126 different lineups while 13 players made 19 visits to the disabled list. But after watching his club get outscored 19-4 by Boston in the sweep, Scioscia vented about the team's need to acquire a power presence, and a few weeks later he found himself in chief position to make that happen.

General manager Bill Stoneman, who led Los Angeles to four playoff appearances in eight years and the only championship in franchise history, stepped down from his post, citing burnout. Owner Arte Moreno introduced Tony Reagins, who joined the Angels as an intern in 1992 and has served as farm director the past six years, as Stoneman's successor. Reagins' most important qualification may have been his strong working relationship with Scioscia. The moves indicated a clear shift in the club's epicenter toward Scioscia, who will have a larger voice in player procurement moving forward.

Los Angeles' first big move on Reagins' watch was the signing of free agent center fielder Torii Hunter to a five-year, $90 million contract. A week later, the Angels traded Orlando Cabera to the White Sox for Jon Garland, but they fell short in their attempts to trade for Miguel Cabrera, as the Tigers struck a deal for the former Marlins slugger.

The silver lining in the failure to land Cabrera is there's an opening for one of baseball's best power prospects, shortstop/third baseman Brandon Wood. Stoneman did a fine job at supplementing the big league roster without sacrificing young talent, but Scioscia's patience with youngsters might be waning. It remains to be seen if Wood will get his shot at an everyday role, as Chone Figgins and Maicer Itzuris are more proven options, albeit with less upside.

The farm system isn't as deep as it has been in

The face of the Angels franchise, manager Mike Scioscia has more say over the roster

TOP 30 PROSPECTS

1. Brandon Wood, 3b/ss	16. Trevor Reckling, lhp
2. Nick Adenhart, rhp	17. Matt Sweeney, 3b
3. Jordan Walden, rhp	18. Terry Evans, of
4. Hank Conger, c	19. Chris Pettit, of
5. Sean O'Sullivan, rhp	20. Barret Browning, lhp
6. Stephen Marek, rhp	21. Mason Tobin, rhp
7. Sean Rodriguez, ss/2b	22. Rich Thompson, rhp
8. Nick Green, rhp	23. Jerremy Haynes, rhp
9. Peter Bourjos, of	24. Jon Bachanov, rhp
10. Anel de los Santos, c	25. Bobby Wilson, c
11. Hainley Statia, ss	26. Jason Bulger, rhp
12. Jose Arredondo, rhp	27. Robert Fish, lhp
13. Young-Il Jung, rhp	28. Andrew Romine, ss
14. Ryan Mount, 2b	29. Mark Trumbo, 1b
15. P.J. Phillips, ss	30. Clay Fuller, of

years past, and Los Angeles was conservative in the 2007 draft, though they did spend $1 million to lock up draft-and-follow righty Jordan Walden. The Angels didn't take any of their trademark gambles and spent just $1.8 million to sign players, the second-lowest total in baseball. Their top pick, supplemental first-round righty Jon Bachanov, tweaked his elbow before he could make his pro debut.

By signing Hunter, the Angels gave up the 27th overall choice in the 2008 draft, leaving them without a first-rounder for the third time four years.

General Manager: Tony Reagins. **Farm Director:** Abe Flores. **Scouting Director:** Eddie Bane.

Class	Team	League	W	L	PCT	Finish*	Manager	Affiliated
Majors	Los Angeles	American	94	68	.580	3rd (14)	Mike Scioscia	—
Triple-A	Salt Lake Bees	Pacific Coast	74	69	.517	7th (16)	Brian Harper	2001
Double-A	Arkansas Travelers	Texas	65	75	.464	7th (8)	Bobby Magallanes	2001
High A	Rancho Cucamonga Quakes	California	69	71	.493	7th (10)	Bobby Mitchell	2001
Low A	Cedar Rapids Kernels	Midwest	78	61	.561	3rd (14)	Ever Magallanes	1993
Rookie	Orem Owlz	Pioneer	37	39	.487	4th (8)	Tom Kotchman	2001
Rookie	AZL Angels	Arizona	33	23	.589	2nd (9)	Ty Boykin	2001
Overall 2007 Minor League Record			356	338	.513	9th		

*Finish in overall standings (No. of teams in league) ^League champion

LAST YEAR'S TOP 30

Player, Pos.		Status
1.	Brandon Wood, ss	No. 1
2.	Nick Adenhart, rhp	No. 2
3.	Erick Aybar, ss	Majors
4.	Young-Il Jung, rhp	No. 13
5.	Stephen Marek, rhp	No. 6
6.	Hank Conger, c	No. 4
7.	Jeff Mathis, c	Majors
8.	Sean Rodriguez, 2b	No. 7
9.	Sean O'Sullivan, rhp	No. 5
10.	Tommy Mendoza, rhp	Dropped out
11.	Kenneth Herndon, rhp	Dropped out
12.	Peter Bourjos, of	No. 9
13.	Jose Arredondo, rhp	No. 12
14.	P.J. Phillips, 3b/ss	No. 15
15.	Hainley Statia, ss	No. 11
16.	Matt Sweeney, 1b	No. 17
17.	Jeremy Haynes, rhp	No. 23
18.	Terry Evans, of	No. 18
19.	Bobby Wilson, c	No. 25
20.	Ryan Mount, 2b	No. 14
21.	Trevor Bell, rhp	Dropped out
22.	Rafael Rodriguez, rhp	Dropped out
23.	Nick Green, rhp	No. 8
24.	Chris Resop, rhp	(Braves)
25.	Richard Aldridge, rhp	Dropped out
26.	Tommy Murphy, of	(Nationals)
27.	Reggie Willits, of	Majors
28.	Barret Browning, lhp	No. 20
29.	Mark Trumbo, 1b	No. 29
30.	Phil Seibel, lhp	Retired

BEST TOOLS

Best Hitter for Average	Hank Conger
Best Power Hitter	Brandon Wood
Best Strike-Zone Discipline	Chris Pettit
Fastest Baserunner	Peter Bourjos
Best Athlete	P.J. Phillips
Best Fastball	Jordan Walden
Best Curveball	Nick Adenhart
Best Slider	Jason Bulger
Best Changeup	Nick Green
Best Control	Sean O'Sullivan
Best Defensive Catcher	Anel de los Santos
Best Defensive Infielder	Andrew Romine
Best Infield Arm	Sean Rodriguez
Best Defensive Outfielder	Peter Bourjos
Best Outfield Arm	Julio Perez

PROJECTED 2011 LINEUP

Catcher	Hank Conger
First Base	Casey Kotchman
Second Base	Howie Kendrick
Third Base	Brandon Wood
Shortstop	Erick Aybar
Left Field	Gary Matthews Jr.
Center Field	Torii Hunter
Right Field	Vladimir Guerrero
Designated Hitter	Kendry Morales
No. 1 Starter	John Lackey
No. 2 Starter	Nick Adenhart
No. 3 Starter	Kelvim Escobar
No. 4 Starter	Jon Garland
No. 5 Starter	Jered Weaver
Closer	Francisco Rodriguez

TOP PROSPECTS OF THE DECADE

Year	Player, Pos.	2007 Org.
1998	Troy Glaus, 3b	Blue Jays
1999	Ramon Ortiz, rhp	Rockies
2000	Ramon Ortiz, rhp	Rockies
2001	Joe Torres, lhp	White Sox
2002	Casey Kotchman, 1b	Angels
2003	Francisco Rodriguez, rhp	Angels
2004	Casey Kotchman, 1b	Angels
2005	Casey Kotchman, 1b	Angels
2006	Brandon Wood, ss	Angels
2007	Brandon Wood, ss	Angels

TOP DRAFT PICKS OF THE DECADE

Year	Player, Pos.	2007 Org.
1998	Seth Etherton, rhp	Marlins
1999	John Lackey, rhp (2nd round)	Angels
2000	Joe Torres, lhp	White Sox
2001	Casey Kotchman, 1b	Angels
2002	Joe Saunders, lhp	Angels
2003	Brandon Wood, ss	Angels
2004	Jered Weaver, rhp	Angels
2005	Trevor Bell, rhp (1st round supp.)	Angels
2006	Hank Conger, c	Angels
2007	Jon Bachanov, rhp (1st round supp.)	Angels

LARGEST BONUSES IN CLUB HISTORY

Jered Weaver, 2004	$4,000,000
Kendry Morales, 2004	$3,000,000
Troy Glaus, 1997	$2,250,000
Joe Torres, 2000	$2,080,000
Casey Kotchman, 2001	$2,075,000

LOS ANGELES ANGELS

Top 2008 Rookie: Brandon Wood, ss/3b. Provided he gets a chance, he finally should show what he's capable of this season.

Breakout Prospect: Trevor Reckling, lhp. A projectable athlete who's still learning how to pitch, he has intriguing upside.

Sleeper: Jose Perez, rhp. After a strong showing in instructional league, the durable Dominican has the makings of becoming a middle-of-the-rotation workhorse.

SOURCE OF TOP 30 TALENT			
Homegrown	28	Acquired	2
College	3	Trades	2
Junior college	2	Rule 5 draft	0
High school	14	Independent leagues	0
Draft-and-follow	5	Free agents/waivers	0
Nondrafted free agents	0		
International	4		

Numbers in parentheses indicate prospect rankings.

LF
Terry Evans (18)
Chris Pettit (19)
Nathan Haynes

CF
Peter Bourjos (9)
Clay Fuller (30)
Jeremy Moore
Angel Castillo
Bradley Coon

RF
Anthony Norman
Tyler Mann
Julio Perez

3B
P.J. Phillips (15)
Matt Brown
Jay Brossman

SS
Brandon Wood (1)
Hainley Statia (11)
Andrew Romine (28)
Darwin Perez
Jean Segura
Norbito Ortiz

2B
Sean Rodriguez (7)
Ryan Mount (14)
Ivan Contreras
Nate Sutton
Tadd Brewer

1B
Matt Sweeney (17)
Mark Trumbo (29)

C
Hank Conger (4)
Anel de los Santos (10)
Bobby Wilson (25)
Ryan Budde
Ben Johnson
Ikko Sumi
Jose Lopez

RHP

Starters	Relievers
Nick Adenhart (2)	Jose Arredondo (12)
Jordan Walden (3)	Rich Thompson (22)
Sean O'Sullivan (5)	Jon Bachanov (24)
Stephen Marek (6)	Jason Bulger (26)
Nick Green (8)	Bobby Mosebach
Young-Il Jung (13)	Tommy Mendoza
Mason Tobin (21)	Rafael Rodriguez
Jeremy Haynes (23)	Darren O'Day
Jose Perez	Brok Butcher
Trevor Bell	Marc Albano
Kenneth Herndon	Ryan Brasier
Anthony Ortega	
Bobby Cassevah	

LHP

Starters	Relievers
Trevor Reckling (16)	Barret Browning (20)
Robert Fish (27)	Michael Anton
Nate Boman	Leonardo Calderon
	Chris Armstrong

2007   SIGNING BUDGET: $1.3 MILLION

Best Pro Debut: LHP Michael Anton (12) led the Rookie-level Arizona League in strikeouts with 82 in 62 innings. RHP Mason Tobin (16) went 4-1, 2.08 between the AZL and Rookie-level Orem. 3B Jay Brossman (36), Utah product, batted .346/.388/.474 for the Owlz.

Best Athlete: Unsigned OF Pat White (27) is West Virginia's starting quarterback and a Heisman trophy candidate; the Angels also drafted him in the fourth round out of high school in 2004. Raw OF Terrell Alliman (43) lacks playing experience but has plenty of tools.

Best Pure Hitter: DH Justin Bass (21) has a sound swing and hit .275 despite needing arm surgery; he could end up at second base or left field.

Best Power Hitter: OF Trevor Pippin (4) has raw power potential from the left side but hit just .188/.269/.203 in his debut.

Fastest Runner: SS Andrew Romine (5) and and Alliman (43) are above-average runners.

Best Defensive Player: Orem manager Tom Kotchman called Romine the best defender he's coached. Romine's strong, accurate arm, plus range and nimble feet make him a 70 defender.

Best Fastball: RHP Jon Bachanov (1s) hit 96 mph when at his best this spring. The Angels shut him down in August with a tender elbow.

Best Secondary Pitch: Anton's plus changeup has screwball action. LHP Trevor Reckling (8) throws a curveball so good, the Angels limited him to one per outing in instructional league so he would work on other pitches.

Most Intriguing Background: Anton pitched two seasons at Virginia Military Institute, but a car accident in December 2004 interrupted his career for two seasons. Scout John Gracio saw him working out in Arizona with Angels farmhand Jesse Smith and helped give Anton's career a second chance. Bass' father Kevin played 14 seasons in the big leagues. Romine's dad Kevin played in the big leagues; brother Austin was drafted in the second round by the Yankees. Unsigned C Matt Scioscia (41), attending Notre Dame, is the son of Angels manager Mike.

Closest To The Majors: Tobin has plus command of his 89-92 mph fastball, a slider than can be a plus pitch and a developing changeup.

Best Late-Round Pick: Tobin.

The One Who Got Away: RHP Matt Harvey (3) has first-round talent, but Los Angeles opted not to buy him away from North Carolina. LHP Tanner Robles (14), now at Oregon State, has reached 94 mph.

Assessment: The Angels let too much talent get away, and Bachanov's injury added to the disappointing early returns. However, draft-and-follow signee Jordan Walden has a first-round arm, and second-day selections such as Anton, Reckling and Tobin could supplement an otherwise uninspiring draft.

2006   BUDGET: $2.4 MILLION

This was an especially deep crop, and there's also some blue-chip talent too, highlighted by C Hank Conger (1) and RHP Jordan Walden (12), who cost $1 million as a draft-and-follow.

GRADE: B+

2005   BUDGET: $3.4 MILLION

RHP Sean O'Sullivan (3), another draft-and-follow, has tremendous pitchability. The Angels drafted several athletes who have yet to truly assert themselves, led by OF Peter Bourjos (10)

GRADE: C+

2004   BUDGET: $4.7 MILLION

RHP Jered Weaver (1) already has won 24 games in the majors. Drafting RHP Nick Adenhart (14) despite his blown-out elbow was a brilliant move, as was locking up draft-and-follow RHP Stephen Marek (40).

GRADE: B+

2003   BUDGET: $3.2 MILLION

The Angels are just about ready to tap into 3B/SS Brandon Wood's (1) prodigious power. OF Reggie Willits (7) has been a pleasant surprise, and SS Sean Rodriguez (3) could be a top-notch utility player.

GRADE: B+

Draft analysis by John Manuel (2007) and Jim Callis (2003-06). Numbers in parentheses indicate draft rounds. Budgets are bonuses in first 10 rounds.

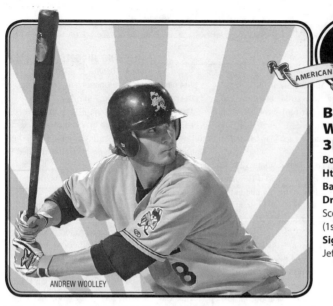
ANDREW WOOLLEY

BRANDON WOOD, 3B/SS

Born: March 2, 1985.
Ht.: 6-3. **Wt.:** 185.
Bats: R. **Throws:** R.
Drafted: HS—Scottsdale, Ariz. 2003 (1st Round).
Signed by: Jeff Scholzen.

Just two years removed from high school, Wood went on a power binge for the ages, clobbering 58 home runs between the minors, the Arizona Fall League and a stint with Team USA in 2005. He ascended to the top of this list after the season and has held the No. 1 spot ever since. With Chone Figgins and Maicer Izturis on the shelf in Anaheim with injuries, Wood made his major league debut last April but received just nine starts during four separate big league callups during the season. He collected his first major league hit off Bobby Jenks on April 29. He led Angels minor leaguers with 23 home runs while learning a new position at Triple-A Salt Lake. A shortstop his whole career, Wood slid over to third base during spring training and played there most of the season, though he returned to shortstop during the Pacific Coast League playoffs.

Wood can do some serious damage with the bat. He profiles as a middle-of-the-order run producer with 25-30 or more homers per year while being capable of handling shortstop. Comparisons range from Cal Ripken because of his tall, lean build and deceptively smooth defense, to Troy Glaus for his light-tower power and aggressive approach. Wood hits from an upright stance and feasts on fastballs early in counts. He generates exceptional bat speed and his swing has lots of leverage. Balls jump off his bat to all fields with loft, carry and backspin. He's slowly making adjustments in his approach and becoming a better all-around hitter. Defensively, his range is unexceptional, but he fits the mold of the modern offensive-minded shortstop with the actions, body control, hands and plus arm to handle the position just fine. He was solid if unspectacular at third base. He's an average runner with good instincts and has a gamer attitude that enhances his skills.

While Wood cut down on his strikeouts from once every 3.0 at-bats in 2006 to once every 3.6 at-bats last season, his greatest deficiency remains his lack of plate discipline. His pitch selection is below-average, and when he falls behind in the count, he'll punch out by chasing balls off the plate and above his hands. He falls into pull-happy modes that make him vulnerable to pitches on the outer half. He must shorten his swing and hone his two-strike approach in order to hit for a higher average and make more consistent contact. He also can tighten his defense at third base, where he made 16 errors in 74 Triple-A games.

With Orlando Cabrera traded to the White Sox, the door again swung open for Wood to play his way into the big league lineup as a shortstop. Erick Aybar, Figgins and Izturis and remain shortstop options as well, so Wood might wind up at third base, either in Anaheim or at Salt Lake.

Year	Club (League)	Class	AVG	G	AB	R	H	2B	3B	HR	RBI	BB	SO	SB	OBP	SLG
2003	Angels (AZL)	R	.308	19	78	14	24	8	2	0	13	4	15	3	.349	.462
	Provo (Pio)	R	.278	42	162	25	45	13	2	5	31	16	48	1	.348	.475
2004	Cedar Rapids (MWL)	A	.251	125	478	65	120	30	5	11	64	46	117	21	.322	.404
2005	Rancho Cucamonga (Cal)	A	.321	130	536	109	172	51	4	43	115	48	128	7	.383	.672
	Salt Lake (PCL)	AAA	.316	4	19	1	6	2	1	0	1	0	6	0	.316	.526
2006	Arkansas (TL)	AA	.276	118	453	74	125	42	4	25	83	54	149	19	.355	.552
2007	Salt Lake (PCL)	AAA	.272	111	437	73	119	27	1	23	77	45	120	10	.338	.497
	Los Angeles (AL)	MLB	.152	13	33	2	5	1	0	1	3	0	12	0	.152	.273
MINOR LEAGUE TOTALS			.282	549	2163	361	611	173	19	107	384	213	583	61	.350	.528
MAJOR LEAGUE TOTALS			.152	13	33	2	5	1	0	1	3	0	12	0	.152	.273

2 NICK ADENHART, RHP

Born: Aug. 24, 1986. **B-T:** R-R. **Ht.:** 6-3. **Wt.:** 185. **Drafted:** HS—Williamsport, Md., 2004 (14th round). **Signed by:** Dan Radcliff.

BILL MITCHELL

Since having Tommy John surgery in high school but still signing for $710,000, Adenhart has logged more than 300 innings in the last two minor league seasons. He impressed in spring training with a 1.84 ERA in four appearances in big league camp, then went 3-0, 1.54 in April to begin a solid, if streaky season that included a short disabled-list stint with a sore shoulder. He's pitched on big stages his entire career, earning Baseball America's Youth Player of the Year honors in 2003, a trip to the Futures Game in 2006 and a spot on the U.S. Olympic qualifying team following the '06 season. Adenhart has outstanding stuff. His fastball sits at 91-92 mph on most nights and ranges from 88-94. The ball jumps out of his hand and explodes at the plate with late, riding life and finish. His slider has hard three-quarter tilt at 75-77 mph. His changeup is a legitimate third weapon and usually more effective than his breaking ball, with plus fade and sink. He maintains his hand speed and sells the pitch well. His delivery isn't picture perfect but he pitches downhill and his arm works easily from a natural three-quarters arm slot. He's a good all-around athlete. While Adenhart shows an ability to throw all three of his pitches for strikes, his command escaped him at times last season. Angels minor league pitching coordinator Kernan Ronan made pitching to contact a point of emphasis for Adenhart because he tries to be too fine. His breaking ball lacks consistent shape and command. Adenhart looks like a future front-of-the-rotation stud who could be ready for a major league job in 2008. But the Angels don't have an opening in their rotation, so he's most likely going to spend the entire season in Triple-A.

Year	Club (League)	Class	W	L	ERA	G	GS	CG	SV	IP	H	R	ER	HR	BB	SO	AVG
2005	Angels (AZL)	R	2	3	3.68	13	12	1	0	44	39	26	18	0	24	52	.245
	Orem (Pio)	R	1	0	0.00	3	1	0	0	6	3	1	0	0	0	7	.143
2006	Cedar Rapids (MWL)	A	10	2	1.95	16	16	1	0	106	84	33	23	2	26	99	.215
	Rancho Cucamonga (Cal)	A	5	2	3.78	9	9	0	0	52	51	23	22	1	16	46	.258
2007	Arkansas (TL)	AA	10	8	3.65	26	26	0	0	153	158	72	62	7	65	116	.273
MINOR LEAGUE TOTALS			28	15	3.11	65	64	2	0	361	335	155	125	10	131	320	.249

3 JORDAN WALDEN, RHP

Born: Nov. 16, 1987. **B-T:** R-R. **Ht.:** 6-5. **Wt.:** 220. **Drafted:** Grayson County (Texas) CC, D/F 2006 (12th round). **Signed by:** Arnold Braithwaite.

BILL MITCHELL

The No. 1 prep prospect in the nation entering his senior season, Walden saw his velocity dip to the mid-80s and he fell to the 12th round of the 2006 draft. He rebounded at Grayson County (Texas) CC in 2007 and signed for $1 million a few hours before the deadline for draft-and-follows. He capped his pro debut by striking out 10 in eight innings during Rookie-level Orem's league championship game. The night Orem won the league title, Walden touched 100 mph and was still flashing 97s in the seventh inning. His fastball is the easily the best in the system. His slurvy 80-81 mph slider grades as a future plus pitch because of its velocity and occasional late bite. His delivery isn't effortless, but his arm action is relatively clean. He's a good athlete. Walden can pound the zone with his fastball, but his overall command, especially of his secondary pitches, can improve. His slider lacks depth and consistency. He has a rudimentary feel for pitching and has a lot to learn about the craft, such as making his changeup more than just a usable pitch. With wide shoulders, big hands and wrists, Walden figures to fill out into a workhorse No. 2 or 3 starter. The cream of the Angels' promising rising crop of pitching prospects, Walden should spend 2008 at low Class A Cedar Rapids.

Year	Club (League)	Class	W	L	ERA	G	GS	CG	SV	IP	H	R	ER	HR	BB	SO	AVG
2007	Orem (Pio)	R	1	1	3.08	15	15	0	0	64	49	27	22	3	17	63	.209
MINOR LEAGUE TOTALS			1	1	3.08	15	15	0	0	64	49	27	22	3	17	63	.209

4 HANK CONGER, C

Born: Jan. 29, 1988. **B-T:** B-R. **Ht.:** 6-1. **Wt.:** 220. **Drafted:** HS—Huntington Beach, Calif., 2006 (1st round). **Signed by:** Bobby DeJardin.

BILL MITCHELL

Like Nick Adenhart, Conger was a high profile amateur player long before he started to shave. A second-generation Korean, his given name is Hyun and his Atlanta-based grandfather nicknamed him after Hank Aaron. He has had repeated injuries since signing for $1.35 million in 2006, missing much of his pro debut with a broken hamate bone in his right wrist. He missed another six weeks in 2007 because of lower-back and hamstring issues, and he tweaked the same hamstring in his first game of instructional league, which cost him the rest of the year. Conger has a good feel for hitting and plus power from both sides of the plate. He has above-average bat speed and a willingness to use all fields. He tracks balls deep into the hitting zone and controls the strike zone adequately for a young hitter. His defensive package has a long ways to go, but he has plus arm strength that elicits 1.9-second home-to-second times. Strong makeup and work ethic are just two reasons to believe he'll improve defensively. Improving his righthanded swing was on top of Conger's instructional league to-do list, as he's significantly better from the left side (.304 with a .866 OPS in 2007 versus .250 and .647 from the right). His swing is looser with better plate coverage from the left side. He's a well-below-average runner and needs to improve his flexibility. He doesn't have quick feet, which inhibits his release and explains why he threw out just 21 percent of basestealers last season. Conger has all the tools to become a frontline, switch-hitting run producer in the big leagues. If he can stay healthy, 2008 could be a monster year for him as he's ticketed to spend the season about an hour from his hometown in high Class A Rancho Cucamonga.

Year	Club (League)	Class	AVG	G	AB	R	H	2B	3B	HR	RBI	BB	SO	SB	OBP	SLG
2006	Angels (AZL)	R	.319	19	69	11	22	3	4	1	11	7	11	1	.382	.522
2007	Angels (AZL)	R	.267	3	15	2	4	1	0	0	3	0	3	0	.267	.333
	Cedar Rapids (MWL)	A	.290	84	290	33	84	20	0	11	48	21	48	9	.336	.472
MINOR LEAGUE TOTALS			.294	106	374	46	110	24	4	12	62	28	62	10	.342	.476

5 SEAN O'SULLIVAN, RHP

Born: Sept. 1, 1987. **B-T:** R-R. **Ht.:** 6-1. **Wt.:** 220. **Drafted:** Grossmont (Calif.) JC, D/F 2005 (3rd round). **Signed by:** Tim Corcoran.

O'Sullivan's development from overpowering amateur to cerebral, calculating pro is intriguing. His velocity plummeted during his senior high school season in 2005 and he fell to the Angels in the third round. He signed the following spring for $500,000 after one season at Grossmont (Calif.) JC. He has won ERA titles in each of his two pro seasons, with a 2.14 mark in the Rookie-level Pioneer League in 2006 and a 2.22 mark in the low Class A Midwest League last year. His younger brother Ryan is a top-five-round high school talent in the 2008 draft class. O'Sullivan has plus control of four solid-average pitches. He adds and subtracts off his 87-91 mph fastball and spots it to all four quadrants of the strike zone. His changeup, curveball and slider aren't knee-bucklers, but they have plenty of deception to get the job done. He'll mix in a two-seam fastball as well. He's durable, repeats his delivery and pitches with poise and guile. Because he doesn't possess plus raw stuff, O'Sullivan will have to maximize his command and pitchability as he faces more advanced hitters. He was generating 95-mph fastballs as a high school underclassman, but it's a stretch to project additional velocity because of his thick, maxed-out body, which earned him the nickname "Nacho" during his debut season. O'Sullivan earned the organization's pitcher of the year award in 2007 and profiles as an innings-eating No. 4 starter in the big leagues. This season will be an important one for him, as he'll be tested in the hitter's haven that is the high Class A California League.

Year	Club (League)	Class	W	L	ERA	G	GS	CG	SV	IP	H	R	ER	HR	BB	SO	AVG
2006	Orem (Pio)	R	4	0	2.14	14	14	0	0	71	65	23	17	2	7	55	.239
2007	Cedar Rapids (MWL)	A	10	7	2.22	25	25	0	0	158	136	58	39	6	40	125	.227
MINOR LEAGUE TOTALS			14	7	2.19	39	39	0	0	229	201	81	56	8	47	180	.231

6 STEPHEN MAREK, RHP

Born: Sept. 3, 1983. **B-T:** L-R. **Ht.:** 6-2. **Wt.:** 220. **Drafted:** San Jacinto (Texas) JC, D/F 2004 (40th round). **Signed by:** Chad McDonald.

The Angels inked Marek in May 2005 for an $800,000 bonus as a draft-and-follow. A reliever at San Jacinto (Texas) JC, he became a starter in pro ball and led the Midwest League with a 1.96 ERA in his first full season. He stayed in extended spring training when camp broke last year, but finished strong with four earned runs allowed in his final four starts in high Class A. Marek comes after hitters with a powerful three-pitch mix. His fastball ranges from 88-94 mph. His 74-77 mph curveball has 11-to-5 shape and grades as a second plus pitch thanks to his knack for locating it. He made improvements to his changeup, which has hard, late sink at times and helped him limit lefthanders to a .183 average in 2007. Marek's mechanics are a work in progress. He doesn't repeat his release point, and when his arm slot gets too high, he loses life on his fastball, especially when he misses up in the zone. He pitches in the middle of the zone too frequently. Angels coaches say his mental focus is also an area they'd like to see improve. Provided he stays healthy, Marek profiles as a middle-of-the-rotation starter. He'll spend 2008 in the Double-A Arkansas rotation.

Year	Club (League)	Class	W	L	ERA	G	GS	CG	SV	IP	H	R	ER	HR	BB	SO	AVG
2005	Orem (Pio)	R	1	3	4.50	15	14	0	0	66	74	37	33	7	25	55	.292
2006	Cedar Rapids (MWL)	A	10	2	1.96	19	19	1	0	119	95	27	26	8	24	100	.216
	Rancho Cucamonga (Cal)	A	2	3	3.94	6	6	0	0	32	26	14	14	4	13	33	.230
2007	Rancho Cucamonga (Cal)	A	8	10	4.30	25	25	1	0	134	133	78	64	17	49	106	.257
MINOR LEAGUE TOTALS			21	18	3.51	65	64	2	0	351	328	156	137	36	111	294	.248

7 SEAN RODRIGUEZ, SS/2B

Born: April 26, 1985. **B-T:** R-R. **Ht.:** 6-0. **Wt.:** 195. **Drafted:** HS—Miami, 2003 (3rd round). **Signed by:** Mike Silvestri.

STEVE MOORE

Rodriguez followed up his breakout 2006 with a solid if inconsistent season in Double-A. The son of longtime Marlins minor league coach Johnny Rodriguez, Sean grew up around the game, watching his dad throw batting practice to Alex Rodriguez (no relation). Los Angeles added him to its 40-man roster in November despite his tepid Arizona Fall League showing. Rodriguez has good tools across the board that play up because of his inherent feel for the game. He has above-average bat speed that produces plus raw power with a quick, whippy swing. He uses the entire field and is beginning to make adjustments effectively. He has solid-average hands and a plus arm, with a solid first step that helps him make up for fringy range up the middle. A below-average runner with a bulky build, Rodriguez lacks strong defensive fundamentals and is expected to move to second base, where he could become an average defender. He swings and misses too often and chases fastballs behind in the count. The Angels would like to see him become more consistent, which starts with improving his plate discipline. A November addition to the 40-man roster, Rodriguez is expected to spend most of 2008 at second base in Triple-A. Because of his bat, he profiles as a reliable utiltyman with some punch, and he could play his way into an everyday role if he reduces his empty swings.

Year	Club (League)	Class	AVG	G	AB	R	H	2B	3B	HR	RBI	BB	SO	SB	OBP	SLG
2003	Angels (AZL)	R	.269	54	216	30	58	8	5	2	25	14	37	11	.332	.380
2004	Cedar Rapids (MWL)	A	.250	57	196	35	49	8	4	4	17	18	54	14	.333	.393
	Provo (Pio)	R	.338	64	225	64	76	14	4	10	55	51	62	9	.486	.569
2005	Cedar Rapids (MWL)	A	.250	124	448	86	112	29	3	14	45	78	85	27	.371	.422
2006	Rancho Cucamonga (Cal)	A	.301	116	455	78	137	29	5	24	77	47	124	15	.377	.545
	Arkansas (TL)	AA	.354	18	65	16	23	5	0	5	9	11	18	0	.462	.662
	Salt Lake (PCL)	AAA	.000	1	2	0	0	0	0	0	0	0	2	0	.000	.000
2007	Arkansas (TL)	AA	.254	136	508	84	129	31	2	17	73	54	132	15	.345	.423
MINOR LEAGUE TOTALS			.276	570	2115	393	584	124	23	76	301	273	514	91	.375	.464

8 NICK GREEN, RHP

Born: Aug. 20, 1984. **B-T:** R-R. **Ht.:** 6-4. **Wt.:** 200. **Drafted:** Darton (Ga.) JC, 2004 (35th round). **Signed by:** Chris McAlpin.

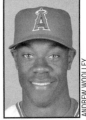

ANDREW WOOLLEY

One of the cheapest prospects on any list, Green turned down $80,000 from the Astros as an 11th-rounder out of high school only to sign with the Angels two years later for $1,500. He took home Double-A Texas League all-star honors last year before taking the series-ending loss in the Pacific Coast League playoffs. He took the biggest step forward of any Los Angeles prospect in 2007, earning a spot on the 40-man roster. Green pounds the zone with an 86-93 mph fastball, mid-70s curve and a dastardly changeup. His changeup graded as a 70 pitch for more than one TL scout, with late sink resembling that of a screwball. He works quickly, pitches to contact and is efficient, spotting his stuff to both sides of the plate. He repeats his simple yet deceptive delivery well. He's durable and hasn't missed a turn in his rotation in two years. Green doesn't have the upside of some of the Angels' bigger arms. He gets a lot of flyball outs and can be prone to homers. His fastball and changeup are not swing-and-miss pitches, and he already has maximized his feel for pitching. Green's sleeper status has expired, and he has a ceiling as a reliable No. 4 starter. He'll spend 2008 in the Triple-A rotation.

Year	Club (League)	Class	W	L	ERA	G	GS	CG	SV	IP	H	R	ER	HR	BB	SO	AVG
2004	Provo (Pio)	R	4	3	4.03	17	10	0	0	51	56	28	23	4	20	44	.275
2005	Cedar Rapids (MWL)	A	3	3	3.58	26	8	1	2	100	95	47	40	11	14	74	.249
2006	Rancho Cucamonga (Cal)	A	5	3	4.15	11	11	1	0	65	77	31	30	9	19	57	.291
	Arkansas (TL)	AA	8	5	4.41	17	17	0	0	112	115	64	55	23	21	77	.268
2007	Arkansas (TL)	AA	10	8	3.68	28	28	2	0	178	164	80	73	17	32	107	.243
MINOR LEAGUE TOTALS			30	22	3.92	99	74	4	2	507	507	250	221	64	106	359	.259

LOS ANGELES ANGELS

9 PETER BOURJOS, OF

BILL MITCHELL

Born: March 31, 1987. **B-T:** R-R. **Ht.:** 6-1. **Wt.:**175. **Drafted:** HS—Scottsdale, Ariz., 2005 (10th round). **Signed by:** John Gracio.

The Angels took a chance on Bourjos in the 10th round in 2005 and signed him for $325,000. On the second day of the 2007 season, he ruptured the ligament between the middle and ring finger on his left hand and fractured the ring finger taking a swing on a cold night. He tried to play with the injury before having surgery in May, missing more than two months. His father Chris played briefly in the majors and now scouts for the Brewers. Bourjos is an above-average runner who glides from gap to gap in the outfield with long, even strides and tremendous acceleration. He has a solid-average arm to complete the defensive package. He has plenty of bat speed and the makings of average power. He has good instincts and has made strides in his bunting and bat control, two elements he needs to add to his game. The biggest question on Bourjos is a big one: Will he hit? His approach vacillates from at-bat to at-bat, he's busy in his setup and he often lacks balance through his swing. His bad habit of drifting toward the pitcher, failing to keep his hands and weight back, makes him particularly vulnerable to offspeed stuff. Bourjos has the tools to impact the game in many ways while playing a premium position. The Angels were pleased with his showing in instructional league and should give him a shot at high Class A at some point in 2008.

Year	Club (League)	Class	AVG	G	AB	R	H	2B	3B	HR	RBI	BB	SO	SB	OBP	SLG
2006	Orem (Pio)	R	.292	65	250	42	73	16	7	5	28	22	67	13	.354	.472
2007	Angels (AZL)	R	.313	4	16	3	5	0	1	0	2	1	2	0	.353	.438
	Cedar Rapids (MWL)	A	.274	63	237	37	65	9	6	5	29	20	53	19	.335	.426
MINOR LEAGUE TOTALS			.284	132	503	82	143	25	14	10	59	43	122	32	.345	.449

10 ANEL DE LOS SANTOS, C

Born: June 19, 1988. **B-T:** R-R. **Ht.:** 6-0. **Wt.:** 180. **Signed:** Dominican Republic, 2005. **Signed by:** Leo Perez.

The Angels originally signed de los Santos as a third baseman but decided to move him behind the plate during his second season in his native Dominican. He took to the position immediately, and adds to the organization's considerable depth behind the plate. De los Santos has the prototype tools package to be a premium defensive catcher. He's athletic and agile with quick-twitch muscles that allow him to bounce around behind the plate. He has a quiet setup, soft hands and sets a good, low target. His feet and arm action work efficiently during throws to second, and his throws have tremendous carry and hit their target. He nabbed 35 percent of basestealers last season and routinely records 1.78-1.80 second times from home to second base. He has solid-average bat speed and enough leverage to his swing to project to hit for at least average power. He's an average runner under way. Occasionally, de los Santos will take a smooth swing with balance and rhythm, but his approach at the plate is inconsistent and he doesn't repeat his swing. He'll chase breaking balls in the dirt and doesn't work counts well. He's primarily a pull hitter. De los Santos' prospect status is based largely on his defensive skills, so anything he contributes offensively will be a plus. He has athleticism and bat speed, so there's reason to believe he can develop into a .250-.265 hitter with 15-20 homers per year. He'll make his full-season debut this spring at Cedar Rapids.

Year	Club (League)	Class	AVG	G	AB	R	H	2B	3B	HR	RBI	BB	SO	SB	OBP	SLG
2005	Angels (DSL)	R	.226	35	124	15	28	6	1	3	14	3	33	4	.256	.363
2006	Angels (AZL)	R	.250	29	104	12	26	4	3	1	11	6	28	2	.295	.375
2007	Orem (Pio)	R	.255	50	188	19	48	8	4	6	37	4	44	0	.268	.436
MINOR LEAGUE TOTALS			.245	114	416	46	102	18	8	10	62	13	105	6	.271	.399

11 HAINLEY STATIA, SS

Born: Jan. 19, 1986. **B-T:** B-R. **Ht.:** 5-11. **Wt.:** 162. **Drafted:** HS—Lake Worth, Fla., 2004 (9th round). **Signed by:** Mike Silverstri.

The Angels have some of the best amateur scouts in the business, and before he was promoted to East Coast supervisor, Mike Silvestri signed Statia for $90,000 out of high school. Statia was born and raised in Curacao, and he earned best defensive player honors during the World Cup in Taiwan last fall, playing with the Netherlands. He took home the organization's same honor in 2007 as well. A live-body, high-energy player lauded for his makeup and attention to detail, Statia's modest offense and a general lack of strength keep him from being a premium prospect. He makes consistent contact and puts the ball in play. He's a better hitter from the left side of the plate, though his lefthanded swing can get long, and it's choppy from the right. His power is below-average, but he knows his game and can drive balls from gap to gap adequately. Statia's a below-average runner but goes first to third well, and his instincts help him have average range at shortstop. His actions are easy and loose, his hands are exceptional and he makes online throws with average arm strength. He profiles to hit at the bottom of an order, and his athleticism and defense could make him a valuable utilityman. He'll spend 2008 in Double-A.

Year	Club (League)	Class	AVG	G	AB	R	H	2B	3B	HR	RBI	BB	SO	SB	OBP	SLG
2005	Rancho Cucamonga (Cal)	A	.245	23	106	12	26	2	0	1	8	5	13	6	.286	.292
	Orem (Pio)	R	.300	68	277	44	83	17	6	2	41	23	40	12	.360	.426
2006	Cedar Rapids (MWL)	A	.297	111	417	68	124	31	1	1	38	52	54	23	.379	.384
	Rancho Cucamonga (Cal)	A	.300	18	60	8	18	2	1	0	8	8	7	1	.386	.367
2007	Rancho Cucamonga (Cal)	A	.288	135	549	86	158	27	7	3	74	48	79	29	.344	.379
MINOR LEAGUE TOTALS			.290	355	1409	218	409	79	15	7	169	136	193	71	.356	.383

12 JOSE ARREDONDO, RHP

Born: March 30, 1984. **B-T:** R-R. **Ht.:** 6-0. **Wt.:** 170. **Signed:** Dominican Republic, 2002. **Signed by:** Leo Perez.

The Angels had hoped for better things from Arredondo, whom they added to the 40-man roster following the 2006 season. They moved him to the bullpen last spring in an effort to accelerate his development. He racked up saves in eight out of his first nine opportunities in Double-A before being suspended and subsequently demoted for storming off the mound when he was pulled from a game in June. He spent the second half of the year in high Class A, and his maturation from former infielder to pitcher hasn't made much progress. His stuff is big—a well-above-average fastball that touched 97 and can sit near 94, deceptive power slider and splitter—but he doesn't have any feel for the craft. He overthrows, doesn't repeat his delivery and works deep in counts. This will be a crucial season for Arredondo, who remains on the 40-man roster. He should begin the season in Double-A.

Year	Club (League)	Class	W	L	ERA	G	GS	CG	SV	IP	H	R	ER	HR	BB	SO	AVG
2004	Angels (AZL)	R	0	0	2.92	8	0	0	1	12	14	10	4	1	4	14	.280
2005	Arkansas (TL)	AA	0	0	3.38	5	0	0	0	5	5	2	2	0	4	4	.278
	Orem (Pio)	R	5	0	4.19	15	13	0	0	68	76	34	32	4	20	60	.285
2006	Rancho Cucamonga (Cal)	A	5	6	2.30	15	15	0	0	90	62	28	23	4	35	115	.198
	Arkansas (TL)	AA	2	3	6.53	11	11	1	0	60	80	47	44	8	22	48	.317
2007	Arkansas (TL)	AA	0	1	2.52	23	0	0	10	25	16	10	7	2	12	28	.184
	Rancho Cucamonga (Cal)	A	2	4	6.43	28	0	0	4	35	46	31	25	5	11	34	.317
	Salt Lake (PCL)	AAA	0	0	3.00	2	0	0	0	3	2	1	1	0	2	1	.222
MINOR LEAGUE TOTALS			14	14	4.14	107	39	1	15	300	301	163	138	24	110	304	.264

13 YOUNG-IL JUNG, RHP

Born: Nov. 16, 1988. **B-T:** R-R. **Ht.:** 6-2. **Wt.:** 190. **Signed:** Korea, 2006. **Signed by:** Charlie Kim/Clay Daniel.

Jung went from the talk of Angels instructional league in 2006 to a $1 million question mark by midseason. He was shut down after just three appearances in Rookie ball with elbow soreness, but general manager Tony Reagins said Jung's right forearm was the culprit. The organization was hopeful the arm trouble was just the residual effect of a heavy workload from Jung's high school career in Korea, which reportedly included one 242-pitch outing. When he's right, Jung has feel for three pitches and a relatively sound delivery. His fastball sits at 89-92 mph, but its life and movement make it even better. He ditched a split-finger fastball and curveball, and whittled his repertoire to a changeup and slider. His change has above-average deception with sinking action at 82 mph. Jung's slider sits near 83 mph with short, late tilt. He gets rotational in his delivery, which leads to below-average command. His body is thick and mature, which means he has little room for projection. His drop-and-drive delivery makes it difficult for him to maintain a downhill plane on his pitches. If he's healthy, Jung could climb to low Class A sometime in 2008.

Year	Club (League)	Class	W	L	ERA	G	GS	CG	SV	IP	H	R	ER	HR	BB	SO	AVG
2007	Orem (Pio)	R	0	1	9.00	3	3	0	0	9	10	12	9	1	6	9	.263
MINOR LEAGUE TOTALS			0	1	9.00	3	3	0	0	9	10	12	9	1	6	9	.263

14 RYAN MOUNT, 2B

Born: Aug. 17, 1986. **B-T:** L-R. **Ht.:** 6-1. **Wt.:** 180. **Drafted:** HS—Chino Hills, Calif., 2005 (2nd round). **Signed by:** Tim Corcoran.

When Mount made a late surge as a high school senior, the Angels drafted him in the second round and signed him for $615,000 in 2005. He was raw defensively and at the plate, but he had tools and projected to hit for power, and he has taken steps in fulfilling his promise. He injured his hamstring in spring training and just as he was starting to hit his stride at the plate, missed a month near midseason with an injured quadriceps muscle. An aggressive hitter with a penchant for squaring up the ball, Mount's best tool is his bat. He can really drop the bat head, with easy power from gap to gap that could translate to 20 homers a year in the big leagues. His approach must improve in order for him to reach that potential. He did a better job of controlling the strike zone last season but tends to get out front and swing and miss on offspeed stuff. He improved his approach and results against lefthanded pitchers (.172 in 2006, .254 in '07). He made the move from shortstop to second base last season and showed improvement defensively. He's not light on his feet, but his hands are adequate and he makes the routine play. He has plenty of arm strength to turn the backside of the double play. Mount is a fringe-average runner. He should spend this season in high Class A.

Year	Club (League)	Class	AVG	G	AB	R	H	2B	3B	HR	RBI	BB	SO	SB	OBP	SLG
2005	Angels (AZL)	R	.216	29	102	15	22	7	1	1	17	17	31	4	.325	.333
2006	Orem (Pio)	R	.285	69	277	54	79	14	2	9	38	36	67	10	.370	.448
2007	Angels (AZL)	R	.333	3	12	0	4	0	0	0	0	1	1	0	.429	.333
	Cedar Rapids (MWL)	A	.251	85	303	47	76	11	3	7	36	29	70	19	.320	.376
MINOR LEAGUE TOTALS			.261	186	694	116	181	32	6	17	91	83	169	33	.343	.398

15 P.J. PHILLIPS, SS

Born: Sept. 23, 1986. **B-T:** R-R. **Ht.:** 6-3. **Wt.:** 170. **Drafted:** HS—Stone Mountain, Ga., 2005 (2nd round). **Signed by:** Chris McAlpin.

Phillips hails from the same suburban Atlanta high school (Redan) as former Angels great Wally Joyner and Rockies prospect Chris Nelson. His sister Porsha plays college basketball at Georgia, and his brother Brandon is the Reds' second baseman. Phillips has as much upside as anyone on this list, but he isn't progressing as quickly as the Angels would like. He finished a frustrating first full season with a 3-for-40 slide that capped a forgettable year in the Midwest League. Phillips will show plus-plus raw power and a smooth swing, but he's still learning how to hit. He has poor strike-zone discipline, which seems to stem from poor pitch recognition, among other things. He needs to sit back and let balls travel deeper. He also has a tendency to lock out his front leg, which causes him to pull off the ball and creates length in swing. He has good hands and a plus arm but doesn't read hops well and needs to improve his footwork. He's a fluid, solid-average runner, but his actions are a little long for a middle infielder. He also isn't finished filling out his long, lean frame, which means a move to third base is forthcoming. He could return to Cedar Rapids to begin 2008 and he remains a long way from being ready for the majors.

Year	Club (League)	Class	AVG	G	AB	R	H	2B	3B	HR	RBI	BB	SO	SB	OBP	SLG
2005	Angels (AZL)	R	.291	49	182	25	53	6	6	1	24	9	53	13	.328	.407
2006	Orem (Pio)	R	.240	69	263	36	63	12	1	6	27	20	75	11	.298	.361
2007	Cedar Rapids (MWL)	A	.245	119	436	67	107	11	8	13	37	15	154	34	.283	.397
MINOR LEAGUE TOTALS			.253	237	881	128	223	29	15	20	88	44	282	58	.297	.388

16 TREVOR RECKLING, LHP

Born: May 22, 1989. **B-T:** L-L. **Ht.:** 6-3. **Wt.:** 190. **Drafted:** HS—Newark, N.J., 2007 (8th round). **Signed by:** Greg Morhardt.

There was plenty of buzz in New Jersey about a high school prospect last spring, but the pitcher everyone wanted to see was Tigers first-rounder Rick Porcello, not Reckling. East Coast supervisor Mike Silvestri saw Reckling in tournaments in Florida and followed him last summer after the Angels took him in the eighth round. The Angels signed him away from his commitment to High Point for $123,300. A good athlete who also played on St. Benedict Prep's nationally ranked high school basketball team, Reckling is a little raw but has plenty of projection. He has a quick arm with a smooth delivery and high three-quarters arm slot. He'll flash three quality offerings and shows the early signs of feel for his craft. His fastball sits between 86-89 mph, touching 92. His curveball projects as above-average, with good spin and hard tilt. His changeup could be a third weapon. Pitching coordinator Kernan Ronan encouraged Reckling to pitch off his fastball instead of leaning on his breaking ball to get outs. Reckling tends to rush toward the plate, causing him to pitch uphill. Reckling could prove to be an eighth-round steal, and he'll begin his level-by-level ascent in Orem next season with a shot to pitch in Cedar Rapids with a strong spring training.

Year	Club (League)	Class	W	L	ERA	G	GS	CG	SV	IP	H	R	ER	HR	BB	SO	AVG
2007	Angels (AZL)	R	3	1	2.75	9	5	0	2	36	33	13	11	2	7	55	.236
MINOR LEAGUE TOTALS			3	1	2.75	9	5	0	2	36	33	13	11	2	7	55	.236

17 MATT SWEENEY, 3B

Born: April 14, 1988. **B-T:** L-R. **Ht.:** 6-3. **Wt.:** 212. **Drafted:** HS—Rockville, Md., 2006 (8th round). **Signed by:** Dan Radcliff.

Sweeney's $75,000 signing bonus was a pittance considering the upside he offers at the plate. A standout football player in high school, Sweeney shed 30 pounds during his senior season in 2006 and got off to a blistering beginning in his first full professional season. He hit safely in his first 17 games, posting a .349/.324/.458 April before finishing fifth in the Midwest League with 18 home runs. Only Brandon Wood and Hank Conger rival Sweeney's thunder with the bat among Halos prospects. Balls fly off his barrel with loft and carry to all fields, and one scout described his approach as smart and fearless. He hit .272 with three homers off lefties. His aggressiveness often leads to empty swings. Sweeney gets rotational and has a habit of using his arms and shoulders too much during his swing. He's pull-happy at times, too. He doesn't run well and he's a rigid defender. Sweeney's .862 fielding percentage was the lowest of any of the league's regular third basemen, and he's more likely to break into the big leagues as a first baseman or DH. His solid-average arm will play fine wherever he winds up. He needs to make conditioning more of a priority, and Sweeney was sent home from instructional league for undisclosed reasons. He's ticketed for high Class A this season.

Year	Club (League)	Class	AVG	G	AB	R	H	2B	3B	HR	RBI	BB	SO	SB	OBP	SLG
2006	Angels (AZL)	R	.341	44	170	38	58	11	7	5	39	23	27	4	.431	.576
	Orem (Pio)	R	.167	2	6	0	1	0	0	0	0	0	2	0	.286	.167
2007	Cedar Rapids (MWL)	A	.260	119	439	64	114	29	2	18	72	38	88	7	.324	.458
MINOR LEAGUE TOTALS			.281	165	615	102	173	40	9	23	111	61	117	11	.354	.488

18 TERRY EVANS, OF

Born: Jan. 19, 1982. **B-T:** R-R. **Ht.:** 6-4. **Wt.:** 211. **Drafted:** Middle Georgia JC, D/F 2001 (47th round). **Signed by:** Roger Smith (Cardinals).

Evans' remarkable resurgence led him to the big leagues in June, and he homered in his first major league start. A career .239 hitter with 40 home runs in 398 games before 2006, Evans posted career highs in average (.309), homers (33) and stolen bases (37) between two levels and two organizations as a 24-year-old in 2006. He came over from the Cardinals for Jeff Weaver that summer, and fortified his reputation in 2007 during his first tour of Triple-A. Like Chris Pettit, Evans is a mature hitter with great makeup, but his tools and raw strength are better than Pettit's. He has good plate coverage and uses the entire field well. He shows plus power, and he understands that in order to drive the ball, he has to muscle it to the opposite field with his arms and upper body, because he doesn't have tremendous bat speed. Pitchers can bust Evans in with good fastballs, and he'll expand the strike zone and swing and miss on soft stuff as well. He's much better against lefthanders. An average defender with average speed, he takes good routes and hustles in the outfield. He has a solid-average, accurate arm. Evans is a good all-around player with juice in his bat. He doesn't profile as an everyday center fielder on a contending club, so his shot may have to come with another organization. There's no room for him in the Angels' crowded outfield, so he's ticketed for a return trip to Triple-A with a chance for a callup anytime.

Year	Club (League)	Class	AVG	G	AB	R	H	2B	3B	HR	RBI	BB	SO	SB	OBP	SLG
2002	Johnson City (Appy)	R	.287	60	230	42	66	22	2	7	41	29	67	17	.364	.491
2003	Peoria (MWL)	A	.246	104	382	35	94	28	1	10	41	19	86	13	.286	.403
2004	Peoria (MWL)	A	.222	101	365	48	81	21	1	13	59	35	105	8	.301	.392
	Palm Beach (FSL)	A	.224	19	58	7	13	4	0	2	7	4	16	1	.281	.397
2005	Palm Beach (FSL)	A	.221	114	385	34	85	16	1	8	47	29	110	12	.285	.330
2006	Palm Beach (FSL)	A	.311	60	238	43	74	10	1	15	45	20	50	21	.373	.550
	Springfield (TL)	AA	.307	21	75	13	23	4	0	7	20	3	21	5	.369	.640
	Arkansas (TL)	AA	.309	52	188	48	58	9	2	11	22	18	56	11	.385	.553
2007	Salt Lake (PCL)	AAA	.316	120	475	70	150	40	4	15	75	26	119	24	.352	.512
	Los Angeles (AL)	MLB	.091	8	11	3	1	0	0	1	2	2	4	0	.231	.364
MINOR LEAGUE TOTALS			.269	651	2396	340	644	154	12	88	357	183	630	112	.328	.453
MAJOR LEAGUE TOTALS			.091	8	11	3	1	0	0	1	2	2	4	0	.231	.364

19 CHRIS PETTIT, OF

Born: Aug. 15, 1984. **B-T:** R-R. **Ht.:** 6-0. **Wt.:** 190. **Drafted:** Loyola Marymount, 2006 (19th round). **Signed by:** Bobby DeJardin.

Just one year removed from signing as a senior in the 19th round out of Loyola Marymount, Pettit enjoyed one of the minors' most surprising seasons in 2007, which earned him the organization's minor league player of the year award. He brings a gritty, gamer attitude to the park every day, with makeup that's off the charts. Comparisons range from Eric Byrnes to a poor man's Jason Bay. Pettit doesn't have a plus tool, but he does everything well. He has tremendous plate discipline and works counts in every at-bat. He has enough bat speed to drive balls out of the park in left and left-center field and could hit 10-14 home runs annually in the big leagues. He tends to work around the ball instead of through it, making him vulnerable to pitches away, and he's primarily a pull hitter. He's a fringe-average runner who doesn't cover enough ground to profile as an everyday center fielder, but he can handle all three outfield positions in a utility role. He did not make an error in 123 chances in high Class A last season, and his arm is average and accurate. Pettit put himself on the map last season, and he'll have a chance to climb to Double-A by midseason.

Year	Club (League)	Class	AVG	G	AB	R	H	2B	3B	HR	RBI	BB	SO	SB	OBP	SLG
2006	Orem (Pio)	R	.336	68	226	41	76	25	3	7	54	31	48	5	.445	.566
2007	Cedar Rapids (MWL)	A	.346	64	228	47	79	24	1	9	41	23	41	17	.429	.579
	Rancho Cucamonga (Cal)	A	.309	69	265	54	82	20	2	9	54	36	48	13	.395	.502
MINOR LEAGUE TOTALS			.330	201	719	142	237	69	6	25	149	90	137	35	.422	.547

20 BARRET BROWNING, LHP

Born: Dec. 28, 1984. **B-T:** L-L. **Ht.:** 6-1. **Wt.:** 170. **Drafted:** Florida State, 2006 (28th round). **Signed by:** Tom Kotchman.

Browning's stock was at its highest when he was a sixth-round pick by the Red Sox out of high school in 2002. He didn't sign, and the Cubs drafted him in 2003 after he pitched at Middle Georgia Junior College. He again didn't sign and instead went to Florida State. He fell to the 38th round to the Rockies as a junior in 2005, went back to school and finally signed as a senior for $1,000 in the 28th round of the 2006 draft. Angels instructors improved the tempo of his delivery and got him more downhill. The results have been spectacular, as Browning dominated at times out of Cedar Rapids' bullpen last season, capping his season with 14 consecutive innings without an earned run. His fastball has plus run and life at 88-91 mph. His slurvy breaking ball is a second weapon, thanks largely to his ability to vary his arm slot and shape of the pitch. He works anywhere from three-quarters to low three-quarters, and the angle he creates makes him tough on lefthanders (.132 in 91 at-bats). His changeup is a serviceable third offering. Browning's command could improve, and he doesn't have an overpowering pitch. He holds runners well and has one of the best pickoff moves in the system. He profiles as a middle reliever, and at the least figures to serve as a lefty specialist. He'll open in high Class A but could jump to Double-A at midseason.

Year	Club (League)	Class	W	L	ERA	G	GS	CG	SV	IP	H	R	ER	HR	BB	SO	AVG
2006	Orem (Pio)	R	3	2	3.05	23	0	0	1	41	33	17	14	3	13	40	.220
2007	Cedar Rapids (MWL)	A	9	4	2.80	48	0	0	8	74	54	25	23	2	26	74	.201
MINOR LEAGUE TOTALS			12	6	2.89	71	0	0	9	115	87	42	37	5	39	114	.208

21 MASON TOBIN, RHP

Born: July 8, 1987. **B-T:** R-R. **Ht.:** 6-3. **Wt.:** 200. **Drafted:** Everett (Wash.) CC, 2007 (16th round). **Signed by:** Casey Harvie.

Atlanta controlled Tobin's rights for two years as a draft-and-follow, first at Western Nevada CC and later at Everett (Wash.) CC. The Braves never signed him, so the Angels drafted Tobin in the 16th round last June and signed him for $120,000. He ranked among the Rookie-level Arizona League's top prospects following a splendid debut. Tobin's fastball hums along at 89-92 mph with plus sink and occasional armside run. The ball jumps on hitters from his deceptive, low three-quarters arm slot. It will always be a challenge for him to stay on top of his slider from that slot, but he'll flash a hard slider with late bite occasionally. His changeup is a distant third offering for now. Concerns about Tobin's work ethic raised questions as an amateur. More than one club official commented on his intimidating demeanor on the mound in a positive way, however. He could make his full-season debut in low Class A provided he has a good showing this spring. He profiles as a back-of-the-rotation starter.

Year	Club (League)	Class	W	L	ERA	G	GS	CG	SV	IP	H	R	ER	HR	BB	SO	AVG
2007	Angels (AZL)	R	2	0	0.95	8	7	0	0	28	17	5	3	1	7	32	.177
	Orem (Pio)	R	2	1	3.21	6	6	0	0	28	23	10	10	0	7	23	.230
MINOR LEAGUE TOTALS			4	1	2.08	14	13	0	0	56	40	15	13	1	14	55	.204

22 RICH THOMPSON, RHP

Born: July 1, 1984. **B-T:** R-R. **Ht.:** 6-1. **Wt.:** 180. **Signed:** Australia, 2002. **Signed by:** Grant Weir.

Thompson took a significant step forward last year after a couple of seasons when it looked like he had stagnated. He signed as a 17-year-old out of Australia in 2002, and spent parts of three seasons in high Class A before pitching in Double-A in 2006 and 2007. He helped Australia win a silver medal at the 2004 Olympics and was named to the Futures Game last season after a phenomenal first half back in Double-A. He also appeared in the World Cup after the 2007 season. He opened the season in extended spring training with a sore shoulder, but by the end of April he was a regular in the Travelers bullpen and received a September callup to Anaheim. His fastball velocity spiked, reaching 94 mph at times with solid-average life. Thompson has always had feel for a plus breaking ball, and the low-70s downer has tight spin and 12-to-6 shape. He added a split-finger fastball to his repertoire, and throws a changeup. Thompson's bounced from the bullpen to the rotation, but his fastball plays up in shorter stints and he could become a reliable middle reliever or No. 5 starter. He'll compete for a big league bullpen job this spring.

Year	Club (League)	Class	W	L	ERA	G	GS	CG	SV	IP	H	R	ER	HR	BB	SO	AVG
2002	Angels (AZL)	R	2	0	2.70	15	0	0	1	23	14	12	7	0	9	29	.167
2003	Cedar Rapids (MWL)	A	1	2	0.24	31	0	0	9	37	18	5	1	1	13	54	.140
	Rancho Cucamonga (Cal)	A	2	2	4.91	24	0	0	8	29	28	19	16	4	18	33	.246
2004	Rancho Cucamonga (Cal)	A	3	2	3.94	41	5	0	4	77	76	36	34	9	33	71	.252
2005	Rancho Cucamonga (Cal)	A	6	8	5.27	42	15	0	3	121	132	76	71	20	53	92	.277
2006	Arkansas (TL)	AA	3	4	5.13	42	0	0	10	66	52	39	38	13	27	60	.218
	Salt Lake (PCL)	AAA	0	1	12.46	4	0	0	1	4	9	6	6	1	4	3	.500
2007	Rancho Cucamonga (Cal)	A	0	0	0.00	1	0	0	0	2	1	0	0	0	0	3	.125
	Arkansas (TL)	AA	2	3	2.01	21	3	0	0	49	34	15	11	5	14	50	.193
	Salt Lake (PCL)	AAA	3	0	2.19	16	0	0	1	24	17	7	6	2	6	32	.193
	Los Angeles (AL)	MLB	0	0	10.80	7	0	0	0	6	10	8	8	4	3	9	.345
MINOR LEAGUE TOTALS			22	22	3.92	237	23	0	37	436	381	215	190	55	177	427	.233
MAJOR LEAGUE TOTALS			0	0	10.80	7	0	0	0	6	10	8	8	4	3	9	.345

23 JEREMY HAYNES, RHP

Born: May 28, 1986. **B-T:** R-R. **Ht.:** 6-2. **Wt.:** 180. **Drafted:** Tallahassee (Fla.) CC, D/F 2005 (37th round). **Signed by:** Tom Kotchman.

Haynes was a two-way player who was used primarily as a center fielder in junior college before signing for $100,000 as a 2005 draft-and-follow. He's just scratching the surface of his potential, and he's unrefined overall. He missed two starts in Cedar Rapids rotation in May with a torn fingernail on his right hand and was shut down in mid-August with tendinitis in his right shoulder. Haynes has a great body, athleticism and arm strength. He reverted to a full windup in instructional league in 2006, and it improved his balance and ability to repeat his release point. He projects to pitch with at least average command, but he's erratic presently. In Cedar Rapids last season, for example, he tossed 17 consecutive innings without a walk, but also walked nine in two bookend starts. His bread and butter is his fastball, which has been up to 94 mph with plus sink. His out pitch is a hard curveball that has occasional two-plane break at 76-82 mph. His changeup is below-average, and he has a tendency to slow his arm on his offspeed stuff. He's a long way from being ready to contribute in the big leagues, but has all the tools to pitch at the back of a rotation or serve as a quality reliever. He'll spend 2008 in high Class A.

Year	Club (League)	Class	W	L	ERA	G	GS	CG	SV	IP	H	R	ER	HR	BB	SO	AVG
2006	Orem (Pio)	R	3	1	2.76	16	14	0	1	58	46	21	18	5	41	68	.217
2007	Cedar Rapids (MWL)	A	5	6	3.06	19	19	0	0	94	98	40	32	3	41	75	.266
MINOR LEAGUE TOTALS			8	7	2.95	35	33	0	1	152	144	61	50	8	82	143	.248

24 JON BACHANOV, RHP

Born: Jan. 30, 1989. **B-T:** R-R. **Ht.:** 6-5. **Wt.:** 220. **Drafted:** HS—Orlando, 2007 (1st round supplemental). **Signed by:** Tom Kotchman.

Bachanov's MySpace page was popular among area scouts heading into the 2007 draft, featuring his "countdown 'til I get paid" clock. The big righthander became the only player the Angels signed in the first three rounds when he received a $553,300 bonus as the 58th overall pick. His elbow flared up between his predraft outing in the Florida high school all-star game and his arrival at the Angels' facility in Arizona, however, and he never made it to the mound. His arm strength has always been evident, and he shows glimpses of greatness, like his 15-strikeout performance in the 6-A regional quarterfinals in May. Angels scouting director Eddie Bane and East Coast supervisor Mike Silvestri were at the game and watched him paint both corners with a 93-95 mph fastball that touched 96. Bachanov throws two breaking balls, and his low-80s slider has occasional plus break. He also has a curveball and changeup that could become usable offerings. His delivery improved last spring, but it's far from fluid, which leads to inconsistent command. He projects as a potential closer, but the Angels were hopeful he'd be healthy and make his debut as a starter this spring.

Year	Club (League)	Class	W	L	ERA	G	GS	CG	SV	IP	H	R	ER	HR	BB	SO	AVG
2007	Did Not Play—Injured																

25 BOBBY WILSON, C

Born: April 8, 1983. **B-T:** R-R. **Ht.:** 6-0. **Wt.:** 205. **Drafted:** St. Petersburg (Fla.) JC, D/F 2002 (48th round). **Signed by:** Tom Kotchman.

Wilson played on the same high school and summer league teams as Angels first baseman Casey Kotchman, whose father Tom signed him. Wilson's portly build and unorthodox swing mechanics make many scouts ambivalent about him, but he's got major league catch-and-throw tools and a track record of offensive performance. He missed most of May with a back injury last season but climbed to Triple-A for the final two months of the season. Wilson doesn't have a lightning-quick bat, but he has improved his approach and uses good hand-eye coordination to put his barrel on the ball consistently. He's at his best when he sprays line drives to all fields, but he gets pull-happy occasionally. He has a nose for the RBI and batted .387 with runners in scoring position in Triple-A last year. He's much more nimble behind the plate than his build would lead you to believe. His hands are soft, he has good range on balls in the dirt and he gets the most out of his average arm strength. He threw out at least 43 percent of basestealers in 2005 and '06 before erasing just 23 percent in Triple-A last year. He's a well-below-average runner. With Jeff Mathis and Mike Napoli ahead of him, Wilson's probably stuck in Triple-A, but his package is better than Ryan Budde's, and he could be the next catcher on Kotchman's list of big league alumni in 2008.

Year	Club (League)	Class	AVG	G	AB	R	H	2B	3B	HR	RBI	BB	SO	SB	OBP	SLG
2003	Provo (Pio)	R	.284	57	236	36	67	12	0	6	62	18	31	0	.329	.411
2004	Cedar Rapids (MWL)	A	.268	105	396	45	106	23	0	8	64	30	55	5	.320	.386
2005	Rancho Cucamonga (Cal)	A	.290	115	466	66	135	32	1	14	77	30	61	2	.333	.453
2006	Arkansas (TL)	AA	.286	103	374	45	107	26	0	9	53	33	47	1	.350	.428
2007	Arkansas (TL)	AA	.271	50	181	24	49	9	0	6	27	22	26	5	.348	.420
	Salt Lake (PCL)	AAA	.295	40	132	15	39	13	1	3	22	8	18	1	.336	.477
MINOR LEAGUE TOTALS			.282	470	1785	231	503	115	2	46	305	141	238	14	.335	.426

26 JASON BULGER, RHP

Born: Dec. 6, 1978. **B-T:** R-R. **Ht.:** 6-4. **Wt.:** 215. **Drafted:** Valdosta State (Ga.), 2001 (1st round). **Signed by:** Mike Valarezo (Diamondbacks).

The Angels shipped Alberto Callaspo to the Diamondbacks for Bulger before the 2006 season. He bounced back quickly from a shoulder injury and came to spring training in good shape. A late-rising converted third baseman whom Arizona drafted in the first round in 2001, Bulger became a reliable set-up man in Triple-A last season. When he's right, Bulger flashes two plus pitches in a fastball that reaches 96 mph and a hard slider. His slider has good, late tilt at times and grades as the best in the system. His command has long been his nemesis and grades as below-average. He doesn't repeat his delivery and tends to leave balls out of over the zone. His slider and changeup are inconsistent. At 29, Bulger has had three shots in the big leagues, and might get a fourth this year in spring training. He could pitch near the back of a bullpen if he ever learns how to harness his stuff.

Year	Club (League)	Class	W	L	ERA	G	GS	CG	SV	IP	H	R	ER	HR	BB	SO	AVG
2002	South Bend (MWL)	A	4	9	4.94	20	20	1	0	94	111	65	52	5	39	84	.291
	Lancaster (Cal)	A	1	1	5.40	2	2	0	0	10	11	7	6	0	3	12	.289
2003	Lancaster (Cal)	A	2	1	6.75	4	4	0	0	17	23	13	13	3	5	20	.311
2004	Lancaster (Cal)	A	0	1	1.52	21	0	0	11	23	14	4	4	0	10	31	.165
	El Paso (TL)	AA	0	3	3.91	24	0	0	8	25	24	12	11	0	19	26	.240
2005	Tucson (PCL)	AAA	3	6	3.54	56	0	0	4	56	50	28	22	3	27	55	.244
	Arizona (NL)	MLB	1	0	5.40	9	0	0	0	10	14	6	6	1	5	9	.333
2006	Los Angeles (AL)	MLB	0	0	16.20	2	0	0	0	1	1	3	3	0	3	1	.167
	Salt Lake (PCL)	AAA	2	2	4.72	27	0	0	4	34	30	19	18	0	15	44	.233
2007	Salt Lake (PCL)	AAA	5	2	3.76	49	0	0	10	52	51	24	22	4	24	81	.249
	Los Angeles (AL)	MLB	0	0	2.84	6	0	0	0	6	5	2	2	0	3	8	.227
MINOR LEAGUE TOTALS			17	25	4.24	203	26	1	37	314	314	172	148	15	142	353	.258
MAJOR LEAGUE TOTALS			1	0	5.50	17	0	0	0	18	20	11	11	1	11	18	.286

27 ROBERT FISH, LHP

Born: Jan. 19, 1988. **B-T:** L-L. **Ht.:** 6-2. **Wt.:** 215. **Drafted:** HS—Fontana, Calif., 2006 (6th round). **Signed by:** Tim Corcoran.

Sometimes prospects from inland Southern California are able to fly under the radar, and Fish wasn't a consensus premium pick coming out high school in 2006. The Angels made him a sixth-round choice and signed him for $140,000. He followed an encouraging debut with an excellent season, finishing among Pioneer League leaders with 77 strikeouts in 72 innings and striking out 13 in eight innings in his lone playoff outing. His laborious, funky delivery was the main reason his stock wasn't higher as an amateur. He has a pronounced wrap in the back of his arm action that might make it hard for him to throw strikes, but he showed an ability to pitch to both sides of the plate with his 88-93 mph fastball that has plenty of deception. His breaking ball and changeup are not polished pitches, but he shows feel for them both, and occasionally his curveball shows two-plane break. Fish has a big, soft body, and he needs to take his conditioning seriously. He should hold down a spot in the Cedar Rapids rotation this season.

Year	Club (League)	Class	W	L	ERA	G	GS	CG	SV	IP	H	R	ER	HR	BB	SO	AVG
2006	Angels (AZL)	R	1	0	3.21	10	1	0	0	14	13	5	5	0	12	16	.245
2007	Rancho Cucamonga (Cal)	A	0	1	6.00	1	1	0	0	3	3	2	2	1	4	4	.273
	Orem (Pio)	R	3	4	3.27	16	15	0	0	71	62	33	26	4	31	77	.239
MINOR LEAGUE TOTALS			4	5	3.35	27	17	0	0	88	78	40	33	5	47	97	.241

28 ANDREW ROMINE, SS

Born: Dec. 24, 1985. **B-T:** R-R. **Ht.:** 6-2. **Wt.:** 180. **Drafted:** Arizona State, 2007 (5th round). **Signed by:** John Gracio.

In a 2007 draft that was thin on competent college infielders, Romine might have been a steal in the fifth round. He's the son of former Arizona State all-American and seven-year major league outfielder Kevin Romine, and his brother Austin signed with the Yankees as a second-rounder last year. Andrew was drafted in the 36th round by the Phillies in 2004, but instead succeeded Dustin Pedroia as Arizona State's shortstop. Romine signed for $128,700 last June as a fifth-rounder. He's a high-energy player who has plus range, hands and actions to go along with the ability to make the spectacular play. His arm is plus and precise, prompting Angels scouting guru Tom Kotchman to say, "He probably has a bunch of stuffed animals at his house from winning stuff at the fair." Romine posted meager .300/.390/.380 numbers with a metal bat last spring in college, and his offensive package is modest. He sticks to the little-man's game well, showing plus barrel control and bunting skills. He needs to add strength, some of which he lost due to surgery in January 2006 to have a rib removed, and he doesn't drive the ball. His righthanded swing is littered with holes, while he stays inside the ball and shows some snap in his wrist from the left side. He batted .188/.188/.250 from the right side in his debut. Romine is a plus runner who goes from first to third well. His defense and mature approach make him a candidate to move quickly, though he'll never be much more than a No. 8 or 9 hitter in a big league lineup. He'll likely start the season in the Midwest League.

Year	Club (League)	Class	AVG	G	AB	R	H	2B	3B	HR	RBI	BB	SO	SB	OBP	SLG
2007	Orem (Pio)	R	.286	56	231	38	66	6	6	5	35	16	38	12	.337	.429
MINOR LEAGUE TOTALS			.286	56	231	38	66	6	6	5	35	16	38	12	.337	.429

29 MARK TRUMBO, 1B

Born: Jan. 16, 1986. **B-T:** R-R. **Ht.:** 6-4. **Wt.:** 220. **Drafted:** HS—Villa Park, Calif., 2004 (18th round). **Signed by:** Tim Corcoran.

Trumbo was a premium two-way talent bound for Southern California when the Angels signed him for $1.425 million in the 18th round in 2004. Most scouts liked him better as a pitcher, but the Angels preferred him as a corner infielder because of his plus raw power. After a forgettable 2006 season, Trumbo returned to Cedar Rapids last year and showed significant improvement. When he gets his arms extended, he can launch balls out of the park with backspin. He tightened his two-strike approach in an effort to reduce his strikeouts. He worked diligently with hitting coordinator Todd Takayoshi to use the middle and right side of the field, something he still struggles to do. He's a slow-twitch player who doesn't have a lot of energy to his game, but an offseason agility program helped his footwork at first base, where he's a below-average defender. He doesn't run well. While Trumbo once had a plus arm, it's apparent his arm strength has waned since high school. Trumbo will get a taste of home with a season at Rancho Cucamonga on tap for '08.

Year	Club (League)	Class	AVG	G	AB	R	H	2B	3B	HR	RBI	BB	SO	SB	OBP	SLG
2005	Orem (Pio)	R	.274	71	299	45	82	23	1	10	45	21	67	2	.322	.458
2006	Cedar Rapids (MWL)	A	.220	118	428	43	94	19	0	13	59	44	99	5	.293	.355
2007	Cedar Rapids (MWL)	A	.272	128	471	57	128	27	2	14	76	34	98	10	.326	.427
MINOR LEAGUE TOTALS			.254	317	1198	145	304	69	3	37	180	99	264	17	.313	.409

30 CLAY FULLER, OF

Born: June 17, 1987. **B-T:** B-R. **Ht.:** 6-2. **Wt.:** 180. **Drafted:** HS—Spring Branch, Texas, 2006 (4th round). **Signed by:** Kevin Ham.

There were more than a half-dozen prospects off the Arizona League team who received consideration for this Top 30 list. Fuller earned notice as a toolsy outfielder with some projection, though he was repeating the league at age 20. He was also learning how to switch-hit. Fuller has table-setting ability and top-of-the-order tools. He led the league with 55 runs and did a much better job of making consistent hard contact his second time through the league. Power isn't a major part of his game, but he he's strong enough to project to hit 10-14 home runs annually in the big leagues. He's a natural righthander and understandably struggles with his swing at times from the left side. He's a plus runner with above-average range in center field, and has shown the early signs of feel for the position. He has an average arm. Fuller had a lower back injury that hampered him in 2007, but he was expected to be ready to move to Cedar Rapids with a strong showing in spring training.

Year	Club (League)	Class	AVG	G	AB	R	H	2B	3B	HR	RBI	BB	SO	SB	OBP	SLG
2006	Angels (AZL)	R	.268	45	157	28	42	3	5	0	10	25	47	14	.383	.350
	Orem (Pio)	R	.000	1	2	0	0	0	0	0	0	1	2	1	.333	.000
2007	Angels (AZL)	R	.301	45	183	55	55	10	4	5	30	24	52	21	.398	.481
MINOR LEAGUE TOTALS			.284	91	342	83	97	13	9	5	40	50	101	36	.391	.418

Los Angeles Dodgers

BY ALAN MATTHEWS

If the Rockies proved anything during the 2007 season, it was that timing is everything. On Sept. 18, the Dodgers were fresh off series wins against the Padres and Diamondbacks and sat just 2½ games back in the National League wild card race. But when Todd Helton hit a two-out, two-strike, two-run homer in the bottom of the ninth inning off Takashi Saito, Colorado had completed a doubleheader sweep of L.A.

The wins were the second and third of 11 straight for the Rockies, who went on to win the NL pennant. They also marked the beginning of the end for the Dodgers, who lost eight of their next 11 games and finished fourth in the NL West.

As Colorado's blend of youth and experience peaked at the perfect time, Los Angeles' was spoiling like month-old milk. Jeff Kent was outspoken about a clubhouse rift between disgruntled veterans and hungry up-and-comers.

Second-year general manager Ned Colletti chose in the 2006 offseason to re-sign Nomar Garciaparra and bring in free agents Luis Gonzalez, Juan Pierre, Jason Schmidt and Randy Wolf at a total cost of $124.85 million. What resulted was a patchwork lineup that finished 10th in the NL in runs and a patchwork pitching staff that wound up with David Wells and Esteban Loaiza taking the ball every fifth day in September.

Though he officially resigned, manager Grady Little was shown the door following the season and replaced by Joe Torre. A cohesive clubhouse was an underpinning of Torre's time with the Yankees, and replicating that serenity in L.A. is a top priority.

During his introductory press conference, Torre waxed about the continuity of the great Dodgers teams he watched growing up in Brooklyn in the 1940s and '50s. Los Angeles could have a similar homegrown nucleus, as it's evident that the future of the franchise lies with its youth.

Catcher Russ Martin won the first of what figure to be multiple Gold Gloves and made the NL all-star team. Matt Kemp recovered from an early-season wrist injury to hit .342/.373/.521 while showing improvement almost daily. After James Loney was left off the Opening Day roster, he eventually pushed Garciaparra to third base and hit .331/.381/.538.

When Schmidt registered only one win before requiring season-ending shoulder surgery, Chad Billingsley entered the rotation and went 8-5, 3.38 in 20 starts.

The next batch of prospects is ready to contribute. Tony Abreu, Chin-Lung Hu and Andy LaRoche all

LARRY GOREN

The hiring of Joe Torre could promote a healthier atmosphere in the L.A. clubhouse

TOP 30 PROSPECTS

1. Clayton Kershaw, lhp	16. Ramon Troncoso, rhp
2. Andy LaRoche, 3b	17. Lucas May, c
3. Chin-Lung Hu, ss	18. Greg Miller, lhp
4. Scott Elbert, lhp	19. James Adkins, lhp
5. Blake DeWitt, 3b	20. Javy Guerra, rhp
6. Chris Withrow, rhp	21. Mario Alvarez, rhp
7. James McDonald, rhp	22. Justin Miller, rhp
8. Jonathan Meloan, rhp	23. Xavier Paul, of
9. Delwyn Young, of	24. Tim Sexton, rhp
10. Pedro Baez, 3b	25. Carlos Santana, c
11. Josh Bell, 3b	26. Cory Wade, rhp
12. Bryan Morris, rhp	27. Justin Orenduff, rhp
13. Ivan DeJesus Jr., ss	28. Preston Mattingly, 2b/of
14. Andrew Lambo, of/1b	29. Alfredo Silverio, of
15. Josh Wall, rhp	30. Geison Aguasviva, lhp

have gotten a taste of the majors and could give the Dodgers a fully homegrown infield, though it may be 2009 before that transition is complete. Clayton Kershaw, who ascended to Double-A in his first full pro season, could join the rotation late in 2008.

Stability was a reason the Dodgers were named Baseball America's Organization of the Year in 2006, but they have gone through massive changes since.

The margin for error in the division has suddenly shrunk, but the Dodgers have the pieces in place to be a part of the party in the future.

General Manager: Ned Colletti. **Farm Director:** DeJon Watson. **Scouting Director:** Logan White.

Class	Team	League	W	L	PCT	Finish*	Manager	Affiliated
Majors	Los Angeles	National	82	80	.506	9th (16)	Grady Little	—
Triple-A	Las Vegas 51s	Pacific Coast	67	77	.465	13th (16)	Lorenzo Bundy	2001
Double-A	Jacksonville Suns	Southern	80	60	.571	2nd (10)	John Shoemaker	2002
High A	Inland Empire 66ers	California	72	67	.518	6th (10)	Dave Collins	2007
Low A	Great Lakes Loons	Midwest	57	82	.410	12th (14)	Lance Parrish	2007
Rookie	Ogden Raptors	Pioneer	34	41	.453	6th (8)	Jeff Carter	2003
Rookie	GCL Dodgers	Gulf Coast	40	15	.727	1st (16)	Juan Bustabad	2001

Overall 2007 Minor League Record · 350 342 .506 · 11th

*Finish in overall standings (No. of teams in league) ^League champion

LAST YEAR'S TOP 30

Player, Pos.		Status
1.	Andy LaRoche, 3b	No. 2
2.	Clayton Kershaw, lhp	No. 1
3.	Scott Elbert, lhp	No. 4
4.	James Loney, 1b/of	Majors
5.	Tony Abreu, 2b	Majors
6.	Ivan DeJesus Jr., ss	No. 13
7.	Jonathan Meloan, rhp	No. 8
8.	Blake DeWitt, 2b/3b	No. 5
9.	Josh Bell, 3b	No. 11
10.	Preston Mattingly, ss	No. 28
11.	Chin-Lung Hu, ss	No. 3
12.	Bryan Morris, rhp	No. 12
13.	Delwyn Young, of	No. 9
14.	Justin Orenduff, rhp	No. 27
15.	Zach Hammes, rhp	Dropped out
16.	Steven Johnson, rhp	Dropped out
17.	Greg Miller, lhp	No. 18
18.	Brent Leach, lhp	Dropped out
19.	Cory Dunlap, 1b	Dropped out
20.	Mark Alexander, rhp	Dropped out
21.	Mike Megrew, lhp	Dropped out
22.	Ramon Troncoso, rhp	No. 16
23.	Carlos Santana, c	No. 25
24.	Cody White, lhp	Dropped out
25.	Kyle Orr, 1b	Dropped out
26.	Xavier Paul, of	No. 23
27.	Casey Hoorelbeke, rhp	Dropped out
28.	Miguel Sanfler, lhp	Dropped out
29.	Josh Wall, rhp	No. 15
30.	Wesley Wright, lhp	(Astros)

BEST TOOLS

Best Hitter for Average	Delwyn Young
Best Power Hitter	Andy LaRoche
Best Strike-Zone Discipline	Ivan DeJesus Jr.
Fastest Baserunner	Jovanny Rosario
Best Athlete	Scott Elbert
Best Fastball	Clayton Kershaw
Best Curveball	James McDonald
Best Slider	Greg Miller
Best Changeup	Cody White
Best Control	James McDonald
Best Defensive Catcher	A.J. Ellis
Best Defensive Infielder	Chin-Lung Hu
Best Infield Arm	Pedro Baez
Best Defensive Outfielder	Jamie Hoffmann
Best Outfield Arm	Xavier Paul

PROJECTED 2011 LINEUP

Catcher	Russell Martin
First Base	James Loney
Second Base	Tony Abreu
Third Base	Andy LaRoche
Shortstop	Chin-Lung Hu
Left Field	Andre Ethier
Center Field	Andruw Jones
Right Field	Matt Kemp
No. 1 Starter	Clayton Kershaw
No. 2 Starter	Chad Billingsley
No. 3 Starter	Brad Penny
No. 4 Starter	Scott Elbert
No. 5 Starter	Derek Lowe
Closer	Jonathan Broxton

TOP PROSPECTS OF THE DECADE

Year	Player, Pos.	2007 Org.
1998	Paul Konerko, 1b	White Sox
1999	Angel Pena, c	Camden (Atlantic)
2000	Chin-Feng Chen, of	La New (Taiwan)
2001	Ben Diggins, rhp	Out of baseball
2002	Ricardo Rodriguez, rhp	Pirates
2003	James Loney, 1b	Dodgers
2004	Edwin Jackson, rhp	Devil Rays
2005	Joel Guzman, ss/of	Devil Rays
2006	Chad Billingsley, rhp	Dodgers
2007	Andy LaRoche, 3b	Dodgers

TOP DRAFT PICKS OF THE DECADE

Year	Player, Pos.	2007 Org.
1998	Bubba Crosby, of	Yankees
1999	Jason Repko, ss/of	Dodgers
2000	Ben Diggins, rhp	Out of baseball
2001	Brian Pilkington, rhp (2nd round)	Out of baseball
2002	James Loney, 1b	Dodgers
2003	Chad Billingsley, rhp	Dodgers
2004	Scott Elbert, lhp	Dodgers
2005	*Luke Hochevar, rhp (1st round supp.)	Royals
2006	Clayton Kershaw, lhp	Dodgers
2007	Chris Withrow, rhp	Dodgers

*Did not sign.

LARGEST BONUSES IN CLUB HISTORY

Clayton Kershaw, 2006	$2,300,000
Joel Guzman, 2001	$2,250,000
Ben Diggins, 2000	$2,200,000
Hideo Nomo, 1995	$2,000,000
Scott Elbert, 2004	$1,575,000

LOS ANGELES DODGERS

Top 2008 Rookie: Andy LaRoche, 3b. The Dodgers have Nomar Garciaparra at third base, but LaRoche finally should get the chance to show what he can do.

Breakout Prospect: Javy Guerra, rhp. He should have improved command to go with his quality stuff now that he's two years removed from Tommy John surgery.

SOURCE OF TOP 30 TALENT			
Homegrown	30	Acquired	0
College	4	Trades	0
Junior college	5	Rule 5 draft	0
High school	13	Independent leagues	0
Draft-and-follow	1	Free agents/waivers	0
Nondrafted free agents	0		
International	7		

Sleeper: Jaime Pedroza, ss. A ninth-round pick in 2007, he batted .360 with eight homers in his pro debut, though he eventually may have to move to second base.

Numbers in parentheses indicate prospect rankings.

LF
Andrew Lambo (14)
Preston Mattingly (28)
Anthony Raglani
Bridger Hunt
Scott Van Slyke
Andrew Locke

CF
Jovanny Rosario
Jamie Hoffmann
Erik Kanaby
Trayvon Robinson
Ryan Rogowski
Tommy Giles

RF
Delwyn Young (9)
Xavier Paul (23)
Alfredo Silverio (29)

3B
Andy LaRoche (2)
Blake DeWitt (5)
Pedro Baez (10)
Josh Bell (11)
Austin Gallagher
Brian Mathews
Pedro Guerrero

SS
Chin-Lung Hu (3)
Ivan DeJesus Jr. (13)
Joe Becker
Francisco Lizzaraga

2B
Jaime Pedroza
Juan Gonzalez
Justin Fuller

1B
Chris Jacobs
Kyle Orr
Cory Dunlap
Jamie Ortiz
Russ Mitchell

C
Lucas May (17)
Carlos Santana (25)
Kenley Jansen
Gabriel Gutierrez
A.J. Ellis

RHP
Starters
Chris Withrow (6)
James McDonald (7)
Bryan Morris (12)
Josh Wall (15)
Javy Guerra (20)
Justin Miller (22)
Tim Sexton (24)
Justin Orenduff (27)
Steven Johnson
Carlos Frias
Jesus Castillo
Kyle Smit
Daigoro Rondon

Relievers
Jonathan Meloan (8)
Ramon Troncoso (16)
Mario Alvarez (21)
Cory Wade (26)
Brian Akin
Kyle Wilson
Francisco Felix
Jhonny Caraballo
Zach Hammes
Casey Hoorelbeke

LHP
Starters
Clayton Kershaw (1)
Scott Elbert (4)
James Adkins (19)
Geison Aguasviva (30)
Leoenel Beras
Cody White
Mike Megrew
Miguel Sanfler
Michael Watt
Bolivar Medina

Relievers
Greg Miller (18)
Brent Leach
Garrett White
Jacobo Meque
Luis Gonzalez

Best Pro Debut: OF/1B Andrew Lambo (4) ranked second in the Rookie-level Gulf Coast League in on-base percentage (.440) and third in batting (.343). SS Jaime Pedroza (9) and OF Erik Kanaby (10) were Rookie-level Pioneer League all-stars, with Pedroza batting .360 with eight homers and Kanaby hitting .338 with a league-high .427 OBP.

Best Athlete: RHP Chris Withrow (1) could have been a two-way player as a third baseman or corner outfielder had he attended Baylor.

Best Pure Hitter: Lambo. A lot of teams wrote him off after he was kicked out of one high school and developed a reputation for immaturity, but his bat warranted more than fourth-round draft status.

Best Power Hitter: The most raw power belongs to 1B Chris Jacobs (17), a massive 6-foot-5, 260-pounder who's still figuring out how to carry over his batting-practice bombs into game action.

Fastest Runner: Few players get down the line quicker than Kanaby, a lefthanded hitter with an Ichiro-style jailbreak swing that enables him to get to first base in 3.8 seconds.

Best Defensive Player: C Jessie Mier (12), whose catch-and-throw skills are well ahead of his bat.

Best Fastball: Withrow ranged from 92-98 mph in a two-inning start in the GCL playoffs, generating velocity with a clean delivery and little effort.

Best Secondary Pitch: LHP James Adkins (1s) has two nasty breaking balls, a hard curveball and a slider that has topped out at 91 mph. They help his high-80s fastball play up because hitters can't sit on it.

Most Intriguing Background: OF Joris Bert (19) is the first Frenchman and the first product of MLB International's European academy ever drafted. 2B Parker Dalton (24) was diagnosed with malignant melanoma on the first day of his senior year at Texas A&M, but beat the cancer and hit a career-high .356 in the spring.

Closest To The Majors: Both Adkins and RHP Timothy Sexton (25) went straight to low Class A and succeeded. Adkins has a chance to start 2008 in Double-A, while Sexton will open in high Class A.

Best Late-Round Pick: Sexton came out of nowhere, then suddenly scared teams off with a $500,000 asking price, but the Dodgers landed him

for $123,000. He has a solid four-pitch repertoire, a deceptive delivery and a nice feel for pitching.

The One Who Got Away: Two-time High School All-American RHP Kyle Blair (5), who wound up at San Diego, has a low-90s fastball and a plus curveball. He wanted first-round money, which is why he slid and ultimately didn't sign.

Assessment: The Dodgers are excited about Withrow, Adkins, LHP Michael Watt (2) and Miller. Getting Lambo in the fourth round was a coup, though signing Blair in the fifth would have been a bigger one.

2006   BUDGET: $5.5 MILLION

LHP Clayton Kershaw (1) is the best lefty pitching prospect in the game. RHP Bryan Morris (1) needed Tommy John surgery after his pro debut, while 2B/SS Preston Mattingly (1s) has been a bust so far.

GRADE: B+

2005   BUDGET: $2.2 MILLION

The Dodgers didn't have a true first-rounder and failed to sign RHP Luke Hochevar (1s), who went No. 1 overall in 2006. At least RHP Jon Meloan (5) will help the bullpen soon, and 3B Josh Bell (4) has tremendous power.

GRADE: C+

2004   BUDGET: $5.6 MILLION

LHP Scott Elbert (1) and 3B Blake DeWitt (1) remain among the system's top prospects. Unsigned LHPs Joe Savery (15) and David Price (19) blossomed into 2007 first-rounders, with Price going No. 1 overall.

GRADE: B

2003   BUDGET: $3.4 MILLION

This is one of the decade's best drafts. RHP Chad Billingsley (1) and OF Matt Kemp (6) are already playing key roles in Los Angeles, and 3B Andy LaRoche (39) will join them in 2008.

GRADE: A

Draft analysis by Jim Callis. Numbers in parentheses indicate draft rounds. Budgets are bonuses in first 10 rounds.

NATIONAL LEAGUE WEST 1

CLAYTON KERSHAW, LHP

Born: March 19, 1988.
Ht.: 6-3. **Wt.:** 210.
Bats: L. **Throws:** L.
Drafted: HS—
Dallas, 2006
(1st round).
Signed by:
Calvin Jones.

As an underclassman in high school, Kershaw had the benefit of pitching on high-profile travel teams, but teammates Shawn Tolleson (now at Baylor) and Jordan Walden (Angels) got most of the attention. Kershaw pitched just four innings out of the U.S. junior team's bullpen at the 2005 Pan American Championships in Mexico, buried at the time behind harder throwers such as Tolleson, Brett Anderson (Athletics) and Josh Thrailkill (Clemson). But it was Kershaw who blossomed into the best high school prospect in the 2006 draft after he gained velocity on his fastball and tightened his curveball. The Tigers were set to take him with the sixth overall pick before Andrew Miller unexpectedly fell in their laps, allowing Kershaw to drop one more spot to the Dodgers. He ranked as the No. 1 prospect in the Rookie-level Gulf Coast League in 2006 and in the low Class A Midwest League in 2007. He also pitched in the Futures Game and jumped to Double-A Jacksonville a month later in just his first full pro season.

Kershaw pitches off a fastball that rests comfortably at 93-94 mph. He touched 99 a handful of times last summer, including once with Los Angeles general manager Ned Colletti in the stands (the Great Lakes scoreboard posted a reading of 101 on the pitch). Kershaw's heater has late, riding life with explosive finish at the plate. His 71-77 mph curveball has hard 1-to-7 tilt from his high-three-quarters arm slot. He made strides with his circle changeup during the year, and it too grades as a third plus future offering. He generates his stuff with a loose, clean arm action. At 6-foot-3 and 210 pounds, he has an ideal pitcher's frame that exudes durability as well as athleticism. He eventually should pitch with above-average command, though he didn't show it in 2007. Kershaw is a little slow to the plate, but is cognizant of baserunners. He employs a slide-step effectively and has a good pickoff move. His makeup and competitiveness are off the charts, and he's lauded for his humility off the field.

After Kershaw posted a 54-5 strikeout-walk mark in his pro debut, he failed to maintain his focus and delivery during 2007, which led to erratic command. He's working on improving the timing of his shoulder tilt. He tends to load his left shoulder late, causing his arm to drag during his follow-through, a correctable flaw. It makes him misfire up in the strike zone, and when he overcompensates, he begins to bury his pitches in the dirt. Because of the exceptional life on his fastball and the fact it gained velocity in 2007, learning to harness it will be an important step. His focus also wavers at times. The shape of his breaking ball is somewhat inconsistent, and he'll need to continue to work on sharpening his secondary pitches.

Kershaw offers a promising combination of front-of-the-rotation stuff and the work ethic to reach his ceiling as an ace. Some in the organization say his stuff is more advanced than Chad Billingsley's and Jonathan Broxton's at the same stage of their development. Now he has to apply the polish. He'll most likely open what could be his last season in the minors in Double-A.

Year	Club (League)	Class	W	L	ERA	G	GS	CG	SV	IP	H	R	ER	HR	BB	SO	AVG
2006	Dodgers (GCL)	R	2	0	1.95	10	8	0	1	37	28	10	8	0	5	54	.201
2007	Great Lakes (MWL)	A	7	5	2.77	20	20	0	0	97	72	39	30	5	50	134	.203
	Jacksonville (SL)	AA	1	2	3.65	5	5	0	0	24	17	13	10	4	17	29	.193
MINOR LEAGUE TOTALS			10	7	2.72	35	33	0	1	159	117	62	48	9	72	217	.201

2 ANDY LaROCHE, 3B

Born: Sept. 13, 1983. **B-T:** R-R. **Ht.:** 6-1. **Wt.:** 200. **Drafted:** Grayson County (Texas) CC, 2003 (39th round). **Signed by:** Mike Leuzinger.

The Dodgers took a 39th-round flier on LaRoche in 2003 and signed him for $1 million after he tore up the Cape Cod League that summer. He's the son of former major league all-star Dave and the brother of Pirates first baseman Adam. Andy entered spring training in competition for Los Angeles' third-base job, but went 11-for-51 without a homer in big league camp and spent most of the season at Triple-A Las Vegas. He had left shoulder surgery after the 2006 season, which might have precipitated his slow start, and he battled back soreness in 2007 as well. LaRoche has plus raw power and a good feel for hitting. When he gets his arms extended, balls fly off his bat to all fields. He lets balls travel deep and has the bat speed to catch up to the best of fastballs. He has advanced pitch recognition and commands the strike zone well when he stays within himself. He's a slightly below-average defender with a solid-average arm. LaRoche's approach was inconsistent last season. He was overly patient at times when he first got to the majors in May, then chased balls out of the zone in his second try with the Dodgers in September. He also gets pull-happy at the plate. He's a below-average runner with unexceptional range defensively. Los Angeles would like to see him take his preparation more seriously. His injury history is more extensive than he or the club would like. LaRoche profiles as an everyday third baseman with the potential to bat in the middle of a lineup. The Dodgers haven't been able to fill the hole at third base since Adrian Beltre left in 2005, and LaRoche should finally get his opportunity this season.

Year	Club (League)	Class	AVG	G	AB	R	H	2B	3B	HR	RBI	BB	SO	SB	OBP	SLG
2003	Ogden (Pio)	R	.211	6	19	1	4	1	0	0	5	1	4	0	.238	.263
2004	Columbus (SAL)	A	.283	65	244	52	69	20	0	13	42	29	30	12	.375	.525
	Vero Beach (FSL)	A	.237	62	219	26	52	13	0	10	34	17	42	2	.295	.434
2005	Vero Beach (FSL)	A	.333	63	249	54	83	14	1	21	51	19	38	6	.380	.651
	Jacksonville (SL)	AA	.273	64	227	41	62	12	0	9	43	32	54	2	.367	.445
2006	Jacksonville (SL)	AA	.309	62	230	42	71	13	0	9	46	41	32	6	.419	.483
	Las Vegas (PCL)	AAA	.322	55	202	35	65	14	1	10	35	25	32	3	.400	.550
2007	Las Vegas (PCL)	AAA	.309	73	265	55	82	18	1	18	48	39	42	2	.399	.589
	Los Angeles (NL)	MLB	.226	35	93	16	21	5	0	1	10	20	24	2	.365	.312
MINOR LEAGUE TOTALS			.295	450	1655	306	488	105	3	90	304	203	274	33	.376	.525
MAJOR LEAGUE TOTALS			.226	35	93	16	21	5	0	1	10	20	24	2	.365	.312

3 CHIN-LUNG HU, SS

Born: Feb. 2, 1984. **B-T:** R-R. **Ht.:** 6-0. **Wt.:** 165. **Signed:** Taiwan, 2003. **Signed by:** Pat Kelly/Vincent Liao.

While high-profile Pacific Rim signees Chin-Feng Chen and Hong-Chi Kuo didn't pan out for Los Angeles, Hu has persevered and developed into a valuable prospect. After a poor offensive season in 2006, he came to camp 10 pounds heavier and produced the best numbers of his career. He was the MVP of the Futures Game, the Dodgers' minor league hitter of the year and a September callup. A line-drive hitter with good barrel awareness, Hu cleaned up mechanical flaws in his swing and improved his plate coverage and ability to make hard contact. He has a tendency to step in the bucket with his front foot, but when he remains closed he hits the top half of the ball consistently and uses all fields. He likes fastballs early in counts, but shows good pitch recognition and plate discipline. His well-above-average defensive package—with the arm strength, footwork and hands of a Gold Glover—always will be his best asset. He has slightly above-average speed and runs the bases well. He's a hard worker with strong makeup. Hu had a career .397 slugging percentage entering 2007, and even with the improvements, his power grades as below-average. Avoiding bad habits with his swing will be vital to his ability to produce against more advanced pitchers. Rafael Furcal is entering the final year of his contract, so Hu will compete with Tony Abreu for a utility-infield job in spring training. Hu could spend most of the season in Triple-A and will be poised to take over in 2009 if he can replicate his offensive success.

Year	Club (League)	Class	AVG	G	AB	R	H	2B	3B	HR	RBI	BB	SO	SB	OBP	SLG
2003	Ogden (Pio)	R	.305	53	220	34	67	9	5	3	23	14	33	5	.343	.432
2004	Columbus (SAL)	A	.298	84	332	58	99	15	4	6	25	20	50	17	.342	.422
	Vero Beach (FSL)	A	.307	20	75	12	23	4	1	0	10	5	6	3	.350	.387
2005	Vero Beach (FSL)	A	.313	116	470	80	147	29	1	8	56	19	40	23	.347	.430
2006	Jacksonville (SL)	AA	.254	125	488	71	124	20	2	5	34	49	63	11	.326	.334
2007	Jacksonville (SL)	AA	.329	82	325	56	107	30	5	6	34	26	33	12	.380	.508
	Las Vegas (PCL)	AAA	.318	45	192	33	61	10	1	8	28	6	18	3	.337	.505
	Los Angeles (NL)	MLB	.241	12	29	5	7	0	1	2	5	0	8	0	.241	.517
MINOR LEAGUE TOTALS			.299	525	2102	344	628	117	19	36	210	139	243	74	.345	.424
MAJOR LEAGUE TOTALS			.241	12	29	5	7	0	1	2	5	0	8	0	.241	.517

4 SCOTT ELBERT, LHP

STEVE MOORE

Born: May 13, 1985. **B-T:** L-L. **Ht.:** 6-2. **Wt.:** 190. **Drafted:** HS—Seneca, Mo., 2004 (1st round). **Signed by:** Mitch Webster.

Elbert entered 2007 among the minors' elite pitching prospects, but he made just three starts before being shut down with a shoulder injury in April. He had surgery to remove scar tissue from his labrum in June and missed the rest of the season. He was throwing at 75 percent up to 70 feet off flat ground by November. A talented athlete who was an all-Missouri running back in high school, Elbert has outstanding arm strength and two plus pitches. When he's healthy, his fastball sits at 90-92 mph and touches 96. His two-plane curveball has the spin, shape and deception of a legitimate wipeout pitch against both lefties and righties. His work ethic and competitiveness should aid in his recovery effort. Elbert's delivery has some effort and his mechanics may cause stress on his shoulder. He has a tendency to rush through his windup, which causes his arm to drag and contributes to below-average command. His secondary stuff is inconsistent, and he needs to improve the feel of his changeup. He had displayed durability in the past and his mechanical flaws are correctable, so there's reason to believe Elbert will recover his status. He profiles as a No. 2 or 3 starter, and he could wind up as a top-flight closer if moved to the bullpen. If he's healthy, he'll begin 2008 in Double-A.

Year	Club (League)	Class	W	L	ERA	G	GS	CG	SV	IP	H	R	ER	HR	BB	SO	AVG
2004	Ogden (Pio)	R	2	3	5.26	12	12	0	0	49	47	33	29	5	30	45	.270
2005	Columbus (SAL)	A	8	5	2.66	25	24	1	0	115	83	37	34	8	57	128	.200
2006	Vero Beach (FSL)	A	5	5	2.37	17	15	0	0	83	57	27	22	4	41	97	.193
	Jacksonville (SL)	AA	6	4	3.61	11	11	0	0	62	40	26	25	11	44	76	.187
2007	Jacksonville (SL)	AA	0	1	3.86	3	3	0	0	14	6	6	6	0	10	24	.128
MINOR LEAGUE TOTALS			21	18	3.22	68	65	1	0	324	233	129	116	28	182	370	.203

5 BLAKE DeWITT, 3B

STEVE MOORE

Born: Aug. 20, 1985. **B-T:** L-R. **Ht.:** 5-11. **Wt.:** 195. **Drafted:** HS—Sikeston, Mo., 2004 (1st round). **Signed by:** Mitch Webster.

DeWitt followed Scott Elbert as the second of two first-rounders the Dodgers drafted out of Missouri high schools in 2004. After a season at second base, DeWitt moved back to third base in 2007 and got back on track offensively. He hit .281/.354/.404 in the Arizona Fall League following the season. DeWitt has a smooth, repeatable, lefthanded swing that creates consistent hard contact and enables him to keep his hands inside the ball. He can let balls travel deep and get enough extension to drive them out of the park. His pitch recognition and plate discipline also contribute to his above-average feel for hitting. He's an adequate defender with a solid-average arm. He has an even temperament and good makeup. Some scouts don't see DeWitt developing the power to play third base every day in the big leagues. He's streaky as a hitter and his approach vacillates. He can get himself out by expanding the strike zone, though it's usually by hitting pitcher's pitches as opposed to swinging and missing. He has 35 speed on the 20-80 scouting scale but runs better once underway. DeWitt's supporters cite the development of James Loney, who also didn't consistently hit for power in the minors. If he continues to improve, DeWitt could compete for a major league role in 2009 and develop into a .280-.290 hitter with 15-20 homers per year.

Year	Club (League)	Class	AVG	G	AB	R	H	2B	3B	HR	RBI	BB	SO	SB	OBP	SLG
2004	Ogden (Pio)	R	.284	70	299	61	85	19	3	12	47	28	78	1	.350	.488
2005	Columbus (SAL)	A	.283	120	481	61	136	31	3	11	65	34	79	0	.333	.428
	Vero Beach (FSL)	A	.419	8	31	4	13	3	0	1	7	1	3	0	.438	.613
2006	Vero Beach (FSL)	A	.268	106	425	61	114	18	1	18	61	45	79	8	.339	.442
	Jacksonville (SL)	AA	.183	26	104	6	19	1	0	1	6	8	21	0	.241	.221
2007	Inland Empire (Cal)	A	.298	83	339	48	101	29	2	8	46	20	42	2	.338	.466
	Jacksonville (SL)	AA	.281	45	178	20	50	13	1	6	20	7	26	0	.306	.466
MINOR LEAGUE TOTALS			.279	458	1857	261	518	114	10	57	252	143	328	11	.332	.443

6 CHRIS WITHROW, RHP

CLIFF WELCH

Born: Apr. 1, 1989. **B-T:** R-R. **Ht.:** 6-3. **Wt.:** 195. **Drafted:** HS—Midland, Texas, 2007 (1st round). **Signed by:** Calvin Jones.

A year after taking Clayton Kershaw with their first-round choice, the Dodgers went back for another Texas high school pitcher and drafted Withrow at No. 20. Withrow's father Mike pitched in the minors with the White Sox and was Chris' pitching coach in high school. Signed for $1.35 million, Withrow was used sparingly in his debut but touched 98 mph in the Gulf Coast League playoffs while striking out five in two innings. A pure projection pitcher, Withrow steadily gained velocity as an amateur and there's likely more to come. Last spring his fastball sat between 88-92 with good life when it was down in the strike zone. His 74-78 mph curveball has 11-to-5 shape with tight spin. He has feel for his changeup. His crisp, compact delivery is picture-perfect and his arm works easily. He's athletic and would have been a two-way player had he attended Baylor. In his first pro season, Withrow will focus on consistency with his secondary stuff and command. His feel for pitching is rudimentary at this stage of his development. Withrow projects to pitch with above-average command of three solid-average to plus pitches. He won't zoom through the minors, but he can become a future No. 2 or 3 starter. He'll most likely start 2008 in extended spring training but could make his way to low Class A Great Lakes sometime this summer.

Year	Club (League)	Class	W	L	ERA	G	GS	CG	SV	IP	H	R	ER	HR	BB	SO	AVG
2007	Dodgers (GCL)	R	0	0	5.00	6	4	0	0	9	5	5	5	0	4	13	.167
MINOR LEAGUE TOTALS			0	0	5.00	6	4	0	0	9	5	5	5	0	4	13	.167

7 JAMES McDONALD, RHP

ROBERT GURGANUS

Born: Oct. 19, 1984. **B-T:** L-R. **Ht.:** 6-5. **Wt.:** 195. **Drafted:** Golden West (Calif.) JC, D/F 2002 (11th round). **Signed by:** Bobby Darwin.

A draft-and-follow who signed for $150,000, McDonald's path to prospect status has been an uncommon one. The Dodgers liked him as a two-way player and moved him to the outfield when he came down with arm trouble after his 2003 pro debut, but he returned to the mound at the end of 2005 when he didn't hit. The son of former NFL tight end James and the cousin of big leaguers Darnell and Donzell McDonald, he has athletic bloodlines. McDonald has above-average command of three average to plus offerings. His curveball is the best in the system, with depth and 11-to-5 shape, and he has the feel to throw it in any count. His 87-93 mph fastball plays up because of deception in his delivery and his ability to add and subtract velocity. He effectively sells his changeup, which shows occasional plus sink and fade. He always has had a loose, clean arm action, and has improved his extension, which gave him better command and life on his pitches. McDonald still is honing the consistency of his stuff and his mechanics, and growing into his slender frame. A possible No. 3 starter, McDonald most likely will open 2008 in Double-A with a chance to move to Triple-A at midseason.

Year	Club (League)	Class	AVG	G	AB	R	H	2B	3B	HR	RBI	BB	SO	SB	OBP	SLG
2004	Dodgers (GCL)	R	.224	46	125	15	28	2	1	0	10	12	44	3	.291	.256
2005	Odgen (Pio)	R	.229	28	83	12	19	3	1	0	8	9	25	3	.312	.289
MINOR LEAGUE TOTALS			.226	74	208	27	47	5	2	0	18	21	69	6	.299	.269

Year	Club (League)	Class	W	L	ERA	G	GS	CG	SV	IP	H	R	ER	HR	BB	SO	AVG
2003	Dodgers (GCL)	R	2	4	3.33	12	9	0	0	48	39	20	18	3	15	47	.220
2005	Ogden (Pio)	R	0	0	1.50	4	0	0	0	6	4	3	1	0	2	9	.174
2006	Columbus (SAL)	A	5	10	3.98	30	22	2	0	142	119	72	63	15	65	146	.229
2007	Inland Empire (Cal)	A	6	7	3.95	16	15	0	0	82	79	37	36	8	21	104	.253
	Jacksonville (SL)	AA	7	2	1.71	10	10	0	0	52	42	14	10	5	16	64	.218
MINOR LEAGUE TOTALS			20	23	3.47	72	56	2	0	331	283	146	128	31	119	370	.231

8 JONATHAN MELOAN, RHP

Born: July 11, 1984. **B-T:** R-R. **Ht.:** 6-3. **Wt.:** 225. **Drafted:** Arizona, 2005 (5th round). **Signed by:** Brian Stephenson.

After going 27-2 as a starter in his last two years at Arizona, Meloan has become a dominant pro reliever with remarkable consistency. He spent the first half of 2007 dealing in Double-A before climbing to Triple-A and eventually Los Angeles. A ferocious competitor with championship makeup, Meloan has an aggressive approach to pitching, pounding the zone with four offerings. His 89-94 mph fastball and mid-80s slider are his bread and butter. His fastball has occasional plus sink. It shows armside run at times and he can cut it with action away from righthanders as well. His plus slider has tight spin and filthy bite. He also throws a curveball and changeup as complementary offerings. He gets ahead with his fastball and has above-average command. Meloan's tightly bound frame lacks looseness. His delivery has flaws, including recoil. He missed time in 2006 with elbow soreness, and his durability might determine his ultimate value. A potential power set-up man with the consistency managers love, Meloan will report to spring training with an opportunity to win a role in the Los Angeles bullpen. The Dodgers have been pleased with his resiliency, and they've discussed moving him back to the rotation if he returns to Triple-A.

Year	Club (League)	Class	W	L	ERA	G	GS	CG	SV	IP	H	R	ER	HR	BB	SO	AVG
2005	Ogden (Pio)	R	0	2	3.69	16	6	0	1	39	30	16	16	4	18	54	.210
2006	Columbus (SAL)	A	1	1	1.54	12	0	0	1	23	9	5	4	2	7	41	.118
	Vero Beach (FSL)	A	1	0	2.50	4	3	0	0	18	15	6	5	2	4	27	.221
	Jacksonville (SL)	AA	1	0	1.69	5	0	0	0	10	3	2	2	1	5	23	.086
2007	Jacksonville (SL)	AA	5	2	2.18	35	0	0	19	45	24	13	11	3	18	70	.155
	Las Vegas (PCL)	AAA	2	0	1.69	14	0	0	1	21	12	5	4	2	9	21	.158
	Los Angeles (NL)	MLB	0	0	11.05	5	0	0	0	7	8	9	9	1	8	7	.286
MINOR LEAGUE TOTALS			10	5	2.40	86	9	0	22	157	93	47	42	14	61	236	.168
MAJOR LEAGUE TOTALS			0	0	11.05	5	0	0	0	7	8	9	9	1	8	7	.286

9 DELWYN YOUNG, OF

Born: June 30, 1982. **B-T:** B-R. **Ht.:** 5-10. **Wt.:** 209. **Drafted:** Santa Barbara (Calif.) CC, 2002 (4th round). **Signed by:** James Merriweather.

Young's father Delwyn Sr. played pro ball and served as a hitting coach in the Mariners system. He taught his son well, as Delwyn Jr. has hit .303 in the minors and hit .382 during a September callup. He was drafted twice by the Braves before signing with the Dodgers. Young has electric bat speed and an above-average feel for hitting. He lets balls travel deep and they jump off his bat. He'll pepper both alleys with line drives from both sides of the plate. He made strides against lefthanders in 2007, improving his average against them in Triple-A to .365, up from .198 the year before. He has average power, coming more in the form of doubles than home runs. A former second baseman, his defense has improved and his arm is solid-average. Minor holes in his stroke and a free-swinging approach ultimately could make Young an extra outfielder. With below-average speed, he lacks the range to play up the middle. Comparisons range from Matt Stairs to Lenny Harris, but the consensus is that Young will hit enough to have a significant major league career. It's likely as a reserve in Los Angeles, but he could carve out an everyday role with a second-division team down the road.

Year	Club (League)	Class	AVG	G	AB	R	H	2B	3B	HR	RBI	BB	SO	SB	OBP	SLG
2002	Great Falls (Pio)	R	.300	59	240	42	72	18	1	10	41	27	60	4	.380	.508
2003	South Georgia (SAL)	A	.323	119	443	67	143	38	7	15	73	36	87	5	.381	.542
2004	Vero Beach (FSL)	A	.281	129	470	76	132	36	3	22	85	57	134	11	.364	.511
2005	Jacksonville (SL)	AA	.296	95	371	52	110	25	1	16	62	27	86	1	.346	.499
	Las Vegas (PCL)	AAA	.325	36	160	23	52	12	0	4	14	8	35	0	.361	.475
2006	Las Vegas (PCL)	AAA	.273	140	532	76	145	42	1	18	98	42	104	3	.326	.457
	Los Angeles (NL)	MLB	.000	8	5	0	0	0	0	0	0	0	1	0	.000	.000
2007	Las Vegas (PCL)	AAA	.337	121	490	107	165	54	5	17	97	38	105	4	.384	.571
	Los Angeles (NL)	MLB	.382	19	34	4	13	1	1	2	3	2	5	1	.417	.647
MINOR LEAGUE TOTALS			.303	699	2706	443	819	225	18	102	470	235	611	28	.362	.512
MAJOR LEAGUE TOTALS			.333	27	39	4	13	1	1	2	3	2	6	1	.366	.564

10 PEDRO BAEZ, 3B

Born: Mar. 11, 1988. **B-T:** R-R. **Ht.:** 6-2. **Wt.:** 199. **Signed:** Dominican Republic, 2007. **Signed by:** Elvio Jiminez.

The Dodgers signed Baez for $200,000 just before his 19th birthday and allowed him to make his pro debut in the United States. In August, he slugged a three-run home run off a rehabbing Pedro Martinez. Baez has four tools that could grade as future pluses, with his power and defense projecting as well-above-average for some scouts. He has a fluid swing with good bat speed and the early signs of barrel awareness. He can launch towering blasts when he squares up pitches. He's a confident, adroit defender with good actions and body control. He has good range to both sides. Los Angeles has clocked his throws across the diamond up to 94 mph. Baez' plate discipline and pitch recognition are in need of improvement. He tends to muscle up during his swing and get pull-oriented rather than letting his hands do the work. He's a below-average runner. Baez will likely spend 2008 in low Class A at age 20.

Year	Club (League)	Class	AVG	G	AB	R	H	2B	3B	HR	RBI	BB	SO	SB	OBP	SLG
2007	Dodgers (GCL)	R	.274	53	201	35	55	14	2	3	39	17	40	3	.341	.408
MINOR LEAGUE TOTALS			.274	53	201	35	55	14	2	3	39	17	40	3	.341	.408

BILL MITCHELL

11 JOSH BELL, 3B

Born: Nov. 13, 1986. **B-T:** B-R. **Ht.:** 6-1. **Wt.:** 205. **Drafted:** HS—Lantana, Fla., 2005 (4th round). **Signed by:** Manny Estrada.

After a substandard senior high school season in 2005, Bell saw his stock slip and he fell to the Dodgers in the fourth round, where he signed for $212,000. Following 407 at-bats in Rookie ball, he opened 2007 in low Class A where he was batting below the Mendoza line a month into the season. He turned it around and ranked as one of the Midwest League's best power prospects before being promoted to high Class A for the final month. Bell comes to the park with one thing in mind—to hit. He has a loose, lively swing with serious juice. His bat speed is above-average and balls jump off his barrel to all fields. His approach needs fine-tuning, as he falls into free-swinging modes that hinder his batting average. Sixteen of his 17 home runs came from the left side of the plate, as his swing gets long from the right side and he makes less consistent contact against lefties. He's a below-average runner and defender, albeit with a plus arm. His feet are heavy and his range is below-average, but he's a good enough athlete that he could develop into an adequate defender with some determination and hard work. He profiles as a run-producing No. 5 hitter who won't hit for a high average. He'll continue his development in high Class A in 2008.

Year	Club (League)	Class	AVG	G	AB	R	H	2B	3B	HR	RBI	BB	SO	SB	OBP	SLG
2005	Dodgers (GCL)	R	.318	45	157	26	50	7	1	1	21	20	33	5	.399	.395
2006	Ogden (Pio)	R	.308	64	250	45	77	17	3	12	53	23	72	4	.367	.544
2007	Great Lakes (MWL)	A	.289	108	398	65	115	21	3	15	62	39	109	5	.354	.470
	Inland Empire (Cal)	A	.173	20	75	4	13	2	1	2	9	3	19	0	.203	.307
MINOR LEAGUE TOTALS			.290	237	880	140	255	47	8	30	145	85	233	14	.354	.464

12 BRYAN MORRIS, RHP

Born: March 28, 1987. **B-T:** R-R. **Ht.:** 6-3. **Wt.:** 175. **Drafted:** Motlow State (Tenn.) CC, 2006 (1st round). **Signed by:** Marty Lamb.

Originally drafted by the Rays in the third round out of high school in 2005, Morris agreed to a $1.4 million bonus but Tampa Bay's ownership failed to finalize the well above-slot deal. So he elected to play under his father Ricky, a pitching coach at Motlow State (Tenn.) CC, where he dominated, then signed with L.A. for $1.325 million. The knock on Morris as an amateur was his delivery, as he pitched with a stiff front side and threw across his body. Sure enough, he had an elbow injury that required Tommy John surgery shortly after the end of his pro debut. Morris missed all of the 2007 season but made it back to the mound by instructional league. Dodgers officials said that his fastball was up to 95 mph there, and they worked on cleaning up his mechanics. During his debut, Morris pitched at 93 mph with good life and cutting action to his fastball. His hammer curveball also graded as a plus pitch with tight, hard spin. He showed some feel for his changeup and mixed in a below-average slider. He could begin 2008 in low Class A and has a ceiling of a No. 3 starter.

Year	Club (League)	Class	W	L	ERA	G	GS	CG	SV	IP	H	R	ER	HR	BB	SO	AVG
2006	Ogden (Pio)	R	4	5	5.13	14	14	0	0	60	64	44	34	3	40	79	.267
2007	Did Not Play—Injured																
MINOR LEAGUE TOTALS			4	5	5.13	14	14	0	0	60	64	44	34	3	40	79	.267

13 IVAN DeJESUS JR., SS

Born: May 1, 1987. **B-T:** R-R. **Ht.:** 5-11. **Wt.:** 182. **Drafted:** HS—Guaynabo, P.R., 2005 (2nd round). **Signed by:** Manny Estrada.

The son of former 15-year major league veteran Ivan Sr., the younger DeJesus has a game that profiled better during his father's era. He's a mature hitter with good barrel awareness and an ability to spray the ball to all fields. His defense is above-average and ahead of his offensive tools. He has easy, natural actions up the middle, terrific hands and body control when making plays on the run. His arm is solid-average and plays up because of his clean, quick exchanges. He's an average runner, and his instincts enhance his all-around game. DeJesus is patient to a fault at the plate. He falls in love with waiting on pitches when he could be more aggressive on balls he can pull. He has wiry strength but projects to hit for no better than below-average power. He'll likely bat at the bottom of an order, but a team that values defense and intangibles enough to live with his modest offense could find an everyday spot for DeJesus in the big leagues. He was unable to attend instructional league because of an injured thumb, but should open 2008 in Double-A.

Year	Club (League)	Class	AVG	G	AB	R	H	2B	3B	HR	RBI	BB	SO	SB	OBP	SLG
2005	Dodgers (GCL)	R	.339	33	121	18	41	5	0	0	11	10	22	8	.389	.380
	Ogden (Pio)	R	.208	20	72	4	15	1	0	0	3	6	18	3	.296	.222
2006	Columbus (SAL)	A	.277	126	483	65	134	17	2	1	44	63	85	16	.361	.327
2007	Inland Empire (Cal)	A	.287	121	428	69	123	22	3	4	52	57	64	11	.371	.381
MINOR LEAGUE TOTALS			.284	300	1104	156	313	45	5	5	110	136	189	38	.364	.347

14 ANDREW LAMBO, OF/1B

Born: Aug. 11, 1988. **B-T:** L-L. **Ht.:** 6-3. **Wt.:** 190. **Drafted:** HS—Newbury Park, Calif., 2007 (4th round). **Signed by:** Mark Sheehy.

Based on ability alone, Lambo would have been long gone by the time the Dodgers drafted him in the fourth round last year. The part-Greek, part-Italian three-sport standout found himself in off-field trouble as an underclassman at Cleveland High in Reseda, Calif., where he was caught smoking marijuana in a classroom. He turned up at Newbury Park High for his final two seasons and continued to show the hitting prowess that makes him a prospect. He signed for $164,250 and raked in his debut, ranking second in the Gulf Coast League in on-base percentage (.440) and third in batting (.343). He drew rave reviews from Los Angeles for his showing during instructional league, earning comparisons to James Loney. For a hitter straight out of high school, Lambo has an advanced feel for hitting. He has leverage and the early signs of lift in his smooth lefthanded stroke. He laces line drives from foul pole to foul pole, keeping his hands inside the ball well. He projects to hit for at least average power. He has a plus arm and good hands that would make him an above-average defensive first baseman, but the Dodgers believe he has a chance to handle a corner outfield position. He's a well below-average runner, but reads balls well off the bat and takes proper routes in the outfield. He probably could handle a full-season assignment following spring training.

Year	Club (League)	Class	AVG	G	AB	R	H	2B	3B	HR	RBI	BB	SO	SB	OBP	SLG
2007	Dodgers (GCL)	R	.343	54	181	38	62	15	1	5	32	29	34	1	.440	.519
MINOR LEAGUE TOTALS			.343	54	181	38	62	15	1	5	32	29	34	1	.440	.519

15 JOSH WALL, RHP

Born: Jan. 21, 1987. **B-T:** R-R. **Ht.:** 6-6. **Wt.:** 190. **Drafted:** HS—Walker, La., 2005 (2nd round). **Signed by:** Dennis Moeller.

From James McDonald to 18-year-old Dominican Carlos Frias, the Dodgers system is deep in projectable pitchers, one of assistant GM Logan White's most coveted commodities. Wall fits the same mold, and he made as much improvement from 2006 to 2007 as any of the system's young arms. His velocity always has vacillated, which was part of the reason he lasted 74 picks in the 2005 draft. He touched 95 mph early his senior year in high school, but had dipped to the high 80s by the time the draft rolled around. His velocity spiked at 96 mph last summer and sat at 92-93 when his mechanics were in sync. He flashes a plus breaking ball that has hard bite at 82 mph and an average circle changeup. Wall is tall and lean, and his arm works well. He doesn't repeat his delivery and tends to land on his left heel, spinning off the mound to his glove side, leading to below-average command and inconsistent secondary stuff. When he's right, his fastball has good downhill plane with boring action. He made strides with his mental approach to pitching, but he gets frustrated during funks and needs to mature. He'll likely open 2008 in high Class A.

Year	Club (League)	Class	W	L	ERA	G	GS	CG	SV	IP	H	R	ER	HR	BB	SO	AVG
2005	Dodgers (GCL)	R	1	3	3.86	5	4	0	0	14	13	8	6	2	8	5	.245
2006	Ogden (Pio)	R	3	5	5.86	14	14	0	0	66	80	56	43	5	33	41	.305
2007	Great Lakes (MWL)	A	6	10	4.18	26	24	1	1	129	136	71	60	8	48	103	.269
MINOR LEAGUE TOTALS			10	18	4.69	45	42	1	1	209	229	135	109	15	89	149	.279

16 RAMON TRONCOSO, RHP

Born: Feb. 16, 1983. **B-T:** R-R. **Ht.:** 6-2. **Wt.:** 197. **Signed:** Dominican Republic, 2002. **Signed by:** Pablo Peguero.

Troncoso capped 2006 with 13 consecutive scoreless innings at high Class A and was scintillating in instructional league, earning a return to the California League to begin last season. He moved up to Double-A and worked as Jonathan Meloan's setup man before inheriting the closer role when Meloan went to Triple-A. Troncoso has a repeatable delivery, loose arm and plenty of arm strength. His fastball ranges from 91-95 mph with heavy sink and late life. He tends to leave it up in the strike zone, and though he has average control, his command is slightly below-average. Troncoso made strides with his secondary stuff last season, and his slider shows occasional plus shape with late bite. He powers through it and gets around it. His changeup is no more than a show-me pitch, though he usually maintains his arm speed when throwing it. With his sinking fastball and durability, Troncoso has a chance to become a middle reliever or setup man. He was added to the 40-man roster and could open 2008 in Triple-A with a shot at a callup at any time.

Year	Club (League)	Class	W	L	ERA	G	GS	CG	SV	IP	H	R	ER	HR	BB	SO	AVG
2002	Dodgers E (DSL)	R	2	4	2.27	11	7	0	0	39	47	23	10	0	14	29	.287
2003	Dodgers E (DSL)	R	2	2	2.47	11	7	0	0	47	39	23	13	1	13	38	.228
2004	Dodgers 1 (DSL)	R	2	0	0.00	9	0	0	3	11	9	0	0	0	3	8	.220
	Dodgers 2 (DSL)	R	0	3	5.73	8	0	0	2	22	27	17	14	0	9	21	.293
2005	Columbus (SAL)	A	2	3	6.69	13	6	0	1	37	58	33	28	2	13	27	.360
	Ogden (Pio)	R	6	2	3.68	29	0	0	13	36	40	19	15	0	12	30	.278

2006	Columbus (SAL)	A	4	0	2.41	23	0	0	15	33	28	11	9	1	7	22	.241
	Vero Beach (FSL)	A	1	3	6.75	18	0	0	0	29	43	27	22	1	14	31	.347
2007	Inland Empire (Cal)	A	3	1	1.04	16	0	0	7	26	18	6	3	0	3	30	.194
	Jacksonville (SL)	AA	7	3	3.12	35	0	0	7	52	52	19	18	3	18	39	.263
MINOR LEAGUE TOTALS			29	21	3.54	173	20	0	48	336	361	178	132	8	106	275	.277

17 LUCAS MAY, C

Born: Oct. 24, 1984. **B-T:** R-R. **Ht.:** 6-0. **Wt.:** 190. **Drafted:** HS—Baldwin, Mo., 2002 (8th round). **Signed by:** Mitch Webster.

No prospect elicits the type of satisfaction in Dodgers officials that May does. An athletic grinder who was drafted as a shortstop out of high school in 2002, May moved to third base before converting to catcher during instructional league in 2006. He was added to the 40-man roster after he showed steady improvement in his first full season behind the dish last season. May always had intriguing juice in his bat, and it came alive as he slugged a career-high 25 home runs in 2007, albeit as a 22-year-old in the hitter's haven that is the California League. He generates plus bat speed and can backspin balls with loft and carry, especially to the pull side. He feasts on fastballs, but has a habit of swinging and missing too often against offspeed stuff. His swing plane often causes him to work around the ball. He's a solid-average runner who takes nothing for granted on the basepaths and could steal 8-15 bases a year. May is agile and nimble with good hip flexibility behind the plate. Though he led Cal League catchers with a .994 fielding percentage and threw out 29 percent of basestealers, his 31 passed balls were the most in the minors. His throws have carry and accuracy, with solid-average arm strength that plays up because of a quick release. His receiving is his greatest defensive deficiency presently, but his hands are adequate. May's pull-happy approach might not elicit high batting averages, so his ability to hit for power and improve defensively are the keys to his value. May's status within the organization is at an all-time high, and he'll try to replicate his success in Double-A this year.

Year	Club (League)	Class	AVG	G	AB	R	H	2B	3B	HR	RBI	BB	SO	SB	OBP	SLG
2003	Dodgers (GCL)	R	.252	48	159	19	40	8	0	0	10	19	38	11	.350	.302
2004	Ogden (Pio)	R	.286	34	147	25	42	5	2	5	30	8	37	4	.329	.449
2005	Columbus (SAL)	A	.229	99	385	46	88	14	2	9	53	16	92	5	.267	.345
2006	Columbus (SAL)	A	.273	119	450	76	123	27	9	18	82	35	130	14	.332	.493
2007	Inland Empire (Cal)	A	.256	128	507	81	130	25	3	25	89	36	107	5	.313	.465
MINOR LEAGUE TOTALS			.257	428	1648	247	423	79	16	57	264	114	404	39	.313	.428

18 GREG MILLER, LHP

Born: Nov. 3, 1984. **B-T:** L-L. **Ht.:** 6-5. **Wt.:** 195. **Drafted:** HS—Yorba Linda, Calif., 2002 (1st round supplemental). **Signed by:** Scott Groot.

As a 19-year-old, Miller's name was spoken in the same breath as Cole Hamels and Scott Kazmir as the minors' best lefthanded pitching prospects. But then he missed the 2004 season and half of '05 with a shoulder injury that required two surgeries, and he never has been the same since. His stuff isn't far from what it was, but a lack of consistency and command are preventing him from reaching his potential. Miller struggled to find the strike zone in Triple-A at the start of 2007, resulting in a demotion, and had a 12.79 ERA with 23 hits and 16 walks in 13 innings in the Arizona Fall League following the season. His arm action is deeper in back than it once was, and though he showed better durability last year, his fastball command was nonexistent at times. He still pitches in the low 90s and touches 95 mph, and his 83-87 mph slider grades as a plus-plus pitch at times, giving him the weapons to profile at least as a situational reliever if he rediscovers his feel for the strike zone. He shows much better command of his slider than he does his fastball. He also throws a curveball, cutter and changeup, but doesn't get to them often because he's too frequently behind in counts. Miller remains on the Dodgers' 40-man roster, and they're optimistic he'll fill a role in their major league bullpen. That will come as soon as he figures out how to consistently throw strikes.

Year	Club (League)	Class	W	L	ERA	G	GS	CG	SV	IP	H	R	ER	HR	BB	SO	AVG
2002	Great Falls (Pio)	R	3	2	2.37	11	7	0	0	38	27	14	10	1	13	37	.199
2003	Vero Beach (FSL)	A	11	4	2.49	21	21	1	0	115	103	40	32	5	41	111	.240
	Jacksonville (SL)	AA	1	1	1.01	4	4	0	0	26	15	5	3	1	7	40	.156
2005	Dodgers (GCL)	R	0	0	2.25	4	3	0	0	12	7	5	3	0	4	14	.150
	Vero Beach (FSL)	A	1	0	0.93	5	3	0	0	9	4	1	1	0	7	10	.138
	Jacksonville (SL)	AA	0	0	2.77	12	0	0	2	13	14	6	4	1	15	17	.275
2006	Jacksonville (SL)	AA	1	0	0.79	11	0	0	1	22	12	8	2	0	13	24	.154
	Las Vegas (PCL)	AAA	3	0	4.38	33	0	0	0	37	33	19	18	1	33	32	.243
2007	Las Vegas (PCL)	AAA	1	1	7.85	14	7	0	0	28	19	31	25	1	46	32	.200
	Jacksonville (SL)	AA	1	2	4.69	20	7	0	1	48	46	31	25	2	43	65	.247
MINOR LEAGUE TOTALS			22	10	3.15	135	52	1	4	351	280	160	123	12	222	382	.219

19 JAMES ADKINS, LHP

Born: Nov. 26, 1985. **B-T:** L-L. **Ht.:** 6-5. **Wt.:** 195. **Drafted:** Tennessee, 2007 (1st round supplemental). **Signed by:** Marty Lamb.

After topping Tennessee's all-time strikeouts list during a terrific three-year career for the Vols, Adkins signed for a $787,500 bonus when the Dodgers made him the 39th overall pick last June. He had shoulder surgery to relieve an impingement before his sophomore season, but logged more than 120 innings as a junior and 350 in his career, one reason the Dodgers limited his outings to three innings or less last summer. Adkins' slider is on par with Greg Miller's as the best in the system. It ranges between 79-82 mph with depth and deception. It would grade as a plus pitch based on its shape alone, but Adkins' knack for spotting it anywhere he wants—in or out of the zone—in any count makes it even better. His 76-78 mph curveball has its moments as well, though it's less consistent. His fastball sits at 88 mph and bumps 91, but as he learns to pitch off his heater, he could add velocity. He also throws a fringe-average changeup. Adkins' arm works well, though he needs to stay online and could improve his extension. He could move quickly and profiles as a durable back-of-the-rotation starter. He could start the season in Double-A with a strong spring.

Year	Club (League)	Class	W	L	ERA	G	GS	CG	SV	IP	H	R	ER	HR	BB	SO	AVG
2007	Great Lakes (MWL)	A	0	1	2.42	11	11	0	0	26	17	7	7	1	10	30	.181
MINOR LEAGUE TOTALS			0	1	2.42	11	11	0	0	26	17	7	7	1	10	30	.181

20 JAVY GUERRA, RHP

Born: Oct. 31, 1985. **B-T:** R-R. **Ht.:** 6-1. **Wt.:** 185. **Drafted:** HS—Denton, Texas, 2004 (4th round). **Signed by:** Mike Leuzinger.

Los Angeles slowly has amassed a nice stock of power arms from Texas, and while Guerra doesn't have the ceiling of Clayton Kershaw or Chris Withrow, his raw stuff at times is every bit as awe-inspiring. He had Tommy John surgery in 2005, and like so many others who had the operation, his velocity has returned but his command has not. He took the ball every fifth day in high Class A last season and consistently pumped 89-95 mph heat, touching 97 on occasion. Guerra generates his velocity and breaking ball with a lightning-quick arm. His 74-78 mph curve has hard, sharp downer action. He'll mix in a slider and changeup that presently grade as below-average. His delivery has been reconstructed from the ground up. He has ironed out the exaggerated crow hop he used as an amateur, but he still struggles to repeat his release point. His command is well below-average, and he's slow to make adjustments in his plan of attack. When he tries to throw harder, his fastball flattens out. He's a long ways from a finished product, but he could develop into a middle-of-the-rotation starter or a setup man with two plus pitches if he moves to the bullpen. He's ticketed for Double-A in 2008.

Year	Club (League)	Class	W	L	ERA	G	GS	CG	SV	IP	H	R	ER	HR	BB	SO	AVG
2004	Dodgers (GCL)	R	4	1	3.38	11	9	0	0	40	31	18	15	3	19	36	.214
2005	Columbus (SAL)	A	2	5	4.96	11	11	0	0	52	51	35	29	3	23	40	.249
2006	Ogden (Pio)	R	1	3	4.82	7	7	0	0	28	37	18	15	1	20	22	.330
2007	Inland Empire (Cal)	A	6	9	6.27	27	24	0	1	117	139	98	82	10	80	121	.296
MINOR LEAGUE TOTALS			13	18	5.32	56	51	0	1	238	258	169	141	17	142	219	.277

21 MARIO ALVAREZ, RHP

Born: Mar. 26, 1984. **B-T:** R-R. **Ht.:** 6-0. **Wt.:** 194. **Signed:** Dominican Republic, 2003. **Signed by:** Pablo Peguero and Ezequiel Sepulveda.

Alvarez could have gotten lost in the mix of Inland Empire's stout pitching staff because of his mediocre performance as a 23-year-old. But his upside was enough to prompt the Dodgers to protect him on the 40-man roster following the season. A converted position player, Alvarez began 2007 in the 66ers bullpen before moving into the rotation in June. His fastball ranges from 90-96 mph, and though he's just 6 feet tall, Alvarez is able to pitch downhill from a high-three-quarters arm slot. His arm is loose and quick. His command is well below-average and he often found himself throwing fastballs in predictable counts. He'll flash the makings of a fair slider, plus curveball and serviceable changeup, but he's inconsistent with all of them. His curve has occasional hard, sharp downer action at 76-81 mph, and easily could become a legitimate weapon if he improves his command and feel of it. He's ticketed for Double-A in 2008, and Los Angeles might opt to move him permanently to the bullpen in an effort to accelerate his arrival in the majors.

Year	Club (League)	Class	W	L	ERA	G	GS	CG	SV	IP	H	R	ER	HR	BB	SO	AVG
2004	Dodgers 2 (DSL)	R	4	3	1.24	13	12	0	0	65	42	19	9	2	12	48	.176
2005	Ogden (Pio)	R	3	3	6.14	12	12	0	0	55	63	39	38	8	22	53	.290
2006	Columbus (SAL)	A	7	10	5.89	27	25	0	0	128	155	101	84	8	56	102	.303
2007	Inland Empire (Cal)	A	7	10	5.60	33	14	0	0	107	123	83	67	11	48	103	.291
MINOR LEAGUE TOTALS			21	26	4.99	85	63	0	0	357	383	242	198	29	138	306	.275

22 JUSTIN MILLER, RHP

Born: Aug. 2, 1987. **B-T**: R-R. **Ht.**: 6-3. **Wt.**: 190. **Drafted**: Johnson County (Kan.) CC, 2007 (6th round). **Signed by**: Mitch Webster.

Many scouts didn't get to see Miller pitch much last spring at Johnson County (Kan.) CC because he threw just 18 innings out of the bullpen while doubling as a right fielder. It didn't help that the Major League Scouting Bureau's video on Miller was a few poor-quality frames of him throwing in a gymnasium. Area scout Mitch Webster liked him all along, however, and when he and assistant GM Logan White saw him touch 93 mph in his final outing of the spring after he had missed a month with a tender arm, Miller was destined to be a Dodger. He signed for $120,000 after going in the sixth round. Clocked from 89-94 mph during his pro debut, he relies heavily on his fastball, which plays up because of its sink. During the GCL playoffs, he induced 16 groundouts and allowed just three hits in a seven-inning relief outing—during which he threw only one breaking ball. He's not polished and looks like a position player trying to pitch, but he has the makings of a second plus pitch in a low-80s slider. He hasn't developed a third offering yet. Miller lands on a stiff front leg and has a habit of not following through completely. He projects to have average command. He has a ceiling as a middle-of-the-rotation starter or a setup man. He'll most likely spend 2008 in low Class A.

Year	Club (League)	Class	W	L	ERA	G	GS	CG	SV	IP	H	R	ER	HR	BB	SO	AVG
2007	Dodgers (GCL)	R	2	1	3.57	7	4	0	1	17	22	10	7	0	2	12	.306
MINOR LEAGUE TOTALS			2	1	3.57	7	4	0	1	17	22	10	7	0	2	12	.306

23 XAVIER PAUL, OF

Born: Feb. 25, 1985. **B-T**: L-R. **Ht.**: 6-0. **Wt.**: 200. **Drafted**: HS—Slidell, La., 2003 (4th round). **Signed by**: Clarence Johns.

Part of Los Angeles' banner draft class of 2003 that included Chad Billingsley, Matt Kemp and Andy LaRoche, Paul hasn't moved as quickly as that trio, but he has made strides in his development the last two seasons. He moved to Double-A last season and played his way onto the 40-man roster. He has above-average bat speed and average power with a line-drive swing that's conducive to hard contact. He'll pepper both alleys with line drives, though he drives the ball best to his pull side. His strike-zone discipline is below-average, and a proclivity to swing and miss figures to prevent him from batting atop a lineup. He's an above-average runner who has worked diligently on his defense. He can handle all three outfield positions, but his speed and plus arm profile best in right field. Paul was considered a five-tool talent as an amateur, but his hit and power tools have been the slowest to show up in game action. At the least, he'll have value as an extra outfielder who can steal a base and deliver some power off the bench. He'll keep working on his approach in Triple-A this season.

Year	Club (League)	Class	AVG	G	AB	R	H	2B	3B	HR	RBI	BB	SO	SB	OBP	SLG
2003	Ogden (Pio)	R	.307	69	264	60	81	15	6	7	47	34	58	11	.384	.489
2004	Columbus (SAL)	A	.262	128	465	69	122	26	6	9	72	56	127	10	.341	.402
2005	Vero Beach (FSL)	A	.247	85	288	42	71	15	3	7	41	32	81	1	.328	.392
2006	Vero Beach (FSL)	A	.285	120	470	62	134	23	3	13	49	38	114	22	.343	.430
2007	Jacksonville (SL)	AA	.291	118	422	64	123	21	2	11	50	48	112	17	.366	.429
MINOR LEAGUE TOTALS			.278	520	1909	297	531	100	20	47	259	208	492	61	.351	.425

24 TIM SEXTON, RHP

Born: June 10, 1987. **B-T**: R-R. **Ht.**: 6-6. **Wt.**: 185. **Drafted**: Miami-Dade (Fla.) CC, 2007 (25th round). **Signed by**: Manny Estrada.

Sexton transferred from George Washington to Miami-Dade (Fla.) CC prior to 2007 and expected to continue his college career at Charleston before going 8-1, 2.07 with 91 strikeouts in 78 innings last spring. He threw out signing bonus demands of $500,000 that caused him to slide to the 25th round. He spent his summer in the college Valley League before eventually signing for $123,000. Because of an unorthodox delivery and long, thin frame, Sexton draws comparisons to Bronson Arroyo. He has an exaggerated drop-and-drive delivery, in which his right knee almost scrapes the mound before he vaults over his front side. His fastball ranges from 87-91 mph and he pitched at 88 deep into games last spring. His fastball has average life with fair downward plane despite his delivery. He's more polished than fellow 2007 Dodgers juco draftee Justin Miller, showing feel for two breaking balls and a changeup that has occasional plus fade. He needs to pitch off his fastball, as he has a tendency to fall in love with his curveball and slider. His delivery is unconventional but he repeats it, and shows average command with plenty of deception. He's ticketed for high Class A in 2008.

Year	Club (League)	Class	W	L	ERA	G	GS	CG	SV	IP	H	R	ER	HR	BB	SO	AVG
2007	Great Lakes (MWL)	A	3	1	3.57	5	0	0	0	22	24	11	9	2	5	25	.270
MINOR LEAGUE TOTALS			3	1	3.57	5	0	0	0	22	24	11	9	2	5	25	.270

25 CARLOS SANTANA, C

Born: April 8, 1986. **B-T:** B-R. **Ht.:** 5-11. **Wt.:** 170. **Signed:** Dominican Republic, 2004. **Signed by:** Andres Lopez.

After spending most of 2006 in the Ogden outfield, Santana joined Lucas May in converting to catcher during instructional league following that season. Like Dodgers all-star Russell Martin, who moved from third base, May and Santana are both athletes with agility and flexibility, which bodes well for their long-term futures behind the plate. Santana's bat is behind May's, but he's a better receiver and projects as a better all-around defender. He has good hands and quick lateral movement, with a real knack for blocking balls. Santana has a plus arm and clean release, helping him erase 38 percent of basestealers in his first season behind the dish. A switch-hitter with fair bat speed, Santana doesn't project to hit for a high average, but he can sting balls from gap to gap and could develop average power. His swing gets long and he tends to work around the ball rather than through it. He shows some feel for the strike zone and consistently puts the ball in play, but he just doesn't do it with the impact May does. A switch-hitter, Santana batted just .213 versus righthanders last year. He'll advance to high Class A.

Year	Club (League)	Class	AVG	G	AB	R	H	2B	3B	HR	RBI	BB	SO	SB	OBP	SLG
2005	Dodgers (GCL)	R	.295	32	78	14	23	4	1	1	14	16	8	0	.412	.410
2006	Vero Beach (FSL)	A	.268	54	198	16	53	10	2	3	18	23	43	0	.345	.384
	Ogden (Pio)	R	.303	37	132	31	40	5	1	7	27	30	19	4	.423	.515
2007	Great Lakes (MWL)	A	.223	86	292	32	65	20	1	7	36	40	45	5	.318	.370
MINOR LEAGUE TOTALS			.259	209	700	93	181	39	5	18	95	109	115	9	.358	.406

26 CORY WADE, RHP

Born: May 28, 1983. **B-T:** R-R. **Ht.:** 6-2. **Wt.:** 170. **Drafted:** Kentucky Wesleyan, 2004 (10th round). **Signed by:** Marty Lamb.

After setting the career record for strikeouts at Indianapolis' Ripple High, Wade spent three years pitching and playing shortstop at Kentucky Wesleyan. His athleticism, clean arm action and remaining projection had several teams interested in drafting him following his junior season. Wade always had good control and a feel for pitching, but last year his stuff improved enough to prompt Los Angeles to add him to its 40-man roster. He dealt out of the bullpen between two levels last year and then pitched well in a 10-inning stint in the Arizona Fall League. Wade's fastball ranges from 86-93 mph and sits at 88. He can spot it to both sides of the plate, and he complements it with three secondary pitches. Inland Empire pitching coach Charlie Hough helped Wade with his curveball, and the pitch shows occasional plus movement with depth and three-quarter shape. He can throw it for a strike in any count. His cutter and changeup are fringy offerings, but he mixes his stuff and keeps hitters guessing. He might make it to the big leagues as a back-of-the-rotation starter, and at worst he'll have some value as an innings-eating middle reliever. His makeup is outstanding. Wade should open the season in Double-A with a chance to move to Triple-A by the all-star break.

Year	Club (League)	Class	W	L	ERA	G	GS	CG	SV	IP	H	R	ER	HR	BB	SO	AVG
2004	Ogden (Pio)	R	1	2	5.14	8	0	0	0	14	24	9	8	0	4	19	.364
	Dodgers (GCL)	R	2	1	3.03	11	2	0	1	32	28	12	11	2	1	26	.228
2005	Columbus (SAL)	A	0	2	4.05	12	0	0	2	20	29	19	9	2	10	14	.341
	Ogden (Pio)	R	2	3	4.35	16	11	1	0	72	81	42	35	12	19	60	.291
2006	Columbus (SAL)	A	6	5	4.96	23	14	1	2	94	101	56	52	9	11	94	.269
	Vero Beach (FSL)	A	2	4	8.24	7	7	0	0	39	52	40	36	9	13	32	.317
2007	Inland Empire (Cal)	A	7	0	2.45	25	2	0	6	66	50	19	18	6	17	67	.207
	Jacksonville (SL)	AA	0	1	1.36	14	0	0	0	33	22	5	5	2	11	33	.182
MINOR LEAGUE TOTALS			20	18	4.21	116	36	2	11	371	387	202	174	42	86	345	.266

27 JUSTIN ORENDUFF, RHP

Born: May 27, 1983. **B-T:** R-R. **Ht.:** 6-4. **Wt.:** 205. **Drafted:** Virginia Commonwealth, 2004 (1st round supplemental). **Signed by:** Clair Rierson.

The two pitchers who might have the least exciting stuff yet remain among the system's mix of pitching prospects because of their command and consistency are Orenduff and Steven Johnson. Orenduff suffered from shoulder inflammation in 2005 before missing most of 2006 with a shoulder injury that required surgery that August. He showed signs of recovering in 2007, but pitched past the fifth inning just six times in 23 starts and had a 5.12 ERA after the all-star break. Orenduff can cruise through a lineup once thanks to a fringe-average fastball, plus slider and average changeup, but the second time through he often had a hard time missing bats. His durability and lack of pure stuff might not allow him to remain a starter in the big leagues. His fastball sat near 88 and touched 92 last season. He has good feel for pitching and solid-average control. Orenduff could develop into a back-of-the-rotation starter if the Dodgers don't make a middle reliever out of him, which could happen as soon as this season.

Year	Club (League)	Class	W	L	ERA	G	GS	CG	SV	IP	H	R	ER	HR	BB	SO	AVG
2004	Ogden (Pio)	R	2	3	4.74	13	10	0	0	43	46	26	23	4	25	57	.272
2005	Vero Beach (FSL)	A	5	3	2.24	12	12	1	0	60	35	21	15	3	26	81	.167
	Jacksonville (SL)	AA	5	2	4.07	14	13	0	0	66	59	33	30	6	24	65	.241
2006	Jacksonville (SL)	AA	4	2	3.40	10	10	0	0	50	40	24	19	4	19	54	.217
2007	Jacksonville (SL)	AA	8	5	4.21	27	23	0	0	109	112	58	51	16	45	113	.265
MINOR LEAGUE TOTALS			24	15	3.77	76	68	1	0	329	292	162	138	33	139	370	.238

28 PRESTON MATTINGLY, 2B/SS/OF

Born: Aug. 28, 1987. **B-T:** R-R. **Ht.:** 6-3. **Wt.:** 205. **Drafted:** HS—Evansville, Ind., 2006 (1st round supplemental). **Signed by:** Marty Lamb.

Despite his bloodlines, Mattingly wasn't a consensus baseball prospect entering his senior high school season in 2006. The son of new Dodgers hitting coach Don Mattingly, Preston was a three-sport star and leaned toward playing basketball in college before Los Angeles popped him with the 31st overall pick and signed him for $1 million. His athleticism hasn't translated on the baseball diamond through 590 professional at-bats, and he batted .157/.204/.196 after the all-star break in a forgettable first full season in 2007. Mattingly's approach at the plate is raw, as he swings and misses, expands the strike zone and fails to make consistent hard contact. He flashes plus bat speed and raw power in batting practice, and Los Angeles hopes his athleticism will help him make adjustments as he matures. Mattingly lacks the range and arm for the left side of the infield, and though he's a solid-average runner underway, his best position might be left field. He held his own at second base last season after playing shortstop as an amateur. He likely will repeat low Class A in 2008 and move up as soon as he shows improvement.

Year	Club (League)	Class	AVG	G	AB	R	H	2B	3B	HR	RBI	BB	SO	SB	OBP	SLG
2006	Dodgers (GCL)	R	.290	47	186	22	54	12	3	1	29	9	39	12	.322	.403
2007	Great Lakes (MWL)	A	.210	107	404	42	85	12	7	3	40	22	119	11	.251	.297
MINOR LEAGUE TOTALS			.236	154	590	64	139	24	10	4	69	31	158	23	.273	.331

29 ALFREDO SILVERIO, OF

Born: May 6, 1987. **B-T:** R-R. **Ht.:** 6-1. **Wt.:** 185. **Signed:** Dominican Republic, 2003. **Signed by:** Angel Santana.

Few young players look the part more than Silverio, who draws physical comparisons to a young George Bell. After three-peating the Rookie-level Dominican Summer League, he won the GCL batting title with a .373 average last summer, helping the Dodgers to a league-best 40-15 mark and a berth in the championship series. He's an exciting player with a good package of tools. Silverio has a sound approach at the plate and projects to hit for slightly above-average power. He shows the makings of pitch recognition and plate discipline. Silverio is a 40 runner on the 20-80 scouting scale, but better under way. He played all three outfield positions in 2007 and figures to settle into a corner spot. His routes and reads are advanced for his age in the outfield, and he has a solid-average arm. Silverio could begin 2008 in low Class A.

Year	Club (League)	Class	AVG	G	AB	R	H	2B	3B	HR	RBI	BB	SO	SB	OBP	SLG
2004	Dodgers2 (DSL)	R	.240	59	192	18	46	6	2	1	16	7	36	5	.273	.307
2005	Dodgers (DSL)	R	.244	25	82	11	20	2	0	1	14	10	15	2	.316	.305
2006	Dodgers (DSL)	R	.276	61	225	36	62	12	6	6	48	18	44	6	.335	.462
2007	Dodgers (GCL)	R	.373	51	193	38	72	9	3	6	46	11	32	5	.406	.544
MINOR LEAGUE TOTALS			.289	196	692	103	200	29	11	14	124	46	127	18	.336	.423

30 GEISON AGUASVIVA, LHP

Born: Aug. 3, 1987. **B-T:** L-L. **Ht.:** 6-2. **Wt.:** 166. **Signed:** Dominican Republic, 2005. **Signed by:** Victor Baez/Eddie D'Oleo.

The Dodgers' 2007 Dominican Summer League pitching staff had more than a handful of prospects, the most polished of whom was Aguasviva. He ranked eighth in the DSL with a 1.50 ERA and posted a 2.6 groundout/flyout ratio. Lefthanders went just 3-for-23 against him. Aguasviva has a free and easy arm action and shows good body control over the rubber. There's projection remaining in his 6-foot-2 frame as well as his stuff. He presently tops out at 91 mph with his fastball, and he shows feel for his breaking ball, which projects as a second plus pitch. He toyed with young Latin hitters at times, setting up his curve by hitting both corners of the plate with his fastball. He has shown durability in his two seasons in the DSL, and the Dodgers are contemplating jumping him to low Class A to start 2008.

Year	Club (League)	Class	W	L	ERA	G	GS	CG	SV	IP	H	R	ER	HR	BB	SO	AVG
2006	Dodgers (DSL)	R	3	3	5.17	14	8	0	0	47	57	32	27	5	21	41	.297
2007	Dodgers (DSL)	R	8	2	1.50	12	12	0	0	66	43	14	11	0	14	69	.183
MINOR LEAGUE TOTALS			11	5	3.03	26	20	0	0	113	100	46	38	5	35	110	.234

Milwaukee Brewers

BY TOM HAUDRICOURT

No team has advanced more impact players to the major leagues over the last few years than the Brewers.

On any given night in the final weeks of the 2007 season, you could find 21-year-old Yovani Gallardo on the mound, backed by an infield of Prince Fielder (23), Rickie Weeks (25), Ryan Braun (23) and J.J. Hardy (25), with Corey Hart (25) in right field. All except Hart were first- or second-round draft picks, which is how Milwaukee rebuilt a sagging franchise.

That young nucleus of players kept the Brewers atop the National League Central before pitching problems finally caused them to slip to second place. Still, at 83-79, they posted their first winning season since 1992.

A year ago, Gallardo and Braun ranked 1-2 atop Milwaukee's Top 10 Prospects list. It was easy to see why they held such lofty status when they were summoned to the big leagues, Braun in late May and Gallardo in mid-June.

All Braun did was post the highest slugging percentage (.634) of any rookie in big league history, batting .324/.370/.634 with 34 home runs and 97 RBIs in just 113 games to win BA's Rookie of the Year award. Gallardo settled in, went 9-5 and posted the lowest ERA in the rotation at 3.67, including a 3-1, 1.36 mark in September.

Fielder became the youngest player ever to sock 50 home runs in the majors, knocking Willie Mays from that perch. Hardy was named by his peers to the NL all-star team and totaled 26 homers and 80 RBIs. Weeks finished with a flourish after his surgically repaired right wrist healed, socking nine homers in September. Hart had a breakthrough season. He hit .295/.353/.539 with 24 homers, 81 RBIs and 23 steals.

As a sign of their big league breakthrough, the Brewers did something they had not done in the past—trade prospects for a veteran. They sent pitchers Will Inman, Joe Thatcher and Steve Garrison—all ranked among the organization's Top 30 prospects—to the Padres for reliever Scott Linebrink before the July 31 deadline.

Graduating so many highly ranked prospects to the majors in such a short time and trading three pitching prospects would wipe out some farm systems. But Milwaukee's six U.S.-based affiliates combined for a 387-298 (.565) record, the best among NL organizations, and five of them reached the

Yovani Gallardo emerged as the Brewers' best homegrown pitcher since Ben Sheets

JOHN WILLIAMSON

TOP 30 PROSPECTS

1. Matt LaPorta, of	16. Jonathan Lucroy, c
2. Manny Parra, lhp	17. Taylor Green, 3b
3. Alcides Escobar, ss	18. Cody Scarpetta, rhp
4. Jeremy Jeffress, rhp	19. Nick Tyson, rhp
5. Mat Gamel, 3b	20. Alexandre Periard, rhp
6. Cole Gillespie, of	21. Darren Ford, of
7. Brent Brewer, ss	22. Lee Haydel, of
8. Angel Salome, c	23. Eric Farris, 2b
9. Lorenzo Cain, of	24. Michael Brantley, of/1b
10. Caleb Gindl, of	25. Stephen Chapman, of
11. Rob Bryson, rhp	26. Hernan Iribarren, 2b
12. Mark Rogers, rhp	27. Steve Hammond, lhp
13. Zach Braddock, lhp	28. Charlie Fermaint, of
14. Luis Pena, rhp	29. Chris Errecart, 1b
15. R.J. Seidel, rhp	30. Brendan Katin, of

playoffs. Most of the Brewers' notable picks were high first-rounders, yet they've done well in the later rounds and had more than their share of success with the now-extinct draft-and-follow system.

Those trends continued in 2007. New No. 1 Matt LaPorta was taken seventh overall and was followed by three more position players who hit .300 or better in their debuts: catcher Jonathan Lucroy, second baseman Eric Farris and outfielder Caleb Gindl. They also had an impressive final class of draft-and-follows, led by righthander Rob Bryson.

General Manager: Doug Melvin. **Farm Director:** Reid Nichols. **Scouting Director:** Jack Zduriencik.

Class	Team	League	W	L	PCT	Finish*	Manager	Affiliated
Majors	Milwaukee	Majors	83	79	.512	8th (16)	Ned Yost	—
Triple-A	Nashville Sounds	Pacific Coast	89	55	.618	1st (16)	Frank Kremblas	2005
Double-A	Huntsville Stars	Southern	75	62	.547	3rd (10)	Don Money	1999
High A	Brevard County Manatees	Florida State	74	62	.544	4th (12)	John Tamargo	2005
Low A	West Virginia Power	South Atlantic	82	54	.603	3rd (16)	Mike Guerrero	2005
Rookie	Helena Brewers	Pioneer	48	28	.632	2nd (8)	Jeff Isom	2003
Rookie	AZL Brewers	Arizona	19	37	.339	9th (9)	Rene Gonzales	2001
Overall 2007 Minor League Record			387	298	.565	2nd		

*Finish in overall standings (No. of teams in league) ^League champion

LAST YEAR'S TOP 30

Player, Pos.		Status
1.	Yovani Gallardo, rhp	Majors
2.	Ryan Braun, 3b	Majors
3.	Will Inman, rhp	(Padres)
4.	Jeremy Jeffress, rhp	No. 4
5.	Mark Rogers, rhp	No. 12
6.	Lorenzo Cain, of	No. 9
7.	Steve Hammond, lhp	No. 27
8.	Cole Gillespie, of	No. 6
9.	Alcides Escobar, ss	No. 3
10.	Mat Gamel, 3b	No. 5
11.	Angel Salome, c	No. 8
12.	Charlie Fermaint, of	No. 28
13.	Darren Ford, of	No. 21
14.	Yohannis Perez, ss	Dropped out
15.	Tim Dillard, rhp	Dropped out
16.	Zach Jackson, lhp	Dropped out
17.	Tony Gwynn Jr., of	Majors
18.	Manny Parra, lhp	No. 2
19.	Brent Brewer, ss	No. 7
20.	Chris Errecart, of/1b	No. 29
21.	Hernan Iribarren, 2b	No. 26
22.	Dennis Sarfate, rhp	(Orioles)
23.	Joe Thatcher, lhp	(Padres)
24.	Robert Hinton, rhp	Dropped out
25.	R.J. Seidel, rhp	No. 15
26.	Brendan Katin, of	No. 30
27.	Steve Garrison, lhp	(Padres)
28.	Stephen Chapman, of	No. 25
29.	Vinny Rottino, 3b/c/of	Dropped out
30.	Rolando Pascual, rhp	Dropped out

BEST TOOLS

Best Hitter for Average	Mat Gamel
Best Power Hitter	Matt LaPorta
Best Strike-Zone Discipline	Michael Brantley
Fastest Baserunner	Darren Ford
Best Athlete	Brent Brewer
Best Fastball	Jeremy Jeffress
Best Curveball	Nick Tyson
Best Slider	Robert Hinton
Best Changeup	R.J. Seidel
Best Control	Manny Parra
Best Defensive Catcher	Lou Palmisano
Best Defensive Infielder	Alcides Escobar
Best Infield Arm	Alcides Escobar
Best Defensive Outfielder	Darren Ford
Best Outfield Arm	Brendan Katin

PROJECTED 2011 LINEUP

Catcher	Angel Salome
First Base	Prince Fielder
Second Base	Rickie Weeks
Third Base	J.J. Hardy
Shortstop	Alcides Escobar
Left Field	Matt LaPorta
Center Field	Ryan Braun
Right Field	Corey Hart
No. 1 Starter	Yovani Gallardo
No. 2 Starter	Ben Sheets
No. 3 Starter	Manny Parra
No. 4 Starter	Jeremy Jeffress
No. 5 Starter	Carlos Villanueva
Closer	Rob Bryson

TOP PROSPECTS OF THE DECADE

Year	Player, Pos.	2007 Org.
1998	Valerio de los Santos, lhp	Mexico
1999	Ron Belliard, 2b	Nationals
2000	Nick Neugebauer, rhp	Out of baseball
2001	Ben Sheets, rhp	Brewers
2002	Nick Neugebauer, rhp	Out of baseball
2003	Brad Nelson, 1b	Brewers
2004	Rickie Weeks, 2b	Brewers
2005	Rickie Weeks, 2b	Brewers
2006	Prince Fielder, 1b	Brewers
2007	Yovani Gallardo, rhp	Brewers

TOP DRAFT PICKS OF THE DECADE

Year	Player, Pos.	2007 Org.
1998	J.M. Gold, rhp	Out of baseball
1999	Ben Sheets, rhp	Brewers
2000	Dave Krynzel, of	Diamondbacks
2001	Mike Jones, rhp	Brewers
2002	Prince Fielder, 1b	Brewers
2003	Rickie Weeks, 2b	Brewers
2004	Mark Rogers, rhp	Brewers
2005	Ryan Braun, 3b	Brewers
2006	Jeremy Jeffress, rhp	Brewers
2007	Matt LaPorta, of	Brewers

LARGEST BONUSES IN CLUB HISTORY

Rickie Weeks, 2003	$3,600,000
Ben Sheets, 1999	$2,450,000
Ryan Braun, 2005	$2,450,000
Prince Fielder, 2002	$2,400,000
Mark Rogers, 2004	$2,200,000

MILWAUKEE BREWERS

Top 2008 Rookie: Manny Parra, lhp. He might have made the difference in the National League Central race had he not broken his thumb trying to bunt in his second big league start.

Breakout Prospect: Zach Braddock, lhp. He dominated when he was on the mound in 2007, but he missed much of the year with shoulder and elbow problems that didn't need surgery. He's also battling some emotional issues.

Sleeper: Chad Robinson, rhp. A $500,000 draft-and-follow, he can touch 95 mph and should get untracked after a lackluster pro debut.

SOURCE OF TOP 30 TALENT			
Homegrown	30	Acquired	0
College	7	Trades	0
Junior college	1	Rule 5 draft	0
High school	10	Independent leagues	0
Draft-and-follow	8	Free agents/waivers	0
Nondrafted free agents	0		
International	4		

Numbers in parentheses indicate prospect rankings

LF
Matt LaPorta (1)
Cole Gillespie (6)
Caleb Gindl (10)
Michael Brantley (24)
Drew Anderson
Chuckie Caufield

CF
Darren Ford (21)
Lee Haydel (22)
Charlie Fermaint (28)
Steve Moss
Mike Goetz

RF
Lorenzo Cain (9)
Stephen Chapman (25)
Brendan Katin (30)
Freddy Parejo

3B
Mat Gamel (5)
Taylor Green (17)
Adam Heether
Vinny Rottino

SS
Alcides Escobar (3)
Brent Brewer (7)
Yohannis Perez
Ozzie Chavez

2B
Eric Farris (23)
Hernan Iribarren (26)
Ryan Crew
Mike Bell

1B
Chris Errecart (29)
Brad Nelson
Steffan Wilson

C
Angel Salome (8)
Jonathan Lucroy (16)
Lou Palmisano
Shawn Zarraga
Carlos Corporan

RHP

Starters	Relievers
Jeremy Jeffress (4)	Luis Pena (14)
Rob Bryson (11)	Tim Dillard
Mark Rogers (12)	Robert Hinton
R.J. Seidel (15)	Steve Bray
Cody Scarpetta (18)	Omar Aguilar
Nick Tyson (19)	
Alexandre Periard (20)	
Chad Robinson	
Mike McClendon	
Roque Mercedes	
Jose Garcia	
Rolando Pascual	

LHP

Starters	Relievers
Manny Parra (2)	Mitch Stetter
Zach Braddock (13)	Jeff Housman
Steve Hammond (23)	Jeremy Lewis
Derek Miller	Dan Merklinger
Zach Jackson	
Sam Narron	
David Welch	
Brae Wright	

2007   SIGNING BUDGET: $3.2 MILLION

Best Pro Debut: The Brewers' first four picks—OF Matt LaPorta (1), C Jonathan Lucroy (3), 2B Eric Farris (4) and OF Caleb Gindl (5)—all hit .300 or better. LaPorta slugged 12 homers, while the other three were Rookie-level Pioneer League all-stars. Gindl won the PL batting title at .372.

Best Athlete: Most of Milwaukee's position players would be classified as bats rather than athletes. Farris has decent tools across the board, though his power is more of the gap variety. OF Erik Miller (17) is similarly athletic and not particularly powerful.

Best Pure Hitter: LaPorta or Gindl.

Best Power Hitter: LaPorta, though 3B Stefan Wilson (28) isn't far behind. C Shawn Zarraga (44) won a national high school home run derby in 2006 with a power display that included six straight homers, one of them a 506-foot blast.

Fastest Runner: Draft-and-follow Lee Haydel (19 in 2006) has top-of-the-line speed and can cover 60 yards in 6.35 seconds. Farris has plus speed and very good baserunning instincts.

Best Defensive Player: Farris, who saw time at shortstop in college and should be an above-average defender at second base.

Best Fastball: Draft-and-follows RHPs Robert Bryson (31 in 2006) and Chad Robinson (12 in 2006) both touch 95 mph. So does RHP Cody Scarpetta (11), who would have gone in the first three rounds if he hadn't torn a tendon in his right index finger in April.

Best Secondary Pitch: Draft-and-follow RHP Nick Tyson (32 in 2006) has the best curveball in the system, followed closely by Scarpetta's power breaker.

Most Intriguing Background: 1B Joey Paciorek's (15) father Jim and uncles John and Tom all played in the majors, as did LHP Casey Baron's (34) grandfather Ray and unsigned RHP Jordan Tanner's (40, now at LaRoche, Pa., College) dad Bruce (now a Tigers advance scout) and grandfather Chuck. Milwaukee drafted Scarpetta's father Dan in the third round in June 1982 and included him with current Brewers manager Ned Yost in a trade for Jim Sundberg.

Closest To The Majors: The Brewers plan on skipping LaPorta a level and starting him in Double-A in 2008.

Best Late-Round Pick: Scarpetta. A native

Aruban, Zarraga has power in his arm as well as his bat. He plummeted in the draft after asking for $500,000 and signed for $230,000.

The One Who Got Away: SS Rick Hague (37) had better all-around tools and defensive prowess than any draftee the Brewers signed. They couldn't sway him from attending Rice.

Assessment: Milwaukee pulled the first surprise of the draft at No. 7, taking LaPorta as an outfielder though he never played the position in college. That was a harbinger of offensive-minded picks to come, though the Brewers landed three high-ceiling pitchers in Scarpetta and draft-and-follows Robinson and Bryson.

2006   BUDGET: $3.4 MILLION

RHP Jeremy Jeffress (1) has a big-time arm but has failed four drug tests for marijuana. SS Brent Brewer (2) and OF Cole Gillespie (3) are keepers, as are sleeper RHP R.J. Seidel (16) and a strong draft-and-follow crop led by RHP Rob Bryson (31).

GRADE: C+

2005   BUDGET: $3.8 MILLION

3B Ryan Braun (1) set a rookie record with a .634 slugging percentage last year. 3B Mat Gamel (5) also has a potent bat, while RHP Will Inman (3) and LHP Steve Garrison (10) were used in the Scott Linebrink trade.

GRADE: A

2004   BUDGET: $4.3 MILLION

RHP Mark Rogers (1) has had injury and command issues, but the Brewers found an ace in RHP Yovani Gallardo (2). C Angel Salome (5) and OF Lorenzo Cain (17) could push for regular jobs in the future.

GRADE: B+

2003   BUDGET: $6.1 MILLION

2B Rickie Weeks (2) is showing signs of why he was the No. 2 overall pick. OF Tony Gwynn (2), LHP Mitch Stetter (16), since-traded RHP Ty Taubenheim (19) and OF Drew Anderson (24) all have made big league cameos.

GRADE: B

Draft analysis by Jim Callis. Numbers in parentheses indicate draft rounds. Budgets are bonuses in first 10 rounds.

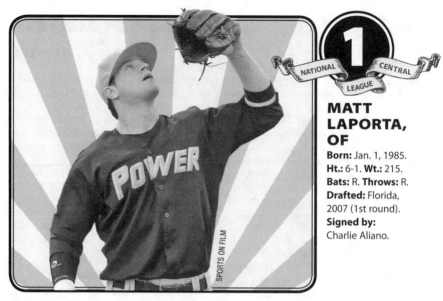

NATIONAL LEAGUE — 1 — CENTRAL

MATT LAPORTA, OF

Born: Jan. 1, 1985.
Ht.: 6-1. **Wt.:** 215.
Bats: R. **Throws:** R.
Drafted: Florida, 2007 (1st round).
Signed by: Charlie Aliano.

The Brewers pulled the first surprise in the 2007 draft when they called out LaPorta's name with the seventh overall selection in the first round. They already had a young, slugging first baseman by the name of Prince Fielder emerging as a superstar in the majors, and no one figured they'd take another. But they had another plan in mind for LaPorta. Milwaukee believed that his advanced bat was a steal at No. 7 and that he could make the transition to left field, having evaluated him in predraft workouts. He wasn't even supposed to be available in the 2007 draft. After leading NCAA Division I hitters with 26 homers as a sophomore at Florida, he figured to be a first-round pick in 2006. But when he was bothered that spring by an oblique injury, he hit just .259 with 14 homers and dropped to the Red Sox in the 14th round of the draft. LaPorta returned to the Gators and batted .402 with 20 homers as a senior, leading Division I with a .582 on-base percentage and 1.399 on-base plus slugging. The first-ever two-time Southeastern Conference player of the year, he signed quickly with the Brewers for $2 million, though he didn't make his pro debut until the end of July because he had an injured quadriceps muscle. LaPorta hit a homer in his first game at Rookie-level Helena and mashed 12 in 115 at-bats overall. Milwaukee sent LaPorta to the Arizona Fall League in an effort to give him more at-bats and work in left field while also showing confidence he could adapt to advanced competition.

LaPorta has game-changing power and doesn't have to pull the ball to get it out of the park. Area scouts who covered him said his approach improved in 2007, and he also kept his hands inside the ball better and made more consistent hard contact. He also has a good eye at the plate and will take a walk if he doesn't get a pitch to hammer. The Brewers also like his poise and maturity, which is why they weren't nervous about challenging him with the AFL assignment. LaPorta's willingness to move from first base to left field and his work ethic in doing so also impressed club officials. Milwaukee isn't asking LaPorta to be anything more than an average left fielder. After all, they committed to Carlos Lee in left a few years back, and as one club official noted, "This guy's better than Carlos Lee."

LaPorta still has to learn how to handle breaking balls, both quality pitches for strikes and those off the plate. He's a below-average athlete and runner, and his arm strength is fringy. He doesn't have the speed to run down many balls in the gap, but he has shown improved instincts in left field. He still needs to work on getting the ball to the cutoff man quickly and mastering the other nuances of outfield play. He spent a lot of time in the AFL learning to read balls off the bat.

LaPorta's AFL experience may allow him to bypass high Class A Brevard County and start 2008 at Double-A Huntsville. As with 2005 first-rounder Ryan Braun, LaPorta shouldn't need much more than a full season in the minors before becoming an impact hitter in Milwaukee.

Year	Club (League)	Class	AVG	G	AB	R	H	2B	3B	HR	RBI	BB	SO	SB	OBP	SLG
2007	Helena (Pio)	R	.259	7	27	4	7	1	0	2	4	1	8	0	.286	.519
	West Virginia (SAL)	A	.318	23	88	18	28	8	0	10	27	7	22	0	.392	.750
MINOR LEAGUE TOTALS			.304	30	115	22	35	9	0	12	31	8	30	0	.369	.696

2 MANNY PARRA, LHP

Born: Oct. 30, 1982. **B-T:** L-L. **Ht.:** 6-3. **Wt.:** 200. **Drafted:** American River (Calif.) JC, D/F 2001 (26th round). **Signed by:** Justin McCray.

The highest-priced draft-and-follow in club history at $1.55 million, Parra got sidetracked by surgery to repair a torn rotator cuff in August 2005. He re-established himself in 2007, tossing a perfect game in his second Triple-A start and reaching the big leagues. He broke his left thumb trying to bunt in his second start with the Brewers. Parra has regained his arm strength and is back throwing his fastball in the low- to mid-90s on a regular basis. He mixes in a changeup and curveball to keep hitters off balance and pounds the strike zone. His return to health restored his confidence and he pitched with a purpose. Parra mainly needs to show he can stay healthy, and his 137 innings was two shy of his career best. He pitched tentatively at times in the majors; he's at his best when he pitches aggressively off his fastball. Parra will get the chance to crack Milwaukee's rotation in spring training. If he can't find a spot, he could shift to the bullpen or return to Triple-A. He eventually should settle in as a No. 3 starter.

Year	Club (League)	Class	W	L	ERA	G	GS	CG	SV	IP	H	R	ER	HR	BB	SO	AVG
2002	Brewers (AZL)	R	0	0	4.50	1	1	0	0	2	1	1	1	1	0	4	.143
	Ogden (Pio)	R	3	1	3.21	11	10	0	0	47	59	30	17	3	10	51	.298
2003	Beloit (MWL)	A	11	2	2.73	23	23	1	0	138	127	50	42	9	24	117	.243
2004	High Desert (Cal)	A	5	2	3.48	13	12	1	0	67	76	41	26	3	19	64	.290
	Huntsville (SL)	AA	0	1	3.00	3	3	0	0	6	5	3	2	0	0	10	.217
2005	Huntsville (SL)	AA	5	6	3.96	16	16	0	0	91	111	47	40	4	21	86	.295
2006	Brevard County (FSL)	A	1	3	2.96	15	14	0	0	54	47	29	18	4	32	61	.235
	Huntsville (SL)	AA	3	0	2.87	6	6	0	0	31	26	13	10	0	8	29	.232
2007	Huntsville (SL)	AA	7	3	2.68	13	13	0	0	80	70	28	24	2	26	81	.234
	Nashville (PCL)	AAA	3	1	1.73	4	4	1	0	26	15	6	5	1	7	25	.172
	Milwaukee (NL)	MLB	0	1	3.76	9	2	0	0	26	25	13	11	1	12	26	.255
MINOR LEAGUE TOTALS			38	19	3.05	105	102	3	0	545	537	248	185	27	147	528	.257
MAJOR LEAGUE TOTALS			0	1	3.76	9	2	0	0	26	25	13	11	1	12	26	.255

3 ALCIDES ESCOBAR, SS

Born: Dec. 16, 1986. **B-T:** R-R. **Ht.:** 6-1. **Wt.:** 175. **Signed:** Venezuela, 2003. **Signed by:** Epy Guerrero.

Escobar played the entire 2007 season at age 20 and thrived during the second half. Consistently one of the youngest players at his level, he batted a career-high .306 overall while finishing strong in Double-A. Escobar could play defense in the big leagues right now. He's a smooth shortstop, with nice range, soft hands and a strong throwing arm. He has gotten stronger, which has stopped pitchers from knocking the bat out of his hands, and the Brewers believe he'll have gap power as he continues to develop. He's an above-average runner. Though he has matured physically over the past year, Escobar still needs to get stronger. He'll never have a lot of pop, and he needs to improve his plate discipline to reach his offensive ceiling. He's a free swinger who settles for merely putting the ball in play too often. He must improve his basestealing aptitude after getting caught 13 times in 35 overall attempts. When Escobar's bat is big league ready, he'll be hard to hold back. He's ticketed to spend 2008 at Triple-A Nashville.

CLIFF WELCH

Year	Club (League)	Class	AVG	G	AB	R	H	2B	3B	HR	RBI	BB	SO	SB	OBP	SLG
2004	Helena (Pio)	R	.281	68	231	38	65	8	0	2	24	20	44	20	.348	.342
2005	West Virginia (SAL)	A	.271	127	520	80	141	25	8	2	36	20	90	30	.305	.362
2006	Brevard County (FSL)	A	.257	87	350	47	90	9	1	2	33	19	56	28	.296	.306
2007	Brevard County (FSL)	A	.325	63	268	37	87	8	3	0	25	7	35	18	.345	.377
	Huntsville (SL)	AA	.283	62	226	27	64	5	4	1	28	11	36	4	.314	.354
MINOR LEAGUE TOTALS			.280	407	1595	229	447	55	16	7	146	77	261	100	.317	.348

4 JEREMY JEFFRESS, RHP

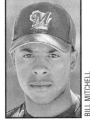

Born: Sept. 21, 1987. **B-T:** R-R. **Ht.:** 6-1. **Wt.:** 185. **Drafted:** HS—South Boston, Va., 2006 (1st round) **Signed by:** Tim McIlvaine.

Jeffress has the best arm in the system, but he drew a 50-game suspension near the end of the 2007 season for testing positive for a drug of abuse. He failed another drug test administered by the team during instructional league, marking the fourth time he has been flagged for marijuana. Jeffress is one of the few pitchers who can actually hit triple digits on the radar gun. He regularly throws his fastball from 93-95 mph and has made progress with his curveball and changeup, making his heater even more

BILL MITCHELL

devastating. A standout basketball player in high school, he's a good athlete with smooth mechanics and a strong lower body. Jeffress' biggest issue is committing to being a professional after failing four drug tests. On the mound, his control is still erratic, in part because he overstrides in his delivery. Jeffress will start 2008 serving his Minor League Baseball suspension, and the Brewers could impose further discipline for his latest failed test. He could remain a starter as he refines his curve and change, but many scouts believe his fastball velocity makes him a better fit as a closer down the road.

Year	Club (League)	Class	W	L	ERA	G	GS	CG	SV	IP	H	R	ER	HR	BB	SO	AVG
2006	Brewers (AZL)	R	2	5	5.88	13	4	0	0	33	30	26	22	0	25	37	.227
2007	West Virginia (SAL)	A	9	5	3.13	18	18	0	0	86	62	43	30	8	44	95	.201
MINOR LEAGUE TOTALS			11	10	3.90	31	22	0	0	120	92	69	52	8	69	132	.209

5 MAT GAMEL, 3B

Born: July 26, 1985. **B-T:** L-R. **Ht.:** 6-0. **Wt.:** 205. **Drafted:** Chipola (Fla.) JC, 2005 (4th round). **Signed by:** Doug Reynolds.

CLIFF WELCH

The Brewers locked onto Gamel while evaluating junior college teammate Darren Ford as a draft-and-follow in 2005. Gamel put together a 33-game hitting streak in 2007, the longest in the high Class A Florida State League in 56 years. He led the minors with 53 errors in 128 games at third base. A professional hitter, Gamel knows the strike zone, sprays balls to all fields and is developing more home run power. His pop was improving rapidly as he challenged for the triple crown in Hawaii Winter Baseball. He has decent speed, runs the bases well and has the arm strength to play third base. Gamel's arm isn't as accurate as it is strong, so he makes a lot of throwing errors, often related to poor footwork. The volume of errors gets in his head at times; he must stop thinking too much in the field and just react. The Brewers think he'll eventually figure it out. He was working on his defense in Hawaii, and Milwaukee has no plans to move Gamel off third base despite his defensive struggles and the presence of Ryan Braun in the majors. He'll make the jump to Double-A in 2008.

Year	Club (League)	Class	AVG	G	AB	R	H	2B	3B	HR	RBI	BB	SO	SB	OBP	SLG
2005	West Virginia (SAL)	A	.174	8	23	2	4	0	0	1	1	5	9	0	.321	.304
	Helena (Pio)	R	.327	50	199	34	65	15	2	5	37	12	49	7	.375	.497
2006	West Virginia (SAL)	A	.288	129	493	65	142	28	5	17	88	52	81	9	.359	.469
2007	Brevard County (FSL)	A	.300	128	466	78	140	37	8	9	60	58	98	14	.378	.472
MINOR LEAGUE TOTALS			.297	315	1181	179	351	80	15	32	186	127	237	30	.368	.472

6 COLE GILLESPIE, OF

Born: June 20, 1984. **B-T:** R-R. **Ht.:** 6-1. **Wt.:** 205. **Drafted:** Oregon State, 2006 (3rd round). **Signed by:** Brandon Newell.

CLIFF WELCH

After Gillespie helped Oregon State win the College World Series and led the Rookie-level Pioneer League with a .464 on-base percentage in his pro debut in 2006, the Brewers jumped him to high Class A for his first full season. The winds at Brevard County cut into his production but he maintained his polished approach at the plate. Gillespie, who has drawn comparisons to Tim Salmon, works counts until he gets a pitch he likes. Milwaukee projects him as a .300 hitter with 20-plus homers per season. His athleticism, speed and left-field range are all average, and he also shows good defensive instincts and an accurate arm. He's a leader on the field and in the clubhouse. His power may be short for a corner outfielder, so Gillespie will have to make up the difference with doubles and RBI production. His arm isn't strong, but it doesn't have to be in left field. With 2007 first-rounder Matt LaPorta targeted as the franchise's left fielder of the future, Gillespie may not have a long-term role with the Brewers. But they think he'll hit enough to be a big league regular. He'll move up to Double-A in 2008.

Year	Club (League)	Class	AVG	G	AB	R	H	2B	3B	HR	RBI	BB	SO	SB	OBP	SLG
2006	Helena (Pio)	R	.344	51	186	49	64	12	1	8	31	40	34	18	.464	.548
2007	Brevard County (FSL)	A	.267	129	438	75	117	25	3	12	62	72	95	16	.378	.420
MINOR LEAGUE TOTALS			.290	180	624	124	181	37	4	20	93	112	129	34	.405	.458

7 BRENT BREWER, SS

SPORTS ON FILM

Born: Dec. 19, 1987. **B-T:** R-R. **Ht.:** 6-2. **Wt.:** 190. **Drafted:** HS—Tyrone, Ga., 2006 (2nd round). **Signed by:** Doug Reynolds.

Brewer has the potential to be the best all-around player in the system. He had a scholarship to play wide receiver for Florida State, but gave up football for a $600,000 signing bonus in 2006. The Brewers pushed him to low Class A for his first full season because they had confidence in his athleticism and determination. Brewer has well-above-average speed and athleticism, and plus power potential. He has tremendous range at shortstop and the strong arm to make plays from deep in the hole. Some scouts believe he profiles even better as a center fielder. Club officials love his leadership skills and work ethic. Lack of experience is Brewer's main shortcoming, and it shows. He topped the South Atlantic League with 170 strikeouts and led all minor league shortstops with 48 errors in 127 games. He needs to improve his discipline at the plate and his footwork in the field. He tries to do too much defensively at times and makes wild throws. The more he plays, the better he'll get. While J.J. Hardy and Alcides Escobar loom as large obstacles ahead of him, Brewer will play in high Class A Brevard County at age 20 in 2008.

Year	Club (League)	Class	AVG	G	AB	R	H	2B	3B	HR	RBI	BB	SO	SB	OBP	SLG
2006	Brewers (AZL)	R	.264	45	182	25	48	3	6	3	22	16	53	10	.328	.396
2007	West Virginia (SAL)	A	.251	127	518	86	130	25	7	11	49	46	170	42	.315	.390
MINOR LEAGUE TOTALS			.254	172	700	111	178	28	13	14	71	62	223	52	.319	.391

8 ANGEL SALOME, C

STEVE MOORE

Born: Oct. 11, 1985. **B-T:** R-R. **Ht.:** 5-7. **Wt.:** 195. **Drafted:** HS—New York, 2004 (5th round). **Signed by:** Tony Blengino.

Salome missed time in 2007 early, as he recovered from ankle surgery, and late, when he was suspended 50 games after testing positive for performance-enhancing drugs. In between, he raised his career batting average to .309. Salome has an unorthodox swing yet makes consistent contact and generates solid power, especially from gap to gap. With a compact body and very little body fat, he's much stronger than he looks and has earned the nickname "Pocket Pudge." Milwaukee believes Salome has legitimate power and that he won't use PEDs again. His arm is well above average. Despite his arm strength, Salome threw out just 6-of-46 basestealers (13 percent) in 2007 due to inaccurate throws. He still struggles with most subtle aspects of catching, such as receiving, blocking balls in the dirt and calling pitches. He's often too aggressive at the plate and is a below-average runner. Salome tried to make up for lost time by going to instructional league and then winter ball in Venezuela. He may return to high Class A to open 2008, after finishing his suspension.

Year	Club (League)	Class	AVG	G	AB	R	H	2B	3B	HR	RBI	BB	SO	SB	OBP	SLG
2004	Brewers (AZL)	R	.235	20	81	7	19	7	0	0	8	4	14	2	.271	.321
2005	West Virginia (SAL)	A	.254	29	118	15	30	7	1	4	21	8	17	1	.302	.432
	Helena (Pio)	R	.415	37	159	34	66	17	0	8	50	15	16	6	.469	.673
2006	West Virginia (SAL)	A	.292	105	418	63	122	31	2	10	85	39	63	7	.349	.447
2007	Brevard County (FSL)	A	.318	68	258	33	82	20	0	6	53	12	32	1	.341	.465
MINOR LEAGUE TOTALS			.309	259	1034	152	319	82	3	28	217	78	142	17	.354	.475

9 LORENZO CAIN, OF

JERRY HALE

Born: April 13, 1986. **B-T:** R-R. **Ht.:** 6-2. **Wt.:** 175. **Drafted:** Tallahassee (Fla.) CC, D/F 2004 (17th round). **Signed by:** Doug Reynolds.

A draft-and-follow who won MVP honors in the Rookie-level Arizona League in his 2005 pro debut, Cain continues to show all-around tools. Like many Brewers prospects, his production suffered going from West Virginia to Brevard County, where prevailing winds hold down offense, but Cain adjusted nicely. Cain's power is mostly to the gaps now, but the Brewers expect him to develop above-average home run pop as he develops physically and gets more game experience. He's a plus runner who's a threat on the bases. A solid defender in right field with a decent arm, he can play center in a pinch. Cain needs to continue working on his plate discipline so he can draw more walks and put himself in position to get pitches he can hammer. He's still wiry and needs to add weight and strength. He didn't play baseball until high school and still is honing his baseball instincts. Cain's numbers should rebound at Double-A in 2008. Some Brewers officials liken him to Corey Hart, who had a breakthrough season in 2007, and think he's on the verge of making a similar move in the minors.

MILWAUKEE BREWERS

Year	Club (League)	Class	AVG	G	AB	R	H	2B	3B	HR	RBI	BB	SO	SB	OBP	SLG
2005	Brewers (AZL)	R	.356	50	205	45	73	18	5	5	37	20	32	12	.418	.566
	Helena (Pio)	R	.208	6	24	4	5	0	0	0	1	1	6	0	.321	.208
2006	West Virginia (SAL)	A	.307	132	527	91	162	36	4	6	60	58	104	34	.384	.425
2007	Brevard County (FSL)	A	.276	126	482	67	133	21	3	2	44	37	97	24	.338	.344
MINOR LEAGUE TOTALS			.301	314	1238	207	373	75	12	13	142	116	239	70	.371	.413

10 CALEB GINDL, OF

BILL MITCHELL

Born: Aug. 31, 1988. **B-T:** L-L. **Ht.:** 5-9. **Wt.:** 185. **Drafted:** HS—Milton, Fla., 2007 (5th round). **Signed by:** Doug Reynolds.

The Brewers don't often send new high school draft picks to the Pioneer League, but they thought Gindl was very advanced for an 18-year-old hitter after they signed him for $144,900 as a fifth-round pick in June. Gindl vindicated the organization's scouting reports as he won the league batting title at .372. Gindl has tremendous pitch recognition for a young hitter, enabling him to hit both fastballs and breaking balls. His stocky build and line-drive power remind some of Brian Giles. Some clubs considered drafting him as a lefthanded pitcher, so his arm plays well in right field. The Brewers like his makeup and maturity. Whether Gindl will have enough home run power to play an outfield corner in the majors remains to be seen. He's close to maxed out physically and limited in terms of speed and athleticism. He came down with elbow tendinitis toward the end of the summer and an MRI revealed a bone chip, though it is not considered a serious problem. Gindl has earned a trip to low Class A for 2008, where the Brewers will get a better indication of his offensive ceiling.

Year	Club (League)	Class	AVG	G	AB	R	H	2B	3B	HR	RBI	BB	SO	SB	OBP	SLG
2007	Helena (Pio)	R	.372	55	207	40	77	22	3	5	42	20	38	4	.420	.580
MINOR LEAGUE TOTALS			.372	55	207	40	77	22	3	5	42	20	38	4	.420	.580

11 ROB BRYSON, RHP

Born: Dec. 11, 1987. **B-T:** R-R. **Ht.:** 6-1. **Wt.:** 200. **Drafted:** Seminole (Fla.) CC, D/F 2006 (31st round). **Signed by:** Charlie Aliano.

The Brewers have worked the draft-and-follow process extremely well, and they hauled in another strong crop in the final year of the rule's existence. Before the 2007 draft, they signed five of their 2006 draftees. While 12th-round righthander Chad Robinson ($500,000) and 19th-rounder Lee Haydel ($624,000) had higher profiles and bigger bonuses, Bryson shined brighter at Helena in their first pro summer. Signed for $300,000, Bryson was tired after a heavy workload at Seminole (Fla.) CC and spent most of his debut working out of the bullpen. Nevertheless, he nearly led the Pioneer League in strikeouts, logging 70 in 54 innings. Bryson's best pitch is his fastball, which usually sits in the low 90s and hits 95 mph, though his velocity was down slightly in his debut. His 78-82 mph slider got better as the season progressed, though he needs considerable work on his changeup. He liked pitching with games on the line, converting all eight of his save opportunities with an aggressive, attacking mentality. Bryson has some delivery issues to work out, mostly in his rhythm and timing, but he does throw strikes and the ball comes out of his hand with little effort. He's not big and ultimately may wind up as a two-pitch reliever, but the Brewers will give him a chance to start when he's at full strength in 2008. He'll move up to low Class A.

Year	Club (League)	Class	W	L	ERA	G	GS	CG	SV	IP	H	R	ER	HR	BB	SO	AVG
2007	Helena (Pio)	R	3	0	2.67	18	4	0	8	54	49	19	16	2	12	70	.245
MINOR LEAGUE TOTALS			3	0	2.67	18	4	0	8	54	49	19	16	2	12	70	.245

12 MARK ROGERS, RHP

Born: Jan. 30, 1986. **B-T:** R-R. **Ht.:** 6-2. **Wt.:** 205. **Drafted:** HS—Mount Ararat, Maine, 2004 (1st round). **Signed by:** Tony Blengino.

The fifth overall pick in the 2004 draft, Rogers missed the entire 2007 season after having surgery to repair some fraying and tighten a ligament in his shoulder in January. The Brewers loved his athleticism (he was also a hockey and soccer star in high school) and makeup, and they passed on Homer Bailey to select him—a decision they may rue in the long run. Before hurting his shoulder, Rogers threw his fastball regularly in the mid- to high 90s and had a sharp, over-the-top curveball that kept hitters off balance. He also was making progress with his changeup. But his control and command were highly erratic, as he had trouble repeating his delivery and threw across his body too much. Milwaukee altered his mechanics to correct those flaws, and the tinkering possibly could have caused his shoulder problems. Rogers has kept an upbeat attitude during his long rehab process. Once he returns to the mound, he must realize that it's not enough to just throw his fastball by hitters. He needs to keep his pitch counts down and gain more consistency with his secondary pitches. He's still just 22 and continues to have the upside of a No. 1 starter if he can get healthy and develop as a pitcher. Rogers did some bullpen work during instructional league and should be ready to pitch at the start of the 2008 season. The Brewers could send him to high Class A so he can take advantage of warm weather in the Florida State League.

Year	Club (League)	Class	W	L	ERA	G	GS	CG	SV	IP	H	R	ER	HR	BB	SO	AVG
2004	Brewers (AZL)	R	0	3	4.73	9	6	0	0	26	30	21	14	0	14	35	.294
2005	West Virginia (SAL)	A	2	9	5.11	25	20	0	1	98	87	65	56	11	70	109	.238
2006	Brevard County (FSL)	A	1	2	5.07	16	16	0	0	71	68	46	40	6	53	96	.253
	Brewers (AZL)	R	0	0	2.25	3	3	0	0	4	5	1	1	0	2	5	.294
2007	Did Not Play—Injured																
MINOR LEAGUE TOTALS			3	14	4.99	53	45	0	1	200	190	133	111	17	139	245	.252

13 ZACH BRADDOCK, LHP

Born: Aug. 23, 1987. **B-T:** L-L. **Ht.:** 6-4. **Wt.:** 230. **Drafted:** Burlington (N.J.) CC, D/F 2005 (18th round). **Signed by:** Tony Blengino.

Some scouts thought Braddock was the best pitcher they saw in the South Atlantic League in the first half of the season. "He had a month and a half that was off the charts," West Virginia pitching coach John Curtis says. But Braddock missed three weeks starting in mid-May with shoulder tendinitis, came back and made two abbreviated starts, then didn't pitch after June 15 because of a shoulder strain. When healthy, Braddock showed an 89-92 mph fastball, a sharp slider and an improving changeup. He demonstrated consistent command and didn't allow more than two runs in any of his 10 outings. Big and strong, Braddock has a smooth, fluid delivery that makes him sneaky fast. Like many young pitchers, he relies too much on his fastball at times but should gain more trust in his secondary pitches with experience. Braddock had Tommy John surgery in high school, so he has bounced back from a more serious injury in the past. He didn't require surgery in 2007, but he also is dealing with emotional issues that are being treated with medication. Braddock has obstacles to overcome, but the Brewers believe he has a very high ceiling. He'll pitch in high Class A this year.

Year	Club (League)	Class	W	L	ERA	G	GS	CG	SV	IP	H	R	ER	HR	BB	SO	AVG
2006	Helena (Pio)	R	2	2	5.49	14	8	0	0	39	32	26	24	3	31	30	.227
2007	West Virginia (SAL)	A	3	1	1.15	10	9	0	0	47	28	6	6	1	15	68	.168
MINOR LEAGUE TOTALS			5	3	3.13	24	17	0	0	86	60	32	30	4	46	98	.195

14 LUIS PENA, RHP

Born: Jan. 10, 1983. **B-T:** R-R. **Ht.:** 6-5. **Wt.:** 200. **Signed:** Venezuela, 1999. **Signed by:** Epy Guerrero.

Finally recovered from shoulder surgery that shortened his 2005 and 2006 seasons, Pena flashed the form that had the Brewers excited about him when they signed him out of Venezuela in 1999. He no longer is a starting pitcher, however, having made a successful transition to the bullpen. Pena is all about power, as he regularly throws in the mid-90s with good life on his fastball and backs it up with a sharp, late-breaking 88-90 mph slider. He has a great pitcher's body that allows him to throw on a downhill plane. No longer having to pace himself or worry about a changeup, Pena just turned the ball loose and reached Double-A for the first time in 2007. He didn't miss a beat in Huntsville, converting 12-of-14 save opportunities and limiting opponents to a .211 average. At times, he struggles with the command of his slider. But he improved his stock so dramatically that he was added to the 40-man roster in November and might find his way into the Milwaukee bullpen as early as this year. He eventually could become a set-up man or possibly a closer.

Year	Club (League)	Class	W	L	ERA	G	GS	CG	SV	IP	H	R	ER	HR	BB	SO	AVG
2000	San Joaquin (VSL)	R	2	3	4.02	20	7	0	2	53	35	31	24	7	30	41	.190
2001	Brewers (AZL)	R	3	4	4.63	11	2	0	0	35	42	23	18	2	13	20	.300
2002	Brewers (AZL)	R	4	1	3.49	11	7	0	0	49	45	28	19	1	24	52	.239
2003	Beloit (MWL)	A	2	6	3.90	23	18	1	0	90	92	51	39	6	46	53	.267
2004	Beloit (MWL)	A	9	3	3.92	21	16	0	0	98	101	50	43	7	35	76	.268
2005	Brevard County (FSL)	A	2	6	4.26	15	12	0	0	76	72	39	36	6	28	51	.258
2006	Brevard County (FSL)	A	4	6	4.41	23	11	0	1	65	68	34	32	6	33	59	.274
2007	Brevard County (FSL)	A	5	0	2.08	16	0	0	6	21	14	5	5	1	7	27	.184
	Huntsville (SL)	AA	0	4	2.89	35	0	0	12	46	36	15	15	1	14	42	.211
MINOR LEAGUE TOTALS			31	33	3.88	175	73	1	21	536	505	276	231	37	230	421	.252

15 R.J. SEIDEL, RHP

Born: Sept. 3, 1987. **B-T:** R-R. **Ht.:** 6-6. **Wt.:** 190. **Drafted:** HS—LaCrosse, Wis., 2006 (16th round). **Signed by:** Harvey Kuenn Jr.

One of the best Wisconsin high school pitchers to come along in recent years, Seidel dropped to the 16th round of the 2006 draft because of a strong commitment to Arkansas. He signed late in the summer for $415,000, the equivalent of third-round money, and made a solid pro debut in 2007. With a great pitching frame that he's still growing into, Seidel already throws his fastball at 88-91 mph, has good movement and should add velocity as he matures physically. He still needs work on his curveball, but his changeup is advanced for his age and rates as the best in the system. He also has precocious feel for pitching, in part because of the lessons learned from his father Dick, who pitched in the Yankees system in the early 1980s. Seidel is a good athlete who starred in football and basketball in high school. Mostly as a precaution, the Brewers shut him down for much of July with biceps tendinitis, and he wasn't the same pitcher afterward. To make up for some of that lost time, he went to instructional league to get more work and focus on his secondary pitches. Seidel will pitch the entire 2008 season at age 20, so Milwaukee won't rush him. He'll spend the year in low Class A.

Year	Club (League)	Class	W	L	ERA	G	GS	CG	SV	IP	H	R	ER	HR	BB	SO	AVG
2007	Helena (Pio)	R	4	0	3.07	12	8	0	0	41	30	20	14	2	16	36	.207
MINOR LEAGUE TOTALS			4	0	3.07	12	8	0	0	41	30	20	14	2	16	36	.207

16 JONATHAN LUCROY, C

Born: June 13, 1986. **B-T:** R-R. **Ht.:** 6-1. **Wt.:** 206. **Drafted:** Louisiana-Lafayette, 2007 (3rd round). **Signed by:** Brian Sankey.

The Brewers didn't have a second-round pick in 2007, so they had to wait 94 choices after taking Matt LaPorta seventh overall. They thought Lucroy surely would be gone by then and they were delighted to land him with the No. 101 pick and $340,000. An offensive-minded catcher, he demonstrates good plate coverage, taking outside pitches the other way and handling both fastballs and breaking balls. Lucroy drove the ball well in the gaps during his pro debut, and with strong hands and a good swing path, he should develop some home run power over time. He knows the strike zone well and is aggressive at the plate. Though Lucroy isn't known for his defensive prowess, he did throw out 43 percent of basestealers in the Pioneer League. His arm is average at best, however, and his throws sometimes tail away from the bag. His receiving and game-calling skills are decent, and his best attribute as a catcher may be the leadership he exudes. He's a below-average runner. Milwaukee isn't exactly brimming with catching prospects, so it sent Lucroy to Hawaii Winter Baseball to expedite his development. He could move quickly and see high Class A at some point in 2008.

Year	Club (League)	Class	AVG	G	AB	R	H	2B	3B	HR	RBI	BB	SO	SB	OBP	SLG
2007	Helena (Pio)	R	.342	61	234	35	80	18	2	4	39	16	37	0	.383	.487
MINOR LEAGUE TOTALS			.342	61	234	35	80	18	2	4	39	16	37	0	.383	.487

17 TAYLOR GREEN, 3B

Born: Nov. 2, 1986. **B-T:** L-R. **Ht.:** 5-10. **Wt.:** 180. **Drafted:** Cypress (Calif.) JC, D/F 2005 (25th round). **Signed by:** Bruce Seid.

After the Brewers drafted Green out of Cypress (Calif.) JC in 2005, he returned for his sophomore season and signed as draft-and-follow after improving tremendously. Limited by a foot injury during his 2006 pro debut, he broke out in 2007 and Milwaukee named him its minor league player of the year. His tools aren't impressive, but he has great instincts and knows how to play the game. His maturity and work ethic rate highly. Green has good plate discipline, works the count and takes walks if he doesn't get his pitch. He drives the ball well to the gaps but projects to have average power at best. His speed is slightly below average, and his range and arm strength at third base are just adequate. But as farm director Reid Nichols says, "He catches it and throws it and the guy is out. That's the bottom line." Originally drafted as a second baseman, Green has a Ron Cey-like build and handles himself decently around the bag. He'll have to prove he can stick at third base and hit for the power desired at that position, but he's off to a good start and will advance to high Class A this year.

Year	Club (League)	Class	AVG	G	AB	R	H	2B	3B	HR	RBI	BB	SO	SB	OBP	SLG
2006	Helena (Pio)	R	.231	62	221	36	51	12	1	1	23	29	35	0	.328	.308
2007	West Virginia (SAL)	A	.327	111	397	68	130	29	2	14	86	51	65	0	.406	.516
MINOR LEAGUE TOTALS			.293	173	618	104	181	41	3	15	109	80	100	0	.378	.442

18 CODY SCARPETTA, RHP

Born: Aug. 25, 1988. **B-T:** R-R. **Ht.:** 6-2. **Wt.:** 220. **Drafted:** HS—Rockford, Ill., 2007 (11th round). **Signed by:** Harvey Kuenn Jr.

The Brewers drafted Scarpetta's father Dan in the third round out of an Illinois high school in 1982, and later included him and their current manager, Ned Yost, in a trade for Jim Sundberg. Cody figured to match his dad's draft status until he tore the flexor tendon at the base of his right index finger while pitching in late April. He had the finger operated on in mid-May and wasn't able to pitch again before the Aug. 15 signing deadline. An 11th-rounder, Scarpetta initially signed for $325,000, but the Brewers voided their initial deal and re-signed him for $125,000 when he needed to have the surgery. Before he got hurt, Scarpetta showed a plus fastball every time he took the mound during the spring, usually parking at 92-94 mph. He worked hard in the offseason to get in the best shape of his life, which not only added velocity to his fastball but also helped him turn his breaking ball into a true power curve. He also added a changeup, though it's still in the developmental stages. His two plus pitches and his strong 6-foot-2 build have earned him comparisons to John Wetteland, though Milwaukee plans to deploy him as a starter. He should be 100 percent by spring training, though he figures to begin the season in extended spring training before moving to Helena in June.

Year	Club (League)	Class	W	L	ERA	G	GS	CG	SV	IP	H	R	ER	HR	BB	SO	AVG
2007	Did Not Play—Injured																

19 NICK TYSON, RHP

Born: June 13, 1988. **B-T:** R-R. **Ht.:** 6-2. **Wt.:** 175. **Drafted:** Lake City (Fla.) CC, D/F 2006 (32nd round). **Signed by:** Charlie Aliano.

Tyson was New Jersey's best two-way prospect in 2006, doubling as a projectable outfielder and right-hander. Most teams preferred him on the mound, including the Brewers, who took him in the 32nd round—one pick after Rob Bryson—and signed him as a draft-and-follow last spring. They thought he threw too many innings at Lake City (Fla.) CC, so they monitored his workload closely in his pro debut. Tyson throws his fastball at 90-92 mph and his velocity could improve as he gets stronger. His sharp curveball—the best in the system—gives him another strikeout pitch. He shows good presence and poise on the mound, as well as command of his pitches. His changeup is a distant third offering and will be a point of emphasis. As with Bryson, Milwaukee is anxious to see what Tyson can do in his first full season, which he'll spend in low Class A. He has improved significantly from high school to junior college to his initial taste of pro ball, and the Brewers believe he'll move steadily through the system.

Year	Club (League)	Class	W	L	ERA	G	GS	CG	SV	IP	H	R	ER	HR	BB	SO	AVG
2007	Helena (Pio)	R	4	1	2.48	17	3	0	2	40	29	14	11	3	7	36	.196
MINOR LEAGUE TOTALS			4	1	2.48	17	3	0	2	40	29	14	11	3	7	36	.196

20 ALEXANDRE PERIARD, RHP

Born: June 15, 1987. **B-T:** L-R. **Ht.:** 6-1. **Wt.:** 185. **Drafted:** HS—St. Eustache, Quebec, 2004 (16th round). **Signed by:** Jay Lapp.

The Brewers knew it would take Periard time to develop when they drafted him as a 16-year-old out of high school in Canada. He played in the Rookie-level Arizona League for two years before moving up to low Class A and making major strides last season. He touched the mid-90s and pitched regularly in the low 90s with his fastball, backing it up with a curveball and a solid changeup. His velocity has jumped 5-6 mph since he turned pro and his command improved considerably. Periard pitches to contact, keeping the ball down and getting a lot of groundouts. He has strong legs that allow him to drop, drive and keep the ball down in the strike zone. The Brewers also like the aggressiveness and confidence he shows on the mound. The only thing that slowed him down in 2007 was an inner-ear infection that shut him down for a month. By the end of the season, Periard had re-established himself as the No. 1 pitcher in West Virginia's rotation during the South Atlantic League playoffs. Still young and filling out, he could be ready for a breakout this year in high Class A.

Year	Club (League)	Class	W	L	ERA	G	GS	CG	SV	IP	H	R	ER	HR	BB	SO	AVG
2005	Brewers (AZL)	R	0	1	5.08	11	4	0	1	28	43	23	16	1	10	22	.358
2006	Brewers (AZL)	R	3	1	4.64	13	4	0	1	42	45	31	22	1	18	25	.266
2007	West Virginia (SAL)	A	7	7	3.55	23	18	0	2	109	115	49	43	8	21	55	.271
MINOR LEAGUE TOTALS			10	9	4.05	47	26	0	4	180	203	103	81	10	49	102	.284

21 DARREN FORD, OF

Born: Oct. 1, 1985. **B-T:** R-R. **Ht.:** 6-1. **Wt.:** 195. **Drafted:** Chipola (Fla.) JC, D/F 2004 (18th round). **Signed by:** Tony Blengino.

Ford has the one tool that can't be taught—blazing speed. The former New Jersey high school track star is one of the fastest runners in the minor leagues, going from the right side of the plate to first base in 3.8 seconds. He stole 67 bases in 83 attempts in 2007. The question is whether Ford can develop the rest of his game to the point where he can become a useful big leaguer. He played very well when he repeated low Class A to start last season but had trouble following a mid-June promotion. He draws walks, but he needs to bunt more often and cut down on his strikeouts. He can turn ordinary groundballs into base hits with his extraordinary speed. "All he has to do," scouting director Jack Zduriencik says, "is make contact." Ford has a little pop in his bat but the Brewers just want him to concentrate on getting on base. An outstanding defender, he could play center field in the big leagues right now. His arm is below average and he must improve his consistency after making 20 errors during the last two seasons. Ford will be 22 all season, so returning to high Class A isn't a setback.

Year	Club (League)	Class	AVG	G	AB	R	H	2B	3B	HR	RBI	BB	SO	SB	OBP	SLG
2005	Helena (Pio)	R	.271	61	236	57	64	4	3	1	24	33	70	18	.365	.326
2006	West Virginia (SAL)	A	.283	125	491	93	139	24	3	7	54	56	133	69	.361	.387
2007	West Virginia (SAL)	A	.335	51	224	48	75	15	4	5	33	23	56	31	.398	.504
	Brevard County (FSL)	A	.231	72	273	46	63	7	1	4	27	35	67	36	.317	.308
MINOR LEAGUE TOTALS			.279	309	1224	244	341	50	11	17	138	147	326	154	.358	.379

22 LEE HAYDEL, OF

Born: July 15, 1987. **B-T:** L-R. **Ht.:** 6-1. **Wt.:** 190. **Drafted:** Delgado (La.) CC, D/F 2006 (19th round). **Signed by:** Joe Mason.

The two fastest players in the system both signed as draft-and-follows. Haydel, who can run the 60-yard dash in 6.35 seconds, intrigued scouts as a Louisiana high schooler in 2006. But his raw bat, desire for a $250,000 bonus and intent to attend Louisiana State rendered him unsignable. The Brewers took a flier on him in the 19th round and caught a break when he opted to attend Delgado (La.) CC after LSU forced out head coach Smoke Laval. Haydel got stronger as a freshman at Delgado, reducing the questions about his bat, and he signed for $624,000 rather than re-entering the 2007 draft, in which he might have gone as high as the supplemental first round. Haydel's hitting is still a work in progress, but he's doing a better job of handling quality fastballs and hanging in against offspeed pitches. He has little power, so he needs to do a better job of controlling the strike zone and getting on base. Haydel has plus range in center field and a solid arm that ranks as above average for his position. He'll need time to develop, but his ceiling is high enough that one scout compared his potential to Jacoby Ellsbury's. Haydel will spend his first full pro season in low Class A.

Year	Club (League)	Class	AVG	G	AB	R	H	2B	3B	HR	RBI	BB	SO	SB	OBP	SLG
2007	Helena (Pio)	R	.276	62	254	42	70	12	5	0	20	12	44	12	.311	.362
MINOR LEAGUE TOTALS			.276	62	254	42	70	12	5	0	20	12	44	12	.311	.362

23 ERIC FARRIS, 2B

Born: March 3, 1986. **B-T:** R-R. **Ht.:** 5-10. **Wt.:** 170. **Drafted:** Loyola Marymount, 2007 (4th round). **Signed by:** Cory Rodriguez.

Farris didn't receive as much attention as Helena teammates such as Matt LaPorta and Caleb Gindl, but the Brewers really liked the way he handled himself at the plate and in the field during his pro debut. A fourth-round pick who signed for $207,000, he earned comparisons to Junior Spivey and Tony Womack by club officials. Scouts saw him perform well in the Cape Cod League, so it didn't surprise them when he easily made the adjustments to wood bats as a first-year pro. Farris doesn't walk or strike out much, preferring to put the ball in play. He hit only one homer at Helena but drives the ball into the gaps on occasion. Though not a blazing runner, he has plus speed, gets good breaks on the bases and swiped 21 bags in 26 attempts. Farris has a strong arm and good instincts in the field. He has good range to both sides, which allowed him to play shortstop at Loyola Marymount without difficulty. He could get some time at shortstop in 2008, and he could reach high Class A before the end of the season.

Year	Club (League)	Class	AVG	G	AB	R	H	2B	3B	HR	RBI	BB	SO	SB	OBP	SLG
2007	Helena (Pio)	R	.326	63	239	34	78	16	2	1	34	16	22	21	.369	.423
MINOR LEAGUE TOTALS			.326	63	239	34	78	16	2	1	34	16	22	21	.369	.423

24 MICHAEL BRANTLEY, OF/1B

Born: May 15, 1987. **B-T:** L-L. **Ht.:** 6-2. **Wt.:** 180. **Drafted:** HS—Fort Pierce, Fla., 2005 (7th round). **Signed by:** Larry Pardo.

Brantley played so well in his return to low Class A last year that the Brewers jumped him to Double-A at midseason. He had a .321 career average in pro ball to that point, and though he hit just .251 after the double promotion, he was just 20. Brantley is a patient hitter who has a gameplan at the plate and waits until he gets what he wants. He hits balls where they're pitched and doesn't offer at much out of the strike zone. He's a reliable contact hitter who draws walks and is a threat to steal any time he reaches base. The problem for Brantley is that he doesn't profile well at any position. His plus speed doesn't translate well to his outfield play. He often gets bad breaks on balls and has a below-average arm, which makes him more of a left fielder than a center fielder. With just two homers in three pro seasons, he doesn't have the power to play regularly in left. He also handled himself well around the bag when Milwaukee gave him some exposure to first base in 2007, but more power is required at that position. Ticketed for a return to Double-A, Brantley looks like a fourth outfielder who can be a useful pinch-hitter.

Year	Club (League)	Class	AVG	G	AB	R	H	2B	3B	HR	RBI	BB	SO	SB	OBP	SLG
2005	Brewers (AZL)	R	.347	44	173	34	60	3	1	0	19	22	13	14	.426	.376
	Helena (Pio)	R	.324	10	34	8	11	2	0	0	3	6	4	2	.425	.382
2006	West Virginia (SAL)	A	.300	108	360	47	108	10	2	0	42	61	51	24	.402	.339
2007	West Virginia (SAL)	A	.335	56	218	41	73	15	1	2	32	31	22	18	.413	.440
	Huntsville (SL)	AA	.251	59	187	28	47	6	1	0	21	29	25	17	.353	.294
MINOR LEAGUE TOTALS			.308	277	972	158	299	36	5	2	117	149	115	75	.400	.361

25 STEPHEN CHAPMAN, OF

Born: Oct. 12, 1985. **B-T:** L-L. **Ht.:** 6-0. **Wt.:** 180. **Drafted:** HS—Marianna, Fla., 2004 (6th round). **Signed by:** Doug Reynolds.

Selected to the inaugural Aflac All-American game in 2003, Chapman turned down Auburn to sign for $159,000 as a sixth-round pick the following June. He didn't make it to full-season ball for good until his fourth year of pro ball, and continued to make steady improvements in 2007 by exceeding his previous career totals with 24 homers and 89 RBIs. Chapman's tools are all average to a tick above, but his bat was slow to develop. He has bat speed and power, though his swing gets long at times and he's sometimes slow to make adjustments. He lacks discipline at the plate and gets himself out too often. He has solid-average speed to go with average range and arm strength in the outfield. Chapman played mostly left field in 2007, though he's capable of playing in right. West Virginia is a haven for hitters, and it will be interesting to see how he adapts at more pitcher-friendly Brevard County this year. He continues to have a high ceiling but still needs a considerable amount of polish.

Year	Club (League)	Class	AVG	G	AB	R	H	2B	3B	HR	RBI	BB	SO	SB	OBP	SLG
2004	Brewers (AZL)	R	.229	49	192	33	44	7	7	4	18	17	50	4	.290	.401
2005	Helena (Pio)	R	.269	54	167	25	45	9	1	6	25	20	38	10	.352	.443
2006	West Virginia (SAL)	A	.176	6	17	3	3	0	0	0	0	1	6	0	.222	.176
	Helena (Pio)	R	.308	70	276	50	85	18	8	6	40	29	63	20	.387	.496
2007	West Virginia (SAL)	A	.262	126	455	77	119	25	6	24	89	36	137	12	.326	.501
MINOR LEAGUE TOTALS			.267	305	1107	188	296	59	22	40	172	103	294	46	.338	.469

26 HERNAN IRIBARREN, 2B

Born: June 29, 1984. **B-T:** L-R. **Ht.:** 6-1. **Wt.:** 175. **Signed:** Venezuela, 2002. **Signed by:** Epy Guerrero.

Iribarren hits everywhere he goes. Owner of a career .324 batting average, he has a compact, line-drive stroke and plus speed. The key for Iribarren will be to develop a more well-rounded game. He can drive the ball into the gaps but doesn't have much power, so he needs to focus on being a table-setter. He hasn't shown the discipline to be a true leadoff man, and he hasn't shown good instincts as a basestealer, getting caught 16 times in 34 attempts last season. He's an effective bunter, forcing defenses to play in at the corners. Though he's a solid second baseman, Iribarren lacks the arm strength to play shortstop. The Brewers are loaded with young infielders in the majors, including Rickie Weeks at second base, so they tried to increase Iribarren's versatility by having him play center field in instructional league. It will be a boost for Iribarren's career if he proves he can handle center this year in Triple-A.

MILWAUKEE BREWERS

Year	Club (League)	Class	AVG	G	AB	R	H	2B	3B	HR	RBI	BB	SO	SB	OBP	SLG
2002	Brewers (DSL)	R	.314	66	223	35	70	13	2	2	34	19	43	7	.383	.417
2003	Brewers (DSL)	R	.344	64	227	43	78	12	7	2	27	24	36	17	.403	.485
2004	Brewers (AZL)	R	.439	46	189	40	83	6	9	4	36	19	23	15	.490	.630
	Beloit (MWL)	A	.373	15	67	12	25	6	5	1	10	5	16	1	.411	.657
2005	West Virginia (SAL)	A	.290	126	486	72	141	15	8	4	48	51	99	38	.360	.379
2006	Brevard County (FSL)	A	.319	108	398	50	127	12	4	2	50	39	57	19	.376	.384
2007	Huntsville (SL)	AA	.307	124	479	72	147	23	12	4	53	44	109	18	.363	.430
MINOR LEAGUE TOTALS			.324	549	2069	324	671	87	47	19	258	201	383	115	.384	.439

27 STEVE HAMMOND, LHP

Born: April 30, 1982. **B-T:** R-L. **Ht.:** 6-2. **Wt.:** 205. **Drafted:** Long Beach State, 2005 (6th round). **Signed by:** Bruce Seid.

No pitcher in the system slipped more in 2007 than Hammond, who ranked No. 7 on this list a year ago after pitching effectively in Double-A in his first full pro season. According to the Brewers, his slide had a unique cause—Hammond worked too hard. He spent too much time in the weight room, bulking up and slowing down his delivery. He wasn't a power pitcher to begin with, succeeding while throwing 88-92 mph, but his fastball lost some velocity last year. His command wasn't as sharp with his fastball, slider or changeup. His secondary pitches are both average at best and were less consistent than in the past. In an effort to help Hammond sharpen his pitches, the Brewers sent him to the Arizona Fall League, but he got hit hard there as well. It's becoming increasingly likely that Hammond's future will be as a reliever than as a starter. He would have advanced to Triple-A had he put together a strong first half in 2007. Now he must prove in the spring that he belongs at that level to begin this season. He'll turn 26 early in the season, so he needs to regroup quickly.

Year	Club (League)	Class	W	L	ERA	G	GS	CG	SV	IP	H	R	ER	HR	BB	SO	AVG
2005	Helena (Pio)	R	1	0	1.06	4	2	0	0	17	13	5	2	1	0	23	.206
	West Virginia (SAL)	A	3	0	2.45	4	1	0	0	14	12	4	4	0	5	11	.235
	Brevard County (FSL)	A	1	3	2.78	8	7	0	0	35	33	17	11	2	9	30	.244
2006	Brevard County (FSL)	A	6	5	2.53	14	14	0	0	85	68	32	24	7	23	70	.215
	Huntsville (SL)	AA	5	6	2.93	13	13	1	0	73	63	29	24	7	25	58	.229
2007	Huntsville (SL)	AA	7	9	4.69	29	26	2	1	142	163	85	74	19	43	109	.292
MINOR LEAGUE TOTALS			23	23	3.40	72	63	3	1	368	352	172	139	36	105	301	.252

28 CHARLIE FERMAINT, OF

Born: Oct. 11, 1985. **B-T:** R-R. **Ht.:** 5-10. **Wt.:** 170. **Drafted:** HS—Dorado, P.R., 2003 (4th round). **Signed by:** Larry Pardo.

Fermaint is one of the most gifted athletes in the system. Now it's time for him to do something with those skills. The only time he has truly lived up to his tools came in 2005 with a torrid stretch when he repeated the Pioneer League. Unhappy about being sent to high Class A for the second straight season in 2007, he performed so poorly that he was demoted to low Class A, where he continued to struggle. His production fell off so sharply from 2006 that the Brewers aren't sure what to make of him, making 2008 a critical year for Fermaint. He has a quick bat but hasn't tapped into the power potential Milwaukee expected. If he's not going to hit for power, he has to get on base more and make things happen. Fermaint still strikes out far too often and doesn't walk enough, which negates his speed factor. And even with plus speed, he gets caught stealing too often (12 times in 39 tries last year), exposing his lack of instincts. He gets inconsistent jumps in center field and made 12 errors in 2007, though he did continue to show a solid-average arm. Other outfield prospects in the system are passing him by, so it's time for Fermaint to apply himself and get the Brewers excited about him again. He'll probably open his third consecutive year at Brevard County.

Year	Club (League)	Class	AVG	G	AB	R	H	2B	3B	HR	RBI	BB	SO	SB	OBP	SLG
2003	Brewers (AZL)	R	.300	25	100	16	30	3	3	1	9	3	19	6	.327	.420
2004	Helena (Pio)	R	.229	58	218	30	50	14	2	5	39	19	83	8	.300	.381
2005	Helena (Pio)	R	.364	31	129	46	47	9	2	12	32	15	28	11	.419	.744
	West Virginia (SAL)	A	.248	27	113	18	28	7	0	5	17	8	39	4	.301	.442
2006	Brevard County (FSL)	A	.276	110	424	67	117	20	4	7	33	42	119	27	.349	.392
2007	Brevard County (FSL)	A	.210	47	167	12	35	3	1	2	17	6	40	7	.236	.275
	West Virginia (SAL)	A	.248	75	294	43	73	10	1	3	20	26	68	20	.313	.320
MINOR LEAGUE TOTALS			.263	373	1445	232	380	66	13	35	167	119	396	83	.323	.399

29 CHRIS ERRECART, 1B

Born: Feb. 11, 1985. **B-T:** R-L. **Ht.:** 6-1. **Wt.:** 210. **Drafted:** California, 2006 (5th round). **Signed by:** Justin McCray.

Errecart had a disappointing junior season at California, enabling the Brewers to get him in the fifth round of the 2006 draft. He led the Pioneer League with 61 RBIs and finished second with 13 homers that summer, so Milwaukee felt comfortable advancing him to high Class A for his first full season. Errecart has legitimate power that should continue to develop. That aspect of his game was thwarted somewhat last year by the incoming breezes at Brevard County. He needs to work on his plate discipline and draw more walks. He gets pull-happy and is susceptible to breaking balls, but he will punish pitchers if they make a mistake inside with a fastball. He's also tough to back off the plate, as he got hit by 13 pitches in 2007. Possessing no speed to speak of, he's prone to grounding into double plays. With a glut of outfielders in the system, the Brewers moved him to first base full-time last year after he played more in the outfield in his debut. First base is a better fit for him. He won't win any Gold Gloves but handles himself well enough around the bag and isn't a liability. Milwaukee had hoped to accelerate his development by sending Errecart to Hawaii Winter Baseball, but he was hit by a pitch in his second game and broke his right wrist. The Brewers hope he'll be ready for spring training and an assignment to Double-A.

Year	Club (League)	Class	AVG	G	AB	R	H	2B	3B	HR	RBI	BB	SO	SB	OBP	SLG
2006	Helena (Pio)	R	.316	70	272	49	86	16	0	13	61	25	56	5	.406	.518
2007	Brevard County (FSL)	A	.262	116	424	63	111	23	1	10	55	33	91	1	.331	.392
MINOR LEAGUE TOTALS			.283	186	696	112	197	39	1	23	116	58	147	6	.361	.441

30 BRENDAN KATIN, OF

Born: Jan. 28, 1983. **B-T:** R-R. **Ht.:** 6-1. **Wt.:** 235. **Drafted:** Miami, 2005 (23rd round). **Signed by:** Larry Pardo.

Katin has more raw power than any hitter in the system, with the exception of Matt LaPorta. The problem is that he has shown little else to get excited about and has been an all-or-nothing player. A teammate of Ryan Braun at Miami, Katin has similar pop but lags far behind in plate coverage and pitch selection. He's particularly susceptible to breaking balls because of his long swing, and his lack of discipline resulted in a Double-A Southern League-leading 163 strikeouts last year. He has to revise his two-strike approach, cut down his swing and put the ball in play more often. Katin is a good athlete for his size. He has decent speed to go with average range and arm strength in right field. The Brewers don't have many true power prospects, so they'll keep giving Katin the chance to show that he can do more than hit homers and strike out. He should get his first taste of Triple-A in 2008.

Year	Club (League)	Class	AVG	G	AB	R	H	2B	3B	HR	RBI	BB	SO	SB	OBP	SLG
2005	Helena (Pio)	R	.386	33	114	30	44	6	0	8	26	17	25	3	.471	.649
	West Virginia (SAL)	A	.202	23	84	7	17	1	0	1	5	8	29	0	.287	.250
2006	Brevard County (FSL)	A	.289	116	450	64	130	34	3	13	75	34	112	4	.349	.464
	Huntsville (SL)	AA	.224	15	58	11	13	2	0	4	8	1	11	0	.250	.466
2007	Huntsville (SL)	AA	.258	128	450	72	116	24	0	24	94	41	163	3	.329	.471
MINOR LEAGUE TOTALS			.277	315	1156	184	320	67	3	50	208	101	340	10	.345	.470

Minnesota Twins

BY JOHN MANUEL

A decade that had been rolling along smoothly suddenly went off course in 2007.

For the first time since being a contraction candidate in the winter of 2000-01, Minnesota finished with a losing record. Starting in late August, the Twins lost 10 of 12 games, fell completely out of the American League playoff chase and never got over .500 after Sept. 4. The offense ranked 12th in the league in scoring despite a career year by Torii Hunter, who signed with the Angels as a free agent after the season.

A first-round pick in 1993, Hunter wasn't the longest-tenured Twin to leave his job. Club employees were asked to come to a morning meeting Sept. 12, and most didn't know what to expect. Many wept with sadness and surprise when told general manager Terry Ryan was stepping aside after 13 seasons. Ryan cited burnout and stress for wanting to accept his new role as senior adviser to his successor, former assistant GM Bill Smith. Ryan will be one of Minnesota's top talent evaluators in a role one club official called "GM Lite."

Smith's ascension had a domino effect. One of those promoted was Mike Radcliff, the longest-tenured scouting director in the industry, who as vice president of player personnel effectively becomes Minnesota's top talent evaluator (along with Ryan) on the pro side as well as the amateur draft. West Coast crosschecker Deron Johnson succeeds Radcliff as scouting director.

Smith and Co. got right to work. The Twins moved to improve their offense in November, dealing Matt Garza, Jason Bartlett and pitching prospect Eduardo Morlan to Tampa Bay for Delmon Young, Brendan Harris and outfield prospect Jason Pridie. The No. 1 overall pick in the 2003 draft, Young was the key piece for Minnesota with his superstar potential.

The acquisitions of Harris and Pridie were important as well, because the Twins haven't had success with the hitters they have drafted highly since Joe Mauer in 2001. First-round picks Denard Span (2002) and Matt Moses (2003) were supposed to be ready for big league jobs by now, yet are far from that point. Harris could take the third-base job that the Twins once envisioned going to Moses, who wasn't protected on the 40-man roster after the season. Pridie will get the chance to replace Hunter in center field because Span hit a soft .267 in Triple-A.

The Young-Garza trade can't be Smith's last bold move, though. The Twins have Johan Santana and

Five years since being a first-round pick, Denard Span still isn't ready for prime time

TOP 30 PROSPECTS

1. Nick Blackburn, rhp	16. Ryan Mullins, lhp
2. Joe Benson, of	17. Estarlin de los Santos, ss
3. Wilson Ramos, c	18. Mike McCardell, rhp
4. Tyler Robertson, lhp	19. Loek Van Mil, rhp
5. Anthony Swarzak, rhp	20. Denard Span, of
6. Ben Revere, of	21. Alex Burnett, rhp
7. Jason Pridie, of	22. Danny Valencia, 3b
8. Brian Duensing, lhp	23. Oswaldo Sosa, rhp
9. Jeff Manship, rhp	24. Rene Tosoni, of
10. Trevor Plouffe, ss	25. Julio DePaula, rhp
11. Jose Mijares, lhp	26. Dan Berlind, rhp
12. Chris Parmelee, of	27. Erik Lis, of/1b
13. Deibinson Romero, 3b	28. Anthony Slama, rhp
14. Glen Perkins, lhp	29. Brian Bass, rhp
15. David Bromberg, rhp	30. Bradley Tippett, rhp

Joe Nathan—arguably the best starter and best closer in the game—signed through 2008 but no longer. Despite a new ballpark scheduled to arrive in 2010, Minnesota still lacks the financial commitment from owner Carl Pohlad to keep both players, not to mention Joe Mauer and Justin Morneau once they approach free agency. Santana rejected a four-year, $80 million offer from the Twins, spurring trade talks that dominated the Winter Meetings. Minnesota's eventual resolution with Santana likely will set the course for the franchise for the rest of the decade.

General Manager: Bill Smith. **Farm Director:** Jim Rantz. **Scouting Director:** Deron Johnson.

Class	Team	League	W	L	PCT	Finish*	Manager	Affiliated
Majors	Minnesota	American	79	83	.488	8th (14)	Ron Gardenhire	—
Triple-A	Rochester Red Wings	International	77	67	.535	5th (14)	Stan Cliburn	2003
Double-A	New Britain Rock Cats	Eastern	69	72	.489	9th (12)	Riccardo Ingram	1995
High A	Fort Meyers Miracle	Florida State	70	70	.500	7th (12)	Kevin Boles	1993
Low A	Beloit Snappers	Midwest	79	61	.564	2nd (14)	Jeff Smith	2005
Rookie	Elizabethton Twins	Appalachian	50	18	.735	1st (9)^	Ray Smith	1974
Rookie	GCL Twins	Gulf Coast	37	19	.661	3rd (16)	Nelson Prada	1989
Overall 2007 Minor League Record			382	307	.554	4th		

*Finish in overall standings (No. of teams in league) ^League champion

LAST YEAR'S TOP 30

Player, Pos.		Status
1.	Matt Garza, rhp	(Rays)
2.	Glen Perkins, lhp	No. 14
3.	Kevin Slowey, rhp	Majors
4.	Chris Parmelee, of/1b	No. 12
5.	Anthony Swarzak, rhp	No. 5
6.	Pat Neshek, rhp	Majors
7.	Alexi Casilla, ss/2b	Majors
8.	Joe Benson, of	No. 2
9.	Paul Kelly, ss	Dropped out
10.	J.D. Durbin, rhp	(Phillies)
11.	Oswaldo Sosa, rhp	No. 23
12.	Matt Moses, 3b	Dropped out
13.	Denard Span, of	No. 20
14.	Jeff Manship, rhp	No. 9
15.	Alexander Smit, lhp	(Diamondbacks)
16.	Jay Rainville, rhp	Dropped out
17.	David Winfree, 3b	Dropped out
18.	Brian Duensing, lhp	No. 8
19.	Trevor Plouffe, ss/3b	No. 10
20.	Kyle Waldrop, rhp	Dropped out
21.	Eduardo Morlan, rhp	(Rays)
22.	Jose Mijares, lhp	No. 11
23.	Whit Robbins, 3b	Dropped out
24.	Tyler Robertson, lhp	No. 4
25.	Erik Lis, 1b	No. 27
26.	Brandon Roberts, of	Dropped out
27.	Yohan Pino, rhp	Dropped out
28.	Alex Burnett, rhp	No. 21
29.	David Shinskie, rhp	Dropped out
30.	Alex Romero, of	(Released)

BEST TOOLS

Best Hitter for Average	Ben Revere
Best Power Hitter	Danny Rams
Best Strike-Zone Discipline	Brian Dinkelman
Fastest Baserunner	Ben Revere
Best Athlete	Joe Benson
Best Fastball	Nick Blackburn
Best Curveball	Mike McCardell
Best Slider	Tyler Robertson
Best Changeup	Brian Duensing
Best Control	Nick Blackburn
Best Defensive Catcher	Wilson Ramos
Best Defensive Infielder	Deibinson Romero
Best Infield Arm	Deibinson Romero
Best Defensive Outfielder	Jason Pridie
Best Outfield Arm	Angel Morales

PROJECTED 2011 LINEUP

Catcher	Joe Mauer
First Base	Justin Morneau
Second Base	Alexi Casilla
Third Base	Brendan Harris
Shortstop	Trevor Plouffe
Left Field	Michael Cuddyer
Center Field	Joe Benson
Right Field	Delmon Young
Designated Hitter	Jason Kubel
No. 1 Starter	Johan Santana
No. 2 Starter	Francisco Liriano
No. 3 Starter	Kevin Slowey
No. 4 Starter	Nick Blackburn
No. 5 Starter	Scott Baker
Closer	Joe Nathan

TOP PROSPECTS OF THE DECADE

Year	Player, Pos.	2007 Org.
1998	Luis Rivas, ss	Indians
1999	Michael Cuddyer, 3b	Twins
2000	Michael Cuddyer, 3b	Twins
2001	Adam Johnson, rhp	Out of baseball
2002	Joe Mauer, c	Twins
2003	Joe Mauer, c	Twins
2004	Joe Mauer, c	Twins
2005	Joe Mauer, c	Twins
2006	Francisco Liriano, lhp	Twins
2007	Matt Garza, rhp	Twins

TOP DRAFT PICKS OF THE DECADE

Year	Player, Pos.	2007 Org.
1998	Ryan Mills, lhp	Out of baseball
1999	B.J. Garbe, of	Out of baseball
2000	Adam Johnson, rhp	Out of baseball
2001	Joe Mauer, c	Twins
2002	Denard Span, of	Twins
2003	Matt Moses, 3b	Twins
2004	Trevor Plouffe, ss	Twins
2005	Matt Garza, rhp	Twins
2006	Chris Parmelee, of/1b	Twins
2007	Ben Revere, of	Twins

LARGEST BONUSES IN CLUB HISTORY

Joe Mauer, 2001	$5,150,000
B.J. Garbe, 1999	$2,750,000
Adam Johnson, 2000	$2,500,000
Ryan Mills, 1998	$2,000,000
Michael Cuddyer, 1997	$1,850,000

MINNESOTA TWINS

Top 2008 Rookie: Nick Blackburn, rhp. Now that he's finally healthy, he's primed to earn a spot in Minnesota's rotation—and keep it.

Breakout Prospect: Deibinson Romero, 3b. He has the chance to provide a plus bat and glove at third base, long a problem spot for the Twins.

Sleeper: Brian Dinkelman, 2b/of. A versatile hitter, he could be Minnesota's answer to Frank Menechino.

SOURCE OF TOP 30 TALENT

Homegrown	28	Acquired	2
College	8	Trades	1
Junior college	1	Rule 5 draft	0
High school	8	Independent leagues	0
Draft-and-follow	3	Free agents/waivers	1
Nondrafted free agents	0		
International	8		

Number in parentheses indicate prospect rankings.

LF
Dustin Martin
Ozzie Lewis
Andrew Schmiesing

CF
Joe Benson (2)
Ben Revere (6)
Jason Pridie (7)
Denard Span (20)
Brandon Roberts

RF
Rene Tosoni (24)
Angel Morales

3B
Deibinson Romero (13)
Danny Valencia (22)
Brian Buscher
Matt Macri
Matt Moses
David Winfree
Reggie Williams

SS
Trevor Plouffe (10)
Estarlin de los Santos (17)
Paul Kelly
James Beresford

2B
Matt Tolbert
Brian Dinkelman
Steven Tolleson
Juan Portes

1B
Chris Parmelee (12)
Erik Lis (27)
Brock Peterson
Rene Leveret
Henry Sanchez

C
Wilson Ramos (3)
Jose Morales
Danny Rams
Alexander Soto
Drew Butera
Dan Rohlfing

RHP

Starters	Relievers
Nick Blackburn (1)	Loek Van Mil (19)
Anthony Swarzak (5)	Julio DePaula (25)
Jeff Manship (9)	Anthony Slama (28)
David Bromberg (15)	Rob Delaney
Mike McCardell (18)	Zach Ward
Alex Burnett (21)	Frank Mata
Oswaldo Sosa (23)	Charles Nolte
Dan Berlind (26)	Tom Stuifbergen
Brian Bass (29)	
Bradley Tippett (30)	
Michael Allen	
Jay Rainville	
Kyle Waldrop	
Brian Kirwan	
Yohan Pino	
Liam Hendriks	

LHP

Starters	Relievers
Tyler Robertson (4)	Jose Mijares (11)
Brian Duensing (8)	Carmen Cali
Glen Perkins (14)	Kyle Aselton
Ryan Mullins (16)	Errol Simonitsch
Henry Reyes	
Jarrad Eacott	
Martire Garcia	

DRAFT ANALYSIS

SIGNING BUDGET: $1.8 MILLION

Best Pro Debut: OF Ben Revere (1) got off to a running start in the Rookie-level Gulf Coast League, batting .325/.388/.461 with 21 steals, and leading the league with 46 runs and 10 triples. OF Ozzie Lewis (21) earned Rookie-level Appalachian League MVP honors while hitting .323/.375/.523 with nine homers and 50 RBIs. RHP Dan Berlind (7) was a GCL all-star after a 6-2, 1.93 effort.

Best Athlete: Revere led his baseball and football teams (as a defensive back, wide receiver and return specialist) to state championships as a senior. OF Angel Morales (3) is a lean, graceful athlete with strength, coordination and speed. OF Andrew Schmiesing (11) missed instructional league to finish his football career as a receiver at Division III St. Olaf (Minn.).

Best Pure Hitter: The Twins wouldn't have picked Revere where they did if they didn't believe he could hit. He has a quick bat to go with his quick feet, and they even project him to hit for average power.

Best Power Hitter: C/1B Danny Rams (2) had as much raw power as any drafted player. He'll need to refine his approach after going homerless in his first 97 pro at-bats.

Fastest Runner: Revere was the fastest runner in the draft, timed at 6.28 seconds over 60 yards at his best.

Best Defensive Player: Morales and Revere project as plus defenders in center field; Morales' arm is at least one grade better, if not more.

Best Fastball: RHP Charles Nolte (24) has flashed 96 mph gas; he sits in the low 90s. He could throw harder more consistently as he gets further away from Tommy John surgery. RHP Mike McCardell (6) is more consistent currently, sitting in the 90-92 mph range with life and command.

Best Secondary Pitch: McCardell, who was a two-way player and primarily a closer in college, has a second potential plus pitch in his curveball.

Most Intriguing Background: Danny Lehmann (8), a potentially plus defender behind the plate, is the nephew of reality TV star Duane Chapman, a.k.a. "Dog the Bounty Hunter." Schmiesing, who started every game during his college baseball career at St. Olaf, followed the football footsteps of his father Mike, drafted by the Philadelphia Eagles in 1969 (seventh round).

Closest To The Majors: RHP Blair Erickson (10), the NCAA's career saves leader with 53, will move quickly if he regains the low-90s fastball he flashed as a freshman at UC Irvine.

Best Late-Round Pick: Nolte or Schmiesing.

The One Who Got Away: The Twins wanted to sign RHP Nate Striz (5), a power arm with mid-90s heat, but couldn't keep him from attending North Carolina.

Assessment: The Twins bucked the consensus in taking Revere so high. They did so in several other instances but like the upside of one of the game's youngest draft classes.

2006 — BUDGET: $3.2 MILLION

OF/1B Chris Parmelee (1) is off to a slow start, but OF Joe Benson (2), LHP Tyler Robertson (3) and RHP Jeff Manship (4) all made our Twins Top 10 list.

GRADE: C+

2005 — BUDGET: $5.2 MILLION

RHP Matt Garza (1) was a revelation, and then Minnesota parlayed him into Delmon Young. RHP Kevin Slowey (2) raced to the majors, and LHP Brian Duensing (3) isn't far behind. Injuries have hampered the careers of 1B Henry Sanchez (1s), SS Paul Kelly (2) and 2B Drew Thompson (2).

GRADE: B+

2004 — BUDGET: $7.5 MILLION

Minnesota had five picks before the second round, but none looks as good as RHP Anthony Swarzak (2). LHP Glen Perkins (1) could help the Twins in a swing role, while SS Trevor Plouffe (1) made some nice progress last year.

GRADE: C+

2003 — BUDGET: $3.2 MILLION

Matt Moses (1) was supposed to be ready to take over third base by now, but he was left off the Twins' 40-man roster in November. RHP Scott Baker (2) is this crop's best bet at this point.

GRADE: C

Draft analysis by John Manuel (2007) and Jim Callis (2003-06). Numbers in parentheses indicate draft rounds. Budgets are bonuses in first 10 rounds.

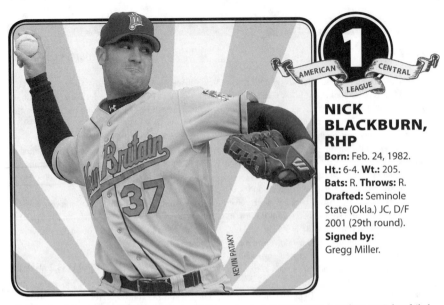

1
AMERICAN CENTRAL
LEAGUE

NICK BLACKBURN, RHP

Born: Feb. 24, 1982.
Ht.: 6-4. **Wt.:** 205.
Bats: R. **Throws:** R.
Drafted: Seminole State (Okla.) JC, D/F 2001 (29th round).
Signed by: Gregg Miller.

The Devil Rays drafted Blackburn in the 34th round out of Del City (Okla.) High in 2000, but failed to land him as a draft-and-follow after he spent a year at Seminole State (Okla.) JC. The Twins made him a 29th-rounder in 2001 and signed him in May 2002. He's had two surgeries on his right knee as a pro to try to fix a cartilage problem along the way. Blackburn's knee problems limited his ability to do conditioning drills, and as he added weight, his fastball lost its zip. Blackburn started to get healthier toward the end of 2006, regaining some velocity, and came to camp in the best shape of his career last spring. Blackburn regained his velocity, his secondary stuff improved and his career took off. He had a streak of 41⅓ innings without giving up an earned run and finished the season in the major leagues.

Blackburn got better in every phase in 2007. With less weight to carry, he got stronger and was able to work with Twins coaches to lengthen his stride, get better extension out front and improve the qualify of his stuff. His two-seam fastball sits at 90-91 mph, and as he has regained velocity, he has run his four-seamer as high as 95. Blackburn's cutter, which sits in the upper 80s and has real depth at times, helped him limit lefthanders to a .226 average in 261 minor league at-bats. Sent to the Arizona Fall League specifically to improve his offspeed pitches, he showed a solid-average curve and improved his feel for a changeup that scouts now grade as a plus pitch. Blackburn repeats his low-maintenance delivery and has average big league command, if not a tick above. His mound demeanor always has endeared him to club officials, who said he never stopped competing even when his stuff was short.

Blackburn has to learn to pitch with better stuff, when to pitch to contact and when to go for strikeouts. Scouts say his curveball could become a strikeout pitch if he threw it more and relied less on the cutter. He doesn't have a truly outstanding pitch, which probably limits his ceiling to that of No. 3 starter. The Twins laud his durability and believe he's over his past knee troubles.

Minnesota stuck with Blackburn, and he rewarded them with a tremendous comeback season, finishing with a dominant turn in the AFL. The Twins will enter spring training with at least seven candidates for their rotation, and Blackburn's command and repertoire could give him a leg up for the No. 5 job.

Year	Club (League)	Class	W	L	ERA	G	GS	CG	SV	IP	H	R	ER	HR	BB	SO	AVG
2002	Elizabethton (Appy)	R	3	3	5.00	13	13	0	0	66	70	41	37	6	21	62	.261
2003	Quad City (MWL)	A	2	9	4.86	16	10	2	1	76	78	44	41	13	18	40	.268
2004	Quad City (MWL)	A	6	4	2.77	20	13	1	1	84	69	37	26	3	23	66	.223
	Fort Myers (FSL)	A	3	3	6.27	9	7	0	0	37	51	30	26	7	7	21	.327
2005	Fort Myers (FSL)	A	7	5	3.36	15	15	1	0	93	95	43	35	5	16	55	.265
	Rochester (IL)	AAA	0	0	5.14	3	3	0	0	14	20	11	8	2	3	7	.328
	New Britain (EL)	AA	2	4	1.84	7	7	2	0	49	35	16	10	1	10	27	.206
2006	New Britain (EL)	AA	7	8	4.42	30	19	2	0	132	141	72	65	11	37	81	.275
2007	New Britain (EL)	AA	3	1	3.08	8	7	0	0	38	36	21	13	1	7	18	.240
	Rochester (IL)	AAA	7	3	2.11	17	17	3	0	110	96	32	26	7	12	57	.232
	Minnesota (AL)	MLB	0	2	7.71	6	0	0	0	11	19	12	10	2	2	8	.365
MINOR LEAGUE TOTALS			40	40	3.68	138	111	11	2	702	691	347	287	56	154	434	.257
MAJOR LEAGUE TOTALS			0	2	7.71	6	0	0	0	11	19	12	10	2	2	8	.365

2 JOE BENSON, OF

PAUL GIERHART

Born: March 5, 1988. **B-T:** R-R. **Ht.:** 6-1. **Wt.:** 205. **Drafted:** HS—Joliet, Ill., 2006 (2nd round). **Signed by:** Billy Milos.

Benson could have played both baseball and football (as a running back) at Purdue but opted to sign with the Twins as a second-round pick for $575,000. He got off to a terrible start in his first full season, batting .175 in April, but rallied to hit .273 after the all-star break. Benson's tools are as prodigious as anyone's in the system. Once he settled into the routine of the season, he let his athletic ability take over and showed a short, quick swing and above-average power potential to all fields. He's a well above-average runner (4.0 seconds to first from the right side) who can handle center field despite his size and football build. His arm is strong enough to play in any outfield spot. It's never good when your weakest tool is your bat, but that's the case with Benson. Even in his strong second half, he struck out once every 3.2 at-bats. He'll need plenty of time to polish his overall offensive approach. His basestealing savvy also needs work after he was caught 16 times in 34 basestealing attempts. Benson has the highest ceiling in the system because of his power-speed combo and ability to play a premium position, but his bat might be three or more years away. He'll start 2008 at high Class A Fort Myers.

Year	Club (League)	Class	AVG	G	AB	R	H	2B	3B	HR	RBI	BB	SO	SB	OBP	SLG
2006	Twins (GCL)	R	.260	52	196	30	51	11	5	5	28	21	41	9	.335	.444
	Beloit (MWL)	A	.263	8	19	2	5	0	0	0	1	0	6	1	.263	.263
2007	Beloit (MWL)	A	.255	122	432	73	110	18	8	5	38	49	124	18	.347	.368
MINOR LEAGUE TOTALS			.257	182	647	105	166	29	13	10	67	70	171	28	.341	.388

3 WILSON RAMOS, C

Born: Aug. 10, 1987. **B-T:** R-R. **Ht.:** 6-0. **Wt.:** 178. **Signed:** Venezuela, 2004. **Signed by:** Jose Leon.

Ramos' season almost went unnoticed, but not by the Twins and not by scouts of rival clubs, who called him the best position prospect on low Class A Beloit's roster. He didn't get there until June after beginning the year in extended spring training, then had his season ended in late August when he hurt his right thumb on an errant slide. Ramos blends catch-and-throw talent and offensive upside in a manner rare among current minor leaguers. He has excellent strength, helping produce above-average bat speed and power to all fields. A solid-average runner for now, Ramos rounds out his tools with an accurate, above-average arm and the hands to be a sound receiver. He threw out 41 percent of basestealers in 2007. He has yet to play a full season, and Ramos needs experience to refine his tools into skills. His swing plane lends itself more to line drives rather than home runs, and he won't maximize his power if he's not more selective at the plate. As he gets older, he'll be a below-average runner. One Twins official described Ramos as nearly a five-tool catcher, while another termed him untouchable. He's young enough to return to low Class A while still being ready to jump on the fast track.

Year	Club (League)	Class	AVG	G	AB	R	H	2B	3B	HR	RBI	BB	SO	SB	OBP	SLG
2005	Twins (DSL)	R	.252	39	127	16	32	5	1	1	15	8	13	1	.295	.331
2006	Twins (GCL)	R	.286	46	154	18	44	12	1	3	26	12	14	4	.339	.435
2007	Beloit (MWL)	A	.291	73	292	40	85	17	1	8	42	19	61	1	.345	.438
MINOR LEAGUE TOTALS			.281	158	573	74	161	34	3	12	83	39	88	6	.332	.414

4 TYLER ROBERTSON, LHP

Born: Dec. 23, 1987. **B-T:** L-L. **Ht.:** 6-5. **Wt.:** 225. **Drafted:** HS—Fair Oaks, Calif., 2006 (3rd round). **Signed by:** Kevin Bootay.

Robertson's father Jay, a longtime scout, is a special assistant to Rangers general manager Jon Daniels. The Twins started Tyler in extended spring training in 2007, but when a rotation spot opened in low Class A, he seized the opportunity and became Beloit's ace. He struck out 20 in two Midwest League playoff starts spanning 12 innings. Big and physical, Robertson attacks hitters with two average or better pitches. His sinking fastball touches 92-93 mph and his hard slider is the best in the system. His delivery adds deception. Minnesota says his makeup separates Robertson, a baseball rat who studies hitters but doesn't overthink. Robertson's fastball velocity was inconsistent all year, often sitting at 86-90 mph with his fastball, and even the Twins agree his stiff arm action precludes significant projection. They don't consider his delivery stressful, however. He's still searching for a consistent third pitch. His advocates contend Robertson proved he could dominate without his best stuff. Skeptical scouts have turned him in as a lefty reliever. Minnesota is confident that he'll reach his No. 2 or 3 starter ceiling due to his makeup, and that he'll move quickly after starting 2008 in high Class A.

Year	Club (League)	Class	W	L	ERA	G	GS	CG	SV	IP	H	R	ER	HR	BB	SO	AVG
2006	Twins (GCL)	R	4	2	4.25	11	10	0	0	48	54	23	23	2	15	54	.280
2007	Beloit (MWL)	A	9	5	2.29	18	16	2	1	102	87	33	26	3	33	123	.226
MINOR LEAGUE TOTALS			13	7	2.92	29	26	2	1	151	141	56	49	5	48	177	.244

5 ANTHONY SWARZAK, RHP

KEVIN PATAKY

Born: Sept. 10, 1985. **B-T:** R-R. **Ht.:** 6-3. **Wt.:** 195. **Drafted:** HS—Fort Lauderdale, Fla., 2004 (2nd round). **Signed by:** Brad Weitzel.

Swarzak's season started inauspiciously, as he made two brutal starts, then was suspended after two brutal starts for 50 games for violating MLB's drug policy. It was for a recreational drug, not a performance enhancer, and he returned from the suspension to post a solid season, capped by a solid stint in the Arizona Fall League. After he worked through 2006 with modest stuff, Swarzak's fastball and curveball ranked among the best in the system last year. At its best, his fastball sits at 91-93 mph and touches 94, and he stays tall in his delivery and pitches with a good downhill angle. His curveball can be a true hammer with power and depth, and he has improved his ability to throw strikes with it. Swarzak lacks the feel for a true changeup. He'll keep throwing it, but he likely will have to use his curve as his offspeed pitch while adding a cutter or slider to give hitters a different look. The Twins were impressed with how he came back from his suspension and believe it forced him to mature. Minnesota has enough pitching options ahead of Swarzak that he could return to Double-A New Britain. He's more likely to push his way up to Triple-A and could make his big league debut later in the year.

Year	Club (League)	Class	W	L	ERA	G	GS	CG	SV	IP	H	R	ER	HR	BB	SO	AVG
2004	Twins (GCL)	R	5	3	2.63	11	9	0	1	48	46	20	14	1	6	42	.251
2005	Beloit (MWL)	A	9	5	4.04	18	18	0	0	91	81	48	41	7	32	101	.238
	Fort Myers (FSL)	A	3	4	3.66	10	10	0	0	59	72	25	24	3	11	55	.300
2006	Fort Myers (FSL)	A	11	7	3.27	27	27	2	0	145	131	56	53	8	60	131	.242
2007	Fort Myers (FSL)	A	0	0	2.30	3	3	0	0	15	14	6	4	0	5	18	.241
	New Britain (EL)	AA	5	4	3.23	15	14	1	0	86	78	34	31	6	23	76	.241
MINOR LEAGUE TOTALS			33	23	3.37	84	81	3	1	446	422	189	167	25	137	423	.250

6 BEN REVERE, OF

CLIFF WELCH

Born: May 3, 1988. **B-T:** L-R. **Ht.:** 5-9. **Wt.:** 152. **Drafted:** HS—Lexington, Ky., 2007 (1st round). **Signed by:** Billy Corrigan.

Revere has a lot to live up to. His father John played (and coached) football at Eastern Kentucky and played baseball there, while older brother J.R. was a two-sport athlete at Georgia Southern at the turn of the decade. Revere wasn't a consensus first-rounder, but the Twins believed in him, drafted him 28th overall and signed him for $750,000. That was the lowest guarantee for a first-round hitter since Adam Kennedy got $650,000 from the Cardinals in 1997. Revere was the fastest player in the draft, covering 60 yards in around 6.3 seconds. He swings the bat with authority and conviction, lashing line drives to the gaps. He has all the tools to be an above-average center-field defender. His confidence and work ethic push his makeup into the elite range. If the power doesn't develop, Revere's ceiling will be a bit limited. His arm is just fringe-average, though that's not much of a liability for a center fielder. If Revere hits his ceiling, his overall game could resemble Ichiro's, minus the game-changing arm. He has a chance to move quickly and will start the season in low Class A.

Year	Club (League)	Class	AVG	G	AB	R	H	2B	3B	HR	RBI	BB	SO	SB	OBP	SLG
2007	Twins (GCL)	R	.325	50	191	46	62	6	10	0	29	13	20	21	.388	.461
MINOR LEAGUE TOTALS			.325	50	191	46	62	6	10	0	29	13	20	21	.388	.461

7 JASON PRIDIE, OF

Born: Oct. 9, 1983. **B-T:** L-R. **Ht.:** 6-1. **Wt.:** 190. **Drafted:** HS—Prescott, Ariz., 2002 (2nd round). **Signed by:** Craig Weissmann (Rays).

The prospect world almost forgot Pridie, whom the Rays drafted sandwiched between B.J. Upton and Elijah Dukes in 2002. Sidetracked by knee problems and by getting Rule 5ed by the Twins—he nearly made their 2006 roster—he didn't reach Triple-A until 2007. Pridie, whose brother Jon once was a Minnesota farmhand, was a crucial piece in the six-player Delmon Young-Matt Garza trade in November. Pridie is a well-rounded player, and his best present tool is his center-field defense. He has plus speed and range to go with a solid, accurate arm. Offensively, he has a smooth swing that generates at least average pop to all fields. He's a good teammate who plays with energy. A career .327 on-base percentage and high caught-stealing totals (10 in 36 tries last year) reflect how Pridie's aggressiveness can get the best of him at times. His home run totals could jump if he becomes more selective. Pridie has more present ability and upside than Denard Span, the other in-house candidate to replace Torri Hunter. If it all comes together, Pridie has a chance to make good on his early-career comparisons to Steve Finley.

Year	Club (League)	Class	AVG	G	AB	R	H	2B	3B	HR	RBI	BB	SO	SB	OBP	SLG
2002	Princeton (Appy)	R	.368	67	285	60	105	12	9	7	33	19	35	13	.410	.547
	Hudson Valley (NYP)	A	.344	8	32	4	11	1	1	1	1	3	6	0	.400	.531
2003	Charleston, S.C. (SAL)	A	.260	128	530	75	138	28	10	7	48	30	113	26	.302	.391
2004	Charleston, S.C. (SAL)	A	.276	128	515	103	142	27	11	17	86	37	114	17	.327	.470
2005	Visalia (Cal)	A	.500	1	2	0	1	0	0	0	0	0	0	0	.500	.500
	Montgomery (SL)	AA	.213	28	94	15	20	4	2	3	8	8	29	5	.275	.394
2006	Montgomery (SL)	AA	.230	132	460	39	106	11	4	5	34	31	93	16	.281	.304
2007	Montgomery (SL)	AA	.290	71	279	42	81	16	7	4	27	14	45	14	.331	.441
	Durham (IL)	AAA	.318	63	245	47	78	16	4	10	39	22	47	12	.375	.539
MINOR LEAGUE TOTALS			.279	626	2442	385	682	115	48	54	276	164	482	103	.327	.432

8 BRIAN DUENSING, LHP

Born: Feb. 22, 1983. **B-T:** L-L. **Ht.:** 5-11. **Wt.:** 195. **Drafted:** Nebraska, 2005 (3rd round). **Signed by:** Mark Wilson.

KEVIN PATAKY

A survivor of Tommy John surgery while in college, Duensing reached Triple-A in his second full season. He led the system with 167 innings, then tacked on a stint with Team USA at the World Cup in Taiwan. He started against Cuba in the gold-medal game and was chased one out shy of earning the victory. Duensing rivals Jeff Manship for having the most polish of any Twins farmhand. He throws strikes with four quality pitches, spotting, sinking and cutting his 87-91 mph fastball to all four quadrants of the strike zone. His changeup grades as above average, helping him combat righthanders, and his average slider yields groundouts. Short and stocky, Duensing will have to monitor his conditioning to make sure he doesn't lose any velocity. He's not particularly athletic, limiting his ability to field his position. His curveball is fringy, though he can spot it for strikes early in the count. Duensing respects hitters but believes he's better than each one who steps to the plate. That makeup has the Twins believing he'll become a solid No. 4 starter, sooner rather than later. If he doesn't force his way into the big league rotation, he'll return to Triple-A to start 2008.

Year	Club (League)	Class	W	L	ERA	G	GS	CG	SV	IP	H	R	ER	HR	BB	SO	AVG
2005	Elizabethton (Appy)	R	4	3	2.32	12	9	0	0	50	49	19	13	4	16	55	.249
2006	Beloit (MWL)	A	2	3	2.94	11	11	0	0	70	68	26	23	3	14	55	.257
	Fort Myers (FSL)	A	2	5	4.24	7	7	0	0	40	47	25	19	4	8	33	.296
	New Britain (EL)	AA	1	2	3.65	10	9	0	0	49	51	29	20	6	18	30	.277
2007	New Britain (EL)	AA	4	1	2.66	9	9	0	0	50	47	19	15	2	7	38	.240
	Rochester (IL)	AAA	11	5	3.24	19	19	3	0	116	115	54	42	13	30	86	.261
MINOR LEAGUE TOTALS			24	19	3.15	68	64	3	0	377	377	172	132	32	93	297	.262

9 JEFF MANSHIP, RHP

Born: Jan. 16, 1985. **B-T:** B-R. **Ht.:** 6-0. **Wt.:** 165. **Drafted:** Notre Dame, 2006 (14th round). **Signed by:** Billy Milos.

PAUL GIERHART

After his senior season of high school, Manship pitched for Team USA in the World Junior Championship and hurt his elbow on a substandard pitching mound in Curacao. He had Tommy John surgery, redshirted as a freshman and had two good seasons at Notre Dame. The Twins paid him $300,000 as a 14th-round pick, and he has gone 15-6, 2.20 in $1^1/_2$ pro seasons. Manship's older brother Matt, a former Stanford pitcher, got the size, but Jeff got the stuff in the family. His curveball ranks among the system's best, a 12-to-6 pitch that he can throw for strikes or bury. His fastball usually sits at 90-91 mph, and his command rivals the organization's models of Brad Radke and Kevin Slowey. Manship throws his solid-average changeup and his slider for strikes. Despite his short frame, he keeps his pitches down and is durable. Manship's repertoire lacks power, giving him less margin for error. When his command is off—on the rare occasions when he overthrows, or when he tires, as he did late in the season—he's quite hittable. Manship profiles as a No. 3 or 4 starter at best, and he'll begin what should be his last full minor league season in Double-A. Even with Minnesota's backlog of starters, he could force his way into the rotation equation by 2009.

Year	Club (League)	Class	W	L	ERA	G	GS	CG	SV	IP	H	R	ER	HR	BB	SO	AVG
2006	Twins (GCL)	R	0	0	0.00	2	0	0	0	5	3	0	0	0	1	10	.150

		Class	W	L	ERA	G	GS	CG	SV	IP	H	R	ER	HR	BB	SO	AVG
	Fort Myers (FSL)	A	0	0	2.08	4	3	0	0	8	7	3	2	0	2	12	.212
2007	Beloit (MWL)	A	7	1	1.51	13	13	0	0	77	51	15	13	4	9	77	.185
	Fort Myers (FSL)	A	8	5	3.15	13	13	0	0	71	77	38	25	5	25	59	.270
MINOR LEAGUE TOTALS			15	6	2.20	32	29	0	0	163	138	56	40	9	37	158	.225

10 TREVOR PLOUFFE, SS

Born: June 15, 1986. **B-T:** R-R. **Ht.:** 6-2. **Wt.:** 175. **Drafted:** HS—Northridge, Calif., 2004 (1st round). **Signed by:** Bill Mele.

The Twins have taken high school hitters with their first pick in seven of the last nine drafts, and with the exception of Joe Mauer, they've developed slowly. Plouffe finally made significant progress in 2007, setting career highs in most categories. When he's playing well, Plouffe shows four or five average tools. He has some feel for hitting and is developing power as he learns to use the leverage in his swing. A good prospect as a pitcher in high school, he has plenty of arm to make plays at shortstop and to handle third base if needed. He has average speed. His professional makeup serves him well. Plouffe doesn't stand out in any phase of the game. He figures to bat at the bottom of a big league order. An inconsistent defender, he made 32 errors last season and must improve his footwork to remain a shortstop. His quickness is below-average for his position. After starting his first Double-A season at age 20, Plouffe will consolidate his gains and go back to New Britain to start the season. He has similar tools but lacks the results of recently traded Jason Bartlett, and he could factor into Minnesota's shortstop mix in 2009 if he can become more consistent.

Year	Club (League)	Class	AVG	G	AB	R	H	2B	3B	HR	RBI	BB	SO	SB	OBP	SLG
2004	Elizabethton (Appy)	R	.283	60	237	29	67	7	2	4	28	19	34	2	.340	.380
2005	Beloit (MWL)	A	.223	127	466	58	104	18	0	13	60	50	78	8	.300	.345
2006	Fort Myers (FSL)	A	.246	125	455	60	112	26	4	4	45	58	93	8	.333	.347
2007	New Britain (EL)	AA	.274	126	497	75	136	37	2	9	50	38	89	12	.326	.410
MINOR LEAGUE TOTALS			.253	438	1655	222	419	88	8	30	183	165	294	30	.323	.370

11 JOSE MIJARES, LHP

Born: Oct. 29, 1984. **B-T:** L-L. **Ht.:** 6-0. **Wt.:** 230. **Signed:** Venezuela, 2002. **Signed by:** Jose Leon.

Mijares remains a favorite of scouts and player-development personnel from other organizations, because his stuff is just so fun to watch. But they don't have to deal with him every day like the Twins do. Minnesota officials also know Mijares comes from a poor background in Caracas' slums, however, and give him credit for small steps of maturity in 2007. Still, he's not ranked higher because his makeup makes it hard to know whether his stuff will play in the big leagues. The Twins protected him on the 40-man roster, an easy call because he's lefthanded and can show three plus pitches. Mijares' four-seam fastball has touched 98 mph and averaged 94 at times. At others, he'll sit at 87-89s. His power curveball and mid-80s slider both have tilt and depth. He even breaks out a changeup from time to time. Mijares' fastball gets straight and he doesn't throw consistent strikes, sometimes a function of not being in shape and being able to repeat his delivery. He averaged 6.9 walks per nine innings in 2007, but he didn't issue a walk in his first 12 innings in winter ball in Venezuela. Ticketed to start the year in Triple-A, Mijares will dictate his own timetable. His stuff will play at any level if he throws strikes.

Year	Club (League)	Class	W	L	ERA	G	GS	CG	SV	IP	H	R	ER	HR	BB	SO	AVG
2002	Cagua (VSL)	R	2	5	3.91	13	9	0	0	53	51	29	23	2	27	42	.264
2003	Tronconero 1 (VSL)	R	2	4	1.05	11	7	0	0	51	28	17	6	1	15	58	.159
2004	Twins (GCL)	R	4	0	2.43	19	0	0	5	29	22	9	8	1	15	25	.208
2005	Beloit (MWL)	A	6	3	4.31	20	6	0	2	54	43	28	26	6	40	78	.219
	Fort Myers (FSL)	A	0	0	1.50	5	1	0	0	12	5	4	2	1	5	17	.116
2006	Fort Myers (FSL)	A	3	5	3.57	27	5	0	0	63	52	30	25	10	27	77	.226
2007	Rochester (IL)	AAA	0	1	6.23	5	0	0	0	8	9	7	6	3	5	6	.265
	New Britain (EL)	AA	5	3	3.54	46	0	0	9	61	40	26	24	7	48	75	.183
MINOR LEAGUE TOTALS			22	21	3.24	146	28	0	16	333	250	150	120	31	182	378	.209

12 CHRIS PARMELEE, OF

Born: Feb. 24, 1988. **B-T:** L-L. **Ht.:** 6-1. **Wt.:** 200. **Drafted:** HS—Chino Hills, Calif., 2006 (1st round). **Signed by:** John Leavitt.

Among the high school hitters the Twins have drafted with their top choice in seven of the last years, Parmelee most closely resembles infielder Matt Moses, a 2003 first-rounder taken more for his bat than for filling Minnesota's usual all-around-tools profile. Signed for $1.5 million as the 20th overall pick in 2006, Parmelee had a modestly disappointing first full pro season. He didn't show the feel for hitting and ability

BaseballAmerica.com

to hit for average the Twins expected, and never got comfortable, tinkering with his setup and showing modest bat speed. Lefthanders handled him easily, holding him to a .549 OPS. His power was evident, as he used a smooth, pretty swing to crush offspeed stuff in the zone. Parmelee's body never has been his strength, and he needs to stay in better shape. His lack of athleticism and already below-average speed may make it difficult for him to stay in right field, which would waste his plus arm at first base or DH. Minnesota has misjudged one-dimensional hitters in the past—see Ortiz, David—and will be patient with Parmelee, who should move up to high Class A for 2008.

Year	Club (League)	Class	AVG	G	AB	R	H	2B	3B	HR	RBI	BB	SO	SB	OBP	SLG
2006	Twins (GCL)	R	.279	45	154	29	43	7	4	8	32	23	47	3	.369	.532
	Beloit (MWL)	A	.227	11	22	2	5	1	0	0	2	5	9	0	.370	.273
2007	Beloit (MWL)	A	.239	128	447	56	107	23	5	15	70	46	137	8	.313	.414
MINOR LEAGUE TOTALS			.249	184	623	87	155	31	9	23	104	74	193	11	.330	.438

13 DEIBINSON ROMERO, 3B

Born: Sept. 24, 1986. **B-T:** R-R. **Ht.:** 6-1. **Wt.:** 170. **Signed:** Dominican Republic, 2004. **Signed by:** Fred Guerrero.

Romero was part of the Rookie-level Elizabethton juggernaut that went 50-18, and he moved up for the Midwest League playoffs at season's end. He has the combination of offensive upside and defensive ability at a key position to be a big league regular. Romero's bat speed jumps out and gives him above-average power potential. He hadn't gone deep in his first 15 Appalachian League games last year, then blasted three homers and drove in 10 runs in a single contest. He stayed hot and finished third in the league in the triple-crown categories while tying for the league lead with 60 runs and 78 hits. Romero enhances his offensive value by being selective at the plate. He has solid athleticism and speed. He projects to be an above-average defender at third base, with agility and above-average arm strength. Some scouts are more confident in his glove than his bat, expressing concern about Romero's feel for hitting. He's the latest prospect to take up the challenge of filling the Twins' void at third base, but he's two or three years away from the majors. He'll begin 2008 in low Class A.

Year	Club (League)	Class	AVG	G	AB	R	H	2B	3B	HR	RBI	BB	SO	SB	OBP	SLG
2005	Twins (DSL)	R	.206	49	175	21	36	4	0	1	12	12	36	7	.286	.246
2006	Twins (GCL)	R	.313	50	176	37	55	10	2	4	38	13	37	6	.365	.460
2007	Elizabethton (Appy)	R	.316	66	247	60	78	16	2	9	52	34	47	9	.406	.506
	Beloit (MWL)	A	.300	2	10	2	3	1	0	0	3	1	4	0	.364	.400
MINOR LEAGUE TOTALS			.283	167	608	120	172	31	4	14	105	60	124	22	.360	.416

14 GLEN PERKINS, LHP

Born: March 2, 1983. **B-T:** L-L. **Ht.:** 5-11. **Wt.:** 200. **Drafted:** Minnesota, 2004 (2nd round). **Signed by:** Mark Wilson.

Born in St. Paul and a product of the University of Minnesota, Perkins was on his way to becoming a hometown hero, earning a spot on the 2006 playoff roster. Then injury and indecision sidetracked him. He began 2007 with one Triple-A start before joining the big league bullpen, where he pitched somewhat effectively before straining a muscle behind his shoulder. After a brief return to the mound in July, he was out until August. The Twins still have mixed opinions on whether he'll be a starter or reliever. His stuff fits the starter profile, with a solid fastball and changeup to go with a plus curveball. At his best, Perkins can touch 94 mph with his fastball and ride it on righthanders. His curve has been a true hammer at times. His stuff usually is a grade lower when he works out of the rotation, however, and while he was hurt, other starters moved forward. Minnesota would like Perkins to begin the year as a starter in Triple-A so it can evaluate him in that role. If a need arises in the major league bullpen, however, he could go back to relief.

Year	Club (League)	Class	W	L	ERA	G	GS	CG	SV	IP	H	R	ER	HR	BB	SO	AVG
2004	Elizabethton (Appy)	R	1	0	2.25	3	3	0	0	12	8	3	3	0	4	22	.186
	Quad City (MWL)	A	2	1	1.30	9	9	0	0	48	33	9	7	2	12	49	.205
2005	Fort Myers (FSL)	A	3	2	2.13	10	9	2	0	55	41	14	13	2	13	66	.205
	New Britain (EL)	AA	4	4	4.90	14	14	0	0	79	80	45	43	4	35	67	.263
2006	New Britain (EL)	AA	4	11	3.91	23	23	2	0	117	109	60	51	11	45	131	.243
	Rochester (IL)	AAA	0	1	2.08	1	1	0	0	4	6	1	1	0	5	3	.333
	Minnesota (AL)	MLB	0	0	1.59	4	0	0	0	5	3	1	1	0	0	6	.150
2007	Rochester (IL)	AAA	0	0	1.50	1	1	0	0	6	2	1	1	1	1	2	.105
	Minnesota (AL)	MLB	0	0	3.14	19	0	0	0	28	23	10	10	2	12	20	.232
	Twins (GCL)	R	0	0	1.80	3	3	0	0	5	3	1	1	0	2	6	.167
	Fort Myers (FSL)	A	0	0	27.00	1	1	0	0	1	3	3	3	1	0	0	.500
	New Britain (EL)	AA	0	2	11.05	3	3	0	0	7	11	9	9	4	7	7	.344
MINOR LEAGUE TOTALS			14	21	3.54	68	67	4	0	335	296	146	132	25	124	353	.237
MAJOR LEAGUE TOTALS			0	0	2.88	23	0	0	0	34	26	11	11	2	12	26	.218

15 DAVID BROMBERG, RHP

Born: Sept. 14, 1987. **B-T:** L-R. **Ht.:** 6-5. **Wt.:** 230. **Drafted:** Santa Ana (Calif.) JC, D/F 2005 (32nd round). **Signed by:** Dan Cox.

The Twins first saw Bromberg playing with Alex Burnett and Curtis Leavitt in a Los Angeles wood-bat event, and all three are now Twins, with Bromberg and Leavitt playing together at Elizabethton last season. After starring at Palisades High in Los Angeles, Bromberg signed as a draft-and-follow after a year at Santa Ana (Calif.) JC, where he pitched with Braves prospect Kris Medlen. Bromberg had a solid pro debut while getting into better shape, then broke out as the Appalachian League pitcher of the year in 2007, averaging 12.5 strikeouts per nine innings. Bromberg attacks hitters confidently with two pitchers, a 90-92 mph fastball and a high-70s power slurve that he improved after working with Elizabethton pitching coach Jim Shellenback. There's probably more velocity to come because he has a projectable frame with a narrow torso and long legs. Bromberg's changeup needs work, as lefthanders (.844 OPS) fared much better against him than righthanders (.566 OPS), and his slurve could use refinement as well. He's still working to repeat his delivery and throw more quality strikes. Bromberg may have a ways to go, but his ceiling is considerable. He's expected to earn a spot in Beloit's 2008 rotation.

Year	Club (League)	Class	W	L	ERA	G	GS	CG	SV	IP	H	R	ER	HR	BB	SO	AVG
2006	Twins (GCL)	R	3	3	2.66	10	10	2	0	50	42	21	15	2	18	31	.230
2007	Elizabethton (Appy)	R	9	0	2.78	13	11	0	0	58	45	19	18	4	32	81	.211
MINOR LEAGUE TOTALS			12	3	2.72	23	21	2	0	109	87	40	33	6	50	112	.220

16 RYAN MULLINS, LHP

Born: Nov. 13, 1983. **B-T:** L-L. **Ht.:** 6-6. **Wt.:** 180. **Drafted:** Vanderbilt, 2005 (3rd round). **Signed by:** Tim O'Neil.

Mullins' profile has risen to its highest point since he was a teammate of current Indians big leaguers Jensen Lewis and Jeremy Sowers at Vanderbilt. All three were in the same rotation in 2004, and Mullins was supposed to be the ace and a possible first-rounder in '05. A drunken-driving arrest and six-game suspension, followed by a subpar season, dropped him to the third round. Mullins has had a solid pro career since then, reaching Triple-A at the end of 2007 and finishing with a solid Arizona Fall League stint. He's a four-pitch lefty with a long, lanky frame and somewhat deceptive arms-and-legs delivery. Mullins' fastball sits in the upper 80s and touches 91. His big, slow curve was his go-to pitch in college, and he's added power to it and learned to throw it for strikes more as he has matured. He has added a slider to help him get inside on righthanders and also owns an effective changeup. Mullins hasn't added velocity as scouts hoped he might, but he knows his limits and executes well. He's ready for another shot at Triple-A, where he was hammered late last year, and profiles as a back-of-the-rotation starter.

Year	Club (League)	Class	W	L	ERA	G	GS	CG	SV	IP	H	R	ER	HR	BB	SO	AVG
2005	Elizabethton (Appy)	R	3	0	2.18	11	11	0	0	53	34	16	13	4	13	60	.182
2006	Beloit (MWL)	A	5	8	3.86	27	26	1	0	156	157	85	67	14	53	139	.257
2007	Fort Myers (FSL)	A	3	3	1.98	10	9	0	0	54	50	17	12	4	12	56	.238
	New Britain (EL)	AA	4	3	3.99	14	14	1	0	85	87	43	38	5	23	68	.264
	Rochester (IL)	AAA	0	3	10.57	4	4	0	0	15	28	23	18	2	5	11	.400
MINOR LEAGUE TOTALS			15	17	3.64	66	64	2	0	365	356	184	148	29	106	334	.253

17 ESTARLIN DE LOS SANTOS, SS

Born: Jan. 20, 1987. **B-T:** B-R. **Ht.:** 5-10. **Wt.:** 155. **Signed:** Dominican Republic, 2005. **Signed by:** Fred Guerrero.

The Twins haven't developed a homegrown shortstop since Pat Meares in the late 1990s, acquiring the likes of Cristian Guzman and Jason Bartlett in trades. De los Santos is the toolsiest shortstop in the system and has made major strides offensively to put himself on the prospect map before reaching full-season ball. He tied for the Appalachian League lead with 60 runs and ranked third with 27 steals last year, even though he tired and finished the season in a 2-for-42 slump (including the playoffs). A slashing switch-hitter, de los Santos takes advantage of his line-drive swing from the left side, using his plus-plus speed, and he has decent raw power. He's just not selective enough to get pitches he can drive yet. Defensively, de los Santos needs better footwork and may not have soft enough hands to stay at shortstop. However, his arm rates an easy 70 on the 20-80 scouting scale. His overall defensive package might profile better in center field, but the Twins could use him at shortstop, so he'll have ample opportunity to stick there. He should open 2008 in low Class A.

Year	Club (League)	Class	AVG	G	AB	R	H	2B	3B	HR	RBI	BB	SO	SB	OBP	SLG
2005	Twins (DSL)	R	.261	42	138	25	36	8	0	0	19	16	33	11	.373	.319
2006	Twins (GCL)	R	.195	24	82	12	16	1	2	0	2	8	18	8	.290	.256
2007	Elizabethton (Appy)	R	.264	67	284	60	75	13	6	1	41	26	66	27	.341	.363
MINOR LEAGUE TOTALS			.252	133	504	97	127	22	8	1	62	50	117	46	.342	.333

18 MIKE McCARDELL, RHP

Born: April 13, 1985. **B-T:** R-R. **Ht.:** 6-5. **Wt.:** 220. **Drafted:** Kutztown (Pa.), 2007 (5th round). **Signed by:** John Wilson.

Area scout John Wilson had seen McCardell as a closer and standout defensive third baseman for Division II power Kutztown (Pa.), but his interest was piqued when McCardell moved into the Golden Bears' rotation late in 2007. He didn't play as much third base as a senior, either, and his velocity jumped into the low 90s, peaking with an outstanding playoff start in which he struck out 13 against Slippery Rock (Pa.). After signing for $75,000 as fifth-round pick, he posted a stunning 102-9 K-BB ratio (including a playoff start). While he signed as a college senior and was old for Rookie ball, McCardell has the Twins thinking he's legitimate. He's athletic and has a pitcher's frame, with excellent control of his fastball. His best pitch is an outstanding curveball, one he can throw for strikes or bury as a chase pitch, and he uses an unusual grip that makes it tougher for hitters to identify. He's learning a changeup. McCardell has to prove his debut was no fluke while adjusting to a full season as a starter. His fastball/curveball combo profiles him as at least a setup man right now. He's expected to get on the fast track and jump to high Class A.

Year	Club (League)	Class	W	L	ERA	G	GS	CG	SV	IP	H	R	ER	HR	BB	SO	AVG
2007	Twins (GCL)	R	2	0	2.50	4	2	0	1	18	11	5	5	2	3	25	.177
	Elizabethton (Appy)	R	5	1	2.00	8	8	0	0	45	29	12	10	3	5	70	.179
MINOR LEAGUE TOTALS			7	1	2.14	12	10	0	1	63	40	17	15	5	8	95	.179

19 LOEK VAN MIL, RHP

Born: Sept. 15, 1984. **B-T:** R-R. **Ht.:** 7-1. **Wt.:** 225. **Signed:** Netherlands, 2005. **Signed by:** Howard Norsetter.

The Twins have been trying to mine Europe for talent for years, and with enigmatic lefty Alexander Smit lost on a waiver claim to the Reds, the 7-foot-1 Van Mil has succeeded him as the organization's top Euro prospect. He might have surpassed Smit anyway because he has one of the Twins' biggest fastballs, which was on display for the Netherlands in the World Cup in November. Van Mil closed for the Dutch and dominated with a 0.71 ERA in 13 innings, topping out at 97 mph and sitting at 94. As a teen, Van Mil had a clean arm action but an awkward delivery, and Minnesota worked with him before signing him. Former special assistant Larry Corrigan (now with the Pirates) was instrumental in getting the fairly athletic and coordinated Van Mil to stay tall in his delivery and use a higher arm slot. His slider touches 88 mph at times, and with his arm action, it's not unthinkable that he could reach 100 with his fastball and 90 with his slider down the line. He's not just a relief prospect either. He has flashed a changeup and curveball with potential, though all his offerings need to find the strike zone more often. Holding runners and fielding are weaknesses for Van Mil, who hadn't pitched until age 17 while growing up about 60 miles south of Amsterdam. Attempting to become the tallest big leaguer ever, he appears to be putting it all together. He'll start the year in low Class A—a long reach, even for him, from the majors.

Year	Club (League)	Class	W	L	ERA	G	GS	CG	SV	IP	H	R	ER	HR	BB	SO	AVG
2006	Twins (GCL)	R	1	2	3.30	10	8	0	0	43	51	31	16	3	17	24	.290
2007	Elizabethton (Appy)	R	2	2	2.63	13	0	0	0	24	14	10	7	0	17	23	.171
MINOR LEAGUE TOTALS			3	4	3.06	23	8	0	0	67	65	41	23	3	34	47	.252

20 DENARD SPAN, OF

Born: Feb. 27, 1984. **B-T:** L-L. **Ht.:** 6-0. **Wt.:** 195. **Drafted:** HS—Tampa, 2002 (1st round). **Signed by:** Brad Weitzel.

The Twins drafted Span and Matt Moses in back-to-back years in the first round, and expected them to be ready to fill holes in the big league team by now. Span got an extra year to develop when the Twins signed Torii Hunter to a one-year contract extension last offseason, but he proved he still wasn't ready for the majors with a poor start in Triple-A. He finished strong, however, hitting .306 after the all-star break with improved plate discipline. Span's offensive ceiling appears to be lower than Minnesota had hoped. He's an outstanding bunter and is more effective when he does that, draws walks and keeps the ball on the ground. His swing lacks a load needed to hit for power. More disappointing is his grasp of baserunning. His poor instincts keep him from putting his excellent speed to work offensively. Defensively, his speed helps him outrun his mistakes and make plays, but he's not smooth. His fringy arm plays well enough in center for him to be an average big league defender. The acquisition of Jason Pridie in the Delmon Young trade with the Rays means Span will need a huge spring training to win the Twins' center-field job. Otherwise, he's headed back to Triple-A.

MINNESOTA TWINS

Year	Club (League)	Class	AVG	G	AB	R	H	2B	3B	HR	RBI	BB	SO	SB	OBP	SLG
2003	Elizabethton (Appy)	R	.271	50	207	34	56	5	1	1	18	23	34	14	.355	.319
2004	Quad Cities (MWL)	A	.267	64	240	29	64	4	3	0	14	34	49	15	.363	.308
2005	Fort Myers (FSL)	A	.339	49	186	38	63	3	3	1	19	22	25	13	.410	.403
	New Britain (EL)	AA	.285	68	267	47	76	6	5	0	26	22	41	10	.355	.345
2006	New Britain (EL)	AA	.285	134	536	80	153	16	6	2	45	40	78	24	.340	.349
2007	Rochester (IL)	AAA	.267	139	487	59	130	20	7	3	55	40	90	25	.323	.355
MINOR LEAGUE TOTALS			.282	504	1923	287	542	54	25	7	177	181	317	101	.349	.347

21 ALEX BURNETT, RHP

Born: July 26, 1987. **B-T:** R-R. **Ht.:** 6-0. **Wt.:** 190. **Drafted:** HS—Huntington, Calif., 2005 (12th round). **Signed by:** John Leavitt.

Minnesota's track record for developing pitchers is mixed of late. The Twins have preferred taller, big-bodied righthanders such as Nick Blackburn, since-traded Matt Garza and 2004 first-rounder Kyle Waldrop, though they've had more success with shorter, more athletic pitchers such as Jesse Crain and Kevin Slowey. Burnett fits into the latter category, and some club officials call him a poor man's Roy Oswalt. Burnett's fastball rivals any in the system because it jumps out of his hand and has good sinking life at 88-92 mph. He has shown more velocity in the past, touching 94-95 in high school. He complements his fastball with a curveball that gives him a second strikeout pitch. Besides his size, the Oswalt comparison also stems from his ability to change speeds on his breaking ball, using it as either a power pitch or as a changeup when he throws a slower version. He also has an average true changeup, and his feel for changing speeds helped him dominate lefthanded hitters (.525 OPS) in 2007. He's prone to missing up in the strike zone with his fastball, which at times is pretty straight. Burnett profiles as a No. 4 starter down the line and will continue his climb this season in high Class A.

Year	Club (League)	Class	W	L	ERA	G	GS	CG	SV	IP	H	R	ER	HR	BB	SO	AVG
2005	Twins (GCL)	R	4	2	4.10	13	8	0	0	48	50	25	22	6	14	33	.267
2006	Elizabethton (Appy)	R	4	3	4.04	13	13	1	0	71	66	41	32	6	13	71	.242
2007	Beloit (MWL)	A	9	8	3.02	27	27	1	0	155	140	60	52	9	38	117	.239
MINOR LEAGUE TOTALS			17	13	3.47	53	48	2	0	274	256	126	106	21	65	221	.245

22 DANNY VALENCIA, 3B

Born: Sept. 19, 1984. **B-T:** R-R. **Ht.:** 6-2. **Wt.:** 200. **Drafted:** Miami, 2006 (19th round). **Signed by:** Hector Otero.

The Twins went hard after third basemen in the 2006 draft, just as they had three years earlier. In those drafts, they acquired players such as Matt Moses, Garrett Olson, Whit Robbins, Valencia and David Winfree, and most of them haven't met expectations. That has prompted them to add Brian Buscher (minor league Rule 5 draft) and Matt Macri (trade) to buttress the big league club at the hot corner, but there's still hope Valencia can be part of the equation. He's one of the system's better run producers, with a pull-oriented approach and good strength and leverage in his swing, producing above-average power. While Valencia sells out too much and is prone to strikeouts, he has some feel for hitting. Defensively, he lacks the range to be a quality defender, but his solid hands and above-average arm should keep him at third base. His makeup hasn't endeared him to the Twins, and similar concerns cropped up in his college career, split between UNC Greensboro and Miami. Despite the organization's logjam of mediocrity on its third-base depth chart, Valencia should move up a step to Double-A.

Year	Club (League)	Class	AVG	G	AB	R	H	2B	3B	HR	RBI	BB	SO	SB	OBP	SLG
2006	Elizabethton (Appy)	R	.311	48	190	30	59	13	0	8	29	15	34	0	.365	.505
2007	Beloit (MWL)	A	.302	66	242	44	73	15	0	11	35	28	54	3	.374	.500
	Fort Myers (FSL)	A	.291	61	230	28	67	8	2	6	31	16	48	1	.332	.422
MINOR LEAGUE TOTALS			.301	175	662	102	199	36	2	25	95	59	136	4	.357	.474

23 OSWALDO SOSA, RHP

Born: Sept. 19, 1985. **B-T:** R-R. **Ht.:** 6-4. **Wt.:** 225. **Signed:** Venezuela, 2002. **Signed by:** Jose Leon.

Twins officials were high on Sosa coming into 2007, particularly after he tore through the Venezuelan League as a 21-year-old, going 5-0, 2.30 for Aragua. His 47 winter innings pushed him past 200 for 2006, counting the minor league regular season and one playoff start. It was too much for Sosa's stuff to hold up over last season. After sitting at 89-94 mph the previous year, his fastball rarely got over 91 in 2007 and usually parked at 88-90. He had pitched with similar stuff in the past before physically maturing and improving his delivery, and he figured out a way to succeed, pounding the bottom of the zone with two-seamers, cut fastballs and sliders to try to get groundballs. While he nibbled too much and didn't attack hitters as much as Minnesota wants him to, he kept the ball in the ballpark and competed well. Some Twins officials believe his velocity will return with a fresher arm, but Sosa frustrated club officials by again pitching in winter ball, albeit with a reduced workload. Just 22, Sosa already has claimed a spot on the 40-man roster and has reached Double-A, and he'll return there for 2008.

Year	Club (League)	Class	W	L	ERA	G	GS	CG	SV	IP	H	R	ER	HR	BB	SO	AVG
2003	Tronconero 1 (VSL)	R	1	2	3.02	11	10	0	0	53	44	24	18	0	18	40	.221
2004	Twins (GCL)	R	1	2	2.20	8	5	0	0	28	27	13	7	0	4	30	.239
2005	Elizabethton (Appy)	R	6	5	4.95	12	11	0	0	56	59	37	31	4	21	40	.265
2006	Beloit (MWL)	A	9	7	2.75	20	20	1	0	117	102	44	36	1	36	95	.233
	Fort Myers (FSL)	A	4	1	2.08	6	6	0	0	34	23	12	8	1	18	27	.189
2007	Fort Myers (FSL)	A	5	5	2.23	19	19	0	0	105	94	30	26	2	36	82	.238
	New Britain (EL)	AA	1	4	4.50	9	9	0	0	48	45	28	24	4	22	35	.251
MINOR LEAGUE TOTALS			27	26	3.04	85	80	1	0	444	394	188	150	12	155	349	.236

24 RENE TOSONI, OF

Born: July 2, 1986. **B-T:** L-R. **Ht.:** 6-0. **Wt.:** 185. **Drafted:** Chipola (Fla.) JC, D/F 2005 (36th round). **Signed by:** Jim Ridley.

The Twins have had success with sweet-swinging Canadians, such as Corey Koskie and Justin Morneau. Tosoni may not have their upside, but he's one of the system's most intriguing hitters. Minnesota liked him enough to draft him twice, in 2004 out of high school and in 2005 after a year at Chipola (Fla.) JC, which alma mater of Canadians such as Adam Loewen and Russell Martin. He's somewhat raw and was exposed a bit in the Midwest League playoffs, but Tosoni has the sweetest swing in the organization. Even when he hit just .192 in the postseason, four of his five hits were doubles. Tosoni has a compact lefthanded stroke, and he keeps the bat in the hitting zone a long time. He has a line-drive approach, centers the ball on the barrel regularly and has shown good plate discipline, making the Twins optimistic that his power will develop. He has average speed, range and arm strength, and he can become an above-average corner fielder with repetitions and work. Tosoni finished the year in low Class A and will go back there for the 2008 season.

Year	Club (League)	Class	AVG	G	AB	R	H	2B	3B	HR	RBI	BB	SO	SB	OBP	SLG
2007	Elizabethton (Appy)	R	.301	63	236	58	71	13	4	3	31	32	48	13	.407	.428
	Beloit (MWL)	A	.273	2	11	1	3	1	0	0	1	0	2	0	.273	.364
MINOR LEAGUE TOTALS			.300	65	247	59	74	14	4	3	32	32	50	13	.402	.425

25 JULIO DePAULA, RHP

Born: Dec. 31, 1982. **B-T:** R-R. **Ht.:** 6-0. **Wt.:** 180. **Signed:** Dominican Republic, 1999. **Signed by:** Johnny Sierra.

When DePaula signed with the Twins, he was a smallish middle infielder. They wanted him as a pitcher, though, and he has worked hard to get stronger over eight years in the system. His one-stop-a-year approach finally paid off with a late-season big league promotion in 2007. DePaula doesn't have the breaking ball to start, but he has two above-average pitches that should make him an effective middle reliever. His low-90s fastball touches 95-96 mph and features good life down in the zone, and his changeup once rated as the best in the organization. It's still a plus pitch, and because of it, DePaula can get lefthanders out (.542 OPS last year). He has enough stuff and durability to extend his outings, with 10 of his Triple-A appearances lasting at least three innings. DePaula gets in trouble when he leaves his fastball up. His lack of confidence in his breaking ball makes him more vulnerable against righthanders. DePaula pitched in the Dominican Winter League and was expected to come to compete for a spot in the big league bullpen.

Year	Club (League)	Class	W	L	ERA	G	GS	CG	SV	IP	H	R	ER	HR	BB	SO	AVG
2000	Indians/Twins (DSL)	R	4	2	4.11	19	4	0	2	46	52	30	21	0	19	37	.277
2001	Twins (DSL)	R	5	3	1.98	19	7	1	2	68	51	25	15	0	23	49	.199
2002	Twins (GCL)	R	3	2	1.82	7	6	1	0	39	39	16	8	0	5	21	.255
	Elizabethton (Appy)	R	0	2	9.13	5	5	0	0	23	40	25	24	1	9	15	.381
2003	Elizabethton (Appy)	R	2	3	1.71	22	0	0	5	26	19	7	5	1	8	24	.200
2004	Quad City (MWL)	A	12	7	3.05	49	0	0	9	91	81	37	31	4	39	88	.229
2005	Fort Myers (FSL)	A	4	3	2.24	36	0	0	4	64	52	18	16	0	25	51	.226
2006	Fort Myers (FSL)	A	1	1	0.00	8	0	0	3	15	8	4	0	1	6	10	.145
	New Britain (EL)	AA	2	2	2.57	43	0	0	7	66	58	25	19	1	27	43	.230
2007	Rochester (IL)	AAA	12	5	2.90	49	0	0	2	83	66	33	27	8	27	63	.226
	Minnesota (AL)	MLB	0	1	8.55	16	0	0	0	20	30	20	19	5	10	8	.357
MINOR LEAGUE TOTALS			45	30	2.84	257	22	2	34	525	466	220	166	16	188	401	.235
MAJOR LEAGUE TOTALS			0	1	8.55	16	0	0	0	20	30	20	19	5	10	8	.357

26 DAN BERLIND, RHP

Born: Dec. 3, 1987. **B-T:** R-R. **Ht.:** 6-7. **Wt.:** 210. **Drafted:** Pierce (Calif.) JC, 2007 (7th round). **Signed by:** Dan Cox.

Berlind was predominantly a catcher in middle and high school before growing too tall for the position and moving to the mound as a prep junior. He was a sought-after recruit who chose Cal Poly, but he spent only the fall semester there before transferring to Pierce (Calif.) JC after Poly assistant coach Jerry Weinstein left the program. Berlind had a solid year at Pierce, signed for $80,000 as a seventh-rounder, then was the Rookie-level Gulf Coast League pitcher of the year in his pro debut. He has imposing size and good athletic ability, showing a three-pitch mix. His fastball sits at 89-90 mph and touches 93, and between his age and body, he has plenty of projection. His hard slider and changeup both have shown potential to be solid-average pitches, if not better. Most encouraging, Berlind challenges hitters and fills up the strike zone, showing coordination and a relatively compact delivery for his size. He's polished enough to jump over Elizabethton and start 2008 in low Class A if he has a good spring.

Year	Club (League)	Class	W	L	ERA	G	GS	CG	SV	IP	H	R	ER	HR	BB	SO	AVG
2007	Twins (GCL)	R	6	2	1.93	11	9	0	0	56	37	16	12	4	20	52	.186
MINOR LEAGUE TOTALS			6	2	1.93	11	9	0	0	56	37	16	12	4	20	52	.186

27 ERIK LIS, OF/1B

Born: March 4, 1984. **B-T:** L-L. **Ht.:** 6-1. **Wt.:** 220. **Drafted:** Evansville, 2005 (9th round). **Signed by:** Billy Milos.

Lis hopes his home run against Roger Clemens in a May 18 game in high Class A isn't his career highlight. Of course, he already has others. He led the organization in batting (.326) in 2006, then topped it in homers (18) and RBIs (97) last year while playing in the Florida State League, a difficult environment for hitters. The Twins aren't sold on Lis because he's not a typical Twins player. His tools other than his bat stand out as negatives, and he's not a well-rounded player, with below-average running, throwing and defensive tools. He played more left field than any other position in 2007, but he hit much better as a first baseman or DH (.293, 12 homers in 225 at-bats) than while playing left (.261, six homers in 264 at-bats). Lis hits with a stiff setup, and his swing is far from classic or fluid, but it works because he has above-average bat speed. FSL managers noted his improvement in handling offspeed pitches. He hangs in well against lefthanders and is a good situational hitter. Lis' efforts to become passable in left field and to hit his way into the Minnesota's plans will continue this year in Double-A.

Year	Club (League)	Class	AVG	G	AB	R	H	2B	3B	HR	RBI	BB	SO	SB	OBP	SLG
2005	Elizabethton (Appy)	R	.315	49	168	29	53	12	1	10	41	9	35	0	.356	.577
2006	Beloit (MWL)	A	.326	105	411	69	134	37	3	16	70	51	83	4	.402	.547
2007	Fort Myers (FSL)	A	.274	132	492	58	135	34	4	18	97	41	109	3	.334	.470
MINOR LEAGUE TOTALS			.301	286	1071	156	322	83	8	44	208	101	227	7	.364	.516

28 ANTHONY SLAMA, RHP

Born: Jan. 6, 1984. **B-T:** R-R. **Ht.:** 6-3. **Wt.:** 205. **Drafted:** San Diego, 2006 (39th round). **Signed by:** John Leavitt.

Slama redshirted as a freshman due to arm trouble at UC Riverside, then transferred to Santa Ana (Calif.) JC for two seasons before joining San Diego. The Twins drafted him in 2006, then followed him in 2007 as Slama closed for the West Coast Conference champion Toreros. Slama was expected to re-enter the draft, but when San Diego went 0-2 in regional play, his college career was done and the Twins moved in to sign him before the 2007 draft. He was still eligible to sign with Minnesota because he was a fifth-year senior. Slama quickly showed he was too good for Elizabethton and dominated in low Class A, striking out 13.9 batters per nine innings between the two stops. He picked up three saves in the Midwest League playoffs, relying on a low 90s fastball that has heavy sink. When he commands the fastball to both sides of the plate, he's tough to elevate. Slama gave up just two homers over the last two years between college and pro ball. He throws from a low three-quarters arm slot and gets groundballs with his heater and solid-average slider. Slama's profile marks him as a middle reliever and he's quite old for a first-year player, but he's primed to move quickly, perhaps even jumping to Double-A in 2008.

Year	Club (League)	Class	W	L	ERA	G	GS	CG	SV	IP	H	R	ER	HR	BB	SO	AVG
2007	Elizabethton (Appy)	R	0	0	2.45	6	0	0	4	7	2	2	2	0	1	10	.091
	Beloit (MWL)	A	1	1	1.48	21	0	0	10	24	15	4	4	0	9	39	.172
MINOR LEAGUE TOTALS			1	1	1.71	27	0	0	14	31	17	6	6	0	10	49	.156

29 BRIAN BASS, RHP

Born: Jan. 6, 1982. **B-T:** R-R. **Ht.:** 6-0. **Wt.:** 215. **Drafted:** HS—Montgomery, Ala., 2000 (6th round). **Signed by:** Dennis Woody (Royals).

Bass has been around, making appearances on Royals prospect lists since he was drafted in 2000, ranking as high as No. 8 after the 2003 season. Shoulder problems interrupted his 2004 and 2006 campaigns, and the Royals let him depart as a minor league free agent. Though he had just four career relief appearances against 140 starts, Minnesota signed him for its Triple-A bullpen. Bass struggled, both with the new role and with shoulder tenderness. As the season went along, he got a chance to start, and his work ethic put him in position to take advantage of it. He showed his old fastball, sitting in the low 90s and touching plenty of 94s and 95s. His slider was a plus pitch late in the year, a hard mid-80s breaking ball with depth. His changeup was fringe-average but played up because he threw quality strikes with everything. The Twins added him to the 40-man roster after the season and he pitched winter ball in Venezuela. Depending on how the big league roster shakes out, Bass will have a chance to make the Opening Day rotation.

Year	Club (League)	Class	W	L	ERA	G	GS	CG	SV	IP	H	R	ER	HR	BB	SO	AVG
2000	Royals (GCL)	R	3	5	3.89	12	9	0	0	44	36	27	19	0	18	44	.211
	Charleston, W.Va. (SAL)	A	0	0	6.75	1	1	0	0	4	6	3	3	0	0	1	.333
2001	Burlington (MWL)	A	3	10	4.65	26	26	1	0	139	138	82	72	16	53	75	.257
2002	Burlington (MWL)	A	5	7	3.83	20	20	1	0	110	103	57	47	8	31	60	.246
2003	Wilmington (Car)	A	9	8	2.84	26	26	2	0	152	129	59	48	7	43	119	.229
2004	Wichita (TL)	AA	0	4	7.43	10	10	0	0	36	53	30	30	4	22	20	.351
	Royals (AZL)	R	0	1	2.55	5	5	0	0	17	17	6	5	0	3	23	.246
2005	Wichita (TL)	AA	12	8	5.24	27	27	0	0	165	185	106	96	14	53	102	.286
2006	Omaha (PCL)	AAA	1	5	7.59	7	7	0	0	32	49	35	27	7	14	11	.348
	Wichita (TL)	AA	4	1	4.00	6	5	1	0	27	29	14	12	2	6	18	.269
	Royals (AZL)	R	1	1	4.50	3	3	0	0	12	15	7	6	0	0	9	.294
2007	Rochester (IL)	AAA	7	3	3.48	37	10	1	1	103	96	45	40	8	24	80	.246
MINOR LEAGUE TOTALS			45	53	4.32	180	149	6	1	843	856	471	405	66	267	562	.262

30 BRADLEY TIPPETT, RHP

Born: Feb. 11, 1988. **B-T:** R-R. **Ht.:** 6-2. **Wt.:** 176. **Signed:** Australia, 2006. **Signed by:** Howard Norsetter.

The Twins have been active in Australia for years, with several players breaking through to the majors (Grant Balfour, Mike Nakamura, Brad Thomas) but none making a major impact. Tippett and fellow Aussie righthander Liam Hendriks are the best of the organization's current crew from Down Under. Hendriks, whose father was an Australian Rules Football star, has better present stuff and is a gifted athlete. However, he has had knee trouble that has led to other nagging injuries, and he has a below-average fastball. Tippett rates as the better long-term prospect because he has similar 84-88 mph velocity—touching 90 at times—but already owns a devastating changeup, a true major league plus pitch. Lefthanders were helpless against Tippett last year, going 0-for-36 with no walks and 19 strikeouts. His curveball has the potential to be an average pitch, and he pounds the strike zone with everything. His low-maintenance delivery makes his command project to be major league average, if not a tick above. If his fastball comes along, Tippett could develop into a middle-of-the-rotation starter. He'll need a good spring to break through Minnesota's glut of young pitchers and make the Beloit rotation, but a return to extended spring training shouldn't be considered a major setback.

Year	Club (League)	Class	W	L	ERA	G	GS	CG	SV	IP	H	R	ER	HR	BB	SO	AVG
2006	Twins (GCL)	R	3	5	2.53	19	0	0	10	21	27	8	6	1	5	18	.303
2007	Elizabethton (Appy)	R	7	1	0.93	21	0	0	3	38	20	4	4	1	4	51	.155
MINOR LEAGUE TOTALS			10	6	1.50	40	0	0	13	60	47	12	10	2	9	69	.216

New York Mets

BY JOHN MANUEL

dvance scouts descended on the Mets in September, as other contenders sent in their top evaluators to check out the team bound to win the National League East. As late as Sept. 12, New York led the Phillies by seven games. But the team scouts saw in September wasn't a playoff team.

A listless team that played without enough energy, a manager in Willie Randolph who couldn't find the right spark for his team, a bullpen constructed by general manager Omar Minaya that gave Randolph few if any reliable middle-relief options . . . the Mets were a mess. A team that spent 140 days in first place didn't finish there, as Philadelphia won 13 of its last 17 games while New York was going 5-12.

It was a historic collapse, but the Mets didn't suddenly become a bad team in September. In fact, they had been a .500 team since the calendar turned to June. New York went 34-18 in the season's first two months and just 54-56 the rest of the way.

The Mets faltered in part because they got old in a hurry. Carlos Delgado and Paul Lo Duca had the worst full-season numbers of their careers. Moises Alou remained productive but couldn't stay healthy. On the mound, Tom Glavine got bombed in his final three starts and Billy Wagner blew three saves down the stretch.

More disconcerting, however, was that some of New York's young building blocks struggled. Jose Reyes wilted in the second half, hitting just .251 after the all-star break. Mike Pelfrey, who signed for a club-record $3.55 million bonus as a first-round pick in 2005, went 3-8, 5.57 and failed to keep the No. 5 starter's job. Philip Humber, a first-rounder whose $3 million bonus ranks second in club history, got hammered by the Nationals in his lone start during the season's final week.

Scouts from other organizations say the Mets have little immediate help on the way in the farm system. The jury is still out on Pelfrey and Humber, and there's not much in the way of upper-level position players behind outfielder Carlos Gomez.

The lack of talent in part reflects New York's decision not to wield its large-market resources to acquire talent the last two years, particularly in the draft. The Mets have surrendered their first-round choice as free-agent compensation in each of the past two drafts, and haven't tried to compensate by exceeding MLB's bonus guidelines with other picks. Minaya said that could change.

Jose Reyes batted just .251 in the second half as the Mets fell out of the playoffs

TOP 30 PROSPECTS

1. Fernando Martinez, of	16. Greg Veloz, 2b
2. Deolis Guerra, rhp	17. Wilmer Flores, 3b/ss
3. Carlos Gomez, of	18. Ruben Tejada, ss/2b
4. Kevin Mulvey, rhp	19. Mike Carp, 1b
5. Eddie Kunz, rhp	20. Nick Evans, 1b
6. Brant Rustich, rhp	21. Francisco Pena, c
7. Philip Humber, rhp	22. Phillips Orta, rhp
8. Jon Niese, lhp	23. Adam Bostick, lhp
9. Nathan Vineyard, lhp	24. Emmanuel Garcia, 2b/ss
10. Robert Parnell, rhp	25. Steven Register, rhp
11. Joe Smith, rhp	26. Mike Antonini, lhp
12. Scott Moviel, rhp	27. Jefry Marte, 3b
13. Steven Clyne, rhp	28. Juan Lagares, ss
14. Nick Carr, rhp	29. Lucas Duda, 1b/of
15. Danny Murphy, 3b	30. Elvin Ramirez, rhp

"We've adhered to the commissioner's slot recommendations," Minaya said. "We've been good citizens. But not all the teams have done that, and the competitive balance is not fair. We have to take that position under review as an organization."

New York did sign 15 players internationally in the summer of 2007, more than any other organization, and has aggressively pushed prospects such as Dominican outfielder Fernando Martinez and Venezuelan righthander Deolis Guerra—the top two prospects on this list.

General Manager: Omar Minaya. **Farm Director:** Adam Wogan. **Scouting Director:** Rudy Terrasas.

Class	Team	League	W	L	PCT	Finish*	Manager	Affiliated
Majors	New York	National	88	74	.543	5th (16)	Willie Randolph	—
Triple-A	New Orleans Zephyrs	Pacific Coast	75	69	.521	6th (16)	Ken Oberkfell	2007
Double-A	Binghamton Mets	Eastern	61	81	.430	11th (12)	Mako Oliveras	1992
High A	St. Lucie Mets	Florida State	68	71	.489	8th (12)	Frank Cacciatore	1988
Low A	Savannah Sand Gnats	South Atlantic	41	94	.304	16th (16)	Tim Teufel	2007
Short-season	Brooklyn Cyclones	New York-Penn	49	25	.662	1st (14)	Edgar Alfonzo	2001
Rookie	Kingsport Mets	Appalachian	35	33	.515	3rd (9)	Donovan Mitchell	1980
Rookie	GCL Mets	Gulf Coast	20	35	.364	13th (16)	Juan Lopez	2004
Overall 2007 Minor League Record			349	408	.461	27th		

*Finish in overall standings (No. of teams in league) ^League champion

LAST YEAR'S TOP 30

Player, Pos.		Status
1.	Mike Pelfrey, rhp	Majors
2.	Fernando Martinez, of	No. 1
3.	Carlos Gomez, of	No. 3
4.	Philip Humber, rhp	No. 7
5.	Deolis Guerra, rhp	No. 2
6.	Kevin Mulvey, rhp	No. 4
7.	Jon Niese, lhp	No. 8
8.	Mike Carp, 1b	No. 19
9.	Joe Smith, rhp	No. 11
10.	Alay Soler, rhp	(Pirates)
11.	Anderson Hernandez, ss/2b	Dropped out
12.	Francisco Pena, c	No. 21
13.	Adam Bostick, lhp	No. 23
14.	Brett Harper, 1b	Dropped out
15.	Emmanuel Garcia, ss	No. 24
16.	Jose Coronado, ss	Dropped out
17.	Josh Stinson, rhp	Dropped out
18.	Bobby Parnell, rhp	No. 10
19.	Dustin Martin, of	(Twins)
20.	Eddie Camacho, lhp	Dropped out
21.	Nick Evans, 1b	No. 20
22.	Tobi Stoner, rhp	Dropped out
23.	Sean Henry, of	(Reds)
24.	Todd Privett, lhp	Dropped out
25.	Mike Devaney, rhp	Dropped out
26.	John Holdzkom, rhp	Dropped out
27.	Mike Nickeas, c	Dropped out
28.	Eric Brown, rhp	Dropped out
29.	Daniel Stegall, of	Dropped out
30.	Corey Coles, of	Dropped out

BEST TOOLS

Best Hitter for Average	Fernando Martinez
Best Power Hitter	Fernando Martinez
Best Strike-Zone Discipline	Ruben Tejada
Fastest Baserunner	Carlos Gomez
Best Athlete	Carlos Gomez
Best Fastball	Brant Rustich
Best Curveball	Philip Humber
Best Slider	Kevin Mulvey
Best Changeup	Deolis Guerra
Best Control	Dylan Owen
Best Defensive Catcher	Mike Nickeas
Best Defensive Infielder	Jose Coronado
Best Infield Arm	Wilmer Flores
Best Defensive Outfielder	Carlos Gomez
Best Outfield Arm	Carlos Gomez

PROJECTED 2011 LINEUP

Catcher	Brian Schneider
First Base	Carlos Delgado
Second Base	Luis Castillo
Third Base	David Wright
Shortstop	Jose Reyes
Left Field	Fernando Martinez
Center Field	Carlos Gomez
Right Field	Carlos Beltran
No. 1 Starter	John Maine
No. 2 Starter	Oliver Perez
No. 3 Starter	Mike Pelfrey
No. 4 Starter	Deolis Guerra
No. 5 Starter	Kevin Mulvey
Closer	Eddie Kunz

TOP PROSPECTS OF THE DECADE

Year	Player, Pos.	2007 Org.
1998	Grant Roberts, rhp	Out of baseball
1999	Alex Escobar, of	Nationals
2000	Alex Escobar, of	Nationals
2001	Alex Escobar, of	Nationals
2002	Aaron Heilman, rhp	Mets
2003	Jose Reyes, ss	Mets
2004	Kazuo Matsui, ss	Rockies
2005	Lastings Milledge, of	Mets
2006	Lastings Milledge, of	Mets
2007	Mike Pelfrey, rhp	Mets

TOP DRAFT PICKS OF THE DECADE

Year	Player, Pos.	2007 Org.
1998	Jason Tyner, of	Twins
1999	Neil Musser, lhp (2)	Royals
2000	Billy Traber, lhp	Nationals
2001	Aaron Heilman, rhp	Mets
2002	Scott Kazmir, lhp	Devil Rays
2003	Lastings Milledge, of	Mets
2004	Philip Humber, rhp	Mets
2005	Mike Pelfrey, rhp	Mets
2006	Kevin Mulvey, rhp (2)	Mets
2007	Eddie Kunz, rhp (1s)	Mets

LARGEST BONUSES IN CLUB HISTORY

Mike Pelfrey, 2005	$3,550,000
Philip Humber, 2004	$3,000,000
Scott Kazmir, 2002	$2,150,000
Lastings Milledge, 2003	$2,075,000
Geoff Goetz, 1997	$1,700,000

NEW YORK METS

Top 2008 Rookie: Carlos Gomez, of. Gomez will challenge for the right-field job in spring training.

Breakout Prospect: Greg Veloz, 2b. In his second try at full-season ball, Veloz should be able to do a better job of tapping into his power-speed combo.

Sleeper: Cole Abbott, rhp. He's not physically developed, but Abbott has flashed low-90s velocity and the ability to spin a breaking ball.

SOURCE OF TOP 30 TALENT

Homegrown	28	Acquired	2
College	10	Trades	1
Junior college	0	Rule 5 draft	1
High school	5	Independent leagues	0
Draft-and-follow	2	Free agents/waivers	0
Nondrafted free agents	1		
International	10		

Numbers in parentheses indicate prospect rankings

LF
Fernando Martinez (1)
Brahaim Maldonado
Darren Clark

CF
Ezequiel Carrera
Carlos Puello
Dan Stegall

RF
Carlos Gomez (3)
Caleb Stewart

3B
Danny Murphy (15)
Wilmer Flores (17)
Jefry Marte (27)
Richard Lucas
Zach Lutz

SS
Ruben Tejada (18)
Emmanuel Garcia (24)
Juan Lagares (28)
Brandon Richey
Jose Coronado
Matt Bouchard

2B
Greg Veloz (16)
Anderson Hernandez
Hector Pellot
Ignacio Medrano

1B
Mike Carp (19)
Nick Evans (20)
Lucas Duda (29)
Jason Jacobs
Stefan Welch

C
Francisco Pena (21)
Sean McCraw
Mike Nickeas
Hector Alvarez

RHP

Starters	Relievers
Deolis Guerra (2)	Eddie Kunz (5)
Kevin Mulvey (4)	Brant Rustich (6)
Philip Humber (7)	Joe Smith (11)
Robert Parnell (10)	Steven Clyne (13)
Scott Moviel (12)	Nick Carr (14)
Phillips Orta (22)	Steven Register (25)
Dylan Owen	Elvin Ramirez (30)
Eric Brown	Dan McDonald
Tobi Stoner	J.J. Leaper
Josh Stinson	
Michael Olmstead	
Guillaume Leduc	
Cole Abbott	
Pedro P. Martinez	
Mike Devaney	

LHP

Starters	Relievers
Jon Niese (8)	Eric Niesen
Nathan Vineyard (9)	Willie Collazo
Adam Bostick (23)	Eddie Camacho
Mike Antonini (26)	Kevin Tomasiewicz
Angel Calero	
Todd Privett	

2007

Best Pro Debut: RHP Dylan Owen (20) won two-thirds of the short-season New York-Penn League pitching triple crown, leading the league in wins and ERA at 9-1, 1.49. RHP Brant Rustich (2) walked just two in 23 innings while going 3-0, 1.57 overall at two levels.

Best Athlete: RHPs Cole Abbott (25) and Scott Moviel (2) both were fine high school basketball players. Moviel already throws strikes and controls his 6-foot-11, 235-pound body well for his age, while Abbott is projectable at 6-foot-2, 175.

Best Pure Hitter: The Mets brought in 3B **Zach Lutz** (5), a Division III all-American, for a predraft workout at Shea Stadium, and he showed above-average bat speed and a swing he repeats easily. Lutz had his debut cut short (one game) by a hairline fracture in his ankle.

Best Power Hitter: A .275 career hitter at Southern California with just 20 doubles and a .410 slugging percentage, 1B/OF Lucas Duda (7) hit .299/.398/.462 for Brooklyn, with 20 doubles.

Fastest Runner: Raw SS Alonzo Harris (39), the last player the Mets drafted, covers 60 yards in 6.4 seconds. He signed too late to make his debut. SS Matt Bouchard (11) is also a plus runner.

Best Defensive Player: Bouchard used his sure hands, quick feet and above-average range to make just eight errors in 68 games at Brooklyn. His arm is fringe-average.

Best Fastball: Rustich has touched 97 mph with his fastball. RHP Eddie Kunz (1s) often pitched at 94-96 during his Oregon State career from a lower arm slot and with greater movement.

Best Secondary Pitch: LHP Nathan Vineyard's (1s) slider comes in at 80-83 mph with depth. RHP Steven Clyne (3) has a low-80s slider that can be an out pitch, as well.

Most Intriguing Background: Bouchard was the first Georgetown player picked since 1993. Moviel has two brothers, Paul (Devil Rays) and Greg (Mariners), who have played pro ball. The Mets failed to sign SS/3B Glen Johnson (36), son of big league coach and former 30-30 Met Howard Johnson.

Closest To The Majors: Kunz is on the Joe Smith development path. He's off to the Arizona Fall League; then, like the '06 third-rounder, he will get a shot to win a big league job in spring training.

Best Late-Round Pick: LHP Michael Antonini (18) throws an average 88-91 mph fastball and has good sink and fade on his plus changeup.

The One Who Got Away: Just 5-foot-11, 165 pounds, RHP Brandon Efferson (17) has big stuff, touching 94 mph and flashing a plus curve and changeup. He stuck to his Southeastern Louisiana commitment.

Assessment: The Mets were pleased to get plenty of power arms, though most of them project to be relievers. The organization clearly could bring its revenue advantages to bear in the draft, but apparently has not found the right match of player, pick and bonus since signing Mike Pelfrey in 2005.

2006 BUDGET: $1.9 MILLION

The Mets didn't have a first-rounder, but RHP Joe Smith (3) already has helped the big league club and RHP Kevin Mulvey (2) could bolster the 2008 rotation.

GRADE: C+

2005 BUDGET: $4.7 MILLION

RHP Mike Pelfrey (1) hasn't lived up to his $5.25 million contract yet, and New York forfeited its second- and third-rounders. LHP Jon Niese (7) and RHP Robert Parnell (9) were nice mid-round finds.

GRADE: C+

2004 BUDGET: $5.3 MILLION

Like Pelfrey, RHP Philip Humber (1) hasn't helped as fast as expected, though Tommy John surgery didn't help his cause. RHP Gaby Hernandez (3) was part of the Paul LoDuca trade.

GRADE: C

2003 BUDGET: $3.0 MILLION

OF Lastings Milledge is still supremely talented, but the Mets finally gave up on him and traded him to the Nationals. RHP Brian Bannister (7) won 12 games as a rookie last year—for the Royals, who stole him in a deal for Ambiorix Burgos.

GRADE: B+

Draft analysis by John Manuel (2007) and Jim Callis (2003-06). Numbers in parentheses indicate draft rounds. Budgets are bonuses in first 10 rounds.

NATIONAL LEAGUE 1 EAST

FERNANDO MARTINEZ, OF

Born: Oct. 10, 1988.
Ht.: 6-1. **Wt.:** 190.
Bats: L. **Throws:** R.
Signed: Dominican Republic, 2005.
Signed by: Rafael Bournigal/ Sandy Johnson/ Eddy Toledo.

Martinez was the most coveted Latin American free agent on the market in 2005, and the Mets were positioned perfectly to land him. He received a $1.4 million bonus both for his present and future hitting ability and as a statement that New York intended to be a leader in Latin America and not a follower. The impact of Martinez' signing and that commitment continues, as the Mets led all organizations by signing 15 international amateurs in the July-August 2007 signing period. He became the youngest player in Arizona Fall League history in 2006 and opened 2007 as the youngest player in Double-A by nearly two years. A right hand injury, initially diagnosed as a bruise, lingered and hampered his play at Binghamton. New York finally shut him down in late July after a pair of appearances in the Rookie-level Gulf Coast League. Despite the injury and his tender age, Martinez, 18, ranked as the Double-A Eastern League's No. 3 prospect. He also was the first player selected in the Dominican League draft in October.

Latin American players who get seven-figure bonuses get paid to hit, and scouts believe Martinez will hit. He has excellent bat speed and generates easy power to all fields. One scout who saw him this year said Martinez "can do anything he wants offensively." He spent the year batting leadoff or third as the Mets tried to give him more at-bats, and he began recognizing breaking balls and learning when to lay off and when to attack them. He's learning to trust his hands and stay back against lefthanders as well. Martinez has some athleticism and runs well once he's underway. He has average raw arm strength.

Martinez is heavy on tools and low on present skills, particularly for a Double-A player, though that's typical for a teenager. His approach at the plate is raw, and some scouts disdain his load (too exaggerated) and spread-out stance (he's not strong enough yet). Defensively, he played a below-average center field across the board in 2007. He needs improvement in running routes, picking up cutoff men and getting his body behind his throws. He profiles better in left field, as many scouts had predicted when he signed. Martinez' baserunning skills are another area where his lack of experience holds him back.

Most organizations would have had Martinez in low Class A last season, and the holes in his game were exposed in Double-A. But his upside remains tremendous. From his days as a scout and coach for the Rangers, general manager Omar Minaya learned that Latin American stars usually get to the major leagues at a young age. Minaya says Martinez is on the same track as players such as Juan Gonzalez, Ivan Rodriguez and Sammy Sosa, all of whom reached the majors by age 20. Martinez' 2008 assignment likely will depend on his spring-training performance, as well as the health of his hand. His bat ultimately will be his calling card, and the Mets see him as a future 30-homer threat.

Year	Club (League)	Class	AVG	G	AB	R	H	2B	3B	HR	RBI	BB	SO	SB	OBP	SLG
2006	Mets (GCL)	R	.250	1	4	1	1	0	0	0	0	0	1	0	.250	.250
	Hagerstown (SAL)	A	.333	45	192	24	64	14	2	5	28	15	36	7	.389	.505
	St. Lucie (FSL)	A	.193	30	119	18	23	4	2	5	11	6	24	1	.254	.387
2007	Binghamton (EL)	AA	.271	60	236	32	64	11	1	4	21	20	51	3	.336	.377
	Mets (GCL)	R	.111	3	9	1	1	0	1	0	1	1	6	0	.200	.333
MINOR LEAGUE TOTALS			.273	139	560	76	153	29	6	14	61	42	118	11	.334	.421

2 DEOLIS GUERRA, RHP

STEVE MOORE

Born: April 17, 1989. **B-T:** R-R. **Ht.:** 6-5. **Wt.:** 200. **Signed:** Venezuela, 2005. **Signed by:** Rafael Bournigal.

Last April, many 17-year-old Americans were heading off to high school proms. Guerra, who signed for $700,000 in 2005, was starting on Opening Day for high Class A St. Lucie. He also pitched in the Futures Game in San Francisco, recovering from a bout with shoulder tendinitis that sidelined him for most of May. Guerra has two present above-average pitches that could become well above-average. His fastball had below-average velocity for most of his first season, but now it ranges from 89-94 mph and touches 96. He features excellent arm speed on his changeup, his best offering since he signed, and it should become a big league out pitch once he commands it. While Guerra's curveball remains a below-average pitch, he has shown an ability to spin the ball and it projects as an average offering. At 18, Guerra still is learning the finer arts of pitching, such as holding runners, fielding his position and pitch sequences. Guerra has thrown just 179 pro innings and has plenty of projection in his big-shouldered frame. The Mets have monitored Guerra's workload carefully, and his next goal will be to stay healthy and pass the 100-inning level.

Year	Club (League)	Class	W	L	ERA	G	GS	CG	SV	IP	H	R	ER	HR	BB	SO	AVG
2006	Hagerstown (SAL)	A	6	7	2.20	17	17	0	0	81	59	22	20	3	37	64	.208
	St. Lucie (FSL)	A	1	1	6.14	2	2	0	0	7	9	6	5	1	6	5	.290
2007	St. Lucie (FSL)	A	2	6	4.01	21	20	0	0	89	80	44	40	9	25	66	.240
MINOR LEAGUE TOTALS			9	14	3.27	40	39	0	0	178	148	72	65	13	68	135	.228

3 CARLOS GOMEZ, OF

STEVE MOORE

Born: Dec. 4, 1985. **B-T:** R-R. **Ht.:** 6-4. **Wt.:** 195. **Signed:** Dominican Republic, 2002. **Signed by:** Eddy Toledo.

Gomez finished his fast-track trip to the major leagues in 2007 and was the National League's youngest player when he debuted in May. He broke the hamate bone in his left hand on a checked swing in July, however, and missed two months following surgery. A true five-tool athlete, Gomez has game-changing speed and a well above-average arm, tools that help make him a premium defender in center field. He also has excellent bat speed that leads to projections of at least average power, if not more. Scouts said Gomez brought needed energy to the Mets. Hitting will be the last tool to develop for Gomez. He's still searching for the balance between aggressiveness and plate discipline. While he showed increased patience in 2007, it came at the expense of his power production. Gomez likely will compete with Ryan Church for the right-field job in spring training. Gomez could use more offensive polish, so he could return to Triple-A at the season's outset.

Year	Club (League)	Class	AVG	G	AB	R	H	2B	3B	HR	RBI	BB	SO	SB	OBP	SLG
2003	Mets (DSL)	R	.240	58	208	26	50	1	0	1	10	7	37	13	.283	.288
2004	Kingsport (Appy)	R	.287	38	150	24	43	10	4	1	20	5	29	8	.333	.427
	Mets (GCL)	R	.268	19	71	10	19	7	0	0	11	2	9	9	.303	.366
2005	Hagerstown (SAL)	A	.275	120	487	75	134	13	6	8	48	32	88	64	.331	.376
2006	Binghamton (EL)	AA	.281	120	430	53	121	24	8	7	48	27	97	41	.350	.423
2007	New Orleans (PCL)	AAA	.286	36	140	24	40	8	2	2	13	15	23	17	.363	.414
	St. Lucie (FSL)	A	.154	5	13	1	2	0	0	0	0	1	4	2	.267	.154
	New York (NL)	MLB	.232	58	125	14	29	3	0	2	12	8	27	12	.288	.304
MINOR LEAGUE TOTALS			.273	396	1499	213	409	69	20	19	150	89	287	154	.331	.384
MAJOR LEAGUE TOTALS			.232	58	125	14	29	3	0	2	12	8	27	12	.288	.304

4 KEVIN MULVEY, RHP

RICH ABEL

Born: May 26, 1985. **B-T:** R-R. **Ht.:** 6-1. **Wt.:** 195. **Drafted:** Villanova, 2006 (2nd round). **Signed by:** Scott Hunter.

The Mets' top pick in the 2006 draft, Mulvey reached Triple-A New Orleans at the end of his first full season and pitched 13 scoreless, walk-less innings, including a playoff start. He was the organization's pitcher of the year and a Futures Gamer as well. Mulvey throws four pitches for strikes and keeps everything down. His fastball, which sits at 87-91 mph and touches 94, features good sink and run. He dominated righthanders, limiting them to a .224 average and no homers. His mid-70s curveball with 11-to-5 break and his low-80s slider both are average pitches, and at times his slider is a put-away offering. His changeup shows signs of being average. His competitiveness makes his whole greater than the sum of his parts. Mulvey has trouble against lefthanders because he can't work them inside easily. At times his changeup is too firm. He has lost 2-3 mph off his fastball from his days at Villanova, but he could gain some of that back as he gets accustomed to the pro workload. He'll open 2008 in Triple-A, but Mulvey could get a look in the rotation by midseason. He projects as a No. 3 or 4 starter.

Year	Club (League)	Class	W	L	ERA	G	GS	CG	SV	IP	H	R	ER	HR	BB	SO	AVG
2006	Mets (GCL)	R	0	0	0.00	1	1	0	0	2	1	0	0	0	0	1	.143
	Binghamton (EL)	AA	0	1	1.35	3	3	1	0	13	10	4	2	1	5	10	.217
2007	Binghamton (EL)	AA	11	10	3.32	26	26	0	0	151	145	74	56	4	43	110	.252
	New Orleans (PCL)	AAA	1	0	0.00	1	1	0	0	6	2	0	0	0	0	3	.095
MINOR LEAGUE TOTALS			12	11	3.02	31	31	1	0	173	158	78	58	5	48	124	.243

5 EDDIE KUNZ, RHP

Born: April 8, 1986. **B-T:** R-R. **Ht.:** 6-4. **Wt.:** 250. **Drafted:** Oregon State, 2007 (1st round supplemental). **Signed by:** Jim Reeves.

BILL MITCHELL

Kunz helped Oregon State win a pair of national championships, first as a setup man in 2006 and then as closer in 2007. New York's top pick (42nd overall) in June, he held out for much of the summer before signing for $720,000. With a low, almost sidearm arm slot, Kunz produces heavy sink on a 94-96 mph fastball. He allowed only one college home run, and that came in his freshman season. At times, his slider can be an overpowering pitch with short, late break and above-average 86-87 mph velocity. He features good arm speed on his changeup. Kunz will have to watch his weight to maintain his best stuff and his command. The Mets have worked to improve the consistency of his slider, which is less reliable than his changeup. Kunz may be able to keep lefthanded batters at bay, despite his arm angle, because of his uncommon velocity and his changeup. The Mets have Kunz on the Joe Smith development plan. They sent Kunz to the Arizona Fall League and will invite him to big league camp, where he could win a big league job. He eventually could replace Billy Wagner as their closer.

Year	Club (League)	Class	W	L	ERA	G	GS	CG	SV	IP	H	R	ER	HR	BB	SO	AVG
2007	Brooklyn (NYP)	A	0	1	6.75	12	0	0	5	12	8	9	9	0	8	9	.190
MINOR LEAGUE TOTALS			0	1	6.75	12	0	0	5	12	8	9	9	0	8	9	.190

6 BRANT RUSTICH, RHP

Born: Jan. 23, 1985. **B-T:** R-R. **Ht.:** 6-6. **Wt.:** 225. **Drafted:** UCLA, 2007 (2nd round). **Signed by:** Steve Leavitt.

LARRY GOREN

Rustich dominated in the Cape Cod League in 2005 and got off to a tremendous start at UCLA the following spring, but then he ruptured a tendon in the middle finger on his pitching hand. Following surgery, he struggled as a redshirt junior and lost the Bruins' closer job in 2007. New York drafted him in the second round and landed him for $373,500. Healthy in pro ball, Rustich showed a premium fastball, sitting from 93-97 mph with late life. He pitches inside to righthanders and uses his size well, throwing downhill with his fastball and an 84-87 mph power slider with tilt. His changeup shows flashes of being an average pitch. Control was a huge problem before and after his finger injury, but Rustich threw strikes as a pro as he used his fastball more. His delivery can get out of whack easily. His splitter was a plus pitch before he got hurt, but he hasn't thrown it much since the injury. His slider can be inconsistent. Rustich has enough stuff to start, but the Mets most likely will have him join Eddie Kunz on the fast track as a reliever. Rustich could jump to Double-A in 2008.

Year	Club (League)	Class	W	L	ERA	G	GS	CG	SV	IP	H	R	ER	HR	BB	SO	AVG
2007	Kingsport (Appy)	R	1	0	0.87	5	2	0	0	10	6	1	1	0	1	10	.158
	Brooklyn (NYP)	A	2	0	2.13	10	0	0	2	12	4	3	3	2	1	11	.095
MINOR LEAGUE TOTALS			3	0	1.57	15	2	0	2	23	10	4	4	2	2	21	.125

7 PHILIP HUMBER, RHP

Born: Dec. 21, 1982. **B-T:** R-R. **Ht.:** 6-4. **Wt.:** 225. **Drafted:** Rice, 2004 (1st round). **Signed by:** Dave Lottsfeldt.

STEVE MOORE

Humber won the championship game of the 2003 College World Series and went third overall in the 2004 draft. He made just 15 pro starts before needing Tommy John surgery in July 2005, and he hasn't been the same pitcher since. He made his first big league start in September, giving up five runs in four innings. Humber still has the best curveball in the organization, and he has learned to shorten it up a bit and throw it for quality strikes. He's learning to spot his fastball better down in the zone, where it has more life. His changeup, which he has used since junking the splitter he had in college, has developed into an average pitch. At times Humber still tries to pitch up in the strike zone, and he doesn't have that kind of velocity anymore. His fastball ranges from 87-91 mph after he used to touch 94-95 at Rice. He's still refining his command two years after his elbow reconstruction. Humber is likely ready for on-the-job training in the majors, but he'll have to earn the spot in spring training. He now projects as a back-of-rotation starter.

Year	Club (League)	Class	W	L	ERA	G	GS	CG	SV	IP	H	R	ER	HR	BB	SO	AVG
2005	St. Lucie (FSL)	A	2	6	4.99	14	14	0	0	70	74	41	39	6	18	65	.273
	Binghamton (EL)	AA	0	1	6.75	1	1	0	0	4	4	3	3	0	2	2	.250
2006	Mets (GCL)	R	0	0	6.75	1	1	0	0	4	7	3	3	0	1	7	.389
	St. Lucie (FSL)	A	3	1	2.37	7	7	0	0	38	24	12	10	4	9	36	.178
	Binghamton (EL)	AA	2	2	2.88	6	6	0	0	34	25	12	11	4	10	36	.195
	New York (NL)	MLB	0	0	0.00	2	0	0	0	2	0	0	0	0	1	2	.000
2007	New Orleans (PCL)	AAA	11	9	4.27	25	25	0	0	139	129	70	66	21	44	120	.244
	New York (NL)	MLB	0	0	7.71	3	1	0	0	7	9	6	6	1	2	2	.300
MINOR LEAGUE TOTALS			18	19	4.10	54	54	0	0	289	263	141	132	35	84	266	.240
MAJOR LEAGUE TOTALS			0	0	6.00	5	1	0	0	9	9	6	6	1	3	4	.250

8 JON NIESE, LHP

STEVE MOORE

Born: Oct. 27, 1986. **B-T:** L-L. **Ht.:** 6-3. **Wt.:** 180. **Drafted:** HS—Defiance, Ohio, 2005 (7th round). **Signed by:** Erwin Bryant.

Ohio's first-ever back-to-back state high school player of the year—he attended the same high school as Dodgers righthander Chad Billingsley—Niese signed with New York after a recruiting call from Hall of Fame catcher Gary Carter. After getting hit hard early in the season, Niese went 4-1, 2.18 with 42 strikeouts in 45 innings over his final eight starts, including six innings of one-hit ball in the high Class A Florida State League playoffs. Niese uses a fastball that sits at 91-92 mph early in games, then attacks hitters with an improved curveball that has become a plus pitch as he has learned to locate it. He's figured out how to throw his changeup with the same arm speed he uses for his fastball, and it has similar sink and tailing action. While he has improved his conditioning, Niese remains inconsistent in terms of maintaining his velocity. He's still learning to pitch inside with his fastball and remain aggressive with his changeup. His competitiveness can work against him at times. After his strong finish, Niese is ready to hit Double-A as a 21-year-old. He's still probably two years away from making an impact in New York's rotation.

Year	Club (League)	Class	W	L	ERA	G	GS	CG	SV	IP	H	R	ER	HR	BB	SO	AVG
2005	Mets (GCL)	R	1	0	3.65	7	5	0	0	24	23	10	10	1	10	24	.245
2006	Hagerstown (SAL)	A	11	9	3.93	25	25	1	0	123	121	67	54	7	62	132	.256
	St. Lucie (FSL)	A	0	2	4.50	2	2	0	0	10	8	8	5	0	5	10	.216
2007	St. Lucie (FSL)	A	11	7	4.29	27	27	2	0	134	151	78	64	9	31	110	.285
MINOR LEAGUE TOTALS			23	18	4.09	61	59	3	0	292	303	163	133	17	108	276	.268

9 NATHAN VINEYARD, LHP

DAVID STONER

Born: Oct. 3, 1988. **B-T:** L-L. **Ht.:** 6-3. **Wt.:** 200. **Drafted:** HS—Cartersville, Ga., 2007 (1st round supplemental). **Signed by:** Marlin McPhail.

Vineyard was a fixture on the summer showcase circuit for Georgia's East Cobb program and helped his cause with a strong performance at the World Wood Bat tournament in Jupiter, Fla., during the fall of his senior year. He wasn't as consistent last spring, but still showed enough for the Mets to draft him 47th overall and sign him for $657,000. At his best, Vineyard throws three pitches that presently grade as average or better, with some projection remaining. His fastball sits at 88-91 mph and he should develop more velocity and command as he uses it more as a pro. His slider is a plus pitch at times, with depth and some low-80s power. He also has shown the ability to turn over his changeup and throw it for strikes. Vineyard threw too many sliders as a high schooler and needs to prove he can get hitters out with his fastball in fastball counts. His changeup needs refinement as well. The Mets believe Vineyard can be a future No. 3 starter and has as much upside as anyone in their 2007 draft class. As a high-schooler, he is further from his ceiling than Eddie Kunz or Brant Rustich. He'll open his first full season at low Class A Savannah.

Year	Club (League)	Class	W	L	ERA	G	GS	CG	SV	IP	H	R	ER	HR	BB	SO	AVG
2007	Mets (GCL)	R	0	3	5.27	9	7	0	0	27	30	18	16	4	9	33	.265
MINOR LEAGUE TOTALS			0	3	5.27	9	7	0	0	27	30	18	16	4	9	33	.265

10 ROBERT PARNELL, RHP

CLIFF WELCH

Born: Sept. 8, 1984. **B-T:** R-R. **Ht.:** 6-3. **Wt.:** 180. **Drafted:** Charleston Southern, 2005 (9th round). **Signed by:** Marlin McPhail.

Parnell has one of the system's best success stories. Though he posted 6.82 and 8.86 ERAs in his final two seasons at Charleston Southern, area scout Marlin McPhail liked his arm strength. Parnell led the short-season New York-Penn League with a 1.73 ERA in his pro debut and finished his second full season in Double-A. A former prep shortstop, Parnell has velocity to spare. His fastball sat in the low 90s and regularly hit 95 mph late in games in August. His heater also has heavy sink and generates plenty of groundouts. His hard slider sits in the mid-80s at times and can be a strikeout pitch. The development of his changeup has been an issue since Parnell became a pro. He still needs to trust the pitch more, but he made significant progress with it in 2007, giving the Mets hope he can remain a starter. Too often Parnell works away from contact while trying to strike every hitter out. Parnell still needs polish, but he has improved his profile from middle reliever to middle-of-the-rotation starter. He'll return to Double-A to begin 2008.

Year	Club (League)	Class	W	L	ERA	G	GS	CG	SV	IP	H	R	ER	HR	BB	SO	AVG
2005	Brooklyn (NYP)	A	2	3	1.73	15	14	0	0	73	48	20	14	1	29	67	.185
2006	Hagerstown (SAL)	A	5	10	4.04	18	18	1	0	93	84	50	42	7	40	84	.239
	St. Lucie (FSL)	A	0	1	9.26	3	3	0	0	11	16	13	12	3	9	13	.333
2007	St. Lucie (FSL)	A	3	3	3.25	12	12	0	0	55	56	22	20	0	22	62	.259
	Binghamton (EL)	AA	5	5	4.77	17	17	0	0	88	98	54	47	9	38	74	.276
MINOR LEAGUE TOTALS			15	22	3.77	65	64	1	0	322	302	159	135	20	138	300	.246

11 JOE SMITH, RHP

Born: March 22, 1984. **B-T:** R-R. **Ht.:** 6-2. **Wt.:** 215. **Drafted:** Wright State, 2006 (3rd round). **Signed by:** Erwin Bryant.

The Mets drafted Smith with every intention of moving him quickly through the farm system, and that part worked as planned. He had just 27 pro appearances before making his big league debut on Opening Day 2007, and he quickly established himself as one of New York's most reliable relievers. He didn't give up a run in his first 17 appearances, and when he did give up runs, it was due in part to the fact he hadn't worked in a week. Smith succeeded with a sidearm delivery that pumped fastballs up to 94 mph into the lower half of the strike zone, mostly sitting at 88-91 mph with heavy sink. He got 3.8 groundouts for every flyout, a stat that backs up the scouting report on his sinker. His hard low-80s slider helps him make life difficult for righthanders. However, Smith didn't adjust when big league hitters did. He nibbled more and more as the season went on, and as usual with righty sidearmers, lefthanded hitters feasted on him (.858 OPS). Smith was sent down to Triple-A in July after allowing 19 out of 27 inherited runners to score, and while he was more aggressive in his return, he also was more hittable. His changeup and command could both improve, but the same could be said of many young pitchers. More likely, Smith is what he is: a big leaguer, but probably not anything more than a sixth- or seventh-inning matchup reliever.

Year	Club (League)	Class	W	L	ERA	G	GS	CG	SV	IP	H	R	ER	HR	BB	SO	AVG
2006	Brooklyn (NYP)	A	0	1	0.45	17	0	0	9	20	10	3	1	0	3	28	.141
	Binghamton (EL)	AA	0	2	5.68	10	0	0	0	12	12	8	8	1	11	12	.267
2007	New Orleans (PCL)	AAA	0	0	2.00	8	0	0	2	9	7	3	2	0	4	5	.233
	New York (NL)	MLB	3	2	3.45	54	0	0	0	44	48	18	17	3	21	45	.274
MINOR LEAGUE TOTALS			0	3	2.38	35	0	0	11	41	29	14	11	1	18	45	.199
MAJOR LEAGUE TOTALS			3	2	3.45	54	0	0	0	44	48	18	17	3	21	45	.274

12 SCOTT MOVIEL, RHP

Born: May 7, 1988. **B-T:** R-R. **Ht.:** 6-11. **Wt.:** 235. **Drafted:** HS—Berea, Ohio, 2007 (2nd round). **Signed by:** Erwin Bryant.

Moviel is the youngest of three brothers pitching in pro ball, joining Greg (Mariners) and Paul (Rays). Scott has the highest upside of the trio, in part because he's three inches taller than his brothers. He was set to follow in the footsteps of another 6-foot-11 Cincinnati-area pitcher, Andrew Brackman, and attend North Carolina State when the Mets drafted him in the second round in June and signed him for $414,000. While Brackman, who went 30th overall to the Yankees, has bigger stuff and was a better basketball player, the Mets are happy with Moviel, who has excellent athleticism and coordination for a pitcher his size. He's flexible and repeats his delivery well. His best pitch is his fastball, which sits at 90-92 mph and tops out at 94. He has shown the ability to spot his fastball well and should have average command down the line. He also has feel for his nascent changeup, which he rarely threw as an amateur. His biggest weakness is his breaking ball, which has been slow and slurvy. He has shown the ability to spin the baseball, though, and New York believes he'll eventually have a solid hard slider with work and experience. Moviel has a high ceiling and just needs innings. He's likely to report to extended spring training and then short-season Brooklyn for 2008.

Year	Club (League)	Class	W	L	ERA	G	GS	CG	SV	IP	H	R	ER	HR	BB	SO	AVG
2007	Mets (GCL)	R	0	2	3.38	12	12	0	0	40	45	23	15	2	11	37	.281
MINOR LEAGUE TOTALS			0	2	3.38	12	12	0	0	40	45	23	15	2	11	37	.281

13 STEVEN CLYNE, RHP

Born: Sept. 22, 1984. **B-T:** B-R. **Ht.:** 6-2. **Wt.:** 215. **Drafted:** Clemson, 2007 (3rd round). **Signed by:** Marlin McPhail.

The Mets got Clyne cheap. As a redshirt senior, he had little bargaining power and signed for $100,000, by far the lowest signing bonus of the first three rounds of the 2007 draft. He redshirted as a freshman after having arm problems dating back his high school career, then missed 2004 with Tommy John surgery. But by 2007 he was Clemson's top reliever, allowing lefthander Daniel Moskos (the No. 4 overall pick by the Pirates in June) to move into the rotation. Clyne isn't far removed from the relievers New York drafted ahead of him, Eddie Kunz and Brant Rustich, as he throws hard, reaching up to 94 mph with his low-90s sinker. He also has a strikeout pitch in an above-average, two-plane slider that has depth and power in the low 80s. The Mets see Clyne as a setup man who should move quickly and believe he can reach that ceiling after seeing improvement since he signed. He has cleaned up his somewhat funky arm action a bit, and St. Lucie pitching coach Al Jackson worked on improving Clyne's delivery during instructional league to get all his energy moving toward the plate, rather than side to side. Both changes should improve his command. Mets coaches also are encouraged by the progress of his changeup, which has sink similar to that of his fastball. If he comes out throwing strikes in 2008, Clyne could speed through the system.

Year	Club (League)	Class	W	L	ERA	G	GS	CG	SV	IP	H	R	ER	HR	BB	SO	AVG
2007	Brooklyn (NYP)	A	1	1	2.05	20	0	0	8	26	21	9	6	0	19	30	.214
MINOR LEAGUE TOTALS			1	1	2.05	20	0	0	8	26	21	9	6	0	19	30	.214

14 NICK CARR, RHP

Born: April 19, 1987. **B-T:** R-R. **Ht.:** 6-1. **Wt.:** 195. **Drafted:** JC of Southern Idaho, D/F 2005 (41st round). **Signed by:** Jim Reeves.

The Mets drafted Carr in 2005, when he was the top prep arm in Idaho, and followed him for a year at the JC of Southern Idaho before signing him. While evaluating Carr, they also saw lefthander Todd Privett at Southern Idaho and wound up drafting and signing him as well. Carr hasn't made it to full-season ball as Privett has, but Carr has had more pro success and has the better arm. He holds his fastball velocity well and maintains his stuff both in games and throughout the season. Carr's fastball sits at 91-94 mph and touches 96, and it has some life. His slider can be a plus pitch with power and tilt, reaching 84-88 mph at times. New York was most encouraged with Carr's improved changeup in instructional league and he focused on the pitch during his stint in Hawaii Winter Baseball. It's still below-average, though, and to be a starter, he'll have to be able to change speeds more effectively. He has trimmed up his body since signing, dropping 15 pounds and becoming stronger and more flexible, allowing him to refine and maintain his improved mechanics. The Mets consider him one of their better arms and hope he can emulate Robert Parnell in honing his change while maintaining his power repertoire. Carr's ready for full-season ball and will pitch in low Class A to open 2008.

Year	Club (League)	Class	W	L	ERA	G	GS	CG	SV	IP	H	R	ER	HR	BB	SO	AVG
2006	Kingsport (Appy)	R	3	3	4.88	12	11	0	0	48	49	29	26	5	23	44	.265
2007	Brooklyn (NYP)	A	5	2	3.80	14	14	0	0	66	55	31	28	4	27	74	.224
MINOR LEAGUE TOTALS			8	5	4.25	26	25	0	0	114	104	60	54	9	50	118	.241

15 DANNY MURPHY, 3B

Born: April 1, 1985. **B-T:** L-R. **Ht.:** 6-3. **Wt.:** 210. **Drafted:** Jacksonville, 2006 (13th round). **Signed by:** Steve Barningham.

Murphy played in the same Jacksonville infield with Anthony Bernazard, whose father Tony is the Mets' vice president of player development. The team had an extended look at him and wasn't fazed by knee and arm injuries in his junior season that limited Murphy to DH duties after signing in 2006. His bat always has been his calling card—he hit .398 as a college junior—and allowed him to rank second in the Florida State League with 143 hits in his first full season. He has a steady, contact-oriented approach and a short, balanced swing. He has a feel for RBI situations and for moving runners along. Murphy's defense at third base remains a work in progress. He didn't play the position regularly until midway though his sophomore college season, and he made 35 errors in 135 games for St. Lucie. Footwork is the main culprit, as he's inconsistent with his setup and has somewhat limited mobility. A below-average runner, he is more likely to move to first base than the outfield if his defense and/or David Wright's presence in New York forces the issue at third. The problem is Murphy's gap-to-gap power doesn't profile well at a less challenging position, though optimistic scouts believe he might hit 20 homers annually. After working primarily on his defense in Hawaii Winter Baseball, Murphy is ticketed for Double-A.

Year	Club (League)	Class	AVG	G	AB	R	H	2B	3B	HR	RBI	BB	SO	SB	OBP	SLG
2006	Mets (GCL)	R	.056	8	18	2	1	0	0	0	0	4	3	0	.227	.056
	Kingsport (Appy)	R	.273	9	33	2	9	0	0	2	7	4	1	0	.351	.455
	Brooklyn (NYP)	A	.241	8	29	2	7	1	0	0	3	4	3	0	.324	.276
2007	St. Lucie (FSL)	A	.285	135	502	68	143	34	3	11	78	42	61	6	.338	.430
MINOR LEAGUE TOTALS			.275	160	582	74	160	35	3	13	88	54	68	6	.334	.412

16 GREG VELOZ, 2B

Born: June 3, 1988. **B-T:** B-R. **Ht.:** 6-1. **Wt.:** 175. **Signed:** Dominican Republic, 2005. **Signed by:** Ismael Cruz/Sandy Johnson/Eddy Toledo.

The Mets had high expectations for Veloz entering 2007, as he was the team's MVP at in the Rookie-level Dominican Summer League the year before. He moved with DSL double-play partner Juan Lagares to low Class A to start the season, but neither was ready for the challenge. Veloz is the physically stronger of the pair and rebounded in the second half after moving down to the Rookie-level Appalachian League, which he led with nine triples. Veloz ranked fourth in the Appy League with 18 steals in 25 tries, yet speed isn't his calling card. At 4.2 seconds to first base from the right side, he's an average runner, though he's a tick better underway. Veloz has power from both sides of the plate that excites scouts even though he's quite raw. The ball jumps off his bat, and he could hit 25 homers annually if he learns to temper his aggressiveness and swing at strikes. Defensively, Veloz has average arm strength and could move over to third base. He's a second baseman for now with solid range, and he projects to be above average there if he can improve his footwork. He'll take another shot at low Class A this year.

Year	Club (League)	Class	AVG	G	AB	R	H	2B	3B	HR	RBI	BB	SO	SB	OBP	SLG
2006	Mets (DSL)	R	.262	63	221	50	58	16	1	4	28	33	57	28	.366	.398
2007	Kingsport (Appy)	R	.271	66	258	43	70	13	9	5	28	26	62	18	.344	.450
	Savannah (SAL)	A	.171	66	234	20	40	7	1	2	14	23	73	15	.243	.235
MINOR LEAGUE TOTALS			.236	195	713	113	168	36	11	11	70	82	192	61	.318	.363

17 WILMER FLORES, 3B/SS

Born: Aug. 6, 1991. **B-T:** R-R. **Ht.:** 6-3. **Wt.:** 175. **Signed:** Venezuela, 2007. **Signed by:** Robert Alfonzo/Ismael Cruz.

New York signed 15 players on the international market last summer, more than any other organization. Flores was the top player from that crop in terms of present tools and future potential, and he got the largest bonus at $750,000. He also was the only 2007 Mets international signee playing winter ball in Venezuela's winter minor league (the Parallel League), doing so at age 16. Flores currently lacks strength but has a projectable frame and should grow into his body and become a force with the bat. He has an advanced approach for a young player, not to mention a 16-year-old Latin American, and earns some internal comparisons to Miguel Cabrera for his present pull power and ability to use the whole field. Flores has the bat speed to catch up to good fastballs, though he's tall and may have to refine a swing that at times gets long. Club officials were most encouraged that he held his own against older pitchers in instructional league, never looking overmatched, and one said he had the best at-bats of anyone in camp. The biggest question scouts have on Flores is his future defensive home, and they're not as sold on his bat as the Mets are. He's a big, rangy shortstop who's likely to outgrow the position. He has the hands and arm to remain in the infield, unless his body goes south. Flores is the most likely of New York's 2007 international signees to jump on the fast track and play full-season ball in 2008 despite his tender age, but the system also has a glut of infielders at the lower levels. His assignment largely will depend on his spring-training performance.

Year	Club (League)	Class	AVG	G	AB	R	H	2B	3B	HR	RBI	BB	SO	SB	OBP	SLG
2007	Did Not Play															

18 RUBEN TEJADA, SS/2B

Born: Sept. 1, 1989. **B-T:** R-R. **Ht.:** 5-11. **Wt.:** 165. **Signed:** Panama, 2006. **Signed by:** Alex Zapata.

Tejada is the Mets' top signee from Panama, a nation the organization considers a growth area in terms of prospects. He began his pro career last year in the Rookie-level Venezuelan Summer League, where he batted .364 to earn a callup to the Gulf Coast League as a 17-year-old. Tejada was the best player in a talented infield that included fourth-round pick Richard Lucas at third base and polished Australian hitter

Stefan Welch at first. Tejada's best present tools are on the defensive side, as he has above-average arm strength and range that allow him to make all the plays at shortstop. In his time at second base, he showed an aptitude for turning double plays. He's an above-average runner and has an advanced approach at the plate, as he walked more than he struck out. Tejada also has some strength and gap-to-gap power, and while he doesn't project to hit for more than fringe-average power, he's not a slap hitter either. Tejada's best quality could be his savvy, as he's mature and showed a grinder mentality. He may have pushed his way to a full-season assignment for 2008, pending his spring performance.

Year	Club (League)	Class	AVG	G	AB	R	H	2B	3B	HR	RBI	BB	SO	SB	OBP	SLG
2007	Mets (VSL)	R	.364	32	121	32	44	5	0	3	25	19	19	16	.466	.479
	Mets (GCL)	R	.283	35	120	13	34	4	3	0	16	19	16	2	.401	.367
MINOR LEAGUE TOTALS			.324	67	241	45	78	9	3	3	41	38	35	18	.434	.423

19 MIKE CARP, 1B

Born: June 30, 1986. **B-T:** L-R. **Ht.:** 6-2. **Wt.:** 215. **Drafted:** HS—Lakewood, Calif., 2004 (9th round). **Signed by:** Steve Leavitt.

What began as a promising 2007 for Carp instead became the worst year of his pro career. Injuries to Carlos Delgado and Julio Franco and visa issues for Michel Abreu prompted the Mets to keep Carp around big league camp for most of spring training, and he went 10-for-43 with a homer before he broke his right ring finger sliding into second base. After missing the first seven weeks of the regular season, he reported to Binghamton and got off to a fast start. Then he struggled making adjustments in his first try at Double-A. Carp has some of the best hitting ability in the organization thanks to his willingness to use the entire field, good hand-eye coordination and usually disciplined approach. However, he struggled mightily with lefthanders for the third straight season, posting a lousy .418 OPS in 110 at-bats with just two walks and two extra-base hits. New York thought he had turned the corner in that regard in the spring, but he looks like a platoon player. Carp's defense also remains below average, as he ranked third in the Eastern league in errors with 10 in just 97 games. Carp tried to make up for lost time in the Arizona Fall League, but didn't swing the bat with much confidence or conviction there. He's just 21, so the Mets will give him a mulligan for 2007 and probably promote him to Triple-A this year.

Year	Club (League)	Class	AVG	G	AB	R	H	2B	3B	HR	RBI	BB	SO	SB	OBP	SLG
2004	Mets (GCL)	R	.267	57	191	30	51	12	0	4	26	22	51	2	.358	.393
2005	Hagerstown (SAL)	A	.249	89	313	49	78	12	1	19	63	35	96	2	.358	.476
2006	St. Lucie (FSL)	A	.287	137	491	69	141	27	1	17	88	51	107	2	.379	.450
2007	St. Lucie (FSL)	A	.250	1	4	0	1	0	0	0	0	0	0	0	.250	.250
	Binghamton (EL)	AA	.251	97	359	55	90	16	0	11	48	39	75	2	.337	.387
MINOR LEAGUE TOTALS			.266	381	1358	203	361	67	2	51	225	147	329	8	.360	.431

20 NICK EVANS, 1B

Born: Jan. 30, 1986. **B-T:** R-R. **Ht.:** 6-2. **Wt.:** 180. **Drafted:** HS—Phoenix, 2004 (5th round). **Signed by:** Dave Birecki.

Evans has become exactly what scouts said he would be out of high school: a one-dimensional slugger whose value is tied completely to his bat. A prep third baseman, he has moved to first base and is just a fair defender. One scout with a National League club said he turned in Evans as a prospect despite considering him below-average as a hitter, runner, fielder and thrower. The reason is that fifth tool. Evans has more usable power than any Mets minor leaguer from the draft. He has a swing that can get long, but he has enough bat speed to catch up to good fastballs when he's looking for them. He's exceptionally strong and can drive the ball out of the park to all fields. In fact, using the whole field as well as improving his two-strike approach were key improvements he made in 2007. He's willing to draw walks and absolutely mashed lefthanders (1.036 OPS). Evans had injury problems interrupt his season early and late. He missed most of May with a partially torn ligament in his left ankle and was set to report to Hawaii Winter Baseball before being shut down with a stress fracture in his right hand. He's going to go as far as his bat will take him, but with Carlos Delgado aging less gracefully than the New York had hoped, 2008 could be a huge year for Evans to see if he can move ahead Mike Carp as the system's best hope for a homegrown first baseman of the future. He should replace Carp as Binghamton's first baseman this season.

Year	Club (League)	Class	AVG	G	AB	R	H	2B	3B	HR	RBI	BB	SO	SB	OBP	SLG
2004	Mets (GCL)	R	.258	50	182	36	47	10	3	7	27	14	51	3	.311	.462
2005	Kingsport (Appy)	R	.344	15	64	11	22	7	0	6	22	4	17	1	.382	.734
	Brooklyn (NYP)	A	.252	57	226	30	57	11	3	6	33	17	34	0	.302	.407
2006	Hagerstown (SAL)	A	.254	137	511	55	130	33	3	15	67	45	99	2	.320	.419
2007	St. Lucie (FSL)	A	.286	103	378	65	108	25	1	15	54	53	64	3	.374	.476
MINOR LEAGUE TOTALS			.267	362	1361	197	364	86	10	49	203	133	265	9	.335	.453

21 FRANCISCO PENA, C

Born: Oct. 12, 1989. **B-T:** R-R. **Ht.:** 6-2. **Wt.:** 230. **Signed:** Dominican Republic, 2006. **Signed by:** Ismael Cruz.

Signed for $750,000 in 2006, Pena was put on the same fast track as the Mets' top two prospects, 2005 signees Fernando Martinez and Deolis Guerra. His big league bloodlines—he's the son of former all-star catcher and current Yankees first-base coach Tony Pena and the brother of Royals shortstop Tony Pena Jr.—good-looking swing and powerful, physically mature build seemed to indicate he'd be well-suited to jump into full-season ball at age 17. But Pena simply wasn't ready and had a dreadful season in low Class A. His best tool is raw power, and he just wasn't skilled enough to make consistent enough contact against older pitchers for his power to come into play. None of his other tools is average right now, and for Pena to bring his overall game into line with his potential, he must get into better shape. One scout outside the organization said simply, "He's just fat right now. It's hard to project much with the shape he's in." Mets international scouting director Ismael Cruz, whose father signed Tony Pena Sr., says Francisco resembles Tony the elder physically when he was 17 and isn't worried about the body or Pena's athletic ability. New York acknowledges Pena has work to do and says he put too much pressure on himself to hit for power immediately, leading the rest of his game to sag. He threw out just 23 percent of basestealers despite above-average arm strength. The combination of being the South Atlantic League's youngest player and having to handle the defensive responsibilities of catching were too much for Pena in 2007. The organization remains confident that Pena will get on track this year as an 18-year-old back in low Class A.

Year	Club (League)	Class	AVG	G	AB	R	H	2B	3B	HR	RBI	BB	SO	SB	OBP	SLG
2007	Savannah (SAL)	A	.210	103	367	26	77	12	0	5	30	24	76	1	.263	.283
MINOR LEAGUE TOTALS			.210	103	367	26	77	12	0	5	30	24	76	1	.263	.283

22 PHILLIPS ORTA, RHP

Born: May 9, 1986. **B-T:** R-R. **Ht.:** 6-2. **Wt.:** 175. **Drafted:** Western Nebraska CC, D/F 2006 (10th round). **Signed by:** Larry Chase.

The Mets' top draft-and-follow signee in 2007, Orta turned pro for $135,000 and has one of the better arms in the system. He's still raw after two seasons at Western Nebraska CC and went just 2-7 as a sophomore, though he helped the Cougars get within a game of the Junior College World Series with a team-best 2.61 ERA. One of four Venezuelans on the Western Nebraska roster, he made his pro debut in the Venezuelan Summer League after going back home to get a work visa. He was signed by the same scout who landed A.J. Burnett for the Mets, Arkansas-based Larry Chase, who said Orta has a ceiling of being a No. 2 or No. 3 starter. Chase had to trek about 1,000 miles to see Orta, impressive dedication that landed the Mets a live arm. Orta's fastball sat at 91-94 mph during the spring and touches 96 at times. He worked more at 88-91 mph during his debut. His fastball has armside run and he needs to learn to spot it to the outer half against righthanders. His clean arm action prompts scouts to predict improvement in his velocity and command. Orta's changeup is a solid-average pitch at times and he has flashed a hard curveball. He also loses feel for his curve at times and doesn't consistently throw it with enough power. He might take a while to develop but he has a strong arm and projection, so the Mets will be patient. He'll have to earn a spot in low Class A in spring training.

Year	Club (League)	Class	W	L	ERA	G	GS	CG	SV	IP	H	R	ER	HR	BB	SO	AVG
2007	Mets (VSL)	R	0	0	1.29	4	3	0	0	14	8	4	2	0	3	12	.167
	Kingsport (Appy)	R	2	2	4.58	11	11	0	0	53	62	29	27	3	21	45	.297
	Savannah (SAL)	A	0	0	27.00	1	0	0	0	0	0	2	2	0	5	1	.000
MINOR LEAGUE TOTALS			2	2	4.12	16	14	0	0	67	70	35	31	3	29	58	.270

23 ADAM BOSTICK, LHP

Born: March 17, 1983. **B-T:** L-L. **Ht.:** 6-1. **Wt.:** 220. **Drafted:** HS—Greensburgh, Pa., 2001 (6th round). **Signed by:** Steve Mondile (Marlins).

Bostick came to the Mets with fellow lefty Jason Vargas in the trade that sent righties Henry Owens and Matt Lindstrom to the Marlins. The deal didn't work out well at all for New York in 2007, as Lindstrom blossomed as a hard-throwing middle reliever in Florida while Bostick and Vargas struggled mightily. The Mets believe Bostick started straightening himself out right after the season ended. Before heading to the Arizona Fall League, he lost about 15 pounds to get back to his ideal weight of 220. He also started regaining some of the bite on his curveball, which long has been his best pitch. His trimmer frame allows him to maintain his mechanics better and throw harder. After sitting in the upper 80s for most of the year with his sinking two-seam fastball, Bostick operated at 89-91 mph and touched 93 in the AFL. His fringe-average changeup works better when set against a harder fastball. Despite his athleticism—NCAA Division II Slippery Rock (Pa.) offered him a football scholarship as a quarterback—throwing strikes consistently always has been a problem for Bostick. He can gets swings and misses with his fastball and curve but can't always catch the plate as much as he needs to. Bostick could be in the fifth starter's mix in New York in 2008, but more likely will return to Triple-A.

Year	Club (League)	Class	W	L	ERA	G	GS	CG	SV	IP	H	R	ER	HR	BB	SO	AVG
2001	Marlins (GCL)	R	1	1	4.26	7	1	0	0	12	16	8	6	0	3	13	.302
2002	Did Not Play—Injured																
2003	Greensboro (SAL)	A	0	1	3.77	7	1	0	0	14	12	6	6	1	12	15	.231
	Jamestown (NYP)	A	4	6	5.12	15	15	0	0	77	77	49	44	9	39	76	.263
2004	Greensboro (SAL)	A	2	8	3.79	23	22	0	0	114	100	57	48	10	58	163	.239
2005	Jupiter (FSL)	A	4	5	3.84	17	17	0	0	91	95	47	39	7	36	94	.270
	Carolina (SL)	AA	4	3	4.67	9	9	0	0	44	42	26	23	3	25	39	.250
2006	Carolina (SL)	AA	8	7	3.52	22	22	0	0	115	100	58	45	7	67	109	.235
	Albuquerque (PCL)	AAA	1	2	4.67	5	5	0	0	27	39	20	14	4	13	30	.339
2007	New Orleans (PCL)	AAA	6	7	5.66	21	20	0	0	97	106	66	61	20	45	91	.283
MINOR LEAGUE TOTALS			30	40	4.34	126	112	0	0	593	587	337	286	61	298	630	.261

24 EMMANUEL GARCIA, 2B/SS

Born: March 4, 1986. **B-T:** L-R. **Ht.:** 6-2. **Wt.:** 180. **Signed:** NDFA/HS—Montreal, 2004. **Signed by:** Claude Pelletier.

Garcia, whose father was a professional tennis player from Spain before settling in Canada, didn't get drafted because of the visa shortage baseball experienced post-9/11, but he has made up for lost time and has developed into one of the Mets' most reliable middle-infield options. He made Top 20 Prospects lists in both the Gulf Coast and Appalachian leagues in his first two years, and was productive in his full-season debut in 2007 after jumping a level to high Class A. After the season, he batted .348 in Hawaii Winter Baseball before joining Team Canada for the World Cup in Taiwan. Garcia has no home run power, but he can go gap to gap and uses the whole field. He isn't afraid to draw a walk, hit behind a runner or lay down a bunt, and he's improving his ability to make contact. He has plus speed and is a solid baserunner who's getting better in that aspect of the game, a crucial aspect of his development. Defensively, Garcia makes the routine plays at shortstop and has average tools, but he's probably better suited to second base, where he saw more time last season. The Mets love his energy, and his overall profile screams utility infielder. He's ticketed to start at shortstop in Double-A in 2008.

Year	Club (League)	Class	AVG	G	AB	R	H	2B	3B	HR	RBI	BB	SO	SB	OBP	SLG
2005	Mets (GCL)	R	.339	45	186	43	63	7	0	2	30	21	36	17	.412	.409
	St. Lucie (FSL)	A	.222	2	9	1	2	1	0	0	0	0	2	0	.222	.333
2006	Kingsport (Appy)	R	.291	51	206	35	60	5	2	3	25	27	41	19	.373	.379
	Brooklyn (NYP)	A	.240	13	50	7	12	0	0	0	3	5	13	3	.316	.240
2007	St. Lucie (FSL)	A	.256	130	488	65	125	12	5	0	31	63	103	34	.339	.301
MINOR LEAGUE TOTALS			.279	241	939	151	262	25	7	5	89	116	195	73	.359	.337

25 STEVEN REGISTER, RHP

Born: May 16, 1983. **B-T:** R-R. **Ht.:** 6-1. **Wt.:** 170. **Drafted:** Auburn, 2004 (3rd round). **Signed by:** Damon Iannelli (Rockies).

Register's career has come full circle. He was a reliever at Auburn and led NCAA Division I with 16 saves as a sophomore in 2003, pitching with Team USA as Huston Street's setup man that summer. The next year he struggled a bit more and moved into a starting role, and the Rockies kept him in the rotation after taking him in the third round in 2004. After reaching Double-A as a starter, he moved back to the bullpen there in 2007 and had his best year as a pro, leading the minor leagues with 37 saves. Register still throws a changeup that he picked up as a starter, but in relief he focuses more on using his average fastball and plus slider. His fastball will touch 93 mph but more regularly sits at 90-91 with a little sink. His slider sits at 82 mph and has some life down as well as away from righthanders and helps him get groundballs. Pro scout Jerry Krause, the former Chicago Bulls general manager, recommended him to the Mets as a major league Rule 5 draft pick because of his solid-average command of those pitches. Register will battle Jorge Sosa and Joe Smith for innings and a spot on the roster, and if he doesn't make it, New York must put him on waivers and offer him back to Colorado for half of the $50,000 Rule 5 price before sending him to the minors.

Year	Club (League)	Class	W	L	ERA	G	GS	CG	SV	IP	H	R	ER	HR	BB	SO	AVG
2004	Tri-City (NWL)	A	6	7	3.63	15	15	0	0	79	68	41	32	5	20	63	.234
2005	Modesto (Cal)	A	9	11	4.44	27	27	1	0	156	184	98	77	16	35	108	.291
2006	Tulsa (TL)	AA	4	10	5.57	27	27	2	0	155	189	114	96	25	53	77	.308
2007	Tulsa (TL)	AA	1	3	4.03	60	0	0	37	58	63	27	26	3	16	48	.279
MINOR LEAGUE TOTALS			20	31	4.64	129	69	3	37	448	504	280	231	49	124	296	.286

26 MIKE ANTONINI, LHP

Born: Aug. 6, 1985. **B-T:** R-L. **Ht.:** 6-0. **Wt.:** 190. **Drafted:** Georgia College & State, 2007 (18th round). **Signed by:** Marlin McPhail.

The Mets may have gotten an 18th-round steal last June in Antonini, a college senior who cost them just $2,500 and could move quickly. He attended Gloucester County (N.J.) JC and helped the team to the 2005 Division III juco national championship before moving on to Georgia College & State for two seasons. He spurned his hometown Phillies as a 41st-round pick after his junior season and struggled somewhat as a senior (7-6, 3.97). However, Antonini showed the Mets three potential average big league pitches, and he has an out pitch in his changeup, which has excellent fade and helps neutralize right-handers. Big leaguer Paul LoDuca caught Antonini in an August rehab stint at Brooklyn and proclaimed his changeup big league-ready. His fastball ranges from 88-91 mph and is fairly straight, and he's homer-prone when he leaves it up in the strike zone. His slider grades out as an average pitch because he throws it with some power in the low 80s. Antonini has little room for projection but has the stuff to be a fourth or fifth starter if he can hone his command and avoid the longball. He could skip a level and jump to high Class A this year.

Year	Club (League)	Class	W	L	ERA	G	GS	CG	SV	IP	H	R	ER	HR	BB	SO	AVG
2007	Kingsport (Appy)	R	1	1	3.71	5	3	0	0	17	16	8	7	3	2	18	.239
	Brooklyn (NYP)	A	0	0	0.46	7	2	0	0	19	13	1	1	0	5	12	.194
MINOR LEAGUE TOTALS			1	1	1.96	12	5	0	0	36	29	9	8	3	7	30	.216

27 JEFRY MARTE, 3B

Born: June 21, 1991. **B-T:** R-R. **Ht.:** 6-1. **Wt.:** 187. **Signed:** Dominican Republic, 2007. **Signed by:** Ismael Cruz/Juan Mercado/Marciano Alvarez.

Marte signed with the Mets soon after turning 16 last June, and he received a $550,000 bonus, the ninth-highest of any position player on the international market last summer. International scouting director Ismael Cruz said New York considered Marte's bat the quickest in the international class and projects him to hit for significant power down the line. Top evaluator Sandy Johnson—who has scouted Latin America for 35 years and signed the likes of Juan Gonzalez, Ivan Rodriguez and Sammy Sosa—was heavily involved in scouting Marte, as he was with all the Mets' six-figure international signees the last three years. He's raw but hit some 400-foot shots during instructional league and got further experience in the organization's Dominican instructional program. He's is physical and has some all-around skills, with a solid arm and above-average speed (6.7 seconds over 60 yards). His defense and ability to hit for average are far from polished, befitting a 16-year-old. New York is flush with infielders at the lower levels, so Marte may start his pro career in the Dominican Summer League, though he could debut in the Gulf Coast League.

Year	Club (League)	Class	AVG	G	AB	R	H	2B	3B	HR	RBI	BB	SO	SB	OBP	SLG
2007	Did Not Play															

28 JUAN LAGARES, SS

Born: March 17, 1989. **B-T:** R-R. **Ht.:** 6-1. **Wt.:** 175. **Signed:** Dominican Republic, 2006. **Signed by:** Ismael Cruz/Juan Mercado.

Lagares teamed with Greg Veloz in the Dominican Summer League in 2006 and again at Savannah to start 2007, but in the second half Lagares was worn down and Veloz sent down to Kingsport. Mariners phenom Carlos Triunfel and Savannah teammate Francisco Pena were the only younger players to begin the 2007 season on a full-season club in the minors, and Lagares' youth showed in his statistics. He hit just .210 and ranked second in the South Atlantic League in errors by a shortstop (40) in just 82 games. However, Lagares has some obvious tools. He's a plus runner with excellent athleticism and body control, and he has the quick feet and requisite arm strength to play shortstop. One Mets official insists Lagares' best tool will be his bat, saying he should develop solid gap power and noting that he actually posted a higher slugging percentage than Pena (.317 to .283) at Savannah. Lagares was obviously raw, expanding his strike zone and being too aggressive on the basepaths to take advantage of his speed. He's likely to repeat low Class A in 2008 and should team with Veloz once again in an intriguing middle infield.

Year	Club (League)	Class	AVG	G	AB	R	H	2B	3B	HR	RBI	BB	SO	SB	OBP	SLG
2006	Mets (DSL)	R	.255	57	204	36	52	7	8	3	33	23	48	12	.339	.412
2007	Savannah (SAL)	A	.210	83	281	26	59	12	6	2	16	18	64	11	.262	.317
MINOR LEAGUE TOTALS			.229	140	485	62	111	19	14	5	49	41	112	23	.296	.357

29 LUCAS DUDA, 1B/OF

Born: Feb. 3, 1986. **B-T:** L-R. **Ht.:** 6-4. **Wt.:** 225. **Drafted:** Southern California, 2007 (7th round). **Signed by:** Steve Leavitt.

Duda ranked among the top power hitters in the prep class of 2004 after putting on a show at the 2003 Area Code Games. He also touched 90 mph as a pitcher and was expected to be a two-way impact player at Southern California. That Duda never materialized, however, as he never hit for much power and never pitched in college (in part because he had Tommy John surgery in high school). After slugging just .410 in three seasons for the Trojans, he took off after signing in June for $85,000. His 20 doubles for Brooklyn matched the total of his three college seasons. Duda trimmed up his body and while he still drew walks, he was more aggressive as a pro and his above-average raw power potential finally came to the fore. He can drive the ball to all fields and is still learning how to add loft to his swing. Despite his size, Duda runs well enough to have fringe-average range in left field, and he still has some arm strength. He played mostly left field as a college junior and has a better chance to stick as a reserve player if he can stay there in pro ball. Whether he plays left or first base (where he saw more action during his pro debut), his raw power will have to play more than it did in his amateur career. He's expected to anchor the Savannah lineup in 2008.

Year	Club (League)	Class	AVG	G	AB	R	H	2B	3B	HR	RBI	BB	SO	SB	OBP	SLG
2007	Brooklyn (NYP)	A	.299	67	234	32	70	20	3	4	32	34	45	3	.398	.462
MINOR LEAGUE TOTALS			.299	67	234	32	70	20	3	4	32	34	45	3	.398	.462

30 ELVIN RAMIREZ, RHP

Born: Oct. 10, 1987. **B-T:** R-R. **Ht.:** 6-3. **Wt.:** 182. **Signed:** Dominican Republic, 2005. **Signed by:** Eddy Toledo.

The Mets have signed several promising position players from Latin America since Omar Minaya became general manager, but Deolis Guerra stands out as by far the best of the international pitching signees. New York hopes that more depth is on the way, with Ramirez leading a group of young Latin arms that also includes lefthander Angel Calero, who has projectable arm strength, and righthander Pedro P. Martinez, no relation to the big leaguer and one of the organization's most improved pitchers in instructional league. Ramirez has a big arm, having hit 96 mph regularly and sitting anywhere from 87-94 with a short, deceptive arm action. One scout who saw Ramirez at Kingsport said he'd have more velocity if the Mets could lengthen his delivery out front, and club officials say they had success doing that in instructional league. Ramirez has a wiry-strong body that allows him to generate a quick arm that helps produce a hard breaking ball that's closer to a curveball than a slider. He has a chance to have decent control but too much effort in his delivery to have much command, making him profile as a reliever. New York likely will keep him in the rotation to get more innings in 2008, at either Brooklyn or Savannah.

Year	Club (League)	Class	W	L	ERA	G	GS	CG	SV	IP	H	R	ER	HR	BB	SO	AVG
2005	Mets (DSL)	R	2	6	6.53	16	6	0	0	40	48	38	29	2	23	24	.284
2006	Mets (DSL)	R	0	1	2.63	11	6	0	0	27	16	13	8	0	10	28	.165
2007	Kingsport (Appy)	R	1	4	5.52	12	12	0	0	45	52	34	28	5	29	48	.280
MINOR LEAGUE TOTALS			3	11	5.18	39	24	0	0	113	116	85	65	7	62	100	.257

New York Yankees

BY JOHN MANUEL

For all the back-page news the Yankees made in 2007, the biggest story was the cold, hard fact that they no longer are the preeminent franchise in baseball.

The Red Sox passed them in 2007, winning the American League East—the first time New York hadn't won the division since 1997—and then winning their second World Series of the decade. It's a decade in which the Yankees have yet to win a championship despite consistently maintaining the game's largest payroll.

The Yankees' 2007 season included 94 victories and rallying from a 21-29 start to make the playoffs. It also included superlative individual performances by the likes of BA Player of the Year and AL MVP Alex Rodriguez, a career year from 35-year-old catcher Jorge Posada and the dynamic debut of Joba Chamberlain, the organization's No. 1 prospect.

But 2007 also included a 4.49 team ERA for New York, a figure that ranked just eighth in the AL. A Division Series defeat to the Indians marked the third straight first-round playoff exit for the Yankees, who are 4-13 in the playoffs since taking a 3-0 lead on Boston in the 2004 AL Championship Series.

The string of playoff disappointments, plus the ascendancy of brothers Hank and Hal Steinbrenner to prominent roles in the ownership group as their father George continued to fade into the background, helped shape the franchise's immediate future. Club officials insisted younger Steinbrenners already had become more involved in recent years, and one went so far as to say it was "business as usual around here," but events say otherwise. Manager Joe Torre was ousted after 12 seasons when he rejected a one-year extension, and the Yankees turned to Joe Girardi, their former color analyst on the YES Network and catcher, and the 2006 National League manager of the year with the Marlins.

Girardi's Florida team was built around young pitchers, and he'll have more young talent to work with in New York. Staff ace Chien-Ming Wang, 27, is coming off consecutive 19-win seasons. And the Yankees are counting on Chamberlain, Phil Hughes and Ian Kennedy to claim rotation spots. That trio has undeniable talent, but also has combined for just 16 big league starts and 116 innings.

The farm system has made significant strides in the last four years, with improved talent allowing the system's domestic affiliates to combine for

The Yankees' offense remains robust with veterans such as Jorge Posada

JOHN WILLIAMSON

TOP 30 PROSPECTS

1. Joba Chamberlain, rhp	16. Carmen Angelini, ss
2. Austin Jackson, of	17. George Kontos, rhp
3. Jose Tabata, of	18. Ivan Nova, rhp
4. Ian Kennedy, rhp	19. Colin Curtis, of
5. Alan Horne, rhp	20. Jairo Heredia, rhp
6. Jesus Montero, c	21. Juan Miranda, 1b
7. Jeff Marquez, rhp	22. Austin Romine, c
8. Brett Gardner, of	23. Francisco Cervelli, c
9. Ross Ohlendorf, rhp	24. David Robertson, rhp
10. Andrew Brackman, rhp	25. Mike Dunn, lhp
11. Mark Melancon, rhp	26. J. Brent Cox, rhp
12. Humberto Sanchez, rhp	27. Mitch Hilligoss, 3b
13. Dellin Betances, rhp	28. Scott Patterson, rhp
14. Daniel McCutchen, rhp	29. Edwar Ramirez, rhp
15. Kevin Whelan, rhp	30. Zach McAllister, rhp

four first-place finishes, two league championships and a .597 winning percentage, the best mark in baseball. Scouting director Damon Oppenheimer, who took over in 2005, has the budget to pick aggressively. The Yankees paid more than MLB's bonus recommendations for five draft picks in the first 10 rounds and spent $8.03 million on the draft, more than any other team. They also were as active as any organization internationally, adding high-priced, high-ceiling talents led by Dominican outfielder Kevin DeLeon, who signed for $1.1 million.

General Manager: Brian Cashman. **Farm Director:** Mark Newman. **Scouting Director:** Damon Oppenheimer.

Class	Team	League	W	L	PCT	Finish*	Manager	Affiliated
Majors	New York	American	94	68	.580	3rd (14)	Joe Torre	—
Triple-A	Scranton/W-B Yankees	International	84	59	.587	1st (14)	Dave Miley	2007
Double-A	Trenton Thunder	Eastern	83	59	.585	1st (12)^	Tony Franklin	2003
High A	Tampa Yankees	Florida State	83	56	.597	1st (12)	Luis Sojo	1994
Low A	Charleston RiverDogs	South Atlantic	78	62	.557	5th (16)	Torre Tyson	2005
Short-season	Staten Island Yankees	New York-Penn	47	28	.627	2nd (14)	Mike Gillespie	1999
Rookie	GCL Yankees	Gulf Coast	42	17	.712	1st (16)^	Jody Reed	1980
Overall 2007 Minor League Record			417	281	.597	1st		

*Finish in overall standings (No. of teams in league) ^League champion

LAST YEAR'S TOP 30

Player, Pos.		Status
1.	Philip Hughes, rhp	Majors
2.	Jose Tabata, of	No. 3
3.	Humberto Sanchez, rhp	No. 12
4.	Dellin Betances, rhp	No. 13
5.	Joba Chamberlain, rhp	No. 1
6.	Ian Kennedy, rhp	No. 4
7.	Tyler Clippard, rhp	(Nationals)
8.	J. Brent Cox, rhp	No. 26
9.	Kevin Whelan, rhp	No. 15
10.	Brett Gardner, of	No. 8
11.	Marcos Vechionacci, 3b	Dropped out
12.	Jeff Marquez, rhp	No. 7
13.	Eric Duncan, 1b/3b	Dropped out
14.	Chris Garcia, rhp	Dropped out
15.	Mark Melancon, rhp	No. 11
16.	Alan Horne, rhp	No. 5
17.	Angel Reyes, lhp	Dropped out
18.	Austin Jackson, of	No. 2
19.	Chase Wright, lhp	Dropped out
20.	George Kontos, rhp	No. 17
21.	Jesus Montero, c	No. 6
22.	Steven White, rhp	Dropped out
23.	T.J. Beam, rhp	Dropped out
24.	Zach McAllister, rhp	No. 30
25.	Colin Curtis, of	No. 19
26.	Jeff Karstens, rhp	Majors
27.	Josue Calzado, of	Dropped out
28.	Bronson Sardinha, of	Dropped out
29.	Tim Norton, rhp	Dropped out
30.	Daniel McCutchen, rhp	No. 14

BEST TOOLS

Best Hitter for Average	Jose Tabata
Best Power Hitter	Jesus Montero
Best Strike-Zone Discipline	Brett Gardner
Fastest Baserunner	Brett Gardner
Best Athlete	Austin Jackson
Best Fastball	Joba Chamberlain
Best Curveball	Joba Chamberlain
Best Slider	Joba Chamberlain
Best Changeup	Edwar Ramirez
Best Control	Ian Kennedy
Best Defensive Catcher	Francisco Cervelli
Best Defensive Infielder	Alberto Gonzalez
Best Infield Arm	Marcos Vechionacci
Best Defensive Outfielder	Austin Jackson
Best Outfield Arm	Seth Fortenberry

PROJECTED 2011 LINEUP

Catcher	Austin Romine
First Base	Jesus Montero
Second Base	Robinson Cano
Third Base	Alex Rodriguez
Shortstop	Derek Jeter
Left Field	Brett Gardner
Center Field	Austin Jackson
Right Field	Jose Tabata
Designated Hitter	Bob Abreu
No. 1 Starter	Joba Chamberlain
No. 2 Starter	Phil Hughes
No. 3 Starter	Chien-Ming Wang
No. 4 Starter	Ian Kennedy
No. 5 Starter	Alan Horne
Closer	Mark Melancon

TOP PROSPECTS OF THE DECADE

Year	Player, Pos.	2007 Org.
1998	Eric Milton, lhp	Reds
1999	Nick Johnson, 1b	Nationals
2000	Nick Johnson, 1b	Nationals
2001	Nick Johnson, 1b	Nationals
2002	Drew Henson, 3b	Out of baseball
2003	Jose Contreras, rhp	White Sox
2004	Dioner Navarro, c	Devil Rays
2005	Eric Duncan, 3b	Yankees
2006	Phil Hughes, rhp	Yankees
2007	Phil Hughes, rhp	Yankees

TOP DRAFT PICKS OF THE DECADE

Year	Player, Pos.	2007 Org.
1998	Andy Brown, of	Out of baseball
1999	David Walling, rhp	Out of baseball
2000	David Parrish, c	Pirates
2001	John-Ford Griffin, of	Blue Jays
2002	Brandon Weeden, rhp (2nd)	Out of baseball
2003	Eric Duncan, 3b	Yankees
2004	Phil Hughes, rhp	Yankees
2005	C.J. Henry, ss	Phillies
2006	Ian Kennedy, rhp	Yankees
2007	Andrew Brackman, rhp	Yankees

LARGEST BONUSES IN CLUB HISTORY

Hideki Irabu, 1997	$8,500,000
Jose Contreras, 2002.	$6,000,000
Andrew Brackman, 2007	$3,350,000
Willy Mo Pena, 1999	$2,440,000
Ian Kennedy, 2006	$2,250,000

NEW YORK YANKEES

Top 2008 Rookie: Joba Chamberlain, rhp. Lights out as a reliever, there's no reason he shouldn't dominate as a starter.

Breakout Prospect: Mark Melancon, rhp. If he's finally healthy, he'll be on the fast track to New York's bullpen.

Sleeper: Abe Almonte, of/2b. One of the organization's fastest players is primed for his first full season.

SOURCE OF TOP 30 TALENT

Homegrown	25	Acquired	5
College	12	Trades	3
Junior college	1	Rule 5 draft	0
High school	5	Independent leagues	2
Draft-and-follow	1	Free agents/waivers	0
Nondrafted free agents	0		
International	6		

Numbers in parentheses indicate prospect rankings

LF
Colin Curtis (19)
Taylor Grote

CF
Austin Jackson (2)
Brett Gardner (8)
Abraham Almonte
Austin Krum

RF
Jose Tabata (3)
Josue Calzado
Seth Fortenberry

3B
Mitch Hilligoss (27)
Bradley Suttle
Brandon Laird
Marcos Vechionacci
Braedyn Pruitt

SS
Carmen Angelini (16)
Ramiro Pena
Jose Pirela
Eduardo Nunez

2B
Damon Sublett
Justin Snyder
Reegie Corona

1B
Juan Miranda (21)
Shelley Duncan
Eric Duncan
Chris Malec
Wady Rufino

C
Jesus Montero (6)
Austin Romine (22)
Francisco Cervelli (23)
Chase Weems
Kyle Anson

RHP

Starters	Relievers
Joba Chamberlain (1)	Ross Ohlendorf (9)
Ian Kennedy (4)	Mark Melancon (11)
Alan Horne (5)	Kevin Whelan (15)
Jeff Marquez (7)	David Robertson (24)
Andrew Brackman (10)	J. Brent Cox (26)
Humberto Sanchez (12)	Scott Patterson (28)
Dellin Betances (13)	Edwar Ramirez (29)
Daniel McCutchen (14)	Tim Norton
George Kontos (17)	Anthony Claggett
Ivan Nova (18)	Grant Duff
Jairo Heredia (20)	Eric Wordekemper
Zach McAllister (30)	
Chris Garcia	
Steven White	
Brett Smith	
Ryan Pope	
Adam Olbrychowski	
Eric Hecker	
Ryan Zink	
Nick Chigges	

LHP

Starters	Relievers
Mike Dunn (25)	Edgar Soto
Chase Wright	Zack Kroenke
Angel Reyes	
Phil Coke	

2007 SIGNING BUDGET: $7.4 MILLION

Best Pro Debut: 2B Justin Snyder (21) played four positions and led the short-season New York-Penn League in hits (87), on-base percentage and runs (68) while batting .335/.459/.477. 3B/1B Brandon Laird (27) and Braedyn Pruitt (14) ranked among league batting leaders in the Rookie-level Gulf Coast League and NY-P, respectively.

Best Athlete: RHP Andrew Brackman (1) averaged 7.6 points and 3.5 rebounds in 2005-06 for North Carolina State's basketball team, and with mobility and touch at close to 7-feet tall, he would potentially have a career as a reserve in the NBA. OF Taylor Grote (5) was a three-year starter at wide receiver for The Woodlands (Texas) High and is an all-around athlete.

Best Pure Hitter: The Yankees paid big money to 3B Bradley Suttle (4, $1.3 million bonus) and SS Carmen Angelini (10, $1 million bonus) because of their offensive polish.

Best Power Hitter: The consensus held that C Austin Romine (2) was better defensively than offensively; the Yankees see it the other way, hoping to tidy up rough receiving edges but banking on his above-average raw power.

Fastest Runner: Grote's above-average speed is the best of the lot; speed was not an emphasis of the class.

Best Defensive Player: Romine has a plus-plus arm and should be an above-average defender eventually. Angelini is smooth and instinctive and the best present defender.

Best Fastball: Brackman has touched 100 mph and at times pitches in the upper-90s. He had Tommy John surgery after signing a major league contract that included a $3.35 million bonus, so he won't debut until 2009.

Best Secondary Pitch: Brackman's spike curveball is an out pitch. RHP Nick Chigges (13) used the tight spin and feel for his curveball to strike out 62 in 55 NY-P innings.

Most Intriguing Background: Between his size, hoops past and surgery, Brackman has plenty going on. Laird followed his older brother Gerald, now the Rangers' catcher, at Cypress (Calif.) JC. 1B Luke Murton (40, unsigned) likewise followed older brother and Cubs outfielder Matt at Georgia Tech.

Closest To The Majors: Suttle has a polished college profile but bombed in Hawaii Winter Baseball. A healthy 2B Damon Sublett (7), a lefthanded hitter with speed, also could move quickly in a utility role.

Best Late-Round Pick: Snyder or Laird; Snyder is more complete and polished, but Laird has the higher ceiling.

The One Who Got Away: The Yankees made futile runs at RHPs Greg Peavey (24, Oregon State) and Drew Storen (34, Stanford). RHP Chris Carpenter (17), who has a plus fastball but is coming off Tommy John surgery, returned to Kent State.

Assessment: The Yankees continue to be more aggressive in the draft and spent money on players they believe in, like Brackman. Players like Angelini don't fit the Yankees profile as future stars, but they are all ballplayers who can hit.

2006 BUDGET: $6.3 MILLION

The Yankees wouldn't have made the playoffs last year without RHPs Ian Kennedy (1) and Joba Chamberlain (1s). RHP Dellin Betances (8) still has as much upside as just about anyone in the system.

GRADE: A

2005 BUDGET: $3.7 MILLION

OF Austin Jackson (8) turned his career around in 2007 and is now New York's best position prospect. RHP Alan Horne (11) was another late-round coup, and it doesn't matter that OF/3B C.J. Henry (1) has fizzled.

GRADE: B+

2004 BUDGET: $4.8 MILLION

With a solid rookie season in 2007, RHP Phil Hughes (1) continued to look like a future frontline starter. RHP Jeff Marquez (1s) is on the verge of helping the Yankees, but OF Jon Poterson (1s) has been relegated to independent ball.

GRADE: B+

2003 BUDGET: $3.8 MILLION

Once-hyped 1B Eric Duncan (1) is now a forgotten man. This crop doesn't get any better than fringy RHPs Tyler Clippard (9, since traded), T.J. Beam (10) and Jeff Karstens (19).

GRADE: C

Draft analysis by John Manuel (2007) and Jim Callis (2003-06). Numbers in parentheses indicate draft rounds. Budgets are bonuses in first 10 rounds.

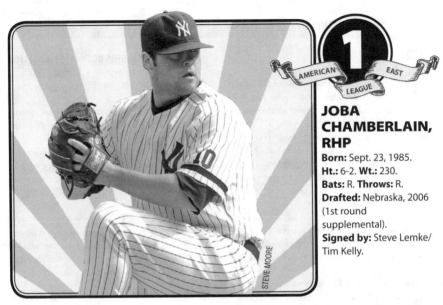

JOBA CHAMBERLAIN, RHP

Born: Sept. 23, 1985.
Ht.: 6-2. **Wt.:** 230.
Bats: R. **Throws:** R.
Drafted: Nebraska, 2006 (1st round supplemental).
Signed by: Steve Lemke/ Tim Kelly.

In 2004, Chamberlain was a 272-pound starter at NCAA Division II Nebraska-Kearney, and he went just 3-6, 5.23. Chamberlain started getting in shape, though, and his fastball started reaching the low 90s by the end of his freshman season. He then transferred to Nebraska, where he kept improving and led his hometown Cornhuskers to the 2005 College World Series. While his talent made him a consensus top prospect for the 2006 draft, his stock fell because of concerns about a knee injury that required surgery in the fall of 2004. He fell to the Yankees with the 41st overall pick and signed for $1.15 million. A member of the Winnebago tribe, he became the second-highest Native American ever drafted, behind only Jacoby Ellsbury. After signing, Chamberlain reported to Hawaii Winter Baseball, where he ranked as the No. 1 prospect in his first pro action. Chamberlain had a mild hamstring pull last spring and didn't make his pro debut until May, then made the minor leagues look easy. After breezing through high Class A Tampa and Double-A Trenton, Chamberlain moved to the bullpen to help the Yankees fill a big league need. He made the majors look easy too. Only Mother Nature could stop him. He coughed up a 2-1 lead against the Indians in Game Three of the Division Series after he was swarmed by midges and lost his focus.

Scouts chuckle with delight discussing Chamberlain's raw stuff, and several give him 70 or 80 grades on the 20-80 scouting scale for three different pitches. He reached 100 mph with his fastball 100 mph as a reliever, and more impressively can sit at 96-97 mph when he starts. His fastball command grades at least major league average, if not higher. He also commands two breaking balls—a mid-80s slider with depth and a nasty power curveball in the low 80s. Both are strikeout pitches, and he's adept at keeping his hand on top of the curve and behind the slider. He showed a solid-average changeup as a starter. Chamberlain's arm action is clean, and his personality and confidence make him well-suited for New York.

Chamberlain will need to keep his weight in check, which would help him avoid any recurrence of his past knee, hamstring or triceps tendinitis issues. He needs to maintain the mechanical improvements he has made as a pro, which keep him more balanced and direct his energy toward the plate, rather than side-to-side. There's almost no room for improvement with his pitches, though he must prove he can maintain his stuff through a full season. His career high for innings remains the 119 he threw for Nebraska as a sophomore.

While he could become an elite closer almost immediately, Chamberlain fits the No. 1 starter profile in nearly every way except for his durability. If the Yankees were only thinking of his development, they would limit him to 170 innings or so. He's likely to pitch so well as to tempt new manager Joe Girardi to use him more than that, however. If he remains healthy, Chamberlain has multiple all-star appearances in his future.

Year	Club (League)	Class	W	L	ERA	G	GS	CG	SV	IP	H	R	ER	HR	BB	SO	AVG
2007	Tampa (FSL)	A	4	0	2.03	7	7	0	0	40	25	10	9	0	11	51	.181
	Trenton (EL)	AA	4	2	3.35	8	7	0	0	40	32	15	15	4	15	66	.218
	Scranton/W-B (IL)	AAA	1	0	0.00	3	1	0	0	8	5	0	0	0	1	18	.179
	New York (AL)	MLB	2	0	0.38	19	0	0	1	24	12	2	1	1	6	34	.145
MINOR LEAGUE TOTALS			9	2	2.45	18	15	0	0	88	62	25	24	4	27	135	.198
MAJOR LEAGUE TOTALS			2	0	0.38	19	0	0	1	24	12	2	1	1	6	34	.145

2 AUSTIN JACKSON, OF

STEVE MOORE

Born: Feb. 1, 1987. **B-T:** R-R. **Ht.:** 6-1. **Wt.:** 185. **Drafted:** HS—Denton, Texas, 2005 (8th round). **Signed by:** Mark Batchko.

For nearly the first two years since Jackson bypassed a Georgia Tech basketball scholarship to sign for $800,000, Jackson's progress was slow. He began 2007 by returning to low Class A Charleston but took off when pushed to high Class A. He finished the season on a roll, helping Trenton win the Double-A Eastern League title and ranking as the No. 2 prospect in Hawaii Winter Baseball. The best athlete in the system, Jackson stopped fighting himself and let the game and his talent flow last season. He takes a big, aggressive swing, and his quick bat and strength give him solid-average raw power. He uses the whole field and feasts on pitches on the inner half. He has developed above-average range in center field as his instincts and reactions have improved, and his plus arm has become more consistent and accurate. Jackson takes a healthy cut and doesn't have great times to first base out of the batter's box, but he has average speed and has improved his first step considerably. He's still gaining baseball experience, which shows in his pitch recognition and baserunning acumen. Jackson still has more room to grow, and the Yankees consider him a future all-star candidate. He'll try to continue his progress in Double-A in 2008 and could challenge for a big league job as soon as 2009.

Year	Club (League)	Class	AVG	G	AB	R	H	2B	3B	HR	RBI	BB	SO	SB	OBP	SLG
2005	Yankees (GCL)	R	.304	40	148	32	45	11	2	0	14	18	26	11	.374	.405
2006	Charleston, S.C. (SAL)	A	.260	134	535	90	139	24	5	4	47	61	151	37	.340	.346
2007	Charleston, S.C. (SAL)	A	.260	60	235	33	61	16	1	3	25	24	59	19	.336	.374
	Tampa (FSL)	A	.345	67	258	53	89	15	6	10	34	22	48	13	.398	.566
	Scranton/W-B (IL)	AAA	.333	1	3	2	1	1	0	0	0	2	2	1	.600	.667
MINOR LEAGUE TOTALS			.284	302	1179	210	335	67	14	17	120	127	286	81	.357	.408

3 JOSE TABATA, OF

STEVE MOORE

Born: Aug. 12, 1988. **B-T:** R-R. **Ht.:** 5-11. **Wt.:** 160. **Signed:** Venezuela, 2005. **Signed by:** Ricardo Finol.

Tabata was rolling along as one of the minors' brightest prospects until being hit on the right wrist by a pitch in July 2006. While he played some late that season and again in winter ball in Venezuela, he was never quite right and saw five different hand specialists to find a solution. He finally had surgery last August to remove the hamate bone in his right wrist. Despite his hand injury, Tabata was one of the high Class A Florida State League's top hitters, and he has a natural knack for making consistent hard contact. His wrist problem sapped some of his power, but scouts still project Tabata to have at least average pop, and some even see him more as a slugger than hitter. While he flashes plus speed, he projects as an average runner and right fielder with a solid average arm. Tabata's offensive future still involves some projection, and there's some concern his thickening body could lose some athleticism, rendering him more one-dimensional. Scouts outside the organization chide him for failing to give a consistent effort. While he has flaws, Tabata also has upside and will play in Double-A as a teenager this year. Ideally, he'd be ready to replace Bob Abreu in right field in 2009, but that might be too ambitious a timetable if his power doesn't develop.

Year	Club (League)	Class	AVG	G	AB	R	H	2B	3B	HR	RBI	BB	SO	SB	OBP	SLG
2005	Yankees (GCL)	R	.314	44	156	30	49	5	1	3	25	15	14	22	.382	.417
2006	Charleston, S.C. (SAL)	A	.298	86	319	50	95	22	1	5	51	30	66	15	.377	.420
2007	Tampa (FSL)	A	.307	103	411	56	126	16	2	5	54	33	70	15	.371	.392
MINOR LEAGUE TOTALS			.305	233	886	136	270	43	4	13	130	78	150	52	.375	.406

4 IAN KENNEDY, RHP

STEVE MOORE

Born: Dec. 19, 1984. **B-T:** R-R. **Ht.:** 6-0. **Wt.:** 190. **Drafted:** Southern California, 2006 (1st round). **Signed by:** Bill Mele/Jeff Patterson.

A high school teammate of Rockies third-base prospect Ian Stewart, Kennedy went to Southern California while Stewart signed out of high school. They both made their big league debuts in 2007 after Kennedy ranked third in the minors in ERA (1.91) in his first full season. Though he pitched well in three starts with the Yankees, they left him off their postseason roster because he had a minor back injury. That was a sort of blessing for Kennedy, who married former Trojans basketball player Allison Jaskowiak on an off day during the Division Series. Kennedy has mound presence and moxie to go with above-average major league command, and that helps all his pitches play up. His 88-92 mph fastball, his curveball and his slider (which he added since turning pro) all are average pitches. His plus changeup is his best offering, featuring late fade. He repeats his compact delivery like a machine. With only one above-average pitch, Kennedy has to hit his spots, but he usually does. At times his curve is too slow, dipping to 69-72 mph, and lacks sharpness. Some club officials compare him to Mike Mussina because of his bend-at-the-waist stretch delivery, but Kennedy lacks the plus stuff from Mussina had at the same age. Kennedy fits a No. 3 or No. 4 starter profile, and New York expects him to fulfill that role in 2008.

Year	Club (League)	Class	W	L	ERA	G	GS	CG	SV	IP	H	R	ER	HR	BB	SO	AVG
2006	Staten Island (NYP)	A	0	0	0.00	1	1	0	0	2	2	0	0	0	2	2	.200
2007	Tampa (FSL)	A	6	1	1.29	11	10	1	0	63	39	9	9	2	22	72	.183
	Trenton (EL)	AA	5	1	2.59	9	9	0	0	48	27	14	14	2	17	57	.163
	Scranton/W-B (IL)	AAA	1	1	2.08	6	6	0	0	34	25	8	8	2	11	34	.205
	New York (AL)	MLB	1	0	1.89	3	3	0	0	19	13	6	4	1	9	15	.191
MINOR LEAGUE TOTALS			12	3	1.87	27	26	1	0	149	93	31	31	6	52	165	.182
MAJOR LEAGUE TOTALS			1	0	1.89	3	3	0	0	19	13	6	4	1	9	15	.191

5 ALAN HORNE, RHP

KEVIN PATAKY

Born: Jan. 5, 1983. **B-T:** R-R. **Ht.:** 6-4. **Wt.:** 195. **Drafted:** Florida, 2005 (11th round). **Signed by:** Brian Barber.

Horne was a first-round pick out of Marianna (Fla.) High in 2001, when he was a teammate of Angels catcher Jeff Mathis. He turned down the Indians and embarked on a three-stop college career, pitching for Mississippi, Chipola (Fla.) Junior College (where his dad played) and Florida, which he helped lead to the 2005 College World Series finals. He had Tommy John surgery along the way but has stayed healthy as a pro, leading the EL in ERA (3.11) and strikeouts (165 in 153 innings) in 2007. At times, Horne shows four above-average pitches, starting with a fastball that usually sits at 92-93 mph but also can park at 94-95. He flashes a power slider and curveball, and he throws his changeup with good arm speed. Horne's arm action is long, leading to inconsistent release points and below-average command, and it likely contributed to his past elbow injury. The Yankees have shortened his delivery in other ways to compensate, but it's not a correctable flaw and limits Horne's ceiling. He doesn't field his position or hold runners particularly well. While he has frontline stuff, Horne's command issues relegate him to a No. 3 or 4 starter profile. He'll head to Triple-A Scranton/Wilkes-Barre for 2008 but give the Yankees another homegrown starter soon thereafter.

Year	Club (League)	Class	W	L	ERA	G	GS	CG	SV	IP	H	R	ER	HR	BB	SO	AVG
2006	Tampa (FSL)	A	6	9	4.84	28	26	0	0	122	105	72	66	10	61	122	.230
2007	Trenton (EL)	AA	12	4	3.11	27	27	0	0	153	149	68	53	10	57	165	.256
MINOR LEAGUE TOTALS			18	13	3.88	55	53	0	0	276	254	140	119	20	118	287	.244

6 JESUS MONTERO, C

CLIFF WELCH

Born: Nov. 28, 1989. **B-T:** R-R. **Ht.:** 6-4. **Wt.:** 225. **Signed:** Venezuela, 2006. **Signed by:** Carlos Rios/Ricardo Finol.

Montero signed for $2 million, the highest bonus of any international free agent in the summer of 2006. He had a difficult fall, however, struggling in instructional league and having his signing bonus reduced to $1.6 million. Industry chatter about the reasons for the reduction hasn't been officially confirmed. Montero has exceptional raw power to all fields, coupling a discerning eye for a young player with brute strength and bat speed. He has plenty of arm strength for his position and natural leadership ability, with an effusive personality and improving knowledge of English. At 6-foot-4 and 225 pounds, Montero already has grown very large for an 18-year-old. The Yankees say he has lower-body flexibility, necessary for blocking balls in the dirt, and he has worked hard to become a solid receiver. There are mixed opinions about his ability to stay at catcher, and he'll have to keep working on his body and catch-and-throw skills to stay behind the plate. He threw out just three of 32 basestealers (9 percent) in the Rookie-level Gulf Coast League in his pro debut. If Montero can remain a catcher, he profiles as a future all-star. He has a leg up on 2007 second-round pick Austin Romine, who has yet to play as a pro, for the starting catching job at short-season Staten Island.

Year	Club (League)	Class	AVG	G	AB	R	H	2B	3B	HR	RBI	BB	SO	SB	OBP	SLG
2007	Yankees (GCL)	R	.280	33	107	13	30	6	0	3	19	12	18	0	.366	.421
MINOR LEAGUE TOTALS			.280	33	107	13	30	6	0	3	19	12	18	0	.366	.421

7 JEFF MARQUEZ, RHP

KEVIN PATAKY

Born: Aug. 10, 1984. **B-T:** L-R. **Ht.:** 6-2. **Wt.:** 175. **Drafted:** Sacramento CC, 2004 (1st round supplemental). **Signed by:** Jeff Patterson.

Drafted with the compensation pick the Yankees received when David Wells left as a free agent after the 2003 season, Marquez has progressed steadily and was a workhorse for Trenton in 2007. He led the Eastern League with 15 wins and ranked second with 155 innings. Known as a groundball guy, Marquez works off his power 89-93 mph sinker. His fastball has as much life as any in the system, with excellent run to go with its sink. His changeup and curveball have improved to be solid-average pitches. He commands his changeup better, making it his preferred secondary pitch. He has the best pickoff move of any righthander in the system. Marquez doesn't have enough power or bite to his curveball for it to be a strikeout pitch, and he's dependent on his defense because he doesn't miss a lot of bats. He'll have to continue to refine his fastball command and have that pitch play up if his curve doesn't improve. Marquez has the chance to become a workhorse groundball machine who fills the No. 3 or 4 slot in a rotation. Because of New York's pitching depth, he'll start 2008 in Triple-A and won't challenge for a big league job until the following year.

Year	Club (League)	Class	W	L	ERA	G	GS	CG	SV	IP	H	R	ER	HR	BB	SO	AVG
2004	Yankees (GCL)	R	2	0	0.63	4	2	0	0	14	10	1	1	0	4	18	.189
	Staten Island (NYP)	A	2	4	3.02	11	11	0	0	50	51	26	17	2	20	36	.267
2005	Charleston, S.C. (SAL)	A	9	13	3.42	27	27	1	0	139	138	64	53	4	61	107	.257
2006	Yankees (GCL)	R	0	1	3.18	2	2	0	0	5	7	2	2	1	1	8	.304
	Tampa (FSL)	A	7	5	3.61	18	17	0	0	92	102	56	37	4	29	82	.279
2007	Trenton (EL)	AA	15	9	3.65	27	27	2	0	155	166	80	63	11	44	94	.270
MINOR LEAGUE TOTALS			35	32	3.40	89	86	3	0	458	474	229	173	22	159	345	.266

8 BRETT GARDNER, OF

STEVE MOORE

Born: Aug. 24, 1983. **B-T:** L-L. **Ht.:** 5-10. **Wt.:** 180. **Drafted:** Charleston, 2005 (3rd round). **Signed by:** Steve Swail.

A former walk-on who became the highest-drafted player ever from the College of Charleston, Gardner reached Triple-A in his second full pro season. After missing a month when an errant pitch broke his right hand, he finished 2007 by hitting .343 in the Arizona Fall League, leading the league with 27 runs and 16 steals. The fastest prospect in the system, Gardner rates as a 70 runner on the 20-80 scouting scale and is an adept basestealer, succeeding on 84 percent of his 116 attempts the last two seasons. He uses his speed well defensively and has above-average range in center field. Offensively, he evokes Brett Butler by bunting, slashing line drives and taking walks. Gardner has hit one homer the last two years and doesn't have the swing path or strength to hit for much more. He'll have to prove he won't be overpowered in the majors, and he needs to hang in better against lefthanders to avoid becoming a platoon player. His arm is below average yet playable in center. The Yankees believe Gardner will hit enough to be a regular and some club officials compare him to Jacoby Ellsbury, which is a stretch. Unlike Ellsbury, Gardner needs to start 2008 in Triple-A and hone his offensive game. Then he can challenge Melky Cabrera for the center-field job in the Bronx—with Austin Jackson gaining ground from behind.

Year	Club (League)	Class	AVG	G	AB	R	H	2B	3B	HR	RBI	BB	SO	SB	OBP	SLG
2005	Staten Island (NYP)	A	.284	73	282	62	80	9	1	5	32	39	49	19	.377	.376
2006	Tampa (FSL)	A	.323	63	232	46	75	12	5	0	22	43	51	30	.433	.418
	Trenton (EL)	AA	.272	55	217	41	59	4	3	0	13	27	39	28	.352	.318
2007	Trenton (EL)	AA	.300	54	203	43	61	14	5	0	17	33	32	18	.392	.419
	Scranton/W-B (IL)	AAA	.260	45	181	37	47	4	3	1	9	21	43	21	.343	.331
MINOR LEAGUE TOTALS			.289	290	1115	229	322	43	17	6	93	163	214	116	.381	.374

9 ROSS OHLENDORF, RHP

Born: Aug. 8, 1982. **B-T:** R-R. **Ht.:** 6-4. **Wt.:** 235. **Drafted:** Princeton, 2004 (4th round). **Signed by:** Greg Lonigro (Diamondbacks).

As his senior thesis at Princeton, Ohlendorf broke down the economics of baseball's draft. The key prospect in the trade that sent Randy Johnson to Arizona, Ohlendorf began his Yankees career by getting hammered as a Triple-A starter. He missed two months with back problems, but thrived once he was moved to the bullpen after returning and finished the year on the New York's playoff roster. A sinker-slider pitcher who relied on groundout as a starter, Ohlendorf became a power pitcher as a reliever. His fastball jumped at least a grade, sitting at 94 mph and topping out at 97 with excellent sink. His slider also jumped a grade, adding velocity and depth when thrown in the mid-80s. He seemed to think less and just let his pitches go more coming out of the bullpen, and that approach suits him. Lefthanders owned Ohlendorf when he was a starter because his changeup was fringy. He's added a splitter to see if that will help. His command slipped at the outset of 2007 but improved dramatically once he moved to the bullpen and hadn't been an issue in the past. Even with his improved stuff as a reliever, he still allowed a .297 opponent average in that role. Ohlendorf could be the sinkerballing setup man the Yankees haven't had since Jeff Nelson's departure as a free agent in 2000. A big league relief job is his to lose come spring training.

Year	Club (League)	Class	W	L	ERA	G	GS	CG	SV	IP	H	R	ER	HR	BB	SO	AVG
2004	Yakima (NWL)	A	2	3	2.79	7	7	0	0	29	22	14	9	1	19	28	.210
2005	South Bend (MWL)	A	11	10	4.53	27	26	1	0	157	181	97	79	10	48	144	.286
2006	Tennessee (SL)	AA	10	8	3.29	27	27	4	0	177	180	70	65	13	29	125	.271
	Tucson (PCL)	AAA	0	0	1.80	1	1	0	0	5	6	1	1	0	0	4	.300
2007	Yankees (GCL)	R	1	1	3.94	4	4	0	0	16	13	8	7	2	1	17	.206
	Scranton/W-B (IL)	AAA	3	3	5.02	21	9	0	0	66	86	39	37	7	24	48	.320
	New York (AL)	MLB	0	0	2.84	6	0	0	0	6	5	2	2	1	2	9	.208
MINOR LEAGUE TOTALS			27	25	3.95	87	74	5	0	451	488	229	198	33	121	366	.278
MAJOR LEAGUE TOTALS			0	0	2.84	6	0	0	0	6	5	2	2	1	2	9	.208

10 ANDREW BRACKMAN, RHP

Born Dec. 4, 1985. **B-T:** R-R. **Ht.:** 6-10. **Wt.:** 240. **Drafted:** North Carolina State, 2007 (1st round). **Signed by:** Steve Swail.

CARL KLINE

Brackman played both basketball and baseball at North Carolina State, averaging 7.6 points per game as a sophomore to help the Wolfpack reach the NCAA tournament's Sweet 16. After ranking as the top pitching prospect in the Cape Cod League in 2006, he gave up basketball to focus on baseball, but his junior season ended in May with an elbow injury. New York drafted him 30th overall anyway and signed him to a major league contract with a $3.35 million bonus—the biggest in franchise history for a draftee—and $4.55 million in total guarantees. With incentives, he could earn as much as $13 million. A premium athlete, Brackman has as high an upside as any player in the '07 draft class. He has reached 100 mph with his fastball, which generally sits at 94, and uses his size to drive it downhill. His filthy spike curveball can be a strikeout pitch and has the potential to be an 80 pitch on the 20-80 scouting scale. Brackman's elbow injury turned out to be a torn ligament, and he had Tommy John surgery immediately after signing in mid-August. He won't pitch in his first pro game until 2009, which is even more of a setback because he worked just 149 innings in three years at N.C. State. The Yankees are willing to wait on Brackman's upside. They believe he could become a No. 1 starter.

Year	Club (League)	Class	W	L	ERA	G	GS	CG	SV	IP	H	R	ER	HR	BB	SO	AVG
2007	Did Not Play—Injured																

11 MARK MELANCON, RHP

Born: March 28, 1985. **B-T:** R-R. **Ht.:** 6-2. **Wt.:** 215. **Drafted:** Arizona, 2006 (9th round). **Signed by:** Andy Stankiewicz.

Normally, pitchers with Melancon's track record don't get ranked so highly: ninth-round pick, seven pro innings, Tommy John surgery in November 2006, college reliever who'll be 23 before the season begins. However, he's far from ordinary, indicated in part by the $600,000 signing bonus he received in 2006. Yankees officials joined the chorus of amateur scouts who knew Melancon as a Colorado prep or as Arizona's closer and loved his off-the-charts makeup. Melancon is fearless on the mound, is a tremendous teammate off it and a monster in terms of work ethic and in the weight room. Oh, and he has two above-average pitches. Both were showing flashes of being at their pre-surgery peak in the fall, when Melancon headed up a contingent of Yankees prospects who traveled to the Dominican Republic for the organization's Latin instructional league. Melancon picked up some Spanish language skills, showed 89-92 mph velocity on his fastball (which sat at 92-95 in the past) and didn't hold back throwing his power curveball. Melancon has a max-effort delivery that New York has tried to harness in order to keep him healthy. In a best-case scenario, club officials imagine Melancon having a strong spring, starting 2008 in high Class A to get his legs under him, then getting challenged with a promotion to Double-A. With Mariano Rivera re-signed for three more seasons, Melancon has time to develop, and the Yankees see him as Rivera's eventual successor.

Year	Club (League)	Class	W	L	ERA	G	GS	CG	SV	IP	H	R	ER	HR	BB	SO	AVG
2006	Staten Island (NYP)	A	0	1	3.52	7	0	0	2	8	9	7	3	0	2	8	.281
2007	Did Not Play—Injured																
MINOR LEAGUE TOTALS			0	1	3.52	7	0	0	2	8	9	7	3	0	2	8	.281

12 HUMBERTO SANCHEZ, RHP

Born: May 28, 1983. **B-T:** R-R. **Ht.:** 6-6. **Wt.:** 230. **Drafted:** Connors State (Okla.) JC, D/F 2001 (31st round). **Signed by:** Rob Guzik/Buddy Paine (Tigers).

The most highly regarded prospect the Yankees got from the Tigers in the November 2006 Gary Sheffield trade, Sanchez joined their ranks of injured pitchers soon after being acquired. He had missed the end of 2006 with elbow inflammation and he came down with forearm tightness in spring training. Finally, in mid-April, Sanchez had Tommy John surgery. In the fall, he was sticking to his throwing program—even during his honeymoon. He was back to playing catch at the Yankees' Tampa complex in December and wasn't expected to get into game shape until mid-2008. Exactly what shape he's in will be crucial for Sanchez, who signed for $1 million as a draft-and-follow in 2002 but teased Detroit with premium stuff and a lack of durability. At his best he has has shown easy velocity, sitting in the low 90s and dialing up as high as 97. His slider was a plus pitch before he got hurt, and he had a passable changeup and curveball. His control was always erratic, as was his conditioning. He has reached as high as 40 pounds above his listed weight, and he never has pitched more than 123 innings in a minor league season. With New York's starting-pitching depth at the upper levels, Sanchez could be ticketed for a long-relief or setup role in the minors this year, both to see how he takes to relieving and to protect his arm.

Year	Club (League)	Class	W	L	ERA	G	GS	CG	SV	IP	H	R	ER	HR	BB	SO	AVG
2002	Oneonta (NYP)	A	2	2	3.62	9	9	0	0	32	29	18	13	1	21	26	.244
2003	West Michigan (MWL)	A	7	7	4.42	23	23	0	0	116	107	71	57	3	78	96	.249
2004	Lakeland (FSL)	A	7	11	5.21	19	19	3	0	105	103	67	61	9	51	115	.263
	Erie (EL)	AA	1	0	2.13	2	2	0	0	12	10	5	3	1	6	15	.213
2005	Erie (EL)	AA	3	5	5.57	15	11	0	0	64	72	42	40	10	27	65	.283
2006	Erie (EL)	AA	5	3	1.76	11	11	0	0	71	47	17	14	2	27	86	.190
	Toledo (IL)	AAA	5	3	3.86	9	9	0	0	51	50	23	22	2	20	43	.260
2007	Did Not Play—Injured																
MINOR LEAGUE TOTALS			30	31	4.16	88	84	3	0	454	418	243	210	28	230	446	.249

13 DELLIN BETANCES, RHP

Born: March 23, 1988. **B-T:** R-R. **Ht.:** 6-7. **Wt.:** 185. **Drafted:** HS—New York, 2006 (8th round). **Signed by:** Cesar Presbott/Brian Barber.

Some scouts and Yankees officials were so enamored with Betances after they signed him for $1 million in the summer of 2006, they talked about him as a future No. 1 starter. Optimism remains high regarding the New York prep product, but his prospect stock took a hit as he pitched just 25 innings at Staten Island before being shut down with forearm tightness—a telltale sign of impending elbow surgery. When asked if Betances would require Tommy John surgery, one club official merely replied, "We're confident in all our guys and in our doctors and in our rehab guys." Betances joined Melancon and 2006 second-round pick Zach McAllister at instructional league in the Dominican and hit some mid-90s with his fastball while flashing his plus curveball. Regardless of whether he'll need surgery, he must to continue to make his delivery more compact and repeatable, even though he lacks the athleticism of a similarly tall pitcher such as Andrew Brackman. Still growing into his body, Betances had little semblance of command or control last year. New York just hopes Betances is healthy enough so they can get a long look at him this season.

Year	Club (League)	Class	W	L	ERA	G	GS	CG	SV	IP	H	R	ER	HR	BB	SO	AVG
2006	Yankees (GCL)	R	0	1	1.16	7	7	0	0	23	14	5	3	1	7	27	.173
2007	Staten Island (NYP)	A	1	2	3.60	6	6	0	0	25	24	11	10	0	17	29	.255
MINOR LEAGUE TOTALS			1	3	2.42	13	13	0	0	48	38	16	13	1	24	56	.217

14 DANIEL McCUTCHEN, RHP

Born: Sept. 26, 1982. **B-T:** R-R. **Ht.:** 6-2. **Wt.:** 195. **Drafted:** Oklahoma, 2006 (13th round). **Signed by:** Mark Batchko.

The Yankees love McCutchen's competitiveness and stuff, and were willing to believe his claims about the 50-game suspension he drew for violating MLB's performance-enhancing drug policy shortly after signing in 2006. He blamed the positive test on ephedra contained in a prescription drug he took during his college career at Oklahoma. With that behind him, he ranked second in the system with 14 wins and a 2.47 ERA in 2007, and he won two starts (including the championship clincher) in the Eastern League playoffs. McCutchen pitches aggressively, which shows in his delivery at times and in his mound demeanor. The Yankees have worked to tone him down somewhat, and his velocity hardly suffered, as he still sat in the low 90s with his four-seam fastball (which hits 94) and was around 89-91 mph with his two-seamer. McCutchen's best pitch remains his overhand curveball, and he has gained confidence in his tailing, fading changeup. Some in the organization want to channel his aggressiveness into the bullpen, believing his stuff will play up as was the case with Ross Ohlendorf. But others see McCutchen as having more value as a

No. 3 or 4 starter role. He'll likely begin the year back in the Double-A rotation, with an outside shot of breaking camp in Triple-A.

Year	Club (League)	Class	W	L	ERA	G	GS	CG	SV	IP	H	R	ER	HR	BB	SO	AVG
2006	Staten Island (NYP)	A	1	0	1.13	2	2	0	0	8	4	1	1	1	1	11	.148
	Charleston, S.C. (SAL)	A	1	0	2.14	7	0	0	1	21	13	5	5	2	5	18	.186
2007	Tampa (FSL)	A	11	2	2.50	17	16	0	0	101	86	29	28	7	21	67	.236
	Trenton (EL)	AA	3	2	2.41	7	7	0	0	41	30	11	11	2	12	36	.205
MINOR LEAGUE TOTALS			16	4	2.37	33	25	0	1	171	133	46	45	12	39	132	.219

15 KEVIN WHELAN, RHP

Born: Jan. 8, 1984. **B-T:** R-R. **Ht.:** 6-0. **Wt.:** 200. **Drafted:** Texas A&M, 2005 (4th round). **Signed by:** Tim Grieve (Tigers).

Scouts don't know why Whelan is a slow starter—they just know that he is. It happened at Texas A&M, where he failed to capitalize as a junior on his strong 2004 Cape Cod League showing and fell from first-round consideration down to the fourth round. While his results were solid early last season—his first in the Yankees system since coming over in the Gary Sheffield trade with Detroit in November 2006—his stuff was not as sharp. He was working with a high-80s fastball and decent splitter as a reliever, then was sent down to high Class A to get some work starting. New York hoped to build up his arm strength and work on his breaking ball, a decent slider that remains his third pitch. When he came back to Double-A, it took Whelan a while to get going but he eventually put it all together and was throwing 92-94 mph with a plus-plus splitter, one he could bury or throw in the strike zone. That Whelan could be in the majors as soon as 2008, but the former catcher just converted to pitching full-time in 2005 and likely will need another year in the minors. He still seeks consistency and is learning nuances of the game such as holding runners, who take advantage of his slow delivery to the plate. Basestealers went 19-for-20 against him last year. Whelan left the Arizona Fall League with a sore arm but was expected to be fully healthy by spring training.

Year	Club (League)	Class	W	L	ERA	G	GS	CG	SV	IP	H	R	ER	HR	BB	SO	AVG
2005	Oneonta (NYP)	A	1	1	2.25	11	0	0	4	12	2	4	3	1	6	19	.051
	West Michigan (MWL)	A	0	0	0.73	14	0	0	11	12	4	1	1	0	2	22	.098
2006	Lakeland (FSL)	A	4	1	2.67	51	0	0	27	54	33	20	16	1	29	69	.178
2007	Tampa (FSL)	A	2	0	1.93	7	7	0	0	28	11	6	6	2	12	28	.117
	Trenton (EL)	AA	4	2	2.98	31	1	0	4	54	34	18	18	2	42	68	.180
MINOR LEAGUE TOTALS			11	4	2.46	114	8	0	46	160	84	49	44	6	91	206	.153

16 CARMEN ANGELINI, SS

Born: Sept. 22, 1988. **B-T:** R-R **Ht.:** 6-1 **Wt.:** 185. **Drafted:** HS—Lake Charles, La., 2007 (10th round). **Signed by:** Steve Boros/Tim Kelly.

The Yankees are betting $1 million—the highest bonus ever for a 10th-round pick who wasn't a draft-and-follow—that Angelini will wind up being the best Louisiana Mr. Baseball out of Barbe High (Lake Charles) in the last few years. The other winners are a Who's Who list of flameouts, including Joe Lawrence (a first-rounder who had 150 big league at-bats with the Blue Jays in 2002), Nick Bourgeois (an ex-Phillies minor leaguer whose career peaked at Tulane) and Austin Nagle (a former Athletics farmhand). The Yankees wooed Angelini away from his Rice commitment with the bonus and, more subtly, by bringing him to Yankee Stadium during the Subway Series with the Mets and working him out alongside Alex Rodriguez and Derek Jeter. Angelini could be the homegrown shortstop to eventually replace Jeter, who will be 34 this season. Scouts like Angelini's range and arm for the position, and the Yankees love his hands, which they believe will work for him in the field and at the plate. At his best, he's a line-drive machine with gap power to all fields and good plate discipline, particularly for a player his age. He's also a plus runner, covering 60 yards in 6.7 seconds. Other teams who scouted Angelini as an amateur weren't as sold on his bat as New York is, liking Angelini more for his energy and athleticism and profiling him more as a utility player. He's polished enough to be able to earn a spot as a starting shortstop in low Class A this year.

Year	Club (League)	Class	AVG	G	AB	R	H	2B	3B	HR	RBI	BB	SO	SB	OBP	SLG
2007	Yankees (GCL)	R	.000	1	1	0	0	0	0	0	0	0	1	0	.000	.000
MINOR LEAGUE TOTALS			.000	1	1	0	0	0	0	0	0	0	1	0	.000	.000

17 GEORGE KONTOS, RHP

Born: June 12, 1985. **B-T:** R-R. **Ht.:** 6-3. **Wt.:** 215. **Drafted:** Northwestern, 2006 (5th round). **Signed by:** Steve Lemke.

Kontos spent eight weeks on the disabled list from mid-April to mid-June, though that stint likely had less to do with injury and more with his arrest in Tampa on April 19. He was charged with trespassing and obstruction after he failed to leave the Green Iguana Bar & Grill when it was closing. Kontos was inconsistent after he came back, a problem that plagued him throughout his college career at Northwestern, where his stuff rarely produced good results. His command was shaky, he gave up too many homers and he relied too much on his plus slider. It's one of the system's best sliders, a two-plane pitch with depth and tilt that he throws in the low 80s. Kontos had a good offseason, making progress with his 90-93 mph sinker and solid changeup in Hawaii Winter Baseball. While he was there, the Yankees made him use his changeup as many as 15 times a game, and now it has more depth and more separation from his fastball than in the past. He also worked on commanding his fastball and solid-average curve, using his slider only sparingly. Kontos still needs to mature and let bad breaks go rather than letting them eat him up. He has strikeout stuff and could take off if he harnesses his sinker. He's headed for Double-A and has a No. 3 starter's ceiling, but he has a long track record of not living up to expectations.

Year	Club (League)	Class	W	L	ERA	G	GS	CG	SV	IP	H	R	ER	HR	BB	SO	AVG
2006	Staten Island (NYP)	A	7	3	2.64	14	14	0	0	78	64	25	23	3	19	82	.227
2007	Tampa (FSL)	A	4	6	4.02	19	17	0	0	94	95	51	42	15	30	101	.260
MINOR LEAGUE TOTALS			11	9	3.39	33	31	0	0	172	159	76	65	18	49	183	.246

18 IVAN NOVA, RHP

Born: January 12, 1987. **B-T:** R-R. **Ht.:** 6-4. **Wt.:** 210. **Signed:** Dominican Republic, 2005. **Signed by:** Victor Mata/Carlos Rios.

While Nova is moving more slowly than the Yankees expect their star Latin American players to develop, he has continued to open eyes with his pure stuff and projectable body. He'll show three plus pitches at times but was far too hittable in low Class A. He began 2007 in extended spring training to keep his workload down, went 4-2, 1.75 in his first six starts, then fell into a 2-6, 6.82 tailspin the rest of the way. Nova must get stronger to maintain his stuff, and he also needs to begin showing better aptitude and ability to make in-game adjustments. His pitches don't need much help, as his fastball sits at 90-94 mph and he has a solid-average curveball and changeup as well. But he doesn't trust his secondary stuff and throws a lot of hittable 0-2 pitches, indicating his lack of mound savvy. Now 21, Nova is a prime breakout candidate for 2008, when he'll repeat low Class A.

Year	Club (League)	Class	W	L	ERA	G	GS	CG	SV	IP	H	R	ER	HR	BB	SO	AVG
2005	Yankees1 (DSL)	R	0	1	2.29	11	7	0	0	39	29	11	10	2	11	38	.200
2006	Yankees (GCL)	R	3	0	2.72	10	5	0	1	43	36	13	13	5	7	36	.229
2007	Charleston, S.C. (SAL)	A	6	8	4.98	21	21	0	0	99	121	64	55	8	31	54	.306
MINOR LEAGUE TOTALS			9	9	3.86	42	33	0	1	181	186	88	78	15	49	128	.266

19 COLLIN CURTIS, OF

Born: Feb. 1, 1985. **B-T:** L-L. **Ht.:** 6-0. **Wt.:** 190. **Drafted:** Arizona State, 2006. **Signed by:** Andy Stankiewicz.

One Yankees official laments that the organization misses out on players such as Dustin Pedroia because they don't profile. While Pedroia's tools didn't scream "big leaguer," it's apparent now that scouts underestimated him. Curtis, Pedroia's teammate at Arizona State, has a somewhat similar resume, though scouts liked Curtis more as an amateur because of his well-rounded tools. However, he doesn't profile well either. Curtis played primarily left field in 2007 and is a better defensive fit there with his average speed, range and arm, but he lacks corner-outfield power. His bat would play better in center field, though he's just an adequate defender there. New York rates him as a plus hitter and pro scouts like his approach, but he wasn't ready for Double-A last season. A cancer survivor who was diagnosed with testicular cancer in 1999, Curtis has tremendous makeup that makes the Yankees confident he'll make the adjustments needed when he repeats Double-A in 2008. He looks like a fourth outfielder.

Year	Club (League)	Class	AVG	G	AB	R	H	2B	3B	HR	RBI	BB	SO	SB	OBP	SLG
2006	Yankees (GCL)	R	.500	3	8	3	4	2	0	1	4	1	0	1	.600	1.125
	Staten Island (NYP)	A	.302	44	159	25	48	9	2	1	18	12	19	4	.362	.403
2007	Tampa (FSL)	A	.298	65	245	37	73	9	2	5	26	29	43	4	.378	.412
	Trenton (EL)	AA	.242	61	240	32	58	10	1	3	15	17	47	1	.298	.329
MINOR LEAGUE TOTALS			.281	173	652	97	183	30	5	10	63	59	109	10	.348	.388

20 JAIRO HEREDIA, RHP

Born: Oct. 8, 1989. **B-T:** R-R **Ht.:** 6-1 **Wt.:** 190. **Signed:** Dominican Republic, 2006. **Signed by:** Victor Mata/Carlos Rios.

The Yankees have remained aggressive internationally throughout this decade, even when they were conservative in the draft in the early part. Of the players in New York's 2006 Dominican signing class, Heredia is off to the fastest start. An easy indication of the Yankees' confidence in a young Latin player is whether they hold him back to play in the Rookie-level Dominican Summer League, and both Heredia and Jesus Montero skipped that level in 2007. So did Robinson Cano and Mariano Rivera in past years. Heredia has a quick, live arm that already produces 90-92 mph four-seam fastballs. He has shown some feel for pitching, especially for varying his fastball, that's uncanny for his age. His curveball remains slurvy but has plus potential, and he worked hard in the Dominican instructional league to learn a changeup as well as English. A strong spring will enable Heredia to jump straight to low Class A.

Year	Club (League)	Class	W	L	ERA	G	GS	CG	SV	IP	H	R	ER	HR	BB	SO	AVG
2007	Yankees (GCL)	R	2	2	2.72	11	6	0	0	46	39	15	14	4	11	52	.228
MINOR LEAGUE TOTALS			2	2	2.72	11	6	0	0	46	39	15	14	4	11	52	.228

21 JUAN MIRANDA, 1B

Born: April 25, 1983. **B-T:** L-L. **Ht.:** 6-0 **Wt.:** 220. **Signed:** Cuba, 2006. **Signed by:** Ramon Valdivia.

The Yankees signed Miranda to a four-year, $4 million contract in 2006, when the Cuban national was made a free agent after two years in limbo. While the Yankees list him with an April 1983 birthdate, several Cuban sources show a 1981 birthdate (some say March, some say April). Whether he's 24 or 26, Miranda is part of New York's first-base picture, which has been cloudy since Jason Giambi's became a defensive liability. Miranda isn't likely to win any Gold Gloves either—his stocky body and fringy defense evoke Tino Martinez, the last Yankee to start 100 games in a season at first base. He's a fringy runner as well, but Miranda can hit. While his swing can get long, which leads to strikeouts, he's shown a feel for the barrel of the bat and raw above-average power to all fields. He was particularly impressive in the Arizona Fall League, where he was patient and showed prodigious power. He doesn't hit lefthanders too well (.223 with two homers in 112 at-bats in 2007), so Miranda and 28-year-old rookie Shelley Duncan could form New York's first-base platoon of the near future, particularly after Giambi's contract expires following 2008.

Year	Club (League)	Class	AVG	G	AB	R	H	2B	3B	HR	RBI	BB	SO	SB	OBP	SLG
2007	Tampa (FSL)	A	.264	67	250	35	66	17	3	9	50	29	60	1	.348	.464
	Trenton (EL)	AA	.265	55	196	29	52	17	2	7	46	23	46	0	.352	.480
MINOR LEAGUE TOTALS			.265	122	446	64	118	34	5	16	96	52	106	1	.350	.471

22 AUSTIN ROMINE, C

Born: Nov. 22, 1988. **B-T:** R-R **Ht.:** 6-1 **Wt.:** 195. **Drafted:** HS—El Toro, Calif., 2007 (2nd round). **Signed by:** David Keith.

The sons of former big leaguer Kevin Romine were both selected on the first day of the 2007 draft. Older brother Andrew helped lead Arizona State to the 2005 and 2007 College World Series as a shortstop and went in the fifth round to the Angels. Younger brother Austin is the better prospect, whether one believes the scouting consensus in southern California or the Yankees' reports. The two accounts differ. New York signed him for $500,000 as a second-round because it believes he has significant offensive potential, with at least solid-average power to the gaps and perhaps above-average home run juice. Most scouts who saw him in showcases or in high school thought his athleticism and defensive tools were better than his bat, admitting he was raw as a receiver but gushing over his plus-plus arm strength that helped Romine occasionally serve as a high school closer. Scouts have recorded his pop times to second base as quick as 1.78 seconds. He has below-average speed but runs decently for a catcher. A ligament tear in Romine's left thumb ended his prep catching career early—he just pitched after the injury—so it was good for Romine to get back on the field in August. The Yankees sent him to their September minicamp and Dominican instructional program in November as well. The fall work should pave the way for Romine to start next season in low Class A, as he's more advanced and older than Jesus Montero, though Montero remains the better prospect.

Year	Club (League)	Class	AVG	G	AB	R	H	2B	3B	HR	RBI	BB	SO	SB	OBP	SLG
2007	Yankees (GCL)	R	.500	1	2	2	1	1	0	0	1	1	1	0	.667	1.000
MINOR LEAGUE TOTALS			.500	1	2	2	1	1	0	0	1	1	1	0	.667	1.000

23 FRANCISCO CERVELLI, C

Born: March 6, 1986. **B-T:** R-R **Ht.:** 6-1 **Wt.:** 170. **Signed:** Venezuela, 2003. **Signed by:** Hector Rincones.

Organizations like to have depth up the middle in the minors. While the Yankees lack second basemen and shortstops (other than Carmen Angelini), they like their center fielders and catchers. Cervelli is by far the closest to the majors of the three catchers ranked on this Top 30 list, but he has the lowest ceiling because he lacks offensive upside. He skipped a level last year and held his own in high Class A until he was sidelined in August after hurting his knee in a home-plate collision. He returned to play winter ball in Venezuela. Cervelli evokes former Yankees prospect Dioner Navarro, who now starts for the Rays, because his above-average catch-and-throw skills are ahead of his bat at this stage of his career. He led the FSL by throwing out 41 percent of basestealers, has a feel for handling pitchers and impressed scouts with his toughness and ability to grind through a season. While he has a good swing, he lacks the premium bat speed or strength to hit for power. The ball doesn't jump off his bat. He does draw some walks, but more advanced pitchers will be more likely to challenge him without fear of reprisal. He's a below-average runner. Cervelli profiles as a backup unless he provides more offensive production. Added to the 40-man roster in November, he's likely to jump to Double-A in 2008 and should soon become Jorge Posada's understudy.

Year	Club (League)	Class	AVG	G	AB	R	H	2B	3B	HR	RBI	BB	SO	SB	OBP	SLG
2003	Yankees1 (DSL)	R	.239	52	155	14	37	4	1	0	14	24	25	0	.379	.277
2004	Yankees1 (DSL)	R	.216	40	88	14	19	2	0	1	14	19	18	1	.392	.273
2005	Yankees (GCL)	R	.190	24	58	10	11	2	0	1	9	8	13	1	.300	.276
2006	Staten Island (NYP)	A	.309	42	136	21	42	10	0	2	16	13	30	0	.397	.426
2007	Tampa (FSL)	A	.279	89	290	34	81	24	2	2	32	36	59	4	.387	.397
MINOR LEAGUE TOTALS			.261	247	727	93	190	42	3	6	85	100	145	6	.381	.352

24 DAVID ROBERTSON, RHP

Born: April 9, 1985. **B-T:** R-R **Ht.:** 5-11 **Wt.:** 180. **Drafted:** Alabama, 2006 (17th round). **Signed by:** D.J. Svihlik/Jeff Patterson.

The Yankees have a plethora of middle-relief prospects coming through the system. Robertson is similar to J. Brent Cox, who was close to the big leagues before 2007 Tommy John surgery caused him to miss the season, and Robertson ranks higher here because he has a better fastball and two above-average breaking balls. Robertson, whose older brother Connor reached the majors with the Athletics last year, was a closer at Alabama and signed as a draft-eligible sophomore after starring in the Cape Cod League in 2006. New York drafted him in the 17th round that June, liked what it saw on the Cape and gave him a $200,000 bonus. In his pro debut last year. Robertson dazzled with a curveball that he didn't throw in college. It's a plus downer with bite, angle and depth, and he can throw it for strikes or bury it. His slider already was a plus pitch, and his 90-92 mph fastball has natural cut action on it. Despite his small frame, he makes his mistakes down in the strike zone and has yet to give up a homer in pro ball. Robertson proved durable in his first pro season and could challenge for a big league role after finishing last year in Double-A. His size seems to be the only reason scouts don't project him as a future closer.

Year	Club (League)	Class	W	L	ERA	G	GS	CG	SV	IP	H	R	ER	HR	BB	SO	AVG
2007	Charleston, S.C. (SAL)	A	5	2	0.77	24	0	0	3	47	25	5	4	0	15	67	.151
	Tampa (FSL)	A	3	1	1.08	18	0	0	1	33	18	6	4	0	15	37	.159
	Trenton (EL)	AA	0	0	2.25	2	0	0	0	4	2	1	1	0	2	9	.143
MINOR LEAGUE TOTALS			8	3	0.96	44	0	0	4	84	45	12	9	0	32	113	.154

25 MIKE DUNN, LHP

Born: Mary 23, 1985. **B-T:** L-L. **Ht.:** 6-1 **Wt.:** 185. **Drafted:** CC of Southern Nevada, D/F 2004 (33rd round). **Signed by:** Jeff Patterson.

Dunn was a two-way player in junior college, and the Yankees knew he had ability to do both when they signed him away from Texas A&M as a draft-and-follow in 2005. When he hit .160 over parts of two seasons as an outfielder, they put him on the mound in mid-2006. A year later, he has emerged as their top lefthanded pitching prospect. Granted, it's an uninspiring lot that includes Chase Wright, a No. 5 starter at best; hard-throwing Angel Reyes, who disappointed New York with his poor command and lack of toughness last season; and sleeper Edgar Soto, a relief candidate with big stuff but poor command. Dunn relies—perhaps too much—on his plus slider, which he throws with low-80s velocity and pretty good depth. He's athletic and repeats his delivery well, giving him solid control of his 88-92 mph fastball, which touches 94. Befitting a converted position player, he's still working to deepen his repertoire, toying with a cutter and a changeup. The changeup works when he finishes off the pitch, uses all his fingers and keeps it low and slow, the way pitching coordinator Nardi Contreras wants it. Dunn will try to do all that and remain a starter as part of the high Class A rotation this year.

Year	Club (League)	Class	AVG	G	AB	R	H	2B	3B	HR	RBI	BB	SO	SB	OBP	SLG
2005	Yankees (GCL)	R	.194	24	62	4	12	2	2	0	9	8	16	0	.284	.290
	Tampa (FSL)	A	.167	28	90	8	15	5	0	0	6	11	28	2	.265	.222
2006	Charleston (SAL)	A	.086	14	35	7	3	2	0	0	2	8	13	1	.256	.143
MINOR LEAGUE TOTALS			.160	66	187	19	30	9	2	0	17	27	57	3	.269	.230

Year	Club (League)	Class	W	L	ERA	G	GS	CG	SV	IP	H	R	ER	HR	BB	SO	AVG
2006	Yankees (GCL)	R	3	0	0.73	11	0	0	4	24	13	2	2	0	9	26	.155
	Staten Island (NYP)	A	0	0	5.68	3	0	0	0	6	3	6	4	0	7	7	.125
2007	Charleston, S.C. (SAL)	A	12	5	3.42	27	27	0	0	144	136	69	55	14	45	138	.253
MINOR LEAGUE TOTALS			15	5	3.13	41	27	0	4	175	152	77	61	14	61	171	.235

26 J. BRENT COX, RHP

Born: May 13, 1984. **B-T:** L-R **Ht.:** 6-3 **Wt.:** 205. **Drafted:** Texas, 2005 (2nd round). **Signed by:** Steve Boros.

When Cox came to the Yankees fresh off being the closer for Texas' 2005 College World Series champions, Yankees fans jumped on his bandwagon as the replacement for Mariano Rivera. However, Cox always has profiled better as a setup man, and after losing the 2007 season to Tommy John surgery, he has fallen back into a large pack of New York middle-relief candidates. Cox's strong suits long have been his plus slider and his command of that pitch and his fastball. His heater touches 92 but sits at 88-89 mph with good sinking life. His fearlessness and willingness to throw strikes have long endeared him to coaches and scouts alike. Coming back from Tommy John surgery could be tough initially for Cox, because command is usually the last thing to return and he needs it to thrive. He was throwing light bullpens in Tampa in December at 30-foot distances, trying to build up arm strength. He wasn't expected to be ready for spring training and probably won't see game action until midsummer. If he adds velocity like a lot of Tommy John survivors have, that will be a bonus.

Year	Club (League)	Class	W	L	ERA	G	GS	CG	SV	IP	H	R	ER	HR	BB	SO	AVG
2005	Tampa (FSL)	A	1	2	2.60	16	0	0	0	28	20	9	8	1	5	27	.206
2006	Trenton (EL)	AA	6	2	1.75	41	0	0	3	77	54	21	15	2	24	60	.196
2007	Did Not Play—Injured																
MINOR LEAGUE TOTALS			7	4	1.98	57	0	0	3	105	74	30	23	3	29	87	.199

27 MITCH HILLIGOSS, 3B/SS

Born: June 17, 1985. **B-T:** L-R **Ht.:** 6-1 **Wt.:** 195. **Drafted:** Purdue, 2006 (6th round). **Signed by:** Mike Gibbons/Tim Kelly.

Hilligoss set a low Class A South Atlantic League record with a 38-game hitting streak in 2007. He's another Yankees prospect without at toolsy profile, but he's such a good hitter that he'll likely reach the big leagues. He had an excellent track record at Purdue, where he won the Big 10 Conference batting title (.404) in 2005 and finished second (.386) in 2006. A dead low-ball hitter, Hilligoss has excellent plate coverage and can drive any pitch below the thigh to all fields, spraying line drives from pole to pole. His approach keeps him from hitting for power, and his confidence in his hitting ability keeps his walk totals low, but it also contributes to his excellent two-strike approach and sheer volume of hits—he led the SAL with 161. Hilligoss is a grinder with excellent makeup, as evidenced by his teammates' delighted reactions every time he extended his hitting streak. He cut across all social groups in the Charleston clubhouse to become a team leader. Defensively, he fits best at third base, where his hands and arm are average or a tick above. He played shortstop at season's end, but lacks the range for the position. With his lefthanded bat and ability to play anywhere in the infield, he could be a useful utility player. If everything comes together, he could be a regular along the lines of Adam Kennedy. Hilligoss could skip a level up to Double-A with a strong spring training.

Year	Club (League)	Class	AVG	G	AB	R	H	2B	3B	HR	RBI	BB	SO	SB	OBP	SLG
2006	Staten Island (NYP)	A	.292	67	267	40	78	8	1	2	36	24	47	12	.357	.352
2007	Charleston, S.C. (SAL)	A	.310	128	520	83	161	35	4	4	53	33	65	35	.352	.415
MINOR LEAGUE TOTALS			.304	195	787	123	239	43	5	6	89	57	112	47	.354	.394

28 SCOTT PATTERSON, RHP

Born: June 20, 1979. **B-T:** R-R **Ht.:** 6-6 **Wt.:** 230. **Signed:** Atlantic League (independent), 2006. **Signed by:** Troy Caradonna.

New York has two pitchers on its 40-man roster whom it signed out of independent leagues. Both Patterson and Edward Ramirez put up video-game numbers in the minors, and while Ramirez reached the majors, the Yankees believe Patterson has more upside. A West Virginia native who attended NCAA Division II West Virginia State, he spent four years in the independent Frontier League and another with the indy Atlantic League's homeless Barnstormers before the Yankees discovered and signed him. Patterson has drawn some comparisons to Adam Wainwright because he's tall and lanky, drives his low-90s fastball downhill and owns a big, low-70s curveball. While scouts would love to see him throw his curve with more power, it has deception and he commands it well, spotting it all over the strike zone or burying it as a chase pitch. Patterson's deceptive high release point adds to his overall package. A six-year minor league free agent at season's end, he re-signed with New York and was added to the 40-man roster in November after not giving up a run in his first 13 outings in the Venezuelan Winter League. He'll contend for a big league middle-relief role in the spring.

Year	Club (League)	Class	W	L	ERA	G	GS	CG	SV	IP	H	R	ER	HR	BB	SO	AVG
2002	Gateway (Fron)	IND	2	2	3.40	13	2	1	1	42	33	18	16	4	13	51	.208
2003	Gateway (Fron)	IND	8	3	2.92	20	18	3	0	129	119	45	42	6	24	120	.242
2004	Gateway (Fron)	IND	11	2	4.30	20	20	1	0	129	127	67	62	18	31	120	.259
2005	Gateway (Fron)	IND	1	1	1.65	19	0	0	9	27	21	5	5	4	8	41	.210
	Lancaster (Atl)	IND	4	2	4.76	28	9	0	6	73	85	40	39	16	20	62	.289
2006	Trenton (EL)	AA	0	1	2.33	26	0	0	1	38	26	11	10	6	8	44	.186
2007	Trenton (EL)	AA	4	2	1.09	43	3	0	2	74	45	13	9	1	15	91	.170
	Scranton/W-B (IL)	AAA	0	0	0.00	1	0	0	0	3	0	0	0	0	0	1	.000
MINOR LEAGUE TOTALS			4	3	1.47	70	3	0	3	116	71	24	19	7	23	136	.171

29 EDWAR RAMIREZ, RHP

Born: March 28, 1981. **B-T:** R-R **Ht.:** 6-3 **Wt.:** 150. **Signed:** Dominican Republic, 2001. **Signed by:** Leo Perez (Angels).

Ramirez' story would have been outstanding if he'd never reached the majors. Discarded by the Angels in spring training in 2004, he pitched in two independent leagues before the Yankees noted his gaudy numbers in the independent league United League in 2006. Scout Mark Batchko, working on a tip from pro scouting assistant John Coppolella (now with the Braves), drove six hours to see Ramirez pitch and kindly asked the Edinburg manager to use Ramirez. Based on that one look—during which Batchko saw a major league changeup—the Yankees signed him. Ramirez has dominated ever since, at least until he got to the majors. Former manager Joe Torre used him erratically, and while he continued to pile up strikeouts, Ramirez made too many mistakes and got hit hard. He proved that he can fool big league hitters with his top-of-the-scale changeup, and he can locate it well and vary the velocity as need. He's liable to throw three in a row if hitters don't catch on. The rest of his package, however, is fringy, starting with a scrawny frame that has scouts doubting his durability over a full big league season. His 90-91 mph fastball lacks life. His below-average slider must improve if he's to become anything more than a sixth-inning long man—and a great story.

Year	Club (League)	Class	W	L	ERA	G	GS	CG	SV	IP	H	R	ER	HR	BB	SO	AVG
2002	Angels (AZL)	R	2	5	3.69	13	7	0	0	46	47	22	19	1	13	45	.263
	Provo (Pio)	R	1	0	9.31	2	1	0	0	9	14	10	10	0	4	4	.368
2003	Rancho Cucamonga (Cal)	A	0	2	8.10	4	4	0	0	16	29	16	15	5	7	9	.387
	Cedar Rapids (MWL)	A	1	1	3.32	6	1	0	0	19	17	7	7	2	8	15	.233
2005	Pensacola (Cen)	IND	2	2	1.45	43	0	0	11	62	37	12	10	4	15	93	.170
	Salt Lake (PCL)	AAA	0	0	0.00	1	0	0	0	2	0	0	0	0	0	2	.000
2006	Edinburg (UL)	IND	1	0	1.07	25	0	0	0	25	14	6	3	2	10	46	.163
	Tampa (FSL)	A	4	1	1.17	19	0	0	3	30	14	4	4	0	6	47	.133
2007	Trenton (EL)	AA	3	0	0.54	9	0	0	1	16	6	1	1	1	8	33	.103
	Scranton/W-B (IL)	AAA	1	0	0.90	25	0	0	6	40	20	4	4	0	14	69	.149
	New York (AL)	MLB	1	1	8.14	21	0	0	1	21	24	19	19	6	14	31	.286
MINOR LEAGUE TOTALS			12	9	2.98	79	13	0	10	181	147	64	60	9	60	224	.220
MAJOR LEAGUE TOTALS			1	1	8.14	21	0	0	1	21	24	19	19	6	14	31	.286

30 ZACH McALLISTER, RHP

Born: Dec. 8, 1987. **B-T:** R-R **Ht.:** 6-5 **Wt.:** 230. **Drafted:** HS—Chillicothe, Ill., 2006 (3rd round). **Signed by:** Steve Lemke.

McAllister was one of the American farmhands the Yankees took to instructional league in the Dominican Republic in November, a group ranging from high-profile prospects such as Mark Melancon and Austin Romine to rehabbing righthander Lance Pendleton. McAllister, whose father Steve is a crosschecker for the Diamondbacks, needed the extra work because the Yankees have changed him since drafting him in the third round in 2006. They've raised his arm slot to make him more of a power pitcher, and added a curveball while taking away his slider. The curve didn't take, however, and in the fall New York switched him back to a slider. His four-seam fastball reaches the low 90s and his two-seamer has become more consistent with its sink and 89-91 mph velocity. He also has taken to a changeup. The Yankees project that McAllister will throw harder in the future and become a three-pitch workhorse. After ranking third in the short-season New York-Penn League with 75 strikeouts in 71 innings, he'll help anchor the low Class A rotation this year.

Year	Club (League)	Class	W	L	ERA	G	GS	CG	SV	IP	H	R	ER	HR	BB	SO	AVG
2006	Yankees (GCL)	R	5	2	3.09	11	1	0	0	35	35	14	12	1	12	28	.259
2007	Staten Island (NYP)	A	4	6	5.17	16	15	0	0	71	80	42	41	3	28	75	.286
MINOR LEAGUE TOTALS			9	8	4.49	27	16	0	0	106	115	56	53	4	40	103	.277

Oakland Athletics

BY CHRIS KLINE

In 2006, the Athletics again showed they could win with different players and different styles, taking the American League West and advancing to the AL Championship Series. It was their eighth straight winning season and fifth playoff trip during the stretch.

So even after losing Barry Zito, Frank Thomas and Jay Payton as free agents last offseason and getting rid of manager Ken Macha, Oakland was banking on a core of players led by Joe Blanton, Eric Chavez, Dan Haren, Huston Street and Nick Swisher to make yet another playoff push in 2007.

That never happened.

Injuries depleted the club in spring training and never stopped. A's players combined to miss 1,259 games. Losing Street was the most significant blow, crippling a bullpen that converted just 59 percent of save opportunities and tied for the AL lead in blown saves. Oakland went 76-86 and finished in third place, 18 games behind the Angels.

The A's were forced to turn to their farm system to fill holes. Nine rookies made their major league debuts. Most notable among them were first baseman Daric Barton, outfielder Travis Buck and catcher Kurt Suzuki, all of whom have futures as starters for Oakland.

The problem, however, is that the farm system isn't nearly as deep as it once was, containing complementary players rather than blue-chip prospects. That left general manager Billy Beane contemplating the future direction of his ballclub. Beane vowed either to make a full effort to contend or undertake a massive rebuilding, saying that he wouldn't sit in the middle and accept mediocrity.

Quality pitching at affordable prices is baseball's most precious commodity, yet the A's spent the Winter Meetings exploring the possibility of dealing Blanton, Haren or Street to restock the system.

Oakland's bright spot in the minors in 2007 was the continued success of its Triple-A Sacramento affiliate. The only A's farm club with a winning record, the River Cats went 84-60 before winning the Pacific Coast League playoffs and the Bricktown Showdown. Barton hit .550 with four homers in the PCL's first round before being called up to Oakland.

The A's haven't drafted well in recent years. After emphasizing high school pitchers in 2005-06, they went back to their previous focus on college players who have a chance to move quickly. Their first 14

Eric Chavez was just one of a host of A's who missed significant time in 2007

TOP 30 PROSPECTS

1. Daric Barton, 1b	16. Matt Sulentic, of
2. Trevor Cahill, rhp	17. Kevin Melillo, 2b
3. James Simmons, rhp	18. Vin Mazzaro, rhp
4. Henry Rodriguez, rhp	19. Sam Demel, rhp
5. Andrew Bailey, rhp	20. Dan Meyer, lhp
6. Corey Brown, of	21. Jeff Baisley, 3b
7. Landon Powell, c	22. Andrew Carignan, rhp
8. Jermaine Mitchell, of	23. Brad Kilby, lhp
9. Javier Herrera, of	24. Cliff Pennington, ss
10. Sean Doolittle, 1b	25. Travis Banwart, rhp
11. Jerry Blevins, lhp	26. Josh Horton, ss
12. Grant Desme, of	27. Anthony Recker, c
13. Gregorio Petit, ss/2b	28. Graham Godfrey, rhp
14. Justin Sellers, 2b/ss	29. Fernando Hernandez, rhp
15. Richie Robnett, of	30. Craig Italiano, rhp

picks were collegians and they didn't sign a single high schooler. Righthanders James Simmons (first round), Sam Demel (third) and Andrew Carignan (fifth) all have a chance to join the big league staff within two years.

If Oakland does decide to go the rebuilding route, it probably will tie its return to contention to the planned opening of its new ballpark for the 2011 season. Cisco Field will contain 32,000 seats and be located in Fremont, about 20 miles south of the club's current McAfee Coliseum site.

General Manager: Billy Beane. **Farm Director:** Keith Lieppman. **Scouting Director:** Eric Kubota.

Class	Team	League	W	L	PCT	Finish*	Manager	Affiliated
Majors	Oakland	American	76	86	.469	9th (14)	Bob Geren	—
Triple-A	Sacramento River Cats	Pacific Coast	84	60	.583	2nd (16)^	Tony DeFrancesco	2000
Double-A	Midland RockHounds	Texas	67	70	.489	5th (8)	Todd Steverson	1999
High A	Stockton Ports	California	64	76	.457	9th (10)	Darren Bush	2005
Low A	Kane County Cougars	Midwest	63	76	.453	10th (14)	Aaron Nieckula	2003
Short-season	Vancouver Canadians	Northwest	37	38	.493	2nd (8)	Rick Magnante	1979
Rookie	AZL Athletics	Arizona	25	31	.446	7th (9)	Ruben Escalera	1988
Overall 2007 Minor League Record			340	351	.492	17th		

*Finish in overall standings (No. of teams in league) ^League champion

LAST YEAR'S TOP 30

Player, Pos.		Status
1.	Travis Buck, of	Majors
2.	Daric Barton, 1b	No. 1
3.	Kurt Suzuki, c	Majors
4.	Matt Sulentic, of	No. 16
5.	Jermaine Mitchell, of	No. 8
6.	Javier Herrera, of	No. 9
7.	Jason Windsor, rhp	Dropped out
8.	Marcus McBeth, rhp	(Reds)
9.	Justin Sellers, ss	No. 14
10.	Trevor Cahill, rhp	No. 2
11.	Richie Robnett, of	No. 15
12.	Cliff Pennington, ss	No. 24
13.	Kevin Melillo, 2b	No. 17
14.	Shane Komine, rhp	Dropped out
15.	Jared Lansford, rhp	Dropped out
16.	Danny Putnam, of	Dropped out
17.	Myron Leslie, 3b/of	Dropped out
18.	Vin Mazzaro, rhp	No. 18
19.	Ryan Goleski, of	(Indians)
20.	Landon Powell, c	No. 7
21.	Jeff Baisley, 3b	No. 21
22.	Craig Italiano, rhp	No. 30
23.	Anthony Recker, c	No. 27
24.	Mike Mitchell, rhp	Dropped out
25.	Jason Ray, rhp	Dropped out
26.	Ryan Webb, rhp	Dropped out
27.	Ben Jukich, lhp	(Reds)
28.	Andrew Bailey, rhp	No. 5
29.	Chad Lee, rhp	Dropped out
30.	Larry Cobb, 2b/of	Dropped out

BEST TOOLS

Best Hitter for Average	Daric Barton
Best Power Hitter	Richie Robnett
Best Strike-Zone Discipline	Daric Barton
Fastest Baserunner	Jermaine Mitchell
Best Athlete	Corey Brown
Best Fastball	Henry Rodriguez
Best Curveball	Trevor Cahill
Best Slider	Sam Demel
Best Changeup	James Simmons
Best Control	James Simmons
Best Defensive Catcher	Landon Powell
Best Defensive Infielder	Gregorio Petit
Best Infield Arm	Gregorio Petit
Best Defensive Outfielder	Javier Herrera
Best Outfield Arm	Javier Herrera

PROJECTED 2011 LINEUP

Catcher	Kurt Suzuki
First Base	Nick Swisher
Second Base	Mark Ellis
Third Base	Eric Chavez
Shortstop	Bobby Crosby
Left Field	Travis Buck
Center Field	Corey Brown
Right Field	Richie Robnett
Designated Hitter	Daric Barton
No. 1 Starter	Dan Haren
No. 2 Starter	Rich Harden
No. 3 Starter	Joe Blanton
No. 4 Starter	Trevor Cahill
No. 5 Starter	James Simmons
Closer	Huston Street

TOP PROSPECTS OF THE DECADE

Year	Player, Pos.	2007 Org.
1998	Ben Grieve, of	Out of baseball
1999	Eric Chavez, 3b	Athletics
2000	Mark Mulder, lhp	Cardinals
2001	Jose Ortiz, 2b	Saltillo (Mexico)
2002	Carlos Pena, 1b	Rays
2003	Rich Harden, rhp	Athletics
2004	Bobby Crosby, ss	Athletics
2005	Nick Swisher, of	Athletics
2006	Daric Barton, 1b	Athletics
2007	Travis Buck, of	Athletics

TOP DRAFT PICKS OF THE DECADE

Year	Player, Pos.	2007 Org.
1998	Mark Mulder, lhp	Cardinals
1999	Barry Zito, lhp	Giants
2000	Freddie Bynum, ss (2nd)	Orioles
2001	Bobby Crosby, ss	Athletics
2002	Nick Swisher, of	Athletics
2003	Brad Sullivan, rhp	Athletics
2004	Landon Powell, c	Athletics
2005	Cliff Pennington, ss	Athletics
2006	Trevor Cahill, rhp (2nd)	Athletics
2007	James Simmons, rhp	Athletics

LARGEST BONUSES IN CLUB HISTORY

Mark Mulder, 1998	$3,200,000
Nick Swisher, 2002	$1,780,000
Barry Zito, 1999	$1,625,000
Cliff Pennington, 2005	$1,475,000
Joe Blanton, 2002	$1,400,000

OAKLAND ATHLETICS

Top 2008 Rookie: Daric Barton, 1b. The Mark Mulder trade keeps on giving to the A's, who watched Barton hit .347 as a September callup.

Breakout Prospect: Josh Horton, ss. A perennial winner in college, he has a chance to move quickly and will open his first full season in high Class A.

Sleeper: Alex Valdez, inf. A switch-hitter with power potential, he's also a versatile defender with soft hands, range and arm strength.

SOURCE OF TOP 30 TALENT			
Homegrown	27	Acquired	3
College	18	Trades	2
Junior college	0	Rule 5 draft	1
High school	6	Independent leagues	0
Draft-and-follow	0	Free agents/waivers	0
Nondrafted free agents	0		
International	3		

Number in parentheses indicates prospect rankings.

LF
Matt Sulentic (16)
Danny Putnam
Jason Perry
Jose Pineda

CF
Corey Brown (6)
Jermaine Mitchell (8)
Toddric Johnson

RF
Javier Herrera (9)
Grant Desme (12)
Richie Robnett (15)
Myron Leslie

3B
Jeff Baisley (21)
Alex Valdez
Frank Martinez

SS
Gregorio Petit (13)
Cliff Pennington (24)

2B
Justin Sellers (14)
Kevin Melillo (17)
Josh Horton (26)
Brian Snyder
Larry Cobb

1B
Daric Barton (1)
Sean Doolittle (10)
Vasili Spanos
Tommy Everidge

C
Landon Powell (7)
Anthony Recker (27)
Jeremy Brown
J.D. Closser

RHP		LHP	
Starters	**Relievers**	**Starters**	**Relievers**
Trevor Cahill (2)	Sam Demel (19)	Dan Meyer (20)	Jerry Blevins (11)
James Simmons (3)	Andrew Carignan (22)	James Heuser	Brad Kilby (23)
Henry Rodriguez (4)	Fernando Hernandez (29)	Brad Hertzler	Derrick Gordon
Andrew Bailey (5)	Connor Robertson		Bradley Davis
Vin Mazzaro (18)	Brad Ziegler		
Travis Banwart (25)	Jeff Gray		
Graham Godfrey (28)	Jason Ray		
Craig Italiano (30)			
Scott Hodsdon			
Jason Fernandez			
Ryan Webb			
Shane Komine			
Michael Madsen			

2007

Best Pro Debut: 1B Danny Hamblin (10) ranked second in the short-season Northwest League in RBIs (62) and fifth in doubles (21) and hit .275/.365/.494 with 11 home runs. RHP James Simmons (1) held his own in 30 innings in the Double-A Texas League, posting a 3.94 ERA.

Best Athlete: OFs Corey Brown (1s) and Grant Desme (2) both have all-around tools. Brown was recruited as a wide receiver in high school.

Best Pure Hitter: 1B Sean Doolittle (1s) reminds scouts of Dave Magadan as a first baseman who will hit for average but not premium power. He has excellent plate discipline and an advanced approach, and should improve now that he no longer has to pitch as he did at Virginia.

Best Power Hitter: Brown and Hamblin tied for fourth in NCAA Division I this spring with 22 homers, and both hit 11 for Vancouver. Desme was keeping pace with 15 before a May wrist injury, and has the most usable power.

Fastest Runner: SS Michael Richard (11) is a well-above-average runner who stole 76 bases between Prairie View A&M and Vancouver.

Best Defensive Player: Doolittle could be a Gold Glover at first base with smooth actions and agility around the bag.

Best Fastball: RHP Andrew Carignan (5) and RHP Sam Demel (3) pitch at 92-94 mph and touch 96; both profile in the back of the bullpen. Simmons doesn't throw as hard, though in shorter outings he can bump 93-94. His 89-90 mph heater with UC Riverside featured 70 command at times.

Best Secondary Pitch: Demel has a plus slider and a changeup with late sink. Simmons commands his changeup as well as his fastball. LHP Aaron Jenkins (22) produces a hellacious curveball from his 5-foot-8, 180-pound frame.

Most Intriguing Background: Brown's younger brother Dylan played with him at Oklahoma State and could be a top prospect for the 2009 draft. Unsigned LHP Daniel Schlereth (9) is the son of ex-NFL player and current TV analyst Mark. The A's drafted two sons of ex-big leaguers: RHP Brent Lysander (16), son of Rick; and unsigned RHP Trent Abbott (36), son of Paul.

Closest To The Majors: Simmons, with Carignan and Demel close behind.

Best Late-Round Pick: Jenkins could be a lefty specialist with his curveball. RHP Lee Land (28) went to three colleges in three seasons but impressed in the Cape Cod League this summer, at times pitching at 92-94 mph.

The One Who Got Away: OF/2B Gary Brown (12) would have brought speed and athleticism to this class. He's at Cal State Fullerton. Schlereth and fellow LHP Eric Berger (8), who missed the spring after Tommy John surgery, returned to Arizona.

Assessment: Oakland went back to what it has done well recently—drafting college players—and found good talent from that pool. The organization needs an infusion of impact players, though, and this draft class didn't provide that.

2006

BUDGET: $1.6 MILLION

RHP Trevor Cahill (2) already has emerged as the A's top pitching prospect, and RHP Andrew Bailey (6) isn't far behind. OF Jermaine Mitchell (5) is a multitooled speedster.

GRADE: C+

2005

BUDGET: $4.8 MILLION

OF Travis Buck (1s) already has hit his way into the big league lineup, but SS Cliff Pennington (1) has fallen apart since a strong debut. Unsigned 1B Justin Smoak (16) is a candidate to go No. 1 overall in the 2008 draft.

GRADE: B

2004

BUDGET: $6.3 MILLION

Oakland had six picks in the first two rounds and scored with RHP Huston Street (1s) and C Kurt Suzuki (2), and possibly C Landon Powell (1) and OF Richie Robnett (1). Four other players have reached the majors.

GRADE: A

2003

BUDGET: $4.9 MILLION

RHP Brad Sullivan (1), 3B Brian Snyder (1) and 2B/SS Omar Quintanilla (1s) have all fizzled. Oakland traded its best pick, OF Andre Ethier (2), for Milton Bradley.

GRADE: C

Draft analysis by John Manuel (2007) and Jim Callis (2003-06). Numbers in parentheses indicate draft rounds. Budgets are bonuses in first 10 rounds.

BILL NICHOLS

DARIC BARTON, 1B

Born: Aug. 16, 1985.
Ht.: 6-0. **Wt.:** 205.
Bats: L. **Throws:** R.
Drafted: HS—
Huntington Beach
Calif., 2003
(1st round).
Signed by:
Dan Ontiveros
(Cardinals).

After the Athletics acquired Barton from the Cardinals in the Mark Mulder deal in December 2004, he quickly established himself as the organization's top prospect while moving from catcher to first base. But his path was derailed just two months into the 2006 season at Triple-A Sacramento, when an infield collision with Tony Womack left Barton with a broken left elbow. He returned briefly in the Rookie-level Arizona League in August before reporting to the Dominican League, where his elbow flared up again and he left after just 14 at-bats. Finally healthy again in 2007, Barton had a streaky year in Triple-A. He was on fire in June, when he batted .454 with 17 extra-base hits. He hit .550 with four homers in the first round of the Pacific Coast League playoffs before getting his first major league callup in September.

Oakland general manager Billy Beane called Barton the best hitter in the minors when the Athletics acquired him, and he's easily the system's top pure hitter. He has a sweet, fluid stroke and repeats it well. He has incorporated more and more loft as he has moved up the ladder, giving him more power. He has outstanding bat control, and his quick hands allow him to punish pitches all over the strike zone. Barton uses the whole field and has little difficulty shortening his swing to fire line drives into the left-center gap. His biggest strength, and obviously something the Athletics value highly, is his strike-zone discipline. He works deep counts and consistently makes hard contact. He has exceptional hand-eye coordination that has allowed him to amass more walks than strikeouts every year since his pro debut in 2003.

Scouts aren't sold on Barton's power, though several point to how similar he is to James Loney, who also didn't show much pop in the minors. The difference is that Loney has a bigger body than Barton. During his catching days, the main knock on Barton was his lack of athleticism and his slow feet. Now that he's at first base, the questions remain the same. He has worked hard on his footwork around the bag and his reactions at first base, but he's still a slightly below-average defender with a tick below average arm strength. He also doesn't run well at all and his heavy lower half isn't an asset. His work ethic was brought into question by scouts who saw him at Sacramento, as he seemed to just be cruising until he got called up.

Barton's lack of raw power and defensive concerns could limit his overall ceiling. Unless he improves defensively, he won't be suited for anything but DH duty. Barring a resurgence from Dan Johnson, however, Barton should be Oakland's first baseman in 2008.

Year	Club (League)	Class	AVG	G	AB	R	H	2B	3B	HR	RBI	BB	SO	SB	OBP	SLG
2003	Johnson City (Appy)	R	.294	54	170	29	50	10	0	4	29	37	48	0	.420	.424
2004	Peoria (MWL)	A	.313	90	313	63	98	23	0	13	77	69	44	4	.445	.511
2005	Stockton (Cal)	A	.318	79	292	60	93	16	2	8	52	62	49	0	.438	.469
	Midland (TL)	AA	.316	56	212	38	67	20	1	5	37	35	30	1	.410	.491
2006	Sacramento (PCL)	AAA	.259	43	147	25	38	6	4	2	22	32	26	1	.389	.395
	Athletics (AZL)	R	.200	2	5	1	1	1	0	0	2	0	0	0	.200	.400
2007	Sacramento (PCL)	AAA	.293	136	516	84	151	38	5	9	70	78	69	3	.389	.438
	Oakland (AL)	MLB	.347	18	72	16	25	9	0	4	8	10	11	1	.429	.639
MINOR LEAGUE TOTALS			.301	460	1655	300	498	114	12	41	289	313	266	9	.414	.459
MAJOR LEAGUE TOTALS			.347	18	72	16	25	9	0	4	8	10	11	1	.429	.639

2 TREVOR CAHILL, RHP

BILL MITCHELL

Born: March 1, 1988. **B-T:** R-R. **Ht.:** 6-3. **Wt.:** 195. **Drafted:** HS—Vista, Calif., 2006 (2nd round). **Signed by:** Craig Weissmann.

With limited experience and a commitment to Dartmouth clouding his availability prior to his high school senior season, Cahill was somewhat of an unknown commodity early in 2006. But he pitched his way into first-round consideration until he was slowed by a bout with strep throat. Oakland was glad to take him with its top pick (second round) and sign him for $560,000. He opened 2007 in extended spring training and struggled early after reporting to low Class A Kane County, but he was one of the Midwest League's top pitchers in August, going 5-0, 0.74 with 44 strikeouts and just 20 hits allowed in 37 innings. Extremely mature for his age, Cahill showed good mound presence and poise as a 19-year-old in the MWL. He has good downward life and natural sink on his 88-92 mph fastball, but his upper-70s curveball rates as his best pitch. Hitters have a tough time picking up the rotation on it out of his hand, and he'll use it in any count. His changeup took a major step forward. He's a good athlete with a simple, compact delivery that he repeats well. As good as his curveball is, Cahill is reluctant to throw it in the strike zone, preferring to bury it. He needs to have consistent confidence in both his curve and changeup in order to reach his potential. He also could use another breaking ball to vary his looks—possibly a slider to give him another weapon against lefthanders. Cahill has the size, strength, makeup and stuff to project as a No. 2 or 3 starter down the road and draws comparisons to former A's righthander Mike Moore. He'll begin his first full season at high Class A Stockton in 2008.

Year	Club (League)	Class	W	L	ERA	G	GS	CG	SV	IP	H	R	ER	HR	BB	SO	AVG
2006	Athletics (AZL)	R	0	0	3.00	4	4	0	0	9	2	4	3	0	7	11	.071
2007	Kane County (MWL)	A	11	4	2.73	20	19	0	0	105	85	38	32	3	40	117	.220
MINOR LEAGUE TOTALS			11	4	2.76	24	23	0	0	114	87	42	35	3	47	128	.210

3 JAMES SIMMONS, RHP

BILL MITCHELL

Born: Sept. 29, 1986. **B-T:** R-R. **Ht.:** 6-4. **Wt.:** 220. **Drafted:** UC Riverside, 2007 (1st round). **Signed by:** Craig Weissmann.

Simmons emerged as a top prospect when he posted a 1.18 ERA in the Cape Cod League in 2006, then solidified his status by going 11-3, 2.40 at UC Riverside last spring. The A's drafted him 25th overall and signed him for $1.192 million, then sent him to Double-A Midland and used him primarily in relief because he had worked 124 innings in college. He also went to the Arizona Fall League, where he posted a 2.89 ERA and helped the Phoenix Desert Dogs win their fourth consecutive league title. Simmons consistently worked at 93-94 mph in relief in the AFL, but as a starter he's a strike-thrower who pitches from 88-92. His two-seam fastball worked well against lefthanders in his pro debut. His command is exquisite, grading as a 70 on the 20-80 scouting scale. His changeup is his best pitch, ranking as tops in the system, and he also throws a slider and curveball. He's a good athlete who fields his position well and maintains his velocity into the late innings. The major question with Simmons is his lack of a true breaking ball. He gets around on his slider often, which reduces its bite and limits his ability to throw it for strikes. His curveball is too soft and loopy at times, and he didn't use it much in the AFL. If Simmons can develop a consistent breaking ball, he profiles as a solid No. 3 starter. If not, he'll be a quality bullpen arm. He'll return to Double-A, this time in a starting role.

Year	Club (League)	Class	W	L	ERA	G	GS	CG	SV	IP	H	R	ER	HR	BB	SO	AVG
2007	Midland (TL)	AA	0	0	3.94	13	2	0	0	29	36	16	13	2	8	23	.308
MINOR LEAGUE TOTALS			0	0	3.94	13	2	0	0	29	36	16	13	2	8	23	.308

4 HENRY RODRIGUEZ, RHP

Born: Feb. 25, 1987. **B-T:** R-R. **Ht.:** 6-1. **Wt.:** 175. **Signed:** Venezuela, 2003. **Signed by:** Julio Franco.

Signed out of Venezuela in 2003, Rodriguez didn't make his pro debut until 2005 because of a nagging groin injury. The injury continued to bother him in his U.S. debut in 2006, the highlight of which was a combined no-hitter with Trevor Cahill in the Rookie-level Arizona League. That outing seemed to turn him around, as his confidence soared and he has been much more effective ever since. Rodriguez owns the best fastball in the system, consistently working at 92-96 mph. His heater has outstanding late life in the zone, riding in on righthanders and down and away from lefties. He has hit 100 mph, though he has bought into the philosophy that command is more important that lighting up radar guns. His changeup shows signs of being a plus pitch. He shows little concern for throwing inside and is aggressive on the mound. He's athletic, repeats his delivery and fields his position well. Rodriguez has tinkered with both a curveball and slider, but he still lacks a consistent breaking ball. He settled on a slider last year, which fits his repertoire much better, but it's still well-below-average. Though he has toned down his emotions on the mound, he still needs to mature. He can fall out of his mechanics easily, leading to erratic command of all three pitches at times. The lack of a breaking ball has some scouts targeting Rodriguez as a future reliever, but the A's will remain patient. If his slider comes around, he has the makings of a middle-of-the-rotation starter. If not, he'll be a power reliever. He'll be challenged to keep the ball down and throw consistent strikes in high Class A this season.

Year	Club (League)	Class	W	L	ERA	G	GS	CG	SV	IP	H	R	ER	HR	BB	SO	AVG
2005	Athletics1 (DSL)	R	0	2	4.03	8	3	0	0	22	14	19	10	1	14	27	.163
2006	Athletics (AZL)	R	5	2	7.42	15	4	0	1	43	46	39	36	1	50	59	.284
2007	Kane County (MWL)	A	6	8	3.07	20	18	1	0	99	75	38	34	2	58	106	.214
MINOR LEAGUE TOTALS			11	12	4.35	43	25	1	1	165	135	96	80	4	122	192	.225

5 ANDREW BAILEY, RHP

Born: May 31, 1984. **B-T:** R-R. **Ht.:** 6-3. **Wt.:** 220. **Drafted:** Wagner, 2006 (6th round). **Signed by:** Jeff Bittiger.

The A's nearly drafted Bailey in 2005 before he was shut down with an elbow injury and needed Tommy John surgery. When he returned and showed his normal low-90s fastball the next spring, Oakland popped him in the sixth round and signed him for $135,000. In his first full pro season, he averaged 10.0 strikeouts per nine innings and made a one-game cameo in Triple-A. Strong and physical, Bailey goes right after hitters with his 90-93 mph fastball, topping out at 95. He's shown the ability to cut it, sink it or run it when he wants, with 60 command on the 20-80 scouting scale. He also features a power spike curveball that he'll throw in any count. Nearly three years removed from surgery, he has worked hard to improve his durability and to maintain his velocity and the sharpness of his curveball late into games. Bailey's changeup still needs major improvement so he'll have a useful weapon against lefthanders. He slows down his arm speed too much when he throws the changeup, and he had trouble commanding it in 2007. His delivery isn't ideal, as he still throws somewhat across his body and struggles with finding his release point at times. Bailey will work on developing his changeup in Double-A. If he can't, he'll be destined for the bullpen. But if he can, he'll profile as a durable innings-eater.

Year	Club (League)	Class	W	L	ERA	G	GS	CG	SV	IP	H	R	ER	HR	BB	SO	AVG
2006	Vancouver (NWL)	A	2	5	2.02	13	10	0	0	58	39	20	13	2	20	53	.187
2007	Kane County (MWL)	A	1	4	3.35	11	10	1	0	51	42	25	19	6	22	74	.219
	Stockton (Cal)	A	3	4	3.82	11	11	0	0	66	56	31	28	8	31	72	.239
	Sacramento (PCL)	AAA	1	0	1.13	1	1	0	0	8	3	1	1	0	1	4	.115
MINOR LEAGUE TOTALS			7	13	3.00	36	32	1	0	183	140	77	61	16	74	203	.212

6 COREY BROWN, OF

Born: Nov. 26, 1985. **B-T:** L-L. **Ht.:** 6-1. **Wt.:** 200. **Drafted:** Oklahoma State, 2007 (1st round supplemental). **Signed by:** Blake Davis.

Football programs recruited Brown as a wide receiver out of high school, but he opted to play baseball at Oklahoma State. One of the best college athletes available in the 2007 draft, he went 59th overall and signed for $544,500. His younger brother Dylan, a sophomore at Oklahoma State, should be a top prospect for the 2009 draft. Power, speed and athleticism are Brown's biggest assets. He possesses plus bat speed with natural loft and leverage that produces plus-plus raw juice. His football mentality makes all his tools play up a level, and while he has the range to play center field, he might profile better in right with above-average arm strength. Brown can get overly aggressive at times and go into pull mode. He has a history of not making consistent contact with wood bats. He hurt his hand late in his pro debut and it cost him the majority of instructional league, though he's healthy now. Brown will see time at all three outfield spots in low Class A in 2008. He's at least two years away but has the potential to be a 20-20 player in the majors.

Year	Club (League)	Class	AVG	G	AB	R	H	2B	3B	HR	RBI	BB	SO	SB	OBP	SLG
2007	Vancouver (NWL)	A	.268	59	213	31	57	18	4	11	48	37	77	5	.379	.545
MINOR LEAGUE TOTALS			.268	59	213	31	57	18	4	11	48	37	77	5	.379	.545

7 LANDON POWELL, C

Born: March 19, 1982. **B-T:** B-R. **Ht.:** 6-3. **Wt.:** 230. **Drafted:** South Carolina, 2004 (1st round). **Signed by:** Michael Holmes.

Though Powell has been on the prospect radar since his sophomore year of high school and has a solid history of performing at the prep level, college and the pros, scouts always have questioned his body and his ability to stay at catcher. He reported to spring training having shed 30 pounds and in the best shape of his career last year, but he tore the anterior-cruciate ligament in his left knee in July, and required surgery on the knee for the second time in three years. Powell stands out with his bat and his catch-and-throw ability. He has a line-drive approach with above-average power. A switch-hitter, he's adept at using the whole field and has good plate discipline. Before he went down with the knee injury, he threw out 54 percent of runners while flashing consistent 1.85-second pop times in Double-A. His soft hands make him an ideal receiver, and his plus arm strength makes up for any deficiencies in his lower half. Powell's knee is a huge concern relating to his ability to remain a catcher. He first had knee surgery to repair a torn lateral meniscus during spring training in 2005. His weight and conditioning fluctuate wildly, and the A's kept on him to work out a dietary plan during this latest rehab. He's a liability on the basepaths, though he did steal the first base of his career last year. Few scouts believe Powell can reach his full potential because of his injury history and his weight. If he can't catch, his value will take a huge hit. That said, he was one of the top catchers in the minors prior to his latest surgery.

Year	Club (League)	Class	AVG	G	AB	R	H	2B	3B	HR	RBI	BB	SO	SB	OBP	SLG
2004	Vancouver (NWL)	A	.237	38	135	24	32	6	1	3	19	26	22	0	.362	.363
2005	Did Not Play—Injured															
2006	Stockton (Cal)	A	.264	90	326	44	86	12	0	15	47	43	77	0	.350	.439
	Midland (TL)	AA	.268	12	41	4	11	0	0	1	4	3	12	0	.333	.341
2007	Midland (TL)	AA	.292	60	219	46	64	9	2	11	39	36	40	1	.391	.502
	Sacramento (PCL)	AAA	.294	4	17	3	5	0	0	3	3	0	4	0	.294	.824
MINOR LEAGUE TOTALS			.268	204	738	121	198	27	3	33	112	108	155	1	.363	.447

8 JERMAINE MITCHELL, OF

Born: Nov. 2, 1984. **B-T:** L-L. **Ht.:** 6-0. **Wt.:** 200. **Drafted:** UNC Greensboro, 2006 (5th round). **Signed by:** Neil Avent.

PAUL GIERHART

After spending two years at Texarkana (Texas) JC, Mitchell transferred to UNC Greensboro as a junior and the A's signed him for $155,000 as a fifth-round pick. He broke a bone in his right foot during his pro debut, but returned last year to turn in a solid season in low Class A. The fastest runner in the system, Mitchell has 70 speed on the 20-80 scouting scale. He uses a level stroke and controls the strike zone well. He has good pop for a speedster. Defensively, he covers a lot of ground in center field. Mitchell gets too aggressive and sells out his approach for power at times, leading to a longer swing and more strikeouts. Pitch recognition, especially with quality breaking balls, is an area of concern. He's still raw with his reads and jumps on the bases and in center field. His arm strength is below-average and his throws need to be more accurate. Though his athleticism is his bread and butter, he could lose that edge if he doesn't keep himself in better shape. Mitchell's performance needs to catch up to his natural ability. He's already 23 yet will open 2008 in high Class A. He has upside as an everyday center fielder but could wind up as a fourth outfielder.

Year	Club (League)	Class	AVG	G	AB	R	H	2B	3B	HR	RBI	BB	SO	SB	OBP	SLG
2006	Vancouver (NWL)	A	.362	37	138	23	50	7	2	3	23	22	27	14	.460	.507
2007	Kane County (MWL)	A	.288	122	431	79	124	20	5	8	58	74	115	24	.390	.413
MINOR LEAGUE TOTALS			.306	159	569	102	174	27	7	11	81	96	142	38	.407	.436

9 JAVIER HERRERA, OF

Born: April 9, 1985. **B-T:** R-R. **Ht.:** 5-10. **Wt.:** 175. **Signed:** Venezuela, 2001. **Signed by:** Julio Franco.

STEVE MOORE

Herrera was highly touted after ranking as the short-season Northwest League's top prospect in 2004, but was suspended for two weeks in 2005 for testing positive for a performance-enhancing substance, then missed all of 2006 recovering from Tommy John surgery. Herrera didn't return until spring training last year and hamstring problems limited him to just 82 games. When he's healthy, Herrera's tools still rank among the best in the system. He's a five-tool player with exceptional bat speed, power, speed, defense and arm strength. His strong wrists help his righthanded stroke produce hard contact to all fields. Herrera's work ethic first came into question when he wasn't fully committed to his rehab from Tommy John surgery. Scouts are critical about his lackadaisical demeanor on the field, as he appears to do what he wants to do and not what's expected of him. His hamstring issues have reduced his speed and limited his range in center field. He never had a lot of plate discipline, and it regressed last season. Herrera might be destined for a corner spot if he can't keep his legs healthy, in which case he'd have to show more power. He's still just 22 and relatively raw from all the missed time, and he'll try to put in a full season in Double-A this year.

Year	Club (League)	Class	AVG	G	AB	R	H	2B	3B	HR	RBI	BB	SO	SB	OBP	SLG
2002	Athletics E (DSL)	R	.286	65	227	40	65	14	5	5	47	23	56	21	.359	.458
2003	Athletics (AZL)	R	.230	17	61	12	14	3	1	2	13	7	19	3	.329	.410
2004	Vancouver (NWL)	A	.331	65	263	50	87	15	4	12	47	24	59	23	.392	.555
2005	Sacramento (PCL)	AAA	.417	5	12	5	5	1	0	1	3	1	1	1	.533	.750
	Kane County (MWL)	A	.275	94	360	70	99	18	2	13	62	47	110	26	.374	.444
2006	Did Not Play—Injured															
2007	Stockton (Cal)	A	.274	62	252	45	69	17	0	9	39	19	60	11	.337	.448
	Midland (TL)	AA	.254	20	71	13	18	5	0	3	13	4	13	1	.316	.451
MINOR LEAGUE TOTALS			.287	328	1246	235	357	73	12	45	224	125	318	86	.364	.473

10 SEAN DOOLITTLE, 1B

Born: Sept. 26, 1986. **B-T:** L-L. **Ht.:** 6-3. **Wt.:** 195. **Drafted:** Virginia, 2007 (1st round supplemental). **Signed by:** Neil Avent.

A standout two-way player in high school, Doolittle was a 39th-round pick of the Braves in 2004, when he was New Jersey's player of the year. He continued to star both ways at Virginia, where he was the Atlantic Coast Conference player of the year as a sophomore. The A's drafted him for his bat, taking him 41st overall last June and signing him for $742,500. Doolittle has a sound approach with a smooth, economical swing, making consistent line-drive contact to all fields. His strike-zone judgment is also a plus. He's an above-average defender with smooth actions and soft hands at first base. Doolittle hit 11 home runs during his freshman year, but showed little power the following two years at Virginia or during his pro debut. His swing lacks loft and leverage, and strength was another issue as he significantly wore down over the course of the year. He still needs to incorporate more of his lower half in his swing. He's more athletic than Daric Barton, but he's also a below-average runner. The A's bumped Doolittle to low Class A after just two weeks at short-season Vancouver, and he struggled at times. He'll likely repeat the Midwest League to start 2008.

Year	Club (League)	Class	AVG	G	AB	R	H	2B	3B	HR	RBI	BB	SO	SB	OBP	SLG
2007	Vancouver (NWL)	A	.283	13	46	6	13	3	0	0	4	9	10	0	.421	.348
	Kane County (MWL)	A	.233	55	193	23	45	10	0	4	29	24	40	1	.320	.347
MINOR LEAGUE TOTALS			.243	68	239	29	58	13	0	4	33	33	50	1	.341	.347

11 JERRY BLEVINS, LHP

Born: Sept. 6, 1983. **B-T:** L-L. **Ht.:** 6-6. **Wt.:** 190. **Drafted:** Dayton, 2004 (17th round). **Signed by:** Brian Williams (Cubs).

Blevins was steadily climbing through the Cubs system when they packaged him with catcher Rob Bowen and shipped him to Oakland for catcher Jason Kendall in July. While he made just five appearances above high Class A when he was traded, Blevins shot through the A's system, whiffed 20 in nine postseason innings for Sacramento and finished the season in the big leagues. A tall lefthander whose fastball tops out in the mid-90s, Blevins creates good deception and downward angle, taking advantage of his 6-foot-6 frame. His changeup has good depth and is his second-best pitch, giving him a weapon against righthanders. His sweepy curveball showed flashes of being an average offering, but still needs work. The A's admittedly rushed Blevins after the trade to help their depleted bullpen. He'll have a shot to win a relief job in spring training, but probably will begin the season back in Triple-A.

Year	Club (League)	Class	W	L	ERA	G	GS	CG	SV	IP	H	R	ER	HR	BB	SO	AVG
2004	Boise (NWL)	A	6	1	1.62	23	0	0	5	33	17	7	6	1	21	42	.145
2005	Peoria (MWL)	A	3	7	5.54	48	2	0	14	76	75	51	47	6	38	96	.260
2006	Daytona (FSL)	A	0	1	9.00	8	0	0	1	11	18	12	11	0	4	9	.367
	Boise (NWL)	A	1	2	6.04	16	0	0	0	22	27	22	15	3	8	19	.287
	West Tenn (SL)	AA	0	0	1.42	5	0	0	1	6	5	1	1	0	1	8	.217
2007	Daytona (FSL)	A	1	0	0.38	15	0	0	6	23	13	1	1	0	5	32	.159
	Tennessee (SL)	AA	2	2	1.53	23	0	0	3	29	23	5	5	1	8	37	.215
	Midland (TL)	AA	1	3	3.32	17	0	0	1	21	18	10	8	2	5	29	.234
	Sacramento (PCL)	AAA	1	0	0.00	1	0	0	0	2	1	0	0	0	0	4	.111
	Oakland (AL)	MLB	0	1	9.64	6	0	0	0	4	8	6	5	1	2	3	.348
MINOR LEAGUE TOTALS			15	16	3.73	156	2	0	31	226	197	109	94	13	90	276	.233
MAJOR LEAGUE TOTALS			0	1	9.64	6	0	0	0	4	8	6	5	1	2	3	.348

12 GRANT DESME, OF

Born: April 4, 1986. **B-T:** R-R. **Ht.:** 6-2. **Wt.:** 205. **Drafted:** Cal Poly, 2007 (2nd round). **Signed by:** Rick Magnante.

Desme was zooming up draft boards in the spring until he broke a bone in his wrist late in the college season. He still went in the second round, where he signed for $432,000. He played shortstop in high school and during his freshman year of college at San Diego State before transferring to Cal Poly, where he moved to the outfield. Desme's best tool is plus raw power. He hit 23 homers and 29 doubles in two seasons for the Mustangs, has tremendous bat speed and gets good leverage in his swing. Desme is one of the better athletes in the system, but doesn't run well enough to play center field. He's destined for either corner, and his arm strength should be enough for right. Desme wore down in his pro debut, and things got worse when his wrist flared up. He also sustained a nagging shoulder injury and missed the bulk of instructional league. The missed time likely means Desme begins 2008 in low Class A, but he could move quickly if he's healthy.

Year	Club (League)	Class	AVG	G	AB	R	H	2B	3B	HR	RBI	BB	SO	SB	OBP	SLG
2007	Vancouver (NWL)	A	.261	12	46	6	12	3	0	1	6	6	21	2	.358	.391
MINOR LEAGUE TOTALS			.261	12	46	6	12	3	0	1	6	6	21	2	.358	.391

13 GREGORIO PETIT, SS/2B

Born: Dec. 10, 1984. **B-T:** R-R. **Ht.:** 5-10. **Wt.:** 190. **Signed:** Venezuela, 2001. **Signed by:** Julio Franco.

Left unprotected in the 2006 Rule 5 draft because of questions about his bat, clubs apparently missed out on Petit a year ago. Signed out of Venezuela in 2001, Petit's offense finally blossomed in 2007, as he moved up to Triple-A as well as the top of the A's depth chart at shortstop. Defense has never been an issue for Petit, whom managers rated as the best defensive shortstop and best infield arm in the Double-A Texas League. He has plus range to both sides, outstanding first-step quickness and gets good reads off the bat. He has soft hands and makes all the throws with plus arm strength. Petit still needs to work on some of the little things offensively—he doesn't bunt particularly well or work deep counts to draw walks. He's a contact hitter who puts the ball in play. He's more of a line-drive singles hitter who can shorten his stroke and go the other way. He likely profiles as a utility player in the long run, with the ability to play either middle infield spot. Added to the 40-man roster in November, he'll start 2008 as the everyday shortstop in Triple-A.

Year	Club (League)	Class	AVG	G	AB	R	H	2B	3B	HR	RBI	BB	SO	SB	OBP	SLG
2002	Athletics W (DSL)	R	.280	63	218	44	61	11	5	1	21	39	44	5	.392	.390
2003	Athletics (AZL)	R	.265	32	117	13	31	6	0	0	12	10	22	3	.323	.316
2004	Vancouver (NWL)	A	.256	68	254	34	65	9	2	4	35	20	67	3	.315	.354
2005	Kane County (MWL)	A	.289	87	287	55	83	10	4	9	33	26	44	8	.349	.446
2006	Stockton (Cal)	A	.256	137	519	71	133	25	7	8	63	38	96	22	.310	.378
2007	Midland (TL)	AA	.306	66	268	33	82	14	0	4	31	25	44	9	.366	.403
	Sacramento (PCL)	AAA	.277	67	235	20	65	12	0	2	28	16	48	1	.327	.353
MINOR LEAGUE TOTALS			.274	520	1898	270	520	87	18	28	223	174	365	51	.338	.383

14 JUSTIN SELLERS, 2B/SS

Born: Feb. 1, 1986. **B-T:** R-R. **Ht.:** 5-10. **Wt.:** 170. **Drafted:** HS—Huntington Beach, Calif., 2005 (6th round). **Signed by:** Randy Johnson.

A high school teammate of Daric Barton, Sellers is the son of former big league righthander Jeff Sellers. He opted to sign with Oakland for $150,000, bypassing a commitment to play at Cal State Fullerton. Sellers is a natural defender at shortstop, with soft hands and above-average range. His arm strength isn't great, but it's enough to get the job done and plays up because of his ability to read balls off the bat and get a quick first step. Sellers has exceptional instincts that translate in the field as well as on the bases. Offense is the question. Sellers led the organization in fly outs in 2006 and he still hits too many balls in the air. He drops his back shoulder and pulls off pitches, minimizing his ability to drive balls. He needs to stay to the middle of the field and work to his strengths and not try to sell out for power, mostly because there simply isn't much power there. He went 9-for-16 to finish his Hawaii Winter Baseball stint on a roll, batting .281 there overall. Sellers profiles as a solid-average defender who'll hit at the bottom of a lineup. While he improved some areas of his approach, he needs more maturity and added strength when he reports to Double-A this spring.

Year	Club (League)	Class	AVG	G	AB	R	H	2B	3B	HR	RBI	BB	SO	SB	OBP	SLG
2005	Vancouver (NWL)	A	.274	47	175	31	48	8	1	0	13	19	24	8	.369	.331
2006	Kane County (MWL)	A	.241	119	411	75	99	21	2	5	46	58	65	17	.346	.338
2007	Stockton (Cal)	A	.274	114	434	72	119	25	4	4	37	46	69	11	.350	.378
	Midland (TL)	AA	.156	14	45	2	7	1	0	0	3	3	10	2	.224	.178
MINOR LEAGUE TOTALS			.256	294	1065	180	273	55	7	9	99	126	168	38	.347	.346

15 RICHIE ROBNETT, OF

Born: Sept. 17, 1983. **B-T:** L-L. **Ht.:** 5-10. **Wt.:** 195. **Drafted:** Fresno State, 2004 (1st round). **Signed by:** Scott Kidd.

Robnett's name surfaces frequently during trade talks, as other clubs obviously value his wide base of skills. The Dodgers were unsuccessful in signing Robnett out of high school as a 32nd-rounder in 2002, and he increased his stock at Fresno State, going in the first round to the A's for $1.325 million two years later. Robnett's best tool is his huge raw power. He's not tall, but stocky and strong, and his quick hands and powerful forearms produce enough juice to leave any ballpark. He's a good athlete who runs well, but will be limited to a corner outfield spot because of suspect routes and poor reads and jumps. He has above-average arm strength, and right field is the best fit. He still swings and misses too much, for a variety of reasons—lack of pitch recognition, lack of patience and a poor two-strike approach are key contributors. After being added to the 40-man roster, Robnett will head to big league camp this spring with an outside chance to make the club, but Triple-A seems a more likely destination.

Year	Club (League)	Class	AVG	G	AB	R	H	2B	3B	HR	RBI	BB	SO	SB	OBP	SLG
2004	Vancouver (NWL)	A	.299	43	164	26	49	14	1	4	36	28	43	1	.395	.470
2005	Stockton (Cal)	A	.243	115	457	77	111	30	0	20	74	56	151	8	.324	.440
2006	Stockton (Cal)	A	.266	69	267	46	71	8	2	11	38	35	73	4	.358	.434
	Sacramento (PCL)	AAA	.091	5	11	0	1	1	0	0	0	0	3	0	.091	.182
	Midland (TL)	AA	.357	5	14	5	5	1	0	1	2	4	4	0	.474	.643
2007	Midland (TL)	AA	.267	120	490	73	131	39	2	18	74	34	130	4	.316	.465
	Sacramento (PCL)	AAA	.152	10	33	6	5	0	0	0	1	4	16	0	.263	.152
MINOR LEAGUE TOTALS			.260	367	1436	233	373	93	5	54	225	161	420	17	.335	.444

16 MATT SULENTIC, OF

Born: Oct. 6, 1987. **B-T:** L-R. **Ht.:** 5-10. **Wt.:** 190. **Drafted:** HS—Dallas, Texas, 2006 (3rd round). **Signed by:** Blake Davis.

After winning the high school triple crown in the Dallas Metroplex during his senior year, Sulentic went to the A's in the third round in 2006 and signed for $395,000. He was an immediate success story in his pro debut, hitting .354/.409/.479 in the Northwest League and ranking as the circuit's No. 3 prospect. Sulentic was promoted to low Class A for a bite-sized stint at the end of 2006, and his numbers served as a warning of what was to come. Sulentic simply had trouble making consistent contact and driving balls in 2007. He'd spin off pitches trying to go too much with a pull-oriented approach, and he'd cut off his swing through the zone at times, not showing the full extension he had in his debut. While his performance improved somewhat after he was sent down to Vancouver, his strikeout rate remained high. Sulentic did show some improvements defensively, however, and he profiles as a corner outfielder. The A's thought it would be tough for Sulentic to duplicate his 2006 success and have tried to slow things down for him developmentally. They rave about the way Sulentic handled failure, however, and he worked hard through adversity. He'll head back to low Class A in 2008.

Year	Club (League)	Class	AVG	G	AB	R	H	2B	3B	HR	RBI	BB	SO	SB	OBP	SLG
2006	Vancouver (NWL)	A	.354	38	144	24	51	10	1	2	22	14	30	3	.409	.479
	Kane County (MWL)	A	.235	30	98	12	23	4	1	1	13	12	19	1	.327	.327
2007	Kane County (MWL)	A	.175	56	206	14	36	6	0	1	16	13	37	2	.234	.218
	Vancouver (NWL)	A	.261	71	276	41	72	19	2	4	40	42	79	2	.362	.388
MINOR LEAGUE TOTALS			.251	195	724	91	182	39	4	8	91	81	165	8	.332	.349

17 KEVIN MELILLO, 2B/3B

Born: May 14, 1982. **B-T:** L-R. **Ht.:** 6-0. **Wt.:** 190. **Drafted:** South Carolina, 2004 (5th round). **Signed by:** Michael Holmes.

After a breakout year offensively in 2005 and a year of defensive improvements in 2006, Melillo made the next step to becoming a more complete player last season. The A's moved him over to third base in Triple-A in August to deepen his versatility defensively, and he proved an adequate defender on the corner. He's not an everyday third baseman by any stretch—his range and footwork were graded as below-average by several scouts—but getting the experience could hasten his path as a lefthanded utility bat with some power. But he hasn't shown the same pop he had in 2005 for the last two seasons, and that's a concern. Melillo isn't going to take Mark Ellis' job anytime soon, but he provides a decent insurance policy for now as he continues to build his defensive resume. Big leaguer Donnie Murphy offers a similar package with less power but more defensively ability and versatility, limiting Melillo's big league chances for 2008. He'll be back in Triple-A to start the year.

Year	Club (League)	Class	AVG	G	AB	R	H	2B	3B	HR	RBI	BB	SO	SB	OBP	SLG
2004	Vancouver (NWL)	A	.340	22	94	22	32	11	2	2	21	11	16	2	.422	.564
2005	Kane County (MWL)	A	.286	78	280	47	80	18	3	8	36	53	40	10	.399	.457
	Stockton (Cal)	A	.400	22	90	21	36	7	1	9	23	12	18	2	.471	.800
	Midland (TL)	AA	.282	35	131	33	37	10	0	7	34	14	23	9	.347	.519
2006	Midland (TL)	AA	.280	136	500	73	140	31	3	12	73	68	98	14	.367	.426
2007	Oakland (AL)	MLB	—	1	0	0	0	0	0	0	0	1	0	0	1.000	—
	Sacramento (PCL)	AAA	.262	98	382	63	100	27	6	10	55	54	100	8	.355	.442
MINOR LEAGUE TOTALS			.288	391	1477	259	425	104	15	48	242	212	295	45	.378	.476
MAJOR LEAGUE TOTALS			—	1	0	0	0	0	0	0	0	1	0	0	1.000	—

18 VIN MAZZARO, RHP

Born: Sept. 27, 1986. **B-T:** R-R. **Ht.:** 6-2. **Wt.:** 190. **Drafted:** HS—Rutherford, N.J., 2005 (3rd round). **Signed by:** Jeff Bittiger.

Mazzaro was the third high school pitcher the A's took in the 2005 draft, and he's always been ahead of his peers. Jared Lansford has the best sinker of the trio, but Mazzaro has good natural sink to his fastball as well. It's a heavy, 90-92 mph fastball that can touch 95 with late explosion through the zone. His best secondary option remains his changeup, but he struggled to command it as he rushed through the lower half of his delivery often leaving it up in the zone, and high Class A hitters pounced on his mistakes. His power breaking ball is below-average, though it shows flashes of at least being an average pitch with some definition. Mazzaro needs to add something to his power arsenal to keep hitters off-balance. Right now, everything is hard without much differential in his velocity. He'll move to Double-A for 2008 and profiles better for the bullpen now until he shows consistent command of the breaking ball or a feel for changing speeds.

Year	Club (League)	Class	W	L	ERA	G	GS	CG	SV	IP	H	R	ER	HR	BB	SO	AVG
2006	Kane County (MWL)	A	9	9	5.05	24	24	0	0	119	146	81	67	7	42	81	.310
2007	Stockton (Cal)	A	9	12	5.33	28	28	0	0	153	159	97	91	13	71	115	.271
MINOR LEAGUE TOTALS			18	21	5.21	52	52	0	0	273	305	178	158	20	113	196	.289

19 SAM DEMEL, RHP

Born: Oct. 23, 1985. **B-T:** R-R. **Ht.:** 6-0. **Wt.:** 210. **Drafted:** Texas Christian, 2007 (3rd round). **Signed by:** Blake Davis.

Demel was a big deal as a prep star at Spring (Texas) High, where he set a school record with 15 wins in a season and broke Josh Beckett's single-season strikeout record with 188 whiffs. He added to his resume for the Horned Frogs, setting a career mark for saves (20), and he had a lot of success as a starter as well. Because of his small frame, most scouts projected him as power reliever. That's the role the A's used him in after signing him for $238,500 as a third-rounder last June. Demel is all effort in his delivery but produces power stuff. His 92-94 mph fastball touched 96 during his pro debut and has very good armside run. Demel's slider rates as the best in the system, with good depth and late bite. His changeup has splitter-like downward tumble, giving him a weapon to attack lefties. Despite his violent delivery, Demel carries no medical baggage. He can rely on his slider and changeup too much, especially when he's in trouble. Demel is one of the most advanced pitchers the A's got in the 2007 draft, but his struggles in high Class A could earn him a ticket back there this season. He could move quickly if he has some success.

Year	Club (League)	Class	W	L	ERA	G	GS	CG	SV	IP	H	R	ER	HR	BB	SO	AVG
2007	Stockton (Cal)	A	0	0	7.07	11	0	0	0	14	16	16	11	2	15	13	.302
	Kane County (MWL)	A	0	1	0.96	9	0	0	4	9	3	2	1	0	4	10	.107
MINOR LEAGUE TOTALS			0	1	4.63	20	0	0	4	23	19	18	12	2	19	23	.235

20 DAN MEYER, LHP

Born: July 3, 1981. **B-T:** R-L. **Ht.:** 6-3. **Wt.:** 210. **Drafted:** James Madison, 2002 (1st round). **Signed by:** J.J. Picollo (Braves).

Meyer was considered a key part of the 2004 deal that sent Tim Hudson to Atlanta, but continued shoulder problems prevented him from making an immediate impact in the system. He struggled in back-to-back years in Triple-A while trying to pitch through the injury before the A's shut him down in late May of 2006. Meyer had surgery to remove a small piece of bone from his left shoulder, and he returned somewhat to form in 2007. His velocity came back to 91-92 mph and his slider again showed flashes of being a plus pitch. His breaking ball will flatten out at times, but the further he's gotten away from surgery, the more bite and depth have returned. He's also trying to regain the feel on his changeup, which was solid-average at its best in the past. Meyer has a chance to make the big league rotation out of spring training, and will see time in the majors one way or another in 2008 if he remains healthy.

OAKLAND ATHLETICS

Year	Club (League)	Class	W	L	ERA	G	GS	CG	SV	IP	H	R	ER	HR	BB	SO	AVG
2002	Danville (Appy)	R	3	3	2.74	13	13	1	0	65	47	22	20	4	18	77	.198
2003	Rome (SAL)	A	4	4	2.87	15	15	0	0	81	76	35	26	6	15	95	.248
	Myrtle Beach (Car)	A	3	6	2.87	13	13	0	0	78	69	29	25	7	17	63	.236
2004	Greenville (SL)	AA	6	3	2.22	14	13	0	0	65	50	17	16	1	12	86	.216
	Richmond (IL)	AAA	3	3	2.79	12	11	0	0	61	62	23	19	6	25	60	.270
	Atlanta (NL)	MLB	0	0	0.00	2	0	0	0	2	2	0	0	0	1	1	.286
2005	Sacramento (PCL)	AAA	2	8	5.36	19	17	0	0	89	101	64	53	15	43	63	.286
2006	Sacramento (PCL)	AAA	3	3	5.07	10	10	0	0	49	63	32	28	10	20	29	.315
2007	Midland (TL)	AA	0	0	6.75	1	1	0	0	4	5	3	3	2	4	2	.357
	Sacramento (PCL)	AAA	8	2	3.28	21	21	0	0	115	103	44	42	12	51	105	.243
	Oakland (AL)	MLB	0	2	8.82	6	3	0	0	16	20	19	16	2	9	11	.294
MINOR LEAGUE TOTALS			32	32	3.42	118	114	1	0	610	576	269	232	63	205	580	.252
MAJOR LEAGUE TOTALS			0	2	7.85	8	3	0	0	18	22	19	16	2	10	12	.293

21 JEFF BAISLEY, 3B

Born: Dec. 19, 1982. **B-T:** R-R. **Ht.:** 6-3. **Wt.:** 210. **Drafted:** South Florida, 2005 (12th round). **Signed by:** Steve Barningham.

As a 23-year-old in the Midwest League, Baisley was named to the midseason all-star team and won league MVP honors. After skipping high Class A in 2007, Baisley performed well enough to make the initial Futures Game roster, but was eventually replaced because of a knee injury. The injury cost him a month and he finished up in the Arizona Fall League to make up for lost time. A solid defender with good hands, footwork and arm strength on the corner, Baisley doesn't excel in any department, and scouts have questioned his bat speed and power ability in the past. He hit for decent pop in Double-A, and in a system devoid of righthanded power bats, Baisley will keep getting chances to prove himself. He's a below-average runner, and after a poor performance in the AFL, coupled with the lost development time, Baisley likely returns to Double-A in 2008.

Year	Club (League)	Class	AVG	G	AB	R	H	2B	3B	HR	RBI	BB	SO	SB	OBP	SLG
2005	Vancouver (NWL)	A	.252	61	218	28	55	15	1	6	38	27	27	3	.362	.413
2006	Kane County (MWL)	A	.298	124	466	86	139	35	1	22	110	62	86	6	.382	.519
2007	Midland (TL)	AA	.257	101	404	60	104	22	3	11	46	29	84	4	.308	.408
MINOR LEAGUE TOTALS			.274	286	1088	174	298	72	5	39	194	118	197	13	.351	.457

22 ANDREW CARIGNAN, RHP

Born: July 23, 1986. **B-T:** R-R. **Ht.:** 5-11. **Wt.:** 215. **Drafted:** North Carolina, 2007 (5th round). **Signed by:** Neil Avent.

The A's were obviously focused on taking college arms that could move quickly in the 2007 draft, taking pitchers in three of the first five rounds. They nabbed Carignan in the fifth round for $126,900. Carignan's great-grandfather, Augustine "Lefty" Dugas, was an outfielder in the big leagues from 1930-34. Carignan racked up 33 saves in his last two seasons to help North Carolina reach back-to-back College World Series finals, using his 92-94 mph fastball, two slurvy breaking balls and changeup. Carignan gets good velocity on his fastball, but it lacks true natural life. But he's shown the ability to cut it, run it or elevate effectively in the zone at times. He commands the fastball to both sides of the plate and is seemingly always working ahead in counts. Carignan throws two different types of breaking balls, though neither one has much definition at this point. His changeup is below-average, and it's easy to pick up because of how much his arm speed decreases. He was effective in his pro debut but needs to develop a breaking ball to induce ground balls on a consistent basis. He'll likely move to high Class A for his first full season.

Year	Club (League)	Class	W	L	ERA	G	GS	CG	SV	IP	H	R	ER	HR	BB	SO	AVG
2007	Kane County (MWL)	A	1	1	2.03	12	0	0	4	13	6	7	3	0	11	19	.136
MINOR LEAGUE TOTALS			1	1	2.03	12	0	0	4	13	6	7	3	0	11	19	.136

23 BRAD KILBY, LHP

Born: Feb. 19, 1983. **B-T:** L-L. **Ht.:** 6-1. **Wt.:** 240. **Drafted:** San Jose State, 2005 (29th round). **Signed by:** Scott Kidd.

Kilby has quietly moved up the organizational ladder with more strikeouts than innings pitched in every pro season, which mirrors what he did as an amateur at San Jose State. The stocky lefthander creates excellent deception in his easily repeatable delivery and has outstanding moxie. His fastball sits anywhere from 87-91, but he has good sink and can pitch to all four quadrants of the strike zone. Kilby's breaking ball still needs some minor tinkering, but it has good depth and bite at times. He can rush somewhat with his delivery out of the stretch with runners on base, causing him to over-rotate and lose command. Kilby finished off the season in the Arizona Fall League, where he didn't miss a lot of bats and gave up a ton of fly balls, but he has the stuff to be a solid relief lefty if he can develop a true secondary pitch to attack righthanders effectively.

Year	Club (League)	Class	W	L	ERA	G	GS	CG	SV	IP	H	R	ER	HR	BB	SO	AVG
2005	Vancouver (NWL)	A	2	0	1.95	23	0	0	14	27	20	7	6	2	11	38	.194
2006	Kane County (MWL)	A	5	1	1.63	49	0	0	9	60	38	13	11	0	23	73	.179
2007	Stockton (Cal)	A	0	0	3.24	7	0	0	3	8	6	5	3	0	6	16	.176
	Midland (TL)	AA	3	3	2.88	47	0	0	0	65	63	24	21	6	22	69	.258
MINOR LEAGUE TOTALS			10	4	2.27	126	0	0	26	162	127	49	41	8	62	196	.214

24 CLIFF PENNINGTON, SS

Born: June 15, 1984. **B-T:** B-R. **Ht.:** 5-11. **Wt.:** 185. **Drafted:** Texas A&M, 2005 (1st round). **Signed by:** Blake Davis.

Scouts loved Pennington in college, when he was a third-team All-American in 2005, but his overall tools have yet to translate in pro ball. He seemed ready to break out in 2006 after spending half a year in the Midwest League and earning an invite to big league spring training, but he struggled defensively, slightly injured his right knee and lost confidence that apparently has yet to return. A torn hamstring cost him a good chunk of 2006, but a completely healthy Pennington struggled again in 2007. Like Justin Sellers, Pennington tries to hit for power too much, and the result is a lot of fly ball outs. He drops his back shoulder and was constantly in pull-mode last year. He was atrocious from the right side, hitting .174 in 149 at-bats counting the Arizona Fall League. While several front-office executives still think he can play shortstop, others are not happy with his defense, questioning his overall effort to get better. One positive is Pennington's plus arm and the advanced strike-zone discipline he showed in the AFL, but he's got a lot to prove and is in danger of falling off the map. He'll likely be in Double-A for all of 2008.

Year	Club (League)	Class	AVG	G	AB	R	H	2B	3B	HR	RBI	BB	SO	SB	OBP	SLG
2005	Kane County (MWL)	A	.276	69	290	49	80	15	0	3	29	39	47	25	.364	.359
2006	Stockton (Cal)	A	.203	46	177	36	36	7	0	2	21	24	35	7	.302	.277
	Athletics (AZL)	R	.464	9	28	3	13	3	1	0	6	4	2	0	.531	.643
2007	Stockton (Cal)	A	.255	68	286	50	73	17	3	6	36	43	54	9	.348	.399
	Midland (TL)	AA	.251	70	271	41	68	13	2	2	21	38	35	8	.343	.336
MINOR LEAGUE TOTALS			.257	262	1052	179	270	55	6	13	113	148	173	49	.348	.357

25 TRAVIS BANWART, RHP

Born: Feb 14, 1986. **B-T:** R-R. **Ht.:** 6-4. **Wt.:** 205. **Drafted:** Wichita State, 2007 (4th round). **Signed by:** Jeremy Scheid.

Banwart was a three-year member of Wichita State's rotation and developed an outstanding feel for pitching in that time. However, he doesn't have the big arm that characterizes past Shockers stars who have reached the big leagues, such as Darren Dreifort, Braden Looper and Mike Pelfrey. Banwart is one of the most intelligent pitchers in the organization, twice making the honor roll in college, and upped his stock as an all-star performer in the Cape Cod League in 2006. He signed for $155,250 as a fourth-rounder last June. His plus changeup is his best pitch, and he commands all four pitches in the strike zone. His fastball comes in at 88-91 mph and he also throws a curveball and slider, but his 60 command on the 20-to-80 scouting scale helps everything play up a notch. He's big, strong and durable and profiles as a back-of-the-rotation starter in the big leagues. Banwart was very effective in his pro debut, though he had trouble getting consistent ground balls. He might be better off scrapping one of his breaking balls in the long term and focusing on improving his slider to give him a weapon with two-plane break. He'll likely move up to the high Class A rotation in 2008.

Year	Club (League)	Class	W	L	ERA	G	GS	CG	SV	IP	H	R	ER	HR	BB	SO	AVG
2007	Kane County (MWL)	A	2	1	2.60	12	6	0	1	45	36	21	13	2	10	41	.206
MINOR LEAGUE TOTALS			2	1	2.60	12	6	0	1	45	36	21	13	2	10	41	.206

26 JOSH HORTON, SS

Born: Feb. 19, 1986. **B-T:** L-R. **Ht.:** 6-1. **Wt.:** 195. **Drafted:** North Carolina, 2007 (2nd round). **Signed by:** Neil Avent.

Horton has a wide base of tools, but his reputation for being a winner pushed him into the second round of the draft in 2007 and the A's signed him for $380,250. His track record speaks for itself. Horton played on back-to-back College World Series teams, was a second-team All-American as a sophomore and won the Atlantic Coast Conference batting title with a .395 mark. Horton has an unorthodox approach but has a knack for hitting and benefits greatly from his ability to control the strike zone. There isn't much power, but Horton uses his quick hands to square up balls on the barrel and uses the whole field consistently. He struggled in the Cape Cod League in 2006 but showed the ability to make adjustments with wood bats in his pro debut. He's an average runner and has a chance to stay at shortstop, though his range will never be anything more than average. Horton has solid-average arm strength, but he doesn't get on top of the ball at times, throwing off his accuracy. He had some soreness in his left hand that limited him during instructional league but will likely move straight to high Class A to begin 2008.

Year	Club (League)	Class	AVG	G	AB	R	H	2B	3B	HR	RBI	BB	SO	SB	OBP	SLG
2007	Vancouver (NWL)	A	.268	14	41	7	11	2	0	1	6	8	7	1	.426	.390
	Kane County (MWL)	A	.279	38	122	28	34	6	0	1	15	28	27	3	.417	.352
MINOR LEAGUE TOTALS			.276	52	163	35	45	8	0	2	21	36	34	4	.419	.362

27 ANTHONY RECKER, C

Born: Aug. 29, 1983. **B-T:** R-R. **Ht.:** 6-3. **Wt.:** 230. **Drafted:** Alvernia (Pa.), 2005 (18th round). **Signed by:** Jeff Bittiger.

Not many clubs other than the Phillies and Mets were on Recker, a standout prep catcher from Allentown, Pa., who went on to star at Division II Alvernia. A's area scout Jeff Bittiger liked the athleticism, power and chiseled physique of Recker, and convinced the club to pop him in the 18th round. Recker is arguably the strongest player in the organization and has plus-plus raw power. He started to develop more opposite-field pop last year in high Class A, but then struggled with the bat in his first exposure to Double-A pitching. Well-disciplined for a power hitter, Recker will work deep counts and showed the ability to shorten his swing last year, but he still has a ways to go to stay to the center of the diamond consistently. His arm strength is above-average, but he carried his offensive woes with him to the field in Double-A, where he threw out just 18 percent of runners. Recker also needs to continue to work on his game-calling skills, blocking balls and receiving to effectively control the running game. He lost development time and an AFL assignment due to a broken hamate bone that sidelined him late in the season. If the bat doesn't come along at the upper levels, Recker profiles as a big league backup. But his defense took a hit last year and he'll go back to Double-A in 2008.

Year	Club (League)	Class	AVG	G	AB	R	H	2B	3B	HR	RBI	BB	SO	SB	OBP	SLG
2005	Vancouver (NWL)	A	.233	43	150	16	35	8	0	5	18	16	40	0	.315	.387
2006	Kane County (MWL)	A	.287	109	407	52	117	24	3	14	57	42	115	5	.358	.464
2007	Stockton (Cal)	A	.319	56	207	39	66	17	2	13	47	27	48	2	.402	.609
	Midland (TL)	AA	.204	58	201	16	41	12	0	4	20	17	63	0	.269	.323
MINOR LEAGUE TOTALS			.268	266	965	123	259	61	5	36	142	102	266	7	.343	.454

28 GRAHAM GODFREY, RHP

Born: Aug. 9, 1984. **B-T:** R-R. **Ht.:** 6-3. **Wt.:** 205. **Drafted:** Charleston, 2006 (34th round). **Signed by:** Marc Tramuta (Blue Jays).

A draft-eligible sophomore who signed for $200,000 as a 34th-rounder in 2006, Godfrey was a junior college all-American in 2005 at Wallace State (Ala.) Community College, where he fashioned a 41-inning scoreless streak as a freshman. After transferring to College of Charleston, he helped the Cougars win the first NCAA regional tournament in the mid-major program's history. The A's got him from Toronto in the Marco Scutaro trade in the fall. Godfrey throws a firm 90-92 mph sinker that touches 94, and he made strides commanding the pitch during the season by staying tall on the back side of his delivery and getting the ball out over his front leg. Prior to that, the pitch tended to run to his arm side, up and out of the zone. Godfrey didn't have much of a changeup when he became a pro, but it morphed into his second pitch with his improved delivery. Likewise, he's developed a slider where previously he had a curveball. The pitch showed improved tilt and velocity, up to 84, over the course of the season. A poised and serious pitcher, Godfrey will need to continue to improve his secondary offerings to stick as a starter. He'll make his A's debut in high Class A this year.

Year	Club (League)	Class	W	L	ERA	G	GS	CG	SV	IP	H	R	ER	HR	BB	SO	AVG
2007	Lansing (MWL)	A	6	7	3.98	21	21	0	0	110	132	63	49	8	36	74	.302
MINOR LEAGUE TOTALS			6	7	3.98	21	21	0	0	110	132	63	49	8	36	74	.302

29 FERNANDO HERNANDEZ, RHP

Born: July 31, 1984. **B-T:** R-R. **Ht.:** 5-11. **Wt.:** 190. **Drafted:** Broward (Fla.) JC, 2002 D/F (49th round). **Signed by:** Jose Ortega (White Sox).

Signed as a draft and follow in 2003, Hernandez climbed to the top of the White Sox farm system even though he lacks both size and a plus fastball. He compensates by being the rare crafty righthander, throwing a variety of breaking balls for strikes in any count. He challenges hitters to beat him and would rather walk a hitter than give in to him with a fastball when behind in the count. He put himself on the radar with a strong season in the Carolina League in 2006, striking out nearly 11 per nine innings and compiling a 1.93 ERA. Often compared to Matt Guerrier for his command and control rather than pure stuff, Hernandez is also an innings-eater with an above-average curveball. Hernandez boosted his stock further after not allowing an earned run in 11 innings in the Arizona Fall League, and the A's swiped him in the major league phase of the Rule 5 draft. He must remain on the active 25-man roster all season or be offered back to the White Sox for $25,000. While his managers in the minor leagues were never afraid to use him as a closer, Hernandez profiles best as a middle reliever or set-up man.

Year	Club (League)	Class	W	L	ERA	G	GS	CG	SV	IP	H	R	ER	HR	BB	SO	AVG
2003	Great Falls (Pio)	R	1	3	2.70	24	0	0	7	23	23	10	7	0	10	14	.261
2004	Kannapolis (SAL)	A	3	3	2.98	28	0	0	4	45	43	20	15	2	16	59	.240
	Winston-Salem (Car)	A	0	0	0.00	2	0	0	0	2	1	0	0	0	1	1	.143
2005	Monterrey (Mex)	AAA	2	2	5.28	6	6	0	0	30	33	18	18	2	16	10	.300
	Aguascalientes (Mex)	AAA	2	1	5.82	16	4	0	0	38	51	28	25	9	20	19	.317
	Winston-Salem (Car)	A	4	1	5.14	45	0	0	1	70	83	44	40	6	30	59	.303
2006	Winston-Salem (Car)	A	7	5	1.93	57	0	0	13	65	50	24	14	4	32	81	.207
2007	Birmingham (SL)	AA	1	3	3.06	60	0	0	9	85	73	30	29	4	23	84	.230
MINOR LEAGUE TOTALS			16	15	3.24	216	0	0	34	291	273	128	105	16	112	298	.247

30 CRAIG ITALIANO, RHP

Born: July 22, 1986. **B-T:** R-R. **Ht.:** 6-3. **Wt.:** 195. **Drafted:** HS—Flower Mound, Texas, 2005 (2nd round). **Signed by:** Blake Davis.

Italiano held a lot of promise when the A's signed him away from Texas Christian for $725,500 in 2005, but the last two years have essentially been lost seasons for the righthander. Italiano lasted just four starts in 2006 before his shoulder broke down and needed labrum surgery. In 2007, he lasted six starts before being struck in the head with a line drive by Mariners' shortstop Carlos Triunfel and spent three days in a Chicago hospital with a skull fracture. He has pitched just 54 innings as a pro in three seasons. Italiano has one of the best fastballs in the system when healthy, topping out at 98 mph, and his curveball has shown signs of being a second plus pitch. But he's a max-effort righthander with a short arm action who's lost a ton of development time. Italiano was back pitching again during instructional league, but there is some concern in the organization about him getting past the mental residue of being hit by the line drive. He should be ready to return to low Class A when camp breaks in late March.

Year	Club (League)	Class	W	L	ERA	G	GS	CG	SV	IP	H	R	ER	HR	BB	SO	AVG
2005	Athletics (AZL)	R	1	2	6.75	8	3	0	0	18	20	17	14	0	8	27	.267
2006	Kane County (MWL)	A	0	1	3.50	4	4	0	0	18	18	12	7	1	9	23	.261
2007	Kane County (MWL)	A	0	3	12.71	6	6	0	0	17	32	25	24	3	16	24	.416
MINOR LEAGUE TOTALS			1	6	7.55	18	13	0	0	54	70	54	45	4	33	74	.317

Philadelphia Phillies

BY CHRIS KLINE

Jimmy Rollins predicted it in spring training, but the Phillies' chances of overtaking the Mets and winning the National League East seemed bleak on Sept. 12. Philadelphia stood seven games back with 17 to play and looked destined for its fifth straight season with a winning record yet no playoff berth.

But as New York stumbled down the stretch, the Phillies went on a 13-4 run to lock up their first division title since 1993. The impetus behind the playoff push was a trio of homegrown infielders, Ryan Howard, Jimmy Rollins and Chase Utley. Howard won the 2006 NL MVP award and Rollins took home the same hardware this year. Utley was a leading contender in the MVP race until he missed a month after an errant pitch broke his right hand.

Howard, Rollins and Utley have formed the heart of the franchise since mid-2005. The farm system made more contributions in 2007, most notably with Kyle Kendrick. Signed away from a Washington State football scholarship as a seventh-round pick in 2003, Kendrick stepped into an injury-riddled rotation in mid-June and won 10 games with a 3.87 ERA that ranked second among Philadelphia starters.

Carlos Ruiz, who signed for a mere $8,000 out of Panama in 1998, took over at catcher and provided steady offense and defense. Michael Bourn provided defense and speed off the bench, then was included in the November trade for Brad Lidge. Philadelphia also used lefthander Matt Maloney, a third-round pick in 2005, to plug a rotation hole by trading him to the Reds for Kyle Lohse.

The Phillies led the NL with 892 runs in 2007 and have all of their key hitters locked up for the near future. On the other hand, their 4.76 ERA was the fourth-worst in the league and their rotation is full of questions behind Cole Hamels and Kendrick. So their player-development focus is going to be on pitching.

In the next two years, Carlos Carrasco and Josh Outman should be able to help the rotation. Both finished last season in Double-A and figure to return there to open 2008. Carrasco ranks as the system's No. 1 prospect for the second straight year, while Outman is more advanced and could beat him to Citizen's Bank Park. Shoulder issues were the only reason that Joe Savery fell to the 19th pick of the 2007 draft, and if he's healthy he should rush through the minors.

Shortstop Jimmy Rollins helped lead the Phillies to their first division title since 1993

DAVID SCHOFIELD

TOP 30 PROSPECTS

1. Carlos Carrasco, rhp	16. Travis d'Arnaud, c
2. Adrian Cardenas, 2b	17. Heitor Correa, rhp
3. Joe Savery, lhp	18. Travis Mattair, 3b
4. Josh Outman, lhp	19. Julian Sampson, rhp
5. Kyle Drabek, rhp	20. Brad Harman, ss
6. Dominic Brown, of	21. D'Arby Myers, of
7. Greg Golson, of	22. Carlos Monasterios, rhp
8. Lou Marson, c	23. Quintin Berry, of
9. Drew Carpenter, rhp	24. Joe Bisenius, rhp
10. Jason Jaramillo, c	25. Tyler Mach, 2b
11. J.A. Happ, lhp	26. Antonio Bastardo, lhp
12. Scott Mathieson, rhp	27. Mike Zagurski, lhp
13. Freddy Galvis, ss	28. Matt Spencer, of
14. Edgar Garcia, rhp	29. Drew Naylor, rhp
15. Jason Donald, ss	30. Lincoln Holdzkom, rhp

Philadelphia took home one championship in the minors, as high Class A Clearwater won the Florida State League behind the continued emergence of catcher Lou Marson and the strong pitching of righthander Drew Carpenter.

The 2008 season figures to be the last for general manager Pat Gillick. Gillick, who won two World Series titles with the Blue Jays, signed a three-year contract in November 2005. When it expires, assistant GMs Ruben Amaro and Mike Arbuckle will be among the top candidates to replace him.

General Manager: Pat Gillick. **Farm Director:** Steve Noworyta. **Scouting Director:** Marti Wolever.

Class	Team	League	W	L	PCT	Finish*	Manager	Affiliated
Majors	Philadelphia	National	89	73	.549	3rd (16)	Charlie Manuel	—
Triple-A	Ottawa Lynx	International	55	88	.385	14th (14)	John Russell	2007
Double-A	Reading Phillies	Eastern	70	71	.496	7th (12)	P.J. Forbes	1967
High A	Clearwater Threshers	Florida State	83	57	.593	2nd (12)^	Dave Huppert	1985
Low A	Lakewood BlueClaws	South Atlantic	69	65	.515	6th (16)	Steve Roadcap	2001
Short-season	Williamsport Crosscutters	New York-Penn	34	42	.447	9th (14)	Gregg Legg	2007
Rookie	GCL Phillies	Gulf Coast	28	32	.467	9th (16)	Roly DeArmas	1999
Overall 2007 Minor League Record			339	355	.488	20th		

*Finish in overall standings (No. of teams in league) ^League champion

LAST YEAR'S TOP 30

Player, Pos.		Status
1.	Carlos Carrasco, rhp	No. 1
2.	Kyle Drabek, rhp	No. 5
3.	Adrian Cardenas, 2b	No. 2
4.	Edgar Garcia, rhp	No. 14
5.	Scott Mathieson, rhp	No. 12
6.	Josh Outman, lhp	No. 4
7.	Michael Bourn, of	(Astros)
8.	J.A. Happ, lhp	No. 11
9.	Matt Maloney, lhp	(Reds)
10.	Greg Golson, of	No. 7
11.	D'Arby Myers, of	No. 21
12.	Mike Costanzo, 3b	(Orioles)
13.	Carlos Ruiz, c	Majors
14.	Zack Segovia, rhp	Dropped out
15.	Kyle Kendrick, rhp	Majors
16.	Joe Bisneius, rhp	No. 24
17.	Drew Carpenter, rhp	No. 9
18.	Brad Harman, ss	No. 20
19.	Lou Marson, c	No. 8
20.	C.J. Henry, ss	(Yankees)
21.	Wellinson Baez, 3b	Dropped out
22.	Dan Brauer, lhp	Dropped out
23.	Pat Overholt, rhp	Dropped out
24.	Jason Jaramillo, c	No. 10
25.	Jim Ed Warden, rhp	(Indians)
26.	Jeremy Slayden, of	Dropped out
27.	Jason Donald, ss	No. 15
28.	Heitor Correa, rhp	No. 17
29.	Alfredo Simon, rhp	(Rangers)
30.	Matt Smith, lhp	Dropped out

BEST TOOLS

Best Hitter for Average	Adrian Cardenas
Best Power Hitter	Greg Golson
Best Strike-Zone Discipline	Quintin Berry
Fastest Baserunner	Greg Golson
Best Athlete	Greg Golson
Best Fastball	Carlos Carrasco
Best Curveball	Kyle Drabek
Best Slider	Josh Outman
Best Changeup	Carlos Carrasco
Best Control	Drew Carpenter
Best Defensive Catcher	Travis D'Arnaud
Best Defensive Infielder	Freddy Galvis
Best Infield Arm	Freddy Galvis
Best Defensive Outfielder	Greg Golson
Best Outfield Arm	Greg Golson

PROJECTED 2011 LINEUP

Catcher	Lou Marson
First Base	Ryan Howard
Second Base	Chase Utley
Third Base	Travis Mattair
Shortstop	Jimmy Rollins
Left Field	Pat Burrell
Center Field	Dominic Brown
Right Field	Adrian Cardenas
No. 1 Starter	Cole Hamels
No. 2 Starter	Brett Myers
No. 3 Starter	Carlos Carrasco
No. 4 Starter	Joe Savery
No. 5 Starter	Josh Outman
Closer	Brad Lidge

TOP PROSPECTS OF THE DECADE

Year	Player, Pos.	2007 Org.
1998	Ryan Brannan, rhp	Out of baseball
1999	Pat Burrell, 1b	Phillies
2000	Pat Burrell, 1b/of	Phillies
2001	Jimmy Rollins, ss	Phillies
2002	Marlon Byrd, of	Rangers
2003	Gavin Floyd, rhp	White Sox
2004	Cole Hamels, lhp	Phillies
2005	Ryan Howard, 1b	Phillies
2006	Cole Hamels, lhp	Phillies
2007	Carlos Carrasco, rhp	Phillies

TOP DRAFT PICKS OF THE DECADE

Year	Player, Pos.	2007 Org.
1998	Pat Burrell, 1b	Phillies
1999	Brett Myers, rhp	Phillies
2000	Chase Utley, 2b	Phillies
2001	Gavin Floyd, rhp	White Sox
2002	Cole Hamels, lhp	Phillies
2003	Tim Moss, 2b (3rd round)	Out of baseball
2004	Greg Golson, of	Phillies
2005	Mike Costanzo, 3b (2nd round)	Phillies
2006	Kyle Drabek, rhp	Phillies
2007	Joe Savery, lhp	Phillies

LARGEST BONUSES IN CLUB HISTORY

Gavin Floyd, 2001	$4,200,000
Pat Burrell, 1998	$3,150,000
Brett Myers, 1999	$2,050,000
Cole Hamels, 2002	$2,000,000
Chase Utley, 2000	$1,780,000

PHILADELPHIA PHILLIES

Top 2008 Rookie: Josh Outman, lhp. The Phillies don't have an obvious rookie candidate, but Outman could crack the rotation at mid-season.

Breakout Prospect: Freddy Galvis, ss. His bat is still a work in progress, but he already excites scouts with his shortstop wizardry.

Sleeper: Freddy Ballestas, rhp. After leading the Venezuelan Summer League in ERA and strikeouts, he's ready to bring his 90-93 mph fastball to the United States.

SOURCE OF TOP 30 TALENT			
Homegrown	28	Acquired	2
College	11	Trades	1
Junior college	0	Rule 5 draft	1
High school	10	Independent leagues	0
Draft-and-follow	0	Free agents/waivers	0
Nondrafted free agents	0		
International	7		

Numbers in parentheses indicate prospect rankings.

LF
T.J. Warren

CF
Greg Golson (7)
D'Arby Myers (21)
Quintin Berry (23)
Leandro Castro

RF
Dominic Brown (6)
Matt Spencer (28)
Gus Milner
Michael Taylor

3B
Travis Mattair (18)
Welinson Baez
Patrick Sellers

SS
Freddy Galvis (13)
Fidel Hernandez

2B
Adrian Cardenas (2)
Jason Donald (15)
Brad Harman (20)
Tyler Mach (25)
Luke Appert

1B
Michael Durant
Matt Rizzotti

C
Lou Marson (8)
Jason Jaramillo (10)
Travis d'Arnaud (16)

RHP		LHP	
Starters	**Relievers**	**Starters**	**Relievers**
Carlos Carrasco (1)	Scott Mathieson (12)	Joe Savery (3)	Antonio Bastardo (26)
Kyle Drabek (5)	Joe Bisenius (24)	Josh Outman (4)	Mike Zagurski (27)
Drew Carpenter (9)	Lincoln Holdzkom (30)	J.A. Happ (11)	Dan Brauer
Edgar Garcia (14)	Francisco Rosario	Jacob Diekman	
Heitor Correa (17)	Pat Overholt	Travis Blackley	
Julian Sampson (19)	Will Savage		
Carlos Monasterios (22)	Andrew Cruse		
Drew Naylor (29)	Ben Pfinsgraff		
Freddy Ballestas	Jordan DeFratus		
Zack Segovia	Luke Wertz		
Darren Byrd			
Chance Chapman			
Jiwan James			
Brian Schlitter			

2007 SIGNING BUDGET: $3.3 MILLION

Best Pro Debut: RHP Chance Chapman (8) went 5-3, 2.09 with 67 strikeouts in 78 New York-Penn League innings. In more limited NY-P action, LHP Joe Savery (1) was just as effective, going 2-3, 2.73 with 22 whiffs in 26 frames.

Best Athlete: RHP Jiwan James (22) and 3B Travis Mattair (2) were three-sport stars in high school. James, who some teams preferred as an outfielder, gave up a baseball scholarship from Florida, where the defending national champion football and basketball programs expressed some interest in him.

Best Pure Hitter: 2B Tyler Mach (4) batted .364 and .386 in two seasons at Oklahoma State, then hit .287 in his pro debut. He's not flashy, but he makes consistent quality contact.

Best Power Hitter: OF Matt Spencer (3) opened eyes by hitting two long homers in the season-opening Houston College Classic. He has more usable power than OF Michael Taylor (5) and 1B Matt Rizzotti (6).

Fastest Runner: OF Cedric Johnson (19) has plus-plus speed, but the Phillies voided his contract because of knee problems. He's now at Chandler-Gilbert (Ariz.) CC. James is an above-average runner.

Best Defensive Player: Travis d'Arnaud (1s) was one of the top defensive catchers in the draft. He regularly records 1.9-second pop times to second base.

Best Fastball: Savery and RHPs Justin DeFratus (11), Luke Wertz (13) and Brian Schlitter (16) all touch 94-95 mph. Wertz had a labrum tear that required surgery, and while Philadelphia didn't void his contract, he'll miss all of 2008.

Best Secondary Pitch: Chapman has a big league slider. Savery has the best changeup.

Most Intriguing Background: 1B Karl Bolt (15) will try to juggle baseball and his Air Force obligations. The second Air Force player ever drafted, he was able to play in the Gulf Coast League while stationed at MacDill Air Force Base in Tampa this summer. Unsigned LHP Mark Adzick's (18, now at Wake Forest) father Scott is a pioneering pediatric surgeon. Johnson has two older brothers in pro ball, Elliott with the Devil Rays and Leon with the Cubs.

Closest To The Majors: Savery, if he's over the shoulder problems that caused him to slide in the first round.

Best Late-Round Pick: RHP Julian Sampson (12) works at 90-92 mph with a 6-foot-5, 200-pound frame with plenty of projection remaining. Schlitter, James and low-90s LHP Jacob Diekman (30) are three more promising late-round arms.

The One Who Got Away: RHP Brandon Workman (3) has a plus fastball, but the Phillies couldn't lure him from Texas.

Assessment: If Savery regains his Rice freshman form, then he was a steal at No. 19. The last time Philadelphia took a lefty with medical issues in the middle of the first round, it came away with Cole Hamels.

2006 BUDGET: $4.3 MILLION

RHP Kyle Drabek (1) could be a steal—if he can overcome makeup issues and Tommy John surgery. 2B Adrian Cardenas (1s), RHP Drew Carpenter (2) and SS Jason Donald (3) are all progressing nicely.

GRADE: B

2005 BUDGET: $1.8 MILLION

The Phillies didn't have a first-rounder, and they've used their top two picks, 3B Mike Costanzo (2) and LHP Matt Maloney (3), as trade fodder. LHP Josh Outman (4) may be the best of the bunch.

GRADE: C+

2004 BUDGET: $3.4 MILLION

OF Greg Golson (1) still has wondrous tools and little clue how to use them. RHP Joe Bisenius (12) was the first member of this class to reach the majors.

GRADE: D

2003 BUDGET: $1.2 MILLION

Philadelphia's first choice came in the third round, and 2B Tim Moss washed out. But RHP Kyle Kendrick (7) exceeded expectations as a rookie last year and OF Michael Bourn (4) helped land Brad Lidge in an offseason trade.

GRADE: C+

Draft analysis by Jim Callis. Numbers in parentheses indicate draft rounds. Budgets are bonuses in first 10 rounds.

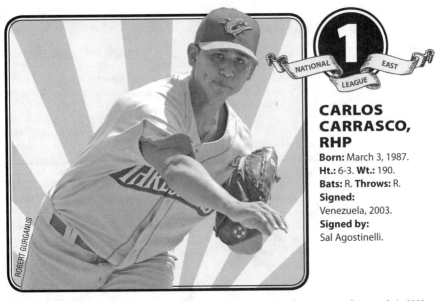

1
NATIONAL LEAGUE EAST

CARLOS CARRASCO, RHP

Born: March 3, 1987.
Ht.: 6-3. **Wt.:** 190.
Bats: R. **Throws:** R.
Signed: Venezuela, 2003.
Signed by: Sal Agostinelli.

Phillies international supervisor Sal Agostinelli signed Carrasco for $300,000 out of Venezuela in 2003, and the young righthander made a successful debut in the Rookie-level Gulf Coast League a year later as a 17-year-old. Philadelphia admittedly rushed him in 2005, pushing Carrasco to low Class A Lakewood, where he was hit hard. But after honing both his mechanics and his mental approach during instructional league, Carrasco turned the corner in a return trip to Lakewood in 2006 and blossomed into the best starter in the system. He also added the Futures Game and the organization's minor league pitcher of the year award to his résumé. After going through a dead-arm period last April when his velocity was down and his secondary pitches lacked their normal bite, Carrasco hit a groove in 2007 and was promoted to Double-A Reading in June. He was inconsistent as a 20-year-old in the Eastern League, however, mixing brilliance (a six-inning no-hitter against Altoona in August) with inconsistency (he allowed five or more runs in five of his 13 starts with Reading). He struggled to get ground balls and command the strike zone.

Carrasco has the makings of two plus pitches with the potential for a third. His fastball has outstanding late life, and is at its best when he works between 89-93 mph. When he needs it, he can touch 94-95. He complements the fastball with the best changeup in the system, and he commands it to both sides of the plate with good depth and fade. His curveball continued to make strides in 2007, ranging from a soft 71-72 mph breaker to a harder 76-78 mph offering that more resembles a slider. His body allows him to unleash all his pitches from a steep downhill plane, and when he's on, he pounds the strike zone.

As good as Carrasco's pure stuff is, he struggled with runners on base in 2007. When he'd get into trouble, he'd rush through his delivery with his lower half and drag his arm behind his body. That would cause his front shoulder to fly open, costing him command. The Phillies attribute these problems to Carrasco's youth, though he did show signs of improvement later in the year. He'll need to make quicker adjustments as he moves along, especially with pitch selection. With the quality of his secondary pitches, Carrasco should profile as a groundball pitcher with enough power in his fastball to miss bats when he has to. Yet in Double-A, his groundout/airout ratio was a mere 0.7.

After a half-season of learning in the Eastern League, Carrasco likely will return there to begin 2008. Some Phillies officials believe that Carrasco was rushed again in 2007, but they were also impressed with how he responded in instructional league afterward. He could debut in the majors in 2009.

Year	Club (League)	Class	W	L	ERA	G	GS	CG	SV	IP	H	R	ER	HR	BB	SO	AVG
2004	Phillies (GCL)	R	5	4	3.56	11	8	0	0	48	53	23	19	2	15	34	.276
2005	Lakewood (SAL)	A	1	7	7.04	13	13	1	0	62	78	50	49	11	28	46	.302
	Batavia (NYP)	A	0	3	13.50	4	4	0	0	15	29	25	23	8	5	12	.392
	Phillies (GCL)	R	0	0	1.80	2	2	0	0	5	3	1	1	0	1	2	.176
2006	Lakewood (SAL)	A	12	6	2.26	26	26	2	0	159	103	50	40	6	65	159	.182
2007	Clearwater (FSL)	A	6	2	2.84	12	12	1	0	69	49	22	22	8	22	53	.199
	Reading (EL)	AA	6	4	4.86	14	13	1	0	70	65	42	38	9	46	49	.247
MINOR LEAGUE TOTALS			**30**	**26**	**4.02**	**82**	**78**	**5**	**0**	**430**	**380**	**213**	**192**	**44**	**182**	**355**	**.235**

2 ADRIAN CARDENAS, 2B

RODGER WOOD

Born: Oct. 10, 1987. **B-T:** L-R. **Ht.:** 5-11. **Wt.:** 190. **Drafted:** HS—Miami, 2006 (1st round supplemental). **Signed by:** Miguel Machado.

Baseball America's 2006 High School Player of the Year, Cardenas had little trouble adjusting to pro ball and switching positions in his first full season. A supplemental first-round pick as a shortstop, he moved to second base and played his way into the Futures Game. He also earned low Class A South Atlantic League all-star honors after doing the same in the Gulf Coast League in his debut. Thick and strong, Cardenas has an easy, compact stroke from the left side that produces consistent line drives with good loft power. He squares up breaking balls and fastballs equally well, and he makes hard contact to all fields. He exhibits above-average arm strength at his new position. Cardenas moved off shortstop because his range was just adequate and figured to diminish as he filled out and grew older. He doesn't cover a lot of ground at second base and his footwork needs improvement. A fringe-average runner, he lacks first-step quickness and his lateral movement also leaves something to be desired. Cardenas will move to high Class A Clearwater for 2008, but his bat could push him to Double-A by midseason. He has middle-of-the-order potential, though the Phillies already are set at second base with Chase Utley.

Year	Club (League)	Class	AVG	G	AB	R	H	2B	3B	HR	RBI	BB	SO	SB	OBP	SLG
2006	Phillies (GCL)	R	.318	41	154	22	49	5	4	2	21	17	28	13	.384	.442
2007	Lakewood (SAL)	A	.295	127	499	70	147	30	2	9	79	47	80	20	.354	.417
MINOR LEAGUE TOTALS			.300	168	653	92	196	35	6	11	100	64	108	33	.361	.423

3 JOE SAVERY, LHP

MIKE JANES

Born: Nov. 4, 1985. **B-T:** L-L. **Ht.:** 6-3. **Wt.:** 215. **Drafted:** Rice, 2007 (1st round). **Signed by:** Steve Cohen.

After starring as a freshman at Rice in 2005, Savery looked like he'd be a top-five draft pick just like fellow Lamar High (Houston) alumnus Jeff Niemann. But like a lot of Owls pitchers, Savery came down with medical issues. He had minor surgery after his sophomore season to shave down a bone growth in the back of his shoulder that was causing some fraying in his labrum. He wasn't at his best last spring, which allowed him to slide to the Phillies at No. 19. He signed for $1,372,500. As a lefty two-way player in college, he garnered comparisons to Mark Mulder. While his fastball velocity was down for much of the spring, Savery flashed 90-94 mph heaters by May and pitched at 88-92 mph in his pro debut. He also can be effective at 86-89 mph. His changeup has the potential to be an above-average pitch and his slurvy breaking ball grades as average to plus. The Phillies rave about his work ethic. Just a year removed from surgery, Savery predictably struggled with the command of all his pitches in his pro debut. He didn't repeat his delivery well, in part because he was worn down. The last four Rice starting pitchers drafted in the first round have had major arm surgeries, a track record that scared a lot of clubs. Philadelphia sent Savery to the Arizona Fall League because they thought his makeup was well-suited for the challenge, which should expedite his development. He'll open 2008 in low Class A and could move quickly if he performs well and shows the ability to maintain his mechanics and velocity deep into games. He could make his big league debut by 2009.

Year	Club (League)	Class	W	L	ERA	G	GS	CG	SV	IP	H	R	ER	HR	BB	SO	AVG
2007	Williamsport (NYP)	A	2	3	2.73	7	7	0	0	26	22	9	8	0	13	22	.214
MINOR LEAGUE TOTALS			2	3	2.73	7	7	0	0	26	22	9	8	0	13	22	.214

4 JOSH OUTMAN, LHP

CLIFF WELCH

Born: Sept. 14, 1984. **B-T:** L-L. **Ht.:** 6-1. **Wt.:** 190. **Drafted:** Central Missouri State, 2005 (10th round). **Signed by:** Jerry Lafferty.

After transferring from St. Louis CC-Forest Park to Central Missouri State, Outman performed an extreme makeover on his mechanics and starred as a two-way player for the Mules. A key contributor to Lakewood's 2006 championship run in 2006, he set the tone early for Clearwater's 2007 title run. Outman won 10 of his 18 starts before being promoted to Double-A. Despite his revamped delivery, deception remains Outman's biggest strength on the mound. Hitters can't get good reads on his 90-94 mph fastball, his late-biting 83-84 mph slider or his changeup. He scrapped his curveball in 2007, and his arm speed and his location with his changeup improved dramatically as he concentrated on a three-pitch mix. He's a good athlete and fields his position well. The patience of Double-A hitters was a wake-up call for Outman, who walked six in his Reading debut. He fell behind in counts after often overthrowing his fastball and elevating it in the strike zone. While he repeats his mechanics well, he throws with some effort and has a slight head jerk, especially when he throws his slider. Outman will begin 2008 back in Double-A, but he could make his debut at Citizen's Bank Park before September. He profiles as a No. 3 starter.

Year	Club (League)	Class	W	L	ERA	G	GS	CG	SV	IP	H	R	ER	HR	BB	SO	AVG
2005	Batavia (NYP)	A	2	1	2.76	11	4	0	0	29	23	14	9	1	14	31	.207
2006	Lakewood (SAL)	A	14	6	2.95	27	27	1	0	155	119	61	51	5	75	161	.213
2007	Clearwater (FSL)	A	10	4	2.45	20	18	0	0	117	104	35	32	7	54	117	.236
	Reading (EL)	AA	2	3	4.50	7	7	1	0	42	38	25	21	5	23	34	.242
MINOR LEAGUE TOTALS			28	14	2.96	65	56	2	0	344	284	135	113	18	166	343	.224

5 KYLE DRABEK, RHP

Born: Dec. 8, 1987. **B-T:** R-R. **Ht.:** 6-1. **Wt.:** 180. **Drafted:** HS—The Woodlands, Texas, 2006 (1st round). **Signed by:** Steve Cohen.

CLIFF WELCH

Several clubs thought Drabek had better stuff than any pitcher in the 2006 draft, but makeup concerns scared them away until Philadelphia took him 18th overall and signed him for $1.55 million. The son of former Cy Young Award winner Doug Drabek, he had a rocky pro debut as field staff and scouts criticized his lack of composure. He kept it together on and off the field in 2007, but Tommy John surgery ended his season in June, and he won't pitch again before August 2008. Drabek has better raw stuff than his father, starting with a mid-90s fastball that touches 97 mph. Despite all that velocity, his best pitch remains an upper-70s spike curveball with hard, late, downward movement. He made strides with his changeup before going down with the elbow injury, both with arm speed and command. He lowered his leg kick in his delivery between high school and pro ball, and now incorporates more of a turn as he goes into his windup. Drabek's makeup is the biggest concern, as his drinking and temper have gotten him into trouble in the past. The Phillies believed that he'd mature like any other teenager once they got him into a routine. Having to overcome elbow reconstruction may help his cause, as he'll have to develop better work habits. The track record of pitchers coming back from Tommy John surgery is strong, so that's not a huge worry. A potential frontline starter, Drabek has been right on schedule with his rehab program. He should return to the mound with short-season Williamsport, and Philadelphia won't push him.

Year	Club (League)	Class	W	L	ERA	G	GS	CG	SV	IP	H	R	ER	HR	BB	SO	AVG
2006	Phillies (GCL)	R	1	3	7.71	6	6	0	0	23	33	24	20	2	11	14	.333
2007	Lakewood (SAL)	A	5	1	4.33	11	10	0	0	54	50	29	26	9	23	46	.239
MINOR LEAGUE TOTALS			6	4	5.35	17	16	0	0	77	83	53	46	11	34	60	.269

6 DOMINIC BROWN, OF

Born: Sept. 3, 1987. **B-T:** L-L. **Ht.:** 6-5. **Wt.:** 205. **Drafted:** HS—Redan, Ga., 2006 (20th round). **Signed by:** Chip Lawrence.

MIKE JANES

Brown is a product of Redan (Ga.) High, the same school that produced 30-30 man Brandon Phillips. Brown first emerged as a prospect as a pitcher and was an even bigger star as a wide receiver, turning down a football scholarship from Miami to sign for $200,000 as a 20th-round pick in 2006. But his future now is as a slugger, as scouts have compared him to a young Darryl Strawberry. While Greg Golson, Quintin Berry and D'Arby Myers can match or exceed his above-average speed, Brown has a bigger and more physical presence. He has gap power now and plenty of home run potential for the future. He's not one-dimensional at the plate, as he uses the whole field and has advanced plate discipline and pitch recognition for his age. He's also adept at bunting. A plus defender with enough range and closing speed to play center field, he fits in right field with his above-average arm strength. Brown is still raw in some phases of the game. He needs to improve as a basestealer (he got caught in seven of 21 attempts), and he can take better routes and make more accurate throws in the outfield. As he continues to grow into his huge 6-foot-5 frame, he's likely to slow down somewhat and lose his plus speed. He opened 2007 with three games in high Class A, and Brown might return there to begin 2008 based on how he handled the initial experience. He's Philadelphia's right fielder of the future, though he's probably at least two or three years away from the majors.

Year	Club (League)	Class	AVG	G	AB	R	H	2B	3B	HR	RBI	BB	SO	SB	OBP	SLG
2006	Phillies (GCL)	R	.214	34	117	13	25	3	0	1	7	12	30	13	.292	.265
2007	Clearwater (FSL)	A	.444	3	9	2	4	1	0	1	7	2	0	0	.545	.889
	Williamsport (NYP)	A	.295	74	285	43	84	11	5	3	32	27	49	14	.356	.400
MINOR LEAGUE TOTALS			.275	111	411	58	113	15	5	5	46	41	79	27	.343	.372

7 GREG GOLSON, OF

Born: Sept. 17, 1985. **B-T:** R-R. **Ht.:** 6-0. **Wt.:** 190. **Drafted:** HS—Austin, 2004 (1st round). **Signed by:** Steve Cohen.

The Phillies have preached patience with Golson since signing him for $1.475 million as the 21st overall pick in 2004. While he still has a long way to go before he's a finished product, he took another step in the right direction in 2007. He finally reached Double-A in late July, and set career in hits, doubles, homers, RBIs and steals. Golson's five-tool package makes him the system's top athlete. His plus-plus speed stands out the most, as he can get from the right side of the plate to first base in less than 4.0 seconds. He also provides above-average raw power, center-field defense and arm strength. Golson's ability to recognize pitches remains his biggest liability. He especially struggles with breaking balls, and tends to get tangled up thinking about what he should do at the plate rather than just seeing the ball and cutting loose. His 49-2 strikeout-walk ratio in Double-A is indicative of his problems, and he led the minors with 173 strikeouts. Golson possesses the tools of a young Ron Gant, but he'll need to show he can make consistent hard contact and take pitches if he's going to move beyond Double-A. The Phillies think he can play a big league center field right now, and if everything clicks offensively, he could make the final leap quickly.

Year	Club (League)	Class	AVG	G	AB	R	H	2B	3B	HR	RBI	BB	SO	SB	OBP	SLG
2004	Phillies (GCL)	R	.295	47	183	34	54	8	5	1	22	10	54	12	.345	.410
2005	Lakewood (SAL)	A	.264	89	375	51	99	19	8	4	27	26	106	25	.322	.389
2006	Lakewood (SAL)	A	.220	93	387	56	85	15	4	7	31	19	107	23	.258	.333
	Clearwater (FSL)	A	.264	40	159	31	42	11	2	6	17	11	53	7	.324	.472
2007	Clearwater (FSL)	A	.285	99	418	66	119	27	3	12	52	21	124	25	.322	.450
	Reading (EL)	AA	.242	37	153	20	37	5	2	3	16	2	49	5	.255	.359
MINOR LEAGUE TOTALS			.260	405	1675	258	436	85	24	33	165	89	493	97	.304	.399

8 LOU MARSON, C

Born: July 26, 1986. **B-T:** R-R. **Ht.:** 6-1. **Wt.:** 195. **Drafted:** HS—Scottsdale, Ariz., 2004 (4th round). **Signed by:** Theron Brockish.

Marson had dreams of playing quarterback in college until he broke his collarbone as a high school senior. He struggled for most of his first three years in pro ball, not hitting for average or power and showing just average defensive tools. Diligence and hard work paid off for him in 2007, when he broke through with the bat and was part of a second straight Class A championship. Marson has an easily repeatable stroke that produces line drives to all fields. In 2007, he shortened his swing and developed a much more consistent two-strike approach. Defensively, Marson's game-calling and receiving skills are above-average. His arm grades as average to slightly above, and he ranked third in the high Class A Florida State League by throwing out 36 percent of basestealers. His arm action sometimes can get long, as he'll lead with his elbow—likely the result of his days as a high school quarterback. He'll be an everyday catcher in Double-A in 2008 and could move up to Triple-A if Jason Jaramillo claims a big league role. The Phillies suddenly have several options behind the plate, so there's no reason to push Marson.

Year	Club (League)	Class	AVG	G	AB	R	H	2B	3B	HR	RBI	BB	SO	SB	OBP	SLG
2004	Phillies (GCL)	R	.257	38	113	18	29	3	0	4	8	13	18	4	.333	.389
2005	Batavia (NYP)	A	.245	60	220	25	54	11	3	5	25	27	52	0	.329	.391
2006	Lakewood (SAL)	A	.243	104	350	44	85	16	5	4	39	49	82	4	.343	.351
2007	Clearwater (FSL)	A	.288	111	393	68	113	24	1	7	63	52	80	3	.373	.407
MINOR LEAGUE TOTALS			.261	313	1076	155	281	54	9	20	135	141	232	11	.350	.384

9 DREW CARPENTER, RHP

Born: May 18, 1985. **B-T:** R-R. **Ht.:** 6-3. **Wt.:** 230. **Drafted:** Long Beach State, 2006 (2nd round). **Signed by:** Tim Kissner.

Carpenter transferred from Sacramento City College to Long Beach State for 2006 and improved his draft stock considerably under 49ers pitching coach Troy Buckley, going to the Phillies with the 65th overall pick. Philadelphia limited his workload in his first pro summer but turned him loose in 2007. He tied for the minor league lead with 17 wins, including a seven-inning perfect game, and the organization named him its minor league pitcher of the year. A finesse righthander, Carpenter makes his pitches more effective because he throws them on a steep, downhill angle. He commands his 89-92 mph fastball to all four quadrants of the strike zone. He has two breaking balls, a plus slider with good tilt and an average curveball, and has added a changeup and splitter since turning pro. His splitter has quickly emerged as his out pitch. He has an easy, simple delivery he repeats well. Carpenter's changeup still has a long way to go to be consistently effective. His arm speed lags behind his body at times and his command of the changeup can be erratic. The Phillies aren't looking to take a pitch away form him yet, but if his changeup doesn't improve, he may just use his splitter to keep hitters off his fastball. Carpenter can get stiff on his front side, which makes him fly open in his delivery and elevate his fastball. Many Phillies officials compare Carpenter's rise to that of Kyle Kendrick, and he could wind up in the big leagues as early as 2008 if the need should arise. Until then, Carpenter will head to Double-A, just like Kendrick did in 2007.

Year	Club (League)	Class	W	L	ERA	G	GS	CG	SV	IP	H	R	ER	HR	BB	SO	AVG
2006	Phillies (GCL)	R	0	0	0.00	2	1	0	0	3	2	0	0	0	0	4	.200
	Batavia (NYP)	A	0	0	0.77	3	3	0	0	11	10	1	1	0	5	12	.250
2007	Clearwater (FSL)	A	17	6	3.20	27	24	3	1	163	150	65	58	16	53	116	.242
MINOR LEAGUE TOTALS			17	6	2.99	32	28	3	1	177	162	66	59	16	58	132	.242

10 JASON JARAMILLO, C

MIKE JANES

Born: Oct. 9, 1982. **B-T:** B-R. **Ht.:** 6-0. **Wt.:** 200. **Drafted:** Oklahoma State, 2004 (2nd round). **Signed by:** Paul Scott.

The Phillies first took Jaramillo out of a Wisconsin high school as a 42nd-round pick in 2001, then signed him three years later as a second-rounder out of Oklahoma State. He hit .304 in his first full pro season, then had 2006 ruined by a broken right hand. He bounced back in 2007, holding his own offensively and defensively at Triple-A Ottawa. A solid hitter from both sides of the plate, Jaramillo has gap-to-gap power and sprays line drives to all fields. He also has a sound approach. Defensively, he has slightly above-average arm strength and quick feet. He threw out 30 percent of basestealers in the International League. Jaramillo has below-average power and well below-average speed. His receiving and game-calling skills got sloppy in 2006, but he righted the ship in Triple-A. He doesn't have the offensive or defensive ceiling of Lou Marson, but Jaramillo can become a reliable backup in the major leagues. He has a chance to serve in that role behind Carlos Ruiz in 2008.

Year	Club (League)	Class	AVG	G	AB	R	H	2B	3B	HR	RBI	BB	SO	SB	OBP	SLG
2004	Phillies (GCL)	R	.667	1	3	1	2	0	0	0	1	0	0	0	.667	.667
	Batavia (NYP)	A	.223	31	112	11	25	5	0	1	14	12	21	0	.299	.295
2005	Lakewood (SAL)	A	.304	119	448	46	136	28	4	8	63	44	72	2	.368	.438
2006	Reading (EL)	AA	.248	93	322	35	80	25	1	6	39	32	55	0	.320	.388
	Scranton/W-B (IL)	AAA	.167	2	6	0	1	0	0	0	1	0	1	0	.143	.167
2007	Ottawa (IL)	AAA	.271	118	435	52	118	13	4	6	56	50	79	0	.350	.361
MINOR LEAGUE TOTALS			.273	364	1326	145	362	71	9	21	174	138	234	2	.344	.388

11 J.A. HAPP, LHP

Born: Oct. 19, 1982. **B-T:** L-L. **Ht.:** 6-5. **Wt.:** 205. **Drafted:** Northwestern, 2004 (3rd round). **Signed by:** Bob Szymkowski.

The Phillies thought Happ had a chance to make an impact in the big leagues last season, but elbow problems lingered throughout the year and his command was inconsistent throughout. His 5.02 ERA in Triple-A was more than double his previous career mark of 2.49. When Happ is healthy, hitters have a hard time getting looks at his low-90s fastball because of his natural deception. Happ's fastball has good life and finish through the zone with some armside run. His 82-85 mph changeup was his most improved offering in 2007, as he increased its depth and was able to locate it well against righthanders. Happ's slider remains too soft and loopy, and he really got into trouble when his stuff tended to flatten out late in games. He repeats his delivery well, but he needs to get stronger to maintain his delivery. Happ likely will return to Triple-A and could be a valuable spot starter if needed in Philadelphia this season. He projects as a No. 3 or 4 starter.

Year	Club (League)	Class	W	L	ERA	G	GS	CG	SV	IP	H	R	ER	HR	BB	SO	AVG
2004	Batavia (NYP)	A	1	2	2.02	11	11	0	0	35	22	8	8	1	18	37	.185
2005	Lakewood (SAL)	A	4	4	2.36	14	12	0	0	72	57	26	19	3	26	70	.213
	Reading (EL)	AA	1	0	1.50	1	1	0	0	6	3	1	1	0	2	8	.150
2006	Clearwater (FSL)	A	3	7	2.81	13	13	0	0	80	63	35	25	9	19	77	.216
	Reading (EL)	AA	6	2	2.65	12	12	0	0	74	58	27	22	2	29	81	.214
	Scranton/W-B (IL)	AAA	1	0	1.50	1	1	0	0	6	3	1	1	1	1	4	.136
2007	Philadelphia (NL)	MLB	0	1	11.25	1	1	0	0	4	7	5	5	3	2	5	.368
	Ottawa (IL)	AAA	4	6	5.02	24	24	0	0	118	118	74	66	12	62	117	.265
MINOR LEAGUE TOTALS			20	21	3.25	76	74	0	0	393	324	172	142	28	157	394	.226
MAJOR LEAGUE TOTALS			0	1	11.25	1	1	0	0	4	7	5	5	3	2	5	.368

12 SCOTT MATHIESON, RHP

Born: Feb. 27, 1984. **B-T:** R-R. **Ht.:** 6-4. **Wt.:** 195. **Drafted:** HS—Aldergrove, B.C., 2002 (17th round). **Signed by:** Tim Kissner.

Mathieson had one of the most promising arms in the system, but an extreme workload caught up to him and he has had a hard time recovering. After pitching 122 innings during the 2005 regular season, he also worked at the World Cup, the Arizona Fall League and then the World Baseball Classic, giving him little time off. He piled on another 164 innings in 2006, making the jump from Double-A to the big leagues, before blowing out his elbow and needing Tommy John surgery in August. Mathieson returned late in 2007, but after just eight innings at three different stops, the Phillies had to shut him down for more elbow surgery, this time the transposition of his elbow nerve. Though Philadelphia considers the second surgery to be a minor setback, his future remains clouded. Before he got hurt, Mathieson pitched with his fastball anywhere from 90-97 mph and also featured a hard slider and a changeup. The Phillies planned on using him as a starter before he got hurt, but now his future role likely will come in relief. That way he would be limited to short stints and could concentrate on a two-pitch power mix. Mathieson is expected to be ready for spring training and probably will begin 2008 in Double-A.

Year	Club (League)	Class	W	L	ERA	G	GS	CG	SV	IP	H	R	ER	HR	BB	SO	AVG
2002	Phillies (GCL)	R	0	2	5.40	7	2	0	0	16	24	11	10	0	6	14	.338
2003	Phillies (GCL)	R	2	7	5.52	11	11	0	0	58	59	42	36	5	13	51	.247
	Batavia (NYP)	A	0	0	0.00	2	0	0	1	6	0	0	0	0	0	7	.000
2004	Lakewood (SAL)	A	8	9	4.32	25	25	1	0	131	130	73	63	7	50	112	.260
2005	Clearwater (FSL)	A	3	8	4.14	23	23	1	0	121	111	62	56	17	34	118	.241
2006	Reading (EL)	AA	7	2	3.21	14	14	0	0	92	73	35	33	8	29	99	.221
	Scranton/W-B (IL)	AAA	3	1	3.93	5	5	0	0	34	26	16	15	2	10	36	.208
	Philadelphia (NL)	MLB	1	4	7.47	9	8	0	0	37	48	36	31	8	16	28	.312
2007	Phillies (GCL)	R	0	0	0.00	2	2	0	0	2	0	0	0	0	1	3	.000
	Clearwater (FSL)	A	0	0	4.50	3	2	0	0	4	3	3	2	0	3	5	.214
	Reading (EL)	AA	0	0	9.00	2	0	0	0	2	3	3	2	1	2	1	.333
MINOR LEAGUE TOTALS			23	29	4.16	94	84	2	1	469	429	245	217	40	148	446	.242
MAJOR LEAGUE TOTALS			1	4	7.47	9	8	0	0	37	48	36	31	8	16	28	.312

13 FREDDY GALVIS, SS

Born: Nov. 14, 1989. **B-T:** B-R. **Ht.:** 5-10. **Wt.:** 160. **Signed:** Venezuela, 2006. **Signed by:** Sal Agostinelli.

Wherever the Phillies' minor league affiliates played during spring training, opposing field staffs gravitated to watch Galvis playing in the middle of the diamond. Since signing out of Venezuela in 2006, Galvis has achieved notoriety with his soft, quick hands, his outstanding range to either side and his plus arm. Scouts compare him to a young Omar Vizquel. Galvis didn't hit much in the short-season New York-Penn League as a 17-year-old making his pro debut, yet he still impressed the managers and scouts who saw him. He was shut down in late July after separating his left (non-throwing) shoulder trying to break up a double play. The question remains whether Galvis will hit enough, but Philadelphia believes he just needs more experience. He won't ever have much power, but he's a switch-hitter with a compact stroke. He has plus speed and some bunting ability, so his emphasis will be getting on base. He'll move up to low Class A this year and could be the South Atlantic League's youngest regular at age 18.

Year	Club (League)	Class	AVG	G	AB	R	H	2B	3B	HR	RBI	BB	SO	SB	OBP	SLG
2007	Williamsport (NYP)	A	.203	38	143	20	29	5	1	0	7	10	20	9	.255	.252
MINOR LEAGUE TOTALS			.203	38	143	20	29	5	1	0	7	10	20	9	.255	.252

14 EDGAR GARCIA, RHP

Born: Sept. 20, 1987. **B-T:** R-R. **Ht.:** 6-2. **Wt.:** 190. **Signed:** Dominican Republic, 2004. **Signed by:** Sal Agostinelli/Will Tejeda.

Ranked No. 4 on this list a year ago, Garcia showed up out of shape in spring training and encountered several minor injuries that nagged him at Lakewood and he never got fully untracked. Signed for $500,000 out of the Dominican Republic in 2004, Garcia has pure stuff on par with Carrasco's. He has excellent life on his fastball and though his velocity was down for much of last season, it returned to its usual low 90s during instructional league. After throwing two variations of curveballs, Garcia settled on a hard-breaking 81-83 mph bender that resembles a slider at times. He hasn't made strides with his changeup, and might be better suited in a relief role. His delivery is simple and repeatable, allowing him to throw strikes with ease. That was a rarity for much of 2007, however, and Garcia needs to command the fastball more effectively. The Phillies have questionined his work ethic, and he'll have to maintain a strict work regimen if he's going to reach his ultimate ceiling of a middle-of-the-rotation starter. Still just 20, he should advance to high Class A at some point this year.

Year	Club (League)	Class	W	L	ERA	G	GS	CG	SV	IP	H	R	ER	HR	BB	SO	AVG
2005	Phillies (GCL)	R	4	4	3.56	10	10	0	0	55	63	26	22	4	13	42	.284
2006	Batavia (NYP)	A	3	5	2.98	12	12	1	0	66	62	28	22	5	10	46	.243
2007	Williamsport (NYP)	A	1	0	2.16	2	1	0	0	8	6	2	2	0	2	11	.200
	Lakewood (SAL)	A	4	9	4.12	20	20	0	0	113	119	61	52	10	32	83	.268
MINOR LEAGUE TOTALS			12	18	3.61	44	43	1	0	244	250	117	98	19	57	182	.263

15 JASON DONALD, SS

Born: Sept. 8, 1984. **B-T:** R-R. **Ht.:** 6-1. **Wt.:** 200. **Drafted:** Arizona, 2006 (3rd round). **Signed by:** Theron Brockish.

A 20th-round pick of the Angels out of high school, Donald turned down a reported $1 million bonus to attend Arizona. After signing for $400,000 as a third-round pick in 2006, he has proven himself with the bat. Last year, he raked in low Class A in the first half before playing a key role in Clearwater's Florida State League championship run. Donald has a short, compact stroke that produces gap power. He draws walks and has slightly above-average speed, though he won't be a basestealing threat. Scouts question his range and arm strength at shortstop, but Donald makes up for his deficiencies with outstanding positioning. The Phillies aren't completely sold on him staying at shortstop, and he might be better suited as a utilityman who can play both middle-infield spots and provide a line-drive bat off the bench. He'll move up to Double-A in 2008.

Year	Club (League)	Class	AVG	G	AB	R	H	2B	3B	HR	RBI	BB	SO	SB	OBP	SLG
2006	Batavia (NYP)	A	.263	63	213	33	56	14	2	1	24	23	42	12	.347	.362
2007	Lakewood (SAL)	A	.310	51	197	41	61	9	3	4	30	29	39	2	.409	.447
	Clearwater (FSL)	A	.300	83	293	48	88	22	5	8	41	35	70	3	.386	.491
MINOR LEAGUE TOTALS			.292	197	703	122	205	45	10	13	95	87	151	17	.381	.440

16 TRAVIS D'ARNAUD, C

Born: Feb. 10, 1989. **B-T:** R-R. **Ht.:** 6-2. **Wt.:** 195. **Drafted:** HS—Lakewood, Calif., 2007 (1st round supplemental). **Signed by:** Tim Kissner.

D'Arnaud's older brother Chase is a third baseman at Pepperdine and will be an early-round pick in the 2008 draft. Travis also committed to play for the Waves, but he never made it to Malibu because the Phillies took him in the supplemental first round last June and signed him for $832,500. One of the best defensive backstops in the draft, d'Arnaud has above-average catch-and-throw skills. He threw out just 24 percent of basestealers in his pro debut, but his arm strength is unquestionable as he regularly gets the ball from mitt to second base in 1.9 seconds. His game-calling still needs work, but he improved in that regard during the summer. Scouts weren't entirely sold on d'Arnaud's bat and he didn't light up Gulf Coast League pitching, but he did show some ability to stay inside balls and drive them to the opposite field. He has a quick swing with the potential for some loft power. He's more athletic and has more speed than most catchers. There's no need to rush d'Arnaud, who will begin the year in low Class A.

Year	Club (League)	Class	AVG	G	AB	R	H	2B	3B	HR	RBI	BB	SO	SB	OBP	SLG
2007	Phillies (GCL)	R	.241	41	141	18	34	3	0	4	20	4	23	4	.278	.348
MINOR LEAGUE TOTALS			.241	41	141	18	34	3	0	4	20	4	23	4	.278	.348

17 HEITOR CORREA, RHP

Born: Aug. 25, 1989. **B-T:** R-R. **Ht.:** 6-2. **Wt.:** 180. **Signed:** Brazil, 2006. **Signed by:** Sal Agostinelli.

Of the four players the Phillies signed out of Brazil for a combined $200,000 in 2006, Correa is the best. He more than held his own in the Gulf Coast League last year, cutting his ERA from 7.83 in his pro debut to 3.74 while still being one of the youngest players in the Rookie circuit at age 17. Correa features a 90-93 mph fastball, a hard 73-77 mph curveball and good feel for his changeup. His fastball has outstanding late life and finish with sink that produces a lot of grounders. He's a strike-thrower who pounds all quadrants of the strike zone. He sometimes gets around on his curve, and while his changeup has above-average potential, he needs to refine his command to make it an effective third pitch. Likened by many in the organization to a young Carlos Carrasco, he might even show more maturity than Carrasco did at the same level. Correa speaks three languages and the Phillies rave about his makeup. He's wiry strong and repeats his delivery well. He could have the makings of a frontline starter if everything comes together. He'll start 2008 in low Class A.

Year	Club (League)	Class	W	L	ERA	G	GS	CG	SV	IP	H	R	ER	HR	BB	SO	AVG
2006	Phillies (GCL)	R	0	3	7.83	8	4	0	0	23	35	21	20	1	7	14	.365
2007	Phillies (GCL)	R	3	3	3.74	13	11	0	0	65	58	33	27	4	20	49	.230
MINOR LEAGUE TOTALS			3	6	4.81	21	15	0	0	88	93	54	47	5	27	63	.267

18 TRAVIS MATTAIR, 3B

Born: Dec. 21, 1988. **B-T:** R-R. **Ht.:** 6-5. **Wt.:** 210. **Drafted:** HS—Southridge, Wash., 2007 (2nd round). **Signed by:** Dave Ryles.

Mattair was considered a better basketball player for much of his high school career, but once he decided to concentrate on baseball full-time, he took off and emerged as Washington's top prep prospect for the 2007 draft. A series of strong workouts for clubs helped his stock, and he went 83rd overall and signed for $395,000. Strong and extremely athletic, Mattair has outstanding leverage in his swing that could produce 25-30 homers annually. He has plus bat speed with a lot of strength. His lack of experience showed when he had problems hitting with wood bats during his debut, but he still has enormous upside. The natural comparison in Philadelphia is to that of Scott Rolen for Mattair's outstanding athleticism, arm strength, power and work ethic. He's a potential plus defender on the corner and could be the Phillies' third baseman of the future, though it could take him time to develop. Mattair's struggles offensively will play a part in where he starts 2008. He wasn't much better with the bat during instructional league, and might wind up in extended spring to open the season.

Year	Club (League)	Class	AVG	G	AB	R	H	2B	3B	HR	RBI	BB	SO	SB	OBP	SLG
2007	Phillies (GCL)	R	.235	54	200	19	47	10	1	3	21	12	58	3	.297	.340
MINOR LEAGUE TOTALS			.235	54	200	19	47	10	1	3	21	12	58	3	.297	.340

19 JULIAN SAMPSON, RHP

Born: Jan. 21, 1989. **B-T:** R-R. **Ht.:** 6-5. **Wt.:** 210. **Drafted:** HS—Skyline, Wash., 2007 (12th round). **Signed by:** Dave Ryles.

Clubs shied away from Sampson in the 2007 draft because of signability concerns, but the Phillies were able to nab him for $390,000 with their 12th-round pick. An outstanding athlete who also played basketball in high school, Sampson has a projectable body with good stuff already in place. Sampson's fastball sits at 90-92 mph, and his loose, easy arm makes it easy to project an increase in velocity as he physically matures. He touched 94 mph with his heater during instructional league. Sampson used two different breaking balls during his amateur career, but his plus hard slider has two-plane break and suits his arsenal better than his softer curveball. The Phillies are leaving both breaking balls on the table for now, and he made strides with tightening the spin on his curveball in instructional league. Sampson has feel for a changeup, but it's easily his fourth-best pitch. Philadelphia raves about his presence and poise, as well as his ability to repeat his relatively simple delivery. He works downhill well. Sampson will be in the mix for a low Class A rotation spot, though he could open 2008 in extended training.

Year	Club (League)	Class	W	L	ERA	G	GS	CG	SV	IP	H	R	ER	HR	BB	SO	AVG
2007	Phillies (GCL)	R	0	0	0.00	1	0	0	0	2	0	0	0	0	0	1	.000
MINOR LEAGUE TOTALS			0	0	0.00	1	0	0	0	2	0	0	0	0	0	1	.000

20 BRAD HARMAN, 2B/SS

Born: Nov. 19, 1985. **B-T:** R-R. **Ht.:** 6-1. **Wt.:** 190. **Signed:** Australia, 2003. **Signed by:** Kevin Hooker.

Harman became the Phillies' top middle-infield prospect after a strong first full season in 2005, but he couldn't recapture that magic the following year. His poor numbers at Clearwater in 2006 are attributed to his inability to make adjustments as well as an illness his father was going through back home in Australia. Harman returned to Clearwater in 2007, switching positions to second base. A line-drive hitter with gap power, he handled high Class A much better the second time around, raising his batting average by 40 points and his slugging percentage by 144. Harman also proved himself at second base. He showed up in spring training in great shape and made all the plays. After going through intense core-strength training, Harman was back playing shortstop and some third base during instructional league. He has average speed and range, slightly above-average arm strength and good hands. The Phillies added him to the 40-man roster in November and have several different options with him for 2008. The most likely is that Harman will start at second base in Double-A.

Year	Club (League)	Class	AVG	G	AB	R	H	2B	3B	HR	RBI	BB	SO	SB	OBP	SLG
2004	Clearwater (FSL)	A	—	1	0	1	0	0	0	0	0	1	0	0	1.000	—
	Phillies (GCL)	R	.230	51	183	23	42	10	0	2	19	11	41	2	.281	.317
2005	Lakewood (SAL)	A	.303	105	419	63	127	23	1	11	58	45	89	5	.380	.442
2006	Clearwater (FSL)	A	.241	119	423	59	102	19	1	2	25	48	102	6	.322	.305
2007	Clearwater (FSL)	A	.281	122	448	63	126	26	5	13	62	40	105	1	.341	.449
MINOR LEAGUE TOTALS			.270	398	1473	209	397	78	7	28	164	145	337	14	.340	.389

21 D'ARBY MYERS, OF

Born: Dec. 12, 1988. **B-T:** R-R. **Ht.:** 6-3. **Wt.:** 180. **Drafted:** HS—Los Angeles, 2006 (4th round). **Signed by:** Tim Kissner.

After a surprising debut pro debut in 2006, Myers took a step back at Williamsport last year. He batted .391 in the first two weeks before pitchers adjusted and he couldn't counter. He hit just .145 the rest of the way before his season ended in mid-August with a slight fracture in his right pinky, though he was healthy for instructional league. His pitch recognition is a liability, as he scuffles with soft breaking balls away from him. Lefthanders exploited this weakness, holding him to a .458 OPS. He's similar to Greg Golson in that he has a huge ceiling but is a long ways from reaching it because he's still raw in many phases of the game. Myers is a plus runner with the potential to hit for average and emerging power. He also has the tools to become an above-average defender in center field, including a solid arm. He needs to improve his instincts in all phases of the game, however. He doesn't control the strike zone or bunt as well as he needs to if he's going to profile as a leadoff hitter. He also has to do a better job of getting jumps on the bases and in the outfield. Myers will work on those aspects of the game in low Class A this season.

Year	Club (League)	Class	AVG	G	AB	R	H	2B	3B	HR	RBI	BB	SO	SB	OBP	SLG
2006	Phillies (GCL)	R	.313	31	128	20	40	7	1	2	13	7	32	11	.353	.430
2007	Williamsport (NYP)	A	.240	46	179	28	43	7	0	1	17	11	34	11	.286	.296
MINOR LEAGUE TOTALS			.270	77	307	48	83	14	1	3	30	18	66	22	.314	.352

22 CARLOS MONASTERIOS, RHP

Born: March 21, 1986. **B-T:** R-R. **Ht.:** 6-2. **Wt.:** 175. **Signed:** Venezuela, 2004. **Signed by:** Ricardo Finol (Yankees).

One of four pieces the Phillies received in return from the Yankees in the Bobby Abreu trade in 2006, Monasterios has the most upside of the group. Infielder C.J. Henry asked for his release from Philadelphia and re-signed with New York; catcher Jesus Sanchez hit just .208 while repeating the Gulf Coast League; and lefthanded reliever Matt Smith had Tommy John surgery in July. Monasterios, meanwhile, won 11 games in his first taste of full-season ball. He has great life and sink on his 90-94 mph fastball and one of the best changeups in the organization. His breaking pitches remain under construction. He's inconsistent with both his hard slider and loopy curveball, and he might wind up scrapping the latter during spring training to concentrate on a three-pitch mix. His sinker gets a lot of ground balls, but he doesn't repeat his delivery very well, making all his pitches hittable when he flies open with his front shoulder and elevates them in the strike zone. Monasterios will continue to move one level at a time, opening this season in high Class A.

Year	Club (League)	Class	W	L	ERA	G	GS	CG	SV	IP	H	R	ER	HR	BB	SO	AVG
2005	Yankees2 (DSL)	R	1	1	0.59	13	5	0	0	45	10	1	3	1	0	0	.054
2006	Yankees (GCL)	R	1	2	2.97	7	3	0	0	30	23	12	10	2	3	24	.207
	Phillies (GCL)	R	0	2	3.68	4	3	0	0	14	18	7	6	1	3	11	.295
2007	Lakewood (SAL)	A	11	11	4.62	26	26	1	0	156	155	93	80	13	55	114	.261
MINOR LEAGUE TOTALS			13	16	3.61	50	37	1	0	246	206	113	99	17	61	149	.216

23 QUINTIN BERRY, OF

Born: Nov. 21, 1984. **B-T:** L-L. **Ht.:** 6-1. **Wt.:** 170. **Drafted:** San Diego State, 2006 (5th round). **Signed by:** Darrell Conner.

Berry has a lot in common with Brewers outfielder Anthony Gwynn. Both are wiry center fielders who standout out most with their quickness, and both played at San Diego State for Hall of Famer Tony Gwynn, Anthony's father. Speed is Berry's best tool, and he can get from the left side of the plate to first base in 3.9 seconds on bunts. He led the system with 55 steals in 73 attempts during his first full season, but the Phillies were more pleased that he honed his approach at the plate and topped their minor leaguers with a .312 batting average as well. Berry has a compact stroke and sprays line drives to all fields. He showed much better plate discipline in his debut, and some club officials believe he could move to Double-A in 2008 without missing a beat. His biggest offensive liability is his lack of strength, but Berry knows his focus is on getting on base and doesn't get caught trying to hit for power. For as much impact as he has on the bases, he's still considered a raw talent in reading pitchers and getting good jumps. His route-running in the outfield is suspect at times, though he has the closing speed to make up for mistakes. He has an average arm. Berry could see Double-A this year, but he'll probably spend at least half the season in high Class A beforehand.

Year	Club (League)	Class	AVG	G	AB	R	H	2B	3B	HR	RBI	BB	SO	SB	OBP	SLG
2006	Batavia (NYP)	A	.219	62	210	34	46	2	2	0	13	25	51	19	.314	.248
2007	Lakewood (SAL)	A	.312	126	487	86	152	19	4	3	44	61	85	55	.395	.386
MINOR LEAGUE TOTALS			.284	188	697	120	198	21	6	3	57	86	136	74	.371	.344

24 JOE BISENIUS, RHP

Born: Sept. 18, 1982. **B-T:** R-R. **Ht.:** 6-5. **Wt.:** 210. **Drafted:** Oklahoma City, 2004 (12th round). **Signed by:** Paul Scott.

The Phillies had tabbed Bisenius as a potential bullpen contributor in 2007 when they sent him to the Arizona Fall League after the 2006 season, and he didn't disappoint. He allowed just six hits and struck out 11 over 12 innings in big league camp in the spring and opened the season in Philadelphia. He was sent out when Tom Gordon returned from the disabled list in early April and spent the remainder of the year in Triple-A, enduring a six-week stint on the DL with elbow soreness. Some in the organization point to overuse as the potential cause for the injury, as he was sent to Venezuela after the AFL and had just a month off before spring training. When healthy, Bisenius regularly touches 95 mph and operates at 92-93 with his fastball. He also features a hammer curveball with devastating late action. His control and command were off in 2007, and he'll have to solve that issue before he returns to the majors. Bisenius went to the AFL for a second straight season to make up for lost time, and the Phillies will give him another look in spring training.

Year	Club (League)	Class	W	L	ERA	G	GS	CG	SV	IP	H	R	ER	HR	BB	SO	AVG
2004	Batavia (NYP)	A	0	1	1.43	11	11	0	0	50	39	12	8	5	14	38	.219
2005	Lakewood (SAL)	A	6	4	5.88	40	4	1	4	64	66	45	42	5	37	56	.264
2006	Clearwater (FSL)	A	4	1	1.93	35	0	0	2	60	48	17	13	4	22	62	.216
	Reading (EL)	AA	4	2	3.09	16	0	0	5	23	14	9	8	2	8	33	.182
2007	Philadelphia (NL)	MLB	0	0	0.00	2	0	0	0	2	2	0	0	0	2	3	.286
	Ottawa (IL)	AAA	3	4	5.48	35	0	0	0	46	52	29	28	5	31	41	.301
MINOR LEAGUE TOTALS			17	12	3.64	137	15	1	11	244	219	112	99	21	112	230	.243
MAJOR LEAGUE TOTALS			0	0	0.00	2	0	0	0	2	2	0	0	0	2	3	.286

25 TYLER MACH, 2B

Born: Dec. 11, 1984. **B-T:** R-R. **Ht.:** 6-1. **Wt.:** 195. **Drafted:** Oklahoma State, 2007 (4th round). **Signed by:** Paul Scott.

Mach isn't a tools guy, but he can hit and attracted the Phillies with his offensive ability. After beginning his college career with a year each at Washington and Edmonds (Wash.) CC, he transferred to Oklahoma State prior to the 2006 season. He hit .364 and led the Big 12 Conference with 16 homers, sharing league player-of-the-year honors with Texas outfielder Drew Stubbs. While Stubbs went with the eighth overall pick to the Reds, Mach wasn't taken until the 40th round by the Cardinals. He returned to the Cowboys for his senior season, hit .386 with another 16 homers and went in the fourth round of the 2007 draft, turning pro for $95,000. Mach has the plus bat speed to turn around fastballs at any velocity. He has good raw power and uses the whole field. But he struggles with quality breaking balls, both in recognizing them and making any kind of decent contact. A fringe-average runner, Mach is a question mark defensively. Though he played better at second base than Philadelphia expected, his footwork needs improvement and he has below-average range. He especially struggles with balls to his right. The Phillies put him on a core-strength program to loosen up his hips more to gain flexibility, something that ultimately could help his swing as well. He played third base as a college junior but his bat would have to pull even more weight at that position. Because he's 23 and polished at the plate, Mach could skip a level and begin 2008 in high Class A.

Year	Club (League)	Class	AVG	G	AB	R	H	2B	3B	HR	RBI	BB	SO	SB	OBP	SLG
2007	Williamsport (NYP)	A	.287	65	247	33	71	19	2	5	38	21	33	1	.362	.441
MINOR LEAGUE TOTALS			.287	65	247	33	71	19	2	5	38	21	33	1	.362	.441

26 ANTONIO BASTARDO, LHP

Born: Sept. 21, 1985. **B-T:** L-L. **Ht.:** 5-11. **Wt.:** 180. **Signed:** Dominican Republic, 2005. **Signed by:** Sal Agostinelli.

Signed out of the Dominican Republic in 2005, Bastardo was slowed by shoulder tendinitis in his 2005 pro debut and by a pulled groin in 2006. Though he had pitched just 23 innings in the United States, the Phillies jumped him to low Class A in June, in part because he was 21. Despite his lack of experience, Bastardo put up the most spectacular numbers in the system last season. He went 10-0, 2.14 with 110 strikeouts in 97 innings while flashing promising stuff. His best pitch is a changeup with good action and depth, and he sets it up with an 87-91 mph fastball. His breaking ball is a slurvy mid-80s pitch, and he struggles to command it effectively at times. He's small and wiry, which combined with his injury history leads to questions about his durability. He ultimately may become more of a middle reliever than a back-of-the-rotation starter. He should remain a starter in the high Class A this year.

PHILADELPHIA PHILLIES

Year	Club (League)	Class	W	L	ERA	G	GS	CG	SV	IP	H	R	ER	HR	BB	SO	AVG
2005	Phillies (DSL)	R	2	2	2.13	11	5	0	1	38	22	14	9	0	22	63	.162
2006	Phillies (GCL)	R	1	2	3.91	9	2	0	0	23	20	16	10	1	14	27	.220
2007	Lakewood (SAL)	A	9	0	1.87	15	15	0	0	91	63	23	19	3	42	98	.189
	Clearwater (FSL)	A	1	0	7.20	1	1	0	0	5	5	4	4	0	3	12	.250
MINOR LEAGUE TOTALS			13	4	2.40	36	23	0	1	157	110	57	42	4	81	200	.190

27 MIKE ZAGURSKI, LHP

Born: Jan. 27, 1983. **B-T:** L-L. **Ht.:** 6-0. **Wt.:** 225. **Drafted:** Kansas, 2005 (12th round). **Signed by:** Jerry Lafferty.

Assistant general manager Mike Arbuckle and the Phillies' staff refer to Zagurski as "Mini-Me" because his thick, barrel-chested body resembles Arbuckle's. That frame didn't create much pro interest in Zagurski until he shut down Texas in front of several scouts in May of his senior year at Kansas. Philadelphia still has lingering concerns about his body, but his arm works well, pumping out fastballs from 89-92 mph with good life. He also throws a plus slider with sharp, late-breaking action. After throwing shutout ball in 11 of his 12 outings in high Class A to open the 2007 season, he jumped three levels and made his major league debut on May 25. He doesn't have much of a changeup, a weakness big league righthanders exploited by tattooing him for a .340 average and a 1.051 OPS, but he was effective against lefties (.216, .502 OPS). Though he could nibble a little less at the higher levels, Zagurski is pretty much all that he's going to be. However, he has enough stuff to carve out a role as a lefty specialist. Shut down in mid-August with a severe hamstring injury, he's expected to be ready to compete for a big league job in spring training.

Year	Club (League)	Class	W	L	ERA	G	GS	CG	SV	IP	H	R	ER	HR	BB	SO	AVG
2005	Batavia (NYP)	A	3	4	4.60	15	8	0	0	45	47	29	23	2	15	43	.266
2006	Lakewood (SAL)	A	4	4	3.51	42	0	0	1	56	46	22	22	0	22	75	.224
2007	Clearwater (FSL)	A	0	0	1.10	12	0	0	5	16	6	2	2	0	4	30	.113
	Reading (EL)	AA	0	0	1.29	6	0	0	0	7	2	1	1	0	2	8	.083
	Ottawa (IL)	AAA	0	0	2.00	7	0	0	0	9	7	2	2	0	6	11	.212
	Philadelphia (NL)	MLB	1	0	5.91	25	0	0	0	21	25	14	14	3	11	21	.287
MINOR LEAGUE TOTALS			7	8	3.37	82	8	0	6	133	108	56	50	2	49	167	.220
MAJOR LEAGUE TOTALS			1	0	5.91	25	0	0	0	21	25	14	14	3	11	21	.287

28 MATT SPENCER, OF

Born: Jan. 27, 1986. **B-T:** L-L. **Ht.:** 6-4. **Wt.:** 225. **Drafted:** Arizona State, 2007 (3rd round). **Signed by:** Theron Brockish.

Spencer went to North Carolina for his first two college seasons, where he showed good athleticism despite his large frame and helped the Tar Heels finish second at the College World Series in 2006. But after he hit just .197 in the Cape Cod League last summer, he lost his starting job in fall ball, so he transferred to Arizona State for his junior season. In front of a crowd of scouts at the season-opening Houston College Classic at Minute Maid Park, Spencer drilled two homers, and it was his power that attracted the Phillies. They drafted him in the third round in June and signed him for $261,000. Much like his college career, Spencer's pro debut was filled with inconsistencies. He hit for good power and a decent average, but didn't control the strike zone. Despite having slightly above-average speed, he wasn't much of a factor on the bases. With his above-average pop and arm strength—he topped out at 94 mph as a reliever for the Sun Devils—he best profiles as a right fielder. Spencer will begin his first full season in low Class A, and could move quickly once he adapts to the everyday routine of pro ball.

Year	Club (League)	Class	AVG	G	AB	R	H	2B	3B	HR	RBI	BB	SO	SB	OBP	SLG
2007	Williamsport (NYP)	A	.263	51	179	21	47	10	0	9	26	11	46	3	.320	.469
MINOR LEAGUE TOTALS			.263	51	179	21	47	10	0	9	26	11	46	3	.320	.469

29 DREW NAYLOR, RHP

Born: May 31, 1986. **B-T:** R-R. **Ht.:** 6-4. **Wt.:** 210. **Signed:** Australia, 2004. **Signed by:** Sal Agostinelli.

His father Geoff played professional rugby for the Balmain Tigers in Australia for two seasons, and Naylor was more interested in Australian rules football in high school before finally settling on baseball. Naylor pitched in the Australian Summer League in 2005 before making his U.S. debut a year later. He pounds the strike zone with three pitches, beginning with an 88-92 mph fastball that he commands to both sides of the plate. His 12-to-6 curveball grades as average to above-average at times. His biggest area of growth has come with his changeup, which has outstanding depth and fade. He still needs to improve his arm speed on his changeup, however. The Phillies rave about Naylor's body and athleticism, which allow him to repeat his delivery well. He has a strong lower half that he uses to get on top of his pitches and drive downhill. He could be poised for a breakout season in low Class A this year.

Year	Club (League)	Class	W	L	ERA	G	GS	CG	SV	IP	H	R	ER	HR	BB	SO	AVG
2006	Phillies (GCL)	R	2	3	4.66	12	2	0	1	36	43	26	19	2	9	22	.297
2007	Williamsport (NYP)	A	8	6	3.28	14	14	2	0	93	78	39	34	3	28	97	.228
MINOR LEAGUE TOTALS			10	9	3.67	26	16	2	1	130	121	65	53	5	37	119	.248

30 LINCOLN HOLDZKOM, RHP

Born: March 23, 1982. **B-T:** R-R. **Ht:** 6-5. **Wt:** 245. **Drafted:** Arizona Western CC, 2001. **Signed by:** David Finley (Marlins).

The Phillies hit paydirt when they were the second team to make Shane Victorino a major league Rule 5 draft pick, and they're hoping for similar good fortune with Holdzkom. Philadelphia plucked Holdzkom from the Red Sox at the Winter Meetings in December. A year earlier, the Astros had taken him from the Cubs, who had acquired him in a deal that sent Todd Wellemeyer to the Marlins. Holdzkom didn't last long in Houston's big league camp. He walked three batters in two innings and the final straw came when he wondered out loud if he could collect his major league salary if he quit, prompting his release. His spring experience was Holdzkom in a nutshell—he always struggled with his command and created headaches wherever he has gone. At the same time, he has a seductive arm that never fails to attract another suitor. At his best, he can sit at 93-94 mph with a fastball that has vicious cut at times and heavy sink at others. He'll also flash a wipeout slider. He has regained his stuff after missing the entire 2004 season because of Tommy John surgery. Batters struggle to lift the ball against him and he didn't surrender his first homer in pro ball until 2007, his sixth season. Holdzkom still needs to throw a lot more strikes and prove he can maintain his stuff for more than an inning at a time. Taking his considerable talent more seriously would be a first step. The Phillies were sold on Holdzkom when they scouted him in the Arizona Fall League, and they'll give him every chance to make their bullpen. If he fails, he has to be put on waivers and be offered back to Boston for half his $50,000 draft price.

Year	Club (League)	Class	W	L	ERA	G	GS	CG	SV	IP	H	R	ER	HR	BB	SO	AVG
2001	Marlins (GCL)	R	1	3	2.49	12	7	0	2	43	26	18	12	0	27	43	.176
2002	Kane County (MWL)	A	1	5	2.53	30	0	0	11	32	21	11	9	0	29	42	.181
2003	Greensboro (SAL)	A	1	4	2.84	43	0	0	4	57	36	24	18	0	27	74	.182
	Jupiter (FSL)	A	0	2	3.07	13	0	0	2	14	9	6	5	0	7	20	.167
2004	Did Not Play—Injured																
2005	Marlins (GCL)	R	0	0	2.25	3	0	0	0	4	5	3	1	0	1	6	.313
	Jupiter (FSL)	A	0	1	5.79	9	0	0	1	9	7	6	6	0	5	9	.206
2006	Cubs (AZL)	R	0	0	2.08	5	1	0	0	8	11	4	2	0	3	10	.324
	Daytona (FSL)	A	0	0	0.00	2	0	0	0	5	3	0	0	0	2	6	.167
	West Tenn (SL)	AA	2	3	1.95	18	0	0	0	32	25	7	7	0	10	27	.221
2007	Portland (EL)	AA	4	1	3.47	30	0	0	1	46	35	23	18	5	30	41	.211
	Pawtucket (IL)	AAA	1	0	1.59	12	0	0	0	17	19	5	3	0	14	13	.279
MINOR LEAGUE TOTALS			10	19	2.70	177	8	0	21	270	197	107	81	5	155	291	.204

Pittsburgh Pirates

BY JOHN PERROTTO

The Pirates finally blew up their organization following the 2007 season, after years of poor drafts and the farm system's failure to produce star-quality players contributed to a continuing downward spiral for the franchise.

Team president Kevin McClatchy, who put together the group that bought the team in 1995, was nudged aside by majority owner Bob Nutting and replaced by Frank Coonelly, who had been a Major League Baseball vice president and chief labor counsel. Nutting, whose family had quietly taken over majority interest in the Pirates many years earlier, also became the public face of the franchise when he assumed the role of controlling owner.

General manager Dave Littlefield was fired after six unsuccessful years on the job, capped by a bizarre deal at the trade deadline. He acquired Matt Morris, who had $13.7 million left on his three-year, $27 million contract and was winless in his previous eight starts, from the Giants for a pair of marginal prospects in outfielder Rajai Davis and righthander Steven MacFarland.

Neal Huntingon, a special assistant to Indians GM Mark Shapiro, was hired to replace Littlefield. Huntington jettisoned manager Jim Tracy, who compiled a 135-189 record in two years, and hired John Russell, manager of Phillies' Triple-A farm club and a former Pirates third-base coach, to replace him.

Huntington also fired farm director Brian Graham and scouting director Ed Creech, who in six years together couldn't produce the talent necessary to end a string of 15 straight losing seasons, one short of the major league record set by the Phillies from 1933-48. After a long search, Huntington named Indians assistant farm director Kyle Stark to replace Graham and former Tigers scouting director Greg Smith to take over for Creech.

"We need to change the culture of the organization," Huntington said. "It's not always easy to make changes. I had to let go some very good baseball people and that was very difficult. However, it has become fairly obvious that we need a fresh start here, new people and some new ideas."

Huntington believes player development and scouting will be the lifeblood of the small-market franchise. He also plans to hire more area scouts in an effort to improve the flow of talent into a farm system that hasn't developed an impact hitter since third baseman Aramis Ramirez was signed out of

The Pirates' puzzling trade for Matt Morris signaled the end of the Dave Littlefield era

BILL NICHOLS

TOP 30 PROSPECTS

1. Andrew McCutchen, of	16. Olivo Astacio, rhp
2. Neil Walker, 3b	17. Jimmy Barthmaier, rhp
3. Steve Pearce, 1b/of	18. Josh Sharpless, rhp
4. Brad Lincoln, rhp	19. Evan Meek, rhp
5. Daniel Moskos, lhp	20. Andrew Walker, c
6. Shelby Ford, 2b	21. Austin McClune, of
7. Jamie Romak, of	22. Quincy Latimore, of
8. Brian Bixler, ss/2b	23. Dave Davidson, lhp
9. Duke Welker, lhp	24. Pat Bresnehan, rhp
10. Brad Corley, of	25. Yoslan Herrera, rhp
11. Tony Watson, lhp	26. Marcus Davis, of
12. Brian Friday, ss	27. Todd Redmond, rhp
13. Romulo Sanchez, rhp	28. Justin Byler, 1b
14. Bryan Bullington, rhp	29. Jason Delaney, 1b/of
15. Nyjer Morgan, of	30. Luis Munoz, rhp

the Dominican Republic in 1995.

Pittsburgh has been somewhat better at producing pitchers in recent years. They drafted each of their top three starters in 2007—Ian Snell, Tom Gorzelanny and Paul Maholm—as well as closer Matt Capps.

"I feel we're building an organization that is going to be very cohesive, with the scouting and player development departments on the same page in their goal of finding talent, developing and sending it to the major leagues," Huntington said.

General Manager: Neil Huntington. **Farm Director:** Kyle Stark. **Scouting Director:** Greg Smith.

Class	Team	League	W	L	PCT	Finish*	Manager	Affiliatd
Majors	Pittsburgh	National	68	94	.420	16th (16)	Jim Tracy	—
Triple-A	Indianapolis Indians	International	70	73	.490	8th (14)	Trent Jewett	2005
Double-A	Altoona Curve	Eastern	73	68	.518	4th (12)	Tim Leiper	1999
High A	Lynchburg Hillcats	Carolina	55	82	.401	8th (8)	Jeff Branson	1995
Low A	Hickory Crawdads	South Atlantic	70	66	.515	6th (16)	Gary Green	1999
Short-season	State College Spikes	New York-Penn	36	39	.480	8th (14)	Turner Ward	2007
Rookie	GCL Pirates	Gulf Coast	26	30	.464	11th (16)	Tom Prince	1967

Overall 2007 Minor League Record   330 358 .480   22nd

*Finish in overall standings (No. of teams in league) ^League champion

LAST YEAR'S TOP 30

Player, Pos.		Status
1.	Andrew McCutchen, of	No.1
2.	Neil Walker, c	No. 2
3.	Brad Lincoln, rhp	No. 4
4.	Brent Lillibridge, ss	(Braves)
5.	Yoslan Herrera, rhp	No. 25
6.	Josh Sharpless, rhp	No. 18
7.	Steve Pearce, 1b	No. 3
8.	Brian Bixler, ss	No. 8
9.	Brad Corley, of	No. 10
10.	Todd Redmond, rhp	No. 27
11.	Mike Felix, lhp	Dropped out
12.	John Van Benschoten, rhp	Majors
13.	Bryan Bullington, rhp	No. 14
14.	Wardell Starling, rhp	Dropped out
15.	Jonah Bayliss, rhp	Majors
16.	Pat Bresnehan, rhp	No. 24
17.	Dave Davidson, lhp	No. 23
18.	James Boone, of	Dropped out
19.	Josh Shortslef, lhp	Dropped out
20.	Joe Bauserman, rhp	Retired
21.	Shelby Ford, 2b	No. 6
22.	Brandon Holden, rhp	Dropped out
23.	Steve Lerud, c	Dropped out
24.	Jesse Chavez, rhp	Dropped out
25.	Franquelis Osoria, rhp	Majors
26.	Brian Rogers, rhp	Dropped out
27.	Rajai Davis, of	(Giants)
28.	Jim Negrych, 2b	Dropped out
29.	Jared Hughes, rhp	Dropped out
30.	Romulo Sanchez, rhp	No. 13

BEST TOOLS

Best Hitter for Average	Steve Pearce
Best Power Hitter	Steve Pearce
Best Strike-Zone Discipline	Steve Pearce
Fastest Baserunner	Pedro Powell
Best Athlete	Andrew McCutchen
Best Fastball	Daniel Moskos
Best Curveball	Dave Davidson
Best Slider	Daniel Moskos
Best Changeup	Tony Watson
Best Control	Todd Redmond
Best Defensive Catcher	Andrew Walker
Best Defensive Infielder	Brian Friday
Best Infield Arm	Brian Bixler
Best Defensive Outfielder	Andrew McCutchen
Best Outfield Arm	Austin McClune

PROJECTED 2011 LINEUP

Catcher	Ronny Paulino
First Base	Adam LaRoche
Second Base	Freddy Sanchez
Third Base	Neil Walker
Shortstop	Jack Wilson
Left Field	Jason Bay
Center Field	Andrew McCutchen
Right Field	Steve Pearce
No. 1 Starter	Tom Gorzelanny
No. 2 Starter	Ian Snell
No. 3 Starter	Brad Lincoln
No. 4 Starter	Paul Maholm
No. 5 Starter	Zach Duke
Closer	Matt Capps

TOP PROSPECTS OF THE DECADE

Year	Player, Pos.	2007 Org.
1998	Kris Benson, rhp	Orioles
1999	Chad Hermansen, of	Marlins
2000	Chad Hermansen, of	Marlins
2001	J.R. House, c	Orioles
2002	J.R. House, c	Orioles
2003	John Van Benschoten, rhp	Pirates
2004	John Van Benschoten, rhp	Pirates
2005	Zach Duke, lhp	Pirates
2006	Neil Walker, c	Pirates
2007	Andrew McCutchen, of	Pirates

TOP DRAFT PICKS OF THE DECADE

Year	Player, Pos.	2007 Org.
1998	Clint Johnston, lhp/of	Northern Lg.
1999	Bobby Bradley, rhp	Out of baseball
2000	Sean Burnett, lhp	Pirates
2001	John Van Benschoten, rhp	Pirates
2002	Bryan Bullington, rhp	Pirates
2003	Paul Maholm, lhp	Pirates
2004	Neil Walker, c	Pirates
2005	Andrew McCutchen, of	Pirates
2006	Brad Lincoln, rhp	Pirates
2007	Daniel Moskos, lhp	Pirates

LARGEST BONUSES IN CLUB HISTORY

Bryan Bullington, 2002	$4,000,000
Brad Lincoln, 2006	$2,750,000
Daniel Moskos, 2007	$2,475,000
John Van Benschoten, 2001	$2,400,000
Bobby Bradley, 1999	$2,225,000

PITTSBURGH PIRATES

Top 2008 Rookie: Steve Pearce, 1b/of. He has hit his way through the system and now the offensively challenged Pirates need to find a place for him in the lineup.

Breakout Prospect: Marcus Davis, of. The potential five-tool talent is very raw but is a hard worker and has a chance to be an impact player.

Sleeper: Phil Dumatrait, lhp. Lefthanders historically develop late, and Pittsburgh thinks he can be the latest example after claiming the former Red Sox first-rounder off waivers from the Reds.

SOURCE OF TOP 30 TALENT

Homegrown	25	Acquired	5
College	15	Trades	1
Junior college	0	Rule 5 draft	1
High school	5	Independent leagues	0
Draft-and-follow	3	Free agents/waivers	3
Nondrafted free agents	0		
International	2		

Numbers in parentheses indicate prospect rankings.

LF
Vonelvy Canal
Butch Biela
Albert Laboy
Ciro Rosero

CF
Andrew McCutchen (1)
Nyjer Morgan (15)
Austin McCune (21)
Quincy Latimore (22)
Marcus Davis (26)
Keanon Simon

RF
Steve Pearce (3)
Jamie Romak (7)
Brad Corley (10)

3B
Neil Walker (2)
Jared Keel
Eddie Prasch

SS
Brian Friday (12)
Angel Gonzalez
Andury Acevedo

2B
Shelby Ford (6)
Brian Bixler (8)
Jim Negrych
Matt Cavagnaro
Caleb Fields

1B
Justin Byler (28)
Jason Delaney (29)
Kent Sakamoto

C
Andrew Walker (20)
Steve Lerud
Kris Watts

RHP

Starters	Relievers
Brad Lincoln (4)	Romulo Sanchez (13)
Duke Welker (9)	Olivo Astacio (16)
Bryan Bullington (14)	Josh Sharpless (18)
Jimmy Barthmaier (17)	Evan Meek (19)
Yoslan Herrera (25)	Pat Bresnehan (24)
Ty Taubenheim	Todd Redmond (27)
Kyle McPherson	Luis Munoz (30)
Ryan Kelly	Jesse Chavez
Serguey Linares	Kevin Roberts
Mike Crotta	Tom Boleska
Jared Hughes	Brandon Holden
Blair Johnson	Chris Hernandez
Matthew Foust	Justin Vaclavik
Brad Clapp	Wardell Starling
Nic Suero	Matt Swanson
	Kyle Pearson
	Marino Salas

LHP

Starters	Relievers
Tony Watson (11)	Daniel Moskos (5)
Nelson Pereira	Dave Davidson (23)
Shane Youman	Charles Benoit
Phil Dumatrait	Mike Felix
Rudy Owens	Brian Holliday
Josh Shortslef	
Kyle Bloom	

2007   SIGNING BUDGET: $4.2 MILLION

Best Pro Debut: LHP Tony Watson (9) went 7-2, 2.79 with a 58-8 K-BB ratio in 68 innings, including three solid starts in low Class A. OF Keanon Simon (25) hit .335 with nine steals in the New York-Penn League.

Best Athlete: OF Marcus Davis (18) hit eight homers and stole 15 bases in the NY-P (albeit with a .231 average). He's raw, but he's loaded with athleticism and also flashed a low-90s fastball as a college closer. OF Quincy Latimore (4) also offers power and speed.

Best Pure Hitter: C Andrew Walker (5) and OF Butch Biela (13) both topped .300 in their pro debuts. Biela, who has a compact swing, caught in high school but may stay in the outfield to expedite his offensive development.

Best Power Hitter: Davis led the Southwest Athletic Conference with 16 homers in the spring. Walker has promising power for a catcher.

Fastest Runner: SS Brian Friday (3), Latimore, Davis and Simon all have plus speed, though none is a burner. Friday was slowed by an ankle injury during his first pro summer.

Best Defensive Player: Friday is a good all-around shortstop with range, arm strength and a quick release. Walker's work behind the plate encouraged the Pirates after he slumped defensively during the spring.

Best Fastball: LHP Daniel Moskos (1) works at 91-95 mph and peaks at 97 out of the bullpen. RHP Duke Welker (2) regularly pitches at 91-94 mph as a starter.

Best Secondary Pitch: Moskos had one of the most unhittable sliders in the draft. Watson has a quality changeup that helped him limit pro lefthanders to a .226 average.

Most Intriguing Background: RHP Brian Tracy's (20) father Jim played in the majors and was fired as Pittsburgh's manager after the season, while his brother Chad is a catcher in the Rangers system. RHP Taylor Cameron's (31) dad Brad was a Pirates area scout but was also fired after the season.

Closest To The Majors: With his stuff and fierce competitiveness, Moskos could quickly get to Pittsburgh's bullpen. Welker has a plus fastball and improved secondary stuff, so he could be on the fast track as well.

Best Late-Round Pick: Davis has the most potential. The Pirates also are high on Biela; McPherson, who skipped a couple of grades early and signed as a 19-year-old college junior; and RHP Tom Boleska (35), who has plus velocity and a power curveball.

The One Who Got Away: Athletic OF Runey Davis (11), who was also a star running back, opted to play college baseball at Texas.

Assessment: The Pirates took a lot of heat for taking Moskos at No. 4 rather than Matt Wieters, who had a higher price tag and went with the next pick to the Orioles. Many clubs also rated Ross Detwiler (No. 6 to the Nationals) ahead of Moskos among college lefties, and some would try Moskos as a starter. New GM Neal Huntington fired scouting director Ed Creech in October.

2006   BUDGET: $4.9 MILLION

RHP Brad Lincoln (1) didn't pitch at all in 2007 after having Tommy John surgery in April. 2B Shelby Ford (3) had a nice first full season, but the success of this draft ultimately rests on Lincoln.

GRADE: C

2005   BUDGET: $3.7 MILLION

This draft could produce three big league regulars in OF Andrew McCutchen (1), the system's best prospect; SS Brent Lillibridge (4), who yielded Adam LaRoche in a trade with the Braves; and 1B/OF Steve Pearce (8).

GRADE: B+

2004   BUDGET: $4.1 MILLION

3B Neil Walker (1) still has a lot of upside despite moving from catcher. SS/2B Brian Bixler (2) is on the verge of claiming a big league job.

GRADE: C+

2003   BUDGET: $4.4 MILLION

Pittsburgh found two-fifths of its big league rotation in LHPs Paul Maholm (1) and Tom Gorzelanny (2). RHP Josh Sharpless (24) is a local product made good, though he took a step back last season.

GRADE: B+

Draft analysis by Jim Callis. Numbers in parentheses indicate draft rounds. Budgets are bonuses in first 10 rounds.

1

NATIONAL LEAGUE CENTRAL

ANDREW McCUTCHEN, OF

Born: Oct. 10, 1986.
Ht.: 5-11. **Wt.:** 170.
Bats: R. **Throws:** R.
Drafted: HS —
Fort Meade, Fla., 2005
(1st round).
Signed by: Rob Sidwell.

McCutchen was such a prodigy that he led Polk County, Fla., high schoolers in hitting with a .507 average as an eighth-grader. As a senior, he won state player of the year and national All-America honors after hitting a mind-boggling .709 with 16 homers. The Pirates drafted him 11th overall and signed him for $1.9 million. McCutchen ranked as the No. 1 prospect in the Rookie-level Gulf Coast and low Class A South Atlantic leagues in his first two pro seasons, and reached Double-A Altoona at age 19 at the end of 2006. He struggled for the first time as a pro in 2007, getting off to a poor start while fighting cold early-season weather when he returned to the Eastern League. But he recovered and produced as he had in the past during the second half, which included a late-season promotion to Triple-A Indianapolis. McCutchen is a multi-talented individual who writes poetry and freestyle rap and is an outstanding singer and artist. He comes from athletic bloodlines, as his father was a running back at small-college power Carson Newman (Tenn.) and his mother was a standout volleyball player at Polk County Community College.

McCutchen is an outstanding athlete with a quick bat, speed, instincts and intelligence. He sprays the ball from gap to gap and also has enough power to hit home runs. He has first-step quickness that helps him both in the field and on the bases, where he has succeeded in 81 percent of his pro steal attempts. he has above-average range in center field and he gets to balls that few other outfielders can reach. His arm strength is average, which makes it better than most center fielders'. After hitting .184 in April, he didn't panic, raising his batting average in each subsequent month and thriving in his first taste of Triple-A.

McCutchen's power potential may already be topping out. He has good bat speed but lacks the size of most power hitters. He can be made to chase breaking balls off the plate, particularly from righthanders. The plate discipline he showed when he first came into pro ball is eroding as he moves higher in the farm system. He projects more as No. 1 or 2 hitter than someone who'll bat in the middle of a major league order, so he'll need to show more patience and draw more walks. With his speed, he could steal more bases than the 61 he has swiped in 327 pro games. He also can improve his outfield instincts, as his quickness allows him to make up for a relative lack of savvy.

Despite his subpar 2007, McCutchen remains on the fast track as the Pirates' one true impact prospect. He'll be given a chance to win the starting job in center field despite being 21 and having just 17 games of experience above Double-A. If he doesn't win it, he still should make his big league debut later in the year.

Year	Club (League)	Class	AVG	G	AB	R	H	2B	3B	HR	RBI	BB	SO	SB	OBP	SLG
2005	Pirates (GCL)	R	.297	45	158	36	47	9	3	2	30	29	24	13	.411	.430
	Williamsport (NYP)	A	.346	13	52	12	18	3	1	0	5	8	6	4	.443	.442
2006	Hickory (SAL)	A	.291	114	453	77	132	20	4	14	62	42	91	22	.356	.446
	Altoona (EL)	AA	.308	20	78	12	24	4	0	3	12	8	20	1	.379	.474
2007	Altoona (EL)	AA	.258	118	446	70	115	20	3	10	48	44	83	17	.327	.383
	Indianapolis (IL)	AAA	.313	17	67	7	21	4	0	1	5	4	11	4	.347	.418
MINOR LEAGUE TOTALS			.285	327	1254	214	357	60	11	30	162	135	235	61	.358	.422

2 NEIL WALKER, 3B

RODGER WOOD

Born: Sept. 10, 1985. **B-T:** B-R. **Ht.:** 6-3. **Wt.:** 210. **Drafted:** HS—Gibsonia, Pa., 2004 (1st round). **Signed by:** Jon Mercurio.

In 2004, the Pirates made Walker their first-ever first-round pick from the Pittsburgh area. He moved from catcher to third base on the first day of spring training in 2007 because the Bucs wanted to get his bat to the big leagues quickly. Walker has worked hard to become productive from both sides of the plate. He has good power and should hit more home runs as he matures. He also improved his plate discipline greatly. His makeup is off the charts and he is a popular figure in the clubhouse. His arm strength plays well at third base. A college football prospect as a wide receiver, he's a good athlete and has average speed. Walker still is getting the hang of playing third base and has some trouble with difficult plays such as slow rollers and balls to his backhand side. He also seems to have lost a bit of pop in his bat since tearing a ligament in his left wrist while in the Arizona Fall League in 2005. The Pirates could use help at third base, and Walker has an outside chance to make the club in spring training. He'll more likely work on his defense in Triple-A before a midseason callup to Pittsburgh.

Year	Club (League)	Class	AVG	G	AB	R	H	2B	3B	HR	RBI	BB	SO	SB	OBP	SLG
2004	Pirates (GCL)	R	.271	52	192	28	52	12	3	4	20	10	33	3	.313	.427
	Williamsport (NYP)	A	.313	8	32	2	10	3	0	0	7	2	1	1	.343	.406
2005	Hickory (SAL)	A	.301	120	485	78	146	33	2	12	68	20	71	7	.332	.452
	Lynchburg (Car)	A	.262	9	42	4	11	2	1	0	12	0	12	0	.244	.357
2006	Lynchburg (Car)	A	.284	72	264	32	75	22	1	3	35	19	41	3	.345	.409
	Altoona (EL)	AA	.161	10	31	5	5	0	0	2	3	1	4	0	.188	.355
2007	Altoona (EL)	AA	.288	117	431	77	124	30	3	13	66	53	73	9	.362	.462
	Indianapolis (IL)	AAA	.203	19	64	7	13	3	0	0	0	2	13	1	.261	.250
MINOR LEAGUE TOTALS			.283	407	1541	233	436	105	10	34	211	107	248	24	.333	.430

3 STEVE PEARCE, 1B/OF

KEVIN PATAKY

Born: April 13, 1983. **B-T:** R-R. **Ht.:** 5-11. **Wt.:** 209. **Drafted:** South Carolina, 2005 (8th round). **Signed by:** Jack Powell.

Pittsburgh drafted Pearce as a college senior after he hit 42 homers in two years at South Carolina and turned down the Red Sox as a 10th-rounder in 2004. He has 64 longballs as a pro, including 31 in a breakout 2007 season in which he also hit .333 with 113 RBIs in the minors and made his big league debut. Pearce is an aggressive hitter with power to all fields. He always looks fastball first but has learned to adjust to breaking and offspeed pitches. He's a solid defensive first baseman with decent range, good hands and rare arm strength for the position. He has slightly below-average speed but good baserunning instincts and stole 16 bases last season. With Adam LaRoche at first base, the Pirates started to deploy Pearce in right field once he reached Triple-A. He's a little shaky in chasing fly balls, but he did show considerable improvement. Pearce's bat is ready for the major leagues. He just needs to show he can handle right field to open the season with Pittsburgh.

Year	Club (League)	Class	AVG	G	AB	R	H	2B	3B	HR	RBI	BB	SO	SB	OBP	SLG
2005	Williamsport (NYP)	A	.301	72	272	48	82	26	0	7	52	35	43	2	.381	.474
2006	Hickory (SAL)	A	.288	41	160	35	46	13	1	12	38	15	32	1	.363	.606
	Lynchburg (Car)	A	.265	90	328	48	87	27	1	14	60	34	65	7	.348	.482
2007	Lynchburg (Car)	A	.347	19	75	19	26	4	1	11	24	8	13	2	.412	.867
	Altoona (EL)	AA	.334	81	290	57	97	27	2	14	72	33	45	7	.400	.586
	Indianapolis (IL)	AAA	.320	34	122	18	39	9	1	6	17	6	12	5	.366	.557
	Pittsburgh (NL)	MLB	.294	23	68	13	20	5	1	0	6	5	12	2	.342	.397
MINOR LEAGUE TOTALS			.302	337	1247	225	377	106	6	64	263	131	210	24	.375	.551
MAJOR LEAGUE TOTALS			.294	23	68	13	20	5	1	0	6	5	12	2	.342	.397

4 BRAD LINCOLN, RHP

STEVE MOORE

Born: May 25, 1985. **B-T:** L-R. **Ht.:** 6-0. **Wt.:** 216. **Drafted:** Houston, 2006 (1st round). **Signed by:** Everett Russell.

The Pirates were happy to get Lincoln with the fourth overall pick in the 2006 draft, but after he signed for $2.75 million, he worked just 24 innings in his pro debut because of an oblique injury. The medical news got worse in 2007, as he followed in the footsteps of recent Pirates first-round pitchers in needing major arm surgery. He had Tommy John surgery in April. Before he got hurt, Lincoln had a four-seam fastball that routinely sat at 92-94 mph and topped out at 98, as well as a two-seamer with plus sink. He also had a hard curveball that many scouts graded as his best pitch.

He's aggressive and willing to challenge hitters. A two-way star in college, he is a better athlete and hitter than most pitchers. Lincoln's changeup has good sink, but he has trouble commanding it at times. Though the track record of Tommy John survivors is encouraging, he won't arrive in Pittsburgh as fast as the team hoped. The Pirates projected Lincoln as a possible No. 1 starter before he got hurt, and they'll be cautious with his comeback. He was throwing at distances of up to 150 feet by the end of instructional league and was on course to begin working off a mound in January.

Year	Club (League)	Class	W	L	ERA	G	GS	CG	SV	IP	H	R	ER	HR	BB	SO	AVG
2006	Pirates (GCL)	R	0	0	0.00	2	2	0	0	8	6	1	0	0	1	9	.222
	Hickory (SAL)	A	1	2	6.75	4	4	0	0	16	25	15	12	2	6	10	.368
2007	Did Not Play—Injured																
MINOR LEAGUE TOTALS			1	2	4.56	6	6	0	0	24	31	16	12	2	7	19	326

5 DANIEL MOSKOS, LHP

Born: April 28, 1986. **B-T:** R-L. **Ht.:** 6-1. **Wt.:** 210. **Drafted:** Clemson, 2007 (1st round). **Signed by:** Greg Schilz.

BILL MITCHELL

Pittsburgh created quite a stir by selecting Moskos with the fourth overall pick in the 2007 draft, passing up Georgia Tech catcher Matt Wieters because of his price tag. Then-GM Dave Littlefield caused more outrage when he announced Moskos, who signed for $2.475 million, would be a reliever. Clemson moved him into its rotation during the spring and several clubs believed he has the pitches to start as a pro. Moskos has a live arm with a fastball that touched 97 mph in college and was consistently in the 91-95 range. He has a wipeout slider that reaches 87 mph, along with a decent curveball and a changeup with good fade. He wins high marks for his competitiveness. In his pro debut, Moskos' fastball rarely hit 90 mph until his last few outings. The Pirates insist the loss of velocity was a matter of fatigue and not something more serious. His curveball and changeup need polish, though that's less of an issue if he's not a starter. His fastball and slider are major league pitches, so Moskos will ride the fast track if he remains a reliever. He'll likely open at high Class A Lynchburg and should reach the majors by no later than 2009.

Year	Club (League)	Class	W	L	ERA	G	GS	CG	SV	IP	H	R	ER	HR	BB	SO	AVG
2007	Pirates (GCL)	R	0	0	0.00	2	0	0	0	3	4	0	0	0	0	3	.333
	State College (NYP)	A	0	0	4.26	11	0	0	1	12	19	8	6	1	6	13	.328
MINOR LEAGUE TOTALS			0	0	3.45	13	0	0	1	15	23	8	6	1	6	16	.329

6 SHELBY FORD, 2B

Born: Dec. 15, 1984. **B-T:** B-R. **Ht.:** 6-3. **Wt.:** 173. **Drafted:** Oklahoma State, 2006 (3rd round). **Signed by:** Mike Leuzinger.

RODGER WOOD

Ford was a three-time all-state selection as the son of a high school coach in Fort Worth, then stayed home to begin his college career at Texas Christian before transferring to Oklahoma State. He put together a strong first full pro season in 2007 before missing the final month with a strained muscle in his lower back. Ford has good pop for a middle infielder and the ability to hit for power to the opposite field. While he has a slightly better swing lefthanded, there's virtually no dropoff when he bats from the right side. He's a good second baseman with decent range and an above-average arm. If he winds up as a utilityman, he already has experience at shortstop from high school and third base from TCU. His speed is average. Ford can be made to chase pitches out of the strike zone, though he showed better plate discipline last season. His footwork is a bit shaky on the double-play pivot, though he has improved in pro ball. Ford will begin 2008 in Double-A, and he's advanced enough that he could make his major league debut at some point in 2009. However, he's blocked by all-star second baseman Freddy Sanchez, who has two more years before he can become a free agent.

Year	Club (League)	Class	AVG	G	AB	R	H	2B	3B	HR	RBI	BB	SO	SB	OBP	SLG
2006	Williamsport (NYP)	A	.400	7	25	3	10	3	0	0	2	3	3	1	.483	.520
	Hickory (SAL)	A	.265	55	223	43	59	16	3	6	27	14	51	4	.329	.444
2007	Lynchburg (Car)	A	.281	94	360	64	101	26	7	5	55	34	68	14	.360	.433
MINOR LEAGUE TOTALS			.280	156	608	110	170	45	10	11	84	51	122	19	.354	.441

7 JAMIE ROMAK, OF

Born: Sept. 30, 1985. **B-T:** R-R. **Ht.:** 6-2. **Wt.:** 220. **Drafted:** HS—London, Ontario, 2003 (4th round). **Signed by:** Lonnie Goldberg (Braves).

Romak had the lowest profile among the players in the January 2007 trade that brought him and Adam LaRoche from the Braves for Mike Gonzalez and shortstop prospect Brent Lillibridge. Despite missing three weeks with a bruised left hand after getting hit by a pitch, Romak increased his home run production for the fourth straight season. Romak has outstanding raw power and can hit the ball out of the park to all fields. He also has an exceptionally strong arm, which makes him a pro-totypical right fielder. He's willing to work counts and take a walk. Romak has holes in his swing and can be fooled by offspeed and breaking pitches off the plate. He's too passive at the plate at times and will take hittable pitches. Romak offers little speed or range. Though he's still rather raw, Romak is one of the few power-hitting prospects in the system. He'll spend 2008 in Double-A, and his ability to make adjustments when he doesn't get fastballs will tell the tale of his long-term chances in the majors.

Year	Club (League)	Class	AVG	G	AB	R	H	2B	3B	HR	RBI	BB	SO	SB	OBP	SLG
2003	Braves (GCL)	R	.176	19	51	5	9	2	0	0	4	9	10	0	.300	.216
2004	Danville (Appy)	R	.190	48	158	25	30	5	1	5	22	14	56	1	.287	.329
2005	Danville (Appy)	R	.274	34	124	25	34	10	1	7	27	14	38	2	.368	.540
2006	Rome (SAL)	A	.247	108	348	55	86	26	2	16	68	59	102	3	.369	.471
2007	Hickory (SAL)	A	.275	20	69	16	19	4	0	5	15	9	24	0	.393	.551
	Lynchburg (Car)	A	.252	85	294	49	74	21	1	15	45	55	90	2	.380	.483
MINOR LEAGUE TOTALS			.241	314	1044	175	252	68	5	48	181	160	320	8	.359	.454

8 BRIAN BIXLER, SS/2B

Born: Oct. 22, 1982. **B-T:** R-R. **Ht.:** 6-1. **Wt.:** 196. **Drafted:** Eastern Michigan, 2004 (2nd round). **Signed by:** Duane Gustavson.

BILL MITCHELL

Bixler was slated to begin 2007 in Double-A but jumped to Triple-A after an impressive showing during his first major league spring training. The International League named him to its postseason all-star team, and he played for Team USA in the World Cup in November. He has shown the ability to hit for average since nearly winning the NCAA Division I batting title with a .453 average in 2004, and Bixler is developing gap power as he gets older. He's an above-average runner and a high-percentage basestealer with good awareness on the basepaths. He has outstanding instincts and makeup, understands the nuances of the game and is a hard worker. Bixler strikes out too much, especially for someone with only modest power. He also can be inconsistent in the field, especially with his throws. His range and arm are fringy, so he'll likely wind up at second base in the long run. There are a number of different scenarios for Bixler in 2008. He could be the Pirates' starting shortstop if Jack Wilson is traded, their utility infielder or their Triple-A shortstop.

Year	Club (League)	Class	AVG	G	AB	R	H	2B	3B	HR	RBI	BB	SO	SB	OBP	SLG
2004	Williamsport (NYP)	A	.276	59	228	40	63	7	4	0	21	15	51	14	.321	.342
2005	Hickory (SAL)	A	.281	126	502	74	141	23	2	9	50	38	134	21	.343	.388
2006	Lynchburg (Car)	A	.303	73	267	46	81	16	2	5	33	35	58	18	.402	.434
	Altoona (EL)	AA	.301	60	226	36	68	13	1	3	19	16	57	6	.363	.407
2007	Indianapolis (IL)	AAA	.274	129	475	77	130	23	10	5	51	54	131	28	.368	.396
MINOR LEAGUE TOTALS			.284	447	1698	273	483	82	19	22	174	158	431	87	.359	.394

9 DUKE WELKER, RHP

Born: Feb. 10, 1986. **B-T:** L-R. **Ht.:** 6-7. **Wt.:** 220. **Drafted:** Arkansas, 2007 (2nd round). **Signed by:** Mike Leuzinger.

RODGER WOOD

Welker missed most of his senior high school season in Washington with back problems, then had his freshman season at Seminole State (Okla.) Junior College shortened by arthroscopic shoulder surgery. He blossomed after transferring to Arkansas in 2007, then signed with the Pirates for $477,000. Pittsburgh shut him down in mid-August with elbow soreness. Welker has a projectable pitcher's body with a long, loose frame. His fastball sits at 91-92 mph and he uses his height to get a good downward plane. He can dial the heater up to 95 mph on occasion, giving hope he could add velocity. He made progress with his secondary pitches during the spring. He has a reputation for being soft, but the Pirates say Welker has a bad rap and that his mound presence is fine. His curveball and changeup still need work. His curve tends to get loopy and his changeup sometimes lacks deception. He has been healthy for just one of the last four years, though Pittsburgh isn't worried about his elbow. Welker will begin the season in low Class A with a chance for a midseason promotion. He projects as a possible No. 3 starter with a major league ETA of 2010.

Year	Club (League)	Class	W	L	ERA	G	GS	CG	SV	IP	H	R	ER	HR	BB	SO	AVG
2007	State College (NYP)	A	2	2	2.35	7	7	0	0	30	29	9	8	2	10	27	.259
MINOR LEAGUE TOTALS			2	2	2.35	7	7	0	0	30	29	9	8	2	10	27	.259

10 BRAD CORLEY, OF

CARL KLINE

Born: Dec. 28, 1983. **B-T:** R-R. **Ht.:** 6-2. **Wt.:** 216. **Drafted:** Mississippi State, 2005 (2nd round). **Signed by:** Everett Russell.

Corley was Kentucky's high school player of the year in 2002 and a first-team All-American as a sophomore two years later at Mississippi State. His statistics slipped as a junior while he recovered from a broken thumb, yet the Pirates took him in the second round. He has registered 193 RBIs in his two full pro seasons. Corley can pull inside pitches over the fence and has good gap power to the opposite field. He has short-ened his swing since turning pro. He also has a strong arm, fitting for a guy who was used as a closer in college. He owns solid speed and right-field range. He believes his aggressiveness helps him be a run producer, but swinging at everything is going to hurt Corley as he moves up the ladder. He has drawn just 32 walks while striking out 214 times in full-season leagues. He's a sucker for high fastballs. Corley will begin 2008 in Double-A after finishing there last season. His career could stall if he doesn't exhibit some semblance of plate discipline against more advanced pitchers.

Year	Club (League)	Class	AVG	G	AB	R	H	2B	3B	HR	RBI	BB	SO	SB	OBP	SLG
2005	Williamsport (NYP)	A	.279	68	265	29	74	10	6	4	35	16	56	3	.331	.408
2006	Hickory (SAL)	A	.281	134	534	87	150	32	2	16	100	18	109	9	.323	.438
2007	Lynchburg (Car)	A	.285	126	485	73	138	36	4	14	89	14	99	3	.319	.462
	Altoona (EL)	AA	.256	10	39	3	10	2	0	0	4	0	6	1	.256	.308
MINOR LEAGUE TOTALS			.281	338	1323	192	372	80	12	34	228	48	270	16	.321	.437

11 TONY WATSON, LHP

Born: May 30, 1985. **B-T:** L-L. **Ht.:** 6-4. **Wt.:** 210. **Drafted:** Nebraska, 2007 (9th round). **Signed by:** Mike Leuzinger.

Watson posted a microscopic 0.10 ERA and won the Bob Feller Award as the top prep pitcher in Iowa as a high school senior. But he also tore the labrum in his shoulder, so he turned down the Marlins as a 23rd-round pick and headed to Nebraska, where he redshirted in 2004. Draft-eligible as a sophomore in 2006, he turned down a six-figure offer from the Orioles in the 17th round and then regressed last spring, signing for $85,000 as a ninth-rounder. Watson has a good feel for pitching, and he knows how to work both sides of the plate and mix his pitches. His fastball sat at 86-88 mph in 2007, a tick or two down from the previous year, and he has lost some velocity since having his labrum repaired. But it plays up because of a changeup that drops off the table. He also has a slurvy breaking ball that has its moments. Watson has to be fine with his control in order to succeed and may run into problems when he faces more advanced hitters. He'll begin this season in low Class A, where he ended 2007 on a good note, and a promotion could be on the docket at some point during the summer.

Year	Club (League)	Class	W	L	ERA	G	GS	CG	SV	IP	H	R	ER	HR	BB	SO	AVG
2007	State College (NYP)	A	6	1	2.52	10	10	0	0	53	47	17	15	4	7	40	.230
	Hickory (SAL)	A	1	1	3.86	3	3	0	0	14	14	6	6	2	1	18	.264
MINOR LEAGUE TOTALS			7	2	2.79	13	13	0	0	67	61	23	21	6	8	58	.237

12 BRIAN FRIDAY, SS

Born: Dec. 16, 1985. **B-T:** R-R. **Ht.:** 5-11. **Wt.:** 180. **Drafted:** Rice, 2007 (3rd round). **Signed by:** Everett Russell.

After hitting just .256 with one home run as a freshman at Rice, Friday blossomed into one of the best shortstops in college baseball. A third-round pick last June, he signed for $355,500. He has outstanding instincts and exceptional leadership skills, making up for his lack of size. He plays the little man's game well, as he's an outstanding directional bunter who's a threat to lay one down for a hit any time the bases are empty. He showed outstanding plate discipline in college, but pro pitchers got him to chase more pitches out of the strike zone and he'll have to prove that won't be a long-term problem. He has plus speed and an aggressive mentality on the bases. Friday has good range in the field to go with a strong arm and reliable hands. He needs to get stronger, though, or risk being overpowered by hard throwers as moves up the ladder. Friday should begin his first full season in low Class A.

Year	Club (League)	Class	AVG	G	AB	R	H	2B	3B	HR	RBI	BB	SO	SB	OBP	SLG
2007	State College (NYP)	A	.295	40	156	31	46	10	1	2	13	10	33	6	.371	.410
MINOR LEAGUE TOTALS			.295	40	156	31	46	10	1	2	13	10	33	6	.371	.410

13 ROMULO SANCHEZ, RHP

Born: April 28, 1984. **B-T:** R-R. **Ht.:** 6-5. **Wt.:** 243. **Signed:** Venezuela, 2002. **Signed by:** Camilo Pascual/ Doug Carpenter (Dodgers).

Once a trailblazer in the region, the Pirates have had a woeful track record of signing players from Latin America in recent seasons. They're slowly reversing the trend under the auspices of Latin American scouting director Rene Gayo. In the meantime, they made quite a find in Sanchez, whom they signed after he was released by the Dodgers in spring training in 2004 after pitching two years in the Rookie-level Venezuelan Summer League. Sanchez promptly threw a no-hitter with 12 strikeouts for the Pirates' VSL team that summer. He's a big, hard thrower who can run his fastball up to 96 mph and routinely hits 92-93 mph. If he can keep improving his curveball, Sanchez could be a dominant late-inning reliever. He held his own in his first taste of the major leagues last season and showed good mound presence. Though he finished the season in the majors after making the jump from Double-A, he could use a little time in Triple-A to tighten up his curveball and add polish to his game.

Year	Club (League)	Class	W	L	ERA	G	GS	CG	SV	IP	H	R	ER	HR	BB	SO	AVG
2002	Dodgers E (DSL)	R	1	4	4.44	15	0	0	1	24	24	16	12	4	10	22	.242
2003	Dodgers E (DSL)	R	2	3	4.46	9	9	0	0	38	40	25	19	1	10	21	.255
2004	San Joaquin (VSL)	R	4	2	1.03	21	2	1	6	43	33	9	5	0	7	49	.202
2005	Pirates (GCL)	R	1	0	1.80	2	1	0	0	10	7	2	2	1	4	7	.206
	Altoona (EL)	AA	1	0	3.60	2	2	0	0	10	11	4	4	2	4	5	.282
	Hickory (SAL)	A	3	3	4.70	10	10	0	0	53	59	34	28	5	19	24	.292
2006	Hickory (SAL)	A	0	3	7.08	21	3	0	4	40	51	36	32	4	18	28	.302
	Lynchburg (Car)	A	0	0	1.04	8	0	0	1	8	7	1	1	0	4	6	.212
	Altoona (EL)	AA	0	0	5.00	8	0	0	0	9	8	5	5	1	8	5	.242
2007	Altoona (EL)	AA	6	3	2.81	40	0	0	1	57	43	24	18	8	17	52	.204
	Pittsburgh (NL)	MLB	1	0	5.00	16	0	0	0	18	16	10	10	2	8	11	.254
MINOR LEAGUE TOTALS			18	18	3.83	136	27	1	13	296	283	156	126	26	101	219	.248
MAJOR LEAGUE TOTALS			1	0	5.00	16	0	0	0	18	16	10	10	2	8	11	.254

14 BRYAN BULLINGTON, RHP

Born: Sept. 30, 1980. **B-T:** R-R. **Ht.:** 6-4. **Wt.:** 220. **Drafted:** Ball State, 2002 (1st round). **Signed by:** Duane Gustavson.

Bullington has been a disappointment since the Pirates made him the first overall pick in the 2002 draft, as seven pitchers drafted after him beat him to the major leagues, including four from the high school ranks. Bullington got to Pittsburgh at the end of the 2005 season, then tore the labrum in his shoulder during his debut and missed all of 2006 after undergoing surgery. He had an up-and-down season at Indianapolis last year, though he did get the win in the Triple-A all-star game. He also created some optimism at the end of the season with two solid major league starts. Bullington's fastball now usually tops out at 90 mph, a far cry from the 95 mph scouts clocked him at in college. He does have a good slider, decent changeup and a solid feel for pitching to make up for a lack of a great heater. It's clear now that he won't be a star, but Bullington has shown great resiliency and can still carve out a major league career as a back-of-the-rotation starter. He'll likely start the 2008 season back in Triple-A

Year	Club (League)	Class	W	L	ERA	G	GS	CG	SV	IP	H	R	ER	HR	BB	SO	AVG
2003	Hickory (SAL)	A	5	1	1.39	8	7	0	0	45	25	10	7	3	11	46	.155
	Lynchburg (Car)	A	8	4	3.05	17	17	2	0	97	101	39	33	5	27	67	.270
2004	Altoona (EL)	AA	12	7	4.10	26	26	0	0	145	160	77	66	18	47	100	.289
2005	Indianapolis (IL)	AAA	9	5	3.38	18	18	1	0	109	104	48	41	11	26	82	.251
	Pittsburgh (NL)	MLB	0	0	13.50	1	0	0	0	1	1	2	2	0	1	1	.250
2006	Did Not Play—Injured																
2007	Indianapolis (IL)	AAA	11	9	4.00	26	26	0	0	150	146	70	67	10	59	89	.262
	Pittsburgh (NL)	MLB	0	3	5.29	5	3	0	0	17	24	11	10	3	5	7	.343
MINOR LEAGUE TOTALS			45	26	3.52	95	94	3	0	547	536	244	214	47	170	384	.260
MAJOR LEAGUE TOTALS			0	3	5.89	6	3	0	0	18	25	13	12	3	6	8	.338

15 NYJER MORGAN, OF

Born: July 2, 1980. **B-T:** L-L. **Ht.:** 6-0. **Wt.:** 172. **Drafted:** Walla Walla (Wash.) CC, D/F 2002 (33rd round). **Signed by:** Kevin Clouser.

Morgan played four years of junior hockey in Alberta before turning his focus to baseball. He had a slow and injury-filled climb through the system, after shoulder surgery cost him much of the 2005 season and a torn thumb ligament limited him to 44 games in Triple-A in 2007. However, he did enough in his limited minor league time in 2007 to get a September callup to the major leagues and make an impression. Former manager Jim Tracy played Morgan regularly in center field and the leadoff spot, and he responded by getting on base at a .359 clip and making highlight-reel plays. His strength is game-changing speed that he uses both on the bases and in the field. While he does not always get the best jumps on balls, Morgan's wheels allow him to close quickly and make catches like the jaw-dropping over-the-shoulder grab he made while running into the wall in right-center at Houston's Minute Maid Park. While he can be overeager on the bases at times, he's an excellent bunter who uses that skill as a means to get on base. On the downside, he offers little power and his arm is just playable in center field. More important, he's already 27. Nevertheless, Morgan will be the favorite to win Pittsburgh's starting center-field job when spring training begins.

Year	Club (League)	Class	AVG	G	AB	R	H	2B	3B	HR	RBI	BB	SO	SB	OBP	SLG
2003	Williamsport (NYP)	A	.343	72	268	49	92	7	4	0	23	33	44	26	.439	.399
2004	Hickory (SAL)	A	.255	134	514	83	131	16	7	4	41	53	120	55	.358	.337
2005	Lynchburg (Car)	A	.286	60	252	36	72	12	3	0	24	11	40	24	.328	.357
2006	Lynchburg (Car)	A	.303	61	228	43	69	7	3	0	22	20	40	38	.390	.360
	Altoona (EL)	AA	.306	56	219	39	67	6	5	1	10	15	28	21	.359	.393
2007	Indianapolis (IL)	AAA	.305	44	164	30	50	4	2	0	10	15	28	26	.374	.354
	Pirates (GCL)	R	.308	4	13	3	4	0	0	1	1	2	3	0	.438	.538
	Pittsburgh (NL)	MLB	.299	28	107	15	32	3	4	1	7	9	19	7	.359	.430
MINOR LEAGUE TOTALS			.293	431	1658	283	485	52	24	6	131	149	303	190	.374	.364
MAJOR LEAGUE TOTALS			.299	28	107	15	32	3	4	1	7	9	19	7	.359	.430

16 OLIVO ASTACIO, RHP

Born: July 28, 1984. **B-T:** R-R. **Ht:** 6-6. **Wt.:** 242. **Signed:** Dominican Republic, 2002. **Signed by:** Jesus Alou (Red Sox).

The Pirates signed Astacio off the scrap heap in March 2006, after he had been released by the Cubs two months earlier. Chicago had acquired him from the Red Sox for Mike Remlinger in 2005, when he missed the entire season for violating a team rule. Now that he's healthy again, Astacio is a prototypical power reliever with a large frame, a live fastball and a big breaking pitch. He can routinely dial his fastball up to 96 mph and it has decent movement. His curveball is an out pitch, a hammer that falls off the table. His changeup is also serviceable, though he doesn't need it much working in short relief. Astacio's biggest problem is control, as he has averaged 5.4 walks per nine innings as a pro. He also lacks experience against quality hitters, as he didn't pitch in a full-season league until 2007 and made just one appearance in Double-A before falling in the shower and breaking his pitching hand. Added to the 40-man roster in November, Astacio will return to Double-A in 2008 and could see his first major league action later in the year if he throws more strikes.

Year	Club (League)	Class	W	L	ERA	G	GS	CG	SV	IP	H	R	ER	HR	BB	SO	AVG
2002	Red Sox (GCL)	R	0	2	6.35	6	3	0	0	17	26	17	12	1	15	7	.377
	Red Sox (DSL)	R	0	0	6.95	7	7	0	0	22	26	18	17	1	21	14	.321
2003	Red Sox E (DSL)	R	3	5	3.19	9	9	0	0	42	31	25	15	1	21	42	.203
2004	Red Sox (GCL)	R	3	4	3.13	12	8	1	0	46	46	27	16	1	18	32	.256
	Red Sox (DSL)	R	1	0	5.25	4	4	0	0	12	8	7	7	0	8	15	.190
2005	Did Not Play—Restricted List																
2006	Williamsport (NYP)	A	2	3	3.49	22	0	0	9	28	16	12	11	0	15	39	.162
2007	Hickory (SAL)	A	1	1	3.54	30	0	0	11	48	39	22	19	0	28	71	.217
	Lynchburg (Car)	A	0	1	8.22	7	0	0	1	15	14	16	14	3	12	19	.241
	Altoona (EL)	AA	0	0	0.00	1	0	0	0	2	0	0	0	0	2	1	.000
MINOR LEAGUE TOTALS			10	16	4.28	98	31	1	21	233	206	144	111	7	140	240	.237

17 JIMMY BARTHMAIER, RHP

Born: Jan. 6, 1984. **B-T:** R-R. **Ht.:** 6-5. **Wt.:** 230. **Drafted:** HS—Roswell, Ga., 2003 (13th round). **Signed by:** Ellis Dungan (Astros).

Barthmaier had ranked as one of the Astros' top pitching prospects since turning down offers to play quarterback at major programs to sign for a 13th-round record $750,000 in 2003. But he came down with a nerve problem in his elbow toward the end of spring training and pitched only sparingly until mid-May, after which he was so inconsistent that Houston removed him from its 40-man roster. His 9.69 ERA in the Arizona Fall League cemented that decision but didn't deter the Pirates from claiming Barthmaier on waivers. At his best, he'll show a low-90s sinker, a four-seam fastball that can touch 96 mph and a big-breaking curveball. But his stuff was down for most of 2007, as his fastball was mostly average and his curve was flat. His changeup, command and consistency never developed as the Astros hoped, leaving some in that organization to question his aptitude and desire. He'll pitch backward at times and doesn't trust his fastball-curve combo as much as he should. Barthmaier still has a big, strong body and the potential for a live arm, and he may benefit from a move to the bullpen, where he could narrow his focus. The Pirates will try to get him back on track this year in Double-A.

Year	Club (League)	Class	W	L	ERA	G	GS	CG	SV	IP	H	R	ER	HR	BB	SO	AVG
2003	Martinsville (Appy)	R	1	1	2.49	8	3	0	0	21	19	9	6	0	7	18	.226
2004	Greeneville (Appy)	R	4	3	3.78	13	13	0	0	69	70	32	29	3	22	65	.262
2005	Lexington (SAL)	A	11	6	2.27	25	25	0	0	134	108	41	34	3	55	142	.220
	Salem (Car)	A	1	0	1.50	1	0	0	0	6	4	4	1	1	1	6	.167
2006	Salem (Car)	A	11	8	3.62	27	27	0	0	146	137	64	59	6	67	134	.252
2007	Corpus Christi (TL)	AA	2	9	6.20	24	16	0	0	90	116	73	62	11	44	73	.312
MINOR LEAGUE TOTALS			30	27	3.67	98	84	0	0	468	454	223	191	24	196	438	.255

18 JOSH SHARPLESS, RHP

Born: Jan. 26, 1981. **B-T:** R-R. **Ht.:** 6-5. **Wt.:** 242. **Drafted:** Allegheny (Pa.), 2003 (24th round). **Signed by:** Jon Mercurio.

Former Pirates scout and baseball-operations direction Jon Mercurio discovered Sharpless as local college senior playing at the NCAA Division III level in the North Coast Athletic Conference. He pitched just 19 innings as a senior while battling mononucleosis, and Mercurio signed him for $1,500 as a 24th-rounder. Sharpless ascended through the system and was nearly unhittable in his first four pro years by using a big-breaking slider and a 90-mph fastball that got on hitters quickly because of his straight overhand delivery. That earned him a promotion to the major leagues, and he pitched well for the Pirates in the final two months of the 2006 season. However, he struggled with mechanical changes former pitching coach Jim Colborn made with his delivery last spring, lost the release point on his slider and struggled to throw strikes throughout 2007 as he lost confidence. A change in regimes in Pittsburgh should help as Sharpless tries to regain his old form, though he will likely begin 2008 in Triple-A after not getting a September callup.

Year	Club (League)	Class	W	L	ERA	G	GS	CG	SV	IP	H	R	ER	HR	BB	SO	AVG
2003	Williamsport (NYP)	A	1	1	2.59	22	0	0	5	31	19	9	9	2	17	45	.173
2004	Hickory (SAL)	A	6	2	3.03	44	0	0	4	74	42	28	25	4	55	109	.158
2005	Lynchburg (Car)	A	3	0	0.00	17	0	0	5	27	7	1	0	0	11	46	.081
	Altoona (EL)	AA	1	0	2.89	7	0	0	0	9	6	3	3	0	3	13	.171
2006	Altoona (EL)	AA	2	0	0.86	14	0	0	8	21	8	2	2	0	9	30	.114
	Indianapolis (IL)	AAA	1	1	2.45	23	0	0	1	33	32	11	9	1	15	30	.250
	Pittsburgh (NL)	MLB	0	0	1.50	14	0	0	0	12	7	2	2	0	11	7	.175
2007	Pittsburgh (NL)	MLB	0	1	12.46	6	0	0	0	4	7	6	6	3	1	1	.368
	Indianapolis (IL)	AAA	2	1	4.34	43	0	0	3	64	61	36	31	10	39	69	.249
MINOR LEAGUE TOTALS			15	9	2.73	170	0	0	26	260	175	90	79	17	149	342	.186
MAJOR LEAGUE TOTALS			0	1	4.41	20	0	0	0	16	14	8	8	3	12	8	.237

19 EVAN MEEK, RHP

Born: May 12, 1983. **B-T:** R-R. **Ht.:** 6-0. **Wt.:** 215. **Drafted:** Bellevue (Wash.) CC, D/F 2002 (11th round). **Signed by:** Bill Lohr (Twins).

The Pirates took Meek with the No. 2 overall pick in the 2007 major league Rule 5 draft, making them his fourth organization in four years since he signed with the Twins as a draft-and-follow in 2003. Minnesota released him in mid-2005 after his control and attitude deteriorated, and the Padres signed him. San Diego then sent him to the Devil Rays in a deal for Russell Branyan in August 2006. Now Pittsburgh will see if he can crack their big league bullpen in 2008. If not, they have to place him on waivers and offer him back to the Devil Rays for half his $50,000 draft price before they can send him to the minors. Using a low-90s fastball that has good sink and run, Meek picks up strikeouts and groundballs. He has been clocked as high as 97 mph, but he loses command and life when he overthrows. His splitter complements his fastball well, and he'll also mix in some sliders. He has made some progress with his control and command but still suffers through bouts of wildness. Bothered by shoulder stiffness early, Meek finished strong with a 1.45 ERA in the season's final month and a 0.93 ERA in the Arizona Fall League.

Year	Club (League)	Class	W	L	ERA	G	GS	CG	SV	IP	H	R	ER	HR	BB	SO	AVG
2003	Elizabethton (Appy)	R	7	1	2.47	14	8	0	1	51	33	15	14	2	24	47	.178
2004	Quad City River Bandits (MWL)	A	0	0	11.12	3	3	0	0	5	7	7	7	0	15	3	.333
	Elizabethton (Appy)	R	1	2	8.06	12	3	0	0	22	18	26	20	1	25	23	.228
2005	Beloit (MWL)	A	0	1	10.00	13	0	0	0	18	15	26	20	0	36	11	.231
2006	Lake Elsinore (Cal)	A	6	6	4.98	26	25	0	0	119	136	80	66	5	62	113	.288
	Visalia (Cal)	A	0	1	9.00	2	0	0	0	5	6	5	5	0	4	7	.300
2007	Montgomery (SL)	AA	2	1	4.30	44	0	0	1	67	74	36	32	2	34	69	.287
MINOR LEAGUE TOTALS			16	12	5.12	114	39	0	2	288	289	195	164	10	200	273	.263

20 ANDREW WALKER, C

Born: Jan. 22, 1986. **B-T:** R-R. **Ht.:** 6-0. **Wt.:** 210. **Drafted:** Texas Christian, 2007 (5th round). **Signed by:** Mike Leuzinger.

Walker had a fine career at Texas Christian, earning Freshman All-America honors in 2005 and all-Conference USA accolades in his last two seasons. After setting career highs with a .328 average and 12 homers last spring, he signed for $147,600 as a fifth-round pick. Walker has good power potential, especially for a catcher, and the ability to hit for a decent average. He gets high marks for his knowledge of the game and take-charge attitude behind the plate, and he won the 10th Man Award in the Cape Cod League in 2006 for his blend of talent and intangibles. Walker's receiving and throwing skills went backward in his final college season, but he appeared to get back on track by the end of his first pro season. However, he threw out just 25 percent of basestealers in pro debut. Walker will start the season in low Class A but has a clear shot to the major leagues by 2010 as the Pirates have no prime catching prospects ahead of him after converting Neil Walker (no relation) to a third baseman last season.

Year	Club (League)	Class	AVG	G	AB	R	H	2B	3B	HR	RBI	BB	SO	SB	OBP	SLG
2007	State College (NYP)	A	.317	46	161	17	51	12	1	2	24	18	36	1	.390	.441
MINOR LEAGUE TOTALS			.317	46	161	17	51	12	1	2	24	18	36	1	.390	.441

21 AUSTIN McCLUNE, OF

Born: Nov. 15, 1987. **B-T:** R-R. **Ht.:** 6-2. **Wt.:** 180. **Drafted:** HS—Edmond, Okla., 2006 (7th round). **Signed by:** Mike Leuzinger.

McClune was the MVP of the Oklahoma state American Legion tournament in 2005 and also starred as a cornerback in football. Yet he was overshadowed in both sports by Santa Fe High (Edmond, Okla.) teammate Ty Weeden, now a catching prospect in the Red Sox system. McClune has plenty of raw tools, chief among them plus speed and an outstanding arm that already make him an above-average outfielder who has a chance to be a top-of-the-order hitter. Like many young hitters, McClune struggles to stay back on offspeed and breaking pitches, so he has yet to hit the ball with much authority. He needs to tighten his strike zone as well as his routes on fly balls. Though he has the range and offensive profile to play center field, the Pirates used him primarily in right field last season to take advantage of his strong arm. McClune has plenty of upside and Pittsburgh will decide in spring training whether he's ready for his first exposure to a full-season league.

Year	Club (League)	Class	AVG	G	AB	R	H	2B	3B	HR	RBI	BB	SO	SB	OBP	SLG
2006	Pirates (GCL)	R	.291	42	148	17	43	7	0	0	10	5	32	2	.321	.338
2007	State College (NYP)	A	.260	59	196	20	51	3	3	0	19	5	32	15	.281	.306
MINOR LEAGUE TOTALS			.273	101	344	37	94	10	3	0	29	10	64	17	.298	.320

22 QUINCY LATIMORE, OF

Born: Feb. 3, 1989. **B-T:** R-R. **Ht.:** 5-10. **Wt.:** 175. **Drafted:** HS—Apex, N.C., 2007 (4th round). **Signed by:** Greg Schilz.

The Pirates drafted more than their share of low-ceiling college players in the early rounds of the final two drafts of the Dave Littlefield regime. They did use their fourth-round pick on a toolsy high school outfielder in 2007, however, taking Latimore and then signing him for $220,000 to persuade him to pass on a scholarship to North Carolina State. Latimore had a solid pro debut, showing above-average speed both on the bases and while tracking down balls in both gaps in center field. He also has power potential, which should manifest itself as he gains more experience and his body continues to fill out. The biggest concern is whether Latimore will lose some of his speed as he puts on more muscle. If he can maintain his wheels and develop a good hitting approach, then he has a chance to become an above-average player with the potential to hit 20 homers and steal 20 bases per season. Like most young players, Latimore needs to add polish to his game, particularly when it comes to handling breaking pitches and running clean routes in the outfield. Spring training will determine his assignment to begin 2008, as he will either be sent to low Class A or stay in extended spring training before reporting to short-season State College.

Year	Club (League)	Class	AVG	G	AB	R	H	2B	3B	HR	RBI	BB	SO	SB	OBP	SLG
2007	Pirates (GCL)	R	.257	45	171	29	44	9	2	3	17	16	25	13	.352	.386
MINOR LEAGUE TOTALS			.257	45	171	29	44	9	2	3	17	16	25	13	.352	.386

23 DAVE DAVIDSON, LHP

Born: April 23, 1984. **B-T:** L-L. **Ht.:** 6-1. **Wt.:** 195. **Drafted:** HS—Thorold, Ont., 2002 (10th round). **Signed by:** Charlie Sullivan.

A 10th-rounder in 2002, Davidson is the highest-drafted Canadian ever taken by the Pirates. He logged just 62 innings in his first three pro seasons because of a variety of injuries and a shoulder operation. Finally healthy in 2006, he had a breakout season and posted a combined 2.01 ERA at three levels, earning him a spot on the 40-man roster at the end of that year. He maintained that status and made his big league debut in 2007. Davidson's fastball usually tops out at 90 mph, but he has an outstanding curveball that's particularly effective against lefthanders. He has had trouble consistently throwing strikes throughout his career, and that could limit him to being a situational reliever in the major leagues. He was overmatched in his first taste of the majors but followed that up with a good showing in the Arizona Fall League. Davidson has a great love for the game and owns a baseball training facility with former Pirates outfielder Scott Bullett in Welland, Ontario. He likely will begin the season in Triple-A but is close to a finished product despite his lack of experience.

Year	Club (League)	Class	W	L	ERA	G	GS	CG	SV	IP	H	R	ER	HR	BB	SO	AVG
2003	Pirates (GCL)	R	0	2	12.91	7	0	0	0	7	10	12	11	0	7	8	.357
2004	Pirates (GCL)	R	1	0	3.44	7	1	0	0	18	16	11	7	0	14	24	.235
2005	Hickory (SAL)	A	1	2	9.78	10	2	0	0	19	16	22	21	4	21	23	.225
	Williamsport (NYP)	A	1	1	3.18	5	4	0	0	17	14	7	6	0	8	23	.226
2006	Hickory (SAL)	A	2	1	1.93	27	0	0	0	56	39	18	12	2	21	72	.195
	Lynchburg (Car)	A	0	0	2.16	5	0	0	0	8	6	2	2	0	2	11	.194
	Altoona (EL)	AA	1	1	2.31	10	1	0	0	11	8	4	3	0	10	13	.186
2007	Altoona (EL)	AA	3	1	4.22	39	0	0	2	59	44	30	28	3	30	55	.205
	Indianapolis (IL)	AAA	1	0	1.17	6	0	0	0	7	6	2	1	0	3	9	.214
	Pittsburgh (NL)	MLB	0	0	22.50	2	0	0	0	2	6	6	5	1	2	0	.462
MINOR LEAGUE TOTALS			10	8	3.98	116	8	0	2	205	159	108	91	9	116	238	.213
MAJOR LEAGUE TOTALS			0	0	22.50	2	0	0	0	2	6	6	5	1	2	0	.462

24 PAT BRESNEHAN, RHP

Born: April 23, 1985. **B-T:** R-R. **Ht.:** 6-2. **Wt.:** 211. **Drafted:** Arizona State, 2006 (5th round). **Signed by:** Ted Williams.

A high school standout in Massachusetts, Bresnehan turned down the Royals as a 23rd-rounder to attend Arizona State. He had an inconsistent three years with the Sun Devils, going 10-9, 5.01. The Pirates initially used Bresnehan as a starter during his 2006 pro debut, but he took off after he moved to the bullpen, finishing the summer with 34 consecutive scoreless innings. Working in relief allows Bresnehan to concentrate on throwing just two pitches: a low-90s fastball and a sharp-breaking slider. He closed games last season in high Class A, but his long-term future appears as a set-up man because of his stuff and because he's capable of working multiple innings thanks to his background as a starter. He needs to refine his control and command as he climbs the ladder. Bresnehan will return to Double-A after finishing 2007 there. He's moving quickly and could see Triple-A before the end of the year.

Year	Club (League)	Class	W	L	ERA	G	GS	CG	SV	IP	H	R	ER	HR	BB	SO	AVG
2006	Williamsport (NYP)	A	4	5	2.25	15	10	0	0	68	50	21	17	3	17	59	.201
2007	Lynchburg (Car)	A	4	3	4.18	34	0	0	6	60	54	37	28	3	32	63	.232
	Altoona (EL)	AA	1	0	4.50	3	0	0	0	6	5	3	3	0	2	3	.217
MINOR LEAGUE TOTALS			9	8	3.22	52	10	0	6	134	109	61	48	6	51	125	.216

25 YOSLAN HERRERA, RHP

Born: April 28, 1981. **B-T:** R-R. **Ht.:** 6-2. **Wt.:** 195. **Signed:** Cuba, 2006. **Signed by:** Rene Gayo/ Louie Eljaua.

The Pirates gave Herrera a three-year, $1.92 million major league contract that included a $750,000 bonus after the 2006 season, their first foray into the Cuban market since Fidel Castro rose to power more than four decades earlier. Herrera defected because he was left off Cuba's 2004 Olympic team because of injury. Though he had performed well with the powerful Cuban national team, Herrera didn't show that same kind of ability in his pro debut last season. His fastball sat at 84-86 mph, six mph slower than his heyday in Cuba, and his curveball and splitter lacked sharpness. He also lost confidence in his fastball and kept throwing his curve early in the count instead of trying to establish his heater. The Pirates attributed Herrera's poor season to having not pitched competitively since defecting in 2004, then getting caught up in political red tape in Dominican Republic while awaiting a work visa. Herrera is already 26 and needs to move fast. Unless he shows marked improvement in spring training, he's likely headed back to Double-A to start this season.

Year	Club (League)	Class	W	L	ERA	G	GS	CG	SV	IP	H	R	ER	HR	BB	SO	AVG
2007	Altoona (EL)	AA	6	9	4.69	25	25	1	0	128	151	72	67	11	38	70	.296
MINOR LEAGUE TOTALS			6	9	4.69	25	25	1	0	128	151	72	67	11	38	70	.296

26 MARCUS DAVIS, OF

Born: Nov. 11, 1984. **B-T:** R-R. **Ht.:** 6-3. **Wt.:** 200. **Drafted:** Alcorn State, 2007 (18th round). **Signed by:** Darren Mazeroski.

Davis dominated as a college player in the Southwestern Athletic Conference, where he was an all-conference pick in each of his two seasons at Alcorn State, but he lasted until the 18th round of the 2007 draft because scouts were skeptical of his level of competition. Signed for a mere $2,000, he showed plenty to like in his pro debut, flashing five-tool potential and earning some Andre Dawson comps from the Pirates. Davis' best tools are his outstanding raw power (he led the SWAC with 16 homers in 2007), above-average speed and strong throwing arm. He threw 94 mph as a closer at East Central (Miss.) CC, prompting the Marlins to draft him in the 21st round as a freshman in 2004. Davis understands his skills are still raw but is a willing learner and wants to get better. He has a tendency to swing at bad pitches, especially breaking balls outside the strike zone, but he did show a foundation to build plate discipline last season. Davis has the tools to be a good defensive outfielder but doesn't take good routes to the ball and needs to harness his arm. He'll start this season in low Class A.

Year	Club (League)	Class	AVG	G	AB	R	H	2B	3B	HR	RBI	BB	SO	SB	OBP	SLG
2007	State College (NYP)	A	.232	48	155	27	36	8	3	8	20	18	46	15	.322	.477
MINOR LEAGUE TOTALS			.232	48	155	27	36	8	3	8	20	18	46	15	.322	.477

27 TODD REDMOND, RHP

Born: May 17, 1985. **B-T:** R-R. **Ht.:** 6-3. **Wt.:** 210. **Drafted:** St. Petersburg (Fla.) JC, D/F 2004 (39th round). **Signed by:** Rob Sidwell.

Redmond was taken in the 40th round of the 2003 draft as a draft-and-follow by the Royals out of high school, but he didn't sign after his freshman year at St. Petersburg (Fla.) JC. The Pirates took him in 2004, again as a draft-and-follow, and Redmond led St. Petersburg to a second-place finish in its first appearance in the Junior College World Series in 2005. He was the Suncoast Conference pitcher of the year in both of his junior college seasons, and the Pirates signed him before the 2005 draft. Redmond was dominant during his first two pro seasons but struggled against high Class A hitters at Lynchburg last season. He has outstanding control and needs to have pinpoint command in order to succeed because he lacks an overpowering pitch. His best pitches are a 90-mph fastball and a curveball, though his changeup is improving. The Pirates want Redmond to be more aggressive with his fastball and use it more often to get ahead early in the count. Better hitters showed they could punish him if he's too fine. While Redmond may lack dominant pure stuff, he wins high marks for his competitiveness. He'll return to Double-A, where he made a three-game cameo last season. In the long run, he's likely more of a middle reliever than a starter.

Year	Club (League)	Class	W	L	ERA	G	GS	CG	SV	IP	H	R	ER	HR	BB	SO	AVG
2005	Williamsport (NYP)	A	1	2	1.98	15	14	0	0	72	62	22	16	2	21	63	.232
2006	Hickory (SAL)	A	13	6	2.75	27	27	0	0	160	137	64	49	13	33	148	.227
2007	Lynchburg (Car)	A	7	12	4.54	25	25	0	0	142	151	82	72	13	32	95	.275
	Altoona (EL)	AA	1	1	3.12	3	3	0	0	17	15	6	6	2	3	12	.227
MINOR LEAGUE TOTALS			22	21	3.27	70	69	0	0	393	365	174	143	30	89	318	.245

28 JUSTIN BYLER, 1B

Born: Aug. 12, 1985. **B-T:** R-R. **Ht.:** 6-1. **Wt.:** 219. **Drafted:** Gulf Coast (Fla.) CC, D/F 2005 (36th round). **Signed by:** Duane Gustavson.

The Pirates drafted Byler in the 33rd round out of an Ohio high school in 2004, then again three rounds later after his freshman season at Gulf Coast (Fla.) CC in 2005, signing him as a draft-and-follow before the 2006 draft. Byler played catcher, third base and the outfield in junior college but has been primarily a first baseman as a pro. His best tool is above-average power, as he's strong enough to hit the ball out to all fields and finished last season with six home runs in the final month at State College. Like many power hitters, Byler has a big swing with holes that need to be closed up. He runs OK for a big man but is subpar defensively, as all the changing of positions suggests. He does show the potential to at least become an adequate first baseman. Byler is ready for low Class A in 2008.

Year	Club (League)	Class	AVG	G	AB	R	H	2B	3B	HR	RBI	BB	SO	SB	OBP	SLG
2006	Pirates (GCL)	R	.306	42	147	22	45	13	1	5	28	9	24	5	.360	.510
	Williamsport (NYP)	A	.184	12	38	5	7	1	0	0	7	6	10	1	.311	.211
2007	State College (NYP)	A	.312	69	263	41	82	18	2	8	43	17	68	1	.362	.487
MINOR LEAGUE TOTALS			.299	123	448	68	134	32	3	13	78	32	102	7	.357	.471

29 JASON DELANEY, 1B/OF

Born: Nov. 9, 1982. **B-T:** R-R. **Ht.:** 6-3. **Wt.:** 220. **Drafted:** Boston College, 2005 (12th round). **Signed by:** Buddy Paine.

Delaney earned his degree in finance at Boston College and aspires to be a general manager or perhaps even a club president when his playing days are over. He also stood out on the field with the Eagles, winning all-Big East Conference honors twice and setting a school record with 256 career hits. Delaney's strength is his ability to put the bat on the ball. Following a disappointing pro debut, he has batted .302 the past two seasons, using a level stroke to spray the ball to all fields. He also developed some power last season, which he'll need to continue developing as he moves up through the farm system as a first baseman or left fielder. Delaney is adequate at both positions, though his lack of speed and arm strength hurts him in the outfield. He'll likely return to Double-A after spending the second half of 2007 there.

Year	Club (League)	Class	AVG	G	AB	R	H	2B	3B	HR	RBI	BB	SO	SB	OBP	SLG
2005	Williamsport (NYP)	A	.213	55	197	19	42	8	0	0	13	19	33	2	.281	.254
2006	Hickory (SAL)	A	.300	128	456	64	137	27	3	9	75	56	79	5	.379	.432
2007	Lynchburg (Car)	A	.340	72	250	39	85	16	3	9	44	38	52	2	.432	.536
	Altoona (EL)	AA	.265	65	223	25	59	10	0	7	35	38	52	0	.370	.404
MINOR LEAGUE TOTALS			.287	320	1126	147	323	61	6	25	167	151	216	9	.373	.418

30 LUIS MUNOZ, RHP

Born: Jan. 10, 1982. **B-T:** R-R. **Ht.:** 6-2. **Wt.:** 183. **Signed:** Dominican Republic, 2000. **Signed by:** Jose Luna.

Munoz began his career under the name Renaldo Reyes in 2000 but his true identity and age were revealed when the U.S. government began cracking down on fake passports and birth certificates in 2002. Though Munoz was found to be more than two years older than the Pirates originally thought, they decided to keep him and he has made a slow climb through the system. Pittsburgh finally may see a payoff on its patience now, as he pitched well enough last season to be placed on the 40-man roster. Munoz is a sinker/slider pitcher who tops out in the low 90s, but he has learned to hit his spots and showed enough last year at the higher levels to make the Pirates think he's a legitimate major league prospect. He was particularly impressive in three spot starts in Triple-A. Munoz will go back to Indianapolis to start this season and has a chance to see major league action at some point during the year in an organization short on starting pitching depth. Though he led the system with 14 wins in 2007, he projects more a middle reliever than a starter in the long term.

Year	Club (League)	Class	W	L	ERA	G	GS	CG	SV	IP	H	R	ER	HR	BB	SO	AVG
2001	Pirates (DSL)	R	0	4	4.33	11	7	0	0	35	40	27	17	0	15	26	.276
2002	Pirates (DSL)	R	3	2	3.38	18	0	0	1	42	42	20	16	2	16	41	.246
2003	Pirates (GCL)	R	2	1	4.89	9	5	2	0	38	38	23	21	5	11	29	.247
2004	Williamsport (NYP)	A	2	4	4.57	15	8	0	0	61	80	40	31	7	14	36	.327
2005	Hickory (SAL)	A	0	0	0.00	1	0	0	0	2	2	1	0	0	1	4	.182
	Williamsport (NYP)	A	6	3	3.81	16	13	0	0	78	69	41	33	8	22	46	.240
2006	Hickory (SAL)	A	6	2	3.28	16	14	0	0	85	82	39	31	5	20	55	.255
	Lynchburg (Car)	A	4	3	3.82	11	11	1	0	66	66	32	28	4	29	36	.261
2007	Indianapolis (IL)	AAA	2	1	3.12	3	3	0	0	17	22	8	6	2	4	16	.319
	Altoona (EL)	AA	12	5	3.63	25	23	1	0	136	130	63	55	11	32	89	.250
MINOR LEAGUE TOTALS			37	25	3.80	125	84	4	1	563	571	294	238	44	164	378	.262

St. Louis Cardinals

BY DERRICK GOOLD

A disappointing season that revealed a divided Cardinals front office spurred a radical change that has placed a public emphasis on player development. After years of plucking key players from other organizations, the new leadership has been charged with producing them through the farm system.

Shortly after their first losing season since 1999, the Cardinals fired general manager Walt Jocketty. The highly regarded and trade-savvy Jocketty watched over one of the greatest eras of St. Louis baseball, building a World Series champion in 2006 to highlight a run that included two National League pennants and seven playoff berths in 13 years.

But behind the winning at the big league level, there was a threadbare minor league system. Ownership had instructed vice president of amateur scouting and player development Jeff Luhnow to restock the supply of young talent. He reports directly to chairman Bill DeWitt Jr., and a fissure developed between Jocketty's people and Luhnow's. By firing Jocketty, the Cardinals made it clear the direction in which they want to go.

Other player-development changes followed Jocketty's dismissal. Field coordinator Jim Riggleman departed to become the Mariners' bench coach. Minor league pitching coordinator and former big league pitching coach Mark Riggins, who had spent 29 years in the organization, became the minor league pitching coordinator for the Cubs.

After assistant GMs Chris Antonetti (Indians) and Rick Hahn (White Sox) withdrew their names from consideration, St. Louis named John Mozeliak to replace Jocketty in November. Mozeliak had been Jocketty's assistant for five seasons and in the organization for 12, developing on the same track as a prospect. He began in amateur scouting and worked his way up to scouting director before making contributions at the major league level. He quickly integrated Luhnow's staff and their analytic and development work with the rest of the baseball operations department.

The pipeline Mozeliak and Luhnow started to build in 2005 is on the verge of producing players who should diminish the Cardinals' reliance on free agents and trades. The first five players on this prospect list, all products of the 2005 and 2006 drafts, should be contributing by 2009. Center fielder Colby Rasmus and closer-in-waiting Chris

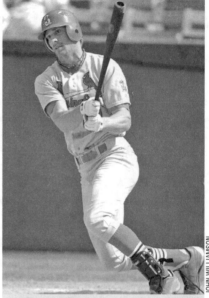

Outfielder Joe Mather was part of a Springfield team filled with intriguing talent

TOP 30 PROSPECTS

1. Colby Rasmus, of	16. P.J. Walters, rhp
2. Chris Perez, rhp	17. Jose Martinez, ss
3. Bryan Anderson, c	18. Brad Furnish, lhp
4. Brian Barton, of	19. Kyle McClellan, rhp
5. Jaime Garcia, lhp	20. Blake Hawksworth, rhp
6. Adam Ottavino, rhp	21. Jarrett Hoffpauir, 2b
7. Pete Kozma, ss	22. Mark Worrell, rhp
8. Clayton Mortensen, rhp	23. Mike Parisi, rhp
9. Mitchell Boggs, rhp	24. Jason Motte, rhp
10. Tyler Herron, rhp	25. Mark McCormick, rhp
11. John Jay, of	26. Blake King, rhp
12. Jess Todd, rhp	27. Mark Hamilton, 1b
13. Joe Mather, of/1b	28. Luke Gregerson, rhp
14. Kenny Maiques, rhp	29. Tyler Greene, ss
15. Allen Craig, 3b/1b	30. Luis de la Cruz, c

Perez are just about ready to take over for Jim Edmonds and Jason Isringhausen, while catcher Bryan Anderson will push Yadier Molina. Jaime Garcia and Adam Ottavino almost are set to reinforce a shaky rotation.

The 2007 draft holds promise. The Cardinals spent their first choice (18th overall) on Pete Kozma, the best all-around shortstop in the draft. Their next three picks were righthanders—Clayton Mortensen, David Kopp and Jess Todd—who could advance quickly through the system.

General Manager: John Mozeliak. **Farm and Scouting Director:** Jeff Luhnow.

Class	Team	League	W	L	PCT	Finish*	Manager	Affiliated
Majors	St. Louis	National	78	84	.481	10th (16)	Tony LaRussa	—
Triple-A	Memphis Redbirds	Pacific Coast	56	88	.389	16th (16)	Chris Maloney	1998
Double-A	Springfield Cardinals	Texas	73	63	.537	2nd (8)	Ron Warner	2005
High A	Palm Beach Cardinals	Florida State	71	69	.507	6th (12)	Gaylen Pitts	2003
Low A	Swing of the Quad Cities	Midwest	78	61	.561	3rd (14)	Keith Mitchell	2005
Short-season	Batavia Muckdogs	New York-Penn	31	43	.419	12th (14)	Mark DeJohn	2007
Rookie	Johnson City Cardinals	Appalachian	28	40	.412	7th (9)	Joe Almaraz	1974
Rookie	GCL Cardinals	Gulf Coast	24	30	.444	12th (16)	Enrique Brito	2007

Overall 2007 Minor League Record   361   394   .478   23rd

*Finish in overall standings (No. of teams in league) ^League champion

LAST YEAR'S TOP 30

	Player, Pos.	Status
1.	Colby Rasmus, of	No. 1
2.	Jaime Garcia, lhp	No. 5
3.	Chris Perez, rhp	No. 2
4.	Blake Hawksworth, rhp	No. 20
5.	Jon Jay, of	No. 11
6.	Bryan Anderson, c	No. 3
7.	Adam Ottavino, rhp	No. 6
8.	Mark McCormick, rhp	No. 25
9.	John Kinney, rhp	Majors
10.	Daryl Jones, of	Dropped out
11.	Mitchell Boggs, rhp	No. 9
12.	Brendan Ryan, ss	Majors
13.	Mark Hamilton, 1b	No. 27
14.	Chris Lambert, rhp	Tigers
15.	Chris Narveson, lhp	Dropped out
16.	Cody Haerther, of	Dropped out
17.	Tyler Greene, ss	No. 29
18.	Tyler Herron, rhp	No. 10
19.	Tyler Johnson, lhp	Majors
20.	Nick Stavinoha, of	Dropped out
21.	Trey Hearne, rhp	Dropped out
22.	Tommy Pham, of	Dropped out
23.	Brad Furnish, lhp	No. 18
24.	Mark Worrell, lhp	No. 22
25.	Dennis Dove, rhp	Dropped out
26.	Mike Sillman, rhp	Dropped out
27.	Jon Edwards, of	Dropped out
28.	Shane Robinson, of	Dropped out
29.	Skip Schumaker, of	Majors
30.	Amaury Cazana-Marti, of	Dropped out

BEST TOOLS

Best Hitter for Average	Colby Rasmus
Best Power Hitter	Colby Rasmus
Best Strike-Zone Discipline	Jarrett Hoffpauir
Fastest Baserunner	Daryl Jones
Best Athlete	Colby Rasmus
Best Fastball	Chris Perez
Best Curveball	Jaime Garcia
Best Slider	Chris Perez
Best Changeup	P.J. Walters
Best Control	P.J. Walters
Best Defensive Catcher	Nick Derba
Best Defensive Infielder	Pete Kozma
Best Infield Arm	Tyler Greene
Best Defensive Outfielder	Colby Rasmus
Best Outfield Arm	Jon Edwards

PROJECTED 2011 LINEUP

Catcher	Yadier Molina
First Base	Albert Pujols
Second Base	Brendan Ryan
Third Base	Scott Rolen
Shortstop	Pete Kozma
Left Field	Chris Duncan
Center Field	Colby Rasmus
Right Field	Rick Ankiel
No. 1 Starter	Chris Carpenter
No. 2 Starter	Adam Wainwright
No. 3 Starter	Jaime Garcia
No. 4 Starter	Adam Ottavino
No. 5 Starter	Clayton Mortensen
Closer	Chris Perez

TOP PROSPECTS OF THE DECADE

Year	Player, Pos.	2007 Org.
1998	Rick Ankiel, lhp	Cardinals
1999	J.D. Drew, of	Red Sox
2000	Rick Ankiel, lhp	Cardinals
2001	Bud Smith, lhp	Golden League
2002	Jimmy Journell, rhp	Out of baseball
2003	Dan Haren, rhp	Athletics
2004	Blake Hawksworth, rhp	Cardinals
2005	Anthony Reyes, rhp	Cardinals
2006	Anthony Reyes, rhp	Cardinals
2007	Colby Rasmus, of	Cardinals

TOP DRAFT PICKS OF THE DECADE

Year	Player, Pos.	2007 Org.
1998	J.D. Drew, of	Red Sox
1999	Chance Caple, rhp	Out of baseball
2000	Shaun Boyd, of	Phillies
2001	Justin Pope, rhp	Yankees
2002	Calvin Hayes, ss (3rd)	Out of baseball
2003	Daric Barton, c	Athletics
2004	Chris Lambert, rhp	Tigers
2005	Colby Rasmus, of	Cardinals
2006	Adam Ottavino, rhp	Cardinals
2007	Pete Kozma, ss	Cardinals

LARGEST BONUSES IN CLUB HISTORY

J.D. Drew, 1998	$3,000,000
Rick Ankiel, 1997	$2,500,000
Chad Hutchinson, 1998	$2,300,000
Shaun Boyd, 2000	$1,750,000
Braden Looper, 1996	$1,675,000

ST. LOUIS CARDINALS

Top 2008 Rookie: Chris Perez, rhp. The heir apparent to Jason Isringhausen will have a chance to spend some time as the late-inning apprentice to the Cardinals' closer.

Breakout Prospect: Kyle McClellan, rhp. After putting two elbow surgeries behind him and moving to the bullpen, he quietly posted a 1.81 ERA last season and could sneak into the big league bullpen this year.

Sleeper: D'Marcus Ingram, of. A draft-and-follow who burst into pro ball last summer appears primed to take off as a leadoff hitter with electric athleticism.

SOURCE OF TOP 30 TALENT			
Homegrown	29	Acquired	1
College	17	Trades	0
Junior college	1	Rule 5 draft	1
High school	7	Independent leagues	0
Draft-and-follow	2	Free agents/waivers	0
Nondrafted free agents	0		
International	2		

Numbers in parentheses indicate prospect rankings.

LF
Jon Jay (11)
Nick Stavinoha
Amaury Cazana-Marti
Cody Haerther
Beau Riportella

CF
Colby Rasmus (1)
Brian Barton (4)
D'Marcus Ingram
Daryl Jones
Shane Robinson
Tyler Henley
Nathan Southard

RF
Joe Mather (13)
Jon Edwards
Mark Shorey
Reid Gorecki
Tommy Pham

3B
Allen Craig (15)
Tyler Greene (29)
Travis Hanson
Tony Cruz
Daniel Descalso

SS
Pete Kozma (7)
Oliver Marmol

2B
Jose Martinez (17)
Jarrett Hoffpauir (21)
Isa Garcia
Juan Lucena

1B
Mark Hamilton (27)
Steven Hill
Brandon Buckman
Mike Ferris

C
Bryan Anderson (3)
Luis de la Cruz (30)
Brandon Yarbrough
Nick Derba
Matt Pagnozzi

RHP

Starters	Relievers
Adam Ottavino (6)	Chris Perez (2)
Clayton Mortensen (8)	Jess Todd (12)
Mitchell Boggs (9)	Kenny Maiques (14)
Tyler Herron (10)	Kyle McClellan (19)
P.J. Walters (16)	Mark Worrell (22)
Blake Hawksworth (20)	Jason Motte (24)
Mike Parisi (23)	Mark McCormick (25)
Stuart Pomeranz	Blake King (26)
David Kopp	Luke Gregerson (28)
Deryk Hooker	Josh Kinney
Brett Zawacki	Dennis Dove
Trey Hearne	Mike Sillman
Eddie Degerman	Adam Reifer
Gary Daley	Josh Dew
Cory Rauschenberger	

LHP

Starters	Relievers
Jaime Garcia (5)	Eric Haberer
Brad Furnish (18)	Zach Zuercher
Tyler Norrick	
Adam Daniels	

2007 — SIGNING BUDGET: $3.8 MILLION

Best Pro Debut: OF/1B/C Steven Hill (12) spent most of the summer in low Class A and hit .320 with 12 homers. RHP Josh Dew (14) had 15 saves and a 1.80 ERA in the New York-Penn League.

Best Athlete: Speed is OF Beau Riportella's (10) best attribute, and he has some power as well. SS Pete Kozma's (1) tools all rate as average to plus except for his power, while OF Tyler Henley (8) is solid across the board. OF Adron Chambers (38) played defensive back for Mississippi State's football team.

Best Pure Hitter: Hill or 3B/2B Daniel Descalso. Also keep an eye on 3B Arnoldi Cruz (26), who hit .299 with seven homers while moving quickly to low Class A.

Best Power Hitter: Hill broke Stephen F. Austin State records for season (24) and career (38 in just two years) homers. If he can be serviceable as a catcher, he could be a versatile and powerful bat off the bench.

Fastest Runner: Riportella ran a 6.3-second 60-yard dash in a predraft workout. He set a JC of the Sequoias (Calif.) mark with 31 steals (in 32 tries) during the spring, then swiped 10 in 12 attempts as a pro.

Best Defensive Player: C Nick Derba (30) has outstanding catch-and-throw skills and led all catchers in full-season leagues by throwing out 53 percent of basestealers. He also showed more bat than the Cardinals expected.

Best Fastball: For the total package, it's RHP Clayton Mortensen (1s), who commands a 90-93 mph sinker that bottoms out at the plate. For pure velocity, it's RHP Adam Riefer (11), who touched 96 mph before sustaining a stress fracture in his elbow.

Best Secondary Pitch: RHP Jess Todd's (2) slider is an out pitch. St. Louis will use him as a starter for now, but he could be a late-inning force as a reliever working with just his fastball and slider.

Most Intriguing Background: Three signees have fathers who work for the Cardinals. RHP Chuck Fick's (15) dad Chuck is a crosschecker, RHP Dylan Gonzalez' (31) father Charlie is a scout and LHP Davis Bilardello's (43) dad Dann is a roving catching instructor.

Closest To The Majors: Mortensen generates a lot of groundballs and strikeouts, a formula for success.

Best Late-Round Pick: RHP Brett Zawacki (12) is the best of a deep group of sleepers for whom the Cardinals have high hopes.

The One Who Got Away: OF Kyle Russell (4) hit a school-record 28 homers, but his shaky track record with wood bats and big bonus demands scared most teams off. He returned to Texas.

Assessment: The Cardinals' best recent drafts have come when they've blended high school talent rather than focusing solely on collegians. With players like Kozma and Zawacki, they added talented prepsters to go with their usual collection of college players with strong statistical performances.

2006 — BUDGET: $4.2 MILLION

This grade will rise if RHPs Adam Ottavino (1), Chris Perez (1s) and P.J. Walters (11), LHP Brad Furnish (2) and OF Jon Jay (2) continue to develop. Keep an eye on athletic OF D'Marcus Ingram (25).

GRADE: C+

2005 — BUDGET: $5.6 MILLION

OF Colby Rasmus (1), RHP Tyler Herron (1s), C Bryan Anderson (4), RHP Mitchell Boggs (5) and LHP Jaime Garcia (22) all rank among the system's 10 best prospects. That takes the edge off injuries to SS Tyler Greene (1) and RHP Mark McCormick (1s).

GRADE: B+

2004 — BUDGET: $3.2 MILLION

"Moneyball" begat a waste of money, as the Cardinals signed only college players with disastrous results. Disappointing RHP Chris Lambert (1) was traded, leaving 2B Jarrett Hoffpauir (6) as the best player from this draft still in the system.

GRADE: F

2003 — BUDGET: $2.8 MILLION

St. Louis drafted future first-round RHPs Ian Kennedy (14), Brett Sinkbeil (38) and Max Scherzer (43), but didn't sign any of them. They did land since-traded 1B Daric Barton (1), SS Brendan Ryan (7) and RHP Anthony Reyes (15).

GRADE: B

Draft analysis by Jim Callis. Numbers in parentheses indicate draft rounds. Budgets are bonuses in first 10 rounds.

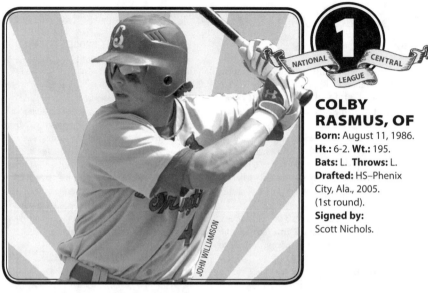

COLBY RASMUS, OF

Born: August 11, 1986.
Ht.: 6-2. **Wt.:** 195.
Bats: L. **Throws:** L.
Drafted: HS–Phenix City, Ala., 2005.
(1st round).
Signed by: Scott Nichols.

As a senior, Rasmus teamed with brother Cory (who became a Braves supplemental first-rounder in 2006) and Kasey Kiker (the Rangers' 2006 first-round pick) to lead Alabama's Russell County High to the national high school championship. Colby broke Bo Jackson's state record for homers with 24 that spring. St. Louis plucked Rasmus with the 28th pick in the 2005 draft and a $1 million signing bonus. When he arrived at his first big league camp in 2007, he found hype waiting for him. That's what comes with being an elite prospect for a franchise that, in the words of farm and scouting director Jeff Luhnow, has been lacking a true No. 1 prospect. Cardinals manager Tony LaRussa privately wondered if the lofty expectations would hamper Rasmus, but that hasn't come close to happening. He blossomed as a bona fide five-tool star in 2007, leading the Double-A Texas League with 93 runs, 29 homers and 69 extra-base hits. Managers voted him the TL's most exciting player and he was the league's No. 1 prospect. He also had a strong showing for Team USA at the World Cup in November.

Rasmus has the head-turning ability of a potential big league all-star, and the swagger too. He has a smooth, balanced lefthanded swing that packs plenty of punch. His wiry frame hints some of his doubles are going to be homers by the time he reaches the majors. Disciplined at the plate, he was able to hit in the middle of the Springfield lineup as a 20-year-old. He also excelled as the leadoff hitter for Team USA. His speed and savvy on the basepaths could mean 20-20 seasons for St. Louis. In center field, he jumped from capable to outstanding in 2007. Scouts who once wondered if he would move to a corner spot said he could be an everyday center fielder in the majors and possibly win Gold Gloves. Even when slumping at the plate, he changed games with his range, and he has the strong arm that made him a standout high school pitcher.

Rasmus kicked his habit of slow starts in 2007, but he still tended to be streaky. Scouts and coaches see the same thing he does: that he goes through stretches where he becomes too pull-conscious. He has shown more willingness to hit to all fields, but he still can become more consistent. The Cardinals have prevailed upon Rasmus to refine a pregame routine that not only will sculpt his developing strength but help sustain it over a long season.

Rasmus is keeping pace with the Cardinals' schedule for him and may speed it up. He's scheduled to open the season at Triple-A Memphis but probably won't need another full season in the minors. "We can expect him to hold up to what everybody expects from him because he has the drive," Springfield manager Pop Warner said. "I know he's the kid who can handle it."

Year	Club (League)	Class	AVG	G	AB	R	H	2B	3B	HR	RBI	BB	SO	SB	OBP	SLG
2005	Johnson City (Appy)	R	.296	62	216	47	64	16	5	7	27	21	73	13	.362	.514
2006	Quad Cities (MWL)	A	.310	78	303	49	94	22	3	11	50	29	55	17	.373	.512
	Palm Beach (FSL)	A	.254	53	193	22	49	4	5	5	35	27	35	11	.351	.404
2007	Springfield (TL)	AA	.275	128	472	93	130	37	3	29	72	70	108	18	.381	.551
MINOR LEAGUE TOTALS			.285	321	1184	211	337	79	16	52	184	147	271	59	.371	.510

2 CHRIS PEREZ, RHP

STEVE MOORE

Born: July 1, 1985. **B-T:** R-R. **Ht.:** 6-4. **Wt.:** 225. **Drafted:** Miami, 2006 (1st round supplemental). **Signed by:** Steve Turco.

When the Cardinals pulled Perez out of Miami with the 42nd pick of the 2006 draft, they earmarked him for a swift climb through the organization. He hasn't disappointed. He opened his first full season in Double-A and botched his first save opportunity, then converted his next 27 before a promotion to Triple-A. Perez has the best fastball in the system, rifling it consistently in the mid-90s with natural sink. Yet his best pitch may be an 85-87 mph slider with sudden bite that he's willing to throw in any count. The combination made him nearly unhittable, as he held righthanders to a .115 average and lefties to a .151 mark last season. He has the guts for the closer role. The only thing that could keep Perez from the majors in 2008 is his command. He also makes mistakes up in the strike zone, leaving him vulnerable to extra-base hits. St. Louis would like to see more consistent mechanics and increased dedication to conditioning. Ticketed for the Triple-A bullpen after a tour with Team USA's World Cup team, Perez could pitch his way into the big league bullpen with a strong spring. Closer Jason Isringhausen is signed through 2008, and Perez could replace him as early as 2009.

Year	Club (League)	Class	W	L	ERA	G	GS	CG	SV	IP	H	R	ER	HR	BB	SO	AVG
2006	Quad Cities (MWL)	A	2	0	1.84	25	0	0	12	29	20	9	6	0	19	32	.198
2007	Springfield (TL)	AA	2	0	2.43	39	0	0	27	40	17	11	11	3	28	62	.126
	Memphis (PCL)	AAA	0	1	4.50	15	0	0	8	14	6	7	7	2	13	15	.143
MINOR LEAGUE TOTALS			4	1	2.57	79	0	0	47	84	43	27	24	5	60	109	.155

3 BRYAN ANDERSON, C

STEVE MOORE

Born: Dec. 16, 1986. **B-T:** L-R. **Ht.:** 6-1. **Wt.:** 190. **Drafted:** HS—Simi Valley, Calif., 2005 (4th round). **Signed by:** Jay North.

Anderson leapfrogged high Class A and became the youngest all-star in the Texas League in 2007, edging Colby Rasmus by two months. He joined Rasmus at the Futures Game and narrowly missed hitting .300 for the third time in three pro seasons. He also played with Rasmus and Chris Perez on Team USA. Anderson has a mature approach at the plate and a keen sense of the strike zone to go with a smooth, uppercut lefthanded swing. He should be able to hit for average with gap power in the majors. Pitchers laud his ability to call and control a game behind the plate, while managers praise his leadership. His arm strength is average. The power Anderson is expected to develop hasn't arrived yet, as he cracked only 22 extra-base hits in 389 at-bats. He has odd throwing mechanics, which costs him accuracy and limited him to throwing out just 27 percent of basestealers in 2007. He's improving behind the plate, but needs work with his receiving and footwork. He has below-average speed. Anderson will be 21 when he reports to his third big league camp this spring. He has a higher offensive ceiling than St. Louis incumbent Yadier Molina, though his defense isn't as stout. If Anderson can't take his job after time in Triple-A, he should make a nice complement to Molina.

Year	Club (League)	Class	AVG	G	AB	R	H	2B	3B	HR	RBI	BB	SO	SB	OBP	SLG
2005	Johnson City (Appy)	R	.331	51	154	28	51	8	1	6	36	15	29	6	.383	.513
2006	Quad Cities (MWL)	A	.302	109	381	50	115	29	3	3	51	42	66	2	.377	.417
2007	Springfield (TL)	AA	.298	103	389	51	116	15	1	6	53	32	77	0	.350	.388
MINOR LEAGUE TOTALS			.305	263	924	129	282	52	5	15	140	89	172	8	.367	.421

4 BRIAN BARTON, OF

RODGER WOOD

Born: April 25, 1982. **B-T:** R-R. **Ht.:** 6-3. **Wt.:** 190. **Signed:** NDFA /Miami, 2004. **Signed by:** Jorge Diaz (Indians).

Few clubs gave Barton a serious look in the 2004 draft because of his academic background, but the Indians signed him as a nondrafted free agent for $100,000 plus another $100,000 in college funds after seeing him in the Cape Cod League. An aerospace engineering major who once interned at Boeing, Barton came into the Tribe system having to prove himself at every level, and broke out in 2006 by hitting .323 with 19 homers and 41 steals. But he quietly injured his right knee on Opening Day that season, and while he had no difficulty playing through it in 2006, the knee problems lingered last season. He wasn't as explosive and ultimately had surgery to clean up the knee in September while finishing his degree at Miami. Cleveland gambled by leaving Barton off its 40-man roster, and the Cardinals snatched him up for $50,000 in the major league Rule 5 draft at the Winter Meetings. They'll have to keep him on their big league roster throughout 2008 or place him on waivers and offer him back to the Indians for half his draft price. Barton had legitimate five-tool potential before his injury. The worst-case scenario is that he becomes just an average runner, and all his other tools grade out as future pluses. He can get a little stiff on his front side on pitches over the inner half of the plate, though that's his only weakness. His plate discipline slipped a bit in 2007 but should be fine. Barton has the ability to play all three outfield spots with above-average arm strength. He should be able to stick in St. Louis as a reserve and should challenge for an everyday job in 2009, if not sooner.

Year	Club (League)	Class	AVG	G	AB	R	H	2B	3B	HR	RBI	BB	SO	SB	OBP	SLG
2005	Lake County (SAL)	A	.414	35	133	31	55	14	1	4	32	18	21	7	.506	.624
	Kinston (Car)	A	.274	64	223	42	61	15	6	3	32	34	57	13	.404	.435
2006	Kinston (Car)	A	.308	82	295	56	91	16	3	13	57	39	83	26	.410	.515
	Akron (EL)	AA	.351	42	151	32	53	5	0	6	26	13	26	15	.415	.503
2007	Akron (EL)	AA	.314	106	389	56	122	18	2	9	59	41	99	20	.416	.440
	Buffalo (IL)	AAA	.264	25	87	9	23	3	0	1	7	7	18	1	.333	.333
MINOR LEAGUE TOTALS			.317	354	1278	226	405	71	12	36	213	152	304	82	.417	.476

5 JAIME GARCIA, LHP

Born: June 2, 1986. **B-T:** L-L. **Ht.:** 6-1. **Wt.:** 200. **Drafted:** Mission, Texas, 2005 (22nd round). **Signed by:** Joe Almaraz.

Area scout Joe Almaraz felt so strongly about Garcia that he persuaded two teams to draft him: the Orioles (who didn't sign him) in 2004 and the Cardinals in 2005. Garcia starred as a two-way player on Mexico's junior national team and was set to play pro ball in his native country before St. Louis signed him. The only negative in two years of pro ball is an elbow injury that ended his 2007 season in mid-July. Garcia has two plus pitches and striking poise on the mound. His fastball hums in the low 90s and he has a down-breaking curveball that he can use as a knockout pitch. His delivery is consistent and smooth. Garcia had trouble with his command at times last season, though that could have been connected to his sore elbow. After several evaluations, he was diagnosed with a sprained ligament that didn't require surgery. Garcia leans on his curveball too much at times and needs to use his changeup more often so he can gain more consistency with it. A potential No. 3 starter, Garcia is expected to be healthy for spring training and primed to continue his sprint from the 22nd round to the majors. Opening the season back in Double-A wouldn't be seen as a setback, and it's unlikely he would remain in Springfield for long.

Year	Club (League)	Class	W	L	ERA	G	GS	CG	SV	IP	H	R	ER	HR	BB	SO	AVG
2006	Quad Cities (MWL)	A	5	4	2.90	13	13	1	0	77	67	28	25	1	18	80	.229
	Palm Beach (FSL)	A	5	4	3.84	12	12	0	0	77	84	33	33	3	16	51	.282
2007	Springfield (TL)	AA	5	9	3.75	18	18	0	0	103	93	47	43	14	45	97	.245
MINOR LEAGUE TOTALS			15	17	3.52	43	43	1	0	258	244	108	101	18	79	228	.252

STEVE MOORE

6 ADAM OTTAVINO, RHP

Born: Nov. 22, 1985. **B-T:** R-R. **Ht.:** 6-5. **Wt.:** 215. **Drafted:** Northeastern, 2006 (1st round). **Signed by:** Kobe Perez.

Ottavino broke the Northeastern single-season strikeout record as a sophomore and again as a junior before signing for $950,000 as the 30th overall pick in 2006. He has ditched the rose-colored sunglasses that were his signature in college, but he has continued to produce. Sent to high Class A Palm Beach for his first full season, he ranked second in the Florida State League with 12 wins and third with a 3.08 ERA and 128 strikeouts. Ottavino has a power mindset and a power build, and he blazed through college with a four-seam fastball that he can still fire in the mid-90s, reaching as high as 94 mph in the late innings. At the urging of the Cardinals, he also has dusted off a running two-seamer in the low 90s. He confidently works both sides of the plate. He has a tight slider and gained traction with his curveball in 2007. He can get carried away with his fastball and becomes too reliant on trying to overpower hitters up in the strike zone. His breaking ball is still slurvy, and his changeup is still a pitch in progress. He needs to become more efficient and cut down on his walks and high pitch counts. Ottavino will begin 2008 in the Double-A rotation. There once was talk of turning him into a reliever, but those plans have shifted to the back burner.

DAVID STONER

Year	Club (League)	Class	W	L	ERA	G	GS	CG	SV	IP	H	R	ER	HR	BB	SO	AVG
2006	State College (NYP)	A	2	2	3.14	6	6	0	0	28	23	12	10	1	13	26	.211
	Quad Cities (MWL)	A	2	3	3.44	8	8	0	0	36	28	21	14	3	19	38	.211
2007	Palm Beach (FSL)	A	12	8	3.08	27	27	1	0	143	130	63	49	10	63	128	.239
MINOR LEAGUE TOTALS			16	13	3.15	41	41	1	0	208	181	96	73	14	95	192	.231

7 PETE KOZMA, SS

Born: April 11, 1988. **B-T:** R-R. **Ht.:** 6-0. **Wt.:** 170. **Drafted:** HS—Owasso, Okla., 2007 (1st round). **Signed by:** Steve Gossett.

SPORTS ON FILM

Picking 18th in 2007, the Cardinals had their highest draft choice since 2000, when they blew the 13th choice on Shaun Boyd, and took Kozma, the best shortstop available. He led Owasso High to the Oklahoma 6-A state championship with a three-homer game in one playoff contest and a solo shot that provided all the scoring in the title game, then signed for $1.395 million. Kozma has four average or better tools. He has good plate coverage and uses the whole field better than most teenage hitters. He has tremendous range and a smooth glide to his play at shortstop. He has a solid arm and enhances it with a quick transfer and release. He's a solid-average runner. His instincts and work ethic are exceptional. He hit just .233 in his debut, but the Cardinals believe Kozma will improve with experience. They like his swing, though with his size and line-drive approach, it's not clear how much power he'll develop. A bone bruise near his right thumb limited Kozma offensively during instructional league, but St. Louis still has enough faith in his bat to send him to low Class A Quad Cities to start 2008. He'll need at least three years in the minors.

Year	Club (League)	Class	AVG	G	AB	R	H	2B	3B	HR	RBI	BB	SO	SB	OBP	SLG
2007	Cardinals (GCL)	R	.154	4	13	4	2	0	0	0	0	2	2	0	.267	.154
	Johnson City (Appy)	R	.264	30	106	16	28	8	0	2	9	12	21	3	.350	.396
	Batavia (NYP)	A	.148	8	27	1	4	0	1	0	2	1	7	1	.179	.222
MINOR LEAGUE TOTALS			.233	42	146	21	34	8	1	2	11	15	30	4	.313	.342

8 CLAYTON MORTENSEN, RHP

Born: April 10, 1985. **B-T:** R-R. **Ht.:** 6-4. **Wt.:** 180. **Drafted:** Gonzaga, 2007 (1st round supplemental). **Signed by:** Jay North.

PAUL GIERHART

After Tampa Bay drafted him in the 25th round in 2005, Mortensen opted to go from junior college to Gonzaga to boost his draft status. He flopped, going 6-8, 5.89 and undrafted as a junior. Mortensen recovered to win the West Coast Conference's pitcher of the year award as a senior. The Cardinals drafted him 36th overall in June, making him the highest June draft pick in school history, and signed him for $650,000. Mortensen has a biting 90-93 mph sinker and a hard slider. He had an outstanding 3.3 groundout/airout ratio and permitted just two homers in 60 pro innings. He throws with little effort and has ironed out his delivery, reducing the control woes that plagued him at Gonzaga in 2006. His gangly frame can handle increased strength. He had little difficulty throwing strikes in low Class A, but Mortensen still can improve his command. His changeup has some deception and projects as a solid third pitch, but it's a lot like he was until this spring—all promise and sparse effectiveness. Mortensen could begin 2008 in Double-A and will be the quickest climber from his Cardinals draft class. As with Adam Ottavino, he could make an intriguing reliever but will be developed as a starter.

Year	Club (League)	Class	W	L	ERA	G	GS	CG	SV	IP	H	R	ER	HR	BB	SO	AVG
2007	Batavia (NYP)	A	1	1	1.77	6	4	0	0	20	13	4	4	0	11	23	.188
	Quad Cities (MWL)	A	0	2	3.12	10	10	0	0	40	44	17	14	2	8	45	.275
MINOR LEAGUE TOTALS			1	3	2.67	16	14	0	0	60	57	21	18	2	19	68	.249

9 MITCHELL BOGGS, RHP

Born: Feb. 15, 1984. **B-T:** R-R. **Ht.:** 6-3. **Wt.:** 195. **Drafted:** Georgia, 2005 (5th round). **Signed by:** Roger Smith.

STEVE MOORE

Boggs was a two-sport athlete who tried his hand as a quarterback at Tennessee-Chattanooga before transferring to Georgia and sticking with baseball. Primarily a set-up man with the Bulldogs, he became a starter after turning pro and has had no trouble adjusting. He was the glue of a Texas League division championship rotation in 2007. Boggs still can reach the mid-90s with his four-seam fastball, but his low-90s two-seamer with sink and bore is his ticket to quicker innings. He has ditched his curveball and developed a wipeout slider that ranks as one of the best in the system. Few Cardinals pitching prospects have been as consistent or durable. Boggs reported to the Arizona Fall League with the goals of improving his command and developing a changeup. Though he has a quality fastball/slider combination, he doesn't miss as many bats as he could because he doesn't locate his pitches with precision. One of his best assets is his competitiveness, but that sometimes leads to overthrowing. The next step in Boggs' progression is Triple-A, but he's not far away from being able to plug a hole in St. Louis' leaky rotation. It's possible that in the long term he'll return to where he came from and become a lockdown reliever.

ST. LOUIS CARDINALS

Year	Club (League)	Class	W	L	ERA	G	GS	CG	SV	IP	H	R	ER	HR	BB	SO	AVG
2005	New Jersey (NYP)	A	4	4	3.89	15	14	0	0	71	77	38	31	5	24	61	.271
2006	Palm Beach (FSL)	A	10	6	3.41	27	27	1	0	145	153	69	55	7	51	126	.271
2007	Springfield (TL)	AA	11	7	3.84	26	26	0	0	152	167	86	65	15	62	117	.279
MINOR LEAGUE TOTALS			25	17	3.68	68	67	1	0	369	397	193	151	27	137	304	.274

10 TYLER HERRON, RHP

PAUL GIERHART

Born: Aug. 5, 1986. **B-T:** R-R. **Ht.:** 6-3. **Wt.:** 190. **Drafted:** HS—Wellington, Fla, 2005 (1st round supplemental). **Signed by:** Steve Turco.

The 46th overall pick in 2005 out of the powerhouse Wellington High program in Florida, Herron went winless in his pro debut and couldn't advance past short-season ball in his first two seasons. He hinted at a breakout by going 4-1, 2.67 in his final five starts in 2006, then delivered by emerging as the best pitching prospect on a deep low Class A Quad Cities staff. Herron has three pitches that are or should be average or better. He throws a sinking fastball in the low 90s and can spot it anywhere he wants in the strike zone. His changeup has become a reliable second pitch and his curveball has good break. He's cool and athletic on the mound and has consistently won praise for his maturity. Herron needs more consistency with his pitches. His fastball can straighten out at times, and he'll also hang his curveball. He needs to add strength to his slender frame, though he did hold up well over his first year in full-season ball. Herron will continue a slow and steady rise in the organization. He'll jump to high Class A, where he'll no longer be protected by the tandem rotation system that worked so well at Quad Cities. He has a ceiling as a No. 3 starter.

Year	Club (League)	Class	W	L	ERA	G	GS	CG	SV	IP	H	R	ER	HR	BB	SO	AVG
2005	Johnson City (Appy)	R	0	3	5.62	13	13	0	0	49	47	35	31	11	27	49	.245
2006	Johnson City (Appy)	R	5	6	4.13	13	13	1	0	69	69	41	32	6	22	54	.259
	State College (NYP)	A	0	1	3.00	1	1	1	0	6	7	2	2	1	1	3	.318
2007	Quad Cities (MWL)	A	10	7	3.74	30	22	0	1	137	123	62	57	7	26	130	.240
MINOR LEAGUE TOTALS			15	17	4.18	57	49	2	1	262	246	140	122	25	76	236	.248

11 JON JAY, OF

Born: March 15, 1985. **B-T:** L-L. **Ht.:** 6-0. **Wt.:** 200. **Drafted:** Miami, 2006 (2nd round). **Signed by:** Steve Turco.

Jay had the best debut among the Cardinals' 2006 draft picks, hitting .342 in low Class A, to earn a jump to Double-A for his first full season. But it became a lost year because of three trips to the disabled list, two for a shoulder injury and one for wrist pain, and he never got untracked at the plate. After watching him in his pro debut, some St. Louis coaches predicted Jay would win a major league batting title. He has a balanced, line-drive stroke and generally controls the strike zone well. He's a solid center fielder with a decent arm, and he runs well enough to steal a few bases. Jay doesn't have the power to profile as a corner outfielder, which is a problem with Colby Rasmus ahead of him. Scouts from other organizations focus on Jay's lack of a standout tool more than his lack of a glaring weakness. They question his quirky hand pumps and bat waggles at the plate and wonder whether he'll hit at the upper levels. Jay likely will return to Double-A. He'll have to produce in all facets of the game to start for the Cardinals, because he can't approach the power of big league starters Rick Ankiel and Chris Duncan.

Year	Club (League)	Class	AVG	G	AB	R	H	2B	3B	HR	RBI	BB	SO	SB	OBP	SLG
2006	Quad Cities (MWL)	A	.342	60	234	42	80	13	3	3	45	28	27	9	.416	.462
2007	Springfield (TL)	AA	.235	26	102	17	24	4	2	2	11	11	19	4	.333	.373
	Cardinals (GCL)	R	.500	1	2	0	1	0	0	0	0	0	1	0	.500	.500
	Palm Beach (FSL)	A	.286	32	126	19	36	8	0	2	10	5	25	5	.321	.397
MINOR LEAGUE TOTALS			.304	119	464	78	141	25	5	7	66	44	72	18	.373	.425

12 JESS TODD, RHP

Born: April 20, 1986. **B-T:** R-R. **Ht.:** 5-11. **Wt.:** 210. **Drafted:** Arkansas, 2007 (2nd round). **Signed by:** Roger Smith.

Todd set an Arkansas school record with 17 strikeouts in his 10th start, a complete-game win over South Carolina in the Southeastern Conference tournament, after he opened the season as the Razorbacks' closer. He became part of a formidable rotation at Arkansas that featured fellow early-round draft picks Nick Schmidt (first round, Padres) and Duke Welker (second round, Pirates). Todd, who spent the first two years of his college career at Navarro (Texas) JC, led the group with 128 strikeouts in 93 innings before signing for $400,000 as a second-rounder. The stocky righthander has a fastball that zipped from 90-94 mph when he was with Arkansas but touched the lower end of that range in his pro debut at short-season Batavia.

His drop in velocity was attributed to a tired arm that caused him to miss a couple of turns in Batavia's piggyback rotation. Todd's heater has nice movement, and while he prefers to jam hitters by cutting it, he also can throw a sinker. He follows the fastball with a plus slider, and he can throw both pitches for strikes. He has little experience with a changeup, though he may not need it if his long-term role is in the bullpen. A clenched-jaw competitor lacking the size to handle a starter's workload, Todd should reach the majors as a late-inning reliever after expanding his game as a minor league starter. He'll likely open 2008 in high Class A.

Year	Club (League)	Class	W	L	ERA	G	GS	CG	SV	IP	H	R	ER	HR	BB	SO	AVG
2007	Batavia (NYP)	A	4	1	2.78	16	7	0	0	58	48	23	18	2	14	69	.223
MINOR LEAGUE TOTALS			4	1	2.78	16	7	0	0	58	48	23	18	2	14	69	.223

13 JOE MATHER, OF/1B

Born: July 23, 1982. **B-T:** R-R. **Ht.:** 6-5. **Wt.:** 210. **Drafted:** HS—Mount Point, Idaho, 2001 (3rd round). **Signed by:** Manny Guerra.

Mather reached Class A in 2004, and for three seasons and more than 1,000 at-bats he stayed at that level, wondering each spring if he was making progress or about to be released. Cardinals officials always recognized the potential in his swing, and in 2007 he blossomed. He hit 31 home runs as he climbed to Double-A and then Triple-A. Mather used to gobble ice cream and other high-calorie delights to pack the weight on his lithe frame. By last year, he had filled out by 15 pounds and his game matured. Scouts saw the same raw ability in Mather, but they wondered if he ever would add the necessary polish. He put it together when he settled into a comfortable stance and approach at the plate, which led to better strike-zone awareness and more consistent power to all fields. He now has the best power in the system this side of Colby Rasmus, and he doesn't strike out excessively for a slugger. Mather is no burner but has stolen 23 bases without being caught once over the last three seasons. He may be better at first base, but he runs well enough and has enough athleticism and arm strength to play a corner outfield position. The versatility that once kept him playing when he struggled with the bat now opens an alternate avenue to the majors, and he's now just a phone call away. Added to the 40-man roster in November, he'll probably open 2008 back in Triple-A.

Year	Club (League)	Class	AVG	G	AB	R	H	2B	3B	HR	RBI	BB	SO	SB	OBP	SLG
2001	Johnson City (Appy)	R	.248	45	165	25	41	3	0	5	21	7	60	2	.288	.358
2002	Johnson City (Appy)	R	.232	62	224	29	52	15	2	8	39	27	57	9	.320	.424
2003	New Jersey (NYP)	A	.230	65	196	23	45	12	1	2	22	18	38	4	.314	.332
2004	New Jersey (NYP)	A	.125	3	8	0	1	0	0	0	0	0	2	2	.125	.125
	Peoria (MWL)	A	.253	65	241	34	61	18	2	7	31	24	70	3	.333	.432
2005	Quad Cities (MWL)	A	.220	54	209	30	46	15	2	9	33	20	49	0	.295	.440
	Palm Beach (FSL)	A	.275	57	200	37	55	12	2	8	27	12	39	4	.342	.475
2006	Palm Beach (FSL)	A	.269	124	443	64	119	33	1	16	74	36	91	9	.332	.456
2007	Springfield (TL)	AA	.303	64	234	48	71	17	0	18	46	29	32	4	.387	.607
	Memphis (PCL)	AAA	.241	70	253	32	61	10	1	13	31	23	51	6	.329	.443
MINOR LEAGUE TOTALS			.254	609	2173	322	552	135	11	86	324	196	489	43	.329	.445

14 KENNY MAIQUES, RHP

Born: June 25, 1985. **B-T:** R-R. **Ht.:** 6-1. **Wt.:** 185. **Drafted:** Rio Hondo (Calif.) JC, 2005 (37th round). **Signed by:** Anup Sinha.

After showing a 95-mph fastball in the Alaska League in the summer of 2004, Maiques transferred from pitching-rich Long Beach State to Rio Hondo (Calif.) JC so he'd be eligible for the 2005 draft. The move looked like it would pay off when he threw two seven-inning perfect games and went 49 innings without allowing a run, but he blew out his elbow shortly before the draft. The Cardinals, who had planned to use a supplemental first-rounder on Maiques, took him instead in the 37th round and offered to cover his Tommy John surgery and wait. The investment began paying dividends last season, as the undersized righthander set a Quad Cities franchise record with 31 saves. His second half was particularly strong, as he allowed two earned runs while striking out 29 innings. Maiques' fastball has returned to its previous 93-94 mph level, touching 96. Low Class A hitters couldn't touch his slider, which is deceptive and features wicked turn. Maiques is chiseled and he held up well in the closer's job, but some still question his durability. He'll also need sharper command at higher levels. But Maiques has the two pitches he needs to advance rapidly and could jump to the Double-A bullpen to open 2008.

Year	Club (League)	Class	W	L	ERA	G	GS	CG	SV	IP	H	R	ER	HR	BB	SO	AVG
2006	State College (NYP)	A	0	0	6.75	1	1	0	0	4	3	3	3	0	3	4	.231
2007	Quad Cities (MWL)	A	1	5	1.53	52	0	0	31	53	34	16	9	3	20	57	.186
MINOR LEAGUE TOTALS			1	5	1.89	53	1	0	31	57	37	19	12	3	23	61	.189

15 ALLEN CRAIG, 3B/1B

Born: July 18, 1984. **B-T:** R-R. **Ht.:** 6-2. **Wt.:** 190. **Drafted:** California, 2006 (8th round). **Signed by:** Dane Walker.

Craig was the shortstop on Baseball America's Summer All-America Team in 2005, though he never really had a permanent position at California. He played shortstop, left field, first base and third base at various times, but his bat was a constant. He continued that production in his first full pro season in 2007, finishing among the Florida State League leaders in several offensive categories and winning the MVP award at the circuit's all-star game. He also may have found a defensive home at third base. Craig generates great speed and leverage with his swing and has pop to all fields. His power numbers were deflated by the big ballparks in the FSL, but he continued to make consistent contact without reducing his aggressive approach at the plate. He's a below-average runner. After his promotion to Double-A, Craig became Springfield's third base-man for the Texas League playoffs. His range is limited, his arm is no better than average and he doesn't look smooth when throwing, but he makes plays and the Cardinals think he can stay at the hot corner. Craig's bat puts him atop the system's depth chart at third. He'll return to Double-A to start the season.

Year	Club (League)	Class	AVG	G	AB	R	H	2B	3B	HR	RBI	BB	SO	SB	OBP	SLG
2006	State College (NYP)	A	.257	48	175	21	45	13	0	4	29	13	28	0	.325	.400
2007	Palm Beach (FSL)	A	.312	112	423	77	132	25	2	21	77	35	79	8	.370	.530
	Springfield (TL)	AA	.292	7	24	5	7	2	0	3	3	1	6	0	.320	.750
MINOR LEAGUE TOTALS			.296	167	622	103	184	40	2	28	109	49	113	8	.355	.502

16 P.J. WALTERS, RHP

Born: March 3, 1985. **B-T:** R-R. **Ht.:** 6-4. **Wt.:** 200. **Drafted:** South Alabama, 2006 (11th round). **Signed by:** Scott Nichols.

After going 11-3, 3.20 with 166 strikeouts for South Alabama in 2006, Walters was a third-team All-American and an 11th-round pick for the Cardinals. In his first full pro season, he led St. Louis minor leaguers in ERA (2.55) and strikeouts (147) and tied for second in wins (12). Walters followed his uncanny control and unnerving changeup through three levels in 2007, finishing as one of Springfield's starters in the Texas League playoffs. His best pitch defies batters and at times defies description, with Walters labeling it a run-of-the-mill changeup and some scouts calling it a screwball. Combine that offering with Walters' strong command and great life on his pitches, and he's able to succeed without throwing hard. His fastball regularly clocks at 86-89 mph, though he can touch the low 90s. His delivery is deceptive enough that it covers for his fastball's lack of velocity, and his changeup breaks against intuition. He spots both pitches well. His breaking ball is still a work in progress, though that didn't stop him from succeeding in Double-A. The beneficiary of aggressive promotions, Walters doesn't have a high ceiling and will have to prove himself at each new level. But nothing's slowed him so far and he could reach Triple-A or even the majors in 2008.

Year	Club (League)	Class	W	L	ERA	G	GS	CG	SV	IP	H	R	ER	HR	BB	SO	AVG
2006	State College (NYP)	A	2	1	3.56	26	0	0	8	30	29	15	12	1	9	31	.242
2007	Quad Cities (MWL)	A	6	1	2.62	17	10	0	1	68	59	25	20	2	12	73	.229
	Palm Beach (FSL)	A	3	1	2.67	5	5	0	0	33	29	10	10	2	6	37	.225
	Springfield (TL)	AA	3	4	2.37	8	8	1	0	49	42	13	13	4	15	37	.228
MINOR LEAGUE TOTALS			14	7	2.72	56	23	1	9	182	159	63	55	9	42	178	.230

17 JOSE MARTINEZ, SS

Born: Jan. 24, 1986. **B-T:** R-R. **Ht.:** 5-11. **Wt.:** 175. Signed: Venezuela, 2004. **Signed by:** Enrique Brito.

Martinez is at the forefront of the Cardinals' attempt to strengthen their presence in Latin America. They have a new facility in the Dominican Republic, and a campus is coming in Venezuela, but their first prospect is already here. A favorite of his managers, Martinez recovered from a slow start in high Class A to earn a promotion and establish himself as a cornerstone of a Texas League contender. Needed for his glove at the higher level, he also found his offensive groove in Double-A. The contact hitter turned in a .300 average with a surprising 10 homers in 66 games, and he continued to play well this winter in Venezuela. He doesn't have the speed to steal bases, so providing some pop makes him valuable. He has no trouble putting the bat on the ball but needs to work deeper counts and draw more walks. Managers praise his situational hitting and reliability in the field. Martinez doesn't have the ideal range to play shortstop at the higher levels, but his hands, athleticism and instincts are good enough to compensate. He's versatile enough to play all over the infield. At one point he projected as a utility infielder, but if Martinez continues to progress offensively he could become a starting second baseman in the majors. He figures to open 2008 as a shortstop in Triple-A.

Year	Club (League)	Class	AVG	G	AB	R	H	2B	3B	HR	RBI	BB	SO	SB	OBP	SLG
2005	Johnson City (Appy)	R	.300	55	150	28	45	8	2	6	31	20	15	9	.387	.500
2006	Quad Cities (MWL)	A	.270	91	326	47	88	20	2	8	36	18	26	7	.320	.417
2007	Palm Beach (FSL)	A	.248	62	226	22	56	9	1	2	19	10	20	4	.285	.323
	Springfield (TL)	AA	.300	66	250	37	75	13	0	10	46	14	24	0	.339	.472
MINOR LEAGUE TOTALS			.277	274	952	134	264	50	5	26	132	62	85	20	.328	.422

18 BRAD FURNISH, LHP

Born: Jan. 19, 1985. **B-T:** B-L. **Ht.:** 6-1. **Wt.:** 185. **Drafted:** Texas Christian, 2006 (2nd round). **Signed by:** Joe Almaraz.

With more quality starters than they had starts at Quad Cities, the Cardinals opted to go with a tandem system in which pairs of pitchers alternated between starting and relieving. Furnish prospered in the piggyback rotation, and he earned a promotion to high Class A after going 3-0, 2.06 with a save in his final 10 appearances. Furnish has solid stuff, beginning with an 88-92 mph fastball and a classic overhand curveball with a waterfall break. His changeup is still rudimentary, and he remains a flyball pitcher in a groundball organization, so getting comfortable with the lower reaches of the strike zone is a must. As he worked to improve his approach in high Class A, his control short-circuited. Furnish has the ingredients to make it as a starter, but he'll have to re-establish the assertiveness he showed in the piggyback rotation during a second turn in high Class A.

Year	Club (League)	Class	W	L	ERA	G	GS	CG	SV	IP	H	R	ER	HR	BB	SO	AVG
2006	State College (NYP)	A	3	6	3.94	15	15	0	0	75	65	36	33	5	19	68	.234
2007	Quad Cities (MWL)	A	3	3	2.42	21	12	0	2	81	56	31	22	7	27	76	.191
	Palm Beach (FSL)	A	3	3	4.91	8	5	0	0	36	33	22	20	3	22	24	.237
MINOR LEAGUE TOTALS			9	12	3.49	44	32	0	2	193	154	89	75	15	68	168	.217

19 KYLE McCLELLAN, RHP

Born: June 12, 1984. **B-T:** R-R. **Ht.:** 6-2. **Wt.:** 185. **Drafted:** HS—Hazelwood, Mo., 2002 (25th round). **Signed by:** Scott Melvin.

After giving up a scholarship offer from Missouri to sign with his hometown Cardinals, McClellan struggled in his first three pro seasons, going 7-20, 5.24 without advancing past low Class A. It got worse in 2005, when he flipped a curveball that would shred his elbow and radically change his career path. Following Tommy John surgery, McClellan was limited to three starts and seven innings in 2006 before his elbow stiffened on him, requiring another operation to transpose his ulnar nerve. Last season, he ditched starting, embraced relieving and saw his career take off. As his arm regained its strength, McClellan's fastball reached 94 mph with diving sink. Before surgery, he threw mostly in the upper 80s. Now his slider climbs that high at times, and he's willing to throw it in any count to lefties and righties. With his enhanced stuff, he has maintained the ability to throw strikes and locate his pitches. He doesn't have much of a changeup but doesn't require one in his new role. McClellan got bruised a bit by better hitters in the Arizona Fall League and he's still searching for his true niche, as he's more than a specialist but not quite a closer. He went from local kid to full-blown prospect in 2007, pitching his way onto the 40-man roster. McClellan has similar stuff and a similar background as Josh Kinney, and the Cardinals believe he can follow the path Kinney blazed in 2006, opening the year in Triple-A before making major contributions down the stretch.

Year	Club (League)	Class	W	L	ERA	G	GS	CG	SV	IP	H	R	ER	HR	BB	SO	AVG
2002	Johnson City (Appy)	R	0	2	11.25	7	3	0	0	12	17	17	15	3	7	8	.327
2003	Johnson City (Appy)	R	3	6	3.99	12	12	0	0	67	74	34	30	4	16	44	.269
2004	Peoria (MWL)	A	4	12	5.34	24	24	1	0	128	143	85	76	12	34	84	.283
2005	Quad Cities (MWL)	A	1	4	4.83	17	8	0	1	54	59	33	29	4	26	36	.286
2006	Johnson City (Appy)	R	0	1	9.45	3	3	0	0	6	7	7	7	0	3	4	.259
2007	Palm Beach (FSL)	A	4	1	1.24	16	1	0	0	29	22	4	4	0	4	24	.210
	Springfield (TL)	AA	2	0	2.35	24	0	0	0	30	24	9	8	2	6	30	.214
MINOR LEAGUE TOTALS			14	26	4.64	103	51	1	1	328	346	189	169	25	96	230	.270

20 BLAKE HAWKSWORTH, RHP

Born: March 1, 1983. **B-T:** R-R. **Ht.:** 6-3. **Wt.:** 195. **Drafted:** Bellevue (Wash.) CC, D/F 2001 (28th round). **Signed by:** Dane Walker.

If 2006 was Hawksworth's chance to show he was healthy and back in the prospect picture, 2007 was a reminder of how far he had to go. The $1.475 million draft-and follow had an erratic year in his first taste of Triple-A, floundering through the middle of the summer. He described himself as hesitant, even timid, and the results showed it. He feathered his fastball instead of firing it, even though it has returned to its pre-surgery low-90s velocity. He leaned heavily on a changeup that's among the best in the system, but it can't be his only reliable weapon. He gave up 24 home runs and lefthanders torched him for a .518 slugging percentage. To combat better hitters, Hawksworth will have to sharpen either his curveball or slider. After pitching just 25 innings in 2004-05 because of bone spurs in his right ankle and a partially torn labrum, he has made 52 starts during the last two seasons. He gave up just 10 runs over his final four outings in 2007, and the Cardinals hope that's a sign that he'll be able to solve Triple-A this season. Getting stronger and more aggressive would help.

Year	Club (League)	Class	W	L	ERA	G	GS	CG	SV	IP	H	R	ER	HR	BB	SO	AVG
2002	Johnson City (Appy)	R	2	4	3.14	13	12	0	0	66	58	31	23	8	18	61	.232
	New Jersey (NYP)	A	1	0	0.00	2	2	0	0	9	6	0	0	0	2	8	.171
2003	Peoria (MWL)	A	5	1	2.30	10	10	0	0	54	37	16	14	0	12	57	.187
	Palm Beach (FSL)	A	1	3	3.94	6	6	0	0	32	28	14	14	2	11	32	.235
2004	Palm Beach (FSL)	A	1	0	5.91	2	2	0	0	10	10	7	7	2	3	11	.250
2005	New Jersey (NYP)	A	0	3	7.98	7	6	0	0	14	18	18	13	0	10	12	.321
2006	Palm Beach (FSL)	A	7	2	2.47	14	14	0	0	83	75	23	23	0	19	55	.247
	Springfield (TL)	AA	4	2	3.39	13	13	0	0	79	72	34	30	8	31	66	.248
2007	Memphis (PCL)	AAA	4	13	5.28	25	25	0	0	129	150	82	76	24	41	88	.295
MINOR LEAGUE TOTALS			25	28	3.74	92	90	0	0	480	454	225	200	44	147	390	.252

21 JARRETT HOFFPAUIR, 2B

Born: June 18, 1983. **B-T:** R-R. **Ht.:** 5-9. **Wt.:** 165. **Drafted:** Southern Mississippi, 2004 (6th round). **Signed by:** Scott Nichols.

The 2004 draft is essentially a lost one for the Cardinals, who adhered to a strict college-first philosophy in order to save money and restock an organization so thin it just needed an infusion of organization players if nothing else. That's about the way it has worked out, with first-round pick Chris Lambert getting traded to the Tigers for Mike Maroth in 2007, and Hoffpauir left as the standard-bearer for this class. A year after hitting just .249 in Double-A, he returned to that level and was competing for the Texas League batting title when he got promoted last summer, and he continued to flash a level swing and astute strike-zone judgment in Triple-A. Hoffpauir always has been willing to take a walk, and that and his ability to put the bat on the ball are his offensive trademarks. He plays a mistake-free second base, though his speed, range and arm are fringy tools. He took on the added challenge of playing some shortstop and third base in Triple-A. Freshly added to the 40-man roster, he'll report to his first big league camp with a chance to make the team as a utility infielder. If Hoffpauir keeps hitting, he could end up as the homegrown second baseman St. Louis has sought since it traded Adam Kennedy to get Jim Edmonds in March 2000.

Year	Club (League)	Class	AVG	G	AB	R	H	2B	3B	HR	RBI	BB	SO	SB	OBP	SLG
2004	New Jersey (NYP)	A	.361	9	36	8	13	3	0	3	6	3	2	1	.410	.694
	Peoria (MWL)	A	.268	62	231	34	62	20	1	5	30	29	21	2	.363	.429
2005	Quad Cities (MWL)	A	.313	61	227	27	71	15	1	2	28	21	14	5	.376	.414
	Palm Beach (FSL)	A	.257	63	226	23	58	10	1	0	19	32	26	11	.346	.310
2006	Springfield (TL)	AA	.249	119	393	55	98	20	1	7	46	54	41	8	.345	.359
2007	Springfield (TL)	AA	.345	61	203	23	70	16	0	7	33	26	18	3	.420	.527
	Memphis (PCL)	AAA	.300	55	190	27	57	10	0	4	24	29	21	2	.394	.416
MINOR LEAGUE TOTALS			.285	430	1506	197	429	94	4	28	186	194	143	32	.370	.408

22 MARK WORRELL, RHP

Born: March 8, 1983. **B-T:** R-R. **Ht.:** 6-1. **Wt.:** 190. **Drafted:** Florida International, 2004 (12th round). **Signed by:** Steve Turco.

Worrell led the minors with 35 saves in 2005, then topped the Texas League with 27 in 2006. As he neared the majors in 2007, he didn't get many opportunities to close games. Cast as a setup man, he no longer racked up saves but continued to produce. He was Memphis' lone Pacific Coast League midseason all-star and was consistent throughout the season. Worrell has a conventional repertoire, with a low-90s fastball, a good slider and a usable changeup. It's his unusual mechanics that continue to confound scouts as well as batters, though. He always works from the stretch, steps toward first base and keeps his front shoulder closed until his right arm swings and forces it open. His delivery virtually hides the ball until its release, and then he comes at hitters from a variety of arm angles. The Cardinals have resisted the temptation to alter Worrell's mechanics, mainly because they work. He continues to dominate righthanders (.208 average) more than lefties (.283), so he may start off as a righty specialist when he makes his first visit to the majors. That should come sometime this season after he was added to the 40-man roster in November.

Year	Club (League)	Class	W	L	ERA	G	GS	CG	SV	IP	H	R	ER	HR	BB	SO	AVG
2004	Johnson City (Appy)	R	1	0	1.21	17	0	0	6	22	12	3	3	1	7	35	.152
	Peoria (MWL)	A	0	2	4.30	12	0	0	6	14	9	10	7	2	6	20	.170
2005	Palm Beach (FSL)	A	2	3	2.25	53	0	0	35	56	38	20	14	6	19	53	.191
2006	Springfield (TL)	AA	3	7	4.52	57	0	0	27	61	52	34	31	10	20	75	.226
2007	Memphis (PCL)	AAA	3	2	3.09	50	0	0	4	67	58	25	23	6	25	66	.236
MINOR LEAGUE TOTALS			9	14	3.17	189	0	0	78	221	169	92	78	25	77	249	.209

23 MIKE PARISI, RHP

Born: April 18, 1983. **B-T:** R-R. **Ht.:** 6-3. **Wt.:** 215. **Drafted:** Manhattan, 2004 (9th round). **Signed by:** Joe Rigoli.

Parisi cruised through his first two pro seasons, flipping his dandy curveball with abandon. When he arrived in Double-A in 2006 and struggled, he pulled out a pen and started keeping notes. He realized he couldn't thrive on a curve and a desire to strike everyone out. His numbers in Triple-A are a bit deceiving, as they reflect a pitcher undone by a weak team, and a season featuring a few terrible performances rather than consistently mediocre outings. Parisi can fire his fastball in the low 90s, and he has become willing to give up velocity in order to gain downward movement on his sinker. He still has the plunging curve that was his hammer as a strikeout king for Manhattan—he holds the Jaspers career record with 272 in 244 innings—and his changeup showed progress last season. He has yet to miss a scheduled start as a pro and has thrown at least 150 innings in three consecutive seasons. Parisi still finds too much of the strike zone with too many of his pitches, but durability and overall effectiveness have him on a short list to get the call from Triple-A if the big league club needs a starter. St. Louis added him to its 40-man roster in November.

Year	Club (League)	Class	W	L	ERA	G	GS	CG	SV	IP	H	R	ER	HR	BB	SO	AVG
2004	New Jersey (NYP)	A	4	2	4.46	7	7	0	0	36	40	18	18	3	6	26	.292
	Peoria (MWL)	A	1	1	3.28	6	6	0	0	35	30	16	13	1	15	36	.238
2005	Quad Cities (MWL)	A	5	5	4.08	14	14	0	0	86	98	42	39	5	25	66	.286
	Palm Beach (FSL)	A	5	6	3.23	13	13	1	0	78	79	31	28	6	22	63	.264
2006	Springfield (TL)	AA	9	8	4.60	27	27	0	0	150	168	92	77	13	63	107	.291
2007	Memphis (PCL)	AAA	8	13	4.91	28	28	0	0	165	192	100	90	21	65	111	.298
MINOR LEAGUE TOTALS			32	35	4.32	95	95	1	0	551	607	299	265	49	196	409	.283

24 JASON MOTTE, RHP

Born: June 22, 1982. **B-T:** R-R. **Ht.:** 6-0. **Wt.:** 200. **Drafted:** Iona, 2003 (19th round). **Signed by:** Joe Rigoli.

The Cardinals loved Motte's defense behind the plate, but when his career average dropped to .190 in May 2006, they decided enough was enough. He moved to the mound in what has proven to be much more than a desperation move and resulted in his addition to St. Louis' 40-man roster after the 2007 season. In his first full year as a pitcher, he reached Double-A and posted a 1.98 ERA with 69 strikeouts in 59 innings. When he first took the mound, Motte just pulled the ball back to his ear and fired, as if he were still a catcher. The Cardinals added a little arm circle, but that's the only major change they've made to his delivery. He throws a heavy fastball that sits at 95-96 mph and regularly touches 98. He couples it with a slider that's improving, and he plans to add a splitter to the mix. Motte was dominant as a Double-A set-up man, so he'll likely find himself in the same role at St. Louis this season. With not even 100 innings under his belt, he's one step away from the majors.

Year	Club (League)	Class	AVG	G	AB	R	H	2B	3B	HR	RBI	BB	SO	SB	OBP	SLG
2003	Johnson City (Appy)	R	.310	9	29	2	9	3	0	0	5	0	9	1	.300	.414
	Peoria (Mid)	A	.203	48	133	8	27	1	0	0	10	10	44	1	.257	.211
2004	Palm Beach (FSL)	A	.174	108	287	22	50	5	0	1	24	6	94	1	.193	.202
	Memphis (PCL)	AAA	.200	3	5	0	1	0	0	0	0	0	4	0	.200	.200
2005	Springfield (TL)	AA	.333	1	3	1	1	0	0	0	1	1	1	0	.500	.333
	Palm Beach (FSL)	A	.172	40	122	7	21	4	0	3	10	4	41	1	.198	.279
MINOR LEAGUE TOTALS			.188	209	579	40	109	13	0	4	50	21	193	4	.217	.231

Year	Club (League)	Class	W	L	ERA	G	GS	CG	SV	IP	H	R	ER	HR	BB	SO	AVG
2006	State College (NYP)	A	1	2	3.08	21	0	0	8	26	30	12	9	1	4	25	.280
	Quad Cities (MWL)	A	1	1	4.97	8	0	0	0	12	16	8	7	1	3	13	.296
2007	Palm Beach (FSL)	A	1	0	0.90	9	0	0	3	10	7	2	1	0	1	6	.184
	Springfield (TL)	AA	3	3	2.20	44	0	0	8	49	36	13	12	3	22	63	.208
MINOR LEAGUE TOTALS			6	6	2.66	82	0	0	19	98	89	35	29	5	30	107	.239

25 MARK McCORMICK, RHP

Born: Oct. 15, 1982. **B-T:** R-R. **Ht.:** 6-2. **Wt.:** 195. **Drafted:** Baylor, 2005 (1st round supplemental). **Signed by:** Joe Almaraz.

McCormick once was prized as the most powerful arm in the system, but that was a couple of summers and several injuries ago. He blazed out of Baylor with a 95-mph fastball but has thrown only 64 innings the past two seasons, including just eight in 2007 as he rehabbed his shoulder. He had shoulder surgery after pitching through soreness for most of the 2006 season. When healthy, McCormick can still bring it—but he just can't control it. He regularly throws in the mid-90s with his fastball and has cranked it even higher on occasion. He also has a hard curveball that rates as above-average. His control is lacking, however, and his delivery isn't as polished as might be expected from a college pitcher. Developing a third pitch will take a back seat for now to staying healthy. Despite plus stuff, McCormick rarely has dominated hitters, thanks to too many walks and too many high pitch counts. He'll stay with starting because his stuff is too electric not to give him every opportunity to make the most of it, but relieving looms as a more likely use of his talent. He'll likely open the season back in high Class A.

Year	Club (League)	Class	W	L	ERA	G	GS	CG	SV	IP	H	R	ER	HR	BB	SO	AVG
2005	New Jersey (NYP)	A	0	0	0.00	2	2	0	0	6	1	0	0	0	3	10	.053
	Quad Cities (MWL)	A	1	2	5.48	9	9	0	0	42	41	27	26	4	28	45	.253
2006	Quad Cities (MWL)	A	2	4	3.78	11	11	0	0	52	38	25	22	3	38	63	.207
	Palm Beach (FSL)	A	0	0	11.25	2	2	0	0	4	5	5	5	0	3	5	.294
2007	Cardinals (GCL)	R	0	0	1.93	3	3	0	0	4	1	2	1	0	2	4	.067
	Palm Beach (FSL)	A	0	0	0.00	1	1	0	0	3	2	0	0	0	0	2	.222
MINOR LEAGUE TOTALS			3	6	4.31	28	28	0	0	112	88	59	54	7	74	129	.217

26 BLAKE KING, RHP

Born: April 11, 1987. **B-T:** R-R. **Ht.:** 6-1. **Wt.:** 195. **Drafted:** Eastern Oklahoma State JC, D/F 2005 (44th round). **Signed by:** Steve Gossett.

When King signed with the Cardinals as a draft-and-follow in 2006, he was surrounded by family and it was big local news because of a famous relative—he's the great-nephew of Mickey Mantle. King turned pro after leading national junior college pitchers with 123 strikeouts in 86 innings at Eastern Oklahoma State. He's still striking people out in pro ball, but he's also walking too many batters, which is why he has yet to taste success in a full-season league. He opened last year in low Class A but went back to Batavia after walking nearly a batter per inning. King can push his fastball into the mid-90s and has developed a hard slurve that resembles a slider more than a curve and arrives in the mid-80s. He throws his breaking ball with the same force as his fastball, and it's as effective as it is deceptive. He has no changeup to speak of at this point. King has called himself effectively wild, while scouts call him just plain wild. The stuff is there for him to advance, but he won't make it far until he establishes better control. He'll give low Class A another shot this spring.

Year	Club (League)	Class	W	L	ERA	G	GS	CG	SV	IP	H	R	ER	HR	BB	SO	AVG
2006	Johnson City (Appy)	R	4	3	3.02	13	13	0	0	62	37	25	21	3	29	74	.167
2007	Quad Cities (MWL)	A	2	3	5.21	19	9	0	0	57	44	36	33	3	44	62	.214
	Batavia (NYP)	A	1	4	4.70	16	9	0	0	53	48	28	28	3	34	65	.240
MINOR LEAGUE TOTALS			7	10	4.26	48	31	0	0	173	129	89	82	9	107	201	.205

27 MARK HAMILTON, 1B

Born: July 29, 1984. **B-T:** L-L. **Ht.:** 6-3. **Wt.:** 220. **Drafted:** Tulane, 2006 (2nd round supplemental). **Signed by:** Scott Nichols.

With three swings of the bat, Hamilton underscored his claim as one of the best power prospects in the Cardinals system. He ripped three home runs and drove in seven runs in a 16-8 victory that clinched Springfield's berth in the Texas League championship series, adding to the 19 home runs he hit during the regular season. No matter the level, Hamilton has always had a hammer. He hit 20 home runs in his final year at Tulane in 2006, then tied for the short-season New York-Penn League lead with eight homers in just 30 games. He uses a muscular frame and an authoritative lefthanded swing to generate plus raw power, getting most of his energy from his upper body. He has a selective approach but also some definite holes in his swing. While Hamilton is a threat at the plate, he offers little else. First base is his lone defensive option because of his below-average arm and speed, and he's not especially adept as a defender. With Albert Pujols at first base in St. Louis, Hamilton's best-case scenario may be to hit his way into a trade to an American League team for whom he could DH.

Year	Club (League)	Class	AVG	G	AB	R	H	2B	3B	HR	RBI	BB	SO	SB	OBP	SLG
2006	State College (NYP)	A	.264	30	106	18	28	3	1	8	24	13	24	1	.347	.538
	Quad Cities (MWL)	A	.254	38	142	16	36	8	0	3	25	10	32	0	.307	.373
2007	Palm Beach (FSL)	A	.290	60	221	31	64	12	0	13	49	20	48	1	.348	.520
	Springfield (TL)	AA	.250	68	248	32	62	15	0	6	41	24	54	1	.318	.383
MINOR LEAGUE TOTALS			.265	196	717	97	190	38	1	30	139	67	158	3	.330	.446

28 LUKE GREGERSON, RHP

Born: May 14, 1984. **B-T:** L-R. **Ht.:** 6-3. **Wt.:** 200. **Drafted:** St. Xavier (Ill.), 2006 (28th round). **Signed by:** Scott Melvin.

Gregerson inherited one of the most relished roles for relievers in the system when he took over as Palm Beach's closer in April. The previous two Palm Beach closers had led the minors in saves in 2005 (Mark Worrell) and finished second in 2006 (Mike Sillman). Gregerson finished with 29 saves while holding batters to a .188 average (.188 by lefties, .189 by righties). He was a two-way threat at St. Xavier (Ill.), an NAIA school, winning the Chicagoland Conference player of the year award in 2006 after batting .335 as a right fielder and posting a 0.68 ERA as a closer. Exclusively a reliever as a pro, he has devastated lower-level hitters with his sinker/slider combo. Gregerson's hard sinker has good movement and comes in the low 90s, and a vicious slider that Palm Beach teammate Adam Ottavino called "out of this world" is his strikeout pitch. Gregerson earned a promotion in August, finished the season as Springfield's closer in the Texas League playoffs and pitched briefly in the Arizona Fall League. He'll likely return to Double-A to open 2008, and he could ascend quickly as a setup man.

Year	Club (League)	Class	W	L	ERA	G	GS	CG	SV	IP	H	R	ER	HR	BB	SO	AVG
2006	Johnson City (Appy)	R	0	1	3.86	15	0	0	5	16	14	10	7	0	6	24	.222
	State College (NYP)	A	6	1	1.72	12	0	0	4	15	9	5	3	0	9	22	.164
2007	Palm Beach (FSL)	A	3	4	1.97	53	0	0	29	64	42	14	14	0	20	69	.188
	Springfield (TL)	AA	0	0	0.00	1	0	0	0	1	1	0	0	0	0	3	.250
MINOR LEAGUE TOTALS			9	6	2.23	81	0	0	38	97	66	29	24	0	35	118	.191

29 TYLER GREENE, SS

Born: Aug. 17, 1983. **B-T:** R-R. **Ht.:** 6-2. **Wt.:** 185. **Drafted:** Georgia Tech, 2005 (1st round). **Signed by:** Roger Smith.

Taken two picks after Colby Rasmus in the 2005 draft, Greene was a decorated college player who received a $1.1 million bonus. His pro career has been uneven to say the least, as he has hit just .233 above low Class A. If there's an element of his game that has translated easily to pro ball, it's his speed. Greene led the system with 33 steals in 2006. But even his speed is a question now, as Greene has to recover from knee surgery. He went on the disabled list with knee pain in June, then returned only to crumple in pain during his first at-bat. Surgery in July cleaned up his knee and ended his season. Greene needs to start making progress with his bat. He began driving the ball more to all fields before his injury, and half of his 54 hits were for extra bases. He still exhibits poor plate discipline and chases too many bad pitches, however. Greene has the arm strength to play shortstop, but his size, footwork and erratic play (64 miscues in 244 pro games) may make him a better fit at third base. He'd have to step up his offensive game even more if he moved to the hot corner. The Cardinals say things were just starting to click for Greene when he got hurt, and at 24 he needs to start moving. He'll start 2008 back in Double-A

Year	Club (League)	Class	AVG	G	AB	R	H	2B	3B	HR	RBI	BB	SO	SB	OBP	SLG
2005	New Jersey (NYP)	A	.261	35	138	28	36	12	0	1	18	15	37	13	.352	.370
	Palm Beach (FSL)	A	.271	20	85	17	23	4	0	2	5	5	28	6	.326	.388
2006	Palm Beach (FSL)	A	.224	71	268	38	60	10	1	5	19	29	90	22	.308	.325
	Quad Cities (MWL)	A	.287	59	223	42	64	8	3	15	47	20	65	11	.375	.552
2007	Springfield (TL)	AA	.244	65	221	41	54	17	2	8	25	16	62	10	.309	.448
MINOR LEAGUE TOTALS			.253	250	935	166	237	51	6	31	114	85	282	62	.333	.420

30 LUIS DE LA CRUZ, C

Born: May 6, 1989. **B-T:** R-R. **Ht.:** 5-10. **Wt.:** 164. Signed: Dominican Republic, 2006. **Signed by:** Maximo Alvarez.

Signed as part of the Cardinals' growing initiative in the Dominican Republic in 2006 as a 17-year-old, de la Cruz made a promising U.S. debut in the Rookie-level Gulf Coast League last season. He lashes at the ball with a powerful, easy, line-drive stroke from the right side of the plate. He shows above-average bat speed, leading scouts to think he'll develop power. Behind the plate, he already has shown catch-and-throw skills and leadership ability, including a good feel for calling games. He has a plus arm and threw out 51 percent of basestealers last season. He also blocks balls well. De la Cruz already has drawn comparisons to Ivan Rodriguez, which will be more apt once he taps into his power. He'll also have to improve his handling of pitchers over the course of a season, but that should come with more experience. He could make his full-season debut in low Class A this year.

Year	Club (League)	Class	AVG	G	AB	R	H	2B	3B	HR	RBI	BB	SO	SB	OBP	SLG
2006	Cardinals (DSL)	R	.293	40	99	9	29	5	0	0	13	10	21	6	.360	.343
2007	Cardinals (GCL)	R	.281	39	96	10	27	6	2	0	9	7	16	3	.337	.385
MINOR LEAGUE TOTALS			.287	79	195	19	56	11	2	0	22	17	37	9	.349	.364

San Diego Padres

BY MATT EDDY

Though the Padres came up one game short of qualifying for the playoffs after two consecutive division titles, the organization enjoyed perhaps its most productive season, all things considered, in the last three.

Under first-year manager Bud Black, San Diego won 89 games, its most since the 1998 pennant winners won 98. The team ran out of steam in September, when Chris Young went 0-3, 6.27 while battling a sore back and Milton Bradley and Mike Cameron were lost to injury with a week left in the season. The Padres still controlled their playoff destiny with three games to play, but lost all three, the last one a one-game wild-card playoff at Colorado.

Jake Peavy remained the ace of the pitching staff, winning his first Cy Young Award as well as the National League pitching triple crown. And in another constant, general manager Kevin Towers' shrewd trading made a big impact.

One year after scoring big with trades for Adrian Gonzalez, Young and Cameron, Towers acquired Kevin Kouzmanoff from the Indians for Josh Barfield, who ultimately lost his job to rookie Asdrubal Cabrera. Kouzmanoff hit 18 homers as a rookie. Towers added bullpen depth by shipping Ben Johnson to the Mets as part of a trade for Heath Bell, who led all major league relievers in innings (94) and strikeouts (102).

In late June, Towers picked up Bradley, and he jump-started the offense while healthy. He also made in-season trades for Michael Barrett and Scott Hairston, which paid modest dividends and cost San Diego little in terms of established talent.

When bullpen stalwart Scott Linebrink started to slip, Towers shrewdly traded him to the Brewers for Steve Garrison, Will Inman and Joe Thatcher.

On the minor league side, Double-A San Antonio and high Class A Lake Elsinore made deep playoff runs with teams stocked with prospects from the 2005 and 2006 drafts, the Padres' first two under vice president of scouting and farm director Grady Fuson.

San Antonio, BA's Minor League Team of the Year, won the Texas League title, led by the system's two best prospects, third baseman Chase Headley and second baseman Matt Antonelli.

Towers also wasn't shy about offering arbitration and reaped seven extra picks for the loss of five free agents after the 2006 season. With eight of the top 87 picks in the 2007 draft, the Padres primarily selected

DAVID STONER

Rookie third baseman Kevin Kouzmanoff overcame a poor first half to hit 18 home runs

TOP 30 PROSPECTS

1. Chase Headley, 3b	16. Drew Cumberland, ss
2. Matt Antonelli, 2b	17. Mitch Canham, c
3. Matt Latos, rhp	18. Cesar Ramos, lhp
4. Wade LeBlanc, lhp	19. Joe Thatcher, lhp
5. Drew Miller, rhp	20. Carlos Guevara, rhp
6. Steve Garrison, lhp	21. Matt Buschmann, rhp
7. Will Inman, rhp	22. Chad Huffman, of
8. Cedric Hunter, of	23. Jared Wells, rhp
9. Nick Schmidt, lhp	24. Nick Hundley, c
10. Kyle Blanks, 1b	25. Jeudy Valdez, ss/2b
11. Cesar Carrillo, rhp	26. Rayner Contreras, 3b/2b
12. Cory Luebke, lhp	27. Josh Geer, rhp
13. Yefri Carvajal, of	28. David Freese, 3b
14. Kellen Kulbacki, of	29. Corey Kluber, rhp
15. Will Venable, of	30. Matt Bush, rhp

established college talent, like lefthanders Cory Luebke and Nick Schmidt, outfielder Kellen Kulbacki and catcher Mitch Canham. San Diego also scored by landing the top player from baseball's final class of draft-and-follows. After signing for $1.25 million, righthander Matt Latos ranked as the No. 1 prospect in the short-season Northwest League.

The Padres also were active in Latin America, handing out six-figure bonuses to a pair of Dominicans, shortstop Jonathan Spraut ($750,000) and outfielder Rymer Liriano ($300,000).

General Manager: Kevin Towers. **Farm Director:** Grady Fuson. **Scouting Director:** Bill Gayton.

Class	Team	League	W	L	PCT	Finish*	Manager	Affiliated
Majors	San Diego	National	89	74	.546	4th (16)	Bud Black	—
Triple-A	Portland Beavers	Pacific Coast	58	86	.403	15th (16)	Rick Renteria	2001
Double-A	San Antonio Missions	Texas	73	66	.525	3rd (8)^	Randy Ready	2007
High A	Lake Elsinore Storm	California	74	65	.532	4th (10)	Carlos Lezcano	2001
Low A	Fort Wayne Wizards	Midwest	55	84	.396	13th (14)	Doug Dascenzo	1999
Short-season	Eugene Emeralds	Northwest	34	42	.447	6th (8)	Greg Riddoch	2001
Rookie	AZL Padres	Arizona	28	28	.500	4th (9)	Tony Muser	2004
Overall 2007 Minor League Record			322	371	.465	26th		

*Finish in overall standings (No. of teams in league) ^League champion

LAST YEAR'S TOP 30

Player, Pos.		Status
1.	Cedric Hunter, of	No. 8
2.	Cesar Carrillo, rhp	No. 11
3.	Matt Antonelli, 3b	No. 2
4.	Kevin Kouzmanoff, 3b	Majors
5.	Will Venable, of	No. 15
6.	Chase Headley, 3b	No. 1
7.	Chad Huffman, of	No. 22
8.	Nick Hundley, c	No. 24
9.	Jared Wells, rhp	No. 23
10.	Cesar Ramos, lhp	No. 18
11.	Aaron Breit, rhp	Dropped out
12.	Drew Miller, rhp	No. 5
13.	Yefri Carvajal, of	No. 13
14.	Kyler Burke, of	(Cubs)
15.	David Freese, 3b	No. 28
16.	Wade LeBlanc, lhp	No. 4
17.	Kevin Cameron, rhp	Majors
18.	Paul McAnulty, 1b/3b	Dropped out
19.	Matt Bush, ss	No. 30
20.	Luis Cruz, 2b/ss	Dropped out
21.	Felix Carrasco, 3b	Dropped out
22.	Andrew Brown, rhp	(Athletics)
23.	Sean Thompson, lhp	(Rockies)
24.	Matt Buschmann, rhp	No. 21
25.	Mike Ekstrom, rhp	Dropped out
26.	Colt Morton, c	Dropped out
27.	Pablo Menchaca, rhp	Dropped out
28.	Simon Castro, rhp	Dropped out
29.	Kyle Blanks, 1b	No. 10
30.	John Hussey, rhp	Dropped out

BEST TOOLS

Best Hitter for Average	Chase Headley
Best Power Hitter	Kyle Blanks
Best Strike-Zone Discipline	Matt Antonelli
Fastest Baserunner	Luis Durango
Best Athlete	Matt Antonelli
Best Fastball	Matt Latos
Best Curveball	Drew Miller
Best Slider	Mike Ekstrom
Best Changeup	Wade LeBlanc
Best Control	Josh Geer
Best Defensive Catcher	Jose Lobaton
Best Defensive Infielder	Jesus Lopez
Best Infield Arm	Jesus Lopez
Best Defensive Outfielder	Drew Macias
Best Outfield Arm	Drew Macias

PROJECTED 2011 LINEUP

Catcher	Mitch Canham
First Base	Adrian Gonzalez
Second Base	Matt Antonelli
Third Base	Kevin Kouzmanoff
Shortstop	Khalil Greene
Left Field	Chase Headley
Center Field	Drew Cumberland
Right Field	Cedric Hunter
No. 1 Starter	Jake Peavy
No. 2 Starter	Chris Young
No. 3 Starter	Matt Latos
No. 4 Starter	Wade LeBlanc
No. 5 Starter	Drew Miller
Closer	Heath Bell

TOP PROSPECTS OF THE DECADE

Year	Player, Pos.	2007 Org.
1998	Matt Clement, rhp	Red Sox
1999	Matt Clement, rhp	Red Sox
2000	Sean Burroughs, 3b	Mariners
2001	Sean Burroughs, 3b	Mariners
2002	Sean Burroughs, 3b	Mariners
2003	Xavier Nady, of	Pirates
2004	Josh Barfield, 2b	Indians
2005	Josh Barfield, 2b	Indians
2006	Cesar Carrillo, rhp	Padres
2007	Cedric Hunter, of	Padres

TOP DRAFT PICKS OF THE DECADE

Year	Player, Pos.	2007 Org.
1998	Sean Burroughs, 3b	Mariners
1999	Vince Faison, of	Athletics
2000	Mark Phillips, lhp	Newark (Atlantic)
2001	Jake Gautreau, 3b	Mets
2002	Khalil Greene, ss	Padres
2003	Tim Stauffer, rhp	Padres
2004	Matt Bush, ss	Padres
2005	Cesar Carrillo, rhp	Padres
2006	Matt Antonelli, 3b	Padres
2007	Nick Schmidt, lhp	Padres

LARGEST BONUSES IN CLUB HISTORY

Matt Bush, 2004	$3,150,000
Mark Phillips, 2000	$2,200,000
Sean Burroughs, 1998	$2,100,000
Jake Gautreau, 2001	$1,875,000
Matt Antonelli, 2006	$1,575,000

SAN DIEGO PADRES

Top 2008 Rookie: Chase Headley, 3b. The Padres will try to convert him to left field, which would allow him and Kevin Kouzmanoff to play in the same lineup.

Breakout Prospect: Rayner Contreras, 3b/2b. His intriguing power-speed combination could blossom in the hitter-friendly California League.

Sleeper: Danny Payne, of. An instinctive center fielder, he already has plate discipline but needs to find swing path that works for him.

SOURCE OF TOP 30 TALENT

Homegrown	26	Acquired	4
College	16	Trades	3
Junior college	0	Rule 5 draft	1
High school	3	Independent leagues	0
Draft-and-follow	4	Free agents/waivers	0
Nondrafted free agents	0		
International	3		

Numbers in parentheses indicate prospect rankings.

LF
Cedric Hunter (8)
Kellen Kulbacki (14)
Will Venable (15)
Chad Huffman (22)
Paul McAnulty

CF
Danny Payne
Brad Chalk
Drew Macias
Luis Durango

RF
Yefri Carvajal (13)
Rymer Liriano

3B
Chase Headley (1)
Rayner Contreras (26)
David Freese (28)
Edinson Rincon
Felix Carrasco

SS
Jeudy Valdez (25)
Jonathan Spraut
Jesus Lopez
Lance Zawadzki

2B
Matt Antonelli (2)
Drew Cumberland (16)
Eric Sogard
Callix Crabbe
Craig Stansberry

1B
Kyle Blanks (10)
Craig Cooper
Brian Myrow
Daryl Jones

C
Mitch Canham (17)
Nick Hundley (24)
Colt Morton
Jose Lobaton
Luis Martinez

RHP

Starters	Relievers
Matt Latos (3)	Carlos Guevara (20)
Drew Miller (5)	Jared Wells (23)
Will Inman (7)	Matt Bush (30)
Cesar Carrillo (11)	Michael Gardner
Matt Buschmann (21)	Mauro Zarate
Josh Geer (27)	Jeremy McBryde
Corey Kluber (29)	Pablo Menchaca
Aaron Breit	Wilton Lopez
Simon Castro	Ernesto Frieri
Jeremy Hefner	Manny Ayala
Mike Ekstrom	John Madden
John Hussey	Rolando Valdez

LHP

Starters	Relievers
Wade LeBlanc (4)	Joe Thatcher (19)
Steve Garrison (6)	Will Startup
Nick Schmidt (9)	Matt Teague
Cory Luebke (12)	Pascual Juan
Cesar Ramos (18)	Colt Hynes
Euclides Viloria	Allen Harrington
Nate Culp	

2007 SIGNING BUDGET: $5.8 MILLION

Best Pro Debut: OF Kellen Kulbacki (1s) hit .301 with eight homers in the Northwest League. LHP Cory Luebke (1s) reached high Class A and went 5-3, 3.07 with a 61-8 K-BB ratio in 69 innings.

Best Athlete: SS Drew Cumberland (1s) was an all-state defensive back and running back in Florida. He has plus-plus speed, a knack for making highlight plays on defense and even gap power. SS Lance Zawadski (4) has plus raw power and speed, not to mention a well-above-average arm. C Mitch Canham (1s) is athletic for his position.

Best Pure Hitter: Kulbacki hit .400 in three seasons at James Madison, including .464 as a sophomore. He has good balance and his bat stays in the strike zone for a long time, so he should continue to hit for average.

Best Power Hitter: Kulbacki led NCAA Division I with 24 homers and a .943 slugging percentage in 2006, and his 51 career homers are a James Madison record.

Fastest Runner: Cumberland gets from the left side to first base in 3.9-4.0 seconds. OF Brad Chalk (2) and Zawadski have plus speed.

Best Defensive Player: Chalk was slowed by a back injury in his pro debut, but he's an outstanding center fielder when healthy. His solid arm strength is better than most center fielders have. Danny Payne (1s) also gets the job done in center field, more with instincts than tools.

Best Fastball: Draft-and-follow RHP Matt Latos (11 in 2006), can sit in the mid-90s and maxes out at 98 mph. Among the 2007 draftees, RHP Wynn Pelzer has a 92-96 mph four-seamer but still is recovering from a broken kneecap sustained in the Cape Cod League.

Best Secondary Pitch: LHP Nick Schmidt's (1) curveball and changeup are solid pitches, which along with his competitive edge help his average fastball play up. He'll miss all of 2008 after blowing out his elbow and requiring Tommy John surgery.

Most Intriguing Background: RHP Dylan Axelrod's (30) uncle Barry is a prominent agent whose clients include Padres general manager Kevin Towers.

Closest To The Majors: Luebke throws strikes with an average fastball and slider, and being lefthanded doesn't hurt.

Best Late-Round Pick: LHP Allen Harrington (13) pitches aggressively with an 88-91 mph fastball. He posted a 2.09 ERA and 52 strikeouts in as many innings while advancing to low Class A.

The One Who Got Away: RHP Tommy Toledo (3) earned comparisons to Padres 2005 first-rounder Cesar Carrillo, but San Diego couldn't sign him away from a Florida scholarship.

Assessment: Three of the Padres' last four top draft choices (Schmidt, Carrillo, Matt Bush) had Tommy John surgery in 2007, but they still brought in a lot of talent with five supplemental first-round picks and Latos as a draft-and-follow.

2006 BUDGET: $4.7 MILLION

2B Matt Antonelli (1) is ready to take over the starting job in San Diego. He, RHP Matt Latos (11) and LHP Wade LeBlanc (2) rank 2-3-4 on this prospect list.

GRADE: B+

2005 BUDGET: $3.0 MILLION

3B Chase Headley (1) also has developed quickly and is the system's top prospect. RHP Cesar Carrillo (1) is recovering from Tommy John surgery, but there's still depth, led by RHP Drew Miller (37).

GRADE: C+

2004 BUDGET: $4.5 MILLION

No. 1 overall pick Matt Bush (1) is showing more promise as a reliever than he did as a shortstop, though he quickly succumbed to Tommy John surgery. For now, 1B Kyle Blanks (42) ranks as a better prospect.

GRADE: D

2003 BUDGET: $2.8 MILLION

RHP Tim Stauffer (1) hasn't been the same since coming down with a shoulder injury that was undiagnosed before the draft. C Colt Morton (3) might be the best of this crop, which isn't saying much.

GRADE: F

Draft analysis by Jim Callis. Numbers in parentheses indicate draft rounds. Budgets are bonuses in first 10 rounds.

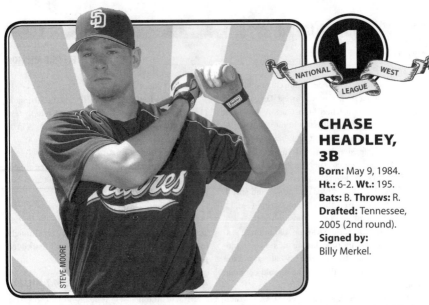

STEVE MOORE

CHASE HEADLEY, 3B

Born: May 9, 1984.
Ht.: 6-2. **Wt.:** 195.
Bats: B. **Throws:** R.
Drafted: Tennessee,
2005 (2nd round).
Signed by:
Billy Merkel.

Headley finished second in NCAA Division I in walks (63) as a junior at Tennessee in 2005, then signed with the Padres for $560,000 as a second-round pick. Headley continued to show outstanding pitch recognition in his first two pro seasons, allowing him to hit for average and draw walks. For all his hitting ability, though, Headley slugged just an aggregate .431 in the hitter-friendly Northwest and Cal leagues. Last offseason, he embarked on a rigorous weight-training program that added 15 pounds of muscle, which he worked hard to retain through the summer months. The returns were immediate. Headley turned in one of the finest seasons in the minors in 2007, taking home Double-A Texas League MVP honors while leading the league in average (.330), on-base percentage (.437) and slugging percentage (.580). He made his major league debut in mid-June when starting third baseman Kevin Kouzmanoff missed time with a back injury. After returning to San Antonio, Headley led the Missions to the TL title.

Like most everybody drafted on vice president of scouting and player development Grady Fuson's watch, Headley is an instinctive player with plus makeup who plays above his tools. A switch-hitter with a sweet swing and power to all fields from both sides of the plate, Headley was noticeably shorter and quicker to the ball in 2007, and observers made note of his improved physique. Already blessed with well-above-average hand-eye coordination and confidence, Headley learned to pick his spots to hit for power without selling out. He wasn't helped by San Antonio's Wolff Municipal Stadium, which ranks among the TL's most difficult power parks, and slugged .624 on the road compared to .528 at home. He also markedly improved his two-strike approach in 2007. Prior to 2007, Headley had struggled from the right side of the plate, as his right elbow would get too high during his load and create a longer, loopier swing. He has overcome that flaw and actually was more productive as a righty last season. An average defender at third base with a solid-average arm, Headley has made strides with both his reads off the bat and his throwing accuracy.

A below-average runner, Headley has a slow body and isn't a factor on the bases. His lack of athleticism could become an issue, because he's just about major league-ready but is blocked by Kouzmanoff. A move to an outfield corner could be in order, but scouts wonder whether Headley or Kouzmanoff has the quickness to be more than playable out there.

Headley has all the qualities required of a third baseman on a first-division team, so the Padres eventually will find a way to get him into their lineup. Because of the presence of Kouzmanoff and the Padres' general lack of outfield depth, Headley may begin his career in left field, where he worked in the offseason.

Year	Club (League)	Class	AVG	G	AB	R	H	2B	3B	HR	RBI	BB	SO	SB	OBP	SLG
2005	Eugene (NWL)	A	.268	57	220	29	59	14	3	6	33	34	48	1	.375	.441
	Fort Wayne (MWL)	A	.200	4	15	2	3	0	0	0	1	1	4	0	.250	.200
2006	Lake Elsinore (Cal)	A	.291	129	484	79	141	33	0	12	73	74	96	4	.389	.434
2007	San Antonio (TL)	AA	.330	121	433	82	143	38	5	20	78	74	114	1	.437	.580
	San Diego (NL)	MLB	.222	8	18	1	4	1	0	0	0	2	4	0	.333	.278
MINOR LEAGUE TOTALS			.300	311	1152	192	346	85	8	38	185	183	262	6	.403	.487
MAJOR LEAGUE TOTALS			.222	8	18	1	4	1	0	0	0	2	4	0	.333	.278

2 MATT ANTONELLI, 2B

STEVE MOORE

Born: April 8, 1985. **B-T:** R-R. **Ht.:** 6-0. **Wt.:** 203. **Drafted:** Wake Forest, 2006 (1st round). **Signed by:** Ash Lawson.

The Padres selected Antonelli with the 17th overall pick in 2006 and signed him for $1.575 million after he showed steady improvement each season at Wake Forest and turned in two strong summers in the Cape Cod League. Prior to that, as a high school senior, he was the Massachusetts state player of the year in football and hockey—and the runner-up in baseball. Drafted as a third baseman, he slugged just .356 and didn't homer in 205 at-bats during his pro debut. Great makeup and competitiveness are the two most common attributes ascribed to Antonelli. He's an overachiever who grinds counts and understands how to hit, using all fields and letting his home runs come naturally instead of muscling up on the ball. Antonelli has average bat speed and his power comes mostly to left field and left-center. San Diego introduced Antonelli to second base in 2006 instructional league and while he's not a flashy defender there, he has good first step reactions, solid-average range, the fortitude to hang in on double plays and more than enough arm. He has plus speed and baserunning instincts. Because he's still learning second base, Antonelli tends to sit back on balls and come up early when fielding. While he runs well, he might not have the explosiveness to steal bases at the highest level. Though he's athletic and offers a wide base of skills, he's a max-effort player who sometimes verges on playing out of control. The Padres signed Tadahito Iguchi to a one-year contract, which allows them to give Antonelli some time in Triple-A if he needs it. He should develop into an offensive second baseman with the potential to be an all-star.

Year	Club (League)	Class	AVG	G	AB	R	H	2B	3B	HR	RBI	BB	SO	SB	OBP	SLG
2006	Eugene (NWL)	A	.286	55	189	38	54	12	1	0	22	46	31	9	.426	.360
	Fort Wayne (MWL)	A	.125	5	16	3	2	1	1	0	0	2	6	0	.222	.313
2007	Lake Elsinore (Cal)	A	.314	82	347	89	109	14	4	14	54	53	58	18	.409	.499
	San Antonio (TL)	AA	.294	49	187	34	55	11	1	7	24	30	36	10	.395	.476
MINOR LEAGUE TOTALS			.298	191	739	164	220	38	7	21	100	131	131	37	.406	.453

3 MATT LATOS, RHP

BILL MITCHELL

Born: Dec. 9, 1987. **B-T:** R-R. **Ht.:** 6-5. **Wt.:** 210. **Drafted:** Broward (Fla.) CC, D/F 2006 (11th round). **Signed by:** Joe Bochy.

Latos had one of the best pure arms in the 2006 draft, but he fell to the 11th round because of questionable maturity and unrealistic bonus demands. After initially committing to Oklahoma, he kept his draft options open by attending Broward (Fla.) CC. He agreed to a $1.25 million bonus as a draft-and-follow just hours before the signing deadline. Though raw, Latos shows the potential for three plus pitches. It all begins with a 92-97 mph fastball that he throws with excellent leverage and downhill plane, affording him plus life down in the zone. He delivers his hard breaking ball, which most closely resembles a curveball, from a high three-quarters arm slot. He spikes his changeup with the knuckle of his forefinger and uses the offering as a chase pitch. His mound presence improved dramatically during his pro debut. Though he gets good rotation on his curveball, Latos tends to throw it too hard and loses his release point. The Padres left his spike changeup alone this summer, but they're teaching him a straight change grip. The effort in his delivery offers some natural deception but also costs him control and command. Latos has the stuff and competitiveness to pitch at the front of a big league rotation, and all he lacks is feel. If he doesn't find it, his stuff will play just as well at the back of a bullpen. He'll advance to low Class A Fort Wayne in 2008.

Year	Club (League)	Class	W	L	ERA	G	GS	CG	SV	IP	H	R	ER	HR	BB	SO	AVG
2007	Eugene (NWL)	A	1	4	3.83	16	13	0	0	56	58	30	24	1	22	74	.266
MINOR LEAGUE TOTALS			1	4	3.83	16	13	0	0	56	58	30	24	1	22	74	.266

4 WADE LeBLANC, LHP

BILL MITCHELL

Born: Aug. 7, 1984. **B-T:** L-L. **Ht.:** 6-3. **Wt.:** 202. **Drafted:** Alabama, 2006 (2nd round). **Signed by:** Bob Filotei.

LeBlanc earned BA's Freshman of the Year honors in 2004, missed much of his sophomore season, then led Alabama to super-regionals as a junior in 2006. In his first full pro season, LeBlanc led all Padres farmhands with 145 strikeouts while finishing second with 13 wins and third with a 2.95 ERA. LeBlanc is a classic college lefty with command who pitches above his raw stuff. His smooth, repeatable delivery allows him to throw three pitches for strikes, and the finish on those pitches improved in 2007. While he generally works backward, LeBlanc gained confidence in fastball and used it to better effect setting up his secondary pitches. His changeup is a true 80 pitch on the

20-80 scouting scale at times, and he delivers it with deceptive arm speed. As the season progressed, he improved his feel for locating his solid-average curveball down in the zone. LeBlanc's fastball leaves him little margin for error. It sits at 86-88 mph and tops out at 90, and it's a bit too true. He's working to develop a two-seamer he can throw to the outer half of the plate with life. Improved fastball command would make his offspeed offerings that much deadlier. LeBlanc sometimes rushes the delivery of his fastball and his body gets ahead of his arm, causing him to miss up and away to righthanders. His command, durability and competitiveness mark him as a future No. 3 starter.

Year	Club (League)	Class	W	L	ERA	G	GS	CG	SV	IP	H	R	ER	HR	BB	SO	AVG
2006	Eugene (NWL)	A	1	0	4.29	7	3	0	0	21	19	10	10	0	6	20	.250
	Fort Wayne (MWL)	A	4	1	2.20	7	7	0	0	32	31	8	8	1	10	27	.250
2007	Lake Elsinore (Cal)	A	6	5	2.64	16	16	0	0	92	72	32	27	5	17	90	.212
	San Antonio (TL)	AA	7	3	3.45	12	11	0	0	57	48	22	22	8	19	55	.225
MINOR LEAGUE TOTALS			18	9	2.97	42	37	0	0	203	170	72	67	14	52	192	.226

5 DREW MILLER, RHP

Born: Feb. 24, 1986. **B-T:** R-R. **Ht.:** 6-4. **Wt.:** 190. **Drafted:** Seminole State (Okla.) JC, D/F 2005 (37th round). **Signed by:** Lane Decker.

BILL MITCHELL

Miller posted dominant strikeout totals in junior college, but struggled to a 4.29 ERA in his sophomore year. The Padres gave him early fourth-round money ($300,000) to sign as a draft-and-follow in 2006. Miller was a model of inconsistency in low Class A last year, averaging more than a strikeout per inning but also posting a 5.28 ERA in the second half while missing time with shoulder soreness and a strained oblique. Miller's athleticism, arm strength and three-pitch mix give him a ceiling to rival that of Matt Latos, but he's only beginning to scratch the surface of his abilities. He pitches at 90-94 with his fastball, and his plus curveball gives him a second swing-and-miss pitch at his disposal. His smooth delivery allows him to repeat his mechanics and throw strikes, and his body still has room for projection. If the Padres didn't make Miller throw his changeup, he probably wouldn't use it, though it's a major league-average pitch at times. In fact, the pitch was the culprit on many of the 12 homers he surrendered in the pitcher-friendly Midwest League. Even with his potent fastball-curveball combo, he can't always put hitters away because he doesn't locate his pitches well in the strike zone. He sometimes loses his composure when he gets into jams. Added strength and durability would benefit Miller in 2008, when he'll navigate the pitcher's rite of passage that is the California League. Continued improvement and trust in his changeup could propel Miller to front-of-the-rotation status, but a No. 3 profile is more likely.

Year	Club (League)	Class	W	L	ERA	G	GS	CG	SV	IP	H	R	ER	HR	BB	SO	AVG
2006	Padres (AZL)	R	3	0	3.47	7	4	0	0	23	19	15	9	1	10	14	.218
	Eugene (NWL)	A	2	1	3.62	9	8	0	0	37	39	24	15	0	20	23	.267
2007	Fort Wayne (MWL)	A	4	6	4.69	16	16	0	0	80	74	45	42	12	24	87	.244
MINOR LEAGUE TOTALS			9	7	4.20	32	28	0	0	141	132	84	66	13	54	124	.246

6 STEVE GARRISON, LHP

Born: Sept. 12, 1986. **B-T:** B-L. **Ht.:** 6-1. **Wt.:** 185. **Drafted:** HS—Ewing, N.J., 2005 (10th round). **Signed by:** Tony Blengino (Brewers).

CLIFF WELCH

As might be expected from a player who went to the elite Hun School of Princeton in New Jersey, Garrison is a smart, poised pitcher with an effervescent personality. He slipped to the 10th round in 2005 due to signability questions, but agreed to terms with the Brewers for $160,000. The Padres acquired him in July, along with Will Inman and Joe Thatcher, in exchange for Scott Linebrink. One Padres official described Garrison as an artist on the mound, one who pitches well above his average stuff. He works to both sides of the plate and stays out of the middle. His curveball and changeup are plus pitches most of the time. He adeptly mixes his offerings and knows how to attack hitters. A good athlete, he repeats his delivery and controls the running game almost as well as he does the strike zone. With an 86-88 mph fastball, Garrison walks a fine line. Anything he leaves up and over the plate is susceptible to being hit a long way, though he has surrendered just 18 homers in 270 minor league innings. He can't get out of jams with a strikeout and must rely on his defense to make plays for him. Garrison tamed the California League after the trade, suggesting he's quite ready for Double-A in 2008. He projects as a No. 4 starter.

Year	Club (League)	Class	W	L	ERA	G	GS	CG	SV	IP	H	R	ER	HR	BB	SO	AVG
2005	Brewers (AZL)	R	2	2	2.86	11	4	0	2	34	39	13	11	0	5	28	.300
2006	West Virginia (SAL)	A	7	6	3.45	17	16	0	0	88	86	38	34	10	22	77	.253
2007	Brevard County (FSL)	A	8	4	3.44	20	20	1	0	104	105	58	40	6	28	74	.253
	Lake Elsinore (Cal)	A	2	3	2.79	7	7	0	0	42	32	15	13	2	6	28	.205
MINOR LEAGUE TOTALS			19	15	3.27	55	47	1	2	270	262	124	98	18	61	207	.252

7 WILL INMAN, RHP

Born: Feb. 6, 1987. **B-T:** R-R. **Ht.:** 6-0. **Wt.:** 200. **Drafted:** HS—Dry Fork, Va., 2005 (3rd round). **Signed by:** Grant Brittain (Brewers).

BILL MITCHELL

After leading Tunstall High to back-to-back Virginia state titles and setting the state record for career strikeouts, Inman spurned Auburn to sign with the Brewers for $500,000. He posted the second-best ERA (1.71) in the minors in 2006 and followed that up with a runner-up finish for in strikeouts (180) in 2007. He joined the Padres, along with minor league lefties Steve Garrison and Joe Thatcher, in a midseason trade for Scott Linebrink. While not overpowering, Inman can command his average fastball to any part of the strike zone. At his best, he pitches at 88-93 mph with a solid-average curveball and an average changeup. He added shape to his curveball last season, as it had previously resembled a slurve, and used more changeups. He's a fierce competitor who works ahead in the count and understands how to set up hitters. Inman tired badly down the stretch and his velocity dipped to 85-88 mph. This after missing time at the end of the 2006 season with shoulder fatigue. Though he locates it well, Inman's fastball is straight, and when he rushes his delivery, he loses velocity on the pitch. The quality of his secondary stuff varies wildly from start to start. Inman profiles as a No. 3 or 4 starter, and his success hinges on command. He breezed through the lower minors before stumbling a bit in Double-A. He may return to San Antonio to begin 2008, but he's still well ahead of most 21-year-olds.

Year	Club (League)	Class	W	L	ERA	G	GS	CG	SV	IP	H	R	ER	HR	BB	SO	AVG
2005	Brewers (AZL)	R	0	0	0.00	1	0	0	0	2	0	0	0	0	1	1	.000
	Helena (Pio)	R	6	0	2.00	13	5	0	1	45	29	11	10	5	11	58	.182
2006	West Virginia (SAL)	A	10	2	1.71	23	20	0	0	110	75	22	21	3	24	134	.190
2007	Brevard County (FSL)	A	4	3	1.72	13	13	0	0	78	56	17	15	4	23	98	.198
	Huntsville (SL)	AA	1	5	5.45	8	8	0	0	39	38	24	24	7	16	42	.259
	San Antonio (TL)	AA	3	3	4.17	7	7	0	0	41	33	19	19	6	19	40	.224
MINOR LEAGUE TOTALS			24	13	2.53	65	53	0	1	317	231	93	89	25	94	373	.203

8 CEDRIC HUNTER, OF

Born: March 10, 1988. **B-T:** L-L. **Ht.:** 6-0. **Wt.:** 185. **Drafted:** HS—Decatur, Ga., 2006 (3rd round). **Signed by:** Pete DeYoung.

STEVE MOORE

Hunter earned first-team All-America honors as a high school senior in 2006 before signing for $415,000 as a third-round pick. He delivered right out of the gate, reaching base in his first 49 pro games and winning the Rookie-level Arizona League's MVP award. In his less-impressive encore, he still produced numbers above the league averages in the pitching-dominated Midwest League. Hunter's hand-eye coordination is his best asset, and he has very good contact skills and the ability to line the ball into the gaps. He commands the strike zone like a much more experienced hitter and he projects to hit .280-.300 at the big league level because he puts the bat on the ball and is geared to use all fields. His tick above-average speed translates into average range in center field, where his arm is also average. His all-around game continues to draw comparisons with that of Jacque Jones. Hunter's swing got loopy in 2007 and he struggled to stay back on pitches, severely limiting his power to the pull side. Because he lacks first-step quickness, he doesn't get out of the box or steal bases well, and it also hampers him in center field. Some MWL observers thought Hunter lacked energy and perhaps fell victim to reading his own press clippings after ranking No. 1 on this list a year ago. The Padres believe Hunter can fix the quirks in his swing and learn to turn on pitches. If he does so, a future job awaits him on one of Petco Park's spacious outfield corners. He should find the going much easier at high Class A Lake Elsinore in 2008.

Year	Club (League)	Class	AVG	G	AB	R	H	2B	3B	HR	RBI	BB	SO	SB	OBP	SLG
2006	Padres (AZL)	R	.371	52	213	46	79	13	4	1	44	40	22	17	.467	.484
	Eugene (NWL)	A	.267	5	15	0	4	0	0	0	0	1	3	0	.313	.267
2007	Fort Wayne (MWL)	A	.282	129	496	53	140	20	2	7	58	47	78	8	.344	.373
	Portland (PCL)	AAA	.500	3	4	1	2	0	0	1	3	1	1	0	.600	1.250
MINOR LEAGUE TOTALS			.309	189	728	100	225	33	6	9	105	89	104	25	.384	.408

9 NICK SCHMIDT, LHP

PAUL GIERHART

Born: Oct. 10, 1985. **B-T:** L-L. **Ht.:** 6-5. **Wt.:** 220. **Drafted:** Arkansas, 2007 (1st round). **Signed by:** Lane Decker.

A polished, durable lefthander who became a No. 1 starter in the rugged Southeastern Conference as a freshman, Schmidt went 23rd overall in the 2007 draft and signed for $1.26 million. After pitching 241 innings in his final two college seasons, not including a stint with Team USA, he tossed just seven innings in pro ball before coming down with elbow soreness. His elbow didn't respond to rest, and he had Tommy John surgery in October. While he doesn't have a swing-and-miss pitch, Schmidt is adept at using his 6-foot-5 frame to drive his pitches down in the zone. He can touch 91 mph but more often pitches at 86-89, and he backs up his fastball with an above-average curveball and solid-average changeup. He's competitive, has fine control and changes speeds well. He also has an advanced feel for reading batters' swings and adjusting accordingly. Schmidt has some effort to his delivery and he shows the open face of his glove to the batter before he delivers his pitches. He stays online to the plate well, however, and his delivery quirks do add deception. His velocity is fringy, though the rest of his game makes his fastball play up. While the track record of pitchers recovering from elbow reconstruction is impressive, he won't be able to return to the mound until 2009. Following Matt Bush and Cesar Carrillo, Schmidt is the third Padres first-round pick in the last four years to succumb to Tommy John surgery. Despite the setback, he shouldn't require much minor league time once he returns and still should have a ceiling as a No. 3 starter.

Year	Club (League)	Class	W	L	ERA	G	GS	CG	SV	IP	H	R	ER	HR	BB	SO	AVG
2007	Fort Wayne (MWL)	A	0	1	6.43	3	1	0	0	7	8	5	5	0	6	6	.286
MINOR LEAGUE TOTALS			0	1	6.43	3	1	0	0	7	8	5	5	0	6	6	.286

10 KYLE BLANKS, 1B

STEVE MOORE

Born: Sept. 11, 1986. **B-T:** R-R. **Ht.:** 6-6. **Wt.:** 281. **Drafted:** Yavapai (Ariz.) JC, D/F 2004 (42nd round). **Signed by:** Jake Wilson.

Blanks led the wood-bat Arizona Community College Athletic Conference in batting (.440), doubles (25) and RBIs (47) in 2004, after which the Padres signed him for $260,000 as a draft-and-follow. A serious leg infection limited him to 86 games with low Class A Fort Wayne in 2006, when the 6-foot-6 Blanks had trouble keeping his playing weight under 300 pounds, but he rebounded nicely in 2007. Possessing the most raw power in the system, Blanks slugged 24 home runs for Lake Elsinore, where the ball doesn't carry to left or left-center field. He became the first righthanded batter to top 20 since Xavier Nady hit 26 for the Storm in 2001. Blanks improved his pitch selection and weight shift in 2007, adding a stride instead of just turning and rotating, which gave him a sense of timing at the plate, not to mention more in-game power. He's agile for his size and has good hands at first base, and he has a plus arm for his position. Blanks' power is almost entirely to the pull side and he would do well to use the opposite field more often. Despite his success, he still was susceptible to hard stuff up and in, and to sliders off the plate when he cheated on fastballs. His footwork and reactions still need cleaning up at first base, and he's a below-average runner. Keeping his weight in check won't be easy. Blanks is a different animal, as one Padres official put it, and with his body type and right-right profile he'll always have to prove himself against the competition. His next step is Double-A.

Year	Club (League)	Class	AVG	G	AB	R	H	2B	3B	HR	RBI	BB	SO	SB	OBP	SLG
2005	Padres (AZL)	R	.299	48	164	33	49	10	1	7	30	25	49	3	.420	.500
2006	Fort Wayne (MWL)	A	.292	86	308	41	90	20	0	10	52	36	79	2	.382	.455
2007	Lake Elsinore (Cal)	A	.301	119	465	94	140	31	4	24	100	44	98	11	.380	.540
MINOR LEAGUE TOTALS			.298	253	937	168	279	61	5	41	182	105	226	16	.388	.505

11 CESAR CARRILLO, RHP

Born: April 29, 1984. **B-T:** R-R. **Ht.:** 6-3. **Wt.:** 175. **Drafted:** Miami, 2005 (1st round). **Signed by:** Joe Bochy.

Carrillo's strong commitment to Miami and a bout with biceps tendinitis dropped him into the 33rd round of the 2002 draft, when the Royals took him out of a Chicago high school. After sitting out 2003 in a dispute between Miami and the NCAA over his ACT score, he won the first 24 decisions of his college career, two shy of the NCAA Division I record. The 18th overall pick in 2005 and the recipient of a $1.55 million bonus, Carrillo made it to Double-A in his 2005 debut, but made just 10 starts in 2006 before straining an elbow ligament in June. The condition did not improve in 2007 and Carrillo had Tommy John surgery in June after five ineffective starts in Triple-A. When healthy he throws an above-average 90-94 mph fastball that can reach 96 and features late life and natural sink. His curveball has tight downward break and the potential to become a plus pitch. Using a three-quarters delivery, he pitches in on righthanders as well as anyone in the system. He doesn't command his fastball to the other side of the plate with the same aplomb. He also needs to improve his changeup to reach his ceiling as a mid-rotation starter, though he also could be used as a power reliever. Carrillo's delivery is a little herky-jerky, but the deception it provides makes it tough for hitters to pick the ball up. He experienced no setbacks in his rehab and should return to the mound by mid-2008.

Year	Club (League)	Class	W	L	ERA	G	GS	CG	SV	IP	H	R	ER	HR	BB	SO	AVG
2005	Mobile (SL)	AA	4	0	3.23	5	5	0	0	30	23	11	11	2	7	35	.204
	Lake Elsinore (Cal)	A	1	2	7.01	7	7	0	0	25	30	21	20	3	9	29	.280
2006	Mobile (SL)	AA	1	3	3.02	9	9	0	0	50	45	23	17	5	15	43	.239
	Portland (PCL)	AAA	0	0	6.75	1	1	0	0	2	2	2	2	0	3	1	.222
2007	Portland (PCL)	AAA	0	2	8.62	5	5	0	0	15	22	16	15	2	14	8	.338
MINOR LEAGUE TOTALS			6	7	4.67	27	27	0	0	125	122	73	65	12	48	116	.253

12 CORY LUEBKE, LHP

Born: March 4, 1985. **B-T:** R-L. **Ht.:** 6-4. **Wt.:** 200. **Drafted:** Ohio State, 2007 (1st round supplemental). **Signed by:** Jeff Stewart.

Luebke turned down the Rangers as a 22nd-round pick in 2006 as a draft-eligible sophomore, and instead spent the summer in the Cape Cod League. He returned to Ohio State in 2007 and led the Big 10 Conference with a 1.95 regular season ERA. The Padres took Luebke 40 picks after Nick Schmidt, and they have similar profiles as big, polished college lefties. Luebke signed for $515,000. He dominated in his pro debut, showing firmer stuff than Schmidt, while generating plenty of strikeouts and groundouts. He reached high Class A and went 1-1, 3.18 in three California League playoff starts. Luebke's fastball comes in at 87-91 mph and touches 93 with good armside run, and he commands it to both sides of the plate. His hard slider is an average pitch with more tilt than depth. Luebke commands his average changeup to the outer half of the plate against right-ies. He works ahead of most hitters because of his repeatable mechanics and competitive demeanor. Though he's already 6-foot-4 and 200 pounds, he still has room to add strength. Luebke commands three pitches but doesn't have overwhelming stuff, and he'll likely improve his sequences with experience. Like the three lefthanders ranked ahead of him, Luebke is durable, has a great feel for pitching and profiles as a possible mid-rotation starter in the major leagues. He should reach Double-A at some point in 2008.

Year	Club (League)	Class	W	L	ERA	G	GS	CG	SV	IP	H	R	ER	HR	BB	SO	AVG
2007	Eugene (NWL)	A	3	0	1.46	8	3	0	0	24	18	6	4	2	2	26	.194
	Fort Wayne (MWL)	A	1	2	3.33	5	5	0	0	27	29	13	10	2	5	30	.269
	Lake Elsinore (Cal)	A	1	1	7.71	2	1	0	0	7	10	6	6	1	1	5	.357
MINOR LEAGUE TOTALS			5	3	3.07	15	9	0	0	58	57	25	20	5	8	61	.249

13 YEFRI CARVAJAL, OF

Born: Jan. 22, 1989. **B-T:** R-R. **Ht.:** 5-11. **Wt.:** 190. **Signed:** Dominican Republic, 2005. **Signed by:** Felix Francisco.

The vanguard of the organization's renewed international movement, Carvajal signed for $350,000 out of the Dominican Republic in 2005 and debuted Stateside the next season. He missed time with shin splints and a hamate bone injury in 2006, and his hitting seemed to suffer. With bat speed that can't be taught, Carvajal makes consistent, loud contact while being aggressive at the plate. His swing can get long, but when he con-nects he has as much power as anybody in the system. He shows extra load in his swing now, which leads to wrapping the bat and pulling his head off the ball. Carvajal saw time in center field in 2007, but because he's already physically mature and projects as a below-average runner he'll likely move to right field because he has solid-average arm strength. The Padres remain excited by Carvajal's potential because he loves to play and takes instruction well, and he could earn an assignment to low Class A with a strong showing in spring training. He'll be just 19 all season, however, so a return to short-season Eugene is a distinct possibility.

Year	Club (League)	Class	AVG	G	AB	R	H	2B	3B	HR	RBI	BB	SO	SB	OBP	SLG
2006	Padres (AZL)	R	.253	19	75	14	19	3	0	2	9	3	16	2	.288	.373
2007	Padres (AZL)	R	.340	25	100	27	34	13	0	1	22	10	22	5	.404	.500
	Eugene (NWL)	A	.262	31	122	15	32	5	1	2	19	5	39	2	.291	.369
MINOR LEAGUE TOTALS			.286	75	297	56	85	21	1	5	50	18	77	9	.330	.414

14 KELLEN KULBACKI, OF

Born: Nov. 21, 1985. **B-T:** L-L. **Ht.:** 5-11. **Wt.:** 185. **Drafted:** James Madison, 2007 (1st round supplemental). **Signed by:** Ash Lawson.

Kulbacki hit .464 and led NCAA Division I with 24 homers and a .943 slugging percentage as a sophomore at James Madison in 2006, yet scouts still questioned his wood-bat power and his athleticism—questions that became louder after a mediocre showing in the Cape Cod League. He repeated as a first-team All-American in

2007, this time after finishing 14th in the nation with 19 homers and eighth with a .785 slugging percentage. The Padres took him with their second selection in the draft, 40th overall, and signed him for $765,000. After a 4-for-31 start at Eugene, Kulbacki hit as San Diego expected. He has good plate coverage and a knack for putting the barrel of the bat on the ball, two ingredients that could allow him to hit for above-average power in the future. Kulbacki has good hands but had trouble getting around on good fastballs in his debut because of average bat speed, and he tended to hit with more authority to the opposite field. All of his value lies in his bat, as he's a below-average defender and thrower on an outfield corner, and he has fringe-average speed. He'll move up to high Class A to start 2008, with a good chance to reach Double-A later in the year.

Year	Club (League)	Class	AVG	G	AB	R	H	2B	3B	HR	RBI	BB	SO	SB	OBP	SLG
2007	Eugene (NWL)	A	.301	61	226	33	68	13	3	8	39	27	56	1	.382	.491
MINOR LEAGUE TOTALS			.301	61	226	33	68	13	3	8	39	27	56	1	.382	.491

15 WILL VENABLE, OF

Born: Oct. 29, 1982. **B-T:** L-L. **Ht.:** 6-2. **Wt.:** 205. **Drafted:** Princeton, 2005 (7th round). **Signed by:** Jim Bretz.

Venable focused on basketball in high school and college, and was an all-Ivy League selection in both hoops and baseball as a senior at Princeton. As the son of former big leaguer Max Venable, Will had more exposure to baseball than most two-sport stars, however. In 2006, his first full season, he led the Midwest League in runs (86) while ranking second in hitting (.314) and third in on-base percentage (.389). The Padres love Venable's makeup, and his pure lefthanded stroke and bat speed produce plenty of line drives, as he showed when he won the 2006 Hawaii Winter Baseball batting title (.330). He jumped to Double-A in 2007, but he never really got going. Part of Venable's problem was a toe tap he added to his stride in the offseason in an attempt to improve his rhythm. Instead of helping him, it took his legs out of his swing, destroying his leverage and power potential. Venable eliminated the toe tap in the second half, began working deeper counts and hit seven of his eight homers. He put his average speed to good use, swiping 21 bases in 23 tries, and he's an average defender on an outfield corner, albeit with a below-average arm. He plays under control, often giving the impression he's not hustling. Venable could challenge for big league playing time in 2008.

Year	Club (League)	Class	AVG	G	AB	R	H	2B	3B	HR	RBI	BB	SO	SB	OBP	SLG
2005	Padres (AZL)	R	.322	15	59	13	19	4	2	1	12	2	9	4	.385	.508
	Eugene (NWL)	A	.216	42	139	17	30	5	2	2	14	14	38	2	.295	.324
2006	Fort Wayne (MWL)	A	.314	124	472	86	148	34	5	11	91	55	81	18	.389	.477
2007	San Antonio (TL)	AA	.278	134	515	66	143	19	3	8	68	38	84	21	.337	.373
MINOR LEAGUE TOTALS			.287	315	1185	182	340	62	12	22	185	109	212	45	.355	.415

16 DREW CUMBERLAND, SS

Born: Jan. 13, 1989. **B-T:** L-R. **Ht.:** 5-10. **Wt.:** 175. **Drafted:** HS—Pace, Fla., 2007 (1st round supplemental). **Signed by:** Bob Filotei.

An all-state selection as a defensive back and running back in football and a plus-plus runner—he can get down the first-base line in 3.9-4.0 seconds—Cumberland offers premium quickness, speed and athleticism. The brother of Reds outfield prospect Shaun Cumberland, Drew went 46th overall in the 2007 draft and signed for $661,500. With live hands and a quick, short swing, he has the strength and bat speed to drive balls from gap to gap and already is an above-average hitter. He has more work to do defensively, as he made 13 errors in 23 games at shortstop and worked in instructional league to improve his arm path. He tended to use an exaggerated load to his throws and cut his arm action off in front of his body. His actions and range are average, as is his arm strength. He could fit at second base or center field if he can't handle shortstop. Cumberland hurt his hamstring late in the high school season, then missed time after signing when he dislocated a finger while trying to catch a pop-up. A high-effort player, he's ticketed for low Class A, where he'll need every ounce of his energy to grind through the tough hitting environments of the Midwest League.

Year	Club (League)	Class	AVG	G	AB	R	H	2B	3B	HR	RBI	BB	SO	SB	OBP	SLG
2007	Padres (AZL)	R	.318	21	85	16	27	2	1	0	7	7	9	6	.389	.365
	Eugene (NWL)	A	.333	4	18	6	6	1	0	0	0	2	2	0	.429	.389
MINOR LEAGUE TOTALS			.320	25	103	22	33	3	1	0	7	9	11	6	.397	.369

17 MITCH CANHAM, C

Born: Sept. 25, 1984. **B-T:** L-R. **Ht.:** 6-2. **Wt.:** 215. **Drafted:** Oregon State, 2007 (1st round supplemental). **Signed by:** Josh Boyd.

Canham's championship-caliber makeup and offensive prowess were a big part of Oregon State's back-to-back College World Series titles in 2006 and 2007. Draft-eligible as a sophomore in 2006, Canham fell to Cardinals in the 41st round but didn't sign. The Padres selected him 57th overall last June and signed him for $552,500. Canham's bat was his best tool throughout his college career, and his athleticism helps him repeat his short lefthanded stroke. He controls the strike zone and has solid-average power. He's an average runner, though above-average for a catcher. A third baseman in high school, Canham has subpar defensive skills at this point, but he has the agility and aptitude to become at least an adequate catcher. He has fringe-average arm strength with a fair release, and he lacks explosion when coming out of his crouch. He threw out 29 percent of basestealers in his debut. Canham required testicular surgery after being struck in his protective cup in mid-July, but he returned to the field two weeks later and played in the California League playoffs. He projects as a regular catcher if he makes just modest improvements to his throwing.

Year	Club (League)	Class	AVG	G	AB	R	H	2B	3B	HR	RBI	BB	SO	SB	OBP	SLG
2007	Eugene (NWL)	A	.293	28	116	20	34	4	1	2	18	11	35	5	.379	.397
	Lake Elsinore (Cal)	A	.000	2	7	0	0	0	0	0	1	0	2	0	.000	.000
MINOR LEAGUE TOTALS			.276	30	123	20	34	4	1	2	19	11	37	5	.357	.374

18 CESAR RAMOS, LHP

Born: June 22, 1984. **B-T:** L-L. **Ht.:** 6-2. **Wt.:** 190. **Drafted:** Long Beach State, 2005 (1st round supplemental). **Signed by:** Brendan Hause.

Ramos turned down the Devil Rays as a sixth-round pick out of high school, then became the winningest lefthander in Long Beach State history. He struggled to a 5.01 ERA in his pro debut, but rebounded to post the second-best ERA (3.70) in the California League in 2006. He nearly turned the trick again in 2007, finishing third in the Texas League in wins (13), ERA (3.41) and innings (163). Ramos doesn't have put-away stuff, but all three of his pitches showed improvement, beginning with his 88-92 mph fastball, which was a couple of ticks quicker than in 2006. The added velocity allowed him to better attack righthanders inside, which meant he could come in even further with his cutter. Both Ramos' slider and changeup are solid-average pitches most of the time. His slider gets too big at times and he needs to use his changeup more, especially on the outer half of the plate. He throws strikes with his full repertoire but gets in trouble when he leaves his stuff up in the zone. Durability has never been an issue for Ramos, who got in better shape last year, and he appears well on his way to his ceiling as a No. 4 or 5 starter. He's ready for Triple-A in 2008.

Year	Club (League)	Class	W	L	ERA	G	GS	CG	SV	IP	H	R	ER	HR	BB	SO	AVG
2005	Eugene (NWL)	A	0	1	6.53	6	4	0	0	20	27	21	15	3	7	13	.303
	Fort Wayne (MWL)	A	3	2	4.19	7	7	1	0	38	42	19	18	0	7	32	.282
2006	Lake Elsinore (Cal)	A	7	8	3.70	26	24	0	0	141	161	72	58	9	44	70	.292
2007	San Antonio (TL)	AA	13	9	3.41	27	27	2	0	163	153	69	62	15	43	90	.249
MINOR LEAGUE TOTALS			23	20	3.78	66	62	3	0	364	383	181	153	27	101	205	.273

19 JOE THATCHER, LHP

Born: Oct. 4, 1981. **B-T:** L-L. **Ht.:** 6-2. **Wt.:** 230. **Signed:** River City (Frontier League), 2005. **Signed by:** Brad Del Barba (Brewers).

Thatcher went undrafted after going 4-8, 5.60 as an Indiana State senior in 2004, so he signed with River City of the independent Frontier League. Scouts noticed him at the league's all-star game and he ultimately signed with the Brewers in 2005. The Padres targeted him in the July trade that also netted them Steve Garrison and Will Inman in exchange for Scott Linebrink. Thatcher began the year in Double-A and finished it as San Diego's top lefthanded reliever. He's tough to hit because of his funky, crossfire delivery, which closes off his front shoulder to the batter. He's aggressive and almost always works ahead of hitters, using a cutting 88-91 mph fastball and a sweeping slider from a low three-quarters arm slot. He's especially tough on lefthanders. The Padres identify successful, unheralded relievers as well as any organization—hitting big on Heath Bell, Kevin Cameron, Linebrink and Cla Meredith in recent years—and seem to have done it again with Thatcher. Barring a poor spring training, he'll be on the big league staff in 2008.

Year	Club (League)	Class	W	L	ERA	G	GS	CG	SV	IP	H	R	ER	HR	BB	SO	AVG
2004	River City (Fron)	IND	2	3	2.98	29	0	0	5	42	38	15	14	3	15	55	.239
2005	River City (Fron)	IND	4	2	1.27	18	0	0	5	21	18	5	3	0	4	27	.228
	Helena (Pio)	R	2	0	3.52	6	0	0	2	7	8	3	3	1	1	10	.258
	Brevard County (FSL)	A	0	0	0.00	7	0	0	2	9	6	0	0	0	0	14	.188
2006	West Virginia (SAL)	A	1	3	2.43	26	0	0	10	29	28	13	8	2	6	42	.243
	Brevard County (FSL)	A	3	1	0.29	16	0	0	2	30	12	6	1	1	9	32	.119
	Huntsville (SL)	AA	1	0	1.69	4	0	0	0	5	2	2	1	0	2	6	.111
2007	Huntsville (SL)	AA	1	0	0.55	14	0	0	2	16	11	1	1	0	2	20	.193
	Nashville (PCL)	AAA	2	1	2.08	24	0	0	1	21	19	5	5	0	7	33	.226
	Portland (PCL)	AAA	1	0	1.04	8	0	0	0	8	10	4	1	0	1	11	.278
	San Diego (NL)	MLB	2	2	1.29	22	0	0	0	21	13	6	3	1	6	16	.167
MINOR LEAGUE TOTALS			11	5	1.40	105	0	0	17	129	96	34	20	4	28	168	.203
MAJOR LEAGUE TOTALS			2	2	1.29	22	0	0	0	21	13	6	3	1	6	16	.167

20 CARLOS GUEVARA, RHP

Born: March 18, 1982. **B-T:** R-R. **Ht.:** 5-11. **Wt.:** 190. **Drafted:** St. Mary's (Texas), 2003 (7th round). **Signed by:** Jimmy Gonzales (Reds).

The Padres were more active during the major league phase of the Rule 5 draft than any other club, adding Guevara (Reds), righthander Michael Gardner (Yankees) and second baseman/outfielder Callix Crabbe (Brewers). All three players would have to remain on the 25-man roster this season, or else they have to clear waivers and be offered back to their original clubs. While that seems like a longshot, San Diego could have room in its bullpen for both Guevara and Gardner. General manager Kevin Towers made it no secret that Guevara was the club's No. 1 target in the Rule 5 draft. Though the Padres didn't select Guevara—the Marlins took him fifth overall—they acquired him after the draft for cash considerations. Guevara repeated Double-A in 2007 despite a solid campaign there the year before, and he was even more impressive the second time around. His fastball, which sits 86-88 mph and touches 90, and curveball are fringe-average offerings, but his screwball gives him a true plus pitch. He learned it in college from from St. Mary's (Texas) pitching coach John Maley, who was a disciple of Mike Marshall's pitching methods. Because Guevara relies on the screwball to strike batters out, some scouts dismiss him as a trick-pitch artist. But because the Padres' track record with other teams' discarded pitchers, such as 2006 Rule 5 pick Kevin Cameron, is so enviable, Guevara seems like a safe bet to crack the Opening Day roster.

Year	Club (League)	Class	W	L	ERA	G	GS	CG	SV	IP	H	R	ER	HR	BB	SO	AVG
2003	Billings (Pio)	R	1	0	0.82	2	2	0	0	11	4	1	1	0	3	14	.108
	Dayton (MWL)	A	0	1	3.43	12	3	0	0	39	37	17	15	4	14	39	.247
2004	Dayton (MWL)	A	3	4	2.86	44	0	0	9	56	47	22	18	6	24	90	.221
2005	Sarasota (FSL)	A	4	3	2.45	44	0	0	14	51	39	17	14	2	14	65	.203
2006	Chattanooga (SL)	AA	2	3	3.72	49	0	0	1	77	74	35	32	6	27	89	.247
2007	Chattanooga (SL)	AA	1	2	2.32	51	0	0	16	62	51	17	16	4	23	87	.226
MINOR LEAGUE TOTALS			11	13	2.90	202	5	0	40	297	252	109	96	22	105	384	.225

21 MATT BUSCHMANN, RHP

Born: Feb. 13, 1984. **B-T:** R-R. **Ht.:** 6-3. **Wt.:** 209. **Drafted:** Vanderbilt, 2006 (15th round). **Signed by:** Ash Lawson.

Buschmann stepped into Vanderbilt's rotation as a senior in 2006 and thrived as the Friday starter when lefthander David Price (who would become the No. 1 overall pick in 2007) hit a slump. Buschmann exceeded expectations by making it to high Class A in his pro debut, and he was even more impressive in his return engagement with Lake Elsinore in 2007. He ranked second in the California League with 12 wins and a 2.89 ERA for a Storm squad that advanced to the league finals. Buschmann offers durability, efficiency and average command of three lively pitches. A competitor with good feel for his pitches down in the strike zone, he touches 92 mph with his two-seam fastball and pitches at 86-90 from a three-quarters arm slot, generating good sink and bore. His natural crossfire delivery adds deception. Buschmann showed improvement in commanding his fastball to the outer half of the plate, which aided in setting up his offspeed offerings. His sharp slider can be a plus pitch at times, but it gets big—and his fastball flattens out—when he rushes his delivery and ends up throwing sidearm. He made strides with his changeup, but it's a third pitch for him. Buschmann, who profiles as a back-of-the-rotation starter or middle reliever, is ready for Double-A.

Year	Club (League)	Class	W	L	ERA	G	GS	CG	SV	IP	H	R	ER	HR	BB	SO	AVG
2006	Eugene (NWL)	A	3	4	3.12	15	10	0	0	60	54	26	21	5	11	63	.242
	Lake Elsinore (Cal)	A	1	0	3.55	2	2	0	0	12	9	5	5	0	4	5	.205
2007	Lake Elsinore (Cal)	A	12	6	2.89	28	25	0	0	149	153	60	48	9	26	115	.270
MINOR LEAGUE TOTALS			16	10	2.99	45	37	0	0	222	216	91	74	14	41	183	.259

22 CHAD HUFFMAN, OF

Born: April 29, 1985. **B-T:** R-R. **Ht.:** 6-1. **Wt.:** 217. **Drafted:** Texas Christian, 2006 (2nd round). **Signed by:** Tim Holt.

Like his two older brothers, Scott and Royce, Huffman played both college baseball and football. And like Royce, a first baseman who played for Triple-A Portland in the Padres system in 2007, Chad was a quarterback and infielder at Texas Christian. He led the short-season Northwest League with a .439 on-base percentage in his pro debut, while finishing second in hitting (.343) and slugging (.576). He tore up the hitter-friendly California League in 2007 before leveling off in Double-A. A physical player with above-average power, Huffman knows the strike zone and plays like his hair is on fire, as one club official puts it. With his long stride, his swing can collapse, which hinders the amount of damage he can do to the opposite field. A second baseman in college, he showed improvement in left field but still has below-average range and arm strength. He's an average runner at best. His athleticism and reflexes may not be enough to allow him to hit for both power and average at the major league level, though he should have enough bat for a platoon or part-time role. He'll get another crack at Double-A to begin 2008.

Year	Club (League)	Class	AVG	G	AB	R	H	2B	3B	HR	RBI	BB	SO	SB	OBP	SLG
2006	Eugene (NWL)	A	.343	54	198	41	68	17	1	9	40	25	34	2	.439	.576
	Fort Wayne (MWL)	A	.214	5	14	2	3	0	1	0	0	2	2	0	.313	.357
2007	Lake Elsinore (Cal)	A	.307	84	316	63	97	19	2	15	76	42	56	0	.402	.522
	San Antonio (TL)	AA	.269	49	167	28	45	4	1	7	28	22	44	0	.362	.431
MINOR LEAGUE TOTALS			.306	192	695	134	213	40	5	31	144	91	136	2	.401	.512

23 JARED WELLS, RHP

Born: Oct. 31, 1981. **B-T:** R-R. **Ht.:** 6-4. **Wt.:** 200. **Drafted:** San Jacinto (Texas) JC, D/F 2002 (31st round). **Signed by:** Jay Darnell.

After struggling with consistency early in his career, Wells made strides in 2005, leading the California League with a 3.44 ERA. After a rough introduction to Double-A at the end of that season, he rebounded to pitch well there in 2006. But after getting shelled at the end of 2006, he couldn't repeat the pattern—at least not until he was converted to relief. After going 3-15, 7.26 in 25 Triple-A starts, he moved to the bullpen for good in June and posted a 2.93 ERA with 47 strikeouts in 43 innings. Wells generates 90-93 mph fastballs and touches 95 from a sturdy pitcher's frame. When he's going well, he features good sink on his two-seamer and nice depth on a hard slider that grades as average. As a reliever he got by without his changeup, which is below-average. Though he had inconsistent control and still worked up in the zone too much, he was more comfortable in one- or two-inning stints. Wells is on the 40-man roster, so he's a candidate for a callup if a major league job opens up.

Year	Club (League)	Class	W	L	ERA	G	GS	CG	SV	IP	H	R	ER	HR	BB	SO	AVG
2003	Eugene (NWL)	A	4	6	2.75	14	14	0	0	78	77	34	24	6	32	53	.256
2004	Fort Wayne (MWL)	A	4	6	4.09	14	14	1	0	81	91	42	37	6	19	72	.283
	Lake Elsinore (Cal)	A	4	6	4.52	13	12	0	0	71	81	44	36	5	30	38	.290
2005	Lake Elsinore (Cal)	A	11	3	3.44	19	19	2	0	120	116	51	46	6	26	80	.257
	Mobile (SL)	AA	2	5	4.40	7	7	0	0	43	51	25	21	3	16	22	.307
2006	Mobile (SL)	AA	4	3	2.64	12	12	1	0	61	53	20	18	4	27	49	.235
	Portland (PCL)	AAA	2	9	7.27	15	15	0	0	73	87	66	59	8	46	55	.296
2007	Portland (PCL)	AAA	3	7	5.24	47	10	0	9	92	107	59	54	9	48	87	.294
MINOR LEAGUE TOTALS			34	45	4.27	141	103	4	9	622	663	341	295	47	244	456	.276

24 NICK HUNDLEY, C

Born: Sept. 8, 1983. **B-T:** R-R. **Ht.:** 6-1. **Wt.:** 210. **Drafted:** Arizona, 2005 (2nd round). **Signed by:** Dave Lottsfeldt.

A fifth-round pick by the Marlins out of high school, Hundley went three rounds earlier in 2005 after establishing himself as one of college baseball's best all-around catchers. His father Tim is the defensive coordinator for Texas-El Paso's football team. Hundley has struggled to find consistency since turning pro, but he turned it up a notch in the second half last year and finished fourth in the Texas League with 20 homers. He has strength and solid-average power, with just enough bat to profile as a backup catcher on a good team or a regular on a second-division club. When he's going well, Hundley uses the entire field, but he's geared for power and is a below-average hitter. His swing still lacks consistency, as he often cuts it off out in front instead of getting his arms extended. Defense doesn't come easy to him either, and at his best he's an average receiver, blocker and game-caller. He threw out 36 percent of TL basestealers with his strong, accurate arm, but he frequently flies open, causing his throws to tail away from the bag. He's a below-average runner but fine for a catcher. Hundley and Colt Morton could vie to be Josh Bard's backup in the near future.

Year	Club (League)	Class	AVG	G	AB	R	H	2B	3B	HR	RBI	BB	SO	SB	OBP	SLG
2005	Eugene (NWL)	A	.250	43	148	30	37	7	1	7	22	33	35	1	.391	.453
	Fort Wayne (MWL)	A	.222	10	36	2	8	2	0	0	5	4	9	0	.310	.278
2006	Fort Wayne (MWL)	A	.274	57	215	29	59	19	0	8	44	25	45	1	.355	.474
	Lake Elsinore (Cal)	A	.278	47	176	18	49	13	0	3	23	20	44	1	.357	.403
2007	San Antonio (TL)	AA	.247	101	373	55	92	23	1	20	72	42	74	0	.324	.475
MINOR LEAGUE TOTALS			.258	258	948	134	245	64	2	38	166	124	207	3	.348	.450

25 JEUDY VALDEZ, SS/2B

Born: May 5, 1989. **B-T:** R-R. **Ht.:** 5-11. **Wt.:** 155. **Signed:** Dominican Republic, 2005. **Signed by:** Felix Francisco.

Valdez signed with the Padres in November 2005 and he made his debut in the Rookie-level Dominican Summer League the following year. He came to the United States at age 18 last season, showing a short, quick stroke with good gap power. Valdez is strong for his size and offers quick wrists and above-average bat speed that could translate into 15-20 home runs per year down the line. He's also an above-average runner who can get down the line in 4.1 seconds from the right side. A former switch-hitter, he gave that up during the 2006 season. Valdez has plus arm strength at shortstop, enough to make plays in the hole, but he has a funky throwing action that might force a move to second base if he doesn't iron it out. Because he's so young, Valdez probably won't reach full-season ball until 2009.

Year	Club (League)	Class	AVG	G	AB	R	H	2B	3B	HR	RBI	BB	SO	SB	OBP	SLG
2006	Padres (DSL)	R	.238	47	168	29	40	7	2	0	10	15	44	12	.319	.304
2007	Padres (AZL)	R	.281	47	192	31	54	7	4	3	30	15	44	11	.346	.406
MINOR LEAGUE TOTALS			.261	94	360	60	94	14	6	3	40	30	88	23	.333	.358

26 RAYNER CONTRERAS, 3B/2B

Born: Sept. 21, 1985. **B-T:** R-R. **Ht.:** 6-0. **Wt.:** 167. **Signed:** Dominican Republic, 2004. **Signed by:** Felix Francisco.

After two nondescript years in the Dominican Summer League, Contreras took one of the biggest steps forward among the Padres' international prospects in 2006. He led the Arizona League with 52 RBIs and finished seventh in the batting race at .316. After earning an assignment to low Class A in 2007, Contreras held his own until an ankle injury sidelined him for the final six weeks. He has a wiry, projectable body—he already has added 17 pounds since signing—with a chance to add significant strength as he matures. He also has shown the ability to make hard contact with line-drive power to all fields, though he still has a long way to go with his pitch recognition. His swing is loose and fluid, if a little long at times, and he gets great carry on the ball. He has slightly above-average speed but isn't a basestealing threat. Contreras has solid-average defensive tools and arm strength, with the ability to play either second or third base. His agility isn't quite up to second-base standards, but he may be able to stick there because of his offensive profile. Contreras is on track to reach high Class A in 2008, but he might need a tuneup at Fort Wayne first.

Year	Club (League)	Class	AVG	G	AB	R	H	2B	3B	HR	RBI	BB	SO	SB	OBP	SLG
2004	Padres (DSL)	R	.260	53	154	15	40	8	1	2	22	13	27	5	.325	.364
2005	Padres (DSL)	R	.277	28	112	21	31	2	2	0	19	6	18	7	.322	.330
2006	Fort Wayne (MWL)	A	.105	12	38	2	4	0	0	0	1	2	9	0	.150	.105
	Padres (AZL)	R	.316	44	171	36	54	9	3	2	52	20	34	4	.389	.439
2007	Fort Wayne (MWL)	A	.276	73	268	26	74	12	2	7	37	22	53	7	.330	.414
MINOR LEAGUE TOTALS			.273	210	743	100	203	31	8	11	131	63	141	23	.333	.381

27 JOSH GEER, RHP

Born: June 2, 1983. **B-T:** R-R. **Ht.:** 6-3. **Wt.:** 190. **Drafted:** Rice, 2005 (3rd round). **Signed by:** Bob Laurie.

After Rice lost Philip Humber, Jeff Niemann and Wade Townsend in the first eight picks of the 2004 draft, Geer transferred from Navarro (Texas) JC and led the Owls with 12 victories. He has continued his winning ways in the minors, going 34-14 in 2½ pro seasons and taking home Texas League pitcher of the year honors in 2007 for his league-leading 16 wins and 3.20 ERA. Double-A hitters were unable to solve Geer, though his overall stuff grades as average at best. His changeup is a plus pitch and he can touch 92 mph with his fastball, but he predominantly throws 86-88 mph sinkers. He flawlessly repeats his delivery and began registering more low-90s readings in 2007 than he had in either of his first two pro seasons. Geer's slurvy curveball is usable, but he might be better served with a cutter or slider instead. Though he has no wipeout pitch, he's a competitor and strike thrower who offers a little deception and a whole lot of pitchability. He might be a fit at the back end of a rotation, and he has nothing left to prove in Double-A.

Year	Club (League)	Class	W	L	ERA	G	GS	CG	SV	IP	H	R	ER	HR	BB	SO	AVG
2005	Eugene (NWL)	A	3	1	3.69	7	6	0	0	31	35	13	13	5	4	13	.285
	Fort Wayne (MWL)	A	1	1	4.25	5	5	0	0	29	29	16	14	3	9	23	.259
2006	Fort Wayne (MWL)	A	6	2	3.10	12	11	0	0	72	72	27	25	3	13	46	.263
	Lake Elsinore (Cal)	A	7	4	4.96	15	15	0	0	89	116	60	49	7	16	56	.316
2007	Portland (PCL)	AAA	1	0	3.00	1	1	0	0	6	6	2	2	0	1	6	.286
	San Antonio (TL)	AA	16	6	3.20	26	26	2	0	171	163	67	61	9	27	102	.252
MINOR LEAGUE TOTALS			34	14	3.69	66	64	3	0	400	421	185	164	27	70	246	.273

28 DAVID FREESE, 3B

Born: April 28, 1983. **B-T:** R-R. **Ht.:** 6-2. **Wt.:** 217. **Drafted:** South Alabama, 2006 (9th round). **Signed by:** Bob Filotei.

As a fifth-year senior in 2006, Freese could have signed as a free agent before the draft, but South Alabama qualified for the NCAA regionals and shrunk his window to one day. He opted to take his chances in the draft, where he signed for $6,000 as a ninth-round pick. Freese has turned in two solid seasons since turning pro, and his strength, bat speed and strike-zone judgment all are above average. He shows the ability to stay inside the ball and drive it the other way with authority. He can turn on inside pitches, too, though his home run power was muted by Lake Elsinore's tough left-center field power alley. His two-strike approach could use more consistency, as he often gets himself out by chasing breaking balls. San Diego has been pleased with Freese's consistency at third base, where he has shown solid-average range, hands and actions to go with an average throwing arm. Because of the organizational logjam at third base, however, he spent time at catcher in instructional league, where he showed solid blocking skills and a plus arm at times. He would need at least a season of work behind the plate if he's to make the switch, so his 2008 assignment will be up in the air until spring training. His bat is ready for Double-A if he stays at third base.

Year	Club (League)	Class	AVG	G	AB	R	H	2B	3B	HR	RBI	BB	SO	SB	OBP	SLG
2006	Eugene (NWL)	A	.379	18	58	19	22	8	0	5	26	7	12	0	.465	.776
	Fort Wayne (MWL)	A	.299	53	204	27	61	13	3	8	44	21	44	1	.374	.510
2007	Lake Elsinore (Cal)	A	.302	128	503	104	152	31	6	17	96	69	99	6	.400	.489
MINOR LEAGUE TOTALS			.307	199	765	150	235	52	9	30	166	97	155	7	.399	.516

29 COREY KLUBER, RHP

Born: April 10, 1986. **B-T:** R-R. **Ht.:** 6-4. **Wt.:** 215. **Drafted:** Stetson, 2007 (4th round). **Signed by:** Joe Bochy.

After a stress fracture in his throwing arm in high school required surgery and the insertion of a screw that remains in his arm, Kluber developed into a reliable starter for Stetson. The 2007 Atlantic Sun Conference pitcher of the year after going 12-2, 2.05, he signed for $200,000. At 6-foot-4 and 215 pounds, he's an intimidating presence on the mound, and Kluber pounds the zone with three pitches. He pitches at 88-92 mph, touching 94 with above-average life, and he holds his velocity late in outings. His slider and changeup are average at times. Though Kluber lacks a legitimate put-away pitch, he reads swings well and understands how to attack batters. He joined fellow 2007 draftees Cory Luebke and Mitch Canham for Lake Elsinore's playoff run. A return engagement to high Class A to open 2008 isn't out of the question, and Kluber could develop into a No. 4 starter in time.

Year	Club (League)	Class	W	L	ERA	G	GS	CG	SV	IP	H	R	ER	HR	BB	SO	AVG
2007	Eugene (NWL)	A	1	1	3.51	10	7	0	0	33	28	16	13	1	15	33	.230
MINOR LEAGUE TOTALS			1	1	3.51	10	7	0	0	33	28	16	13	1	15	33	.230

30 MATT BUSH, RHP

Born: Feb. 8, 1986. **B-T:** R-R. **Ht.:** 5-10. **Wt.:** 189. **Drafted:** HS—El Cajon, Calif., 2004 (1st round). **Signed by:** Tim McWilliam.

Bush finally made the conversion from shortstop to pitcher that long had been predicted, and while he showed promise as a reliever, his momentum was derailed when he had Tommy John surgery in September. He was the No. 1 overall pick in the 2004 draft because he agreed to a $3.15 million bonus, after the Padres decided they didn't want to pay the asking price for college stars Stephen Drew, Jeff Niemann and Jered Weaver. They gave Bush nearly three full years to settle in at shortstop, but he hit just .221/.291/.276 and his defensive range went backward, the result of ankle and hamstring injuries and poor work habits. His arm strength never wavered—his arm rated a pure 80 on the 20-80 scouting scale in high school—and San Diego switched him to the mound last June. The conversion was an immediate success, with Bush flashing mid-90s velocity, an impressive slider and surprisingly good mechanics. In fact, he struck out 16 of the 29 Arizona League batters he faced, walking just two, prompting a promotion to low Class A in early August. One batter later, Bush's season was done. He twice hit 99 mph in that brief outing, but he also tore the ulnar collateral ligament in his elbow. Though he never has received high marks for his work ethic, Bush appeared to be motivated to pitch, lending optimism to the notion that he could be ready for instructional league in 2008.

Year	Club (League)	Class	AVG	G	AB	R	H	2B	3B	HR	RBI	BB	SO	SB	OBP	SLG
2004	Padres (AZL)	R	.181	21	72	12	13	2	1	0	10	11	17	4	.302	.236
	Eugene (NWL)	A	.222	8	27	1	6	2	0	0	3	2	9	0	.276	.296
2005	Fort Wayne (MWL)	A	.221	126	453	56	100	13	3	2	32	33	76	8	.279	.276
2006	Padres (AZL)	R	.000	1	1	1	0	0	0	0	1	3	0	0	.750	.000
	Fort Wayne (MWL)	A	.268	21	71	8	19	3	0	0	7	6	13	2	.333	.310
MINOR LEAGUE TOTALS			.221	177	624	78	138	20	4	2	53	55	115	14	.291	.276

Year	Club (League)	Class	W	L	ERA	G	GS	CG	SV	IP	H	R	ER	HR	BB	SO	AVG
2007	Padres (AZL)	R	1	0	1.23	6	0	0	0	7	5	1	1	0	2	16	.192
	Fort Wayne (MWL)	A	0	0	0.00	1	0	0	0	0	0	0	0	0	0	0	.000
MINOR LEAGUE TOTALS			1	0	1.17	7	0	0	0	7	5	1	1	0	2	16	.185

San Francisco Giants

BY ANDY BAGGARLY

For the first time since 1993, the Giants must build a baseball team without Barry Bonds as their cornerstone. The front office finally signaled this new direction in late September, announcing it would not deign to the 43-year-old slugger's wishes to bring him back for one more season.

So Bonds leaves San Francisco as the all-time home run king and general manager Brian Sabean,

who signed a two-year extension in July, is charged with rebuilding a club while knowing that ticket holders and his own bosses aren't blessed with infinite patience.

Sabean says he's committed to rebuilding San Francisco's farm system and churning out homegrown position players to match the constant stream of pitching talent the organization has produced. The Giants haven't signed a player who has developed into a homegrown all-star since drafting Matt Williams with the third pick in 1986.

Since the season ended, San Francisco has made several front-office changes that will affect scouting and player development. Longtime minor league instructor Fred Stanley was promoted to farm director, replacing the retiring Jack Hiatt. The Giants also hired John Barr away from the Dodgers and appointed him scouting director. Barr's arrival freed up resident pitching guru Dick Tidrow to assist Sabean more actively on the major league level.

San Francisco begins the rebuilding process fully aware that National League West rivals Arizona and Colorado rode impressive young talent to the NL Championship Series. The rival Dodgers have a young nucleus and can match the Giants' financial resources, while San Diego has an improving farm system and is the only NL West team with three straight winning seasons.

If San Francisco has a saving grace, it's the best crop of young pitchers in the division. Matt Cain's 7-16 record belied an outstanding season. Rookie Tim Lincecum brought his Cirque du Soleil delivery to the major leagues in May and led all major league rookies with 150 strikeouts. Though Barry Zito didn't live up to his $126 million contract in his first season as a Giant, he brought reliability to the rotation and is still just 29. Kevin Correia emerged in a late-season audition as a starter, and while Noah Lowry couldn't finish the season because of a bone spur in his elbow, he led the staff with 14 victories.

San Francisco planned to dangle one or more arms as trade bait as it attempts to form a competitive

Tim Lincecum heads a pitching staff that gives the Giants their post-Bonds identity

LARRY GOREN

TOP 30 PROSPECTS

1. Angel Villalona, 3b/1b	16. Nick Pereira, rhp
2. Tim Alderson, rhp	17. Osiris Matos, rhp
3. Madison Bumgarner, lhp	18. Jackson Williams, c
4. Nate Schierholtz, of	19. Wilber Bucardo, rhp
5. Henry Sosa, rhp	20. Erick Threets, lhp
6. Nick Noonan, 2b	21. Ben Snyder, lhp
7. Eugenio Velez, 2b/of	22. Pat Misch, lhp
8. Wendell Fairley, of	23. Kelvin Pichardo, rhp
9. John Bowker, of	24. Merkin Valdez, rhp
10. Emmanuel Burriss, ss	25. Brett Pill, 1b
11. Brian Bocock, ss	26. Brian Anderson, rhp
12. Clayton Tanner, lhp	27. Travis Denker, 2b
13. Mike McBryde, of	28. Sergio Romo, rhp
14. Charlie Culberson, ss	29. Brian Horwitz, of
15. Waldis Joaquin, rhp	30. Ben Copeland, of

lineup. While hitters such as Nate Schierholtz and Dan Ortmeier had some big league success in their 2007 trials, the Giants don't have any near-ready position prospects who project as surefire regulars.

The Giants were able to restock the system with six of the first 51 picks the 2007 draft, but spent five of them on high school players who won't help anytime soon. If it hopes to contend in the near term, San Francisco must place some faith in its homegrown players, be creative in acquiring more talent—and get a bit lucky, too.

ORGANIZATION OVERVIEW

General Manager: Brian Sabean. **Farm Director:** Fred Stanley. **Scouting Director:** John Barr.

Class	Team	League	W	L	PCT	Finish*	Manager	Affiliated
Majors	San Francisco	National	71	91	.438	14th (16)	Bruce Bochy	—
Triple-A	Fresno Grizzlies	Pacific Coast	77	67	.535	4th (16)	Dan Rohn	1998
Double-A	Connecticut Defenders	Eastern	63	78	.447	10th (12)	Dave Machemer	2003
High A	San Jose Giants	California	73	67	.521	5th (10)^	Lenn Sakata	1988
Low A	Augusta GreenJackets	South Atlantic	89	51	.636	1st (16)	Roberto Kelly	2005
Short-season	Salem-Keizer Volcanoes	Northwest	57	19	.750	1st (8)^	Steve Decker	1997
Rookie	AZL Giants	Arizona	33	23	.589	2nd (9)	Bert Hunter	2000

Overall 2007 Minor League Record — 392 305 .562 — 3rd

*Finish in overall standings (No. of teams in league) ^League champion

LAST YEAR'S TOP 30

Player, Pos.		Status
1.	Tim Lincecum, rhp	Majors
2.	Jonathan Sanchez, lhp	Majors
3.	Angel Villalona, 3b	No. 1
4.	Emmanuel Burriss, ss	No. 10
5.	Brian Wilson, rhp	Majors
6.	Kevin Frandsen, 2b	Majors
7.	Fred Lewis, of	Majors
8.	Nate Schierholtz, of	No. 4
9.	Eddy Martinez-Esteve, of	Dropped out
10.	Billy Sadler, rhp	Dropped out
11.	Travis Ishikawa, 1b	Dropped out
12.	Mike McBryde, of	No. 13
13.	Clayton Tanner, lhp	No. 12
14.	Osiris Matos, rhp	No. 17
15.	Nick Pereira, rhp	No. 16
16.	Marcus Sanders, ss	Dropped out
17.	Dan Griffin, rhp	Dropped out
18.	Merkin Valdez, rhp	No. 24
19.	Brian Anderson, rhp	No. 26
20.	Joey Martinez, rhp	Dropped out
21.	Sharlon Schoop, ss	Dropped out
22.	Thomas Neal, of	Dropped out
23.	Justin Hedrick, rhp	Dropped out
24.	Erick Threets, lhp	No. 20
25.	Ben Copeland, of	No. 30
26.	Brian Bocock, ss	No. 11
27.	David Quinowski, lhp	Dropped out
28.	Dan Ortmeier, of	Majors
29.	Jose Valdez, rhp	Dropped out
30.	Brian Horwitz, of/1b	No. 29

BEST TOOLS

Best Hitter for Average	Nick Noonan
Best Power Hitter	Angel Villalona
Best Strike-Zone Discipline	Nick Noonan
Fastest Baserunner	Emmanuel Burriss
Best Athlete	Wendell Fairley
Best Fastball	Henry Sosa
Best Curveball	Tim Alderson
Best Slider	Steve Edlefsen
Best Changeup	Erick Threets
Best Control	Tim Alderson
Best Defensive Catcher	Jackson Williams
Best Defensive Infielder	Brian Bocock
Best Infield Arm	Brian Bocock
Best Defensive Outfielder	Antoan Richardson
Best Outfield Arm	Mike McBryde

PROJECTED 2011 LINEUP

Catcher	Jackson Williams
First Base	Dan Ortmeier
Second Base	Nick Noonan
Third Base	Angel Villalona
Shortstop	Emmanuel Burriss
Left Field	Fred Lewis
Center Field	Aaron Rowand
Right Field	Nate Schierholtz
No. 1 Starter	Matt Cain
No. 2 Starter	Tim Lincecum
No. 3 Starter	Barry Zito
No. 4 Starter	Tim Alderson
No. 5 Starter	Madison Bumgarner
Closer	Brian Wilson

TOP PROSPECTS OF THE DECADE

Year	Player, Pos.	2007 Org.
1997	Joe Fontenot, rhp	Out of baseball
1998	Jason Grilli, rhp	Tigers
1999	Jason Grilli, rhp	Tigers
2000	Kurt Ainsworth, rhp	Out of baseball
2001	Jerome Williams, rhp	Twins
2002	Jerome Williams, rhp	Twins
2003	Jesse Foppert, rhp	Giants
2004	Merkin Valdez, rhp	Giants
2005	Matt Cain, rhp	Giants
2006	Matt Cain, rhp	Giants
2007	Tim Lincecum, rhp	Giants

TOP DRAFT PICKS OF THE DECADE

Year	Player, Pos.	2007 Org.
1997	Jason Grilli, rhp	Tigers
1998	Tony Torcato, of	Out of baseball
1999	Kurt Ainsworth, rhp	Out of baseball
2000	Boof Bonser, rhp	Twins
2001	Brad Hennessey, rhp	Giants
2002	Matt Cain, rhp	Giants
2003	David Aardsma, rhp	White Sox
2004	Eddy Martinez-Esteve, of (2nd round)	Giants
2005	Ben Copeland, of (4th round)	Giants
2006	Tim Lincecum, rhp	Giants
2007	Madison Bumgarner, lhp	Giants

LARGEST BONUSES IN CLUB HISTORY

Angel Villalona, 2006	$2,100,000
Tim Lincecum, 2006	$2,025,000
Madison Bumgarner, 2007	$2,000,000
Jason Grilli, 1997	$1,875,000
David Aardsma, 2003	$1,425,000

SAN FRANCISCO GIANTS

Top 2008 Rookie: Nate Schierholtz, of. With his ability to hit for average and power while playing an above-average right field, the Giants have no excuse not to hand Schierholtz an everyday job.

Breakout Prospect: Waldis Joaquin, rhp. After missing a year recovering from Tommy John surgery, Joaquin roared back with an upper-90s fastball and a wicked slider in the Northwest League playoffs.

Sleeper: Adam Cowart, rhp. Armed with a sidearm delivery and impeccable command, Cowart has a 24-8, 1.96 record in the minors and has upside as a Chad Bradford-style setup man.

SOURCE OF TOP 30 TALENT			
Homegrown	26	Acquired	4
College	12	Trades	3
Junior college	2	Rule 5 draft	1
High school	6	Independent leagues	0
Draft-and-follow	0	Free agents/waivers	0
Nondrafted free agents	1		
International	5		

Numbers in parentheses indicate prospect rankings

LF
John Bowker (9)
Brian Horwitz (29)
Ben Copeland (30)
Eddy Martinez-Esteve
James Simmons

CF
Wendell Fairley (8)
Mike McBryde (13)
Antoan Richardson
Clay Timpner

RF
Nate Schierholtz (4)
Thomas Neal

3B
Ryan Rohlinger
Matthew Downs
David Maroul
Andrew Davis

SS
Brian Bocock (11)
Charlie Culberson (14)

2B
Nick Noonan (6)
Eugenio Velez (7)
Emmanuel Burriss (10)
Travis Denker (27)
Sharlon Schoop
Marcus Sanders

1B
Angel Villalona (1)
Brett Pill (25)
Travis Ishikawa
Andy D'Alessio

C
Jackson Williams (18)
Pablo Sandoval
Adam Witter
Todd Jennings

RHP

Starters	Relievers
Tim Alderson (2)	Osiris Matos (17)
Henry Sosa (5)	Kelvin Pichardo (23)
Waldis Joaquin (15)	Merkin Valdez (24)
Nick Pereira (16)	Brian Anderson (26)
Wilber Bucardo (19)	Sergio Romo (28)
Kevin Pucetas	Adam Cowart
Joey Martinez	Billy Sadler
Dan Griffin	Steve Edlefsen
Jose Valdez	David Newton
Garrett Broshuis	Justin Hedrick
	Manny Cabeza
	Danny Otero
	Dan Turpen
	Juan Trinidad

LHP

Starters	Relievers
Madison Bumgarner (3)	Erick Threets (20)
Clayton Tanner (12)	Pat Misch (22)
Ben Snyder (21)	Jose Capellan
Paul Oseguera	Wilmin Rodriguez
	Jesse English
	David Quinowski
	Alex Hinshaw
	Jared Cranston

Best Pro Debut: As a college senior, 1B Andy D'Alessio (19) was too old for the Arizona League, but he still batted .306 and topped the circuit in homers (14), RBIs (51), extra-base hits (30) and slugging percentage (.624). He was an AZL all-star, as was more appropriately aged 2B/SS Nick Noonan (1s), who hit .316 with 18 steals. RHPs Danny Otero (21) and T.J. Brewer (35) were Northwest League all-stars, as Otero had a 1.21 ERA and a league-best 19 saves and Brewer went 9-1, 3.05. Brewer shared the win lead with LHP Andy de la Garza (18).

Best Athlete: The top prep athlete in the draft, OF Wendell Fairley (1s) has well-above-average power potential and speed to go with legitimate center-field ability. He also showed a low-90s fastball on the mound. Several Southeastern Conference football programs recruited him as a wide receiver.

Best Pure Hitter: Noonan is sophisticated for a high school hitter and already has proven he can hit quality fastballs.

Best Power Hitter: D'Alessio, who tied Jeff Baker's Clemson record with 59 career homers, has the most present power. Fairley has the raw strength to surpass him in the future.

Fastest Runner: Fairley can cover 60 yards in 6.5 seconds. OF Bruce Edwards (15) is a plus runner.

Best Defensive Player: C Jackson Williams (1s) led the NWL by throwing out 43 percent of base-stealers and has all the skills a catcher needs. The Giants believe strong-armed Charlie Culberson (1s) can stay at shortstop.

Best Fastball: Madison Bumgarner (1) was the hardest-throwing high school lefty in the draft, operating at 92-94 mph and touching 97. RHP Tim Alderson (1) pitches in the low 90s and had the best command of any prep pitcher in the 2007 crop.

Best Secondary Pitch: Alderson has a low-80s curveball with late, hard break. RHP Steve Edlefsen (16) has the best slider in the system, though it isn't as good as Alderson's curve.

Most Intriguing Background: Culberson's grandfather Leon played in the majors, and he's related to Hall of Famer George Sisler, former all-star Dick and ex-big leaguer Dave.

Closest To The Majors: Alderson's stuff, command and desire could make him the first 2007 high school draftee to get to the big leagues.

Bumgarner and Noonan are also more advanced than most prep players.

Best Late-Round Pick: Edlefsen, who also has heavy sink on his 88-92 mph fastball, and D'Alessio. Otero is the best of the NWL pitching standouts, with a fastball that creeps into the low 90s.

The One Who Got Away: The Giants signed the first 29 players they drafted. They made a run at SS Tyler Ladendorf (34), who turned down a six-figure offer from the Yankees before the draft and returned to Howard (Texas) JC.

Assessment: San Francisco had more first-rounders than any club and landed three high-ceiling high schoolers in Bumgarner, Alderson and Fairley. Noonan, the first of three sandwich picks, is another prepster with a lot of upside.

2006   BUDGET: $4.3 MILLION

RHP Tim Lincecum (1) made just 13 starts in the minors before jumping to San Francisco. The Giants hope either Emmanuel Burris (1) or Brian Bocock (9) is their shortstop of the future.

GRADE: B+

2005   BUDGET: $0.5 MILLION

San Francisco gave up its first three choices as free-agent compensation and its top pick, OF Ben Copeland (4) has been slow to develop.

GRADE: F

2004   BUDGET: $1.5 MILLION

Again without a first-round pick, the Giants dug deep to find LHP Jonathan Sanchez (27). OF John Bowker (3) and 2B/SS Kevin Frandsen (12) could be big league role players.

GRADE: C

2003   BUDGET: $4.4 MILLION

RHPs David Aardsma (1) and Craig Whitaker (1s) haven't worked out, but San Francisco landed a possible impact hitter in OF Nate Schierholtz (2) and a possible closer in RHP Brian Wilson (24). Four other draftees have reached the majors, most notably since-traded OF-turned-LHP Jon Coutlangus (19).

GRADE: C+

Draft analysis by Jim Callis. Numbers in parentheses indicate draft rounds. Budgets are bonuses in first 10 rounds.

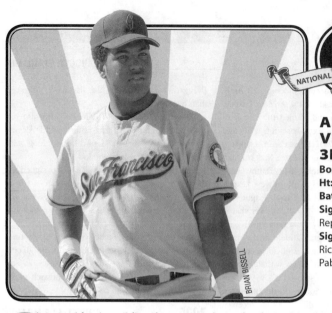

BRIAN BISSELL

NATIONAL LEAGUE 1 WEST

ANGEL VILLALONA, 3B/1B

Born: Aug. 13, 1990.
Ht:. 6-3. **Wt:.** 210.
Bats: R. **Throws:** R.
Signed: Dominican Republic, 2006.
Signed by: Rick Ragazzo/ Pablo Peguero.

Giants special assistant Felipe Alou spent nearly two decades in player development with the Expos and considers Andres Galarraga the best young power hitter he ever came across. When Alou watched Villalona take batting practice for the first time, he had visions of the Big Cat dancing in his head. With a barrel chest and a strapping body, Villalona looks like a premier power-hitting prospect and he takes batting practice to match. He doesn't look like he's 17, which is what the Giants must keep reminding themselves as they develop their $2.1 million bonus baby out of the Dominican Republic. "If he's a 17-year-old high school player right now, I don't know how much money he'd get," retiring farm director Jack Hiatt said. "He's got unbelievable power." Though his major league debut is years away, San Francisco fans already consider Villalona the shining savior in a system that hasn't produced an impact position player since Will Clark and Matt Williams in the mid-1980s. Villalona made his pro debut in the Rookie-level Arizona League, where he was both the youngest player and the No. 1 prospect, and earned a late callup to short-season Salem-Keizer.

The Giants wanted Villalona to concentrate on developing good habits as he acclimated to life in the United States, including basics like taking productive batting practice and learning to compete. They noticed major improvements from his first instructional league in 2006 to the next, especially with his hitting approach. He's able to hang in tougher on breaking balls, has shown the ability to hit to the opposite field with runners on base and no longer swings out of his shoes at every pitch. San Francisco is so enamored with his powerful bat that it isn't concerned yet about where it will play. Villalona is athletic for his size, and he has good hands and a well above-average arm at third base. He's shy but easily likable and coaches say he is eager to learn.

Villalona is still growing and his weight bears watching. He is an average runner now but will rate below average as he gets older. The Giants already acknowledge that he'll probably be a first baseman down the road, perhaps as soon as 2008. Special assistant J.T. Snow, a former Gold Glove first baseman, worked with Villalona during instructional league and he picked up first base quickly. He tends to throw from a low arm angle, leading to errors. Villalona didn't react well at first when he wasn't assigned to Salem to start the summer and he remains unschooled when it comes to the subtle nuances of the game such as bunt plays and cutoffs, but all that's to be expected of someone who could be a high school junior.

In 2008, Villalona will log his first full pro season and almost certainly will be the youngest regular in the low Class A South Atlantic League. He's talented enough to reach the majors before his 20th birthday—which won't come until August 2010—but the Giants insist they have no timetable. "When he's ready and can do the right things consistently in front of crowds, he'll get there and stay there a long time," Hiatt said.

Year	Club (League)	Class	AVG	G	AB	R	H	2B	3B	HR	RBI	BB	SO	SB	OBP	SLG
2007	Giants (AZL)	R	.285	52	200	40	57	12	3	5	37	15	42	1	.344	.450
	Salem-Keizer (NWL)	A	.167	5	12	1	2	0	0	0	1	0	2	1	.231	.167
MINOR LEAGUE TOTALS			.278	57	212	41	59	12	3	5	38	15	44	2	.338	.434

2 TIM ALDERSON, RHP

BILL MITCHELL

Born: Nov. 3, 1988. **B-T:** R-R. **Ht.:** 6-7. **Wt.:** 217. **Drafted:** HS—Scottsdale, Ariz., 2007 (1st round). **Signed by:** Lee Carballo.

Pitching exclusively from the stretch, Alderson was a two-time Arizona player of the year and helped Horizon High to a pair of state 5-A championships. He showed unbelievable command for a high school senior, let alone one who's 6-foot-7, issuing just four walks while striking out 111 in 73 innings. He was drafted 22nd overall and signed for $1.29 million. Alderson had the best command of any high school pitcher in recent memory. His fastball sits in the low 90s and tops out at 94 mph, and San Francisco projects that he'll throw harder. His low-80s curveball already ranks as the best in the system. He can change planes with it, taking some velocity off to achieve a bigger break. He had no problems throwing out of an easy windup in instructional league, and he repeated those mechanics well. Alderson's herky-jerky delivery leads to concerns about his durability as a starter. The Giants think he gets his body in a good position to throw and won't have any problem staying in a rotation. He's made progress with his rudimentary changeup. The Giants won't be afraid to push Alderson due to his uncanny command. Low Class A Augusta is the logical next step, but don't be surprised if Alderson opens 2008 at high Class A San Jose.

Year	Club (League)	Class	W	L	ERA	G	GS	CG	SV	IP	H	R	ER	HR	BB	SO	AVG
2007	Giants (AZL)	R	0	0	0.00	3	2	0	0	5	4	0	0	0	0	12	.211
MINOR LEAGUE TOTALS			0	0	0.00	3	2	0	0	5	4	0	0	0	0	12	.211

3 MADISON BUMGARNER, LHP

BILL MITCHELL

Born: Aug, 1, 1989. **B-T:** L-R. **Ht.:** 6-4. **Wt.:** 215. **Drafted:** HS—Hudson, N.C., 2007 (1st round). **Signed by:** Pat Portugal.

The hardest-throwing high school lefthander in the 2007 draft, Bumgarner also was a fine righthanded hitter who helped South Caldwell High win two North Carolina 4-A state championships. He became the first prep southpaw drafted in the first round by the Giants since Mike Remlinger in 1987. The 10th overall pick, Bumgarner signed for $2 million. Bumgarner has everything the Giants look for in a pitching prospect—size, athleticism and velocity. His fastball works at 92-94 mph and hits 97 on occasion. It has good, boring action and often runs in on the hands of right-handers. A tremendous athlete, he showed flashes of dominance in instructional league. Bumgarner went higher in the draft but grades below Tim Alderson because his command and breaking ball aren't nearly as good. When Bumgarner stays on top of the pitch, it's a hard slurve that sweeps away from lefthanders. His changeup is in the experimental stages and he throws it too hard, but should be a useful pitch in time. Coming from rural western North Carolina, Bumgarner had a tougher task acclimating to Arizona and his first pro experience. While he might not move as quickly as Alderson, Bumgarner has a higher ceiling. He figures to make his pro debut in low Class A.

Year	Club (League)	Class	W	L	ERA	G	GS	CG	SV	IP	H	R	ER	HR	BB	SO	AVG
2007	Did Not Play—Signed Late																

4 NATE SCHIERHOLTZ, OF

Born: Feb. 15, 1984. **B-T:** L-R. **Ht.:** 6-2. **Wt.:** 215. **Drafted:** Chabot (Calif.) JC, 2003 (2nd round). **Signed by:** Matt Nerland.

Schierholtz led Giants minor leaguers with a career-high .333 average, made his major league debut in June and earned another callup in September. He did his best work at Triple-A Fresno in between his two big league stints, hitting .317 with 12 homers in 51 games. He capped his year by batting .348/.363/.596 in the Arizona Fall League. For a player with 30-homer potential, Schierholtz makes excellent contact. His strikeouts have dropped from 132 to 81 to 77 over the past three seasons as he has leveled out his lefthanded swing. He plays a strong right field and has an above-aver-age, accurate arm. He's a good runner for his size if not a pure basestealer. His body is all sculpted muscle. Schierholtz must learn to work counts, improve his on-base percentage and be more aggressive when he gets ahead of pitchers. San Francisco challenged him to swing for the fences and he responded at Fresno, then appeared much more comfortable in September. Schierholtz is the youngest member of the Giants' projected 2008 outfield corps, and aside from $60 million free agent Aaron Rowand, he's also the most talented.

Year	Club (League)	Class	AVG	G	AB	R	H	2B	3B	HR	RBI	BB	SO	SB	OBP	SLG
2003	Giants (AZL)	R	.400	11	45	5	18	0	2	0	5	3	8	4	.449	.489
	Salem-Keizer (NWL)	A	.306	35	124	23	38	6	2	3	29	12	15	0	.382	.460

2004	Hagerstown (SAL)	A	.296	58	233	41	69	22	0	15	53	18	52	1	.353	.584
	San Jose (Cal)	A	.295	62	258	39	76	18	9	3	31	15	41	3	.338	.469
2005	San Jose (Cal)	A	.319	128	502	83	160	37	8	15	86	32	132	5	.363	.514
2006	Connecticut (EL)	AA	.270	125	470	55	127	25	7	14	54	27	81	8	.325	.443
2007	Fresno (PCL)	AAA	.333	109	411	67	137	31	7	16	68	17	58	10	.365	.560
	San Francisco (NL)	MLB	.304	39	112	9	34	5	3	0	10	2	19	3	.316	.402
MINOR LEAGUE TOTALS			.306	528	2043	313	625	139	35	66	326	124	387	31	.354	.505
MAJOR LEAGUE TOTALS			.304	39	112	9	34	5	3	0	10	2	19	3	.316	.402

5 HENRY SOSA, RHP

BILL MITCHELL

Born: July 28, 1985. **B-T:** R-R. **Ht.:** 6-2. **Wt.:** 180. **Signed:** Dominican Republic, 2004. **Signed by:** Rick Ragazzo/Pablo Peguero.

Signed for just $15,000, Sosa was scheduled to remain in extended spring and pitch in the Arizona League in 2007. But Orlando Yntema tore a knee ligament in the final week of spring training and Sosa replaced him at Augusta. He made the most of his chance, winning more games (six) than he allowed earned runs (five) before earning a trip to the Futures Game and a promotion to high Class A. Sosa pitches consistently in the mid-90s and tops out at 97 mph with his fastball. His hard curveball is a strikeout pitch. He repeats his delivery well while throwing from a high three-quarters slot. He's among the more durable high-profile arms in the system. He's still more thrower than pitcher, and Sosa at times has trouble finding the strike zone and keeping his fastball down. He's trying to learn a changeup, and it remains a distant third pitch. If Sosa can harness his stuff, his upside is huge, and his changeup is the key for him to remain a starter. He probably will get more experience in high Class A at the start of 2008.

Year	Club (League)	Class	W	L	ERA	G	GS	CG	SV	IP	H	R	ER	HR	BB	SO	AVG
2004	Giants (DSL)	R	0	5	5.30	13	7	0	0	35	40	28	21	2	19	25	.282
2005	Giants (DSL)	R	5	6	3.58	13	12	0	0	55	53	30	22	4	46	.250
2006	Giants (AZL)	R	2	1	3.90	9	6	0	0	32	20	15	14	3	12	41	.177
2007	Augusta (SAL)	A	6	0	0.73	13	10	0	1	62	30	8	5	2	25	61	.144
	San Jose (Cal)	A	5	5	4.38	14	14	0	0	63	66	36	31	8	36	78	.262
MINOR LEAGUE TOTALS			18	17	3.36	62	49	0	1	249	209	117	93	19	100	251	.225

6 NICK NOONAN, 2B/SS

BILL MITCHELL

Born: May 4, 1989. **B-T:** L-R. **Ht.:** 6-0. **Wt.:** 180. **Drafted:** HS—San Diego, 2007 (1st round supplemental). **Signed by:** Ray Krawczyk.

The 32nd overall pick in June, Noonan turned down a Clemson scholarship and signed quickly for $915,750. He earned Arizona League all-star honors and hit over .500 for most of instructional league. Noonan made a brilliant first impression with his sweet lefthanded swing and polished baseball acumen. He quickly earned a reputation for having the best pure hitting skills and soundest strike-zone judgment in the system. He makes steady, line-drive contact in the mold of Robin Ventura, and he's also an excellent bunter. Despite a loopy stride, Noonan has above-average speed, and his fine instincts helped him steal 18 bases in 21 pro attempts. There's a smooth quality to everything he does on the field. Though some scouts have compared him to Chase Utley, Noonan doesn't have the same power potential. He prefers to play shortstop but fellow supplemental first-rounder Charlie Culberson has a stronger arm, so Noonan will move up the ladder at second base. He's still working on his skills around the bag, especially turning the double play. Noonan could advance quickly thanks to his polished approach and instincts.

Year	Club (League)	Class	AVG	G	AB	R	H	2B	3B	HR	RBI	BB	SO	SB	OBP	SLG
2007	Giants (AZL)	R	.316	52	206	33	65	11	4	3	40	12	20	18	.357	.451
MINOR LEAGUE TOTALS			.316	52	206	33	65	11	4	3	40	12	20	18	.357	.451

7 EUGENIO VELEZ, OF/2B

STEVE MOORE

Born: May 16, 1982. **B-T:** B-R. **Ht.:** 6-1. **Wt.:** 160. **Signed:** Dominican Republic, 2001. **Signed by:** Tony Arias (Blue Jays).

Velez was a utilityman in the Blue Jays system, but he has been an electric difference-maker since the Giants plucked him in the Triple-A phase of the 2005 Rule 5 draft. He was the South Atlantic League MVP in 2006, though he was 24 in low Class A. For an encore, he led the Double-A Eastern League with 49 steals, reached the majors and hit .303 with 15 swipes in 17 Arizona Fall League games. It's fitting that Velez' first big league hit was a triple because he flies around the bases with well above-average speed. He has some gap power, especially as a lefthanded hitter. His best defensive tool is his plus arm strength. A wrist sprain cost Velez the first month of the season. San Francisco moved him to the outfield to get him back on the field quicker. The one-time shortstop would fit best as a second baseman, but he tends to field balls too upright, which hardens up his hands. He lacks finesse on the infield. Offensively, his biggest need is patience. The Giants see Velez as a high-energy utility player. His value would increase as a dependable infielder. San Francisco likely will field a speed-oriented lineup in 2008, enhancing his chances of making the team.

Year	Club (League)	Class	AVG	G	AB	R	H	2B	3B	HR	RBI	BB	SO	SB	OBP	SLG
2002	Blue Jays (DSL)	R	.301	69	259	33	78	13	7	1	56	25	50	28	.372	.417
2003	Pulaski (Appy)	R	.258	50	186	20	48	7	2	2	24	8	49	3	.291	.349
	Auburn (NYP)	A	.192	7	26	2	5	2	0	1	7	1	10	0	.222	.385
2004	Auburn (NYP)	A	.263	10	19	5	5	0	0	0	2	3	5	0	.391	.263
	Pulaski (Appy)	R	.292	44	168	27	49	14	4	1	27	12	32	1	.339	.440
2005	Lansing (MWL)	A	.285	67	239	25	68	11	3	4	34	9	40	7	.311	.406
2006	Augusta (SAL)	A	.315	126	460	90	145	29	20	14	90	34	81	64	.369	.557
2007	Connecticut (EL)	AA	.298	96	376	55	112	17	9	1	25	26	66	49	.344	.399
	Fresno (PCL)	AAA	.278	4	18	5	5	0	0	0	0	2	3	5	.381	.278
	San Francisco (NL)	MLB	.273	14	11	5	3	0	2	0	2	2	3	4	.385	.636
MINOR LEAGUE TOTALS			.294	473	1751	262	515	93	45	24	265	120	336	157	.344	.440
MAJOR LEAGUE TOTALS			.273	14	11	5	3	0	2	0	2	2	3	4	.385	.636

8 WENDELL FAIRLEY, OF

BILL MITCHELL

Born: March 17, 1988. **B-T:** L-R. **Ht.:** 6-0. **Wt.:** 190. **Drafted:** HS—Lucedale, Miss., 2007 (1st round). **Signed by:** Andrew Jefferson.

The best all-around high school athlete in the 2007 draft, Fairley hit .538 with nine home runs, went 9-2 as a pitcher and drew interest from Division I football programs as a wide receiver. He remained something of a wild card because he didn't participate in many showcases, and lasted until the Giants took him 29th overall and signed him for $1 million. Fairley generates tremendous bat speed, reminiscent of a young Fred Lewis, and has the tools to hit for average and power. He didn't let many fastballs get past him in instructional league. He has easily above-average speed, the range to play center field and an above-average arm. Fairley is still very raw at the plate and will need time to develop. He'll have to learn to recognize and react to offspeed pitches. He couldn't do much in instructional league because he was slowed by shoulder tendinitis. The Giants aren't concerned about his past, which includes a misdemeanor conviction for contributing to the delinquency of a minor. His attorney is appealing the conviction. He also faced assault charges after a prank on a high school bus, but that case was dismissed. He has the highest ceiling among Giants hitters after Villalona, but Fairley likely will move slowly and probably won't see the majors before 2011 at the earliest. He'll make his pro debut in low Class A.

Year	Club (League)	Class	AVG	G	AB	R	H	2B	3B	HR	RBI	BB	SO	SB	OBP	SLG
2007	Did Not Play—Signed Late															

9 JOHN BOWKER, OF

STEVE MOORE

Born: July 8, 1983. **B-T:** L-L. **Ht.:** 6-2. **Wt.:** 190. **Drafted:** Long Beach State, 2004 (3rd round). **Signed by:** Lee Carballo.

Bowker held his own over his first three minor league seasons, but hadn't flashed the power San Francisco expected when it drafted him in the third round. The power arrived at an unlikely place last season, as Bowker finished third in the pitching-dominated Eastern League with a .523 slugging percentage. Bowker arrived in spring training last year with added muscle and began to flourish when coaches suggested he stand closer to the plate. He combines the ability to hit for average—he's a career .296 hitter—with pull power. He has strong hands and can hit good fastballs. The Giants loves his aggressive approach and work ethic. He's limited to left field because he has below-average speed and his range and arm are adequate at best. San Francisco pulled the plug quickly after trying Bowker in center field. He has played right field as well, but it would be a stretch for him to man that position at spacious AT&T Park. Because dead-pull lefty hitters seldom fare well there, he'd be well served to work on driving the ball to all fields. His breakthrough earned Bowker a spot on the Giants' 40-man roster. Because they have a glut of young outfielders, including several lefthanded hitters, he'll need to continue putting up strong numbers to earn a permanent role in San Francisco.

SAN FRANCISCO GIANTS

Year	Club (League)	Class	AVG	G	AB	R	H	2B	3B	HR	RBI	BB	SO	SB	OBP	SLG
2004	Giants (AZL)	R	.512	10	43	14	22	7	1	2	11	7	11	1	.580	.860
	Salem-Keizer (NWL)	A	.323	31	127	23	41	9	2	4	16	8	25	1	.390	.520
2005	San Jose (Cal)	A	.267	121	464	66	124	27	1	13	67	36	108	3	.319	.414
2006	Fresno (PCL)	AAA	.500	2	4	0	2	0	0	0	0	0	0	0	.500	.500
	San Jose (Cal)	A	.284	112	462	61	131	32	6	7	66	37	100	6	.337	.424
2007	Connecticut (EL)	AA	.307	139	522	79	160	35	6	22	90	41	103	3	.363	.523
MINOR LEAGUE TOTALS			.296	415	1622	243	480	110	16	48	250	129	347	14	.352	.472

10 EMMANUEL BURRISS, SS

Born: Jan. 17, 1985. **B-T:** B-R. **Ht.:** 6-0. **Wt.:** 170. **Drafted:** Kent State, 2006 (1st round supplemental). **Signed by:** Sean O'Connor.

After hitting .307 in his pro debut, Burriss struggled so badly in high Class A that the Giants demoted him after 36 games. He said he wasn't mentally prepared when the 2007 season began. He regained his focus and confidence against younger competition in the South Atlantic League, finishing third in steals (51) and fifth in batting (.321). It's no surprise that Burriss led a system full of burners with 68 stolen bases. In addition to his pure speed, he has fine basestealing skills and was encouraged to use them by aggressive Augusta manager Roberto Kelly. Burriss is a contact hitter who works counts better than his walk totals would indicate. He has good range and instincts at shortstop. Burriss has no power and will have to prove he can handle quality fastballs at higher levels. After making 30 errors in 123 games in 2007, he needs to be more consistent on defense. Caught stealing 18 times last season, he can become more efficient on the bases. Burriss, who hit .365 in 17 Arizona Fall League games, says he learned his lesson and will be ready to start 2008. He'll take another crack at San Jose, likely playing some second base next to Brian Bocock. The Giants hope one can be their shortstop by 2010.

Year	Club (League)	Class	AVG	G	AB	R	H	2B	3B	HR	RBI	BB	SO	SB	OBP	SLG
2006	Salem-Keizer (NWL)	A	.307	65	254	50	78	8	2	1	27	27	22	35	.384	.366
2007	San Jose (Cal)	A	.165	36	139	23	23	2	0	0	8	12	20	17	.237	.180
	Augusta (SAL)	A	.321	89	365	64	117	14	4	0	38	28	49	51	.374	.381
MINOR LEAGUE TOTALS			.288	190	758	137	218	24	6	1	73	67	91	103	.352	.339

11 BRIAN BOCOCK, SS

Born: March 9, 1985. **B-T:** R-R. **Ht.:** 5-11. **Wt.:** 185. **Drafted:** Stetson, 2006 (9th round). **Signed by:** Glenn Tufts.

The Giants absolutely love Bocock's playmaking ability on the infield and didn't hesitate to name him the host club's U.S. representative in the Futures Game. It was a gutsy move, considering he was a ninth-rounder and they took another shortstop, Emmanuel Burriss, with a supplemental first-round pick in the same draft. But Burriss said he didn't feel slighted, nor was he upset when San Francisco swapped the two players in early May, promoting Bocock to high Class A and demoting Burriss to low Class A. Bocock started hot but struggled as the summer wore on, finishing with a .220 average and .293 OBP at San Jose. The Giants knew developing his bat would be a challenge, and while he's a 65 runner on the 20-80 scouting scale, he doesn't get on base or stay consistent enough to project as a top-of-the-order presence. His swing path makes it tough for him to hit breaking balls, as his bat doesn't stay in the strike zone for long. But club officials can't stop gushing about Bocock's superior defensive skills, including plus range and arm strength that allow him to make difficult plays in the hole look easy. Bocock, whose uncle Mike is the winningest coach in the history of the summer collegiate Valley League, had minor elbow surgery after the season but should be ready for spring training. The Giants must find a place for Burriss and Bocock to play every day this season and were expected to pair them at San Jose, with Burriss likely sliding to second base.

Year	Club (League)	Class	AVG	G	AB	R	H	2B	3B	HR	RBI	BB	SO	SB	OBP	SLG
2006	Salem-Keizer (NWL)	A	.223	39	103	12	23	6	0	0	7	12	29	6	.305	.282
	Augusta (SAL)	A	.000	2	1	1	0	0	0	0	0	0	0	0	.000	.000
2007	Augusta (SAL)	A	.292	39	161	24	47	9	1	1	20	16	19	26	.354	.379
	San Jose (Cal)	A	.220	87	345	42	76	19	3	4	37	35	105	15	.293	.328
MINOR LEAGUE TOTALS			.239	167	610	79	146	34	4	5	65	63	153	47	.310	.333

12 CLAYTON TANNER, LHP

Born: Dec. 5, 1987. **B-T:** R-L. **Ht.:** 6-1. **Wt.:** 180. **Drafted:** HS—Concord, Calif., 2006 (3rd round). **Signed by:** Keith Snider.

Tanner competed well as a 19-year-old in low Class A last year, earning a spot in the South Atlantic

League all-star game before fading down the stretch. The Giants expected that, considering it was his first full pro season and Augusta gets as hot as the surface of the sun in late summer. Tanner has an advanced sense of how to attack hitters. His fastball hits 91 mph but he usually pitches in the upper 80s with late life. Because his delivery is so easy, his fastball tends to sneak up on hitters. San Francisco believes he'll add velocity as he matures, too. His changeup and slider aren't anything special yet, but he has above-average command and both pitches should improve. Tanner threw over the top in the spring but the Giants lowered his arm slot a bit to a high three-quarters delivery, which he easily repeats. He's competitive, studies hitters and surprised Augusta pitching coach Ross Grimsley by keeping detailed notes on each opposing player. Tanner patterns himself after Barry Zito, and because Zito's contract runs through at least 2013, there's a good chance he'll make his major league debut alongside his idol.

Year	Club (League)	Class	W	L	ERA	G	GS	CG	SV	IP	H	R	ER	HR	BB	SO	AVG
2006	Salem-Keizer (NWL)	A	2	2	3.46	13	0	0	1	26	17	11	10	1	8	25	.183
2007	Augusta (SAL)	A	12	8	3.59	27	23	1	0	135	147	61	54	5	44	104	.282
MINOR LEAGUE TOTALS			14	10	3.57	40	23	1	1	161	164	72	64	6	52	129	.267

13 MIKE McBRYDE, OF

Born: March 22, 1985. **B-T:** R-R. **Ht.:** 6-2. **Wt.:** 170. **Drafted:** Florida Atlantic, 2006 (5th round). **Signed by:** Steve Arnieri.

McBryde committed 15 errors in low Class A, but it didn't reflect on his ability to play center field. He picked up most of those errors because of his cannon arm, which is well above average and is easily the strongest among outfielders in the system. "He tried to throw out everyone trying to go first to third," one Giants coach said. "If he hit the runner or short-hopped the third baseman, that was his error." Fully recovered from a hamstring injury that short-circuited his junior year at Florida Atlantic, McBryde also grades out as a plus-plus runner, ranking behind Emmanuel Burriss, Eugenio Velez and Antoan Richardson as the fastest players in the system. Yet he stole just 14 bases and was caught 11 times last year, suggesting that he hasn't learned to use his speed yet. The big question with McBryde is his bat. He shows signs of 15-20 homer potential and is also a good bunter, but he needs to make better contact. Once he develops better strike-zone awareness, he could turn a corner quickly. McBryde, who has the tools to become an elite prospect, will take the step up to high Class A in 2008.

Year	Club (League)	Class	AVG	G	AB	R	H	2B	3B	HR	RBI	BB	SO	SB	OBP	SLG
2006	Salem-Keizer (NWL)	A	.276	71	225	38	62	9	5	3	34	22	59	16	.344	.400
2007	Augusta (SAL)	A	.276	119	417	71	115	17	4	7	61	27	100	14	.328	.386
MINOR LEAGUE TOTALS			.276	190	642	109	177	26	9	10	95	49	159	30	.334	.391

14 CHARLIE CULBERSON, SS

Born: April 10, 1989. **B-T:** R-R. **Ht.:** 6-0. **Wt.:** 175. **Drafted:** HS—Calhoun, Ga., 2007 (1st round supplemental). **Signed by:** Sean O'Connor.

Culberson went 51st overall in the 2007 draft, higher than most draft experts expected, but the Giants didn't have another selection until the fifth round and didn't figure he'd still be around. He got extra exposure as a Calhoun (Ga.) High teammate of lefthander Josh Smoker, picked 31st overall by the Nationals. Signed for $607,500, Culberson teamed with Angel Villalona and Nick Noonan to form a prospect-studded infield for the Arizona League Giants, who reached the league title game. San Francisco plans on continuing to bring the three of them up together. In the best-case scenario, they make it all the way to the major leagues like the 1970s Dodgers infield of Steve Garvey, Davey Lopes, Bill Russell and Ron Cey. Russell would be a pretty good role model for Culberson, who isn't flashy but manages to make plays in spite of average range and an unorthodox, sidearm release. The Giants grade his arm as above-average, with the drawback being that he tries to make every play, no matter how impossible. Culberson has a metal-bat swing and lacks a true load to generate power, but he got plenty of work with wood in his pro debut after signing quickly and showed signs of making adjustments. Culberson has a stocky build and some pull power that helped him mash 15 homers as a prep senior, but power isn't expected to be a major part of his game. He'll move up with Villalona and Noonan to low Class A.

Year	Club (League)	Class	AVG	G	AB	R	H	2B	3B	HR	RBI	BB	SO	SB	OBP	SLG
2007	Giants (AZL)	R	.286	46	161	32	46	8	5	1	16	19	38	19	.374	.416
MINOR LEAGUE TOTALS			.286	46	161	32	46	8	5	1	16	19	38	19	.374	.416

15 WALDIS JOAQUIN, RHP

Born: Dec. 25. 1986. **B-T:** R-R. **Ht.:** 6-2. **Wt.:** 190. **Signed:** Dominican Republic, 2003. **Signed by:** Rick Ragazzo/Pablo Peguero.

Joaquin missed all of 2006 after Tommy John surgery, but upon returning to the mound he didn't take long to show the Giants that he still had his electric stuff. On Sept. 9, Joaquin threw six shutout innings, allowed just two hits and struck out seven as Salem-Keizer defeated Tri-City in a Northwest League playoff game. And he did it all with a strict limit of 70 pitches. Joaquin made 15 appearances for the Volcanoes during the regular season and showed improvement each time out. By the end, he was throwing an easy 95-mph fastball along with a power slider—the stuff that made him such an intriguing prospect two years earlier. San Francisco believes Joaquin could become a frontline starter, though like most young pitchers, he's prone to overthrowing and flying open with his shoulder. Like many Tommy John survivors, he struggled with command in his first season back. His changeup has a long ways to go as well. Though it'll be a few years before he would arrive in the majors, the Giants are ecstatic at the progress Joaquin made in 2007 and want to see how he holds up in full-season ball this year.

Year	Club (League)	Class	W	L	ERA	G	GS	CG	SV	IP	H	R	ER	HR	BB	SO	AVG
2004	Giants (DSL)	R	6	1	1.61	14	13	0	0	61	51	21	11	0	28	44	.229
2005	Giants (AZL)	R	1	1	3.64	10	5	0	1	29	28	17	12	1	10	37	.241
2006	Did Not Play—Injured																
2007	Salem-Keizer (NWL)	A	3	0	2.84	15	5	0	0	38	24	13	12	2	16	30	.176
MINOR LEAGUE TOTALS			10	2	2.44	39	23	0	1	129	103	51	35	3	54	111	.217

16 NICK PEREIRA, RHP

Born: Sept. 22, 1982. **B-T:** R-R. **Ht.:** 6-1. **Wt.:** 190. **Drafted:** San Francisco, 2005 (10th round). **Signed by:** Matt Nerland.

Pereira literally wrote the book on pitching. He and fellow Giants minor leaguer Dave McKae authored and self-published a 63-page manual titled "In Pursuit of Pitching Perfection." The book includes diagrams and photos that demonstrate basic mechanics, grips, exercises and other techniques. Pereira must practice what he preaches, because he ranks as the system's best upper-level pitching prospect. He spent all of 2007 at Double-A Connecticut, got stronger in the second half and carried his success into a solid showing in the Arizona Fall League. Club officials were happy with his steady progress one year after he jumped from high Class A to Triple-A and was San Francisco's representative in the 2006 Futures Game. Pereira thrives with his ability to locate his upper-80s fastball, his changeup and his curveball. None of his pitches stand out, but he gets outs and keeps lefthanders at bay with his changeup. He's one of the most athletic pitchers in the system and compares favorably to Brad Hennessey, who has been valuable to the Giants as both a starter and reliever. Pereira's next stop will be a longer engagement in Triple-A than he had in the second half of 2006.

Year	Club (League)	Class	W	L	ERA	G	GS	CG	SV	IP	H	R	ER	HR	BB	SO	AVG
2005	Salem-Keizer (NWL)	A	5	3	3.04	14	9	0	0	50	54	21	17	0	14	41	.277
2006	San Jose (Cal)	A	7	1	2.06	13	13	0	0	78	65	21	18	1	16	76	.222
	Fresno (PCL)	AAA	4	3	5.92	15	15	0	0	79	87	55	52	10	48	60	.281
2007	Connecticut (EL)	AA	9	9	3.39	26	26	1	0	143	124	64	54	15	65	123	.231
MINOR LEAGUE TOTALS			25	16	3.61	68	63	1	0	351	330	161	141	26	143	300	.247

17 OSIRIS MATOS, RHP

Born: Nov. 6, 1984. **B-T:** R-R. **Ht.:** 6-1. **Wt.:** 180. **Drafted:** Dominican Republic, 2002. **Signed by:** Rick Ragazzo.

Matos appeared to be on the fast track to the big leagues, but he traveled in a few circles in 2007 while trying to hone a consistent breaking ball. He spent most of the season in middle relief in Double-A, where he showed more consistency with his two-seam fastball as well as a mid-90s four-seamer. But he struggled against lefthanders, who hit .277 against him, and went to low Class A to work on throwing a slider. From there, the Giants sent him to help San Jose's playoff push. Matos got minimal work in the Dominican Winter League and was expected to report to Triple-A for 2008. San Francisco loves the way he comes after hitters and remains open-minded to his future role, believing he could move back onto a starter's development track if he can keep his arm fresh. He looks like at least a future contributor out of the bullpen with the equipment to mow down righthanders.

Year	Club (League)	Class	W	L	ERA	G	GS	CG	SV	IP	H	R	ER	HR	BB	SO	AVG
2002	Giants (AZL)	R	4	2	4.65	13	13	0	0	62	63	35	32	3	22	51	.266
2003	Giants (AZL)	R	2	2	4.67	9	6	0	0	34	35	21	18	1	10	28	.261
2004	Giants (AZL)	R	2	0	2.44	11	8	0	1	48	43	23	13	1	20	47	.230
2005	Augusta (SAL)	A	8	8	4.99	29	22	0	0	135	162	83	75	12	31	79	.297
2006	Connecticut (EL)	AA	0	0	3.72	6	0	0	2	9	11	4	4	0	2	5	.282
	Augusta (SAL)	A	7	3	1.76	44	0	0	13	61	42	13	12	3	12	81	.193
2007	Connecticut (EL)	AA	5	0	2.89	35	0	0	4	56	50	20	18	3	21	43	.239
	Augusta (SAL)	A	0	0	0.00	7	0	0	4	9	1	0	0	0	1	9	.036
MINOR LEAGUE TOTALS			28	15	3.72	154	49	0	24	416	407	199	172	23	119	343	.255

18 JACKSON WILLIAMS, C

Born: May 14, 1986. **B-T:** R-R. **Ht.:** 5-11. **Wt.:** 200. **Drafted:** Oklahoma, 2007 (1st round supplemental). **Signed by:** Todd Thomas.

Most scouts thought San Francisco overdrafted Williams because they had six selections among the first 51 picks and needed to watch their bonus money. While his bat certainly didn't merit the 43rd overall selection or a $708,750 bonus, the Giants are captivated by his skills behind the plate and think he'll be a big leaguer if they can make him just a serviceable hitter. As a bonus, his first pro manager at Salem-Keizer happened to be former big league catcher Steve Decker, who knew he was watching something special the first time Williams threw to second base. He has a slightly above-average arm but his lightning-quick release helps him get a pop time consistently below 1.95 seconds on throws to second base. He was able to control the running without pitchers even bothering with a slide-step, leading the Northwest League by throwing out 43 percent of opposing basestealers. Williams also has terrific footwork, blocks everything in the dirt and runs well for a catcher. He works hard on his line-drive swing, has a bit of gap power and does a decent job putting the ball in play. Williams had a tender elbow in instructional league, where he was limited to DH duty. Considering the dearth of catchers in the system, he'll move fast as long as his bat is playable, with a jump to high Class A likely for 2008.

Year	Club (League)	Class	AVG	G	AB	R	H	2B	3B	HR	RBI	BB	SO	SB	OBP	SLG
2007	Salem-Keizer (NWL)	A	.231	42	130	20	30	3	0	5	20	16	27	0	.338	.369
MINOR LEAGUE TOTALS			.231	42	130	20	30	3	0	5	20	16	27	0	.338	.369

19 WILBER BUCARDO, RHP

Born: Nov. 20, 1987. **B-T:** R-R. **Ht.:** 6-2. **Wt.:** 175. **Signed:** Nicaragua, 2005. **Signed by:** Rick Ragazzo.

Bucardo was the best pitcher on the Giants' Rookie-level Dominican Summer League club for two seasons, and his success translated to the Arizona League last year. The native Nicaraguan throws a low-90s fastball with heavy sink, giving up just one home run in 60 innings and posting a 3.14 groundout/flyout ratio. Bucardo also has a promising slider and is just beginning to throw a changeup, which he'll need against lefthanders. He pounds the strike zone and had enough polish to earn a late callup to Salem-Keizer. But Bucardo might have made his biggest contribution when he helped convince his younger brother Jorge to spurn a larger offer from the Yankees and sign with the Giants. Jorge Bucardo, who went 7-2, 1.35 in the DSL as a 17-year-old, has a similar build and repertoire as Wilber but is further along at a younger age and will be a player to watch when he makes his U.S. debut. Wilber should make his full-season debut in low Class A this year.

Year	Club (League)	Class	W	L	ERA	G	GS	CG	SV	IP	H	R	ER	HR	BB	SO	AVG
2005	Giants (DSL)	R	5	2	2.72	13	11	0	0	56	54	23	17	2	7	28	.239
2006	Giants (DSL)	R	3	2	1.82	27	0	0	12	34	27	13	7	1	11	31	.213
2007	Giants (AZL)	R	6	2	1.94	11	11	0	0	60	46	16	13	1	10	34	.213
	Salem-Keizer (NWL)	A	1	0	3.60	1	1	0	0	5	7	3	2	0	1	3	.292
MINOR LEAGUE TOTALS			15	6	2.25	52	23	0	12	156	134	55	39	4	29	96	.226

20 ERICK THREETS, LHP

Born: Nov. 4, 1981. **B-T:** L-L. **Ht.:** 6-5. **Wt.:** 240. **Drafted:** Modesto (Calif.) JC, 2000 (7th round). **Signed by:** Matt Nerland.

Threets finally climbed the mountain in 2007, earning a September callup after pitching effectively out of the Triple-A bullpen for a second consecutive season. He sat and waited nearly two weeks before making his major league debut, and his nerves probably contributed to a 19.29 ERA over three appearances with the Giants. But his promotion was a success story nonetheless, considering his colorful seven-year ride through the minors. Threets once was clocked at 104 mph, and while he jokes that "those days are long gone," there are plenty of major league lefthanders who would kill for his 95-mph fastball. Shoulder and back injuries derailed Threets in the past, but he finally got enough consistent mound time to address his once-considerable command issues. He still doesn't throw enough strikes, but he pitched effectively and showed improved command in the Mexican Pacific League this winter. While learning to pitch without his old velocity, he has gained a better feel for his cutter, and he also flashes a plus changeup. If Threets has a consistent spring, he'll be a candidate for the major league bullpen.

Year	Club (League)	Class	W	L	ERA	G	GS	CG	SV	IP	H	R	ER	HR	BB	SO	AVG
2001	San Jose (Cal)	A	0	10	4.25	14	14	0	0	59	49	34	28	2	40	60	.224
	Hagerstown (SAL)	A	2	0	0.75	12	0	0	1	24	13	3	2	1	9	32	.155
2002	San Jose (Cal)	A	0	1	6.67	26	0	0	0	28	23	24	21	2	28	43	.225
2003	Norwich (EL)	AA	0	0	15.88	11	0	0	0	11	15	20	20	1	21	16	.306
	Hagerstown (SAL)	A	2	3	3.26	22	0	0	0	49	26	20	18	2	42	47	.159
2005	Norwich (EL)	AA	1	2	5.06	30	0	0	2	42	43	28	24	2	31	35	.259

2006	Fresno (PCL)	AAA	2	1	2.87	49	0	0	0	62	51	26	20	4	44	51	.223
2007	Fresno (PCL)	AAA	3	1	3.46	40	3	0	1	54	46	26	21	4	35	40	.235
	San Francisco (NL)	MLB	0	0	19.29	3	0	0	0	2	5	5	5	0	3	1	.417
MINOR LEAGUE TOTALS			10	18	4.17	204	17	0	4	332	266	181	154	18	250	324	.220
MAJOR LEAGUE TOTALS			0	0	19.29	3	0	0	0	2	5	5	5	0	3	1	.417

21 BEN SNYDER, LHP

Born: July 20, 1985. **B-T:** L-L. **Ht.:** 6-2. **Wt.:** 205. **Drafted:** Ball State, 2006 (4th round). **Signed by:** Steve Arnieri.

As a pitcher with collegiate experience who knows how to change speeds, Snyder was expected to do well in low Class A. He didn't disappoint, leading San Francisco farmhands with 16 victories and becoming a key figure in the minor leagues' most dominant rotation. In fact, Snyder was the only member of Augusta's starting five who wasn't selected to the South Atlantic League all-star game—despite ranking fourth in the league with 75 strikeouts and sixth with a 2.15 ERA at the break. Snyder, whose older brother Brad preceded him at Ball State and is an outfielder in the Indians organization, is a true starting pitching prospect with a fastball, curve, changeup and slider. He can hit 90 mph but usually pitches in the upper 80s and isn't afraid to throw inside to lefthanders, whom he limited to a .180 average last season. One Giants coach said Snyder is ahead of where Noah Lowry was in his first pro season. Snyder's changeup might not be as good as Lowry's, but it has potential to be a plus pitch. Snyder reported to Hawaii Winter Baseball and got pounded for a 9.39 ERA, mostly because of fatigue. He's a strong athlete who fields his position well. Because he repeats his delivery well and throws strikes, Snyder could move through the system quickly. He'll open in high Class A this year.

Year	Club (League)	Class	W	L	ERA	G	GS	CG	SV	IP	H	R	ER	HR	BB	SO	AVG
2006	Salem-Keizer (NWL)	A	4	1	3.66	15	12	0	0	66	60	30	27	6	17	58	.242
2007	Augusta (SAL)	A	16	5	2.09	28	25	0	1	151	128	49	35	12	32	145	.225
MINOR LEAGUE TOTALS			20	6	2.57	43	37	0	1	217	188	79	62	18	49	203	.230

22 PAT MISCH, LHP

Born: Aug. 18, 1981. **B-T:** R-L. **Ht.:** 6-2. **Wt.:** 170. **Drafted:** Western Michigan, 2003 (7th round). **Signed by:** Steve Arnieri.

No matter when he's handed the ball, Misch competes and throws strikes. While he'll never intimidate out of the bullpen with his mid-80s fastball and mild-mannered appearance, he was much appreciated by Giants manager Bruce Bochy as other pitchers labored in deep counts or issued walks. Misch became more than just a September callup last season, and made himself the answer to a trivia question when he started the Aug. 4 game at San Diego in which Barry Bonds hit his 755th career home run to tie Hank Aaron. Misch should have earned his first major league victory in that game—he struck out eight and allowed two runs over five innings—but the bullpen blew his decision. His best pitches are a slow curveball and an above-average changeup, both of which he commands and will throw in any count. While Misch's big league ceiling appears limited, he has a few things going for him: He's durable, versatile and athletic. He originally committed to play soccer at Miami (Ohio) before the school dropped the sport. Misch's development of a cut fastball has helped him combat righthanders to the point that he could be a candidate to start again, though he fared poorly in that role in the big leagues, going 0-2, 6.41 in four outings. He has an excellent chance of opening the season as a long man in the San Francisco bullpen.

Year	Club (League)	Class	W	L	ERA	G	GS	CG	SV	IP	H	R	ER	HR	BB	SO	AVG
2003	Salem-Keizer (NWL)	A	7	5	2.18	14	14	0	0	86	78	33	21	3	20	61	.247
2004	Norwich (EL)	AA	7	6	3.06	26	26	4	0	159	138	61	54	13	35	123	.243
2005	Fresno (PCL)	AAA	3	9	6.35	19	19	1	0	102	135	80	72	18	40	69	.325
	Norwich (EL)	AA	4	2	3.52	9	9	1	0	61	63	25	24	7	7	43	.270
2006	Connecticut (EL)	AA	5	4	2.26	18	17	0	0	103	95	32	26	7	24	79	.247
	Fresno (PCL)	AAA	4	2	4.02	10	10	1	0	65	74	32	29	7	11	57	.287
	San Francisco (NL)	MLB	0	0	0.00	1	0	0	0	1	2	0	0	0	0	1	.400
2007	Fresno (PCL)	AAA	2	5	2.30	34	3	0	1	66	54	24	17	4	19	74	.227
	San Francisco (NL)	MLB	0	4	4.24	18	4	0	0	40	47	21	19	3	12	26	.296
MINOR LEAGUE TOTALS			32	33	3.39	130	98	7	1	644	637	287	243	59	156	506	.264
MAJOR LEAGUE TOTALS			0	4	4.14	19	4	0	0	41	49	21	19	3	12	27	.299

23 KELVIN PICHARDO, RHP

Born: Oct. 13, 1985. **B-T:** R-R. **Ht.:** 6-0. **Wt.:** 160. **Signed:** Dominican Republic, 2003. **Signed by:** Sal Agostinelli (Phillies).

The Giants can find power arms anywhere—high schools, colleges, internationally, position players they convert, small colleges, and, yes, in trades. They obtained Pichardo from the Phillies in an August 2005 deal for Michael Tucker and toyed with Pichardo in a starter's role in 2006. He battled arm issues that season and was moved to the bullpen full-time last year. As a reliever, he stayed healthy while showing significant improvement and good durability. Pichardo flashes three quality pitches, the best of which is a fastball that at times sits at 94-96 mph with good life. His delivery requires lots of effort and he tends to overthrow, with his command suffering as a result. When he throws strikes and gets ahead of hitters, though, he can finish them off with his power breaking ball that's a cross between a curveball and slider. Double-A hitters didn't chase the pitch as frequently when it was out of the zone. He has flashed a decent changeup with good arm speed as well. The Giants protected Pichardo on their 40-man roster in the offseason, and with a strong start at Triple-A, he'll be on the verge of making his big league debut at age 22.

Year	Club (League)	Class	W	L	ERA	G	GS	CG	SV	IP	H	R	ER	HR	BB	SO	AVG
2004	Phillies (GCL)	R	5	5	2.79	12	11	0	0	58	41	21	18	5	15	62	.202
2005	Phillies (GCL)	R	3	2	4.17	10	9	0	0	54	59	28	25	4	3	37	.273
2006	Salem-Keizer (NWL)	A	2	0	4.60	6	0	0	1	15	17	10	8	2	4	24	.266
	Augusta (SAL)	A	2	4	3.19	12	5	0	0	36	31	15	13	1	17	35	.226
2007	San Jose (Cal)	A	2	3	3.09	29	0	0	3	46	37	24	16	2	17	71	.218
	Connecticut (EL)	AA	2	2	3.86	17	0	0	2	21	14	9	9	2	16	16	.194
MINOR LEAGUE TOTALS			16	16	3.45	86	25	0	6	232	199	107	89	16	72	245	.231

24 MERKIN VALDEZ, RHP

Born: Nov. 10, 1981. **B-T:** R-R. **Ht.:** 6-3. **Wt.:** 220. **Signed:** Dominican Republic, 1999. **Signed by:** Felix Francisco (Braves).

There was a time the Giants envisioned a rotation anchored by Valdez (acquired from the Braves in a December 2002 trade for Russ Ortiz) as the ace with Matt Cain as a solid No. 2 starter. When those plans didn't quite materialize, San Francisco watched Valdez blow his 99-mph fastball past hitters in spring training and thought he'd become a lethal force in the late innings. But he couldn't keep his fastball down in the zone, had trouble developing an offspeed pitch and was dispatched to the bullpen early in a disastrous 2006 season. He might have been hurt all year, as his season ended when he grabbed his arm in the third inning of a late-August start. On the day he was injured, club officials said Valdez was throwing with the best combination of command and velocity that they had seen in two years. He had Tommy John surgery, missed all of the 2007 season and returned to the mound in short stints for Escogido in the Dominican Winter League. It speaks to Valdez' talent that he remains one of the most prized arms in the system. His health will determine where he starts 2008, though he's out of options and San Francisco will have to sneak him through waivers if he doesn't make the 25-man roster.

Year	Club (League)	Class	W	L	ERA	G	GS	CG	SV	IP	H	R	ER	HR	BB	SO	AVG
2000	Braves (DSL)	R	1	5	1.57	14	7	0	0	57	52	27	10	2	14	32	.234
2001	Braves 2 (DSL)	R	6	7	2.93	15	14	1	0	92	93	41	30	0	18	48	.258
2002	Braves (GCL)	R	7	3	1.98	12	8	1	0	68	47	18	15	0	12	76	.193
2003	Hagerstown (SAL)	A	9	5	2.25	26	26	2	0	156	119	42	39	11	49	166	.213
2004	Fresno (PCL)	AAA	0	0	7.20	1	1	0	0	5	6	4	4	0	4	5	.316
	San Jose (Cal)	A	3	1	2.52	7	7	0	0	35	30	12	10	4	5	44	.219
	San Francisco (NL)	MLB	0	0	27.00	2	0	0	0	1	4	5	5	1	3	2	.444
	Norwich (EL)	AA	1	4	4.32	10	7	0	1	41	35	21	20	3	15	31	.229
2005	Norwich (EL)	AA	5	6	3.53	24	19	1	0	107	99	48	42	7	45	96	.252
2006	Fresno (PCL)	AAA	0	4	5.80	46	3	0	5	49	52	42	32	6	39	48	.268
2007	Did Not Play—Injured																
MINOR LEAGUE TOTALS			32	35	2.97	155	92	5	6	612	533	255	202	33	201	546	.234
MAJOR LEAGUE TOTALS			0	0	27.00	2	0	0	0	1	4	5	5	1	3	2	.444

25 BRETT PILL, 1B

Born: Sept. 9, 1984. **B-T:** R-R. **Ht.:** 6-4. **Wt.:** 200. **Drafted:** Cal State Fullerton, 2006 (7th round). **Signed by:** Ray Krawczyk.

A former Cal State Fullerton standout whose pinch-hit triple ignited the winning rally in the 2004 College World Series clincher against Texas, Pill made major strides in his first full pro season to supplant Travis Ishikawa as the most promising first base prospect in the system. While Ishikawa regressed at the plate, crashing from the big leagues all the way back to high Class A, Pill racked up 10 homers and a South Atlantic League-leading 47 doubles while playing in a pitcher's park one level lower. The Giants believe he has serious power potential and put him on a strength program to add muscle to his long, lean frame. Most of his homers came from left-center to the left-field pole, but with added strength he could put many of those doubles over the wall. His long arms generate leverage in his swing, and he also makes surprisingly consistent contact for a big man. Coaches consider Pill the best defensive first baseman in the system, quite a statement considering Ishikawa's solid glove. Pill has outstanding hands, good instincts and average speed. Playing in the more hitter-friendly high Class A California League should boost his numbers this year.

SAN FRANCISCO GIANTS

Year	Club (League)	Class	AVG	G	AB	R	H	2B	3B	HR	RBI	BB	SO	SB	OBP	SLG
2006	Salem-Keizer (NWL)	A	.220	60	223	37	49	16	0	5	35	22	39	3	.296	.359
2007	Augusta (SAL)	A	.269	137	536	72	144	47	1	10	91	38	81	4	.321	.416
MINOR LEAGUE TOTALS			.254	197	759	109	193	63	1	15	126	60	120	7	.314	.399

26 BRIAN ANDERSON, RHP

Born: May 25, 1983. **B-T:** R-R. **Ht.:** 6-3. **Wt.:** 210. **Drafted:** Long Beach State, 2005 (14th round). **Signed by:** Ray Krawczyk.

Anderson doesn't have eye-popping stuff, but he competes so well and has such terrific poise that he seems destined to make a contribution in the San Francisco bullpen, perhaps in the near future. A year after topping the minor leagues and setting a California League record with 37 saves, he reported to Double-A and recorded 29 saves to tie for the Eastern League lead. As a pro, he has 85 saves in just 128 appearances. Anderson commands a fastball in the upper 80s, can cut it to get in on lefthanders and paints corners, often recording three outs on 10 pitches or less. Because of his efficiency and his size, he's able to pitch on multiple days without any durability issues. He's not afraid of pitching to contact. Anderson also throws a slider, and he could use a changeup or splitter to better combat lefthanders, who hit .293 against him in 2007. The Giants sent Anderson to the Arizona Fall League after the season, and he didn't allow an earned run and walked just one batter in 12 innings. He's a good bet to open the season closing games in Triple-A, with a shot to move up whenever San Francisco needs him.

Year	Club (League)	Class	W	L	ERA	G	GS	CG	SV	IP	H	R	ER	HR	BB	SO	AVG
2005	Salem-Keizer (NWL)	A	3	1	1.95	27	0	0	19	27	16	6	6	2	3	42	.162
2006	San Jose (Cal)	A	1	1	1.86	54	0	0	37	67	44	14	14	5	17	85	.183
2007	Connecticut (EL)	AA	1	5	3.93	47	0	0	29	50	55	27	22	4	20	46	.275
MINOR LEAGUE TOTALS			5	7	2.59	128	0	0	85	145	115	47	42	11	40	173	.213

27 TRAVIS DENKER, 2B

Born: Aug. 5, 1985. **B-T:** R-R. **Ht.:** 5-9. **Wt.:** 170. **Drafted:** HS—Brea, Calif., 2003 (21st round). **Signed by:** Scott Groot (Dodgers).

The Giants acquired Denker as the player to be named in the trade that sent pinch-hitter Mark Sweeney to the Dodgers in August. Denker made an immediate impression with his new club, hitting a grand slam and a two-run double in his first game for San Jose. He remained a major force as San Jose scrapped to the California League title, hitting .480 in the playoffs despite a strained quad. Denker is a fireplug who generates plenty of power despite his size. However, as he has faced better pitching moving up the minor league ladder, his homer totals have declined from 23 in 2005 to 16 in 2006 to 11 last year. Denker can hit in any count and has drawn 272 walks against 318 strikeouts over his minor league career—numbers not often seen among San Francisco's position prospects. He turns the double play well enough and has average range and arm strength but stiff infield actions. His speed is average at best. The Dodgers had planned to send Denker to the Arizona Fall League, and the Giants might have done the same but already had their rosters set when the trade went down in August. His value lies in his bat and his tenacity, and he'll probably jump all the way to Triple-A this season.

Year	Club (League)	Class	AVG	G	AB	R	H	2B	3B	HR	RBI	BB	SO	SB	OBP	SLG
2003	Dodgers (GCL)	R	.270	39	122	17	33	8	1	3	13	20	16	2	.382	.426
	South Georgia (SAL)	A	.227	8	22	2	5	2	0	1	2	6	0	.292	.318
2004	Ogden (Pio)	R	.311	57	225	44	70	17	1	12	43	24	52	2	.372	.556
2005	Columbus (SAL)	A	.310	101	358	65	111	23	1	21	68	67	78	2	.417	.556
	Vero Beach (FSL)	A	.185	31	108	14	20	3	0	2	9	15	26	1	.296	.269
2006	Vero Beach (FSL)	A	.220	54	191	24	42	6	0	5	25	24	36	0	.309	.330
	Columbus (SAL)	A	.268	75	250	47	67	11	1	11	45	65	37	2	.420	.452
2007	Inland Empire (Cal)	A	.294	111	402	65	118	27	3	10	57	48	65	8	.369	.450
	San Jose (Cal)	A	.400	7	25	7	10	3	0	1	9	7	2	1	.531	.640
MINOR LEAGUE TOTALS			.280	483	1703	285	476	100	7	65	270	272	318	18	.379	.461

28 SERGIO ROMO, RHP

Born: March 4, 1983. **B-T:** R-R. **Ht.:** 5-11. **Wt.:** 185. **Drafted:** Mesa State (Colo.), 2005 (28th round). **Signed by:** Joe Strain.

Romo spent two years at Arizona Western JC, then went 24-4 in two NCAA Division II seasons, one at North Alabama and one at Mesa State. He has put up eye-popping numbers as a pro as well, and after starting part-time in 2006, he moved full-time to the bullpen last season and showed excellent control and a durable arm. Romo led all full-season relievers by striking out 14.4 batters per nine innings despite a lack of true power stuff. Instead, he relies on a tremendous feel for pitching, using different angles and a five-pitch arsenal to baffle batters. His fastball has reached 93 mph and sits at 88-90 mph regardless of his arm slot, and he spots it with confidence and plenty of guts. He'll show hitters both a curveball and slider, and mix speeds with a changeup and splitter. Romo kept boosting his profile with another fearless performance in the Arizona Fall League, where he allowed just one run in 14 innings. His feel for changing speeds and ability to throw strikes with any pitch in any count keeps hitters off balance. He has been extremely effective against lefthanders, who hit .153 with 45 strikeouts in 111 at-bats against him last year (including the AFL). Short and far from imposing on the mound, Romo gives up a lot of fly balls, and his fringe-average fastball and trickery may not work against advanced hitters on a consistent basis. He'll report to Connecticut to see if he passes the Double-A test.

Year	Club (League)	Class	W	L	ERA	G	GS	CG	SV	IP	H	R	ER	HR	BB	SO	AVG
2005	Salem-Keizer (NWL)	A	7	1	2.75	15	14	0	0	68	70	24	21	7	9	65	.261
2006	Augusta (SAL)	A	10	2	2.53	31	10	0	4	103	78	33	29	9	19	95	.208
2007	San Jose (Cal)	A	6	2	1.36	41	0	0	9	66	35	12	10	4	15	106	.155
MINOR LEAGUE TOTALS			23	5	2.27	87	24	0	13	238	183	69	60	20	43	266	.211

29 BRIAN HORWITZ, OF

Born: Nov. 7, 1982. **B-T:** R-R. **Ht.:** 6-1. **Wt.:** 180. **Signed:** NDFA/California, 2004. **Signed by:** Matt Nerland.

Scouts never will rave about Horwitz, but all he does is spray hits wherever he plays. He won batting titles in his first two pro seasons and didn't slow down once he landed in Triple-A last year, hitting .326 after a midseason promotion. Every manager for whom he has played has become his biggest fan. Horwitz has a great two-strike approach, loves the opposite field and doesn't strike out despite a swing that can get a bit long and choppy. He has little power to speak of and is better suited defensively for left field, so he doesn't fit the profile of a starting big leaguer. His arm is decent and his speed is below-average, so basically all he provides is a high batting average. But it's hard to find a more dedicated worker than Horwitz, who made the most of his invitation to big league camp last spring. He usually arrived before 7 a.m. for early hitting, even beating the coaches to the cage. He'll probably return to Triple-A this year.

Year	Club (League)	Class	AVG	G	AB	R	H	2B	3B	HR	RBI	BB	SO	SB	OBP	SLG
2004	Salem-Keizer (NWL)	A	.347	71	268	41	93	24	1	2	44	21	34	3	.407	.466
2005	Augusta (SAL)	A	.349	123	470	77	164	38	4	2	88	50	39	6	.415	.460
2006	San Jose (Cal)	A	.324	56	207	26	67	11	2	2	31	30	23	0	.414	.425
	Connecticut (EL)	AA	.286	78	269	23	77	9	1	2	29	31	35	3	.365	.349
	Fresno (PCL)	AAA	.281	5	16	1	2	1	0	0	1	2	2	0	.222	.188
2007	Connecticut (EL)	AA	.309	35	136	17	42	5	0	2	10	13	10	2	.371	.390
	Fresno (PCL)	AAA	.326	84	264	32	86	21	2	1	21	21	22	2	.383	.432
MINOR LEAGUE TOTALS			.326	452	1630	217	531	109	10	11	224	168	165	16	.395	.425

30 BEN COPELAND, OF

Born: Dec. 17, 1983. **B-T:** L-L. **Ht.:** 6-1. **Wt.:** 195. **Drafted:** Pittsburgh, 2005 (4th round). **Signed by:** Sean O'Connor.

The Giants gave up their first three picks in the 2005 draft for signing free agents Armando Benitez, Mike Matheny and Omar Vizquel. That was the best draft of the decade, and Copeland was San Francisco's first pick—which came in the fourth round. While he doesn't compare to the outfielders drafted early that year—a list that includes No. 1 overall pick Justin Upton, 2007 Minor League Player of the Year Jay Bruce, World Series hero Jacoby Ellsbury and other potential studs such as Cameron Maybin and Colby Rasmus— Copeland still should be able to help San Francisco down the line. He profiles best as a fourth outfielder, as he has no true standout tool. His biggest weakness is power, as his line-drive stroke isn't conducive to hitting homers. He has a quick bat and is a tick above-average as a runner, though he's just a fair baserunner. Copeland also ranks as perhaps the Giants' most patient minor league hitter. After hitting better against lefties than righties in 2006, he struggled significantly against them in 2007, posting a .433 OPS against southpaws (compared to .903 against righties). While he can play center field, Copeland fits better in left, and his fringy throwing arm would be exposed in right. He's ready to jump to Double-A this year.

Year	Club (League)	Class	AVG	G	AB	R	H	2B	3B	HR	RBI	BB	SO	SB	OBP	SLG
2005	Giants (AZL)	R	.333	18	60	16	20	4	2	1	14	5	14	2	.388	.517
	Salem-Keizer (NWL)	A	.306	29	121	25	37	5	4	4	23	11	25	2	.364	.512
2006	Augusta (SAL)	A	.281	135	527	90	148	29	12	5	71	73	90	30	.368	.410
2007	San Jose (Cal)	A	.280	106	404	68	113	22	6	7	50	70	77	14	.387	.416
MINOR LEAGUE TOTALS			.286	288	1112	199	318	60	24	17	158	159	206	48	.376	.429

Seattle Mariners

BY MATT EDDY

To say the Mariners had a season of ups and downs would be an understatement.

They won 88 games, fifth-most in the American League, and held the lead for the wild-card berth deep into the season. Yet they were outscored by 19 runs on the year, and they lost 13 of 14 games to close August and open September, ruining their playoff chances.

Seattle had an eight-game winning streak earlier in the year—during which manager Mike Hargrove resigned. He was replaced by bench coach John McLaren, who guided the team as high as 20 games over .500 before its collapse.

At least the season was a step in the right direction after the franchise's precipitous decline in the last few seasons. The Mariners haven't made the playoffs since 2001 and averaged just 70 wins a year from 2004-06—their worst three-year stretch since the dark days of the 1980s.

The team's success in 2007 was built around three players: Ichiro Suzuki, who led the AL in hits for the fourth time and kept his Gold Glove and All-Star Game streaks alive at seven years; Felix Hernandez, who went 14-7, 3.92 and took another step toward superstardom at age 21; and J.J. Putz, who saved 40 games with a 1.38 ERA.

The farm system helped the bullpen significantly. Brandon Morrow, the fifth overall pick in the 2006 draft, stuck in Seattle all year and posted 18 holds. Sean Green, 28 and in his first full big league season, contributed 13. Two other rookies, Eric O'Flaherty and Ryan Rowland-Smith, gave Seattle a pair of dependable lefty options.

One year after landing Morrow, Chris Tillman and Tony Butler in the draft, the Mariners again went for pure arm strength, taking Canadian righthander Phillippe Aumont with the 11th overall pick.

Seattle also continued to show a pronounced open-mindedness in all areas of player development, drafting players equally from the college and high school ranks and committing fully to the international market. Aside from the United States, Mariners prospects hail from Australia, Canada, Curacao, the Dominican Republic, Italy, the Netherlands, Nicaragua, Taiwan and Venezuela.

The Mariners invested $2.9 million—a sum surpassed only by the Yankees—on 10 players during the international signing period. They landed Dominican shortstop Jharmidy DeJesus ($1 million), Venezuelan shortstop Gabriel Noriega ($800,000)

Brandon Morrow was a fixture in Seattle's bullpen just a year after going fifth overall

BILL MITCHELL

TOP 30 PROSPECTS

1. Jeff Clement, c	16. Jharmidy DeJesus, ss
2. Phillippe Aumont, rhp	17. Rob Johnson, c
3. Chris Tillman, rhp	18. Kam Mickolio, rhp
4. Carlos Triunfel, ss	19. Bryan LaHair, 1b
5. Wladimir Balentien, of	20. Yung-Chi Chen, 2b
6. Michael Saunders, of	21. Danny Carroll, of
7. Juan Ramirez, rhp	22. Edward Paredes, lhp
8. Mark Lowe, rhp	23. Mario Martinez, ss/3b
9. Ryan Rowland-Smith, lhp	24. Denny Almonte, of
10. Matt Tuiasosopo, 3b	25. Nolan Gallagher, rhp
11. Carlos Peguero, of	26. Justin Thomas, lhp
12. Tony Butler, lhp	27. Robert Rohrbaugh, lhp
13. Greg Halman, of	28. Nick Hill, lhp
14. Matt Mangini, 3b	29. Alex Liddi, 3b
15. Adam Moore, c	30. Anthony Varvaro, rhp

and Dominican outfielder Efrain Nunez ($450,000) for six-figure bonuses.

Seattle continued to aggressively push its prospects through the system, regardless of age. Their top five affiliates were younger than average for their leagues, in terms of both hitters and pitchers. Thus it shouldn't be surprising that none of those teams made the playoffs. In fact, not one finished with a winning record, though the Rookie-level Arizona League Mariners had the AZL's best record and won the league title.

General Manager: Bill Bavasi. **Farm Director:** Greg Hunter. **Scouting Director:** Bob Fontaine.

Class	Team	League	W	L	PCT	Finish*	Manager	Affiliated
Majors	Seattle	American	88	74	.543	5th (14)	Hargrove/McLaren	—
Triple-A	Tacoma Rainiers	Pacific Coast	68	76	.472	12th (16)	Darren Brown	1995
Double-A	West Tenn Diamond Jaxx	Southern	60	79	.432	9th (10)	Eddie Rodriguez	2007
High A	High Desert Mavericks	California	54	86	.386	10th (10)	Scott Steinmann	2007
Low A	Wisconsin Timber Rattlers	Midwest	53	85	.384	14th (14)	Jim Horner	1993
Short-season	Everett AquaSox	Northwest	35	41	.461	5th (8)	Mike Tosar	1995
Rookie	AZL Mariners	Arizona	37	19	.661	1st (9)^	Jose Moreno	2001

Overall 2007 Minor League Record   307   386   .443   28th

*Finish in overall standings (No. of teams in league) ^League champion

LAST YEAR'S TOP 30

Player, Pos.	Status
1. Adam Jones, of	Majors
2. Jeff Clement, c	No. 1
3. Brandon Morrow, rhp	Majors
4. Tony Butler, lhp	No. 12
5. Ryan Feierabend, lhp	Majors
6. Wladimir Balentien, of	No. 5
7. Mark Lowe, rhp	No. 8
8. Chris Tillman, rhp	No. 3
9. Yung-Chi Chen, 2b	No. 20
10. Eric O'Flaherty, lhp	Majors
11. Carlos Triunfel, ss	No. 4
12. Justin Thomas, lhp	No. 26
13. Jon Huber, rhp	Dropped out
14. Michael Wilson, of	Dropped out
15. Rob Johnson, c	No. 17
16. Bryan LaHair, 1b	No. 19
17. Matt Tuiasosopo, 3b/ss	No. 10
18. Stephen Kahn, rhp	Dropped out
19. Anthony Varvaro, rhp	No. 30
20. Luis Valbuena, 2b	Dropped out
21. Jose de la Cruz, rhp	Dropped out
22. Travis Blackley, lhp	(Phillies)
23. Robert Rohrbaugh, lhp	No. 27
24. Michael Saunders, of	No. 6
25. Greg Halman, of	No. 13
26. Alex Liddi, 3b	No. 29
27. Carlos Peguero, of	No. 11
28. Cesar Jimenez, lhp	Dropped out
29. Oswaldo Navarro, ss	Dropped out
30. Michael Garciaparra, ss	(Phillies)

BEST TOOLS

Best Hitter for Average	Carlos Triunfel
Best Power Hitter	Jeff Clement
Best Strike-Zone Discipline	Jeff Clement
Fastest Baserunner	Danny Carroll
Best Athlete	Greg Halman
Best Fastball	Phillippe Aumont
Best Curveball	Chris Tillman
Best Slider	Mark Lowe
Best Changeup	Cesar Jimenez
Best Control	Robert Rohrbaugh
Best Defensive Catcher	Rob Johnson
Best Defensive Infielder	Juan Diaz
Best Infield Arm	Carlos Triunfel
Best Defensive Outfielder	Michael Saunders
Best Outfield Arm	Wladimir Balentien

PROJECTED 2011 LINEUP

Catcher	Kenji Johjima
First Base	Jeff Clement
Second Base	Carlos Triunfel
Third Base	Adrian Beltre
Shortstop	Yuniesky Betancourt
Left Field	Michael Saunders
Center Field	Ichiro Suzuki
Right Field	Adam Jones
Designated Hitter	Wladimir Balentien
No. 1 Starter	Felix Hernandez
No. 2 Starter	Brandon Morrow
No. 3 Starter	Phillippe Aumont
No. 4 Starter	Chris Tillman
No. 5 Starter	Juan Ramirez
Closer	J.J. Putz

TOP PROSPECTS OF THE DECADE

Year	Player, Pos.	2007 Org.
1998	Ryan Anderson, lhp	Out of baseball
1999	Ryan Anderson, lhp	Out of baseball
2000	Ryan Anderson, lhp	Out of baseball
2001	Ryan Anderson, lhp	Out of baseball
2002	Ryan Anderson, lhp	Out of baseball
2003	Rafael Soriano, rhp	Braves
2004	Felix Hernandez, rhp	Mariners
2005	Felix Hernandez, rhp	Mariners
2006	Jeff Clement, c	Mariners
2007	Adam Jones, of	Mariners

TOP DRAFT PICKS OF THE DECADE

Year	Player, Pos.	2007 Org.
1998	Matt Thornton, lhp	White Sox
1999	Ryan Christianson, c	Cardinals
2000	Sam Hayes, lhp (4th)	Out of baseball
2001	Michael Garciaparra, ss (1st supp.)	Phillies
2002	*John Mayberry Jr., of	Rangers
2003	Adam Jones, ss/rhp (1st supp.)	Mariners
2004	Matt Tuiasosopo, ss (3rd)	Mariners
2005	Jeff Clement, c	Mariners
2006	Brandon Morrow, rhp	Mariners
2007	Phillippe Aumont, rhp	Mariners

*Did not sign.

LARGEST BONUSES IN CLUB HISTORY

Ichiro Suzuki, 2000	$5,000,000
Jefff Clement, 2005	$3,400,000
Brandon Morrow, 2006	$2,450,000
Matt Tuiasosopo, 2004	$2,290,000
Ryan Anderson, 1997	$2,175,000

SEATTLE MARINERS

Top 2008 Rookie: Jeff Clement, c. His bat is ready, though big league playing time could be hard to come by unless he gets time at first base and DH.

Breakout Prospect: Carlos Peguero, of. His big lefty power should play nicely in the hitter-friendly California League.

Sleeper: Kalian Sams, of. A product of the Netherlands, like Greg Halman, he has above-average power and runs and defends well.

SOURCE OF TOP 30 TALENT			
Homegrown	30	Acquired	0
College	11	Trades	0
Junior college	0	Rule 5 draft	0
High school	6	Independent leagues	0
Draft-and-follow	2	Free agents/waivers	0
Nondrafted free agents	0		
International	11		

Numbers in parentheses indicate prospect rankings.

LF
Michael Wilson
Kuo-Hui Lo

CF
Michael Saunders (6)
Greg Halman (13)
Danny Carroll (21)
Denny Almonte (24)
James McOwen

RF
Wladimir Balentien (5)
Carlos Peguero (11)
Kalian Sams
Efrain Nunez

3B
Matt Tuiasosopo (10)
Matt Mangini (14)
Jharmidy DeJesus (16)
Mario Martinez (23)
Alex Liddi (29)

SS
Juan Diaz
Oswaldo Navarro
Gabriel Noriega

2B
Carlos Triunfel (4)
Yung-Chi Chen (20)
Luis Valbuena
Tug Hulett

1B
Bryan LaHair (19)
Joe Dunigan

C
Jeff Clement (1)
Adam Moore (15)
Rob Johnson (17)
Jeff Dunbar

RHP

Starters	Relievers
Phillippe Aumont (2)	Mark Lowe (8)
Chris Tillman (3)	Kam Mickolio (18)
Juan Ramirez (7)	Joe Woerman
Nolan Gallagher (25)	Aaron Brown
Anthony Varvaro (30)	Brodie Downs
Ricky Orta	Jon Huber
Nathan Adcock	Stephen Kahn
Marwin Vega	Jose de la Cruz
Jake Wild	Justin Souzo
	Austin Bibens-Dirkx
	Andrew Barb

LHP

Starters	Relievers
Ryan Rowland-Smith (9)	Cesar Jimenez
Tony Butler (12)	Fabian Williamson
Edward Paredes (22)	
Justin Thomas (26)	
Robert Rohrbaugh (27)	
Nick Hill (28)	
Donnie Hume	

2007

Best Pro Debut: LHP Nick Hill (7), Army's all-time wins leader, dominated the short-season Northwest League, posting a 0.51 ERA and 45 strikeouts in 35 innings for Everett. Hill set up closer RHP Aaron Brown (9), who went 2-1, 1.95 with six saves and a 49-15 K-BB ratio in 37 innings. RHP Jake Wild (26) struck out 76 in 56 innings in the Rookie-level Arizona League, including 14 in the championship game.

Best Athlete: OF Denny Almonte (2) had a rough debut, hitting .145/.226/.197. The Mariners will be patient because he has a wiry, athletic body, with raw power, above-average speed and plus range in center field.

Best Pure Hitter: 3B Matt Mangini (1s) finished the year in high Class A because of his polished approach and line-drive swing. He won the Cape Cod League batting title in 2006.

Best Power Hitter: OF Joe Dunigan (5) has above-average bat speed and good size, though he remains raw after three years at Oklahoma.

Fastest Runner: Almonte and OFs Danny Carroll (3) and James McOwen (6) are all above-average runners under way.

Best Defensive Player: Almonte has elicited comparisons to Devon White for his easy range and closing ability in center field. C Jeff Dunbar (11) has excellent athleticism for the position, and 70 arm strength.

Best Fastball: RHP Phillippe Aumont (1) touches 98 mph and lives at 89-93 mph with heavy sink at his best.

Best Secondary Pitch: Aumont's slider can be hard (low 80s) and dirty at times, but it's inconsistent. LHPs Hill and Donnie Hume (8) have above-average changeups.

Most Intriguing Background: Hill is the highest-drafted Army player ever. RHP Brodie Downs (23) was the oldest player drafted at 27 (he's now 28). He became a land surveyor after graduating from high school in 1997, but was seen by Rangers scout Butch Metzger playing for a Ceres (Calif.) adult recreational league team. Metzger told Downs he was throwing 94 mph, and Downs decided to give baseball a shot at Modesto (Calif.) Junior College, where he went 6-4, 2.55 with 101 strikeouts in 98 innings.

Closest To The Majors: Downs has reached Triple-A; only Nationals LHP Ross Detwiler advanced further from this year's draft. Mangini's bat should put him on the fast track.

Best Late-Round Pick: Downs and Wild. Wild commanded an 89-93 mph fastball in the AZL and has projection at 6-foot-5.

The One Who Got Away: RHP Cole Cook (36), at 6-foot-6 and already touching 90 mph, could be a high pick after three years at Pepperdine.

Assessment: The Mariners signed just eight position players, as opposed to 21 pitchers. Aumont hasn't made his debut but was a pleasant surprise at No. 11 overall. In an organization that likes to push prospects, Almonte and Aumont may have the most upside in the class but may need the most time.

2006   **BUDGET: $4.4 MILLION**

RHP Brandon Morrow (1) provided immediate bullpen help and now will try to become a starter. RHP Chris Tillman (2) and LHP Tony Butler (3) could join him in Seattle in a few years.

GRADE: B

2005   **BUDGET: $4.1 MILLION**

C Jeff Clement's (1) bat is ready for the big leagues, though the Mariners have to figure out how to get him in the lineup. Not having second- and third-round picks limited their ability to do much else in this draft.

GRADE: C+

2004   **BUDGET: $3.2 MILLION**

3B Matt Tuiasosopo's (3) career is on the upswing, though he's still far from justifying his $2.29 million bonus as Seattle's top pick. RHP Mark Lowe (5) was a revelation in 2006 before getting hurt, while OF Michael Saunders (11) made a breakthrough last season.

GRADE: C

2003   **BUDGET: $2.8 MILLION**

OF Adam Jones (1s) is an all-around talent who made a smooth transition from a shortstop and probably could have made it as a pitcher. LHPs Ryan Feierabend (3) and Eric O'Flaherty (6) went from high school to the Mariners in three years.

GRADE: B+

Draft analysis by John Manuel (2007) and Jim Callis (2003-06).
Numbers in parentheses indicate draft rounds. Budgets are
bonuses in first 10 rounds.

1

AMERICAN WEST LEAGUE

JEFF CLEMENT, C

Born: Aug. 21, 1983.
Ht.: 6-1. **Wt.:** 210.
Bats: L. **Throws:** R.
Drafted:
Southern California,
2005 (1st round).
Signed by:
Greg Whitworth.

Clement turned down the Twins as a 12th-round pick out of an Iowa high school in 2002, opting to attend Southern California instead. After the draft, Clement finished his prep career by breaking Drew Henson's national high school career home run record with 75. With the Trojans, he hit 46 home runs in three years, eight short of Mark McGwire's career mark, prompting the Mariners to take him with the third pick in the 2005 draft. Seattle signed him for $3.4 million, a club record for a drafted player. Clement's first full pro season, 2006, was interrupted for seven weeks when he needed operations to repair a torn meniscus in his left knee and remove a bone chip from his left elbow. Upon his return, the Mariners jumped Clement from Double-A San Antonio to Triple-A Tacoma, where he struggled to gain his footing. He caught his breath in 2007, turning in his best pro season, and clubbed two home runs 16 at-bats during his big league debut in September. Clement headed to the Arizona Fall League in October, his third winter ball stint in three years since signing, but missed the final two games after being sidelined with a sore left elbow that didn't require surgery.

Clement offers rare above-average lefthanded power from the catcher position. He stays inside the ball well and makes consistent, hard contact to all fields. Clement worked to slow the game down in 2007. Where previously he would look to pull everything, he now shows a mature approach, extending at-bats by working pitchers for his pitch or for walks. Clement gets such good backspin and carry on the ball that he can drive it out of any part of the park. A natural leader with work ethic to spare, he offers average arm strength to go with solid receiving, blocking and game-calling abilities behind the plate.

Clement has worked extensively with roving catching instructor Roger Hansen on getting his feet to work with his arm on throws. Hansen is convinced that Clement will catch in the big leagues because he's dedicated to putting in the necessary work to improve. Scouts outside the organization are less optimistic, though, believing Clement will always struggle to throw out runners because of below-average release times and accuracy. He has caught 29, 26 and 27 percent of basestealers in three pro seasons. Typical for a catcher, he's a below-average runner.

Despite running hot and cold in Triple-A and having to contend with a timeshare arrangement with fellow catching prospect Rob Johnson, Clement's bat is ready for the big leagues. But with 31-year-old Kenji Johjima entrenched as the Mariners' catcher—not to mention Johnson's plus defensive tools—Clement may have to work his way into the lineup at DH or by learning first base.

Year	Club (League)	Class	AVG	G	AB	R	H	2B	3B	HR	RBI	BB	SO	SB	OBP	SLG
2005	Everett (NWL)	A	.273	4	11	4	3	1	0	0	1	1	2	0	.400	.364
	Wisconsin (MWL)	A	.319	30	113	17	36	5	0	6	20	12	25	1	.386	.522
2006	San Antonio (TL)	AA	.288	15	59	7	17	6	1	2	10	7	8	0	.386	.525
	Tacoma (PCL)	AAA	.257	67	245	23	63	10	0	4	32	16	53	0	.321	.347
2007	Tacoma (PCL)	AAA	.275	125	455	76	125	35	3	20	80	61	88	0	.370	.497
	Seattle (AL)	MLB	.375	9	16	4	6	1	0	2	3	3	3	0	.474	.813
MINOR LEAGUE TOTALS			.276	241	883	127	244	57	4	32	143	97	176	1	.360	.459
MAJOR LEAGUE TOTALS			.375	9	16	4	6	1	0	2	3	3	3	0	.474	.813

2 PHILLIPPE AUMONT, RHP

BILL MITCHELL

Born: Jan. 7, 1989. **B-T:** R-R. **Ht.:** 6-7. **Wt.:** 230. **Drafted:** HS—Gatineau, Quebec, 2007 (1st round). **Signed by:** Wayne Norton.

The best Canadian prospect since Adam Loewen, Aumont caught the attention of scouting directors while pitching for traveling teams, primarily the Canadian national team, because his Quebec high school didn't offer baseball. He gained prominence in 2006 at a high school all-star game in Cape Cod and at the East Coast Showcase, after which he was viewed as a potential first-round pick. The Mariners made him the 11th overall choice in June and signed him for $1.9 million. Aumont, who is reluctant to discuss his parents or his past with the media, has lived with legal guardians since 2003. Because Aumont signed too late to pitch, the Mariners put him on a five-day rotation schedule in instructional league. He pitches at 92-94 mph with his plus-plus power sinker that bores in on righthanders and features the best movement in the system. He also throws a four-seam fastball that touches 98. The athletic 6-foot-7, 230-pounder carves an intimidating presence on the mound, and his low three-quarters arm slot gives batters an uncomfortable look. His hard slider has above-average potential at 80-82 mph. Though he offers plus arm strength, Aumont doesn't have the polish or experience of other first-round high school arms. In fact, he didn't start playing baseball until age 11 and didn't start pitching until 14. Though he throws a lot of strikes, he needs to fine-tune his command of the strike zone. Repeating his delivery and staying balanced would allow him to more consistently stay on top of his breaking ball. He doesn't have much of a changeup—he threw a splitter as an amateur—but he'll get plenty of practice seeing as Mariners farmhands are required to throw the pitch 10 percent of the time. Despite his inexperience, Aumont will move as quickly as his command allows. He profiles as a front-of-the-rotation starter because his ball is so lively and because he has such a knack for avoiding the barrel of the bat. He figures to begin his pro career with low Class A Wisconsin.

Year	Club (League)	Class	W	L	ERA	G	GS	CG	SV	IP	H	R	ER	HR	BB	SO	AVG
2007	Did Not Play—Signed Late																

3 CHRIS TILLMAN, RHP

DAVID STONER

Born: April 15, 1988. **B-T:** R-R. **Ht.:** 6-5. **Wt.:** 195. **Drafted:** HS—Fountain Valley, Calif., 2006 (2nd round). **Signed by:** Tim Reynolds.

An inconsistent senior season dropped Tillman into the second round of the 2006 draft, where the Mariners pounced, adding him to a haul that also included Brandon Morrow and Tony Butler. Seattle bumped the 19-year-old Tillman to high Class A High Desert after just eight low Class A starts. He struggled initially as he got used to more advanced California League competition and an unforgiving home park, but went 5-4, 4.75 with 89 strikeouts in 78 innings in the second half. The lanky Tillman still is growing into his 6-foot-5 frame, and the leverage in his clean delivery gives extra life to an above-average 91-94 mph four-seam fastball. He's aggressive with the pitch, throwing it to all four quadrants of the strike zone. Tillman throws a true 11-to-5 curveball with tight rotation and late break that functions as his strikeout pitch. He has a loose arm and could grow into more strength and velocity as he matures. He shows aptitude for a changeup, but it's still his third pitch. Tillman didn't live up to expectations as a senior, leading some scouts to question his mental toughness. While he's around the strike zone, he sometimes struggles to throw his curveball for strikes because of its big break. Like most young pitchers, he needs to tighten his command and improve his pitches sequences. Tillman learned a valuable lesson in the Cal League. Because the ball carries so well, the parks are so small and the ground so fast, he tried to avoid contact—and he paid for it. But after a few starts he realized that his stuff plays anywhere and he began to attack hitters. He has enough stuff to start in the middle of a big league rotation, or higher, as evidenced by the fact that he'll pitch in Double-A at age 20.

Year	Club (League)	Class	W	L	ERA	G	GS	CG	SV	IP	H	R	ER	HR	BB	SO	AVG
2006	Mariners (AZL)	R	2	0	0.82	5	0	0	1	11	9	4	1	0	5	16	.214
	Everett (NWL)	A	1	3	7.78	5	5	0	0	19	25	17	17	4	15	29	.325
2007	Wisconsin (MWL)	A	1	4	3.55	8	8	0	0	33	31	21	13	1	13	34	.238
	High Desert (Cal)	A	6	7	5.26	20	20	0	0	102	107	79	60	12	48	105	.266
MINOR LEAGUE TOTALS			10	14	4.92	38	33	0	1	166	172	121	91	17	81	184	.264

4 CARLOS TRIUNFEL, SS

Born: Feb. 27, 1990. **B-T:** R-R. **Ht.:** 5-11. **Wt.:** 175. **Signed:** Dominican Republic, 2006. **Signed by:** Patrick Guerrero/Franklin Tavares/Bob Engle.

BILL MITCHELL

Last year, we wrote that the Mariners couldn't wait to see what Triunfel would do in his debut. The results are in: He hit his way to high Class A at age 17. While other clubs offered him more money to sign as an amateur, he chose the Mariners because of his comfort with the organization. He got $1.3 million to sign, more than all but three 2006 Latin American free agents. Triunfel broke his right thumb in May and upon his return, the Mariners pushed the young shortstop up a level. Two things elevate Triunfel above most prospects his age—his hitting instincts and his makeup. He has the hand-eye coordination, contact ability and strength to sting the ball from gap to gap. He makes rapid adjustments to the way pitchers work him, marking him as an above-average hitter. Unlike most young players, Triunfel is unfazed by mistakes and has the utmost confidence in his abilities. He had one of the strongest throwing arms in the two leagues in which he played. The Mariners don't take for granted that Triunfel acclimated himself to 40-degree April weather in the low Class A Midwest League. Only one Cal League player came to the plate more often without homering than Triunfel, though his first instructional league homer traveled 450 feet. The Mariners firmly believe he'll develop average power once he learns to turn on pitches, because his hands are quick, he hits the ball hard the other way and gets such good backspin. Nearly physically mature, Triunfel is thick-legged and has below-average running speed. He lacks classic shortstop actions and range, and almost certainly will have to find a new position once he fills out. Because he throws well, Triunfel could find a home at third base, and the Mariners tried him at second base in instructional league in an effort to keep him in the middle of the field. His future position may depend largely on the needs of the big league club and Seattle hasn't figured out what positon he'll play when he returns to high Class A in 2008.

Year	Club (League)	Class	AVG	G	AB	R	H	2B	3B	HR	RBI	BB	SO	SB	OBP	SLG
2007	Wisconsin (MWL)	A	.309	43	152	18	47	8	2	0	14	5	23	4	.342	.388
	Mariners (AZL)	R	.273	3	11	1	3	0	0	0	3	0	1	0	.231	.273
	High Desert (Cal)	A	.288	50	208	32	60	10	2	0	22	12	31	3	.333	.356
MINOR LEAGUE TOTALS			.296	96	371	51	110	18	4	0	39	17	55	7	.333	.367

5 WLADIMIR BALENTIEN, OF

Born: July 2, 1984. **B-T:** R-R. **Ht.:** 6-2. **Wt.:** 190. **Signed:** Curacao, 2000. **Signed by:** Karel Williams.

Balentien arrived in the United States by hitting a Rookie-level Arizona League-record 16 home runs in 2004. He has done nothing but mash since, averaging 22 homers in each of the past four seasons. After winning team MVP honors at San Antonio in 2006, he showed improvement across the board in his first taste of Triple-A. He homered off Fausto Carmona in one of three September at-bats for the Mariners. Few players in the game can match Balentien's immense raw power to all fields. Though he still wildly chases pitches out of the strike zone, he did show increased pitch recognition and selectivity in first half of last season. He slashed his strikeout rate from one every 3.2 at-bats in 2006 to one every 4.5. He has average speed and good baserunning instincts. An average defender in right field, he charges the ball well and has a plus arm he used to register 15 assists last year. Balentien spins off pitches a lot, though he can still drive the ball when he does. He frequently has come under scrutiny for his lackadaisical play and though he still has lapses, he showed more focus and maturity in 2007. Balentien missed a week in August with a left pinky injury and hit just .209/.281/.318 in 148 at-bats in the second half. Balentien accomplished his goal of making more contact without sacrificing power, bringing him to the cusp of being big league ready. The Mariners, though, are committed to Ichiro Suzuki and Adam Jones in center and right field, and Raul Ibanez has played well in left, meaning Balentien may have to wait for a spot to open in Seattle. He could use more Triple-A time to further refine his game.

Year	Club (League)	Class	AVG	G	AB	R	H	2B	3B	HR	RBI	BB	SO	SB	OBP	SLG
2001	Aguirre (VSL)	R	.206	53	131	27	27	2	1	0	9	25	48	7	.333	.237
2002	Aguirre (VSL)	R	.279	59	197	41	55	13	4	10	39	34	52	6	.390	.538
2003	Mariners (AZL)	R	.283	50	187	42	53	12	5	16	52	22	55	4	.363	.658
2004	Wisconsin (MWL)	A	.277	76	260	39	72	12	3	15	46	12	77	10	.315	.519
	Inland Empire (Cal)	A	.289	10	38	5	11	1	0	2	5	4	10	1	.357	.474
2005	Inland Empire (Cal)	A	.291	123	492	76	143	38	8	25	93	33	160	9	.338	.553
2006	San Antonio (TL)	AA	.230	121	444	76	102	23	1	22	82	70	140	14	.337	.435
2007	Tacoma (PCL)	AAA	.291	124	477	77	139	24	4	24	84	54	105	15	.362	.509
	Seattle (AL)	MLB	.667	3	3	1	2	1	0	1	4	0	0	0	.500	2.000
MINOR LEAGUE TOTALS			.270	616	2226	383	602	125	26	114	410	254	647	66	.347	.504
MAJOR LEAGUE TOTALS			.667	3	3	1	2	1	0	1	4	0	0	0	.500	2.000

6 MICHAEL SAUNDERS, OF

Born: Nov. 19, 1986. **B-T:** L-R. **Ht.:** 6-4. **Wt.:** 205. **Drafted:** Tallahassee (Fla.) CC, D/F 2004 (11th round). **Signed by:** Phil Geisler.

A visa shortage in baseball would have made it impossible for Saunders to start his pro career in 2004, when the Mariners drafted him out of a British Columbia high school. So he headed to junior college for a year before signing as a draft-and-follow for $237,500. Saunders showed NHL potential in hockey and also starred in basketball, lacrosse and soccer as an amateur. After being unprepared physically or mentally for the rigors of the low Class A in 2006, Saunders put to rest any doubts about his potential by reaching Double-A at age 20. A potential five-tool talent with as much athleticism as any Seattle farmhand, he generates good loft with a fluid lefthanded stroke. Still growing into his 6-foot-4 frame, he could mature into a 20-homer hitter with the above-average speed required to steal bases and play a plus center field. He has a strong arm, having touched 91 mph as an amateur pitcher. Experience is the missing ingredient to Saunders' game. The Mariners believe the Double-A promotion was the best thing for him, as it forced him to hone his baseball instincts—everything from stealing bases to playing defense to working pitchers. Though his patience is encouraging for a young player, he piles up an excessive number of strikeouts. While added bulk probably would help Saunders hit for more power, it might detract from his speed, making a future move to right field possible. Regardless, he'll get the chance to master Double-A in 2008.

Year	Club (League)	Class	AVG	G	AB	R	H	2B	3B	HR	RBI	BB	SO	SB	OBP	SLG
2005	Everett (NWL)	A	.270	56	196	24	53	13	3	7	39	27	74	2	.361	.474
2006	Wisconsin (MWL)	A	.240	104	359	48	86	10	8	4	39	48	103	22	.329	.345
2007	High Desert (Cal)	A	.299	108	431	91	129	25	4	14	77	60	116	27	.392	.473
	West Tenn (SL)	AA	.288	15	52	8	15	1	2	1	7	7	20	2	.373	.442
MINOR LEAGUE TOTALS			.273	283	1038	171	283	49	17	26	162	142	313	53	.364	.428

7 JUAN RAMIREZ, RHP

Born: Aug. 16, 1988. **B-T:** R-R. **Ht.:** 6-3. **Wt.:** 175. **Signed:** Nicaragua, 2005. **Signed by:** Luis Molina/Nemesio Porras.

With just 65 innings in the Rookie-level Venezuelan Summer League under his belt, Ramirez made his U.S. debut in the short-season Northwest League at age 18. He had his share of rough outings and struggled with his command, but he also had one of the league's best arms. Ramirez finished second in the NWL in opponent average (.211) and fourth in strikeouts per nine innings (8.7). Ramirez has a prototypical pitcher's body and compares favorably with former Mariners prospect Rafael Soriano for his build and his delivery. He has a loose, easy arm and the ball jumps out of his hand from a three-quarters arm slot. His plus four-seam fastball ranges from 91-95 mph and sits at 93 with life and occasional armside run. Batters simply don't look comfortable facing him, nor do they get good swings on his fastball. Ramirez will rush his delivery and miss up in the zone, which leads to walks. His breaking ball is a work in progress, but he'll flash tight spin on a 75-mph curveball. He has some feel for a changeup but it also needs refinement. At present, he has below-average command of all three of his pitches. Ramirez likely will team with 2007 first-round pick Phillippe Aumont in the low Class A rotation this year. With improved command, he would have front-of-the-rotation stuff. If not, he'd profile as power reliever.

Year	Club (League)	Class	W	L	ERA	G	GS	CG	SV	IP	H	R	ER	HR	BB	SO	AVG
2006	Mariners (VSL)	R	5	1	1.66	14	13	1	0	65	43	16	12	0	35	56	.191
2007	Everett (NWL)	A	3	7	4.30	15	15	0	0	75	61	49	36	3	43	73	.211
MINOR LEAGUE TOTALS			8	8	3.08	29	28	1	0	140	104	65	48	3	78	129	.202

8 MARK LOWE, RHP

Born: June 7, 1983. **B-T:** R-R. **Ht.:** 6-3. **Wt.:** 190. **Drafted:** Texas-Arlington, 2004 (5th round). **Signed by:** Mark Lummus.

Lowe took off after a move to the bullpen in 2006, winning Seattle's minor league pitcher of the year award for his three-month trek from high Class A to the majors. His breakthrough season was cut short that August with what was believed to be elbow tendinitis. Doctors instead found that he had no cartilage in the joint and had to perform a drastic, unprecedented microfracture operation in an effort to regenerate it. Lowe's stuff jumped a grade as a reliever. Prior to elbow surgery, his fastball reached a consistent 94-96 mph with quality life. His hard slider had late, quick break and chews up righthanders. He also had a changeup for lefties, and all three of his pitches were plus at times. His command and control also improved in short stints when he could cut loose. In addition to his elbow woes, Lowe also missed three weeks in 2006 with a shoulder impingement. Limited to just 13 innings last year, he didn't cut loose, couldn't pitch on consecutive days and threw only bullpens in instructional league. Team doctors told the Mariners that Lowe will be under no restrictions in spring training, so that's when they'll get a better idea if his stuff will come back. If Lowe is healthy, he'll be an asset as a late-inning reliever, possibly filling Brandon Morrow's role if Morrow moves to the rotation as planned.

Year	Club (League)	Class	W	L	ERA	G	GS	CG	SV	IP	H	R	ER	HR	BB	SO	AVG
2004	Everett (NWL)	A	1	2	4.93	18	3	0	7	38	42	22	21	4	14	38	.276
2005	Wisconsin (MWL)	A	6	6	5.47	22	22	0	0	103	107	72	63	12	49	72	.264
2006	Inland Empire (Cal)	A	1	0	1.84	13	2	0	2	29	14	10	6	0	11	46	.132
	San Antonio (TL)	AA	0	2	2.16	11	0	0	4	16	14	4	4	1	3	14	.233
	Seattle (AL)	MLB	1	0	1.93	15	0	0	0	18	12	4	4	1	9	20	.190
2007	Everett (NWL)	A	0	0	0.00	1	1	0	0	1	0	0	0	0	0	0	.000
	West Tenn (SL)	AA	0	0	3.38	3	1	0	0	3	2	1	1	0	2	1	.222
	Seattle (AL)	MLB	0	0	6.75	4	0	0	0	3	2	2	2	1	3	3	.200
	Tacoma (PCL)	AAA	0	0	5.68	7	3	0	0	6	12	4	4	1	3	5	.387
MINOR LEAGUE TOTALS			8	10	4.50	75	32	0	13	198	191	113	99	18	82	176	.249
MAJOR LEAGUE TOTALS			1	0	2.53	19	0	0	0	21	14	6	6	2	12	23	.192

9 RYAN ROWLAND-SMITH, LHP

Born: Jan. 26, 1983. **B-T:** L-L. **Ht.:** 6-3. **Wt.:** 205. **Signed:** Australia, 2000. **Signed by:** Barry Holland.

The first player ever signed from Newcastle, Australia, Rowland-Smith pitched for his nation in the 2004 Olympics. The Twins took him the major league Rule 5 draft at the 2004 Winter Meetings but returned him to the Mariners the following spring. Rowland-Smith, who spent the second half of last season in Seattle's bullpen, has worked predominantly as a reliever in his seven years in the system. However, the Mariners want him to start in 2008 and sent him to the Venezuelan Winter League to prepare for that assignment. With a fastball that reaches 93-94 mph and three other pitches, Rowland-Smith never was typical lefty-specialist material. He relied on his slider as a reliever, and the pitch is a tick above average, but he's more comfortable with throwing his average curveball and deceptive changeup. He's a physical pitcher who offers power stuff from the left side and has a plan on the mound. Rowland-Smith never has started more than 17 games or pitched more than 122 innings in any pro season, leading to questions about how he'll adapt to the rigors of his new role. Despite his size, he doesn't get a lot of downward plane on his fastball, and his curve can be a little big and early at times. With no knockout pitch, he's probably a No. 4 or 5 starter. Rowland-Smith won't have an easy time cracking the rotation, seeing as Seattle has three other lefty candidates in Jarrod Washburn, Horacio Ramirez and Ryan Feierabend.

Year	Club (League)	Class	W	L	ERA	G	GS	CG	SV	IP	H	R	ER	HR	BB	SO	AVG
2001	Mariners (AZL)	R	1	1	2.97	17	0	0	5	33	25	11	11	1	9	39	.216
2002	Wisconsin (MWL)	A	1	2	6.75	12	8	0	0	41	50	39	31	7	19	38	.289
	Everett (NWL)	A	4	1	2.77	18	6	0	2	61	58	22	19	2	22	58	.246
2003	Wisconsin (MWL)	A	3	0	1.11	13	0	0	1	32	22	13	4	0	14	37	.182
	Inland Empire (Cal)	A	0	1	3.20	15	0	0	0	19	12	9	7	0	8	15	.182
2004	Inland Empire (Cal)	A	5	3	3.79	29	12	0	3	99	107	50	42	10	30	119	.278
2005	San Antonio (TL)	AA	6	7	4.35	33	17	0	0	122	133	72	59	7	51	102	.283
2006	Inland Empire (Cal)	A	0	1	5.68	7	0	0	0	6	8	7	4	1	2	9	.308
	San Antonio (TL)	AA	1	3	2.83	23	1	0	4	41	38	18	13	2	18	48	.241
2007	Tacoma (PCL)	AAA	3	4	3.67	25	0	0	1	41	35	20	17	2	22	50	.226
	Seattle (AL)	MLB	1	0	3.96	26	0	0	0	38	39	19	17	4	15	42	.269
MINOR LEAGUE TOTALS			24	23	3.73	192	44	0	16	499	488	261	207	32	195	515	.256
MAJOR LEAGUE TOTALS			1	0	3.96	26	0	0	0	38	39	19	17	4	15	42	.269

10 MATT TUIASOSOPO, 3B

Born: May 10, 1986. **B-T:** R-R. **Ht.:** 6-2. **Wt.:** 210. **Drafted:** HS—Woodinville, Wash., 2004 (3rd round). **Signed by:** Phil Geisler.

Tuiasosopo was on a football path, like his father Manu and brother Marques (who both played in the NFL), when he accepted a scholarship to play quarterback at Washington. He changed course when the Mariners took him with their top pick in the 2004 draft and signed him for a third round-record $2.29 million bonus. After three years of mostly struggling, Tuiasosopo's bat came alive in Double-A last season and he continued to hit in the Arizona Fall League. The Mariners rave about Tuiasosopo's makeup, noting that he never lost focus despite bombing in his first crack at Double-A in 2006. He got off to a fast start with West Tenn in 2007 and ran with it, showing above-average bat speed and solid pitch recognition and plate coverage. His power is strictly gap to gap now, but he has the strength and athleticism to drive the ball once he learns to identify his pitch. A converted shortstop, Tuiasosopo has the makings of a big league third baseman with soft hands, arm strength and agility. He has good speed for his size. Tuiasosopo still uses an inside-out swing and takes most balls the other way, cutting into his power potential. He started to correct that, turning on inside pitches in the second half and in the AFL. Tuiasosopo's stroke is long and he has a high leg kick that throws his timing off. Even four years into his pro career, Tuiasosopo remains raw because of his football background. He has no standout tool, but if his bat develops as the Mariners expect, he could be a solid big league regular. He'll probably never be a middle-of-the-order hitter.

Year	Club (League)	Class	AVG	G	AB	R	H	2B	3B	HR	RBI	BB	SO	SB	OBP	SLG
2004	Mariners (AZL)	R	.412	20	68	18	28	5	2	4	12	13	14	1	.528	.721
	Everett (NWL)	A	.248	29	101	18	25	6	1	2	14	10	36	4	.336	.386
2005	Wisconsin (MWL)	A	.276	107	409	72	113	21	3	6	45	44	96	8	.359	.386
2006	Inland Empire (Cal)	A	.306	59	232	31	71	14	0	1	34	14	58	5	.359	.379
	San Antonio (TL)	AA	.185	62	216	16	40	4	0	1	10	20	64	2	.259	.218
2007	West Tenn (SL)	AA	.260	129	446	74	116	27	5	9	57	76	113	4	.371	.404
MINOR LEAGUE TOTALS			.267	406	1472	229	393	77	11	23	172	177	381	24	.356	.381

11 CARLOS PEGUERO, DH/OF

Born: Feb. 22, 1987. **B-T:** L-L. **Ht.:** 6-5. **Wt.:** 210. **Signed:** Dominican Republic, 2005. **Signed by:** Patrick Guerrero/Bob Engle.

Peguero led the Rookie-level Arizona League in slugging (.649) and tied two other Mariners farmhands for the home run crown (seven) in 2006. And he accomplished it even after moving to short-season Everett with a month left in the season. At 6-foot-5 and 210 pounds, Peguero has the power to match anyone in the system, and he slugged a well-above-average .465 in the tough Midwest League in 2007. He can lift and drive any ball he can reach, and his swing, though long, can be pretty at times. Peguero's not entirely a one-dimensional masher, though. He's an above-average runner for his size (he has covered 60 yards in 6.6 seconds) and he has an above-average right-fielder's arm—though he spent most of his time at DH with Wisconsin while he recovered from surgery to remove bone chips from his elbow. Peguero doesn't have much of a plan at the plate yet, and he's got a lot of work to do cleaning up his reads and routes in the outfield, but his huge lefty power alone makes him a potential impact hitter. He'll see time with high Class A High Desert in 2008, where the California League's favorable conditions should bring Peguero's power to the fore.

Year	Club (League)	Class	AVG	G	AB	R	H	2B	3B	HR	RBI	BB	SO	SB	OBP	SLG
2005	Mariners (DSL)	R	.251	59	179	31	45	8	4	6	30	22	66	1	.337	.441
2006	Mariners (AZL)	R	.313	34	134	27	42	10	7	7	30	13	49	3	.380	.649
	Everett (NWL)	A	.204	25	93	7	19	4	1	2	9	2	34	0	.221	.333
2007	Wisconsin (MWL)	A	.263	79	297	35	78	21	6	9	50	16	97	4	.315	.465
MINOR LEAGUE TOTALS			.262	197	703	100	184	43	18	24	119	53	246	8	.322	.477

12 TONY BUTLER, LHP

Born: Nov. 18, 1987. **B-T:** L-L. **Ht.:** 6-7. **Wt.:** 205. **Drafted:** HS—Oak Creek, Wis., 2006 (3rd round). **Signed by:** Joe Bohringer.

After sitting at 86-87 mph and touching 90 for much of his senior year, Butler's velocity peaked in the mid-90s right before the draft, prompting the Mariners to invest a third-round pick in the projectable lefty. He dominated in the Northwest League in his debut, but slumped at low Class A Wisconsin in his sophomore season, getting out of the gates at 0-6, 7.02 with 30 walks, 29 strikeouts and six home runs in 33 first-half innings. Butler spent time on the disabled list twice with a dead arm. His above-average 88-92 mph four-seam fastball features late life, and he uses his 6-foot-7 frame to leverage it down in the strike zone. He also can buckle knees with his 76-80 mph curveball, which is one of the system's best. Butler has feel for a changeup with late fade and deception. Pitching in Appleton may have posed distractions to Butler, whose hometown is nearby Oak Creek, Wis. He was not prepared to pitch every five days and he'll need to improve his endurance. Butler was hit hard, especially in the first half, as he struggled to command his fastball. His arm action is not fluid, which provides deception but also puts stress on his shoulder and makes it difficult to maintain velocity. In fact, Midwest League observers were impressed that Butler got so much bite on his curveball with his slinging delivery. Though he didn't live up to expectations in 2007, Butler still is a physical lefty with stuff who projects as a mid-rotation starter or reliever. He recovered in the second half, going 4-1, 3.29 with 44 strikeouts and 16 walks in 52 innings, but the Mariners may opt to send Butler back to Wisconsin to catch his breath. He'll be ready for high Class A at some point in 2008.

Year	Club (League)	Class	W	L	ERA	G	GS	CG	SV	IP	H	R	ER	HR	BB	SO	AVG
2006	Mariners (AZL)	R	2	0	2.57	5	3	0	0	14	5	4	4	0	9	25	.116
	Everett (NWL)	A	1	2	2.76	9	9	0	0	42	23	16	13	2	25	52	.160
2007	Wisconsin (MWL)	A	4	7	4.75	20	18	1	0	85	78	52	45	10	46	73	.247
MINOR LEAGUE TOTALS			7	9	3.94	34	30	1	0	141	106	72	62	12	80	150	.211

13 GREG HALMAN, OF

Born: Aug. 26, 1987. **B-T:** R-R. **Ht.:** 6-4. **Wt.:** 192. **Signed:** Netherlands, 2004. **Signed by:** Peter Van Dalen.

A long-limbed, high-waisted athlete, Halman signed after winning the MVP award in the Dutch league as a 17-year-old. With a projectable frame and wiry strength, especially in his wrists and forearms, Halman has drawn physical comparisons with Andre Dawson and Alfonso Soriano. Because he had played well in a few big league spring training games, Halman was unhappy with his Opening Day assignment to low Class A Wisconsin. He fared so poorly, failing to make adjustments, that he was demoted to Everett in June. He said the experience has humbled him. Halman dominated in his return to the Northwest League, leading all batters in slugging (.597) and finishing second with 16 home runs. With the power came bushels of strikeouts, as Halman struggled with pitch recognition and continued to sell out for power. With plus bat speed and above-average power, the home runs will come naturally if he lets them. A long-strider who runs well for his size, Halman is capable in center field but probably will shift to right, where his plus arm also plays. Few Seattle prospects have as many raw tools as Halman, but he still has a long way to go to harness his ability. Shortening his swing and focusing on contact—as Wladimir Balentien had to do as he advanced—should be on his to-do list as he heads back to Wisconsin.

Year	Club (League)	Class	AVG	G	AB	R	H	2B	3B	HR	RBI	BB	SO	SB	OBP	SLG
2005	Mariners (AZL)	R	.258	26	89	17	23	2	3	3	11	10	19	1	.350	.449
2006	Everett (NWL)	A	.259	28	116	19	30	6	4	5	15	3	32	10	.295	.509
2007	Wisconsin (MWL)	A	.182	52	187	26	34	5	0	4	15	8	77	15	.234	.273
	Everett (NWL)	A	.307	62	238	37	73	19	1	16	37	21	85	16	.371	.597
MINOR LEAGUE TOTALS			.254	168	630	99	160	32	8	28	78	42	213	42	.314	.463

14 MATT MANGINI, 3B

Born: Dec. 21, 1985. **B-T:** L-R. **Ht.:** 6-4. **Wt.:** 220. **Drafted:** Oklahoma State, 2007 (1st round supplemental). **Signed by:** Dan Wright.

Since he won the Cape Cod League batting title with a .310 average in the summer of 2006, things haven't gone as smoothly for Mangini. After transferring from North Carolina State to Oklahoma State for his junior year, he didn't perform as hoped and slid out of the first round of the draft—but not too far. The Mariners took him with the 52nd overall pick and gave him a $603,000 bonus. A hard-nosed player who puts together good at-bats, Mangini's line-drive approach has served him well as a hitter for average, though it has cost him leverage in his swing. He projects to have no more than average power because of a lack of loft in his swing, and back soreness that hampered him in his pro debut didn't help. Scouts who have history with Mangini say he always has hit better with wood than metal and that he has solid-average bat speed. He hangs in against lefties and isn't afraid to use the opposite field. At third base, Mangini has fringe-average range, which the Mariners are trying to clean up with improved footwork, and an average arm. He's not a great athlete and offers below-average running speed. Mangini figures to see plenty of action at High Desert in 2008 and could reach Double-A.

Year	Club (League)	Class	AVG	G	AB	R	H	2B	3B	HR	RBI	BB	SO	SB	OBP	SLG
2007	Everett (NWL)	A	.291	22	79	12	23	4	0	2	9	13	18	3	.398	.418
	Mariners (AZL)	R	.000	2	6	0	0	0	0	0	0	2	1	0	.250	.000
	High Desert (Cal)	A	.226	17	62	7	14	1	2	2	8	6	21	1	.304	.403
MINOR LEAGUE TOTALS			.252	41	147	19	37	5	2	4	17	21	40	4	.353	.395

15 ADAM MOORE, C

Born: May 8, 1984. **B-T:** R-R. **Ht.:** 6-3. **Wt.:** 215. **Drafted:** Texas-Arlington, 2006 (6th round). **Signed by:** Mark Lummus.

Moore missed the entire 2005 college season at Nebraska after tearing the meniscus in his left knee just before the season started. After transferring to Texas-Arlington, he became the Mavericks' best hitter and led them to the Southland Conference tournament title. Moore has come on strong since turning pro for $140,000, putting up 22 homers and 102 RBIs in 2007, taking full advantage of the favorable conditions at high Class A High Desert. In fact, above-average power is Moore's most pronounced tool, but he also impressed the Mariners with his leadership qualities and game-calling technique. At his best, he's a solid-average receiver and thrower, but his bat always will have to carry him. That should be no problem in terms of power production, but while Moore has good pitch recognition skills, he may lack the reflexes to hit for a high average. A sturdily-built 6-foot-3 and 215 pounds, he has enough arm to stick at catcher, but his footwork can get out of sync while blocking and throwing. He erased 32 percent of basestealers last season. Roving catching instructor Roger Hansen will focus on cleaning up Moore's footwork—as he has Jeff Clement's—as he moves to Double-A.

Year	Club (League)	Class	AVG	G	AB	R	H	2B	3B	HR	RBI	BB	SO	SB	OBP	SLG
2006	Everett (NWL)	A	.317	16	63	8	20	9	0	0	9	2	10	0	.348	.460
	Wisconsin (MWL)	A	.267	44	165	21	44	6	0	7	24	14	38	0	.342	.430
2007	High Desert (Cal)	A	.307	115	433	74	133	30	3	22	102	41	84	1	.371	.543
MINOR LEAGUE TOTALS			.298	175	661	103	197	45	3	29	135	57	132	1	.362	.507

16 JHARMIDY DeJESUS, SS

Born: Aug. 30, 1989. **B-T:** R-R. **Ht.:** 6-3. **Wt.:** 185. **Signed:** Dominican Republic, 2007. **Signed by:** Franklin Taveras.

By inking three Latin American prospects to bonuses of six figures or more, the Mariners reiterated their commitment to international scouting. Seattle signed DeJesus for $1 million, while also adding shortstop Gabriel Noriega (Venezuela) and outfielder Efrain Nunez (Dominican Republic) during the 2007 international signing period. DeJesus was eligible in 2006, too, but teams did not meet his asking price. Added strength garnered him more attention in 2007, and many scouts thought he offered one of the better, more polished bats in the Dominican. DeJesus reminds the Mariners of his countryman Carlos Triunfel, in whom they invested $1.3 million in 2006. Like Triunfel, DeJesus is supremely confident in his abilities, but will have to move off shortstop as he matures. Already 6-foot-3 and 185 pounds, DeJesus has above-average potential as a hitter and as a power hitter. He's a slightly below-average runner who profiles as a plus defensive third baseman with a strong arm. The Mariners like to challenge their prospects, so DeJesus stands a good chance of making his pro debut with Wisconsin at age 18.

Year	Club (League)	Class	AVG	G	AB	R	H	2B	3B	HR	RBI	BB	SO	SB	OBP	SLG
2007	Did Not Play															

17 ROB JOHNSON, C

Born: July 22, 1983. **B-T:** R-R. **Ht.:** 6-1. **Wt.:** 2000. **Drafted:** Houston, 2004 (4th round). **Signed by:** Kyle Van Hook.

Johnson rated as the best defensive catcher in the Midwest League in 2005, his full-season debut, and reached high Class A later that year. He hasn't served as a full-time catcher since then, as he's had to share playing time at Triple-A Tacoma with Guillermo Quiroz in 2006 (catching 74 games) and Jeff Clement in 2007 (69 games). The Mariners felt comfortable rushing him because of his leadership qualities and strong arm—though he threw out just 24 percent of basestealers in 2007. An outfielder in junior college, Johnson runs very well for a catcher but is an inconsistent receiver. As a hitter, he's struggled with advanced breaking balls and has batted just .252/.301/.348 through 209 Triple-A games. He has good hand-eye coordination and raw power, but could add more pop with increased loft in his swing and a better plan at the plate. Johnson is the best defensive catcher the Mariners have on the farm, but with Kenji Johjima and Clement ahead of him on the depth chart, he'll have to bide his time in Tacoma. He profiles as a backup catcher in the big leagues but could start if his bat comes along.

Year	Club (League)	Class	AVG	G	AB	R	H	2B	3B	HR	RBI	BB	SO	SB	OBP	SLG
2004	Everett (NWL)	A	.234	20	77	17	18	3	1	1	7	4	10	6	.286	.338
	Mariners (AZL)	R	.222	8	27	4	6	1	0	0	1	3	7	1	.323	.259
2005	Wisconsin (MWL)	A	.272	77	305	41	83	19	1	9	51	20	31	10	.319	.430
	Inland Empire (Cal)	A	.314	19	70	15	22	3	0	2	12	10	14	2	.381	.443
2006	Tacoma (PCL)	AAA	.231	97	337	28	78	9	4	4	33	13	74	14	.261	.318
2007	Tacoma (PCL)	AAA	.268	112	422	57	113	26	0	6	40	39	62	7	.331	.372
	Seattle (AL)	MLB	.333	6	3	1	1	0	0	0	0	0	0	1	.333	.333
MINOR LEAGUE TOTALS			.258	333	1238	162	320	61	6	22	144	89	198	40	.310	.371
MAJOR LEAGUE TOTALS			.333	6	3	1	1	0	0	0	0	0	0	1	.333	.333

18 KAM MICKOLIO, RHP

Born: May 10, 1984. **B-T:** R-R. **Ht.:** 6-9. **Wt.:** 256. **Drafted:** Utah Valley State, 2006 (18th round). **Signed by:** Phil Geisler.

A native of Montana, where there's no high school baseball, the 6-foot-9 Mickolio played only basketball until the summer before his senior year of high school, when he began playing American Legion ball. He showed enough promise in his first year at Eastern Utah Junior College in 2003 that the Cardinals drafted him in the 35th round, and he made even more progress after transferring to Utah Valley State. A true scouting success story, Mickolio jumped from 18th-round pick in 2006 to Triple-A in 2007. The definition of uncomfortable to hit, Mickolio throws his power sinker at 92-97 mph from a low three-quarters arm slot. The ball bores in on righthanders and his cross-body throwing motion gives him plenty of deception. Mickolio needs to find more consistency with his slider, which shows good depth at times, but as a reliever he can get by if the pitch is merely average because his fastball is so good. He'll also need to improve his changeup to combat lefthanders, and he still needs to do a better job commanding his stuff in the strike zone. All the ingredients are present for Mickolio to be a big league reliever, potentially an eighth-inning guy if he slightly improves his three pitches.

Year	Club (League)	Class	W	L	ERA	G	GS	CG	SV	IP	H	R	ER	HR	BB	SO	AVG
2006	Everett (NWL)	A	1	0	2.78	21	0	0	4	32	34	14	10	1	7	26	.264
2007	West Tenn (SL)	AA	3	1	1.82	18	0	0	2	29	24	9	6	0	12	27	.224
	Tacoma (PCL)	AAA	3	3	3.75	14	0	0	1	24	19	12	10	3	10	28	.213
MINOR LEAGUE TOTALS			7	4	2.72	53	0	0	7	86	77	35	26	4	29	81	.237

19 BRYAN LaHAIR, 1B

Born: Nov. 5, 1982. **B-T:** L-R. **Ht.:** 6-5. **Wt.:** 215. **Drafted:** St. Petersburg (Fla.) JC, D/F 2002 (39th round). **Signed by:** Mark Leavitt.

LaHair won Seattle minor league player of the year honors in 2006 and followed that up by hitting 46 doubles in 2007, a mark good enough to rank second in the Pacific Coast League and seventh in the minors. His resurgence began in 2005 when he started to drive the ball more regularly during games. LaHair uses the entire field and has good plate coverage, but his upside is probably closer to Sean Casey than a true impact bat. He could improve his home run output by learning to pull the inside pitch, which the Mariners believe he will do with more Triple-A experience. LaHair's work ethic is strong, but he tends to be too hard on himself. Drafted as a corner outfielder/third baseman, he isn't very athletic and is limited to first base, where he has below-average speed and defensive skills. Unless he improves dramatically against lefthanders—against whom he has hit .209 and slugged .316 in two Triple-A seasons—LaHair profiles more as a part-time player. Weakness against lefty pitching is preferable to the opposite, though, so LaHair could carve out a career as a platoon first baseman/DH, possibly as early as 2008 if Richie Sexson gets hurt or is traded.

Year	Club (League)	Class	AVG	G	AB	R	H	2B	3B	HR	RBI	BB	SO	SB	OBP	SLG
2003	Everett (NWL)	A	.244	57	201	26	49	14	0	2	20	11	40	4	.286	.343
2004	Everett (NWL)	A	.440	7	25	5	11	6	0	1	7	1	3	0	.464	.800
	Wisconsin (MWL)	A	.279	67	262	30	73	24	0	5	28	16	66	0	.323	.427
2005	Inland Empire (Cal)	A	.310	126	509	81	158	28	2	22	113	51	125	0	.373	.503
2006	San Antonio (TL)	AA	.293	60	222	22	65	12	0	6	30	24	52	0	.371	.428
	Tacoma (PCL)	AAA	.327	54	202	36	66	10	0	10	44	23	49	3	.393	.525
2007	Tacoma (PCL)	AAA	.275	138	552	79	152	46	2	12	81	49	126	0	.332	.431
MINOR LEAGUE TOTALS			.291	509	1973	279	574	140	4	58	323	175	461	7	.350	.454

20 YUNG-CHI CHEN, 2B

Born: July 13, 1983. **B-T:** R-R. **Ht.:** 5-11. **Wt.:** 170. **Signed:** Taiwan, 2004. **Signed by:** Jamey Storvick.

Chen led Taiwan with one homer and five RBIs at the inaugural World Baseball Classic in 2006, and played in that year's Futures Game. Chen failed to build on that momentum in 2007 when he dislocated his shoulder five games into the Triple-A Tacoma season and missed the rest of the year. He returned to hit .339/.444/.424 in 59 at-bats in the Arizona Fall League. Chen's best tool is his bat. He has a knack for contact, knows how to work pitchers and uses the whole field. Quality breaking balls give him trouble, and he has below-average power—though his buggy-whip swing generates surprising gap power for his size. Chen doesn't run all that well and he's just an average defender who still has to answer questions about his footwork and range at second base. His arm is average. Chen tends to sit back on balls instead of getting his weight up front, but his exchange on double plays is above-average. Added to the 40-man roster in November, Chen will get another shot at Triple-A in 2008, but he'll have to perform. Otherwise the organization's infield depth, like the fast-rising Carlos Triunfel, might catch up to him.

Year	Club (League)	Class	AVG	G	AB	R	H	2B	3B	HR	RBI	BB	SO	SB	OBP	SLG
2004	Everett (NWL)	A	.300	49	200	37	60	13	1	3	34	16	36	25	.353	.420
2005	Wisconsin (MWL)	A	.292	121	503	77	147	27	7	7	80	37	76	15	.339	.416
2006	Inland Empire (Cal)	A	.342	67	278	49	95	17	3	5	48	22	40	21	.388	.478
	Mariners (AZL)	R	.273	3	11	1	3	1	1	0	2	1	0	0	.385	.545
	San Antonio (TL)	AA	.295	40	149	22	44	9	2	3	22	18	23	5	.365	.443
2007	Tacoma (PCL)	AAA	.333	5	15	2	5	2	0	0	3	0	3	1	.294	.467
MINOR LEAGUE TOTALS			.306	285	1156	188	354	69	14	18	189	94	178	67	.357	.437

21 DANNY CARROLL, OF

Born: Jan. 6, 1989. **B-T:** R-R. **Ht.:** 6-1. **Wt.:** 175. **Drafted:** HS—Moreno Valley, Calif., 2007 (3rd round). **Signed by:** Tim Reynolds.

Not many teams rated Carroll highly enough to draft him in the third round like the Mariners did, but his early returns have Seattle excited. He signed for $315,000, eschewing his commitment to UC Irvine, and finished in the top five in the Arizona League in batting (.323), hits (65), steals (27) and on-base percentage (.415). Teammates nicknamed him "Machine" for his ability to repeat his swing with ease and for his high-energy disposition. Simply put, Carroll is a baseball player. What he lacks in present strength, he makes up for with above-average pitch recognition, contact ability and speed. Carroll is an above-average runner with plus instincts both on the bases and in center field. His arm is strong enough that he could handle right field. Carroll could be an ideal No. 2 hitter, using the whole field and having potential gap power as he gets stronger. He's ready for an assignment to Wisconsin.

Year	Club (League)	Class	AVG	G	AB	R	H	2B	3B	HR	RBI	BB	SO	SB	OBP	SLG
2007	Mariners (AZL)	R	.323	53	201	39	65	9	6	0	24	27	56	27	.415	.428
	Everett (NWL)	A	.176	4	17	0	3	0	0	0	0	0	6	2	.176	.176
MINOR LEAGUE TOTALS			.312	57	218	39	68	9	6	0	24	27	62	29	.398	.408

22 EDWARD PAREDES, LHP

Born: Sept. 30, 1986. **B-T:** L-L. **Ht.:** 6-0. **Wt.:** 175. **Signed:** Dominican Republic, 2005. **Signed by:** Patrick Guerrero/Bob Engle.

Paredes' first official U.S. appearance came for Triple-A Tacoma when he was used as an emergency reliever in mid-June, and he tossed five hitless innings. He had spent the previous two seasons as a reliever in the Rookie-level Dominican Summer League, but the Mariners stretched Paredes out by putting him in Everett's rotation. They were pleased with the results. The lean, 6-foot lefty has a quick, loose arm action, and he led the Northwest League in innings (86) and walks (48). Paredes struggles to repeat his low-three-quarters arm slot, which is the root of his command issues. His fastball ranges from 88-93 mph with armside run and occasional plus life at the plate. His 78 mph slurve was at times a legitimate out pitch with 2-to-8 tilt. It gets sweepy, lacks depth and hangs when he drops his arm angle, which was the case during his final few starts. His changeup is below-average. Paredes will work to refine his command issues in Wisconsin's rotation in 2008.

Year	Club (League)	Class	W	L	ERA	G	GS	CG	SV	IP	H	R	ER	HR	BB	SO	AVG
2005	Mariners (DSL)	R	3	0	2.03	12	0	0	1	26	16	11	6	1	13	28	.163
2006	Mariners (DSL)	R	3	3	2.63	24	2	0	14	41	21	18	12	1	19	45	.147
2007	Tacoma (PCL)	AAA	0	0	0.00	1	0	0	0	5	0	0	0	0	1	5	.000
	Everett (NWL)	A	7	6	3.99	16	15	0	0	86	75	47	38	2	48	61	.235
MINOR LEAGUE TOTALS			13	9	3.18	53	17	0	15	158	112	76	56	4	81	139	.195

23 MARIO MARTINEZ, SS/3B

Born: Nov. 13, 1989. **B-T:** R-R. **Ht.:** 6-2. **Wt.:** 175. **Signed:** Venezuela, 2006. **Signed by:** Bob Engle/Emilio Carrasquel.

The Mariners made a splash on the international market in 2006, signing Martinez and Carlos Triunfel for a combined $1.9 million. Martinez received $600,000, and while he didn't make it to high Class A in his debut, as Triunfel did, he more than held his own in the Arizona League, where he ranked as the No. 10 prospect. He made the game look easy with a sound swing he repeated easily and smooth actions in the field. His 6-foot-2, 175-pound frame leaves scouts plenty of room to project future power potential as Martinez adds strength. Signed as a shortstop, he already has outgrown the position, but he offers soft hands and a strong arm at third base. An aggressive hitter, Martinez can look foolish on one pitch then absolutely crush the next offering. He has plus power potential to all fields and the ball just sounds different off his bat. Martinez is a fluid athlete who runs well, but may lose some speed as he adds strength. The Mariners are encouraged by Martinez' tools, instincts and work habits and probably will push the 18-year-old to Wisconsin.

Year	Club (League)	Class	AVG	G	AB	R	H	2B	3B	HR	RBI	BB	SO	SB	OBP	SLG
2007	Mariners (AZL)	R	.281	53	196	36	55	9	1	1	26	6	31	3	.311	.352
MINOR LEAGUE TOTALS			.281	53	196	36	55	9	1	1	26	6	31	3	.311	.352

24 DENNY ALMONTE, OF

Born: Sept. 24, 1988. **B-T:** B-R. **Ht.:** 6-2. **Wt.:** 187. **Drafted:** HS—Miami, 2007 (2nd round). **Signed by:** Mike Tosar.

Though just one round separated them in the 2007 June, Almonte and third-rounder Danny Carroll are practically polar opposites of one another. Where Carroll is a pure baseball player without overwhelming tools, Almonte oozes tools but has struggled to put all five together. Case in point: he hit .145 in his debut with strikeouts in nearly half his at-bats. Taken 75th overall and signed for $427,500, Almonte has strong wrists and forearms, but the switch-hitter's swing is going to take a lot of repetitions to iron out. His swing is more compact and natural from the right side, but he has a pronounced uppercut from the left side, which the Mariners believe can be refined because of Almonte's athleticism and fluidity. He has some feel for the strike zone and offers plus power projection and well above-average speed. He also is an above-average center fielder with a quick first step and good body control. Rounding out his tool set, Almonte has a plus arm. Even though the Mariners like to challenge their young players, their low-level outfield situation already is crowded with the likes of Greg Halman, Danny Carroll, Joe Dunigan and Kalian Sams, meaning Almonte may return to Everett in 2008.

Year	Club (League)	Class	AVG	G	AB	R	H	2B	3B	HR	RBI	BB	SO	SB	OBP	SLG
2007	Mariners (AZL)	R	.161	18	56	11	9	2	1	0	5	6	26	3	.254	.232
	Everett (NWL)	A	.100	5	20	0	2	0	0	0	1	1	11	1	.143	.100
MINOR LEAGUE TOTALS			.145	23	76	11	11	2	1	0	6	7	37	4	.226	.197

25 NOLAN GALLAGHER, RHP

Born: Dec. 20, 1985. **B-T:** R-R. **Ht.:** 6-3. **Wt.:** 190. **Drafted:** Stanford, 2007 (4th round). **Signed by:** Stacey Pettis.

Gallagher entered the year as Stanford's ace, and at times showed the form he displayed in the 2006 Cape Cod League, but inconsistent command caused him to leave his pitches up in the zone and he got blitzed for a 7.39 ERA. He wasn't in the Cardinal's rotation during Pacific-10 Conference play. A potential supplemental first-round pick coming into the year, Gallagher fell to the fourth round where the Mariners signed him for $193,500. In his pro debut, the Montana native showed flashes of the 88-92 mph fastball, hard curveball and ability to change speeds that he had as a sophomore. He started pitching inside more to pro hitters and the Mariners noticed a marked improvement in Gallagher's mound presence. His plus curveball features tight rotation, and he throws it for strikes. That pitch and his clean, effortless delivery make him a potential mid-rotation starter, but he'll need to improve his below-average changeup. An abdominal strain slowed Gallagher when he moved to Wisconsin, but he should be ready for the challenges of high Class A in 2008.

Year	Club (League)	Class	W	L	ERA	G	GS	CG	SV	IP	H	R	ER	HR	BB	SO	AVG
2007	Everett (NWL)	A	1	1	0.84	6	6	0	0	32	19	5	3	2	6	24	.167
	Wisconsin (MWL)	A	0	2	4.58	4	4	0	0	19	23	13	10	3	14	15	.303
MINOR LEAGUE TOTALS			1	3	2.26	10	10	0	0	51	42	18	13	5	20	39	.221

26 JUSTIN THOMAS, LHP

Born: Jan. 18, 1984. **B-T:** L-L. **Ht.:** 6-3. **Wt.:** 220. **Drafted:** Youngstown State, 2005 (4th round). **Signed by:** Ken Madeja.

Everything Thomas throws moves, and he has the type of durable frame to absorb innings. He struggled in Double-A West Tenn a year after dominating in the California League playoffs, where he struck out 17 and didn't allow a run in 12 innings. Thomas lost a few ticks off his 88-92 mph fastball as he tried to pitch through pain brought on by bone chips in his left elbow. He shut things down in April and never got on track afterward in the Southern League. Thomas has the raw stuff to rival any lefthander in Seattle's system, with a lively fastball, a solid slider that breaks laterally and a fading changeup. His command isn't as impressive as his control, and he needs to do a better job of staying on top of his slider and changeup. The Mariners love his makeup, though, and he's a mid-rotation starter if everything clicks, a power lefty reliever if it doesn't. Thomas will reach Triple-A by the end of the 2008 season, but with the big league club's bevy of lefty pitching, the Mariners can afford to take it slow.

Year	Club (League)	Class	W	L	ERA	G	GS	CG	SV	IP	H	R	ER	HR	BB	SO	AVG
2005	Everett (NWL)	A	3	3	3.81	18	6	0	0	59	63	31	25	2	20	48	.272
2006	Wisconsin (MWL)	A	5	5	3.10	11	11	0	0	61	69	29	21	4	17	51	.286
	Inland Empire (Cal)	A	9	4	4.10	17	17	1	0	105	108	58	48	10	45	111	.269
2007	West Tenn (SL)	AA	4	9	5.51	24	24	0	0	119	147	82	73	11	61	100	.308
MINOR LEAGUE TOTALS			21	21	4.36	70	58	1	0	344	387	200	167	27	143	310	.286

27 ROBERT ROHRBAUGH, LHP

Born: Dec. 28, 1983. **B-T:** R-L. **Ht.:** 6-2. **Wt.:** 195. **Drafted:** Clemson, 2005 (7th round). **Signed by:** Craig Bell.

Rohrbaugh reached Double-A in his first full pro season and Triple-A in his second, largely because of his mature mound presence. He's an athletic strike-throwing machine with a simple delivery that he repeats well. Rohrbaugh's stuff is just average to a tick above, but he's not afraid to pitch to contact. His cutting 86-90 mph fastball generates lots of awkward swings and misses, and he throws on a good downward plane from a high three-quarters angle. Rohrbaugh's curveball has slurvy action that doesn't impress scouts or same-side batters. For the second year in a row, Southern League lefties hit him harder than did right-handers. Rohrbaugh's changeup has some fade and sink. Despite leading the organization in wins (13) and innings (170) in 2007, Rohrbaugh is a No. 5 starter if everything breaks right. He'll start at Tacoma, but he's behind other young, upper-level lefties like Ryan Feierabend, Ryan Rowland-Smith and Justin Thomas.

Year	Club (League)	Class	W	L	ERA	G	GS	CG	SV	IP	H	R	ER	HR	BB	SO	AVG
2005	Everett (NWL)	A	5	2	3.84	14	12	0	0	68	68	33	29	7	18	71	.262
2006	Inland Empire (Cal)	A	7	1	1.46	10	9	1	0	55	43	11	9	2	8	47	.214
	San Antonio (TL)	AA	5	5	3.78	14	14	0	0	85	87	37	36	9	27	64	.268
2007	West Tenn (SL)	AA	7	5	3.28	15	15	0	0	85	84	35	31	5	21	62	.257
	Tacoma (PCL)	AAA	6	3	2.95	13	13	2	0	85	84	31	28	10	26	49	.258
MINOR LEAGUE TOTALS			30	16	3.16	66	63	3	0	379	366	147	133	33	100	293	.255

28 NICK HILL, LHP

Born: Jan. 30, 1985. **B-T:** L-L. **Ht.:** 6-0. **Wt.:** 190. **Drafted:** Army, 2007 (7th round). **Signed by:** Rob Mummau.

The Red Sox drafted Hill as a junior in 2006 just to honor him, even though U.S. Military Academy rules prevented him from signing. He received permission to put off his active duty to pursue his professional baseball career in 2007, and the Mariners signed him for $70,000 after taking him in the seventh round. He's the highest-drafted player ever out of Army. Though his stuff is fringy, Hill has all kinds of pitchability and was one of the fiercest competitors available in the 2007 draft. He attacks with three pitches and loves pitching inside, two reasons why Everett's coaching staff immediately took to him. For a pitcher who stands 6-feet tall, Hill gets surprisingly good plane on an 87 mph fastball with riding life, occasionally scraping 90. His slurvy curveball is average and his changeup slightly above, and he locates them both well to both sides of the plate. Because his stuff leaves him little margin for error, Hill will need to continue mixing and locating his pitches with aplomb as he takes on high Class A in 2008.

Year	Club (League)	Class	W	L	ERA	G	GS	CG	SV	IP	H	R	ER	HR	BB	SO	AVG
2007	Everett (NWL)	A	1	3	0.51	18	0	0	2	35	24	6	2	0	9	45	.197
MINOR LEAGUE TOTALS			1	3	0.51	18	0	0	2	35	24	6	2	0	9	45	.197

29 ALEX LIDDI, 3B

Born: Aug. 14, 1988. **B-T:** R-R. **Ht.:** 6-4. **Wt.:** 176. **Signed:** Italy, 2005. **Signed by:** Wayne Norton/ Mario Mazzotti.

Liddi made his pro debut in 2006, hitting .313 and finishing fifth in Arizona League batting race as a 17-year-old. A year older and wiser, he held his own at Wisconsin, especially considering his youth and inexperience. With a sound swing, natural power to center and right-center field and a slender 6-foot-4, 176-pound frame, Liddi offers plenty of room to project power. The Mariners were encouraged that he recovered from a lousy first half to hit .262/.314/.398—or essentially league average—in the second. He has an unrefined grasp of the strike zone, struggling with pitch recognition and selection. He could outgrow third base as he fills out, but he has a plus arm, soft hands and enough agility to make plays. In the long term, he's probably a below-average runner. Critics of Liddi's noted that he was among the league's most awkward athletes and that he needed to stress strength and conditioning. The Mariners rave about his energy and work ethic, and he'll be one of the youngest players in his league, whether he repeats the MWL or heads to high Class A.

Year	Club (League)	Class	AVG	G	AB	R	H	2B	3B	HR	RBI	BB	SO	SB	OBP	SLG
2006	Mariners (AZL)	R	.313	47	182	31	57	13	6	3	25	12	48	9	.355	.500
	Wisconsin (MWL)	A	.184	11	38	4	7	1	0	0	2	1	8	0	.200	.211
2007	Wisconsin (MWL)	A	.240	113	400	41	96	28	3	8	52	36	123	5	.308	.385
MINOR LEAGUE TOTALS			.258	171	620	76	160	42	9	11	79	49	179	14	.315	.408

30 ANTHONY VARVARO, RHP

Born: Oct. 31, 1984. **B-T:** R-R. **Ht.:** 6-0. **Wt.:** 180. **Drafted:** St. John's, 2005 (12th round). **Signed by:** David May.

Varvaro blew out his elbow in May 2005 and fell to the 12th round of that year's draft, where the Mariners gambled $500,000 on his upside. Prior to the injury, he had a 92-94 mph fastball, a hard curveball and a chance to go as high as the supplemental first round. The Mariners have eased Varvaro back into action after he recovered from Tommy John surgery, as he averaged fewer than five innings per start for Wisconsin and was shut down with two weeks left in the season. Though he showed flashes of two plus pitches with Wisconsin, Varvaro's fastball ranged from 86-90 mph, reaching 92 on occasion. His curveball showed good depth at times but mostly was inconsistent. The Mariners took away Varvaro's slider when he signed and added a changeup, but it's strictly a third pitch. Some Midwest League observers didn't like the effort in Varvaro's drop-and-drive delivery, but the Mariners are optimistic that he'll make a full recovery and reach his upside as a No. 3 starter.

Year	Club (League)	Class	W	L	ERA	G	GS	CG	SV	IP	H	R	ER	HR	BB	SO	AVG
2006	Mariners (AZL)	R	0	2	1.64	5	3	0	0	11	7	3	2	0	5	15	.184
2007	Wisconsin (MWL)	A	4	11	4.69	22	21	0	1	103	94	67	54	7	51	112	.233
MINOR LEAGUE TOTALS			4	13	4.40	27	24	0	1	114	101	70	56	7	56	127	.229

Tampa Bay Rays

BY BILL BALLEW

Shortly after the 2007 season concluded, Tampa Bay officials announced that their franchise was undergoing an extreme makeover. The club dropped "Devil" from its name and will henceforth be known simply as the Rays. The team adopted a brighter blue and yellow color scheme, while switching to a logo that includes a yellow starburst, presumably to focus more on sunshine—and a brighter future.

On the field, the Rays hope to follow in the footsteps of their 1998 expansion brethren, the Diamondbacks, and ride a group of young and promising players to the postseason. Tampa Bay has quite a hill to climb after placing last in the American League East for the ninth time in its 10 seasons, and finishing with the worst record in baseball for the fourth time. In doing so, the Rays become the first team ever to own the No. 1 overall pick in consecutive drafts.

On the positive side, Tampa Bay has spent many of its early choices wisely, grabbing B.J. Upton in 2002, Delmon Young in 2003 and Evan Longoria in 2006. The Rays had the second-youngest team in the majors in 2007, with an average age of 26.7 years, and didn't have a single regular in their lineup or rotation who was 30. They caught lightning in a bottle with the signing of Carlos Pena, who hit 46 homers, as well as Japanese infielder Akinori Iwamura.

Though Tampa Bay had the game's lowest payroll in 2007 ($24.1 million on Opening Day), it will have a better chance of holding its own by solidifying the franchise's traditional weakness: pitching. James Shields emerged as a legitimate second starter behind ace Scott Kazmir, and lefthanders David Price (the No. 1 overall pick in 2007) and Jake McGee and righty Wade Davis lead a wave of arms who are nearly ready for the majors.

To further shore up their pitching, the Rays parted with Young in a November trade after he had hit .288 with 13 homers in his rookie season. But they wanted to get a potential frontline starter, so they sent Young, Brendan Harris and outfield prospect Jason Pridie to the Twins for Matt Garza, Jason Bartlett and pitching prospect Eduardo Morlan.

The deal also signaled that Tampa Bay is putting a higher premium on makeup and becoming less tolerant of gifted players with petulant attitudes. Young, who was suspended 50 games for tossing a bat at an umpire in the minors, had a sense of entitlement and had a couple of run-ins with man-

CLIFF WELCH

Staff ace Scott Kazmir shows off the road uniform for the new-look Rays

TOP 30 PROSPECTS

1. Evan Longoria, 3b	16. Josh Butler, rhp
2. David Price, lhp	17. Nick Barnese, rhp
3. Jake McGee, lhp	18. James Houser, lhp
4. Wade Davis, rhp	19. Heath Rollins, rhp
5. Reid Brignac, ss	20. Matt Walker, rhp
6. Desmond Jennings, of	21. Mitch Talbot, rhp
7. Jeff Niemann, rhp	22. Mike McCormick, c
8. Jeremy Hellickson, rhp	23. Will Kline, rhp
9. Ryan Royster, of	24. Wade Townsend, rhp
10. Chris Mason, rhp	25. Fernando Perez, of
11. Glenn Gibson, lhp	26. Nevin Ashley, c
12. Juan Salas, rhp	27. Justin Ruggiano, of
13. John Jaso, c	28. Rhyne Hughes, 1b
14. Alex Cobb, rhp	29. Joel Guzman, 3b/1b
15. Eduardo Morlan, rhp	30. D.J. Jones, of

ager Joe Maddon. Five days after trading Young, the Rays dealt Elijah Dukes—one of the game's most gifted and most troubled players—to the Nationals for minor league lefty Glenn Gibson.

While the Rays have yet to reach the 70-win mark, they should crack that barrier soon and could contend in the near future. And the commitment to homegrown talent continued, as they signed their first 16 draft picks, fielded a team in the Rookie-level Dominican Summer League for the first time since 2001 and opened an academy in Venezuela.

General Manager: Andrew Friedman. **Farm Director:** Mitch Lukevics. **Scouting Director:** R.J. Harrison.

Class	Team	League	W	L	PCT	Finish*	Manager	Affiliated
Majors	Tampa Bay	American	66	96	.407	14th (14)	Joe Maddon	—
Triple-A	Durham Bulls	International	80	63	.559	3rd (14)	Charlie Montoyo	1998
Double-A	Montgomery Biscuits	Southern	81	59	.579	1st (10)^	Billy Gardner Jr.	2004
High A	Vero Beach Devil Rays	Florida State	59	79	.428	10th (12)	Joe Szekely	2007
Low A	Columbus Catfish	South Atlantic	82	53	.607	2nd (16)^	Jim Morrison	2007
Short-season	Hudson Valley Renegades	New York-Penn	34	42	.447	9th (14)	Matt Quatraro	1996
Rookie	Princeton Devil Rays	Appalachian	33	35	.485	5th (9)	Jamie Nelson	1997
Overall 2007 Minor League Record			369	331	.527	7th		

*Finish in overall standings (No. of teams in league) ^League champion

LAST YEAR'S TOP 30

Player, Pos.		Status
1.	Delmon Young, of	(Twins)
2.	Evan Longoria, 3b	No. 1
3.	Reid Brignac, ss	No. 5
4.	Jeff Niemann, rhp	No. 7
5.	Jacob McGee, lhp	No. 3
6.	Elijah Dukes, of	(Nationals)
7.	Akinori Iwamura, 3b	Majors
8.	Wade Davis, rhp	No. 4
9.	Matt Walker, rhp	No. 20
10.	Jeremy Hellickson, rhp	No. 8
11.	Joel Guzman, of/1b/3b	No. 29
12.	Jason Hammel, rhp	Majors
13.	Mitch Talbot, rhp	No. 21
14.	Juan Salas, rhp	No. 12
15.	Fernando Perez, of	No. 25
16.	Shawn Riggans, c	Dropped out
17.	Andy Sonnanstine, rhp	Majors
18.	John Jaso, c	No. 13
19.	Jeff Ridgway, lhp	Dropped out
20.	Elliot Johnson, 2b	Dropped out
21.	James Houser, lhp	No. 18
22.	Wes Bankston, 1b/3b	(Athletics)
23.	Chris Mason, rhp	No. 10
24.	Jonathan Barratt, lhp	Dropped out
25.	Josh Butler, rhp	No. 16
26.	Wade Townsend, rhp	No. 24
27.	Sergio Pedroza, of	Dropped out
28.	Chris Nowak, 1b	Dropped out
29.	Shaun Cumberland, of	(Reds)
30.	Desmond Jennings, of	No. 6

BEST TOOLS

Best Hitter for Average	Evan Longoria
Best Power Hitter	Evan Longoria
Best Strike-Zone Discipline	John Jaso
Fastest Baserunner	Fernando Perez
Best Athlete	Desmond Jennings
Best Fastball	Jake McGee
Best Curveball	Wade Davis
Best Slider	David Price
Best Changeup	Mitch Talbot
Best Control	Chris Mason
Best Defensive Catcher	Christian Lopez
Best Defensive Infielder	Reid Brignac
Best Infield Arm	Jairo de la Rosa
Best Defensive Outfielder	Fernando Perez
Best Outfield Arm	Justin Ruggiano

PROJECTED 2011 LINEUP

Catcher	Dioner Navarro
First Base	Carlos Pena
Second Base	Akinori Iwamura
Third Base	Evan Longoria
Shortstop	Reid Brignac
Left Field	Carl Crawford
Center Field	Desmond Jennings
Right Field	B.J. Upton
Designated Hitter	Rocco Baldelli
No. 1 Starter	David Price
No. 2 Starter	Scott Kazmir
No. 3 Starter	Matt Garza
No. 4 Starter	Wade Davis
No. 5 Starter	James Shields
Closer	Jake McGee

TOP PROSPECTS OF THE DECADE

Year	Player, Pos.	2007 Org.
1998	Matt White, rhp	Out of baseball
1999	Matt White, rhp	Out of baseball
2000	Josh Hamilton, of	Reds
2001	Josh Hamilton, of	Reds
2002	Josh Hamilton, of	Reds
2003	Rocco Baldelli, of	Devil Rays
2004	B.J. Upton, ss	Devil Rays
2005	Delmon Young, of	Devil Rays
2006	Delmon Young, of	Devil Rays
2007	Delmon Young, of	Devil Rays

TOP DRAFT PICKS OF THE DECADE

Year	Player, Pos.	2007 Org.
1998	Josh Pressley, 1b (4th round)	Atlantic Lg.
1999	Josh Hamilton, of	Reds
2000	Rocco Baldelli, of	Devil Rays
2001	Dewon Brazelton, rhp	Pirates
2002	B.J. Upton, ss	Devil Rays
2003	Delmon Young, of	Devil Rays
2004	Jeff Niemann, rhp	Devil Rays
2005	Wade Townsend, rhp	Devil Rays
2006	Evan Longoria, 3b	Devil Rays
2007	David Price, lhp	Devil Rays

LARGEST BONUSES IN CLUB HISTORY

Matt White, 1996	$10,200,000
Rolando Arrojo, 1997	$7,000,000
David Price, 2007	$5,600,000
B.J. Upton, 2002	$4,600,000
Dewon Brazelton, 2001	$4,200,000

TAMPA BAY RAYS

Top 2008 Rookie: Evan Longoria, 3b. Having raced through the organization in a season and a half, he'll win the Opening Day third-base job unless he falters in spring training.

Breakout Prospect: Alex Cobb, rhp. He has three legitimate pitches, and if he maintains his uncanny feel for a curveball, he'll hop on the fast track.

SOURCE OF TOP 30 TALENT			
Homegrown	25	Acquired	5
College	10	Trades	5
Junior college	3	Rule 5 draft	0
High school	11	Independent leagues	0
Draft-and-follow	0	Free agents/waivers	0
Nondrafted free agents	0		
International	1		

Sleeper: Christian Lopez, c. The Rays are starting to develop some catching prospects, and Lopez could jump toward the top of that list if he can add offensive consistency to his strong defensive skills.

Numbers in parentheses indicate prospect rankings.

LF
Ryan Royster (9)
Sergio Pedroza
Reid Fronk
K.D. Kang
Stephen Vogt

CF
Desmond Jennings (6)
Fernando Perez (25)
D.J. Jones (30)
Emeel Salem
Dustin Biell

RF
Justin Ruggiano (27)
Quinn Stewart
Justin Reynolds

3B
Evan Longoria (1)
Joel Guzman (29)

SS
Reid Brignac (5)
Jairo de la Rosa
Shawn O'Malley

2B
Elliot Johnson
Cody Cipriano
Michael Ross

1B
Rhyne Hughes (28)
Chris Nowak
Matt Fields
Gabe Martinez
Eli Sonoqui

C
John Jaso (13)
Mike McCormick (22)
Nevin Ashley (26)
Christian Lopez
Shawn Riggans
Mark Thomas

RHP	
Starters	**Relievers**
Wade Davis (4)	Juan Salas (12)
Jeff Niemann (7)	Eduardo Morlan (15)
Jeremy Hellickson (8)	Matt Walker (17)
Chris Mason (10)	Wade Townsend (24)
Alex Cobb (14)	Ryan Reid
Josh Butler (16)	Richard de los Santos
Nick Barnese (17)	Dale Thayer
Heath Rollins (19)	
Mitch Talbot (21)	
Will Kline (23)	
Woods Fines	
Frank de los Santos	
Tyree Hayes	
Joseph Cruz	

LHP	
Starters	**Relievers**
David Price (2)	Jeff Ridgway
Jacob McGee (3)	Brian Henderson
Glenn Gibson (11)	Jino Gonzalez
James Houser (18)	
David Newmann	
Michael Wlodarczyk	

2007

Best Pro Debut: OFs Reid Fronk (7) and Emeel Salem (6) were short-season Hudson Valley's top hitters. Fronk started late after helping North Carolina to a runner-up finish in the College World Series and posted a .961 OPS; Salem ranked among New York-Penn League leaders in batting, runs (41) and steals (28) while hitting .311/.384/.436.

Best Athlete: OF D.J. Jones (11) fits the organization's profile—toolsy outfielders—and was an excellent high school football player due to his speed and strong build. Besides outstanding make-up and stuff, LHP David Price (1) has excellent athleticism for a pitcher.

Best Pure Hitter: Fronk and C/1B Stephen Vogt (12) both control the strike zone and have advanced approaches at the plate to go with solid lefthanded swings. Vogt was primarily a catcher at NAIA Azusa Pacific but played some outfield this summer and took to it well.

Best Power Hitter: Fronk has solid-average power and led North Carolina in home runs this spring, but the class lacks a masher. Draft-and-follow OF K.D. Kang (15, 2006) has better bat speed and above-average raw juice.

Fastest Runner: Jones and Salem are above-average runners.

Best Defensive Player: Salem's instincts, speed and arm suit him well in center field; 3B Greg Sexton (10) impressed Hudson Valley's coaches with his hands and arm strength.

Best Fastball: Price commands his fastball in the 90-93 mph range and can go get 95 whenever he wants.

Best Secondary Pitch: Price's hard (87 mph), two-plane slider overmatched college hitters. The Rays considered RHP Will Kline (2) to have one of the draft's best changeups, and see similarities between him and big leaguer James Shields.

Most Intriguing Background: Price was the 2007 College Player of the Year. Kang is a Korean immigrant who recruited himself to Atlanta's Parkview High, and was discovered by the coaching staff while playing pickup games on the school's field. His parents (who have since moved back to Korea) have business interests in Atlanta, and Kang knew about Parkview through the career of alumnus Jeff Francoeur.

Closest To The Majors: Price signed a major league deal. It wouldn't be a shock to see him in St. Petersburg in 2008.

Best Late-Round Pick: Jones' athleticism and Auburn commitment prompted a $330,000 bonus. The Rays gave RHP Joseph Cruz (30) $100,000 because he has a projectable 6-foot-4 frame and throws 92-94 mph at times.

The One Who Got Away: RHP Ryan Turner (22) has thrown 94 mph at times and is at Arkansas after missing much of the spring with mononucleosis.

Assessment: Price could make this draft special on his own. Kline and RHP Nick Barnese (3) could give the game's top farm system even more pitching depth. The Rays are just as excited about their draft-and-follows like Kang.

2006
BUDGET: $5.0 MILLION

3B Evan Longoria (1) has lived up to his billing as the best hitter in the entire 2006 draft. OF Desmond Jennings (10) developing into a potential five-tool player has been a much bigger surprise.

GRADE: A

2005
BUDGET: $3.4 MILLION

RHP Wade Townsend (1) has battled injuries and been passed by RHPs Chris Mason (2) and Jeremy Hellickson (4).

GRADE: C

2004
BUDGET: $6.3 MILLION

RHP Jeff Niemann (1) has developed slower than hoped, but that doesn't matter. Not with SS Reid Brignac (2), RHP Wade Davis (3) and LHP Jake McGee (5) looking like future stars; OF Ryne Royster (6) and 1B Rhyne Hughes (8) breaking out in 2007; and RHP Andy Sonnanstine (13) already speeding to the majors.

GRADE: A

2003
BUDGET: $5.7 MILLION

OF Delmon Young (1) had an impressive rookie season at age 21, then was dispatched in a six-player trade for Matt Garza. Unsigned LHP Andrew Miller (3) became the top prospect in the 2006 draft and was involved in a blockbuster of his own this offseason.

GRADE: B+

Draft analysis by John Manuel (2007) and Jim Callis (2003-06). Numbers in parentheses indicate draft rounds. Budgets are bonuses in first 10 rounds.

AMERICAN LEAGUE EAST

1

EVAN LONGORIA, 3B

Born: Oct. 7, 1985.
Ht.: 6-2. **Wt.:** 190.
Bats: R. **Throws:** R.
Drafted: Long Beach State, 2006 (1st round).
Signed by: Fred Repke.

SPORTS ON FILM

Longoria has blistered professional pitching since he unexpectedly fell to the Rays as the third overall pick in the 2006 draft and signed for $3 million. The 2005 Cape Cod League MVP and Troy Tulowitzki's successor as Long Beach State's shortstop, he moved to third base, hit .315 with 18 homers in 62 games and reached Double-A Montgomery in his 2006 pro debut. That was just a warmup for 2007, when he was named Southern League MVP. Longoria was leading the Double-A circuit in runs, homers and RBIs when he was promoted to Triple-A Durham in late July, and his 21 homers set a Montgomery franchise record. He did top the SL in slugging percentage (.528) and home run percentage (5.5). A Futures Game selection, he ranked as the No. 2 prospect in the league behind Justin Upton. Longoria continued to rake in the International League, hitting .375 with two homers in the playoffs.

Longoria displays a great feel for hitting, with a disciplined approach and impressive raw power. Both his bat and his power rate as 70 tools on the 20-80 scouting scale. With quick hands and strong wrists, he has a loose and easy swing, producing great leverage and exceptional bat speed. He hits through the ball with his strong follow-through and finish. When Double-A pitchers began to pitch around Longoria last season, he showed improved patience. Even so, he's an aggressive hitter who will swing at any time in the count if he gets his pitch. With his solid pitch recognition, he rarely misses a mistake, and he's capable of hitting tape-measure shots to all fields. Defensively, Longoria is an above-average third baseman with soft hands and solid body control. His footwork is a plus, both with his lateral movement and with charging the ball on slow rollers. His arm strength is another plus, and his throws have good carry and accuracy. He has taken quickly to his new position, making just 19 errors in 177 games at third. He competes hard and has good makeup.

There are times when Longoria's aggressiveness gets the best of him, particularly when it comes to chasing sliders down and away in the strike zone. He doesn't have a classic swing but there's no question that it gets the job done. His biggest shortcoming is his speed, which grades as slightly below average and led to just adequate range at shortstop, prompting his position switch. He does, however, run the bases well with his impressive instincts.

The Rays should have a rookie-of-the-year candidate at third base for the second straight season. Longoria has little to prove in the minors and will push Akinori Otsuka to second base when he's ready. Longoria's spring-training performance will determine whether he makes the Opening Day roster, but there's not question he'll be playing for Tampa on a full-time basis at some point in 2008. He gives every indication of becoming an all-star, hitting .300 with 30-plus homers on an annual basis.

Year	Club (League)	Class	AVG	G	AB	R	H	2B	3B	HR	RBI	BB	SO	SB	OBP	SLG
2006	Hudson Valley (NYP)	A	.424	8	33	5	14	1	1	4	11	5	5	1	.487	.879
	Visalia (Cal)	A	.327	28	110	22	36	8	0	8	28	13	19	1	.402	.618
	Montgomery (SL)	AA	.267	26	105	14	28	5	0	6	19	1	20	2	.266	.486
2007	Montgomery (SL)	AA	.307	105	381	78	117	21	0	21	76	51	81	4	.403	.528
	Durham (IL)	AAA	.269	31	104	19	28	8	0	5	19	22	29	0	.398	.490
MINOR LEAGUE TOTALS			.304	198	733	138	223	43	1	44	153	92	154	8	.388	.546

2 DAVID PRICE, LHP

CLIFF WELCH

Born: Aug. 26, 1985. **B-T:** L-L. **Ht.:** 6-6. **Wt.:** 225. **Drafted:** Vanderbilt, 2007 (1st round). **Signed by:** Brad Matthews.

The Rays pegged Price as the first overall pick in the 2007 draft in October 2006 and he never budged from their plans. Price shattered most of Vanderbilt's pitching records while going 11-1, 2.63 and leading NCAA Division I with 194 strikeouts in 133 innings as a junior. He led the Commodores to their first-ever Southeastern Conference regular-season championship and No. 1 ranking, and he received numerous individual honors, including the Baseball America College Player of the Year and the Golden Spikes awards. He signed on the Aug. 15 deadline, agreeing to an $8.5 million big league contract that included a backloaded $5.6 million bonus. Price is the complete package with outstanding athleticism, stuff and makeup. His fastball has great late life and armside run while sitting in the low 90s and touching 95 mph. He throws a plus-plus slider that reaches 87 mph and has a late, sharp bite. His changeup is also a plus pitch with excellent deception and fade. He uses the entire strike zone and is adept at adding or subtracting velocity with all of his pitches to keep hitters completely baffled. There's no knock on Price. While he still needs to make the adjustment to pro ball, Tampa Bay doesn't see him having any difficulties after he fared well against tough competition in the SEC and with Team USA. He has yet to make his pro debut and spent just two weeks in instructional league before returning to Vanderbilt to work toward his sociology degree, but that shouldn't prevent him from moving rapidly through the system. He has legitimate No. 1 stuff, and he has a deeper repertoire and more polish than Scott Kazmir. Price likely will break into pro ball at high Class A Vero Beach or Double-A, and he could reach Tampa before the end of the season.

Year	Club (League)	Class	W	L	ERA	G	GS	CG	SV	IP	H	R	ER	HR	BB	SO	AVG
2007	Did Not Play—Signed Late																

3 JAKE McGEE, LHP

RICK BATTLE

Born: Aug. 6, 1986. **B-T:** L-L. **Ht.:** 6-3. **Wt.:** 190. **Drafted:** HS—Sparks, Nev., 2004 (5th round). **Signed by:** Fred Repke.

After leading the low Class A Midwest League with 171 strikeouts in 134 innings during a breakout 2006, McGee followed up by ranking fourth in the minors with 175 whiffs in 140 innings. He continued his friendly rivalry with fellow 2004 draftee Wade Davis, though Davis beat him to Double-A. Once McGee got to Montgomery in August, he had no trouble overpowering hitters there. McGee has a nasty fastball that managers rated as the best in the high Class A Florida State League. His heater sits at 93-95 mph and touches 98 with impressive movement. His slider has good tilt and he has improved the depth and fade on his changeup. He dominates lefthanders, who hit just .147 with two homers against him in 2007. McGee is still working on mastering his secondary pitches, though both have the makings of becoming plus offerings. He was erratic with his changeup early last season and doesn't fully trust it. He struggles with the command of his slider and also has trouble locating his fastball when he overthrows. Scouts believe McGee could be a power reliever if he can't refine his changeup. At this point, he'll remain a potential No. 2 starter and keep the Rays dreaming about the day they'll have three power lefties in David Price, Scott Kazmir and McGee in their rotation. He'll likely return to Double-A to open 2008.

Year	Club (League)	Class	W	L	ERA	G	GS	CG	SV	IP	H	R	ER	HR	BB	SO	AVG
2004	Princeton (Appy)	R	4	1	3.97	12	12	0	0	56	49	30	25	5	25	53	.244
2005	Hudson Valley (NYP)	A	5	4	3.64	15	14	0	0	76	64	32	31	4	23	89	.226
2006	Southwest Michigan (MWL)	A	7	9	2.96	26	26	0	0	134	103	54	44	7	65	171	.211
2007	Vero Beach (FSL)	A	5	4	2.93	21	21	0	0	116	86	45	38	8	39	145	.203
	Montgomery (SL)	AA	3	2	4.24	5	5	0	0	23	19	11	11	2	13	30	.224
MINOR LEAGUE TOTALS			24	20	3.29	79	78	0	0	407	321	172	149	26	165	488	.217

4 WADE DAVIS, RHP

JERRY HALE

Born: Sept. 7, 1985. **B-T:** R-R. **Ht.:** 6-5. **Wt.:** 220. **Drafted:** HS—Lake Wales, Fla., 2004 (3rd round). **Signed by:** Kevin Elfering.

The Rays' minor league pitcher of the year, Davis led the system with a 2.50 ERA and ranked seventh in the minors with 169 strikeouts in 158 innings. He tossed the minors' first no-hitter of 2007 on May 4, the second such gem of his career. He was Montgomery's Game One starter in both rounds of the Southern League playoffs. Davis attracts raves for his stuff, command and competitiveness. He relies heavily on a four-seam fastball that sits at 92-94 mph and touches 96. He also throws a hard 11-to-5 curveball in the upper 70s with occasional two-plane break. His changeup can become an above-average pitch, as can his cutter. He works both sides of the plate, and he became more aggressive on the inner half as last season progressed. He uses his height to his advantage by getting good downward plane on his pitches. Davis needs to fine-tune the command of his fastball and his overall feel for pitching in order to mix his offerings more consistently. He still needs to hone a third pitch, which is just a matter of sharpening his promising changeup and cutter. He runs deep into counts when he tries to be too fine with his pitches. Davis has a bulldog mentality and the potential to become a frontline starter. He could open 2008 in Triple-A unless the Rays want to team him with McGee again in Double-A at the start of the season.

Year	Club (League)	Class	W	L	ERA	G	GS	CG	SV	IP	H	R	ER	HR	BB	SO	AVG
2004	Princeton (Appy)	R	3	5	6.09	13	13	0	0	57	71	46	39	8	19	38	.301
2005	Hudson Valley (NYP)	A	7	4	2.72	15	15	0	0	86	75	35	26	5	23	97	.234
2006	Southwest Michigan (MWL)	A	7	12	3.02	27	27	1	0	146	124	61	49	5	64	165	.234
2007	Vero Beach (FSL)	A	3	0	1.84	13	13	0	0	78	54	20	16	5	21	88	.196
	Montgomery (SL)	AA	7	3	3.15	14	14	0	0	80	74	37	28	3	30	81	.249
MINOR LEAGUE TOTALS			27	24	3.17	82	82	2	0	448	398	199	158	26	157	469	.240

5 REID BRIGNAC, SS

BRIAN BISSELL

Born: Jan. 16, 1986. **B-T:** L-R. **Ht.:** 6-3. **Wt.:** 180. **Drafted:** HS—St. Amant, La., 2004 (2nd round). **Signed by:** Benny Latino.

After breaking out and winning the Rays' minor league player of the year award and high Class A California League MVP honors in 2006, Brignac continued to make impressive strides last year despite not maintaining the same gaudy numbers. He played all season in Double-A at age 21 and paced the Southern League with 91 runs, 52 extra-base hits and 228 total bases. Brignac's advanced approach to the game makes him a solid contributor in all phases. He improved his plate discipline and bettered his ability to hit offspeed pitches by making adjustments with his setup and load. He uses the entire field and has plus power that really stands out for a shortstop. His speed and defense are solid. Brignac reduced his whiffs by shortening his swing with two strikes last year, but he needs to continue to trust his hands and resist a tendency to become pull-happy. Though he has good body control, his range is just adequate at shortstop and he struggles at times with balls hit right at him. He's still growing into his body and making improvements with his footwork and quickness. Tampa Bay's trade for Jason Bartlett eliminated any need to push Brignac even more aggressively. Projecting as an offensive-minded shortstop, he'll get a full season at Triple-A before challenging for a big league starting job in 2009.

Year	Club (League)	Class	AVG	G	AB	R	H	2B	3B	HR	RBI	BB	SO	SB	OBP	SLG
2004	Princeton (Appy)	R	.361	25	97	16	35	4	2	1	25	9	10	2	.413	.474
	Charleston, S.C. (SAL)	A	.500	3	14	3	7	1	0	0	5	1	2	0	.533	.571
2005	Southwest Michigan (MWL)	A	.264	127	512	77	135	29	2	15	61	40	131	5	.319	.416
2006	Visalia (Cal)	A	.326	100	411	82	134	26	3	21	83	35	82	12	.382	.557
	Montgomery (SL)	AA	.300	28	110	18	33	6	2	3	16	7	31	3	.355	.473
2007	Montgomery (SL)	AA	.260	133	527	91	137	30	5	17	81	55	94	15	.328	.433
MINOR LEAGUE TOTALS			.288	416	1671	287	481	96	14	57	271	147	350	37	.347	.464

6 DESMOND JENNINGS, OF

SPORTS ON FILM

Born: Oct. 30, 1986. **B-T:** R-R. **Ht.:** 6-2. **Wt.:** 200. **Drafted:** Itawamba (Miss.) CC, 2006 (10th round). **Signed by:** Rickey Drexler.

Jennings planned on playing football at Alabama but wound up at Itawamba (Miss.) CC, where he earned juco all-America honors in 2005 as a wide receiver who led all juco players with 6.75 catches per game. Signed for $150,000 as a 10th-rounder, he ranked as the No. 1 prospect in the low Class A South Atlantic League in his first full pro season. The lone negative was arthroscopic surgery to repair the lateral meniscus in his knee, which ended his season in August. His most obvious tool is his speed, which rates near the top of the 20-80 scouting scale. At the plate, Jennings has a discerning eye with the ability to make contact and drive the ball in the gaps. He has all the tools to become a top-flight leadoff hitter. Managers rated Jennings as the SAL's best defensive outfielder, and he has an average arm. In order for Jennings to make the most of his speed, he needs to improve his jumps and reads. He tends to hesitate ever so slightly in the outfield, and he'll become an even better defender as he hones his ability to read the ball off the bat. The Rays have a knack for developing outfielders, and Jennings is their latest find. He's headed to high Class A in 2008 and has a big league ETA of mid-2010.

Year	Club (League)	Class	AVG	G	AB	R	H	2B	3B	HR	RBI	BB	SO	SB	OBP	SLG
2006	Princeton (Appy)	R	.277	56	213	48	59	10	1	4	20	22	39	32	.360	.390
2007	Columbus (SAL)	A	.315	99	387	75	122	21	5	9	37	45	53	45	.401	.465
MINOR LEAGUE TOTALS			.302	155	600	123	181	31	6	13	57	67	92	77	.387	.438

7 JEFF NIEMANN, RHP

Born: Feb. 8, 1983. **B-T:** R-R. **Ht.:** 6-9. **Wt.:** 280. **Drafted:** Rice, 2004 (1st round). **Signed by:** Jonathan Bonifay.

For the first time since signing a $5.2 million big league contract as the fourth overall pick in the 2004 draft, Niemann turned in a completely healthy season. He worked 131 innings after totaling just 108 in his first two years, and he drew the start for the U.S. team in the Futures Game. After ranking third in the International League with 12 victories, he won two more games in the playoffs. At 6-foot-9, Niemann has an intimidating presence on the mound. His long body and arms, plus the length of his stride, gives hitters little time to decide whether they want to swing. He pounds the strike zone with his 91-94 mph fastball, and he mixes it well with an above-average power curveball that has hard downward break. He's intelligent and does a solid job of keeping batters off balance. Niemann is a slow worker who has little deception. He tends to leave pitches up in the strike zone when he stabs in the back of his delivery. He added a splitter last season that he uses a changeup, but it's still a fringy pitch. He still has to prove that he's durable after having arthroscopic elbow surgery in 2003 and a minor shoulder operation in 2006. He pitched through some shoulder pain last August and had a small bone spur removed after the season. The Rays aren't worried about Niemann's shoulder, and they'll give him the chance to make their rotation in spring training. He still has the stuff to be a No. 2 or 3 starter, even if he has developed more slowly than Tampa Bay hoped.

Year	Club (League)	Class	W	L	ERA	G	GS	CG	SV	IP	H	R	ER	HR	BB	SO	AVG
2005	Visalia (Cal)	A	0	1	3.98	5	5	0	0	20	12	10	9	3	10	28	.167
	Montgomery (SL)	AA	0	1	4.35	6	3	0	0	10	7	7	5	0	5	14	.184
2006	Montgomery (SL)	AA	5	5	2.68	14	14	0	0	77	56	24	23	6	29	84	.202
2007	Durham (IL)	AAA	12	6	3.98	25	25	0	0	131	144	69	58	13	46	123	.277
MINOR LEAGUE TOTALS			17	13	3.58	50	47	0	0	239	219	110	95	22	90	249	.242

8 JEREMY HELLICKSON, RHP

Born: April 8, 1987. **B-T:** R-R. **Ht.:** 6-1. **Wt.:** 185. **Drafted:** HS—Des Moines, Iowa, 2005 (4th round). **Signed by:** Tom Couston.

Drafted out of an Iowa high school after serving as the staff ace of the gold medal-winning U.S. national team at the 2004 World Youth Championship, Hellickson has been brought along slowly by the Rays. Rated as the top prospect in the short-season New York-Penn League in 2006, he came down with a sore arm and missed the first couple of weeks last season. He got on a roll in the second half, allowing just 20 runs over his last 14 starts, including two in the playoffs as low Class A Columbus won the South Atlantic League crown. Hellickson commands a fastball that sits at 92-93 mph and touches 95. He has good feel for a curveball that jumps on hitters. He tries to emulate Greg Maddux, albeit with more electric stuff, and has a great feel for pitching. He has terrific arm action with an excellent release point, and he works down in the strike zone. A 6-foot-1 and 185 pounds, Hellickson lacks projectability. That's not as much of a concern as his durability. While he has the same release point for all of his pitches, he needs to repeat his delivery in order to throw quality strikes with more consistency. An improved changeup would go a long way toward making him a complete pitcher. He has worked just 195 innings since signing, but the Rays are pleased with his progress. They'll continue to advance him one level per year, which makes high Class A his next stop.

Year	Club (League)	Class	W	L	ERA	G	GS	CG	SV	IP	H	R	ER	HR	BB	SO	AVG
2005	Princeton (Appy)	R	0	0	6.00	4	0	0	0	6	6	4	4	1	1	11	.240
2006	Hudson Valley (NYP)	A	4	3	2.43	15	14	0	0	77	55	24	21	3	16	96	.193
2007	Columbus (SAL)	A	13	3	2.67	21	21	1	0	111	87	36	33	7	34	106	.214
MINOR LEAGUE TOTALS			17	6	2.68	40	35	1	0	195	148	64	58	11	51	213	.207

9 RYAN ROYSTER, OF

Born: July 25, 1986. **B-T:** R-R. **Ht.:** 6-2. **Wt.:** 210. **Drafted:** HS—Eugene, Ore., 2004 (6th round). **Signed by:** Paul Kirsch.

After three years in short-season leagues, Royster had a breakthrough season in 2007 and was named the Rays' minor league player of the year. He won the system's triple crown and led the South Atlantic League with 30 homers, 65 extra-base hits and a .601 slugging percentage. He homered in six straight games in August and finished the season with a double and homer in the clinching game of the SAL championship series. Royster is a classic country boy with tremendous bat speed and plus-plus raw power to all fields. He cut down on his swing midway through the season and displayed

TOM PRIDDY

improved patience at the plate. His hands work exceptionally well, enabling him to control the bat head and put the barrel on the ball with impressive consistency. His swing is particularly effective from the point of contact through the finish. He has surprising speed for his size and good instincts on the bases. Though he moves well, Royster needs to upgrade his routes to balls in left field as well as the accuracy of his throws. His arm strength is fringy. Offensively, he's working on covering the outer half of the plate better and upgrading his strike zone discipline. Royster has the righthanded power to play at the game's top level. The Rays are interested to see how his pop will play in 2008 in the pitching-friendly Florida State League.

Year	Club (League)	Class	AVG	G	AB	R	H	2B	3B	HR	RBI	BB	SO	SB	OBP	SLG
2004	Princeton (Appy)	R	.273	52	176	25	48	10	2	5	26	5	47	3	.297	.438
2005	Princeton (Appy)	R	.246	51	187	30	46	8	0	12	37	13	48	6	.300	.481
2006	Hudson Valley (NYP)	A	.247	63	231	20	57	15	1	8	29	9	65	5	.286	.424
2007	Columbus (SAL)	A	.329	125	474	90	156	31	4	30	98	36	121	17	.380	.601
MINOR LEAGUE TOTALS			.287	291	1068	165	307	64	7	55	190	63	281	31	.333	.515

10 CHRIS MASON, RHP

Born: July 1, 1984. **B-T:** R-R. **Ht.:** 6-1. **Wt.:** 190. **Drafted:** UNC Greensboro, 2005 (2nd round). **Signed by:** Brad Matthews.

TOM PRIDDY

Mason bounced back from a disappointing 2006 season by leading the Southern League with 15 wins and a 2.57 ERA. The league's pitcher of the year, he also led Montgomery with 161 innings and 136 strikeouts and helped the Biscuits win the SL championship. Mason controls the game with his tempo on the mound. He works fast with an unorthodox delivery and fills the strike zone, with managers rating his control the best in the SL. Last year, he learned how to stay over the rubber better in order to give his arm a chance to catch up with his body and produce some deception. His best pitch is a changeup with late sink that he throws at any time in the count. His slider has the makings of a plus pitch, sitting at 78-81 mph with sharp break. Mason's fastball is a fringe-average pitch with a comfort zone of 88-89 mph, and it had more velocity and life when he came out of college. Even with a quality changeup, he struggles against lefthanders, who have batted .326 and .282 against him the last two seasons. He has little difficulty throwing strikes but can do a better job of locating his pitches in the zone. Moving methodically through the system, Mason will spend most of 2008 in Triple-A. His stuff could play up significantly as a reliever, and he has the competitiveness needed for the late innings, but he'll remain a starter for now.

Year	Club (League)	Class	W	L	ERA	G	GS	CG	SV	IP	H	R	ER	HR	BB	SO	AVG
2005	Hudson Valley (NYP)	A	1	1	2.40	9	0	0	2	15	11	4	4	0	8	14	.220
	Southwest Michigan (MWL)	A	1	0	1.45	10	0	0	0	18	17	8	3	0	5	16	.246
2006	Visalia (Cal)	A	12	10	5.02	28	27	0	0	152	177	96	85	17	44	111	.289
2007	Montgomery (SL)	AA	15	4	2.57	28	28	1	0	161	147	52	46	7	44	136	.241
MINOR LEAGUE TOTALS			29	15	3.58	75	55	1	2	347	352	160	138	24	101	277	.262

11 GLENN GIBSON, LHP

Born: Sept. 21, 1987. **B-T:** L-L. **Ht.:** 6-4. **Wt.:** 195. **Drafted:** HS—Center Moriches, N.Y., 2006 (4th round). **Signed by:** Guy Mader (Nationals).

When the Rays decided they'd had enough of Elijah Dukes, they shipped him to the Nationals in December and received Gibson in return. The son of former major league lefthander Paul Gibson, he might have been the New-York Penn League's best pitcher last summer until his final two starts, when he tried to pitch while sick and saw his ERA balloon from 1.74 to 3.10. It was later discovered he had mononucleosis, which caused him to drop about 20 pounds and reversed his solid progress in the weight room. Gibson's savvy makes his stuff play up. He pores over hitting and pitching charts before every start so he can exploit weaknesses, and he mixes speeds and locations well. He can throw his plus changeup in any count for strikes, his slow downer curveball can be above-average at times, and his fastball can touch 91 mph and has late movement. Gibson's fastball sits in the high 80s and isn't overpowering, which limits his upside and margin for error. He still needs to add strength to his frame, particularly his lower half, to improve his durability and velocity. Gibson is ready for a full-season league and should begin 2008 in low Class A. He looks like a safe bet to reach the big leagues as a back-of-the-rotation starter.

Year	Club (League)	Class	W	L	ERA	G	GS	CG	SV	IP	H	R	ER	HR	BB	SO	AVG
2006	Vermont (NYP)	A	0	0	0.00	3	3	0	0	6	2	0	0	0	0	7	.100
2007	Vermont (NYP)	A	4	3	3.10	12	12	0	0	58	47	23	20	3	15	58	.223
MINOR LEAGUE TOTALS			4	3	2.81	15	15	0	0	64	49	23	20	3	15	65	.212

12 JUAN SALAS, RHP

Born: Nov. 7, 1978. **B-T:** R-R. **Ht.:** 6-2. **Wt.:** 230. **Signed:** Dominican Republic, 1998. **Signed by:** Rudy Santin.

Salas has spent parts of the past two seasons in the big leagues and has shown hints of success in 46 innings, just shy of MLB's rookie and BA's prospect limits. He broke camp with the Rays last year before being suspended for 50 games in May after testing positive for a performance-enhancing substance. After the suspension he tuned up in Double-A and Triple-A, then returned to the big leagues in late July and pitched well during the last two months. Signed for $600,000 as a third baseman, Salas hit an unimpressive .264 in his first six pro seasons. He also aged three years when his birthdate proved to be falsified, and he was suspended in 2004 after an encounter with an umpire. Upon his return, Salas moved to the mound and had extraordinary success, including a run of 48⅓ straight innings without allowing an earned run to open the 2006 season. Salas is a power pitcher who features a mid-90s fastball with natural cutting action and a hard slider that sits in the mid-80s. His arm is loose and works easily, but he tends to lose consistency with his delivery, which affects his command. Still, Salas has low mileage on his arm and offers plenty of power in relief. He should be a mainstay in Tampa Bay bullpen this year.

Year	Club (League)	Class	W	L	ERA	G	GS	CG	SV	IP	H	R	ER	HR	BB	SO	AVG
2004	Princeton (Appy)	R	1	0	4.82	8	0	0	0	9	10	7	5	2	6	6	.263
2005	Visalia (Cal)	A	2	1	3.52	25	0	0	1	38	30	19	15	6	18	47	.216
	Montgomery (SL)	AA	1	0	3.68	15	0	0	0	22	25	12	9	2	12	18	.281
2006	Montgomery (SL)	AA	3	0	0.00	23	0	0	14	34	13	4	0	0	14	52	.110
	Durham (IL)	AAA	1	1	1.57	27	0	0	3	28	15	5	5	3	11	33	.149
	Tampa Bay (AL)	MLB	0	0	5.40	8	0	0	0	10	13	7	6	1	3	8	.295
2007	Montgomery (SL)	AA	0	0	27.00	2	0	0	0	1	4	4	4	0	2	2	.500
	Durham (IL)	AAA	1	0	2.08	7	0	0	1	8	5	2	2	0	3	12	.161
	Tampa Bay (AL)	MLB	1	1	3.72	34	0	0	0	36	36	19	15	7	17	26	.248
MINOR LEAGUE TOTALS			9	2	2.52	107	0	0	19	143	102	53	40	13	66	170	.195
MAJOR LEAGUE TOTALS			1	1	4.08	42	0	0	0	46	49	26	21	8	20	34	.259

13 JOHN JASO, C

Born: Sept. 19, 1983. **B-T:** L-R. **Ht.:** 6-2. **Wt.:** 205. **Drafted:** Southwestern (Calif.) CC, 2003 (12th round). **Signed by:** Craig Weissmann.

The Rays have known for a while that Jaso could be a special player if he can stay healthy. He achieved that feat in 2007 and earned a spot on Baseball America's year-end Double-A all-star team. He showed his hitting ability by ranking fourth in Double-A and second in the Southern League with a .316 average. A much-desired lefthanded-hitting catcher, Jaso also has some pop. His swing is far from textbook and could even be described as ugly, but he makes it work with his outstanding plate discipline and willingness to battle every time he steps in the box. Jaso's long-term potential centers on whether he can hold up behind the plate. While shoulder ailments have limited his development, he's more than adequate defensively. His arm strength is a tick below-average, especially when he gets long in his release, but he did throw out 35 percent of basestealers last season. He moves well behind the plate and does a solid job of blocking balls and calling a game. He's a good athlete for a catcher and runs better than most, though his speed is below-average. Expected to move up to Triple-A in 2008 after being added to the 40-man roster in the offseason, Jaso could push Dioner Navarro in Tampa Bay if he can stay in the lineup on a regular basis.

Year	Club (League)	Class	AVG	G	AB	R	H	2B	3B	HR	RBI	BB	SO	SB	OBP	SLG
2003	Hudson Valley (NYP)	A	.227	47	154	20	35	7	0	2	20	25	26	2	.344	.312
2004	Hudson Valley (NYP)	A	.302	57	199	34	60	17	2	2	35	22	32	1	.378	.437
2005	Southwest Michigan (MWL)	A	.307	92	332	61	102	25	1	14	50	42	53	3	.383	.515
2006	Visalia (Cal)	A	.309	95	366	58	113	22	0	10	55	31	48	1	.362	.451
2007	Montgomery (SL)	AA	.316	109	380	62	120	24	2	12	71	59	49	2	.408	.484
MINOR LEAGUE TOTALS			.300	400	1431	235	430	95	5	40	231	179	208	9	.380	.458

14 ALEX COBB, RHP

Born: Oct. 7, 1987. **B-T:** R-R. **Ht.:** 6-1. **Wt.:** 180. **Drafted:** HS—Vero Beach, Fla., 2006 (4th round). **Signed by:** Kevin Elfering.

As a 19-year-old last season, Cobb was one of the youngest pitchers in the New York-Penn League, yet he was Hudson Valley's pitcher of the year after leading the team in starts (16), strikeouts (62) and innings (81). He drew college recruiting interest as both a pitcher and a quarterback, leading to a scholarship offer from Clemson and inquiries from some Ivy League schools, but he turned pro for $400,000 as a fourth-round pick. Cobb isn't overpowering, with a fastball that tops out at 91 mph with some sink. His best pitch is an 11-to-5 curveball that he feels comfortable throwing at any time in the count. Normally a pitcher with good command, he lost the feel for his curve at the end of last season before regaining it in instructional league. His third pitch is a decent splitter that he uses as a changeup. His intelligence, competitiveness and mound savvy are all above average. Cobb is a solid athlete but doesn't offer much projection for a young righthander. Some scouts question his strength and durability, though those haven't become been an issue yet. He'll get his first taste of full-season ball this year in low Class A.

Year	Club (League)	Class	W	L	ERA	G	GS	CG	SV	IP	H	R	ER	HR	BB	SO	AVG
2006	Princeton (Appy)	R	0	0	5.19	6	1	0	0	8	9	7	5	3	3	8	.265
2007	Hudson Valley (NYP)	A	5	6	3.54	16	16	0	0	81	78	36	32	4	31	62	.259
MINOR LEAGUE TOTALS			5	6	3.70	22	17	0	0	90	87	43	37	7	34	70	.260

15 EDUARDO MORLAN, RHP

Born: March 1, 1986. **B-T:** R-R. **Ht.:** 6-2. **Wt.:** 220. **Drafted:** HS—Miami, 2004 (3rd round). **Signed by:** Hector Otero (Twins).

Born in Cuba, Morlan moved with his parents to Spain and then at age 12 to Miami, where he emerged as one of south Florida's top high school pitchers. While he flashed three pitches in high school, the Twins moved him to the bullpen in 2006. He had one of the biggest arms in the Minnesota system, with a fastball that touches 97 mph and a mid-80s slider. He loses fastball command when he works in the mid-90s, however, and the Twins had him focus on command and averaging 92-93 mph. His fastball lacks life, and Morland still struggles to command the strike zone because of persistent overthrowing and over-rotating in his delivery. His slider remains a plus pitch, and at times it has excellent two-plane depth, making it a true strikeout offering. While he had success in the Arizona Fall League, with 12 scoreless outings, he walked six in 13 innings, and Minnesota believed his command issues limit his ceiling to setup man rather than closer. That's a key reason why the Twins included him in the six-player trade that centered around Delmon Young and Matt Garza in the offseason. Morlan should have a chance to make Tampa Bay's big league bullpen in the spring, but more likely he's headed for Double-A to continue work on his command.

Year	Club (League)	Class	W	L	ERA	G	GS	CG	SV	IP	H	R	ER	HR	BB	SO	AVG
2004	Twins (GCL)	R	1	2	2.84	11	2	0	1	25	25	14	8	1	10	28	.245
2005	Elizabethton (Appy)	R	2	0	0.82	4	4	0	0	22	6	2	2	0	6	30	.085
	Beloit (MWL)	A	4	4	4.38	10	10	0	0	51	39	25	25	5	31	55	.207
2006	Beloit (MWL)	A	5	5	2.29	28	18	1	2	106	78	31	27	6	38	125	.202
2007	Fort Myers (FSL)	A	4	3	3.15	41	0	0	18	65	55	25	23	7	17	92	.218
	New Britain (EL)	AA	1	0	2.25	2	0	0	0	4	3	1	1	0	3	7	.200
MINOR LEAGUE TOTALS			17	14	2.82	96	34	1	21	274	206	98	86	19	105	337	.203

16 JOSH BUTLER, RHP

Born: Dec. 11, 1984. **B-T:** R-R. **Ht.:** 6-5. **Wt.:** 200. **Drafted:** San Diego, 2006 (2nd round). **Signed by:** Dan Drake.

Butler reached high Class A in his first full pro season, continuing to show filthy stuff even after a sprained thumb cost him three weeks starting in mid-July. The 47th overall pick in 2006, he had his pro debut cut short by biceps tendinitis. His arm strength returned last season, and he has one of the best repertoires among Tampa Bay pitching prospects. Butler owns a 92-95 mph fastball with outstanding movement, including late sinking action. He also has an overhand curveball with tight spin and a hard, sharp slider. His changeup continues to show improvement, though he tends to abandon the pitch too readily. The Rays like Butler's competitive streak and his work ethic. He simply needs innings against better competition so he can become more consistent with his changeup and his release. Tampa Bay has worked with him to incorporate his legs more in his delivery. He'll open the season back in high Class A and should move up to Double-A at some point in 2008.

Year	Club (League)	Class	W	L	ERA	G	GS	CG	SV	IP	H	R	ER	HR	BB	SO	AVG
2006	Hudson Valley (NYP)	A	0	3	5.40	5	2	0	0	13	13	9	8	0	7	12	.265
2007	Columbus (SAL)	A	5	1	2.33	13	13	0	0	77	63	25	20	3	20	54	.224
	Vero Beach (FSL)	A	4	3	4.93	10	9	1	0	49	51	31	27	9	21	34	.273
MINOR LEAGUE TOTALS			9	7	3.54	28	24	1	0	140	127	65	55	12	48	100	.246

17 NICK BARNESE, RHP

Born: Jan. 11, 1989. **B-T:** R-R. **Ht.:** 6-2. **Wt.:** 170. **Drafted:** HS—Simi Valley, Calif., 2007 (3rd round). **Signed by:** Robbie Moen.

Barnese twirled a shutout in his first start as a high school junior in 2006, then was suspended for the rest of the season for violating an unspecified team rule. He returned to the mound last spring and pitched himself into the third round of the draft, turning pro for $366,000. He showed absolutely no fear in his debut, averaging a strikeout per inning and limited opponents to a .216 average. His control was exceptional, as he issued just four walks in 36 innings. In addition to having the cockiness of a gunslinger, Barnese owns a plus fastball that sits at 91-93 mph and shows good life, particularly down in the strike zone. His breaking ball is primarily a slurve with good depth and a late, sharp break. He has a quick arm and works both sides of the plate with consistency. His changeup needs work, though he has shown a good feel for the pitch. Barnese demonstrated a focused attitude throughout his senior year that led to his being a top recruit for Cal State Fullerton and a premium draft pick. The Rays are usually conservative in the development of high school arms, but a jump to low Class A isn't out of the question for Barnese.

Year	Club (League)	Class	W	L	ERA	G	GS	CG	SV	IP	H	R	ER	HR	BB	SO	AVG
2007	Princeton (Appy)	R	2	2	3.22	9	8	0	0	36	30	19	13	1	4	37	.216
MINOR LEAGUE TOTALS			2	2	3.22	9	8	0	0	36	30	19	13	1	4	37	.216

18 JAMES HOUSER, LHP

Born: Dec. 15, 1984. **B-T:** L-L. **Ht.:** 6-4. **Wt.:** 185. **Drafted:** HS—Sarasota, Fla., 2003 (2nd round). **Signed by:** Kevin Elfering.

Houser was following up his solid 2006 showing with a similar performance in Double-A last year, but it came to an abrupt halt when he was suspended for 50 games in August for testing positive for a performance-enhancing substance. He's one of the highest-profile prospects ever nabbed by the minor league testing program. The Rays questioned the results because Houser has a heart condition that requires medication, and he took an amphetamine that resulted in the positive showing. The suspension also prevented him from competing in the Arizona Fall League, which Tampa Bay had hoped would give him a jump on 2008, but didn't stop the club from protecting him on its 40-man roster. Houser throws four pitches for strikes, though none of his offerings is dominant. His fastball touches 91 mph and resides comfortably around 88, and he's able to add and subtract from it while maintaining solid armside run. He has the most confidence in his curveball, which features good tilt. His changeup is solid average, while his cutter sits at 83-85 mph and serves as his out pitch against lefthanders. Houser also unveils a slider on occasion, but he's not consistent with it. His total package may not make him more than a bottom-of-the-rotation starter. After completing his suspension, he'll resume his career in Double-A.

Year	Club (League)	Class	W	L	ERA	G	GS	CG	SV	IP	H	R	ER	HR	BB	SO	AVG
2003	Princeton (Appy)	R	0	4	3.73	10	10	0	0	41	43	23	17	1	13	44	.262
2004	Charleston, S.C. (SAL)	A	3	1	2.20	7	7	0	0	32	27	9	8	1	13	27	.239
2005	Southwest Michigan (MWL)	A	8	8	3.76	22	22	0	0	115	100	50	48	12	31	109	.239
2006	Visalia (Cal)	A	12	4	4.41	28	27	0	0	151	140	80	74	20	46	137	.246
2007	Montgomery (SL)	AA	5	4	3.65	20	20	0	0	103	88	51	42	10	39	90	.230
MINOR LEAGUE TOTALS			28	21	3.84	87	86	0	0	443	398	213	189	44	142	407	.242

19 HEATH ROLLINS, RHP

Born: May 25, 1985. **B-T:** L-R. **Ht.:** 6-1. **Wt.:** 185. **Drafted:** Winthrop, 2006 (11th round). **Signed by:** Brad Matthews.

A two-way player in college, Rollins had one of the best seasons of any pitcher in the minor leagues last year, establishing a Rays system record with 17 wins, which tied for tops in the minors. He had a string of six straight starts without allowing an earned run early in the season, finished second in the South Atlantic League in strikeouts (149 in 159 innings) and fourth in ERA (2.54), then went 2-0, 1.38 in the postseason to help Columbus win the league crown. Rollins' strength centers on his ability to change speeds while pounding the strike zone with all four of his offerings. He keeps his 88-92 mph fastball down in the zone. His slider is a true out pitch, and he spins the ball well with his quick arm action. He has a good feel for moving the ball in and out, and he keeps his offerings to lefthanders down and in—though they did hit .272 against him. He can add and subtract velocity with all of his pitches without affecting his plus command. His changeup is fringy and needs more polish and consistency. Rollins' clean delivery is efficient, and he repeats it with ease. He has excellent baseball sense, which can be attributed in part to his experience as an everyday player. He also competes well and is a true student of the game. Considered by many within the organization to be a clone of Jamie Shields, Rollins will get his next challenge in high Class A.

Year	Club (League)	Class	W	L	ERA	G	GS	CG	SV	IP	H	R	ER	HR	BB	SO	AVG
2006	Hudson Valley (NYP)	A	1	3	4.08	12	10	0	0	46	44	25	21	3	14	48	.249
2007	Columbus (SAL)	A	17	4	2.54	27	27	1	0	159	132	57	45	11	38	149	.223
MINOR LEAGUE TOTALS			18	7	2.89	39	37	1	0	205	176	82	66	14	52	197	.229

20 MATT WALKER, RHP

Born: Aug. 16, 1986. **B-T:** R-R. **Ht.:** 6-3. **Wt.:** 195. **Drafted:** HS—Baton Rouge, La., 2004 (10th round). **Signed by:** Benny Latino.

The 2007 season was one to forget for Walker. His best friend was killed in a house fire, and he had difficulty finding the strike zone all season. He spent the first half in the rotation at high Class A and went 2-6, 5.97 before moving to the bullpen. He had a little more success in relief, yet he still finished the season ranked fourth in the minors with 82 walks. Fortunately for Walker, the light seemed to come back on during instructional league. He has one of the best breaking balls in the organization, a 12-to-6 overhand curveball. His heavy low-90s fastball is also a plus pitch with its impressive sinking action. After his changeup showed the potential to be an above-average offering in the past, he started to establish it earlier in games last year. Command has always been the biggest issue for Walker, and he bottomed out in that regard last year. His mechanics were out of sync, and he'd fly open after rushing with his lower half, causing his arm to drag. Walker also learned that he can't overpower more advanced hitters, particularly if he abandons his secondary offerings. Unless his overall repertoire develops, he's likely to remain in the bullpen and could become a setup man. If he shows better command in spring training, Walker could open the 2008 season in Double-A.

Year	Club (League)	Class	W	L	ERA	G	GS	CG	SV	IP	H	R	ER	HR	BB	SO	AVG
2005	Princeton (Appy)	R	2	3	5.31	13	12	0	1	57	63	39	34	2	22	71	.274
	Hudson Valley (NYP)	A	0	0	10.80	1	1	0	0	3	5	4	4	0	4	5	.357
2006	Southwest Michigan (MWL)	A	5	5	3.18	15	15	0	0	82	66	34	29	5	41	68	.223
2007	Vero Beach (FSL)	A	4	9	5.55	31	15	0	0	95	96	75	59	8	82	76	.264
MINOR LEAGUE TOTALS			11	17	4.75	60	43	0	1	238	230	152	126	15	149	220	.255

21 MITCH TALBOT, RHP

Born: Oct. 17, 1983. **B-T:** R-R. **Ht.:** 6-2. **Wt.:** 200. **Drafted:** HS—Cedar City, Utah, 2002 (2nd round). **Signed by:** Doug Deutsch (Astros).

After initially exciting the Rays following his acquisition in a mid-2006 deal that sent Aubrey Huff to Houston, Talbot had an up-and-down 2007 season in Triple-A. He struggled at times with the command of all three of his pitches while trying to deal with the high expectations he created during his initial stint in the system, when he showed a consistent plus fastball and threw two complete-game shutouts in the Southern League playoffs. Though he didn't live up to those expectations, he still managed to win 13 games and made adjustments as he continued to learn about himself as a pitcher. Talbot pitched at 89-91 mph with his fastball while mixing in a solid changeup and a slider. An excellent athlete, he has a clean delivery that he repeats well. He's capable of dialing up his fastball a few extra notches when needed, and the effectiveness of his slider, which has late cutting action, has improved. Talbot continues to mature as a pitcher and could be a long-term solution in the back half of the major league rotation. He could make that jump in 2008, though he figures to return to Triple-A to open the slate.

Year	Club (League)	Class	W	L	ERA	G	GS	CG	SV	IP	H	R	ER	HR	BB	SO	AVG
2003	Martinsville (Appy)	R	4	4	2.83	12	12	0	0	54	45	26	17	1	11	46	.224
2004	Lexington (SAL)	A	10	10	3.83	27	27	1	0	152	145	78	65	16	49	115	.252
2005	Salem (Car)	A	8	11	4.34	27	27	1	0	151	169	90	73	15	46	100	.280
2006	Corpus Christi (TL)	AA	6	4	3.39	18	17	0	1	90	94	49	34	4	29	96	.269
	Montgomery (SL)	AA	4	3	1.90	10	10	0	0	66	51	16	14	2	18	59	.214
2007	Durham (IL)	AAA	13	9	4.53	29	29	1	0	161	169	89	81	13	59	124	.274
MINOR LEAGUE TOTALS			45	41	3.78	123	122	3	1	675	673	348	284	51	212	540	.260

22 MIKE McCORMICK, C

Born: Sept. 6, 1986. **B-T:** R-R. **Ht.:** 6-2. **Wt.:** 200. **Drafted:** HS—Eugene, Ore., 2005 (5th round). **Signed by:** Paul Kirsch.

A position change proved to be the catalyst that allowed McCormick to blossom as a prospect. After playing third base his first two seasons of pro ball, he moved behind the plate in 2007 and impressed. McCormick had shown pop in his bat since signing in 2005, and he continued to display solid raw power last year. He needs to develop more patience at the plate, but he can make pitchers pay when they throw him a mistake. McCormick's bat can slow down at times due to the rigors of catching, and his tendency to wrap the bat head toward the pitcher makes him susceptible to pitches up and in under his hands. In his first season as a catcher, McCormick showed a strong and accurate arm with a quick release that produced pop times as low as 1.8 seconds. He also threw out 31 percent of basestealers. His footwork is solid, and he shifts and blocks balls in the dirt well. His speed is below average but he's not a baseclogger and he runs better than most catchers. McCormick continues to learn the nuances of calling a game and receiving, but the early returns and his tremendous work ethic has the Rays encouraged. He'll open 2008 in low Class A, finally reaching full-season ball in his fourth pro year.

Year	Club (League)	Class	AVG	G	AB	R	H	2B	3B	HR	RBI	BB	SO	SB	OBP	SLG
2005	Princeton (Appy)	R	.252	32	111	15	28	10	1	3	16	11	31	3	.339	.441
2006	Princeton (Appy)	R	.275	62	222	34	61	18	0	10	39	26	64	7	.364	.491
2007	Hudson Valley (NYP)	A	.276	67	239	35	66	20	1	8	44	27	66	3	.352	.469
MINOR LEAGUE TOTALS			.271	161	572	84	155	48	2	21	99	64	161	13	.354	.472

23 WILL KLINE, RHP

Born: Sept. 10, 1984. **B-T:** R-R. **Ht.:** 6-2. **Wt.:** 210. **Drafted:** Mississippi, 2007 (2nd round). **Signed by:** Rickey Drexler.

Shortly after signing for $513,000 last June as a second-round pick, Kline described himself as "an unpolished tool ready to be polished." That might have been a little modest after he had gone 7-3, 3.75 with 134 strikeouts in 125 innings during his final season at Mississippi. Kline has worked less than the typical college pitcher, because he had Tommy John surgery during his senior year of high school and it took him a couple of seasons to fully regain his arm strength. He pitched well in nine starts in low Class A, save for an outing in which he allowed 11 of his 16 earned runs. Kline does an excellent job of working ahead in the count and keeping hitters off balance by mixing his pitches and moving the ball around the strike zone. He also shows impressive determination and wants the ball in key situations. His repertoire is far from overwhelming, though he did have one of the best changeups available in the 2007 draft. Kline also has an 89-92 mph fastball and a slurvy breaking ball, both of which rate as average to slightly above. Some scouts were concerned about Kline's long arm action, but he repeats his delivery well and his mechanics are sound. Spring training will determine whether he moves up to high Class A to start his first full pro season.

Year	Club (League)	Class	W	L	ERA	G	GS	CG	SV	IP	H	R	ER	HR	BB	SO	AVG
2007	Columbus (SAL)	A	0	4	4.97	9	9	0	0	29	38	19	16	4	11	27	.309
MINOR LEAGUE TOTALS			0	4	4.97	9	9	0	0	29	38	19	16	4	11	27	.309

24 WADE TOWNSEND, RHP

Born: Feb. 22, 1983. **B-T:** R-R. **Ht.:** 6-4. **Wt.:** 230. **Drafted:** Rice, 2005 (1st round). **Signed by:** Jonathan Bonifay.

Townsend endured another tough season in 2007, though this one at least started out on the mound. The eighth overall pick in the 2005 draft, he missed all of the following season after having Tommy John surgery. He allowed 11 runs in his first eight starts in 2007 but struggled thereafter and gradually pitched worse. He was shut down in early August and had a small bone spur removed from his elbow. To his credit, Townsend tried to pitch through the pain and demonstrated a bulldog tenacity that should bode well for the future. He approached his rehab with similar intensity and is expected to be healthy in spring training. Before the latest injury, he showed more than a glimpse of the form that made him a star at Rice and a two-time first-round pick. Townsend's fastball resides in the low 90s with decent movement. He also has a spike curveball that should become a plus pitch, and his changeup could become an above-average offering as well. Townsend has pitched just 142 innings since his college career ended in 2004—negotiations with the Orioles broke down swiftly after they took him eighth overall that June—and he needs more time to iron out the kinks in his delivery and improve his pitch sequence. Some scouts see his future in the bullpen, but he'll aim for a healthy year as a starter in high Class A.

Year	Club (League)	Class	W	L	ERA	G	GS	CG	SV	IP	H	R	ER	HR	BB	SO	AVG
2005	Hudson Valley (NYP)	A	0	4	5.49	12	10	0	0	39	44	28	24	4	24	33	.275
2006	Did Not Play—Injured																
2007	Columbus (SAL)	A	6	10	5.08	21	21	0	0	102	91	65	58	16	53	92	.238
MINOR LEAGUE TOTALS			6	14	5.20	33	31	0	0	142	135	93	82	20	77	125	.249

25 FERNANDO PEREZ, OF

Born: April 23, 1983. **B-T:** B-R. **Ht.:** 6-1. **Wt.:** 195. **Drafted:** Columbia, 2004 (7th round). **Signed by:** Brad Matthews.

One of the catalysts on Montgomery's championship team in 2007, Perez made the Southern League and Baseball America Double-A all-star teams. The highest-drafted player ever out of Columbia (seventh round), Perez has excellent tools, featuring quick-twitch muscles and above-average athleticism. His speed ranks near the top of the 20-80 scouting scale and he uses his legs to his advantage on the basepaths and in center field. Perez began switch-hitting in 2006 and showed progress last year. While he's capable of driving the ball from his natural right side, he employs a slap-and-run approach from the left side. He has work to do with making more consistent contact and maintaining his balance at the plate, but scouts believe he will be a much better hitter than former Rays speedster Joey Gathright. Perez does a good job of drawing walks. He uses his intelligence in the outfield, where he has plus range with controlled actions and a solid-average arm. A soccer player for most of his life, he continues to learn the nuances of baseball. His success rate on steals dropped to a career-low 64 percent last season, and he has the quickness to do much better than that. With his speed, defense and improving performance at the plate, Perez could be a factor in the major leagues, though the Rays are loaded with outfield options. After being added to the 40-man roster for the first time, he'll begin 2008 in Triple-A.

Year	Club (League)	Class	AVG	G	AB	R	H	2B	3B	HR	RBI	BB	SO	SB	OBP	SLG
2004	Hudson Valley (NYP)	A	.232	69	267	46	62	8	5	2	20	30	70	24	.314	.322
2005	Southwest Michigan (MWL)	A	.289	134	522	93	151	17	13	6	48	58	80	57	.361	.406
2006	Visalia (Cal)	A	.307	133	547	123	168	19	9	4	56	78	134	33	.398	.397
2007	Montgomery (SL)	AA	.308	102	393	84	121	24	10	8	33	76	104	32	.423	.481
MINOR LEAGUE TOTALS			.290	438	1729	346	502	68	37	20	157	242	388	146	.380	.407

26 NEVIN ASHLEY, C

Born: Aug. 14, 1984. **B-T:** R-R. **Ht.:** 6-1. **Wt.:** 215. **Drafted:** Indiana State, 2006 (6th round). **Signed by:** James Bonnici.

Ashley made steady improvements behind the plate in low Class A last year, his first full season in pro ball. He earned his second all-star recognition in as many seasons by displaying a consistent bat and impressive leadership at catcher. Ashley has excellent strength that helps him drive the ball in the gaps. His swing isn't pretty, but it works better with wood as opposed to metal bats, and he has a chance to hit for a solid average with decent power at higher levels. He will strike out but he offsets his whiffs with a healthy amount of walks. He's very athletic for a catcher, has decent speed and managed to steal 20 bases in 2007. Ashley impressed the Columbus coaching staff with his work ethic and desire to win. He spent hours working with pitchers and helped make them better. Ashley's defensive game also improved, particularly in blocking balls, and he paced South Atlantic League catchers with a .992 fielding percentage. He calls a good game, but still needs to improve on his exchange, which in turn will make his throws to second more accurate. Even so, he threw out 52 percent of basestealers in 2006 and 33 percent last season. His next step is high Class A.

Year	Club (League)	Class	AVG	G	AB	R	H	2B	3B	HR	RBI	BB	SO	SB	OBP	SLG
2006	Princeton (Appy)	R	.333	47	153	25	51	8	1	4	28	21	40	7	.440	.477
2007	Columbus (SAL)	A	.280	119	429	76	120	13	8	12	60	49	92	20	.354	.431
MINOR LEAGUE TOTALS			.294	166	582	101	171	21	9	16	88	70	132	27	.377	.443

27 JUSTIN RUGGIANO, OF

Born: April 12, 1982. **B-T:** R-R. **Ht.:** 6-2. **Wt.:** 205. **Drafted:** Texas A&M, 2004 (24th round). **Signed by:** Chris Smith (Dodgers).

Considered a throw-in to a deal that brought Dioner Navarro and Jae Seo to Tampa Bay from the Dodgers for Toby Hall and Mark Hendrickson in mid-2006, Ruggiano put together one of the better all-around campaigns in the system last season. He was Durham's player of the year, leading the Bulls in most offensive categories, as well as an all-star in the International League, where he was the lone 20-20 player. He hit .367 with four homers in the playoffs before making his major league debut in September. Ruggiano has playable tools, and the sum ends up being greater than the individual parts. He's a hard-nosed performer with above-average speed who hits for average and some power. He'll play almost the entire 2008 season at 26, so his ceiling isn't as high as most of the players on this list, but he has the ability to be a capable fourth outfielder in the major leagues. He played all three outfield spots last season, but he fits better on a corner than he does in center. His arm is average and enough for him to play regularly in right field. While he probably will return to Triple-A to open the season, Ruggiano should get the chance to contribute in Tampa at some point.

Year	Club (League)	Class	AVG	G	AB	R	H	2B	3B	HR	RBI	BB	SO	SB	OBP	SLG
2004	Ogden (Pio)	R	.329	46	155	26	51	12	0	7	36	23	38	6	.428	.542
2005	Vero Beach (FSL)	A	.310	71	242	47	75	15	4	9	37	28	65	16	.400	.517
	Jacksonville (SL)	AA	.342	53	161	23	55	10	1	6	29	17	56	8	.422	.528
2006	Jacksonville (SL)	AA	.260	89	292	51	76	18	3	9	45	46	74	10	.367	.435
	Montgomery (SL)	AA	.333	31	108	25	36	14	3	4	27	19	29	4	.442	.630
2007	Durham (IL)	AAA	.309	127	482	78	149	29	2	20	73	53	151	26	.386	.502
	Tampa Bay (AL)	MLB	.214	7	14	2	3	0	0	0	3	1	5	0	.267	.214
MINOR LEAGUE TOTALS			.307	417	1440	250	442	98	13	55	247	186	413	70	.397	.508
MAJOR LEAGUE TOTALS			.214	7	14	2	3	0	0	0	3	1	5	0	.267	.214

28 RHYNE HUGHES, 1B

Born: Sept. 9, 1983. **B-T:** L-L. **Ht.:** 6-2. **Wt.:** 175. **Drafted:** Pearl River (Miss.) CC, 2004 (8th round). **Signed by:** Benny Latino.

Hughes was drafted by the Pirates in the 50th round in 2003 and committed to Mississippi before leading Division II juco players with 18 homers in 2004. After turning down Pittsburgh as a draft-and-follow, he signed with the Rays but hit just .250 with 11 homers in his first two pro seasons. He became one of the system's biggest surprises in 2008, leading the Florida State League in batting until he was promoted to Double-A at the end of July. FSL observers compared him to Keith Hernandez and James Loney, and managers rated him as the best defensive first baseman in the circuit. Hughes works the count until he gets a pitch he can handle, preferring stuff on the outer half that he can drive to the opposite field. He's strong but he may need to pull the ball more often to provide the power teams want at first base. Though he has below-average speed, he moves well and has soft hands at first base. A two-way player in junior college, he also has a strong arm for his position. Hughes was hit in the face by a pitch and missed the last week of the season, but he's fine now and will return to Double-A to start 2008.

Year	Club (League)	Class	AVG	G	AB	R	H	2B	3B	HR	RBI	BB	SO	SB	OBP	SLG
2005	Hudson Valley (NYP)	A	.279	58	219	34	61	18	0	8	30	15	53	3	.335	.470
2006	Southwest Michigan (MWL)	A	.233	114	386	22	90	16	4	3	39	33	102	1	.294	.319
2007	Vero Beach (FSL)	A	.329	94	334	65	110	24	1	12	57	35	62	1	.392	.515
	Montgomery (SL)	AA	.295	21	78	12	23	4	1	2	15	9	23	0	.378	.449
MINOR LEAGUE TOTALS			.279	287	1017	133	284	62	6	25	141	92	240	5	.342	.426

29 JOEL GUZMAN, 3B/1B

Born: Nov. 24, 1984. **B-T:** R-R. **Ht.:** 6-6. **Wt.:** 252. **Signed:** Dominican Republic, 2001. **Signed by:** Pablo Peguero (Dodgers).

Once one of the most coveted prospects in the minors, Guzman did little in his first full season in the Rays system to indicate that he might live up to his previous projections. Signed for a Dominican-record $2.25 million in 2001, Guzman and outfield prospect Sergio Pedroza came to Tampa Bay in a July 2006 trade that sent Julio Lugo to the Dodgers. Guzman has a full toolbox, but he fails to get the most from his talent because he doesn't make adjustments. He doesn't play with much energy and displays an apathetic approach to improving his skills, particularly in controlling the strike zone. He has plus-plus raw power and hit several tape-measure shots for Durham, but he has topped 16 homers just once in six pro seasons. He still struggles with hard stuff on the inner half and remains a tease at the plate. For his size, he's a very good athlete and runs well. A shortstop early in his pro career, Guzman tried to make the move to the outfield but shifted back to the infield at third base last season. The position suits him, as he has quick reactions, relatively soft hands and a strong arm. If he can show some maturity and improve his game, Guzman has a chance to play in the big leagues for a long time. Otherwise, he'll be on the list of classic underachievers.

Year	Club (League)	Class	AVG	G	AB	R	H	2B	3B	HR	RBI	BB	SO	SB	OBP	SLG
2002	Dodgers (GCL)	R	.212	10	33	4	7	2	0	0	2	5	8	1	.316	.273
	Great Falls (Pio)	R	.252	43	151	19	38	8	2	3	27	18	54	5	.331	.391
2003	South Georgia Waves (SAL)	A	.235	58	217	33	51	13	0	8	29	9	62	4	.263	.406
	Vero Beach (FSL)	A	.246	62	240	30	59	13	1	5	24	11	60	0	.279	.371
2004	Vero Beach (FSL)	A	.307	87	329	52	101	22	8	14	51	21	78	8	.349	.550
	Jacksonville (SL)	AA	.280	46	182	25	51	11	3	9	35	13	44	1	.325	.522
2005	Jacksonville (SL)	AA	.287	122	442	63	127	31	2	16	75	42	128	7	.351	.475
2006	Los Angeles (NL)	MLB	.211	9	19	2	4	0	0	0	3	3	2	0	.348	.211
	Las Vegas (PCL)	AAA	.297	85	317	44	94	16	2	11	55	26	72	9	.353	.464
	Durham (IL)	AAA	.193	25	88	7	17	5	0	4	9	4	23	0	.228	.386
2007	Durham (IL)	AAA	.242	110	414	44	100	17	2	16	64	23	117	9	.279	.408
	Tampa Bay (AL)	MLB	.243	16	37	5	9	1	2	0	4	2	10	0	.282	.378
MINOR LEAGUE TOTALS			.267	648	2413	321	645	138	20	86	371	172	646	44	.317	.448
MAJOR LEAGUE TOTALS			.232	24	56	7	13	1	2	0	7	5	12	0	.306	.321

30 D.J. JONES, OF

Born: Dec. 15, 1987. **B-T:** L-L. **Ht.:** 6-1. **Wt.:** 190. **Drafted:** HS—Gulf Shores, Ala., 2007 (11th round). **Signed by:** Milt Hill.

He may be the most raw prospect in the system, but Jones has a huge ceiling. The Rays always have loved athletes and couldn't help but sign him away from an Auburn commitment for a $335,000 bonus as an 11th-round pick in 2007. A star wide receiver and cornerback for his high school football team, Jones was a two-way player in baseball and tossed a no-hitter in the Alabama state playoffs. Jones has a good approach at the plate, though he has a ways to go with his discipline and pitch recognition. The biggest question about his offensive game is his bat speed, which is just fringe average. He uses a level swing to lace line drives to all fields, and he set an Alabama prep record for career triples thanks to his plus speed and his ability to drive the ball in the gaps. Jones is still learning how to put his quickness to use. He has to read pitchers better in order to become a consistent basestealing threat, and he must take better routes on balls in center field. He has an above-average arm that would fit in right field if needed. Jones is definitely a work in progress, but the Rays have a solid history of being able to mold toolsy outfielders into major league contributors. He'll open 2008 in extended spring training before making his pro debut at Rookie-level Princeton.

Year	Club (League)	Class	AVG	G	AB	R	H	2B	3B	HR	RBI	BB	SO	SB	OBP	SLG
2007	Did Not Play—Signed Late															

Texas Rangers

BY AARON FITT

As it became apparent that the Rangers were going to miss the playoffs for the eighth straight season in 2007, second-year general manager Jon Daniels faced some tough decisions and ultimately embraced a true commitment to rebuilding the organization from the ground up.

Texas limped out of the gates under first-year manager Ron Washington, finding itself in last place and 5½ games back of the first-place Angels by the end of April. By the end of May, the Rangers trailed by 13½ games, and when the deficit had stretched to 16½ games by the end of June, Daniels had little choice but to look toward the future. That meant trading franchise player Mark Teixeira to maximize the return for a player who faces free agency after the 2008 season. He did just that by shipping Teixeira to the Braves along with lefthander Ron Mahay for a bounty of five highly regarded prospects: catcher Jarrod Saltalamacchia, shortstop Elvis Andrus, righthander Neftali Feliz and lefties Matt Harrison and Beau Jones.

Texas compounded the move by moving Eric Gagne and Kenny Lofton to the Red Sox and Indians, bringing back more prospects in outfielders Engel Beltre and David Murphy and catcher Max Ramirez, plus a young big league lefty in Kason Gabbard.

Those three deals highlighted the dramatic overhaul of the farm system, as nine of the Rangers' top 30 prospects have now been acquired in trades. The system's transformation was augmented by strong work in the draft by scouting director Ron Hopkins and his staff. The Rangers had five picks before the second round, which they used on a trio of high-upside prep righthanders (Blake Beavan, Michael Main and Neil Ramirez), a safe college righty (Tommy Hunter) and a college center fielder who could be the team's leadoff man of the future (Julio Borbon). And as usual, the Rangers were active in the Latin American market under international scouting director A.J. Preller, landing a solid crop led by Dominican lefthander Martin Perez.

The net result is greatly improved minor league depth, particularly on the mound. Developing impact pitchers long has been a challenge for the Rangers, whose 4.75 ERA ranked 24th in baseball in 2007. Now 17 of their top 30 prospects are pitchers, giving some reason for optimism. However, much of the high-ceiling talent remains in the lower levels of the minors, so it will take another couple of years

Slugging catcher Jarrod Saltalamacchia was the crown jewel of the Mark Teixeira bounty

TOP 30 PROSPECTS

1. Elvis Andrus, ss	16. German Duran, 2b
2. Chris Davis, 3b	17. John Mayberry Jr., of
3. Eric Hurley, rhp	18. Wilmer Font, rhp
4. Taylor Teagarden, c	19. Thomas Diamond, rhp
5. Neftali Feliz, rhp	20. Cristian Santana, c
6. Michael Main, rhp	21. Johnny Whittleman, 3b
7. Kasey Kiker, lhp	22. David Murphy, of
8. Blake Beavan, rhp	23. Max Ramirez, c
9. Julio Borbon, of	24. Luis Mendoza, rhp
10. Engel Beltre, of	25. Warner Madrigal, rhp
11. Omar Poveda, rhp	26. Joaquin Arias, ss
12. Matt Harrison, lhp	27. Zach Phillips, lhp
13. Neil Ramirez, rhp	28. Jose Vallejo, 2b
14. Fabio Castillo, rhp	29. Brennan Garr, rhp
15. Tommy Hunter, rhp	30. Armando Galarraga, rhp

before it will start to surface in Texas.

The Rangers expect to continue their rebuilding process in 2008, field a competitive team by 2009 and make a serious playoff run in 2010. In addition to the foundation in the farm system, Texas has whom it regards as a few core players to build around at the big league level, including Ian Kinsler, Brandon McCarthy, Saltalamacchia, Edinson Volquez and Michael Young. The most significant major league bright spot from a gloomy 2007, Young recorded his fifth straight 200-hit season.

General Manager: Jon Daniels. **Farm Director:** Scott Servais. **Scouting Director:** Ron Hopkins.

Class	Team	League	W	L	PCT	Finish*	Manager	Affiliated
Majors	Texas	American	75	87	.463	10th (14)	Ron Washington	—
Triple-A	Oklahoma RedHawks	Pacific Coast	71	72	.497	10th (16)	Bobby Jones	1983
Double-A	Frisco RoughRiders	Texas	85	55	.607	1st (8)	Dave Anderson	2003
High A	Bakersfield Blaze	California	57	83	.407	9th (10)	Carlos Subero	2005
Low A	Clinton LumberKings	Midwest	70	67	.511	7th (14)	Mike Micucci	2003
Short-season	Spokane Indians	Northwest	33	42	.440	7th (8)	Andy Fox	2003
Rookie	AZL Rangers	Arizona	22	34	.393	8th (9)	Pedro Lopez	2003

Overall 2007 Minor League Record 338 353 .489 19th
*Finish in overall standings (No. of teams in league) ^League champion

LAST YEAR'S TOP 30

Player, Pos.		Status
1.	John Danks, lhp	(White Sox)
2.	Eric Hurley, rhp	No. 3
3.	Edinson Volquez, rhp	Majors
4.	Thomas Diamond, rhp	No. 19
5.	John Mayberry Jr., of	No. 17
6.	Joaquin Arias, ss	No. 26
7.	Kasey Kiker, lhp	No. 7
8.	Nick Masset, rhp	(White Sox)
9.	Jason Botts, of/dh	Majors
10.	Josh Rupe, rhp	Dropped out
11.	Chris Davis, 3b	No. 2
12.	Marcus Lemon, ss	Dropped out
13.	Taylor Teagarden, c	No. 4
14.	Omar Poveda, rhp	No. 11
15.	Armando Galarraga, rhp	No. 30
16.	Chad Tracy, c	Dropped out
17.	Ben Harrison, of	Dropped out
18.	Johnny Whittleman, 3b	No. 21
19.	Fabio Castillo, rhp	No. 14
20.	Francisco Cruceta, rhp	(Tigers)
21.	Wes Littleton, rhp	Majors
22.	Daniel Haigwood, lhp	(Red Sox)
23.	Freddy Guzman, of	(Tigers)
24.	Michael Schlact, rhp	Dropped out
25.	Anthony Webster, of	Dropped out
26.	Jesse Ingram, rhp	Dropped out
27.	Doug Mathis, rhp	Dropped out
28.	Danny Ray Herrera, lhp	Dropped out
29.	Jose Vallejo, 2b	No. 28
30.	Jacob Rasner, rhp	(White Sox)

BEST TOOLS

Best Hitter for Average	German Duran
Best Power Hitter	Chris Davis
Best Strike-Zone Discipline	Johnny Whittleman
Fastest Baserunner	Jose Vallejo
Best Athlete	Michael Main
Best Fastball	Neftali Feliz
Best Curveball	Neil Ramirez
Best Slider	Eric Hurley
Best Changeup	Kasey Kiker
Best Control	Matt Harrison
Best Defensive Catcher	Taylor Teagarden
Best Defensive Infielder	Elvis Andrus
Best Infield Arm	Elvis Andrus
Best Defensive Outfielder	Julio Borbon
Best Outfield Arm	Engel Beltre

PROJECTED 2011 LINEUP

Catcher	Taylor Teagarden
First Base	Jarrod Saltalamacchia
Second Base	Michael Young
Third Base	Chris Davis
Shortstop	Elvis Andrus
Left Field	John Mayberry Jr.
Center Field	Julio Borbon
Right Field	Engel Beltre
No. 1 Starter	Eric Hurley
No. 2 Starter	Neftali Feliz
No. 3 Starter	Michael Main
No. 4 Starter	Edinson Volquez
No. 5 Starter	Blake Beavan
Closer	Kasey Kiker

TOP PROSPECTS OF THE DECADE

Year	Player, Pos.	2007 Org.
1998	Ruben Mateo, of	Brewers
1999	Ruben Mateo, of	Brewers
2000	Ruben Mateo, of	Brewers
2001	Carlos Pena, 1b	Rays
2002	Hank Blalock, 3b	Rangers
2003	Mark Teixeira, 3b	Braves
2004	Adrian Gonzalez, 1b	Padres
2005	Thomas Diamond, rhp	Rangers
2006	Edinson Volquez, rhp	Rangers
2007	John Danks, lhp	White Sox

TOP DRAFT PICKS OF THE DECADE

Year	Player, Pos.	2007 Org.
1998	Carlos Pena, 1b	Rays
1999	Colby Lewis, rhp	Athletics
2000	Scott Heard, c	Out of baseball
2001	Mark Teixeira, 3b	Braves
2002	Drew Meyer, ss	Rangers
2003	John Danks, lhp	White Sox
2004	Thomas Diamond, rhp	Rangers
2005	John Mayberry Jr., of	Rangers
2006	Kasey Kiker, lhp	Rangers
2007	Blake Beavan, rhp	Rangers

LARGEST BONUSES IN CLUB HISTORY

Mark Teixeira, 2001	$4,500,000
John Danks, 2003	$2,100,000
Vincent Sinisi, 2003	$2,070,000
Thomas Diamond, 2004	$2,025,000
Drew Meyer, 2002	$1,875,000

TEXAS RANGERS

Top 2008 Rookie: Luis Mendoza, rhp. With a sinker/slider repertoire that should be a good fit for hitter-friendly Arlington, Mendoza is likely to earn a job as a back-end starter or swingman.

Breakout Prospect: Cristian Santana, c. Finally healthy after shoulder surgery caused him to miss all of 2006, he hinted at his enormous potential in 2007.

SOURCE OF TOP 30 TALENT			
Homegrown	20	**Acquired**	**10**
College	6	Trades	9
Junior college	2	Rule 5 draft	0
High school	6	Independent leagues	0
Draft-and-follow	1	Free agents/waivers	1
Nondrafted free agents	0		
International	5		

Sleeper: Derek Holland, lhp. A strike-thrower with a lively 90-94 mph fastball, a quality changeup and a promising slider, he could make the Rangers look good for signing him as a draft-and-follow prior to the 2007 draft.

Numbers in parentheses indicate prospect rankings.

LF
Chad Tracy
Kevin Mahar
Tim Smith
K.C. Herren
J.T. Restko

CF
Julio Borbon (9)
Engel Beltre (10)
David Murphy (22)
Brandon Boggs
David Paisano
Craig Gentry

RF
John Mayberry (17)
Ben Harrison

3B
Chris Davis (2)
Johnny Whittleman (21)
Matt West
Emmanuel Solis
Johan Yan

SS
Elvis Andrus (1)
Joaquin Arias (26)
Marcus Lemon

2B
German Duran (16)
Jose Vallejo (28)

1B
Nate Gold
Mitch Moreland
Ian Gac

C
Taylor Teagarden (4)
Cristian Santana (20)
Max Ramirez (23)
Manuel Pina

RHP

Starters	Relievers
Eric Hurley (3)	Warner Madrigal (25)
Neftali Feliz (5)	Brennan Garr (29)
Michael Main (6)	Andrew Laughter
Blake Beavan (8)	Kea Kometani
Omar Poveda (11)	Alexi Ogando
Neil Ramirez (13)	Josh Rupe
Fabio Castillo (14)	Josh Lueke
Tommy Hunter (15)	Jesse Ingram
Wilmer Font (18)	Clayton Hamilton
Thomas Diamond (19)	
Luis Mendoza (24)	
Armando Galarraga (30)	
Evan Reed	
Omar Beltre	
Jacob Brigham	
Michael Schlact	
Doug Mathis	

LHP

Starters	Relievers
Kasey Kiker (7)	Beau Jones
Matt Harrison (12)	A.J. Murray
Zach Phillips (27)	Danny Ray Herrera
Derek Holland	
Martin Perez	
Geuris Grullon	
Glenn Swanson	

2007   SIGNING BUDGET: $6.1 MILLION

Best Pro Debut: RHP Michael Main (1) struck out 34 in 28 innings over two levels and went 8-for-30 as a hitter in the Rookie-level Arizona League. LHP Ryan Falcon (29) dominated in middle relief for short-season Spokane, posting a 62-6 K-BB ratio and 2.68 ERA in 47 innings. Spokane closer RHP Andrew Laughter (10) had 11 saves and 2.03 ERA. RHP Evan Reed (3) went 1-1, 1.91 in 11 games (eight starts) between Spokane and low Class A Clinton.

Best Athlete: Main's fast-twitch athleticism made him a possible first-rounder as both a switch-hitting center fielder and a pitcher. OF Julio Borbon (1s) has strength and speed, and the Rangers considered Borbon and Main two of the draft's top athletes overall.

Best Pure Hitter: Borbon struggled all spring after breaking his ankle in January. At his best, he generates above-average bat speed. 3B Matt West (2) hit .301 in his debut and has good hands, but the Rangers aren't sure what they have in him after he was suspended 50 games for violating MLB's performance-enhancing drugs testing program.

Best Power Hitter: OF/1B Mitch Moreland (17) won the Cape Cod League home run derby in 2006 and lost in the finals in '07. The Rangers figure his above-average raw power will play better now that he's given up pitching.

Fastest Runner: Borbon and Main are 70 runners on the 20-to-80 scale.

Best Defensive Player: Borbon has a below-average arm but should be an excellent center fielder.

Best Fastball: Main has touched 97 mph; he and fellow prep RHPs Blake Beavan (1) and Neil Ramirez (1s) all pitch at 92-94 mph and flash 96s.

Best Secondary Pitch: Some scouts considered Beavan's two-plane slider a better pitch than his fastball. Main's curveball is a hard breaker with power, and Ramirez also throws a sharp breaking ball.

Most Intriguing Background: West is the highest-drafted player to be suspended in his debut season.

Closest To The Majors: RHP Tommy Hunter (1s) ranked among the top prospects in the NWL. The 6-foot-2, 250-pounder is far more athletic than he looks and has live stuff in a low-90s fastball and

hard breaking stuff.

Best Late-Round Pick: RHP Josh Lueke (16) jumped straight to Clinton from Division II Northern Kentucky. His fastball touched 95 mph in a relief role.

The One Who Got Away: Texas wasn't as sorry to lose speedy IF/OF Garrett Nash (4, Oregon State) as it was LHP Drew Pomeranz (12, Mississippi) or LHP John Gast (5), who will recover from Tommy John surgery at Florida State.

Assessment: The Rangers had a good second half, and the draft was part of it, as Beavan, Borbon and Ramirez signed at the last minute to give the organization some high-ceiling arms and a potential star in the middle of the field in Borbon.

2006   BUDGET: $3.6 MILLION

LHP Kasey Kiker (1) has a lightning arm, but 3B Chris Davis (5) is an even better prospect thanks to his huge power.

GRADE: B

2005   BUDGET: $3.9 MILLION

If C Taylor Teagarden (3) can stay healthy, he has the all-around tools to be an all-star. OF John Mayberry Jr. (1), 3B Johnny Whittleman (2) and 2B German Duran (6) all made nice progress last season.

GRADE: C+

2004   BUDGET: $5.0 MILLION

Of Texas' two first-round pitchers, RHP Eric Hurley (1) has lived up to expecations, while RHP Thomas Diamond (1) has not while battling injuries. 3B Travis Metcalf (11) filled in for an injured Hank Blalock last year.

GRADE: C+

2003   BUDGET: $5.5 MILLION

OF Vincent Sinisi (2) was a $2.07 million bust, but he's counterbalanced by 2B Ian Kinsler (17), one of the biggest heists in recent draft memory. LHP John Danks (1) still has potential but is now with the White Sox.

GRADE: B+

Draft analysis by John Manuel (2007) and Jim Callis (2003-06). Numbers in parentheses indicate draft rounds. Budgets are bonuses in first 10 rounds.

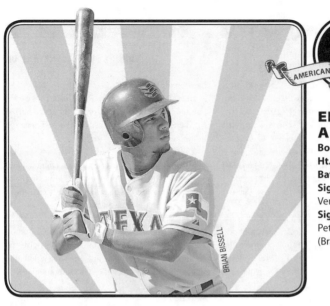

BRIAN BISSELL

ELVIS ANDRUS, SS

Born: Aug. 26, 1988.
Ht.: 6-0. **Wt.:** 185.
Bats: R. **Throws:** R.
Signed:
Venezuela, 2005.
Signed by: Rolando
Petit/Julian Perez
(Braves).

A s the younger brother of Rays minor leaguer Erold Andrus, Elvis was on the prospect landscape at an early age. The Rangers had a chance to sign him during international scouting director A.J. Preller's first week on the job in 2005, when the club had Andrus at its Dominican complex for a workout. But Andrus was hampered by a leg injury and Texas couldn't justify blowing 70 percent of their then-modest international budget on him. Instead, he signed with the Braves for nearly $600,000 and held his own against much older competition in his first three years in the United States. Last July, he and Jarrod Saltalamacchia were the centerpieces of a five-prospect package Atlanta surrendered for Mark Teixeira and Ron Mahay. After changing organizations, Andrus thrived in the hitter-friendly high Class A California League and then batted .353 as the youngest player in the Arizona Fall League.

After his regular season ended, Andrus arrived early at instructional league and had dinner with Preller and farm director Scott Servais. He dazzled the pair with his desire to lead, telling them that his favorite shortstop is Derek Jeter because "he's a leader and a winner, and that's what I am." He also picked Sammy Sosa's brain about how to get other players to respect him as a leader. That makeup sets Andrus apart, not just off the field but on it, where he has a unique ability to slow the game down and always put himself in the right position to make plays. He long has been regarded as a naturally gifted defensive shortstop, with sure hands to go with plus range and plus arm strength, which is especially evident when he goes into the hole or on relay throws from the outfield. He's an above-average runner who's improving as a basestealer, and he shows the ability to make adjustments at the plate. A gap-to-gap hitter with a mature approach for his age, Andrus has a short, direct swing path and enough strength to project to hit 10-20 homers per year in the big leagues.

Andrus remains somewhat raw offensively, but he has made progress with the Rangers, who wanted him to narrow his wide, spread-out stance to get more weight transfer and drive the ball better. His inconsistent stride causes him to get out of rhythm at times, but he showed improvement in the fall. Texas gave Andrus the green light to run whenever he wanted, and he's still refining his technique and picking up nuances such as when he can steal third base. Though he has an accurate arm and gets plenty of carry on his throws, he sometimes makes careless throwing errors.

Andrus' all-around game draws comparisons to an in-his-prime Edgar Renteria's. As with Renteria, defense will always be Andrus' calling card, but he has a chance to be a solid No. 2 hitter in the big leagues if he's given more at-bats to develop. He figures to get a shot at playing at Double-A Frisco as a teenager in 2008.

Year	Club (League)	Class	AVG	G	AB	R	H	2B	3B	HR	RBI	BB	SO	SB	OBP	SLG
2005	Braves (GCL)	R	.295	46	166	26	49	6	1	3	20	19	28	7	.377	.398
	Danville (Appy)	R	.278	6	18	3	5	1	0	0	1	4	4	1	.409	.333
2006	Rome (SAL)	A	.265	111	437	67	116	25	4	3	50	36	91	23	.324	.362
2007	Myrtle Beach (Car)	A	.244	99	385	59	94	20	3	3	37	44	88	25	.330	.335
	Bakersfield (Cal)	A	.300	27	110	19	33	2	0	2	12	10	19	15	.369	.373
MINOR LEAGUE TOTALS			.266	289	1116	174	297	54	8	11	120	113	230	71	.340	.358

2 CHRIS DAVIS, 3B

BILL MITCHELL

Born: March 17, 1986. **B-T:** L-R. **Ht.:** 6-3. **Wt.:** 210. **Drafted:** Navarro (Texas) JC, 2006 (5th round). **Signed by:** Randy Taylor.

A two-way star in high school who also pitched some after transferring from Texas to Navarro (Texas) JC, Davis has taken off as a power hitter in pro ball. He followed up his solid 2006 debut with a monstrous first full season, finishing second in the minors with 36 homers and 118 RBIs and setting a California League record with a 35-game hitting streak. Not only does Davis possess well above-average power, but he knows how to use it, thanks to a balanced approach and willingness to use the whole field. He has improved against lefthanders, shortened up his swing somewhat and showed an ability to make adjustments against more advanced pitching as he has moved through the minors. Despite a plus arm, Davis is a below-average defender at third base, with poor footwork and actions. He played right field in his pro debut but is a below-average runner who likely will be limited to first base down the road. Though he has a good feel for hitting, he swings and misses a lot. He tends to start his hands high then drop them down before the pitch, making him vulnerable against pitches above the belt. Davis could be an impact middle-of-the-lineup bat in the big leagues even if he is limited to first base. He needs another season in the minors to see more quality pitching, and he figures to split 2008 between Double-A and Triple-A Oklahoma.

Year	Club (League)	Class	AVG	G	AB	R	H	2B	3B	HR	RBI	BB	SO	SB	OBP	SLG
2006	Spokane (NWL)	A	.277	69	253	38	70	18	1	15	42	23	65	2	.343	.534
2007	Bakersfield (Cal)	A	.298	99	386	69	115	28	3	24	93	22	123	3	.340	.573
	Frisco (TL)	AA	.294	30	109	21	32	7	0	12	25	13	27	0	.371	.688
MINOR LEAGUE TOTALS			.290	198	748	128	217	53	4	51	160	58	215	5	.345	.576

3 ERIC HURLEY, RHP

BILL MITCHELL

Born: Sept. 17, 1985. **B-T:** R-R. **Ht.:** 6-4. **Wt.:** 195. **Drafted:** HS—Jacksonville, 2004 (1st round). **Signed by:** Guy DeMutis.

At the lower levels of the minors, Hurley was often able to dominate hitters simply by overpowering them, but he has had to learn how to adjust to hitters at higher levels. When he began overmatching Double-A batters in the first half of 2007, the Rangers moved him up to Triple-A, where he wore down late and experienced his first real taste of adversity. Hurley has a pair of plus offerings in his sinking 92-95 mph fastball that runs down and in and his firm slider with good depth. He refined his command of both pitches in 2007, and Texas forced him to focus on developing his changeup in Triple-A. He made some progress with the changeup early, flashing some turnover fade. As Hurley ran out of gas down the stretch, his changeup wasn't as comfortable coming out of his hand and he struggled to locate it. He also got hit hard when he left his fastball up in the zone. It usually takes him a few innings to get his velocity up, as he works at 88-92 mph early in games. Hurley will likely get a chance to crack the big league rotation in spring training, but a return to Triple-A and a midseason callup seems more likely. He projects as a mid-rotation starter in the Kevin Millwood mold.

Year	Club (League)	Class	W	L	ERA	G	GS	CG	SV	IP	H	R	ER	HR	BB	SO	AVG
2004	Rangers (AZL)	R	0	1	2.35	6	2	0	0	15	20	8	4	1	4	15	.317
	Spokane (NWL)	A	0	2	5.40	8	6	0	0	28	31	18	17	6	6	21	.295
2005	Clinton (MWL)	A	12	6	3.77	28	28	0	0	155	135	72	65	11	59	152	.234
2006	Bakersfield (Cal)	A	5	6	4.11	18	18	1	0	100	92	60	46	12	32	106	.239
	Frisco (TL)	AA	3	1	1.95	6	6	0	0	37	21	9	8	4	11	31	.168
2007	Frisco (TL)	AA	7	2	3.25	15	14	1	0	88	71	39	32	13	27	76	.219
	Oklahoma (PCL)	AAA	4	7	4.91	13	13	0	0	73	65	45	40	13	28	59	.236
MINOR LEAGUE TOTALS			31	25	3.83	94	87	2	0	498	435	251	212	60	167	460	.235

4 TAYLOR TEAGARDEN, C

BILL MITCHELL

Born: Dec. 21, 1983. **B-T:** R-R. **Ht.:** 6-1. **Wt.:** 200. **Drafted:** Texas, 2005 (3rd round). **Signed by:** Randy Taylor.

After leading Texas to the College World Series and posting a solid pro debut in 2005, Teagarden ended his year with Tommy John surgery. He worked his way back as a DH late in 2006 and entered 2007 mostly healthy, but elbow fatigue in late April set him back. He wound up catching just two or three games per week the rest of the way and serving as a DH the rest of the time. Most Rangers officials regard Teagarden as a major league-ready defensive catcher already, thanks to his soft hands, solid footwork and feel for the game. His arm is slightly above average but plays up further thanks to his footwork, quick release and accuracy. He threw out 33 percent of basestealers in 2007. Offensively, he entered pro ball with a rather flat swing path at times, but he since has improved his load and been able to generate more loft and backspin, giving him solid-average pull power and doubles pop to the opposite field. He has natural leadership skills. Teagarden still needs a little more work calling games, but his intelligence should expedite that process as he gets more work behind the plate. Because of his patient offensive approach, he takes his share of strikeouts. The Rangers took the reins off Teagarden in the fall, and he should be ready to catch nearly every day in 2008—likely back at Double-A to start the year. Texas may not need him thanks to Saltalamacchia, but Teagarden should be ready to be an everyday catcher by 2009.

Year	Club (League)	Class	AVG	G	AB	R	H	2B	3B	HR	RBI	BB	SO	SB	OBP	SLG
2005	Spokane (NWL)	A	.281	31	96	23	27	5	4	7	16	23	32	1	.426	.635
2006	Rangers (AZL)	R	.050	7	20	4	1	0	0	0	1	9	7	1	.345	.050
2007	Bakersfield (Cal)	A	.315	81	292	75	92	25	0	20	67	65	89	2	.448	.606
	Frisco (TL)	AA	.294	29	102	19	30	3	0	7	16	10	39	0	.357	.529
MINOR LEAGUE TOTALS			.294	148	510	121	150	33	4	34	100	107	167	4	.422	.575

5 NEFTALI FELIZ, RHP

BILL MITCHELL

Born: May 2, 1988. **B-T:** R-R. **Ht.:** 6-3. **Wt.:** 180. **Signed:** Dominican Republic, 2005. **Signed by:** Julian Perez/Roberto Aquino (Braves).

Feliz lacked the name recognition of the other youngsters the Braves gave up in the Mark Teixeira trade last July, but he could wind up as the crown jewel of the haul. Rather than blowing hitters away with his fastball after the trade, he focused on developing his secondary stuff and still struck out 27 in just 15 innings. With some time to refine his command, Feliz' fastball could rate as an 80 on the 20-80 scouting scale. With a smooth, effortless arm action, he pumps heaters that sit at 94-97 mph and touches 99, exploding on hitters. He stays on a good line to the plate and throws strikes. He has an athletic build and he's a hard worker. Feliz flashes a promising three-quarters breaking ball in the high 70s, but it's inconsistent. One day he'll show a plus curve with very good depth, and the next day he'll drop his arm, causing the pitch to flatten out and spin but not bite. He tends to throw his changeup too hard, right into hitters' bat speeds, but he has some feel for the pitch and made progress with it in instructional league. His command currently lags behind his control. Feliz has a chance to open 2008 as a 19-year-old at low Class A Clinton, but he's still a long way from the majors. If it all comes together for him, he has the potential to be a true No. 1 starter, though some scouts see him as a flamethrowing closer down the road.

Year	Club (League)	Class	W	L	ERA	G	GS	CG	SV	IP	H	R	ER	HR	BB	SO	AVG
2005	Braves1 (DSL)	R	0	0	3.60	10	0	0	0	10	7	4	4	0	11	8	.184
2006	Braves (GCL)	R	0	2	4.03	11	5	0	2	29	20	13	13	0	14	42	.192
2007	Danville (Appy)	R	2	0	1.98	8	7	0	0	27	18	8	6	0	12	28	.191
	Spokane (NWL)	A	0	2	3.60	8	1	0	0	15	13	8	6	2	12	27	.228
MINOR LEAGUE TOTALS			2	4	3.21	37	13	0	2	81	58	33	29	2	49	105	.198

6 MICHAEL MAIN, RHP

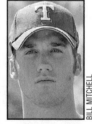

BILL MITCHELL

Born: Dec. 14, 1988. **B-T:** R-R. **Ht.:** 6-2. **Wt.:** 170. **Drafted:** HS—Deland, Fla., 2007 (1st round). **Signed by:** Guy DeMutis.

Since he was named Baseball America's top 15-year-old prospect in 2004, Main has generated buzz for his lightning-quick arm and supreme athleticism. A number of clubs thought hard about drafting him as a center fielder, and the Rangers even let him DH for eight games in his debut in the Rookie-level Arizona League, where he batted .267. Main evokes Bret Saberhagen for his slight build, plus-plus arm strength, intelligence and determination. He pitches with minimal effort at 92-97 mph with a lively fastball, and he did a much better job keeping the pitch down in the zone in 2007 than he did in high school in 2006. Main's 75-78 mph downer curveball has tight rotation and good depth. It's an average pitch at times and could wind up better than that. He has good command for his age. He has plus-plus speed and the athleticism to field his position well. Main has the makings of an average changeup but needs to develop the pitch, which he used infrequently in high school. He also must get more consistent with his curveball. Added strength would improve his long-term durability. Main could wind up as a legitimate front-of-the-rotation starter in the big leagues. He figures to follow Kasey Kiker's development plan and start 2008 in extended spring training before going to low Class A around mid-May.

Year	Club (League)	Class	W	L	ERA	G	GS	CG	SV	IP	H	R	ER	HR	BB	SO	AVG
2007	Rangers (AZL)	R	0	1	1.42	5	5	0	0	12	9	2	2	1	6	16	.196
	Spokane (NWL)	A	2	0	4.70	5	5	0	0	15	14	11	8	1	7	18	.237
MINOR LEAGUE TOTALS			2	1	3.21	10	10	0	0	28	23	13	10	2	13	34	.219

7 KASEY KIKER, LHP

Born: Nov. 19, 1987. **B-T:** L-L. **Ht.:** 5-10. **Wt.:** 170. **Drafted:** HS—Seale, Ala., 2006 (1st round). **Signed by:** Jeff Wood.

The Rangers have been careful with the undersized Kiker, first keeping him on a strict pitch count in his pro debut after his standout career as a workhorse at national powerhouse Russell County High (Seale, Ala.), then holding him back in extended spring training to start his first full pro season. The idea was to keep him to 20 starts in 2007, and Texas preferred to have him peaking at the end of the season rather than in July. It worked perfectly, as he repeatedly dialed his fastball up to 97 mph in a Midwest League playoff game. A bulldog who wants the ball in big spots, Kiker has the stuff and competitiveness to make up for his slight build. With a clean arm action from a high three-quarters slot, he pitches comfortably at 91-93 mph and has the ability to elevate the ball in the zone to get strikeouts when needed. He has a plus changeup with some tail to it. He always has thrown the changeup with good arm speed and commanded it much better in 2007, even using it when he was behind in the count. Kiker's 75-78 mph curveball has tight downward rotation and is a plus pitch at times, but it remains inconsistent. Though he has a strong lower half and keeps himself in great shape, his size raises questions about his ability to shoulder a starter's heavy workload over the long term. Kiker will start 2008 in the hitter-friendly California League, which will be a major test for him as a flyball pitcher. His three-pitch mix gives him a shot to be a mid-rotation starter in the big leagues by 2010.

Year	Club (League)	Class	W	L	ERA	G	GS	CG	SV	IP	H	R	ER	HR	BB	SO	AVG
2006	Spokane (NWL)	A	0	7	4.13	16	15	0	0	52	44	34	24	5	35	51	.232
2007	Clinton (MWL)	A	7	4	2.90	20	20	0	0	96	84	35	31	10	41	112	.237
MINOR LEAGUE TOTALS			7	11	3.33	36	35	0	0	148	128	69	55	15	76	163	.235

8 BLAKE BEAVAN, RHP

Born: Jan. 17, 1989. **B-T:** R-R. **Ht.:** 6-7. **Wt.:** 210. **Drafted:** HS—Irving, Texas, 2007 (1st round). **Signed by:** Jay Eddings.

Beavan was Baseball America's 2006 Youth Player of the Year after serving as the ace for the U.S. junior national team, which included striking out 11 in a shutout against Cuba on Cuban soil. He followed his standout summer with a dominating senior season, which included an 18-strikeout perfect game, and bypassed a commitment to Oklahoma to sign with the Rangers for $1,497,500 right before the Aug. 15 signing deadline. Beavan has an imposing, workhorse frame and a swagger on the mound. He pounds the strike zone with an above-average heavy fastball that sits at 92-94 mph and reaches 96 when he needs it. His mid-80s slider can be a plus pitch at times as well. Beavan tends to use a lower arm slot with his slider than he does with his fastball, causing it to flatten out. He should be able to tighten the pitch by cleaning up his delivery, and his velocity could climb if he learns to finish pitches instead of cutting himself off. He'll need to develop his nascent changeup to stick as a starter. He can be too brash at times, and he got a taste of humble pie in instructional league. Some scouts think Beavan profiles best as a two-pitch bullpen ace with a nasty streak, but the Rangers will give him every chance to start. He figures to make his pro debut at short-season Spokane in June.

Year	Club (League)	Class	W	L	ERA	G	GS	CG	SV	IP	H	R	ER	HR	BB	SO	AVG
2007	Did Not Play—Signed Late																

9 JULIO BORBON, OF

Born: Feb. 20, 1986. **B-T:** L-L. **Ht.:** 6-1. **Wt.:** 190. **Drafted:** Tennessee, 2007 (1st round supplemental). **Signed by:** Jeff Wood.

Tennessee coach Rod Delmonico discovered Borbon almost by accident while recruiting another player in the Dominican Republic, and Borbon helped lead the Volunteers to the College World Series as a freshman before exploding onto the prospect landscape with a standout summer for Team USA in 2006. He missed the first eight weeks of his junior year after fracturing his ankle while sliding awkwardly during an intrasquad game, and though he never fully got on track during the season, the Rangers signed him to a major league contract worth $1.3 million, including an $800,000 signing bonus. Borbon garners comparisons to Johnny Damon for his prototypical center-field tools. His 70 speed on the 20-80 scale and his good instincts make him a plus defender in center. He has a strong, physical frame with gap-to-gap power, and he projects to hit 10-20 homers annually in the big leagues. He makes consistent, line-drive contact, is a good bunter and isn't afraid to work the count. He's also a natural leader. Like Damon, Borbon has a below-average arm, though Texas thinks it could become average if he can improve his exchange from his glove and retrain his muscle memory. Offensively, the Rangers want him to narrow his stance to get more weight transfer. He also needs to use the opposite field more and work on getting better jumps on the basepaths. He'll have to be more patient as a pro than he was as an amateur (37 walks in 155 games) to be a leadoff hitter. Borbon has the tool set to be an everyday center fielder in the big leagues. He should open 2008 in low Class A and could move fairly quickly.

Year	Club (League)	Class	AVG	G	AB	R	H	2B	3B	HR	RBI	BB	SO	SB	OBP	SLG
2007	Spokane (NWL)	A	.172	7	29	1	5	0	0	0	2	2	3	3	.226	.172
	Rangers (AZL)	R	.250	2	8	0	2	1	0	0	0	1	1	0	.333	.375
MINOR LEAGUE TOTALS			.189	9	37	1	7	1	0	0	2	3	4	3	.250	.216

10 ENGEL BELTRE, OF

Born: Nov. 1, 1989. **B-T:** L-L. **Ht.:** 6-1. **Wt.:** 169. **Signed:** Dominican Republic, 2006. **Signed by:** Pablo Lantigua (Red Sox).

The Red Sox signed Beltre for $600,000 in 2006 and traded him to Texas along with Kason Gabbard and David Murphy for Eric Gagne last July. After shining in his Rangers debut, Beltre reported early to instructional league, where the gifted athlete further impressed by bowling a strike in the first roll of his life during the club's bowling tournament. Scouts drooled over Beltre's legitimate five-tool potential after he signed with Boston, with one even comparing him to a young Barry Bonds. The Rangers liken his wiry-strong frame to that of a young Kenny Lofton, and like Lofton he's an above-average runner who gets good jumps and reads in center field to go along with a plus arm. Beltre has a loose swing and quick wrists and projects to hit for above-average power as he fills out. Though Beltre has good bat control and isn't afraid to work the count, he tends to get jumpy with runners on base. His swing can get too big and he's prone to chasing pitches in the dirt. He's raw in every phase of the game and hasn't yet figured out how to use his speed on the basepaths. Given time and at-bats, Beltre could blossom into a true five-tool superstar, but he's a long way off. He'll likely start 2008 in extended spring training before heading back to Spokane.

Year	Club (League)	Class	AVG	G	AB	R	H	2B	3B	HR	RBI	BB	SO	SB	OBP	SLG
2007	Red Sox (GCL)	R	.208	34	125	20	26	3	3	5	13	12	44	6	.310	.400
	Rangers (AZL)	R	.310	22	84	19	26	3	4	4	15	8	21	3	.388	.583
	Spokane (NWL)	A	.211	9	38	3	8	0	0	0	1	2	10	2	.250	.211
MINOR LEAGUE TOTALS			.243	65	247	42	60	6	7	9	29	22	75	11	.329	.433

11 OMAR POVEDA, RHP

Born: Sept. 28, 1987. **B-T:** R-R. **Ht.:** 6-4. **Wt.:** 215. **Signed:** Venezuela, 2004. **Signed by:** Andres Espinosa/Manny Batista.

After holding his own in the Midwest League as an 18-year-old in his 2006 U.S. debut, Poveda returned to the MWL and mastered it in '07 before earning a late promotion. Though he's still officially listed at 200 pounds, the Rangers say Poveda is finally starting to fill out his angular frame and is now closer to a more durable 215 pounds. That build evokes fellow Venezuelan Freddy Garcia and Yankees righty Carl Pavano, and like those former No. 3 starters, Poveda is a strike-thrower with a good work ethic and solid mound presence. His solid-average fastball sits at 89-92 mph and occasionally touches 93, and he might have a touch more projection left. His straight changeup is a plus offering that can sometimes be plus-plus, and he throws it in any count to righties as well as lefties. He has developed his downer curveball into an average offering that he can sometimes get hitters to chase in the dirt. He still needs to continue refining the pitch and learn how to attack advanced hitters, but he figures to continue his rapid climb through the system in 2008, starting back at high Class A Bakersfield. He could reach Double-A by midseason and could be a mid-rotation starter in the big leagues by 2010.

Year	Club (League)	Class	W	L	ERA	G	GS	CG	SV	IP	H	R	ER	HR	BB	SO	AVG
2005	Rangers (AZL)	R	2	6	5.71	14	9	0	0	52	64	38	33	1	12	56	.305
2006	Frisco (TL)	AA	0	1	1.80	1	1	0	0	5	4	2	1	0	5	1	.222
	Clinton (MWL)	A	4	13	4.88	26	26	0	0	149	167	92	81	12	37	133	.286
2007	Clinton (MWL)	A	11	4	2.79	21	21	0	0	125	94	44	39	10	32	120	.208
	Bakersfield (Cal)	A	1	2	5.14	5	5	0	0	28	27	18	16	4	13	33	.250
MINOR LEAGUE TOTALS			18	26	4.25	67	62	0	0	360	356	194	170	27	99	343	.260

12 MATT HARRISON, LHP

Born: Aug. 16, 1985. **B-T:** L-L. **Ht.:** 6-5. **Wt.:** 205. **Drafted:** HS—Stern, N.C., 2003 (3rd round). **Signed by:** Billy Best (Braves).

Harrison did not pitch for the Rangers after being acquired as part of last July's Mark Teixeira trade with the Braves because he had developed a nasty case of turf toe that affected his delivery, leading to shoulder irritation. He changed from a no-windup delivery to a full windup in an effort to add velocity, but the

Rangers decided to shut him down until the Arizona Fall League, where a healthy Harrison went 5-0, 2.00 in 27 innings. Harrison's biggest strength is his excellent feel for pitching and ability to work all quadrants of the strike zone. His four-pitch mix includes an average 88-93 mph fastball and an average changeup that he throws in any count. He also throws two breaking balls: a slurve with darting three-quarters break and a big, slow 71-75 curveball that is more of a show pitch. Harrison has a big, physical frame and pitches downhill from a three-quarters arm slot. He's not a great athlete and his body is maxed out, so his ceiling is probably as a No. 3 starter, though he's more likely a No. 4 or No. 5. Added to the 40-man roster in November, he figures to advance to Triple-A to start the season and could see the big leagues sometime in 2008.

Year	Club (League)	Class	W	L	ERA	G	GS	CG	SV	IP	H	R	ER	HR	BB	SO	AVG
2003	Braves (GCL)	R	3	1	3.69	11	6	0	1	39	40	18	16	2	9	33	.263
2004	Danville (Appy)	R	4	4	4.09	13	12	1	0	66	72	36	30	3	10	49	.278
2005	Rome (SAL)	A	12	7	3.23	27	27	2	0	167	151	65	60	17	30	118	.239
2006	Myrtle Beach (Car)	A	8	4	3.10	13	13	2	0	81	77	30	28	6	16	60	.252
	Mississippi (SL)	AA	3	4	3.61	13	12	1	0	77	83	36	31	6	17	54	.272
2007	Mississippi (SL)	AA	5	7	3.39	20	20	0	0	116	118	51	44	6	34	78	.264
MINOR LEAGUE TOTALS			35	27	3.44	97	90	6	1	547	541	236	209	40	116	392	.258

13 NEIL RAMIREZ, RHP

Born: May 25, 1989. **B-T:** R-R. **Ht.:** 6-4. **Wt.:** 190. **Drafted:** HS—Kempsville, Va., 2007 (1st round supplemental). **Signed by:** Russ Ardolina.

In the summer of 2006, Ramirez held his own against players up to three years older than him in the Cal Ripken Sr. League, a summer college wood-bat league where he ranked as the No. 1 prospect. An up-and-down senior season caused him to slip to the Rangers at No. 44 overall in the draft, and he passed up a scholarship at Georgia Tech to sign for a $1 million bonus right before the Aug. 15 signing deadline. He was still working his way into game shape in instructional league, but he flashed the electric stuff that has garnered comparisons to John Smoltz and A.J. Burnett. Ramirez oozes projection, but he already pitches at 92-94 mph with his high-riding four-seam fastball, which he ran up to 96 in instructs. His short, tight, low-to-mid-80s power curveball projects as a potential plus-plus offering, but he's still learning to command it consistently. Ramirez is just starting to develop his changeup, and he still struggles to repeat his delivery, often opening his front side and changing his release point, causing the ball to go all over the place. He's got plenty of time to smooth all of that out, and if it comes together for him, he could be a bona fide top-of-the-rotation starter. He figures to open 2008 in extended spring training before heading to the Arizona League.

Year	Club (League)	Class	W	L	ERA	G	GS	CG	SV	IP	H	R	ER	HR	BB	SO	AVG
2007	Did Not Play—Signed Late																

14 FABIO CASTILLO, RHP

Born: Feb. 19, 1989. **B-T:** R-R. **Ht.:** 6-3. **Wt.:** 220. **Signed:** Dominican Republic, 2005. **Signed by:** Danilo Troncoso/Don Welke/Manny Bautista.

Castillo had thrown just three innings in the U.S. before heading to Spokane in 2007, and though he took his lumps against much older competition, he still ranked as the No. 5 prospect in the league. During instructional league in 2006 and in extended spring last year, Castillo showed three quality pitches, highlighted by a plus fastball that parks at 92-95 mph and touches 97. His breaking ball was a true power curveball at 81-82 mph, and his 78-80 mph changeup had some split-finger action. But while Castillo still showed that lively, sinking fastball and promising changeup in Spokane, he struggled to get around his breaking ball, causing it to flatten out and look like a slider that spun but lacked action. He worked on correcting the problem in instructs after the season, but he'll need to focus on the curveball and becoming more consistent with his changeup in the spring. Though Castillo has some feel for pitching, he needs to improve his command. He has the potential to be a No. 2 starter or a closer in the big leagues down the road, but he'll likely get a shot at low Class A Clinton in 2008.

Year	Club (League)	Class	W	L	ERA	G	GS	CG	SV	IP	H	R	ER	HR	BB	SO	AVG
2006	Rangers (AZL)	R	0	0	0.00	1	1	0	0	3	1	0	0	0	2	4	.100
	Rangers (DSL)	R	1	4	3.46	7	6	0	0	26	21	13	10	0	12	37	.216
2007	Spokane (NWL)	A	3	5	5.92	14	14	0	0	62	73	46	41	4	27	46	.289
MINOR LEAGUE TOTALS			4	9	5.03	22	21	0	0	91	95	59	51	4	41	87	.264

15 TOMMY HUNTER, RHP

Born: July 3, 1986. **B-T:** R-R. **Ht.:** 6-2. **Wt.:** 250. **Drafted:** Alabama, 2007 (1st round supplemental). **Signed by:** Jeff Wood.

After earning second-team freshman All-America honors as a starter in 2006, Hunter thrived in the bullpen for Team USA, then split 2007 between the closer role and Friday starter spot for the Crimson Tide. The

Rangers popped the draft-eligible sophomore with their third supplemental first-round pick (No. 54 overall) and signed him for a $585,000 bonus, and he excelled out of the bullpen for Spokane, where he ranked as the No. 7 prospect in the short-season Northwest League. Hunter's hulking, rather soft frame belies his athleticism—he was a two-time junior Olympic judo champion, and he's surprisingly quick off the mound. A leader off the field, Hunter took Rangers top pick Blake Beavan under his wing in instructional league, and his commanding presence carries over to the mound. Hunter pounds the strike zone with a solid-average 90-94 mph fastball, the centerpiece of his quality four-pitch mix. His short, tight, late-breaking curveball is his better breaking ball, a plus pitch at 82-84 mph, but his slider and changeup with split-finger action are usually average offerings, though he sometimes gets around his slider, causing it to flatten out. Some scouts see Hunter as a tenacious late-innings bulldog in the Jonathan Broxton mold, but others envision him as an innings-eating workhorse along the lines of Joe Blanton. In either case, he was one of the most polished pitchers in the 2007 draft class and figures to move very quickly, starting with a likely assignment to high Class A in 2008.

Year	Club (League)	Class	W	L	ERA	G	GS	CG	SV	IP	H	R	ER	HR	BB	SO	AVG
2007	Spokane (NWL)	A	2	3	2.55	10	0	0	1	17	15	7	5	0	1	13	.221
MINOR LEAGUE TOTALS			2	3	2.55	10	0	0	1	17	15	7	5	0	1	13	.221

16 GERMAN DURAN, 2B

Born: Aug. 3, 1984. **B-T:** R-R. **Ht.:** 5-10. **Wt.:** 185. **Drafted:** Weatherford (Texas) JC, 2005 (6th round). **Signed by:** Jay Eddings.

Like Chris Davis in 2006, Duran went into the Rangers' predraft workout in 2005 and really impressed the club, convincing them to take him in the sixth round and award him a $90,000 bonus. He flew under the radar despite solid outputs in his first two pro seasons, but he exploded in 2007 in the Double-A Texas League, where he ranked as the No. 14 prospect after finishing among the leaders in most offensive categories. He held his own in the Arizona Fall League after the season, batting .281/.385/.422 despite spending his mornings in Arizona working with Rangers outfield coordinator Wayne Kirby on learning left field. Versatility figures to be Duran's best ticket to the majors—he's an average defensive second baseman with adequate range and a strong arm that allows him to fill in at third base and shortstop. Offensively, Duran packs some punch into his compact frame, and his short, quick, smooth stroke produces consistent, hard line-drive contact and average pull power. He's a very aggressive hitter who loves to hit early in the count, though a little more patience could do him some good. He used to be a dead pull hitter but has gotten better at knocking pitches on the outer half to the opposite field. Duran profiles as a Placido Polanco type who can play multiple positions but is a good enough hitter to eventually settle in as an everyday second baseman. He could get to the big leagues in 2008.

Year	Club (League)	Class	AVG	G	AB	R	H	2B	3B	HR	RBI	BB	SO	SB	OBP	SLG
2005	Spokane (NWL)	A	.262	62	252	36	66	17	2	4	33	18	56	6	.313	.393
2006	Bakersfield (Cal)	A	.284	114	457	81	130	31	2	13	72	35	89	15	.331	.446
2007	Frisco (TL)	AA	.300	130	480	81	144	32	5	22	84	34	77	11	.352	.525
MINOR LEAGUE TOTALS			.286	306	1189	198	340	80	9	39	189	87	222	32	.336	.467

17 JOHN MAYBERRY JR., OF

Born: Dec. 21, 1983. **B-T:** R-R. **Ht.:** 6-6. **Wt.:** 230. **Drafted:** Stanford, 2005 (1st round). **Signed by:** Tim Fortugno.

During his college career at Stanford, Mayberry played mostly first base like his father, two-time major league all-star John Mayberry. The Rangers drafted him in the first round in 2005 knowing that it would take time to refine his impressive but raw set of tools, and the progress has been slow but steady. He showed power but struggled to make consistent contact while hitting in the three-hole in the first half of the year at Bakersfield, but he was able to relax after a promotion to a more competitive Frisco team, where he batted lower in the lineup. Mayberry has well-above-average raw power that he is still learning to tap into—he's made progress shortening his swing, but he's still vulnerable on the inner half and struggles to authoritatively pull the ball with consistency. He has above-average arm strength but a slow release because of his long levers. Accordingly, he's a long strider and a fringe-average runner underway, but he lacks first-step quickness, making him a fringe-average defender in right field. He's always going to strike out a lot and never will hit for a high average, but he could be an everyday big league right fielder who hits 35 home runs. He'll likely head back to Double-A in 2008.

Year	Club (League)	Class	AVG	G	AB	R	H	2B	3B	HR	RBI	BB	SO	SB	OBP	SLG
2005	Spokane (NWL)	A	.253	71	265	51	67	16	0	11	26	26	71	7	.341	.438
2006	Clinton (MWL)	A	.268	126	459	77	123	26	4	21	77	59	117	9	.358	.479
2007	Bakersfield (Cal)	A	.230	63	244	47	56	15	1	16	45	28	64	9	.314	.496
	Frisco (TL)	AA	.241	69	245	35	59	10	0	14	38	20	62	7	.307	.453
MINOR LEAGUE TOTALS			.251	329	1213	210	305	67	5	62	186	133	314	32	.336	.468

18 WILMER FONT, RHP

Born: May 24, 1990. **B-T:** R-R. **Ht.:** 6-4. **Wt.:** 237. **Signed:** Venezuela, 2006. **Signed by:** Manny Batista/Andres Espinosa.

Font and Fabio Castillo were the jewels of the Rangers' 2006 international haul, and Font held his own in his stateside debut as a 17-year-old in 2007. Despite his youth, Font already has a strong, physical frame, and the Rangers say he finished the year at 237 pounds after starting it at 210. Though he's pigeon-toed when he walks around, he's more athletic than he looks. His arm strength is his best asset, as he runs his fastball up to 97-98 mph and sits at 93-96, though he has a long arm action and some effort in his delivery. He still needs to develop his fastball command, but it's not bad for his age. Font's secondary stuff is a work in progress. He has good feel for a changeup, which is his No. 2 pitch right now, but he's still experimenting with a mid-70s curveball. Some in the Rangers system think his arm action is more suited to a slider, but for now he just needs to learn how to maintain his arm speed when throwing a pitch that spins. Font remains very green, but he has front-of-the-rotation upside. He figures to get a crack at Spokane in 2008.

Year	Club (League)	Class	W	L	ERA	G	GS	CG	SV	IP	H	R	ER	HR	BB	SO	AVG
2007	Rangers (AZL)	R	2	3	4.53	14	10	0	0	45	41	33	23	2	24	61	.238
MINOR LEAGUE TOTALS			2	3	4.53	14	10	0	0	45	41	33	23	2	24	61	.238

19 THOMAS DIAMOND, RHP

Born: April 6, 1983. **B-T:** R-R. **Ht.:** 6-3. **Wt.:** 245. **Drafted:** New Orleans, 2004 (1st round). **Signed by:** Randy Taylor.

Diamond has been one of the Rangers' top prospects ever since they drafted him 10th overall in 2004, and he earned postseason all-star honors in 2005 in the California League and 2006 in the Texas League. But Diamond began feeling elbow discomfort off and on in the Rangers' mini-camp last January, and it flared up after a spring training appearance against the Mariners in early March. He had Tommy John surgery and missed all of 2007, but his recovery was on schedule, and he began throwing off a mound in November. The Rangers expect him to throw simulated games in spring training, but he likely won't return to game action until June 1. When healthy, Diamond attacked hitters with a 91-94 mph fastball that reached 95-96. His plus changeup has always been his No. 2 pitch, and his long arm action caused him to abandon his overhand curveball in favor of a promising 82-83 mph slider in 2006. He needs to get better at putting hitters away. Diamond closed in college and could eventually wind up as a power bullpen arm, but the Rangers protected him on their 40-man roster and will give him every chance to start. Expect him to get a shot at Triple-A by season's end barring any setbacks.

Year	Club (League)	Class	W	L	ERA	G	GS	CG	SV	IP	H	R	ER	HR	BB	SO	AVG
2004	Spokane (NWL)	A	0	2	2.35	5	3	0	1	15	13	5	4	0	5	26	.220
	Clinton (MWL)	A	1	0	2.05	7	7	0	0	30	18	8	7	1	8	42	.175
2005	Bakersfield (Cal)	A	8	0	1.99	14	14	1	0	81	53	20	18	3	31	101	.191
	Frisco (TL)	AA	5	4	5.35	14	14	0	0	69	66	44	41	8	38	68	.249
2006	Frisco (TL)	AA	12	5	4.24	27	27	1	0	129	104	65	61	14	78	145	.219
2007	Did Not Play—Injured																
MINOR LEAGUE TOTALS			26	11	3.62	67	65	2	1	325	254	142	131	26	160	382	.215

20 CRISTIAN SANTANA, C

Born: June 18, 1989. **B-T:** R-R. **Ht.:** 6-0. **Wt.:** 175. **Signed:** Dominican Republic, 2005. **Signed by:** Jesus Ovalle/Don Welke/Manny Batista.

Santana anchored the Rangers' strong 2005 international haul, signing with the Rangers for a $325,000 bonus. He had cleanup surgery in his shoulder that caused him to miss all of 2006, but he finally made his debut in the Arizona League in 2007, though he missed a month after breaking a bone in his thumb on a foul tip. Santana is a premium athlete who drew interest as a center fielder from other clubs, and one Rangers official described him as "Raul Mondesi, if you put him behind the plate." He has a strong, square-shouldered frame and quick hands that give him a short path to the ball. He has yet to tap into his plus raw power, but he demonstrated a maturing offensive approach last summer, hitting with confidence in two-strike counts and using the whole field. Santana is a plus runner, not just for a catcher. He receives well, has good footwork and does a good job blocking balls in the dirt. He has some arm strength, but his arm action is actually too short and could use some more arm swing. If he can straighten out his throwing, he has the ability to be a special catcher in the big leagues, and enough offensive potential that he could still be an impact player at another position. He could get a shot at the Midwest League in '08, but a return to Spokane (where he finished 2007) might do him some good.

Year	Club (League)	Class	AVG	G	AB	R	H	2B	3B	HR	RBI	BB	SO	SB	OBP	SLG
2006	Did Not Play—Injured															
2007	Rangers (AZL)	R	.302	27	96	20	29	7	3	3	15	12	27	3	.427	.531
	Spokane (NWL)	A	.320	6	25	1	8	2	0	1	4	0	6	0	.346	.520
MINOR LEAGUE TOTALS			.306	33	121	21	37	9	3	4	19	12	33	3	.413	.529

21 JOHNNY WHITTLEMAN, 3B

Born: Feb. 11, 1987. **B-T:** L-R. **Ht.:** 6-2. **Wt.:** 195. **Drafted:** HS—Kingswood, Texas, 2005 (2nd round). **Signed by:** Randy Taylor.

After struggling mightily in his first crack at the Midwest League in 2006, Whittleman returned to the circuit with a vengeance in 2007, hitting .343 with nine homers and 30 RBIs in the first two months of the season. That performance earned him a spot in the Futures Game, where he walked and homered against Mets flame-thrower Deolis Guerra in two plate appearances. The Rangers hoped that performance would spark a hot second half, but pitchers began approaching him more cautiously and he started pressing and chasing balls down out of the zone. Whittleman batted just .162 after the MWL all-star break and .240 after Texas gave him a change of scenery with a promotion to high Class A. Whittleman's fall in the instructional league was cut short by a viral infection in his spleen, but the Rangers expect him to be fine by spring training. Whittleman has a smooth lefthanded stroke with average power. He has a patient approach and can spray hard line drives from line to line, although the Rangers would like to see him get more aggressive and pull the ball a little more. Whittleman has improved somewhat at third base, where his strong arm and decent instincts give him a shot, but he committed 34 errors for the second year in a row and needs to become more consistent. He tends to put too much pressure on himself and is still learning to cope with failure. Whittleman should return to Bakersfield in 2008 and could still become an everyday corner bat in the big leagues.

Year	Club (League)	Class	AVG	G	AB	R	H	2B	3B	HR	RBI	BB	SO	SB	OBP	SLG
2005	Rangers (AZL)	R	.279	51	190	31	53	12	8	0	35	35	42	11	.393	.426
2006	Clinton (MWL)	A	.227	130	466	56	106	21	3	9	43	60	97	7	.313	.343
2007	Clinton (MWL)	A	.271	95	336	56	91	25	1	14	57	63	91	5	.382	.476
	Bakersfield (Cal)	A	.240	29	104	18	25	9	0	3	15	23	33	0	.372	.413
MINOR LEAGUE TOTALS			.251	305	1096	161	275	67	12	26	150	181	263	23	.355	.405

22 DAVID MURPHY, OF

Born: Oct. 18, 1981. **B-T:** L-L. **Ht.:** 6-4. **Wt.:** 190. **Drafted:** Baylor, 2003 (1st round). **Signed by:** Jim Robinson (Red Sox).

Murphy's development has been slow and deliberate since the Red Sox drafted him 17th overall in 2003, but he finally broke through to the big leagues for a brief stint in 2006 and was traded to Texas along with Kason Gabbard and Engel Beltre in July's Eric Gagne deal. The Rangers gave him a longer look in the majors after the trade, and he was one of the team's hottest hitters down the stretch. Murphy has plus raw power, but his smooth, easy swing is more tailored to making contact and finding the gaps in games. He has a mature, patient approach and does not strike out often. Defensively, Murphy is adequate in all three outfield positions, thanks to average speed, good instincts and a solid arm. He's not a burner on the base-paths, and he doesn't hit for enough power to hold down a corner outfield spot, but he's a versatile enough defender with enough offensive ability to fit in as a quality fourth outfielder for the Rangers in 2008. Unless he taps into his raw power in his late 20s, Murphy doesn't figure to profile as an everyday outfielder.

Year	Club (League)	Class	AVG	G	AB	R	H	2B	3B	HR	RBI	BB	SO	SB	OBP	SLG
2003	Lowell (NYP)	A	.346	21	78	13	27	4	0	0	13	16	9	4	.453	.397
	Sarasota (FSL)	A	.242	45	153	18	37	5	1	1	18	20	33	6	.329	.307
2004	Red Sox (GCL)	R	.278	5	18	3	5	1	0	0	1	2	1	1	.316	.333
	Sarasota (FSL)	A	.261	73	272	35	71	11	0	4	38	25	46	3	.323	.346
2005	Portland (EL)	AA	.275	135	484	71	133	25	4	14	75	46	83	13	.337	.430
2006	Portland (EL)	AA	.273	42	172	22	47	17	1	3	25	11	29	4	.315	.436
	Pawtucket (IL)	AAA	.267	84	318	45	85	23	5	8	44	45	53	3	.355	.447
	Boston (AL)	MLB	.227	20	22	4	5	1	0	1	2	4	4	0	.346	.409
2007	Boston (AL)	MLB	.500	3	2	1	1	0	1	0	0	0	1	0	.500	1.500
	Pawtucket (IL)	AAA	.280	100	400	50	112	20	5	9	47	41	68	8	.347	.423
	Oklahoma (PCL)	AAA	.286	2	7	0	2	0	0	0	0	0	3	0	.286	.286
	Texas (AL)	MLB	.340	43	103	16	35	12	1	2	14	7	19	0	.382	.534
MINOR LEAGUE TOTALS			.273	507	1902	257	519	106	16	39	261	205	326	42	.343	.407
MAJOR LEAGUE TOTALS			.323	66	127	21	41	13	2	3	16	11	24	0	.377	.528

23 MAX RAMIREZ, C

Born: Oct. 11, 1984. **B-T:** R-R. **Ht.:** 5-11. **Wt.:** 170. **Signed:** Venezuela, 2002. **Signed by:** Rolando Petit (Braves).

Ramirez has been moved prior to the trade deadline two years in a row, first going from the Braves to the Indians for Bob Wickman in 2006, then getting shipped to Texas for Kenny Lofton in 2007. He has hit since his first professional season in 2003, and he continued to do so in high Class A, along the way being voted by managers as the Carolina League player with the best plate discipline. Ramirez is a mature, gifted hitter who maintains his balance and bat control through his swing despite a high leg kick and a lot of hand movement in his trigger. He has good power to the gaps and occasional home run pop, and he could hit enough to play first base or left field if he has to move from behind the plate. He was signed as a third baseman and is still working to shore up his footwork and receiving behind the plate, but he has enough athleticism and arm strength to at least have a chance to catch in the majors. Texas put him on its 40-man roster in the offseason, and he figures to do the bulk of the catching at Double-A in 2008.

Year	Club (League)	Class	AVG	G	AB	R	H	2B	3B	HR	RBI	BB	SO	SB	OBP	SLG
2003	Braves2 (DSL)	R	.305	52	177	27	54	16	1	5	43	20	27	5	.386	.492
2004	Braves (GCL)	R	.275	57	204	20	56	16	1	8	35	19	50	1	.339	.480
2005	Danville (Appy)	R	.347	63	239	45	83	19	0	8	47	31	41	1	.424	.527
2006	Rome (SAL)	A	.285	80	267	50	76	17	0	9	37	54	72	2	.408	.449
	Lake County (SAL)	A	.307	37	127	19	39	6	1	4	26	30	27	0	.435	.465
2007	Kinston (Car)	A	.303	77	277	46	84	20	0	12	62	53	63	1	.418	.505
	Bakersfield (Cal)	A	.307	32	114	16	35	10	0	4	20	21	39	1	.420	.500
MINOR LEAGUE TOTALS			.304	398	1405	223	427	104	3	50	270	228	319	11	.404	.489

24 LUIS MENDOZA, RHP

Born: Oct. 31, 1983. **B-T:** L-R. **Ht.:** 6-3. **Wt.:** 180. **Signed:** Mexico, 2000. **Signed by:** Lee Sigman (Red Sox).

Rangers scout Russ Ardelina recommended Mendoza after seeing him pitch in the Red Sox system, and Texas acquired him in a deal for Bryan Corey in July, 2006. Boston had released him in 2005 and picked him back up off waivers after just two starts in the Padres system. He spent most of 2007 in Double-A, leading the Texas League in complete games and finishing second in wins before earning a September callup to the majors, where he earned his first win with five innings of one-run ball against the Orioles in his second start. Mendoza relies heavily upon his low-90s sinker, which tops out at 93-94 and induces plenty of ground balls when he's right. He has a rubber arm and a durable frame with a barrel chest and long limbs. Mendoza also throws strikes with a slurvy breaking ball and a changeup, but neither is a swing-and-miss pitch, and he does not get many strikeouts, making him very reliant on strong infield defense. His ceiling is limited, but he has a shot to crack the Rangers' Opening Day roster as a back-of-the-rotation starter or a swingman.

Year	Club (League)	Class	W	L	ERA	G	GS	CG	SV	IP	H	R	ER	HR	BB	SO	AVG
2001	San Joaquin (VSL)	R	6	0	2.27	13	9	0	1	67	46	20	17	0	10	61	—
2002	Ciudad Alianza (VSL)	R	0	3	3.03	15	4	0	2	35	44	29	12	2	15	32	.293
	Red Sox (GCL)	R	3	4	4.21	13	10	0	1	57	76	36	27	3	8	21	.329
2003	Red Sox (GCL)	R	0	0	0.00	2	2	0	0	5	4	0	0	0	0	3	.222
	Augusta (SAL)	A	3	3	2.26	13	11	0	0	59	46	19	15	1	14	29	.210
2004	Sarasota (FSL)	A	8	7	3.74	25	25	1	0	137	133	76	57	12	54	51	.255
2005	Lake Elsinore (Cal)	A	0	1	9.28	2	2	0	0	10	18	14	11	1	4	3	.391
	Wilmington (Car)	A	4	9	6.34	23	22	1	0	119	145	91	84	17	36	60	.297
2006	Wilmington (Car)	A	5	4	3.14	13	13	0	0	63	67	26	22	4	14	46	.269
	Portland (EL)	AA	1	5	6.38	9	9	0	0	48	73	35	34	4	14	29	.356
	Frisco (TL)	AA	2	4	7.75	7	7	0	0	38	55	33	33	2	11	21	.333
2007	Frisco (TL)	AA	15	4	3.93	26	25	3	0	148	145	75	65	11	48	93	.255
	Texas (AL)	MLB	1	0	2.25	6	3	0	0	16	13	4	4	1	4	7	.232
MINOR LEAGUE TOTALS			47	44	4.29	161	139	5	4	790	852	454	377	57	228	449	.298
MAJOR LEAGUE TOTALS			1	0	2.25	6	3	0	0	16	13	4	4	1	4	7	.232

25 WARNER MADRIGAL, RHP

Born: March 21, 1984. **B-T:** R-R. **Ht.:** 6-0. **Wt.:** 200. **Signed:** Dominican Republic, 2001. **Signed by:** Leo Perez (Angels).

As a hitter, the powerful Madrigal drew comparisons to Albert Belle for his thick body and swing mechanics, and the Angels signed him as an outfielder for a $150,000 bonus. After he batted just .235/.273/.348 in his third straight season in the low Class A Midwest League in 2006, the Angels decided to convert him to the mound, and he had a breakout season back at Cedar Rapids in '07. But when the Angels inadvertently failed to place him on the 40-man roster before the end of the World Series, Madrigal became a minor league free agent, and the Rangers scooped him up. Madrigal has a strong, durable frame, a good arm action and a repeatable delivery. He mostly overpowered MWL hitters by pounding the strike zone with his plus fastball at 93-96 mph, but he'll flash an average slider at 83-86 in warmups. Madrigal won't be able to get by solely on his fastball in the upper levels, so he'll need to tighten the slider and develop more confidence in the pitch. The Rangers expect him to move quickly and will give him a look in big league camp, though he's more likely to close in Double-A this year.

Year	Club (League)	Class	W	L	ERA	G	GS	CG	SV	IP	H	R	ER	HR	BB	SO	AVG
2006	Angels (AZL)	R	2	1	3.75	12	0	0	5	12	11	5	5	0	3	13	.250
2007	Cedar Rapids (MWL)	A	5	4	2.07	54	0	0	20	61	44	18	14	3	23	75	.202
MINOR LEAGUE TOTALS			7	5	2.34	66	0	0	25	73	55	23	19	3	26	88	.210

26 JOAQUIN ARIAS, SS

Born: Sept. 21, 1984. **B-T:** R-R. **Ht.:** 6-1. **Wt.:** 165. **Signed:** Dominican Republic, 2001. **Signed by:** Victor Mata/Carlos Rios/Freddy Tiburcio (Yankees).

Arias had advanced steadily through the Rangers system since being acquired from the Yankees in the 2004 Alex Rodriguez trade, but 2007 proved to be a lost season for him. With Michael Young entrenched at shortstop in the big leagues, Texas tried Arias out in center field during spring training, but he developed shoulder soreness trying to make outfield throws and was sidelined until late June. After a brief comeback attempt, Arias had arthroscopic surgery on his shoulder and was shut down for the season. He did not have any structural damage, however, and should be ready to compete for a utility job in the majors in spring training. When healthy, Arias is a plus-plus runner with good range and excellent arm strength at shortstop. He has an aggressive, line-drive approach at the plate but needs to improve his selectivity. He's shown little or no power over the course of his minor league career, posting a slugging percentage above .400 only once. Arias has a thin, fragile frame, and some in the organization questioned his toughness in 2007. He'll need to increase his defensive versatility if he's to have any value to the Rangers. As a gifted athlete with multiple standout tools, Arias could still emerge as a valuable everyday shortstop, but it seems unlikely that will happen with the Rangers.

Year	Club (League)	Class	AVG	G	AB	R	H	2B	3B	HR	RBI	BB	SO	SB	OBP	SLG
2002	Yankees (GCL)	R	.300	57	203	29	61	7	6	0	21	12	16	2	.338	.394
2003	Battle Creek (MWL)	A	.266	130	481	60	128	12	8	3	48	26	44	12	.306	.343
2004	Stockton (Cal)	A	.300	123	500	77	150	20	8	4	62	31	53	30	.344	.396
2005	Frisco (TL)	AA	.315	120	499	65	157	23	8	5	56	17	46	20	.335	.423
2006	Oklahoma (PCL)	AAA	.268	124	493	56	132	14	10	4	49	19	64	26	.296	.361
	Texas (AL)	MLB	.545	6	11	4	6	1	0	0	1	1	0	0	.583	.636
2007	Rangers (AZL)	R	.286	2	7	1	2	1	0	0	1	0	2	0	.250	.429
	Oklahoma (PCL)	AAA	.182	3	11	3	2	0	0	0	1	0	2	1	.182	.182
MINOR LEAGUE TOTALS			.288	559	2194	291	632	77	40	16	238	105	227	91	.321	.381
MAJOR LEAGUE TOTALS			.545	6	11	4	6	1	0	0	1	1	0	0	.583	.636

27 ZACH PHILLIPS, LHP

Born: Sept. 21, 1986. **B-T:** L-L. **Ht.:** 6-1. **Wt.:** 200. **Drafted:** Sacramento (Calif.) CC, D/F 2004 (23rd round). **Signed by:** Tim Fortugno.

The Rangers drafted Phillips out of Galt (Calif.) High in 2004 and signed him as a draft-and-follow in 2005. After getting off to a 1-0, 1.19 start in April during his full-season debut in 2006, Phillips struggled with his confidence for three months before getting back on track in August and carrying his progress over to instructional league. He went back to the Midwest League in 2007 and finished third in the league in ERA and second in strikeouts. Phillips is a quick-twitch athlete who got in trouble in the past when he rushed himself, but he made a lot of progress controlling his tempo and delivery in '07. His feel for pitching and command are his best assets, while his stuff is solid if not overwhelming. He works at 87-91 mph with his fringe-average fastball, and his second pitch is a solid-average changeup. He flashes a quick, downer curveball with tight rotation, but it can get slurvy at times. Phillips' upside is limited, but the Rangers feel confident that he will eventually be a back-of-the-rotation starter in the big leagues. He'll advance to high Class A in 2008.

Year	Club (League)	Class	W	L	ERA	G	GS	CG	SV	IP	H	R	ER	HR	BB	SO	AVG
2005	Rangers (AZL)	R	1	3	3.93	14	11	0	0	50	52	26	22	3	13	73	.260
	Clinton (MWL)	A	0	0	6.75	2	0	0	0	4	7	3	3	0	0	4	.389
2006	Clinton (MWL)	A	5	12	5.96	28	28	0	0	142	178	106	94	5	66	126	.315
2007	Clinton (MWL)	A	11	7	2.91	27	27	0	0	151	139	56	49	6	43	157	.247
MINOR LEAGUE TOTALS			17	22	4.34	71	66	0	0	348	376	191	168	14	122	360	.279

28 JOSE VALLEJO, 2B

Born: Sept. 11, 1986. **B-T:** R-R. **Ht.:** 6-0. **Wt.:** 172. **Signed:** Dominican Republic, 2004. **Signed by:** Rodolfo Rosario/Manny Batista.

Vallejo is a model of perseverance. He overcame the deaths of both of his parents, and he rebounded from a rough debut in the Midwest League with a solid performance in his second crack at the circuit in 2007. In just his second season since former Rangers special assistant Terry Shumpert taught him to switch-hit, Vallejo improved his batting average against righthanders from .240 to .260, but he made even more progress against lefties, jumping from .220 to .294. He has more strength from the right side than the left and slugged 85 points higher against lefties, but he profiles as a slasher from both sides of the plate. Vallejo is a well-above-average runner who made huge progress as a basestealer last year, swiping 47 bases in 50 attempts. He's a plus defender at second with excellent range, a strong arm and sure hands. Vallejo is still learning to control the zone and cut down his strikeouts, and he improved his bunting but still has work to do. He'll never hit for power and projects as a speedy, slick-fielding second baseman who could hit in the No. 9 hole or lead off in the majors. There's been talk of skipping Vallejo to Double-A in 2008, but the Rangers want to continue to build up his confidence and will likely send him to high Class A.

Year	Club (League)	Class	AVG	G	AB	R	H	2B	3B	HR	RBI	BB	SO	SB	OBP	SLG
2004	Rangers (DSL)	R	.212	52	170	23	36	4	1	1	19	16	52	9	.302	.265
2005	Rangers (AZL)	R	.291	52	203	28	59	7	2	1	15	19	49	18	.364	.360
2006	Clinton (MWL)	A	.234	127	496	62	116	11	4	2	29	32	104	24	.289	.284
2007	Clinton (MWL)	A	.269	129	513	68	138	17	5	1	46	44	102	47	.326	.327
MINOR LEAGUE TOTALS			.253	360	1382	181	349	39	12	5	109	111	307	98	.316	.309

29 BRENNAN GARR, RHP

Born: Feb. 22, 1984. **B-T:** R-R. **Ht.:** 6-2. **Wt.:** 190. **Drafted:** Northern Colorado, 2006 (9th round). **Signed by:** Rick Schroeder.

Garr spent most of his collegiate career at Northern Colorado as a third baseman, and he led the Bears in batting in his sophomore and junior years while smacking eight homers each year. He also served as Northern Colorado's closer his last two years, registering 12 career saves, though he logged just 35 collegiate innings and had erratic command. Still, he flashed a 93-mph fastball, and the Rangers signed him for a $65,000 bonus as a ninth-round pick. He succeeded as a reliever at three levels during his first full season in 2007, and his heater has climbed to 92-96 mph with heavy life that induces plenty of groundballs. He has a short-arm delivery that provides good deception, and he has a bulldog mentality. He's still developing his secondary stuff, but he has flashed an average slider and average change with split-finger action. He's still learning how to attack hitters, and he seemed to get a little gun-shy against Double-A hitters at the end of the season. Garr will return to Double-A in 2008 and could find his way to the big leagues by season's end. He projects as a solid setup man.

Year	Club (League)	Class	W	L	ERA	G	GS	CG	SV	IP	H	R	ER	HR	BB	SO	AVG
2006	Spokane (NWL)	A	2	0	4.85	17	0	0	0	26	30	20	14	1	14	29	.280
2007	Clinton (MWL)	A	0	3	2.31	25	0	0	5	39	25	13	10	2	16	50	.177
	Bakersfield (Cal)	A	0	0	1.10	10	0	0	0	16	9	2	2	1	6	20	.158
	Frisco (TL)	AA	0	0	2.57	6	0	0	0	7	8	4	2	0	10	5	.267
MINOR LEAGUE TOTALS			2	3	2.85	58	0	0	5	88	72	39	28	4	46	104	.215

30 ARMANDO GALARRAGA, RHP

Born: Jan. 15, 1982. **B-T:** R-R. **Ht.:** 6-4. **Wt.:** 180. **Signed:** Venezuela, 1998. **Signed by:** Fred Ferreira (Expos).

After missing most of 2002 and 2003 with Tommy John surgery, Galarraga's workload increased dramatically in his next two seasons in the Nationals organization, and he was worn out when the Rangers acquired him as part of the Alfonso Soriano trade in December 2005. As a result, he pitched just 70 innings in 2006 while battling shoulder fatigue, but he bounced back with a 160-inning campaign in 2007, culminating in three big league appearances in September. Galarraga works at 89-94 mph with a fastball that he keeps down in the strike zone. His slider is an above-average pitch, and his changeup is an adequate third pitch. He made some adjustments last year to get more downhill plane on his fastball, as he gets into trouble when he leaves the pitch up. Galarraga's stuff is decent but not special, and he profiles as a No. 5 starter and swingman in the majors, though he'll likely head to the Triple-A rotation in 2008.

Year	Club (League)	Class	W	L	ERA	G	GS	CG	SV	IP	H	R	ER	HR	BB	SO	AVG
1999	San Joaquin (VSL)	R	1	2	4.98	21	3	0	2	43	49	37	24	4	28	31	.283
2000	Cagua (VSL)	R	1	5	5.24	14	9	0	1	46	49	35	27	0	22	47	.266
2001	Expos (GCL)	R	1	3	3.12	14	1	0	2	34	37	21	12	2	15	24	.274
2002	Expos (GCL)	R	0	0	2.45	2	2	0	0	3	1	1	1	1	0	1	.083
2003	Expos (GCL)	R	1	1	1.80	5	5	0	0	15	13	5	3	0	5	7	.241
2004	Savannah (SAL)	A	5	5	4.65	23	19	2	0	110	104	64	57	14	31	94	.248
2005	Potomac (Car)	A	3	4	2.48	14	14	0	0	80	69	30	22	7	23	79	.228
	Harrisburg (EL)	AA	3	4	5.19	13	13	1	0	76	80	47	44	10	21	58	.275
2006	Frisco (TL)	AA	1	6	5.49	9	9	0	0	41	56	34	25	5	13	38	.327
	Rangers (AZL)	R	0	2	3.31	6	6	0	0	16	18	8	6	0	6	16	.290
	Spokane (NWL)	A	0	1	4.50	1	1	0	0	4	4	2	2	1	0	3	.250
	Bakersfield (Cal)	A	0	1	6.23	2	2	0	0	8	6	9	6	2	7	7	.176
2007	Frisco (TL)	AA	9	6	4.02	23	22	2	0	127	122	58	57	14	47	114	.255
	Oklahoma (PCL)	AAA	2	2	4.74	4	4	1	0	24	23	13	13	1	11	21	.237
	Texas (AL)	MLB	0	0	6.23	3	1	0	0	8	8	6	6	2	7	6	.250
MINOR LEAGUE TOTALS			27	42	4.26	151	110	6	5	632	631	364	299	61	229	540	.260
MAJOR LEAGUE TOTALS			0	0	6.23	3	1	0	0	8	8	6	6	2	7	6	.250

Toronto Blue Jays

BY MATT EDDY

The Blue Jays' pitching took a giant step forward in 2007 only to be sabotaged by a sagging offense, resulting in a five-game drop in the win column. But more vital to the organization's long-term health, Toronto had the type of draft that could shape its player-development outlook for years to come, the type of draft its farm system desperately needed.

Compensated for the loss of free agents Frank Catalanotto, Ted Lilly and Justin Speier, the Blue Jays held seven of the top 88 picks and put them to good use, selecting high-ceiling prospects at critical defensive positions, such as third baseman Kevin Ahrens (16th overall), catcher J.P. Arencibia (21st), shortstop Justin Jackson (45th) and second baseman John Tolisano (85th). All four shot to the top of Toronto's depth chart at their respective positions, as did center fielder Eric Eiland (88th).

Most talented of all was lefthander Brett Cecil (38th), a closer at Maryland whom Toronto will develop as a starter, as they will righthanders Trystan Magnuson (56th) and Alan Farina (third round), relievers while at Louisville and Clemson. The Blue Jays successfully developed two other college relievers, Shaun Marcum and since-traded David Bush, into major league starters.

At the big league level, Toronto pitching allowed the second fewest runs in the American League—and it wasn't all the doing of Roy Halladay and A.J. Burnett. Dustin McGowan announced his arrival by one-hitting the Rockies on June 24. He ended up taking the second-most starts on the staff and won 12 games. Marcum and Jesse Litsch also took regular turns in the rotation and were similarly effective.

McGowan, Marcum and Litsch all were 25 or younger last season, as were bullpen stalwarts Jeremy Accardo and Casey Janssen. Acquired from the Giants for Shea Hillenbrand in 2006, Accardo thrived in the closer's role after B.J. Ryan succumbed to Tommy John surgery.

The fine work turned in by Marcum, Litsch, Janssen and second baseman Aaron Hill was especially noteworthy, as they represent the only productive players drafted and developed by the Blue Jays since general manager J.P. Ricciardi came aboard in 2002. Outfielder Travis Snider, a first-round pick in 2006, might one day provide an emphatic counterpoint.

Toronto's offense sputtered to a disappointing 10th-place AL finish in scoring, and there are few

Dustin McGowan took the next step, winning 12 games with 144 strikeouts

TOP 30 PROSPECTS

1. Travis Snider, of	16. Brian Wolfe, rhp
2. Brett Cecil, lhp	17. Kyle Ginley, rhp
3. Kevin Ahrens, 3b/ss	18. Brandon Magee, rhp
4. J.P. Arencibia, c	19. Brian Jeroloman, c
5. Ricky Romero, lhp	20. Brad Mills, lhp
6. Justin Jackson, ss	21. Marc Rzepcynski, lhp
7. John Tolisano, 2b	22. Randy Wells, rhp
8. Curtis Thigpen, c/1b	23. Buck Coats, of
9. David Purcey, lhp	24. Balbino Fuenmayor, 3b
10. Ryan Patterson, of	25. Josh Banks, rhp
11. Trystan Magnuson, rhp	26. Zach Dials, rhp
12. Yohermyn Chavez, of	27. Chase Lirette, rhp
13. Robinzon Diaz, c	28. Joel Carreno, rhp
14. Eric Eiland, of	29. Anthony Hatch, 3b/2b
15. Alan Farina, rhp	30. Moises Sierra, of

young players ready to provide the boost the pitching staff got. Adam Lind, the No. 1 prospect on this list a year ago, hit just .238 with 11 homers in 89 games, though he was much better during a September callup. Outside of having Lind live up to expecations, the Jays have to hope the likes of Troy Glaus, Lyle Overbay and Vernon Wells can rebound in 2008.

The Jays signed just one player to a six-figure bonus during the international signing period, but they believe 22-year-old Cuban righthander Kenny Rodriguez can move quickly as a reliever.

General Manager: J.P. Ricciardi. **Farm Director:** Dick Scott. **Scouting Director:** Jon Lalonde.

Class	Team	League	W	L	PCT	Finish*	Manager	Affiliated
Majors	Toronto	American	83	79	.512	7th (14)	John Gibbons	—
Triple-A	Syracuse Chiefs	International	64	80	.444	11th (14)	Doug Davis	1978
Double-A	New Hampshire Fisher Cats	Eastern	70	73	.490	8th (12)	Bill Masse	2003
High A	Dunedin Blue Jays	Florida State	72	68	.514	5th (12)	Omar Malave	1987
Low A	Lansing Lugnuts	Midwest	78	61	.561	3rd (14)	Gary Cathcart	2005
Short-season	Auburn Doubledays	New York-Penn	47	29	.618	3rd (14)^	Dennis Holmberg	2001
Rookie	GCL Blue Jays	Gulf Coast	36	24	.600	4th (16)	Clayton McCullough	2007

Overall 2007 Minor League Record   367   335   .523   8th

*Finish in overall standings (No. of teams in league) ^League champion

LAST YEAR'S TOP 30

Player, Pos.		Status
1.	Adam Lind, of	Majors
2.	Travis Snider, of	No. 1
3.	Ricky Romero, lhp	No. 5
4.	Ryan Patterson, of	No. 10
5.	Curtis Thigpen, c/1b	No. 8
6.	Francisco Rosario, rhp	(Phillies)
7.	Brandon Magee, rhp	No. 18
8.	Jesse Litsch, rhp	Majors
9.	David Purcey, lhp	No. 9
10.	Balbino Fuenmayor, 3b	No. 24
11.	Eric Fowler, lhp	Dropped out
12.	Josh Banks, rhp	No. 25
13.	Chi-Hung Chen, lhp	Dropped out
14.	Ryan Klosterman, ss	Dropped out
15.	Kyle Yates, rhp	Dropped out
16.	Sergio Santos, ss	Dropped out
17.	Anthony Hatch, inf	No. 29
18.	Graham Godfrey, rhp	(Athletics)
19.	Kyle Ginley, rhp	No. 17
20.	Davis Romero, lhp	Dropped out
21.	Paul Phillips, rhp	Dropped out
22.	Brian Pettway, of	Dropped out
23.	Yohermyn Chavez, of	No. 12
24.	Ismael Ramirez, rhp	Dropped out
25.	Ty Taubenheim, rhp	(Pirates)
26.	Ryan Roberts, 2b	Dropped out
27.	Chip Cannon, 1b	Dropped out
28.	Robinzon Diaz, c	No. 13
29.	Chase Lirette, rhp	No. 27
30.	Brian Jeroloman, c	No. 19

BEST TOOLS

Best Hitter for Average	Travis Snider
Best Power Hitter	Travis Snider
Best Strike-Zone Discipline	Brian Jeroloman
Fastest Baserunner	Eric Eiland
Best Athlete	Eric Eiland
Best Fastball	David Purcey
Best Curveball	Ricky Romero
Best Slider	Brett Cecil
Best Changeup	Ricky Romero
Best Control	Josh Banks
Best Defensive Catcher	Brian Jeroloman
Best Defensive Infielder	Luis Sanchez
Best Infield Arm	Sergio Santos
Best Defensive Outfielder	Eric Eiland
Best Outfield Arm	Moises Sierra

PROJECTED 2011 LINEUP

Catcher	J.P. Arencibia
First Base	Adam Lind
Second Base	Aaron Hill
Third Base	Kevin Ahrens
Shortstop	Justin Jackson
Left Field	John Tolisano
Center Field	Vernon Wells
Right Field	Alex Rios
Designated Hitter	Travis Snider
No. 1 Starter	Roy Halladay
No. 2 Starter	A.J. Burnett
No. 3 Starter	Dustin McGowan
No. 4 Starter	Brett Cecil
No. 5 Starter	Shaun Marcum
Closer	Jeremy Accardo

TOP PROSPECTS OF THE DECADE

Year	Player, Pos.	2007 Org.
1998	Roy Halladay, rhp	Blue Jays
1999	Roy Halladay, rhp	Blue Jays
2000	Vernon Wells, of	Blue Jays
2001	Vernon Wells, of	Blue Jays
2002	Josh Phelps, c	Pirates
2003	Dustin McGowan, rhp	Blue Jays
2004	Alex Rios, of	Blue Jays
2005	Brandon League, rhp	Blue Jays
2006	Dustin McGowan, rhp	Blue Jays
2007	Adam Lind, of	Blue Jays

TOP DRAFT PICKS OF THE DECADE

Year	Player, Pos.	2007 Org.
1998	Felipe Lopez, ss	Nationals
1999	Alex Rios, of	Blue Jays
2000	Miguel Negron, of	Mets
2001	Gabe Gross, of	Brewers
2002	Russ Adams, ss	Blue Jays
2003	Aaron Hill, ss	Blue Jays
2004	David Purcey, lhp	Blue Jays
2005	Ricky Romero, lhp	Blue Jays
2006	Travis Snider, of	Blue Jays
2007	Kevin Ahrens, 3b	Blue Jays

LARGEST BONUSES IN CLUB HISTORY

Ricky Romero, 2005	$2,400,000
Felipe Lopez, 1998	$2,000,000
Gabe Gross, 2001	$1,865,000
Russ Adams, 2002	$1,785,000
Travis Snider, 2006	$1,700,000

TORONTO BLUE JAYS

Top 2008 Rookie: David Purcey, lhp. With injuries behind him, the big lefthander could thrive in a short-relief role.

Breakout Prospect: Kyle Ginley, rhp. A 17th-round pick making good, he has swing-and-miss stuff.

Sleeper: Brad Emaus, 3b. Though he has no real position, the 11th-round pick from Tulane grinds out at-bats and is just beginning to tap into power potential.

SOURCE OF TOP 30 TALENT

Homegrown	28	Acquired	2
College	16	Trades	1
Junior college	1	Rule 5 draft	1
High school	6	Independent leagues	0
Draft-and-follow	0	Free agents/waivers	0
Nondrafted free agents	0		
International	5		

Numbers in parentheses indicate prospect rankings.

LF
Ryan Patterson (10)
Jacob Butler
Brian Pettway

CF
Eric Eiland (14)
Buck Coats (23)
Chris Emanuele

RF
Travis Snider (1)
Yohermyn Chavez (12)
Moises Sierra (30)

3B
Kevin Ahrens (3)
Balbino Fuenmayor (24)
Anthony Hatch (29)
Brad Emaus
Sergio Santos

SS
Justin Jackson (6)
Luis Sanchez
Jonathan Diaz
Jesus Gonzalez
Marcos Cabral

2B
John Tolisano (7)
Scott Campbell
Jonathan Del Campo
Darin Mastroianni

1B
Chip Cannon
Matt Lane
Brant Colamarino

C
J.P. Arencibia (4)
Curtis Thigpen (8)
Robinzon Diaz (13)
Brian Jeroloman (19)
Joel Collins
Matt Liuzza

RHP

Starters	Relievers
Trystan Magnuson (11)	Brian Wolfe (16)
Alan Farina (15)	Brandon Magee (18)
Kyle Ginley (17)	Randy Wells (22)
Josh Banks (25)	Zach Dials (26)
Mike MacDonald	Chase Lirette (27)
Orlando Trias	Joel Carreno (28)
Shane Benson	Seth Overbey
	Kenny Rodriguez
	Jordan De Jong
	Adrian Martin
	Kyle Yates
	Sean Stidfole
	Paul Phillips
	Robert Ray
	Brad Cuthbertson

LHP

Starters	Relievers
Brett Cecil (2)	Davis Romero
Ricky Romero (5)	Nathan Starner
David Purcey (9)	Chi-Hung Cheng
Brad Mills (20)	
Marc Rzepcynski (21)	
Luis Perez	
Eric Fowler	

2007 — SIGNING BUDGET: $6.3 MILLION

Best Pro Debut: LHP Brett Cecil (1s) was the top prospect in the short-season New York-Penn League, with a 1.17 ERA in 62 innings (counting playoffs) with 69 strikeouts. A pair of former small-college stars, LHP Brian Letko (19) and RHP Jimmy Dougher (24), dominated the Rookie-level Gulf Coast League, finishing 1-2 in ERA at 1.50 and 1.56.

Best Athlete: OF Eric Eiland (2) is a four-tool athlete (below-average arm) who was an all-state safety at Houston's Lamar High. He had significant Division I football recruiting interest.

Best Pure Hitter: 3B/SS Kevin Ahrens (1) has a feel for his swing from both sides of the plate and controls the strike zone.

Best Power Hitter: C J.P. Arencibia (1) slammed nine homers for Team USA as a college sophomore and has above-average raw power to all fields. 2B/OF John Tolisano (2) led the GCL in home runs (10) despite hitting just .246, and has strength and loft in his swing.

Fastest Runner: Eiland covers 60 yards in just under 6.5 seconds and is a 70 runner. SS Steve Condotta (12) and 2B Daron Mastroianni (16) both run above-average as well.

Best Defensive Player: A pure defender, SS Justin Jackson (1s) has natural infield actions, excellent hands and a strong arm.

Best Fastball: RHP Alan Farina (5) dominated in the NY-P playoffs, striking out 12 in five innings while reaching 95 mph. Cecil ran his heater up to 93-94 mph.

Best Secondary Pitch: Cecil's hard 85-87 mph slider was one of the best breaking balls in the draft. LHP Brad Mills (4) has good arm speed on his plus changeup.

Most Intriguing Background: Tolisano was home-schooled and was Baseball America's top-rated 14-year-old in 2003. RHP Trystan Magnuson (1s), one of four Canadians the Jays signed, comes from a hockey family that features great uncle Keith Magnuson, an 11-year NHL veteran.

Closest To The Majors: Cecil and Farina would move quickly if left in the bullpen, but both are going to be given a chance to start, making Magnuson the best choice.

Best Late-Round Pick: Mastroianni has exceptional energy and can hit. 3B Brad Emaus (11) has a higher profile and started to tap into his raw power with three homers in Auburn's championship run.

The One Who Got Away: The Jays stopped drafting after just 30 rounds and signed the first 21 players they picked. Juco RHP Matt Thomson (22) took his three-pitch mix to be part of San Diego's top-rated recruiting class.

Assessment: The Blue Jays had 10 of the first 175 picks in the draft and hope they restocked a depleted farm system. They took more chances due to their extra picks, with five high school players in the first six rounds. In the first 10 rounds of the previous five drafts, they'd taken one: their top prospect, 2006 first-rounder Travis Snider. Now they have to develop these younger players.

2006 — BUDGET: $2.5 MILLION

OF Travis Snider (1) may have the best bat from the entire 2006 draft when all is said and done. The Blue Jays didn't have second- or third-round choices, so they did little after Snider.

GRADE: B

2005 — BUDGET: $3.6 MILLION

Toronto regrettably passed on Troy Tulowitzki to take LHP Ricky Romero (1), who hasn't moved as quickly as expected. OF Ryan Patterson (4) just keeps hitting.

GRADE: D

2004 — BUDGET: $4.6 MILLION

LHPs David Purcey (1) and Zach Jackson (1s, since traded) have been somewhat disappointing, but this is still a deep draft. RHPs Casey Janssen (4) and Jesse Litsch (24) already are contributing in the majors, and C/1B Curtis Thigpen (2) and OF Adam Lind (3) aren't far behind.

GRADE: B

2003 — BUDGET: $3.6 MILLION

2B Aaron Hill (1) and RHP Shaun Marcum (3) are two more solid contributors in Toronto. RHP Tom Mastny (11) has been surprisingly effective, but he was dealt for John McDonald.

GRADE: B

Draft analysis by John Manuel (2007) and Jim Callis (2003-06). Numbers in parentheses indicate draft rounds. Budgets are bonuses in first 10 rounds.

1

TRAVIS SNIDER, OF
Born: Feb. 2, 1988.

Ht.: 5-11. **Wt.:** 245.
Bats: L. **Throws:** L.
Drafted: HS—Everett,
Wash., 2006 (1st round).
Signed by: Brandon
Mozley.

PAUL GIERHART

Some scouts considered Snider the best hitter in the entire 2006 draft and he has done nothing to dispel that notion since turning pro. As a high school senior, he led Jackson High in Mill Creek, Wash., to a No. 2 national ranking. After signing for $1.7 million as the 14th overall pick, Snider earned MVP honors and No. 1 prospect status in the Rookie-level Appalachian League, where he batted .325 with 11 homers. He might have led the league in homers had he not lost the last week of the season to wrist tendinitis. Snider nearly repeated as MVP of his circuit in 2007, when he led the low Class A Midwest League with 35 doubles, 58 extra-base hits, 93 RBIs and a .525 slugging percentage. That last figure was particularly impressive, seeing as Snider was the only MWL qualifier to slug better than .500. Snider also finished second in the batting race at .313, but MWL voters chose West Michigan outfielder Gorkys Hernandez, who led only in stolen bases, as MVP. Snider hit .405 in April, and after pitchers adjusted to him, he regrouped, batting .333 with eight of his 16 homers in the final month. After the season, the Blue Jays assigned the 19-year-old Snider to the Arizona Fall League. The only younger player in the AFL was Rangers shortstop Elvis Andrus, yet Snider batted .316 with four homers.

Snider is extremely advanced for a young hitter. He has a quick, powerful swing from the left side and already can handle southpaws and offspeed pitches. He has the tools—strength, bat speed and a simple swing—necessary to hit for both average and power in the big leagues. He stays balanced throughout his swing, thanks to a sound hitting base, and shows advanced hitting instincts. When they saw the baby-faced Snider for the first time in the AFL, veteran pitchers tried to blow the ball past him. But after he connected for a few line drives to the gaps, he encouraged opponents to modify their plans of attack. His mental and competitive makeup is off the charts. Though he's already strong for a player his age, some Toronto officials think he has a chance to get even more physical. Snider is more athletic than he appears, and he has improved his reads and routes enough to project as an average defender on an outfield corner. He has enough arm for right field and topped the MWL with 16 outfield assists.

Snider is physically mature with a muscular build that served him well as a high school running back until he broke his leg as a junior. But that frame—he already plays at a weight in the neighborhood of 245 pounds—means he'll have to stress conditioning as he matures, especially with regard to his heavy lower half. He will accumulate some strikeouts, but they don't cost him much in the way of production. He has below-average speed but isn't a bad runner once he gets underway.

Snider has exceeded expectations thus far, and those expectations were high to begin with. He could move more quickly now that he has been exposed to the AFL and has put the MWL, the toughest hitting environment he'll encounter, behind him. Ticketed for high Class A Dunedin in 2008, he'll eventually bat in the middle of Toronto's order and has a big league ETA of 2010.

Year	Club (League)	Class	AVG	G	AB	R	H	2B	3B	HR	RBI	BB	SO	SB	OBP	SLG
2006	Pulaski (Appy)	R	.325	54	194	36	63	12	1	11	41	30	47	6	.412	.567
2007	Lansing (MWL)	A	.313	118	457	72	143	35	7	16	93	49	129	3	.377	.525
MINOR LEAGUE TOTALS			.316	172	651	108	206	47	8	27	134	79	176	9	.388	.538

2 BRETT CECIL, LHP

Born: July 2, 1986. **B-T:** R-L. **Ht.:** 6-3. **Wt.:** 220. **Drafted:** Maryland, 2007 (1st round supplemental). **Signed by:** Tom Burns.

Cecil worked primarily out of the bullpen in three years at Maryland, where his body, arm action and stuff improved significantly during his college career. He turned in a strong Cape Cod League performance in 2006 to cement his draft stock. After the Blue Jays drafted him 38th overall in June and signed him for $810,000, he shifted to a starting role and ranked as the short-season New York-Penn League's top prospect. Cecil has four key ingredients working for him—a 90-92 mph fastball that features sink and tops out at 94, a plus slider, command to both sides of the plate and poise. His knockout 85-87 mph slider was one of the draft's best breaking balls, and he can get the pitch in on righthanders. Turning pro improved Cecil's aggressive nature, seeing as he no longer had to contend with a small home park or metal-bat home runs. With a good move to first and the ability to vary his times to the plate, he already shows a nuanced feel for controlling the running game. Auburn pitching coach Tony Caceres helped Cecil with his changeup grip, and while the pitch is still developing, it's a swing-and-miss offering against righties at times. He also has a fringy curveball that he'll use as a show-me pitch. As he gets acclimated to starting, he'll have to prove he can hold his velocity after it tended to drop off quickly in the NY-P, where he was limited to a 55-pitch maximum in the regular season. Toronto was elated that Cecil fell into the supplemental first round. His frontline stuff and bulldog demeanor should make him at least a No. 3 starter. He'll begin his first full season in high Class A.

RODGER WOOD

Year	Club (League)	Class	W	L	ERA	G	GS	CG	SV	IP	H	R	ER	HR	BB	SO	AVG
2007	Auburn (NYP)	A	1	0	1.27	14	13	0	0	49	36	10	7	1	11	56	.197
MINOR LEAGUE TOTALS			1	0	1.27	14	13	0	0	49	36	10	7	1	11	56	.197

3 KEVIN AHRENS, 3B/SS

Born: April 26, 1989. **B-T:** B-R. **Ht.:** 6-1. **Wt.:** 190. **Drafted:** HS—Houston, 2007 (1st round). **Signed by:** Andy Beene.

The best position player in Texas in another strong draft year in the Lone Star State, Ahrens added power and the ability to bat lefthanded after his junior season, and the returns were immediate. He kept hitting from both sides of the plate as a senior, prompting the Blue Jays to select him with the 16th overall pick. They signed him for $1.44 million. With hand speed, a feel for his swing from both sides of the plate and a firm grasp of the strike zone, Ahrens projects to hit for average and power. A natural righthander, he has more power and better pitch recognition from that side. Drafted as a shortstop, he moved to third base in mid-July, as scouts had predicted. He showed solid hands, good lateral movement and a plus arm. Charging in on balls and making throws on the run posed little challenge. Ahrens may have put too much pressure on himself while debuting in a lineup full of fellow high draft picks. His bat isn't as quick from the left side as it is from the right, but he'll have plenty of time to hone that and adjust to hitting with wood as he moves up the ladder. He's a below-average runner, but not a baseclogger. The selection of Ahrens marked the second straight year Toronto opted for a high school talent with its first pick. He may not make the same splash at low Class A Lansing that Travis Snider did, because Ahrens has to adjust to a new position and refine his lefthanded swing. Regardless, he continues to draw Chipper Jones comparisons and has huge upside at the hot corner.

JERRY HALE

Year	Club (League)	Class	AVG	G	AB	R	H	2B	3B	HR	RBI	BB	SO	SB	OBP	SLG
2007	Blue Jays (GCL)	R	.230	48	165	19	38	6	0	3	21	25	47	3	.339	.321
MINOR LEAGUE TOTALS			.230	48	165	19	38	6	0	3	21	25	47	3	.339	.321

4 J.P. ARENCIBIA, C

Born: Jan. 5, 1986. **B-T:** R-R. **Ht.:** 6-1. **Wt.:** 210. **Drafted:** Tennessee, 2007 (1st round). **Signed by:** Matt Briggs.

Arencibia tied Alex Rodriguez' career record with 17 homers at Miami's Westminster Christian High, and he led USA Baseball's college national team with nine homers in the summer of 2006. A strained muscle in his back contributed to a lackluster junior season at Tennessee, but he still went 21st overall in the 2007 draft and signed for $1,327,500. It took him some time to get comfortable in pro ball, and he was hit by a pitch on his left wrist in midsummer, which sapped his power. Power long has been Arencibia's calling card. He's an aggressive hitter with juice to all fields. He has decent mobility and a strong arm, which he employed to throw out 34 percent of basestealers in his debut. He blocks balls well and made progress calling games. He's a natural leader who's also fluent in Spanish. Arencibia's swing gets long

RODGER WOOD

and he tends to have too much of an uppercut. He'll need to shorten his stroke and tighten his strike zone to hit for average. His receiving skills were rudimentary at best in college. The Blue Jays have worked on his setup to help him better receive the ball to his glove side, with his elbow down instead of out. Though his arm is strong, his footwork often prevents him from getting off quicker throws. He's a below-average runner. With Curtis Thigpen and Robinzon Diaz close to being big league ready, Toronto can afford to take its time with Arencibia. He'll begin his first full season in high Class A.

Year	Club (League)	Class	AVG	G	AB	R	H	2B	3B	HR	RBI	BB	SO	SB	OBP	SLG
2007	Auburn (NYP)	A	.254	63	228	31	58	17	1	3	25	14	56	0	.309	.377
MINOR LEAGUE TOTALS			.254	63	228	31	58	17	1	3	25	14	56	0	.309	.377

5 RICKY ROMERO, LHP

STEVE MOORE

Born: Nov. 6, 1984. **B-T:** R-L. **Ht.:** 6-1. **Wt.:** 200. **Drafted:** Cal State Fullerton, 2005 (1st round). **Signed by:** Demerius Pittman.

The first pitcher selected in the 2005 draft, Romero went sixth overall and signed for a club-record $2.4 million. He missed the first month of the 2006 season with elbow stiffness, then struggled through much of his Double-A stint upon his return. He again had a difficult time at New Hampshire again in 2007, and again missed time with injury, in this case shoulder soreness. At his best, Romero has two offspeed offerings that grade as plus pitches. His changeup, which travels about 10 mph slower than his fastball and bottoms out as it reaches the plate, is a go-to pitch versus right-handers. He also throws an 83-84 mph vulcan change, which behaves like a splitter. His weapon of choice against lefties is his 12-to-6 curveball. He has good life on his fastball, which sits at 89-91 and touches 93. For someone who was supposed to be a polished college pitcher, Romero's command has been disappointing. The Blue Jays have worked to simplify his delivery, trying to make it easier for him to get extension out over his front leg, enabling him to work down and to the corners. When he doesn't, his pitches are elevated and his curveball is flat. He has much more success throwing his curve as a chase pitch than he does throwing it for strikes, mostly because it has such huge break. Often he finds his slider easier to command, but it's not nearly as devastating as his curve. His injuries haven't been serious, but they have limited him to just 218 innings in his two full seasons. Romero has gone 5-13, 4.98 in 30 Double-A starts, and he has taken his pro struggles hard. He'll return to New Hampshire, where a strong first half would give him some needed confidence and put him back on track to become a mid-rotation starter in the big leagues.

Year	Club (League)	Class	W	L	ERA	G	GS	CG	SV	IP	H	R	ER	HR	BB	SO	AVG
2005	Auburn (NYP)	A	0	0	0.00	1	1	0	0	2	2	0	0	0	1	2	.250
	Dunedin (FSL)	A	1	0	3.82	8	8	0	0	30	36	13	13	2	7	22	.283
2006	Dunedin (FSL)	A	2	1	2.47	10	10	1	0	58	48	17	16	5	14	61	.224
	New Hampshire (EL)	AA	2	7	5.08	12	12	0	0	67	65	43	38	7	26	41	.256
2007	Dunedin (FSL)	A	0	0	3.86	1	1	0	0	4	4	2	2	0	1	2	.250
	New Hampshire (EL)	AA	3	6	4.89	18	18	1	0	88	98	57	48	9	51	80	.279
MINOR LEAGUE TOTALS			8	14	4.19	50	50	2	0	251	253	132	117	23	100	208	.261

6 JUSTIN JACKSON, SS

DAVID STONER

Born: Dec. 11, 1988. **B-T:** R-R. **Ht.:** 6-2. **Wt.:** 175. **Drafted:** HS—Asheville, N.C., 2007 (1st round supplemental). **Signed by:** Marc Tramuta.

Hailing from the same Roberson High (Asheville, N.C.) program that produced Marlins No. 1 prospect Cameron Maybin, Jackson started at shortstop for the U.S. junior national team in the fall of 2006. Though his offensive potential was called into question during his senior year, Jackson nevertheless was the third shortstop drafted in June, going 45th overall and signing for $675,000. Like most of the other talented teenagers with the Rookie-level Gulf Coast League Jays, he struggled with the bat in his pro debut. A long-armed, wiry athlete, Jackson has natural infield actions, excellent hands and a strong arm. He could become an even better defender as he becomes more efficient with his footwork, but he already fields the ball out in front. Jackson's simple swing is repeatable and he has a good approach, though his bat speed is just average. He's so physically projectable that he might hit for power down the road. Once he's underway, he has average to slightly above-average speed. Strength is the missing link to Jackson's offensive game, an area he was to address in an offseason conditioning program. High school pitchers were able to exploit holes in his swing and he'll need to use the opposite field more often against pros. Though his first step is good on defense, Jackson is slow to accelerate out of the batter's box. Jackson projects as exactly the type of shortstop defender the Blue Jays haven't developed since trading away the likes of Cesar Izturis, Felipe Lopez and Michael Young earlier in the decade. Jackson may take several years to develop, but he's Toronto's shortstop of the future.

Year	Club (League)	Class	AVG	G	AB	R	H	2B	3B	HR	RBI	BB	SO	SB	OBP	SLG
2007	Blue Jays (GCL)	R	.187	42	166	20	31	1	1	2	13	20	44	7	.274	.241
MINOR LEAGUE TOTALS			.187	42	166	20	31	1	1	2	13	20	44	7	.274	.241

7 JOHN TOLISANO, 2B

DAVID STONER

Born: Oct. 7, 1988. **B-T:** B-R. **Ht.:** 5-11. **Wt.:** 179. **Drafted:** HS—Estero, Fla., 2007 (2nd round). **Signed by:** Joel Grampietro.

Tolisano has been on Baseball America's radar since 2003, when we named him the top 14-year-old player in the United States. Though he was home-schooled, Tolisano played for Estero (Fla.) High, where he was considered one of the nation's top underclassmen as a freshman and sophomore. His stock slipped somewhat afterward and he lasted until the second round last June. Signed for $391,500, he led the Gulf Coast League with 10 homers in his debut. With strength and loft in his swing from both sides of the plate, Tolisano is short to the ball and has average bat speed and solid-average power to all fields. His swing is more fluid from the left side, and he tends to get out on his front side too much as a righty. He commands the strike zone and is more mature than most players his age, suggesting he'll get the most out of his abilities as a hitter. He's an average runner and has a strong arm for a second baseman. Tolisano's days of playing shortstop are behind him, and he still has work to do to stay at second base. His hands don't work particularly well and his footwork has a long way to go. Some scouts suggest he'll end up in right field. While the Blue Jays concede that Tolisano never will be much better than an average defender at second, his bat might be enough to carry him. He'll head to low Class A, where he could continue to provide more immediate returns than Toronto's other early-round high school draftees from 2007.

Year	Club (League)	Class	AVG	G	AB	R	H	2B	3B	HR	RBI	BB	SO	SB	OBP	SLG
2007	Blue Jays (GCL)	R	.246	49	183	35	45	5	0	10	33	26	40	7	.336	.437
MINOR LEAGUE TOTALS			.246	49	183	35	45	5	0	10	33	26	40	7	.336	.437

8 CURTIS THIGPEN, C/1B

Born: April 19, 1983. **B-T:** R-R. **Ht.:** 5-11. **Wt.:** 190. **Drafted:** Texas, 2004 (2nd round). **Signed by:** Andy Beene.

Thigpen was a member of three College World Series teams at Texas from 2002-04. More advanced as a catcher than the Blue Jays thought, he reached Double-A in his first full season and the major leagues in his third. Thigpen commands the strike zone and handles the bat well, spraying line drives all over the field. He exhibited those skills in Toronto, as well, though his gap power wasn't as evident. He gets good backspin on the ball, hinting that the potential to hit for power is there. An agile athlete, he offers mobility, actions and soft hands behind the plate. He has average arm strength and a quick release. His biggest drawback behind the plate is inconsistent footwork, and he has been slow to improve in that regard. He threw out just 17 percent of basestealers at Triple-A Syracuse, but that number rose to 36 percent in Toronto. His power is below-average but in line with the positional demands. He may lack the build to hold up as a catcher over the course of a grueling season. Much of Thigpen's value is tied to him staying behind the plate. But because he's athletic and light on his feet, he often takes ground balls at the infield corners, and he runs well enough to play the outfield corners. He even has gotten minimal exposure to second base. Toronto will give him every opportunity to stay at catcher, though he could become an extremely versatile utilityman.

Year	Club (League)	Class	AVG	G	AB	R	H	2B	3B	HR	RBI	BB	SO	SB	OBP	SLG
2004	Auburn (NYP)	A	.301	45	166	34	50	11	2	7	29	23	32	1	.390	.518
2005	Lansing (MWL)	A	.287	79	293	41	84	18	2	5	35	54	34	5	.397	.413
	New Hampshire (EL)	AA	.284	39	141	18	40	8	0	4	15	9	19	0	.340	.426
2006	New Hampshire (EL)	AA	.259	87	309	49	80	25	5	5	36	52	61	5	.370	.421
	Syracuse (IL)	AAA	.264	13	53	3	14	3	0	1	9	2	9	0	.304	.377
2007	Syracuse (IL)	AAA	.285	50	179	20	51	10	0	3	20	17	23	1	.348	.391
	Toronto (AL)	MLB	.238	47	101	13	24	5	0	0	11	8	17	2	.294	.287
MINOR LEAGUE TOTALS			.280	313	1141	165	319	75	9	25	144	157	178	12	.370	.427
MAJOR LEAGUE TOTALS			.238	47	101	13	24	5	0	0	11	8	17	2	.294	.287

9 DAVID PURCEY, LHP

Born: April 22, 1982. **B-T:** L-L. **Ht.:** 6-5. **Wt.:** 235. **Drafted:** Oklahoma, 2004 (1st round). **Signed by:** Ty Nichols.

The 16th overall pick in 2004, Purcey has yet to pay off on the Blue Jays' $1.6 million investment. But after having surgery in June to remove cysts in his forearm and triceps, he threw as well in the Arizona Fall League as he had since turning pro. He had been plagued by minor maladies throughout his career, and Toronto hopes the surgery will help him turn the corner. Purcey is capable of dialing his fastball up to 93-95 mph, but the Blue Jays have toned him down to the low 90s to improve his location. It also prevents him from maxing out on every pitch. He gets such good spin off his fingers that his fastball has serious life down in the zone. Like his fastball, his biting curveball is a plus pitch when he commands it. He's big and works on a tough downhill plane. With inconsistent mechanics affecting his release point, Purcey often finds command elusive. As a result, he often runs up high pitch counts. His changeup is usually below average, and he uses it mostly to keep batters off his fastball. Toronto has toyed with the idea of moving Purcey to the bullpen, where he wouldn't have to worry about efficiency or setting up batters as much. Despite the strong AFL showing, Purcey has made minimal progress the past two seasons. He'll get another crack at Double-A in 2008, and the Blue Jays still believe he'll blossom into a mid-rotation starter or power lefty reliever.

Year	Club (League)	Class	W	L	ERA	G	GS	CG	SV	IP	H	R	ER	HR	BB	SO	AVG
2004	Auburn (NYP)	A	1	0	1.50	3	2	0	0	12	6	2	2	0	1	13	.158
2005	Dunedin (FSL)	A	5	4	3.63	21	21	0	0	94	80	51	38	8	56	116	.229
	New Hampshire (EL)	AA	4	3	2.93	8	8	1	0	43	32	17	14	2	25	45	.205
2006	Syracuse (IL)	AAA	2	7	5.40	12	12	1	0	51	49	41	31	7	38	45	.249
	New Hampshire (EL)	AA	4	5	5.60	16	16	0	0	88	101	59	55	9	44	81	.287
2007	New Hampshire (EL)	AA	3	5	5.37	11	11	1	0	62	67	41	37	4	16	55	.277
MINOR LEAGUE TOTALS			19	24	4.53	71	70	3	0	351	335	211	177	30	180	355	.251

10 RYAN PATTERSON, OF

MIKE JANES

Born: May 2, 1983. **B-T:** R-R. **Ht.:** 5-11. **Wt.:** 205. **Drafted:** Louisiana State, 2005 (4th round). **Signed by:** Matt Briggs.

Patterson had a successful career at Louisiana State but wasn't drafted as a junior in 2004, nor was he signed as a free agent after winning the Cape Cod League batting title with a .327 mark that summer. Upon turning pro, Patterson led the New York-Penn (.595) and Florida State (.520) leagues in slugging percentage in his first two seasons. His progress was halted in spring training 2007 when he a pitch from Boston's Edgar Martinez shattered his right forearm, requiring the insertion of a metal plate. Originally slated to miss three months, Patterson returned to the field April 30. Patterson stays on the ball well and uses his short, powerful swing to drive the ball to all fields. Most of Patterson's home-run power is to left field. He provides average speed, arm strength and corner-outfield defense. Patterson likes to swing at the first pitch he can handle, and his lack of selectivity hampered him in Double-A. While his unorthodox swing works for him despite a number of moving parts, he can get off balance at times. The Blue Jays have minimized the sink in his load that he displayed in college, in an attempt to keep his eye level steady. Because he never admitted to lingering pain, it's difficult to know how heavily Patterson's gruesome spring-training injury factored into his mediocre Double-A performance. If he comes to spring training in the same physical shape he did last year, he could open 2008 in Triple-A.

Year	Club (League)	Class	AVG	G	AB	R	H	2B	3B	HR	RBI	BB	SO	SB	OBP	SLG
2005	Auburn (NYP)	A	.339	71	274	52	93	23	4	13	65	21	53	5	.386	.595
2006	Dunedin (FSL)	A	.288	84	354	65	102	25	0	19	69	20	61	2	.327	.520
	New Hampshire (EL)	AA	.257	49	187	19	48	14	1	6	20	13	50	2	.310	.439
2007	Dunedin (FSL)	A	.190	5	21	1	4	2	0	0	1	2	3	0	.261	.286
	New Hampshire (EL)	AA	.267	111	446	53	119	27	0	18	68	23	102	1	.302	.448
MINOR LEAGUE TOTALS			.285	320	1282	190	366	91	5	56	223	79	269	10	.328	.495

11 TRYSTAN MAGNUSON, RHP

Born: June 6, 1985. **B-T:** L-R. **Ht.:** 6-7. **Wt.:** 210. **Drafted:** Louisville, 2007 (1st round supplemental). **Signed by:** Steve Miller.

Magnuson walked on at Louisville and helped lead the Cardinals to the College World Series as a closer in 2007. Louisville's postseason success worked against him, because he was a fifth-year senior who would have become a free agent had his season ended before the draft. One of four Canadians drafted by Toronto in 2007, he went 56th overall and signed for $462,500. His uncle Keith Magnuson was an 11-year NHL veteran who appeared in two Stanley Cup finals during the 1970s. The Blue Jays plan to use Magnuson as a starter, but they held him out of action after he signed because of mild elbow soreness. His velocity surged from 88-89 mph into the mid-90s last year. He has learned to take advantage of his 6-foot-7 frame, using it and an easy delivery to drive the ball down in the zone, and he still has room to fill out. He also throws an average slider in the mid-80s. Magnuson will work on sharpening the break on his slider and developing a changeup as he begins his career as a starter in high Class A this year.

Year	Club (League)	Class	W	L	ERA	G	GS	CG	SV	IP	H	R	ER	HR	BB	SO	AVG
2007	Did Not Play—Signed Late																

12 YOHERMYN CHAVEZ, OF

Born: Jan. 26, 1989. **B-T:** R-R. **Ht.:** 6-3. **Wt.:** 200. **Signed:** Venezuela, 2005. **Signed by:** Tony Arias.

Though not as heralded as some of Toronto's other international signees, Chavez has shown the most potential. He made his U.S. debut in advanced Rookie ball at age 17 in 2006 and more than held his own, though a sore wrist at midseason cut into his playing time and hampered his power output. Chavez took a step back when the Blue Jays switched to a Gulf Coast League team in 2007, but that didn't stop him from flashing above-average power, ranking ninth in the league with a .494 slugging percentage. Though he has strength and bat speed, Chavez starts with his hands low—one club official compared his setup to Rondell White's—leading to questions about whether he'll hit for average against better pitching. He would benefit by driving the ball the other way more frequently and by not expanding his strike zone. Already a physical specimen, Chavez has a rangy build that suggests the potential for added muscle. He has enough range, speed and arm for right field, but spent most of the summer in left. He's on the right track and he'll advance to low Class A with a good spring training.

Year	Club (League)	Class	AVG	G	AB	R	H	2B	3B	HR	RBI	BB	SO	SB	OBP	SLG
2006	Pulaski (Appy)	R	.276	36	105	19	29	9	0	0	18	9	23	1	.371	.362
2007	Blue Jays (GCL)	R	.301	50	176	29	53	12	2	6	21	20	50	7	.389	.494
MINOR LEAGUE TOTALS			.292	86	281	48	82	21	2	6	39	29	73	8	.382	.445

13 ROBINZON DIAZ, C

Born: Sept. 19, 1983. **B-T:** R-R. **Ht.:** 5-11. **Wt.:** 220. **Signed:** Dominican Republic, 2000. **Signed by:** Hilario Soriano.

Free of Curtis Thigpen's shadow for the first time since 2004, Diaz thrived in Double-A last year. He had earned postseason all-star honors in the previous four seasons, and he might have done so again in the Eastern League had he not moved up to Triple-A in late July. Both Diaz and Thigpen are athletic receivers and righthanded batters with strong contact skills and good speed for catchers. Diaz is a free swinger with exceptional hand-eye coordination and he rarely strikes out. Though he makes lots of contact, Diaz doesn't drive the ball consistently because of a flat plane to his swing and an inside-out approach. He's also a classic bad-ball hitter who draws few walks. With loose actions and average arm strength, Diaz gets good carry on his throws, and he nailed 32 percent of basestealers in 2007. His game-calling has improved considerably over the past two seasons. Diaz will play every day in Triple-A this season.

Year	Club (League)	Class	AVG	G	AB	R	H	2B	3B	HR	RBI	BB	SO	SB	OBP	SLG
2001	Blue Jays (DSL)	R	.312	65	253	49	79	17	2	2	45	20	19	4	.374	.419
2002	Dunedin (FSL)	A	.120	10	25	3	3	0	0	0	1	1	4	0	.148	.120
	Medicine Hat (Pio)	R	.297	58	192	29	57	9	0	0	20	13	19	7	.345	.344
2003	Pulaski (Appy)	R	.374	48	182	33	68	20	2	1	44	10	14	1	.407	.522
2004	Charleston (SAL)	A	.287	105	407	62	117	20	2	2	42	27	31	10	.341	.361
2005	Dunedin (FSL)	A	.294	100	388	47	114	17	6	1	65	15	28	5	.325	.376
2006	Dunedin (FSL)	A	.306	104	418	59	128	21	1	3	44	20	37	8	.341	.383
2007	New Hampshire (EL)	AA	.316	74	301	33	95	17	1	3	30	11	16	5	.344	.409
	Syracuse (IL)	AAA	.338	19	65	4	22	3	0	1	10	1	6	0	.358	.431
MINOR LEAGUE TOTALS			.306	583	2231	319	683	124	14	13	301	118	174	40	.347	.392

14 ERIC EILAND, OF

Born: Sept. 16, 1988. **B-T:** L-L. **Ht.:** 6-2. **Wt.:** 200. **Drafted:** HS—Houston, 2007 (2nd round). **Signed by:** Andy Beene.

A brilliant performance at the 2006 Area Code Games thrust Eiland into the mix as a possible first-round pick for 2007. An up-and-down senior season ended that talk, though, as he battled left hamstring problems that robbed him of his speed and even forced the natural center fielder to right on occasion. The Blue Jays took Eiland, an all-state safety who drew significant Division I football interest, in the second round and signed him away from a Texas A&M commitment for $384,750. While Eiland is the least-refined early-round pick of general manager J.P. Ricciardi's tenure, he has supreme body control and exciting tools. He has a below-average arm, but the other four tools are present, and one club official likened his body type to that of an NFL cornerback. A 70 runner on the 20-80 scouting scale, Eiland shows the potential to be a plus center fielder. He has a longer way to go with the bat, though he has good bat speed and no glaring flaws in his swing. The Jays will stress adding a more pronounced load and staying through the ball, two techniques to help him add game power. He also needs to figure out how to make consistent contact after whiffing 62 times in his first 51 pro games. If everything clicks, Eiland will become an all-star, though he may move more slowly at first than Toronto's other high school picks from the early rounds of the 2007 draft.

Year	Club (League)	Class	AVG	G	AB	R	H	2B	3B	HR	RBI	BB	SO	SB	OBP	SLG
2007	Blue Jays (GCL)	R	.216	51	176	22	38	7	1	1	14	22	62	16	.315	.284
MINOR LEAGUE TOTALS			.216	51	176	22	38	7	1	1	14	22	62	16	.315	.284

15 ALAN FARINA, RHP

Born: Aug. 9, 1986. **B-T:** R-R. **Ht.:** 5-11. **Wt.:** 195. **Drafted:** Clemson, 2007 (3rd round). **Signed by:** Marc Tramuta.

A power reliever at Clemson, Farina improved his velocity and slider during his junior season when he lengthened his stride and got better extension out front. The Blue Jays invested a third-round pick and $254,250 in him with the intention of making him a starter because they like his arm action and mechanics. He joins Brett Cecil and Trystan Magnuson as 2007 draftees who will go from college relievers to pro starters, a move Toronto successfully pulled off with David Bush and Shaun Marcum. Because he spins the ball so well out of his hand from a high three-quarters arm slot, Farina gets above-average life on his 91-93 mph fastball, which tops out at 95. Listed at 5-foot-11, Farina also can two-seam the ball and shows two above-average breaking balls at times. His two-plane slider reaches as high as 86 mph and has hard tilt, and his downer curveball also shows promise. A turned ankle limited Farina's innings in his pro debut, but he'll take his first steps toward developing a changeup and improving his stamina in Class A this year.

Year	Club (League)	Class	W	L	ERA	G	GS	CG	SV	IP	H	R	ER	HR	BB	SO	AVG
2007	Auburn (NYP)	A	0	2	4.91	6	3	0	0	11	10	7	6	1	10	14	.233
MINOR LEAGUE TOTALS			0	2	4.91	6	3	0	0	11	10	7	6	1	10	14	.233

16 BRIAN WOLFE, RHP

Born: Nov. 29, 1980. **B-T:** R-R. **Ht.:** 6-3. **Wt.:** 220. **Drafted:** HS—Irvine, Calif., 1999 (6th round). **Signed by:** John Leavitt (Twins).

It took him nine years, three organizations and one Tommy John surgery, but Wolfe finally established himself as a major league reliever. Drafted in 1999, he languished for five years in the Twins system before needing elbow surgery in 2004. He returned in 2005 but was released that May, hooking on with the Brewers for the remainder of that season. The Blue Jays acquired him in the January 2006 trade that sent Corey Koskie to Milwaukee. Wolfe established himself as a key late-inning reliever for Toronto in the second half of 2007, after injuries knocked closer B.J. Ryan and setup man Brandon League out of action. With a cutting fastball he throws up to 96 mph, Wolfe doesn't miss many bats but he does get plenty of mis-hits. He held righthanders to a .130 average, the lowest figure among AL relievers. His curveball is average and he uses it as a change of pace. The curve generates plenty of funny swings by batters looking for his fastball. Because of his poise and his cutter, Wolfe should remain a factor in the big league bullpen.

Year	Club (League)	Class	W	L	ERA	G	GS	CG	SV	IP	H	R	ER	HR	BB	SO	AVG
1999	Twins (GCL)	R	4	0	2.84	9	5	2	0	38	33	14	12	2	9	40	.234
2000	Quad City (MWL)	A	5	9	4.74	31	18	0	0	123	148	73	65	13	34	91	.299
2001	Quad City (MWL)	A	13	8	2.81	28	23	2	0	160	128	64	50	11	32	128	.214
2002	Fort Myers (FSL)	A	6	9	4.64	25	23	0	0	132	160	84	68	17	34	85	.300
2003	Fort Myers (FSL)	A	2	1	2.53	7	7	0	0	46	41	15	13	3	6	22	.232
	New Britain (EL)	AA	5	7	6.42	30	10	1	3	82	111	65	59	10	24	42	.326
2004	New Britain (EL)	AA	1	1	8.18	7	0	0	0	11	16	10	10	3	3	6	.348
2005	Rochester (IL)	AAA	0	2	8.53	3	0	0	0	6	10	8	6	1	2	5	.345
	New Britain (EL)	AA	1	0	7.04	5	0	0	0	7	10	6	6	0	7	4	.333
	Brevard County (FSL)	A	1	1	0.79	18	0	0	8	22	19	3	2	0	8	22	.229
	Huntsville (SL)	AA	3	1	3.38	16	0	0	0	24	32	12	9	1	8	19	.311
2006	Dunedin (FSL)	A	1	4	6.00	5	5	0	0	24	33	20	16	3	3	17	.317
	New Hampshire (EL)	AA	1	3	5.74	24	2	0	0	42	54	30	27	5	15	34	.302
2007	Syracuse (IL)	AAA	2	0	1.04	17	0	0	0	26	18	4	3	1	6	23	.191
	Toronto (AL)	MLB	3	1	2.98	38	0	0	0	45	36	17	15	5	9	22	.224
MINOR LEAGUE TOTALS			45	46	4.17	225	93	5	11	746	813	408	346	70	191	538	.275
MAJOR LEAGUE TOTALS			3	1	2.98	38	0	0	0	45	36	17	15	5	9	22	.224

17 KYLE GINLEY, RHP

Born: Sept. 1, 1986. **B-T:** R-R. **Ht.:** 6-2. **Wt.:** 225. **Drafted:** St. Petersburg (Fla.) JC, 2006 (17th round). **Signed by:** Joel Grampietro.

After losing their 2006 second- and third-round picks for signing free agents A.J. Burnett and B.J. Ryan, the Blue Jays tried to compensate by handing out six-figure bonuses to four players drafted after the 15th round. Ginley, who had planned on transferring to NCAA Division II power Florida Southern, signed for $155,000. With a true swing-and-miss fastball that ranges from 91-94 mph, he pitched the entire season in low Class A at age 20, finishing seventh in the Midwest League with 129 strikeouts in 122 innings. Though he lacks a quick arm, Ginley's long arm action generates plenty of power and sink, with the ball jumping out of his hand. He learned to throw an 86-88 mph cutter in 2007 and it instantly became his No. 2 offering. His curveball is a get-me-over pitch at this stage and he needs to continue developing his changeup by throwing it more often. Despite cleaning up his delivery and showing better direction toward the plate, Ginley still saw his command waver throughout the season. He also struggled to pitch deep into games and to put batters away. Shut down at the end of August with shoulder tendinitis, Ginley could receive a bump to high Class A to begin 2008. He profiles as a No. 4 starter or setup man.

Year	Club (League)	Class	W	L	ERA	G	GS	CG	SV	IP	H	R	ER	HR	BB	SO	AVG
2006	Pulaski (Appy)	R	1	1	4.73	8	1	0	0	26	22	14	14	3	11	42	.222
	Auburn (NYP)	A	1	0	0.00	2	1	0	0	10	5	0	0	0	5	6	.147
2007	Lansing (MWL)	A	7	6	4.73	26	26	0	0	122	142	81	64	11	41	129	.292
MINOR LEAGUE TOTALS			9	7	4.43	36	28	0	0	158	169	95	78	14	57	177	.273

18 BRANDON MAGEE, RHP

Born: July 26, 1983. **B-T:** R-R. **Ht.:** 6-5. **Wt.:** 205. **Drafted:** Bradley, 2006 (4th round). **Signed by:** Aaron Jerslid.

Magee began his college career as Bradley's closer but blossomed into a starter and finished with 260 strikeouts, one shy of the school record. He became one of the top senior signs in the 2006 draft, nabbing a $155,000 bonus in the fourth round. After a modest pro debut in 2006, Magee jumped to high Class A and dug himself into a hole, going 0-2, 9.56 in April. Once he stopped overthrowing, he reduced his ERA to 3.91 by season's end and ranked third in the Florida State League with 157 innings. The key for Magee is extension out in front, which is crucial to adding sink and movement to his 91-93 mph fastball down in the zone. He uses his above-average slider as an out pitch. Magee has shown modest aptitude for a changeup, and he's learning to command a cutter to give him a third weapon. Many scouts see him as a reliever because of his sinker/slider repertoire, lack of a reliable third pitch and the effort in his delivery. At best, he profiles as a back-end starter on a good team. Keeping the ball down and getting innings will be Magee's main goals as he moves to Double-A in 2008.

Year	Club (League)	Class	W	L	ERA	G	GS	CG	SV	IP	H	R	ER	HR	BB	SO	AVG
2006	Auburn (NYP)	A	3	1	3.10	11	11	0	0	52	51	23	18	1	19	40	.254
2007	Dunedin (FSL)	A	9	8	3.91	28	27	1	0	157	161	77	68	14	54	76	.267
MINOR LEAGUE TOTALS			12	9	3.70	39	38	1	0	209	212	100	86	15	73	116	.264

19 BRIAN JEROLOMAN, C

Born: May 10, 1985. **B-T:** L-R. **Ht.:** 6-0. **Wt.:** 195. **Drafted:** Florida, 2006 (6th round). **Signed by:** Joel Grampietro.

On the strength of his defensive tools, Jeroloman entered 2006 as the top catching prospect in college baseball. Then he hit just .242 and was just the eighth college catcher drafted that June. Pitchers love throwing to Jeroloman, the top defensive catcher in the system, because he's an above-average receiver and game caller. His average arm plays up because of his athleticism and trigger-fast release, with his throws to second base averaging 1.9 seconds. He threw out 28 percent of basestealers in 2007. Jeroloman has a sound swing but he's actually more valuable when he's not swinging the bat. He led Florida State League batters with 85 walks and finished second with a .421 on-base percentage. He offers little in the way of power or speed, though, and doesn't make enough hard contact to hit for much average. Because of his lefty bat, strike-zone discipline and impeccable defensive tools, he's a safe bet to become at least a big league backup. He'll open 2008 in Double-A.

Year	Club (League)	Class	AVG	G	AB	R	H	2B	3B	HR	RBI	BB	SO	SB	OBP	SLG
2006	Auburn (NYP)	A	.241	45	141	27	34	10	1	0	21	26	38	0	.363	.326
2007	Dunedin (FSL)	A	.259	100	290	32	75	14	0	3	39	85	57	0	.421	.338
MINOR LEAGUE TOTALS			.253	145	431	59	109	24	1	3	60	111	95	0	.404	.334

20 BRAD MILLS, LHP

Born: March 5, 1985. **B-T:** L-L. **Ht.:** 6-0. **Wt.:** 185. **Drafted:** Arizona, 2007 (4th round). **Signed by:** Dan Cholowsky.

The Blue Jays made Mills a 22nd-round pick in 2006, but as expected, the civil-engineering major opted to return to Arizona for his senior year. A former walk-on, he improved his draft status by 18 rounds in 2007 and received $140,000 to sign. Mills excited scouts by touching 92 mph as a junior, but he reverted to his more customary 87-88 last season. It didn't help that he received a cortisone shot late in the spring to help a balky back, then missed time with a strained oblique after turning pro. Deception is Mills' biggest asset as a pitcher, as he leans back in the middle of a herky-jerky, over-the-top delivery, and he perfectly disguises his offspeed offerings. Even playing catch with Mills presents a challenge. He gets tight rotation on his four-seam fastball and his average 12-to-6 curveball, but it's his changeup that's his equalizer pitch. He shows quality arm speed on the changeup, his lone above-average offering. The Blue Jays would like Mills to concentrate on pounding the bottom of the strike zone, which should be easier once he's free of injury this year in Class A. He projects as a back-of-the-rotation starter or middle reliever.

Year	Club (League)	Class	W	L	ERA	G	GS	CG	SV	IP	H	R	ER	HR	BB	SO	AVG
2007	Auburn (NYP)	A	2	0	2.00	6	2	0	0	18	9	4	4	0	6	21	.143
MINOR LEAGUE TOTALS			2	0	2.00	6	2	0	0	18	9	4	4	0	6	21	.143

21 MARC RZEPCYNSKI, LHP

Born: Aug. 29, 1985. **B-T:** L-L. **Ht.:** 6-3. **Wt.:** 205. **Drafted:** UC Riverside, 2007 (5th round). **Signed by:** Demerius Pittman.

One of the top college senior arms in the 2007 draft, Rzepcynski represented a good value after he signed for $110,000 as a fifth-round pick. He rebounded from elbow soreness and a broken left knuckle during the college season to pitch well in the New York-Penn League, where he teamed with fellow lefties Brett Cecil and Luis Perez in a formidable Auburn rotation. At his best, Rzepcynski throws an 87-89 mph fastball with sink and bore (topping out at 92) and a hard slider, giving him one weapon he can command to each side of the plate. His long, slinging arm action from a three-quarters slot generates plenty of life on his pitches. He locates an average changeup down in the zone, and his competitive makeup makes his stuff play up even further. Rzepcynski showed none of the lapses in command with Auburn that he had early in UC Riverside career. Though he lacks an out pitch, he isn't afraid to throw any pitch in any count, and he profiles as a No. 4 or 5 starter. He'll likely open his first full season in high Class A.

Year	Club (League)	Class	W	L	ERA	G	GS	CG	SV	IP	H	R	ER	HR	BB	SO	AVG
2007	Auburn (NYP)	A	5	0	2.76	11	7	0	0	45	33	21	14	2	17	49	.201
MINOR LEAGUE TOTALS			5	0	2.76	11	7	0	0	45	33	21	14	2	17	49	.201

22 RANDY WELLS, RHP

Born: Aug. 28, 1982. **B-T:** R-R. **Ht.:** 6-5. **Wt.:** 230. **Drafted:** Southwestern Illinois CC, 2002 (38th round). **Signed by:** Mark Adair (Cubs).

The Blue Jays selected Wells with the 11th overall pick in major league Rule 5 draft, but his amateur draft experience was much more meager. Drafted by the Cubs in the 38th round as a catcher in 2002, he converted to pitching by the end of 2003, in part because he grew to 6-foot-5. Adding intrigue to the conversion, Wells never had pitched in high school or junior college. But then he didn't hit as a pro, either, batting just .157 with two doubles in 124 at-bats, none above low Class A. Wells pitches at 90-92 mph but can flash 93-94 on occasion. His slider is inconsistent but shows promise, as does his changeup. The Cubs, though, were disappointed that his secondary stuff didn't improve as quickly as they hoped, and that his control regressed in 2007. Interestingly, Chicago left Wells unprotected only to trade up in the Rule 5 draft to select another catcher-turned-reliever, Tim Lahey. With Toronto, Wells will compete for a long-relief role. If he doesn't stick with the big league club, he has to clear waivers and be offered back to the Cubs for half his $50,000 draft price before he could be sent to the minors.

Year	Club (League)	Class	W	L	ERA	G	GS	CG	SV	IP	H	R	ER	HR	BB	SO	AVG
2003	Lansing (MWL)	A	0	0	0.00	1	0	0	0	1	1	0	0	0	0	0	.333
	Cubs (AZL)	R	0	0	3.60	3	0	0	0	5	5	2	2	0	4	4	.250
2004	Lansing (MWL)	A	6	6	4.43	36	15	0	1	107	112	64	53	9	40	121	.269
2005	Daytona (FSL)	A	10	2	2.74	41	10	0	2	98	93	33	30	5	22	106	.245
	West Tenn (SL)	AA	0	1	3.86	6	0	0	1	9	13	4	4	0	7	4	.371
2006	West Tenn (SL)	AA	4	2	1.59	12	12	0	0	62	45	13	11	2	13	54	.199
	Iowa (PCL)	AAA	5	5	4.96	13	12	0	0	69	87	42	38	7	23	59	.309
2007	Iowa (PCL)	AAA	5	6	4.52	40	9	0	2	95	100	54	48	11	41	101	.268
MINOR LEAGUE TOTALS			30	22	3.73	152	58	0	6	448	456	212	186	34	150	449	.263

23 BUCK COATS, OF

Born: June 9, 1982. **B-T:** L-R. **Ht.:** 6-3. **Wt.:** 195. **Drafted:** HS—Valdosta, Ga., 2000 (18th round). **Signed by:** Sam Hughes (Cubs).

The Cubs tried for three years to convert Coats into a shortstop, but it wouldn't take, as the erstwhile outfielder committed 114 errors in 303 games at short from 2003-05. Back in the outfield for the 2007 season, Coats hit well in Triple-A but was traded to the Reds in August, after he'd been designated for assignment, for Class A righthander Marcos Mateo. The Blue Jays acquired him in December for righthander Justin James, who was the club's fifth-round pick in 2003. A good athlete who runs well, Coats has the range and arm to capably play all three outfield spots. He has a sound lefthanded swing, makes reasonable contact, commands the strike zone and has some gap power. But he doesn't do anything particularly well offensively, so it's hard to project him as a regular. His versatility (he has played seven positions as a pro) and modest offensive profile mark him as a strong candidate for a roster spot in 2008.

Year	Club (League)	Class	AVG	G	AB	R	H	2B	3B	HR	RBI	BB	SO	SB	OBP	SLG
2000	Cubs (AZL)	R	.296	30	98	20	29	6	3	0	14	12	24	7	.395	.418
2001	Cubs (AZL)	R	.260	33	123	11	32	3	3	1	18	4	19	3	.292	.358
2002	Lansing (MWL)	A	.257	133	501	65	129	21	4	4	47	31	67	14	.303	.339
2003	Lansing (MWL)	A	.277	132	488	64	135	25	7	1	59	64	93	32	.364	.363
2004	Daytona (FSL)	A	.290	112	414	64	120	22	4	8	55	32	90	28	.340	.420
2005	West Tenn (SL)	AA	.282	127	439	47	124	32	6	1	49	38	80	17	.340	.390
2006	Iowa (PCL)	AAA	.282	124	450	60	127	21	0	7	51	38	87	17	.342	.376
	Chicago (NL)	MLB	.167	18	18	2	3	1	0	1	1	0	6	0	.167	.389
2007	Iowa (PCL)	AAA	.303	123	455	81	138	21	3	11	59	44	74	18	.363	.435
	Louisville (IL)	AAA	.438	4	16	1	7	2	0	4	1	5	2	.471	.563
	Cincinnati (NL)	MLB	.206	20	34	2	7	4	0	0	2	3	15	0	.263	.324
MINOR LEAGUE TOTALS			.282	818	2984	413	841	153	30	33	356	264	539	138	.342	.386
MAJOR LEAGUE TOTALS			.192	38	52	4	10	5	0	1	3	3	21	0	.232	.346

24 BALBINO FUENMAYOR, 3B

Born: Nov. 26, 1989. **B-T:** R-R. **Ht.:** 6-3. **Wt.:** 195. **Signed:** Venezuela, 2006. **Signed by:** Rafael Moncada.

Following an impressive workout at Rogers Centre in front of general manager J.P. Ricciardi, Fuenmayor signed for $725,000 in 2006. Nothing went right for Fuenmayor in his pro debut last year, as he hit .174 and struck out a Gulf Coast League-leading 68 times. In his defense, he was one of the younger players in the GCL, which presents a tough environment for young hitters. Fuenmayor has a compact swing and solid bat speed, but he has yet to show the ability to pull pitches—not even in batting practice. Furthermore, he struggled mightily with his pitch recognition, which led to all the strikeouts. Though he has average arm strength, the athletic Fuenmayor showed below-average lateral movement at third base, which could improve with better footwork. He's a slightly below-average runner and will slow down as he fills out. More was expected of Fuenmayor because of the bonus he received, but the Blue Jays remain optimistic. More than likely, he'll get another shot at the GCL.

Year	Club (League)	Class	AVG	G	AB	R	H	2B	3B	HR	RBI	BB	SO	SB	OBP	SLG
2007	Blue Jays (GCL)	R	.174	48	178	13	31	5	2	1	12	12	68	0	.244	.242
MINOR LEAGUE TOTALS			.174	48	178	13	31	5	2	1	12	12	68	0	.244	.242

25 JOSH BANKS, RHP

Born: July 18, 1982. **B-T:** R-R. **Ht.:** 6-3. **Wt.:** 195. **Drafted:** Florida International, 2003 (2nd round). **Signed by:** Tony Arias.

Banks has been nothing if not durable. He reached Double-A 26 starts into his pro career and has averaged 163 innings over his four full seasons. His control and pitch efficiency have translated to an eye-popping 4.9-1 K-BB ratio in Double-A and Triple-A, though he also has a 4.63 ERA because he may be around the strike zone too much. Banks pitches primarily with a straight 90-91 mph fastball, and he cuts it to get in on lefthanders. He's also tried to sink it more to alleviate some of his longball problems. Banks' splitter remains his best secondary offering, as his curveball never has developed into anything more than a show pitch. He'll also mix in an occasional changeup. While leveling off in Triple-A the last two years, Banks has tumbled down the organizational pecking order. He's headed back to Syracuse and will be ready if injuries strike the big league rotation.

Year	Club (League)	Class	W	L	ERA	G	GS	CG	SV	IP	H	R	ER	HR	BB	SO	AVG
2003	Auburn (NYP)	A	7	2	2.43	15	15	0	0	66	58	21	18	1	10	81	.233
2004	Dunedin (FSL)	A	7	1	1.80	11	11	0	0	60	49	17	12	4	8	60	.225
	New Hampshire (EL)	AA	6	6	5.03	18	17	1	0	91	89	54	51	15	28	76	.256
2005	New Hampshire (EL)	AA	8	12	3.83	27	27	2	0	162	159	76	69	18	11	145	.256
2006	Syracuse (IL)	AAA	10	11	5.17	29	29	0	0	170	184	108	98	35	28	126	.267
2007	Syracuse (IL)	AAA	12	10	4.63	27	27	3	0	169	192	89	87	22	24	101	.284
	Toronto (AL)	MLB	0	0	7.36	3	1	0	0	7	11	6	6	1	2	2	.344
MINOR LEAGUE TOTALS			50	42	4.19	127	126	6	0	720	731	365	335	95	109	589	.261
MAJOR LEAGUE TOTALS			0	0	7.36	3	1	0	0	7	11	6	6	1	2	2	.344

26 ZACH DIALS, RHP

Born: July 22, 1985. **B-T:** R-R. **Ht.:** 6-1. **Wt.:** 205. **Drafted:** Kentucky, 2006 (28th round). **Signed by:** Aaron Jerslid.

From 28th-round afterthought and fledgling minor league starter to power reliever, Dials came as far as any Toronto farmhand in 2007. Because he had trouble staying healthy as a starter, the Blue Jays moved him to the bullpen, where his fastball and slider played up a grade. Where previously his fastball had been 87-90 mph, it sat at 92-95 with incredible sink when he came out of the bullpen. His slider went from 80-83 to 83-86 with late tilt, and he was throwing it for first-pitch strikes. Even as an amateur, Dials struggled to repeat his delivery and stay online to the plate, but his entire mindset changed as a reliever, as he realized he could just air it out. He still has a changeup that he learned as a starter, but it's below average. Dials has yet to pitch above low Class A, but he could move quickly if he keeps improving in 2008.

Year	Club (League)	Class	W	L	ERA	G	GS	CG	SV	IP	H	R	ER	HR	BB	SO	AVG
2006	Pulaski (Appy)	R	0	0	0.00	3	0	0	1	3	1	0	0	0	1	2	.125
	Auburn (NYP)	A	4	3	1.89	15	5	0	3	38	27	14	8	0	11	23	.190
2007	Lansing (MWL)	A	4	6	4.87	22	15	0	2	85	91	55	46	5	23	43	.266
MINOR LEAGUE TOTALS			8	9	3.86	40	20	0	6	126	119	69	54	5	35	68	.242

27 CHASE LIRETTE, RHP

Born: June 9, 1985. **B-T:** R-R. **Ht.:** 6-3. **Wt.:** 210. **Drafted:** South Florida, 2006 (16th round). **Signed by:** Joel Grampietro.

Lirette lasted 16 rounds in the 2006 draft, despite strong performances in the Cape Cod League the previous summer and with South Florida as a junior that spring. He received one of four six-figure bonuses Toronto handed out after the 15th round that year, turning pro for $135,000. Mostly a reliever in college, Lirette had to make mechanical adjustments when the Jays made him a starter. He worked to not stay so tall in his delivery and to become more flexible in his upper body. Lirette is sturdily built yet athletic, and he gets good extension on a 90-91 mph fastball that comes out of his hand cleanly. His changeup is his second pitch and it's above average at times. His slider has a little further to go. Lirette missed the season's final two months with a shoulder injury, but he was feeling well enough to throw side sessions during instructional league. He may get a refresher course in low Class A to begin 2008.

Year	Club (League)	Class	W	L	ERA	G	GS	CG	SV	IP	H	R	ER	HR	BB	SO	AVG
2006	Auburn (NYP)	A	4	1	2.23	10	6	0	1	40	32	11	10	1	7	37	.219
2007	Lansing (MWL)	A	5	5	4.42	10	10	0	0	59	59	38	29	6	19	41	.261
MINOR LEAGUE TOTALS			9	6	3.53	20	16	0	1	99	91	49	39	7	26	78	.245

28 JOEL CARRENO, RHP

Born: March 7, 1987. **B-T:** R-R. **Ht.:** 6-0. **Wt.:** 190. **Signed:** Dominican Republic, 2004. **Signed by:** Hilario Soriano.

On the heels of two productive seasons in the Rookie-level Dominican Summer League, Carreno made a rousing U.S. debut in 2007, leading the Gulf Coast League with 64 strikeouts in 65 innings. He gets above-average movement on his two-seam fastball, which he delivers from a high three-quarters arm slot. He impressed GCL observers with a loose arm and 89-93 mph heat, and his changeup also showed plus potential. His sweeping slider needs to be cleaned up. He repeats his delivery well, but he has a tendency to fly open and sling the ball. A tremendous competitor, Carreno showed improved mound presence as the season progressed. Because he pounds the zone with above-average sink, he might grade out as a reliever down the line. If he has a strong spring, he could make his full-season debut in low Class A this season.

Year	Club (League)	Class	W	L	ERA	G	GS	CG	SV	IP	H	R	ER	HR	BB	SO	AVG
2005	Blue Jays (DSL)	R	2	1	4.15	8	4	0	1	30	29	17	14	0	12	29	.236
2006	Blue Jays (DSL)	R	8	3	1.53	15	15	0	0	82	48	26	14	2	28	86	.168
2007	Blue Jays (GCL)	R	6	4	2.62	12	12	0	0	65	60	27	19	4	13	64	.243
MINOR LEAGUE TOTALS			16	8	2.38	35	31	0	1	178	137	70	47	6	53	179	.209

29 ANTHONY HATCH, 3B/2B

Born: Aug. 30, 1983. **B-T:** L-R. **Ht.:** 6-4. **Wt.:** 195. **Drafted:** Nicholls State, 2005 (13th round). **Signed by:** Matt Briggs.

Hatch provided good value for a 13th-round pick, hitting for average and power in the low Class A in 2006, when he emerged as a sleeper prospect. Injuries have limited him, though, as he was unable to participate in instructional league after the 2005 or '06 seasons. He had surgery on both his wrists in 2006, which hurt his bat speed last season. Still, Hatch nearly doubled his previous career-high for at-bats, showing surprising power that he generates from an angular and wiry 6-foot-4 frame. He stays through the ball well and gets good backspin on it, so the potential for more juice is there. The Blue Jays experimented with Hatch all over the infield in 2006, but abandoned the plan last year, letting him play his natural position of third base, where his range and arm are average. He's an average runner as well. Hatch next will face the challenges of Double-A, where he could see time at second base or in the outfield to increase his versatility.

Year	Club (League)	Class	AVG	G	AB	R	H	2B	3B	HR	RBI	BB	SO	SB	OBP	SLG
2005	Pulaski (Appy)	R	.273	41	128	16	35	11	2	5	26	9	30	0	.331	.508
2006	Dunedin (FSL)	A	.500	3	8	3	4	2	0	0	2	2	0	0	.600	.750
	Lansing (MWL)	A	.314	70	239	46	75	23	3	9	37	35	37	5	.406	.548
2007	Dunedin (FSL)	A	.249	116	481	67	120	24	6	15	53	32	86	5	.305	.418
MINOR LEAGUE TOTALS			.273	230	856	132	234	60	11	29	118	78	153	10	.341	.471

30 MOISES SIERRA, OF

Born: Sept. 24, 1988. **B-T:** R-R. **Ht.:** 6-1. **Wt.:** 185. **Signed:** Dominican Republic, 2005. **Signed by:** Hilario Soriano.

Sierra and Venezuelan outfielder Yohermyn Chavez both received six-figure bonuses from the Jays during the 2005 international signing period. While Chavez made his U.S. debut in 2006, Sierra remained in the Dominican, waiting until 2007 to come over. He didn't do much to distinguish himself and he was overshadowed in instructional league by the Blue Jays' best position-player prospects. But Sierra has two above-average tools that could garner him attention in coming years: a right fielder's arm and raw power. "Raw" might be the best way to describe Sierra's game. He struggles to command the strike zone and comes out of his swing easily, but he has as much upside as any of Toronto's international prospects. Sierra's speed and defensive range are no more than average, but his arm definitely puts him in right field. He'll likely get another go at the Gulf Coast League in 2008.

Year	Club (League)	Class	AVG	G	AB	R	H	2B	3B	HR	RBI	BB	SO	SB	OBP	SLG
2006	Blue Jays (DSL)	R	.253	69	245	35	62	16	1	4	26	24	50	17	.345	.376
2007	Blue Jays (GCL)	R	.203	43	143	17	29	5	1	5	15	5	39	2	.248	.357
MINOR LEAGUE TOTALS			.235	112	388	52	91	21	2	9	41	29	89	19	.311	.369

Washington Nationals

BY AARON FITT

I t's a measure of just how low expectations were for the Nationals in 2007 that they won 73 games and finished 16 games out of first place, yet Manny Acta garnered manager-of-the-year consideration for getting his team to overachieve in his first year at the helm. Washington, in its first full season with the Lerner family installed as owners and Stan Kasten as club president, embraced a youth movement with an eye at fielding a competitive, exciting team when their new Nationals Park opens in 2008.

Ryan Zimmerman turned in his second straight solid season, giving the Nationals confidence that they have a cornerstone player to build a franchise around. Other young players made positive impressions in varying amounts of big league exposure, as rookie Matt Chico led the beleaguered pitching staff in starts (31) and innings (167), Jason Bergmann made a successful conversion from the bullpen to the rotation, and rookies Shawn Hill and John Lannan also showed promise as starters.

Freewheeling general manager Jim Bowden made just one significant trade during the season, acquiring powerful outfielder Wily Mo Pena from the Red Sox. Instead of bolstering the system through trades as it did in 2006, Washington focused on building through the draft, where it had five picks in the first two rounds. The Nationals spent $7.9 million on the draft, the fifth-highest figure in baseball.

The first four players they drafted—lefthanders Ross Detwiler (first round) and Josh Smoker (supplemental first), outfielder Michael Burgess (supplemental first) and righthander Jordan Zimmermann (second)—rank among the top 10 prospects in the system. So does lefthander Jack McGeary—who received a $1.8 million bonus, a record for a sixth-round pick, plus the money and permission from Washington to attend classes at Stanford from September through May for up to three years.

The aggressive approach to the draft paid immediately dividends, as Washington's system is already far deeper and flush with more high-impact talent than it had a year ago, when it ranked as the worst system in baseball. Assistant general manager of baseball operations Mike Rizzo and scouting director Dana Brown have co-existed very well, and there are no signs of a power struggle that some feared when Rizzo joined the organization in mid-2006 after a successful run as the Diamondbacks' scouting director.

The Nationals may not be blessed with many

Ryan Zimmerman emerged as a cornerstone to build around with a good sophomore year

TOP 30 PROSPECTS

1. Chris Marrero, 1b/of	16. Stephen King, 2b/ss
2. Ross Detwiler, lhp	17. Esmailyn Gonzalez, ss
3. Collin Balester, rhp	18. Shairon Martis, rhp
4. Michael Burgess, of	19. Brad Peacock, rhp
5. Jack McGeary, lhp	20. Kory Casto, of/3b
6. Josh Smoker, lhp	21. Matt Whitney, 1b
7. Jordan Zimmermann, rhp	22. Derek Norris, c
8. Justin Maxwell, of	23. Mike Daniel, of
9. Colton Willems, rhp	24. Stephen Englund, of
10. John Lannan, lhp	25. Jhonny Nunez, rhp
11. Jake Smolinski, of	26. Hassan Pena, rhp
12. Tyler Clippard, rhp	27. Martin Beno, rhp
13. Adam Carr, rhp	28. Zech Zinicola, rhp
14. Ian Desmond, ss	29. Rogearvin Bernadina, of
15. Garrett Mock, rhp	30. P.J. Dean, rhp

prospects in the upper levels of their organization, but their player-development system has made strides under farm director Bobby Williams and minor league pitching coordinator Spin Williams. Bowden also was busy making offseason trades to bring in more major league-ready talent, acquiring outfielders Elijah Dukes and Lastings Milledge plus pitching prospect Tyler Clippard at little cost. The only player Bowden gave up who might have played a key part in Washington's future was lefty Glenn Gibson—who has yet to reach full-season ball.

General Manager: Jim Bowden. **Farm Director:** Andy Dunn. **Scouting Director:** Dana Brown.

Class	Team	League	W	L	PCT	Finish*	Manager	Affiliated
Majors	Washington	National	73	89	.451	11th (16)	Manny Acta	—
Triple-A	Columbus Clippers	International	64	80	.444	11th (14)	John Stearns	2007
Double-A	Harrisburg Senators	Eastern	55	86	.390	12th (12)	Scott Little	1991
High A	Potomac Nationals	Carolina	69	68	.504	4th (8)	Rany Knorr	2005
Low A	Hagerstown Suns	South Atlantic	55	81	.404	15th (16)	Tommy Herr	2007
Short-season	Vermont Lake Monsters	New York-Penn	38	37	.507	6th (14)	Darnell Coles	1994
Rookie	GCL Nationals	Gulf Coast	23	31	.426	13th (16)	Bobby Henley	1998
Overall 2007 Minor League Record			304	383	.443	29th		

*Finish in overall standings (No. of teams in league) ^League champion

LAST YEAR'S TOP 30

Player, Pos.		Status
1.	Collin Balester, rhp	No. 3
2.	Chris Marrero, of	No. 1
3.	Colton Willems, rhp	No. 9
4.	Kory Casto, 3b/of	No. 20
5.	Esmailyn Gonzalez, ss	No. 17
6.	Zech Zinicola, rhp	No. 28
7.	Glenn Gibson, lhp	(Rays)
8.	Matt Chico, lhp	Majors
9.	Stephen King, ss	No. 16
10.	Ian Desmond, ss	No. 14
11.	Jesus Flores, c	Majors
12.	Garrett Mock, rhp	No. 15
13.	Emiliano Fruto, rhp	(Diamondbacks)
14.	Jhonny Nunez, rhp	No. 25
15.	Shairon Martis, rhp	No. 18
16.	Larry Broadway, 1b	Dropped out
17.	Stephen Englund, of	No. 24
18.	Justin Maxwell, of	No. 8
19.	Adam Carr, rhp	No. 13
20.	John Lannan, lhp	No. 10
21.	Craig Stammen, rhp	Dropped out
22.	Marco Estrada, rhp	Dropped out
23.	Brian Peacock, c	Dropped out
24.	Clint Everts, rhp	Dropped out
25.	Shawn Hill, rhp	Majors
26.	Devin Ivany, c	Dropped out
27.	Frank Diaz, of	Dropped out
28.	Cory Van Allen, lhp	Dropped out
29.	Levale Speigner, rhp	Dropped out
30.	Mike Hinckley, lhp	Dropped out

BEST TOOLS

Best Hitter for Average	Jake Smolinski
Best Power Hitter	Chris Marrero
Best Strike-Zone Discipline	Josh Whitesell
Fastest Baserunner	Rogearvin Bernadina
Best Athlete	Justin Maxwell
Best Fastball	Ross Detwiler
Best Curveball	Jack McGeary
Best Slider	Zech Zinicola
Best Changeup	Shairon Martis
Best Control	Adrian Alaniz
Best Defensive Catcher	Devin Ivany
Best Defensive Infielder	Ian Desmond
Best Infield Arm	Ian Desmond
Best Defensive Outfielder	Rogearvin Bernadina
Best Outfield Arm	Edgardo Baez

PROJECTED 2011 LINEUP

Catcher	Jesus Flores
First Base	Chris Marrero
Second Base	Stephen King
Third Base	Ryan Zimmerman
Shortstop	Ian Desmond
Left Field	Justin Maxwell
Center Field	Lastings Milledge
Right Field	Michael Burgess
No. 1 Starter	Ross Detwiler
No. 2 Starter	Collin Balester
No. 3 Starter	Jack McGeary
No. 4 Starter	Josh Smoker
No. 5 Starter	Jordan Zimmermann
Closer	Chad Cordero

TOP PROSPECTS OF THE DECADE

Year	Player, Pos.	2007 Org.
1998	Brad Fullmer, 1b	Out of baseball
1999	Michael Barrett, 3b/c	Padres
2000	Tony Armas, rhp	Pirates
2001	Donnie Bridges, rhp	United League
2002	Brandon Phillips, ss	Reds
2003	Clint Everts, rhp	Nationals
2004	Clint Everts, rhp	Nationals
2005	Mike Hinckley, lhp	Nationals
2006	Ryan Zimmerman, 3b	Nationals
2007	Collin Balester, rhp	Nationals

TOP DRAFT PICKS OF THE DECADE

Year	Player, Pos.	2007 Org.
1998	Josh McKinley, ss	Out of baseball
1999	Josh Girdley, lhp	Out of baseball
2000	Justin Wayne, rhp	Out of baseball
2001	Josh Karp, rhp	Out of baseball
2002	Clint Everts, rhp	Nationals
2003	Chad Cordero, rhp	Nationals
2004	Bill Bray, lhp	Reds
2005	Ryan Zimmerman, 3b	Nationals
2006	Chris Marrero, of	Nationals
2007	Ross Detwiler, lhp	Nationals

LARGEST BONUSES IN CLUB HISTORY

Ryan Zimmerman, 2005	$2,975,000
Justin Wayne, 2000	$2,950,000
Josh Karp, 2001	$2,650,000
Clint Everts, 2002	$2,500,000
Ross Detwiler, 2007	$2,150,000

WASHINGTON NATIONALS

Top 2008 Rookie: Collin Balester, rhp. After pitching well in Triple-A at age 21, Balester should crack Washington's rotation by midseason—if not Opening Day.

Breakout Prospect: Hassan Pena, rhp. The Cuban defector flashed three average or better pitches in his pro debut and could take off with a few mechanical adjustments.

Sleeper: Jeff Mandel, rhp. A 19th-round pick out of Baylor in 2007, Mandel can break bats with his 89-92 mph sinker from a low three-quarters arm slot, and his changeup is above average.

SOURCE OF TOP 30 TALENT			
Homegrown	25	Acquired	5
College	9	Trades	4
Junior college	1	Rule 5 draft	1
High school	12	Independent leagues	0
Draft-and-follow	1	Free agents/waivers	0
Nondrafted free agents	0		
International	2		

Numbers in parentheses indicates prospect rankings.

LF
Jake Smolinski (11)
Kory Casto (20)
Mike Daniel (23)
Garrett Guzman
Marvin Lowrance
Dee Brown
Garrett Bass

CF
Justin Maxwell (8)
Stephen Englund (24)
Rogearvin Bernadina (29)
Mark Gildea
Boomer Whiting

RF
Michael Burgess (4)
Edgardo Baez
Aaron Seuss

3B
Steven Souza
Leonard Davis

SS
Ian Desmond (14)
Dan Lyons

2B
Stephen King (16)
Esmailyn Gonzalez (17)
Ofilio Castro

1B
Chris Marrero (1)
Matt Whitney (21)
Josh Whitesell
Larry Broadway
Bill Rhinehart

C
Derek Norris (22)
Devin Ivany
Brian Peacock
Sean Rooney
Sandy Leon
Luke Montz

RHP

Starters	Relievers
Collin Balester (3)	Adam Carr (13)
Jordan Zimmermann (7)	Martin Beno (27)
Colton Willems (9)	Zech Zinicola (28)
Tyler Clippard (12)	Clint Everts
Garrett Mock (15)	Cole Kimball
Shairon Martis (18)	Alexis Morales
Brad Peacock (19)	Bobby Brownlie
Jhonny Nunez (25)	Jose Pinales
Hassan Pena (26)	Alberto Tavarez
P.J. Dean (30)	Randy Matias
Adrian Alaniz	Luke Pisker
Brad Meyers	David Trahan
Jeff Mandel	Chris Lugo
Edulin Abreu	Devin Perrin
Marco Estrada	Josh Wilkie
Craig Stammen	
Luis Atilano	

LHP

Starters	Relievers
Ross Detwiler (2)	Jack Spradlin
Jack McGeary (5)	Yunior Novoa
Josh Smoker (6)	
John Lannan (10)	
Cory Van Allen	
Patrick McCoy	
Mike Hinckley	

Best Pro Debut: OF Michael Burgess (1s) hit .318 with 11 homers, leading the Gulf Coast League in on-base (.442) and slugging (.617) percentage and ranking as the league's No. 1 prospect. RHP Jordan Zimmermann (2) went 5-2, 2.38 with 71 strikeouts in 53 New York-Penn League innings, while polished RHP Adrian Alaniz (8) went 8-2, 2.39 with a 62-8 K-BB ratio in 60 innings in the NY-P.

Best Athlete: OF Jake Smolinski (2), a quarterback in high school, has solid athletic ability and a blue-collar mentality. Zimmermann was a two-way player in college and starred in football and basketball in high school.

Best Pure Hitter: Smolinski, whose pro debut was truncated when a foul ball off his bat cracked a bone in his foot. He has good balance at the plate and a fine approach.

Best Power Hitter: Burgess. C Derek Norris (4) has above-average power potential.

Fastest Runner: Whiting used his plus-plus speed to lead NCAA Division I with 73 steals in the spring.

Best Defensive Player: Nationals assistant GM Bob Boone, who knows a thing or two about catching, raves about Norris' agility and arm strength.

Best Fastball: LHP Ross Detwiler (1) has arm speed and leverage in his 6-foot-5 frame, allowing him to throw 90-96 mph fastballs with nasty sink. Zimmermann worked from 90-94 while recovering from a broken jaw and pulled wisdom teeth this spring. RHP Martin Beno (36) touched 96 during instructional league.

Best Secondary Pitch: LHPs Josh Smoker (1s) and Jack McGeary (6) and Zimmerman all have intriguing curveballs. Smoker also has a quality splitter and may have too many pitches (six) for his own good, so Washington will try to pare down his repertoire.

Most Intriguing Background: OF Garrett Bass' (42) father Kevin was an all-star outfielder, and his brother Justin signed this summer as the Angels' 21st-round pick. RHP Devin Drag (37) beat out Zimmermann for NCAA Division III pitcher of the year honors after going 16-0, 2.41 at Chapman (Calif.).

Closest To The Majors: Detwiler became the first player from the 2007 draft to advance to the big leagues, working a scoreless inning against the Braves.

Best Late-Round Pick: Patrick McCoy (10) is a 6-foot-4 lefty with the potential to have a plus fastball and breaking ball.

The One Who Got Away: It almost wound up being McGeary, who agreed to a $1.8 million bonus minutes before the signing deadline. Washington never got close with LHP David Duncan (23), who could become an early-round pick after returning to Georgia Tech.

Assessment: The Nationals had the best draft in the industry. Landing three lefthanders like Detwiler, Smoker and McGeary is a rare feat, and Washington backed them up with Burgess, Zimmermann, Smolinski and Norris.

2006   BUDGET: $5.1 MILLION

OF/1B Chris Marrero (1), RHP Colten Willems (1) and LHP Glenn Gibson (4) are all a big part of the Nationals' future. Converting RHP Adam Carr (13) from first base looks like a stroke of genius.

GRADE: B

2005   BUDGET: $4.0 MILLION

3B Ryan Zimmerman (1) swiftly became the cornerstone of the big league lineup. OF Justin Maxwell (4) finally stayed healthy, nearly having a 30-30 season in the minors and joining LHP John Lannan (11) in the majors.

GRADE: A

2004   BUDGET: $3.7 MILLION

RHP Collin Balester (4) will bolster Washington's rotation at some point in 2008, and there's still hope for the bat of slick-fielding SS Ian Desmond (3). LHP Bill Bray (1) went to the Reds in the Austin Kearns/Felipe Lopez trade.

GRADE: C+

2003   BUDGET: $3.1 MILLION

Considered a reach at the time, RHP Chad Cordero (1) reached the majors two months after signing and has racked up 128 saves. Since-traded OF Jerry Owens (2) and OF/3B Kory Casto (3) have seen big league duty.

GRADE: B+

Draft analysis by Jim Callis. Numbers in parentheses indicate draft rounds. Budgets are bonuses in first 10 rounds.

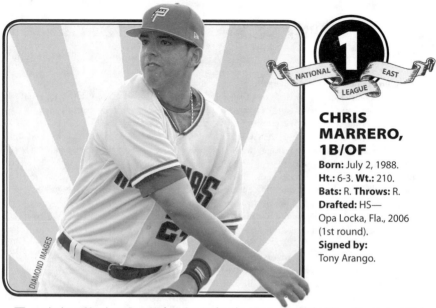

CHRIS MARRERO, 1B/OF

Born: July 2, 1988.
Ht.: 6-3. **Wt.:** 210.
Bats: R. **Throws:** R.
Drafted: HS—
Opa Locka, Fla., 2006
(1st round).
Signed by:
Tony Arango.

As a junior at Monsignor Pace High in Opa Locka, Fla., Marrero established himself as the best high school position prospect for the 2006 draft. But a hamstring injury during his senior year caused Marrero to overcompensate by opening up his front hip and pulling off the ball, making his swing look deceptively long and causing him to wave over the top of breaking balls. He wasn't even the best player on his state championship team, as that distinction fell to Adrian Cardenas, who's now starring in the Phillies system. Nationals scouts surmised that Marrero would return to form if they could fix his stride, and he reinforced their belief that his senior struggles were a fluke by putting on a monstrous pre-draft power display in a workout at RFK Stadium. Washington stole him with the 15th overall pick and signed him for $1.625 million. After the draft, he worked on the mechanical adjustments and began to make progress before viral meningitis cut short his debut in the Rookie-level Gulf Coast League. He was completely healthy by the spring and began his first full professional season at low Class A Hagerstown, where his power exploded with 11 homers and 35 RBIs in May. After a promotion to high Class A Potomac, Marrero tired down the stretch, batting just .220/.311/.418 in August, but rallied in the final two weeks after choking up a bit on the bat.

Marrero's best tool is his well above-average power to all fields. He has a quiet, line-drive stroke, and he's strong enough to hit the ball over the fence from foul pole to foul pole. His swing has tremendous leverage, and his balance and bat speed allow him to square up balls on the barrel consistently. His approach was very mature for a 19-year-old in high Class A, not only because of his willingness to use the opposite field but also because of his ability to make adjustments. He drew more walks and chased fewer pitches in his time at Potomac. Marrero also has an above-average arm. His work ethic receives rave reviews from Nationals personnel.

Despite his arm strength, Marrero isn't a good outfielder, thanks largely to his below-average speed. Washington decided to move him to first base in instructional league. He showed good aptitude for the position, with sufficient lateral range, quick reactions and decent hands. He still needs to get comfortable at first base and work on receiving throws from infielders and picking balls in the dirt. Offensively, Marrero has all the tools but requires more at-bats to learn how to hit advanced pitching. He's better against lefthanded pitching (.312 combined average in 2007) than against righties (.265).

Marrero has a chance to start 2008 as a 19-year-old at Double-A Harrisburg, though he could return to Potomac and move up quickly. He's not far from big league ready as a hitter, and how fast he learns first base could determine how soon he reaches Washington. That could happen as early as the second half of 2008, and by 2009 he figures to be a fixture in the middle of the big league lineup. His massive power gives him a chance to be a star.

Year	Club (League)	Class	AVG	G	AB	R	H	2B	3B	HR	RBI	BB	SO	SB	OBP	SLG
2006	Nationals (GCL)	R	.309	22	81	10	25	9	0	0	16	8	19	0	.374	.420
2007	Hagerstown (SAL)	A	.293	57	222	31	65	14	0	14	53	14	39	0	.337	.545
	Potomac (Car)	A	.259	68	255	40	66	11	3	9	35	32	63	0	.338	.431
MINOR LEAGUE TOTALS			.280	147	558	81	156	34	3	23	104	54	121	0	.343	.475

2 ROSS DETWILER, LHP

Born: March 6, 1986. **B-T:** R-L. **Ht.:** 6-5. **Wt.:** 185. **Drafted:** Missouri State, 2007 (1st round). **Signed by:** Ryan Fox.

After a star turn with Team USA in 2006, Detwiler showed dominant stuff but was plagued by poor run support as a junior at Missouri State, going 4-5, 2.22 with 110 strike-outs and 38 walks in 89 innings. The Nationals made him the highest-drafted player in school history, taking him sixth overall and giving him a $2.15 million bonus. He made a Washington cameo in just his 10th professional appearance, making him the first 2006 draftee to reach the majors. Detwiler's arm is electric. His four-seam fastball sits at 90-93 mph and touches 95-96, and his two-seamer has darting armside run. His hard-breaking spike curveball is a second plus offering that can reach 83 mph. His high-70s changeup can be a third plus pitch at times, with very good arm speed and late fade. His frame always will be wiry, but Detwiler needs to add strength to endure a major league season. He throws strikes but is still learning to command the zone with his fastball and refine his changeup. He throws across his body somewhat despite easy arm action and a mostly sound delivery. With a chance for three above-average pitches, Detwiler has a chance to be a legitimate ace. He figures to start 2008 in Double-A but could force his way to the big leagues for good by the second half.

Year	Club (League)	Class	W	L	ERA	G	GS	CG	SV	IP	H	R	ER	HR	BB	SO	AVG
2007	Nationals (GCL)	R	0	0	2.25	4	4	0	0	12	11	3	3	1	3	15	.234
	Potomac (Car)	A	2	2	4.22	5	4	0	0	21	27	11	10	1	9	13	.310
	Washington (NL)	MLB	0	0	0.00	1	0	0	0	1	0	0	0	0	0	1	.000
MINOR LEAGUE TOTALS			2	2	3.51	9	8	0	0	33	38	14	13	2	12	28	.284
MAJOR LEAGUE TOTALS			0	0	0.00	1	0	0	0	1	0	0	0	0	0	1	.000

3 COLLIN BALESTER, RHP

Born: June 6, 1986. **B-T:** R-R. **Ht.:** 6-5. **Wt.:** 190. **Drafted:** HS—Huntington Beach, Calif., 2004 (4th round). **Signed by:** Tony Arango.

Balester has moved quickly through the system since the Nationals drafted the free-spirited former surfer, and once again he was young for his level in 2007. He pitched well enough in Double-A to warrant a second-half promotion to Triple-A Columbus and held his own without dominating. The long-limbed Balester is growing into his frame, and he maintained 90-93 mph fastball velocity, touching 94 regularly and reaching 96 at the Futures Game. His curveball is often an above-average pitch at 77-81 with hard downward break. Balester excels at pitching to contact, but he needs to get better at putting hitters away, particularly with his swing-and-miss curveball. He tends to throw his changeup too hard at 85-87 mph, and he's better off using it in the low 80s to get more sink and separation from his fastball. He needs to command his fastball down in the strike zone more consistently. A potential middle-of-the-rotation starter with a ceiling as a No. 2, Balester isn't far from breaking into the majors. Barring a standout spring, he'll open 2008 back in Triple-A, but he could be in Washington by midseason.

Year	Club (League)	Class	W	L	ERA	G	GS	CG	SV	IP	H	R	ER	HR	BB	SO	AVG
2004	Expos (GCL)	R	1	2	2.19	5	4	0	0	24	20	8	6	0	5	21	.215
2005	Savannah (SAL)	A	8	6	3.67	24	23	1	0	125	105	62	51	11	42	95	.222
2006	Potomac (Car)	A	4	5	5.20	23	22	0	0	117	126	71	68	12	53	87	.280
	Harrisburg (EL)	AA	1	0	1.83	3	3	0	0	19	15	5	4	0	6	10	.231
2007	Harrisburg (EL)	AA	2	7	3.74	17	17	0	0	98	103	47	41	9	25	77	.268
	Columbus (IL)	AAA	2	3	4.18	10	10	0	0	51	49	27	24	3	23	40	.255
MINOR LEAGUE TOTALS			18	23	3.99	82	79	1	0	437	418	220	194	35	154	330	.252

4 MICHAEL BURGESS, OF

Born: Oct. 20, 1988. **B-T:** L-L. **Ht.:** 5-11. **Wt.:** 195. **Drafted:** HS—Tampa, 2007 (1st round supplemental). **Signed by:** Paul Tinnell.

Like Chris Marrero a year earlier, Burgess established himself as one of the draft's premier power hitters as a junior, batting .512 with 12 homers at Hillsborough High (the same Tampa school that produced Dwight Gooden, Gary Sheffield and Elijah Dukes) and excelling with wood over the summer. Also like Marrero, he slumped as a senior. Inconsistent contact and a perceived lack of focus dropped him to the supplemental first round, but after signing for $630,000 he led the Gulf Coast League in on-base and slugging percentage and ranked as its No. 1 prospect. With a strong, compact frame, a short stroke and a lightning-quick bat, Burgess has well above-average raw power, mostly to right field. He has good plate discipline and isn't afraid to use the opposite field on occasion. He's an average defender in right field with a plus arm. Burgess channels controlled aggression into every at-bat, but he can fall into bad habits mechanically, lengthening his stroke and taking monster hacks. Sometimes he gets out of sync, getting his front foot down too early and then jerking his swing a bit. Though not a base-clogger, he's a below-average runner who'll need to watch his weight to stay in the outfield. In time, Burgess could be a 40-homer man in the big leagues. His next step is to make adjustments against more advanced pitching in low Class A.

Year	Club (League)	Class	AVG	G	AB	R	H	2B	3B	HR	RBI	BB	SO	SB	OBP	SLG
2007	Nationals (GCL)	R	.336	36	128	22	43	6	3	8	32	25	37	1	.442	.617
	Vermont (NYP)	A	.286	19	70	10	20	1	1	3	10	10	23	1	.383	.457
MINOR LEAGUE TOTALS			.318	55	198	32	63	7	4	11	42	35	60	2	.421	.561

5 JACK McGEARY, LHP

Born: March 19, 1989. **B-T:** L-L. **Ht.:** 6-3. **Wt.:** 195. **Drafted:** HS—West Roxbury, Mass. (6th round). **Signed by:** Mike Alberts.

McGeary entered last spring as a potential first-round pick, but he separated his non-throwing shoulder playing basketball. He showed toughness by pitching through the discomfort, though he lost some velocity on his fastball. The Nationals bought him out of a commitment to Stanford by giving him a $1.8 million bonus, a record for the sixth round, and allowing him to be a full-time student for the next three years. McGeary draws comparisons to Andy Pettitte for his size, stuff and smooth, effortless arm action. His power curveball is the best in the system, a tight mid-70s hammer that he can throw for strikes or get hitters to chase out of the zone. When he's healthy, his fastball sits in the 87-90 mph range, and he should add a bit of velocity as he matures. He's an exceptional athlete with a commanding mound presence. The separated right shoulder caused McGeary to get into some bad habits on his front side and led his command to lapse at times in the spring, but he has shown impeccable command in the past. He flashes an average changeup but hasn't had to use it much in high school, so it needs some development. Though he's not overpowering, McGeary is very polished and should move quickly through the system, starting with a likely promotion to low Class A in 2008. He could be a No. 2 or 3 starter down the road.

Year	Club (League)	Class	W	L	ERA	G	GS	CG	SV	IP	H	R	ER	HR	BB	SO	AVG
2007	Vermont (NYP)	A	0	1	13.50	2	1	0	0	2	3	5	4	0	5	4	.273
MINOR LEAGUE TOTALS			0	1	13.50	2	1	0	0	2	3	5	4	0	5	4	.273

6 JOSH SMOKER, LHP

Born: Nov. 26, 1988. **B-T:** L-L. **Ht.:** 6-2. **Wt.:** 195. **Drafted:** HS—Calhoun, Ga., 2007 (1st round supplemental). **Signed by:** Eric Robinson.

The Braves coveted Smoker and he wanted to play for his home-state team, but the Nationals ruined those plans by taking him with the first pick of the supplemental first round, two choices ahead of Atlanta. Though his velocity dipped at the end of the spring, which is why he lasted until the 31st pick, Washington gave him a slightly above-slot $1 million bonus. Smoker's lively fastball can sit in the low 90s and has touched 94 in the past, and he can run it in on righthanders. He flashes a plus curveball in the high 70s with good depth and a promising changeup. He has a clean delivery and a consistent release point that should translate into plus command. He's a fiery, intense competitor. His splitter was his go-to pitch in high school, when he would use as many as six different offerings, but the Nationals want Smoker to focus on his fastball, curveball and changeup. He needs to refine his fastball command and become more consistent with his offspeed pitches. With the potential for a plus fastball and curve, Smoker draws comparisons to Mark Langston. He should be ready to tackle low Class A in 2008 and could move quickly for a prep product.

Year	Club (League)	Class	W	L	ERA	G	GS	CG	SV	IP	H	R	ER	HR	BB	SO	AVG
2007	Vermont (NYP)	A	0	0	4.50	2	2	0	0	4	2	2	2	0	3	5	.167
MINOR LEAGUE TOTALS			0	0	4.50	2	2	0	0	4	2	2	2	0	3	5	.167

7 JORDAN ZIMMERMANN, RHP

Born: May 23, 1986. **B-T:** R-R. **Ht.:** 6-2. **Wt.:** 200. **Drafted:** Wisconsin-Stevens Point, 2007 (2nd round). **Signed by:** Steve Arnieri.

After bursting onto the prospect landscape with a dominant 2006 summer in the Northwoods League, Zimmermann took a line drive off his jaw while throwing batting practice in an offseason workout. That injury, combined with bad weather in Wisconsin and some missed time when he had his wisdom teeth pulled, affected his spring and caused him to drop to the second round. The Nationals, who signed him for $495,000, think he could have been a top-10 pick had he pitched at a higher-profile program. Zimmermann's heavy, boring 90-94 fastball is an above-average pitch.

He entered professional ball with a pair of quality breaking balls, but the Nationals had him shelve his slider for now and focus on his plus downer curveball with sharp, late bite. He has a sturdy frame and strong legs, and his three-quarters delivery is smooth. He's a very good athlete for a pitcher and was named MVP of the 2007 Division III College World Series after starring as a two-way player. Though Zimmermann can command his fastball to both sides of the plate, he sometimes leaves the pitch up in the zone. His secondary stuff needs to get more consistent, particularly his changeup. An intense competitor, he must avoid letting his perfectionist tendencies get the best of him. Zimmermann should skip a level and jump to high Class A to start 2008. He could be a mid-rotation starter by 2009.

Year	Club (League)	Class	W	L	ERA	G	GS	CG	SV	IP	H	R	ER	HR	BB	SO	AVG
2007	Vermont (NYP)	A	5	2	2.38	13	11	0	0	53	45	14	14	2	18	71	.228
MINOR LEAGUE TOTALS			5	2	2.38	13	11	0	0	53	45	14	14	2	18	71	.228

8 JUSTIN MAXWELL, OF

Born: Nov. 5, 1983. **B-T:** R-R. **Ht.:** 6-5. **Wt.:** 225. **Drafted:** Maryland, 2005 (4th round). **Signed by:** Alex Smith.

After injuries plagued his college career and first full pro season in 2006, Maxwell stayed mostly healthy in 2007 and translated his immense talent into the only 25-double, 25-homer, 25-steal performance in the minors. After Potomac's season ended, he got a taste of the big leagues and his first hit was a grand slam in his third at-bat. The best athlete in the system, Maxwell finally started to tap into his above-average raw power in 2007, showing the ability to drive the ball out of the park to all fields. He's an above-average runner who can get good jumps on the basepaths and track down balls in the outfield gaps. Maxwell shortened his swing considerably over the past year, but he doesn't figure to hit for a high average in the majors. He needs to improve his pitch selection and lay off breaking balls in the dirt. He's a solid-average center fielder, but his arm is just fringe-average. He strengthened it last winter by throwing footballs. Maxwell garners comparisons to Mike Cameron for his speed/power mix and his inconsistent ability to hit for average. He could push for a job in Washington's outfield sometime in 2008, but a full year at Double-A to refine his approach would do him good.

Year	Club (League)	Class	AVG	G	AB	R	H	2B	3B	HR	RBI	BB	SO	SB	OBP	SLG
2006	Savannah (SAL)	A	.172	17	58	8	10	2	2	1	7	8	23	1	.294	.328
	Vermont (NYP)	A	.269	74	271	36	73	11	3	4	33	27	61	20	.346	.376
2007	Hagerstown (SAL)	A	.301	56	209	51	63	12	2	14	40	26	57	14	.389	.579
	Potomac (Car)	A	.263	58	228	35	60	13	0	13	43	24	65	21	.338	.491
	Washington (NL)	MLB	.269	15	26	5	7	0	0	2	5	1	8	0	.296	.500
MINOR LEAGUE TOTALS			.269	205	766	130	206	38	7	32	123	85	206	56	.352	.462
MAJOR LEAGUE TOTALS			.269	15	26	5	7	0	0	2	5	1	8	0	.296	.500

9 COLTON WILLEMS, RHP

Born: July 30, 1988. **B-T:** R-R. **Ht.:** 6-3. **Wt.:** 175. **Drafted:** HS—Fort Pierce, Fla., 2006 (1st round). **Signed by:** Tony Arango.

After a sore elbow limited him to 16 innings in his 2006 pro debut, Willems looked strong against older competition in the New York-Penn League. Vermont manager Darnell Coles said Willems grew about two inches over the summer, and he pitches from an imposing downhill plane. Willems worked at 87-93 mph and touched 94-95 this summer, and he ran his fastball up to 97 mph at times in high school. He commands his heater very well down in the zone, and he flashes a promising curveball and changeup. Like Jordan Zimmermann, he has shelved the slider he carried into pro ball. Willems matured quite a bit with Vermont, and his demeanor on the mound never changes no matter the situation. Shaky command of his secondary pitches means Willems works in a lot of unfavorable counts and always seems to be running into jams. He made some progress with his curveball and changeup early in the summer but leveled out in the second half. His 1.84 ERA at Vermont is misleading because 13 of the 25 runs he allowed were unearned. With an athletic frame, a live arm and a loose, easy delivery, Willems has one of the highest ceilings in the system, but he's still very much a work in progress. He should advance to low Class A in 2008.

Year	Club (League)	Class	W	L	ERA	G	GS	CG	SV	IP	H	R	ER	HR	BB	SO	AVG
2006	Nationals (GCL)	R	0	1	3.38	5	5	0	0	16	23	8	6	1	3	8	.338
2007	Vermont (NYP)	A	3	2	1.84	12	12	0	0	58	55	25	12	2	26	31	.251
MINOR LEAGUE TOTALS			3	3	2.17	17	17	0	0	74	78	33	18	3	29	39	.272

10 JOHN LANNAN, LHP

ED WOLFSTEIN

Born: Sept. 27, 1984. **B-T:** L-L. **Ht.:** 6-5. **Wt.:** 200. **Drafted:** Siena, 2005 (11th round). **Signed by:** Dana Brown.

The Nationals hoped Lannan would be a late-blooming Northern arm who would take off in pro ball, and he developed even quicker than they could imagine, going a combined 12-3, 2.31 over three minor league stops in 2007 en route to the organization's minor league pitcher of the year award. He even broke into Washington's rotation, settling down after hitting Chase Utley and Ryan Howard with pitches in his first big league outing, resulting in a broken hand for Utley and an ejection for Lannan. The Nationals shut him down in September as a precaution because his 160 innings were 22 more than his previous season high. Lannan, who has spent the last three offseasons working with former big leaguer Paul Gibson (the father of former Nats lefty Glenn Gibson, who was traded to the Rays), has trained hard to add strength to his wiry frame. As a result his high-80s fastball can touch 90-91 at times. Last year, he added a sinking two-seamer that's very effective against righthanders, and he commands both fastballs well to both sides of the plate. He throws his changeup for strikes, and it projects as an average pitch. His curveball remains below average, but it's not as loopy as it used to be. He still needs to develop both of his secondary pitches, but his feel for pitching and competitiveness give him a chance to be a back-of-the-rotation starter in Washington out of spring training in 2008.

Year	Club (League)	Class	W	L	ERA	G	GS	CG	SV	IP	H	R	ER	HR	BB	SO	AVG
2005	Vermont (NYP)	A	3	5	5.26	14	11	0	0	63	74	46	37	5	31	41	.287
2006	Savannah (SAL)	A	6	8	4.76	27	25	1	0	138	149	83	73	11	54	114	.275
2007	Potomac (Car)	A	6	0	2.13	8	8	0	0	51	31	13	12	3	15	35	.179
	Harrisburg (EL)	AA	3	2	3.25	6	5	0	0	36	31	14	13	2	15	20	.233
	Washington (NL)	MLB	2	2	4.15	6	6	0	0	34	36	17	16	3	17	10	.273
	Columbus (IL)	AAA	3	1	1.66	7	6	0	0	39	30	8	7	1	12	19	.213
MINOR LEAGUE TOTALS			21	16	3.92	62	55	1	0	326	315	164	142	22	127	229	.253
MAJOR LEAGUE TOTALS			2	2	4.15	6	6	0	0	34	36	17	16	3	17	10	.273

11 JAKE SMOLINSKI, OF

Born: Feb. 9, 1989. **B-T:** R-R. **Ht.:** 5-11. **Wt.:** 185. **Drafted:** HS—Rockford, Ill., 2007 (2nd round). **Signed by:** Steve Arnieri.

Smolinski was the best position-player prospect in Illinois in last year, starring as a shortstop and a quarterback for Boylan Catholic High. Some clubs worried about his signability, but the Nationals landed him in the second round for $452,500. He lacks the range to play shortstop in pro ball, so Washington put him in left field after signing him away from Clemson. His solid pro debut was cut short when he fouled a ball off his foot and suffered a small break. Smolinski should be back to 100 percent by the spring and could move fairly quickly, thanks to his polished offensive approach and blue-collar mentality. His setup and stance are quiet and balanced, and he rarely chases pitches out of the strike zone, instead waiting for his pitch and attacking it with his line-drive stroke. Smolinski has good power to the gaps and figures to hit for some home run power as he matures, though his frame lacks projection. He's a fringy runner who might be better suited to third base or second as he fills out, and his arm is solid average. He figures to hit for average at every stop, starting with a likely trip to low Class A in 2008.

Year	Club (League)	Class	AVG	G	AB	R	H	2B	3B	HR	RBI	BB	SO	SB	OBP	SLG
2007	Nationals (GCL)	R	.305	28	105	18	32	8	0	1	16	13	24	7	.387	.410
MINOR LEAGUE TOTALS			.305	28	105	18	32	8	0	1	16	13	24	7	.387	.410

12 TYLER CLIPPARD, RHP

Born: Feb. 14, 1985. **B-T:** R-R. **Ht.:** 6-4. **Wt.:** 170. **Drafted:** HS—Trinity, Fla., 2003 (9th round). **Signed by:** Steve Boros (Yankees).

Clippard finally reached the majors in 2007, striking out six in six innings while winning his big league debut May 20 against the Mets. That was the peak of his season, however, as major league hitters caught up with his finesse approach and he failed to make adjustments. His confidence took a beating and he faltered at Triple-A after his return to the minors. He finished the year in Double-A before being traded to the Nationals for Jonathan Albaladejo during the Winter Meetings. Clippard can throw his curveball and changeup, both slightly above-average pitches, for quality strikes, and he does a good job of spotting his 87-91 mph fastball, which tops out at 94. His long arms and lanky body add deception to his delivery. With a pedestrian fastball in terms of both velocity and life, Clippard can't afford to miss his spots. He struggled to get hitters out when they were looking fastball and turned into a nibbler, leading to more walks, more runners on base and more three-run homers. Clippard will be just 23 this season, but he doesn't figure to add velocity and his upside is limited. He profiles as a back-of-the-rotation starter and could get a shot to fill that role coming out of spring training.

Year	Club (League)	Class	W	L	ERA	G	GS	CG	SV	IP	H	R	ER	HR	BB	SO	AVG
2003	Yankees (GCL)	R	3	3	2.89	11	5	0	0	43	33	16	14	3	5	56	.212
2004	Battle Creek (MWL)	A	10	10	3.44	26	25	1	0	149	153	71	57	12	32	145	.264
2005	Charleston, S.C. (SAL)	A	0	1	7.50	1	1	0	0	6	9	5	5	1	0	10	.333
	Tampa (FSL)	A	10	9	3.18	26	25	0	0	147	118	56	52	12	34	169	.219
	Columbus (IL)	AAA	0	0	0.00	1	0	0	0	1	0	0	0	0	0	2	.000
2006	Trenton (EL)	AA	12	10	3.35	28	28	1	0	166	118	72	62	14	55	175	.200
2007	New York (AL)	MLB	3	1	6.33	6	6	0	0	27	29	19	19	6	17	18	.271
	Scranton/W-B (IL)	AAA	4	4	4.15	14	14	0	0	69	82	40	32	7	35	55	.299
	Trenton (EL)	AA	2	1	5.40	6	6	0	0	26	22	18	16	5	12	28	.227
MINOR LEAGUE TOTALS			41	38	3.52	113	104	2	0	609	535	278	238	54	173	640	.236
MAJOR LEAGUE TOTALS			3	1	6.33	6	6	0	0	27	29	19	19	6	17	18	.271

13 ADAM CARR, RHP

Born: April 1, 1984. **B-T:** R-R. **Ht.:** 6-1. **Wt.:** 185. **Drafted:** Oklahoma State, 2006 (18th round). **Signed by:** Ryan Fox.

Carr pitched just five innings in his two-year career at Oklahoma State, where he mostly played first base and blasted 34 home runs. But Nationals area scout Ryan Fox saw him light up radar guns in fall practice and urged the club to draft him as a pitcher. That looks like a stroke of genius now that Carr, who signed for $1,000 as an 18th-rounder, dominated high Class A and reached Double-A in his first full pro season. His power fastball-slider repertoire made him a feared closer for Potomac, and he has the potential to fill the same role in the big leagues. With a fresh, electric arm, Carr easily pitches at 92-96 mph with his fastball, routinely touching 97. He attacks hitters with the fastball and an 80-82 mph slider that has good tilt and depth when it's on. He's still working on the spin with his slider and sometimes overthrows it, but it has the makings of a plus pitch. Carr is trying to refine his control, but Washington isn't discouraged by his high walk total because his location isn't all over the place. Most of the time, he just misses off the corners. Carr has a well below-average changeup that he seldom uses, but it doesn't figure to be a big part of his future repertoire. He should return to Double-A to start 2008 and could be in the big leagues as a setup man by the second half of the season.

Year	Club (League)	Class	W	L	ERA	G	GS	CG	SV	IP	H	R	ER	HR	BB	SO	AVG
2006	Nationals (GCL)	R	1	0	3.06	10	0	0	1	17	13	6	6	1	7	19	.200
	Savannah (SAL)	A	0	0	2.25	6	0	0	0	8	8	2	2	0	4	8	.267
2007	Potomac (Car)	A	3	1	1.81	41	0	0	10	49	30	12	10	4	38	65	.171
	Harrisburg (EL)	AA	1	0	1.64	7	0	0	2	11	7	2	2	1	9	13	.189
MINOR LEAGUE TOTALS			5	1	2.08	64	0	0	13	86	58	22	20	6	58	105	.189

14 IAN DESMOND, SS

Born: Sept. 20, 1985. **B-T:** R-R. **Ht.:** 6-2. **Wt.:** 185. **Drafted:** HS—Sarasota, Fla., 2004 (3rd round). **Signed by:** Russ Bove.

Desmond was developing slowly but steadily before Washington rushed him to Double-A in 2006, and he struggled mightily and took a full year to get back on track. He was sent back to high Class A in 2007 and batted just .239 before the all-star break, though the Nationals insist it was the hardest .239 you'll ever see. He worked hard to get his hands into a good hitting position and let balls on the outer half travel farther before he knocked them to the opposite field. In the second half, he also made progress turning on inside fastballs and laying off breaking balls in the dirt, and it all clicked in August, when he batted .362/.455/.574. He also drew 57 walks—23 more than his previous season high—illustrating his new, more patient approach. Desmond's quick hands generate plenty of bat speed, which translates into gap power and still could lead to average home run pop. He's a very good defensive shortstop with plus range and arm strength, and he has improved his focus to make routine plays. He has become a very smart baserunner with average speed. He's a confident, hard-working player whose professional manner is contagious. Desmond still has plenty of work to do at the plate, where his stance is too spread out, causing him to dip and get underneath the ball at times. But he's finally ready for Double-A and still has a chance to be Washington's shortstop of the future. After all, he's still just 22.

Year	Club (League)	Class	AVG	G	AB	R	H	2B	3B	HR	RBI	BB	SO	SB	OBP	SLG
2004	Expos (GCL)	R	.227	55	216	28	49	11	0	1	27	10	40	13	.272	.292
	Vermont (NYP)	A	.250	4	12	2	3	0	0	1	1	0	2	0	.308	.500
2005	Savannah (SAL)	A	.247	73	296	37	73	10	2	4	23	13	60	20	.291	.334
	Potomac (Car)	A	.256	55	219	37	56	13	3	3	15	21	53	13	.325	.384
2006	Harrisburg (EL)	AA	.182	37	121	8	22	4	1	0	3	5	35	4	.214	.231
	Potomac (Car)	A	.244	92	365	50	89	20	2	9	45	29	79	14	.313	.384
2007	Potomac (Car)	A	.264	129	458	69	121	30	4	13	45	57	99	27	.357	.432
MINOR LEAGUE TOTALS			.245	445	1687	231	413	88	12	31	159	135	368	91	.311	.366

15 GARRETT MOCK, RHP

Born: April 25, 1983. **B-T:** R-R. **Ht.:** 6-4. **Wt.:** 215. **Drafted:** Houston, 2004 (3rd round). **Signed by:** Trip Couch (Diamondbacks).

A favorite of Nationals assistant general manager Mike Rizzo from the days when both were with the Diamondbacks, Mock was acquired as part of the Livan Hernandez trade in 2006, when he struggled trying to pitch through a knee injury. He had surgery that fall to remove a lesion from a tendon in his left knee, and he pitched just 65 innings in 2007 while trying to work his way back to his previous form. Toward the end of the season and in the Arizona Fall League, Mock once again started to flash electric stuff, showing an 89-94 mph fastball, a power slider that can be a plus pitch, a sharp curveball and a changeup that remains underdeveloped. He has a big, physical frame with strong legs and has the potential to be a workhorse if he can stay healthy. Mock is very good when his command is on, but he needs to become more consistent. He's a fierce competitor but also a little flaky. He talks too much at times and has a tendency to out-think himself. Added to the 40-man roster in November, Mock will compete for a spot in Washington's Opening Day rotation in 2008 but probably will get some more minor league time to refine his command and work on the mental part of his game.

Year	Club (League)	Class	W	L	ERA	G	GS	CG	SV	IP	H	R	ER	HR	BB	SO	AVG
2004	Yakima (NWL)	A	2	0	1.54	5	5	0	0	23	18	8	4	1	4	14	.228
	South Bend (MWL)	A	3	2	3.00	8	8	1	0	54	49	21	18	2	12	37	.251
2005	Lancaster (Cal)	A	14	7	4.18	28	28	0	0	174	202	95	81	19	33	160	.284
2006	Tennessee (SL)	AA	4	8	4.95	23	23	0	0	131	144	81	72	14	50	117	.280
	Harrisburg (EL)	AA	0	4	10.26	4	4	0	0	16	29	21	19	2	5	9	.387
2007	Potomac (Car)	A	1	0	0.00	1	1	0	0	6	3	0	0	0	1	5	.143
	Nationals (GCL)	R	0	2	4.70	3	2	0	0	7	11	7	4	3	1	8	.333
	Harrisburg (EL)	AA	1	5	5.79	11	11	0	0	51	66	41	33	5	28	41	.311
MINOR LEAGUE TOTALS			25	28	4.48	83	82	1	0	464	522	274	231	46	134	391	.284

16 STEPHEN KING, 2B/SS

Born: Oct. 2, 1987. **B-T:** R-R. **Ht.:** 6-2. **Wt.:** 195. **Drafted:** HS—Winter Park, Fla., 2006 (3rd round). **Signed by:** Tony Arango.

King signed for an above-slot $750,000 as a third-rounder in 2006, but the extended negotiations delayed his pro debut until last April. He surprised the Nationals by claiming their Opening Day shortstop job in low Class A, and he hit homered twice in his first week there. Washington believes that early success got into his head, causing him to try to match teammates Chris Marrero and Justin Maxwell homer for homer. As a result, his average plummeted and his strikeouts soared. The Nationals sent him down to the Gulf Coast League and moved him to second base alongside shortstop Esmailyn Gonzalez, and he showed off his solid-average raw power by hitting nine home runs. King hit well in six games after a promotion to Vermont before a pulled hamstring ended his season. King's lower half was too rigid for shortstop, but he has enough range and arm strength to play second base. He's still learning how to turn the double play from that side and correct his footwork. Some scouts project King as an offensive second baseman in the Jeff Kent mold, thanks to his promising line-drive swing and ability to drive the ball up the middle and to the opposite field, but he needs to become a more selective hitter and make more consistent contact. He'll likely get another shot at Hagerstown in 2008.

Year	Club (League)	Class	AVG	G	AB	R	H	2B	3B	HR	RBI	BB	SO	SB	OBP	SLG
2007	Hagerstown (SAL)	A	.180	35	128	16	23	4	0	2	9	13	51	5	.261	.258
	Nationals (GCL)	R	.248	42	161	20	40	6	1	9	30	12	47	1	.315	.466
	Vermont (NYP)	A	.333	6	24	3	8	2	0	0	2	1	7	0	.360	.417
MINOR LEAGUE TOTALS			.227	83	313	39	71	12	1	11	41	26	105	6	.296	.377

17 ESMAILYN GONZALEZ, SS

Born: Sept. 21, 1989. **B-T:** B-R. **Ht.:** 5-11. **Wt.:** 175. **Signed:** Dominican Republic, 2006. **Signed by:** Jose Rijo.

Internally, the Nationals are divided on Gonzalez. Because they signed him for a $1.4 million bonus—far more than anyone else was willing to pay him—many club officials are reluctant to say anything critical about him, but there are serious questions about whether his fringy tools will allow him to stay at shortstop. His soft, sure hands and smooth actions are his best assets defensively, but his range is below average at short, particularly to his right. He played through a minor shoulder injury for most of 2007 and showed below-average arm strength. Even at full strength, his arm is likely better suited for second base. The Nationals tried to sell Gonzalez as a slick-fielding shortstop when they signed him, but in reality he profiles more as a switch-hitting second baseman with a line-drive bat, similar to Jose Vidro. Like most young switch-hitters, Gonzalez is a better hitter from the left side, with a fluid swing that stays inside the ball consistently. He needs to add strength in his wrists and forearms. His lower half has some thickness and he's a below-average runner. At this early stage of his career, Gonzalez is a contact hitter with advanced strike-zone judgment, but he projects for some gap power. He could get a shot at Hagerstown in 2008, though Vermont seems a more likely destination.

Year	Club (League)	Class	AVG	G	AB	R	H	2B	3B	HR	RBI	BB	SO	SB	OBP	SLG
2007	Nationals (GCL)	R	.245	33	106	13	26	3	2	0	11	19	18	4	.382	.311
MINOR LEAGUE TOTALS			.245	33	106	13	26	3	2	0	11	19	18	4	.382	.311

18 SHAIRON MARTIS, RHP

Born: March 30, 1987. **B-T:** R-R. **Ht.:** 6-1. **Wt.:** 175. **Signed:** Curacao, 2004. **Signed by:** Philip Elhage (Giants).

Acquired from the Giants in the 2006 Mike Stanton trade, Martis has made a name for himself in international competition. He threw a seven-inning no-hitter against Panama in the World Baseball Classic, then made two strong starts to help the Netherlands win the European Olympic qualifier tournament in Spain this fall. Martis posted a 0.82 ERA and 15 strikeouts in 11 innings for the Dutch, on the heels of a career-high 151-inning season. He lacks overpowering stuff, but he commands a solid four-pitch repertoire and mixes his pitches and locations well. He works at 89-91 mph with his fastball and uses a sinking two-seamer to induce grounders. He can throw his plus changeup for a strike in any count, though he's still working on his two breaking balls. His slider has more promise, but he's more comfortable with his curveball at this stage. A good athlete with a commanding mound presence and impressive feel for pitching, Martis has a good shot to reach the big leagues as a back-of-the-rotation starter, though his upside is limited. He'll pitch in Double-A as a 21-year-old in 2008.

Year	Club (League)	Class	W	L	ERA	G	GS	CG	SV	IP	H	R	ER	HR	BB	SO	AVG
2004	Giants (DSL)	R	4	3	1.79	14	12	0	0	70	55	15	14	2	17	63	.221
2005	Giants (AZL)	R	2	1	1.85	11	5	0	1	34	28	10	7	1	9	50	.226
2006	Augusta (SAL)	A	6	4	3.64	15	15	0	0	76	76	39	31	3	21	66	.257
	Savannah (SAL)	A	1	1	3.80	4	4	0	0	21	23	9	9	2	4	14	.284
	Potomac (Car)	A	0	2	3.00	2	2	0	0	12	9	5	4	0	3	7	.209
	Harrisburg (EL)	AA	0	1	12.60	1	1	0	0	5	8	7	7	4	3	1	.348
2007	Potomac (Car)	A	14	8	4.23	27	26	1	0	151	150	83	71	9	52	108	.258
MINOR LEAGUE TOTALS			27	20	3.48	74	65	1	1	370	349	168	143	21	109	309	.250

19 BRAD PEACOCK, RHP

Born: Feb. 2, 1988. **B-T:** R-R. **Ht.:** 6-1. **Wt.:** 175. **Drafted:** Palm Beach (Fla.) CC, D/F 2006 (41st round). **Signed by:** Tony Arango.

The athletic Peacock played mostly shortstop in high school and was drafted as a catcher, but he was impressive on the mound at Palm Beach (Fla.) CC in the spring of 2007, prompting the Nationals to sign him as a draft-and-follow for $110,000. He garners comparisons to Tim Hudson for his slight stature, smooth delivery and three-pitch repertoire. Peacock works comfortably at 89-92 mph with his lively fastball and touches 93-94 at times. He dazzled in instructional league with a changeup that was at times well above-average with deception and late armside movement. His curveball has some sharpness and has a chance to be another plus pitch in time. Peacock still needs to add some weight to maintain his fastball velocity, but his stuff, command, advanced feel for pitching and excellent makeup suggest he has a chance to be a No. 3 starter in the big leagues someday. He'll likely skip a level and move to low Class A this year.

Year	Club (League)	Class	W	L	ERA	G	GS	CG	SV	IP	H	R	ER	HR	BB	SO	AVG
2007	Nationals (GCL)	R	1	1	3.89	13	7	0	0	39	38	23	17	1	15	34	.242
MINOR LEAGUE TOTALS			1	1	3.89	13	7	0	0	39	38	23	17	1	15	34	.242

20 KORY CASTO, OF/3B

Born: Dec. 8, 1981. **B-T:** L-R. **Ht.:** 6-1. **Wt.:** 195. **Drafted:** Portland, 2003 (3rd round). **Signed by:** Doug McMillan.

Casto entered 2007 with a tentative grasp on the Nationals' starting left-field job, but he struggled out of the gate and lost his regular playing time. When he got another brief chance to play every in early May, he went 1-for-20 and was sent down to Triple-A. An outfielder in college who was converted to third base in 2004 and then moved back to the outfield after the 2006 all-star break out of respect for Ryan Zimmerman, Casto wound up back at the hot corner with Columbus. The position shuffle and demotion prevented him from ever getting into a rhythm in 2007, and he hit for his lowest average since his pro debut. One problem is that Casto was feeling for his stride, rushing to get his front foot down and losing leverage as a result. In the past, he had shown average power and the ability to use all fields. He always has been a patient hitter, but Washington would like to see him get more aggressive instead of waiting for the perfect pitch. His slightly above-average arm plays at third base or the outfield, though his speed and range are fringy. His future might now be as a utility player, but he could get another shot at the Opening Day left-field job in 2008.

Year	Club (League)	Class	AVG	G	AB	R	H	2B	3B	HR	RBI	BB	SO	SB	OBP	SLG
2003	Vermont (NYP)	A	.239	71	259	26	62	14	2	4	28	30	47	1	.322	.355
2004	Savannah (SAL)	A	.286	124	483	67	138	35	4	16	88	31	70	1	.337	.474
2005	Potomac (Car)	A	.290	135	500	86	145	36	4	22	90	84	98	6	.394	.510
2006	Harrisburg (EL)	AA	.272	140	489	84	133	24	6	20	80	81	104	6	.379	.467
2007	Washington (NL)	MLB	.130	16	54	1	7	2	0	0	3	2	17	0	.158	.167
	Columbus (IL)	AAA	.246	114	411	56	101	20	2	11	55	54	106	4	.334	.384
MINOR LEAGUE TOTALS			.270	584	2142	319	579	129	18	73	341	280	425	18	.358	.450
MAJOR LEAGUE TOTALS			.130	16	54	1	7	2	0	0	3	2	17	0	.158	.167

21 MATT WHITNEY, 1B

Born: Feb. 13, 1984. **B-T:** R-R. **Ht.:** 6-4. **Wt.:** 190. **Drafted:** HS—Palm Beach Gardens, Fla., 2002 (1st round). **Signed by:** Jim Gabella (Indians).

One of the best high school hitters in the 2002 draft, Whitney slipped to the Indians with the 33rd overall pick and signed for $1.25 million. One of the most exciting position players to come into the Tribe system in years, he drew Manny Ramirez comparisons for his raw power after hitting 10 homers in 45 games at Rookie-level Burlington. But Whitney's career was derailed the following spring, when he broke his leg stepping on a water sprinkler on his way to a post-workout hoops session. The leg required several surgeries to repair, and Whitney wasn't fully healthy until 2006. Even then, his range at third base had decreased significantly and his struggles in the field carried over to the plate. The Indians moved him to first base during last spring and he wound up clubbing an organization-high 32 home runs in high Class A. Whitney has outstanding power to all fields, and he showed more ability to allow balls to get deeper in the zone with opposite-field pop in 2007. His swing still can get long at times and he might never hit for a high average. He's a below-average runner, but his defense at first base is adequate. Plucked from Cleveland in the major league phase of the Rule 5 draft, Whitney must remain on the 25-man roster all season or be placed on waivers and then offered back to the Indians for $25,000. The Nationals plan on keeping him, and GM Jim Bowden said Whitney will provide an insurance policy for oft-injured Nick Johnson and battle Tony Batista for major league at-bats. Washington made a second major league Rule 5 pick, taking line-drive hitting outfielder Garrett Guzman from the Twins.

Year	Club (League)	Class	AVG	G	AB	R	H	2B	3B	HR	RBI	BB	SO	SB	OBP	SLG
2002	Burlington (Appy)	R	.286	45	175	33	50	12	1	10	33	18	49	5	.359	.537
	Columbus (SAL)	A	.111	6	18	0	2	0	0	0	0	3	4	0	.238	.111
2003	Did Not Play—Injured															
2004	Lake County (SAL)	A	.256	55	195	21	50	11	0	5	31	23	81	0	.347	.390
2005	Lake County (SAL)	A	.242	74	277	38	67	7	0	6	27	34	64	0	.332	.332
2006	Kinston (Car)	A	.206	96	345	40	71	20	2	10	39	41	131	0	.294	.362
2007	Lake County (SAL)	A	.308	71	286	52	88	19	0	16	64	31	62	0	.377	.542
	Kinston (Car)	A	.288	57	226	43	65	11	0	16	49	22	59	1	.347	.549
MINOR LEAGUE TOTALS			.258	404	1522	227	393	80	3	63	243	172	450	6	.338	.439

22 DEREK NORRIS, C

Born: Feb. 14, 1989. **B-T:** R-R. **Ht.:** 6-0. **Wt.:** 210. **Drafted:** HS—Goddard, Kan., 2007 (4th round). **Signed by:** Ryan Fox.

Norris' high school senior season got off to a slow start in 2007 when an overthrow hit him in the head while he was sitting in the dugout. He recovered to have a solid year and solidify his place as the best prep prospect in Kansas, and he passed up a scholarship from Wichita State to sign with the Nationals for $210,000 as a fourth-round pick. Norris flashed some of his above-average power potential in his pro debut and he has a fairly mature approach for his age. He's not afraid to take walks and shows the ability to hit the ball the other way, though his swing remains raw. Defensively, Norris didn't start catching until his senior year of high school after playing third base his first three seasons, so naturally he needs more experience to refine his skills behind the plate. But former all-star catcher Bob Boone, Washington's vice president of player personnel, likes how Norris approaches catching and sees some softness in his hands and quickness in his feet. He has a strong arm but needs to work on his exchange after throwing out just 24 percent of basestealers in his debut. The Nationals haven't had much luck developing catchers in recent years, but Norris has enough tools to become their catcher of the future, though that future is years away. He figures to get a crack at Vermont at some point in 2008.

Year	Club (League)	Class	AVG	G	AB	R	H	2B	3B	HR	RBI	BB	SO	SB	OBP	SLG
2007	Nationals (GCL)	R	.203	37	123	16	25	6	2	4	15	25	38	2	.344	.382
MINOR LEAGUE TOTALS			.203	37	123	16	25	6	2	4	15	25	38	2	.344	.382

23 MIKE DANIEL, OF

Born: Aug. 17, 1984. **B-T:** L-R. **Ht.:** 6-3. **Wt.:** 180. **Drafted:** North Carolina, 2005 (7th round). **Signed by:** Dana Brown.

Daniel has athletic genes. His father was a triple-jumper at McNeese State, his mother was a dancer who owned her own studio and his younger brother Cyril is a pitcher at North Carolina A&T. Mike caught Nationals scouting director Dana Brown's eye as a raw 20-year-old junior at North Carolina, and he has begun to grow into his lanky, athletic frame. Daniel has wiry strength and occasional pull power, but he's more of a gap-to-gap, line-drive hitter with a mature, patient approach. He has good balance in the box and squares balls up consistently, but he tends to cut off his swing, preventing him from getting good extension and explosion through the ball. That figures to limit his power. Daniel's versatility is an asset. He's a solid-average runner capable of playing all three outfield spots, though his slightly below-average arm makes left field his best position. He has gotten better at reading balls off the bat and taking better angles to the ball, and his range is average. He could be a No. 2 hole-type hitter and a fourth outfielder in the big leagues. Daniel will advance to Double-A this year.

Year	Club (League)	Class	AVG	G	AB	R	H	2B	3B	HR	RBI	BB	SO	SB	OBP	SLG
2005	Vermont (NYP)	A	.260	67	235	41	61	6	4	3	25	29	64	6	.351	.357
2006	Savannah (SAL)	A	.193	52	181	20	35	5	1	4	16	26	52	8	.301	.298
	Vermont (NYP)	A	.304	53	181	29	55	8	3	3	18	16	52	13	.376	.431
2007	Hagerstown (SAL)	A	.290	54	207	38	60	15	1	7	37	19	50	9	.365	.473
	Potomac (Car)	A	.296	71	280	37	83	20	5	4	41	29	62	16	.361	.446
MINOR LEAGUE TOTALS			.271	297	1084	165	294	54	14	21	137	119	280	52	.352	.405

24 STEPHEN ENGLUND, OF

Born: June 6, 1988. **B-T:** R-R. **Ht.:** 6-3. **Wt.:** 190. **Drafted:** HS—Bellevue, Wash., 2006 (2nd round). **Signed by:** Doug McMillan.

Athleticism is Englund's calling card, and it's the reason the Nationals gave him a $515,000 bonus to buy the high school shortstop out of his commitment to Washington State. They knew he'd would be a long-term project with high upside, so they're not overly concerned about his early-career struggles at the plate. Englund was one of the most improved players in Nationals camp during the spring, but he fractured the thumb on his non-throwing hand while making a catch against a chain-link fence in his first game of the season in the Gulf Coast League, causing him to miss a month. When he returned, he showed impressive plate discipline but little pop. Englund has average raw power at this point, but he hasn't begun to carry it into game action. His bat has been questioned since his pedestrian senior year of high school, but he has plenty of hand speed. He also has plenty of work to do, as he gets caught in between with his stride and doesn't make consistent contact. He's a slightly above-average runner underway who has a chance to be a decent center fielder but is more likely to outgrow the position and move to right, where his strong arm will be an asset. Some coaches in the system think Englund has more upside than anyone Washington farmhand, but he's a long ways off and likely to return to Vermont after ending last season there.

Year	Club (League)	Class	AVG	G	AB	R	H	2B	3B	HR	RBI	BB	SO	SB	OBP	SLG
2006	Nationals (GCL)	R	.183	35	115	16	21	3	0	1	12	17	41	5	.307	.235
2007	Nationals (GCL)	R	.253	24	79	18	20	3	0	0	2	28	24	13	.454	.291
	Vermont (NYP)	A	.220	17	59	10	13	4	0	1	7	8	22	0	.319	.339
MINOR LEAGUE TOTALS			.213	76	253	44	54	10	0	2	21	53	87	18	.360	.277

25 JHONNY NUNEZ, RHP

Born: Nov. 26, 1985. **B-T:** R-R. **Ht.:** 6-3. **Wt.:** 185. **Signed:** Dominican Republic, 2003. **Signed by:** Andres Lopez (Dodgers).

The Nationals acquired Nunez from the Dodgers in the Marlon Anderson trade after his stellar U.S. debut in the Gulf Coast League in 2006, and he followed it up with a solid debut in full-season ball in 2007. He runs his fastball up to 94 mph and pitches in the low 90s with sinking life. Washington tried to teach him a curveball like it does with most of its young arms, but his low three-quarters arm slot was more conducive to a slider, so he scrapped the curve. He made progress tightening the slider, and it has a chance to be a plus pitch if he can command it more consistently. The Nationals forced him to throw his nascent changeup throughout the year, and he showed flashes of an average change in the instructional league. He still needs to refine both of his secondary offerings as well as his control, and to continue to learn how to set hitters up. Nunez often struggles to maintain his stuff as he gets deeper into outings, and his future may be in the bullpen. For now, he'll continue to start and advance to high Class A.

Year	Club (League)	Class	W	L	ERA	G	GS	CG	SV	IP	H	R	ER	HR	BB	SO	AVG
2004	Dodgers1 (DSL)	R	2	1	1.73	7	7	0	0	36	30	8	7	1	6	23	.229
	Dodgers2 (DSL)	R	2	0	4.60	4	3	0	0	15	17	9	8	0	4	12	.262

2005	Dodgers (DSL)	R	4	3	1.92	15	8	1	0	51	29	13	11	0	13	40	.153
2006	Dodgers (GCL)	R	6	0	1.58	10	7	0	0	57	35	12	10	0	19	56	.177
2007	Hagerstown (SAL)	A	4	6	4.05	23	22	0	0	106	97	59	48	10	48	86	.239
MINOR LEAGUE TOTALS			18	10	2.83	59	47	1	0	267	208	101	84	11	90	217	.210

26 HASSAN PENA, RHP

Born: March 25, 1985. **B-T:** R-R. **Ht.:** 6-2. **Wt.:** 210. **Drafted:** Palm Beach (Fla.) CC, 2006 (13th round).
Signed by: Tony Arango.

Pena defected from Cuba and spent a year at Palm Beach (Fla.) CC before the Nationals signed him as a 13th-round pick for a $149,500 bonus. He tried to come back too soon from shoulder tendinitis in 2006, causing it to flare up again and preventing him from making his pro debut that summer. Then he had minor offseason surgery to shave off a small spot near his rotator cuff, but he came back strong and showed electric stuff last summer. Pena's best pitch is a sharp-breaking curveball that grades at plus when it's on, and his 90-94 mph fastball has good life. He also has good feel for a changeup that projects as a solid-average offering. Pena walked nearly as many as he struck out in 2007 because he tries too hard to make the perfect pitch and often falls behind in counts. He has a tendency to fly open in his delivery, perhaps because he's trying to overthrow, which puts stress on his shoulder and hurts his command. When he stays balanced and on a straight line toward home plate, he's very effective. Pena has enough stuff to eventually pitch in a big league rotation, perhaps even as a solid No. 3 starter, but he has plenty of work to do. He'll move up to low Class A in 2008.

Year	Club (League)	Class	W	L	ERA	G	GS	CG	SV	IP	H	R	ER	HR	BB	SO	AVG
2007	Vermont (NYP)	A	4	5	4.25	13	13	0	0	59	55	36	28	3	33	36	.256
MINOR LEAGUE TOTALS			4	5	4.25	13	13	0	0	59	55	36	28	3	33	36	.256

27 MARTIN BENO, RHP

Born: Aug. 24, 1986. **B-T:** R-R. **Ht.:** 6-0. **Wt.:** 180. **Drafted:** Oklahoma State, 2007 (36th round). **Signed by:** Ryan Fox.

Beno has been on the prospect landscape since he was Mississippi high schooler and the Royals drafted him in the 28th round in 2004. After his freshman year at Bossier Parish (La.) CC, Beno opened eyes in the Cape Cod League but turned down $100,000 as a free agent and transferred to Mississippi Gulf Coast CC, where the Dodgers drafted him in the seventh round in 2006. He delayed pro ball again, moving on to Oklahoma State and having a disappointing junior year. Beno worked mostly in relief for the Cowboys and dropped to the 36th round, where he finally signed for $10,000. He made a strong first impression by striking out 38 in 22 innings at Vermont and impressed the Nationals further in instructional league by effortlessly running his fastball up to 96 mph and sitting at 90-94 with late life. He also showed an average-plus changeup and flashed a promising but inconsistent curveball. Beno has a short, smooth arm action, though his mechanics aren't textbook. He has a tendency to leave his fastball up in the zone at times and needs to improve his all-around command. Maturity has been an issue for Beno at times in the past, but the Nationals haven't reported any issues with him so far. His lack of size and a reliable breaking ball likely will keep him in the bullpen, but he has a high ceiling if he can put it all together. He'll open his first full season in low Class A.

Year	Club (League)	Class	W	L	ERA	G	GS	CG	SV	IP	H	R	ER	HR	BB	SO	AVG
2007	Nationals (GCL)	R	0	0	0.00	1	0	0	0	1	0	0	0	0	0	2	.000
	Vermont (NYP)	A	2	1	4.15	16	0	0	2	21	9	12	10	0	16	38	.118
MINOR LEAGUE TOTALS			2	1	3.97	17	0	0	2	22	9	12	10	0	16	40	.114

28 ZECH ZINICOLA, RHP

Born: March 2, 1985. **B-T:** R-R. **Ht.:** 6-1. **Wt.:** 220. **Drafted:** Arizona State, 2006 (6th round). **Signed by:** Mitch Sokol.

Zinicola developed a reputation in college for being either eccentric or immature, depending on who you ask. He followed up his stellar pro debut—during which he posted a 1.65 ERA over three levels while reaching Double-A to rank No. 6 on this list a year ago—with a rough sophomore campaign. The Nationals think his struggles had more to do with his head than anything else. He blew a couple of saves early in the season and felt like he was letting his team down, so he started pressing and his command became erratic. He was better in the second half and looked good in instructional league before heading to the Arizona Fall League. When Zinicola commands his fastball down in the zone, he'll pitch at 92-93 mph and touch 95 with heavy sink. He also mixes in a plus 82-85 mph slider with good bite, and he was working to develop a changeup in instructs. Sometimes he falls into patterns where he doesn't use the slider as much as he ought to. Zinicola still has the stuff to be a late-inning reliever in the majors, but he needs to be more consistent with his command and his mental approach. A standout spring could land him in Washington on Opening Day, but he's more likely to head to Triple-A.

Year	Club (League)	Class	W	L	ERA	G	GS	CG	SV	IP	H	R	ER	HR	BB	SO	AVG
2006	Vermont (NYP)	A	0	0	0.00	8	0	0	4	9	6	0	0	0	1	10	.182
	Potomac (Car)	A	3	0	1.98	9	0	0	3	13	11	3	3	0	3	13	.229
	Harrisburg (EL)	AA	1	1	2.70	10	0	0	5	10	11	6	3	0	11	8	.256
2007	Harrisburg (EL)	AA	0	4	5.46	42	0	0	6	57	53	35	35	3	36	45	.248
MINOR LEAGUE TOTALS			4	5	4.08	69	0	0	18	90	81	44	41	3	51	76	.240

29 ROGEARVIN BERNADINA, OF

Born: June 12, 1984. **B-T:** L-L. **Ht.:** 6-0. **Wt.:** 175. **Signed:** Netherlands, 2001. **Signed by:** Fred Ferreira.

The Nationals have been patient with Bernadina, who entered the system as a very raw 17-year-old with a tantalizing toolset, but his progress was frustratingly slow over his first five seasons. He posted a slugging percentage of exactly .369 in three consecutive seasons in Class A, illustrating his inability to translate his decent raw power into results. He hit that magic .369 slugging number again at Double-A in 2007, then exploded at the European Olympic qualifier in Spain in the fall, leading eventual champion Netherlands with a .632/.759/1.052 line in seven games. Afterward, Washington placed him on its 40-man roster. Bernadina is a plus-plus athlete and a 65 runner on the 20-80 scouting scale, and he's a superb defensive center fielder with a strong, accurate arm. He has gotten better at hitting hard line drives to the gaps, but he still tends to get underneath the ball too much and needs to make better use of his speed. To that end, the Nationals had him focus on improving his bunting in instructional league. Washington wanted him to be more aggressive at the plate, so his walk totals were down in 2007, but so were his strikeouts as he did a better job making consistent contact. Bernadina's bat remains a question mark, but his speed and defense give him a good chance to reach the big leagues as an extra outfielder. He should play at Triple-A in 2008.

Year	Club (League)	Class	AVG	G	AB	R	H	2B	3B	HR	RBI	BB	SO	SB	OBP	SLG
2002	Expos (GCL)	R	.276	57	196	22	54	7	0	3	18	19	25	1	.348	.357
2003	Savannah (SAL)	A	.237	77	278	36	66	12	3	4	39	19	53	11	.292	.345
2004	Savannah (SAL)	A	.238	129	450	67	107	24	7	7	66	60	113	24	.338	.369
2005	Savannah (SAL)	A	.233	122	417	64	97	15	3	12	54	75	92	35	.356	.369
2006	Potomac (Car)	A	.270	123	434	60	117	19	3	6	42	56	98	28	.355	.369
2007	Columbus (IL)	AAA	.167	13	42	6	7	3	0	0	1	9	11	0	.327	.238
	Harrisburg (EL)	AA	.270	97	371	58	100	15	2	6	36	38	80	40	.340	.369
MINOR LEAGUE TOTALS			.250	618	2188	313	548	95	18	38	256	276	472	139	.340	.362

30 P.J. DEAN, RHP

Born: Oct. 27, 1988. **B-T:** R-R. **Ht.:** 6-3. **Wt.:** 175. **Drafted:** HS—New Caney, Texas, 2007 (7th round). **Signed by:** Tyler Wilt.

The Nationals bought Dean out of a commitment to Oklahoma with a $120,000 bonus as a seventh-round pick in June. He made a positive first impression in his debut before hitting a wall late in the summer. Washington compares his lean, athletic body and clean arm action to Collin Balester's, and like a younger Balester, Dean needs to get stronger. But he already operates at 89-91 mph and touches 92 with his lively fastball, and there's plenty of room for projection. He throws his fastball and his hard, sharp curveball for strikes, and he flashes a promising changeup. There were questions about Dean's makeup in high school, but he's young and simply needs to mature. His command isn't bad for his age, but it will have to improve as he moves up the ladder. Dean figures to start the year in extended spring training and then advance to Vermont. He could blossom into a mid-rotation starter as he matures physically and mentally.

Year	Club (League)	Class	W	L	ERA	G	GS	CG	SV	IP	H	R	ER	HR	BB	SO	AVG
2007	Nationals (GCL)	R	3	1	4.06	9	5	0	0	31	27	16	14	1	11	26	.225
MINOR LEAGUE TOTALS			3	1	4.06	9	5	0	0	31	27	16	14	1	11	26	.225

These three Japanese players signed too late to be included in other sections of the book, but we add their scouting reports here so you'll have a good idea of what to look for when they take a major league field. Fukudome signed a four-year, $48 million contract with the Cubs; Fukumori inked a two-year, $3 million deal with the Rangers; and Kuroda got a three-year, $35.3 million pact from the Rangers.

KOSUKE FUKUDOME, OF, CUBS

Born: April 26, 1977. **B-T:** L-R. **Ht.:** 6-0. **Wt.:** 190.

The departures of Ichiro Suzuki and Hideki Matsui meant that Fukudome was the best all-around player remaining in Japan. While he doesn't have the same power as Matsui, he's a comparable player and has better all-around tools. The 2006 Central League MVP and two-time batting champ has a strong arm and runs well enough to play center field in a pinch, though he profiles best as a right fielder who hits for average, draws walks and occasionally drives the ball out of the park with a smooth lefthanded swing. The Cubs will play him in right and bat him near the top of the order, perhaps even in the leadoff spot. The biggest concern about Fukudome is his durability. He missed the second half of the 2007 season with bone chips in his throwing elbow and has been bothered by other minor injuries in recent years. Fukudome played third base as a teenager on Japan's silver-medal winning 1996 Olympic team before taking his speed to the outfield. He has plenty of experience on the international stage. He also played for Japan's 2004 Olympic team and was one of the stars of Japan's World Baseball Classic squad, hitting a pinch-hit, two-run home run in the semifinals against Korea and a key two-run single against Cuba in the championship game.

KAZ FUKUMORI, RHP, RANGERS

Born: Aug. 4, 1976. **B-T:** R-R. **Ht.:** 5-11. **Wt.:** 170.

Of the Japanese players making the trip across the Pacific for the 2008 season, Fukumori will carry the most risk. He has closed at times during his Japanese career, but he never has been effective enough to stay in the role for long. He missed time late last season with an elbow injury, though he was showing no ill effects when he came to the States to work out for scouts after the season. The righthander pairs an 88-90 mph fastball with a splitter that's his out pitch, though he's not a strikeout artist. He also uses a below-average curveball to give hitters something else to worry about. Fukumori profiles as a set-up man in the United States, and the Rangers plan on using him in that role. His stuff isn't overpowering, but the track record for Japanese relievers making the jump to the major leagues is pretty good, at least in the short term until hitters learn their strengths and weaknesses.

HIROKI KURODA, RHP, DODGERS

Born: Feb. 10, 1975. **B-T:** R-R. **Ht.:** 6-0. **Wt.:** 190.

A fixture in the Hiroshima Carp rotation since 1997, Kuroda had a chance to head to the United States after an outstanding 2006 season in which he led the Central League with a 1.85 ERA. He decided to remain in Japan for one more year, partly because he needed minor elbow surgery. Kuroda was effective in his swan song, but he did tire as the season went on. He pitches off a 91-93 mph fastball that he works to both sides of the plate. His best asset is his command and his ability to keep the ball down. He wasn't a strikeout pitcher in Japan, but his ability to work his sinker for groundouts allows him to get out of jams, and his deliberate motion makes it difficult to time him. Like many Japanese pitchers, he has a broad assortment of offspeed pitches, but he relies primarily on a slider and forkball. Kuroda has over 1,700 innings on his arm, and his lack of a dominating pitch means he may struggle at times, but his savvy and ability to keep the ball in the park should allow him to be an effective No. 3 or No. 4 starter for the Dodgers.

2007 DRAFT

These are the bonuses and estimated slot recommendations by Major League Baseball for picks in the 2007 draft. MLB has established guidelines for every pick through the first five rounds, and sets a ceiling equal to the final choice in the fifth round for subsequent rounds. Asterisks indicate bonuses that were part of a major league contract:

FIRST ROUND

Pick. Team: Player, Pos.	'07 Bonus	'07 Slot
1. Devil Rays: David Price, lhp	*$5,600,000	$3,600,000
2. Royals: Mike Moustakas, ss/3b	$4,000,000	$3,150,000
3. Cubs: Josh Vitters, 3b	$3,200,000	$2,700,000
4. Pirates: Daniel Moskos, lhp	$2,475,000	$2,475,000
5. Orioles: Matt Wieters, c	$6,000,000	$2,250,000
6. Nationals: Ross Detwiler, lhp	$2,150,000	$2,160,000
7. Brewers: Matt LaPorta, of/1b	$2,000,000	$2,070,000
8. Rockies: Casey Weathers, rhp	$1,800,000	$1,980,000
9. D'backs: Jarrod Parker, rhp	$2,100,000	$1,890,000
10. Giants: Madison Bumgarner, lhp	$2,000,000	$1,800,000
11. Mariners: Phillippe Aumont, rhp	$1,900,000	$1,710,000
12. Marlins: Matt Dominguez, 3b	$1,800,000	$1,620,000
13. Indians: Beau Mills, 3b/1b	$1,575,000	$1,575,000
14. Braves: Jason Heyward, of	$1,700,000	$1,530,000
15. Reds: Devin Mesoraco, c	$1,400,000	$1,485,000
16. Blue Jays: Kevin Ahrens, ss/3b	$1,440,000	$1,440,000
17. Rangers: Blake Beavan, rhp	$1,497,500	$1,417,500
18. Cardinals: Pete Kozma, ss	$1,395,000	$1,395,000
19. Phillies: Joe Savery, lhp	$1,372,500	$1,372,500
20. Dodgers: Chris Withrow, rhp	$1,350,000	$1,350,000
21. Blue Jays: J.P. Arencibia, c	$1,327,500	$1,327,500
22. Giants: Tim Alderson, rhp	$1,290,000	$1,282,500
23. Padres: Nick Schmidt, lhp	$1,260,000	$1,260,000
24. Rangers: Michael Main, rhp	$1,237,500	$1,237,500
25. White Sox: Aaron Poreda, lhp	$1,200,000	$1,215,000
26. Athletics: James Simmons, rhp	$1,192,500	$1,192,500
27. Tigers: Rick Porcello, rhp	*$3,580,000	$1,170,000
28. Twins: Ben Revere, of	$750,000	$1,080,000
29. Giants: Wendell Fairley, of	$1,000,000	$990,000
30. Yankees: Andrew Brackman, rhp	*$3,350,000	$945,000

SUPPLEMENTAL FIRST ROUND

Pick. Team: Player, Pos.	'07 Bonus	'07 Slot
31. Nationals: Josh Smoker, lhp	$1,000,000	$922,500
32. Giants: Nick Noonan, ss/2b	$915,750	$915,750
33. Braves: Jon Gilmore, 3b	$900,000	$900,000
34. Reds: Todd Frazier, ss	$825,000	$877,500
35. Rangers: Julio Borbon, of	*$800,000	$855,000
36. Cards: Clayton Mortensen, rhp	$650,000	$855,000
37. Phillies: Travis d'Arnaud, c	$832,500	$832,500
38. Blue Jays: Brett Cecil, lhp	$810,000	$810,000
39. Dodgers: James Adkins, lhp	$787,500	$787,500
40. Padres: Kellen Kulbacki, of	$765,000	$765,000
41. Athletics: Sean Doolittle, 1b	$742,500	$742,500
42. Mets: Eddie Kunz, rhp	$720,000	$720,000

	'07 Bonus	'07 Slot
43. Giants: Jackson Williams, c	$708,750	$708,750
44. Rangers: Neil Ramirez, rhp	$1,000,000	$697,500
45. Blue Jays: Justin Jackson, ss	$675,000	$675,000
46. Padres: Drew Cumberland, ss	$661,500	$661,500
47. Mets: Nathan Vineyard, lhp	$657,000	$657,000
48. Cubs: Josh Donaldson, c	$652,500	$652,500
49. Nationals: Michael Burgess, of	$630,000	$630,000
50. D'backs: Wes Roemer, rhp	$620,000	$621,000
51. Giants: Charlie Culberson, ss	$607,500	$607,500
52. Mariners: Matt Mangini, 3b	$603,000	$603,000
53. Reds: Kyle Lotzkar, rhp	$594,000	$594,000
54. Rangers: Tommy Hunter, rhp	$585,000	$585,000
55. Red Sox: Nick Hagadone, lhp	$571,500	$571,500
56. Jays: Trystan Magnuson, rhp	$462,500	$567,000
57. Padres: Mitch Canham, c	$552,500	$562,500
58. Angels: Jon Bachanov, rhp	$553,300	$553,500
59. Athletics: Corey Brown, of	$544,500	$544,500
60. Tigers: Brandon Hamilton, rhp	$540,000	$540,000
61. Diamondbacks: Ed Easley, c	$531,000	$531,000
62. Red Sox: Ryan Dent, ss	$571,000	$526,500
63. Padres: Cory Luebke, lhp	$515,000	$522,000
64. Padres: Danny Payne, of	$517,500	$517,500

SECOND ROUND

Pick. Team: Player, Pos.	'07 Bonus	'07 Slot
65. Devil Rays: Will Kline, rhp	$513,000	$513,000
66. Royals: Sam Runion, rhp	$504,000	$504,000
67. Nats: Jordan Zimmermann, rhp	$495,000	$495,000
68. Pirates: Duke Welker, rhp	$477,000	$477,000
69. Braves: Joshua Fields, rhp	Unsigned	$472,500
70. Nationals: Jake Smolinski, 3b	$452,500	$463,500
71. Cardinals: David Kopp, rhp	$459,000	$459,000
72. Rockies: Brian Rike, of	$450,000	$450,000
73. D'backs: Barry Enright, rhp	$441,000	$441,000
74. Athletics: Grant Desme, of	$432,000	$432,000
75. Mariners: Denny Almonte, of	$427,500	$427,500
76. Marlins: Mike Stanton, of	$475,000	$418,500
77. Mets: Scott Moviel, rhp	$414,000	$414,000
78. Braves: Freddie Freeman, 1b	$409,500	$409,500
79. Reds: Zack Cozart, ss	$407,250	$407,250
80. Rangers: Matt West, inf	$405,000	$405,000
81. Padres: Eric Sogard, 2b	$400,000	$400,500
82. Cardinals: Jess Todd, rhp	$400,000	$400,500
83. Phillies: Travis Mattair, 3b	$395,000	$396,000
84. Red Sox: Hunter Morris, 3b	Unsigned	$393,750
85. Blue Jays: John Tolisano, 2b	$391,500	$391,500
86. Dodgers: Michael Watt, lhp	$389,000	$389,250
87. Padres: Brad Chalk, of	$300,000	$387,000
88. Blue Jays: Eric Eiland, of	$384,750	$384,750
89. White Sox: Nevin Griffith, rhp	$382,500	$382,500
90. Athletics: Josh Horton, ss	$380,250	$380,250
91. Tigers: Danny Worth, ss	$378,000	$378,000
92. Twins: Danny Rams, c	$375,000	$375,750
93. Mets: Brant Rustich, rhp	$373,500	$373,500
94. Yankees: Austin Romine, c	$500,000	$369,000

THIRD ROUND

Pick. Team: Player, Pos.	'07 Bonus	'07 Slot
95. Devil Rays: Nick Barnese, rhp	$366,000	$366,750
96. Royals: Danny Duffy, lhp	$365,000	$364,500
97. Cubs: Tony Thomas, 2b	$360,000	$360,000
98. Pirates: Brian Friday, ss	$355,500	$355,500
99. Mets: Eric Niesen, lhp	$351,000	$351,000
100. Nationals: Steven Souza, 3b	$346,000	$346,500
101. Brewers: Jonathan Lucroy, c	$340,000	$342,000
102. Rockies: Lars Davis, c	$337,000	$337,500
103. D'backs: Reynaldo Navarro, ss	$333,000	$333,000
104. Reds: Scott Carroll, rhp	$310,000	$324,000
105. Mariners: Danny Carroll, of	$315,000	$315,000
106. Marlins: Jameson Smith, c	$310,000	$292,500
107. Phillies: Brandon Workman, rhp	Unsigned	$288,000
108. Braves: Brandon Hicks, ss	$283,500	$283,500
109. Reds: Neftali Soto, ss	$279,000	$279,000
110. Rangers: Evan Reed, rhp	$274,500	$274,500
111. Astros: Derek Dietrich, 3b	Unsigned	$270,000
112. Cards: Daniel Descalso, 2b/3b	$255,000	$265,500
113. Phillies: Matt Spencer, of	$261,000	$261,000
114. Red Sox: Brock Huntzinger, rhp	$225,000	$258,750
115. Blue Jays: Alan Farina, rhp	$254,250	$254,250
116. Dodgers: Austin Gallagher, 3b	$252,000	$252,000
117. Padres: Tommy Toledo, rhp	Unsigned	$247,500
118. Angels: Matt Harvey, rhp	Unsigned	$243,000
119. White Sox: John Ely, rhp	$240,750	$240,750
120. Athletics: Sam Demel, rhp	$238,500	$238,500
121. Tigers: Luke Putkonen, rhp	$236,000	$236,250
122. Twins: Angel Morales, of	$234,000	$234,000
123. Mets: Stephen Clyne, rhp	$100,000	$231,750
124. Yankees: Ryan Pope, rhp	$229,500	$229,500

FOURTH ROUND

Pick. Team: Player, Pos.	'07 Bonus	'07 Slot
125. Devil Rays: David Newmann, lhp	$250,000	$227,250
126. Royals: Mitch Hodge, rhp	$225,000	$225,000
127. Cubs: Darwin Barney, ss	$222,750	$222,750
128. Pirates: Quincy Latimore, of	$220,000	$220,500
129. Orioles: Tim Bascom, rhp	$200,000	$218,250
130. Nationals: Derek Norris, c	$210,000	$211,500
131. Brewers: Eric Farris, 2b	$207,000	$207,000
132. Rockies: Isaiah Froneberger, lhp	$200,000	$204,750
133. D'backs: Sean Morgan, rhp	$202,500	$202,500
134. Padres: Corey Kluber, rhp	$200,000	$200,250
135. Mariners: Nolan Gallagher, rhp	$193,500	$193,500
136. Marlins: Bryan Petersen, of	$191,250	$191,250
137. Indians: T.J. McFarland, lhp	$285,000	$189,000
138. Braves: Cory Gearrin, rhp	$186,750	$186,750

139. Reds: Blake Stouffer, 3b/of	Unsigned	$184,500
140. Rangers: Garrett Nash, of	Unsigned	$182,250
141. Astros: Brett Eibner, rhp	Unsigned	$180,000
142. Cardinals: Kyle Russell, of	Unsigned	$177,750
143. Phillies: Tyler Mach, 2b	$95,000	$171,000
144. Red Sox: Chris Province, rhp	$120,000	$168,750
145. Blue Jays: Brad Mills, lhp	$140,000	$166,500
146. Dodgers: Andrew Lambo, of/1b	$164,250	$164,250
147. Padres: Lance Zawadzki, ss	$50,000	$162,000
148. Angels: Trevor Pippin, of	$140,000	$159,750
149. White Sox: Leroy Hunt, rhp	$150,000	$157,500
150. Athletics: Travis Banwart, rhp	$155,250	$155,250
151. Tigers: Charlie Furbush, lhp	$153,000	$153,000
152. Twins: Reggie Williams, ss	$153,000	$153,000
153. Mets: Richard Lucas, 3b	$150,000	$150,750
154. Yankees: Brad Suttle, 3b	$1,300,000	$150,750

FIFTH ROUND

Pick. Team: Player, Pos.	'07 Bonus	'07 Slot
155. Devil Rays: Dustin Biell, of	$150,000	$150,300
156. Royals: Adrian Ortiz, of	$149,400	$149,400
157. Cubs: Brandon Guyer, of	$148,000	$148,500
158. Pirates: Andrew Walker, c	$147,600	$147,600
159. Orioles: Jake Arrieta, rhp	$1,100,000	$146,700
160. Nationals: Brad Meyers, rhp	$145,800	$145,800
161. Brewers: Caleb Gindl, of	$144,900	$144,900
162. Rockies: Connor Graham, rhp	$143,000	$144,000
163. D'backs: Tyrell Worthington, of	$220,000	$143,100
164. Giants: Chance Corgan, rhp	$142,200	$142,200
165. Mariners: Joe Dunigan, of	$140,000	$140,400
166. Marlins: Steven Cishek, rhp	$139,500	$139,500
167. Indians: Jonathan Holt, rhp	$138,500	$138,600
168. Braves: Dennis Dixon, of	$137,700	$137,700
169. Reds: Drew Bowman, rhp	$135,000	$136,800
170. Rangers: John Gast, lhp	Unsigned	$135,900
171. Astros: Collin DeLome, of	$135,000	$135,000
172. Cardinals: Thomas Eager, rhp	$134,000	$134,100
173. Phillies: Michael Taylor, of	$131,000	$133,200
174. Red Sox: Will Middlebrooks, 3b	$925,000	$132,300
175. Jays: Marc Rzepczynski, lhp	$110,000	$131,400
176. Dodgers: Kyle Blair, rhp	Unsigned	$130,500
177. Padres: Jeremy Hefner, rhp	$129,000	$129,600
178. Angels: Andrew Romine, ss	$128,700	$128,700
179. White Sox: Nathan Jones, rhp	$127,800	$127,800
180. Athletics: Andrew Carignan, rhp	$126,900	$126,900
181. Tigers: Casey Crosby, lhp	$748,500	$126,000
182. Twins: Nate Striz, rhp	Unsigned	$125,100
183. Mets: Zach Lutz, 3b	$120,000	$124,200
184. Yanks: Adam Olbrychowski, rhp	$123,000	$123,300

2006 DRAFT

FIRST ROUND

No. Team. Player, Pos.	Bonus
1. Royals. Luke Hochevar, rhp	$3,500,000
2. Rockies. Greg Reynolds, rhp	$3,250,000
3. Devil Rays. Evan Longoria, 3b	$3,000,000
4. Pirates. Brad Lincoln, rhp	$2,750,000
5. Mariners. Brandon Morrow, rhp	$2,450,000
6. Tigers. Andrew Miller, lhp	$3,550,000
7. Dodgers. Clayton Kershaw, lhp	$2,300,000
8. Reds. Drew Stubbs, of	$2,000,000
9. Orioles. Bill Rowell, 3b	$2,100,000
10. Giants. Tim Lincecum, rhp	$2,025,000
11. Diamondbacks. Max Scherzer, rhp	$3,000,000
12. Rangers. Kasey Kiker, lhp	$1,600,000
13. Cubs. Tyler Colvin, of	$1,475,000
14. Blue Jays. Travis Snider, of	$1,700,000
15. Nationals. Chris Marrero, of	$1,625,000
16. Brewers. Jeremy Jeffress, rhp	$1,550,000
17. Padres. Matt Antonelli, 3b	$1,575,000
18. Phillies. Kyle Drabek, rhp/ss	$1,550,000
19. Marlins. Brett Sinkbeil, rhp	$1,525,000
20. Twins. Chris Parmelee, of/1b	$1,500,000
21. Yankees. Ian Kennedy, rhp	$2,250,000
22. Nationals. Colton Willems, rhp	$1,425,000
23. Astros. Max Sapp, c	$1,400,000
24. Braves. Cody Johnson, 1b	$1,375,000
25. Angels. Hank Conger, c	$1,350,000
26. Dodgers. Bryan Morris, rhp	$1,325,000
27. Red Sox. Jason Place, of	$1,300,000
28. Red Sox. Daniel Bard, rhp	$1,550,000
29. White Sox. Kyle McCulloch, rhp	$1,050,000
30. Cardinals. Adam Ottavino, rhp	$950,000

SUPPLEMENTAL FIRST ROUND

31. Dodgers. Preston Mattingly, ss	$1,000,000
32. Orioles. Pedro Beato, rhp	$1,000,000
33. Giants. Emmanuel Burriss, ss	$1,000,000
34. Diamondbacks. Brooks Brown, rhp	$900,000
35. Padres. Kyler Burke, of	$950,000
36. Marlins. Chris Coghlan, 3b	$950,000
37. Phillies. Adrian Cardenas, ss	$925,000
38. Braves. Cory Rasmus, rhp	$900,000
39. Indians. David Huff, lhp	$900,000
40. Red Sox. Kris Johnson, lhp	$850,000
41. Yankees. Joba Chamberlain, rhp	$1,150,000
42. Cardinals. Chris Perez, rhp	$800,000
43. Braves. Steve Evarts, lhp	$800,000
44. Red Sox. Caleb Clay, rhp	$775,000

SECOND ROUND

45. Royals. Jason Taylor, of	$762,500
46. Rockies. David Christensen, of	$750,000
47. Devil Rays. Josh Butler, rhp	$725,000
48. Pirates. Mike Felix, lhp	$725,000
49. Mariners. Chris Tillman, rhp	$680,000

50. Tigers. Ronnie Bourquin, 3b	$690,000
51. Braves. Jeff Locke, lhp	$675,000
52. Reds. Sean Watson, rhp	$670,000
53. Padres. Chad Huffman, of	$660,000
54. Cardinals. Brad Furnish, lhp	$600,000
55. Diamondbacks. Brett Anderson, lhp	$950,000
56. Indians. Steven Wright, rhp	$630,000
57. Indians. Josh Rodriguez, ss	$625,000
58. Orioles. Ryan Adams, 2b	$675,000
59. Nationals. Sean Black, rhp	Did Not Sign
60. Brewers. Brent Brewer, ss	$600,000
61. Padres. Wade LeBlanc, lhp	$590,000
62. Mets. Kevin Mulvey, rhp	$585,000
63. Marlins. Tom Hickman, of	$575,000
64. Twins. Joe Benson, of	$575,000
65. Phillies. Drew Carpenter, rhp	$570,000
66. Athletics. Trevor Cahill, rhp	$560,000
67. Astros. Sergio Perez, rhp	$550,000
68. Braves. Dustin Evans, rhp	$530,000
69. Indians. Wes Hodges, 3b	$1,000,000
70. Nationals. Stephen Englund, of	$515,000
71. Red Sox. Justin Masterson, rhp	$510,000
72. Braves. Chase Fontaine, ss	$500,000
73. White Sox. Matt Long, rhp	$330,000
74. Cardinals. Jon Jay, of	$480,000

SUPPLEMENTAL SECOND ROUND

75. Indians. Matt McBride, c	$445,000
76. Cardinals. Mark Hamilton, 1b	$465,000

THIRD ROUND

77. Royals. Blake Wood, rhp	$460,000
78. Rockies. Keith Weiser, lhp	$455,000
79. Devil Rays. Nick Fuller, rhp	Did Not Sign
80. Pirates. Shelby Ford, 2b	$450,000
81. Mariners. Tony Butler, lhp	$445,000
82. Tigers. Brennan Boesch, of	$445,000
83. Red Sox. Aaron Bates, 1b	$440,000
84. Reds. Chris Valaika, ss	$437,500
85. Orioles. Zach Britton, lhp	$435,000
86. Diamondbacks. Dallas Buck, rhp	$250,000
87. Diamondbacks. Cyle Hankerd, of	$430,000
88. Rangers. Chad Tracy, c	$427,500
89. Giants. Clayton Tanner, lhp	$425,000
90. Marlins. Torre Langley, c	$422,500
91. Nationals. Stephen King, ss	$750,000
92. Brewers. Cole Gillespie, of	$417,500
93. Padres. Cedric Hunter, of	$415,000
94. Mets. Joe Smith, rhp	$410,000
95. Marlins. Scott Cousins, of	$407,500
96. Twins. Tyler Robertson, lhp	$405,000
97. Phillies. Jason Donald, ss	$400,000
98. Athletics. Matt Sulentic, of	$395,000
99. Astros. Nick Moresi, of	$390,000
100. Braves. Chad Rodgers, lhp	$385,000

2005 DRAFT

TOP 100 PICKS

FIRST ROUND

No. Team. Player, Pos.	Bonus
1. Diamondbacks. Justin Upton, ss	$6,100,000
2. Royals. Alex Gordon, 3b	$4,000,000
3. Mariners. Jeff Clement, c	$3,400,000
4. Nationals. Ryan Zimmerman, 3b	$2,975,000
5. Brewers. Ryan Braun, 3b	$2,450,000
6. Blue Jays. Ricky Romero, lhp	$2,400,000
7. Rockies. Troy Tulowitzki, ss	$2,300,000
8. Devil Rays. Wade Townsend, rhp	$1,500,000
9. Mets. Mike Pelfrey, rhp	$3,550,000
10. Tigers. Cameron Maybin, of	$2,650,000
11. Pirates. Andrew McCutchen, of	$1,900,000
12. Reds. Jay Bruce, of	$1,800,000
13. Orioles. Brandon Snyder, c	$1,700,000
14. Indians. Trevor Crowe, of	$1,695,000
15. White Sox. Lance Broadway, rhp	$1,570,000
16. Marlins. Chris Volstad, rhp	$1,600,000
17. Yankees. C.J. Henry, ss	$1,575,000
18. Padres. Cesar Carrillo, rhp	$1,550,000
19. Rangers. John Mayberry, of	$1,525,000
20. Cubs. Mark Pawelek, lhp	$1,750,000
21. Athletics. Cliff Pennington, ss	$1,475,000
22. Marlins. Aaron Thompson, lhp	$1,225,000
23. Red Sox. Jacoby Ellsbury, of	$1,400,000
24. Astros. Brian Bogusevic, lhp	$1,375,000
25. Twins. Matt Garza, rhp	$1,350,000
26. Red Sox. Craig Hansen, rhp	$1,325,000
27. Braves. Joey Devine, rhp	$1,300,000
28. Cardinals. Colby Rasmus, of	$1,000,000
29. Marlins. Jacob Marceaux, rhp	$1,000,000
30. Cardinals. Tyler Greene, ss	$1,100,000

SUPPLEMENTAL FIRST ROUND

31. Diamondbacks. Matt Torra, rhp	$1,025,000
32. Rockies. Chaz Roe, rhp	$1,025,000
33. Indians. John Drennen, of	$1,000,000
34. Marlins. Ryan Tucker, rhp	$975,000
35. Padres. Cesar Ramos, lhp	$950,000
36. Athletics. Travis Buck, of	$950,000
37. Angels. Trevor Bell, rhp	$925,000
38. Astros. Eli Iorg, of	$900,000
39. Twins. Henry Sanchez, 1b	$900,000
40. Dodgers. Luke Hochevar, rhp	Did Not Sign
41. Braves. Beau Jones, lhp	$825,000
42. Red Sox. Clay Buchholz, rhp	$800,000
43. Cardinals. Mark McCormick, rhp	$800,000
44. Marlins. Sean West, lhp	$775,000
45. Red Sox. Jed Lowrie, 2b	$762,500
46. Cardinals. Tyler Herron, rhp	$675,000
47. Red Sox. Michael Bowden, rhp	$730,000
48. Orioles. Garrett Olson, lhp	$650,000

SECOND ROUND

49. Diamondbacks. Matt Green, rhp	$500,000
50. Royals. Jeff Bianchi, ss	$690,000
51. Dodgers. Ivan DeJesus Jr., ss	$675,000
52. Rockies. Daniel Carte, of	$670,000
53. Athletics. Craig Italiano, rhp	$725,500
54. Twins. Paul Kelly, ss	$650,000
55. Rockies. Zach Simons, rhp	$635,000
56. Devil Rays. Chris Mason, rhp	$630,000
57. Red Sox. Jon Egan, c	$625,000
58. Angels. Ryan Mount, ss	$615,000
59. Pirates. Brad Corley, of	$605,000
60. Reds. Travis Wood, lhp	$600,000
61. Orioles. Nolan Reimold, of	$590,000
62. Indians. Stephen Head, 1b	$605,000
63. Yankees. J. Brent Cox, rhp	$550,000
64. Marlins. Kris Harvey, of	$575,000
65. Phillies. Mike Costanzo, 3b	$570,000
66. Padres. Chase Headley, 3b	$560,000
67. Rangers. Johnny Whittleman, 3b	$650,000
68. Cubs. Donald Veal, lhp	$530,000
69. Athletics. Jared Lansford, rhp	$525,000
70. Cardinals. Josh Wilson, rhp	$515,000
71. Angels. P.J. Phillips, ss	$505,000
72. Astros. Ralph Henriquez, c	$485,000
73. Twins. Kevin Slowey, rhp	$490,000
74. Dodgers. Josh Wall, rhp	$480,000
75. Braves. Yunel Escobar, ss	$475,000
76. Padres. Nick Hundley, c	$465,000
77. Braves. Jeff Lyman, rhp	$460,000
78. Cardinals. Nick Webber, rhp	$425,000

SUPPLEMENTAL SECOND ROUND

79. Marlins. Brett Hayes, c	$450,000
80. Twins. Drew Thompson, ss	$475,000

THIRD ROUND

81. Diamondbacks. Jason Neighborgall, rhp	$500,000
82. Royals. Chris Nicoll, rhp	$445,000
83. Diamondbacks. Micah Owings, rhp	$440,000
84. Twins. Brian Duensing, lhp	$400,000
85. Brewers. Will Inman, rhp	$500,000
86. Blue Jays. Brian Pettway, of	$440,000
87. Rockies. Kyle Hancock, rhp	Contract Voided
88. Devil Rays. Bryan Morris, rhp	Did Not Sign
89. Astros. Tommy Manzella, ss	$289,000
90. Tigers. Chris Robinson, c	$422,000
91. Pirates. James Boone, of	$420,000
92. Reds. Zach Ward, rhp	$420,000
93. Orioles. Brandon Erbe, rhp	$415,000
94. Indians. Nick Weglarz, 1b	$435,000
95. White Sox. Ricky Brooks, rhp	$300,000
96. Marlins. Matt Goyen, lhp	$340,000
97. Phillies. Matt Maloney, lhp	$400,000
98. Padres. Josh Geer, rhp	$395,000
99. Rangers. Taylor Teagarden, c	$725,000
100. Cubs. Mark Holliman, rhp	$385,000

COLLEGE TOP 100

Rank	Player	Pos.	Class	B-T	Ht.	Wt.	School
1.	Pedro Alvarez	3b	Jr.	L-R	6-2	225	Vanderbilt
2.	Aaron Crow	rhp	Jr.	R-R	6-2	195	Missouri
3.	Justin Smoak	1b	Jr.	B-L	6-4	215	South Carolina
4.	Brian Matusz	lhp	Jr.	L-L	6-4	193	San Diego
5.	Yonder Alonso	1b	Jr.	L-L	6-2	215	Miami
6.	Christian Friedrich	lhp	Jr.	R-L	6-3	208	Eastern Kentucky
7.	Brett Hunter	rhp	Jr.	R-R	6-4	215	Pepperdine
8.	Jacob Thompson	rhp	Jr.	R-R	6-6	215	Virginia
9.	Dennis Raben	of	Jr.	L-L	6-3	220	Miami
10.	Brandon Crawford	ss	Jr.	L-R	6-2	200	UCLA
11.	Tyson Ross	rhp	Jr.	R-R	6-5	215	California
12.	Scott Green	rhp	Jr.	R-R	6-8	240	Kentucky
13.	Shooter Hunt	rhp	Jr.	R-R	6-3	200	Tulane
14.	Luke Burnett	rhp	Jr.	R-R	6-8	260	Louisiana Tech
15.	Ryan Perry	rhp	Jr.	R-R	6-4	200	Arizona
16.	Gordon Beckham	ss	Jr.	R-R	6-0	181	Georgia
17.	Buster Posey	c	Jr.	R-R	6-2	200	Florida State
18.	Tim Murphy	lhp	Jr.	L-L	6-2	205	UCLA
19.	Jemile Weeks	2b	Jr.	B-R	5-9	165	Miami
20.	Aaron Shafer	rhp	Jr.	L-R	6-4	205	Wichita State
21.	Conor Gillaspie	3b	Jr.	L-R	6-1	200	Wichita State
22.	Roger Kieschnick	of	Jr.	L-R	6-3	210	Texas Tech
23.	Cody Satterwhite	rhp	Jr.	R-R	6-4	205	Mississippi
24.	Allan Dykstra	1b	Jr.	L-R	6-5	225	Wake Forest
25.	James Darnell	3b	Jr.	R-R	6-2	195	South Carolina
26.	Lance Lynn	rhp	Jr.	R-R	6-5	260	Mississippi
27.	Joshua Fields	rhp	Sr.	R-R	6-0	180	Georgia
28.	Brett Wallace	1b	Jr.	L-R	6-1	245	Arizona State
29.	Ryan Flaherty	ss	Jr.	L-R	6-2	205	Vanderbilt
30.	Josh Romanski	lhp/of	Jr.	L-L	6-0	180	San Diego
31.	Preston Guilmet	rhp	Jr.	R-R	6-2	190	Arizona
32.	David Duncan	lhp	Jr.	L-L	6-8	201	Georgia Tech
33.	Brett Jacobson	rhp	Jr.	R-R	6-6	205	Vanderbilt
34.	Reese Havens	ss	Jr.	L-R	6-1	195	South Carolina
35.	Petey Paramore	c	Jr.	B-R	6-2	215	Arizona State
36.	Preston Clark	c	Jr.	R-R	5-11	212	Texas
37.	Logan Forsythe	3b/of	Jr.	R-R	6-0	195	Arkansas
38.	Jordan Danks	of	Jr.	L-L	6-5	209	Texas
39.	Kyle Russell	of	Jr.	L-L	6-5	185	Texas
40.	Scott Barnes	lhp	Jr.	L-L	6-3	185	St. John's
41.	D.J. Mitchell	rhp	Jr.	R-R	6-0	160	Clemson
42.	Stephen Porlier	rhp	Jr.	R-R	6-3	210	Oklahoma
43.	Chris Carpenter	rhp	Jr.	R-R	6-4	210	Kent State
44.	Cole St. Clair	lhp	Sr.	L-L	6-5	225	Rice
45.	Ryan Hinson	lhp	Jr.	L-L	6-2	220	Clemson
46.	Jermaine Curtis	3b	Jr.	R-R	6-1	190	UCLA
47.	Cody Adams	rhp	Jr.	R-R	6-2	180	Southern Illinois
48.	Shane Peterson	of/1b	Jr.	L-L	6-0	185	Long Beach State
49.	Evan Crawford	lhp	Jr.	R-L	6-1	185	Auburn
50.	Eric Surkamp	lhp	Jr.	L-L	6-5	216	North Carolina State

Rank	Player	Pos.	Class	B-T	Ht.	Wt.	School
51.	David Adams	2b	Jr.	R-R	6-2	210	Virginia
52.	Zach Putnam	rhp/of	Jr.	R-R	6-2	215	Michigan
53.	Josh Lindblom	rhp	Jr.	R-R	6-5	240	Purdue
54.	Dominic de la Osa	of	Sr.	R-R	6-0	205	Vanderbilt
55.	David Cooper	1b	Jr.	L-L	6-0	185	California
56.	Mitch Harris	rhp	Sr.	R-R	6-4	215	Navy
57.	Scott Gorgen	rhp	Jr.	R-R	5-10	190	UC Irvine
58.	Tanner Scheppers	rhp	Jr.	R-R	6-4	200	Fresno State
59.	Kyle Weiland	rhp	Jr.	L-R	6-3	190	Notre Dame
60.	Jeremy Bleich	lhp	Jr.	L-L	6-2	190	Stanford
61.	Dan Brewer	of/inf	Jr.	R-R	6-0	180	Bradley
62.	Aaron Weatherford	rhp	Jr.	R-R	6-0	189	Mississippi State
63.	Bryan Shaw	rhp	Jr.	B-R	6-1	172	Long Beach State
64.	Chris Gloor	lhp	Jr.	L-L	6-6	255	Quinnipiac
65.	Jeremy Farrell	3b	Jr.	R-R	6-4	215	Virginia
66.	Tim Federowicz	c/rhp	Jr.	R-R	5-10	198	North Carolina
67.	Mike Bianucci	of	Jr.	R-R	6-1	210	Auburn
68.	Ike Davis	of/lhp	Jr.	L-L	6-4	205	Arizona State
69.	Jason Castro	c/1b/of	Jr.	L-R	6-3	210	Stanford
70.	Stephen Penney	rhp	Jr.	R-R	6-7	240	UC Riverside
71.	Dan Hudson	rhp	Jr.	R-R	6-4	215	Old Dominion
72.	Jordy Mercer	rhp/ss	Jr.	R-R	6-3	192	Oklahoma State
73.	Danny Espinosa	ss	Jr.	B-R	6-0	185	Long Beach State
74.	Nick Buss	of	Jr.	L-R	6-1	180	Southern California
75.	Wade Miley	lhp	Jr.	L-L	6-2	195	Southeastern Louisiana
76.	Nate Newman	rhp	Jr.	R-R	6-5	210	Pepperdine
77.	Blake Stouffer	3b/of	Sr.	B-R	6-1	185	Texas A&M
78.	Ryan Babineau	c	Jr.	R-R	6-2	205	UCLA
79.	Matt Clark	1b	Jr.	L-R	6-5	230	Louisiana State
80.	Matt Hague	3b/of/rhp	Sr.	R-R	6-3	225	Oklahoma State
81.	Mark Sobolewski	of/3b	So.	R-R	6-1	195	Miami
82.	Vance Worley	rhp	Jr.	R-R	6-2	200	Long Beach State
83.	Mike Colla	rhp	Jr.	R-R	6-2	230	Arizona
84.	Austin Wood	lhp	Jr.	L-L	6-2	200	Texas
85.	Beamer Weems	ss	Jr.	B-R	5-10	176	Baylor
86.	Bryce Stowell	rhp	So.	R-R	6-2	205	UC Irvine
87.	Luke Greinke	rhp/of	Jr.	R-R	6-0	187	Auburn
88.	Eric Thames	of	Jr.	L-R	6-1	197	Pepperdine
89.	Jericho Jones	of/rhp	Jr.	R-R	6-5	205	Louisiana Tech
90.	Blake Tekotte	of	Jr.	L-R	6-0	175	Miami
91.	T.J. Steele	of	Jr.	R-R	6-3	200	Arizona
92.	Sam Brown	rhp	So.	R-R	6-3	202	North Carolina State
93.	Dexter Carter	rhp	Jr.	R-R	6-6	198	Old Dominion
94.	Aaron Luna	2b/of	Jr.	R-R	5-11	200	Rice
95.	Brian Pruitt	of	Jr.	R-R	6-1	200	Stetson
96.	Luke Murton	1b	Jr.	R-R	6-4	240	Georgia Tech
97.	Steven Hensley	rhp	Jr.	R-R	6-3	190	Elon
98.	Eddie Burns	rhp	Jr.	R-R	6-8	220	Georgia Tech
99.	Matt Daly	rhp	Jr.	R-R	5-10	185	Hawaii
100.	Chris Dominguez	3b	So.	R-R	6-4	240	Louisville

HIGH SCHOOL TOP 100

(All are seniors who graduate in the Class of 2008)

Rank	Player	Pos.	B-T	Ht.	Wt.	School
1.	Tim Melville	rhp	R-R	6-4	190	Holt High, Wentzville, Mo.
2.	Tim Beckham	ss	R-R	6-1	180	Griffin (Ga.) HS
3.	Harold Martinez	3b	R-R	6-3	195	Braddock HS, Miami
4.	Eric Hosmer	1b	L-L	6-3	210	American Heritage HS, Plantation, Fla.
5.	Alex Meyer	rhp	R-R	6-7	200	Greensburg (Ind.) HS
6.	Sonny Gray	rhp	R-R	6-0	185	Smyrna (Tenn.) HS
7.	Kyle Lobstein	lhp	L-L	6-3	185	Coconino HS, Flagstaff, Ariz.
8.	Kyle Skipworth	c	L-R	6-3	185	Patriot HS, Riverside, Calif.
9.	Gerrit Cole	rhp	R-R	6-2	175	Lutheran HS, Orange, Calif.
10.	Aaron Hicks	of/rhp	B-R	6-1	165	Wilson HS, Long Beach
11.	Isaac Galloway	of	R-R	6-2	190	Los Osos HS, Rancho Cucamonga, Calif.
12.	Jarret Martin	lhp	L-L	6-2	180	Centennial HS, Bakersfield, Calif.
13.	Robbie Grossman	of	B-L	6-0	195	Cy-Fair HS, Cypress, Texas
14.	Adrian Nieto	c	B-R	6-0	195	American Heritage HS, Plantation, Fla.
15.	Casey Kelly	ss	R-R	6-3	190	Sarasota (Fla.) HS
16.	Ethan Martin	3b	R-R	6-3	185	Stephens County HS, Toccoa, Ga.
17.	Robbie Ross	lhp	L-L	5-11	180	Lexington (Ky.) Christian Academy
18.	Brett DeVall	lhp	L-L	6-4	205	Niceville (Fla.) HS
19.	Nick Maronde	lhp	B-L	6-3	195	Lexington (Ky.) Catholic HS
20.	Michael Palazzone	rhp	R-R	6-3	190	Lassiter HS, Marietta, Ga.
21.	Rolando Gomez	2b/ss	L-R	5-9	155	Flanagan HS, Pembroke Pines, Fla.
22.	Anthony Gose	lhp/of	L-L	5-11	160	Bellflower (Calif.) HS
23.	Matt Lollis	rhp	R-R	6-7	210	Rubidoux (Calif.) HS
24.	Zack Cox	3b/c	L-R	6-0	205	Pleasure Ridge Park HS, Lexington, Ky.
25.	Xavier Avery	of	L-L	6-0	160	Cedar Grove HS, Ellenwood, Ga.
26.	Daniel Webb	rhp	R-R	6-2	205	Heath HS, West Paducah, Ky.
27.	Cecil Tanner	rhp	R-R	6-6	190	Ware County HS, Waycross, Ga.
28.	B.J. Hermsen	rhp	R-R	6-6	230	West Delaware HS, Manchester, Iowa
29.	Scott Silverstein	lhp	L-L	6-5	210	St. John's College HS, Washington, D.C.
30.	Bobby Bundy	rhp	R-R	6-2	205	Sperry (Okla.) HS
31.	Tyler Chatwood	of/c	R-R	6-0	175	East Valley HS, Redlands, Calif.
32.	Brian Humphries	of	L-R	6-3	170	Granite Hills HS, El Cajon, Calif.
33.	Austin Dicharry	rhp	R-R	6-2	190	Klein-Collins HS, Spring, Texas
34.	Steven Upchurch	rhp	R-R	6-4	180	Faith Academy, Mobile, Ala.
35.	L.J. Hoes	of	R-R	6-0	175	St. John's College HS, Washington, D.C.
36.	Miles Reagan	rhp	R-R	6-2	190	El Capitan HS, Lakeside, Calif.
37.	Destin Hood	of	R-R	6-2	180	Saint Paul's Episcopal HS, Mobile, Ala.
38.	Andy Burns	3b/2b	R-R	6-1	180	Rocky Mountain HS, Fort Collins, Colo.
39.	T.J. House	lhp	R-L	6-2	190	Picayune (Miss.) HS
40.	Matt Ramsey	c/rhp	R-R	5-11	180	Farragut HS, Knoxville
41.	Cutter Dykstra	2b/ss	R-R	6-0	175	Westlake HS, Westlake Village, Calif.
42.	Donn Roach	rhp	R-R	6-1	175	Bishop Gorman HS, Las Vegas
43.	Mike Montgomery	lhp	L-L	6-4	170	Hart HS, Newhall, Calif.
44.	Zeke Spruill	rhp	R-R	6-3	185	Etowah HS, Woodstock, Ga.
45.	Tyler Yockey	of	L-L	6-1	196	Acadiana HS, Lafayette, La.
46.	Trey Haley	rhp	R-R	6-4	185	San Augustine (Texas) HS
47.	Conner Mach	2b	R-R	6-1	189	Parkway West HS, Ballwin, Mo.
48.	Corban Joseph	ss/2b	L-R	6-0	168	Franklin (Tenn.) HS
49.	Niko Vasquez	ss	R-R	6-0	175	Durango HS, Las Vegas
50.	Ryan Rieger	1b	L-L	6-0	185	Woodcreek HS, Roseville, Calif.

Rank	Player	Pos.	B-T	Ht.	Wt.	School
51.	Tyler Massey	1b/of	L-L	6-0	205	Baylor School, Chattanooga, Tenn.
52.	Garrison Lassiter	ss	L-R	6-2	175	West Forsyth HS, Clemmons, N.C.
53.	Mike Tonkin	rhp	R-R	6-6	185	Palmdale (Calif.) HS
54.	Kyle Long	lhp/1b	L-L	6-7	280	Saint Anne's-Belfield HS, Charlottesville, Va.
55.	Grayson Garvin	lhp	L-L	6-5	180	Wesleyan School, Norcross, Ga.
56.	Riccio Torrez	2b	R-R	6-0	190	Brophy Prep, Phoenix
57.	Austin Wright	lhp	L-L	6-4	195	Conant HS, Hoffman Estates, Ill.
58.	Taylor Jungmann	rhp	R-R	6-5	175	Georgetown (Texas) HS
59.	Bobby Crocker	of/rhp	R-R	6-3	195	Aptos (Calif.) HS
60.	Randall Thorpe	of	R-R	6-0	170	Heritage HS, Colleyville, Texas
61.	Jordan Swagerty	rhp	B-R	6-1	175	Prestonwood Christian Academy, Plano, Texas
62.	Jordan Cooper	rhp	R-R	6-2	195	Shawnee Heights HS, Tecumseh, Kan.
63.	Jason Esposito	3b	R-R	6-2	185	Amity HS, Woodbridge, Conn.
64.	Mac Williamson	rhp	R-R	6-3	202	Wake Forest-Rolesville HS, Wake Forest, N.C.
65.	Shawn Armstrong	rhp	R-R	6-2	181	West Craven HS, Vanceboro, N.C.
66.	Jake Odorizzi	rhp	R-R	6-2	175	Highland (Ill.) HS
67.	Tyler Thompson	of	R-R	6-0	170	Jupiter (Fla.) HS
68.	Ryan O'Sullivan	rhp/ss	R-R	6-1	170	Valhalla HS, El Cajon, Calif.
69.	Chris Amezquita	3b/rhp	R-R	6-1	168	Servite HS, Anaheim
70.	Jarrod McKinney	of/c	R-R	6-0	205	Hughes Springs (Texas) HS
71.	Chase Davidson	1b	L-R	6-5	216	Milton (Ga.) HS
72.	Jeremy Rathjen	of	R-R	6-4	175	Memorial HS, Houston
73.	Brent Warren	of	L-L	6-2	155	Xavier HS, Cedar Rapids, Iowa
74.	J.P. Ramirez	of	L-L	5-11	185	Canyon (Texas) HS
75.	Anthony DeSclafani	rhp	R-R	6-3	175	Colts Neck (N.J.) HS
76.	Tyler Stovall	lhp/of	L-L	6-2	190	Hokes Bluff (Ala.) HS
77.	Ben Grisz	rhp	R-R	6-1	210	St. Mark's School, Dallas
78.	D.J. Hicks	1b	L-R	6-5	205	Lake Brantley HS, Altamonte Springs, Fla.
79.	Quinton Miller	rhp	R-R	6-2	170	Shawnee HS, Medford, N.J.
80.	Matt Marquis	of	R-R	6-2	190	Immaculata HS, Sommerville, N.J.
81.	Ross Seaton	rhp	L-R	6-4	185	Second Baptist HS, Houston
82.	Jason Hanson	2b/ss	R-R	6-0	180	Sabino HS, Tucson, Ariz.
83.	Scott Weismann	rhp	R-R	6-0	172	Acton-Boxborough Regional HS, Acton, Mass.
84.	Tyler Rahmatulla	ss	R-R	5-10	165	Mater Dei HS, Santa Ana, Calif.
85.	Jason Knapp	rhp	R-R	6-5	235	North Hunterdon HS, Annandale, N.J.
86.	Clark Murphy	1b	L-L	6-3	195	Fallbrook (Calif.) HS
87.	Tyler Pastornicky	ss	R-R	5-11	165	Pendleton School, Bradenton, Fla.
88.	Josh Poytress	rhp	R-R	6-0	170	Fowler (Calif.) HS
89.	Taylor Hightower	c	R-R	6-1	190	Cartersville (Ga.) HS
90.	Brian Litwin	of/3b	R-R	6-2	185	St. Stephens HS, Conover, N.C.
91.	Ricky Oropesa	1b	L-R	6-2	215	Etiwanda (Calif.) HS
92.	Jarred Cosart	rhp	R-R	6-3	175	Clear Creek HS, League City, Texas
93.	Ryan Gorton	c/rhp	R-R	6-2	185	Tigard (Ore.) HS
94.	Brennan May	of	R-R	6-0	185	Woodward Academy, Atlanta
95.	Ryan Weber	rhp	R-R	6-0	170	Clearwater (Fla.) Central Catholic HS
96.	Taylor Featherston	ss	R-R	6-0	175	Taylor HS, Katy, Texas
97.	Anthony Rendon	of	R-R	5-11	160	Lamar HS, Houston
98.	Ben McMahan	c	R-R	6-0	192	Bishop Moore HS, Orlando
99.	Bryce Robinson	lhp	L-L	6-0	170	Kokomo (Ind.) HS
100.	Greg Larson	rhp	R-R	6-8	205	Lake Brantley HS, Altamonte Springs, Fla.

FROM EVERY MINOR LEAGUE

As a complement to our organizational prospect rankings, Baseball America also ranks prospects in every minor league after each season. Like the organizational lists, they place more weight on potential than present performance and should not be regarded as minor league all-star teams.

The league lists do differ from the organizational lists, which are taken more from a scouting perspective. The league lists are based on conversations with league managers as well as scouts. They are not strictly polls, though we do try to talk with every manager. Some players on these lists, such as Justin Upton and Yovani Gallardo, were not eligible for our organization prospect lists because they are no longer rookie-eligible. Such players are indicated with an asterisk. Players who have moved from the organizations they are listed with are indicated with a pound sign.

Remember that managers and scouts tend to look at players differently. Managers give more weight to what a player does on the field, while scouts look at what a player might eventually do. We think both perspectives are useful, so we give you both, even though they don't always match up with each other.

For a player to qualify for a league prospect list, he much have spent at least one-third of the season in a league. Position players must have one plate appearance per league game. Pitchers must pitch ⅓ inning per league game. Relievers must make at least 20 appearances in a full-season league or 10 appearances in a short-season league.

TRIPLE-A

INTERNATIONAL LEAGUE

1. Jay Bruce, of, Louisville (Reds)
2. Homer Bailey, rhp, Louisville (Reds)
3. *#Matt Garza, rhp, Rochester (Twins)
4. *Josh Fields, 3b, Charlotte (White Sox)
5. Jed Lowrie, ss, Pawtucket (Red Sox)
6. Jacoby Ellsbury, of, Pawtucket (Red Sox)
7. Brent Lillibridge, ss, Richmond (Braves)
8. *Yunel Escobar, ss, Richmond (Braves)
9. Jeff Niemann, rhp, Durham (Devil Rays)
10. Joey Votto, 1b/of, Louisville (Reds)
11. Adam Miller, rhp, Buffalo (Indians)
12. Garrett Olson, lhp, Norfolk (Orioles)
13. Brandon Moss, of, Pawtucket (Red Sox)
14. Brandon Jones, of, Richmond (Braves)
15. *Adam Lind, of, Syracuse (Blue Jays)
16. Collin Balester, rhp, Columbus (Nationals)
17. *Jason Hammel, rhp, Durham (Devil Rays)
18. *Kevin Slowey, rhp, Rochester (Twins)
19. Aaron Laffey, lhp, Buffalo (Indians)
20. #Jason Pridie, of, Durham (Devil Rays)

PACIFIC COAST LEAGUE

1. *Yovani Gallardo, rhp, Nashville (Brewers)
2. *Adam Jones, of, Tacoma (Mariners)
3. *Billy Butler, of/1b, Omaha (Royals)

4. Andy LaRoche, 3b, Las Vegas (Dodgers)
5. Ian Stewart, 3b, Colorado Springs (Rockies)
6. *Felix Pie, of, Iowa (Cubs)
7. Carlos Gomez, of, New Orleans (Mets)
8. *James Loney, 1b/of, Las Vegas (Dodgers)
9. Brandon Wood, 3b/ss, Salt Lake (Angels)
10. Luke Hochevar, rhp, Omaha (Royals)
11. Jeff Clement, c, Tacoma (Mariners)
12. *Mike Pelfrey, rhp, New Orleans (Mets)
13. *Edinson Volquez, rhp, Oklahoma (Rangers)
14. Wladimir Balentien, of, Tacoma (Mariners)
15. #Troy Patton, lhp, Round Rock (Astros)
16. Eric Hurley, rhp, Oklahoma (Rangers)
17. Billy Buckner, rhp, Omaha (Royals)
18. Chin-Lung Hu, ss, Las Vegas (Dodgers)
19. Daric Barton, 1b, Sacramento (Athletics)
20. Geovany Soto, c/1b, Iowa (Cubs)

DOUBLE-A

EASTERN LEAGUE

1. Clay Buchholz, rhp, Portland (Boston)
2. Andrew McCutchen, of, Altoona (Pirates)
3. Fernando Martinez, of, Binghamton (Mets)
4. *Asdrubal Cabrera, ss, Akron (Indians)
5. Ian Kennedy, rhp, Trenton (Yankees)
6. #Jair Jurrjens, rhp, Erie (Tigers)
7. Alan Horne, rhp, Trenton (Yankees)
8. Jed Lowrie, ss, Portland (Red Sox)
9. Neil Walker, 3b, Altoona (Pirates)
10. Collin Balester, rhp, Harrisburg (Nationals)
11. Jordan Brown, 1b/of, Akron (Indians)
12. Radhames Liz, rhp, Bowie (Orioles)
13. Justin Masterson, rhp, Portland (Red Sox)
14. *Kyle Kendrick, rhp, Reading (Phillies)
15. Chuck Lofgren, lhp, Akron (Indians)
16. Jeff Larish, 1b, Erie (Tigers)
17. #Brian Barton, of, Akron (Indians)
18. Brian Duensing, lhp, New Britain (Twins)
19. #Mike Costanzo, 3b, Reading (Phillies)
20. Nolan Reimold, of, Bowie (Orioles)

SOUTHERN LEAGUE

1. *Justin Upton, of, Mobile (Diamondbacks)
2. Evan Longoria, 3b, Montgomery (Devil Rays)
3. Wade Davis, rhp, Montgomery (Devil Rays)
4. Johnny Cueto, rhp, Chattanooga (Reds)
5. Brandon Jones, of, Mississippi (Braves)
6. Reid Brignac, ss, Montgomery (Devil Rays)
7. Tyler Colvin, of, Tennessee (Cubs)
8. Manny Parra, lhp, Huntsville (Brewers)
9. Gio Gonzalez, lhp, Birmingham (White Sox)
10. Carlos Gonzalez, of, Mobile (Diamondbacks)
11. *Mark Reynolds, 3b, Mobile (Diamondbacks)
12. Chin-Lung Hu, ss, Jacksonville (Dodgers)
13. Brent Lillibridge, ss, Mississippi (Braves)
14. Jonathan Meloan, rhp, Jacksonville (Dodgers)
15. Max Scherzer, rhp, Mobile (Diamondbacks)
16. Jo Jo Reyes, lhp, Mississippi (Braves)
17. Diory Hernandez, ss, Mississippi (Braves)
18. James McDonald, rhp, Jacksonville (Dodgers)
19. Gaby Hernandez, rhp, Carolina (Marlins)
20. Alcides Escobar, ss, Huntsville (Brewers)

TEXAS LEAGUE

1. Colby Rasmus, of, Springfield (Cardinals)
2. Chase Headley, 3b, San Antonio (Padres)
3. Nick Adenhart, rhp, Arkansas (Angels)
4. Greg Reynolds, rhp, Tulsa (Rockies)
5. Luke Hochevar, rhp, Wichita (Royals)
6. Matt Antonelli, 2b, San Antonio (Padres)
7. Franklin Morales, lhp, Tulsa (Rockies)
8. Eric Hurley, rhp, Frisco (Rangers)
9. #Troy Patton, lhp, Corpus Christi (Astros)
10. J.R. Towles, c, Corpus Christi (Astros)
11. Chris Perez, rhp, Springfield (Cardinals)
12. Jaime Garcia, lhp, Springfield (Cardinals)
13. Juan Morillo, rhp, Tulsa (Rockies)
14. German Duran, 2b, Frisco (Rangers)
15. Sean Rodriguez, ss, Arkansas (Angels)
16. Felipe Paulino, rhp, Corpus Christi (Astros)
17. Bryan Anderson, c, Springfield (Cardinals)
18. Richie Robnett, of, Midland (Athletics)
19. Josh Geer, rhp, San Antonio (Padres)
20. Joe Mather, of, Springfield (Cardinals)

FLORIDA STATE LEAGUE

1. Jay Bruce, of, Sarasota (Reds)
2. #Cameron Maybin, of, Lakeland (Tigers)
3. Jake McGee, lhp, Vero Beach (Devil Rays)
4. Wade Davis, rhp, Vero Beach (Devil Rays)
5. Johnny Cueto, rhp, Sarasota (Reds)
6. Carlos Carrasco, rhp, Clearwater (Phillies)
7. Ian Kennedy, rhp, Tampa (Yankees)
8. Deolis Guerra, rhp, St. Lucie (Mets)
9. Jose Tabata, of, Tampa (Yankees)
10. Austin Jackson, of, Tampa (Yankees)
11. Chris Volstad, rhp, Jupiter (Marlins)
12. Alcides Escobar, ss, Brevard County (Brewers)
13. Tyler Colvin, of, Daytona (Cubs)
14. Josh Outman, lhp, Clearwater (Phillies)
15. Adam Ottavino, rhp, Palm Beach (Cardinals)
16. Brett Sinkbeil, rhp, Jupiter (Marlins)
17. Frank Cervelli, c, Tampa (Yankees)
18. #Eduardo Morlan, rhp, Fort Myers (Twins)
19. Jeff Samardzija, rhp, Daytona (Cubs)
20. Rhyne Hughes, 1b, Vero Beach (Devil Rays)

HIGH CLASS A

CALIFORNIA LEAGUE

1. *Justin Upton, of, Visalia (Diamondbacks)
2. Henry Sosa, rhp, San Jose (Giants)
3. Chris Tillman, rhp, High Desert (Mariners)
4. Matt Antonelli, 2b, Lake Elsinore (Padres)
5. Justin Masterson, rhp, Lancaster (Red Sox)
6. Carlos Triunfel, ss, High Desert (Mariners)
7. James McDonald, rhp, Inland Empire (Dodgers)
8. Chris Nelson, ss, Modesto (Rockies)
9. Chris Davis, 3b, Bakersfield (Rangers)
10. Dexter Fowler, of, Modesto (Rockies)
11. Brandon Hynick, rhp, Modesto (Rockies)
12. Wade LeBlanc, lhp, Lake Elsinore (Padres)
13. Taylor Teagarden, c, Bakersfield (Rangers)
14. Eric Young Jr., 2b, Modesto (Rockies)
15. Hainley Statia, ss, Rancho Cucamonga (Angels)
16. Michael Saunders, of, High Desert (Mariners)
17. Andrew Bailey, rhp, Stockton (Athletics)
18. Kelvin Pichardo, rhp, San Jose (Giants)
19. Brooks Brown, rhp, Visalia (Diamondbacks)
20. Bubba Bell, of, Lancaster (Red Sox)

CAROLINA LEAGUE

1. Jordan Schafer, of, Myrtle Beach (Braves)
2. Chris Marrero, of, Potomac (Nationals)
3. #Elvis Andrus, ss, Myrtle Beach (Braves)
4. #Max Ramirez, c, Kinston (Indians)
5. Wes Hodges, 3b, Kinston (Indians)
6. Chorye Spoone, rhp, Frederick (Orioles)
7. Brandon Erbe, rhp, Frederick (Orioles)
8. Tommy Hanson, rhp, Myrtle Beach (Braves)
9. Adam Carr, rhp, Potomac (Nationals)
10. #Matt Whitney, 1b, Kinston (Indians)
11. Mitch Einertson, of, Salem (Astros)
12. Daniel Cortes, rhp, Wilmington (Royals)
13. Josh Rodriguez, ss, Kinston (Indians)
14. Sergio Perez, rhp, Salem (Astros)
15. Brad James, rhp, Salem (Astros)
16. Brad Bergesen, rhp, Frederick (Orioles)
17. Shelby Ford, 2b, Lynchburg (Pirates)
18. Jairo Cuevas, rhp, Myrtle Beach (Braves)
19. Julio Pimentel, rhp, Wilmington (Royals)
20. Kyle McCulloch, rhp, Winston-Salem (White Sox)

FLORIDA STATE LEAGUE

LOW CLASS A

MIDWEST LEAGUE

1. Clayton Kershaw, lhp, Great Lakes (Dodgers)
2. Travis Snider, of, Lansing (Blue Jays)
3. Brett Anderson, lhp, South Bend (Diamondbacks)
4. #Gorkys Hernandez, of, West Michigan (Tigers)
5. Hank Conger, c, Cedar Rapids (Angels)
6. Carlos Triunfel, ss, Wisconsin (Mariners)
7. Jose Ceda, rhp, Peoria (Cubs)
8. Gerardo Parra, of, South Bend (Diamondbacks)
9. Josh Bell, 3b, Great Lakes (Dodgers)
10. Drew Stubbs, of, Dayton (Reds)
11. Tyler Herron, rhp, Quad Cities (Cardinals)
12. Omar Poveda, rhp, Clinton (Rangers)
13. Jeff Manship, rhp, Beloit (Twins)
14. John Whittleman, 3b, Clinton (Rangers)
15. Juan Francisco, 3b, Dayton (Reds)
16. Drew Miller, rhp, Fort Wayne (Padres)
17. Kasey Kiker, lhp, Clinton (Rangers)
18. Sean O'Sullivan, rhp, Cedar Rapids (Angels)
19. Trevor Cahill, rhp, Kane County (Athletics)
20. Tyler Robertson, lhp, Beloit (Twins)

SOUTH ATLANTIC LEAGUE

1. Desmond Jennings, of, Columbus (Devil Rays)
2. Hector Gomez, ss, Asheville (Rockies)
3. Fautino de los Santos, rhp, Kannapolis (White Sox)
4. Lars Anderson, 1b, Greenville (Red Sox)
5. Chris Marrero, of, Hagerstown (Nationals)
6. Jordan Schafer, of, Rome (Braves)
7. Henry Sosa, rhp, Augusta (Giants)
8. Jeremy Hellickson, rhp, Columbus (Devil Rays)
9. Ryan Royster, of, Columbus (Devil Rays)
10. #Chris Carter, 1b, Kannapolis (White Sox)
11. Chris Coghlan, 2b, Greensboro (Marlins)
12. John Raynor, of, Greensboro (Marlins)
13. Adrian Cardenas, ss, Lakewood (Phillies)
14. Tommy Hanson, rhp, Rome (Braves)
15. Brandon Snyder, 1b, Delmarva (Orioles)
16. Jared Goedert, 3b, Lake County (Indians)
17. Daniel Mayora, ss, Asheville (Rockies)
18. Justin Maxwell, of, Hagerstown (Nationals)
19. Josh Reddick, of, Greenville (Red Sox)
20. Billy Rowell, 3b, Delmarva (Orioles)

SHORT-SEASON

NEW YORK-PENN LEAGUE

1. Brett Cecil, lhp, Auburn (Blue Jays)
2. Joe Savery, lhp, Williamsport (Phillies)
3. Hector Correa, rhp, Jamestown (Marlins)
4. Daniel Moskos, lhp, State College (Pirates)
5. Jordan Zimmerman, rhp, Vermont (Nationals)
6. Ryan Kalish, of, Lowell (Red Sox)
7. J.P. Arencibia, c, Auburn (Blue Jays)
8. Oscar Tejeda, ss, Lowell (Red Sox)
9. Glenn Gibson, lhp, Vermont (Nationals)
10. Dellin Betances, rhp, Staten Island (Yankees)
11. Colton Willems, rhp, Vermont (Nationals)
12. Yamaico Navarro, ss/3b, Lowell (Red Sox)
13. Jess Todd, rhp, Batavia (Cardinals)
14. Duke Welker, rhp, State College (Pirates)
15. Dominic Brown, of, Williamsport (Phillies)
16. Nick Carr, rhp, Brooklyn (Mets)
17. Damon Sublett, 2b, Staten Island (Yankees)
18. Zach McAllister, rhp, Staten Island (Yankees)
19. Michael McCormick, c, Hudson Valley (Devil Rays)
20. Brant Rustich, rhp, Brooklyn (Mets)

NORTHWEST LEAGUE

1. Matt Latos, rhp, Eugene (Padres)
2. Josh Donaldson, c, Boise (Cubs)
3. Juan Ramirez, rhp, Everett (Mariners)
4. Tony Thomas, 2b, Boise (Cubs)
5. Fabio Castillo, rhp, Spokane (Rangers)
6. Kellen Kulbacki, of, Eugene (Padres)
7. Tommy Hunter, rhp, Spokane (Rangers)
8. Greg Halman, of, Everett (Mariners)
9. Helder Velazquez, ss, Tri City (Rockies)
10. Matt Mangini, 3b, Everett (Mariners)
11. Corey Brown, of, Vancouver (Athletics)
12. Bruce Billings, rhp, Tri City (Rockies)
13. Cory Riordan, rhp, Tri City (Rockies)
14. Mitch Canham, c, Eugene (Padres)
15. Robinson Fabian, rhp, Tri City (Rockies)
16. Kyler Burke, of, Boise (Cubs)
17. Edward Paredes, lhp, Everett (Mariners)
18. Chris Huseby, rhp, Boise (Cubs)
19. Brian Rike, of, Tri City (Rockies)
20. Jake Brigham, rhp, Spokane (Rangers)

ROOKIE ADVANCED

APPALACHIAN LEAGUE

1. Cole Rohrbough, lhp, Danville (Braves)
2. Cody Johnson, of, Danville (Braves)
3. David Bromberg, rhp, Elizabethton (Twins)
4. #Neftali Feliz, rhp, Danville (Braves)
5. Jeffrey Locke, lhp, Danville (Braves)
6. Nick Barnese, rhp, Princeton (Devil Rays)
7. Pete Kozma, ss, Johnson City (Cardinals)
8. Brandon Hicks, ss, Danville (Braves)
9. Steve Evarts, lhp, Danville (Braves)
10. Mike McCardell, rhp, Elizabethton (Twins)
11. Michael Fisher, ss, Danville (Braves)
12. Jose Martinez, of, Bristol (White Sox)
13. Estarlin de los Santos, ss, Elizabethton (Twins)
14. Loek Van Mil, rhp, Elizabethton (Twins)
15. Deibinson Romero, 3b, Elizabethton (Twins)
16. Ozzie Lewis, of, Elizabethton (Twins)
17. Ebert Rosario, 3b, Greeneville (Astros)
18. Bradley Tippett, rhp, Elizabethton (Twins)
19. Kraig Binick, of, Bluefield (Orioles)
20. Kyle Greenwalt, rhp, Greeneville (Astros)

PIONEER LEAGUE

1. Todd Frazier, ss, Billings (Reds)
2. Caleb Gindl, of, Helena (Brewers)
3. Jordan Walden, rhp, Orem (Angels)
4. Aaron Poreda, lhp, Great Falls (White Sox)
5. Brandon Waring, 3b, Billings (Reds)
6. Jonathan Lucroy, c, Helena (Brewers)
7. Austin Gallagher, 3b, Ogden (Brewers)
8. Robert Bryson, rhp, Helena (Brewers)
9. Reynaldo Navarro, ss, Missoula (Diamondbacks)
10. Christian Marrero, 1b, Great Falls (White Sox)
11. Salvador Sanchez, of, Great Falls (White Sox)
12. Jaime Ortiz, 1b, Ogden (Dodgers)
13. Jhoulys Chacin, rhp, Casper (Rockies)
14. Robert Fish, lhp, Orem (Angels)
15. John Ely, rhp, Great Falls (White Sox)
16. Justin Reed, of, Billings (Reds)
17. Andrew Romine, ss, Orem (Angels)
18. Jimmy Gallagher, of, Great Falls (White Sox)
19. Adrian Ortiz, of, Idaho Falls (Royals)
20. Lyndon Estill, of, Great Falls (White Sox)

ROOKIE

ARIZONA LEAGUE

1. Angel Villalona, 3b, Giants
2. Engel Beltre, of, Rangers
3. Nick Noonan, 2b, Giants
4. Danny Duffy, lhp, Royals
5. Wilmer Font, rhp, Rangers
6. Wilber Bucardo, rhp, Giants
7. Drew Cumberland, ss, Padres
8. Danny Carroll, of, Mariners
9. Cristian Santana, c, Rangers
10. Mario Martinez, ss/3b, Mariners
11. Mason Tobin, rhp, Angels
12. Michael Anton, lhp, Angels
13. Matt Mitchell, rhp, Royals
14. Yefri Carvajal, of, Padres
15. Charlie Culberson, 2b/ss, Giants
16. Larry Suarez, rhp, Cubs
17. Clay Fuller, of, Angels
18. Sam Runion, rhp, Royals
19. Ivan Contreras, 2b, Angels
20. Jacob Wild, rhp, Mariners

GULF COAST LEAGUE

1. Michael Burgess, of, Nationals
2. Jesus Montero, c, Yankees
3. Ben Revere, of, Twins
4. Che-Hsuan Lin, of, Red Sox
5. John Tolisano, 2b, Blue Jays
6. Pedro Baez, 3b, Dodgers
7. Oscar Tejeda, ss, Red Sox
8. Neftali Soto, ss, Reds
9. Luis de la Cruz, c, Cardinals
10. Andrew Lambo, 1b/of, Dodgers
11. Devin Mesoraco, c, Reds
12. Kevin Aherns, 3b/ss, Blue Jays
13. Kyle Lotzkar, rhp, Reds
14. Scott Moviel, rhp, Mets
15. Jairo Heredia, rhp, Yankees
16. D'Marcus Ingram, of, Cardinals
17. Deryk Hooker, rhp, Cardinals
18. Daniel Berlind, rhp, Twins
19. Angel Morales, of, Twins
20. Tyler Kolodny, 3b, Orioles

A

Acosta, Ryan (Cubs) 90
Adenhart, Nick (Angels) 179
Adkins, James (Dodgers) 250
Aguasviva, Geison (Dodgers) 253
Ahrens, Kevin (Blue Jays) 467
Alderson, Tim (Giants) 403
Allen, Brandon (White Sox) 108
Almanzar, Michael (Red Sox) 72
Almonte, Denny (Mariners) 427
Alvarez, Mario (Dodgers) 250
Ambriz, Hector (Diamondbacks) 28
Anderson, Brett (Diamondbacks) 19
Anderson, Brian (Giants) 412
Anderson, Bryan (Cardinals) 371
Anderson, Josh (Braves) 41
Anderson, Lars (Red Sox) 67
Andrus, Elvis (Rangers) 450
Angelini, Carmen (Yankees) 312
Angle, Matt (Orioles) 59
Antonelli, Matt (Padres) 387
Antonini, Mike (Mets) 300
Arencibia, J.P. (Blue Jays) 467
Arias, Joaquin (Rangers) 460
Arredondo, Jose (Angels) 183
Arrieta, Jake (Orioles) 53
Ascanio, Jose (Cubs) 91
Ash, Jonny (Astros) 205
Ashley, Nevin (Rays) 444
Astacio, Olivo (Pirates) 360
Aubrey, Michael (Indians) 138
Aumont, Phillippe (Mariners) 419
Aviles, Mike (Royals) 221

B

Bachanov, Jon (Angels) 187
Baez, Pedro (Dodgers) 246
Bailey, Andrew (Athletics) 308
Bailey, Homer (Reds) 115
Baisley, Jeff (Athletics) 314
Balentien, Wladimir (Mariners) 420
Balester, Collin (Nationals) 483
Banks, Josh (Blue Jays) 475
Banwart, Travis (Athletics) 315
Bard, Daniel (Red Sox) 73
Barnese, Nick (Rays) 440
Barney, Darwin (Cubs) 91
Barrett, Eric (Braves) 44
Barthmaier, Jimmy (Pirates) 360
Barton, Brian (Cardinals) 371
Barton, Daric (Athletics) 306
Bascom, Tim (Orioles) 55
Bass, Brian (Twins) 285
Bastardo, Antonio (Phillies) 347
Bates, Aaron (Red Sox) 74
Bazardo, Yorman (Tigers) 164
Beato, Pedro (Orioles) 53
Beavan, Blake (Rangers) 453
Bell, Bubba (Red Sox) 75
Bell, Josh (Dodgers) 247
Below, Duane (Tigers) 172
Beltre, Engel (Rangers) 454
Beno, Martin (Nationals) 492
Benson, Joe (Twins) 275
Bergesen, Brad (Orioles) 60

Berlind, Dan (Twins) 284
Bernadina, Rogearvin (Nationals) 493
Berry, Quintin (Phillies) 346
Betances, Dellin (Yankees) 311
Bianchi, Jeff (Royals) 217
Bierd, Randor (Orioles) 57
Bisenius, Joe (Phillies) 347
Bixler, Brian (Pirates) 357
Blackburn, Nick (Twins) 274
Blanks, Kyle (Padres) 390
Blevins, Jerry (Athletics) 310
Bocock, Brian (Giants) 406
Boesch, Brennan (Tigers) 171
Boggs, Mitchell (Cardinals) 373
Bogusevic, Brian (Astros) 201
Bonifacio, Emilio (Diamondbacks) 20
Bono, Robert (Astros) 204
Borbon, Julio (Rangers) 453
Bostick, Adam (Mets) 298
Bourjos, Peter (Angels) 230
Bourn, Michael (Astros) 196
Bowden, Michael (Red Sox) 69
Bowker, John (Giants) 405
Brackman, Andrew (Yankees) 310
Braddock, Zach (Brewers) 263
Brantley, Michael (Brewers) 267
Braun, Ryan (Royals) 215
Bresnehan, Pat (Pirates) 363
Brewer, Brent (Brewers) 261
Brignac, Reid (Rays) 436
Brito, Javier (Diamondbacks) 28
Britton, Phillip (Braves) 45
Britton, Zach (Orioles) 58
Broadway, Lance (White Sox) 99
Bromberg, David (Twins) 280
Brown, Brooks (Diamondbacks) 22
Brown, Corey (Athletics) 308
Brown, Dominic (Phillies) 340
Brown, Jordan (Indians) 133
Browning, Barret (Angels) 186
Bruce, Jay (Reds) 114
Bryson, Rob (Brewers) 262
Bucardo, Wilber (Giants) 409
Buchholz, Clay (Red Sox) 66
Buck, Dallas (Diamondbacks) 24
Buckner, Billy (Royals) 211
Bulger, Jason (Angels) 188
Bullington, Bryan (Pirates) 359
Bumgarner, Madison (Giants) 403
Burgess, Michael (Nationals) 483
Burke, Kyler (Cubs) 87
Burnett, Alex (Twins) 282
Burns, Greg (Marlins) 186
Burriss, Emmanuel (Giants) 406
Burton, Jared (Reds) 118
Buschmann, Matt (Padres) 394
Bush, Matt (Padres) 397
Butler, Josh (Rays) 440
Butler, Tony (Mariners) 423
Byler, Justin (Pirates) 364

C

Cahill, Trevor (Athletics) 307
Cain, Lorenzo (Brewers) 261
Campbell, Eric (Bravese) 41
Canham, Mitch (Padres) 392

Cardenas, Adrian (Phillies) 339
Carignan, Andrew (Athletics) 314
Carp, Mike (Mets) 297
Carpenter, Drew (Phillies) 341
Carr, Adam (Nationals) 487
Carr, Nick (Mets) 295
Carrasco, Carlos (Phillies) 338
Carreno, Joel (Blue Jays) 476
Carrillo, Cesar (Padres) 390
Carroll, Brett (Marlins) 186
Carroll, Danny (Mariners) 426
Carter, Chris (Diamondbacks) 21
Carter, Chris (Red Sox) 76
Carvajal, Yefri (Padres) 391
Cassel, Justin (White Sox) 105
Castillo, Fabio (Rangers) 455
Castillo, Welington (Cubs) 88
Castillo, Wilkin (Diamondbacks) 23
Casto, Kory (Nationals) 489
Castro, Jose (Reds) 123
Cecil, Brett (Blue Jays) 467
Ceda, Jose (Cubs) 83
Cervelli, Francisco (Yankees) 314
Chacin, Jhoulys (Rockies) 153
Chamberlain, Joba (Yankees) 306
Chapman, Stephen (Brewers) 267
Chavez, Yohermyn (Blue Jays) 471
Chen, Yung-Chi (Mariners) 426
Ciriaco, Pedro (Diamondbacks) 29
Clarke, Darren (Rockies) 154
Clemens, Koby (Astros) 204
Clement, Jeff (Mariners) 418
Clevenger, Steve (Cubs) 93
Clevlen, Brent (Tigers) 168
Clippard, Tyler (Nationals) 486
Clyne, Steven (Mets) 295
Coats, Buck (Blue Jays) 475
Cobb, Alex (Rays) 439
Coghlan, Chris (Marlins) 181
Colvin, Tyler (Cubs) 83
Conger, Hank (Angels) 179
Conner, Clayton (Diamondbacks) 27
Contreras, Rayner (Padres) 396
Copeland, Ben (Giants) 413
Cordier, Eric (Braves) 42
Corley, Brad (Pirates) 358
Correa, Hector (Marlins) 183
Correa, Heitor (Marlins) 344
Cortes, Daniel (Royals) 211
Costanzo, Mike (Orioles) 54
Cousins, Scott (Marlins) 183
Cox, Bryce (Red Sox) 77
Cox, J. Brent (Yankees) 316
Cozart, Zack (Reds) 121
Craig, Allen (Cardinals) 376
Crosby, Casey (Tigers) 167
Crowe, Trevor (Indians) 135
Cruceta, Francisco (Tigers) 165
Cruz, Fernando (Royals) 218
Cueto, Johnny (Reds) 115
Cuevas, Jairo (Braves) 44
Culberson, Charlie (Giants) 407
Cumberland, Drew (Padres) 392
Cunningham, Aaron (D'backs) 21
Curtis, Collin (Yankees) 313
Cusick, Matt (Astros) 205

D

Daniel, Mike (Nationals) 491
D'Arnaud, Travis (Phillies) 344
Davidson, Dave (Pirates) 362
Davis, Chris (Rangers) 451
Davis, Lars (Rockies) 156
Davis, Marcus (Pirates) 364
Davis, Wade (Rays) 435
Day, Dewon (White Sox) 108
De la Cruz, Eulogio (Marlins) 185
De la Cruz, Luis (Cardinals) 381
De los Santos, Anel (Angels) 182
De los Santos, Estarlin (Twins) 280
De los Santos, Fautino (White Sox) 99
Dean, P.J. (Nationals) 493
DeJesus Jr., Ivan (Dodgers) 247
DeJesus, Jharmidy (Mariners) 425
Delaney, Jason (Pirates) 365
Delgado, Jesus (Marlins) 188
DeLome, Collin (Astros) 198
Demel, Sam (Athletics) 313
Denker, Travis (Giants) 412
Dent, Ryan (Red Sox) 72
DePaula, Julio (Twins) 283
Desme, Grant (Athletics) 311
Desmond, Ian (Nationals) 487
Detwiler, Ross (Nationals) 483
Devine, Joey (Braves) 40
DeWitt, Blake (Dodgers) 244
Dials, Zach (Blue Jays) 476
Diamond, Thomas (Rangers) 457
Diaz, Argenis (Red Sox) 71
Diaz, Robinzon (Blue Jays) 471
Dickerson, Chris (Reds) 124
Dickerson, Joe (Royals) 220
Dlugach, Brent (Tigers) 170
Dolsi, Freddy (Tigers) 173
Dominguez, Matt (Marlins) 181
Donald, Jason (Phillies) 344
Donaldson, Josh (Cubs) 85
Doolittle, Sean (Athletics) 310
Dorn, Danny (Reds) 124
Drabek, Kyle (Phillies) 340
Drennen, John (Indians) 138
Duarte, Jose (Royals) 220
Duda, Lucas (Mets) 301
Duensing, Brian (Twins) 277
Duffy, Danny (Royals) 212
Dunn, Mike (Yankees) 315
Duran, German (Rangers) 456

E

Easley, Ed (Diamondbacks) 25
Egbert, Jack (White Sox) 100
Eiland, Eric (Blue Jays) 471
Einertson, Mitch (Astros) 198
Elbert, Scott (Dodgers) 244
Ellsbury, Jacoby (Red Sox) 67
Ely, John (White Sox) 102
Engel, Reid (Red Sox) 76
Englund, Stephen (Nationals) 491
Enright, Barry (Diamondbacks) 22
Erbe, Brandon (Orioles) 54
Errecart, Chris (Brewers) 268
Escobar, Alcides (Brewers) 259
Estill, Lyndon (White Sox) 109
Estrada, Paul (Astros) 200
Evans, Nick (Mets) 297
Evans, Terry (Angels) 185
Evarts, Steve (Braves) 39

F

Fairley, Wendell (Giants) 405
Farina, Alan (Blue Jays) 472
Farris, Eric (Brewers) 266
Feliz, Neftali (Rangers) 452
Fermaint, Charlie (Brewers) 268
Fiorentino, Jeff (Orioles) 59
Fish, Robert (Angels) 188
Fisher, Brent (Royals) 217
Fisher, Carlos (Reds) 121
Flores, Josh (Astros) 198
Flores, Wilmer (Mets) 296
Flowers, Tyler (Braves) 38
Font, Wilmer (Rangers) 457
Ford, Darren (Brewers) 266
Ford, Shelby (Pirates) 356
Fowler, Dexter (Rockies) 147
Fox, Jake (Cubs) 89
Francisco, Ben (Indians) 133
Francisco, Juan (Reds) 117
Frazier, Todd (Reds) 117
Freeman, Freddie (Braves) 41
Freese, David (Padres) 396
Friday, Brian (Pirates) 358
Fruto, Emiliano (Diamondbacks) 27
Fuenmayor, Balbino (Blue Jays) 475
Fuld, Sam (Cubs) 89
Fuller, Clay (Angels) 189
Furbush, Charlie (Tigers) 170

G

Galarraga, Armando (Rangers) 461
Gallagher, Nolan (Mariners) 428
Gallagher, Sean (Cubs) 84
Galvis, Freddy (Phillies) 343
Gamel, Mat (Brewers) 260
Garcia, Brett (Marlins) 187
Garcia, Edgar (Phillies) 343
Garcia, Emmanuel (Mets) 299
Garcia, Jaime (Cardinals) 372
Gardner, Brett (Yankees) 309
Garr, Brennan (Rangers) 461
Garrison, Steve (Padres) 388
Geer, Josh (Padres) 396
Gerbe, Jeff (Tigers) 169
Gervacio, Samuel (Astros) 200
Getz, Chris (White Sox) 101
Giarratano, Tony (Tigers) 169
Gibson, Glenn (Rays) 438
Gillespie, Cole (Brewers) 260
Gilmore, Jon (Braves) 39
Gindl, Caleb (Brewers) 262
Ginley, Kyle (Blue Jays) 473
Godfrey, Graham (Athletics) 316
Golson, Greg (Phillies) 341
Gomez, Carlos (Mets) 291
Gomez, Hector (Rockies) 147
Gonzalez, Carlos (Diamondbacks) 18
Gonzalez, Esmailyn (Nationals) 488
Gonzalez, Gio (White Sox) 98
Graham, Connor (Rockies) 157
Green, Matt (Diamondbacks) 26
Green, Nick (Angels) 181
Green, Taylor (Brewers) 264
Greene, Tyler (Cardinals) 381
Gregerson, Luke (Cardinals) 381
Griffith, Nevin (White Sox) 103
Guerra, Deolis (Mets) 291
Guerra, Javy (Dodgers) 250
Guevara, Carlos (Padres) 394

Gutierrez, Juan (Astros) 195
Guzman, Freddy (Tigers) 168
Guzman, Joel (Rays) 445

H

Haeger, Charlie (White Sox) 104
Hagadone, Nick (Red Sox) 69
Halman, Greg (Mariners) 424
Hamilton, Brandon (Tigers) 166
Hamilton, Mark (Cardinals) 380
Hammond, Steve (Brewers) 268
Hankerd, Cyle (Diamondbacks) 27
Hansen, Craig (Red Sox) 73
Hanson, Tommy (Braves) 37
Happ, J.A. (Phillies) 342
Hardy, Rowdy (Royals) 221
Harman, Brad (Phillies) 345
Harrell, Lucas (White Sox) 104
Harrison, Matt (Rangers) 454
Hart, Kevin (Cubs) 86
Hatch, Anthony (Blue Jays) 477
Hawksworth, Blake (Cardinals) 377
Haydel, Lee (Brewers) 266
Hayenga, Keaton (Royals) 220
Hayes, Brett (Marlins) 185
Haynes, Jeremy (Angels) 187
Headley, Chase (Padres) 386
Hellickson, Jeremy (Rays) 437
Henson, Tyler (Orioles) 58
Heredia, Jairo (Yankees) 313
Hernandez, David (Orioles) 56
Hernandez, Diory (Braves) 45
Hernandez, Fernando (Athletics) 317
Hernandez, Francisco (White Sox) 106
Hernandez, Gaby (Marlins) 180
Hernandez, Gorkys (Braves) 36
Hernandez, Robert (Cubs) 88
Herrera, Javier (Athletics) 309
Herrera, Jonathan (Rockies) 155
Herrera, Yoslan (Pirates) 363
Herrmann, Frank (Indians) 140
Herron, Tyler (Cardinals) 374
Heyward, Jason (Braves) 35
Hickman, Tom (Marlins) 188
Hicks, Brandon (Braves) 39
Hill, Nick (Mariners) 429
Hilligoss, Mitch (Yankees) 316
Hochevar, Luke (Royals) 211
Hodges, Wes (Indians) 131
Hoey, James (Orioles) 57
Hoffpauir, Jarrett (Cardinals) 378
Holdzkom, Lincoln (Phillies) 349
Holliman, Mark (Cubs) 92
Hollimon, Michael (Tigers) 163
Horne, Alan (Yankees) 308
Horton, Josh (Athletics) 315
Horwitz, Brian (Giants) 413
Houser, James (Rays) 441
Hu, Chin-Lung (Dodgers) 243
Huber, Justin (Royals) 216
Huff, David (Indians) 133
Huffman, Chad (Padres) 394
Hughes, Dusty (Royals) 221
Hughes, Rhyne (Rays) 444
Humber, Philip (Mets) 292
Hundley, Nick (Padres) 395
Hunter, Cedric (Padres) 389
Hunter, Tommy (Rangers) 455
Hurley, Eric (Rangers) 451
Huseby, Chris (Cubs) 87
Hynick, Brandon (Rockies) 149

I

Inman, Will (Padres)	389
Iorg, Cale (Tigers)	163
Iorg, Eli (Astros)	197
Iribarren, Hernan (Brewers)	267
Italiano, Craig (Athletics)	317

J

Jackson, Austin (Yankees)	307
Jackson, Justin (Blue Jays)	468
James, Brad (Astros)	196
Janish, Paul (Reds)	121
Jaramillo, Jason (Phillies)	342
Jaso, John (Rays)	439
Jay, Jon (Cardinals)	374
Jeffress, Jeremy (Brewers)	259
Jennings, Desmond (Rays)	436
Jeroloman, Brian (Blue Jays)	473
Joaquin, Waldis (Giants)	407
Johnson, Blake (Royals)	215
Johnson, Chris (Astros)	199
Johnson, Cody (Braves)	38
Johnson, James (Orioles)	61
Johnson, Kris (Red Sox)	71
Johnson, Rob (Mariners)	425
Jones, Brandon (Braves)	35
Jones, Chris (Indians)	136
Jones, D.J. (Rays)	445
Jones, Hunter (Red Sox)	76
Joyce, Matt (Tigers)	165
Jung, Young-Il (Angels)	183
Jurrjens, Jair (Braves)	35

K

Ka'aihue, Kala (Braves)	43
Kalish, Ryan (Red Sox)	68
Katin, Brendan (Brewers)	269
Kennedy, Ian (Yankees)	307
Kershaw, Clayton (Dodgers)	242
Kiker, Kasey (Rangers)	453
Kilby, Brad (Athletics)	314
King, Blake (Cardinals)	380
King, Stephen (Nationals)	488
Kline, Will (Rays)	443
Kluber, Corey (Padres)	397
Kobayashi, Masahide (Indians)	134
Kolodny, Tyler (Orioles)	60
Kontos, George (Yankees)	312
Koshansky, Joe (Rockies)	152
Kozma, Pete (Cardinals)	373
Kulbacki, Kellen (Padres)	391
Kunz, Eddie (Mets)	292

L

Laffey, Aaron (Indians)	132
Lagares, Juan (Mets)	300
Lahair, Bryan (Mariners)	426
Lahey, Tim (Cubs)	93
Lambo, Andrew (Dodgers)	248
Lannan, John (Nationals)	486
Lansford, Josh (Cubs)	92
LaPorta, Matt (Brewers)	258
Larish, Jeff (Tigers)	164
LaRoche, Andy (Dodgers)	243
Larrison, Preston (Tigers)	173
Laster, Jeramy (Tigers)	171
Latimore, Quincy (Pirates)	362
Latos, Matt (Padres)	387
LeBlanc, Wade (Padres)	387

Lebron, Luis (Orioles)	60
LeCure, Same (Reds)	123
Leroux, Chris (Marlins)	185
Lewis, Jensen (Indians)	134
Lewis, Scott (Indians)	136
Liddi, Alex (Mariners)	429
Lillibridge, Brent (Braves)	36
Lin, Che-Hsuan (Red Sox)	75
Lincoln, Brad (Pirates)	355
Lirette, Chase (Blue Jays)	476
Lis, Erik (Twins)	284
Liz, Radhames (Orioles)	51
Locke, Jeff (Braves)	37
Lofgren, Chuck (Indians)	131
Longoria, Evan (Rays)	434
Lotzkar, Kyle (Reds)	118
Lough, David (Royals)	219
Lowe, Mark (Mariners)	421
Lowrie, Jed (Red Sox)	68
Lubanski, Chris (Royals)	216
Lucroy, Jonathan (Brewers)	264
Lucy, Donny (White Sox)	107
Luebke, Cory (Padres)	391
Lumsden, Tyler (Royals)	215

M

Mach, Tyler (Phillies)	347
Madrigal, Warner (Rangers)	459
Maestri, Alex (Cubs)	91
Magee, Brandon (Blue Jays)	473
Magnuson, Trystan (Blue Jays)	470
Mahalic, Joey (Indians)	141
Maier, Mitch (Royals)	219
Main, Michael (Rangers)	452
Maiques, Kenny (Cardinals)	375
Maloney, Matt (Reds)	118
Mangini, Matt (Mariners)	424
Manship, Jeff (Twins)	277
Manzella, Tommy (Astros)	200
Marceaux, Jacob (Marlins)	188
Marek, Stephen (Angels)	180
Marquez, Jeff (Yankees)	309
Marrero, Chris (Nationals)	482
Marrero, Christian (White Sox)	104
Marson, Lou (Phillies)	341
Marte, Jefry (Mets)	300
Martinez, Fernando (Mets)	290
Martinez, Jose (Cardinals)	376
Martinez, Jose (White Sox)	101
Martinez, Mario (Mariners)	427
Martis, Shairon (Nationals)	489
Mason, Chris (Rays)	438
Masterson, Justin (Red Sox)	67
Mather, Joe (Cardinals)	375
Mathieson, Scott (Phillies)	343
Matos, Osiris (Giants)	408
Mattair, Travis (Phillies)	345
Mattingly, Preston (Dodgers)	253
Maxwell, Justin (Nationals)	485
May, Lucas (Dodgers)	249
Mayberry Jr., John (Rangers)	456
Maybin, Cameron (Marlins)	178
Mayora, Daniel (Rockies)	154
Mazzaro, Vin (Athletics)	313
McAllister, Zach (Yankees)	317
McBride, Matt (Indians)	135
McBryde, Mike (Giants)	407
McCardell, Mike (Twins)	281
McClellan, Kyle (Cardinals)	377
McClune, Austin (Pirates)	362
McConnell, Chris (Royals)	219
McCormick, Mark (Cardinals)	379

McCormick, Mike (Rays)	442
McCrory, Bob (Orioles)	56
McCulloch, Kyle (White Sox)	103
McCutchen, Andrew (Pirates)	354
McCutchen, Daniel (Yankees)	311
McDonald, James (Dodgers)	245
McGeary, Jack (Nationals)	484
McGee, Jake (Rays)	435
McKenry, Michael (Rockies)	152
McLemore, Mark (Astros)	203
Medlen, Kris (Braves)	43
Meek, Evan (Pirates)	361
Melancon, Mark (Yankees)	310
Melillo, Kevin (Athletics)	312
Meloan, Jonathan (Dodgers)	245
Mendoza, Luis (Rangers)	459
Mesoraco, Devin (Reds)	116
Meyer, Dan (Athletics)	313
Mickolio, Kam (Mariners)	425
Middlebrooks, Will (Red Sox)	71
Mijares, Jose (Twins)	278
Miller, Adam (Indians)	130
Miller, Drew (Padres)	388
Miller, Greg (Dodgers)	249
Miller, Jai (Marlins)	189
Miller, Justin (Dodgers)	251
Miller, Ryan (Indians)	138
Mills, Beau (Indians)	131
Mills, Brad (Blue Jays)	474
Miranda, Juan (Yankees)	314
Miranda, Sergio (White Sox)	105
Misch, Pat (Giants)	410
Mitchell, Jermaine (Athletics)	309
Mitchell, Matt (Royals)	213
Mock, Garrett (Nationals)	488
Monasterios, Carlos (Phillies)	346
Montero, Jesus (Yankees)	308
Moore, Adam (Mariners)	424
Moore, Scott (Orioles)	55
Morales, Franklin (Rockies)	146
Morales, Sergio (White Sox)	105
Morgan, Nyjer (Pirates)	359
Morgan, Sean (Diamondbacks)	26
Morillo, Juan (Rockies)	150
Morlan, Eduardo (Rays)	440
Morris, Bryan (Dodgers)	247
Morrison, Logan (Marlins)	184
Mortensen, Clayton (Cardinals)	373
Moskos, Daniel (Pirates)	356
Moss, Brandon (Red Sox)	70
Motte, Jason (Cardinals)	379
Mount, Ryan (Angels)	183
Moustakas, Mike (Royals)	210
Moviel, Scott (Mets)	294
Muecke, Josh (Astros)	204
Mullins, Ryan (Twins)	280
Mulvey, Kevin (Mets)	291
Munoz, Luis (Pirates)	365
Murphy, Danny (Mets)	295
Murphy, David (Rangers)	458
Musser, Neal (Royals)	218
Myers, D'Arby (Phillies)	346

N

Nash, Chris (Indians)	140
Navarro, Reynaldo (Diamondbacks)	21
Navarro, Yamaico (Red Sox)	77
Naylor, Drew (Phillies)	348
Nelson, Chris (Rockies)	149
Nestor, Scott (Marlins)	187
Nickerson, Jonah (Tigers)	170
Niemann, Jeff (Rays)	437

Niese, Jon (Mets) 293
Nix, Jayson (Rockies) 152
Noonan, Nick (Giants) 404
Norris, Bud (Astros) 196
Norris, Derek (Nationals) 490
Nova, Ivan (Yankees) 313
Nunez, Jhonny (Nationals) 491

O

Ohlendorf, Ross (Yankees) 309
Olson, Garrett (Orioles) 54
Omogrosso, Brian (White Sox) 107
Orenduff, Justin (Dodgers) 252
Orta, Phillips (Mets) 298
O'Sullivan, Sean (Angels) 180
Ottavino, Adam (Cardinals) 372
Outman, Josh (Phillies) 339
Owens, Henry (Marlins) 184

P

Paredes, Edward (Mariners) 427
Parisi, Mike (Cardinals) 379
Parker, Jarrod (Diamondbacks) 19
Parmelee, Chris (Twins) 278
Parnell, Robert (Mets) 294
Parra, Gerardo (Diamondbacks) 20
Parra, Manny (Brewers) 259
Parraz, Jordan (Astros) 201
Patterson, Eric (Cubs) 87
Patterson, Ryan (Blue Jays) 470
Patterson, Scott (Yankees) 316
Patton, Troy (Orioles) 51
Paul, Xavier (Dodgers) 251
Paulino, Felipe (Astros) 195
Peacock, Brad (Nationals) 489
Pearce, Steve (Pirates) 355
Peguero, Carlos (Mariners) 423
Pelland, Tyler (Reds) 123
Pena, Francisco (Mets) 298
Pena, Hassan (Nationals) 492
Pena, Luis (Brewers) 263
Pennington, Cliff (Athletics) 315
Pereira, Nick (Giants) 408
Perez, Chris (Cardinals) 371
Perez, Fernando (Rays) 443
Perez, Oneli (White Sox) 107
Perez, Sergio (Astros) 199
Periard, Alexandre (Brewers) 265
Perkins, Glen (Twins) 279
Petit, Gregorio (Athletics) 311
Petrick, Billy (Cubs) 86
Pettit, Chris (Angels) 185
Phillips, P.J. (Angels) 184
Phillips, Zach (Rangers) 460
Pichardo, Kelvin (Giants) 410
Pill, Brett (Giants) 411
Pimentel, Julio (Royals) 213
Place, Jason (Red Sox) 75
Plouffe, Trevor (Twins) 278
Pope, Kieron (Orioles) 61
Pope, Van (Braves) 42
Porcello, Rick (Tigers) 162
Poreda, Aaron (White Sox) 99
Poveda, Omar (Rangers) 454
Powell, Landon (Athletics) 309
Price, David (Rays) 435
Pridie, Jason (Twins) 276
Purcey, David (Blue Jays) 470

R

Ramirez, Edwar (Yankees) 317
Ramirez, Elvin (Mets) 301
Ramirez, Juan (Mariners) 421
Ramirez, Max (Rangers) 458
Ramirez, Neil (Rangers) 455
Ramirez, Wilkin (Tigers) 167
Ramirez, Yordany (Astros) 202
Ramos, Cesar (Padres) 393
Ramos, Wilson (Twins) 275
Rapada, Clay (Tigers) 171
Rasmus, Colby (Cardinals) 370
Rasmus, Cory (Braves) 42
Raynor, John (Marlins) 183
Recker, Anthony (Athletics) 316
Reckling, Trevor (Angels) 184
Reddick, Josh (Red Sox) 70
Redmond, Todd (Pirates) 364
Register, Steven (Mets) 299
Reimold, Nolan (Orioles) 51
Reineke, Chad (Astros) 197
Revere, Ben (Twins) 276
Reynolds, Greg (Rockies) 148
Rhee, Dae-Eun (Cubs) 88
Richardson, Dustin (Red Sox) 74
Rike, Brian (Rockies) 151
Riordan, Cory (Rockies) 157
Rivero, Carlos (Indians) 137
Rizzo, Anthony (Red Sox) 72
Robertson, David (Yankees) 315
Robertson, Tyler (Twins) 275
Robinson, Derrick (Royals) 214
Robnett, Richie (Athletics) 312
Rodgers, Chad (Braves) 40
Rodriguez, Aneury (Rockies) 156
Rodriguez, Henry (Athletics) 307
Rodriguez, Josh (Indians) 137
Rodriguez, Sean (Angels) 181
Roe, Chaz (Rockies) 150
Roemer, Wes (Diamondbacks) 22
Roenicke, Josh (Reds) 117
Rogers, Esmil (Rockies) 151
Rogers, Mark (Brewers) 262
Rohrbaugh, Robert (Mariners) 428
Rohrbough, Cole (Braves) 37
Rollins, Heath (Rays) 441
Romak, Jamie (Pirates) 357
Romero, Alex (Diamondbacks) 28
Romero, Deibinson (Twins) 279
Romero, Ricky (Blue Jays) 468
Romine, Andrew (Angels) 189
Romine, Austin (Yankees) 314
Romo, Sergio (Giants) 412
Rondon, Hector (Indians) 140
Roquet, Rocky (Cubs) 92
Rosa, Carlos (Royals) 213
Rosales, Adam (Reds) 122
Rowell, Bill (Orioles) 52
Rowland-Smith, Ryan (Mariners) 422
Royster, Ryan (Rays) 437
Ruggiano, Justin (Rays) 444
Runion, Sam (Royals) 215
Russell, Adam (White Sox) 103
Russell, James (Cubs) 90
Rustich, Brant (Mets) 292
Rzepczynski, Marc (Blue Jays) 474

S

Safarte, Dennis (Orioles) 58
Salas, Juan (Rays) 439
Salome, Angel (Brewers) 261

Samardzija, Jeff (Cubs) 85
Sammons, Clint (Braves) 44
Sampson, Julian (Phillies) 345
Sanchez, Gaby (Marlins) 182
Sanchez, Humberto (Yankees) 311
Sanchez, Romulo (Pirates) 359
Sanchez, Sal (White Sox) 109
Santana, Carlos (Dodgers) 252
Santana, Cristian (Rangers) 457
Santangelo, Lou (Astros) 203
Santos, Reid (Indians) 141
Sapp, Max (Astros) 201
Saunders, Michael (Mariners) 421
Savery, Joe (Phillies) 339
Scarpetta, Cody (Brewers) 265
Schafer, Jordan (Braves) 24
Scherzer, Max (Diamondbacks) 19
Schierholtz, Nate (Giants) 403
Schmidt, Nick (Padres) 390
Seidel, R.J. (Brewers) 264
Sellers, Justin (Athletics) 311
Septimo, Leyson (Diamondbacks) 29
Sexton, Tim (Dodgers) 251
Sharpless, Josh (Pirates) 361
Shelby Jr., John (White Sox) 102
Sierra, Moises (Blue Jays) 477
Silverio, Alfredo (Dodgers) 253
Silverio, Juan (White Sox) 102
Simmons, James (Athletics) 307
Sinkbiel, Brett (Marlins) 179
Sipp, Tony (Indians) 135
Sizemore, Scott (Tigers) 163
Skelton, James (Tigers) 172
Slama, Anthony (Twins) 284
Slaten, Doug (Diamondbacks) 25
Smith, Greg (Diamondbacks) 23
Smith, Joe (Mets) 294
Smith, Seth (Rockies) 151
Smoker, Josh (Nationals) 484
Smolinski, Jake (Nationals) 486
Snider, Travis (Blue Jays) 466
Snyder, Ben (Giants) 410
Snyder, Brad (Indians) 139
Snyder, Brandon (Orioles) 52
Sosa, Henry (Giants) 404
Sosa, Oswaldo (Twins) 282
Soto, Geovanny (Cubs) 83
Soto, Neftali (Reds) 119
Span, Denard (Twins) 281
Speier, Ryan (Rockies) 153
Spencer, Matt (Phillies) 348
Spoone, Chorye (Orioles) 53
Stange, Daniel (Diamondbacks) 24
Stanton, Mike (Marlins) 182
Statia, Hainley (Angels) 182
Stevens, Jeff (Indians) 137
Stewart, Ian (Rockies) 147
Strieby, Ryan (Tigers) 172
Strop, Pedro (Rockies) 149
Stubbs, Drew (Reds) 116
Suarez, Larry (Cubs) 90
Sulentic, Matt (Athletics) 312
Swarzak, Anthony (Twins) 276
Sweeney, Matt (Angels) 184
Sweeney, Ryan (White Sox) 100

T

Tabata, Jose (Yankees) 307
Talbot, Mitch (Rays) 442
Tanner, Clayton (Giants) 406
Tata, Jordan (Tigers) 166
Tatum, Craig (Reds) 120

Taylor, Graham (Marlins)	189	Valdez, Merkin (Giants)	411	Weglarz, Nick (Indians)	132
Teagarden, Taylor (Rangers)	451	Valencia, Danny (Twins)	282	Weiser, Keith (Rockies)	156
Teheran, Julio (Braves)	38	Valenzuela, Sergio (Reds)	125	Welker, Duke (Pirates)	357
Tejada, Ruben (Mets)	296	Valido, Robert (White Sox)	109	Wells, Jared (Padres)	395
Tejeda, Oscar (Red Sox)	69	Vallejo, Jose (Rangers)	460	Wells, Randy (Blue Jays)	474
Thatcher, Joe (Padres)	393	Van Mil, Loek (Twins)	281	West, Sean (Marlins)	180
Thigpen, Curtis (Blue Jays)	469	Van Ostrand, Jimmy (Astros)	205	Whelan, Kevin (Yankees)	312
Thomas, Clete (Tigers)	167	Varvaro, Anthony (Mariners)	429	Whitney, Matt (Nationals)	490
Thomas, Justin (Mariners)	428	Vasquez, Esmerling (Diamondbacks)	24	Whittleman, Johnny (Rangers)	458
Thomas, Tony (Cubs)	85	Vasquez, Virgil (Tigers)	169	Wieters, Matt (Orioles)	50
Thompson, Aaron (Marlins)	181	Veal, Donald (Cubs)	84	Willems, Colton (Nationals)	485
Thompson, Rich (Angels)	186	Velazquez, Helder (Rockies)	155	Williams, Jackson (Giants)	409
Threets, Erick (Giants)	409	Velez, Eugenio (Giants)	405	Wilson, Bobby (Angels)	187
Tillman, Chris (Mariners)	419	Veloz, Greg (Mets)	296	Wimberly, Corey (Rockies)	155
Tippett, Bradley (Twins)	285	Venable, Will (Padres)	392	Winters, Kyle (Marlins)	186
Tobin, Mason (Angels)	186	Villalona, Angel (Giants)	402	Withrow, Chris (Dodgers)	245
Todd, Jess (Cardinals)	374	Vineyard, Nathan (Mets)	293	Wolfe, Brian (Blue Jays)	472
Tolisano, John (Blue Jays)	469	Vinyard, Chris (Orioles)	59	Wood, Blake (Royals)	212
Toregas, Wyatt (Indians)	139	Viola, Pedro (Reds)	119	Wood, Brandon (Angels)	178
Torrence, Devon (Astros)	203	Vitters, Josh (Cubs)	82	Wood, Travis (Reds)	122
Tosoni, Rene (Twins)	283	Volstad, Chris (Marlins)	179	Worrell, Mark (Cardinals)	378
Towles, J.R. (Astros)	194	Votto, Joey (Reds)	115	Worth, Danny (Tigers)	165
Townsend, Wade (Rays)	443			Worthington, Tyrell (Diamondbacks)	26
Trahern, Dallas (Marlins)	182			Wright, Wesley (Astros)	202
Tripp, Brandon (Orioles)	56				

W

Triunfel, Carlos (Mariners)	420	Wade, Cory (Dodgers)	252
Troncoso, Ramon (Dodgers)	248	Wagner, Mark (Red Sox)	74
Trumbo, Mark (Angels)	189	Walden, Jordan (Angels)	179

Y

Tseng, Sung-Wei (Indians)	136	Walker, Andrew (Pirates)	362
Tucker, Ryan (Marlins)	179	Walker, Matt (Rays)	441	Yabuta, Yasuhiko (Royals)	214
Tuiasosopo, Matt (Mariners)	422	Walker, Neil (Pirates)	355	Young, Delwyn (Dodgers)	246
Turner, Justin (Reds)	125	Wall, Josh (Dodgers)	248	Young Jr., Eric (Rockies)	154
Tyson, Nick (Brewers)	265	Walters, P.J. (Cardinals)	376

Z

		Waring, Brandon (Reds)	122
		Wasserman, Ehren (White Sox)	106	Zagurski, Mike (Phillies)	348

V

		Watson, Sean (Reds)	120	Zimmerman, Jordan (Nationals)	484
		Watson, Tony (Pirates)	358	Zinicola, Zech (Nationals)	492
Valaika, Chris (Reds)	119	Weathers, Casey (Rockies)	148
Valdez, Jeudy (Padres)	395

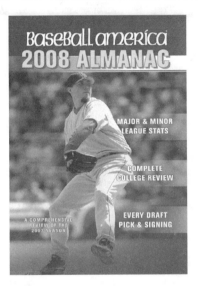

BaseBall america ®

MAJORS ◆ MINORS ◆ PROSPECTS ◆ DRAFT ◆ COLLEGE ◆ HIGH SCHOOL

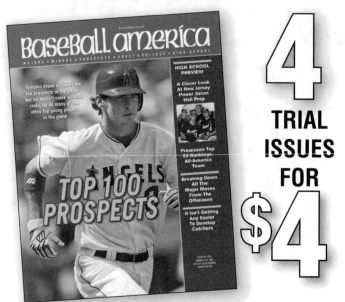

4
TRIAL
ISSUES
FOR
$4